EDUCATION IN THE UNITED STATES
A DOCUMENTARY HISTORY

Edited by
SOL COHEN

UNIVERSITY OF
CALIFORNIA
LOS ANGELES

VOLUME 4

Random House New York

Reference Series Editors:

Fred L. Israel
William P. Hansen

Acknowledgments for use of material covered by
Copyright Conventions appear on pages 3395–99.

Art spots courtesy of Dover Pictorial Archives

FIRST EDITION

9 8 7 6 5 4 3 2 1

MANUFACTURED IN THE UNITED STATES OF AMERICA

Library of Congress Cataloging in Publication Data
Cohen, Sol, comp.
Education in the United States: a documentary history.
1. Education—United States—History—Sources.
1. Title.
LA205.C53   370.973   73-3099
ISBN 0-394-49379-6 (v. 4)

Designed by Marsha Picker
for computer typesetting by Volt Information Sciences, Inc.

VOLUME IV
CONTENTS

BOOK THREE

The Transformation of
American Education 1896–1973

*Whenever we have in mind the discussion of a new movement in
education, it is especially necessary to take the broader, or social,
view. Otherwise, changes in the school institution and tradition
will be looked at as the arbitrary inventions of particular teachers,
at the worst transitory fads, and at the best merely improvements
in certain details—and this is the plane upon which it is too
customary to consider school changes. It is as rational to conceive
of the locomotive or the telegraph as personal devices. The
modification going on in the method and curriculum of education
is as much a product of the changed social situation, and as
much an effort to meet the needs of the new society that is
forming, as are changes in modes of industry and commerce.*

John Dewey, *The School and Society*

a. The 20th century has witnessed a phenomenal expansion of the American educational system. By 1918 elementary education was virtually universal. High schools, in 1890, confined largely to the cities and more affluent rural areas, were by 1918 a well-accepted part of American education. Much the same thing might be said for colleges, universities, and professional schools. New institutions such as the junior high school and the junior college were fashioned to meet the needs of specific groups. In 1890 the classroom teachers and supervisory staff numbered 364,000. School enrollment numbered almost 12,700,000. Total expenditures for schools amounted to about $140 million. By 1918, one contemporary remarked, American education had become "big business." In that year, total expenditures for all schools had reached $763 million. Classroom teachers and supervisory staff numbered over 650,000. More than 25,000,000 students were enrolled at all levels. But the boom was still to come.

In 1946, total school expenditures for all purposes had reached $2.9 billion. The schools at all levels enrolled some 27.8 million students. Classroom teachers and supervisory staff numbered 867,000. In 1956, the schools enrolled some 35.8 million students. Classroom teaching and supervisory staff numbered 1,213,000. School expenditures for all purposes amounted to almost $11 billion. In 1969–70, total school budgets for current expenditures and capital outlay reached almost $65 billion. More than 61,000,000 Americans were engaged full-time as students, teachers, or administrators in the nation's educational enterprise. The schools at all levels enrolled 58.6 million students. This army was serviced or led (or controlled) by some 2,775,000 teachers, 217,000 administrators and supervisors, and another 132,000 school board members. But in 1972–73 total school expenditures amounted to over $90 billion, while 96 million Americans were engaged more or less full-time as pupils, teachers, or school administrators in the educational enterprise.

b. The American school system was not only different quantitatively, but qualitatively. The schools, at all levels, had been transformed. The key role in this transformation, as Lawrence A. Cremin has demonstrated in *The Transformation of the School,* was played by an extraordinary and many-sided complex of educational reform movements which can be subsumed under the rubric, "progressive education." Indeed, mass education was not so much transformed, as it was created, and the professional educator had come into his own.

Progressive education started as the educational phase of the broader Progressive Movement, which, beginning in the late 19th century, attempted to cope with the often baffling and urgent problems created by the rise of the city, the rise of the factory, and the massive influx of immigrants from South and East Europe. Progressive education meant at least this much—that the functions of the public schools were to be extended far beyond their traditional, formal intellectual concerns, extended in any direction in order to meet the needs of the new urban-industrial America.

a. One recent historian has declared that the industrial revolution is the dominant theme of modern world history. In the United States, its impact was swift, powerful, and all-encompassing. It created a new nation. The development of manufacturing, industry, and large scale business enterprise in the period following the Civil War was phenomenal. Even as late as 1860 the bulk of general manufacturing was carried on in homes and small neighborhood shops. By the turn of the century, however, household and neighborhood industries were virtually non-existent, and even the processing of many agricultural products such as butter and cheese had become factory tasks. With dramatic suddenness America emerged as the world's foremost industrial nation and a powerful rival to England and Germany in world trade.

In the last decades of the 19th century, the whole face of the land was made over. Made over, too, were the millions of men and women from rural America and Europe who poured into the new industrial centers to become subjected to the discipline of factory labor. Behind the technological transformation lay a new method of production based on the factory, the machine, standardization of parts, specialization of labor and mass production. The Machine Age created an urgent demand for a small but increasing number of skilled workers and technicians. But the chief need was for an army of semi-skilled labor to man the machines in the factories, go down into the mines. The jack-of-all-trades became a tender of a machine in a factory, and a permanent laboring class, that owned neither its homes nor the tools of its trade, made its appearance, determined to get its share of the bounty. How could Americans adjust to, if not wholly master, the techniques of industrial society? Could the rural and native-born, and the foreign-born of all degrees of ethnic and religious diversity pouring into the new industrial centers learn to accept the imposed discipline of industrial labor? What role would the public schools play in the new industrial society? Urbanization posed equally grave problems for the schools.

b. By the turn of the century we had become a nation of cities. As late as 1860 less than 16% of Americans lived in cities; in 1890, 33%; in 1900, 40%. Between 1880–1900, Chicago grew from 500,000 to 1,500,000; New York City from 1,900,000 to 3,500,000; Philadelphia from 850,000 to 1,000,000. By 1900 St. Louis, Boston, Baltimore, and Washington, D.C. had populations close to 1,000,000, Cincinnati, Buffalo, Pittsburgh about 850,000. The cities grew up unplanned. They were characterized by an enormous density of population. Housing was scarce, land dear. Owners piled floor atop floor, pushed buildings back to back and side to side, and the infamous tenement slum made its appearance—unsanitary, unattractive, overcrowded firetraps, which spread "like a scab" to Boston, Chicago, Pittsburgh, New York, and other large cities. A report on a Boston slum in 1899 applied equally to the slum areas of every big city: "Dirty and battered walls and ceilings, dark cellars with water standing in them, alleys littered with garbage and filth, broken and leaking drainpipes . . . dark and filthy water closets . . ."

Such an environment was hardly conducive to child development. Instead of the traditional experiences of childhood celebrated in song and literature—fields and countryside—now there was the shabby tenement, or alley, or saloon. In the American hierarchy of values, a stable and harmonious family life loomed high. Whatever else failed, the moral influence of the family unit over the individual would maintain the integrity of the community. But in the tenements with its dense overcrowding, what chance did the family have to properly socialize the young? A group of investigators from Albany sent down to report on New York City's tenement districts expressed the widely shared sentiment:

> "They are centres of disease, poverty, vice and crime, where it is a marvel, not that children grow up to be thieves, drunkards, and prostitutes, but that so many should ever grow up to be decent and self-respecting."

When the stability of home and family and neighborhood, taken for granted by an older generation of educators is shaken what happens to the school? Could it go along in its old ways? But perhaps it was immigration more than any other factor which determined the program of school reformers.

c. The growth of the city was fed from two sources—one internal, the other external. Lured by the lights, the noise, the gaiety, the variety, the jobs, the rural population moved to the city in droves. And for the great majority of immigrants venturing to America in the 1880's, the city was their destination. Between 1880 and 1914, by far the greatest and presumably the last of the great waves of European immigrants arrived, some 22,000,000. By 1900, first and second generation immigrants constituted about 60% of the population of the nation's twelve largest cities.

Many Americans began to make invidious distinctions between the "old" and the "new" immigrants. The "old" were the pre-1881 immigrants, 95% of whom came from western and northern Europe. They were largely English-speaking and, with the exception of the Irish, mainly Protestant. The "new" immigrants came from different backgrounds—Italians, Greeks, Slavs, Russians, Poles, from South and Eastern Europe, regions which were considered comparatively backward. They were largely non-English speaking and largely non-Protestant; mostly Italian and central European Catholics, and Russian and Polish Jews. And, unlike the older immigrants, who often headed for the mid-West, the new arrivals clustered conspicuously in the northeastern cities where they recreated the semi-oriental ghettoes of the old world. Many Americans began to urge an end to unrestricted immigration; by 1924 they were successful. In the meantime, what about the immigrants who were already here? By 1909, when the United States Immigration Commission made its massive study, 57.8% of the children in the public schools of 37% of the nation's largest cities were of foreign-born parentage. In Chelsea, Massachusetts, and Duluth, Minnesota, the percentage ran as high as 74%; in New York it was 71.5%, in Chicago 67.3%, and in Boston, 63.5%. What would be their effect on the public schools? Could education proceed in traditional ways?

d. Disorders and discontents plagued the nation in the closing decades of the 19th century. Many developments seemed ominous to Americans— their fears focused on the city, the growth of which destroyed for many Americans the cherished belief that the New World was somehow immune from the sicknesses of the Old. It now had the very proletariat, the very poverty, the very slums, the very social tensions long familiar to Europe. The 1880's and 1890's witnessed cataclysmic warnings that the city, if not tamed, would bring about the downfall of the nation. "What shall we do with our great cities? What will our great cities do with us? These are the two problems which confront every thoughtful American," warned Helen Campbell in 1891. The schools would not be able to escape the challenges posed by massive urban growth.

This sordid picture of the urban-industrial city with its myriads of new immigrants, its squalor, poverty, wretchedness was presented with often brilliant clarity by many of the journalists and muckrakers of the 1890's—Robert A. Woods, William Stead, Benjamin O. Flower. Yet in the forefront stood Jacob Riis, who more than anyone else awakened America to the challenge of the city. His *How the Other Half Lives* (1890) inspired a generation of progressives. In the 1890's, against a background of mounting social crisis, progressives seized upon education and the public schools as the great panacea. "It is all a matter of education," said Riis. The schools would have to help solve the problems of health, hygiene, recreation, vocation, congestion of population, assimilation of the immigrant, and more. For example in 1896, sociologist Albion Small told a meeting of the National Education Association: "Sociology demands of educators, . . . , that they shall not rate themselves as leaders of children but as makers of society. Sociology knows no means for the amelioration or reform of society more radical than those of which teachers hold the leverage . . ." But first the public schools would have to be transformed. Public schools still emphasized formal training in intellectual skills. Progressives would force the schools to meet the challenge of the city. The social settlement movement acted as the spearhead for reform.

||| **a.** In the late 19th century a group of dedicated, socially aware young university men and women in England organized a concerted attack on urban poverty. One of their principal tools was the social settlement house. Social settlements originated in England, in the slums of the late 19th-century London, and soon spread rapidly through England and West Europe, and within a few years came over to the United States. By 1910 there were in this country over 400 settlements, including Henry Street Settlement, New York City; South End House, Boston; and Hull House, Chicago, founded by Jane Addams and Ellen Gates Starr in 1889.

Settlement activities knew no boundaries. As Jane Addams put it: "We were asked to wash the newborn babies, to prepare the dead for burial, to nurse the sick, and to mind the children." Expediency governed their practices. They fought for housing and sanitation reform, elimination of sweatshops and child labor, for parks and playgrounds, for more schools, and for a different kind of school. Always, settlement residents took their cues directly from neighborhood needs. Settlements founded anti-filth societies and junior street cleaning brigades, provided baths and showers, drinking fountains, gymnasiums, and social and recreational facilities of all sorts. They taught health and hygiene, became first aid centers and headquarters for visiting nurses. They functioned as libraries and reading rooms, experimented with vocational education and vocational guidance, and with classes for the physically and mentally handicapped, and introduced kindergartens, day nurseries, and noon lunch programs for children.

By the mid-1890's the settlements had developed a sprawling educational program, which forced them to turn to the public schools for relief. The "new" school would have to be less formal; would have to become, in Cremin's felicitous phrase, a "legatee" institution. Pragmatic and untheoretical at first, the whole movement of school expansion, the major thrust of school reform in America in the 20th century, arose from the social and humanitarian needs of the city. This meant a new role for the school going far beyond its formal, intellectual interests to an active concern with all aspects of child welfare and neighborhood improvement, a concept of the school as a child welfare center, a concept of the school as a social or community center, and a concept of the school as an industrial training agency.

One of the most radical ideas ever advanced in American education is that the school is responsible for the "whole child," that it takes the place of parent and home in caring for every phase of the child's welfare. To settlement residents the city was destructive of home and family. Parents were compelled to work and, therefore, they were unable to properly care for their children, who were left to shift for themselves; the street was a powerful school but one with an alarming pedagogical fare. Settlements undertook the role of surrogate parent and surrogate home in the lives of immigrant children, and then the settlements asked the schools also to assume this responsibility. All the problems of child life, Robert Hunter of New York's University Settlement declared in 1904, were school problems. The school was obliged to conquer them. The question Hunter posed in 1904 was this: "Are we to have the school ignore this larger work of education and remain a sort of dispensary of learning—an inflexible missionary of the three R's? . . . or is it to take as its responsibility the entire problem of child-life and master it? If the school does not assume this responsibility, how shall the work be done?" With these words Hunter struck the keynote of school reform in the Progressive Era. The school would take as its responsibility the entire problem of child-life and master it. Jane Addams described it as "socialized education." Lillian Wald called it "socialized parental control."

From its inception, the settlement was conceived as a vehicle for neighborhood improvement. Settlement residents realized, however, that if "community" is lacking, nothing gets done for the neighborhood; public authority waits upon local initiative. But in the ghetto, there was no "community." According to Jane Addams, one of the most pernicious effects of the city was that it destroyed the sense of community: "The social organism has broken down through the large districts of our great cities. . . . They live for the moment, side by side, many of them without knowledge of each other, without fellowship, without local tradition or public spirit, without social organization of any kind. . . ." Settlement residents hoped that the school, as social center, with its games, classes, lectures, parties, dances, would help restore the cohesiveness which the tenement had wrecked. Then, after an organic unity had been created, the campaign for neighborhood relief and improvement would be launched. Of course, in the meantime, the school would help Americanize the immigrant.

Many social critics, like Jacob Riis, saw Americanization primarily as a rapid initiation into the English language. Some went further, to demand that the immigrant not only learn American ways, but be divested of his past as quickly and as definitively as possible. In 1909, in his *Changing Conceptions of Education*, Ellwood Cubberley called on the public schools to break up the ghettoes and "to assimilate or amalgamate these people as a part of the American race, and to implant in their children, so far as can be done, the Anglo-Saxon conception of righteousness, law, order, and popular government, and to awaken in them reverence for our democratic institutions, and for those things which we as a people hold to be of abiding worth." The social settlements had a broader view. The immigrants had "gifts" to offer America. These were to be fostered, while the immigrant learned American ways. The settlements would bridge the ghetto and the broader world of America. The school as a neighborhood center would simply continue this process. Needless to say, the immigrants' own foreign language newspaper, his *landschaft* and fraternal organizations, his church or synagogue, were also helping him make the transition from the old world to the new.

b. Beginning about 1905 there was a shift in emphasis on the part of school reformers from a concern with the expansion of school functions, and from the expansion of the curriculum to include more subjects to a program calling for the radical reconstruction of the curriculum along vocational lines. The industrial education movement began in a desultory way in the late 1870's as a demand for manual training in the elementary grades and trade training at the high school level. In the 1880's and 1890's a few vocational or manual training high schools were established, some public, more private. Many public high schools began to add vocational courses to their programs, and elementary schools began gradually to expand their offerings in manual training. But it was a case of too little and too late. In 1906, with the organization of the National Society for the Promotion of Industrial Education, the push began in earnest.

Few movements in the history of American education have taken so sudden and so powerful a hold on the minds of school reformers. So far as educators were concerned, particularly those active in the National Education Association and the State Departments of Education, as well as professors of education at the new teachers colleges and schools of education, industrial education was the wave of the future. By 1908 the NEA rang with oratory and resolutions on its behalf. It was truly an amazing phenomenon, whose ramifications were very wide indeed. The industrial education movement involved the child labor and compulsory education movements, the junior high school movement, vocational guidance, the neighborhood school concept and, above all, the very way Americans had traditionally conceived of the public schools.

The connection between the industrial education movement and the child labor and compulsory education movements is extremely close. Until the late 19th century, child labor was not only acceptable but even praiseworthy. But child labor in an industrial society was another matter. For many of the estimated 1,750,000 children between the ages of 10 and 16 employed in gainful occupations in 1900 (some placed the figure much higher), here was no benevolent system of apprenticeship, but rather a system of cheap, easily discarded labor which depressed the wages of adults and broke the spirits and bodies of the children. In the early 1900's spurred on by the muckraking of John Spargo, Robert Hunter, and others, Progressives launched a strenuous crusade against child labor. The point to emphasize is that from the beginning all those concerned with the child labor problem insisted on the centrality of the schools in any reform program. It wasn't enough to shut the child out of the factory, he had to be placed into school. "Compulsory Education, The Solution of the Child Labor Problem," was one of the key planks of the child labor movement. By 1910, child labor reformers could point to some significant gains, as school enrollment figures testify. Public elementary school enrollment climbed from 12,500,000 in 1900 to 17,000,000 in 1910, while the average number of days per pupil per semester rose from 86.3 to 113. But if the schools were to help solve the problems of child labor and child welfare, of immigration and congestion of population, the children had not only to be got into the schools but kept there as long as possible.

But here the schools were failing, as a high dropout rate offset the expansion of school population. Children were leaving school in large numbers, and as soon as they could. It was estimated that only 40–50% finished the eighth grade; only 8–10% completed high school. Between the ages of 13 and 15 more than 50% dropped out of school, most in the sixth and seventh grades. One of the major problems of the pre-World War I generation of school reformers became that of halting this "premature" school leaving. While investigators disagreed on the statistics, all agreed that the school mortality rate was high. And there was surprising unanimity on the cause for this deplorable situation; the curriculum was not meeting the interests and needs of children. The schools holding power would be increased if the schools offered industrial training.

While the needs and interests of children can be overemphasized, the needs and interests of American industrial society no less than those of the children conspired to demand vocational education. As mentioned earlier, with dramatic suddenness, by the last years of the 19th century America emerged as the world's foremost industrial nation, and a powerful rival to England and Germany in world trade. If rivalry in trade and commerce was destined to be the warfare of the future, then Americans were determined to carry off the victor's share of the spoils.

Now the question of the recruitment and proper training of a new-style army, an industrial army, assumed in the United States the same urgency it was assuming in England, and had assumed a generation earlier in Germany. The officers for this new army would be recruited and trained in the engineering and scientific and business schools. But industry desperately needed privates (it was estimated that the country's labor force required at least 1,000,000 additions annually). What the schools had to provide, therefore, was an education with a vocational bias—one which would predispose the children to enter the factories and manual trades, impress them with the "dignity of labor," and equip them with "industrial intelligence"; that is, equip them with some facility in handling tools and machines, basic literacy to enable them to read and understand directions, and discipline enough to enable them to better conform to the requirements of large-scale, rationalized factory routine.

At first, the main thrust of the industrial education movement was aimed at the high schools. Very shortly, however, the limited value of this objective became apparent. Not only had the children to be recruited into the vocational high schools or into vocational tracks in comprehensive high schools, but more important, children weren't staying for the high school course. They were leaving in large numbers before the end of the eighth grade. The problem was one of keeping them in school up to the eighth grade and exposing them to some form of vocational training before they left. In other words, by 1907 or 1908 the problem of vocational training in the public schools had become one of adjusting the work of the elementary school for those who upon graduation, or upon dropping out before graduation, entered the world of work. Out of the search for some solution to this problem came the theory of "differentiation." The upper grades of the elementary were to differentiate between the needs of those children preparing for high school and higher education, and those children whose education would be terminated with the elementary school. Some educators called for the organization of "intermediate industrial schools," or "junior industrial high schools." Others proposed that the upper grades of the elementary schools be devoted solely to "pre-vocational" education. Others, that the upper grades offer alternative courses of study: general, commercial and vocational.

Partisans of vocational training agreed that youngsters in the upper grades or in the junior high school were hardly prepared to choose wisely their course of studies and their life's work. This is where vocational guidance enters the picture. Implicit in the notion of "differentiation" is the elective principle. And implicit in the principle of election (a principle which by 1915 had been in retreat on the college level for at least a decade), is the guidance of children. Children needed direction; industry needed recruits. Out of these imperatives came the vocational guidance movement. The two movements went hand in hand. The same faces were active in both movements; their objectives were identical.

With the drive for industrial education each year gaining more and more momentum, a problem arose. The high school was, or was fast becoming, the educational ideal of the middle class throughout the length and breadth of the land. It was necessary to assure these parents who looked forward to sending their children to academic high schools that vocational training was not intended for their offspring. Vocational guidance was one answer. The "neighborhood school" concept was another. It was as evident then as now that neighborhoods tend to be inhabited by families of roughly similar social rank. Vocational training would not be for all children. The socioeconomic status of a neighborhood would dictate the particular course of study to be followed in the neighborhood school.

In the end, by 1917, advocates of industrial education could point to some successes: The proliferation of public vocational high schools, the proliferation of vocational courses in comprehensive high schools, the development of junior high schools, and the emergence of vocational guidance as a new specialty. They could especially point to the Smith-Hughes Act passed by the Congress and signed into law by President Wilson in February 1917. The act provided federal support for the teaching of agriculture, trade, industrial subjects and home economics on the secondary level in day, part-time, and evening schools. Provision was also made for the preparation of vocational teachers. It would be a rare Congress that would subsequently fail to pass new or supplementary legislation for vocational education.

The movement to redirect the school in the pre-World War I period was not just an urban phenomenon. In the country, rural spokesmen like Seamen A. Knapp and Liberty Hyde Bailey turned to the school as the agency to inculcate rural values, improve farming, and hopefully, to stop the drift to the city. Thus, from Cornell University in the 1890's, and later as chairman of the Country Life Commission (1908), horticulturist Bailey called for a new kind of rural education: "I want to see our country schools," Bailey wrote, "without screwed-down seats and to see children put to work with tools and soils and plants and problems." The public schools of Menominie, Wisconsin, perhaps best illustrated Bailey's ideal in practice. Agricultural clubs, 4-H, and Agricultural Extension Service brought into existence by the Smith-Lever Act (1914) also contributed toward the development of a new rural education. Everywhere, in the country and in the city, the schools were to be agents of social change. Nor was the university immune from pressures to be relevant. Particularly in the Midwest, public higher education quickened during the Progressive era to many of the same influences that were transforming the lower schools. The leading example is Wisconsin University during the La Follette period. There, under the vigorous presidency of Charles Van Hise, the University quickly became the pivotal element in that larger program of reform commonly referred to as "the Wisconsin idea." As Van Hise wrote, "I shall not be content until the beneficent influence of the University reaches every family in the State. This is my ideal of a State University."

IV

a. In the early decades of the 20th century, the public schools gradually, often reluctantly, changed, largely as the result of pressure from social critics, social workers, and social reformers. Although most of the pressure came from outside the educational establishment, there were some members of that establishment who legitimized the long-standing contention of school reformers that public schools had to be rethought in order to meet the needs of the new urban-industrial world.

America believes, as does no other country, that education must be based on a study of psychology. That this is so is due to no small degree to the influence of Edward Thorndike. Few psychologists have had this prodigious impact. For what had been previously vague and generalized descriptions of how people learn, Thorndike attempted to substitute something more specific and "scientific." Beginning in 1898 with the publication of his *Animal Intelligence,* a landmark in the history of psychology, in a brilliant career spanning forty years, Thorndike instructed two generations of American educators in the doctrines of connectionism. With his S→R bond psychology, Thorndike, operating from a base of power at Teachers College, Columbia University, was to deliver the decisive blow against the concepts of mental training, faculty psychology, and formal discipline of the mind. By the turn of the century, advocates of a mind possessed by faculties that could be trained by mental discipline were fighting a losing battle. As against a faculty of memory, or imagination or reason that man was taught to employ, many educators now concluded that man engages only in specific acts of memory, imagination, or reason; habit, rather than intelligence, ruled man's behavior. The old faith in a general or liberal education was now left without adequate foundation. Education became a matter of imparting specific items of information and building up particular habits. That this came about was due in no small measure to Thorndike's efforts.

From his experiments with animals, Thorndike derived his "Laws of Learning," by which S→R bonds or connections are made or broken: The Law of Readiness, The Law of Exercise, and the Law of Effect. The latter especially became a decisive weapon in the arsenal of school reformers, calling forth a new scrutiny of rewards, punishments, motivation, and incentives in education, and complementing the concern with child nature and pupil activity stressed earlier by Francis Parker and G. Stanley Hall. By virtue of the large number of students who studied under him, Thorndike's psychology of learning became for several decades virtually the official psychology in American schools of education.

Thorndike, with James McKeen Cattell and others, also helped launch the movement that goes under the rubric of the educational tests and measurement movement; the effort to express every dimension of the educational enterprise in quantitative form. The intellectual credo of the scientific educators as enunciated by Thorndike was: "Whatever exists, exists in some amount. To measure it is simply to know its varying amounts." With questionnaires, tests, scales, and statistics, American educators explored and sought to measure and evaluate every phase of school practice with typical American zeal and enthusiasm. As Harold Rugg was later to describe it:

> Under the leadership of Thorndike, Judd, Cubberley, Strayer, Terman, Whipple, Freeman, Gray, and others, the quantitative method began to be applied to the solution of educational problems. The fact finding era was launched; it was the day of the question-blank and the school survey. Learning was being experimentally investigated in the laboratory; "tests" had entered the classroom. Thorndike had made available the statistical procedure of the British biometricians (1903); standard deviations and coefficient of correlations were in the air. Promotion plans, the elimination and retardation of children, school building, the relation of efficiency of instruction to size of class, the measurement of educational products, and the objective investigation of educational processes—all these and other matters of administrative importance were being studied by the new quantitative technique.

Rugg summed it all by saying that it was all "one long orgy of tabulation." Efficiency was the desideratum.

Underlying educational efficiency was the need for a more sophisticated administration and management to cope with the incredible expansion in student numbers and the constantly growing range of subjects offered in the schools. The inspiration and model was sought in the technique developed in the industrial sector of the economy. As Cubberley put it: "Our schools are in a sense, factories in which the raw products (children) are to be shaped and fashioned into products to meet the various demands of life. . . . ." If schooling is conceived as a preparation for work, it was only natural to organize it on the model of the factory. School superintendents began to conceive themselves as plant managers, and proposed to treat education as a production process in which children were the raw materials, a development treated thoroughly in Raymond Callahan's *The Cult of Efficiency*.

Efficiency implied devising measures to evaluate performance in the various school subjects. But efficiency also implied the need to eliminate waste and to concentrate on essentials. Another part of the school reform movement took the form of curriculum revision toward the end of overcoming the traditional emphasis on "knowledge," and applying a new emphasis to practical preparation for life's needs. It devoted its energies to basing curricula reform upon the premise that curriculum-making consisted essentially in the analysis of the needs of American life and adjusting curricula to meet those needs. Of particular significance here was the work of the Committee on Economy of Time (in Education).

The Committee on Economy of Time was appointed in 1911 by the Department of Superintendents of the NEA and charged with the specific task of formulating recommendations for the systematic removal of "waste" from the school curriculum. The Committee published four major reports which appeared in the 14th, 15th, 17th, and 18th *Yearbooks* of the National Society for the Study of Education between 1911 and 1919. The Committee began with a detailed study of existing conditions in representative city school systems. The effort was not merely to discover what was actually being taught—itself a revealing enterprise—but also to determine how much students were really learning, as a basis for building norms of performance in each of the subject fields. Having made its survey of what was actually going on, the Committee proceeded to the business of working out the "minimum essentials" of a good education. Since it had defined satisfactory educational results as those which meet "the common needs of life in society," the next step was to specify those needs. The Committee subsequently embarked upon a vast Spencerian attempt to describe what people actually do in the course of "life in society" and to derive from this analysis the content of the school's curriculum. Notable among the Committee members was Franklin Bobbitt who in the 1920's (along with W. W. Charters) would carry out the recommendations of the Committee to their logical conclusion in his "life-activity" curriculum.

b. Thorndike's influence was potent. As mentioned earlier, by reason of the large numbers of students who studied under him, Thorndike's psychology of learning became for many years virtually the official psychology of schools of education throughout the country. Nevertheless, in the history of American education, John Dewey has no serious rival. He is accepted. He is entrenched. He is to American education what Aristotle was to medieval education, not *a* philosopher, but *the* philosopher, the most commanding figure in the history of American education.

Dewey was born in 1859, died in 1952. He was born during the administration of James Buchanan in the small, quiet town of Burlington, Vermont. He died in an apartment house in New York City, in the year that Dwight Eisenhower was elected president. In the intervening nine decades, America had been transformed from a country of farms, small towns, and open frontier into a nation of factories, sprawling metropoli, jet planes, and continental super-highways. In 1894, Dewey moved from the University of Michigan to the University of Chicago to become Chairman of its new Department of Philosophy, Psychology, and Pedagogy. He soon became an habitue of Hull House and a friend of Jane Addams. In 1896, Dewey established an experimental elementary school at the University. "The Laboratory School," as it was called, was one of the earliest experiments in progressive education. At the school the curriculum was organized around the occupations of home and industry; in short, children "learned by doing."

In 1899, Dewey delivered to parents and patrons of the Laboratory School a series of three lectures in which he tried to explain the New Education, especially the introduction of manual training, shopwork, sewing and cooking into elementary education. The talks were published as a tract, *School and Society*, which won immediate recognition and acclaim. Dewey's main thesis was that the traditional cultural and intellectual curriculum no longer met the needs of the new industrial society. The influences of home and community had ceased to be educative as they had been in the old agrarian society. The necessary discipline and character-building forces were no longer at work in the daily life of the child. The school would have to fill these needs. How? Occupations would have to be introduced which trained the child with relation to the physical and social realities of life. Each school must assume, said Dewey, the character of an "embryonic community life, active with occupations that reflect the life of the larger society." Central to this objective was the incorporation of manual training, shopwork, sewing, and cooking, into the elementary school program. Indeed, they were to *be* the school program.

In his 1915 work *Schools of To-Morrow* Dewey amplified and expanded the pedagogical doctrines set forth in *School and Society* and his earlier, too little read *My Pedagogic Creed*. Everywhere Dewey and his daughter traveled in their tour of the "Schools of To-Morrow"—Marietta Johnson's School of Organic Education, Caroline Pratt's Play School, Junius Merriam's Demonstration School, the Kindergarten at Teachers College, Columbia—they portrayed healthy, happy children playing and working in school shops and kitchens, as well as studying nature out of doors. But it was William Wirt's school in Gary, Indiana, that most nearly exemplified Dewey's ideal school and to it Dewey accords the most comprehensive treatment.

The boldly innovative Wirt had, among other innovations, devised a radical scheme of industrial education which started in the fourth grade, employed skilled laborers as instructors, used workshops as classrooms, employed children as apprentices in all the maintenance and repair and construction work needed in the school, and correlated all the subjects of instruction around "occupations." All this, Dewey wrote, furnishes children with a general outlook in life which "will fit them for their place in the world as adults."

The children's health and recreation were looked after. The schools were used as community centers. As Wirt explained, at Gary, children lead a complete life—eight hours a day of work-study-play. As *The New Republic*'s Randolph Bourne put it, the Gary schools represented "the most complete and admirable application yet attempted" of Dewey's educational philosophy. It remained only for Dewey, Bourne and *The New Republic* to speak up for the Gary schools for progressive America to be possessed with enthusiasm bordering on hysteria for Wirt's plan, a hysteria which came to an end only when it became embroiled finally in the New York City mayoralty race of 1917.

Schools of To-Morrow is the most complete and revolutionary break with America's educational past, the most complete and comprehensive attack on America's educational tradition—a tradition which emphasized mental development, academic training, linguistic study, and more. American education had hitherto been considered the most democratic the ingenuity of man could make it. But Dewey repudiated it as undemocratic and medieval, suitable only for the aristocratic and professional elite. American education had been language-oriented. Dewey repudiated it as a fetish: "There is a false educational god whose idolaters are legion, and whose cult influences the entire educational system. This is language-study—the study not of foreign languages, but of English, not in higher, but in primary education. It is almost an unquestioned assumption of educational theory and practice both, that the first three years of a child's school life shall be mainly taken up with learning to read and write his own language. . . ." This regime may have been adapted to past conditions, Dewey stated, but the present has its claims.

What sort of education was suitable for the present? An education built around "occupations." A curriculum centered around occupations fit in with the child-centered pedagogy of Francis Parker and G. Stanley Hall; what the children were interested in were occupations. It found support in the "new psychology" of Thorndike—that learning was specific, a product of action, of doing something. But especially, in formulating a curriculum built around occupations, Dewey was providing an answer to the exigencies of the time. The public schools had to meet the industrial and social needs of the hour. A curriculum organized around occupations would help meet the need of American industry for a pool of industrial labor. More important, it would help meet the need for a new moral and social discipline. Dewey was much concerned about the weakening of the bonds of social discipline and control: As he put it in a 1902 article significantly titled "The School As Social Center," "We might as well frankly recognize that many of the old agencies for moralizing mankind, and of keeping them living decent, responsible, and orderly lives, are losing in efficiency. . . ." Dewey looked to the schools to provide the necessary social discipline and cohesion essential to national unity. Occupations were to be introduced into the school, Dewey stressed, not to provide better seamstresses and cooks, not even as conveyors of education, even industrial education, but as a way of life, as "methods of living . . . not as distinct studies."

Nineteenth century education had been concerned with developing individuality and ambition, but to a generation grown increasingly concerned about the quality of social life, the rampant individualism inherent in the child-centered views of education promulgated by Parker and Hall had to be domesticated. This was Dewey's accomplishment. To him, an education built around occupations best fostered the social traits which schools had to inculcate in children. Where active work is going on, there is developed a spirit of social cooperation and community life. Thus Dewey hoped to bring about the new society where cooperation rather than competition would rule. In his own words, "When the school introduces and trains each child of society into membership within such a little community—saturating him with the spirit of service . . . we shall have the deepest and best guarantee of a larger society which is worthy, lovely, and harmonious."

Dewey is difficult to read. His prose style is ambiguous and frequently opaque. Other innovations like the Montessori Method imported from Italy, and various native forms of individualized instruction involving differentiated curricula, homogeneous grouping, supervised study, and flexible grading and promotion as exemplified by the Pueblo Plan, the Batavia Plan, the Cambridge Plan, and Frederick Burk's fascinating work at San Francisco State Normal School with self-teaching textbooks, were then competing for the American educator's attention. It is interesting to speculate how fundamentally Dewey's thought would have influenced education in this country (and abroad) had he not found in Professor William Heard Kilpatrick of Teachers College, Columbia University, a remarkably persuasive expounder of his philosophy, especially its application in the form of the "project method" of teaching.

V The Gary School Plan was a landmark in the transformation of the elementary school. But between 1893 and 1918, a revolution occurred in American secondary education also, at least in theory. At the beginning stands the NEA's Report of the Committee of Ten, and at the end, the NEA's Report of the Commission on the Reorganization of Secondary Education. At the heart of this revolution lay a shift in the conception of the high school, of what should be its primary goals and responsibilities, its organization, and its curriculum.

In 1893, the secondary school was viewed as an institution designed to prepare students "for the duties of life" via the mastery of academic subject matter. The most memorable document endorsing this view was the NEA's 1893 Report of the Committee of Ten. By 1918, however, the high school was regarded as an institution which should educate *all* youth to the age of eighteen and prepare them for life in a manner deemphasizing intellectual development and academic subjects. The document best representative of this view is another NEA report—the Report of the Commission on the Reorganization of Secondary Education. It set the tone and provided the terminology for all quasi-official educational statements concerning the high school until the early 1950's.

The Committee of Ten reckoned without an awareness of the immigrants and their children, reckoned without an awareness of the new urban-industrial civilization, and without an awareness that after 1890 high school enrollment would rise from 360,000 to 1,115,000 in 1910 to 2,500,000 in 1920! The creation of a system of mass secondary education for the New America would not simply be an extension of the old secondary education system. It would be different in function. It would have its own books, its own teacher-training institutions, its own ideology, its own nomenclature.

By 1913 a new generation of educators was ready to make a complete break with the world of the Committee of Ten. In that year the NEA appointed a twenty-seven-member commission significantly called the "Commission on the Reorganization of Secondary Education," headed by Clarence Kingsley, an official of the Massachusetts State Department of Education. Also on the Commission were representatives of the United States Bureau of Education, the YMCA, the Ethical Culture Society, as well as public school principals or administrators, professors of education, and two college or university presidents. Subjects previously ignored thrust themselves forward in subcommittees; business education, home economics, industrial arts and agricultural education, and physical education. Five years in the making, the Commission reported finally in 1918. The Report was given a quasi-official endorsement by the U. S. Bureau of Education which printed and distributed an edition of 130,000 copies. While it is difficult to judge the importance in practice of the report, it seems clear that it both reflected and shaped a growing consensus among schoolmen on the broad purposes of secondary education. It consummated, at least in theory, a revolution in American secondary education.

The Report was a masterful summary of progressive educational doctrine current at the time. Its opening sentence proclaimed that secondary education should be determined by the needs of society, the character of the students to be educated, and the knowledge of the best educational theory and practice available at the time. The Commission pointed to the changes taking place in these three areas of concern—all of which called for extreme modification of the curriculum and organization of secondary education. The Commission repudiated the goal of mastery of academic subject matter as a goal for American secondary education. In the latter's place it substituted the seven "Cardinal Principles": Health, Command of Fundamental Processes, Worthy Home Membership, Vocation, Citizenship, Worthy Use of Leisure, Ethical Character. All subjects in high school curriculum were now to be reorganized in order to contribute to the achievement of the Cardinal Principles.

That such a change should have taken place in just 20 years is staggering until one remembers the context. The Cardinal Principles testify to the exigencies of American society. The school, the Commission argued, "is the one agency that may be controlled definitely and consciously . . . for the purpose of unifying the people." Schools, the Commission argued, should enable "each member to develop his personality through activities designed for the well-being of his fellow-members and of society as a whole." What the high school had to undertake was a commitment to provide each student with an education for *complete living*: "It is the firm belief of this commission that secondary education in the United States must aim at nothing less than complete and worthy living for all youth . . ."

Increasingly, in the post-World War I period, college and university faculties scornfully turned away from the problems of public secondary education, which they now saw as the preoccupation of some strange and lesser breed of academician. Educationists were happy to see them withdraw. Here, one educational leader asserted of the Cardinal Principles, "was the Declaration of Independence of American secondary education." The field was now left to professional educators with little authoritative criticism or opposition. In the meantime, normal schools became Teachers Colleges and Schools of Education, the latter becoming increasingly specialized, with a high degree of isolation as well as autonomy. The mental world of the professional educationist became increasingly separated from that of the academic scholar, a separation to be rectified only in the 1950's.

VI a. The chief tendency in American school reform in the 20th century may be summed up in one word—more—more money, more teachers, more buildings, and more responsibilities. By World War I school reformers had arrived at a conception of the public school as one whose major functions were vastly expanded beyond formal instruction to encompass responsibilities formerly left to other agencies. Of course, schools varied in infinite ways from the model. At the time of World War I, as the new school system was taking form, 60% of American teachers still worked in rural schools, many of them in one-room schoolhouses. And there was, of course, considerable resistance to the new education. The twenties would bear witness to Fundamentalist hostility to science in the classroom and the efforts to impose a narrow, uncritical patriotism in the classroom. Still, by 1917, many urban public school systems had vastly enlarged their activities to take into account the physical, social, recreational, and vocational needs of children. In the 1920's school reformers went still further by demanding that the school must assume responsibility for the child's social and emotional adjustment, though this aspect of educational innovation in the twenties has been largely neglected or overlooked in favor of the Rousseauistic, romantic ideal of self-expression and child-centered education.

World War I marks a great divide in the history of American education. The war with its carnage, and then the lost peace, were taken as a manifestation of a depraved and bankrupt civilization. In the 1920's, the younger generation especially lost faith in the pre-war political and social organisms. They turned their backs on social salvation to search for personal salvation. The restraints and shackles of Puritanism and Victorianism were to be overthrown. America was to be redeemed by Art and Freud, by Creative Self-Expression and Psychoanalysis.

In the 1920's art took on the aspects of a mystique. The world was to be redeemed by Art—by the creative spirit. Here was something which could not be corrupted by the machine and money, the two reigning gods of American life. "Take the lid off youth" was one of the slogans of the 1920's. Every child was born with the potential to be creative. The task of the school was to surround the child with an environment which would draw out this creative power. At Margaret Naumburg's Walden School and Caroline Pratt's City and Country School, children were encouraged to express through art, music, drama, dance, rhythmics, and creative writing what they had seen, heard, and felt. Which is not to say that some educational innovators in the 20's did not try to keep content and discipline and subject matter categories; as for example, Helen Parkhurst's Dalton Method, and the Winnetka Plan in which Carleton Washburne in the public schools of Winnetka, Illinois, tried to combine the traditional with the progressive.

The impact of art on progressive education is well-known; that of Freud less well known. Freud came to America in 1909 to deliver a general exegesis of psychoanalytic theory at Clark University. His lectures dealt with the phenomena of the neuroses, the unconscious and its mechanisms, problems of infantile sexuality, and the interpretation of dreams. The lectures were carried in the influential medical journals. Thanks to Drs. Abraham A. Brill and Ernest Jones, Freud's work was disseminated to a large American public. With startling speed Freudian doctrines made headway. By World War I, psychoanalysis was a popular topic of conversation among intellectuals and sophisticates.

Freud himself wrote little on education. His work was applied to education by a group of disciples in psychology, in social work, and especially in the mental hygiene movement, a strange compound of Freudian psychoanalysis, Watsonian behaviorism, and Adlerian individual psychology. Even before Hitler annexed Austria and drove Freud and his followers into exile, the theory and practice of psychoanalysis were more widely spread and widely accepted in the United States than in any other country. However, in the process of becoming Americanized, as it were, some important aspects of Freud's original theory were sloughed off, treated as almost nonexistent; for example, Freud's pessimism about the malleability of human nature, and his postulants about the instinctual basis of aggressiveness and hostility in children. As interpreted in America, the child is a *tabula rasa*, and any defects which subsequently develop are the fault of uncontrollable circumstances, or of the ignorance or malice of its parents who mar what would otherwise be a perfect, or at least well-adjusted, human being. Freud was Americanized with the aid of the "individual psychology" of Alfred Adler, and especially John B. Watson's psychology of behaviorism. Behaviorists dispensed with consciousness and introspective methods and studied the human organism in its environment, using the methods of animal psychology. Behaviorism embraced a radical environmentalism most congenial to the American temper and to the American belief in the child as the hope for the future.

In the writings of spokesmen for the mental hygiene movement, like William Alanson White, William Healy, Adolf Meyer, Jessie Taft, and William H. Burnham, the pattern for a new school theory and practice can be found, a pattern in which the following are key strands: (a) the family was a sick institution, a source of neurosis; (b) there was no such thing as a bad child, only bad parents and maladjusted or sick children; (c) maladjustment, anti-social behavior, and neurosis could be prevented or ameliorated; (d) the emotional life of the individual was the key to behavior; (e) the emotions could be molded or trained or controlled if the right environment was supplied in childhood; (childhood, in the notable words of Dr. White, was "the golden period of mental hygiene"); (f) the elementary school was the strategic agency for the training of the emotions and, finally, (g) the school's essential task was the social adjustment of the child. In the words of Dr. White: "Education has been . . . too much confined to teaching; it needs to be developed as a scheme for assisting and guiding the developing personality." But first the principles and practices of the school would have to be transformed.

Teachers were to be taught to recognize that they are the sole agents by which responsible individuals are created out of the debris left by parents, that the classroom was inevitably an emotionally charged situation which only a psychoanalytically sophisticated teacher could really comprehend, and that inhibitions and repression were harmful to the child's development. Teachers would have to provide love and support and a more permissive atmosphere in the classroom. They were also taught that authority was dangerous for the child. Fear of authority makes the child repress his instincts and emotions which will then dominate the unconscious, instead of being acted out and controlled. Especially among persons concerned with maladjustment and neurosis and juvenile delinquency, school failure and nonpromotion were prime targets in the 1920's. Feelings of inferiority were caused by failure. "If the example in arithmetic is not solved," according to Dr. Wilhelm Lay, "the pupil is much more likely to take his gratification from the dream life of the moving picture shows." Reality must not be made too harsh and uncompromising, so that dreams of doing, and introversion or anti-social behavior would be less tempting. Failure and retardation would have to be eliminated by minimizing or abandoning formal courses of instruction, academic standards, and competition and achievement. In their place would be substituted projects, play, and creative self-expression through art and other aesthetic activities.

b. To many, hedonism was the hallmark of the twenties. The labels given to the decade are indicative—the "Age of the Flapper," and the "Roaring Twenties." In the spirit of the time, F. Scott Fitzgerald has Amory Blaine in *This Side of Paradise* declare: "Here was a new generation . . . grown up to find all Gods dead, all wars fought, all faiths in man shaken." All they knew was that "America was going on the greatest, gaudiest spree in history." Everyone wanted to be young and gay. Parents were to be emancipated. Youthful wives wanted to be flappers; to "lead their own lives." Chanting slogans like "come out of the kitchen" and "never darn a sock," they rebelled against the age-old household tasks of women. The new woman was to be freed from the responsibilities of child-rearing;

the school would educate the "whole child." Much of middle class America seemed to be going Greenwich Village, a spirit evoked faithfully in Malcolm Cowley's *Exile's Return.* It all added up to a post-war revolution in manners and morals. School reform movements, as they emerged in the 20's, were in part a faithful reflection of this mood. The child, too, was to be freed—freed from the restraints of the traditional teacher and the shackles of the authoritarian school, freed by Art and Freud.

But it is erroneous to think of the 20's solely in terms of Jazz and Booze and Prosperity. The 20's were also a time of grave internal dissension, of social disorganization, a period of serious division and divisiveness in American life. The 20's were a time of ugly flareups against Negroes, Jews, Roman Catholics, a time of 100% Americanism and intolerance of difference. A time when America's daily reading material concerned crime waves and the revolt of youth and the revolution in manners and morals. A time when the Ku Klux Klan blossomed. A time of the Red Scare, the Sacco-Vanzetti and Scopes trials, of prohibition and immigration restriction, and the too little remembered Americanization Movement. Thus, under the auspices of the National Americanization Committee, and utilizing slogans like "English first" and "Many peoples, but one nation," the immigrants were to be stampeded into citizenship, forced to adopt the English language and to show unquestioned reverence for existing American institutions. It was inevitable that German and other foreign languages would come to be regarded as symptoms of disloyalty. In 1919 the Nebraska Legislature passed a law prohibiting any person or teacher in a private, denominational, parochial or public school to teach any language but English to children who had not successfully passed the 8th grade. But in *Meyer* vs. *State of Nebraska* the Supreme Court in 1923 ruled that such legislation was arbitrary and without reasonable relation to any end within the competence of the state. In 1922 Oregon passed perhaps the last and certainly one of the most severe Americanization laws; a measure requiring parents to send their children to public elementary schools. This too was overturned by the U. S. Supreme Court in *Pierce* vs. *Society of Sisters* (1923). The Court unanimously maintained that the Oregon law unreasonably interfered with the liberty of parents to direct the education of their children. The child was not the "mere creature of the state"; "children belonged primarily to parents and only to a limited extent to the state." With these statutes the Americanization movement peaked.

As a workaday endeavor to teach English and civics to immigrants in public evening schools, and as a stimulus to all phases of adult education, the Americanization movement took root and endured. In the end, while the movement for the redemption of the alien ebbed in the early 20's, the old drive for rejection of the immigrant passed all previous boundaries. After 1924 with the passage of the restrictive "Quota Act" by the Congress, the question of educating the immigrants almost passed from the scene.

c. The 20's were a time then when America felt deeply threatened from within. "They have" observed French visitor, Andre Siegfried, in the 1920's, "a vague, uneasy fear of being overwhelmed from within, and of suddenly finding one day that they are no longer themselves." In a quest for security and homogeneity, some Americans, the 100 percenters and the Ku Kluxers, turned to behavior control through the techniques of restriction, repression, and violence. Other equally perplexed and fearful Americans, including an important segment of liberal thinkers and liberal organizations, eschewing methods of violence or legal coercion, turned to behavior control through the more benign techniques of psychology and the social sciences. For them, mental health, i.e., social and emotional adjustment, was to serve as the new unifying ideal. As usual, all paths led to the schools. Behind a formulistic rhetoric which bowed ceremoniously in the direction of "the needs of the child," there came a powerful school reform movement which aimed at the goal of the prediction and control of behavior for the purpose of directing it into socially approved channels. This was sometimes made explicit. Thus Franklin Bobbitt in 1925 described education as "a carefully conditioned and carefully guided series of normal life-experiences," with the goal of "the right upbringing of human beings." Patty Smith Hill's "conduct curriculum" for the Kindergarten which she directed in the 20's at Teachers College, Columbia, had the same priorities.

But there was something more involved in school reform activities of the 20's than a response to the needs of parents of the new middle class. Something more than a response to the social crises, something more than a quest for security. There was also a utopian element in school reform activities that must be reckoned with. The chiliastic hopes that characterized movements for social reform in the Progressive era survived in the 20's in the field of education. School reformers were like lay or secular preachers who sought to reform the world by means of the reeducation and training of children. School reformers were possessed with a vision of new schools producing a new American man and a new era. Through the right education, every child was to become a happy, well-adjusted, productive individual and a valuable social asset. The pervasive influence of the mental hygiene movement created the climate in which such dreams could thrive.

There is also, in school reform movements of the 20's, one suspects, a conviction that the majority of children would be unable to cope with the demands of an academically rigorous program, a conviction which the IQ movement helped foster. Despite the importance of the IQ movement, we know little as to its beginnings in this country. The Frenchman Alfred Binet's test for measuring intelligence was introduced into the U. S. in 1910 by Henry H. Goddard of the Vineland (N. J.) Training School for the Feeble-Minded. But it was Stanford professor Lewis M. Terman's adaptation of Binet, and popularization of the IQ as an index of relative intelligence, the ratio of mental age to chronological age, in *The Measurement of Intelligence* (1916) and *The Intelligence of School Children* (1919) which really launched the movement in the schools. Terman believed that intelligence was hereditary; that the intelligence test measured "innate intelligence." Terman proceeded to divide children into five groups—very superior, superior, average, inferior, and very inferior, and to call for differentiation of curricula and methods for each group. The critical datum: the superior were only 15%, the rest were average or below.

Initially, intelligence tests met with skepticism. But World War I stimulated the development of the Alpha and Beta group intelligence test, which subsequently made mass testing possible. The War also made intelligence testing respectable. As Professor Robert M. Yerkes put it, psychology had "helped to win the war," and had "demonstrated its right to serious consideration in . . . human engineering." After the War extensive use of the tests began in primary and secondary schools, and even universities adopted them for purposes of screening admission. The tests were used to guide children, to help break the educational lockstep, and to individualize instruction; but they too frequently served to label children as irredeemably stupid or average. In the pages of the *New Republic* in 1922 Walter Lippmann questioned the meaning of the tests, whether intelligence is fixed by heredity, and whether the tests actually measure intelligence. But it was losing cause. The IQ tests with their assumptions of "native intelligence" for many children were to become a modern form of infant damnation.

      d. When the public school emerged as the agency responsible for the deliberate adjustment of personality, school reformers could ask no more. Now they had to implement their vision in the classroom. This meant educating teachers, educating laymen and parents, and reorganizing school principles and practices according to the new point of view. This was one of the tasks of the Progressive Education Association.

Even before World War I there were many progressive schools in existence: Marietta Johnson's School of Organic Education, Fairhope, Alabama; E. R. Smith's Park School, Baltimore; Caroline Pratt's City and Country School, *nee* the Play School, New York City, Margaret Naumburg's Walden School, New York City; A. E. Morgan's Moraine Park School, Dayton, Ohio; Francis Froelicher's Oak Land Country Day School, Philadelphia; William Hocking's Shady Hill School, Cambridge, Massachusetts, and others. The schools differed among themselves. But they shared several characteristics in common: they were overwhelmingly upper middle-class in terms of sponsorship, support, and clientele. And they subscribed to the list of basic principles, the "new Articles of Faith;" Freedom, Child-Initiative, The Active School, Child Interest, Creative Self-Expression, and Personality and Social Adjustment, as catalogued in Harold Rugg and Ann Shumaker, *The Child-Centered School* (1928).

After the war, it was easier than ever to secure a hearing for new educational principles. In the spring of 1919 a small coterie of wealthy Washington matrons, private schoolteachers, and a sprinkling of public school people, under the leadership of Stanwood Cobb, a young English instructor at the U. S. Naval Academy and soon-to-be Headmaster of the Chevy Chase Country Day School, organized the Progressive Education Association. Charles W. Eliot was persuaded to serve as honorary president. What had formerly been a rather loosely joined revolt against pedagogical formalism now gained vigorous organizational voice.

Only a few people were involved, but the PEA was launched as no modest venture. The PEA was not simply to be an association of private school people and patrons to clear and channel private school information or encourage the proliferation of progressive private schools. "It must not be thought," Cobb declared, "that either our purpose or our effort was confined to a group of private schools. Nothing could be farther from the truth. Our aim from the very beginning had in it very little of modesty. We aimed at nothing short of reforming the entire school system in America." From the beginning their something of a religious fervor suffused the Association's activities. Progressive education, as Cobb put it, was "a great humanitarian movement for the benefit of the world's children. . . . It is a Cause—it enlists parents as well as educators in its loyal and aggressive ranks. It is willing to make sacrifices, to endure, to battle for what it considers right." Through the new education, Progressives hoped to secure the final abolition of unhappiness, the final extirpation of all social problems. Through progressive education, every child could become a creative, happy, well-adjusted person.

The Progressive Education Association developed slowly. For about five years informal newsletters and bulletins were its chief means of publicity. For money it depended on individual contributions and even tried a chain letter system. Then in 1924, a wealthy donor made it possible for PEA to publish *Progressive Education*, a handsome, high-quality journal which soon established a national reputation, and the association was on its way. In 1926 the PEA was able to hire a full-time professional executive secretary. In that year John Dewey consented to assume the post of honorary president. Between 1926 and 1928 membership climbed from about 3,500 to 6,600 and the PEA was busy cementing ties abroad with the New Education Fellowship, and A. S. Neill and Beatrice Ensor of England, Dr. Adolphe Ferriere of Switzerland, Dr. Ovide Decroly of Belgium, and Dr. Elizabeth Rotten of Germany, the European wing of progressive education, and at home quickly securing a place in American elementary education. During the summer of 1927 pioneer courses in the behavior problems of children were given to teachers and teachers-in-training at Harvard, the University of Kansas, Michigan, Peabody College for Teachers, and the University of Washington. By 1928, Margaret Naumburg could assert, "anything less than progressive education is quite out of date in America."

Miss Naumburg's boast was a bit premature. The PEA's growth had been impressive, but much work remained to be done, as leaders of progressive education realized. In 1932, Cobb described progressive education as having reached a stage characteristic of the evolution of all successful movements, where in spite of continuing opposition to some of its principles, it was on the whole in a strategic position in regards public opinion. A large group of leaders in the educational world not only accept the most important tenets of the movement—but proclaim them. "Should the Association by some catastrophe cease to exist," Cobb declared, "the principles of progressive education would continue to invade fields of educational theory and practice. This is a tide which nothing can stop."

Yet there was need for much more work. There was no widespread infiltration of public (or private) schools yet. Cobb estimated the number of people committed to progressive education as but one-half of one percent of the population. But this numerically small group "happens to be, fortunately, a superior group as regards intelligence, financial circumstances, and social leadership." There was a need to educate the public as well as still unenlightened educators to the values of progressive education. But here was the problem. The values of progressive education are largely "subtle values of personality . . . not easily discernible to the mediocre and skeptical mentality." Such values, Cobb concluded, "belong to the category of things concerning which Christ remarked succinctly: "Those that have eyes, let them see." In the 1930's, those that had eyes which could see, really see, proliferated. The 30's were the progressives' decade.

VII

a. Progressive education scored some great successes during the Depression. Metaphorically speaking, progressive education had been waiting for just such a moment. Now, more than ever, in the confusion and demoralization bound to follow in the wake of a crisis such as a worldwide depression was the time to turn to the schools and the education of the "whole child"; to turn to the schools and the emotional and personality adjustment of children.

On Thursday, October 24, 1929, scrambling, yelling traders dumped 12,895,000 shares of stock on the New York Stock Exchange. On the Tuesday next, 16,410,000. The stock market collapse marked the beginning of the longest and most severe depression in the nation's history. Unemployment began to mount. A year after the Crash, 6,000,000 men walked the streets. The farmer, who had seen little of the prosperity of the 20's, was devastated by the depression. Fear of the breadline drifted up into the middle-class. At first the country refused to believe what was happening. "Life was just a bowl of cherries, don't take it serious, it's too mysterious," was a refrain from one of the hit songs of the winter of 1931. But soon confidence gave way to worry and worry to bitterness.

As the depression ground past its third year, an unprecedented fear seeped through the nation—fear, gloom, violence, talk of revolution. In the early 30's food riots were common, as was labor violence. Demagogues like Father Coughlin and Francis Townsend and Huey Long made thousands of converts, as did the Khaki Shirts and the Minute Men. "There'll be a revolution for sure," a Los Angeles banker predicted, "the farmers will rise up. So will labor. The Reds will run the country—or maybe the Fascists."

Youth was one of the prime casualties of the Depression. It was estimated as of 1935 that 4,200,000 youths, ages 16–24, were out of school and out of work. Not only high school youth but college youth had little to look forward to but unemployment. In 1934 college graduates organized the Association of Unemployed College Alumni, while undergraduates in increasing numbers became militant in their demands for radical social measures. There were millions of youths, too many of them, idle, broke, brooding, leading a life of "tragic purposelessness," many of them homeless wanderers, boy and girl tramps, "nomads of the depression," a new class of the socially disinherited, and an enormous problem. One of the major accomplishments of the American Youth Commission, appointed by the American Council on Education in 1935, was a survey conducted in Maryland in the 1930's and published as *Youth Tell Their Story* (1938). A nation fearful of Communism and Nazism, struggling with a massive economic depression, finally became aware of the despair of its own youth. By far the most prevalent attitude of youth surveyed was one of discontent and discouragement. "Which way America's youth?" was a question many Americans were asking by the mid-30's, glancing over their shoulders at youth in Europe. In Europe, youth was on the march. "Whoever has the youth has the future," was one of Hitler's oft-repeated phrases. Would an American youth movement develop? If it did, what direction would it take?

Democracy was being challenged within and without. The devotion of America's youth to democracy could no longer be taken for granted. "If someone came along with a line of stuff in which I could really believe," said one youth in the winter of '32, "I'd follow him pretty near anywhere." Youth had to be kept safe and sane and wholesome and well-adjusted. The schools, as one educational leader put it, must assure growth in "socially desirable directions." In this context it was not surprising that school reformers would score some of their greatest breakthroughs during the 30's. Now, more than ever, in the confusion and demoralization bound to follow in the wake of a crisis such as a worldwide depression, was the time to turn to the elementary schools and the education of the "whole child." Most revealing here are a series of publications in the 1930's by the influential Educational Policies Commission of the National Education Association.

Of course the economic crisis produced cutbacks in the schools, with many communities decreasing their school spending severely. Retrenchment was the order of the day: shortened school day and year, reduced expenses for services and curriculum, salaries and equipment, building and repairs, and cutting of "fads and frills." Nevertheless, in the 30's, many Americans turned to the schools to succor the child and preserve the stability of the nation. Thus, in the 30's, the PEA reached its peak membership of over 10,000. And by the mid-30's, thanks to grants from the Carnegie Foundation and especially the General Education Board ($1,500,000 alone from the GEB between 1933 and 1941), the Association was more affluent and active than ever. On October 31, 1938, *Time* magazine featured Frederick L. Redefer, Executive Secretary of the PEA, on its cover; the story was entitled, "Progressive's Progress." *Time* quoted Redefer as saying "We are no longer a rebel group." Twenty years ago, he said, progressive education was mainly a private school affair. Now it was predominantly a public school affair with strongholds in the schools of New York City, Chicago, Los Angeles, Cleveland, Detroit, San Francisco, and elsewhere. It was time to attend to the high school.

b. By 1929–30 about 4.8 million students were enrolled in the high schools, about 51 percent of the age group from 14–17 years old. By the 1930's there was an army of youth in the high school. Indeed, one of the outstanding educational achievements of the 20's and 30's was to make high school education almost as universal as the preceding 100 years had made elementary education. Between 1920–1940 high school enrollment rose from 4,800,000 to 7,100,000. This was an extraordinary accomplishment. Yet all was not well. By 1929 the Lynds in *Middletown* could already describe the high school as a "city within a city," without clear educational purpose. And George S. Courts even earlier, in 1922, could persuasively argue that despite the rapid increase in high school enrollments, inherited indicia of social status played an enormous role in determining entrance to secondary school, the likelihood of remaining in school, and selection to curricula within schools. In surveying the state of education at the secondary level in 1934, E. W. Butterfield, then Commissioner of Education in Connecticut, pointed out the change in social and economic makeup of at least half of the high school population, a group which had not been present in the secondary schools of 1900. This group he termed "The New Fifty Per Cent." In an essay, much discussed and quoted at the time, Butterfield pointed out the needs of this new group, which differed considerably from the former college preparatory makeup of the high school. Most urgent, as mentioned earlier, the isolation and alienation of the adolescent, heightened by economic insecurity, left educators fearful that this condition would be capitalized on by some demagogue, unless they found some alternatives. The high schools would have to serve the social and emotional needs of adolescents while at the same time instill in them democratic ideals. Against this background the PEA was to formulate programs and curricula adjusted to the "needs" of all youth in secondary schools.

In the 1920's, the PEA was concerned with transforming elementary education; finally in the 30's, financed by several millions in foundations money, it turned its attention to reconstructing secondary education according to the "needs of adolescence"; that is, 1920 style mental hygiene principles in 1930 dress.

The PEA's effort to reconstruct the high school was restrained and hampered by college entrance requirements. Consequently, in the early 30's, the PEA created a Commission on the Relation of School and College to conduct an experiment in progressive education at the secondary school level, the so-called "Thirty Schools Study" or "Eight-Year Study." The thirty schools represented a cross-section of American secondary schools, in which preparation for college was a major objective, and which were prepared to undertake "some significant and reasonably thoroughgoing experimentation in a generally progressive direction." Some 300 colleges and universities would waive certain entrance requirements for graduates of the thirty high schools. In the meantime, the PEA created several other commissions: the Commission on Secondary School Curriculum, and the Commission on Human Relations whose goals were to formulate a new program for the high schools. As a criterion for curricula building, each commission built its program on the "needs of youth." And what youth needed was set out in a series of books, such as Vivian T. Thayer, *Reorganizing Secondary Education*, Caroline Zachry, *Emotion and Conduct in Adolescence*, Lois Meek, *The Personal-Social Development of Boys and Girls*, Alice Keliher, *Life and Growth*. Not surprisingly, they were similar to the old Cardinal Principles: instruction in personal living, in personal-social relationships, in social-civic relationships, and in economic relationships. As Thayer put it, ". . . the supreme mission of secondary education at this time is to help people find themselves anew in their personal, social and economic relationships, and to develop a working philosophy of values which will give meaning, zest, and purpose to their living." The question to be put to the secondary school was, in Thayer's words, does it "help the adolescent develop the personality essential to effective living in a democratic society?"

The Thirty Schools Project began in 1933 and terminated in 1941. It reported in five volumes, summarized in Wilford Aiken, *The Story of the Eight Year Study*. The essentials of the plan were carried out; the results inconclusive. Progressive high schools "can prepare students for college with as good or with slightly better results than traditional schools." Still, reformers seized upon the study as a vindication of progressive education. *Time* magazine announced that many considered the final report "a death sentence for the traditional system of high school education." The Commission proposed the following primary objectives for the American high school: that every student should learn to read, write, and speak the English language with skill, and understand mathematics. That textbook teaching should give way to teaching about problems of modern living. That the concerns of youth should be the heart of the curriculum. And finally that the schools should promote the students' physical, mental, and moral health. The report, appearing in the middle of the war, never received much attention, but the same theses would be reiterated in the mid-forties by the American Council on Education, and would culminate finally in "the life adjustment" movement of the late 40's and early 50's, discussed below.

c. The Great Depression alerted the American public schools to the problem of youth. But schools alone couldn't cope with the problem; the federal government was forced to step in through agencies like the Civilian Conservation Corps, the Works Progress Administration, and the National Youth Administration. The Civilian Conservation Corps was originally established in 1933 to relieve unemployment of youth between the ages of 17–23, and to help conserve the country's natural resources. Inevitably, formal and informal educational programs were developed for the corpsmen. Instruction in forestry was the first subject offered through the Forestry Service, then came classes in general and vocational and crafts education conducted by the Army for all enrollees who desired them. Education classes quickly grew and by 1939 attendance was officially estimated at 91.3 percent of the average strength of the Corps. By 1942, almost two-thirds of the enlistees in the C.C.C. had taken part in some sort of job training and about one-third had attended formal classes on every conceivable subject. By 1942, over 100,000 had been taught to read and write; over 5,000 of the men had received eighth-grade certificates; over 5,000 had received high school diplomas; and 96 had actually received college degrees. A total of almost $3 billion was spent on the C.C.C. between 1933 and 1941.

During the Depression years, the federal government also aided education through the Works Progress Administration, which organized thousands of nursery schools, taught well over a million illiterates to read and write, and ran a vast adult educational program. In addition W.P.A. funds purchased school lunches, vocational and recreational equipment, and almost 6,000 new buildings for state public school systems.

For those youth who chose or who were able to remain at home, the government organized the National Youth Administration under the W.P.A. in 1935. By 1942, N.Y.A. had offered part-time employment on public projects to more than 1,750,000 out-of-school youth, and a work program for high school and college students that involved more than 1,800,000 young people. The N.Y.A., like the C.C.C. was abandoned during the early months of the Second World War. However useful the federally-funded programs were, they tended to bypass state and local civic and educational authorities and antagonize professional educators, as well as the National Education Association. World War II quickly put an end to the protests and the programs which simply vanished into history.

   d. It is ironic that the PEA's zenith was so close to its nadir. At the top in the late 20's, within a decade, the Association was moribund. By the late 30's, the PEA was under fire from assorted intellectuals and scholars as the quintessence of anti-intellectualism, and from a ragtag of critics as sentimental or subversive or both. Internecine quarrels further weakened the Association. In the 30's, a group of educators, most of them a Teachers College, Columbia group, including George Counts, William Heard Kilpatrick, Harold Rugg, R. Bruce Raup, Goodwin Watson, John L. Childs, John Dewey, and Theodore Brameld tried to move the PEA in the direction of a radical politics. They called themselves "The Social Reconstructionists" or "The Social Frontiersmen." The first major formulation of the "frontier" position was Counts' *Dare The Schools Build A New Social Order* (1932). In an address to the Progressive Education Association, Counts boldly called on the teachers of the nation to organize and "deliberately reach for power and then make the most of their conquest." The schools were to be transformed into centers for the building of the new society along collectivistic lines. Counts called upon teachers to use peaceful persuasion, but as a last resort, "to follow the method of revolution." The PEA responded in 1933 with a *Call to the Teachers of the Nation* to work for the "new social order." In the meantime, the radicals founded a journal, *The Social Frontier*, (1934) which was to be for ten years the main organ of the reconstructionist faction within the progressive education movement. All of this was an egregious tactical error. The radicals appealed to teachers to usher in the New Order; teachers were frightened. They appealed to labor—the unions scorned them. They appealed to intellectuals—who scoffed at the idea of schools as agents of social reconstruction. In the meantime, the child-centered educators were unable to challenge effectively the rapid politicizing of educational theory by the social reconstructionists or to formulate their own position in a convincing manner.

The social frontiersmen helped dissipate the strength of the PEA and helped discredit it in the eyes of the public. In the late 30's and early 40's, the PEA and progressive education came under increasing fire. More and more its publicized victories called forth a counter-reaction, from college presidents like R. M. Hutchins and liberal intellectuals such as Walter Lippmann for its hostility to liberal culture, from Catholic philosophers like Jacques Maritain for its hostility to religion, and from a handful of educators for its neglect of the fundamentals. Indeed in 1938 a group of educators including Michael John Demiashkevich, Isaac L. Kandel, William Chandler Bagley, Guy Whipple, and Frederick Eby organized the short-lived Essentialist Committee for the Advancement of American Education to fight progressive education and advance the claims of "essentialism" in education. Even a disillusioned John Dewey in 1938 was moved to exclaim that "the fundamental issue is not of new versus old education, nor of progressive versus traditional education, but . . . what anything whatever must be to be worthy of the name *education*."

In the early 40's, the foundations withdrew their support and membership plummeted. The very words "progressive education," in the 20's a talisman of success, had by now become tainted. In 1944 the PEA changed its name to American Education Fellowship (in 1953 the group shifted back to its former name). But now it was all downhill. Originally conceived as a lay organization, the PEA more and more became a clique of professional educators and the PEA was becoming increasingly isolated from sources of lay support. The Association folded in 1955, a casualty of the lacerating attacks of its critics and of its own inadequacies.

For an organization calling itself "progressive," the PEA had become, by the early 1950's, startlingly out of touch with the challenges and tensions of the Space Age, the Cold War, and the revolution in race relations. Despite its decline, however, well trained cadres were waiting in the wings to take up the torch of progressive education. In the 40's leadership in American public education passed from the PEA to more orthodox centers of power—the NEA and its satellite, the U. S. Office of Education. In the late 30's and early 40's, a series of books and pamphlets, all reaffirming the Cardinal Principles of Education, issued forth from the Educational Policies Commission of the NEA, culminating finally in the "life adjustment movement."

e. The problem of youth was lost sight of during World War II. But one legacy of the 30's was a concern with those youth whom the high school wasn't reaching—those who dropped out of school, usually because its programs didn't meet their needs and interests. The development of such programs governed educational discussions of the 40's and was encouraged by the Educational Policies Commission of the NEA whose intentions were well expressed by the title of its 1944 publication *Education For ALL American Youth,* essentially a reformulation of the basic aims stated as early as "The Cardinal Principles of Secondary Education" (1918), and foreshadowing the "life-adjustment" philosophy of the late 40's and 50's.

In the post-war period, youth were brought into the limelight again. Right after the war, in the spring of 1945, there was a meeting of the Division of Vocational Education of the United States Office of Education in Washington, D. C. At the session, Charles A. Prosser, former lobbyist of the National Society for the Promotion of Industrial Education, declared that the high schools were not meeting the needs of the great majority of youth. The high schools were preparing 20% of youth for college, 20% for "desirable skilled occupations." The needs of the other 60% were not being met. What they needed, in Prosser's fateful words, was an education for "life adjustment."

The majority of the nation's high school youth were written off then as being more or less uneducable, unfit not just for academic studies but even for programs of vocational education leading to desirable skilled occupations. What kind of education did the 60% need? An education which equipped them "to live democratically with satisfaction to themselves and profit to society as home members, workers, and citizens." Here, as the authors of *Life Adjustment Education for Every Youth* put it, was "a philosophy of education which places life values above acquisitions of knowledge."

The conception implicit above that knowledge has little or nothing to do with "life values" was an essential premise of the whole movement. Repeatedly, life-adjustment spokesmen were to intimate that intellectual training is of no use in solving the "real life problems of ordinary youth." Thus as the late Richard Hofstadter put it, the life-adjustment movement stated, in extreme form to be sure, the proposition toward which American school reformers had been moving for over four decades—that in a system of mass education, an academically serious training is an impossibility for more than a modest fraction of the student population. Some life-adjustment educators, in the name of democracy, looked forward to the day when "the aristocratic, cultural tradition of education (will be) completely and finally abandoned."

Of course, this was not seen by its advocates as an abandonment of intellectual or cultural standards. Rather it was seen as a "New Deal" for the ordinary boy and girl, teaching them how to get married, how to furnish a home and budget its upkeep, how to drive a car, how to dress and get along with people. They saw themselves as crusaders. Indeed, life-adjustment education was deemed so good that it was applied not merely to the forgotten three-fifths of youth but to "all American youth," a favorite post-war educational slogan. Subsequently a tremendous drive was launched on national, regional, state and local levels to translate life-adjustment principles into curricula practice.

The life adjustment movement has some extraordinary implications. Not only were sixty percent of the future citizens of the United States deemed incapable of benefitting from a serious academic education or even training for skilled and desirable occupations, but as one examines the range and content of the courses the progressives demanded and which they have in some measure succeeded in installing, to cite Professor Hofstadter again, one realizes that the schools were indeed trying to educate the "whole child." And what they aimed to do was not primarily to fit the child to become a disciplined part of the world of production and competition, ambition and vocation, creativity and analytical thought, but rather to help him learn the ways of the world of consumption and hobbies, of enjoyment and style summed up in the significant word "adjustment." To deprecate life-adjustment education however is not to deprecate one of the great unsolved problems of American secondary education. "The unsolved problem, the Jacksonian task, of the high school," in the words of the Harvard Committee's *General Education In A Free Society* (1945) "is to reach students who do not read well yet, are not skilled in hand, whose backgrounds are bad, who in cities especially are prey to a thousand mercenary interests—the kind of young people who . . . in other times would have left school early and found self-respect in work but who now, if they leave school, are simply unemployed," a concern revived in 1961 by James B. Conant in his *Slums and Suburbs*.

VIII **a.** The emergence of the modern university in the late 19th century shattered the unified, if somewhat outmoded, pattern of the old-time college without replacing it with a firm pattern of its own. Throughout this century competing interests—liberal culture, research, service, social action, vocationism—have struggled to fill the lacuna. Some attempts were made to replace the old notion of a liberal education with that of a "general education," e.g., the pioneer effort made at Columbia University in 1917 through its Contemporary Civilization Program, a program widely imitated throughout the country. The most thorough recent investigations of the problem were made at Harvard University in 1945 at the behest of President James B. Conant—The Harvard Committee's *General Education in a Free Society*, and the more recent Columbia University study by Daniel Bell, *The Reforming of General Education* (1966).

The university movement led to an immense liberation of intellectual energies, and ultimately to an immense liberation of social energy in terms of social mobility, a movement greatly stimulated by the federal government. For example, on June 22, 1944, the Seventy-Eighth Congress of the United States passed the Servicemen's Readjustment Act (Public Law 346). This Act, combined with the Vocational Rehabilitation Act of 1943 (Public Law 16), authorized programs of unprecedented scope. Public Law 16 provided for the retraining or reeducation of those whose vocational competencies had been destroyed by service connected disabilities, and Public Law 346 (popularly known as the "G.I. Bill") provided honorably discharged veterans with educational or vocational training for a period of one year plus the number of months served in the armed forces. The cost of the veteran's tuition, books, supplies, and equipment were paid directly to the institution which he attended. Over eight million veterans received benefits under this "G.I. Bill of Rights," at a total cost of approximately $15 billion. (In addition to the more striking examples of direct federal aid given under programs such as the "G.I. Bill," the federal government expanded its educational activities into many other areas and made way for more widespread government participation in the postwar years.)

In 1946, with hundreds of thousands of veterans returning to college, it was clear that the facilities of higher education were being overstrained and that a major turning point loomed ahead. Accordingly, President Harry S. Truman appointed a Presidential Commission on Higher Education in the summer of 1946, urging that "we should now reexamine our system of higher education in terms of its objectives, methods, and facilities; and in the light of the social role it has to play." A commission of 28 educators and laymen, headed by George F. Zook, President of the American Council on Education, went promptly to work and produced at the end of the following year a report consisting of six volumes—*The Report of the President's Commission on Higher Education*, a strongly egalitarian document which aroused much controversy. Many felt that the new numbers of college graduates recommended by the Commission were not viable given the American economy; some felt that the Commission proposed to sacrifice quality to accommodate the multitude of college applicants envisaged. But others turned to the junior college to provide a buffer for the colleges.

The junior college began as an extension of the high school, first at Joliet, Illinois, then at Goshen, Indiana, where six-year academic programs were instituted in 1902. But it was California that took the lead in developing junior colleges. The post-World War II period especially witnessed a tremendous proliferation of junior colleges. Enrollments tripled in the 1960's. In 1971 California's 92 public junior colleges enrolled nearly one third of all community college students in the nation—about 700,000 students—this in less than 9% of all the country's 1100 junior colleges, for post-secondary education, vocational training, and cultural enrichment. As opportunity for higher education was extended to an ever-widening proportion of the population (those enrolled in college in 1900 constituted only 4% of the population aged 18–21; in 1970 well over half this age group was in college), the colleges and universities became a new American frontier. Instead of "Go West, Young Man," it was now "Go to College, Young Man."

b. Critics of the university movement were never lacking. As early as 1930, Abraham Flexner, whose survey of American medical schools 20 years earlier had resulted in the complete reformation of American medical education, attempted a similar critique of the American university, this time with less decisive results. Flexner found in the American university a beehive of triviality and vocationalism, characterized by confusion of purpose, part secondary school, part graduate and professional school, part "service station." The verdicts of defenders of a liberal arts education and critics of the university like Irving Babbitt, Albert Jay Nock, Alexander Meiklejohn, and Robert Maynard Hutchins a few years later were similar.

As universities moved out in areas of "service," they inevitably moved into areas of political and social controversy. The American Association of University Professors was organized in 1915 to provide a channel for the faculty's views on broad questions of university policy. But it soon found its practical work in helping to defend professors in academic freedom cases. Continued violations of academic freedom led the AAUP in 1915 to the formulation of a statement on academic freedom which has remained until recently the classic attempt to codify the principles governing the rights of teachers. But in the mid-60's, youthful militants seized on the service function of the university and insisted that the university serve the causes that *it* holds dear. A series of controversies at the University of California, Berkeley, eventually erupted in 1964 in the Free Speech Movement. Student activism eventually spread east to Cornell and Columbia University and climaxed tragically with the death of four students at Kent State University and of two more at Jackson State in May of 1970. The student revolution even percolated down from the college campuses to the high schools. In the late 1960s, the AAUP was forced to give increased attention to the problems relating to the academic freedom of students, leading to the formulation of its "Joint Statement on Rights and Freedoms of Students" (1967). However, many academicians agreed with Sidney Hook, who was convinced that too much attention was being paid to student rights, not enough to their responsibilities.

The Old-Time College was characterized by Piety, Paternalism, Mental Discipline. It was rife with tension between students and faculty which broke out in the 1880's and 1890's into revolts, riots, trials. The focus of the student discontent was the evangelism, the discipline, the *in loco parentis* view of the college. But whatever the weaknesses of the Old-Time College, it possessed a definiteness, a sharpness of cast, a common denominator. It stood for a common body of Knowledge—"the Classics," a common ethos, the education of "the Whole Man." The demise of the Old-Time College and the emergence of the University meant scholarship, specialization, research, electives, freedom for faculty. And for students, it meant treating the student as a man, and a potential scholar. A price was exacted, however—loss of a sense of direction, of purposefulness, of cohesion. It meant chaos or pluralism, depending upon one's sympathy for the University Movement. It certainly meant conflict. Especially over two major aspects of university life:

I. Academic Goals—which shall have priority?
   A. Research, B. Service, C. Vocationalism, D. Liberal Culture

II. Who shall command?
A. Administration, B. Faculty, C. Students, D. Town, E. Gown

The university movement raised many other profound questions. What are the students—boys or men? What do they want—"college life" and "collegiate values" or a university education? What are their rights, their responsibilities? It raised profound questions concerning the university. What is the responsibility of the university as a social instrument? And it raised profound questions concerning the faculty—what is the proper pattern for the life of a scholar? what is the proper relation between professor and student, between the scholar and the university which employs him. These questions have still not been resolved.

IX **a.** It was only in the early 50's that any large number of Americans became aware of vast changes in the public schools, The ill-named, ill-famed "life-adjustment" movement was one shock. The Korean War, with its inconclusive ending was another. But it was the Soviet Union's launching of Sputnik in 1957 that proved catalytic. Then, against a background of deepening public concern over national security, the voracious demands of an "expert society" for scientists, skilled technicians, and trained manpower, and the emergence of a new generation of parents who possessed the education and the motivation to be concerned with the quality of the education their children were receiving, the dam of criticism burst. In the 50's and 60's a large audience emerged for books like Albert Lynd, *Quackery in the Public Schools*, Mortimer Smith, *The Diminished Mind*, John Keats, *Schools Without Scholars*, Arthur Bestor, *Educational Waste-lands*, James D. Koerner, *The Mis-Education of American Teachers*, Rudolph Flesch, *Why Johnny Can't Read*, as well as the writings of Admiral Hyman Rickover and James B. Conant. It is this same rapidly growing group of concerned laymen who provide the support for organizations like the Council for Basic Education (1956), and who are responsible for the revival of interest in Montessori schools and other private schools which stress the skills and academic disciplines that are considered basic in a precollegiate curriculum.

Unaccustomed to having their programs or objectives, their principles or practices, their competence or judgment called into question, the educational establishment developed standard techniques for dealing with critics. They identified the public schools with the democratic way of life and dismissed all critics of the schools as "enemies" of democracy; even at one time urging a boycott of *Time* and *Life* for articles critical of the public schools. Sometimes educators conceded that there were some defects in the schools, but these were defects in practice not in theory—and practice was unsatisfactory because of the unwillingness of the public to support adequately the schools. Another defensive ploy was to welcome "constructive criticism" or "honest and sincere critics," critics who are "willing to work with the schools." But most Americans agreed with Professor Bestor and Admiral Rickover that education was too important a matter to be left to professional educators, a view which defied half a century of effort on the part of the latter. A word of explanation may be helpful here.

A very significant development in higher education in the early 20th century was the emergence of a serious academic discipline called education. With the beginning of graduate study in education, particularly at Teachers College, Columbia University, The University of Chicago, and Stanford University, a group of scholars began to apply the latest techniques and methods of their disciplines to the educational process. The growing importance of education within universities can be seen from the following list of scholars who found in the study of education a fruitful field for their own research: William James, G. Stanley Hall, Edward L. Thorndike in psychology; John Dewey in philosophy; and Albion Small and Thorstein Veblen in sociology.

Throughout the early decades of the 20th century, the work of the educationist increased in importance within the university. As the number of students attending high school increased phenomenally, the demands upon the universities to train teachers increased, and more and more students enrolled in university education courses. As their enterprise prospered, educators drove for the autonomy of the medical and law schools. They based their claim on "The Science of Education." They believed in the science of education and labored to make their belief come true, especially by appropriating whatever scientific or pseudo-scientific knowledge the social scientist of the late 19th and early 20th century offered. Led by James Earl Russell of Teachers College, Columbia, and Charles Judd of the School of Education at the University of Chicago, they substituted for the older dependence on the history and philosophy of education a new dependence on the social sciences, especially psychology and statistics. It was hoped that the high prestige of science would minimize outside interference, and provide instant legitimacy to the youthful profession. Although educationists would find themselves ultimately at home neither in the academic nor professional camps, they did increasingly establish the autonomy they sought.

The rapid growth of university departments and schools of education at the turn of the century, as well as the expansion of normal schools and teachers colleges, made it feasible for the first time to meet the demand for professionally prepared teachers. Thus, in 1900 no state required graduation from high school and professional training for teacher certification; by 1925, 21 states required both. By the latter date all state teaching certificates demanded at least some knowledge of pedagogy. Educationists helped to set state certification requirements and then helped to establish teacher training programs which conformed to these requirements. The pattern of teacher certification thus became crystallized into legally fixed courses which differed from state to state, but which were fairly uniform within states, a situation which infuriated many academics.

For decades professors of arts and sciences had neglected teacher training. By the 1950's and 1960's they were ready to make up for the years of neglect. Arthur Bestor in 1953 condemned what he called the "Interlocking Public School Directorate," a clique of education professors, school administrators, and state and federal education officials, hostile to scholarship and conspiring to control the training and employment of teachers. Other critics, like James Koerner, one of the founders of the Council for Basic Education, joined the attack. Relying more on diplomacy than the frontal assault in his attempts to obtain reform was James B. Conant. Yet even Conant in 1963 in his *The Education of American Teachers* was moved to score teacher training as a "scandal." Conant called for the abolition of the existing teacher certification system, proposed measures that would make performance in the classroom the sole criterion for licensing teachers, and urged laymen to play a greater role in determining standards. Interestingly, Conant found *all* American higher education at fault, not only the schools of education. This point too warrants elaboration.

The early normal schools were in no way collegiate institutions, and as we have seen it was not intended that they should be. It was the rapid development of the free, public high school which resulted in the development of normal schools into degree-granting colleges. By 1900 normal schools could require a high school diploma for admission; by 1920 many normal schools were offering four-year post-high school courses terminating in a college degree. By the mid-1930's many normal schools had changed their names to teachers colleges or colleges of education, and by 1950 many of the state institutions had dropped the words "teachers" or "education" from their titles and had become general or liberal arts colleges, or, in some cases, universities. The change was by no means in name only. Liberal arts offerings were greatly increased and faculties were strengthened by the addition of graduates of leading graduate schools. If evidence were required for the scholarly respectability of the new breed of professional educator, one might point to the luminaries comprising the National Academy of Education, organized in 1965.

As a result of these changes, and others, as Paul Woodring put it in 1963, the term "teachers college" was fast becoming obsolete. Further there were many colleges, public and private, which prepared teachers along with their other responsibilities. Consequently, much of the criticism of teacher education had missed the mark. Only about 20% of all new teachers entering elementary or secondary schools are trained in teachers colleges. The remainder are trained in public or private liberal arts colleges or universities. It seems clear that if changes are to be made in teacher education, attention must be given to all the institutions that prepare teachers rather than to the teachers colleges alone. This is the point that Conant so astutely made; that it is the quality of the teacher's liberal arts education as much as his professional training that is crucial. There are still sharp conflicts of view between professional educators and academic professors in many an American university over the proper balance between liberal and professional education in the training of teachers, while in recent years, strife has broken out among schoolmen themselves.

The National Education Association has through the years, of course, been the most influential group in the field of public education. But beginning around World War I an increasingly significant body of educators became convinced that the NEA with its grouping together of teachers and administrators could never possibly play a militant role for the improvement of education or of teaching conditions. Only, they felt, as educators allied themselves with labor organizations and other powerful groups could teachers really improve their status. Accordingly, the American Federation of Teachers was organized in April 1916, affiliating with the AFL a month later. After a late start, the progress of AFT in recent years has been remarkable. Thus one of the few questions of substance before a recent convention of the NEA was how to merge with the AFT without being swallowed up by its parent union, the AFL-CIO. A merger of the old NEA with 1.4 million members and the AFT which has grown to a membership of 365,000 seems ultimately inevitable. The two organizations, which once differed sharply in philosophy and tactics, today are almost indistinguishable. The days are long past when the NEA was dominated by school administrators who told the classroom teachers that collective bargaining and strikes were behavior unbecoming to professionals. In recent years, the NEA has been as boastful of successful strikes as the most militant union. With a potential of over two million members, a merged organization of educators would dwarf most other unions; it would be a lobbying force to be reckoned with at national, state, and local levels, and in the AFL-CIO itself.

b. In the 50's a new educational line, a hard line or "counter-progressive" line, made its appearance. Whereas the central thrust of school reform for close to three quarters of a century had been expansionist and sought to extend the functions of the schools, the central effort of the 50's and 60's was rather to define more precisely the schools' responsibility, to delineate those things the school needed to do, because if the school did not do them, they would not get done, namely, as Professor Bestor put it, "the deliberate cultivation of the ability to think." This was one of the major themes of the 1956 White House Conference on Education. It was pointed out that in attempting to provide all manner of services for children, the public school was doing nothing excellently. Appealing to the ideal of equality of opportunity, the conference explicitly warned that the schools must not consider themselves the only agencies in the field of education. The conference called for a new set of educational priorities and stated that "the development of the intellectual powers of young people, each to the limit of his capacity, is the first responsibility of schools." In 1961 the Educational Policies Commission of the NEA published a statement of *The Central Purpose of American Education* which reaffirmed the basic importance of developing the "rational powers" of each student—in language strikingly redolent of Charles Eliot's in the early 1890's.

By the 60's, evidence of the new "hard line" was available on every hand. James B. Conant's massive and influential study of the high school, *The American High School Today* (1959), concluded that talented students were not being worked hard enough, and that they are not offered a wide enough range of academic studies (though he came out squarely in favor of the comprehensive high school). The federal government, through the National Defense Education Act, signed by President Eisenhower in 1958, expended millions of dollars to upgrade or retrain teachers on both elementary and secondary school levels in science, mathematics, and foreign languages. Largely on the initiative of university scientists from such distinguished insititutions as M.I.T., Harvard, and the University of Illinois, and with the support of the Ford Foundation's Fund for the Advancement of Education, a number of studies and programs were initiated expressly to develop new high school courses in the sciences and mathematics and to prepare textbooks and other materials: the Physical Science Study Committee organized by Professor Jerrold Zacharias of M.I.T. in 1956; the School Maths Study Group (1958); the Biological Sciences Curriculum Study (1958); the Chemical Education Material Study (1959); and many others.

In 1960 President Eisenhower appointed eleven distinguished Americans to consider the goals of education. Their deliberations resulted in *Excellence in Education*, a report edited by John W. Gardner. In the meantime in September 1959, under the auspices of the National Academy of Sciences, another distinguished group of scientists and scholars met at Woods Hole on Cape Cod to discuss how education in science might be improved in primary and secondary schools. Included in the meeting were many psychologists concerned with the examination of intelligence, learning, remembering, thinking, and motivation, including Dr. Jerome S. Bruner, Dr. Lee Cronbach, Dr. Robert M. Gagne, and Dr. Barbel Inhelder of Geneva, Jean Piaget's distinguished co-worker. Teaching machines and programmed learning were demonstrated by Professor B. B. Skinner of Harvard. The meeting was chaired by Dr. Bruner, who was also responsible for writing the summary report, *The Process of Education* (1960). Dr. Bruner reflected the thought of most at the conference when he stated the hypothesis: "any subject can be taught effectively in some intellectually honest form to any child at any stage of development." Bruner went on to articulate certain of the leading principles of the curricula reform movement of the 1960's, using concepts like "structure" to characterize the canon of curriculum selection, "discovery" to describe the approach to curriculum method, and "spiraling" to express the view of curriculum sequence. This is not to suggest, however, that the pressures for the reform of education emanate only from those concerned with the continued technical superiority of the nation, or the academics or the foundations or the parents of college-bound children. In the past decade the demands for the strengthening of education have been reinforced by a revolution in race relations.

X **a.** The first generation of emancipated Negroes trusted that education would lead to the promised land of opportunity—a hope soon shattered for a people disenfranchised, economically suppressed, socially barred by rigid rules of caste, and subject to humiliation and terror. The Civil Rights Act of 1875 left the issue of segregated schools up to the several states. By the 1880's, most of the northern states prohibited segregated schools, either by constitutional provision, or statute, or court decision. At the same time the southern and border states as rapidly as they were able, either made segregated schools mandatory or struck all reference to mixed schools from their laws. Thus when the U. S. Supreme Court in *Plessy* v. *Ferguson* (1896), finally spoke in favor of the constitutionality of "separate but equal" train facilities in Louisiana, it merely gave sanction to a long-established situation that had been accepted widely for a generation. *Plessy* v. *Ferguson* took the constitutionality of separate schools for granted, using the widespread tolerance of that practice to justify its opinion that separate railroad accommodations were constitutional. Its formula for constitutionality, "equal but separate," usually recalled as "separate but equal," was ignored by politicians and school administrators who participated in the new era of southern school development which opened shortly after that decision; schools became increasingly "separate and unequal." Thus in 1895, South Carolina spent $3.11 for each white student; $1.05 for each Negro student. In 1911, the figures were, respectively, $13.02 and $1.71.

By 1895 the civil rights of Negroes were overwhelmed in a rising tide of white supremacy—legally enforced in the southern states, unofficially endorsed by the entire nation, and left intact by the U. S. Supreme Court. More than 20 years of post-Reconstruction "progress" had made the country a less promising place for Negroes (as well as Indians and Orientals) than it had been just after the Civil War. At the nadir of Negro life in America, Booker T. Washington emerged as the chief spokesman of the black masses. It was Washington's belief that black people had to learn to crawl before they could walk. He once said during a speech, that instead of starting at the top of the social ladder as many Blacks had done during Reconstruction, black people could start at the bottom as small farmers then work themselves up in society. Washington preached the dignity of common labor, of thrift, and the need for patience. Washington believed that accommodation and not confrontation was the best way to get along with white southerners. For Washington the ultimate goal of education for black people was the acquisition of property and a savings in the bank. By making material gains and improving their lot economically, Washington felt that black people could prove how capable and responsible they were. This in return would lead to acceptance by white America.

Booker T. Washington's ideas were well received by a large segment of America's black belt population. Southern whites liked his ideas because they saw in him a Negro who knew how to stay in his place in their society, while Northern whites saw him as a great man, sincere and dedicated to the advancement of his race without violence. Booker T. Washington was able to obtain large financial gifts for Tuskegee Institute and other black schools because of his "work hard and wait for acceptance philosophy." This is not to say that Washington was without critics in the black community, especially in the Northeast, where William E. B. DuBois led the opposition.

DuBois, the first Negro to earn a Harvard Ph.D., believed in the higher education of a "talented tenth" of Negroes, who through their knowledge and culture could guide the black masses into the modern world. Without educated black leaders, the Negro would have to accept white leadership, and such leadership could not always be trusted to guide the Negro to realize his full potential. In 1903, DuBois published *The Souls of Black Folk*, in which he described the shortcomings of Washington's philosophy. To DuBois, Washington was asking black people to give up three vital things: political power, civil rights, and the higher education of Negro youth. Aided by William Trotter, DuBois organized the first effective black opposition to Washington through the Niagara Movement. DuBois' group of black intellectuals and professionals held a secret meeting near Niagara Falls in 1905, then another national meeting at Harpers Ferry, in 1906. Aside from their verbal protest, the Niagara Movement was unable to accomplish more than making a great number of people in America uneasy. Booker T. Washington successfully persuaded the Negro and white press to ignore the Movement after 1907. Nevertheless, the Niagara Movement laid the ground for the formation of the National Association for the Advancement of Colored People. Beginning in 1910, the NAACP began to publish *The Crisis* magazine. It is interesting to note that the editorial page of the first issue of the *The Crisis* was largely devoted to a discussion of the evils of school segregation.

In 1944 the black cause received another boost when Gunnar Myrdal, a Swedish economist, published his landmark study, *An American Dilemma*. Essentially, Myrdal's argument was that the depressed and segregated condition of the Negro in the United States was a violation of what he called the "American Creed," in which education played an important role. Myrdal maintained that the major factor in the assimilation of white immigrant groups who came to this country was the school. It was the school and the education and skills it transmitted that enabled each immigrant group in turn to rise from the bottom of the economic, social, and political ladder. Education not only opened doors to better jobs but also tended to transform one's life-style and make it more compatible with urban living. Considered in the mass, Myrdal concluded, the Negro's major handicap was his limited education and skills.

During World War II, economic opportunities for the Negro improved. Yet school segregation continued to belie the premises of the common school as it concerned the Negro. Negroes sometimes protested the inequality in education. There were Negro boycotts of segregated schools in Alton, Illinois, in 1897–1908; in East Orange, New Jersey, in 1899–1906: and in Springfield, Ohio, in 1922–1923, and the NAACP won some victories in Atlanta in 1916–1917. Still as late as 1951, twenty-one states and the District of Columbia either compelled or permitted by law the separate education of the races. Then in 1954 after a long, carefully planned legal campaign led by the NAACP, the Supreme Court concluded in *Brown* v. *Board of Education* (of Topeka, Kansas), that segregation is a denial of the equal protection of the laws: "separate educational facilities are inherently unequal." One year later the Court ruled that school districts must desegregate "with all deliberate speed."

The deep South resisted the court's decision bitterly. Whether in open defiance—as at Little Rock, Arkansas, in 1957, and the University of Mississippi in 1962, or through tactics of evasion and delay, the old Confederate states effectively slowed integration. Defiance of the Supreme Court was spurred by the "Southern Manifesto" issued by ninety-six Southern Congressmen in March 1956. It denounced the Brown ruling and called for "all lawful means to bring about a reversal of this decision which is contrary to the Constitution. . . ." The civil rights movement, at first nonviolent and restrained, had by 1964 become more aggressive and violent. And whereas discrimination in education had been formerly defined chiefly as a southern problem, after 1954 more and more attention was turned to the inequality of the educational treatment of Negroes and other nonwhites in all sections of the country.

b. If the attitude of white America towards the Negro's assimilation into the American society has been ambivalent, there was no such ambivalence towards the Indian. The Indian was to be forcibly assimilated. In 1889 T. J. Morgan, the Commissioner of Indian Affairs, reflected the government's intention when he stated: "The Indian must conform to the white man's way peaceably if they will, forcibly if they must. They must adjust themselves to their environment, and conform their mode of living substantially to our civilization. . . . They cannot escape it, and must either conform to it or be crushed by it." As to the end of Indian education in the late 19th century, then, there was little dispute; the means remained in question.

The early 1900's marked the beginning of a change in federal policy for Indian education. In 1916 a uniform course of study was adopted for all Indian schools. *The Course of Study for United States Indian Schools* remained intact until World War II with just minor revision. The policy of building Indian schools off reservations was curtailed, and the manual training emphasis was changed to vocational education. The first six years of instruction in Indian schools were to be academic and would follow those usually found in the public schools. At the junior high school level, "prevocational" training was to be offered in industrial and agricultural arts. At the senior high school level, the course of study became primarily vocational. The goal of Indian education was now "to provide that form of training and instruction which leads directly to self-support and productive efficiency."

In the early 1920's widespread public indignation over a plan to divest the Pueblos of land led to a Senate investigation into the whole problem of Indian administration. The principal fruit of this reexamination of government policies was the decision of Secretary of the Interior Herbert Work to request a private concern, the Institute for Government Research, under the direction of Dr. Lewis Meriam, to make a survey and propose a program. Published in 1928, the Meriam Report provided reformers with some badly needed ammunition. The Meriam Report called upon the Bureau of Indian Affairs (BIA) to expand day schools and to humanize the boarding schools, to stimulate community participation in the schools, and to relate schooling more closely to the postschool needs of Indian youth. A system of federal loans for Indian higher education was also recommended. The Meriam Report declared that "the whole Indian problem is essentially an educational one." The report regarded the role of education as "the training of all Indians for the best type of American citizenship, looking to their eventual absorption into the general citizenship of the nation."

On the heels of the Meriam Report some changes occurred in Indian education. Numerous day schools were founded, while subsidies for boarding schools were reduced markedly. Attendance at public schools was encouraged. The total appropriations for the education of Indian youth increased fourfold. But hampering the efforts to improve the Indian's lot was the Depression which struck in 1929. In the early 1930's the federal government again reoriented its policy towards the Indian. In 1934 the Indian Reorganization Act was passed. The Bureau of Indian Affairs was upgraded under the leadership of Commissioner John Collier, and W. Carson Ryan, Jr., BIA Education Director. Collier called for an end to forced-draft assimilation of the Indian and introduced Indian arts and crafts courses into the reservation schools. He also wanted to make vocational education courses more relevant. Under Collier, the trend away from boarding schools was accelerated; day schools began to provide community welfare services for adults as well as children. But the problem of Indian education remained intractable.

Today nearly a quarter of a million Indian children are in American schools. About half of them are the responsibility of the BIA. Most Indian schools located on reservations are secondary schools with boarding facilities. The majority of elementary schools, both day and boarding schools, are located on reservations. An estimated two thirds of all Indian children entering BIA schools have little or no skill in English. Most Indian schools have few Indian teachers and a high teacher turnover. They offer little familiarity with local cultures, and educate children at levels which are below the national average in the early years, and which get progressively lower. Until recently no college of education in the country offered special training for prospective teachers of Indians. In recent decades many Indians have quietly left their reservations or their isolated rural communities and moved to the cities, where problems of adjustment caused many to return to the reservations. It seems clear that the schools have largely failed to meet the Indian's needs and to help him find his place in American society. After two years of exhaustive hearings, a Senate subcommittee report of the late 60's was entitled "Indian Education: A National Tragedy—A National Challenge." As one historian has commented: Indians are assimilated at last; they share the problems of other poor and disadvantaged minorities in America.

Based on the 1970 census, American Indians are the poorest minority in the country. One point of progress, however, has been in education. The census report indicated that 95% of Indian children between ages of 7–13 attended school in 1970; the number attending college doubled in 1960–1970. Nationally, about 1/3 of all Indians over 25 years of age had completed high school, compared with less than 1/5 in 1960, and median schooling was now 9.8 years, the same as for Blacks (the national median was 12.1 years and 52.3% of the total population had finished high school).

There have recently been some helpful innovations in Indian education. For example, the Teaching English as a Second Language (TESL) programs financed under the Bilingual Education Act (1967) have profited Indian children. Another exciting departure in Indian education is the DINE (Demonstration in Navajo Education) experimental school at Rough Rock, Arizona. Instruction in Navajo language and culture is part of the curriculum, and the school itself is supervised by an all-Navajo school board. The newly organized first Indian college, the Navajo Junior College at Many Farms, Arizona, is also gearing its curriculum to the special needs of Indian students. In 1972 President Nixon proposed a new Indian policy. "The time has come . . . for a new era in which the Indian future is determined by Indian acts and Indian decisions," the president declared in a message to Congress.

Indians, long accustomed to equating silence with dignity, are newly aroused, especially over the continuing paternalistic authority of BIA. The pan-Indian movement offers some evidence that further improvement is in sight. For sure we have entered a new era in the relations of Indians with their fellow Americans.

        c. The prejudice that plagued Negroes and Indians and "inferior breeds" of Europeans in the South, East, and Midwest has been shared in the West and Southwest by Orientals and Mexicans.

        Chinese immigration to the United States became negligible after passage of the Exclusion Act of 1882; but Japanese immigration took up the slack. The immigration of Japanese to California had been insignificant until the late 1890's, but it steadily increased in the early 20th century. The early Japanese immigrants to the West Coast were received fairly well. The California growers liked them; they were young, vigorous, hard workers. However, the Japanese immigrants who came to the West Coast inherited the racial slurs and anti-Chinese precedents of the late 19th century. The "yellow peril" stereotype was transferred to the Japanese when they began to compete economically with the natives. The stunning Japanese victory in the Russo-Japanese War (1905) reinforced the stereotype. The Nisei, or native-born children, though they lived in segregated enclaves, attended public schools and in other ways participated in civic life much more fully than the Chinese ever had. Ironically, the successful "Americanization" of the Japanese, coupled with a very "American" striving for economic success, produced an even more intense hostility from the majority population than had the Chinese.

        The history of the anti-Japanese movement in the United States, particularly on the West Coast, from the turn of the century until after World War II is replete with the hostile actions of labor unions, the press, political organizations, and various other interest groups and individuals. These organizations and individuals often acted in concert with each other against the Japanese. For example, the San Francisco school affair of 1905–1907 was the outcome of a tacit alliance between labor leaders and politicians for the purpose of eventual exclusion of the Japanese from the West Coast. Thus in 1905 San Francisco labor union leaders formed the influential Asiatic Exclusion League to combat Japanese immigration. Under pressure from the League the San Francisco Board of Education announced its intention to segregate Japanese public school children, native or foreign-born, along with Chinese, subsequently creating a major diplomatic issue.

        Recall that California had almost completely excluded Chinese children from the public schools until a California court ruling prohibited this practice in 1885. Subsequently, in San Francisco a separate public school had been provided for them. When this Chinese school was rebuilt after the earthquake and fire, its name was changed to the "Oriental School." On October 11, 1906 the San Francisco Board of Education adopted an order requiring Japanese public school children to attend this school. Protests from the Japanese government led to a diplomatic crisis between Japan and the United States. President Roosevelt ordered an investigation by his Secretary of Commerce and Labor, Victor H. Metcalf, who discovered only 93 Japanese pupils out of a total school population of 28,736 in the 23 public schools of San Francisco.

        Early in 1907 President Roosevelt invited the Mayor of San Francisco and members of the Board of Education to Washington, D. C., where they agreed to a compromise. The Board was to withdraw its segregation order. Only over-age pupils and those not having facility in English might be placed in segregated schools, and the new regulations would apply to all children of alien birth, not to Japanese as such. In return, President Roosevelt promised to place limits on Japanese immigration, eventually negotiating the "Gentlemen's Agreement" (1908), under which the Japanese government promised not to issue passports good for the continental U. S. to laborers, whether skilled or unskilled. Though parents, wives, or children of Japanese already resident in the United States were not covered by this agreement, the latter provided for a virtual halt to Japanese immigration to the United States.

Scarcely a session of the California State Legislature from the turn of the century to World War II was to pass without the introduction of some anti-Japanese bills. The continued series of discriminatory enactments against the resident Japanese affected adversely relations between Japan and the United States and, conversely, disturbances in relations between the two countries aggravated the relations between Japanese and non-Japanese in California. The effect upon the Nisei (an American citizen of Japanese ancestry) coming of age before World War II was devastating. He was a citizen, yet American society, especially in the West, treated him as an undesirable alien. The evacuation of the West Coast Japanese, in the early years of World War II, in the words of Eugene V. Rostow, "our worst wartime mistake" was almost inevitable. Beginning in 1942 more than 110,000 Japanese, citizens and alien alike, were evacuated from the West Coast, confined in the army's assembly centers, and moved into ten guarded camps; "relocation centers," established under the auspices of the War Relocation Authority (WRA), an agency created by executive order of President Franklin D. Roosevelt.

Education was considered one of the functions of the camps, and one of the responsibilities of the WRA. The WRA stipulated that the educational program of the camps should provide standards that would equal those of the schools from which the students came, and that the WRA schools should not later handicap students in transferring to other schools or colleges or in obtaining employment after the war. The schools in the detention centers were also to promote loyalty to American ideals and institutions. There were approximately 27,700 Japanese-American school age pupils in the camps. The schools' attempt to teach principles of Americanism was, of course, contradicted by the forced evaluation, the discriminatory treatment, the denial of rights and responsibilities of citizenship. Still the schools enabled Japanese children to make some educational progress, helped both children and adults retain some contact with the world outside the camps, and helped prepare them for eventual return into normal life. On December 17, 1944 the Western Defense Command revoked the general exclusion order; WRA was to be liquidated by June 30, 1946.

The Japanese-American reaction to the humiliation of the war years has been extraordinary. Most of the Japanese returned to California. Most of those who returned managed to pick up the pieces of their shattered lives. Indeed, in the years since the war, Americans of Japanese descent have established an unrivaled record for good citizenship. Along with the Chinese and Jews, they ranked higher in education and lower in crime and juvenile delinquency than any other ethnic group in the United States, including native whites, today constituting an identifiable American elite.

d. From the American Conquest in 1848 until about 1920 very few Mexicans migrated into California, or into the United States for that matter. But a great fear enveloped the Southwest with the movement of more than half a million

Mexicans into that region during the 1920's. By 1925, the southwestern states produced 40% of the nation's fruits, vegetables, and truck crops, almost all on farms developed in the 20th century, and it was only an enormous influx of Mexican labor that made this production possible. As the Spanish-speaking population of the country grew, it remained highly localized with almost 90% of it located in Texas, New Mexico, Arizona, Colorado, and California. As early as 1930 Mexican-Americans had become the largest ethnic minority in California, a position they still retain.

There are presently more than 5,000,000 persons of Mexican-American descent in the United States, most of them concentrated in the above-named five Southwestern states. There are approximately 2,000,000 Spanish-surnamed pupils in public schools in the U. S., about 70% of them in the five states. Although Mexican-Americans are one of the largest minorities in the United States (again, they are California's largest ethnic minority), and although the Mexican and his ancestor have been present in the Southwest for over 350 years, little is known about them. They have been described as "the forgotten Americans," forgotten in employment, housing, medical care, and education.

Segregation of Mexican-American children in the schools of the Southwest was never rigidly fixed by statute and ordinance as it was for the Negro in the South. Nevertheless, the unwritten laws of many communities in the Southwest resulted in a system that ensured segregated, inadequate education. Most of the Mexican-American children in the Southwest as late as 1947 still attended segregated schools. In that year the U. S. Circuit Court of Appeals for California ruled that segregation of school children of Mexican or Latin extraction was illegal (Westminster School District, et al. *vs.* Mendez, et al.). Furthermore, minimal or no attention was given to the Mexican-American heritage or to contemporary issues in Mexican-American life. It was usual for the schools to ignore the language and cultural heritage of the children as if it didn't exist, or worse, as if it required eradication. In March 1968, the quiet acceptance of inferior education ended. Led by a group of youthful activists, four East Los Angeles high schools erupted in a week of walkouts, picketing, demonstrations, police tactical alerts, and emergency sessions of the Board of Education. The words "blow out," "Brown Power," "Chicano," and "La Raza" entered the language.

Since the mid-60's, La Raza has gradually emerged as a recognized entity on the American scene. Whereas George Sanchez could describe the Mexican-Americans of 1940 as forgotten Americans, by 1970 they were anything but forgotten. And in education there have been some significant improvements. Thanks to the efforts of educators like Sanchez, Herschel Manuel, Julian Samorra and others, bilingual education for Spanish-speaking children is becoming a reality. The Bilingual Education Act (Title VII of The Elementary and Secondary Education Act), passed by Congress in 1967, authorized funds and support for schools to develop programs in which both English and the native language of the student (the Act has profited Puerto Rican and Indian children as well as Mexican-American children) can be used as teaching tools until a mastery of English has been achieved. Still, in 1971 the U. S. Civil Rights Commission reported that Mexican-American school children were severely isolated in the public schools, and that Mexican-American teachers and other members of the professional staff were "under-represented." The report showed that only 4% of the teachers and 3% of the principals in schools with Chicano majorities were Mexican-Americans. Even in California, with its vaunted system of higher education, only about 2% of the four-year college enrollment is

Mexican-American. Mexican-Americans lag two years behind the Negro in scholastic achievement, and four years behind the non-minority citizens of that state.

The predicament of the Mexican-American child brings up again the question of assimilation that has troubled American education from the beginning, a question which has first involved Indians and Negroes, and then immigrant and ethnic groups in turn. From the time of the revolution, substantial numbers of Americans supposed that cultural diversity somehow endangered the country, since it threatened cohesiveness. Others have idealized American society as a place where it was possible to be culturally different and still be "American." The education of the Indian, the Negro, the Oriental, the new immigrants, all pose the problem of diversity within unity; the education of the Mexican-American opens the question once more.

XI The Civil Rights Movement had three major lines of development in relation to the schools. At first, civil rights advocates concentrated on fighting racial segregation in the Old South and the border states. The second line of development concerned the fight against segregated schools of the Northern states, especially in the large cities. In these Northern metropolitan areas the pattern of racial segregation took a more subtle form. Here segregation came to be referred to as *de facto*, having its basis usually in residential patterns rather than actual legislation. The third major area of concern of civil rights advocates became that of improving the quality of public school education in the urban centers of the nation, especially for culturally deprived or disadvantaged children. In the 1960's especially, civil rights advocates and social reformers called upon the schools to provide the kind of compensatory education which could overcome or compensate for the effects of poverty and discrimination and deprivation. By the early 1960's the infusion of excellence and quality into American education now came to be one of the prime concerns of the federal government, reflecting a radical shift in the concept and practice of federal aid to education which occurred in the post-World War II period.

Federal aid to education in the Truman years (1945–1952) was stymied by religious antagonisms over the question of the separation of church and state. Some readers will recall the harsh exchanges between Mrs. Eleanor Roosevelt and New York's Cardinal Spellman in the late 1940's. During the Eisenhower years (1953–1960) the racial issue joined the religious one. With Southern states fearful of the imposition of integrated schooling which might come with federal aid, all federal aid bills in the 50's were doomed. But federal aid emerged as a major issue in the 1959 presidential campaign. Indeed, *both* parties were pledged to federal aid in 1959. In his message to Congress on February 20, 1961, newly-elected President John F. Kennedy called for the enactment of a huge program of educational aid consisting of large-scale grants and loans for school and library construction, teacher salaries, special education needs, and student loans (but aid to elementary and secondary parochial schools was prohibited). Bills were introduced in the House and Senate, but were finally defeated. It remained for President Lyndon B. Johnson, following the assassination of President Kennedy, to make the breakthrough and sign into law some sixty legislative measures providing federal aid to education.

In the late 50's and 60's the federal government responded to the changing climate of opinion with an extraordinary series of laws and a massive influx of funds. First came the passage of the 1958 National Defense Education Act, mentioned earlier, under which the U. S. Office of Education has sponsored efforts to upgrade the teaching of foreign languages, mathematics, and science. During the next seven years the federal government expanded this initial narrow outlook to a concern for the total quality of American education. Congress passed the Higher Education Act, the Library Services Act, the Vocational and Technical Education Act, the Economic Opportunity Act, the Civil Rights Act, the International Education Act, and many others. In 1964, Congress extended the NDEA for a period of three years and expanded the Act to include funds for improving instruction in reading, English, geography, history, and civics. The culmination of this landslide of educational legislation was the far-reaching Elementary and Secondary Education Act of 1965, which committed the government to expenditures of $1.3 billion for 1965 alone, with most of the authorization for programs designed to meet the needs of culturally disadvantaged children from low-income families. President Lyndon B. Johnson put it well: "the first session of the Eighty-Ninth Congress will go down in history as 'The Education Congress.'"

The White House Conference on Education of 1965 provides more dramatic evidence of how far the federal government had moved to becoming a major force in education. In 1955 the federal government was still not involved in education on a major scale; Congress was indifferent if not hostile toward federal aid. By 1965 the federal government was ahead of professional educators and the general public— now providing the backing, money, and inspiration for educational innovation. Between 1958 and 1968 the Office of Education changed radically. It acquired new resources and new responsibilities. In 1965, the Office was reorganized under the direction of Commissioner of Education Francis Keppel. The main effect of this reorganization was the transformation of the Office from a loose confederation of independent activities and projects to a centrally controlled and coordinated agency with authority vested in the office of the commissioner, and extensively involved in the formulation of national educational policy. It is still not a federal *ministry* of education, but it has become a major factor in the determining of national educational policy. For example, after 1961 the Office of Education acquired tremendously increased resources. In 1957, total Office appropriations were $272 million; in 1967; $3.9 *billion.* The research funds of the Office increased from $3 million in 1960 to $129 million in 1967.

Yet paradoxically, where money had once been deemed a cure-all, the massive influx of funds has apparently had little effect. *The Report of the National Advisory Commission on Civil Disorders* (1968) has testified to the bleak record of the public schools. Education in a democratic society, the report begins, must equip children to develop their potential and to participate fully in American life. For the community-at-large, the public schools have discharged this responsibility well. But, the report continued, for many minorities, and particularly for the children of the ghetto, the schools have failed to provide the educational experiences which could overcome the effects of discrimination and deprivation. Indeed, the bleak record for ghetto children, especially Negro children, is getting worse: "In the critical skills— verbal and reading ability—Negro students are falling further behind whites with each year of school completed." In 1969 the U. S. Civil Rights Commission concluded that of the major compensatory education programs it has studied, "none . . . appear to have raised significantly the achievement of participating pupils." In 1970 U. S. Education Commissioner James E. Allen called for an extraordinary "Right to Read" program, to assure every citizen "the right to read" English. But the schools have not totally failed the black child. According to the 1972 census the 727,000 blacks in college almost doubled the 370,000 in 1967. While the proportion of blacks 20-29 years old who were high school graduates rose from 54%

in 1967 to 65% in 1972.

Many liberals, white and black, advocate that singularly controversial and audacious experiment in social engineering—busing—to achieve a racial mix in schools—as the only way to improve the educational standards and opportunities of minorities. On the other hand, some blacks have given up on integration as the panacea for Negro education, and have begun, ironically, to call for decentralized or community schools, really segregated school systems—black schools for black children, taught by black teachers, responsible to the black community. The failure of the inner-city schools is so great that some thoughtful observers like Kenneth Clark and James Coleman are beginning to think the unthinkable, or what at least was unthinkable until recently. They argue that the inner-city schools have failed on so grand a scale that they might well be replaced or radically altered by contracting out education to nonpublic organizations, to private industry or the foundations, for example, the so-called "educational performance contracting." More recently, the "voucher plan" has gained adherents from the vigorous advocacy of Christopher Jencks and the Center for the Study of Public Policy at Harvard. Others, influenced by the work of Benjamin Bloom or Martin Deutsch or Jean Piaget, are turning to the preschool or to early childhood education, as the solution to the problems of urban education. Meanwhile, the large audience attracted to the work of "de-schoolers," free schoolers, and open schoolers, like Paul Goodman, Ivan Illich, A. S. Neill, and Joseph Featherstone among others, give increasing evidence that even the community-at-large is no longer satisfied with the public school's performance. President Nixon spoke for many Americans when in 1970 recommending the establishment of a clearinghouse for research, National Institute of Education, he declared, "we must stop congratulating ourselves for spending nearly as much money on education as does the entire rest of the world . . . when we are not getting as much as we should out of the dollars we spend."

XII For more than 70 years, the swiftly moving currents of social change have placed upon the schools new and enlarged responsibilities. It is these changes which define many of the major problems of American education—the conquest of a continent, mass immigration, incredibly rapid industrialization, two world wars, a worldwide economic depression. More recent pressures have been the impact of technology, the migration of blacks and other poor and minority groups to northern cities, the flight of the white (and increasingly, the black) middle classes and of corporations to the suburbs, the declining tax base of urban areas, regional differences in economic resources, the emergence of the small-family pattern, changes in the age structure of the population, the civil rights revolution, and the impact of the mass media. Another extremely important but overlooked factor has been the increasing role in education of the Supreme Court.

Education is not mentioned in the Constitution and is never, therefore, directly at issue before the Supreme Court. Public education resides as a function of the state and local governments. Thus, the appearance of education before the Court remains always incidental—but not therefore insignificant—to cases adjudicated within the Court's prescribed purview. Indeed, the Supreme Court's decisions, especially in the last 25 years, have increasingly involved education. As early as 1948, Mr. Justice Robert Jackson, speaking in the *McCollum* case, remarked that the Court exhibited tendencies to become the "national school board." This tendency has been even more marked in the years following 1948.

Most of the Supreme Court's decisions affecting education have turned upon the questions of state or federal powers, civil rights under the First and Fifth Amendments, and "due process of law" and "equal protection of the laws" under the Fourteenth Amendment. So far as the field of education is concerned, the cases which the United States Supreme Court has decided fall into three groups. One group deals with the impact of state educational policy on claims to religious liberty. A second group has dealt with the questions of racial segregation in the public schools. The third group of cases, a smaller group, has been concerned with issues of academic freedom. Taken together, Justice Jackson's comment becomes prescient indeed. There is no space here to elaborate on the role of the Court in education. But one observation perhaps will be helpful. Protestant denominations, of course, operate schools. And Jewish schools have proliferated in the past decade, but the religious question affects Catholic parochial schools for the most part. Catholic schools comprise nine-tenths of all private school education in the country. Catholic school enrollment in 1969–70 was about 4.6 million, about 10% of the total public school enrollment. But there are fifteen states in which Catholic schools educated more than 10% of the school children, including New York with 16.3%, Pennsylvania with 17.2%, Illinois with 15.2%, Massachusetts with 14.2%, and Wisconsin with 14.2%. The Catholic schools are almost exclusively financed from private sources. The Catholic school system is caught in a painful financial squeeze between inflation and the decrease in available teaching brothers and nuns. That is why to Catholics the question of federal aid to religious schools, above all other issues, is so pressing.

One could go on. The changes mentioned above and many others have forced a painful rethinking of educational policy. In addition, one should not overlook the problems inherent in the rapid, extensive, and extraordinary expansion of the school system itself. The undue disillusion with public education is the reverse side of the coin of educational utopianism referred to earlier in these volumes. To place sole responsibility at the profession's feet for all the present defects in education is to ignore the relationships which exist between the flow of social events and the school. Among the current crop of school critics and school reformers this point is too often ignored. Much of the criticism and many of the attempts at reform overlook the fact that the schools mirror the society of which they are a part. "Things fall apart," as the great Irish poet, W. B. Yeats, wrote, "the centre cannot hold." Before wide-scale school reforms can succeed, more attention than has hitherto been paid needs to be given to repairing the total fabric of American society.

"We in this country, in this generation, are, by destiny rather than choice, the watchmen on the wall of world freedom," wrote President John F. Kennedy in an undelivered speech released to the press on November 22, 1963, just before his tragic death. Thus in modern terminology, President Kennedy rephrased a constant in our history: America, the City Upon a Hill. This ideal expresses a general belief in America's unique mission in the world. This ideal contains within it a repugnant strain of superiority, but also our noblest aspirations. This pietistic-perfectionist streak in the American temper has produced some of the worst aspects of American self-righteousness, bigotry, and naive stupidity. It has also inspired much of America's dynamic generosity, self-awareness, and social concern. For better or worse, America is, and always has been a nation of pietists. No other nation has yet succeeded in measuring up fully to the high ideal which America has set for itself; only a free society would even attempt such an arduous and noble venture. If it has led to a repugnant feeling of superiority, it has also led to efforts to close the gap between reality and aspiration. It is both the despair and the promise of America, and of American education.

15

IDEAS
FROM
ABROAD

The Continent

THE PSYCHOLOGICAL METHOD OF MEASURING INTELLIGENCE
(**1905**)   From Alfred Binet and Theodore Simon, *The Development of Intelligence in Children*, Elizabeth S. Kite, trans. (Baltimore, 1916), pp. 40–44.

In order to recognize the inferior states of intelligence we believe that three different methods should be employed. We have arrived at this synthetic view only after many years of research, but we are now certain that each of these methods renders some service. These methods are:

1. *The medical method*, which aims to appreciate the anatomical, physiological, and pathological signs of inferior intelligence.

2. *The pedagogical method*, which aims to judge of the intelligence according to the sum of acquired knowledge.

3. *The psychological method*, which makes direct observations and measurements of the degree of intelligence.

From what has gone before it is easy to see the value of each of these methods. The medical method is indirect because it conjectures the mental from the physical. The pedagogical method is more direct; but the psychological is the most direct of all because it aims to measure the state of the intelligence as it is at the present moment. It does this by experiments which oblige the subject to make an effort which shows his capability in the way of comprehension, judgment, reasoning, and invention.

I. The Psychological Method

The fundamental idea of this method is the establishment of what we shall call a measuring scale of intelligence. This scale is composed of a series of tests of increasing difficulty, starting from the lowest intellectual level that can be observed, and ending with that of average normal intelligence. Each group in the series corresponds to a different mental level.

This scale properly speaking does not permit the measure of the intelligence, because intellectual qualities are not superposable, and therefore cannot be measured as linear surfaces are measured, but are on the contrary, a classification, a hierarchy among diverse intelligences; and for the necessities of practice this classification is equivalent to a measure. We shall therefore be able to know, after studying two individuals, if one rises above the other and to how many degrees, if one rises above the average level of other individuals considered as normal, or if he remains below. Understanding the normal progress of intellectual development among normals, we shall be able to determine how many years such an individual is advanced or retarded. In a word we shall be able to determine to what degrees of the scale idiocy, imbecility, and moronity correspond.

The scale that we shall describe is not a theoretical work; it is the result of long investigations, first at the Salpêtrière, and afterwards in the primary schools of Paris, with both normal and subnormal children. These short psychological questions have been given the name of tests. The use of tests is today very common, and there are even contemporary authors who have made a specialty of organizing new tests according to theoretical views, but who have made no effort to patiently try them out in the schools. Theirs is an amusing occupation, comparable to a person's making a colonizing expedition into Algeria, advancing always only upon the map, without taking off his dressing gown. We place but slight confidence in the tests invented by these authors and we have borrowed nothing from them. All the tests which we propose have been repeatedly tried, and have been retained from among many, which after trial have been discarded. We can certify that those which are here presented have proved themselves valuable.

We have aimed to make all our tests simple, rapid, convenient, precise, heterogeneous, holding the subject in continued contact with the experimenter, and bearing principally upon the faculty of judgment. Rapidity is necessary for this sort of examination. It is impossible to prolong it beyond twenty minutes without fatiguing the subject. During this maximum of twenty minutes, it must be turned and turned about in every sense, and at least ten tests must be executed, so that not more than about two minutes can be given to each. In spite of their interest, we were obliged to proscribe long exercises. For example, it would be very instructive to know how a subject learns by heart a series of sentences. We have often tested the advantage of leaving a person by himself with a lesson of prose or verse after having said to him, "Try to learn as much as you can of this in five minutes." Five minutes is too long for our test, because during that time the subject escapes us; it may be that he becomes distracted or thinks of other things; the test loses its clinical character and becomes too scholastic. We have therefore reluctantly been obliged to renounce testing the rapidity and extent of the memory by this method. Several other equivalent examples of elimination could be cited. In order to cover rapidly a wide field of observation, it goes without saying that the tests should be heterogeneous.

Another consideration. Our purpose is to evaluate a level of intelligence. It is understood that we here separate natural intelligence and instruction. It is the intelligence alone that we seek to measure, by disregarding insofar as possible, the degree of instruction which the subject possesses. He should, indeed, be considered by the examiner as a complete ignoramus knowing neither how to read nor write. This necessity forces us to forego a great many exercises having a verbal, literary or scholastic character. These belong to a pedagogical examination. We believe that we have succeeded in completely disregarding the acquired information of the subject. We give him nothing to read, nothing to write, and submit him to no test in which he might succeed by means of rote learning. In fact we do not even notice his inability to read if a case occurs. It is simply the level of his natural intelligence that is taken into account.

But here we must come to an understanding of what meaning to give to that word so vague and so comprehensive, "the intelligence." Nearly all the phenomena with which psychology concerns itself are phenomena of intelligence; sensation, perception, are intellectual manifestations as much as reasoning. Should we therefore bring into our examination the measure of sensation after the manner of the psycho-physicists? Should we put to the test all of his psychological processes? A slight reflection has shown us that this would indeed be wasted time.

It seems to us that in intelligence there is a fundamental faculty, the alteration or the lack of which, is of the utmost importance for practical life. This faculty is judgment, otherwise called good sense, practical sense, initiative, the faculty of adapting one's self to circumstances. To judge well, to comprehend well, to reason well, these are the essential activities of intelligence. A person may be a moron or an imbecile if he is lacking in judgment; but with good judgment he can never be either. Indeed the rest of the intellectual faculties seem of little importance in comparison with judgment. What does it matter, for example, whether the organs of sense function normally? Of what import that certain ones are hyperesthetic, or that others are anesthetic or are weakened? Laura Bridgman, Helen Keller and their fellow-unfortunates were blind as well as deaf, but this did not prevent them from being very intelligent. Certainly this is demonstrative proof that the total or even partial integrity of the senses does not form a mental factor equal to judgment. We may measure the acuteness of the sensibility of subjects; nothing could be easier. But we should do this, not so much to find out the state of their sensibility as to learn the exactitude of their judgment.

The same remark holds good for the study of the memory. At first glance, memory being a psychological phenomenon of capital importance, one would be tempted to give it a very conspicuous part in an examination of intelligence. But memory is distinct from and independent of judgment. One may have good sense and lack memory. The reverse is also common. Just at the present time we are observing a backward girl who is developing before our astonished eyes a memory very much greater than our own. We have measured that memory and we are not deceived regarding it. Nevertheless that girl presents a most beautifully classic type of imbecility.

As a result of all this investigation, in the scale which we present we accord the first place to judgment; that which is of importance to us is not certain errors which the subject commits, but absurd errors, which prove that he lacks judgment. We have even made special provision to encourage people to make absurd replies. In spite of the accuracy of this directing idea, it will be easily understood that it has been impossible to permit of its regulating exclusively our examinations. For example, one can not make tests of judgment on children of less than two years when one begins to watch their first gleams of intelligence. Much is gained when one can discern in them traces of coordination, the first delineation of attention and memory. We shall therefore bring out in our lists some tests of memory; but so far as we are able, we shall give these tests such a turn as to invite the subject to make absurd replies, and thus under cover of a test of memory, we shall have an appreciation of their judgment.

THE MONTESSORI METHOD (1912) From Maria Montessori, *The Montessori Method*, Anne E. George, trans. (New York, 1912), pp. 167, 169–75.

In a pedagogical method which is experimental the education of the senses must undoubtedly assume the greatest importance. Experimental psychology also takes note of movements by means of sense measurements.

Pedagogy, however, although it may profit by psychometry, is not designed to *measure* the sensations, but *educate* the senses. This is a point easily understood, yet one which is often confused. While the proceedings of esthesiometry are not to any great extent applicable to little children, the *education* of the *senses* is entirely possible.

We do not start from the conclusions of experimental psychology. That is, it is not the knowledge of the average sense conditions according to the age of the child which leads us to determine the educational applications we shall make. We start essentially from a method, and it is probable that psychology will be able to draw its conclusions from pedagogy so understood, and not *vice versa*.

The method used by me is that of making a pedagogical experiment with a didactic object and awaiting the spontaneous reaction of the child. This is a method in every way analogous to that of experimental psychology.

* * *

I believe, however, that I have arrived at a *selection of objects* (which I do not here wish to speak of in the technical language of psychology as stimuli) representing the minimum *necessary* to a practical sense education.

These objects constitute the *didactic system* (or set of didactic materials) used by me. They are manufactured by the House of Labour of the Humanitarian Society at Milan.

A description of the objects will be given as the educational scope of each is explained. Here I shall limit myself to the setting forth of a few general considerations.

First. The difference in the reaction between deficient and normal children, in the presentation of didactic material made up of graded stimuli. This difference is plainly seen from the fact that the same didactic material used with deficients *makes education possible*, while with normal children it *provokes auto-education*.

This fact is one of the most interesting I have met with in all my experience, and it inspired and rendered possible the method of *observation* and *liberty*.

Let us suppose that we use our first object,—a block in which solid geometric forms are set. Into corresponding holes in the block are set ten little wooden cylinders, the bases diminishing gradually about ten millimetres. The game consists in taking the cylinders out of their places, putting them on the table, mixing them, and then putting each one back in its own place. The aim is to educate the eye to the differential perception of dimensions.

With the deficient child, it would be necessary to begin with exercises in which the stimuli were much more strongly contrasted, and to arrive at this exercise only after many others had preceded it.

With normal children, this is, on the other hand, the first object which we may present, and out of all the didactic material this is the game preferred by the very little children of two and a half and three years. Once we arrived at this exercise with a deficient child, it was necessary continually and actively to recall his attention, inviting him to look at the block and showing him the various pieces. And if the child once succeeded in placing all the cylinders properly, he stopped, and the game was finished. Whenever the deficient child committed an error, it was necessary to correct it, or to urge him to correct it himself, and when he was able to correct an error he was usually quite indifferent.

Now the normal child, instead, takes spontaneously a lively interest in this game. He pushes away all who would interfere, or offer to help him, and wishes to be alone before his problem.

It had already been noted that little ones of two or three years take the greatest pleasure in arranging small objects, and this experiment in the "Children's Houses" demonstrates the truth of this assertion.

Now, and here is the important point, the normal child attentively observes the relation between the size of the opening and that of the object which he is to place in the mould, and is greatly interested in the game, as is clearly shown by the expression of attention on the little face.

If he mistakes, placing one of the objects in an opening that is small for it, he takes it away, and proceeds to make various trials, seeking the proper opening. If he makes a contrary error, letting the cylinder fall into an opening that is a little too large for it, and then collects all the successive cylinders in openings just a little too large, he will find himself at the last with the big cylinder in his hand while only the smallest opening is empty. The didactic material *controls every error*. The child proceeds to correct himself, doing this in various ways. Most often he feels the cylinders or shakes them, in order to recognise which are the largest. Sometimes, he sees at a glance where his error lies, pulls the cylinders from the places where they should not be, and puts those left out where they belong, then replaces all the others. The normal child always repeats the exercise with growing interest.

Indeed, it is precisely in these errors that the educational importance of the didactic material lies, and when the child with evident security places each piece in its proper place, he has outgrown the exercise, and this piece of material becomes useless to him.

This self-correction leads the child to concentrate his attention upon the differences of dimensions, and to compare the various pieces. It is in just this comparison that the *psycho-sensory* exercise lies.

There is, therefore, no question here of teaching the child the *knowledge* of the dimensions, through the medium of these pieces. Neither is it our aim that the child shall know how to use, *without an error*, the material presented to him thus performing the exercises well.

That would place our material on the same basis as many others, for example that of Froebel, and would require again the *active* work of the *teacher*, who busies herself furnishing knowledge, and making haste to correct every error in order that the child may *learn the use of the objects.*

Here instead it is the work of the child, the auto-correction, the auto-education which acts, for the *teacher must not interfere* in the *slightest* way. No teacher can furnish the child with the *agility which he acquires* through gymnastic *exercises:* it is necessary that the *pupil perfect himself* through his own efforts. It is very much the same with the *education of the senses.*

It might be said that the same thing is true of every form of education; a man is not what he is because of the teachers he has had, but because of what he has done.

One of the difficulties of putting this method into practice with teachers of the old school, lies in the difficulty of preventing them from intervening when the little child remains for some time puzzled before some error, and with his eyebrows drawn together and his lips puckered, makes repeated efforts to correct himself. When they see this, the old-time teachers are seized with pity, and long, with an almost irresistible force, to help the child. When we prevent this intervention, they burst into words of compassion for the little scholar, but he soon shows in his smiling face the joy of having surmounted an obstacle.

Normal children repeat such exercises many times. This repetition varies according to the individual. Some children after having completed the exercise five or six times are tired of it. Others will remove and replace the pieces at least *twenty times*, with an expression of evident interest. Once, after I had watched a little one of four years repeat this exercise sixteen times, I had the other children sing in order to distract her, but she continued unmoved to take out the cylinders, mix them up and put them back in their places.

An intelligent teacher ought to be able to make most interesting individual psychological observations, and, to a certain point, should be able to measure the length of time for which the various stimuli held the attention.

In fact, when the child educates himself, and when the control and correction of errors is yielded to the didactic material, there *remains for the teacher nothing but to observe*. She must then be more of a psychologist than a teacher, and this shows the importance of a scientific preparation on the part of the teacher.

Indeed, with my methods, the teacher teaches *little* and observes *much*, and, above all, it is her function to direct the psychic activity of the children and their physiological development. For this reason I have changed the name of teacher into that of directress.

At first this name provoked many smiles, for everyone asked whom there was for this teacher to direct, since she had no assistants, and since she must leave her little scholars *in liberty*. But her direction is much more profound and important than that which is commonly understood, for this teacher directs *the life and the soul.*

Second. The education of the senses has, as its aim, the refinement of the differential perception of stimuli by means of repeated exercises.

There exists a *sensory culture*, which is not generally taken into consideration, but which is a factor in esthesiometry.

For example, in the mental *tests* which are used in France, or in a series of tests which De Sanctis has established for the *diagnosis* of the intellectual status, I have often seen used *cubes of different sizes placed at varying distances*. The child was to select the *smallest* and the *largest*, while the chronometer measured the time of reaction between the command and the execution of the act. Account was also taken of the errors. I repeat that in such experiments the factor of *culture* is forgotten and by this I mean *sensory culture.*

Our children have, for example, among the didactic material for the education of the senses, a series of ten cubes. The first has a base of ten centimetres, and the others decrease, successively, one centimetre as to base, the smallest cube having a base of one centimetre. The exercise consists in throwing the blocks, which are pink in colour, down upon a green carpet, and then building them up into a little tower, placing the largest cube as the base, and then placing the others in order of size until the little cube of one centimetre is placed at the top.

The little one must each time select, from the blocks scattered upon the green carpet, "the largest" block. This game is most entertaining to the little ones of two years and a half, who, as soon as they have constructed the little tower, tumble it down with little blows of the hand, admiring the pink cubes as they lie scattered upon the green carpet. Then, they begin again the construction, building and destroying a definite number of times.

If we were to place before these tests one of my children from three to four years, and one of the children from the first elementary (six or seven years old), my pupil would undoubtedly manifest a shorter period of reaction, and would not commit errors. The same may be said for the tests of the chromatic sense, etc.

This educational method should therefore prove interesting to students of experimental psychology as well as to teachers.

In conclusion, let me summarize briefly: Our didactic material renders auto-education possible, permits a methodical education of the senses. Not upon the ability of the teacher does such education rest, but upon the didactic system. This presents objects which, first, attract the spontaneous attention of the child, and, second, contain a rational gradation of stimuli.

RULES AND REGULATIONS OF THE MONTESSORI "CHILDREN'S HOUSE" (1912) From Maria Montessori, *The Montessori Method,* Anne E. George, trans. (New York, 1912), pp. 70–71.

Rules and Regulations of the ''Children's Houses''

The Roman Association of Good Building hereby establishes within its tenement house number   , a "Children's House," in which may be gathered together all children under common school age, belonging to the families of the tenants.

The chief aim of the "Children's House" is to offer, free of charge, to the children of those parents who are obliged to absent themselves for their work, the personal care which the parents are not able to give.

In the "Children's House" attention is given to the education, the health, the physical and moral development of the children. This work is carried on in a way suited to the age of the children.

There shall be connected with the "Children's House" a Directress, a Physician, and a Caretaker.

The programme and hours of the "Children's House" shall be fixed by the Directress.

There may be admitted to the "Children's House" all the children in the tenement between the ages of three and seven.

The parents who wish to avail themselves of the advantages of the "Children's House" pay nothing. They must, however, assume these binding obligations:

(a) To send their children to the "Children's House" at the appointed time, clean in body and clothing, and provided with a suitable apron.

(b) To show the greatest respect and deference toward the Directress and toward all persons connected with the "Children's House," and to co-operate with the Directress herself in the education of the children. Once a week, at least, the mothers may talk with the Directress, giving her information concerning the home life of the child, and receiving helpful advice from her.

IDEAS FROM ABROAD

1999

There shall be expelled from the "Children's House":

(a) Those children who present themselves unwashed, or in soiled clothing.

(b) Those who show themselves to be incorrigible.

(c) Those whose parents fail in respect to the persons connected with the "Children's House," or who destroy through bad conduct the educational work of the institution.

FREUD ON THE PSYCHICAL APPARATUS (1919) From Sigmund Freud, *An Outline of Psychoanalysis,* James Strachey, trans. (New York, 1949), pp. 14–21.

We assume that mental life is the function of an apparatus to which we ascribe the characteristics of being extended in space and of being made up of several portions—which we imagine, that is, as being like a telescope or microscope or something of the sort. The consistent carrying through of a conception of this kind is a scientific novelty, even though some attempts in that direction have been made previously.

We have arrived at our knowledge of this psychical apparatus by studying the individual development of human beings. To the oldest of these mental provinces or agencies we give the name of *id.* It contains everything that is inherited, that is present at birth, that is fixed in the constitution—above all, therefore, the instincts, which originate in the somatic organization and which find their first mental expression in the id in forms unknown to us.[1]

*   *   *

Under the influence of the real external world which surrounds us, one portion of the id has undergone a special development. From what was originally a cortical layer, provided with organs for receiving stimuli and with apparatus for protection against excessive stimulation, a special organization has arisen which henceforward acts as an intermediary between the id and the external world. This region of our mental life has been given the name of *ego.*

The principal characteristics of the ego are these. In consequence of the relation which was already established between sensory perception and muscular action, the ego is in control of voluntary movement. It has the task of self-preservation. As regards *external* events, it performs that task by becoming aware of the stimuli from without, by storing up experiences of them (in the memory), by avoiding excessive stimuli (through flight), by dealing with moderate stimuli (through adaptation) and, finally, by learning to bring about appropriate modifications in the external world to its own advantage (through activity). As regards *internal* events, in relation to the id, it performs that task by gaining control over the demands of the instincts, by

[1]This oldest portion of the mental apparatus remains the most important throughout life, and it was the first subject of the investigations of psychoanalysis. [Throughout this book the English word "instinct" is, with some misgivings, used to render the German *"Trieb."* The sense in which Freud uses the term is, in any case, made clear in the following pages.—*Trans.*]

deciding whether they shall be allowed to obtain satisfaction, by postponing that satisfaction to time and circumstances favorable in the external world or by suppressing their excitations completely. Its activities are governed by consideration of the tensions produced by stimuli present within it or introduced into it. The raising of these tensions is in general felt as *unpleasure* and their lowering as *pleasure*. It is probable, however, that what is felt as pleasure or unpleasure is not the *absolute* degree of the tensions but something in the rhythm of their changes. The ego pursues pleasure and seeks to avoid unpleasure. An increase in unpleasure which is expected and foreseen is met by a *signal of anxiety;* the occasion of this increase, whether it threatens from without or within, is called a *danger.* From time to time the ego gives up its connection with the external world and withdraws into the state of sleep, in which its organization undergoes far-reaching changes. It may be inferred from the state of sleep that that organization consists in a particular distribution of mental energy.

The long period of childhood, during which the growing human being lives in dependence upon his parents, leaves behind it a precipitate, which forms within his ego a special agency in which this parental influence is prolonged. It has received the name of *superego.* In so far as the superego is differentiated from the ego or opposed to it, it constitutes a third force which the ego must take into account.

Thus, an action by the ego is as it should be if it satisfies simultaneously the demands of the id, of the superego and of reality, that is to say if it is able to reconcile their demands with one another. The details of the relation between the ego and the superego become completely intelligible if they are carried back to the child's attitude toward his parents. The parents' influence naturally includes not merely the personalities of the parents themselves but also the racial, national, and family traditions handed on through them as well as the demands of the immediate social *milieu* which they represent. In the same way, an individual's superego in the course of his development takes over contributions from later successors and substitutes of his parents, such as teachers, admired figures in public life, or high social ideals. It will be seen that, in spite of their fundamental difference, the id and the superego have one thing in common: they both represent the influences of the past (the id the influence of heredity, the superego essentially the influence of what is taken over from other people), whereas the ego is principally determined by the individual's own experience, that is to say by accidental and current events.

This general pattern of a psychical apparatus may be supposed to apply equally to the higher animals which resemble man mentally. A superego must be presumed to be present wherever, as in the case of man, there is a long period of dependence in childhood. The assumption of a distinction between ego and id cannot be avoided.

※　※　※

The power of the id expresses the true purpose of the individual organism's life. This consists in the satisfaction of its innate needs. No such purpose as that of keeping itself alive or of protecting itself from dangers by means of anxiety can be attributed to the id. That is the business of the ego, which is also concerned with discovering the most favorable and least perilous method of obtaining satisfaction, taking the external world into account. The superego may bring fresh needs to the fore, but its chief function remains the *limitation* of satisfactions.

The forces which we assume to exist behind the tensions caused by the needs of the id are called *instincts*. They represent the somatic demands upon mental life. Though they are the ultimate cause of all activity, they are by nature conservative; the state, whatever it may be, which a living thing has reached, gives rise to a tendency to re-establish that state so soon as it has been abandoned. It is possible to distinguish an indeterminate number of instincts and in common practice this is in fact done. For us, however, the important question arises whether we may not be able to derive all of these various instincts from a few fundamental ones. We have found that instincts can change their aim (by displacement) and also that they can replace one another—the energy of one instinct passing over to another. This latter process is still insufficiently understood. After long doubts and vacillations we have decided to assume the existence of only two basic instincts, *Eros,* and *the destructive instinct.* (The contrast between the instincts of self-preservation and of the preservation of the species, as well as the contrast between ego-love and object-love, fall within the bounds of Eros.) The aim of the first of these basic instincts is to establish ever greater unities and to preserve them thus—in short, to bind together; the aim of the second, on the contrary, is to undo connections and so to destroy things. We may suppose that the final aim of the destructive instinct is to reduce living things to an inorganic state. For this reason we also call it the *death instinct.* If we suppose that living things appeared later than inanimate ones and arose out of them, then the death instinct agrees with the formula that we have stated, to the effect that instincts tend toward a return to an earlier state. We are unable to apply the formula to Eros (the love instinct). That would be to imply that living substance had once been a unity but had subsequently been torn apart and was now tending toward re-union.

In biological functions the two basic instincts work against each other or combine with each other. Thus, the act of eating is a destruction of the object with the final aim of incorporating it, and the sexual act is an act of aggression having as its purpose the most intimate union. This interaction of the two basic instincts with and against each other gives rise to the whole variegation of the phenomena of life. The analogy of our two basic instincts extends from the region of animate things to the pair of opposing forces—attraction and repulsion—which rule in the inorganic world.

FREUD ON PSYCHOANALYSIS AND CHILD TRAINING (1935)   From
Sigmund Freud, Foreword to August Aichhorn, *Wayward Youth* (New York, 1935), pp. v–vii.

Of all the fields in which psychoanalysis has been applied none has aroused so much interest, inspired so much hope, and accordingly attracted so many capable workers as the *theory and practice of child training.* This is easy to understand. The child has become the main object of psychoanalytic research and in this respect has replaced the neurotic with whom the work began. Analysis has revealed that the child lives on almost unchanged in the sick patient as well as in the dreamer and the artist; it has thrown a flood of light on the instinctual forces and impulses which give the childish being its characteristic features; and it has traced the paths of development which proceed to maturity. It is no wonder that expectation was aroused that psychoanalytic work would prove valuable in education, the purpose of which is to guide the child on his way to maturity, to encourage him, and to protect him from taking the wrong path.

My personal share in this application of psychoanalysis has been slight. In my youth, I accepted it as a byword that the three impossible professions are teaching, healing, and governing, and I have been sufficiently busy with the second. This does not mean that I do not appreciate the great social value of the work which attracts my co-workers in the pedagogical field.

August Aichhorn's book deals with one part of the great problem of the application of psychoanalysis to education, namely, that of influencing the dissocial adolescent by means of education. The author had worked for many years in an official position as director of state institutions for the care of delinquents before he became acquainted with psychoanalysis. His treatment of his charges had its source in a warm sympathy for the fate of these unfortunates and was rightly guided by his intuitive understanding of their psychic needs. Psychoanalysis could teach him little that was new to him in a practical way, but it offered him a clear theoretical insight into the justification of his treatment and enabled him to explain his method to others in this field.

We cannot assume that every educator has this intuitive gift. Aichhorn's experience and achievement lead us to two conclusions. One is that the educator should be psychoanalytically trained; otherwise the child, the object of his effort, remains an inaccessible enigma to him. Such training is best achieved when the educator subjects himself to an analysis in order to experience it within himself. Theoretical teaching of analysis does not penetrate deeply enough and brings no conviction.

The second conclusion sounds rather more conservative in its purport, that educational work is *sui generis,* not to be confused with nor exchanged for psychoanalytic means of influence. Psychoanalysis of the child may be drawn upon as a contributory help, but it is not an appropriate substitute for education. This is true not only because of practical reasons, but also because of theoretical considerations. The relation between education and psychoanalytic work will probably be the subject for a detailed investigation in the near future. I shall indicate only a few points here. One must not be led astray by the statement, quite justified in another sense, that psychoanalysis of the adult neurotic may be compared to re-education. The child, even the wayward and delinquent child, should not be compared to the adult neurotic, and re-education is something quite different from the education of the immature. The possibility of exerting influence through psychoanalysis depends on quite definite conditions, which may be described as the "analytic situation"; it requires the formation of certain psychic structures and a special attitude toward the analyst. When these factors are lacking, as in the case of children and young delinquents and, as a rule, in criminals dominated by their instincts, the psychoanalytic method must be adapted to meet the need. The theoretical chapters of this book offer the reader a preliminary orientation in these various considerations.

I add one more conclusion, which has no special significance for the theory of pedagogy but is important for the position of the educator. If a teacher has learned analysis by experiencing it himself and is capable of applying his knowledge as a supplementary aid in his work with borderline and mixed cases, he should obviously be allowed the practice of analysis and should not be hindered in it for narrow-minded reasons.

ANNA FREUD ON PSYCHOANALYSIS AND THE EDUCATION OF THE CHILD (1935)

From "Psychoanalysis and the Training of the Young Child," *Psychoanalytic Quarterly*, vol. IV, pp. 15–16, 18–24.

We are all aware of the difficult position in which the teacher finds himself. To be sure, we frequently hear it stated that one of the most important community tasks is given over to teachers, that the most valuable material at the disposal of society comes under their control, that they determine the destiny of the coming generation, etc. But in actual practice we find little of this high value set on education or on the educator himself. Nor are teachers even so well paid as, let us say, industrialists and bankers, who handle the material resources of the nation. As members of the community they must struggle continually for the esteem of their fellow-men and for recognition from the parents and officials of their district. Although many people believe that the younger the child the more important his education, in actual practice the evaluation of the teacher increases with the age of the pupil. Compare, for example, the esteemed position of the high school teacher with the status of the kindergarten teacher. There is an inconsistency somewhere.

The low evaluation of teachers in general arises from the fact that they are really not independent producers but middlemen, agents, buffers between two generations. They are given raw material and are expected to turn out certain specific products. The only freedom given them is in the choice of pedagogical method. Just because they enjoy so little freedom in other ways, they seize upon this little piece of independence and create out of it the fiction of a great power. . . .

The failures in educational work have always been attributed to the teachers. It has seemed that somehow the individual teacher was at fault rather than education as a whole. I believe, indeed, the reason why teachers of all ages have turned to the science of psychology has been to exonerate themselves from the imputed disgrace of this failure. Psychology, they thought, would teach them the nature of the raw material given over to them. The truth is that not until psychology really does succeed in understanding children will teachers stand in a more favorable relation to society. Only then will they be able to point out the discrepancy of the goal set up by society and the capacity of the child to reach this goal. Only then will they weigh the psychological potentialities of the individual child with the demands made on him by society as factors deserving equal consideration. Only when it becomes clear which educational goals are compatible with mental health and which are attainable only at the expense of this health, will greater justice be done for the child.

*　　*　　*

For practical purposes, knowledge of the child's mental condition, unaccompanied by suggestions for its application to education, brings us no further than we were before. Instead of letting our feelings determine our attitude toward the child's instincts, let us turn to the knowledge gained from psychoanalytic practice. In the treatment of adults we learn to recognize various types of illness. From each type we can draw conclusions about definite relationships which existed between the child and the individuals responsible for his training. We meet with neurotic inhibitions, for instance, which have developed because one of the instinctual impulses has been forcibly repressed at a very early period and consequently denied satisfaction. But the impulse is too powerful and tenacious to be quelled in this manner. An inner conflict arises and eventually the repressed impulse forces its way to the surface, usually in a curiously distorted and disturbing form. On the other hand, we meet with pathological conditions, such as perversions and certain forms of unsocial behavior, which are characterized by an adherence or a regression to an infantile type of instinctual gratification, to the exclusion of all other forms of gratification. In the history of such an illness we usually find traumatic experiences which have allowed the particular instinctual impulse to break through and achieve complete gratification. The child's development remains fixed at this point and does not progress to the desired adult level of instinctual life. However, these two entirely different types of illnesses have something in common. In both the child has been caught and held at an infantile level of development. So we see that such a fixation with its subsequent neurotic illness may occur either when the impulse is allowed full expression or, conversely, when it is entirely denied. The path to mental health lies somewhere between these two extremes. The problem is evidently to find a middle course. The instinctual urge must not be driven into repression, thus preventing its sublimation, nor must it be allowed full satisfaction. It is as if we had to teach the child not to put his hand into the fire because it burns, but dare not express it so directly, lest he become afraid of all fire and be unable in later life to light a match, smoke a cigarette or cook a meal. Our task is to teach the child to keep away from the fire without arousing in him a horror of it.

We can learn something from this simple analogy. Considering the danger of complete instinctual gratification for the child, educators have always found frightening the child to be the easiest way out of the situation. Educators recognized the dangers of instinctual gratification long before they had any formal knowledge of the child's instincts. They have set up boundaries which the child has not dared to overstep and have utilized every means in their power to reinforce these prohibitions. . . . In order to avoid a continual struggle with the child and to make it unnecessary to cry out each time he approached the fire of instinctual gratification, they have said, "Once and for all, that burns!" This has apparently been the simplest solution.

How can the intelligent educator of today find the proper solution? Is a continued struggle the only alternative to absolute prohibition? Must the adult be on hand every time the child approaches an instinctual danger? What means should he use to avoid creating a lasting fear in the child and yet protect him in each individual instance?

*   *   *

There are two ways of looking at the problem. We may say, on the one hand, that whatever we do, the child is going to feel that he is denied and forbidden all satisfaction, so why should we try to avoid being stern? On the other hand, we may say that no matter how much a child may be spared, he still has to be subjected to a great deal, so why not at least reduce our interference to a minimum? But the fact is that we do struggle with the child over his instinctual gratifications. . . .

The situation would really be hopeless for education and for our relations to the little child if he were interested in nothing but the search for pleasure, or instinctual gratification. . . . However, the course of development itself helps to remedy the situation. The period in which the child tries to satisfy his instinctual wishes exclusively on his own person is a relatively short one, whether these wishes are oral, anal or sadistic. The instinctual impulses are very soon directed toward the outer world. The child seeks out the people in his immediate environment who are the most important to him and insistently demands of them the gratification of his wishes. We say that the child now has a love object. . . .

As soon as an external love object is introduced into the situation the child becomes dependent on the good-will of this object. The satisfaction of every wish now depends on the consent or cooperation of the loved being. . . .

Although for the child the situation has thus been complicated, it has been vastly improved for his training and education. Suppose the individual who is training the child and the child's love object are one and the same person. . . . The love object needs only to refuse cooperation to make gratification [of the instincts] impossible. . . . The child's fear is an aid in his training and education. The very first fear tending to make him obedient is that of being left alone and helpless. Another fear arises from the attachment to the love object—the fear of losing this person's love if he fails to obey. . . . Let us recall how hard it is in adult life to give up a love object on whom we have lavished all our affection, whom we have desired to possess completely and, if possible, without rivals. . . . If this is true of a more or less independent and mature adult, whose personality is already formed, we can imagine what the small child must undergo in similar circumstances.

* * *

Every child then suffers the same experience: this love object (the mother) will not or cannot belong to him. She offers him occasional satisfaction, tenderness and care, but never exclusive possession. The child must consent to share her with his brothers and sisters, must recognize that she belongs in the first place to the father. He must learn to renounce the idea of total possession and all that that means to him. . . . It costs too great a price for the child to give up the love object inwardly as well as outwardly; he must at least partially absorb the object, he must modify himself to resemble his mother or father. Strangely enough, the child takes over from the love object the very things which were most unpleasant and disturbing to him, the commands and prohibitions. Thus it comes about that toward the end of the Œdipus situation, the child, although remaining in part unchanged, has taken unto himself the object, the parent or person in charge of his training. This incorporated portion with which, as we express it, the child has identified himself, treats the other part of the child's inner personality in the same way as the parental object actually treated the child. [This identification we call the superego.] It dominates the child's ego just as the parents dominated the child.

The formation of the superego facilitates matters for those who are educating and training the child. . . . The educator of the older child can rely on this superego to support him. . . . The child finds himself confronted by two authorities, the transformed part of his own inner personality, i.e., his new superego, and the ever-present love object of the outer world. He becomes unexpectedly docile and obedient. It is the docility thus achieved, the strict obedience which parents or teachers so often encourage for the sake of making their work easier, that can drive the child into extreme repression, into neurosis.

Of all the modifying processes which determine the child's personality, the formation of the superego, as above described, is the most decisive one. It starts with love for an object and proceeds to identification with this object. . . . The child with this budding or more or less completely developed superego is no longer a small, pre-school child; he has entered the second period of childhood, and has passed from the jurisdiction of the parents or pre-school educators into the hands of other teachers, who undoubtedly have the easier task. And here I bring to those who have the harder, more complicated task, to all who undertake the guidance of small children, the consolation that they, too, have really significant work to accomplish for the future.

ALFRED ADLER ON INFERIORITY FEELINGS IN CHILDREN
(**1920**)   From Alfred Adler, "Demoralized Children," as quoted in *The Practice and Theory of Individual Psychology* (London, 1929), pp. 340–42, 345–50.

Generally when we speak of demoralization we think of the school years. The expert observer will, however, be able to point out a number of cases where the demoralization began before the school days. It is not always possible to attribute them to the bringing-up. Parents must be told that no matter how careful they are that part of the education of which they know or notice nothing and which emanates from other circles, influences the child more than their consciously superior education.

These extraneous influences that find their way into the nursery represent all the events and conditions of life and of the environment. The child is impressed by the difficulties with which he sees his father beset in order to make a living, and he realizes the hostility of life even if he does not speak of it. He will develop a conception with the inadequate means at his disposal, with childish interpretations and experiences. This view of the world then becomes for the child a measure of evaluation; he makes it the basis for his judgments in every position in which he finds himself and will draw the correspondingly necessary inferences. These are in large measure wrong because we are here dealing with an inexperienced child whose reasoning powers are undeveloped and who consequently is liable to make false deductions. But just visualize the tremendous impression made upon a child whose parents live in a poor dwelling under depressing social circumstances, and contrast it with that of a child who does not feel life's hostility so definitely. These two types are so distinct that it is possible to infer from every child's expression and manner of speaking to which group he belongs. How differently will this last-mentioned child's attitude toward life be, with his self-confidence and courage, and how markedly will this be reflected in his whole carriage. The second type makes friends with the world easily because he knows nothing of life's difficulties or can overcome them more easily. I have asked children among the proletariat of what they were most in fear and practically all answered—*of being struck*—in other words, of occurrences taking place in their own family. Children who grow up in fear of a strong father, stepfather or mother, retain this feeling of fear till puberty, and we must remember that on the average the proletarian does not give us the same world-satisfied impression as the average bourgeois who is more courageous. A good deal of this pitiable bearing can be traced back to the fact that he has grown up in an atmosphere of fear of life and punishment. This is the most venomous kind of poison for developing *pessimism* in children, for they retain this perspective throughout life, have no self-confidence and are indecisive. To gain a courageous attitude afterwards requires both time and energy. The children of well-to-do parents generally answered the question of what they feared most, by saying schoolwork. This shows that neither individuals nor their own environment frighten them and they feel themselves to be in the midst of life where tasks and work exist of which they are afraid. This of course makes us assume the existence of untenable conditions in the schools, which instead of training them to face life gladly and courageously merely filled them with fear.

Let us now go back to the question of demoralization before the school-days. We ought not to be surprised to find, in view of the excitable state of the moods called up by all the disturbing relations that create fear of life, and in view of the envisaging of one's neighbour as hostile, that children will make a peristent effort to gain prestige and not to appear as the insignificant personages to which people often try to reduce them. It is one of the most important principles in any educational system to take the child *seriously,* to regard him as *an equal* and not to humiliate and make fun of him; for the child feels and must necessarily feel all those expressions of his immediate surrounding as oppressive, just as the weaker person possesses a sensibility different from that of an individual who finds himself in an assured position of a mental and bodily superiority. We are not even in a position to state exactly how a child is affected by the fact that it cannot do the things that he wonderingly sees his parents and brothers perform daily. This should be remembered. Everyone who has developed a capacity for reading the child's soul, must have realized that every child possesses *an extraordinary craving for power and importance,* for increased self-consciousness; that he wishes to exert influence and appear important. The *young would-be hero* represents but a special case of the power that all wish to have.

✳   ✳   ✳

The formation of bands is so common that it is the first thing that comes to mind when thinking of demoralized youths. But the demoralization of an individual distinct from a group is quite frequent. Such a person's life is similar to that we have described above, though apparently the directly impelling motives are different. Let us keep before us the fact that in the cases of group demoralization described above, the fate of the individuals *is foreshadowed as soon as they have suffered some set-back or expect one.* The same is true of a single individual. The simple, almost unwitting, persons come under this rule to the same extent as the more complicated. It is always some offence to one's *amour propre,* the fear of making a fool of one's self, the feeling of some decline in power or the will to power, that becomes the occasion for a *deviation to some side-line of development.* It looks almost as if these children *were seeking for some subsidiary field of action.* Frequently demoralization shows itself in a special form of laziness, which must then be looked upon neither as hereditary nor as the acquisition of a bad habit, but rather as a method of preventing any of them being put to tests. A lazy child can always fall back upon laziness as an excuse. If he fails in an examination it is the fault of his laziness, and such a child prefers to attribute his failure to laziness than to inability. Thus, like an experienced criminal, he is forced *to prove an alibi;* he must in each case demonstrate that his lack of success is due to laziness. And he succeeds. His laziness covers his failures, and from one point of view, that of sparing his conceit, his psychic situation has improved.

We know the demerits of our schools. The crowded classes, the insufficient training of many of the teachers, occasionally their lack of interest, for they suffer intensely from cramped economic conditions and more is hardly to be expected of them. Primarily, however, the greatest drawback of the school is *the prevailing ignorance about the psychic development of the child;* and that is the reason why hitherto the relations of the teacher and pupil have been so much more hopeless than those existing anywhere else in life. If the pupil makes a mistake he is either punished or given a poor mark. That is about the same as if a doctor called to treat someone who has broken a bone, saying: "You have a bone-fracture! Good-bye!" That assuredly is not the purpose of education! In the main the children take care of themselves under these horrible conditions and progress, but what of the gaps in their development? Children will proceed until they finally come to a point where their deficiencies assume such a form that a halt must be called. It is sad enough to realize how difficult it is even for the best child to progress, how under the weight of the accumulated difficulties he is afflicted with there emerges the painful feeling of being unable to perform the tasks others achieve, and finally to be a witness of his wounded and offended self-esteem! Many pass beyond this stage too, but many prefer to develop for themselves some subsidiary field of action.

Individual demoralization thus develops in the same manner as group demoralization. Here, likewise, the feeling of inferiority, of inadequacy and of humiliation tower above everything else. Let me quote the case of a boy, an only child, whose parents devoted great pains in educating him. At the age of five he already regarded the locking of chests, when the parents were absent, as a great insult and succeeded somehow in procuring a skeleton key and ransacking the chests. He was impelled to this conduct by his striving for independence, his will to power asserting itself in antagonism to his parents and the laws of society. Even to-day, at the age of eighteen, he indulges in household thefts unknown to his parents, although they believe they are aware of all of them. When his father tells him, "Of what use are these acts to you? As often as you steal I discover the fact," then the boy has the proud realization of knowing that his father does not know one in twenty and continues his thefts in the conviction that all that is necessary is to be clever enough to escape detection. Here we have an example of the frequent struggle between a child and its parents that induces the former to resort to acts contrary to the moral code of society. When fully grown-up this young man will undoubtedly provide himself with these psychic aids and supports that will enable him to transgress without feeling any pricks of conscience. His father is a business man, and even though the son is not permitted to visit his father's factories, he knows that the latter is engaged in the manufacture of chains, etc. When conversing with people he calls his father's attacks upon him unjust, because the latter is simply doing what he does, simply on a larger scale. So here again we have an example of the educative influence of the environment of which the parents are totally ignorant.

*   *   *

If we wish to understand clearly both all the interrelations and the position of the children to society we should bear two things in mind. First that their ambition and vanity are signs of their craving for power and superiority so that in consequence they try to obtain prestige along some side-path as soon as the main-line of development is closed to them. Secondly, their relation to their fellows is somehow deficient; they are not good companions, they do not easily adjust themselves to society, have something of the dog-in-the-manger attitude and exhibit little contact with the outer world. At times, nothing but a meaningless pretence or a mere habit is all that remains of their love for their own people; often even this is missing and they may then even attack their own family. They play the role of people whose feeling for society is defective, who have not discovered the point of contact with their fellowmen and look upon them as hostile. Traits of suspicion are very common among them; they are always on guard lest someone take advantage of them and I have often heard these children exclaim that it is necessary to be unscrupulous, *i.e.*, that superiority must be attained.

*   *   *

Evils are also noticeable in the type of attitude taken by society. Both courts and police work to no purpose because they always centre their attention upon questions other than the really radical and determining ones. To improve the situation the first requirement is to have a different and a more humane personnel. Institutions ought to be erected for taking care of these demoralized children, for bringing them back to life; not shutting them off from society, but, on the contrary, making them more adapted for it. That can only happen if we have a full understanding of their peculiarities. Nothing can be accomplished if any kind of person whatsoever (*e.g.* a retired officer or a subaltern) can be appointed director of an institution of this kind merely because he enjoys political protection. Only such people are to be considered for these posts who have a strongly developed community-sense and a full understanding of the people entrusted to their care. The essential point of my argument is this, that in a civilization where one man is the enemy of the other—for this is what our whole industrial system means—demoralization is ineradicable, for demoralization and crime are *by-products of the struggle for existence* as known to our industrialized civilization. The shadows of this struggle fall very early across the soul of the child, destroy its poise, facilitate its craving for greatness and render it craven and incapable of co-operation.

To limit and do away with this demoralization a chair of curative pedagogy should be established. It is indeed hard to understand why such a chair does not already exist. To-day a true understanding of the problem is exceedingly rare. All persons in any way connected with this problem should be compelled to take an active part. The institution itself should be in the nature of a central exchange bureau which would give information on all matters relating to the prevention and combating of demoralization.

In addition, county institutions of an advisory nature should exist for the lighter cases. For the more severe forms the relatives of the patients must suggest a method of treating them, for the patients themselves would never be able to find one.

In conclusion teachers should be made acquainted with individual-psychology and curative pedagogy, so that from the very beginning they might be in a position to recognize the signs of demoralization and to intervene helpfully themselves and nip the danger tactfully and lovingly in the bud. A model school for the practical education of the personnel should also be founded.

THE CONSTITUTION OF THE INTERNATIONAL BUREAU OF
EDUCATION AT GENEVA (1925)   From Pedro Resselló, *Forerunners of the International Bureau of Education,* Marie Butts, trans. (London, 1944), p. 118.

Preamble.—Being convinced that the development of education is an essential factor in the establishment of peace and in the moral and material progress of humanity.

That, with a view to promoting this development, it is important to collect educational data through investigation and research, and to facilitate the exchange of such information for the purpose of encouraging each country to profit by the experience of others,

Article 1.—An institution of universal interest, to be known as the "International Bureau of Education," is hereby created.

Article 2.—The object of the International Bureau of Education is to act as an information centre for all matters relating to education.

The Bureau, which aims to promote international cooperation, maintains a completely neutral position with regard to national, political and religious questions. As an organ of information and investigation, its work is carried on in a strictly scientific and objective spirit. Its activities are of two kinds: (1) the collection of information relating to public and private education; (2) the initiation of scientific investigations within its sphere and the undertaking of statistical enquiries or those relating to experimental projects. The results of these efforts are made available to educators.

Article 3.—The seat of the International Bureau of Education is at Geneva.

WOLFGANG KOHLER ON ANIMAL INTELLIGENCE AND GESTALT
THEORY (1925)   From Wolfgang Kohler, *The Mentality of Apes,* Ella Winter trans. (New York, 1925), pp. 2–5, 130–34, 275–79.

Introduction

There is probably no association psychologist who does not, in his own unprejudiced observations, distinguish, and, to a certain extent, contrast unintelligent behaviour and intelligent. For what is association psychology other than the theory that one can trace back to the phenomena of a generally-known simple association type even occurrences which, according to unbiassed observation, do not at first make the impression of being identical, above all so-called intelligence performances? In short, it is just these differences which are the starting-point of a strict association psychology; it is they which need to be theoretically accounted for; they are well known to the association psychologist. Thus for instance, we find a radical representative of this school (Thorndike) stating the conclusion, drawn from experiments on dogs and cats: "I failed to find any act that even *seemed* due to reasoning." To anyone who can formulate his results thus, other behaviour must already have seemed to be intelligent; he is already acquainted with the contrast in his observations, perhaps of human beings, even if he discards it afterwards in theory.

Accordingly, if we are to inquire whether the anthropoid ape behaves intelligently, this problem can for the present be treated quite independently of theoretical assumptions, particularly those for or against the association theory. It is true that it then becomes somewhat indefinite; we are not to inquire whether anthropoid apes show something well defined, but whether their behaviour approximates to a type rather superficially known by experience, and which we call "intelligence" in contrast to other behaviour—especially in animals. . . .

What seems to us "intelligence" tends to be called into play when circumstances block a course which seems obvious to us, leaving open a roundabout path which the human being or animal takes, so meeting the situation. In unexpressed agreement with this, nearly all those observers who heretofore have sought to solve the problem of animal intelligence, have done so by watching animals in just such predicaments. As in cases below the stage of development of anthropoid apes results are, in general, negative, there arose out of those experiments the view widely held at present, i.e. that there is very little intelligent behaviour in animals; only a small number of such experiments have been carried out on anthropoid apes, and they have not yet led to any very definite results. All the experiments described in the following pages are of one and the same kind: the experimenter sets up a situation in which the direct path to the objective is blocked, but a roundabout way left open. The animal is introduced into this situation, which can, potentially, be wholly surveyed, and so we shall be able to see up to which level of behaviour its capabilities take it, and, particularly, whether it can solve the problem in the possible "roundabout" way.

The experiments were at first applied to chimpanzees only, with the exception of a few cases taken for comparison, in which human beings, a dog, and hens were observed.

Seven of the animals belonged to the old branch of the anthropoid station which the Prussian Academy of Science maintained in Tenerife from 1912 to 1920. Of these seven the oldest, an adult female, was named Tschego, because of several characteristics which made us, perhaps wrongly, consider her a member of the Tschego species. (We are yet far from possessing a clear and systematized classification of the varieties of the chimpanzee.) The oldest of the smaller animals, called Grande, also differs considerably in several respects from its comrades. But as the differences concern its general character rather than the behaviour investigated in the intelligence tests, a detailed description of them would be out of place here. The other five, two males (Sultan and Konsul), three females (Tercera, Rana, and Chica), are of the usual chimpanzee type.

The Making Of Implements

Are the two sticks ever combined so as to become technically useful? This time Sultan is the subject of the experiment. His sticks are two hollow, but firm, bamboo rods, such as the animals often use for pulling along fruit. The one is so much smaller than the other, that it can be pushed in at either end quite easily. Beyond the bars lies the objective, just so far away that the animal cannot reach it with either rod. They are about the same length. Nevertheless, he takes great pains to try to reach it with one stick or the other, even pushing his right shoulder through the bars.[1] When everything proves futile, Sultan commits a "bad error," or, more clearly, a great stupidity, such as he made sometimes on other occasions. He pulls a box from the back of the room towards the bars; true, he pushes it away again at once as it is useless, or rather, actually in the way. Immediately afterwards, he does something which, although practically useless, must be counted among the "good errors": he pushes one of the sticks out as far as it will go, then takes the second, and with it pokes the first one cautiously towards the objective, pushing it carefully from the nearer end and thus slowly urging it towards the fruit. This does not always succeed, but if he has got pretty close in this way, he takes even greater precaution; he pushes very gently, watches the movements of the stick that is lying on the ground, and actually touches the objective with its tip. Thus, all of a sudden, for the first time, the contact "animal-objective" has been established, and Sultan visibly feels (we humans can sympathize) a certain satisfaction in having even so much power over the fruit that he can touch and slightly move it by pushing the stick. The proceeding is repeated; when the animal has pushed the stick on the ground so far out that he cannot possibly get it back by himself, it is given back to him. But although, in trying to steer it cautiously, he puts the stick in his hand exactly to the cut (i.e. the opening) of the stick on the ground, and although one might think that doing so would suggest the possibility of pushing one stick into the other, there is no indication whatever of such a practically valuable solution. Finally, the observer gives the animal some help by putting one finger into the opening of one stick under the animal's nose (without pointing to the other stick at all). This has no effect; Sultan, as before, pushes one stick with the other towards the objective, and as this pseudo-solution does not satisfy him any longer, he abandons his efforts altogether, and does not even pick up the sticks when they are both again thrown through the bars to him. The experiment has lasted over an hour, and is stopped for the present, as it seems hopeless, carried out like this, As we intend to take it up again after a while, Sultan is left in possession of his sticks; the keeper is left there to watch him.

Keeper's report: "Sultan first of all squats indifferently on the box, which has been left standing a little back from the railings; then he gets up, picks up the two sticks, sits down again on the box and plays carelessly with them. While doing this, it happens that he finds himself holding one rod in either hand in such a way that they lie in a straight line; he pushes the thinner one a little way into the opening of the thicker, jumps up and is already on the run towards the railings, to which he has up to now half turned his back, and begins to draw a banana towards him with the double stick. I call the master: meanwhile, one of the animal's rods has fallen out of

[1]In order not to discourage the animal from the very beginning, I put the objective only just out of reach of the single stick.

the other, as he has pushed one of them only a little way into the other; whereupon he connects them again."[2]

The keeper's report covers a period of scarcely five minutes, which had elapsed since stopping the experiment. Called by the man, I continued observation myself: Sultan is squatting at the bars, holding out one stick, and, at its end, a second bigger one, which is on the point of falling off. It does fall. Sultan pulls it to him and forthwith, with the greatest assurance, pushes the thinner one in again, so that it is firmly wedged, and fetches a fruit with the lengthened implement. But the bigger tube selected is a little too big, and so it slips from the end of the thinner one several times; each time Sultan rejoins the tubes immediately by holding the bigger one towards himself in the left and the thinner one in his right hand and a little backwards, and then sliding one into the other. The proceeding seems to please him immensely; he is very lively, pulls all the fruit, one after the other, towards the railings, without taking time to eat it, and when I disconnect the double-stick he puts it together again at once, and draws any distant objects whatever to the bars.

The next day the test is repeated; Sultan begins with the proceeding which is in practice useless, but after he has pushed one of the tubes forward with the other for a few seconds, he again takes up both, quickly puts one into the other, and attains his objective with the double stick.

The objective lies in front of the railings, still farther away; Sultan has three tubes to resort to, the two bigger ones fitting over either end of the third. He tries to reach his objective with two tubes, as before; as the outer one keeps falling off, he takes distinct pains to push the thinner stick farther into the bigger one. Contrary to expectation, he actually attains his objective with the double tube, and pulls it to him. The long tool sometimes get into his way when doing this, by its farther end getting caught between the railings, when being moved obliquely, so the animal quickly separates it into its parts, and finishes the task with one tube only. From now on, he does this every time when the objective is so close that *one* stick is sufficient, and the double-stick awkward. The new objective is placed still farther away. In consequence, Sultan tries which of the bigger tubes is more useful when joined to the thin one; for they do not differ very much in length (64 and 70 cms.), and, of course, the animal does not lay them together in order to compare their lengths. *Sultan never tries to join the two bigger tubes;* once he puts them opposite to each other for a moment, not touching, and looks at the two openings, but puts one aside directly (without trying it) and picks up the third thinner one; the two wide tubes have openings of the same size.[3] The solution follows quite suddenly: Sultan fishes with a double-stick, consisting of the thinner one and one of the bigger ones, holding, as usual, the end of the smaller one in his hand. All of a sudden he pulls the double-stick in, turns it round, so that the thin end is before his eyes and the other towering up in the air behind him, seizes the third tube with his left hand,

---

[2] The keeper's tale seems acceptable to me, especially as, upon inquiries, he emphasized the fact that Sultan had first of all connected the sticks in play and without considering the objective (his task). The animals are constantly poking about with straws and small sticks in holes and cracks in their play, so that it would be more astonishing if Sultan had never done this, while playing about with the two sticks. There need be no suspicion that the keeper quickly "trained the animal"; the man would never dare it. If anybody continues to doubt, even that does not matter, for Sultan continually not only performs this act but shows that he realizes its meaning.

[3] It can be shown that when the chimpanzee connects the double-stick he is guided by the relation between the two thicknesses of the tubes.

and introduces the tip of the double-stick into its opening. With the triple pole he reaches the objective easily; and when the long implement proves a hindrance in pulling the objective to him, it is disconnected as before.

∗   ∗   ∗

Conclusion

The chimpanzees manifest intelligent behaviour of the general kind familiar in human beings. Not all their intelligent acts are externally similar to human acts, but under well-chosen experimental conditions, the type of intelligent conduct can always be traced. This applies, in spite of very important differences between one animal and another, even to the least gifted specimens of the species that have been observed here, and, therefore, must hold good of every member of the species, as long as it is not mentally deficient, in the pathological sense of the word. With this exception, which is presumably rare, the success of the intelligence tests in general will be more likely endangered by the person making the experiment than by the animal. One must know, and, if necessary, establish by preliminary observation, within which limits of difficulty and in which functions the chimpanzee *can possibly* show insight; negative or confused results from complicated and accidentally-chosen test-material, have obviously no bearing upon the fundamental question, and, in general, the experimenter should recognize that every intelligence test is a test, not only of the creature examined, but also of the experimenter himself. I have said that to myself quite often, and yet I have remained uncertain whether the experiments I performed may be considered "satisfactory" in this respect; without theoretical foundations, and in unknown territory, methodological mistakes may quite well have occurred; anyone who continues this work will be able to prevent them more easily.

At any rate, this remains true: Chimpanzees not only stand out against the rest of the animal world by several morphological and, in its narrower sense, physiological, characteristics, but they also behave in a way which counts as specifically human. As yet we know little of their neighbours on the other side, but according to the little we do know, with the results of this report, it is not impossible that, in this region of experimental research, the anthropoid is nearer to man *in intelligence too,* than to many of the lower ape-species. So far, observations agree well with the theories of evolution; in particular, the correlation between intelligence, and the development of the brain, is confirmed.

The positive result of the investigation requires a kind of boundary-line. It is, indeed, confirmed by experiments of a somewhat different nature, which will be recounted later; but a more complete picture should be formed when they are added, and, in so far, our judgment of the intelligence of apes is left some scope. Of much greater importance is the fact that the experiments in which we tested these animals brought them into situations in which all the factors were given, and the solution could be achieved. This method of experimentation is as well adapted to the chief problem of insight as are any which can bring about the decision "yes" or "no"; in fact, it may be the very best method possible at present, as it yields very many, and very clear, results. But we must not forget that it is just in these experimental circumstances that certain factors hardly appear, or appear not at all, which are rightly considered to be of the greatest importance for *human* intelligence. We do not test at all, or rather only once in passing, how far the chimpanzee is influenced by factors not present, whether things "merely thought about" occupy him noticeably at all. And most closely connected with this, is the following problem. In the method adopted so far we have not been able to tell how far back and forward stretches the time "in which the chimpanzee lives"; for we know that, though one can prove some effects of recognition and reproduction after considerable lapses of time—as is actually the case in anthropoids—this is not the same as "life for a longer space of time." A great deal of time spent with chimpanzees leads me to venture the opinion that, beside the lack of speech, it is in extremely narrow limits in *this* direction that the chief difference is to be found between anthropoids and even the most primitive human beings. The lack of an invaluable technical aid (speech) and a great limitation to those very important components of thought, so-called "images," would thus constitute the causes that prevent the chimpanzee from attaining even the smallest beginnings of cultural development. With special reference to the second fact, the chimpanzee, who is easily puzzled by the simplest optical complications, will indeed fare badly in "image-life," where even man has continually to be fighting against the running into one another, and melting together, of certain processes.

In the field of the experiments carried out here the insight of the chimpanzee shows itself to be principally determined by his optical apprehension of the situation; at times he even starts solving problems from a too visual point of view, and in many cases in which the chimpanzee stops acting with insight, it may have been simply that the lie of the land was too much for his visual grasp (relative "weakness of shape perception"). It is therefore difficult to give a satisfactory explanation of all his performances, so long as no detailed theory of shape (*Gestalt*) has been laid as a foundation. The need for such a theory will be felt the more, when one remembers that *solutions* showing insight in this field of intelligence necessarily take part in the nature of the structure of the situations, in so far as they arise in dynamic processes *co-ordinated with* the situation.

It would be less a boundary-line than a standard for the achievements of intelligence described here that would be arrived at by comparing with our experiments the performances of human beings (sick and well) and, above all, human children of different ages. As the results in this book have special reference to a particular method of testing and the special test-material of optically-given situations, it would be those psychological facts established in human beings (especially children), under the same conditions, which would have to be used. But such comparisons cannot be instituted, as, very much to the disadvantage of psychology, not even the most necessary of such facts have been ascertained. Preliminary experiments—some have been mentioned—have given me the impression that we are inclined to overestimate the capabilities of children of all ages up to maturity, and even adults, who have had no special technical training in this type of performance. We are in a region of *terra incognita*. Educational psychology, engaged on the well-known quantitative tests for some time, has not yet been able to test how far normal, and how far mentally-deficient, children can go in certain situations. As experiments of this kind can be performed at the very tenderest age, and are certainly as scientifically valuable as the intelligence tests usually employed, it can be forgiven if they do not become immediately practicable for school and other uses. M. Wertheimer has been expressing this view for some years in his lectures; in this place, where the lack of them makes itself so much felt, I should like to emphasize particularly the importance and—if the anthropoids do not deceive us—the fruitfulness of further work in this direction.

THE CONDITIONED REFLEX (1928) From Ivan P. Pavlov, *Lectures on Conditioned Reflexes*, W. Horsley Gantt, trans. (New York, 1928), pp. 76–80.

During the study of the gastric glands, I became more and more convinced, that the appetite acts not only as a general stimulus of the glands, but that it stimulates them in different degrees according to the object upon which it is directed. For the salivary glands the rule obtains that all the variations of their activity observed in physiological experiments are exactly duplicated in the experiments using a psychical stimulation, *i.e.*, in those experiments in which the stimulus is not brought into direct contact with the mucous membrane of the mouth, but attracts the attention of the animal from some distance. Here are examples of this. The sight of dry bread calls out a stronger salivary secretion than the sight of meat, although the meat, judging by the movement of the animals, excites a much livelier interest. On teasing the dog with meat or other foods, there flows from the submaxillary glands a concentrated saliva rich in mucus (lubricating saliva): on the contrary, the sight of a disagreeable substance produces from these same glands a secretion of very fluid saliva which contains almost no mucus (cleansing saliva). In brief, the experiments with psychical stimuli represent exact miniatures of the experiments with physiological stimulations by the same substances.

Thus, psychology, in relation to the work of the salivary glands, occupies a place close to that of physiology. And even more! On first view the psychological explanation of the activity of the salivary glands seems to be as incontrovertible as the physiological. When any object from a distance attracting the attention of the dog produces a flow of saliva, one has ground for assuming that this is a psychical and not a physiological phenomenon. When, however, after the dog has eaten something or has had something forced into his mouth, saliva flows, it is necessary to prove that in this phenomenon there is actually present a physiological cause, and not only a purely psychical one which, owing to the special conditions, is perhaps reinforced. From the following experiment this conception is seen to correspond in a remarkable way with reality. Most substances which during eating or forceful introduction into the mouth produce a flow of saliva, evoke a secretion after severance of all the sensory nerves of the tongue similar to that which they evoked before this operation. One must resort to more radical measures, such as poisoning of the animal or extirpation of the higher parts of the central nervous system, in order to convince oneself that between a substance stimulating the oral cavity and the salivary glands there exists not only a psychical but a purely physiological connection. Thus we have two series of apparently entirely different phenomena. How must the physiologist treat these psychical phenomena? It is impossible to neglect them, because they are closely bound up with purely physiological phenomena and determine the work of the whole organ. If the physiologist decides to study them, he must answer the question, How?

Following the examples of the study of the lowest representatives of the animal kingdom, and naturally not desiring to abandon physiology for psychology—especially after an entirely unsuccessful trial in this direction—we chose to maintain in our experiments with the so-called psychical phenomena a purely objective position. Above all, we endeavoured to discipline our thoughts and our speech about these phenomena, and not to concern ourselves with the imaginary mental state of the animal; and we limited our task to exact observation and description of the effect on the secretion of the salivary glands of the object acting from a distance. The results corresponded to our expectations—the relations we observed between the external phenomena and the variations in the work of the salivary glands appeared quite regularly, could be reproduced at will again and again as usual physiological phenomena, and were capable of being definitely systematised. To our great joy, we are convinced that we have started along the path which leads to a successful goal. I shall give some examples of the constant relations which have been established by the aid of this new method of research.

If the dog is repeatedly excited by the sight of substances calling forth a salivary secretion from a distance, the reaction of the salivary glands after each stimulation becomes weaker and weaker, and finally falls to zero. The shorter the intervals between separate stimulations, the quicker the reaction reaches zero, and vice versa. These rules are fully manifested only when the conditions of the experiment do not change. The identity of the conditions, however, need be only relative; it may be limited to those phenomena of the outer world with which had been associated the acts of eating or the forceful introduction of the corresponding substances into the animal's mouth; the variation of other conditions may remain without any effect. This relative identity can be easily attained by the experimenter, so that an experiment in which a stimulus is repeatedly applied from a distance gradually loses its effect, can be readily demonstrated in the lecture hall. If a substance, owing to its repeated employment as a distant stimulus, has become ineffective, the influence of other stimulating substances is not thereby annihilated: if milk from a distance ceases to stimulate the salivary glands, the distant action of bread remains clearly effective. After this has lost its influence by repetition, showing the dog acid will produce again a full effect on the salivary glands. These relations also explain the real meaning of the above-mentioned identity of the experimental conditions; every detail of the surrounding objects appears as a new stimulus. When a certain stimulus has lost its efficacy due to repetition, then its action after a certain interval of minutes or of hours is restored without fail.

The effect when temporarily lost, can be restored at any given time, however, by special means. If bread repeatedly shown to the dog fails to stimulate the salivary glands, it is only necessary to give it to the dog to eat and thereupon the full effect of the bread at a distance is at once restored. The same result is obtained when the dog receives some other food. And even more. When some substance producing a salivary secretion, for example, acid, is forced into the dog's mouth, the original distant effect of the bread previously lost is again fully manifested. In general, everything that stimulates the salivary glands restores the lost reaction, and the more fully, the greater has been their activity.

Our reaction can be inhibited by certain influences with the same regularity; if, for example, some stimulus which evokes in the animal a definite motor reaction acts on the eye or ear of the dog.

For the sake of brevity, I shall limit myself to the above-mentioned material, and now pass on to theoretical considerations of the experiments. Our given facts can readily be included in a framework of physiological description. The effects we produced on the salivary glands from a distance may properly be considered and termed reflexes. It is impossible not to see, by close attention, that the activity of the salivary glands, when present, is always excited by some external phenomenon; i.e., in the same way as the usual physiological salivary reflex, it is always produced by an external stimulus. The difference consists chiefly in that the usual reflex is determined by the stimulation from the mouth cavity, whereas the new reflexes are evoked by stimulation of the eye, ear, etc. A further essential difference between the old and the new reflexes is that the former are constant and unconditional, while the latter are subject to fluctuation, and dependent upon many conditions. They, therefore, deserve the name of "conditioned."

Considering the phenomena more closely, I can not fail to see the following distinction between these two kinds of reflexes: in the *unconditioned* reflex, those properties of the substance to which the saliva is physiologically adapted act as the stimulus, for example, the hardness, the dryness, the definite chemical properties, etc.; in the *conditioned* reflex, on the other hand, those properties which bear no direct relation to the physiological role of the saliva act as stimuli, for example, colour, form, and the like. These last properties evidently receive their physiological importance as *signals* for the first ones, *i.e.*, for the essential properties. In their response one can not but notice a further and more delicate adaptation of the salivary glands to the external world. This is seen in the following case. We prepare to put acid into the dog's mouth, and the dog sees it. In the interest of the integrity of the buccal mucous membrane, it is highly desirable that before the acid comes into the mouth, there should be some saliva present; on the one hand, the saliva will hinder the direct contact of the acid with the mucous membrane, and, on the other hand, will serve to dilute the acid and thus weaken its injurious effect. But, of course, in reality the signals can have only a conditional significance, they are readily subject to change, as, for example, when the signalling objects do not come into contact with the mucous membrane. In this way the finer adaptation is based on the fact that the properties of the substances which serve as signals, now stimulate (*i.e.*, call out the reflex), now lose their exciting action. This is what occurs in reality. Any given phenomenon can be made a temporary signal of the object which stimulates the salivary glands, if the stimulation of the mucous membrane by the object has been once or several times associated simultaneously with the action of the stimulating phenomenon on another receptor surface of the body. We are now trying in our laboratory, with great success, to apply many such, and even highly paradoxical, combinations.

On the other hand, closely related and stable signals can be deprived of their stimulating action if they are often repeated without bringing the corresponding object into contact with the mucous membrane. If any food is shown to a dog for days or weeks without giving it to the animal it finally completely loses its distant stimulating effect on the salivary glands. The mechanism of the stimulation of the salivary glands through the signalising properties of objects, *i.e.*, the mechanism of the *"conditioned stimulation,"* may be easily conceived of from the physiological point of view as a function of the nervous system. As we have just said, at the basis of each conditioned reflex, *i.e.*, a stimulation through the signalising properties of an object, there lies an unconditioned reflex, *i.e.*, a stimulation through the essential attributes of the object. Then it must be assumed that the point of the central nervous system which during the unconditioned reflex becomes strongly stimulated, attracts to itself weaker impulses arriving simultaneously from the outer or internal worlds at other points of this system, *i.e.*, thanks to the unconditioned reflex, there is opened for all these stimulations a temporary path leading to the point of this reaction. The circumstances influencing the opening or closing of this path in the brain are the internal mechanism of the action or of the inaction of the signalising properties of the objects, and they represent the physiological basis of the finest reactivity of the living substance, the most delicate adaptation of the animal organism, to the outer world.

I desire to express my deep conviction that physiological research in the direction which I have briefly outlined, will be highly successful and will help us to make great advances.

Only one thing in life is of actual interest for us—our psychical experience. Its mechanism, however, has been, and remains, wrapped in deep mystery. All human resources—art, religion, literature, philosophy, historical science—all these unite to cast a beam of light into this mysterious darkness. Man has at his disposal one more powerful ally—biological science with its strictly objective methods. This study, as we all see and know, is making great advances every day. The facts and conceptions which I have given at the close of this lecture are typical of numerous trials to make use of systematic application of a purely naturalistic method of thinking in the study of the mechanism of the highest vital expression of the dog—this faithful and friendly representative of the animal world.

PIUS XI's ENCYCLICAL LETTER ON CHRISTIAN EDUCATION OF YOUTH (1930)   From *Current History*, vol. XXXI, pp. 1091–92, 1098–99, 1103–4.

Reasons for Treating of Christian Education

Never has there been so much discussion about education as nowadays; never have exponents of new pedagogical theories been so numerous, or so many methods and means devised, proposed and debated, not merely to facilitate education, but to create a new system infallibly efficacious, and capable of preparing the present generations for that earthly happiness which they so ardently desire.

The reason is that men, created by God, to His image and likeness and destined for Him Who is infinite perfection, realize today more than ever amid the most exuberant material progress, the insufficiency of earthly goods to produce true happiness either for the individual or for the nations. And hence they feel more keenly in themselves the impulse towards a perfection that is higher, which impulse is implanted in their rational nature by the Creator Himself. This perfection they seek to acquire by means of education. But many of them with, it would seem, too great insistence on the etymological meaning of the word, pretend to draw education out of human nature itself and evolve it by its own unaided powers. Such easily fall into error, because, instead of fixing their gaze on God, first principle and last end of the whole universe, they fall back upon themselves, becoming attached exclusively to passing things of earth; and thus their restlessness will never cease till they direct their attention and their efforts to God, the goal of all perfection, according to the profound saying of St. Augustine: "Thou didst create us, O Lord, for Thyself, and our heart is restless till it rest in Thee."

It is therefore as important to make no mistake in education, as it is to make no mistake in the pursuit of the last end, with which the whole work of education is intimately and necessarily connected. In fact, since education consists essentially in preparing man for what he must be and for what he must do here below, in order to attain the sublime end for which he was created, it is clear that there can be no true education which is not wholly directed to man's last end, and that in the present order of Providence, since God has revealed Himself to us in the Person of His Only Begotten Son, Who alone is "the way, the truth and the life," there can be no ideally perfect education which is not Christian education.

From this we see the supreme importance of Christian education, not merely for each individual, but for families and for the whole of human society, whose perfection comes from the perfection of the elements that compose it. From these same principles, the excellence, we may well call it the unsurpassed excellence, of the work of Christian education becomes manifest and clear; for after all it aims at securing the Supreme Good, that is, God, for the souls of those who are being educated, and the maximum of well-being possible here below for human society. And this it does as efficaciously as man is capable of doing it, namely by cooperating with God in the perfecting of individuals and of society, inasmuch as education makes upon the soul the first, the most powerful and lasting impression for life, according to the well-known saying of the Wise Man, "A young man according to his way, even when he is old, he will not depart from it." With good reason therefore did St. John Chrysostom say, "What greater work is there than training the mind and forming the habits of the young?"

But nothing discloses to us the supernatural beauty and excellence of the work of Christian education better than the sublime expression of love of Our Blessed Lord, identifying Himself with children, "Whosoever shall receive one such child as this in My name, receiveth Me."

Now in order that no mistake be made in this work of utmost importance, and in order to conduct it in the best manner possible with the help of God's grace, it is necessary to have a clear and definite idea of Christian education in its essential aspects, viz., who has the mission to educate, who are the subjects to be educated, what are the necessary accompanying circumstances, what is the end and object proper to Christian education according to God's established order in the economy of His Divine Providence.

✳   ✳   ✳

Subject of Education

In fact it must never be forgotten that the subject of Christian education is man whole and entire, soul united to body in unity of nature, with all his faculties natural and supernatural, such as right reason and revelation show him to be; man, therefore, fallen from his original estate, but redeemed by Christ and restored to the supernatural condition of adopted son of God, though without the preternatural privileges of bodily immortality or perfect control of appetite. There remain therefore, in human nature the effects of original sin, the chief of which are weakness of will and disorderly inclinations.

"Folly is bound up in the heart of a child and the rod of correction shall drive it away." Disorderly inclinations then must be corrected, good tendencies encouraged and regulated from tender childhood, and above all the mind must be enlightened and the will strengthened by supernatural truth and by the means of grace, without which it is impossible to control evil impulses, impossible to attain to the full and complete perfection of education intended by the Church, which Christ has endowed so richly with divine doctrine and with the Sacraments, the efficacious means of grace.

Naturalism in Education, False and Damaging

Hence every form of pedagogic naturalism which in any way excludes or weakens supernatural Christian formation in the teaching of youth, is false. Every method of education founded, wholly or in part, on the denial or forgetfulness of original sin and of grace, and relying on the sole powers of human nature, is unsound. Such, generally speaking, are those modern systems bearing various names which appeal to a pretended self-government and unrestrained freedom on the part of the child, and which diminish or even suppress the teacher's authority and action, attributing to the child an exclusive primacy of initiative, and an activity independent of any higher law, natural or divine, in the work of his education.

If any of these terms are used, less properly to denote the necessity of a gradually more active cooperation on the part of the pupil in his own education, if the intention is to banish from education despotism and violence, which, by the way, just punishment is not, this would be correct, but in no way new. It would mean only what has been taught and reduced to practise by the Church in traditional Christian education, in imitation of the method employed by God Himself towards His creatures, of whom He demands active cooperation according to the nature of each; for His Wisdom "reacheth from end to end mightily and ordereth all things sweetly."

But alas! It is clear from the obvious meaning of the words and from experience, that what is intended by not a few, is the withdrawal of education from every sort of dependence on the divine law. So today we see, strange sight indeed, educators and philosophers who spend their lives in searching for a universal moral code of education, as if there existed no decalogue, no gospel law, no law even of nature stamped by God on the heart of man, promulgated by right reason, and codified in positive revelation by God Himself in the ten commandments. These innovators are wont to refer contemptuously to Christian education as "heteronomous," "passive," "obsolete," because founded upon the authority of God and His holy law.

Such men are miserably deluded in their claim to emancipate, as they say, the child, while in reality they are making him the slave of his own blind pride and his disorderly affections, which, as a logical consequence of this false system, come to be justified as legitimate demands of a so-called autonomous nature.

But what is worse is the claim, not only vain but false, irreverent and dangerous, to submit to research, experiment and conclusions of a purely natural and profane order, those matters of education which belong to the supernatural order; as for example questions of priestly or religious vocation, and in general the secret workings of grace which indeed elevate the natural powers, but are infinitely superior to them, and may nowise be subjected to physical laws, for "the Spirit breatheth where He will."

✻   ✻   ✻

Hence the true Christian, product of Christian education, is the supernatural man who thinks, judges and acts constantly and consistently in accordance with right reason illumined by the supernatural light of the example and teaching of Christ; in other words, to use the current term, the true and finished man of character. For, it is not every kind of consistency and firmness of conduct based on subjective principles that makes true character, but only constancy in following the eternal principles of justice, as is admitted even by the pagan poet when he praises as one and the same "the man who is just and firm of purpose." And on the other hand, there cannot be full justice except in giving to God what is due to God, as the true Christian does.

The scope and aim of Christian education as here described, appears to the worldly as an abstraction, or rather as something that cannot be attained without the suppression or dwarfing of the natural faculties, and without a renunciation of the activities of the present life, and hence inimical to social life and temporal prosperity, and contrary to all progress in letters, arts and sciences, and all the other elements of civilization. To a like objection raised by the ignorance and the prejudice of even cultured pagans of a former day, and repeated with greater frequency and insistence in modern times, Tertullian has replied as follows: "We are not strangers to life. We are fully aware of the gratitude we owe to God, Our Lord and Creator. We reject none of the fruits of His handiwork; we only abstain from their immoderate or unlawful use. We are living in the world with you; we do not shun your forum, your markets, your baths, your shops, your factories, your stables, your places of business and traffic. We take ship with you and we serve in your armies, we are farmers and merchants with you; we interchange skilled labor and display our works in public for your service. How we can seem unprofitable to you with whom we live and of whom we are, I know not."

The true Christian does not renounce the activities of this life, he does not stunt his natural faculties; but he develops and perfects them, by coordinating them with the supernatural. He thus ennobles what is merely natural in life and secures for it new strength in the material and temporal order, no less than in the spiritual and eternal.

PIAGET ON THE CHILD'S CONCEPTION OF PHYSICAL CAUSALITY

(**1930**)   From Jean Piaget, *The Child's Conception of Physical Causality,* Marjorie Gabain, trans. (New York, 1930), pp. 237, 241–52, 291–94.

We propose in this final section to enquire into the relations existing between the mind of the child and the external world. This should lead us into the very heart of the Problem of Knowledge. . . .

THE CHILD'S REALITY.—How does the idea of reality constitute itself in the child's mind? Any direct analysis of its origin is beyond our power; the earliest stages precede language or are contemporaneous with the first spoken words, and any effort to reach the child's consciousness during these stages is fruitless, if one claims to go beyond mere hypothesis. But if we can content ourselves with conjecture, then it is best to try and extricate the laws according to which the idea of reality develops between the ages of 3 and 11, and to extrapolate the guiding lines thus obtained so as to reconstruct the earliest stages. Moreover, as soon as we put this method into practice, we find that we can learn enough from the laws of evolution between 3 and 11 years, and that there is no need to attach any special importance to the original stage.

Three complementary processes seem to be at work in directing the evolution of reality as it is conceived by the child between the ages of 3 and 11. Child thought moves simultaneously: (1) *from realism to objectivity*, (2) *from realism to reciprocity*, and (3) *from realism to relativity*. By *objectivity* we mean the mental attitude of persons who are able to distinguish what comes from themselves and what forms part of external reality as it can be observed by everybody. We say that there is *reciprocity* when the same value is attributed to the point of view of other people as to one's own, and when the correspondence can be found between these two points of view. We say that there is relativity when no object and no quality or character is posited in the subject's mind with the claim to being an independent substance or attribute.

Let us examine these processes more closely. In order to be objective, one must have become conscious of one's "I." Objective knowledge can only be conceived in relation to subjective, and a mind that was ignorant of itself would inevitably tend to put into things its own pre-notions and prejudices, whether in the domain of reasoning, of immediate judgment, or even of perception. An objective intelligence in no way escapes from this law, but, being conscious of its own "I," it will be on its guard, it will be able to hold back and criticise, in short it will be able to say what, roughly, is fact and what is interpretation.

So that in stating that the child proceeds from realism to objectivity, all we are saying is that originally the child puts the whole content of consciousness on the same plane and draws no distinction between the "I" and the external world. Above all we mean that the constitution of the idea of reality presupposes a progressive splitting-up of this protoplasmic consciousness into two complementary universes—the objective universe and the subjective.

We have met with many examples of this realism of the first kind and of its progressive reduction. Children's ideas about thought may be taken as a first illustration of the phenomenon in question. The feeling of subjectivity and inwardness felt by the adult is, to a great extent, connected with the conviction of being the owner of a thought that is distinct from the things thought about, distinct from the physical world in general, and more internal and intimate than the body itself. This conviction only comes late in the child's development. During the earliest stages, the child believes that he thinks with his mouth, that thought consists in articulating words, and that these words themselves form part of the external things. The voice, being thus identified with thought itself, is regarded as a breath which participates with the surrounding air, and some children go so far as to say that it is identical with the wind in the trees, and that dreams are made of "wind." They are quite incapable of distinguishing between thought and the things thought about. To use the expression chosen by M. H. Delacroix, the sign "adheres" to the thing signified. Later on, the child gives up this realism and localises thought inside his mouth, then in a little voice placed in the head; he then gives up materialising thought and makes of it something *sui generis* which characterises the self as spirit.

The evolution of ideas about names is particularly suggestive from this same point of view. Word and name are about all that the child knows of thought, since he identifies thought with the voice. Now, names are, to begin with, situated in objects. They form part of things in the same way as do colour or form. Things have always had their names. It has always been sufficient to look at things in order to know their names. In some cases, this realism actually turns to magic: to deform the name is to deform the thing. Later on, names are situated in the adjoining air where the voice has uttered them, then in the voice, and finally in thought itself.

Dreams give rise to an equally definite realism. At first, they are thought to be pictures of air or light which come before our eyes from outside. At the earliest stage, the child thinks, naturally enough, that anyone could see the dream come into the room and go out again. Later on, the dream is believed to have an internal origin, but is conceived as coming out of the head or the stomach before appearing before the child. Finally, the child learns to distinguish between "being" and "seeming," and localises the dream, first in the eyes, then in the head.

All these facts show that the localisation of the objects of thought is not inborn. It is through a progressive differentiation that the internal world comes into being and is contrasted with the external. Neither of these two terms is given at the start. The initial realism is not due simply to ignorance of the internal world, it is due to confusion and absence of objectivity.

Consequently, during the gradual and slow differentiation of the initial protoplasmic reality into objective and subjective reality, it is clear that each of the two terms in process of differentiation will evolve in accordance with its own structure. In the case of every object there will be a displacement of values which will modify the character of the object. Take, for example, the notion of "air," or of "wind." During the earliest stages, air is conceived as participating with thought: the voice is air, and, in return, the wind takes notice of us, obeys us, is "good at making us grow," comes when we move our hands, and so on. When thought proper is localised in the self, and the participations between air and thought are broken, the nature of air changes by virtue of this fact alone. Air becomes independent of men, sufficient to itself, and living its own life. But owing to the fact that it is held to participate with the self, it retains at the very moment when it is severing these bonds, a certain number of purely human aspects: it still has consciousness, of a different kind perhaps than formerly, but its own nevertheless. Only very gradually will it be reduced to a mere thing.

This phenomenon is very general. During the early stages the world and the self are one; neither term is distinguished from the other. But when they become distinct, these two terms begin by remaining very close to each other: the world is still conscious and full of intentions, the self is still material, so to speak, and only slightly interiorised. At each step in the process of dissociation these two terms evolve in the sense of the greatest divergence, but they are never in the child (nor in the adult for that matter) entirely separate. From our present point of view, therefore, there is never complete objectivity: at every stage there remain in the conception of nature what we might call "adherences," fragments of internal experience which still cling to the external world.

We have distinguished at least five varieties of adherences defined in this way. There are, to begin with, during a very early stage, feelings of participation accompanied sometimes by magical beliefs; the sun and moon follow us, and if we walk, it is enough to make them move along; things around us notice us and obey us, like the wind, the clouds, the night, etc.; the moon, the street lamps, etc., send us dreams "to annoy us," etc., etc. In short, the world is filled with tendencies and intentions which are in participation with our own. This is what we have called dynamic participation, in contrast to substantial participation, to which, however, it may lead.

A second form of adherence, closely allied to the preceding, is that constituted by animism, which makes the child endow things with consciousness and life.

A third form is artificialism. The reader should be reminded at this point that artificialism in the child is not a theory which after reflection systematically takes man as the point of departure for everything. The terms must be reversed, and that is why artificialism has the same right to be classed among the adherences as animism. The child begins by thinking of things in terms of his own "I": the things around him take notice of man and are made for man; everything about them is willed and intentional, everything is organised for the good of men. If we ask the child, or if the child asks himself how things began, he has recourse to man to explain them. Thus artificialism is based on feelings of participation which constitute a very special and very important class of adherences in the sense that we have defined.

A fourth form is finalism: the starting-point and then the residuum both of animism and of artificialism, the deep and stubborn finalism of the child shows with what difficulty external reality frees itself from schemas due to internal and psychical experience.

A fifth form of adherence is constituted by the notion of force: things make efforts, and their powers imply an internal and substantial energy analogous to our own muscular force.

It is a striking fact that both the area of application and the strength of resistance of these adherences decrease progressively throughout the mental development of the child. And not only do these adherences lose ground little by little in correlation with each other, but their progressive disappearance seems to be proportional to the increasing clarity with which the child becomes conscious of his subjectivity. In other words, the better the child succeeds in dividing off the internal world from the external, the less stubborn are the adherences.

Three groups of facts may be mentioned in this connection. In the first place, as the child comes to notice the existence and the mechanism of his own thought, he separates signs from the things signified: thus, names cease to belong to the things named, thought is interiorised and ceases to participate with wind, dreams are no longer regarded as emanations of objects, and so on. Thus participations are loosened little by little, and even eliminated.

In the second place, in so far as the child discovers the existence and inwardness of his thought, animism, far from being strengthened is, through this alone, compromised and even completely destroyed. The decline of animism brings with it a progressive reduction of child dynamism. For so long as things seem to be alive and consequently active, the forces of nature are multiplied by the child; and the elimination of life leads to a mechanisation of force which means ultimately an impoverishment of the actual notion of force. This very general process of evolution which leads the child from a dynamic to a mechanical view has been dealt with at sufficient length in connection with the details of children's explanations to render any further comment [un]necessary.

Finally, as the child becomes conscious of his subjectivity, he rids himself of his egocentricity. For, after all, it is in so far as we fail to realise the personal nature of our own point of view that we regard this point of view as absolute and shared by all. Whereas, in so far as we discover this purely individual character, we learn to distinguish our own from the objective point of view. Egocentricity, in a word, diminishes as we become conscious of our subjectivity. Now the decrease of egocentricity means the decrease of anthropomorphic finalism, and consequently the decrease of all the feelings of participation that are at the bottom of artificialism.

Progressive separation of the outer from the inner world, and progressive reduction of the adherences, such, in brief, are the two fundamental aspects of the first process which we defined as a passage from realism to objectivity. What we have just said about the relations between egocentricity and artificialism takes us on to the analysis of the second process, for it goes without saying that all these processes are closely related to each other, so much so, indeed, that they may be said to be completely indissociable.

The second characteristic process in the evolution of the idea of reality is the passage *from realism to reciprocity*. This formula means that the child, after having regarded his own point of view as absolute, comes to discover the possibility of other points of view and to conceive of reality as constituted, no longer by what is immediately given, but by what is common to all points of view taken together.

One of the first aspects of this process is the passage from realism of perception to interpretation properly so called. All the younger children take their immediate perceptions as true, and then proceed to interpret them according to their egocentric pre-relations, instead of making allowance for their own perspective. The most striking example we have found is that of the clouds and the heavenly bodies, of which children believe that they follow us. The sun and moon are small globes travelling a little way above the level of the roofs of houses and following us about on our walks. Even the child of 6–8 years does not hesitate to take this perception as the expression of truth, and, curiously enough, he never thinks of asking himself whether these heavenly bodies do not also follow other people. When we ask the captious question as to which of two people walking in opposite directions the sun would prefer to follow, the child is taken aback and shows how new the question is to him. Children of 9–10 years, on the other hand, have discovered that the sun follows everybody. From this they conclude that the truth lies in the reciprocity of the points of view: that the sun is very high up, that it follows no one, and that each sees it as just above him.

What we said just now about dreams is also to a certain extent germane to the present process: the child begins by regarding his own dreams as true, without asking himself whether every one dreams the same as he does.

Side by side with this realism of perception and images, there is a logical realism which is far more important. We met with numerous examples of it in the course of our studies on child logic. Before the age of 10, on the average, the child does not know that he is a brother in relation to his own brothers. The ideas of right and left, of dark and fair, of the points of the compass, etc., are all subject to the law which is occupying us at the moment. These conceptions are at first regarded as absolute, so long as the personal point of view is accepted as the only possible one; after that, the reciprocity of relations gradually begins to make itself felt. In the present volume (as also in *The Child's Conception of the World*) we have pointed to several fresh examples of this process, examples which were of importance in forming the structure of reality.

Such are, above all, the ideas of weight and density. During the earliest stages, an object is heavy or light according to the immediate judgment implied by the child's own point of view: a pebble is light, a boat is heavy. Later on, other points of view are taken into account, and the child will say, for example, that such and such a pebble is light for him but heavy for the water, and that a boat may be light for the lake while it remains heavy for the child.

These last examples bring us to the third process which marks the evolution of the child's idea of reality; thought evolves *from realism to relativity*. This process is closely related to the last, and yet differentiates itself from it on certain points. During the early stage, the child tends to think of everything under the form of absolute substance and quality; after that, bodies and their qualities seem to him more and more dependent upon each other and relative to us. Thus, substances become relations, on the one hand, because the mutual connection of phenomena has been seen, and on the other, because the relativity of our evaluations has been discovered. It would perhaps be as well to distinguish between these two aspects of "relativity," but the second is, as a matter of fact, nothing but a combination of the first with the "reciprocity" of which we spoke just now. It will therefore be enough to point to this connection without complicating our classification.

The most striking example of this process is undoubtedly the evolution of the conceptions about life and movement. During the early stages, every movement is regarded as singular, as the manifestation, that is, of a substantial and living activity. In other words, there is in every moving object a motor substance: the clouds, the heavenly bodies, water, and machines, etc., move by themselves. Even when the child succeeds in conceiving an external motor, which already takes away from the substantiality of movement, the internal motor continues to be regarded as necessary. Thus a leaf is alive, even though it moves with the wind, *i.e.* it retains its spontaneity even though the wind is needed to set it in motion. Similarly, a cloud or one of the heavenly bodies remains master of its movements, even though the wind is necessary to start it on its path. But later on, the movement of every body becomes the function of external movements, which are regarded no longer as necessary collaborators but as sufficient conditions. Thus the movement of clouds comes to be entirely explained by that of the wind. Then these external motors are conceived as themselves dependent upon other external motors, and so on. In this way there comes into being a universe of relations which takes the place of a universe of independent and spontaneous substances.

Closely analogous to this is the evolution of the idea of force, since it is, as we saw, intimately connected with the idea of life.

The idea of weight supplies us with an excellent example of this advance towards relativity, and the evolution in this particular case is closely bound up with the advance towards reciprocity which we spoke of just now. During the earliest stages, weight is synonymous with strength and activity. A pebble sunk in water weighs on the water, even when the latter is motionless, and produces a current towards the surface. An object floats because, being heavy, it has the strength to keep itself up. Weight is an absolute thing: it is a quality possessed by certain bodies, a variant of that life, or substantial force which we have described. Later on, weight is regarded as relative to the surrounding medium: bodies float because they are lighter than water, the clouds, because they are lighter than air, etc. But the relation is still vague: the child simply means that for the water in the lake, such and such a boat is light, but no comparison has been made which introduces proportional volumes. The wood of the boat is regarded as heavier than an equal volume of water. Finally, between the years of 9 and 10, "lighter than the water" begins to mean that the body in question is, taken at equal volume, lighter than water. Thus do the ideas of density and specific weight make their appearance: absolute weight is succeeded, in part at any rate, by relative weight.

The explanation of shadows and of night also offers an example of the progression from substantialism to an explanation founded on relations. During the earliest stages, night and shade are substances that emanate from clouds and bodies in general, and which come and go more or less intentionally. In the later stages, night and shade are nothing but the effects conditioned by the spatial relations which regulate the diffusion of light.

In every domain the substantialist realism of perception is succeeded by explanation through geometrical and cinematic relations. Running parallel with this growing relativity of phenomena in relation to each other, can be seen a growing relativity of ideas and notions in relation to ourselves and our evaluations. Thus the establishment of relativity between phenomena leads to a relativity between the measurer and what is measured. The evolution of the notion of weight brings out very clearly this double development. On the one hand, as we have just seen, the weight of the body becomes relative to the medium constituted by the other bodies, and presupposes the establishment of a relation between weight and volume. On the other hand, the words "light" and "heavy" lose the absolute meaning they had during the earliest stages, and acquire a meaning that is relative to the units of measurement that have been chosen: the pebble is heavy for the water, light for us, etc. The absolute concept has become a relation. In such cases, the advance towards relativity ends by converging absolutely with the advance towards reciprocity of view-points; in other words, the second and third processes as we distinguished them, finally merge into one.

Such, then, is the evolution of the notion of reality in the child. Three processes help to make it emerge from its initial realism and to orientate it towards objectivity. In what relation do these three processes stand to one another? The first is of a purely social nature: the child replaces his own individual and egocentric point of view by the point of view of others and the reciprocity existing between them. The second of these three processes is of a purely intellectual order: substantialism of perception is replaced by the relativism of intelligence. The third process is both social and intellectual in character: in becoming conscious of his "I," the child clears external reality of all its subjective elements, and thus attains to objectivity; but it is, above all, social life that has forced the child to become conscious of his "ego." Are we then to conclude that social factors determine the progress in the understanding of reality, or does this progress itself explain the development of social life? Let us note, in the first place, that the three processes synchronise. All three begin very early, all three are very slow, they remain uncompleted at the close of childhood and survive throughout the intellectual development of the adult. There is therefore every reason to believe that they are interdependent.

As a matter of fact, we have here, as in the case of child logic, to suppose that social life is necessary to rational development, but that it is not sufficient to create the power of reasoning. Without collaboration between his own thought and that of others, the child would not become conscious of the divergences which separate his ego from that of others, and he would take each of his perceptions or conceptions as absolute. He would therefore never attain to objectivity, for lack of having ever discovered his own subjectivity. Without social life, he would never succeed in understanding the reciprocity of view-points, and, consequently, the existence of perspectives, whether geometrical or logical. He would never cease to believe that the sun follows him on his walks. He would be ignorant of the reciprocity of the notions of right and left, of dependence, in short, of relations in general. It is therefore highly probable that the relativity of ideas would elude him.

IDEAS
FROM ABROAD

*   *   *

ORTEGA Y GASSET ON THE COMING OF THE MASSES (1932) From Jose Ortega y Gasset, *The Revolt of the Masses* (New York, 1932), pp. 11–18.

There is one fact which, whether for good or ill, is of utmost importance in the public life of Europe at the present moment. This fact is the accession of the masses to complete social power. As the masses, by definition, neither should nor can direct their own personal existence, and still less rule society in general, this fact means that actually Europe is suffering from the greatest crisis that can afflict peoples, nations, and civilisation. Such a crisis has occurred more than once in history. Its characteristics and its consequences are well known. So also is its name. It is called the rebellion of the masses. In order to understand this formidable fact, it is important from the start to avoid giving to the words "rebellion," "masses," and "social power" a meaning exclusively or primarily political. Public life is not solely political, but equally, and even primarily, intellectual, moral, economic, religious; it comprises all our collective habits, including our fashions both of dress and amusement.

Perhaps the best line of approach to this historical phenomenon may be found by turning our attention to a visual experience, stressing one aspect of our epoch which is plain to our very eyes. This fact is quite simple to enunciate, though not so to analyse. I shall call it the fact of agglomeration, of "plenitude." Towns are full of people, houses full of tenants, hotels full of guests, trains full of travellers, cafés full of customers, parks full of promenaders, consulting-rooms of famous doctors full of patients, theatres full of spectators, and beaches full of bathers. What previously was, in general, no problem, now begins to be an everyday one, namely, to find room.

That is all. Can there be any fact simpler, more patent, more constant in actual life? Let us now pierce the plain surface of this observation and we shall be surprised to see how there wells forth an unexpected spring in which the white light of day, of our actual day, is broken up into its rich chromatic content. What is it that we see, and the sight of which causes us so much surprise? We see the multitude, as such, in possession of the places and the instruments created by civilisation. The slightest reflection will then make us surprised at our own surprise. What about it? Is this not the ideal state of things? The theatre has seats to be occupied—in other words, so that the house may be full—and now they are overflowing; people anxious to use them are left standing outside. Though the fact be quite logical and natural, we cannot but recognize that this did not happen before and that now it does; consequently, there has been a change, an innovation, which justifies, at least for the moment, our surprise.

* * *

Agglomeration, fullness, was not frequent before. Why then is it now? The components of the multitudes around us have not sprung from nothing. Approximately the same number of people existed fifteen years ago. Indeed, after the war it might seem natural that their number should be less. Nevertheless, it is here we come up against the first important point. The individuals who made up these multitudes existed, but not *qua* multitude. Scattered about the world in small groups, or solitary, they lived a life, to all appearances, divergent, dissociate, apart. Each individual or small group occupied a place, its own, in country, village, town, or quarter of the great city. Now, suddenly, they appear as an agglomeration, and looking in any direction our eyes meet with the multitudes. Not only in any direction, but precisely in the best places, the relatively refined creation of human culture, previously reserved to lesser groups, in a word, to minorities. The multitude has suddenly become visible, installing itself in the preferential positions in society. Before, if it existed, it passed unnoticed, occupying the background of the social stage; now it has advanced to the footlights and is the principal character. There are no longer protagonists; there is only the chorus.

The concept of the multitude is quantitative and visual. Without changing its nature, let us translate it into terms of sociology. We then meet with the notion of the "social mass." Society is always a dynamic unity of two component factors: minorities and masses. The minorities are individuals or groups of individuals which are specially qualified. The mass is the assemblage of persons not specially qualified. By masses, then, is not to be understood, solely or mainly, "the working masses." The mass is the average man. In this way what was mere quantity—the multitude—is converted into a qualitative determination: it becomes the common social quality, man as undifferentiated from other men, but as repeating in himself a generic type. What have we gained by this conversion of quantity into quality? Simply this: by means of the latter we understand the genesis of the former. It is evident to the verge of platitude that the normal formation of a multitude implies the coincidence of desires, ideas, ways of life, in the individuals who constitute it. It will be objected that this is just what happens with every social group, however select it may strive to be. This is true; but there is an essential difference. In those groups which are characterised by not being multitude and mass, the effective coincidence of its members is based on some desire, idea, or ideal, which of itself excludes the great number. To form a minority, of whatever kind, it is necessary beforehand that each member separate himself from the multitude for *special*, relatively personal, reasons. Their coincidence with the others who form the minority is, then, secondary, posterior to their having each adopted an attitude of singularity, and is consequently, to a large extent, a coincidence in not coinciding. There are cases in which this singularising character of the group appears in the light of day: those English groups, which style themselves "nonconformists," where we have the grouping together of those who agree only in their disagreement in regard to the limitless multitude. This coming together of the minority precisely in order to separate themselves from the majority is a necessary ingredient in the formation of every minority. Speaking of the limited public which listened to a musician of refinement, Mallarmé wittily says that this public by its presence in small numbers stressed the absence of the multitude.

Strictly speaking, the mass, as a psychological fact, can be defined without waiting for individuals to appear in mass formation. In the presence of one individual we can decide whether he is "mass" or not. The mass is all that which sets no value on itself—good or ill—based on specific grounds, but which feels itself "just like everybody," and nevertheless is not concerned about it; is, in fact, quite happy to feel itself as one with everybody else. Imagine a humble-minded man who, having tried to estimate his own worth on specific grounds—asking himself if he has any talent for this or that, if he excels in any direction—realises that he possesses no quality of excellence. Such a man will feel that he is mediocre and commonplace, ill-gifted, but will not feel himself "mass."

*   *   *

The division of society into masses and select minorities is, then, not a division into social classes, but into classes of men, and cannot coincide with the hierarchic separation of "upper" and "lower" classes. It is, of course, plain that in these "upper" classes, when and as long as they really are so, there is much more likelihood of finding men who adopt the "great vehicle," whereas the "lower" classes, normally comprise individuals of minus quality. But, strictly speaking, within both these social classes, there are to be found mass and genuine minority. As we shall see, a characteristic of our times is the predominance, even in groups traditionally selective, of the mass and the vulgar. Thus, in the intellectual life, which of its essence requires and presupposes qualification, one can note the progressive triumph of the pseudo-intellectual, unqualified, unqualifiable, and, by their very mental texture, disqualified. Similarly, in the surviving groups of the "nobility," male and female. On the other hand, it is not rare to find to-day amongst working men, who before might be taken as the best example of what we are calling "mass," nobly disciplined minds.

There exist, then, in society, operations, activities, and functions of the most diverse order, which are of their very nature special, and which consequently cannot be properly carried out without special gifts. For example: certain pleasures of an artistic and refined character, or again the functions of government and of political judgment in public affairs. Previously these special activities were exercised by qualified minorities, or at least by those who claimed such qualification. The mass asserted no right to intervene in them; they realised that if they wished to intervene they would necessarily have to acquire those special qualities and cease being mere mass. They recognised their place in a healthy dynamic social system.

If we now revert to the facts indicated at the start, they will appear clearly as the heralds of a changed attitude in the mass. They all indicate that the mass has decided to advance to the foreground of social life, to occupy the places, to use the instruments and to enjoy the pleasures hitherto reserved to the few. It is evident, for example, that the places were never intended for the multitude, for their dimensions are too limited, and the crowd is continuously overflowing; thus manifesting to our eyes and in the clearest manner the new phenomenon: the mass, without ceasing to be mass, is supplanting the minorities.

No one, I believe, will regret that people are to-day enjoying themselves in greater measure and numbers than before, since they have now both the desire and the means of satisfying it. The evil lies in the fact that this decision taken by the masses to assume the activities proper to the minorities is not, and cannot be, manifested solely in the domain of pleasure, but that it is a general feature of our time. Thus—to anticipate what we shall see later—I believe that the political innovations of recent times signify nothing less than the political domination of the masses. The old democracy was tempered by a generous dose of liberalism and of enthusiasm for law. By serving these principles the individual is bound himself to maintain a severe discipline over himself. Under the shelter of liberal principles and the rule of law, minorities could live and act. Democracy and law—life in common under the law—were synonymous. To-day we are witnessing the triumphs of a hyperdemocracy in which the mass acts directly, outside the law, imposing its aspirations and its desires by means of material pressure. It is a false interpretation of the new situation to say that the mass has grown tired of politics and handed over the exercise of it to specialised persons. Quite the contrary. That was what happened previously; that was democracy. The mass took it for granted that after all, in spite of their defects and weaknesses, the minorities understood a little more of public problems than it did itself. Now, on the other hand, the mass believes that it has the right to impose and to give force of law to notions born in the cafe. I doubt whether there have been other periods of history in which the multitude has come to govern more directly than in our own. That is why I speak of hyperdemocracy.

The same thing is happening in other orders, particularly in the intellectual. I may be mistaken, but the present-day writer, when he takes his pen in hand to treat a subject which he has studied deeply, has to bear in mind that the average reader, who has never concerned himself with this subject, if he reads does so with the view, not of learning something from the writer, but rather, of pronouncing judgment on him when he is not in agreement with the commonplaces that the said reader carries in his head. If the individuals who make up the mass believed themselves specially qualified, it would be a case merely of personal error, not a sociological subversion. *The characteristic of the hour is that the commonplace mind, knowing itself to be commonplace, has the assurance to proclaim the rights of the commonplace and to impose them wherever it will.* As they say in the United States: "to be different is to be indecent." The mass crushes beneath it everything that is different, everything that is excellent, individual, qualified and select. Anybody who is not like everybody, who does not think like everybody, runs the risk of being eliminated. And it is clear, of course, that this "everybody" is not "everybody." "Everybody" was normally the complex unity of the mass and the divergent, specialised minorities. Nowadays, "everybody" is the mass alone. Here we have the formidable fact of our times, described without any concealment of the brutality of its features.

KURT LEWIN ON THE PSYCHOLOGICAL INFLUENCE OF THE ENVIRONMENT (1933)   From Kurt Lewin, *A Dynamic Theory of Personality; Selected Papers,* Donald K. Adams and Karl E. Zener, trans. (London, 1935), pp. 66, 68, 73, 76–81.

We have here to deal only with the psychological influence of the environment. This does not mean that the somatic effects of environment, for example, of nutrition or climate, do not have great psychological significance. On the contrary, the somatic as well as the psychological influence of the environment is constantly operating on the entire child.

Introduction

It has long been recognized that the psychological influence of environment on the behavior and development of the child is extremely important. Actually, all aspects of the child's behavior, hence instinctive and voluntary behavior, play, emotion, speech, expression, are codetermined by the existing environment. Some recent theories, notably those of Watson and Adler, assign to environment so predominant an influence upon development that hereditary factors are usually neglected. Stern's theory of convergence emphasizes, on the contrary, that a predisposition and an environmental influence must operate in the same direction in order to effect a particular mode of behavior.

*   *   *

Valuable and indispensable as these facts are, they can rarely offer more than hints toward the problem of the forces of the environment. For, in the investigation of the fundamental dynamic relations between the individual and the environment, it is essential to keep constantly in the mind the actual total situation in its concrete individuality. The statistical method is usually compelled to define its groups on the basis not of purely psychological characteristics but of more or less extrinsic ones (such as the number of siblings), so that particular cases having quite different or even opposed psychological structure may be included in the same group. Especially to be emphasized, however, is the following consideration: the calculation of an average (e.g., of "the one-year-old child") is designed to eliminate the "accidents" of the environment; the determination of the "average situation" (e.g., of the average effect of the situation of being an only child) is to exclude individual variations. But the very relation that is decisive for the investigation of dynamics—namely, that of the position of the actual individual child in the actual, concrete, total situation—is thereby abstracted. An inference from the average to the concrete particular case is hence impossible. The concepts of the average child and of the average situation are abstractions that have no utility whatever for the investigation of dynamics . . .

*   *   *

An analysis of environmental factors must start from a consideration of the total situation. Such an analysis hence presupposes an adequate comprehension and presentation in dynamic terms of the total psychological situation as its most important task.

*   *   *

Exactly the same physical object may have quite different sorts of psychological existence for different children and for the same child in different situations. A wooden cube may be one time a missile, again a building block, and a third time a locomotive. What a thing is at any time depends upon the total situation and the momentary condition of the child involved. Similar considerations hold also for the social factors.

In this dependence there becomes clear a matter of fundamental psychological importance, namely, *the direct relationship between the momentary state of the individual and the structure of his psychological environment.* That the psychological environment, even when objectively the same, depends not only upon the individual character and developmental stage of the child concerned but also upon its momentary condition becomes clear when we consider the relation between environment and needs.

Beside the quasi-physical and quasi-social environment, a mental task or a phantasy must sometimes be characterized from the dynamic point of view as environment. Activities (e.g., a game) may have the character of a region into or out of which the child may go. In the same sense a mathematical problem may have this character. The description of the child's environment would be incomplete without including the whole world of phantasy which is so important for the child's behavior and so closely connected with its ideals and with its ideal goals.

In the environment there are, as we have seen, many objects and events of quasi-physical and quasi-social nature, such as rooms, halls, tables, chairs, a bed, a cap, knife and fork, things that fall down, turn over, can start and go of themselves; there are dogs, friends, grown-ups, neighbors, someone who rarely gets cross, and someone who is always strict and disagreeable. There are places where one is safe from rain, others where one is safe from adults, and still others where one may not go under any circumstances. All these things and events are defined for the child partly by their appearance but above all by their *functional possibilities* (the *Wirkwelt* in von Uexküll's sense). The stairs are something that one can (or cannot yet) go up and down, or something that one climbed yesterday for the first time. Thus history, as the child has experienced it, is also a psychologically essential constituent of the things of the environment.

With all these, however, there remain certain critical properties of the psychobiological environment still undescribed. Objects are not neutral to the child, but have an immediate psychological effect on its behavior. Many things attract the child to eating, others to climbing, to grasping, to manipulation, to sucking, to raging at them, etc. These imperative environmental facts—we shall call them valences [*Aufforderungscharaktere*]—determine the direction of the behavior. Particularly from the standpoint of dynamics, the valences, their kind (sign), strength, and distribution, must be regarded as among the most important properties of the environment.

*   *   *

The valence of an object usually derives from the fact that the object is a means to the satisfaction of a need, or has indirectly something to do with the satisfaction of a need. The kind (sign) and strength of the valence of an object or event thus depends directly upon the momentary condition of the needs of the individual concerned; the valence of environmental objects and the needs of the individual are correlative.

*   *   *

Even with objective identity of environment, the strength and the appearance of the valences are quite other for a hungry child than for a satisfied one, for a healthy child than for a sickly one.

The correlation between valence and environment leads to a fundamental change in the latter with the changing needs of increasing age. The objects bearing valences are different for the baby, the toddler, the kindergartener, and the pubescent.

The valences change also with the *momentary state* of the needs. When the need for nourishment, for playing with a doll, or for reading history is in a hungry or unsatisfied condition, a bit of food, a doll, or the history book attracts the child, that is, has a positive valence; whereas, when this need is in a stage or state of satisfaction, the object is indifferent to the child; and, in the stage of oversatiation of the need, it becomes disagreeable to the child, that is, it acquires a negative valence.

Since the psychological environment, especially for the child, is not identical with the physical or social environment, one cannot, in investigating environmental forces, proceed from the physical forces as Loeb, for example, does in biology. If we start primarily from the psychobiological environment and pay due attention to its dependence upon the actual momentary condition of the individual involved, it is quite possible to discover universally valid principles of the dynamic effects of the environment. To be sure, it will always be necessary to keep in mind the total structure of the existing situation.

Psychological environmental forces [*Umweltkräfte*] may be defined empirically and functionally, excluding all metaphysical problems, by their effect upon the behavior of the child. They are equally applicable to the momentary situation and to the permanent environment of the child.

In summary: to understand or predict the psychological behavior (B) one has to determine for every kind of psychological event (actions, emotions, expressions, etc.) the momentary whole situation, that is, the momentary structure and the state of the person (P) and of the psychological environment (E). $B = f(PE)$. Every fact that exists psychobiologically must have a position in this field and only facts that have such position have dynamic effects (are causes of events). The environment is for all of its properties (directions, distances, etc.) to be defined not physically but *psychobiologically*, that is, according to its quasi-physical, quasi-social, and quasi-mental structure.

It is possible to represent the dynamic structure of the person and of the environment by means of mathematical concepts. The coordination between the mathematical representation and its psychodynamic meaning has to be strict and without exception.

We shall first describe the psychological field forces and their mode of operation, without consideration of the question whether the object in any particular case has acquired its valence through some previous experience or in some other way.

The Region of Freedom of Movement. Forces and Fields of Force

The first presupposition for the understanding of the child is the determination of the psychological place at which the child concerned is and of his region of freedom of movement, that is, of the regions that are accessible to him and of those regions that psychologically exist for the child but are inaccessible to him by reason of the social situation (prohibition by the adult, limitation by other children, etc.) or because of the limitations of his own social, physical, and intellectual abilities. Whether his region of freedom of movement is large or small is of decisive significance for the whole behavior of the child.

One can characterize these possible and not possible psychodynamic locomotions (quasi-bodily, quasi-social, and quasi-mental locomotions) at every point of the environment with the help of the concept of topology, which is a nonquantitative discipline about the possible kinds of connections between "spaces" and their parts.

The basis for the coordination between mathematical and psychodynamic concepts so far as environmental questions are concerned is the coordination of topological path and psychodynamic locomotion. The topological description determines which points the different paths lead to and which regions these paths cross. The region which a child cannot reach one can characterize by means of barriers between these regions and their neighboring regions. The barrier corresponds as a dynamic concept to the mathematical concept of boundary. One must distinguish between different strengths of barriers.

To determine not only which locomotions (paths) are possible but which of the possible locomotions will occur at a given moment one has to use the concept of *force*.

A force is defined through three properties: (1) direction, (2) strength, and (3) point of application. The first and second properties are to be represented through the mathematical concept *vector*. The point of application is indicated in the figures (as is the custom in physics) by the point of the arrow.

Dynamically the force is correlated with psychobiological locomotions in a one-to-one correspondence. "The real locomotion must occur in every case according to the direction and the strength of the resultant of the momentary forces" and "In any case of locomotion there exists a resultant of forces in its direction."

The direction which the valence imparts to the child's behavior varies extremely, according to the content of the wants and needs. Nevertheless, one may distinguish two large groups of valences according to the sort of initial behavior they elicit: the positive valences (+), those effecting approach; and the negative (-), or those producing withdrawal or retreat.

The *actions* in the direction of the valence may have the form of uncontrolled impulsive behavior or of directed voluntary activity; they may be "appropriate" or "inappropriate."

Those processes which make an especially goal-striving impression are usually characterized dynamically by a reference to a positive valence.

One has to distinguish between *driving* forces, which correspond to positive or negative valences, and *restraining* forces, which correspond to barriers.

Direction of the Field Force. That the valence is not associated merely with a subjective experience of direction, but that a directed force, determinative of the behavior, must be ascribed to it, may be seen in the fact that a change in the position of the attractive object brings about (other things being equal) a change in the direction of the child's movements.

THE PARENT AS UPBRINGER (1937)   From Anton S. Makarenko, *The Collective Family: A Handbook For Russian Parents*, Robert Daglish, trans. (New York, 1967), pp. 11–17.

A Soviet person cannot be educated by the direct influence of one personality, whatever qualities this personality may possess. Education is a social process in the broadest sense of the term. Everything contributes to education: people, things, events, but first of all and above all—people. Of these, parents and teachers hold first place. The child enters into an infinite number of relationships with the whole complex world of surrounding reality. Each one of these relationships is irresistibly developing, overlapping with other relationships, and becoming more complicated as the physical and moral growth of the child increases.

Nothing in this "chaos" seems to yield to any calculation. Nevertheless at each given moment definite changes are created in the personality of the child. And it is the task of the educator to direct and guide this development.

IDEAS
FROM ABROAD

Senseless and hopeless is the attempt made by some parents to shield the child from the influence of life and substitute individual domestic training for social education. It is bound to end in failure: either the child breaks out of the domestic prison or you produce a freak.

Then it is life that is responsible for the child's upbringing. But where does the family come in?

No, it is the family or, if you like, the parents that are responsible for the child's upbringing. But the training provided by the family collective cannot mold the child out of nothing. A limited assortment of family impressions or pedagogical lectures from Father will not suffice as material for the future man. It is Soviet life in all its multiform variety that provides that material.

In the old days, in well-to-do families children used to be called "angelic souls." In our day it has been said that children are "flowers of life." That is good. But rashminded, sentimental people have not taken the trouble to think over the meaning of these beautiful words. Once children are described as "flowers," it means to such people that we should do nothing but go into raptures over them, make a fuss over them, smell them, sigh over them. Perhaps they even think we should teach the flowers themselves that they are a fragile "luxury" bouquet.

This purely aesthetic and thoughtless enthusiasm contains the seeds of its own failure. The "flowers of life" should not be imagined as a "luxury" bouquet in a Chinese vase on your table. However much you enthuse over such flowers, however much fuss you make over them, these flowers are already dying, they are already doomed and they are sterile. Tomorrow you will simply have them thrown away. At best, if you are incorrigibly sentimental, you will dry them in a bulky volume, but you can expect little joy from that: give yourself up as much as you like to memories, look at them as much as you like, you will still have nothing but hay, just hay.

No, our children are not flowers of that kind at all. Our children blossom on the living trunk of our life; they are not a bouquet, they are a wonderful apple orchard. And this orchard is ours. Here the right of property means something fine, believe me! It is hard, of course, not to admire such an orchard, hard not to rejoice over it, but it is even harder not to work in it. Be so kind as to take on this job: dig, water, get rid of the caterpillars, prune out the dead branches. Remember the words of the great gardener, Comrade Stalin:

"People should be reared with care and attention as a gardener rears his chosen fruit-tree."

Note the word: fruit. Not only fragrance, not only range of colors, but fruit, that is what should interest you especially. And for this reason do not descend upon the flowers with nothing but raptures and kisses—take up your spade, your scissors and watering can, and fetch the ladder. And when the caterpillar appears in your garden, reach for the insecticide. Do not be afraid of it, shake it around a bit, let even the flowers feel a little uncomfortable. By the way, a good gardener never has trouble with caterpillars.

Yes, let us be gardeners. This excellent comparison will help us to explain a few things about the difficult problem of who educates the child—parents or life?

Who cultivates the tree in an orchard?

The soil and the air give it substance, the sun gives it the valuable power of combustion, the winds and storms bring it toughness in battle, its fellow trees save it from sterility. Both in the tree and around it extremely complex chemical processes are always at work.

What can the gardener change in this laborious work of life? Should he just wait helplessly and submissively till the fruit are ripe and he can pluck them and gorge himself on them with greedy indifference?

That is exactly what savages do in the wilds of Tierra del Fuego. And that is what many parents do.

But a real gardener would never act like that.

Man learned long ago to approach nature cautiously and tenderly. Now he has learned to transform nature, to create new natural forms, to apply his powerful corrective to the life of nature. And we should remember that we Soviet educationalists also are no longer "servants of nature," but her masters.

Our education is a similar corrective. And only on these lines is education possible. To lead a child wisely and surely along the rich paths of life, amid its flowers and through its storms and tempests, is a task which every man can accomplish if he really wants to do so.

Nothing annoys me more than the disgusting panic-stricken howl:
"Street urchins!!"
"You see, everything was all right, but then Seryozha got friendly with a lot of urchins in our yard. . . ."

This "lot of urchins" corrupt Seryozha. Seryozha roams off no one knows where. Seryozha has taken a length of worsted from the closet and sold it. Seryozha came home past midnight, smelling of vodka. Seryozha insulted his mother.

Only the most hopeless simpleton can believe that all this was brought about by "a lot of urchins," "street urchins."

Seryozha is not unique. He is perfectly ordinary, a standard type which everybody is quite tired of, and it is not "street urchins" or the "urchins in our yard" but lazy and unscrupulous parents that have made him what he is. He is not produced in a flash; the process is a persistent and patient one, beginning from the time when Seryozha was one and a half years old. A large number of thoroughly disgraceful characteristics in the family's behavior contributed to the making of him: blank idleness, aimless daydreaming, petty tyranny and, above all, unpardonable irresponsibility and an infinitesimal sense of duty.

Seryozha is indeed a real "street urchin," but it was the family, and only the family, that made him one. Perhaps in your yard he does meet failures like himself; together they make up the usual gang of youngsters, all of them equally demoralized and equally "street." But in that same yard you will find dozens of children for whom the family body and the family corrective have created principles and traditions which help them to overcome the influence of the street boys without avoiding them and without barricading themselves off from life within the family walls.

The decisive factor in successful family upbringing lies in the constant, active, and conscious fulfillment by parents of their civic duty toward Soviet society. In those cases where this duty is really felt by parents, where it forms the basis of their daily lives, there it necessarily guides the family's work of upbringing too, there no failures or catastrophes are possible.

But there is, unfortunately, a category of parents, a fairly numerous category, with whom this rule does not work. These people seem to be good citizens, but they suffer either from inability to think consistently, or from a weak sense of direction, or from not being observant enough. And for this reason alone their sense of duty does not operate in the sphere of their family relationships, nor, consequently, does it operate in the sphere of their children's upbringing. And for this reason alone they meet with more or less serious failures, and produce for society human beings of dubious quality.

Others are more honest. They say sincerely: "You have to know how to bring up a child. Perhaps I am not doing it right, really. It takes knowledge to bring up children."

In other words: everybody wants to bring up their children well, but not everyone knows the secret. Some people have discovered it, some people make full use of it, but you are completely in the dark, no one has revealed the mystery to you.

This being so, the eyes of all turn toward the teachers' training colleges and institutes.

Dear Parents!

Between ourselves, in their families our pedagogical brethren produce, proportionately, about the same quantity of defective goods as you do. And, on the contrary, fine children are often brought up by parents who have never seen either the front door or the back door of pedagogical science.

And pedagogical science pays little attention to family upbringing. That is why even the most learned pedagogues, although they know the why and wherefore of things very well, when bringing up their own children try to rely more on common sense and worldly wisdom. But perhaps more often than others they are guilty of a naive belief in the pedagogical "secret."

I once knew such a professor of pedagogics. He would always treat his only son as a problem to be solved with the aid of books and profound psychological analyses. Like many pedagogues he believed that there must exist somewhere in the world some kind of pedagogical trick which would bring complete and delightful satisfaction both to educator and child, satisfy all principles and bring about the reign of peace and quiet and eternal bliss! The son was rude to his mother at dinner. The professor thought for a moment and arrived at an inspired solution:

"Fedya, since you have insulted your mother, it follows that you do not appreciate our home, that you are unworthy to sit at our table. Very well, beginning tomorrow I shall give you five rubles a day—eat your dinner where you like."

The professor was pleased. In his opinion he had reacted to his son's rudeness brilliantly. Fedya was also pleased. But the trick plan did not work. There was a period of peace and quiet, but the eternal bliss was missing.

The professor expected that in three or four days' time Fedya would come and fling his arms round his father's neck, saying: "Father, I was wrong! Don't shut me out from home!"

But it did not happen like that, or rather, not quite like that, Fedya became very fond of visiting cafes and restaurants. The only thing that disconcerted him was the small allowance his father had given him. He made one or two amendments to the scheme; he rooted about the house and showed some initiative. Next morning, the professor's trousers were missing from his closet and in the evening the son came home drunk. In touching tones he proclaimed his love for his mama and papa, but did not raise the question of returning to the family table. The professor took off his belt and waved it in front of his son's face for some minutes.

After a month the professor threw in the sponge and asked for his son to be sent to a labor colony. According to him Fedya had been spoiled by various comrades of his.

"You know what children there are about!"

Some parents, if they heard of this affair, would undoubtedly say: "Very well!

But all the same, how is one supposed to act if one's son is rude to his mother at dinner?"

Comrades! Perhaps you will ask me next how one should act if one loses a purse full of money? Think it over and you will find the answer at once: buy yourself a new purse, earn some more money and put it into the purse.

If a son insults his mother, no tricks will do any good. It means that you have brought up your son very badly and that you have been doing so for a long time. You must begin the work of bringing him up all over again, you must change a lot of things in your family, think over a lot of things, and, above all, put yourself under the microscope. And as for how you should act immediately after rudeness, that is a question to which one cannot give any general answer—it depends on each individual case. One must know what kind of a person you are and how you have acted toward your family. Perhaps you yourself were rude to your wife in the presence of your son. Incidentally, if you treated your wife badly when your son was not at home—take that into consideration too.

No, tricks in family upbringing must be firmly discarded. The care and upbringing of children is a big, a serious, and a terribly responsible task, and it is, of course, also a difficult task. No easy tricks can help you out here. Once you have a child, it means that for many years to come you must give him all your power of concentration, all your attention and all your strength of character. You must be not only father and guardian of your children, you must also be organizer of your own life, because your quality as an educator is entirely bound up with your activities as a citizen and your feelings as an individual.

THE CONSTITUTION OF THE UNITED NATIONS EDUCATIONAL, SCIENTIFIC, AND CULTURAL ORGANIZATION (1945) From *Conference for the Establishment of the United Nations Educational, Scientific, and Cultural Organization* (London, 1946), pp. 93–99.

London, 16th November, 1945

The Governments of the States parties to this Constitution on behalf of their peoples declare, that since wars begin in the minds of men, it is in the minds of men that the defences of peace must be constructed;

that ignorance of each other's ways and lives has been a common cause, throughout the history of mankind, of that suspicion and mistrust between the peoples of the world through which their differences have all too often broken into war;

that the great and terrible war which has now ended was a war made possible by the denial of the democratic principles of the dignity, equality and mutual respect of men, and by the propagation, in their place, through ignorance and prejudice, of the doctrine of the inequality of men and races;

that the wide diffusion of culture, and the education of humanity for justice and liberty and peace are indispensable to the dignity of man and constitute a sacred duty which all the nations must fulfil in a spirit of mutual assistance and concern;

that a peace based exclusively upon the political and economic arrangements of governments would not be a peace which could secure the unanimous lasting and sincere support of the peoples of the world, and that the peace must therefore be founded, if it is not to fail, upon the intellectual and moral solidarity of mankind.

For these reasons, the States parties to this Constitution, believing in full and equal opportunities for education for all, in the unrestricted pursuit of objective truth, and in the free exchange of ideas and knowledge, are agreed and determined to develop and to increase the means of communication between their peoples and to employ these means for the purposes of mutual understanding and a truer and more perfect knowledge of each other's lives;

In consequence whereof they do hereby create the United Nations Educational, Scientific and Cultural Organisation for the purpose of advancing, through the educational and scientific and cultural relations of the peoples of the world, the objectives of international peace and of the common welfare of mankind for which the United Nations Organisation was established and which its Charter proclaims.

Article I

PURPOSES AND FUNCTIONS

1. The purpose of the Organisation is to contribute to peace and security by promoting collaboration among the nations through education, science and culture in order to further universal respect for justice, for the rule of law and for the human rights and fundamental freedoms which are affirmed for the peoples of the world, without distinction of race, sex, language or religion, by the Charter of the United Nations.

2. To realise this purpose the Organisation will:

(a) collaborate in the work of advancing the mutual knowledge and understanding of peoples, through all means of mass communication and to that end recommend such international agreements as may be necessary to promote the free flow of ideas by word and image;

(b) give fresh impulse to popular education and to the spread of culture: by collaborating with Members, at their request, in the development of educational activities; by instituting collaboration among the nations to advance the ideal of equality of educational opportunity without regard to race, sex or any distinctions, economic or social; by suggesting educational methods best suited to prepare the children of the world for the responsibilities of freedom;

(c) maintain, increase and diffuse knowledge: by assuring the conservation and protection of the world's inheritance of books, works of art and monuments of history and science, and recommending to the nations concerned the necessary international conventions; by encouraging co-operation among the nations in all branches of intellectual activity, including the international exchange of persons active in the fields of education, science and culture and the exchange of publications, objects of artistic and scientific interest and other materials of information; by initiating methods of international co-operation calculated to give the people of all countries access to the printed and published materials produced by any of them.

3. With a view to preserving the independence, integrity and fruitful diversity

of the cultures and educational systems of the States Members of this Organisation, the Organisation is prohibited from intervening in matters which are essentially within their domestic jurisdiction.

Article II

MEMBERSHIP

1. Membership of the United Nations Organisation shall carry with it the right to membership of the United Nations Educational, Scientific and Cultural Organisation.

2. Subject to the conditions of the agreement between this Organisation and the United Nations Organisation, approved pursuant to Article X of this Constitution, States not members of the United Nations Organisation, may be admitted to membership of the Organisation, upon recommendation of the Executive Board, by a two-thirds majority vote of the General Conference.

3. Members of the Organisation which are suspended from the exercise of the rights and privileges of membership of the United Nations Organisation shall, upon the request of the latter, be suspended from the rights and privileges of this Organisation.

4. Members of the Organisation which are expelled from the United Nations Organisation shall automatically cease to be members of this Organisation.

Article III

ORGANS

The Organisation shall include a General Conference, an Executive Board and a Secretariat.

VATICAN II ON CHRISTIAN EDUCATION (1964) From "Declaration on Christian Education," Walter M. Abbott, ed., *Documents of Vatican II*, (London, 1966), pp. 637–49.

Introduction

This sacred Ecumenical Synod has carefully considered the paramount importance of education in the life of man, and its ever-mounting influence on the social progress of this age.[1] In fact, the education of the young and even a measure of

---

[1] Among many documents illustrating the importance of education, see especially:
Benedict XV, apostolic letter "Communes Litteras," Apr. 10, 1919: AAS 11 (1919), p. 172.
Pius XI, encyclical letter "Divini Illius Magistri," Dec. 31, 1929: AAS 22 (1930), pp. 49–86.
Pius XII, allocution to the youths of Italian Catholic Action, Apr. 20, 1946: "Discorsi e Radiomessaggi," Vol. 8, pp. 53–57.
Pius XII, allocution to fathers of Families of France, Sept. 18, 1951: "Discorsi e Radiomessagi," Vol. 13, pp. 241–245.
John XXIII, message on the 30th anniversary of the publication of the encyclical letter "Divini Illius Magistri," Dec. 30, 1959: AAS 52 (1960), pp. 57–59.
Paul VI, allocution to members of Federated Institutes Dependent on Ecclestiastical Authority, Dec. 30, 1963: "Encicliche e Discorsi di S.S. Paolo VI." Vol. I, Rome, 1964, pp. 601–603.
In addition, there may be consulted "Acta et Documenta Concilio Oecumenico Vaticano II apparando," series I, "Antepraeparatoria," Vol. III, pp. 363–364, 370–371, 373, 374.

IDEAS
FROM ABROAD

continued instruction for adults have grown both easier and more urgent in the circumstances of our times. For as men grow more conscious of their dignity and calling, they prefer to take an increasingly active part in the life of society, especially in economic and political matters.[2] Enjoying more leisure, as they sometimes do, men find that remarkable developments in technology and in scientific investigation, and new means of social communication offer them readier opportunities for attaining their inheritance of intellectual and spiritual culture, and for fulfilling themselves and

As a result, ever-increasing efforts are being everywhere expended to promote the work of education. The primary rights of men with respect to education, especially those of children and of parents, are being emphasized, and are finding expression in public documents.[3] On every side, as the number of pupils rapidly increases, schools are being multiplied and perfected, and other educational institutions are being established. Techniques of education and training are being refined on the basis of new experiments. Strenuous efforts are being made so that all men can obtain an education, though, admittedly, vast numbers of children and young people are still being deprived of even rudimentary training, and many others lack the suitable kind of education in which truth and love are simultaneously inculcated.

In fulfilling the mandate she has received from her divine Founder to proclaim the mystery of salvation to all men, and to restore all things in Christ, Holy Mother the Church must be concerned with the whole of man's life,[4] even the earthly part of it insofar as that has a bearing on his heavenly calling.[5] Therefore she has her role to play in the progress and spread of education. Hence this sacred Synod enunciates certain basic principles of Christian education, especially those applicable to formal schooling. These principles will have to be developed at greater length by a special postconciliar Commission and applied by episcopal conferences to varying local situations.

1. Since every man of whatever race, condition, and age is endowed with the dignity of a person, he has an inalienable right to an education[6] corresponding to his proper destiny[7] and suited to his native talents, his sex, his cultural background, and his

[2] Cf. John XXIII, encyclical letter "Mater et Magistra," May 15, 1961: AAS 53 (1961), pp. 413, 415–417, 424.
Also his encyclical letter "Pacem in Terris," Apr. 1, 1963: AAS 55 (1963), pp. 278 ff.
[3] Cf. the universal profession of the rights of men ("Declaration des droits de l'homme") of Dec. 10, 1948, adopted by the General Assembly of the United Nations; see also "Declaration des droits de l'enfant" of Nov. 20, 1959; also "Protocole additionnel a la convention de sauvegarde des droits de l'homme et des libertes fondamentales," Paris, Mar. 20, 1952; regarding that universal profession of the rights of man mentioned above, cf. John XXIII, encyclical letter "Pacem in Terris," Apr. 11, 1963: AAS 55 (1963), pp. 295 ff.
[4] The Council here states its basic position with regard to the Declaration on Christian Education. Although the Church is concerned primarily with the spiritual and supernatural destiny of man, it recognizes the intimate connection between that destiny and "the whole of man's life." See introductory notes.
[5] Cf. John XXIII, encyclical letter "Mater et Magistra," May 15, 1961: AAS 53 (1961) p. 402.
See also Second Vatican Council's Dogmatic Constitution on the Church, Art. 17: AAS 57 (1965), p. 21; also the schema of the Pastoral Constitution on the Church in the Modern World (1965), passim.
[6] Pius XII, radio message of Dec. 24, 1942: AAS 35 (1943), pp. 12, 19.
John XXIII, encyclical letter "Pacem in Terris," Apr. 11, 1963: AAS 55 (1963), pp. 259 ff. See also the declarations of the rights of man cited in note (3).
[7] Cf. Pius XI, encyclical letter "Divini Illius Magistri," Dec. 31, 1929: AAS 22 (1930), pp. 50 ff.

ancestral heritage. At the same time, this education should pave the way to brotherly association with other peoples, so that genuine unity and peace on earth may be promoted. For a true education aims at the formation of the human person with respect to his ultimate goal, and simultaneously with respect to the good of those societies of which, as a man, he is a member, and in whose responsibilities, as an adult, he will share.

As a consequence, with the help of advances in psychology and in the art and science of teaching, children and young people should be assisted in the harmonious development of their physical, moral, and intellectual endowments. Surmounting hardships with a gallant and steady heart, they should be helped to acquire gradually a more mature sense of responsibility toward ennobling their own lives through constant effort, and toward pursuing authentic freedom. As they advance in years, they should be given positive and prudent sexual education. Moreover, they should be trained to take their part in social life, so that by proper instruction in necessary and useful skills they can become actively involved in various community organizations, be ready for dialogue with others, and be willing to act energetically on behalf of the common good.

This holy Synod likewise affirms that children and young people have a right to be encouraged to weigh moral values with an upright conscience, and to embrace them by personal choice, and to know and love God more adequately.[8] Hence, it earnestly entreats all who exercise government over peoples or presides over the work of education to see that youth is never deprived of this sacred right. It urges sons of the Church to devote themselves generously to the whole enterprise of education, with the special aim of helping to bring more speedily to all men everywhere the worthy benefits of education and training.[9]

2. Since every Christian has become a new creature[10] by rebirth from water and the Holy Spirit, so that he may be called what he truly is, a child of God, he is entitled to a Christian education. Such an education does not merely strive to foster in the human person the maturity already described. Rather, its principal aims are these:[11] that as the baptized person is gradually introduced into a knowledge of the mystery of salvation, he may daily grow more conscious of the gift of faith which he has received; that he may learn to adore God the Father in spirit and in truth (cf. Jn. 4:23), especially through liturgical worship; that he may be trained to conduct his personal life in righteousness and in the sanctity of truth, according to his new standard of manhood (Eph. 4:22-24).

Thus, indeed, he may grow into manhood according to the mature measure of Christ (cf. Eph. 4:13), and devote himself to the upbuilding of the Mystical Body. Moreover, aware of his calling, he should grow accustomed to giving witness to the

[8]The theme of personal responsibility which has dominated so many of the deliberations of Vatican II comes out very clearly here. Note the insistence on children and young people and their own development in contradistinction to a previous attitude of education as if it were imposed from above. There is an interesting connection between this paragraph and the Declaration on Religious Freedom.

[9]Cf. John XXIII, encyclical letter "Mater et Magistra," May 15, 1961: AAS 53 (1961), pp. 441 ff.

[10]Cf. Pius XI, encyclical letter "Divini Illius Magistri," loc. cit., p. 83.

[11]Here is the most positive statement of the true essence of Christian education. The Christian view of life is simply different and is based on a belief in a supernatural life. The result is that the Christian can never be satisfied with mere material-minded education. It also explains why Christian education is not merely ordinary education with an added dose of religious knowledge.

hope that is in him (1 Pet. 3:15), and to promoting that Christian transformation of the world by which natural values, viewed in the full perspective of humanity as redeemed by Christ, may contribute to the good of society as a whole.[12] Therefore this holy Synod reminds pastors of souls of their acutely serious duty to make every effort to see that all the faithful enjoy a Christian education of this sort, especially young people, who are the hope of the Church.[13]

3. Since parents have conferred life on their children, they have a most solemn obligation to educate their offspring. Hence, parents must be acknowledged as the first and foremost educators of their children.[14] Their role as educators is so decisive that scarcely anything can compensate for their failure in it. For it devolves on parents to create a family atmosphere so animated with love and reverence for God and men that a well-rounded personal and social development will be fostered among the children.[15] Hence, the family is the first school of those social virtues which every society needs.

It is particularly in the Christian family, enriched by the grace and the office of the sacrament of matrimony, that from their earliest years children should be taught, according to the faith received in baptism, to have a knowledge of God, to worship Him, and to love their neighbor. Here, too, they gain their first experience of wholesome human companionship and of the Church. Finally, it is through the family that they are gradually introduced into civic partnership with their fellow men, and into the People of God. Let parents, then, clearly recognize how vital a truly Christian family is for the life and development of God's own people.[16]

While belonging primarily to the family, the task of imparting education requires the help of society as a whole. In addition, therefore, to the rights of parents and of others to whom parents entrust a share in the work of education, certain rights and duties belong to civil society.[17] For this society exists to arrange for the temporal necessities of the common good. Part of its duty is to promote the education of the young in several ways: namely, by overseeing the duties and rights

---

[12]Cf. Second Vatican Council, Dogmatic Constitution on the Church, Art. 36: AAS 57 (1965), pp. 41 ff.

[13]Cf. Second Vatican Council, schema of the Decree on the Apostolate of the Laity (1965), Art. 12.

[14]Cf. Pius XI, encyclical letter "Divini Illius Magistri," loc. cit., pp. 59 ff.: also encyclical letter "Mit brennender Sorge," Mar. 14, 1937: AAS 29 (1937), pp. 164 ff.
Pius XII, allocution to the first national congress of the Italian Association of Catholic Teachers, Sept. 8, 1946: "Discorsi e Radiomessaggi," Vol. 8, p. 218.

[15]The rights of parents are set out very much as they were in the encyclical of Pope Pius XI on Catholic education. However, attention should be drawn here to the spiritual and psychological role of parents. It is a development of the concept that the prime educative force in society is the family.

[16]Cf. Second Vatican Council, Dogmatic Constitution on the Church, Art. 11 and 35: AAS 57 (1965), pp. 16 and 40 ff.

of parents and of others who have a role in education, and by providing them with assistance; by implementing the principle of subsidiarity and completing the task of education, with attention to parental wishes, whenever the efforts of parents and of other groups are insufficient; and, moreover, by building its own schools and institutes, as the common good may demand.[18]

Finally, the office of educating belongs by a unique title to the Church, not merely because she deserves recognition as a human society capable of educating, but most of all because she has the responsibility of announcing the way of salvation to all men, of communicating the life of Christ to those who believe, and of assisting them with ceaseless concern so that they may grow into the fullness of that same life.[19] As a mother, the Church is bound to give these children of hers the kind of education through which their entire lives can be penetrated with the spirit of Christ, while at the same time she offers her services to all peoples by way of promoting the full development of the human person, for the welfare of earthly society and the building of a world fashioned more humanly.[20]

4. In discharging her educative function, the Church is preoccupied with all appropriate means to that end. But she is particularly concerned with the means which are proper to herself, of which catechetical training is foremost.[21] Such instruction gives clarity and vigor to faith, nourishes a life lived according to the spirit of Christ, leads to a knowing and active participation in the liturgical

---

[17]The Declaration limits the powers of the state rather sharply in this paragraph. Note the unusual application of the principle of subsidiarity.

[18]Cf. Pius XI, encyclical letter "Divini Illius Magistri," loc. cit., pp. 63 ff. Pius XII, radio message of June 1, 1941: AAS 33 (1941), p. 200; allocution to the first national congress of the Italian Association of Catholic Teachers, Sept. 8, 1946: "Discorsi e Radiomessaggi," Vol. 8, p. 218.
  Regarding the principle of subsidiarity, cf. John XXIII, encyclical letter "Pacem in Terris," Apr. 11, 1963: AAS 44 (1963), p. 294.

[19]Cf. Pius XI, encyclical letter "Divini Illius Magistra," loc. cit., pp. 53 ff., 56 ff.
  Also his encyclical letter "Non abbiamo bisogno," June 29, 1931: AAS 23 (1931), pp. 311 ff.
  Pius XII, letter of the Secretariate of State to the 28th Italian Social Week, Sept. 20, 1955: "L'Osservatore Romano," Sept. 29, 1955.

[20]The Church praises those local, national, and international civil authorities who, conscious of the more pressing necessities of these times, expend all their energy so that all people may share a fuller education and human culture. Cf. Paul VI's allocution to the General Assembly of the United Nations, Oct. 4, 1965: "L'Osservatore Romano," Oct. 6, 1965.

[21]Cf. Pius XI, motu proprio "Orbem Catholicum," June 29, 1923: AAS 15 (1923), pp. 327–329; decree "Provide Sane," Jan. 12, 1935: AAS 27 (1935), pp. 145–152; Second Vatican Council, Decree on the Bishops' Pastoral Office in the Church, Art. 13 and 14.

mystery,[22] and inspires apostolic action. In her high regard for them, the Church seeks to penetrate and ennoble with her own spirit those other means which belong to the common heritage of mankind, and which contribute mightily to the refinement of spirit and the molding of men. Among these are the media of social communication,[23] many groups devoted to spiritual and physical development, youth associations, and especially schools.

5. Among all the agencies of education the school has a special importance.[24] By virtue of its very purpose, while it cultivates the intellect with unremitting attention, the school ripens the capacity for right judgment, provides an introduction into the cultural heritage won by past generations, promotes a sense of values, and readies for professional life. By creating friendly contacts between students of diverse temperament and background, the school fosters among them a willingness to understand one another. Moreover, the school sets up a kind of center whose operation and progress deserve to engage the joint participation of families, teachers, various kinds of cultural, civic, and religious groups, civil society, and the entire human community.[25]

Beautiful, therefore, and truly solemn is the vocation[26] of all those who assist parents in fulfilling their task, and who represent human society as well, by undertaking the role of school teacher. This calling requires extraordinary qualities of mind and heart, extremely careful preparation, and a constant readiness to begin anew and to adapt.

6. Parents, who have the first and the inalienable duty and right to educate their children, should enjoy true freedom in their choice of schools. Consequently, public authority, which has the obligation to oversee and defend the liberties of citizens, ought to see to it, out of a concern for distributive justice, that public subsidies are allocated[27] in such a way that, when selecting schools for their children, parents are genuinely free to follow their consciences.[28]

For the rest, it is incumbent upon the state to provide all citizens with the opportunity to acquire an appropriate degree of cultural enrichment, and with the proper preparation for exercising their civic duties and rights. Therefore, the state

---

[22]Cf. Second Vatican Council Constitution on the Sacred Liturgy, Art 14: AAS 56 (1964), p. 104.
[23]Cf. Second Vatican Council, Decree on the Instruments of Social Communication, Art. 13 and 14: AAS 56 (1964), pp. 149 ff.

[24]Cf. Pius XI, encyclical letter "Divini Illius Magistri," loc. cit., p. 76; also Pius XII, allocution to the Association of Catholic Teachers of Bavaria, Dec. 31, 1956: "Discorsi e Radiomessaggi," Vol. 18, p. 746.

[25]Although this paragraph gives priority to the development of intellectual values, there is insistence on the universal value of schools. This is not without interest in view of some of the current discussion concerning the role of the school.

[26]The Council is obviously concerned here with restoring the concept of the teaching profession as a vocation as well as an occupation.

[27]Note the connection between the allocation of public money and the rights of parents. There is no attempt to enter the practical field, by discussing how the state should subsidize Catholic education, but the principle that parents should not be handicapped in the exercise of their rights in education is clearly established.

itself ought to protect the right of children to receive an adequate schooling. It should be vigilant about the ability of teachers and the excellence of their training. It should look after the health of students and, in general, promote the whole school enterprise. But it must keep in mind the principle of subsidiarity, so that no kind of school monopoly arises.[29] For such a monopoly would militate against the native rights of the human person, the development and spread of culture itself, the peaceful association of citizens, and the pluralism which exists today in very many societies.[30]

As for the faithful, this sacred Synod exhorts them to offer their services generously to the work of finding suitable methods of education and programs of study, and of forming teachers who can provide young people with an authentic education. Especially through parents' associations, let the faithful make their own contribution to advancing the whole function of the school, above all, its task of providing moral development.[31.]

7. The Church is keenly aware of her very grave obligation to give zealous attention to the moral and religious education of all her children. To those large numbers of them who are being trained in schools which are not Catholic, she needs to be present with her special affection and helpfulness.[32] This she does through the living witness of those who teach and direct such students, through the apostolic activity of their schoolmates,[33] but most of all through the services of the priests and laymen who transmit to them the doctrine of salvation in a way suited to their age and circumstances, and who afford them spiritual assistance through programs which are appropriate under the prevailing conditions of time and setting.

The Church reminds parents of the serious duty which is theirs of taking every opportunity—or of making the opportunity—for their children to be able to enjoy these helps and to pace their development as Christians with their growth as citizens of the world. For this reason, the Church gives high praise to those civil authorities and civil societies that show regard for the pluralistic character of

[28]Cf. Third Provincial Council of Cincinnati (1861): "Collatio Lacensis," Vol. III, col. 1240, c/d; also cf. Pius XI, encyclical letter "Divini Illius Magistri," loc cit., pp. 60 and 63 ff.

[29]Once again there is a strong limitation of state control in educational administration.

[30]Cf. Pius XI, encyclical letter "Divini Illius Magistri," loc. cit., p. 63; also his encyclical letter "Non abbiamo bisogno," June 29, 1931: AAS 23 (1931), p. 305.
Pius XII, letter of the Secretariate of State to the 28th Italian Social Week, Sept. 20, 1955: "L'Osservatore Romano," Sept. 29, 1965.
Paul VI, allocution to the Christian Association of Italian Workers, Oct. 6, 1963: "Encicliche e Discorsi di Paolo VI," Vol. I, Rome, 1964, p. 230.

[31]Cf. John XXIII, message on the 30th anniversary of the publication of the encyclical letter "Divini Illius Magistri," Dec. 30, 1959: AAS 52 (1960), p. 57.

[32]One of the more original parts of the Declaration, this is an unequivocal statement of the responsibility of the Church to children not in Catholic schools.

[33]The Church highly values the apostolic action which Catholic teachers and associates are able to perform also in these schools. Cf. Second Vatican Council, schema of the Decree on the Apostolate of the Laity (1965), Art. 12 and 16.

modern society, and take into account the right of religious liberty, by helping families in such a way that in all schools the education of their children can be carried out according to the moral and religious convictions of each family.[34]

8. The Church's involvement in the field of education is demonstrated especially by the Catholic school.[35] No less than other schools does the Catholic school pursue cultural goals and the natural development of youth. But it has several distinctive purposes. It aims to create for the school community an atmosphere enlivened by the gospel spirit of freedom and charity. It aims to help the adolescent in such a way that the development of his own personality will be matched by the growth of that new creation which he became by baptism. It strives to relate all human culture eventually to the news of salvation, so that the light of faith will illumine the knowledge which students gradually gain of the world, of life, and of mankind.[36]

So it is that while the Catholic school fittingly adjusts itself to the circumstances of advancing times, it is educating its students to promote effectively the welfare of the earthly city, and preparing them to serve the advancement of the reign of God. The purpose in view is that by living an exemplary and apostolic life, the Catholic graduate can become, as it were, the saving leaven of the human family.

Therefore, since it can contribute so substantially to fulfilling the mission of God's people, and can further the dialogue between the Church and the family of man, to their mutual benefit, the Catholic school retains its immense importance in the circumstances of our times too. Consequently, this sacred Synod proclaims anew a right already made clear in numerous documents of the Church's teaching authority,[37] namely, the Church's right freely to establish and to run schools of every kind and at every level. At the same time, the Council recalls that the exercise of this right makes a supreme contribution to freedom of conscience, the protection of parental rights, and the progress of culture itself.

But let teachers realize that to the greatest possible extent they determine whether the Catholic school can bring its goals and undertakings to fruition.[38] They should, therefore, be trained with particular care so that they may be enriched with both secular and religious knowledge, appropriately certified, and may be equipped with an educational skill which reflects modern-day findings. Bound by charity to one another and to their students, and penetrated by an apostolic spirit, let them give witness to Christ, the unique Teacher, by their lives as well as by their teachings.[39]

Above all, let them perform their services as partners of the parents. Together

---

[34]Cf. Second Vatican Council, schema of the Declaration on Religious Freedom (1965), Art. 5.

[35]Catholic schools must: a) have the same cultural aims as all other schools; b) be opened to the contemporary world; c) be illumined by faith.
[36]Cf. First Provincial Council of Westminster (1852): "Collatio Lacensis," Vol. III, col 1334, a/b; cf. also Pius XI, encyclical letter "Divini Illius Magistri," loc. cit., pp. 77 ff.; Pius XII's allocution to the Assocation of Catholic Teachers of Bavaria, Dec. 31, 1956: "Discorsi e Radiomessaggi," Vol. 18, p. 746; Paul VI, allocution to the members of Federated Institutes Dependent on Ecclesiastical Authority, Dec. 30, 1963: "Encicliche e Discorsi de Paolo VI," Vol. 1, Rome, 1964, pp. 602 ff.

[37]Cf. especially the documents cited in note (1); in addition, this right of the Church is proclaimed by many provincial councils and in very recent declarations of very many episcopal conferences.

with them, they should pay due regard in every educational activity to sexual differences and to the special role which divine Providence allots to each sex in family life and in society. Let them work strenuously to inspire personal initiative on their students' part. Even after students have graduated, their teachers should continue to assist them with advice and friendship and also by establishing special groups genuinely inspired by the spirit of the Church. This holy Synod asserts that the ministry of such teachers is a true apostolate which our times make extremely serviceable and necessary, and which simultaneously renders an authentic service to society.

As for Catholic parents, the Council calls to mind their duty to entrust their children to Catholic schools, when and where this is possible, to support such schools to the extent of their ability, and to work along with them for the welfare of their children.[40]

9. To this ideal of a Catholic school, all schools which are in any way dependent on the Church should conform as far as possible, though Catholic schools can take on forms which vary according to local circumstances.[41] Thus the Church feels a most cordial esteem for those Catholic schools, found especially where the Church is newly established, which contain large numbers of non-Catholic students.

In the establishment and direction of Catholic schools, attention must be paid to contemporary needs. Therefore, although primary and intermediate schools must still be fostered as the foundations of education, considerable importance is to be attached to those schools which are demanded in a particular way by modern conditions, such as so-called professional[42] and technical schools, institutes for educating adults and promoting social services, as well as for persons requiring special care as a result of some natural deficiency, and also schools for preparing teachers to give religious instruction and other types of education.

This sacred Synod earnestly entreats pastors of the Church and all the faithful to spare no sacrifice in helping Catholic schools to achieve their purpose in an increasingly adequate way, and to show special concern for the needs of those who are poor in the goods of this world or who are deprived of the assistance and affection of a family or who are strangers to the gift of faith.[43]

---

[38]Cf. Pius XI, encyclical letter "Divini Illius Magistri," loc. cit., pp. 80 ff.; Pius XII, allocution to the Catholic Association of Italian Teachers in Secondary Schools, Jan. 5, 1954: "Discorsi e Radiomessaggi," Vol. 15, pp. 551–556; John XXIII, allocution to the 6th Congress of the Association of Catholic Italian Teachers, Sept. 5, 1959: "Discorsi, Messaggi," Colloqui, Vol. I, Rome, 1960, pp. 427–431.

[39]Further illustration of the personalist principle of Vatican II. The importance of the teacher is stressed in terms of personal impact.

[40]Cf. Pius XII, allocution to the Catholic Association of Italian Teachers in Secondary Schools, Jan. 5, 1954, loc. cit., p. 555.

[41]Cf. Paul VI, allocution to the International Office of Catholic Education, Feb. 25, 1964: "Encicliche e Discorsi di Paolo VI," Vol. II, Rome, 1964, p. 232.

[42]Cf. Paul VI, allocution to the Christian Association of Italian Workers, Oct. 6, 1963: "Encicliche e Discorsi di Paolo VI," Vol. I, Rome, 1964, p. 229.

[43]Again the emphasis on the interpersonal. The value of the teacher is not only intellectual but, above all, human and spiritual.

10. The Church is preoccupied too with schools of higher learning, especially colleges and universities and their faculties. In schools of this sort which are dependent on her, she seeks in a systematic way to have individual branches of knowledge studied according to their own proper principles and methods, and with due freedom of scientific investigation. She intends thereby to promote an ever deeper understanding of these fields, and as a result of extremely precise evaluation of modern problems and inquiries, to have it seen more profoundly how faith and reason give harmonious witness to the unity of all truth.[44] The Church pursues such a goal after the manner of her most illustrious teachers, especially St. Thomas Aquinas.[45] The hoped-for result is that the Christian mind may achieve, as it were, a public, persistent, and universal presence in the whole enterprise of advancing higher culture, and that the students of these institutions may become men truly outstanding in learning, ready to shoulder society's heavier burdens and to witness the faith to the world.[46]

In Catholic colleges and universities lacking a faculty of sacred theology, an institute or chair of sacred theology should be set up so that lectures designed for lay students too can be given. Since the sciences progress chiefly through special investigations of advanced scientific significance, Catholic colleges and universities and their faculties should give the maximum support to institutes which primarily serve the progress of scientific research.

This sacred Synod strongly recommends that Catholic colleges and universities and their faculties be conveniently located in diverse parts of the world, and that they be accorded the kind of support which will distinguish them for their academic pursuits rather than for the size of their enrollment. It urges that their doors open readily to students of special promise, even though of slender means, especially those who come from young nations.

Since the future of society and of the Church herself is closely bound up with the development of young people who engage in higher studies,[47] pastors of the Church should not limit their concern to the spiritual life of students attending Catholic colleges and universities. In their care for the religious development of all their sons, bishops should take appropriate counsel together to see to it that at colleges and universities which are not Catholic there are Catholic residences and centers where priests, religious, and laymen who have been judiciously chosen and trained can serve as on-campus sources of spiritual and intellectual assistance to young college people.

Whether they attend a college or university which is Catholic or otherwise,

---

[44]There is clear refutation here of any anti-intellectualism in the Church. The document evidences preoccupation with a meeting of spiritual and intellectual values.

[45]Cf. Paul VI, allocution before the 6th International Thomistic Congress, Sept. 10, 1965: "L'Osservatore Romano," Sept. 13–14, 1965.

[46]Cf. Pius XII, allocution to the teachers and students of Catholic Higher Institutes of France, Sept. 21, 1950: "Discorsi e Radiomessaggi," Vol. 12, pp. 219–221; Letters to the 22nd Congress of "Pax Romana," Aug. 12, 1952: "Discorsi e Radiomessaggi," Vol. 14, pp. 567–569; John XXIII, allocution to the Federation of Catholic Universities, Apr. 1, 1959: "Discorsi, Messaggi," Colloqui, Vol. I, Rome, 1960, pp. 226–229; Paul VI, allocution to the Academic Senate of the Catholic University of Milan, Apr. 5, 1964: "Encicliche e Discorsi di Paolo VI," Vol. II, Rome, 1964, pp. 438–443.

[47]Cf. Pius XII, allocution to the Academic Senate and students of the University of Rome, June 15, 1952: "Discorsi e Radiomessaggi," Vol. 14, p. 208: "The direction of tomorrow's society is principally placed in the mind and heart of the university students of today."

young people of special ability who appear suited for teaching and research should be trained with particular care and urged to undertake a teaching career.

* * *

THE INTERNATIONAL STUDY OF ACHIEVEMENT IN MATHEMATICS

(1967) From Torsten Husen, ed., *International Study of Achievement in Mathematics* (London, 1967), vol. II, pp. 287–95.

The project reported here is the first large-scale attempt to employ empirical methods in comparative education and thereby to arrive at comparable criterion measures. The construction of internationally valid evaluation instruments—achievement tests—however, did not create the most difficult problem for this study. The main obstacle turned out to be the measurement of certain independent variables, operationally feasible indices of basic characteristics of the school systems. Thus, for instance, the concept of "differentiation" was apparently interpreted in quite a variety of ways by the school principals when asked to rate their own schools according to what extent differentiation was provided. When the students were asked about their course or program, confusion existed as to whether a program should be labeled "academic", "vocational", or "general". In order to arrive at a description of the level of mathematics instruction, the English curriculum had to serve as a reference scale which was not easily translated into the situation in other countries. Even measures that *prima facie* would seem to be easily obtained, such as salary budget for the school, expenditures for equipment, or length of teachers' postsecondary training, were not easily ascertainable. In many instances a lack of comparability stemmed from the difficulties of translating terms like "comprehensive" or "postsecondary". It seems that we still have a long way to go before we will have cross-nationally codified independent variables to describe the most important dimensions of school systems.

As shown in Volume I, Chapter 14, even as regards certain basic statistical information, such as per-pupil expenditures or enrollment figures, there is a lack of uniformity in data reporting.

The difficulties indicated above should be kept in mind when interpreting some inconsistencies that appear in the findings.

The IEA study was not designed to compare countries; needless to say, it is not to be conceived of as an "international contest". As was spelled out in the introduction to Volume I, its main objective is to test hypotheses which have been advanced within a framework of comparative thinking in education. Many of the hypotheses cannot be tested unless one takes into consideration cross-national differences related to the various school systems operating within the countries participating in this investigation.

Certain descriptive statistics relating to the main dependent variables (mathematics test and attitude test scores) have been presented in Chapter 1. The international range among means for the 12 participating countries in total mathematics score for the 13-year-old population covers more than one standard deviation of the combined distribution, and is even larger in the terminal mathematics population (3 a). Thus, students who are much above the average in one country might be regarded as mathematically rather backward in another country. At the lower level (1 a), where 100 percent of the age group is still in full-time schooling, Japan has the highest mean and Sweden the lowest. In the preuniversity year students with terminal mathematics in the United States averaged far below the other countries. It is interesting to note the country means as a percentage of the total number of items in the test. The lowest and highest means expressed as a percent of the total number of items is 22 percent in the United States Population 1 b and 46 percent in Israel also for 1 b. The corresponding percentages for Level 3 a range from a low of 20 percent in the United States to a high of 53 percent in Israel. However, neither the "productivity" of an educational system of a country, nor the effect of the instruction given, can be assessed from national means. The age of school entry varies between countries, and the grade placement of mathematics topics varies considerably. In a dual system with early transfer of the more adept students to the academic secondary school there is a tendency to introduce advanced mathematics topics earlier whereas in countries with a comprehensive system one seeks to introduce them later. Furthermore, the high "retentivity" of the comprehensive systems has the effect that within the terminal mathematics group one can, in spite of the low average, identify an elite comparable both in quality (average) and quantity (proportion of age group) with the entire terminal group in a country with a low retentivity and a high average. Neither the national average at a level where schooling is still compulsory nor the average at a major terminal point would suffice to evaluate the "efficiency" of a whole school system.

Variability among student achievements is also marked, especially at the 13-year-old level where all the students are still in school; in the 1 a population the standard deviation is almost twice as large in England as in Finland.

By means of "bridge" tests the increase in mathematical competence from age 13 to the higher (preuniversity) level could be estimated for the individual countries. This increase was highly related to an index of selectivity, that is, the more selective or exclusive the secondary school, the larger the increase in performance for those who reach the terminal grade.

Partly because the part scores tended to be highly intercorrelated, they did not reveal differences of particular interest between countries.

Total mathematics scores were correlated with 45 other, mostly independent, variables characterizing the school, the teacher, and the student in each country and population. Since the between-country components tend to average each other out, these correlations are rather low, though some of them were rather high for individual countries. Of the variables characterizing the schools, size tends consistently to be positively related to the total scores at the lower level. At the upper level the picture is inconsistent, due probably to selection mechanisms on which we do not possess complete data. Length of teacher training is positively related to the total score and so are teacher ratings of the students' opportunity to learn the topics represented by the test items. Yet, the latter correlation is surprisingly low, on the average .20 and ranging from below zero in Sweden to .50 in England. Of the students' characteristics, fathers' and mothers' education and status of fathers' occupation tended at the lower level consistently to be positively related (on the level of .20) to mathematics score. In the terminal population these correlations varied quite widely due to variations in degrees of social selection and of retentivity. Students' interest in mathematics correlated .30 to .36 with total scores; students' plans and aspirations for futher education correlated with the same scores about .35 to .40.

* * *

By means of five scales the students' attitudes toward mathematics, education, and the environment have been assessed. Students in the terminal program tend to a greater extent to view mathematics as a fixed or "frozen" and less open system than students at the 13-year-old level. Differences in this respect between countries are quite marked with a range of about one standard deviation. Mathematics is perceived as more difficult and demanding by the students in the terminal program than by students at the lower level. The between-country range is almost the same as for the view of mathematics as an open or closed system. Students in the terminal program, that is, among those with the largest exposure to mathematics, tend to have a more pessimistic appraisal of the role of mathematics in contemporary society, but large international differences were found in this variable also. The "I like-dislike" scale on attitudes toward school and school learning disclosed an international range of about one standard deviation. Attitudes were most positive in Japan and least positive in the United States.

Correlations between country means (on the one side mean total score and on the other the means for the 45 other variables) were computed. These correlations reflect the between-country components of the variables and are thus much higher than within country variables where the international differences tend to level out. The fact that per-student expenditure or teacher training displays a sizable negative correlation with total mathematics score on the 13-year-old level is explained by the fact that Sweden and the United States have the lowest score and at the same time the highest perstudent expenditure, while in Japan the opposite is the case. The same logic applies to many other factors, like Gross National Product (GNP), which is negatively correlated with the average mathematics performance at both levels. It should, however, once again be emphasized that neither performance at an age before mandatory school attendance expires nor at the preuniversity level can be used as an assessment index of the "efficiency" of a school system. . . .

Problems Related To School Organization

Mathematics is regarded as a "strategic" subject in present-day technological society. Until recently it was conceived of as central to general education and an essential component in a liberal arts education. Nineteenth century humanism held mathematics in high esteem since, together with Latin, it was considered to contribute in a major way to mental discipline and to a sharpening of the intellect. Today, mathematics is more typically regarded as a major component of a proper education for science and technology. Its new objectives, however, have in most countries collided with rather strongly institutionalized curriculum content and methods of instruction (Dahllöf, 1963). In all countries a shortage of mathematicians and mathematics teachers is strongly felt.

Most of the problems dealt with in hypotheses related to school organization could be put under the general heading of "selective versus comprehensive education". As was indicated in the introduction to Volume I, the cardinal problem in most West European countries is how to adapt the dual or parallel school structure which is a heritage from a society with strong class distinctions to a changing technological society where class differences are leveling out and the public has become more sensitive to waste of talent. But most striking of all is the need in economically highly developed countries for education of progressively larger proportions of youth not only at the secondary but also at the university level. Apart from all ideological considerations about "democratization of higher education" or providing "equality of opportunity", the increasing need for highly trained man-power is a powerful impetus to the rapidly expanding enrollments at the secondary and postsecondary level. There is also the growing appreciation of the individual's need for general education in a world of change and amidst growing social and technological complexities. Mathematics as an instrument to deal with the quantitative aspect of the environment is an increasingly important part of the spectrum of skills the individual needs to possess.

The IEA countries represent a rather broad spectrum of school organizations. In the United States the schools are by tradition more comprehensive, while in Europe most pupils are differentiated at an early age into separate schools and courses. In Europe, on the one side a small intellectual and social elite has been channeled into an academic, university-preparing program and on the other hand, the broad mass, especially from working class homes, has proceeded with a general or semivocational program until the end of compulsory schooling.[1] The United States has by tradition a school structure whereby the secondary school has been added to the primary, not as a parallel but as a continuation school. Under the impact of broadened enrollment and extended curricula the selectivity of European schools has tended to lessen, and more flexibility in terms of transfer from one type of program or school to another has appeared. There is also a growing tendency to postpone selection for academic education and the final choice of program in order to provide a broader general education for all students and to avoid a lengthening of parallelism when compulsory schooling is prolonged and school-leaving age is raised.

"Comprehensive" schools catering for all the students of a given area with all the programs under the same roof have been introduced in some European countries since World War II. Their introduction has in most cases been a political issue since they have been conceived of as a means of "democratizing" secondary education.

The problem of comprehensive education is, however, apart from its social and political implications, regarded by many teachers as a purely pedagogical one, namely that of grouping. How should students be organized into instructional groups so as to provide for optimal learning? Some secondary schoolteachers have conceived of grouping as a fairly simple problem: the academically talented should be grouped together in separate classes (or schools) at an early age in order not to be hampered by their slower-learning non-academic age mates. It is thereby implied that the latter category of students would also profit from the separation because they would not be discouraged by the presence of brighter classmates. "Undifferentiated" classes, embracing the whole range of ability, are supposed to be impractical and unproductive, since the standards of the university-bound students would be lowered and the slow-learning students would lag more behind than they do in separated classes.

Grouping can be executed in two main ways. One can either try to homogenize

[1]This does not deny that for several decades students from manual workers and similar families have made up small fractions of secondary enrollment in some countries.

the students throughout all the academic subjects according to some criterion of scholastic ability, such as marks, teachers' rating, achievement or aptitude test scores. Thereby, one obtains so-called homogeneous grouping. "Streaming", which takes place in most schools in England on the primary level and in the comprehensive schools on the secondary level, is another example of homogeneous grouping. The other type of grouping takes into account the *intra*individual differences and is a way of grouping students according to their varying proficiency in separate subjects; this is usual in English grammar schools and is called "setting". Thus, parallel instructional groups in mathematics on a certain grade level are set up according to the performance in that particular subject. This within-subject grouping does not imply separation of the students over all the subjects even if there might be a quite sizable correlation between subjects. . .

As is pointed out in Chapter 3, the setting up of a comprehensive or selective system and grouping practices are affected not only by the society, which the school is supposed to serve, but also by the teacher's philosophy of his role in that society. The beliefs they hold about what can be accomplished with their students have a strong effect on the outcomes of school instruction over and above the effects of school structure or grouping procedure as decided upon by the educational policy-makers.

When designing the IEA study it was decided to collect data which would enable us to test certain basic assumptions related to the issue of selective versus comprehensive school structure. These problems might be grouped in the following categories. 1. What effects does comprehensive and selective organization have upon the performances in mathematics of high- and low-ability pupils, respectively? What effects do the two school structures have upon the students' interest in school subjects, in this case in mathematics? 2. Does a comprehensive system with a higher retentivity of pupils at the secondary level produce an elite of the same standard as a selective system? Is this elite smaller or larger in the comprehensive system? 3. What is the "yield" of the comprehensive system as compared with the selective in terms of "how many are brought how far"? 4. What are the socio-economic implications of the two systems in terms of equality of opportunity?

As might be expected, the average level of mathematics performance was inversely related to the proportion of the age group in school at the terminal level. When the national scores at this level were adjusted for age at testing, performance at age 13, and retentivity (that is, the proportion of a yeargroup still at school at the preuniversity stage), they became closely concordant as may be seen from Table 3.8.

According to the assumptions many teachers hold about the effects of selection and grouping, students in a system with specialized courses and schools should perform better than those in an undifferentiated, more comprehensive system. Furthermore, it was expected that the variability would be lower in the specialized schools. Apart from the difficulties of classifying schools as comprehensive, academic-selective, etc. and of obtaining relevant information from the students about the program they were following, we were not in a good position to make sensible comparisons between systems within countries because of the differences between comprehensive and selective schools in social class composition and facilities. Thus, in England the students in grammar schools performed much better on average than students in the academic stream of the comprehensive schools. Of course this does not say anything decisive about the relative "productivity" or "efficiency" of the two systems, since the selection mechanisms determining the input to the two types of schools are not under control.

The opportunity to make cross-national comparisons enabled us, however, to shed light on the related important problem, namely, to what extent it is possible to educate an elite within a comprehensive and retentive system. This required that equal proportions of the age groups be analyzed. When the top four percent of the age group in each country were extracted, countries with a more comprehensive and thus a more retentive system then showed the greatest upward shift. The most striking example was provided by the United States. There the total group of mathematics students in the senior high school grade averaged far behind their age-mates in other countries but an elite existed with, on the whole, the same average score as in most of the countries with a much more selective system and with a lower degree of retentivity. This kind of analysis was extended by setting up international percentiles on the basis of the composite distribution of all the countries and determining the proportion of the age group at the terminal level in each country with attainments above given percentile scores. The question "does more mean worse" cannot be answered unequivocally. . . . The increase of the intake into the preuniversity school in general and the mathematics program in particular increases the size of the elite, defined, for instance, by the number of students reaching the 95th international percentile. At the same time, increased intake means an increase in variability, due mainly to increased intake of lower ability students. This, however, is achieved not specifically by the pedagogical qualities of the system, but by its retentivity. In selective systems the students, who do not keep up with the fairly uniform requirements, either drop out or are held back as grade-repeaters.

The opening up of opportunities for preuniversity education for more students and retaining students at school thus produced an elite group comparable and in some cases superior in size and quality to the one accomplished by a selective system. What, then, is happening to the major part of the students, those who by statistical or other criteria are not referred to as the elite? The "productivity" or the "yield" of a system cannot be assessed solely by the size and quality of the elite. The more a society needs highly trained manpower, the more the "yield"; of its schools should be measured by its capacity to promote optimum achievement among *all types* and at *all levels* of aptitude. A selective system with the dual-track school structure succeeds in bringing the few who survive to graduation up to outstanding accomplishments, whereas those who were not selected are left far behind. A system with a high degree of retentivity can bring a larger proportion of the students of average ability up to a higher level of performance than the selective system. An assessment of the "yield" in mathematics would have required a much more extensive testing program than was possible in the present project. Apart from testing representative samples of students at all the terminal points in the primary and secondary school, we would have had to test students who for various reasons dropped out of the secondary level.

Everybody in educational circles pays lip service to the principle of "equal opportunity". But the *conditions* for this principle to operate vary considerably from system to system. Previous research has furnished ample evidence that the criteria employed in evaluating and selecting students for secondary school admission are often loaded with social class factors and so is grade repeating and dropping out. It could therefore be hypothesized that the more marked the selectivity in terms of entrance examinations, grade repeating and "flunking-out", the stronger the social bias in favor of middle-class students. We found, when using the proportion of an age group of students who reached the preuniversity year as a composite index of selectivity, that social bias in favor of upper- or middle-class students was more pronounced in countries with a low retentivity. Furthermore, the earlier the selection, the stronger the social bias at the preuniversity level.

On the basis of previous research it could be hypothesized that students in the selective academic programs would be more interested in mathematics than those in comprehensive and "remaining" programs. Students in selective programs on the average have a more "school-minded" social background, and the selective academic schools have better educational provisions; for instance, they have more qualified teachers. We found that students in the selective academic program showed the greatest interest and the "remainder" the lowest interest, whereas those in the comprehensive courses occupied an intermediate position. This fits into findings from other research, according to which the average or below-average students tend to be better motivated in undifferentiated classes or schools than if they are allocated to separate classes or schools.

THE MARCH 22ND MOVEMENT; FRANCE (1967) From Extract from the *Bulletin of The March 22nd Movement, Nanterre, April, 1968 in The Student Revolt*, Hervé Bourges, comp., B. R. Brewster trans. (London, 1968), pp. 129–33.

I. Historical

In the autumn term in 1967 a strike launched outside the traditional political or trade-union framework united ten thousand of the twelve thousand students in the faculty [of Nanterre] on the issue of an improvement in work conditions. Result: the constitution of equal-representation departmental commissions, which soon admitted their sterility.

In the second term a series of sporadic incidents occurred, expressing a diffuse unrest: a demonstration in solidarity with a student threatened with expulsion ended in a clash with police called in by the Dean; brawls in a few courtyards, etc. Also, the action of the residents of the *Cité Universitaire* made possible the abrogation of the internal regulations.

At the end of March a new phase began:

—psychology students boycotted their preliminary examinations;
—four students distributed a pamphlet attacking the teaching and vocation of sociology *(Pourquoi des Sociologues?)*;
—*on Friday, March 2nd, after the arrest of six anti-imperialist militants, a protest meeting was called, which finally voted to occupy the administration building the same evening. Two hundred and fifty students meeting in the faculty board room discussed a number of political problems until two o'clock in the morning. A day of political discussion on various unrestricted topics was fixed for Friday, March 29th.*

The university authorities were disturbed by the turn of events (the intensive preparation for the 29th: leaflets, speeches, inscriptions on the faculty walls and poster campaigns), and set the administrative staff against the students; the internal library was closed and the laboratory technicians went on strike. On Thursday the 28th, Dean Grappin decreed the suspension of lectures and practicals until the following Monday. A meeting of about three hundred students decided to carry on with the next day's activities, but as a day of preparation for the political discussions, which were postponed until April 2nd.

On Friday, March 29th, while a considerable force of police surrounded the campus, five hundred students took part in the opening meeting in the foyer of the Cité and then set themselves up as a commission to discuss the agreed topics.

On Monday, April 1st, a majority of the sociology students in the second year of the first cycle decided to boycott their preliminary examinations. They then voted in favour of a text denouncing sociology as an ideology. On the other hand, at the teaching level, dissensions appeared between the liberal departments (social sciences and letters) who favoured the concession of a site, and the reactionary ones (history) who demanded the arrest of the 'ringleaders'.

Tuesday, April 22nd, was a success: the administration could not prevent fifteen hundred people occupying the B1 lecture theatre for the opening meeting, nor could corporatists and fascists prevent the meetings of the commissions in rooms in C Building. The final full meeting, in which eight hundred students and a few lecturers participated, decided to carry on with the movement and to publish this bulletin.

2. The Nature of the Movement

The Nanterre movement is a fully politicized one. As opposed to the November strike and its 'corporatist' spirit, it has advanced non-union topics such as 'down with police repression'; 'the critical university'; 'the right to political expression and action in the faculty'. By the same token it has revealed its *minority character*, and it is conscious of this fact: several speakers denounced the illusions behind the slogan 'Defend the common interests of all students.' It is clear that at Nanterre many accept higher studies as an initiation into bourgeois affairs. So a nucleus of three hundred 'extremists' emerged, capable of carrying with it one thousand out of the twelve thousand students in the faculty.

The actions pursued accelerated the emergence of consciousness in some individuals: rather than 'provocation' it was a matter of *forcing latent authoritarianism to manifest itself* (cf. the bus-loads of CRS waiting to intervene) by showing *the true face of the proposed 'dialogue'*. Once certain problems appear, dialogue gives way to truncheons. So there was an increase in political consciousness, and also an active participation of all those who until then had been paralysed by the ineffectiveness of the sects and the routine of traditional demands supported by petitions and silent marches. Finally, students and teachers had to separate when the repressive apparatus got moving. It was interesting to see the UEC call for the efficient running of a bourgeois university in which certain 'left' or even 'Marxist' professors were afraid of a challenge to their status in that bourgeois university.

We must insist on the *novelty of the movement launched*, at least in the French context. First of all, *a common labour has been achieved*, transcending the oppositions between sects; we cannot assert their inanity, but a process has been started in which divergence will arise from theoretical and practical confrontation with reality rather than from verbal quarrels between denominations. Already terminological particularisms have been challenged as rigid and unchanged ideas of reality which act as a means to demarcate one sect from another rather than as an instrument of scientific analysis. On the other hand, we were resolved *to avoid falling into the hands of any particular political group or of the administration* and the liberal teachers, adepts at 'dialogue' and conflict behind closed doors (cf. Grappin's proposal).

New issues were raised, in particular *a more direct and effective rejection of the class university, a denunciation of neutral and objective knowledge as of its parcelization, inquiry into the objective place we are destined to occupy in the present division of labour, union with the struggling workers, etc.*

Simultaneously, original forms of action were developed: improvised meetings in the faculty, occupation of rooms to hold our discussions, interventions in lectures, examination boycotts, political posters and banners in the entrance halls, seizure of the public address system hitherto monopolized by the administration, etc.

Lastly, the movement demonstrated its vitality by two additional characteristics: the *multitude of tendencies,* and the *lag of theory behind practice.* The commission reports are an eloquent testimony to the multiplicity of tendencies, and that besides directly political reflections there should be a text on 'culture and creativity' is not something to be despised. As for the lag of theory behind practice, it is enough to recall that no one yet knows exactly what is happening, while talk of 'folklore' and 'anarchist provocation' does not resolve the problem. The 'student struggle' commission will have to face up to the questions: what is the extent of the contradictions induced in the educational sector by monopoly capitalism? what perspectives are opened up, etc?

In the section on perspectives we shall restrict ourselves to tendencies which can be registered at present.

3. Perspectives

As the movement has defined itself primarily in terms which are negative (rejection of institutionalization, sectarian divisions, black lists) and formal (rights of political expression), if it is to work out a line of action it must examine all the problems raised and reflect on their specific causes. While Dean Grappin is satisfied by arguments worthy of *France-Soir* about emotional isolation and the closed academic atmosphere, we believe deeper realities are hidden behind these apparent causes. Can we explain the events by a melange of chance facts: a band of activists inspired by the German SDS, the uncertainty of others as to their careers, the tense atmosphere in departments divided between professors and junior staff, etc.?

So we must go further and try to work out as scientifically as possible the structural factors that lie behind the agitation.

In the immediate future, the movement's continuity will depend on our ability to establish concrete aims for the summer term and for next year. In this area, several tendencies have already emerged as to the conception of a critical university; should we increase direct action in the universities? Should we be more reformist and unite a more significant proportion of the students behind less radical slogans? Or should we reject the idea of a specifically student agitation and give priority to directly supporting the workers? Finally, should we seek to achieve a union between workers' struggles and an autonomous development of our own actions?

❋   ❋   ❋

England

ESTABLISHMENT OF THE RHODES SCHOLARSHIPS (1899) From W. T. Stead, ed. *The Last Will and Testament of Cecil John Rhodes* (London, 1902), pp. 43–45.

The Scholarships at Oxford

Whereas I consider that the education of young Colonists at one of the Universities in the United Kingdom is of great advantage to them for giving breadth to their views for their instruction in life and manners and for instilling into their minds the advantage to the Colonies as well as to the United Kingdom of the retention of the unity of the Empire.

And whereas in the case of young Colonists studying at a University in the United Kingdom I attach very great importance to the University having a residential system such as is in force at the Universities of Oxford and Cambridge for without it those students are at the most critical period of their lives left without any supervision.

And whereas there are at the present time 50 or more students from South Africa studying at the University of Edinburgh many of whom are attracted there by its excellent medical school and I should like to establish some of the Scholarships hereinafter mentioned in the University but owing to its not having such a residential system as aforesaid I feel obliged to refrain from doing so. And whereas my own University the University of Oxford has such a system and I suggest that it should try and extend its scope so as if possible to make its medical school at least as good as that at the University of Edinburgh.

And whereas I also desire to encourage and foster an appreciation of the advantages which I implicitly believe will result from the union of the English-speaking peoples throughout the world and to encourage in the students from the United States of North America who will benefit from the American Scholarships to be established for the reason above given at the University of Oxford under this my Will an attachment to the country from which they have sprung but without I hope withdrawing them of their sympathies from the land of their adoption or birth.

Now therefore I direct my Trustees as soon as may be after my death and either simultaneously or gradually as they shall find convenient and if gradually then in such order as they shall think fit to establish for male students the Scholarships hereinafter directed to be established each of which shall be of the yearly value of 300 pounds and be tenable at any College in the University of Oxford for three consecutive academical years.

I direct my Trustees to establish certain Scholarships and these Scholarships I sometimes hereinafter refer to as "the Colonial Scholarships." . . .

I further direct my Trustees to establish additional Scholarships sufficient in number for the appropriation in the next following clause hereof directed and those Scholarships I sometimes hereinafter refer to as "the American Scholarships."

I appropriate two of the American Scholarships to each of the present States and Territories of the United States of North America. Provided that if any of the said Territories shall in my lifetime be admitted as a State the scholarships appropriated to such Territory shall be appropriated to such State and that my Trustees may in their uncontrolled discretion withhold for such time as they shall think fit the appropriation of Scholarships to any Territory.

I direct that of the two Scholarships appropriated to a State or Territory not more than one shall be filled up in any year so that at no time shall more than two Scholarships be held for the same State or Territory.

*   *   *

My desire being that the students who shall be elected to the Scholarships shall not be merely bookworms I direct that in the election of a student to a Scholarship regard shall be had to

(i) his literary and scholastic attainments

(ii) his fondness of and success in manly outdoor sports such as cricket football and the like

(iii) his qualities of manhood truth courage devotion to duty sympathy for the protection of the weak kindliness unselfishness and fellowship
and

(iv) his exhibition during school days of moral force of character and of instincts to lead and to take an interest in his school-mates for those latter attributes will be likely in after-life to guide him to esteem the performance of public duty as his highest aim.

As mere suggestions for the guidance of those who will have the choice of students for the Scholarships I record that (i) my ideal qualified student would combine these four qualifications in the proportions of three-tenths for the first two-tenths for the second three-tenths for the third and two-tenths for the fourth qualification so that according to my ideas if the maximum number of marks for any Scholarship were 200 they would be apportioned as follows—60 to each of the first and third qualifications and 40 to each of the second and fourth qualifications (ii) the marks for the several qualifications would be awarded independently as follows (that is to say) the marks for the first qualification by examination for the second and third qualifications respectively by ballot by the fellow-students of the candidates and for the fourth qualification by the head master of the candidate's school and (iii) the results of the wards (that is to say the marks obtained by each candidate for each qualification) would be sent as soon as possible for consideration to the Trustees or to some person or persons appointed to receive the same and the person or persons so appointed would ascertain by averaging the marks in blocks of 20 marks each of all candidates the best ideal qualified students.

No student shall be qualified or disqualified for election to a Scholarship on account of his race or religious opinions.

Except in the cases of the four schools hereinbefore mentioned the election to Scholarships shall be by the Trustees after such (if any) consultation as they shall think fit with the Minister having the control of education in such Colony, Province, State or Territory.

A qualified student who has been elected as aforesaid shall within six calendar months after his election or as soon thereafter as he can be admitted into residence or within such extended time as my Trustees shall allow Commence residence as an undergraduate at some college in the University of Oxford.

The scholarships shall be payable to him from the time when he shall commence such residence.

I desire that the Scholars holding the scholarships shall be distributed amongst the Colleges of the University of Oxford and not resort in undue numbers to one or more Colleges only.

Notwithstanding anything hereinbefore contained my Trustees may in their uncontrolled discretion suspend for such time as they shall think fit or remove any Scholar from his Scholarship.

In order that the Scholars past and present may have opportunities of meeting and discussing their experiences and prospects I desire that my Trustees shall annually give a dinner to the past and present Scholars able and willing to attend at which I hope my Trustees or some of them will be able to be present and to which they will I hope from time to time invite as guests persons who have shown sympathy with the views expressed by me in this my Will.

STATEMENT OF THE PRINCIPLES OF THE NEW EDUCATION FELLOWSHIP (1921)   From *The New Era*, vol. II, p. 252.

Principles

1.—The essential object of all education should be to train the child to desire the supremacy of spirit over matter and to express that supremacy in daily life. The new education should therefore—whatever in other respects may be the point of view of the educator—always aim at preserving and increasing spiritual power in the child.

2.—Particularly should this aim be kept in mind in the sort of discipline applied to the child. The educator must study and respect the child's individuality remembering that that individuality can only develop under a form of discipline which ensures freedom for the child's spiritual faculties.

3.—All the education provided at the schools of the new type—whether it be for the purpose of imparting actual knowledge or for that of preparing the pupil for adult life by the development of character and right feeling—should give fresh rein to the innate interests of the child i.e. those which come from the child himself, arising spontaneously within him. The school curriculum should always furnish an outlet for those interests, whether they be of the intellectual aesthetic or social kind or be the synthesis of all these which are found in properly organised handicrafts.

4.—The government of the school community as a whole should be organised by the children themselves in collaboration with their teachers and that government; as

IDEAS
FROM ABROAD

2065

well as the self discipline which each child must be taught to apply to himself, should be deliberately aimed at rendering external authority unnecessary.

5.—The spirit of selfish competition must be discouraged in every possible way by the new educational system and the child must be taught to substitute for it a spirit of co-operation which will lead him to place himself at the service of the community as a whole.

6.—The Fellowship stands for Co-education in the fullest sense of the term i.e. for the co-operation of the two sexes both in and out of class hours, whereby opportunity may be given to each sex to exercise to the full its beneficial influence on the other.

7.—The new education rightly conducted on the aforesaid principles will develop in the child not only the future citizen ready and able to fulfill his duties towards his neighbours, his nation and Humanity as a whole, but also the man conscious of his own dignity as a human being and recognising that same dignity in every one else.

Aims

1.—To introduce these principles as far as possible into the existing schools, by the methods best calculated to give full effect to them, and also to establish schools for the express purpose of putting them into practice.

2.—To promote closer co-operation between the teachers themselves throughout the different grades of the profession and also between the teachers and the parents in all types of schools and

3.—To promote relations and a sense of solidarity between teachers and others of similar educational ideals in all countries of the world by the organisation of an international congress every second year and by the publication of an international magazine in English, French and German.

The organisers of this New Education Fellowship have sought to establish a very elastic association which can be adapted to the idiosyncracies and methods of each individual country. There are therefore no rules and no application for membership is necessary. Every person who subscribes to any one of the organs published under the auspices of the Fellowship becomes ipso facto a member of it.

A DAY AT SUMMERHILL (1924)   From A. S. Neill, *Summerhill* (New York, 1960), pp. 13–19.

Let me describe a typical day in Summerhill. Breakfast is from 8:15 to 9. The staff and pupils carry their breakfast from the kitchen across to the dining room. Beds are supposed to be made by 9:30, when lessons begin.

At the beginning of each term, a timetable is posted. Thus, Derek in the laboratory may have Class I on Monday, Class II on Tuesday, and so on. I have a similar timetable for English and mathematics; Maurice for geography and history. The younger children (aged seven to nine) usually stay with their own teacher most of the morning, but they also go to Science or the Art Room.

No pupil is compelled to attend lessons. But if Jimmy comes to English on Monday and does not make an appearance again until Friday of the following week, the others quite rightly object that he is holding back the work, and they may throw him out for impeding progress.

Lessons go on until one, but the kindergarteners and juniors lunch at 12:30. The school has to be fed in two relays. The staff and seniors sit down to lunch at 1:30.

Afternoons are completely free for everyone. What they all do in the afternoon I do not know. I garden, and seldom see youngsters about. I see the juniors playing gangsters. Some of the seniors busy themselves with motors and radios and drawing and painting. In good weather, seniors play games. Some tinker about in the workshop, mending their bicycles or making boats or revolvers.

Tea is served at four. At five, various activities begin. The juniors like to be read to. The middle group likes work in the Art Room—painting, linoleum cuts, leather work, basket making. There is usually a busy group in the pottery; in fact, the pottery seems to be a favorite haunt morning and evening. The oldest group works from five onward. The wood and metal workshop is full every night.

On Monday nights, the pupils go to the local movie at their parents' expense. When the program changes on Thursday, those who have the money go again.

On Tuesday night, the staff and seniors hear my talk on psychology. At the same time the juniors have various reading groups. Wednesday night is dance night. Dance records are selected from a great pile. The children are all good dancers, and some visitors say that they feel inferior dancing with them. On Thursday night, there's nothing special on. The seniors go to the movies in Leiston or Aldeburgh. Friday is left for any special event, such as rehearsing for a play.

Saturday night is our most important one, for it is General School Meeting night. Dancing usually follows. During the winter months, Sunday is theater evening.

There is no timetable for handiwork. There are no set lessons in woodworking. Children make what they want to. And what they want to make is nearly always a toy revolver or gun or boat or kite. They are not much interested in elaborate joints of the dovetail variety; even the older boys do not care for difficult carpentry. Not many of them take an interest in my own hobby—hammered brasswork—because you can't attach much of a fantasy to a brass bowl.

On a good day you may not see the boy gangsters of Summerhill. They are in far corners intent on their deeds of derring-do. But you will see the girls. They are in or near the house, and never far away from the grownups.

You will often find the Art Room full of girls painting and making bright things with fabrics. In the main, however, I think that the small boys are more creative; at least I never hear a boy say he is bored because he doesn't know what to do, whereas I sometimes hear girls say that.

Possibly I find the boys more creative than the girls because the school may be better equipped for boys than for girls. Girls of ten and over have little use for a workshop with iron and wood. They have no desire to tinker with engines, nor are they attracted by electricity or radio. They have their art work, which includes pottery, cutting linoleum blocks and painting, and sewing work, but for some that is not enough. Boys are just as keen on cooking as girls are. The girls and boys write and produce their own plays, make their own costumes and scenery. Generally, the acting talent of the pupils is of a high standard, because the acting is sincere and not show-offish.

The girls seem to frequent the chemical lab just as often as the boys do. The workshop is about the only place that does not attract girls from nine up.

The girls take a less active part in school meetings than the boys do, and I have no ready explanation for this fact.

Up to a few years ago, girls were apt to come late to Summerhill; we had lots of failures from convents and girls' schools. I never consider such a child a true example of a free education. These girls who came late were usually children of parents who had no appreciation of freedom, for if they had had, their girls would not have been problems. Then when the girl was cured here in Summerhill of her special failing, she was whisked off by her parents to "a nice school where she will be educated." But in recent years we have been getting girls from homes that believe in Summerhill. A fine bunch they are, too, full of spirit and originality and initiative.

We have lost girls occasionally because of financial reasons; sometimes when their brothers were kept on at expensive private schools. The old tradition of making the son the important one in the family dies hard. We have lost both girls and boys through the possessive jealousy of the parents, who feared that the children might transfer to the school their loyalty toward home.

Summerhill has always had a bit of a struggle to keep going. Few parents have the patience and faith to send their children to a school in which the youngsters can play as an alternative to learning. Parents tremble to think that at twenty-one their son may not be capable of earning a living.

Today, Summerhill pupils are mostly children whose parents want them brought up without restrictive discipline. This is a most happy circumstance, for in the old days I would have the son of a die-hard who sent his lad to me in desperation. Such parents had no interest at all in freedom for children, and secretly they must have considered us a crowd of lunatic cranks. It was very difficult to explain things to those die-hards.

I recall the military gentleman who thought of enrolling his nine-year-old son as a pupil.

"The place seems all right," he said, "but I have one fear. My boy may learn to masturbate here."

I asked him why he feared this.

"It will do him so much harm," he said.

"It didn't do you or me much harm, did it?" I said pleasantly. He went off rather hurriedly with his son.

Then there was the rich mother who, after asking me questions for an hour, turned to her husband and said, "I can't decide whether to send Marjorie here or not."

"Don't bother," I said. "I have decided for you. I'm not taking her."

I had to explain to her what I meant. "You don't really believe in freedom," I said. "If Marjorie came here, I should waste half my life explaining to you what it was all about, and in the end you wouldn't be convinced. The result would be disastrous for Marjorie, for she would be perpetually faced with the awful doubt: Which is right, home or school?"

The ideal parents are those who come down and say, "Summerhill is the place for our kids; no other school will do."

When we opened the school, the difficulties were especially grave. We could only take children from the upper and middle classes because we had to make ends meet. We had no rich man behind us. In the early days of the school, a benefactor, who insisted on anonymity, helped us through one or two bad times; and later one of the parents made generous gifts—a new kitchen, a radio, a new wing on our cottage, a new workshop. He was the ideal benefactor, for he set no conditions and asked for nothing in return. "Summerhill gave my Jimmy the education I wanted for him," he said simply, for James Shand was a true believer in freedom for children.

But we have never been able to take the children of the very poor. That is a pity, for we have had to confine our study to only the children of the middle class. And sometimes it is difficult to see child nature when it is hidden behind too much money and expensive clothes. When a girl knows that on her twenty-first birthday she will come into a substantial amount of money, it is not easy to study child nature in her. Luckily, however, most of the present and past pupils of Summerhill have not been spoiled by wealth; all of them know that they must earn a living when they leave school.

In Summerhill, we have chambermaids from the town who work for us all day but who sleep at their own homes. They are young girls who work hard and well. In a free atmosphere where they are not bossed, they work harder and better than maids do who are under authority. They are excellent girls in every way. I have always felt ashamed of the fact that these girls have to work hard because they were born poor, whereas I have had spoiled girls from well-to-do homes who had not the energy to make their own beds. But I must confess that I myself hated to make my bed. My lame excuse that I had so much else to do did not impress the children. They jeered at my defense that you can't expect a general to pick up rubbish.

I have suggested more than once that the adults in Summerhill are no paragons of virtue. We are human like everyone else, and our human frailties often come into conflict with our theories. In the average home, if a child breaks a plate, father or mother makes a fuss—the plate becoming more important than the child. In Summerhill, if a maid or a child drops a pile of plates, I say nothing and my wife says nothing. Accidents are accidents. But if a child borrows a book and leaves it out in the rain, my wife gets angry because books mean much to her. In such a case, I am personally indifferent, for books have little value for me. On the other hand, my wife seems vaguely surprised when I make a fuss about a ruined chisel. I value tools, but tools mean little to her.

In Summerhill, our life is one of giving all the time. Visitors wear us out more than the children do, for they also want us to give. It may be more blessed to give than to receive, but it certainly is more exhausting.

Our Saturday night General Meetings, alas, show the conflict between children and adults. That is natural, for to have a community of mixed ages and for everyone to sacrifice all to the young children would be to completely spoil these children. The adults make complaints if a gang of seniors keeps them awake by laughing and talking after all have gone to bed. Harry complains that he spent an hour planing a panel for the front door, went to lunch, and came back to find that Billy had converted it into a shelf. I make accusations against the boys who borrowed my soldering outfit and didn't return it. My wife makes a fuss because three small children came after supper and said they were hungry and got bread and jam, and the pieces of bread were found lying in the hallway the next morning. Peter reports sadly that a gang threw his precious clay at each other in the pottery room. So it goes on, the fight between the adult point of view and the juvenile lack of awareness. But the fight never degenerates into personalities; there is no feeling of bitterness against the individual. This conflict keeps Summerhill very much alive. There is always something happening, and there isn't a dull day in the whole year.

Luckily, the staff is not too possessive, though I admit it hurts me when I have bought a special tin of paint at three pounds a gallon and then find that a girl has taken the precious stuff to paint an old bedstead. I am possessive about my car and my typewriter and my workshop tools, but I have no feeling of possession about people. If you are possessive about people, you ought not to be a schoolmaster.

The wear and tear of materials in Summerhill is a natural process. It could be obviated only by the introduction of fear. The wear and tear of psychic forces cannot be obviated in any way, for children ask and must be given. Fifty times a day my sitting room door opens and a child asks a question: "Is this movie night?" "Why don't I get a P.L. [Private Lesson]?" "Have you seen Pam?" "Where's Ena?" It is all in a day's work, and I do not feel any strain at the time, though we have no real private life, partly because the house is not a good one for a school—not good from the adult's point of view, for the children are always on top of us. But by the end of term, my wife and I are thoroughly fatigued.

One noteworthy fact is that members of the staff seldom lose their tempers. That says as much for the children as for the staff. Really, they are delightful children to live with, and the occasions for losing one's temper are very few. If a child is free to approve of himself, he will not usually be hateful. He will not see any fun in trying to make an adult lose his temper.

ALFRED NORTH WHITEHEAD ON THE FUNCTION OF UNIVERSITIES
(1929) From Alfred North Whitehead, *The Aims of Education And Other Essays* (London, 1929), pp. 97-104.

The universities are schools of education, and schools of research. But the primary reason for their existence is not to be found either in the mere knowledge conveyed to the students or in the mere opportunities for research afforded to the members of the faculty.

Both these functions could be performed at a cheaper rate, apart from these very expensive institutions. Books are cheap, and the system of apprenticeship is well understood. So far as the mere imparting of information is concerned, no university has had any justification for existence since the popularisation of printing in the fifteenth century. Yet the chief impetus to the foundation of universities came after that date, and in more recent times has even increased.

The justification for a university is that it preserves the connection between knowledge and the zest of life, by uniting the young and the old in the imaginative consideration of learning. The university imparts information, but it imparts it imaginatively. At least, this is the function which it should perform for society. A university which fails in this respect has no reason for existence. This atmosphere of excitement, arising from imaginative consideration, transforms knowledge. A fact is no longer a bare fact: it is invested with all its possibilities. It is no longer a burden on the memory: it is energising as the poet of our dreams, and as the architect of our purposes.

Imagination is not to be divorced from the facts: it is a way of illuminating the facts. It works by eliciting the general principles which apply to the facts, as they exist, and then by an intellectual survey of alternative possibilities which are consistent with those principles. It enables men to construct an intellectual vision of a new world, and it preserves the zest of life by the suggestion of satisfying purposes.

Youth is imaginative, and if the imagination be strengthened by discipline this energy of imagination can in great measure be preserved through life. The tragedy of the world is that those who are imaginative have but slight experience, and those who are experienced have feeble imaginations. Fools act on imagination without knowledge; pedants act on knowledge without imagination. The task of a university is to weld together imagination and experience.

The initial discipline of imagination in its period of youthful vigor requires that there be no responsibility for immediate action. The habit of unbiased thought, whereby the ideal variety of exemplifications is discerned in its derivation from general principles, cannot be acquired when there is the daily task of preserving a concrete organisation. You must be free to think rightly and wrongly, and free to appreciate the variousness of the universe undisturbed by its perils.

These reflections upon the general functions of a university can be at once translated in terms of the particular functions of a business school. We need not flinch from the assertion that the main function of such a school is to produce men with a greater zest for business. It is a libel upon human nature to conceive that zest for life is the product of pedestrian purposes directed toward the narrow routine of material comforts. Mankind by its pioneering instinct, and in a hundred other ways, proclaims falsehood of that lie.

In the modern complex social organism, the adventure of life cannot be disjoined from intellectual adventure. Amid simpler circumstances, the pioneer can follow the urge of his instinct, directed toward the scene of his vision from the mountain top. But in the complex organisations of modern business the intellectual adventure of analysis, and of imaginative reconstruction, must precede any successful reorganisation. In a simpler world, business relations were simpler, being based on the immediate contact of man with man and on immediate confrontation with all relevant material circumstances. To-day business organisation requires an imaginative grasp of the psychologies of populations engaged in differing modes of occupation; of populations scattered through cities, through mountains, through plains; of populations on the ocean, and of populations in mines, and of populations in forests. It requires an imaginative grasp of conditions in the tropics, and of conditions in temperate zones. It requires an imaginative grasp of the interlocking interests of great organisations, and of the reactions of the whole complex to any change in one of its elements. It requires an imaginative understanding of laws of political economy, not merely in the abstract, but also with the power to construe them in terms of the particular circumstances of a concrete business. It requires some knowledge of the habits of government, and of the variations of those habits under diverse conditions. It requires an imaginative vision of the binding forces of any human organisation, a sympathetic vision of the limits of human nature and of the conditions which evoke loyalty of service. It requires some knowledge of the laws of health, and of the laws of fatigue, and of the conditions for sustained reliability. It requires an imaginative understanding of the social effects of the conditions of factories. It requires a sufficient conception of the role of applied science in modern society. It requires that discipline of character which can say "yes" and "no" to other men, not by reason of blind obstinacy, but with firmness derived from a conscious evaluation of relevant alternatives.

The universities have trained the intellectual pioneers of our civilisation—the priests, the lawyers, the statesmen, the doctors, the men of science, and the men of letters. They have been the home of those ideals which lead men to confront the

confusion of their present times. The Pilgrim Fathers left England to found a state
of society according to the ideals of their religious faith; and one of their earlier
acts was the foundation of Harvard University in Cambridge, named after that
ancient mother of ideals in England, to which so many of them owed their training.
The conduct of business now requires intellectual imagination of the same type as
that which in former times has mainly passed into those other occupations; and the
universities are the organisations which have supplied this type of mentality for the
service of the progress of the European races.

✳   ✳   ✳

In early mediaeval history the origin of universities was obscure and almost
unnoticed. They were a gradual and natural growth. But their existence is the reason
for the sustained, rapid progressiveness of European life in so many fields of
activity. By their agency the adventure of action met the adventure of thought. It
would not have been possible antecedently to have divined that such organisations
would have been successful. Even now, amid the imperfections of all things human,
it is sometimes difficult to understand how they succeed in their work. Of course
there is much failure in the work of universities. But, if we take a broad view of
history, their success has been remarkable and almost uniform. The cultural
histories of Italy, of France, of Germany, of Holland, of Scotland, of England, of the
United States, bear witness to the influence of universities. By "cultural history" I
am not chiefly thinking of the lives of scholars; I mean the energising of the lives of
those men who gave to France, to Germany, and to other countries that impress of
types of human achievement which, by their addition to the zest of life, form the
foundation of our patriotism. We love to be members of society which can do those
things.

There is one great difficulty which hampers all the higher types of human
endeavour. In modern times this difficulty has even increased in its possibilities for
evil. In any large organisation the younger men, who are novices, must be set to
jobs which consist in carrying out fixed duties in obedience to orders. No president
of a large corporation meets his youngest employee at his office door with the offer
of the most responsible job which the work of that corporation includes. The young
men are set to work at a fixed routine, and only occasionally even see the president
as he passes in and out of the building. Such work is a great discipline. It imparts
knowledge, and it produces reliability of character; also it is the only work for
which the young men, in that novice stage, are fit, and it is the work for which they
are hired. There can be no criticism of the custom, but there may be an unfortunate
effect—prolonged routine work dulls the imagination.

The result is that qualities essential at a later stage of a career are apt to be
stamped out in an earlier stage. This is only an instance of the more general fact,
that necessary technical excellence can only be acquired by a training which is apt
to damage those energies of mind which should direct the technical skill. This is the
key fact in education, and the reason for most of its difficulties.

The way in which a university should function in the preparation for an
intellectual career, such as modern business or one of the older professions, is by
promoting the imaginative consideration of the various general principles underlying that career. Its students thus pass into their period of technical apprenticeship
with their imaginations already practised in connecting details with general
principles. The routine then receives its meaning, and also illuminates the principles

which give it that meaning. Hence, instead of a drudgery issuing in a blind rule of thumb, the properly trained man has some hope of obtaining an imagination disciplined by detailed facts and by necessary habits.

Thus the proper function of a university is the imaginative acquisition of knowledge. Apart from this importance of the imagination, there is no reason why business men, and other professional men, should not pick up their facts bit by bit as they want them for particular occasions. A university is imaginative or it is nothing—at least nothing useful.

*   *   *

Imagination is a contagious disease. It cannot be measured by the yard, or weighed by the pound, and then delivered to the students by members of the faculty. It can only be communicated by a faculty whose members themselves wear their learning with imagination. In saying this, I am only repeating one of the oldest of observations. More than two thousand years ago the ancients symbolised learning by a torch passing from hand to hand down the generations. That lighted torch is the imagination of which I speak. The whole art in the organisation of a university is the provision of a faculty whose learning is lighted up with imagination. This is the problem of problems in university education; and unless we are careful the recent vast extension of universities in number of students and in variety of activities—of which we are so justly proud—will fail in producing its proper results, by the mishandling of this problem.

The combination of imagination and learning normally requires some leisure, freedom from restraint, freedom from harassing worry, some variety of experiences, and the stimulation of other minds diverse in opinion and diverse in equipment. Also there is required the excitement of curiosity, and the self-confidence derived from pride in the achievements of the surrounding society in procuring the advance of knowledge. Imagination cannot be acquired once and for all, and then kept indefinitely in an ice box to be produced periodically in stated quantities. The learned and imaginative life is a way of living, and is not an article of commerce.

It is in respect to the provision and utilisation of these conditions for an efficient faculty that the two functions of education and research meet together in a university. Do you want your teachers to be imaginative? Then encourage them to research. Do you want your researchers to be imaginative? Then bring them into intellectual sympathy with the young at the most eager, imaginative period of life, when intellects are just entering upon their mature discipline. Make your researchers explain themselves to active minds, plastic and with the world before them; make your young students crown their period of intellectual acquistion by some contact with minds gifted with experience of intellectual adventure. Education is discipline for the adventure of life; research is intellectual adventure; and the universities should be homes of adventure shared in common by young and old. For successful education there must always be a certain freshness in the knowledge dealt with. It must either be new in itself or it must be invested with some novelty of application to the new world of new times. Knowledge does not keep any better than fish. You may be dealing with knowledge of the old species, with some old truth; but somehow or other it must come to the students, as it were, just drawn out of the sea and with the freshness of its immediate importance.

It is the function of the scholar to evoke into life wisdom and beauty which, apart from his magic, would remain lost in the past. A progressive society depends upon its inclusion of three groups—scholars, discoverers, inventors. Its progress also depends upon the fact that its educated masses are composed of members each with a tinge of scholarship, a tinge of discovery, and a tinge of invention. I am here using the term "discovery" to mean the progress of knowledge in respect to truths of some high generality, and the term "invention" to mean the progress of knowledge in respect to the application of general truths in particular ways subservient to present needs. It is evident that these three groups merge into each other, and also that men engaged in practical affairs are properly to be called inventors so far as they contribute to the progress of society. But any one individual has his own limitation of function, and his own peculiar needs. What is important for a nation is that there shall be a very close relation between all types of its progressive elements, so that the study may influence the market place, and the market place the study. Universities are the chief agencies for this fusion of progressive activities into an effective instrument of progress. Of course they are not the only agencies, but it is a fact that to-day the progressive nations are those in which universities flourish.

It must not be supposed that the output of a university in the form of original ideas is solely to be measured by printed papers and books labeled with the names of their authors. Mankind is as individual in its mode of output as in the substance of its thoughts. For some of the most fertile minds composition in writing, or in a form reducible to writing, seems to be an impossibility. In every faculty you will find that some of the more brilliant teachers are not among those who publish. Their originality requires for its expression direct intercourse with their pupils in the form of lectures, or of personal discussion. Such men exercise an immense influence; and yet, after the generation of their pupils has passed away, they sleep among the innumerable unthanked benefactors of humanity. Fortunately, one of them is immortal—Socrates.

Thus it would be the greatest mistake to estimate the value of each member of a faculty by the printed work signed with his name. There is at the present day some tendency to fall into this error; and an emphatic protest is necessary against an attitude on the part of authorities which is damaging to efficiency and unjust to unselfish zeal.

But, when all such allowances have been made, one good test for the general efficiency of a faculty is that as a whole it shall be producing in published form its quota of contributions of thought. Such a quota is to be estimated in weight of thought, and not in number of words.

This survey shows that the management of a university faculty has no analogy to that of a business organisation. The public opinion of the faculty, and a common zeal for the purposes of the university, form the only effective safeguards for the high level of university work. The faculty should be a band of scholars, stimulating each other, and freely determining their various activities. You can secure certain formal requirements, that lectures are given at stated times and that instructors and students are in attendance. But the heart of the matter lies beyond all regulation.

The question of justice to the teachers has very little to do with the case. It is perfectly just to hire a man to perform any legal services under any legal conditions as to times and salary. No one need accept the post unless he so desires.

The sole question is, What sort of conditions will produce the type of faculty which will run a successful university? The danger is that it is quite easy to produce a faculty entirely unfit—a faculty of very efficient pedants and dullards. The general public will only detect the difference after the university has stunted the promise of youth for scores of years.

The modern university system in the great democratic countries will only be successful if the ultimate authorities exercise singular restraint, so as to remember that universities cannot be dealt with according to the rules and policies which apply to the familiar business corporations. Business schools are no exception to this law of university life. There is really nothing to add to what the presidents of many American universities have recently said in public on this topic. But whether the effective portion of the general public, in America or other countries, will follow their advice appears to be doubtful. The whole point of a university, on its educational side, is to bring the young under the intellectual influence of a band of imaginative scholars. There can be no escape from proper attention to the conditions which—as experience has shown—will produce such a band.

EDUCATION IN THE "BRAVE NEW WORLD" (1932) From Aldous Huxley,
Brave New World (New York, 1932), pp. 1–3, 262–74, 283–84.

A squat grey building of only thirty-four stories. Over the main entrance the words, Central London Hatchery and Conditioning Centre, and, in a shield, the World State's motto, Community, Identity, Stability.

The enormous room on the ground floor faced towards the north. Cold for all the summer beyond the panes, for all the tropical heat of the room itself, a harsh thin light glared through the windows, hungrily seeking some draped lay figure, some pallid shape of academic goose-flesh, but finding only the glass and nickel and bleakly shining porcelain of a laboratory. Wintriness responded to wintriness. The overalls of the workers were white, their hands gloved with a pale corpse-coloured rubber. The light was frozen, dead, a ghost. Only from the yellow barrels of the microscopes did it borrow a certain rich and living substance, lying along the polished tubes like butter, streak after luscious streak in long recession down the work tables.

"And this," said the Director opening the door, "is the Fertilizing Room."

Bent over their instruments, three hundred Fertilizers were plunged, as the Director of Hatcheries and Conditioning entered the room, in the scarcely breathing silence, the absent-minded, soliloquizing hum or whistle, of absorbed concentration. A troop of newly arrived students, very young, pink and callow, followed nervously, rather abjectly, at the Director's heels. Each of them carried a notebook, in which, whenever the great man spoke, he desperately scribbled. Straight from the horse's mouth. It was a rare privilege. The D.H.C. for Central London always made a point of personally conducting his new students round the various departments.

❋   ❋   ❋

Infant Nurseries. Neo–Pavlovian Conditioning Rooms, announced the notice board.

The Director opened a door. They were in a large bare room, very bright and sunny; for the whole of the southern wall was a single window. Half a dozen nurses, trousered and jacketed in the regulation white viscose-linen uniform, their hair aseptically hidden under white caps, were engaged in setting out bowls of roses in a long row across the floor. Big bowls, packed tight with blossom. Thousands of petals, ripe-blown and silkily smooth, like the cheeks of innumerable little cherubs, but of cherubs, in that bright light, not exclusively pink and Aryann but also luminously Chinese, also Mexican, also apoplectic with too much blowing of celestial trumpets, also pale as death, pale with the posthumous whiteness of marble.

The nurses stiffened to attention as the D.H.C. came in.

"Set out the books," he said curtly.

In silence the nurses obeyed his command. Between the rose bowls the books were duly set out—a row of nursery quartos opened invitingly each at some gaily coloured image of beast or fish or bird.

"Now bring in the children."

They hurried out of the room and returned in a minute or two, each pushing a kind of tall dumb-waiter laden, on all its four wire-netted shelves, with eight-month-old babies, all exactly alike (a Bokanovsky Group, it was evident) and all (since their caste was Delta) dressed in khaki.

"Put them down on the floor."

The infants were unloaded.

"Now turn them so that they can see the flowers and books."

Turned, the babies at once fell silent, then began to crawl towards those clusters of sleek colours, those shapes so gay and brilliant on the white pages. As they approached, the sun came out of a momentary eclipse behind a cloud. The roses flamed up as though with a sudden passion from within; a new and profound significance seemed to suffuse the shining pages of the books. From the ranks of the crawling babies came little squeals of excitement, gurgles and twitterings of pleasure.

The Director rubbed his hands. "Excellent!" he said. "It might almost have been done on purpose."

The swiftest crawlers were already at their goal. Small hands reached out uncertainly, touched, grasped, unpetaling the transfigured roses, crumpling the illuminated pages of the books. The Director waited until all were happily busy. Then, "Watch carefully," he said. And, lifting his hand, he gave the signal.

The Head Nurse, who was standing by a switchboard at the other end of the room, pressed down a little lever.

There was a violent explosion. Shriller and ever shriller, a siren shrieked. Alarm bells maddeningly sounded.

The children started, screamed; their faces were distorted with terror.

"And now," the Director shouted (for the noise was deafening), "now we proceed to rub in the lesson with a mild electric shock."

He waved his hand again, and the Head Nurse pressed a second lever. The screaming of the babies suddenly changed its tone. There was something desperate, almost insane, about the sharp spasmodic yelps to which they now gave utterance. Their little bodies twitched and stiffened; their limbs moved jerkily as if to the tug of unseen wires.

"We can electrify that whole strip of floor," bawled the Director in explanation. "But that's enough," he signalled to the nurse.

The explosions ceased, the bells stopped ringing, the shriek of the siren died down from tone to tone into silence. The stiffly twitching bodies relaxed, and what had become the sob and yelp of infant maniacs broadened out once more into a normal howl of ordinary terror.

"Offer them the flowers and the books again."

The nurses obeyed; but at the approach of the roses, at the mere sight of those gaily-coloured images of pussy and cock-a-doodle-doo and baa-baa black sheep, the infants shrank away in horror; the volume of their howling suddenly increased.

"Observe," said the Director triumphantly, "observe."

Books and loud noises, flowers and electric shocks—already in the infant mind these couples were compromisingly linked; and after two hundred repetitions of the same or a similar lesson would be wedded indissolubly. What man has joined, nature is powerless to put asunder.

"They'll grow up with what the psychologists used to call an 'instinctive' hatred of books and flowers. Reflexes unalterably conditioned. They'll be safe from books and botany all their lives." The Director turned to his nurses. "Take them away again."

Still yelling, the khaki babies were loaded on to their dumb-waiters and wheeled out, leaving behind them the smell of sour milk and a most welcome silence.

One of the students held up his hand; and though he could see quite well why you couldn't have lower-caste people wasting the Community's time over books, and that there was always the risk of their reading something which might undesirably decondition one of their reflexes, yet . . . well, he couldn't understand about the flowers. Why go to the trouble of making it psychologically impossible for Deltas to like flowers?

Patiently the D.H.C. explained. If the children were made to scream at the sight of a rose, that was on grounds of high economic policy. Not so very long ago (a century or thereabouts), Gammas, Deltas, even Epsilons, had been conditioned to like flowers—flowers in particular and wild nature in general. The idea was to make them want to be going out into the country at every available opportunity, and so compel them to consume transport.

"And didn't they consume transport?" asked the student.

"Quite a lot," the D.H.C. replied. "But nothing else."

Primroses and landscapes, he pointed out, have one grave defect: they are gratuitous. A love of nature keeps no factories busy. It was decided to abolish the love of nature, at any rate among the lower classes; to abolish the love of nature, but *not* the tendency to consume transport. For of course it was essential that they should keep on going to the country, even though they hated it. The problem was to find an economically sounder reason for consuming transport than a mere affection for primroses and landscapes. It was duly found.

"We condition the masses to hate the country," concluded the Director. "But simultaneously we condition them to love all country sports. At the same time, we see to it that all country sports shall entail the use of elaborate apparatus. So that they consume manufactured articles as well as transport. Hence those electric shocks."

"I see," said the student, and was silent, lost in admiration.

There was a silence; then, clearing his throat, "Once upon a time," the Director began, "while our Ford was still on earth, there was a little boy called Reuben Rabinovitch. Reuben was the child of Polish-speaking parents." The Director interrupted himself. "You know what Polish is, I suppose?"

"A dead language."

"Like French and German," added another student, officiously showing off his learning.

"And 'parent'?" questioned the D.H.C.

There was an uneasy silence. Several of the boys blushed. They had not yet learned to draw the significant but often very fine distinction between smut and pure science. One, at last, had the courage to raise a hand.

"Human beings used to be . . ." he hesitated; the blood rushed to his cheeks. "Well, they used to be viviparous."

"Quite right." The Director nodded approvingly.

"And when the babies were decanted . . ."

" 'Born,' " came the correction.

"Well, then they were the parents—I mean, not the babies, of course; the other ones." The poor boy was overwhelmed with confusion.

"In brief," the Director summed up, "the parents were the father and the mother." The smut that was really science fell with a crash into the boys' eye-avoiding silence. "Mother," he repeated loudly rubbing in the science; and, leaning back in his chair, "These," he said gravely, "are unpleasant facts; I know it. But then most historical facts *are* unpleasant."

He returned to Little Reuben—to Little Reuben, in whose room, one evening, by an oversight, his father and mother (crash, crash!) happened to leave the radio turned on.

("For you must remember that in those days of gross viviparous reproduction, children were always brought up by their parents and not in State Conditioning Centres.")

While the child was asleep, a broadcast programme from London suddenly started to come through; and the next morning, to the astonishment of his crash and crash (the more daring of the boys ventured to grin at one another), Little Reuben woke up repeating word for word a long lecture by that curious old writer ("one of the very few whose works have been permitted to come down to us"), George Bernard Shaw, who was speaking, according to a well-authenticated tradition, about his own genius. To Little Reuben's wink and snigger, this lecture was, of course, perfectly incomprehensible and, imagining that their child had suddenly gone mad, they sent for a doctor. He, fortunately, understood English, recognized the discourse as that which Shaw had broadcasted the previous evening, realized the significance of what had happened, and sent a letter to the medical press about it.

"The principle of sleep-teaching, or hypnopædia, had been discovered." The D.H.C. made an impressive pause.

The principle had been discovered; but many, many years were to elapse before that principle was usefully applied.

"The case of Little Reuben occurred only twenty-three years after Our Ford's first T-Model was put on the market." (Here the Director made a sign of the T on his stomach and all the students reverently followed suit.) "And yet . . ."

Furiously the students scribbled. *"Hypnopædia, first used officially in A.F. 214. Why not before? Two reasons. (a) . . ."*

"These early experimenters," the D.H.C. was saying, "were on the wrong track. They thought that hypnopædia could be made an instrument of intellectual education . . ."

(A small boy asleep on his right side, the right arm stuck out, the right hand hanging limp over the edge of the bed. Through a round grating in the side of a box a voice speaks softly.

"The Nile is the longest river in Africa and the second in length of all the rivers of the globe. Although falling short of the length of the Mississippi-Missouri, the Nile is at the head of all rivers as regards the length of its basin, which extends through 35 degrees of latitude . . ."

At breakfast the next morning, "Tommy," some one says, "do you know which is the longest river in Africa?" A shaking of the head. "But don't you remember something that begins: The Nile is the . . ."

"The - Nile - is - the - longest - river - in - Africa - and - the - second - in - length - of - all - the - rivers - of - the - globe . . ." The words come rushing out. "Although - falling - short - of . . ."

"Well now, which is the longest river in Africa?"

The eyes are blank. "I don't know."

"But the Nile, Tommy."

"The - Nile - is - the - longest - river - in - Africa - and - second . . ."

"Then which river is the longest, Tommy?"

Tommy burst into tears. "I don't know," he howls.)

That howl, the Director made it plain, discouraged the earliest investigators. The experiments were abandoned. No further attempt was made to teach children the length of the Nile in their sleep. Quite rightly. You can't learn a science unless you know what it's all about.

SUSAN ISAACS ON THE FUNCTION OF PLAY IN PERSONALITY DEVELOPMENT (1933)   From Susan Isaacs, *Social Development in Young Children: A Study of Beginnings* (New York, 1933), pp. 425–28.

Play is not only the means by which the child comes to discover the world; it is supremely the activity which brings him psychic equilibrium in the early years. In his play activities, the child externalises and works out to some measure of harmony all the different trends of his internal psychic life. In turn he gives external form and expression, now to the parent, now to the child within himself, and to each of the different aspects of his real parents, as he apprehends these at the different levels of his own development, through his own wishes and impulses. And gradually he learns to relate his deepest and most primitive phantasies to the ordered world of real relations.

Educators have long appreciated the vast significance of play, and many different aspects of its value have been brought out by different thinkers. It has remained for psycho-analysts, and in particular those working with young children, to show in the greatest detail how play is indeed the breath of life to the child, since it is through play activities that he finds mental ease, and can work upon his wishes, fears and phantasies, so as to integrate them into a living personality. The child does much for himself in his play, even without the help of an analyst, who is in any case but an auxiliary to the child's own integrative impulses.

The function of the educator with regard to play lies in the study of the normal interests and activities of the child at different ages, so that he may know how to supply those materials and opportunities and stimuli to play as shall give him the greatest fulfilment along all directions of his growth. It is here that the study of norms of development in the early years, with regard to skill or understanding, is of the greatest possible aid to the educator of little children. But not alone the study of the ordered play in which the child learns skill and knowledge. It is not less important that parents in the home and teachers in the nursery school should leave ample opportunity to the child for quite free, unhindered, unorganised, imaginative play, than that they should provide didactic apparatus and materials for development in physical skill. This passive work of the educator in leaving the child free to make-believe is as valuable a part of his function as his more active services—a point sometimes lost sight of in the modern nursery school.

The third general significance of the psycho-analytic study of young children, which links up with play activities, is that of the great importance of giving opportunities for the sublimations. Here, again, it is the function of the educator to be passive. He should not, for example, introduce a moral element into the teaching of art, as by over-valuing neatness, accuracy, or formal virtues of any kind. He needs to leave the child free with his painting or modelling materials, to develop his own skill of expression as his own inner needs dictate. As the wisest teachers have shown us, we cannot order or control the child's expression in art. We can but give him material and opportunity, and leave him free to his own creative spirit. This is now beginning to be understood in the realm of art; but it has a wider general application, too. Whatever line of real achievement we consider, that indirect expression of unconscious phantasy which we call sublimation can never appear at the behest of the super-ego, whether the primitive internal super-ego or the real external teacher. It is always the fruit of the child's own creative wishes. If we attempt to control and contain it, we simply make it lifeless and formal. It is not here that the active function of the educator as the super-ego should operate; here he must be passive and merely supporting. His active functions lie in maintaining the stable framework of ordered routine, and in the control of aggressive, destructive impulses in their crude forms.

The psycho-analytic study of young children, and especially of the early phantasies and anxieties, thus altogether re-emphasises the importance of respecting the child's individuality, even at an early age. The personality of the child, and of the adult that he is to be, rests in the last resort upon the inner flux of forces within his own mind, which it is beyond our power to affect and control by any deliberate act. The way in which he will resolve his own anxieties, the particular channels he will find for indirect satisfaction of his early wishes, the lines upon which his ego will build up its control of primitive wishes, are largely out of our reach. They are determined by imponderable forces within the child's own psyche, which we can but respect. Where the child is in special difficulties, we can aid him, either by providing a more adequate, more secure and more stable environment, or by strengthening his ego through the special work of analysis. But by neither of these functions can we actually determine the lines upon which his individuality shall develop, and what his actual solution of conflict shall be. The more clearly we ourselves recognise this, the greater support we are likely to be to him. If, from the beginning, we respect not only his early efforts at practical independence, in the way Dr. Montessori has taught us to respect these, but the individual genius of his expression in creative art, in imaginative play, in the special choice of individual skills and achievements, we give him a very real support towards the solution of his own difficulties. If we try to cramp and control him by our own notions of what he ought to be, we may close up the very channels which will bring him value and safety.

Here, then, is another profound reinforcement of the teaching of the best educators of our time, namely, that we need to respect the child's developing personality and to treat him as an individual, with personal rights, even whilst, at the same time, we recognise that other side of our educational responsibility, that need to help his control of the more crudely destructive impulses, and to train him to a settled routine in the fundamental activities of his daily life, as well as to those minimal levels of mutual consideration which make social relations possible.

The fourth general bearing of all the facts of child behavior illustrated and examined here is that of the immense value to the young child of the companionship of his fellows. In our study of early egocentrism, and of group hostility and aggression, we saw how the children are carried on to real independence through discovering the value of other children as allies, against the fear both of real grownups and of the internal super-ego. I need not elaborate this point further here, except to bring it in relation to the child's deeper phantasy life. Through the cooperative expression of phantasy in dramatic play, the child is led out from his deepest rivalries and anxieties to the discovery of the delights of real satisfaction in social life. He is, moreover, carried from his earliest and deepest needs for sensual satisfaction in actual bodily contact, to the non-sensual satisfactions of ordered social life, and the sharing of interests and activities, upon which not only his social adaptation depends, but his sublimatory activities and real achievements also. The children can help each other in their play, by giving each other support against the dread of rivals, as well as by the common pursuit of non-sexual aims. Companionship in play, therefore, is from an early age one of the greatest needs of little children, whatever aspect of their developing life one is considering.

✳   ✳   ✳

In all these directions, then, the psycho-analytic study of young children serves to reinforce the established values of the best practice of modern educators. The value of play, play with companions, free imaginative play as well as play leading to ordered skill and knowledge, is enormously supported and confirmed by this deeper study of children's phantasies. The notion that children must not be interfered with at all, but left to work out their own salvation, without control or guidance, is, however, seen to be without firm basis. In some directions, the child cannot do without our guidance. He needs the help of external restraints in learning to control and deflect his own impulses, particularly the aggressive ones. On the other hand, he needs our *passive* help as educators in giving him opportunity for indirect expression in social activities and the mastering of skill.

KARL MANNHEIM ON EDUCATION AND SOCIAL CONTROL

(1943)   From Karl Mannheim, *Diagnosis of Our Time* (London, 1943), pp. 73–75.

The democratic Governments cannot pride themselves on discovering satisfactory forms of social control to replace a vanishing community culture, or new psychological techniques for dealing with the needs of mass society. A general psychological break-down can only be prevented if we are quick enough to realize the nature of the new situation, and to re-define the aims and means of democratic education accordingly.

This reformation of democratic and liberal aims and methods to fit a new society

IDEAS
FROM ABROAD

calls for a sociological approach to education. I shall specify a few of its implications:

(1) Education does not mould man in the abstract, but in and for a given society.

(2) The ultimate educational unit is never the individual but the group, which may vary in size, aim and function. With them will vary the predominant patterns of action to which the individuals in these groups will have to conform.

(3) The educational aims of society cannot be adequately understood as long as they are severed from the situations that each age is called upon to face and from the social order for which they are framed.

(4) Codes and norms are, to the sociologist, not ends in themselves but always the expression of an interplay between individual and group adjustment. The fact that norms are themselves not absolute but change with the changing social order and help to solve the tasks with which society is faced, cannot be seen from the experience of the single individual. To him they seem to be absolute and unalterable decrees, and without this belief in their stability they cannot be made to work. Their true nature and function in society as a form of collective adaptation reveals itself only if we follow their history through many generations, continuously relating them to the changing social background.

(5) These educational aims in their social context are handed down to the new generation together with the prevailing educational techniques. Educational techniques in their turn do not develop in isolation but always as part in the general development of "social techniques". Thus education is rightly understood only if we consider it as one of the techniques of influencing human behaviour and as one means of social control. The slightest change in these more general techniques and controls reacts upon education in the narrow sense, as it is carried out within the walls of the school.

(6) The more we consider education from the point of view of our recent experience, as only one of the many ways of influencing human behaviour, the more it becomes evident that even the most efficient educational technique is doomed to fail unless it is related to the remaining forms of social control. No educational system is able to maintain emotional stability and mental integrity in the new generation, unless it has a kind of common strategy with the social agencies outside the school. Only through co-operation with them is it possible, particularly in our present age, to hold in check the social influences which otherwise disorganize community life. Only through a co-ordinated attack upon the disorganizing effects of mass society on the mind of the individual can one hope to stem mass psychoses such as developed on the Continent.

T. S. ELIOT ON CULTURE AND ELITES (1948)   From T. S. Eliot, *Notes Toward A Definition of Culture* (New York, 1949), pp. 23, 47–48, 99–100, 104, 108.

We know that good manners, without education, intellect or sensibility to the arts, tends towards mere automatism; that learning without good manners or sensibility is pedantry; that intellectual ability without the more human attributes is admirable only in the same way as the brilliance of a child chess prodigy; and that the arts without intellectual context are vanity. And if we do not find culture in any one of these perfections alone, so we must not expect any one person to be accomplished in all of them; we shall come to infer that the wholly cultured individual is a phantasm; and we shall look for culture, not in any individual or in any one group of individuals, but more and more widely; and we are driven in the end to find it in the pattern of the society as a whole. This seems to me a very obvious reflection: but it is frequently overlooked. People are always ready to consider themselves persons of culture, on the strength of one proficiency, when they are not only lacking in others, but blind to those they lack. An artist of any kind, even a very great artist, is not for this reason alone a man of culture: artists are not only often insensitive to other arts than those which they practice, but sometimes have very bad manners or meagre intellectual gifts. The person who contributes to culture, however important his contribution may be, is not always a "cultured person."

*   *   *

All that concerns me at the moment is the question whether, by education alone, we can ensure the transmission of culture in a society in which some educationists appear indifferent to class distinctions, and from which some other educationists appear to want to remove class distinctions altogether. There is, in any case, a danger of interpreting "education" to cover both too much and too little; too little, when it implies that education is limited to what can be taught; too much, when it implies that everything worth preserving can be transmitted by teaching. In the society desired by some reformers what the family can transmit will be limited to the minimum, especially if the child is to be . . . manipulated by a unified educational system "from the cradle to the grave." And unless the child is classified, by the officials who will have the task of sorting him out, as being just like his father, he will be brought up in a different—not necessarily a better, because all will be equally good, but a different—school environment, and trained on what the official opinion of the moment considers to be "the genuinely democratic lines." The élites, in consequence, will consist solely of individuals whose only common bond will be their professional interest: with no social cohesion, with no social continuity. They will be united only by a part, and that the most conscious part, of their personalities; they will meet like committees. The greater part of their "culture" will be only what they share with all the other individuals composing their nation.

The case for a society with a class structure, the affirmation that it is, in some sense, the "natural" society, is prejudiced if we allow ourselves to be hypnotised by the two contrasted terms *aristocracy* and *democracy*. The whole problem is falsified if we use these terms antithetically. What I have advanced is not a "defence of aristocracy"—an emphasis upon the importance of one organ of society. Rather it is a plea on behalf of a form of society in which an aristocracy should have a peculiar and essential function, as peculiar and essential as the function of any other part of society. What is important is a structure of society in which there will be, from "top" to "bottom," a continuous gradation of cultural levels: it is important to remember that we should not consider the upper levels as possessing *more* culture than the lower, but as representing a more conscious culture and a greater specialisation of culture. I incline to believe that no true democracy can maintain itself unless it contains these different levels of culture. The levels of culture may also be seen as levels of power, to the extent that a smaller group at a higher level will have equal power with a larger group at a lower level; for it may be argued that complete equality means universal irresponsibility; and in such a society as I envisage, each individual would inherit greater or less responsibility towards the commonwealth, according to the position in society which he inherited—each class would have somewhat different responsibilities.

✳　✳　✳

We have already found that the purpose of education has been defined as the making people happier. The assumption that it *does* make people happier needs to be considered separately. That the educated person is happier than the uneducated is by no means self-evident. Those who are conscious of their lack of education are discontented, if they cherish ambitions to excel in occupations for which they are not qualified; they are sometimes discontented, simply because they have been given to understand that more education would have made them happier. Many of us feel some grievance against our elders, our schools or our universities for not having done better by us: this can be a way of extenuating our own shortcomings and excusing our failures. On the other hand, to be educated above the level of those whose social habits and tastes one has inherited, may cause a division within a man which interferes with happiness; even though, when the individual is of superior intellect, it may bring him a fuller and more useful life. And to be trained, taught or instructed above the level of one's abilities and strength may be disastrous; for education is a strain, and can impose greater burdens upon a mind than that mind can bear. Too much education, like too little education, can produce unhappiness.

✳　✳　✳

It follows from what has been said in an earlier chapter about classes and élites, that education should help to preserve the class and to select the élite. It is right that the exceptional individual should have the opportunity to elevate himself in the social scale and attain a position in which he can exercise his talents to the greatest benefit of himself and of society. But the ideal of an educational system which would automatically sort out everyone according to his native capacities is unattainable in practice; and if we made it our chief aim, would disorganise society and debase education. It would disorganise society, by substituting for classes, élites of brains, or perhaps only of sharp wits. Any educational system aiming at a complete adjustment between education and society will tend both to restrict education to what will lead to success in the world, and to restrict success in the world to those persons who have been good pupils of the system. The prospect of a society ruled and directed only by those who have passed certain examinations or satisfied tests devised by psychologists is not reassuring: while it might give scope to talents hitherto obscured, it would probably obscure others, and reduce to impotence some who should have rendered high service. Furthermore, the ideal of a uniform system such that no one capable of receiving higher education could fail to get it, leads imperceptibly to the education of too many people, and consequently to the lowering of standards to whatever this swollen number of candidates is able to reach.

* * *

Besides the motive of giving everyone as much education as possible, because education is in itself desirable, there are other motives affecting educational legislation: motives which may be praiseworthy, or which simply recognise the inevitable, and which we need mention here only as a reminder of the complexity of the legislative problem. One motive, for instance, for raising the age-limit of compulsory schooling is the laudable desire to protect the adolescent, and fortify him against the more degrading influences to which he is exposed on entering the ranks of industry. We should be candid about such a motive; and instead of affirming what is to be doubted, that everyone will profit by as many years of tuition as we can give him, admit that the conditions of life in modern industrial society are so deplorable, and the moral restraints so weak, that we must prolong the schooling of young people simply because we are at our wits' end to know what to do to save them. Instead of congratulating ourselves on our progress, whenever the school assumes another responsibility hitherto left to parents, we might do better to admit that we have arrived at a stage of civilisation at which the family is irresponsible, or incompetent, or helpless; at which parents cannot be expected to train their children properly; at which many parents cannot afford to feed them properly, and would not know how, even if they had the means; and that Education must step in and make the best of a bad job.

* * *

. . . the culture of Europe has deteriorated visibly within the memory of many who are by no means the oldest among us. And we know, that whether education can foster and improve culture or not, it can surely adulterate and degrade it. For there is no doubt that in our headlong rush to educate everybody, we are lowering our standards, and more and more abandoning the study of those subjects by which the essentials of our culture—of that part of it which is transmissible by education— are transmitted; destorying our ancient edifices to make ready the ground upon which the barbarian nomads of the future will encamp in their merchandised caravans.

A MERITOCRATIC UTOPIA (2033)   From Michael Young, *The Rise of the Meritocracy, 1870–2033* (London, 1958), pp. 9–13.

Introduction

What was the connection between the gutting of the Ministry of Education and the attempt on the life of the Chairman of the T.U.C.? Between the unofficial transport strike and the equally unofficial walk-out of domestic servants? All these questions are rendered doubly topical by the general strike which the Populists have called for the coming May, on the first anniversary of the troubles. Will there be a response? Will 2034 repeat 1789 or merely 1848? I would submit that more topical, and more important, a subject could hardly be discussed. It touches on a clear and present danger to the state.

The Prime Minister, in his frank report to the House of Lords, put part of the responsibility for the May Affair upon administrative failings. The wrecking of Wren's store at Stevenage the Prime Minister regards as a local disturbance; its 2,000 shop assistants were undoubtedly incensed by the management's unexpected rejection of the four-day week. Destruction of the atomic station at South Shields might never have happened with a less provocative director. The walk-out of domestic servants was precipitated by the slowness of the Price Review, similar trouble in the other Provinces of Europe being evidence enough for that. Feeling against the Education Ministry was stimulated by the publication in April of the last report of the Standing Commission on the National Intelligence, and so on. All this I readily accept, yet it is not the whole story. We also have to explain why administrative miscalculations, that in an ordinary year would have passed almost unnoticed, should on this occasion have provoked such fierce and concerted protest. To understand what happened, and so be prepared for what is going to happen, we have to take the measure of the Populist movement, with its strange blend of women in the lead and men in the rank and file.

The women's circles have produced evangelists before; their eclipse has usually been as sudden as their rising. Not so the leaders by whom we are now plagued. They have consolidated their strength. The Convention they organized at Leicester shortly before Christmas 2032 was their decisive moment. The women's circles would be mustered—that was well known; the women's sections of the Technicians' Party would be there—that was half allowed for. What was not expected was the attendance of so many representatives, men as well as women, from local branches of the Party and the Unions. In defiance of their leaders, they came from all over the country, and particularly from the North of England and Scotland—this hostility to London and the South is a sinister aspect of the agitation too much played down by government sociologists. Even the Association of Scientific Benefactors was represented. From Leicester sprang the ill-assorted conglomeration which has come to be known as the Populist Movement, with its strange charter. For the only time within living memory a dissident minority from the elite has struck up an alliance with the lower orders, hitherto so isolated and so docile. Their union fomented the local incidents in Kirkcaldy and Stevenage, South Shields and Whitehall, into the national crisis of last May.

What does it all mean? Only the historians of the future will know, perhaps even they will not agree. Close as we are to the crisis, with every day bringing fresh news, it is impossible for anyone to be more than tentative in his opinions. No consensus has yet formed. The official view is that such an alliance across class-lines is a misalliance, the background of leaders and led so different, and the common interest between them so slight, that the movement cannot last. The *Sunday Scientist* has in a much-quoted, if scurrilous, phrase likened some of the leaders to 'Rimsky Korsakov in a Lyons Corner House'. Has Somerville vulgarized itself without finding any deep response? I think not, at least I do not agree about the response. The Populists could not have gathered such momentum, the May Affair reached such dimensions, unless there were more than passing resentments to feed on. My reading is that these resentments have their roots deep in history.

*   *   *

The purpose of this essay is to discuss some of the historical causes of the grievances that erupted in the May risings. My theme is that, whether or not these were explicitly organized by the Populists, they were certainly organized by history. One belief is implicit throughout: there are no revolutions, only the slow accretions of a ceaseless change that reproduces the past while transforming it. I am not thinking of the thousand and one technical innovations which have, from one point of view, made of the last century an aeon. These commonplaces I will not deal with but rather try to show that, however odd our great-grandfathers may now seem, the 21st century is woven on the same loom as neo-Elizabethan times. I shall illustrate my essay with references to the period, between 1914 and 1963, on which I specialized at the Manchester Grammar School. I would like to acknowledge my debt to my sixth-form master, Mr. Woodcock, for first pointing out to me how revealing a study of that time could be for an understanding of the progress man has made in the last century. He first introduced me to historical sociology as it has been developed in the ancient universities.

At the beginning of my special period, 1914, the upper classes had their fair share of geniuses and morons, so did the workers; or, I should say, since a few brilliant and fortunate working men always climbed up to the top despite having been subordinate in society, the inferior classes contained *almost* as high a proportion of superior people as the upper classes themselves. Intelligence was distributed more or less at random. Each social class was, in ability, the miniature of society itself; the part the same as the whole. The fundamental change of the last century, which was fairly begun before 1963, is that intelligence has been re-distributed between the classes, and the nature of the classes changed. The talented have been given the opportunity to rise to the level which accords with their capacities, and the lower classes consequently reserved for those who are also lower in ability. The part is no longer the same as the whole.

The rate of social progress depends upon the degree to which power is matched with intelligence. The Britain of a century ago squandered its resources by condemning even talented people to manual work; and blocked the efforts of members of the lower classes to obtain just recognition for their abilities. But Britain could not be a caste society if it was to survive as a great nation, great, that is, in comparison with others. To withstand international competition the country had to make better use of its human material, above all, of the talent which was even in England, one might say always and everywhere, too scarce. Schools and industries were progressively thrown open to merit, so that the clever children of each generation had opportunity for ascent. The proportion of people with I.Q.s over 130 could not be raised—the task was rather to prevent a fall—but the proportion of such people in work which called upon their full capacities was steadily raised. For every Rutherford there have in modern times been ten such magnates, for every Keynes two, and even Elgar has had a successor. Civilization does not depend upon the stolid mass the *homme moyen sensuel*, but upon the creative minority, the innovator who with one stroke can save the labour of 10,000, the brilliant few who cannot look without wonder, the restless elite who have made mutation a social, as well as a biological, fact. The ranks of the scientists and technologists, the artists and the teachers, have been swelled, their education shaped to their high genetic destiny, their power for good increased. Progress is their triumph; the modern world their monument.

And yet, if we ignore the casualties of progress, we fall victim, in the sphere of human relations, to the insidious complacency which in natural science we so much deplore. In the balanced view of sociology we have to consider the failures as well as the successes. Every selection of one is a rejection of many. Let us be frank and admit that we have failed to assess the mental state of the rejected, and so secure their necessary adjustment. The danger that has settled in upon us since the shock administered by the events of the last year is that the clamouring throng who find the gates of higher education barred against them may turn against the social order by which they feel themselves condemned. Do not the masses, for all their lack of capacity, sometimes behave as though they suffered from a sense of indignity? Do they necessarily see themselves as we see them? We know it is only by giving free rein to well-trained imagination and organized intelligence that humanity can hope to reach, in centuries to come, the fulfilment it deserves. Let us still recognize that those who complain of present injustice *think* they are talking about something real, and try to understand how it is that nonsense to us makes sense to them.

C. P. SNOW ON THE TWO CULTURES (1961)   From C. P. Snow, *The Two Cultures and the Scientific Revolution* (New York, 1961), pp. 4–9, 15–19.

I believe the intellectual life of the whole of western society is increasingly being split into two polar groups. When I say the intellectual life, I mean to include also a large part of our practical life, because I should be the last person to suggest the two can at the deepest level be distinguished. I shall come back to the practical life a little later. Two polar groups: at one pole we have the literary intellectuals, who incidentally while no one was looking took to referring to themselves as 'intellectuals' as though there were no others. I remember G. H. Hardy once remarking to me in mild puzzlement, some time in the 1930's: 'Have you noticed how the word "intellectual" is used nowadays? There seems to be a new definition which certainly doesn't include Rutherford or Eddington or Dirac or Adrian or me. It does seem rather odd, don't y' know.'

Literary intellectuals at one pole—at the other scientists, and as the most representative, the physical scientists. Between the two a gulf of mutual incomprehension—sometimes (particularly among the young) hostility and dislike, but most of all lack of understanding. They have a curious distorted image of each other. Their attitudes are so different that, even on the level of emotion, they can't find much common ground. Non-scientists tend to think of scientists as brash and boastful. They hear Mr. T. S. Eliot, who just for these illustrations we can take as an archetypal figure, saying about his attempts to revive verse-drama, that we can hope for very little, but that he would feel content if he and his co-workers could prepare the ground for a new Kyd or a new Greene. That is the tone, restricted and constrained, with which literary intellectuals are at home: it is the subdued voice of their culture. Then they hear a much louder voice, that of another archetypal figure, Rutherford, trumpeting: 'This is the heroic age of science! This is the Elizabethan age!' Many of us heard that, and a good many other statements beside which that was mild; and we weren't left in any doubt whom Rutherford was casting for the role of Shakespeare. What is hard for the literary intellectuals to understand, imaginatively or intellectually, is that he was absolutely right.

And compare 'this is the way the world ends, not with a bang but a whimper'—

incidentally, one of the least likely scientific prophecies ever made—compare that with Rutherford's famous repartee, 'Lucky fellow, Rutherford, always on the crest of the wave.' 'Well, I made the wave, didn't I?'

The non-scientists have a rooted impression that the scientists are shallowly optimistic, unaware of man's condition. On the other hand, the scientists believe that the literary intellectuals are totally lacking in foresight, peculiarly unconcerned with their brother men, in a deep sense anti-intellectual, anxious to restrict both art and thought to the existential moment. And so on. Anyone with a mild talent for invective could produce plenty of this kind of subterranean back-chat. On each side there is some of it which is not entirely baseless. It is all destructive. Much of it rests on misinterpretations which are dangerous. I should like to deal with two of the most profound of these now, one on each side.

First, about the scientists' optimism. This is an accusation which has been made so often that it has become a platitude. It has been made by some of the acutest non-scientific minds of the day. But it depends upon a confusion between the individual experience and the social experience, between the individual condition of man and his social condition. Most of the scientists I have known well have felt—just as deeply as the non-scientists I have known well—that the individual condition of each of us is tragic. Each of us is alone: sometimes we escape from solitariness, through love or affection or perhaps creative moments, but those triumphs of life are pools of light we make for ourselves while the edge of the road is black: each of us dies alone. Some scientists I have known have had faith in revealed religion. Perhaps with them the sense of the tragic condition is not so strong. I don't know. With most people of deep feeling, however high-spirited and happy they are, sometimes most with those who are happiest and most high-spirited, it seems to be right in the fibres, part of the weight of life. That is as true of the scientists I have known best as of anyone at all.

But nearly all of them—and this is where the colour of hope genuinely comes in—would see no reason why, just because the individual condition is tragic, so must the social condition be. Each of us is solitary: each of us dies alone: all right, that's a fate against which we can't struggle—but there is plenty in our condition which is not fate, and against which we are less than human unless we do struggle.

Most of our fellow human beings, for instance, are underfed and die before their time. In the crudest terms, *that* is the social condition. There is a moral trap which comes through the insight into man's loneliness: it tempts one to sit back, complacent in one's unique tragedy, and let the others go without a meal.

As a group, the scientists fall into that trap less than others. They are inclined to be impatient to see if something can be done: and inclined to think that it can be done, until it's proved otherwise. That is their real optimism, and it's an optimism that the rest of us badly need.

In reverse, the same spirit, tough and good and determined to fight it out at the side of their brother men, has made scientists regard the other culture's social attitudes as contemptible. That is too facile: some of them are, but they are a temporary phase and not to be taken as representative.

I remember being cross-examined by a scientist of distinction. 'Why do most writers take on social opinions which would have been thought distinctly uncivilised and démodé at the time of the Plantagenets? Wasn't that true of most of the famous twentieth-century writers? Yeats, Pound, Wyndham Lewis, nine out of ten of those who have dominated literary sensibility in our time—weren't they not only politically silly, but politically wicked? Didn't the influence of all they represent bring Auschwitz that much nearer?'

I thought at the time, and I still think, that the correct answer was not to defend the indefensible. It was no use saying that Yeats, according to friends whose judgment I trust, was a man of singular magnanimity of character, as well as a great poet. It was no use denying the facts, which are broadly true. The honest answer was that there is, in fact, a connection, which literary persons were culpably slow to see, between some kinds of early twentieth-century art and the most imbecile expressions of anti-social feeling. That was one reason, among many, why some of us turned our backs on the art and tried to hack out a new or different way for ourselves.

But though many of those writers dominated literary sensibility for a generation, that is no longer so, or at least to nothing like the same extent. Literature changes more slowly than science. It hasn't the same automatic corrective, and so its misguided periods are longer. But it is ill-considered of scientists to judge writers on the evidence of the period 1914–50.

✳   ✳   ✳

But what about the other side? They are impoverished too—perhaps more seriously, because they are vainer about it. They still like to pretend that the traditional culture is the whole of 'culture', as though the natural order didn't exist. As though the exploration of the natural order was of no interest either in its own value or its consequences. As though the scientific edifice of the physical world was not, in its intellectual depth, complexity and articulation, the most beautiful and wonderful collective work of the mind of man. Yet most non-scientists have no conception of that edifice at all. Even if they want to have it, they can't. It is rather as though, over an immense range of intellectual experience, a whole group was tone-deaf. Except that this tone-deafness doesn't come by nature, but by training, or rather the absence of training.

As with the tone-deaf, they don't know what they miss. They give a pitying chuckle at the news of scientists who have never read a major work of English literature. They dismiss them as ignorant specialists. Yet their own ignorance and their own specialisation is just as startling. A good many times I have been present at gatherings of people who, by the standards of the traditional culture, are thought highly educated and who have with considerable gusto been expressing their incredulity at the illiteracy of scientists. Once or twice I have been provoked and have asked the company how many of them could describe the Second Law of Thermodynamics. The response was cold: it was also negative. Yet I was asking something which is about the scientific equivalent of: *Have you read a work of Shakespeare's?*

I now believe that if I had asked an even simpler question—such as, What do you mean by mass, or acceleration, which is the scientific equivalent of saying, *Can you read?*—not more than one in ten of the highly educated would have felt that I was speaking the same language. So the great edifice of modern physics goes up, and the majority of the cleverest people in the western world have about as much insight into it as their neolithic ancestors would have had.

Just one more of those questions, that my non-scientific friends regard as being in the worst of taste. Cambridge is a university where scientists and non-scientists meet every night at dinner. About two years ago, one of the most astonishing experiments in the whole history of science was brought off. I don't mean the sputnik—that was admirable for quite different reasons, as a feat of organisation and a triumphant use of existing knowledge. No, I mean the experiment at Columbia by Yang and Lee. It is an experiment of the greatest beauty and originality, but the result is so startling that one forgets how beautiful the experiment is. It makes us think again about some of the fundamentals of the physical world. Intuition, common sense—they are neatly stood on their heads. The result is usually known as the contradiction of the parity. If there were any serious communication between the two cultures, this experiment would have been talked about at every High Table in Cambridge. Was it? I wasn't here: but I should like to ask the question.

There seems then to be no place where the cultures meet. I am not going to waste time saying that this is a pity. It is much worse than that. Soon I shall come to some practical consequences. But at the heart of thought and creation we are letting some of our best chances go by default. The clashing point of two subjects, two disciplines, two cultures—of two galaxies, so far as that goes—ought to produce creative chances. In the history of mental activity that has been where some of the break-throughs came. The chances are there now. But they are there, as it were, in a vacuum, because those in the two cultures can't talk to each other. It is bizarre how very little of twentieth-century science has been assimilated into twentieth-century art. Now and then one used to find poets conscientiously using scientific expressions, and getting them wrong—there was a time when 'refraction' kept cropping up in verse in a mystifying fashion, and when 'polarised light' was used as though writers were under the illusion that it was a specially admirable kind of light.

Of course, that isn't the way that science could be any good to art. It has got to be assimilated along with, and as part and parcel of, the whole of our mental experience, and used as naturally as the rest.

I said earlier that this cultural divide is not just an English phenomenon: it exists all over the western world. But it probably seems at its sharpest in England, for two reasons. One is our fanatical belief in educational specialisation, which is much more deeply ingrained in us than in any country in the world, west or east. The other is our tendency to let our social forms crystallise. This tendency appears to get stronger, not weaker, the more we iron out economic inequalities: and this is specially true in education. It means that once anything like a cultural divide gets established, all the social forces operate to make it not less rigid, but more so.

The two cultures were already dangerously separate sixty years ago; but a prime minister like Lord Salisbury could have his own laboratory at Hatfield, and Arthur Balfour had a somewhat more than amateur interest in natural science. John Anderson did some research in organic chemistry in Würzburg before passing first into the Civil Service, and incidentally took a spread of subjects which is now impossible. None of that degree of interchange at the top of the Establishment is likely, or indeed thinkable, now.

In fact, the separation between the scientists and non-scientists is much less bridgeable among the young than it was even thirty years ago. Thirty years ago the cultures had long ceased to speak to each other: but at least they managed a kind of frozen smile across the gulf. Now the politeness has gone, and they just make faces. It is not only that the young scientists now feel that they are part of a culture on the rise while the other is in retreat. It is also, to be brutal, that the young scientists know that with an indifferent degree they'll get a comfortable job, while their contemporaries and counterparts in English or History will be lucky to earn 60 per cent as much. No young scientist of any talent would feel that he isn't wanted or that his work is ridiculous, as did the hero of *Lucky Jim*, and in fact, some of the disgruntlement of Amis and his associates is the disgruntlement of the under-employed arts graduate.

There is only one way out of all this: it is, of course, by rethinking our education.

THE (LADY) PLOWDEN REPORT (1967)   From Great Britain, Report of the
Central Advisory Council, *Children and Their Primary Schools*, vol.1, pp.13–24, 50–65.

Heredity and Environment

Biologists are now much clearer than they were 30 years ago about the manner in which hereditary and environmental factors interact to produce a characteristic, be that characteristic stature or the score in an intelligence test. What is inherited are the genes. Except in very special instances, such as the blood groups and a few diseases, the chemical substance that any given gene causes to be produced is not directly related to any characteristic of a child or an adult. All characteristics have a history of continuous developmental interactions, first of gene products with other gene products, then of more complex molecules with other molecules, then of cells with cells, of tissues with the environment of the mother's uterus, and finally of a whole complex organism with an equally complex environment during the whole of growth after birth. It is now believed that all characteristics are developed in this way; none is inherited. And none can develop without the necessary genetic endowment to provide the basis, a basis as essential for characteristics which are learned as for those which are apparently not learned. The effect of this new biological outlook is of particular importance when we come to consider the question of changes in measured intelligence.

From an educational point of view the characteristics which have most importance such as intelligence are those which vary in degree in a population rather than being simply present or absent. Stature is a similar example related to physical characteristics. One cannot meaningfully talk of genes for tallness nor of genes for high intelligence. What we can say about such characteristics is that in a given population, growing up under given environmental circumstances, x per cent of the variability in height or intelligence can be attributed to inherited factors (the genotype), y per cent to environmental ones, and z per cent to genotype-environment interaction. The point is that hereditability is not a quantity that belongs to a characteristic but to a population in its environment. Accordingly it varies with the population and the environment. The more uniform the environment, the greater the proportion of variability due to genotype. In England, for example, the differences in height between adults are largely due to hereditary causes, for most children have had enough to eat. But in many underdeveloped countries, where starvation and disease are rife, more of the adult variation will be environmental in origin and a smaller proportion genetic.

The interaction of genes and environment may not be additive; for example, bettering the nutrition by a given amount may not produce a ten per cent increase in height in each person in a population irrespective of his genetic constitution. There may be genotype-environment interaction. Some people may have a rise of 12 per cent, others of eight per cent, depending on whether they carry genes making them react favourably to this new environmental circumstance. A particular environment, in other words, may be highly suitable for a child with certain genes, but highly unsuitable for a child with others. We do not know if such interactions occur in the genesis, for example, of the variations in measured intelligence in our population. If they do, and in principle this seems likely, it would follow that giving everybody the maximum educational opportunity may mean creating individual educational environments for different children. In the same way deprivation would not necessarily mean the same thing for one child as for another.

Genetic factors operate throughout the whole period of growth. Not all genes are active at birth; some only begin to exert their influence after a period of time. Probably this phased effect accounts for the fact that, physically, and perhaps in other respects, children resemble their parents increasingly as they grow older. Some environmental factors, too, may produce little apparent effect when they are most obviously operative, but a larger effect at some later time. This known as the 'sleeper' effect.

*　　*　　*

Educational Priority Areas

In a neighbourhood where the jobs people do and the status they hold owe little to their education it is natural for children as they grow older to regard school as a brief prelude to work rather than an avenue to future opportunities. Some of these neighbourhoods have for generations been starved of new schools, new houses and new investment of every kind. Everyone knows this; but for year after year priority has been given to the new towns and new suburbs, because if new schools do not keep pace with the new houses some children will be unable to go to school at all. The continually rising proportion of children staying on at school beyond the minimum age has led some authorities to build secondary schools and postpone the rebuilding of older primary schools. Not surprisingly, many teachers are unwilling to work in a neighbourhood where the schools are old, where housing of the sort they want is unobtainable, and where education does not attain the standards they expect for their own children. From some neighbourhoods, urban and rural, there has been a continuing outflow of the more successful young people. The loss of their enterprise and skill makes things worse for those left behind. Thus the vicious circle may turn from generation to generation and the schools play a central part in the process, both causing and suffering cumulative deprivation.

We have ourselves seen schools caught in such vicious circles and read accounts of many more. They are quite untypical of schools in the rest of the country. We noted the grim approaches; incessant traffic noise in narrow streets; parked vehicles hemming in the pavement; rubbish dumps on waste land nearby; the absence of green playing spaces on or near the school sites; tiny play grounds; gaunt looking buildings; often poor decorative conditions inside; narrow passages; dark rooms; unheated and cramped cloakrooms; unroofed outside lavatories; tiny staff rooms; inadequate storage space with consequent restriction on teaching materials and therefore methods; inadequate space for movement and P.E.; meals in classrooms; art on desks; music only to the discomfort of others in an echoing building; non-soundproof partitions between classes; lack of smaller rooms for group work; lack of spare room for tuition of small groups; insufficient display space; attractive books kept unseen in cupboards for lack of space to lay them out; no privacy for parents waiting to see the head; sometimes the head and his secretary sharing the same room; and, sometimes all around, the ingrained grime of generations.

We heard from local education authorities of growing difficulty in replacing heads with successors of similar calibre. It is becoming particularly hard to find good heads of infant or deputy heads of junior schools. We are not surprised to hear of the rapid turnover of staff, of vacancies sometimes unfilled or filled with a succession of temporary and supply teachers of one kind or another. Probationary teachers are trained by heads to meet the needs of their schools but then pass on to others where strains are not so great. Many teachers able to do a decent job in a ordinary school are defeated by these conditions. Some become dispirited by long journeys to decaying buildings to see each morning children among whom some seem to have learned only how not to learn. Heads rely on the faithful, devoted and hard working regulars. There may be one or two in any school, or they may be as many as half the staff, who have so much to do in keeping the school running that they are sometimes too tired even to enjoy their own holidays.

We saw admission registers whose pages of new names with so many rapid crossings out told their own story of a migratory population. In one school 111 out of 150 pupils were recent newcomers. We heard heads explain, as they looked down the lines, that many of those who had gone were good pupils, while a high proportion of those who had been long in the school came from crowded, down-at-heel homes.

What these deprived areas need most are perfectly normal, good primary schools alive with experience from which children of all kinds can benefit. . . . But, . . . there are special and additional demands on teachers who work in deprived areas with deprived children. They meet special challenges. Teachers must be constantly aware that ideas, values and relationships within the school may conflict with those of the home, and that the world assumed by teachers and school books may be unreal to the children. There will have to be constant communication between parents and the schools if the aims of the schools are to be fully understood. The child from a really impoverished background may well have had a normal, satisfactory emotional life. What he often lacks is the opportunity to develop intellectual interests. This shows in his poor command of language. It is not, however, with vocabulary that teaching can begin. The primary school must first supply experiences and establish relationships which enable children to discriminate, to reason and to express themselves. Placing such children in the right stance for further learning is a very skilled operation. But those who have done remedial work will be aware of the astonishing rapidity of the progress which can be achieved, particularly in extending vocabulary, once children's curiosity is released. The thrust to learn seems to be latent in every child, at least within a very wide range of normality. But however good the opportunities, some children may not be able to take advantage of them. Failure may have taken away from them their urge to learn.

A teacher cannot and should not give the deep personal love that each child needs from his parents. There are ways he can help:–

(a) He can relieve children of responsibility without dominating them in a way which prevents them from developing independence. Deprived children may have been forced into premature responsibility. They are often given the care of younger children and are free to roam, to go to bed or to stay up, to eat when and where they can. This produces what is often a spurious maturity. Confidence can be encouraged by tasks which are fully within their capacity. A measure of irresponsibility has to be allowed for: it will pretty certainly come later, and in a less acceptable form, if not permitted at the proper time.

(b) A teacher can do much by listening and trying to understand the context of the questions the children ask. It will be much easier if he knows the child's family and the neighbourhood surrounding his home.

(c) Children in deprived neighbourhoods are often backward. There is a risk that an inexperienced teacher will think there is not time for anything but the three Rs if the child is not to be handicapped throughout his life. This is quite wrong. These children need time for play and imaginative and expressive work and may suffer later if they do not get it at school.

(d) Teachers need to use books which make sense to the children they teach. They will often have to search hard for material which is suitable for downtown children.

(e) Record keeping is especially necessary for teachers in schools in deprived neighbourhoods. There is so much coming and going by families that a child's progress may depend very much on the amount and quality of information that can be sent with him from school to school . . .

DESCRIPTION OF THE NEW BRITISH PRIMARY SCHOOL (1967)   From

John Blackie, *Inside the Primary School* (London, 1967), pp. 46–50.

The curriculum, though legally under the control of the Local Education Authority, is in fact the responsibility of the Head Teacher. We must now look a little more closely at it. Many foreign visitors find it almost incredible that we should leave this essential matter to personal taste. In the Iron Curtain countries, of course, the curriculum and the text-book are exactly prescribed and virtually no deviation from either allowed. But in the countries of the west too, including the U.S.A., there is far more central or state control over the choice of subjects and the syllabus to be followed than in England, and to some it appears that we are almost in a state of anarchy. The freedom, and the resultant responsibility are real, but they are not quite as unlimited as might first appear.

The basic legal control is simply Clause 36 of the Education Act of 1944, which states: "It shall be the duty of the parent of every child of compulsory school age to cause him to receive efficient full-time education suitable to his age, ability and aptitude. . . ." The matter has never come into the courts, but it must be presumed that if a head teacher was so eccentric as to omit for instance any trace of mathematics in his syllabus, he or the L.E.A. could be prosecuted for preventing the parents of the children from carrying out their obligations. This possibility is, of course, a piece of pure fantasy. An effective control until recently has perhaps been the II+ examination, which exercised a normalising influence on the primary school curriculum. This control will disappear as comprehensive secondary education increases, though the demands, supposed or expressed, of the secondary schools will continue to have some influence in the primary schools. Probably the strongest control of all is simply that of custom. The curriculum of the old elementary school was originally. . .what was considered necessary and advisable for the children of

IDEAS
FROM ABROAD

2095

the working class. Gradually it was widened, but between 1900 and 1960 it scarcely altered at all. Religious instruction, arithmetic, English, history, geography, nature study, art, music, craft (boys), needlework (girls), physical education. It was rare to find a school in those sixty years which omitted any of these or included anything else. If the same sort of classification is used the curriculum of a modern primary school would include only one additional subject—a modern language—and that would only be true of one in five. Arithmetic would be called Mathematics, Nature Study would be called Science and there would not be a sharp division between Craft for boys and Craft for girls. There would be many internal differences and the whole curriculum would be looked at very differently but the actual *list of subjects* would, a modern language apart, be recognisably the same. There would be little disagreement that these subjects in some form or other should form part of a good general education. The curriculum in that sense is likely to remain much the same for as long as can be imagined.

In the following chapters I shall describe and discuss the curriculum under headings which group some of the traditional subjects together, but which in the main follow them. This is the most convenient way of dealing with them. But a comparison between the time-table that was typical of the old pre-1944 elementary school and that which is found in a modern primary school, will show that the curriculum is now something very different from what it used to be.

The old time-table was divided into compartments which showed exactly what was to be done by each class at every moment of the day. After 30 minutes of religious instruction there followed, almost invariably, 45 or even 50 minutes of arithmetic. English occupied most of the rest of the morning. This was often sub-divided into spelling, grammar, recitation, speech training, reading, composition and dictation, each with its allotted time. The other subjects were treated in the same way. In practice there was often rather more flexibility than the time-table suggested and the Head Teacher always had powers to vary or change it. It had to be signed by H.M.I. This was intended to show only that it complied with the law covering religious instruction (i.e. that this should be either at the beginning or end of a session, so that children who were withdrawn on conscientious grounds could be more conveniently provided for). Unfortunately the signature was sometimes taken as indicating inspectorial approval for the whole time-table and even as an obstacle to changes made without H.M.I.'s approval. For this reason many inspectors in the 1930s refused to sign time-tables even though it was part of their duties.

It was the infants' schools which began the breakaway from the rigid time-table. It became increasingly clear to teachers that such a time-table was totally unsuited to all that was known about the nature of young children and the way in which they learned. But the change came rather slowly. In many country schools the infants were taught by untrained teachers who were sometimes timid about innovations and preferred definite guiding-lines. When the change was made it often consisted only of rather more general headings, still blocked out in precise periods of time— number, reading, activities, written work, oral work, craft and so on. In the junior schools or upper classes of full-range primary schools the change came even more slowly. No head teacher of such a school could entirely ignore the II + examination and many felt themselves obliged to let it influence the work of the school sometimes to a very marked degree. It was all very well, perhaps, to have free time-tables in the infant's schools but time was short and once the children were seven they must 'get down to it'. So the argument ran and 'getting down to it' meant a clearly mapped-out day. Many parents, perhaps the majority, agreed with this and sometimes head teachers with more progressive ideas met with grumblings and complaints from that quarter.

Quite apart from these objections to a flexible time-table, there were some plain practical difficulties. In all but the smaller schools there would probably be some specialisation. A good musician would naturally and properly take the music of more than his own class. Needlework would be taught by a woman and mainly only to girls. The hall, if there was one, would have to be used for physical education at allotted times. If the children went outside for anything, to a swimming bath or to a distant playing field, this would have to be exactly time-tabled. These difficulties obviously still apply and even in the most permissive schools nowadays there are fixed points on the time-table at various times in the day. Apart from these, however, it is becoming increasingly common for the rest of the day to be left entirely to the individual teacher's discretion, to decide when any particular subject is to be studied and how much time is to be spent on it.

How does this work out in practice? Is there not a danger that some things will be neglected and others over-stressed, perhaps according to the teacher's preferences or whims? How can continuity and cohesion be assured? These questions will undoubtedly occur to most readers and, when it is added that the children are likely to be working individually and, for some of the time, be doing quite different things from each other, there may be doubts aroused as to whether the whole thing is not something near the chaos that many foreign visitors suspect.

I have already said. . .that the new approach makes heavier and not lighter demands upon the skill of the teacher. It will be obvious that the flexible time-table is also a great test of his skill and that a careful record has to be kept of what each child does so as to ensure that over a period, say of a term, there is a proper balance between subjects and appropriate progress within subjects. Part of this record will consist of the child's own work. If each child has a folder in which all his written work, in whatever subject, is kept, it will be possible to see quite rapidly whether both these requirements are being met. The teacher will also maintain his own records and these two together will constitute a much more informative and useful account of work done than the old type of teacher's record which was simply a statement of lessons given and set.

**EUROPEAN
VIEWS
OF
AMERICAN
EDUCATION**

SIR MICHAEL SADLER ON AMERICAN EDUCATION (1903)   From

"Impressions of American Education," *Educational Review,* vol. XXV, pp. 217–25.

At rare intervals in the history of a nation there comes a great outburst of physical and intellectual energy which, with overmastering power, carries forward the masses of the people, together with its leaders, in an exhilarating rush of common effort. In the United States of America such a movement is in progress to-day. It reveals its force at three points—the American workshop, the American office, and the American school. Of the tremendous power of the movement no one who has witnessed it can doubt. But whither it will lead he would be a rash man who would dare to prophesy. These great national movements often turn in new and unlooked-for directions with an accumulated force which breaks old bounds and tears entrance into new channels. Those who seem to lead the movement believe that they can guide it toward some chosen goal. But they often find themselves swept along in the flood toward some unexpected issue, thru gaps in ancient barriers which looked immovable, but prove to have been sapped and weakened by slow and hidden changes in national character and in national belief.

The great movement now going forward in American education is but one aspect of the national movement which is stirring to its depth the whole of American life. Hence its profound significance, not only to Americans, but to the Old World, and not least to us who, geographically, politically, and spiritually, are, as it were, the link between the Old World and the New.

It is appropriate for us, here in Glasgow, to consider the meaning of these things. The fame of Glasgow is significant of sea power and of trading enterprise, and in regard to both of these the United States seem destined to play a great part in the world's history.

And it is fitting in a congress of Scottish teachers to consider what American schools and universities are seeking to accomplish for American life, because in the great movement now going forward for the deepening and strengthening of American education, men of Scottish or Scotch-Irish ancestry are bearing a prominent and influential part. These men are proud to trace back their descent to the Covenanters or to those Scottish Presbyterians who, settled in Ulster in the earlier part of the seventeenth century, found themselves driven to emigrate two generations afterward by the hostility of the English Parliament toward the flourishing growth of Irish manufactures.

Before I plunge into the details of my subject, I will venture to say one word as to the point of view from which to approach it. A great and famous Scotch philosopher, once, I believe an unsuccessful candidate for a chair in this University, used to say that the power of seeing the favorable rather than the unfavorable side of things is a turn of mind which is worth as much as being born to an estate of ten thousand a year. The Americans have this turn of mind. They prefer to talk about the bright side. They leave the dark side to one's natural powers of observation and of inference. No one can form a shrewd judgment on American education who merely sees what he is bid to see, and who refrains from employing his critical faculty as well as his organ of admiration. The comparative study of national systems of education is a delicate enterprise. The path to truth lies between Scylla and Charybdis; between harsh, censorious judgments of other people's failings and too ready belief in the superior merits of other people's achievements. But the first requisite for the intelligent study of a foreign system of education is sympathy. We must do as we would be done by. We must endeavor to enter, to the best of our power, into the spirit of patriotism and self-sacrifice which always animates any living and progressive system of national education. Imitate it in any mechanical or literal way we cannot: profit by it we can, but in order to profit we first must sympathize. Look at the favorable side first; then the defects will reveal themselves in due course and in due proportion. Then, and not till then, the way is open to a measured judgment. But it is both good sense and good manners to think first and chiefly of the favorable side of a foreign system to which we are admitted with graceful hospitality and in the spirit of professional comradeship. And I am inclined to think that if we, as a nation, take to heart the favorable side of American education, we shall find it worth a good deal more to us than ten thousand a year.

1. The first thing to which I would draw your attention is the fact that America—progressive America—heartily believes in education. That is the heart of the whole matter. America believes in education. The American school is radiant with a belief in its mission, and it works among people who believe in the reality of its influence, in the necessity for its labors, and in the grandeur of its task. It is the old story. The essential thing is faith. Faith can move mountains of inertia, and ignorance, and class selfishness. This glowing faith in the power of education is the saving grace of modern American life. All witnesses agree on the one point that in education all intelligent Americans heartily and unfeignedly believe. I have even heard it said that they don't really believe in anything else.

The words of Washington in his Farewell Address fell on fruitful ground. "Promote, as an object of primary importance, institutions for the general diffusion of knowledge. In proportion as the structure of a Government gives force to public opinion, it is essential that public opinion should be enlightened." That is one of the first principles of American policy. The Monroe doctrine is the second. Round the frieze of the Public Library of Boston, Mass., there are carved in plain letters fifteen words which sum up this central doctrine of American democracy: "The Commonwealth requires the education of the people as the safeguard of order and liberty."

Thus regarded, education becomes at once a national thing. Its chief power in America is to make Americans. Stand at the Battery in New York and watch the great liners coming up the Narrows from the Old World. That is the gate of America, and thru it pass the poor immigrants of varied nationality, bringing with them a strange medley of discordant ideals, and in some cases not a little anti-social distrust of law and government. These are the raw materials of American democracy. The school is the mill which grinds up these diverse materials into one consistence. Once let that machinery stand idle or fall into disrepair, and the civic unity of America is imperiled.

But national unity is a moral thing. The means of conserving it must therefore make use of moral, as well as of purely intellectual, influences. Patriotism, tho protected by identity of economic interest, has its deepest roots in other than self-regarding instincts. And to those hidden sources of national strength any education, worthy to be called national, makes confident appeal. This is the note of all that is best in the new educational movement in America. It seeks to touch the springs of character. Its ideal is not a selfish and exclusive culture, but scholarship engaged in social service. "It is not scholarship alone," if I may recall those stirring words of Dr. Chalmers, "it is not scholarship alone that tells on the great masses of society, but scholarship impregnated with religion."

2. Thus America believes in education because education is making America.

But the essence of a democratic commonwealth lies in the individuality of its citizenship. This eager belief in individuality is the second characteristic of American education to which I would invite your attention to-day. American firms advertise for "a live man." The American primary school is determined to produce a live child. For some tastes it succeeds only too well, but that is another story. For the work of the earliest grades of American education, the harshest critic would give little else than praise. In the first four years of school life the American child is stimulated to self-expression and self-realization by teachers skillful in their art, and unwearied in their practice of it. The brushwork, the modeling, the simple compositions, the beginnings of scientific education, which distinguish this stage of American education are often excellent. Much is done to produce alertness of mind and body and to cultivate the faculty and habit of self-expression. What is too often lacking, as a background to all this stimulation, is wise restraint and discipline at home. Many American parents, in their desire to give their children a good time, seem to shrink from exercising parental authority in matters in which home and school should work together, and in which the school may fairly claim the help of the home. That, however, is an evil not wholly confined to the western hemisphere.

The atmosphere of the American school and college is an atmosphere of equality and of independence. Energy and self-confidence thrive in it. Whatever else is sacrificed, the individual is encouraged to express himself and to realize his native capacity as best he may. This readiness to encourage individuality is a characteristic of American life. It has profoundly changed the organization of their universities thru the development of what was called "elective studies." The same lesson is working in their secondary schools. And we can see the same principle at work in American industry, where great pains are taken to encourage the individual workmen to make suggestions for the improvement of processes of manufacture or distribution, and where there is almost a passion for hearing new ideas and for experimenting with new appliances.

But thoughtful Americans perceive that to stimulate individuality and self-expression is only half the work of a good school. The other half is discipline. Is there not high authority for the belief that the true beginning of wisdom is desire of discipline? But just as the yearning for individuality implies a philosophical ideal in which the individual plays a determining part, so does the belief in discipline postulate a social ideal—a striving after some ordered organization of society—in which the stress is laid on duties rather than on rights. And here it is that American thinking has been weak, and American life is at present somewhat thin and poor. In old days the strength of American character lay in the discipline of Puritan society. But the bonds of that society burst under the pressure of modern life, and then there rushed out a wonderful energy, which had been long confined within the restraints of the older discipline. This energy, this powerful individuality, carried the descendants of the old Puritan stock thru the chief part of their new task of subduing to settlement and to the needs of agriculture and industry the northern part of the United States as far as the Pacific by means of the adventurous courage of pioneers and the resources of applied science. But this stage is nearly accomplished. What is needed next is a new social discipline, a new social ideal, dominating the lives and inspiring the devotion of the common people. But this is the very point at which chaos reigns. The problem of problems in American education is to foresee the social organization for which the children must be prepared. No American writer discusses this question with a clearer sense of its urgency than Dr. John Dewey, of the University of Chicago. "We must make," he says, in his *School and Society*, "each one of our schools an embryonic community life, active in the types of occupations that reflect the life of the larger society, and permeated thruout with the spirit of art, history, and science. When the school introduces and trains each child of society into membership with such a little community, saturating him with the spirit of service, and providing him with the instruments of effective self-direction, we shall have the deepest and best guarantee of a larger society which is worthy, lovely, and harmonious." Yes; but how shall we set to work to get some clearer notion of what the duties, the relationships, and the extent of these future adult communities are going to be? And what, in preparation for such adult duties, is to be the task of the home as compared with that of the school? Dr. Dewey indicates the drift of the need—a need not confined to America—but he throws little light on the future evolution of American society.

3. Thus the American believes in education, because education equips individuals for the tasks of American citizenship. But those tasks are changing, because applied science has changed some of the fundamental conditions on which rested the old order of society and the balance of power between the great nations of the earth. Applied science, too, has drawn into inevitably closer political relationship the nations of the Old World and the New. The American flag in the Philippines is the symbol of the change. Education therefore must change together with the change in the world conditions, because it is with the new conditions that education must train the rising generation to cope. This conviction that great changes are impending in the subject-matter of education is the third great characteristic of American educational thought to which I would call your attention to-day. In every type of school strenuous American teachers are endeavoring to tear out the non essentials. "Don't be cumbered up with a lot of unnecessary luggage in education," the American teacher pleads, "cut down your transport; don't make your pupils carry an ounce of unnecessary weight; confine yourself to the essentials; revise all your old traditions; lop away all superfluities. There is so much that a man ought to know that we must reduce the cost of the production of knowledge to the lowest possible figure by employing labor-saving appliances in education, and by avoiding to the utmost the waste of precious time."

THE MOSELY COMMISSION VIEWS AMERICAN SCHOOLS (1903)   From

Alfred Mosely, "A British View of American Schools," *The World's Work*, vol. VII, pp. 4484–87.

Together with a commission of thirty English educational experts, I have just completed an investigation of American schools. The most striking facts I have gathered are these:

1. That the people of the United States spend a marvelous amount of money on their public schools, endowing education more lavishly than any other people in the world.

2. They do not spend enough. The salaries to teachers are not sufficient for the service the country desires and should have.

Our tour of investigation began in New York in October of last year. The previous autumn a commission of British trade-union representatives made a tour of the industrial centres of the United States on my invitation to study industrial conditions—a trip the results of which have already been published in this magazine. The investigations by this industrial commission and the recent educational commission were part of a single plan formed a number of years ago.

While in business in South Africa I had unusual opportunities to study the work of English and American engineers. The English engineers were much inferior. They slavishly followed conventional principles. They worked by rule of thumb. They lacked initiative. They showed inability in a sudden emergency to grasp the situation confronting them, to put the right machinery to work, to carry the task in hand in a practical way to completion. Often they attacked engineering problems with no more expert sureness and efficiency than any intelligent business man might have exhibited. The Americans, on the other hand, were alert and up to date, instantly equal to any occasion that might arise. In emergencies they knew at once what to do and what kind of machinery to use; and whenever they attacked a problem, after swiftly arguing the pros and cons they carried the matter through in the straightest way with professional certitude of method. The English engineers had been poorly trained; the American engineers well trained. American business men whom I met were quite as alert as the engineers. A visit to the United States convinced me that the secret of this national efficiency lay in the American schools.

*　　*　　*

My own strongest impression was of the amount of money spent on education. East and West it has become quite the fashion for millionaires to make large gifts to colleges, and in every section I visited I found the people lavishing money on their schools. And the expenditure is appreciated. If the buildings and the equipment are on a much more generous scale than in England, there is greater enthusiasm here also. The very atmosphere of American schoolrooms breathes progress. American teachers are more enthusiatic than English teachers; American pupils have a greater thirst for knowledge than English pupils; and there is a closer bond of sympathy here than in England between pupil and teacher.

In essence, the American people have realized better than European the value of education. They have learned to consider it their primary duty to train themselves for the struggle that modern development entails on the individual. They seem to realize, as the English have not begun to realize, that no boy—and no girl, for that matter—can do without such training.

One especially notable manifestation of enthusiasm I found in New York, Boston, and other large cities. On the East Side in New York and at the North End in Boston the schools in the poorer districts are kept open at night to give the children of the crowded tenements a clean and comfortable place to study their morrow's lessons, with some one to help them on difficult points. The children resort to these evening studyrooms in surprising numbers, and the teachers help them patiently and encouragingly.

Manual training is a very important feature in all the schools of the principal cities for both boys and girls. In England some few schools, laying special stress on the subject, teach manual training. Here in the United States the study is general. And my inquiries serve to show that it helps in the pupil's general development; it offers a change from the other work and it brings out individuality. Serving a need of the United States by turning boys with a mechanical turn of mind to the technical schools, it also develops a practical taste among all the children for the mechanical side of life.

As a whole, the Middle West is more intense in matters of education than the other parts of the country. The schools of the Middle West are newer than the Eastern schools and more modern, because they have no traditions to get rid of. There is an even greater thirst for knowledge there than elsewhere, and money is spent to advantage. The schools of Indianapolis are among the best in the country.

I was much struck with the many colleges for the training of teachers. Both East and West are numerous normal schools and such institutions as the Teachers' College at Columbia University; and in the West especially a large proportion of the women graduates of the State universities enter the teaching profession. This training system assures an endless flow of the best class of teachers. In England the proportion of college-bred women teachers is far lower than in the United States, and, on the whole, the grade of teaching by women is lower. But England is considerably better off in its force of men teachers. My severest criticism of the American school system would be that the teaching force lacks men. Few men in the United States go into school-teaching, and these are not the best. The profession in England attracts a distinctly more capable class.

The trouble lies in the salaries. In many cases the actual money pay of teachers is higher here than in England, but reckoning the difference in the standard of living, especially in those articles that are above necessities, both men and women are paid more there than here. Thus men are attracted to teaching in England, whereas in the United States they find better opportunities in other callings. A larger proportion of men would greatly improve the American teaching force, but there can be no such improvement until American communities match the generosity they exhibit in school equipment with generosity in allotting salaries. Nor are the salaries of the women teachers adequate. The people of the United States have an excellent school system because they spend much money on it; they could have a better system by paying more.

The school system I am referring to is, of course, the public-school system. I am not in favor of private schools conducted for individual profit, of which there are more in England than here, because such schools are likely to be conducted for profit rather than for efficiency. Here all classes go to the public schools, with no harmful results, as far as I can learn, and with many benefits. The poorer boy or girl gets some refinement from the more fortunate children; the more fortunate children are in no way harmed. With no distinctions all classes side by side seek the same advantages. And these are many.

In England the average boy of the poorer class goes to work at an early age after a merely elementary education, entering the trade of his father or a trade his father has chosen for him—often independently of the boy's fitness for it. Here the wonderful opportunities for the masses to go on into higher and higher schools and colleges, securing their education free or practically free, render a boy immeasurably better able to choose a calling for which he is fitted. The manual training, too, discovers latent aptitudes. It is safe to say that an American boy has every opportunity to enter any vocation. In no State can any boy say that he cannot secure all the education he wishes.

The girls, too, have better opportunities here than at home. More of them advance into the higher fields of education. The result is that as a whole American girls are distinctly better educated that English girls—not merely because their parents wish it, but because they have, on their own part, greater appreciation of education and a greater desire for it.

If American teaching fails in any respect, it is in the matter of inculcating the power of correct and accurate English speech. Again and again I heard children in the public schools give ungrammatical answers quite unchecked. The teachers seemed content to receive correct answers to questions in geography or history instead of being dissatisfied until the correct answer had been given in correct language. This was the one serious defect I found in the public schools. The buildings were better in New York and Boston and Chicago than in London; the sanitation and ventilation were better; and I found highly commendable facilities offered in the higher schools for the pupils to purchase healthful food at low prices during the school recesses. The seats and desks are better. Greater attention is devoted to providing such of these as have been scientifically found best fitted for health and comfort. But the speech of the pupil is often bad.

There is, moreover, too little attention paid, in my opinion, to athletics. In England the taste for athletics is carried to extremes. A schoolmaster is not chosen, as here, solely on his academic qualifications: he is asked what his record has been in 'varsity cricket or football, and whether he has taken his "blue." He is expected then to foster the athletic tendencies of his boys. All the boys take part in one sport or another. Here, in the high schools and colleges, small teams and crews of picked youths monopolize the athletics; the other students merely look on. A wider athletic activity would be better.

The most interesting sights we saw on our tour were in the schools of the great cities, especially New York and Chicago, in which the newly arrived immigrant children were receiving their first lessons in Americanism. It was wonderful to see the raw peasant lad from Russia or Germany in a few months after landing sitting in an American school and singing "My Country, 'Tis of Thee." We saw hundreds of these who in a marvelously short time had caught the American spirit and who were daily saluting the flag, considering themselves part and parcel of the American nation. The teachers showed immense enthusiasm in teaching these little atoms of humanity, and the musical marchings in and out of school, and flag salutes, and the songs they taught the children were decidedly effective devices to engender discipline and patriotism. The United States is handling the immigration problem so successfully by assimilating the second generation of immigrants in the public schools that the American people may well relieve themselves of any fear on the score of excessive inpourings of untrained foreigners. It is an achievement the United States has every reason to be proud of.

Whether it is advisable or possible to adopt in Great Britain any parts of this or other features of American education, the delegates will declare with some authority in their reports next spring. As a layman with no claim to expert educational knowledge, I should say that the American excellences are well worthy of being grafted on the present English systems. After all, we must judge by results. The public education of the United States has had a large part in placing the country in the first rank in the world, industrially and commercially, at the same time maintaining a high ideal of civilization. There is some disposition on the part of English observers to attack American materialism. What materialism I have seen is largely ambition. There is no more of the "dollar-hunting" spirit in the United States than in other countries. The humanities, culture, refinement are not neglected in the schools and colleges. Research and scientific inquiry of the more advanced kinds are perhaps not so highly developed here as abroad, but there is no serious deficiency, and swift progress is being made. England might well learn lessons from the way in which the United States has worked out its problem.

In brief, I might sum up my impressions of American education by a single personal note. I have placed my two sons in the Hopkins Grammar School at New Haven to prepare for Yale.

AN ENGLISH HEADMISTRESS DESCRIBES A TYPICAL DAY IN AN AMERICAN HIGH SCHOOL (1908)   From Sara A. Burstall, *Impressions of American Education in 1908* (New York, 1909), pp. 60–65.

Let us try to imagine a typical day in an American high school and contrast it with what is so familiar to some of us in England. There is no assembly of the whole school, first thing in the morning every day, for prayers. The school law of many places does not allow of any religious observance, and as we have seen it would not always be possible to get the whole school into the hall or auditorium; but the principle of an assembly at least once a week for different parts of the school is, so far as we know, universal; some have it twice a week. In the McKinley High School, at St. Louis, numbering 1,500, they assemble first thing on Friday morning for one hour, and music is performed by visitors and pupils; speakers from the city or the university or visitors may deliver addresses, or lantern lectures may be given. In Philadelphia and New York the old custom of the reading of a passage from the Bible by the headmaster continues. A hymn of a simple character, such as one of Whittier's, is sung by the pupils, and at Philadelphia the Lord's Prayer is repeated. This represents, we think, the maximum of religious observance allowed anywhere in the public high school. The writer had the privilege of addressing several assemblies. The order and attention were perfect, and the marching out to music at the close is as fine as anything she had ever seen in England. The way in which the thousands of girls in the Philadelphia High School and the Wadleigh High School, in New York, marched out in under two minutes was wonderful. It was a triumph of discipline and organisation. The wide passages and skilful arrangement of seats make possible what would need much more care and time in the average English school hall.

The hours are from 8:30 to 1:30, or 9 to 2, or 9 to 2:30; roughly, a five hours' session with six or seven periods of forty, forty-five or fifty minutes each and a recess or break of twenty minutes to half an hour, rarely longer, for food and rest. One sees pupils hurrying the first thing in the morning in the familiar way, but they do not wear a school cap or a school-hat ribbon. This is quite contrary to American sentiment and would be resented. The girls do not change their shoes, but they wear rubbers in bad weather, which are slipped off quickly with the other outdoor garments, and the girls proceed at once to the room where they have the first recitation of the day. Here one comes at once upon a difference; the teacher keeps the room and the pupils move about. This has the advantage that the room is arranged for mathematics, for history, for classics, but it is of course impossible to combine this with the Form system. After three-quarters of an hour electric bells ring and the recitation or lesson ends. The pupils gather up their books and go on somewhere else, just as they please. We did not see any general marching about; everything is done quite freely, but quickly, neatly and in perfect order, and though conversation is allowed at the change of lessons, without any loitering and noise;

and this we must remember with 1,500 to 2,000 young people from fourteen to eighteen years of age and no teachers or prefects on duty up and down the stairs and on the corridors. One could only wonder how it is done, and wish all our young people were as quiet and orderly. There will generally be four lesson periods before recess. One may be spent in the gymnasium and one may be a study period, when a pupil is free to go to the library or to a large study hall and work alone. A teacher was always to be found seated on duty in these rooms, which would contain from 40 to 100 or more students—boys and girls. If a pupil has his or her own desk it will be in a study hall. The recitation-rooms often have chairs with a flap to rest a notebook, if they are used for literary subjects. Silence is, of course, observed in periods of private study. There seem to be in some cases the beginnings of a Form system—when a master or a mistress is specially responsible for pupils belonging to one study hall.

An experienced teacher cannot, of course, help noticing boys and girls and formulating opinions about them. The American schoolgirl is very much neater and carries herself much better than the average English one. She wears, in winter, a short, well-made woollen skirt and a white shirt waist or blouse, often daintily trimmed with embroidery. She is, of course, exquisitely shod. Short sleeves were in fashion in the winter of 1907–8, and the arms and hands were obviously very well cared for. A good deal of jewellery is worn, and apparently it would not be possible to make a rule against it, as is the custom in some schools in England. We are speaking, it is understood, of a public high school, attended by all sections of the community, not only by the well-to-do. A private school might forbid jewellery as do some. The hair is always beautifully dressed, and girls seem to put it up at the earliest possible age; the flowing tresses which often have to be tied back according to rule in England do not appear in general. The girls in the first year, at fourteen or fifteen, wear large ribbon-bows and plaits somewhat after the French style. Obviously the ensemble is very different from that one sees in England, where there is a very much greater variety of appearance, unless it should happen that all our girls are wearing gymnastic costume with coloured ribbons.

*   *   *

After lunch work goes on again, two more recitations, or possibly three, filling up the time till 1:30 P.M. or 2 P.M. or later. Then the girls and boys go home. There is no "seeing out" by teachers in any formal way. In a very large school one staircase will be used for ascending and one for descending. Organised games in the afternoon are rare; more study out of school is done than with us, and in the afternoon one sees pupils (students they are called) of the high schools working in public libraries. Teachers complain of the distractions of parties, theatres, bazaars, and amusements generally, which exhaust the strength of the girls in particular and take the energy and time that ought to be given to school work. The boys are affected also.

The good discipline of American schools is always noticed by English observers; the most remarkable thing about it is that it seems to come of itself. It is not maintained by artificial sanctions. Corporal punishment, the inalienable right of the English public school boy, is all but obsolete. There appear to be no small penalties, bad marks, impositions or the like. Detention is rare, and, if it does happen, seems to be unsystematised. As far as one could understand, their school discipline depends on two natural sanctions, the spirit of the nation and the teacher's personal force. When teachers do not possess this, even in good schools the discipline goes to pieces. With members of the other sex present, girls or boys, there is not the same positive disorder in the classroom we should get in such a case, but there is considerable slackness and inattention. A teacher who has not this personal force has before long to leave. There is, however, with difficult pupils, reference to the headmaster, or principal. Boys and girls are sent for, and talked to, and, if the worst comes to the worst, expelled. The personal force of the principal counts for a great deal, as with us, in the maintenance of discipline. While in some ways the work of a teacher is easier in America than here, in others it is more difficult. We have a traditional authority and, in a public school, a reasonable security of tenure and some dignity of status. A weak teacher can get along better here with the strong framework of customary order to help him or her. Apparently in America it would never do for a teacher to assume the official superiority of status, which our young people take as in the natural order of things, and to act as a master or mistress. The very words are unknown in their school terminology.

Social life in an American public high school among the pupils themselves takes forms somewhat different from ours. There is a good deal more of the "party" element, acting, dances, "socials," etc., managed by the boys and girls themselves. They have debating and literary societies, and school magazines managed by committees; glee and mandoline clubs are also very popular. The pupils of a particular year or "class" choose and wear a class pin. Philanthropic school societies for charitable work seem less common than with us. Games exist; in some schools the authorities say they are too popular and cause too much excitement. Girls are prohibited in some cases from playing matches with other schools; they would be so keen on winning that they would do no work. There is much less regular playing of games as a matter of course just as one eats or bathes; a Rhodes scholar says that in England brainworkers must play games to keep in health (what we say of India), but that in America it is not necessary. One difference in the American public high school is obvious: that teachers are not so much in things, games and societies as with us; the pupils run their societies themselves. A curious example of this separation is the existence of secret fraternities and sororities, imitated from the Greek-letter secret fraternities that are so important, so influential, and, it is said, so valuable an element in American college life. . . .

DENNIS BROGAN ON EDUCATION AND THE AMERICAN CHARACTER
(**1944**)   From Dennis Brogan, *The American Character* (New York, 1944), pp. 135–41.

The word "school" in America covers every type of educational institution. Being "at school" may mean being at a kindergarten or at Harvard. School, too, has kept much of its Greek meaning. It is a system of organization and training for leisure as well as work. And it has become more and more adjusted to its environment, undertaking to do more than it can (which is very American) and doing much more than it seems to do (which is also very American).

The social and political role of American education cannot be understood if it is thought of as being primarily a means of formal instruction. If it is so thought of, it will be overrated and underrated. It will be overrated because the figures of two million college students, of seven million high school students, will dazzle the visitor used to seeing opportunities for higher education doled out (except in Soviet Russia) on a combined class-and-intellectual basis. It will be underrated if, at any stage below the highest (that is, below the great universities), the academic standards are compared with those of a good English, French, or pre-Hitler German school. If these millions of boys and girls are to be judged by their academic accomplishments, they will be judged harshly. But they are not to be judged, for their schools are doing far more than instruct them: they are letting them instruct each other in how to live in America.

Of those millions, a large section will be the children of immigrants to whom English is still largely a foreign tongue. Of these millions, a very large proportion will be the children of migrants from different parts of the United States. Others will be the children of rural-bred parents, forced to adjust themselves to the new urban world. They have to learn a common language, common habits, common tolerances, a common political and national faith. And they do. It is this aim and this success that justifies the lavish buildings of the local high school; not merely the classrooms and the laboratories, but the gymnasium, the field-house where basketball can be played in comfort in the depth of the bitter winter, the swimming pools in which the summer heat can be endured.

It is true that the teachers are relatively badly paid and have an inferior social as well as economic standing, insecure tenure and politics making their condition worse. More money spent on men might get better results than more money spent on buildings. But it is easier to get the materials for buildings than the materials for teachers. As long as American society remains individualistic, competitive, confident that the answers to the present are in the future, not in the past, it is going to take more than money to seduce the right men and women in adequate numbers away from the life of action. And, a point too seldom remembered, the necessity for providing teachers for the two million college students hampers recruiting for high schools. In many cases, the colleges are doing what is really high school work and it matters comparatively little where the good teachers are, as long as they are teaching.

The political function of the schools is to teach Americanism, meaning not merely political and patriotic dogma, but the habits necessary to American life. This justifies the most extravagant items in the curriculum. Since the ability to play bridge is one of the marks of Americanism in a suburb, it is reasonable that there should be bridge clubs in schools. The main political achievement of the high schools and grammar schools is to bring together the young of all classes and all origins, to provide, artificially, the common background that in an old, rural society is provided by tradition, by the necessary collaboration of village life. The elementary schools—the "grade" schools—do this, too, but as far as an American town is broken up into racial blocs, the Ethan Allen Public School may have mainly Polish pupils, the Zachary Chandler mainly Welsh. Only in the Warren G. Harding High School is a big enough common pool formed in which Americans can be made.

Some of that Americanization is, of course, done deliberately and formally. Mr. Carlton Hayes pointed out long ago that the ritual of flag worship and oath-taking in an American school is a religious observance. Little boys and girls, in a school from which religion in the old sense is barred, solemnly rising each morning and reciting together the "American's Creed"[1] are performing a religious exercise as truly as if they began the day with "I believe in God the Father Almighty" or asserted that "There is no God but God."

And that these daily rituals are religious has been at last affirmed by the Supreme Court in a series of cases in which the children of a fanatical sect, Jehovah's Witnesses, had been excluded from schools for refusing to give the flag honors that, so their parents had taught them, were due to God alone. In 1940, all the Court except Chief Justice Stone held that flag worship was among the things that were Caesar's. Since that year, however, they have decided by a majority that the religious rights of the children were being infringed. What is significant in the cases is not the Court's reversal of itself but the reality of the issue presented to it. For to the Court, and to the overwhelming majority of the American people, the objections of the Witnesses were as unintelligible as the objections of the Christians to making a formal sacrifice to the Divine Emperor were to Trajan and Pliny. The school board of Minersville, Pennsylvania, was faced with a real problem when it was asked to admit that children refusing to take part in the most sacred rite of the day should be allowed to associate with the believing children of the formally unestablished national church of the United States. So, too, was the state of Oregon when it found Catholic and Lutheran children refusing to go to the schools it provided. But in both cases the Supreme Court held, finally, that compulsory Americanism was not Americanism at all, that coerced belief was not what the American people needed to stay united. This was not Germany or Russia but the country of Jefferson and Justice Holmes.

The flag worship of the American school and the American nation was brought home to the British public in an episode that, if funny, was also very revealing. For the London makers of ladies' underwear who adorned their garments with American flags were innocent of any insulting or even frivolous intention. At the same time, a revue chorus in London was attired in Union Jack handkerchiefs and nothing else— to the public indifference. But the flag, in America, is more than a mere symbol among many others. It is the regimental color of a regiment in which all Americans are enrolled. Its thirteen stripes and forty-eight stars are symbols far better understood than the complicated heraldry of crosses of Saint George, Saint Andrew, and Saint Patrick imposed on each other in a way that only experts understand. It was Lincoln's task to see that the number of stars in the flag was not diminished by eleven during his term of office. It was the discovery that the flag still flew over Fort McHenry, despite the British fleet, that moved Francis Scott key to write:

> Oh, say, can you see by the dawn's early light,
>   What so proudly we hailed at the twilight's last gleaming;
> Whose broad stripes and bright stars, thro' the perilous fight,
>   O'er the ramparts we watched were so gallantly streaming?

What he wrote in 1814, tens of millions of Americans have since sung or tried to sing. And when Barbara Frietchie in Whittier's poem told-off Stonewall Jackson with:

[1] "I believe in the United States of America as a Government of the people, by the people, for the people; whose just powers are derived from the consent of the governed; a democracy in a republic; a sovereign Nation of many sovereign states; a perfect union, one and inseparable; established upon those principles of freedom, equality, justice, and humanity for which American patriots sacrificed their lives and fortunes. I therefore believe it is my duty to my country to love it; to support its Constitution; to obey its laws; to respect its flag, and to defend it against all enemies."

"Shoot if you must this old gray head,
But spare your country's flag," she said,

she was speaking for all Americans for whom the Stars and Stripes was still their country's flag as it had been, till recently, that of General Jackson.

Thus Americanization by ritual is an important and necessary part of the function of the American school. And because it is best carried out in schools, it matters little that the high school curriculum has been so widened that it no longer means a great deal that this boy or that girl has graduated from it—if we are looking for proof of academic achievement. But graduation from high school is reasonable proof that a great deal has been learned about American ways of life, that lessons in practical politics, in organization, in social ease have been learned that could not have been learned in factory or office.

And if the high school seems to devote too much time and money to social life, penalizing the poor boy or girl more than a theoretically less democratic educational system might do, it is thus early impressing an awkward truth on the boy or girl who is both mediocre and poor. It also penalizes the really able boy or girl who is not kept in good enough intellectual training. And if the main business of the school is, in fact, the Americanization of the children of newcomers, the parents of "old American stock" have a good reason (to add to less good ones) for not sending their children to learn what they know already, at the cost of diminishing their chance of learning what they do not know. If English is native to your children and to their home, it is not merely undemocratic to object to having their progress held up and their accent debased by the tone of a high school largely immigrant in composition.

For the task of an American school in many regions is to teach the American language, to enable it to compete with Spanish, with French, with Yiddish, with Polish, with German, with Swedish. Another task is to give, through the language and the literature of the language, a common vocabulary and a common fund of allusion, fable, and sentiment. With a fluid population this has not been easy. And the countless teachers who have labored, pedantically, formally, with complete and erroneous conviction that there were correct standards, have been heroes as important in the mass as was William McGuffey whose *Eclectic Readers* sold over one hundred and twenty million copies and helped to make the Union. The teachers were heroes because, although English won against all its rivals, it was itself going through important changes, in vocabulary, in grammar, in sound, becoming the new tongue we are beginning to call American. The teachers who stuck by the rules, who worshipped at the New England shrines in Concord, were bound to lose, but their struggle was not pure waste. For the common tongue, hammered out by millions of immigrants, by millions of migrants, would have been poor in vocabulary and structure but for the people Mr. Mencken calls the dominies and who call themselves schoolmen. The creation of general literacy and a common written and spoken tongue, intelligible everywhere except possibly in the deep South, is an achievement as remarkable as the creation of Mandarin Chinese or Low Latin or Hellenistic Greek, and this tongue is certain to be the new *lingua franca* of the world.

The making of American has been mixed-up in English minds with the making of American slang. Slang, as we should know, is one of the great sources of language. French is improved Latin slang. And slang has contributed a good deal to American. It is a generation since Mr. Dooley said that when his countrymen had finished with the English language it would look as if it had been run over by a musical comedy. Since then it has been run over by *Hellzapoppin*. But it is possible, indeed very easy, to overestimate the role of slang. It is more and more the creation of professional artists, "makers." The Hollywood prose masters provide a current and often shortlived jargon; the boys and girls, men and women, who wish to be on the beam or in the groove, may murmur with admiration, "I wish I had said that." And Whistler's classical answer to Wilde is certainly appropriate: "You will, Oscar—you will!" But not for long. Some slang will enter the language; some words will lose their meanings or acquire new ones; syntax will be loosened up. But formal speech as taught in schools will still be very important. The high school English teacher, for all her pedantry, is as much a maker of the American language as Messrs. Runyon and O'Hara. Two streams of language may run roughly parallel, but in time they will merge; they will provide America with many interesting variations, do for American what its dual Germanic and Latin character does for English. That time has not yet come, but it is on the way. And the future character of this truly national tongue is foreshadowed in the drawing by Mr. Peter Arno in which an indignant citizen tells another: "I consider your conduct unethical and lousy."

Most American parents do not want, or are not able, to send their children to anything but public high schools, and the life in such a school is a training in life for America. It may be and often is a training in life *against* Europe. For Europe is the background from which many of the children are reacting and from which they must be delivered if they are to be Americanized. For nearly all immigrants, America is promotion, and this promotion is more clearly felt by their children. The old people may hanker after the old country, but the children—whatever sentimental feelings for their ancestral homes they may have, especially when provoked—are, above all else, anxious to be Americans.

Necessarily something is lost here. The least-common-denominator Americanism of the schools is not a complete substitute for a native culture. What the first-generation American children learn to despise may include elements in their moral diet that are not replaced. A new American whose pride in that promotion involves mere contempt for the habits, what Americans call the "folkways" or "mores," of his parents is not necessarily a good American. So attempts are made to instill pride in the ancestral cultures of the European lands from which the immigrants come. The University of Pittsburgh, located in one of the main melting pots of America, has a set of rooms illustrating the culture of various European countries. In the case of the Greeks, the room may instill adequate pride; in the case of the Scots (if any such need is felt) a shrine of Robert Burns may serve. But, for many of the peasant immigrants, the old country is backward though beloved, while for their children it is merely backward.

Americanization comes not from preservation of Slovak or Italian peasant culture, but from speedy assimilation to "American" culture. And that assimilation may take the form of distinction in anything that the American world obviously values. In the narrow sense of culture, there may even be a temptation to go for those courses that have not immigrant stigma on them. Thus I have been told by an eminent Scandinavian American that it is difficult to get good students of Scandinavian literature and language at the University of Minnesota, although most of the students have fairly recent Scandinavian connections. They will study French but not Swedish, for "French is not a servant's language." Latin, emblem of functionless "culture," plays something of the same role; it is a symbol of liberation.

Study is not the only way up to Americanization, to acceptation. Sport is another—and one that does the job more dramatically for the newcomers gifted with what it takes to excel in competitive contests, with what is needed to win personal and community and institutional glory.

THE "ALL-AMERICAN CHILD" (1948)   From Geoffrey Gorer, *The American People* (New York, 1948), pp. 83–89, 94–102.

Because of the great hopes placed on the baby, and because of the necessarily experimental manner in which it is being raised, the mother is anxious, from the very first, to find out if her baby is developing as it should. She has only one guide: comparison with the neighbor's children of similar age and social position, being raised on the same, or parallel, principles. The "science" of pediatrics is changing so rapidly that older children are no guide; they were raised under the disadvantage of old-fashioned, unscientific methods, and what may have been a good enough performance ten years ago may be quite inadequate now. And so from birth (the "correct" weight for a newborn child changes, but there always is a "correct" weight) the child is placed in a competitive position vis-à-vis its age mates. The mother's pride in her child and her self-esteem as a mother depend on her baby's not falling below the average for its group. Its weight, its growth, its acquisition of bodily skills, its time of teething, its time of talking, are all points on the scale by which the baby's success is weighed. As Margaret Mead has pointed out in detail, the mother's love is conditional on the child's success in this competition with its peers; only if it is successful can the mother give it her unconditional love, for it proves she has been a success in her role as mother, that she has done her duty by the hope of the future and can look the world in the face without shame. This does not, of course, mean that the failures in this primal competition are unloved or neglected; on the contrary, even more anxious attention may be paid to their getting the proper diet, to helping them to catch up; but the love for the failures is mixed with a sense of guilt; such children are a constant reproach to the inadequacy of the mother.

As soon as a child has acquired sufficient physical independence to be let out of doors alone—certainly by the age of three, and often earlier—it will leave its family and spend most of its time with its competitors and rivals in the immediate neighborhood. It will have known and played with these children (provided the parents have stayed in the same neighborhood all the time) from the time that it could be safely taken out of the baby carriage; but this earlier sociability has taken place under the watchful and anxious eyes of the mothers. By the time the child is three the mother is likely to be occupied with a younger brother or sister; and even if she were not, even if she had complete leisure, she should be ashamed of keeping a constant eye on the child, keeping it permanently tied to her apron strings. By so doing, she would risk committing the greatest crime that an American parent can commit: she would risk turning her child into a sissy.

This concept of being a sissy is a key concept for the understanding of American character; it has no exact parallel in any other society. It has nowadays become a term of opprobrium which can be applied to anyone, regardless of age or sex; although it is analogous to some English terms of opprobrium (e.g. milksop, cry-baby, nancy, mother's darling) it is more than any of them. Schematically, it means showing more dependence or fear or lack of initiative or passivity than is suitable for the occasion. It can be applied to a gambler hesitant about risking his money, to a mother overanxious about the pain her child may suffer at the hands of a surgeon, to a boy shy about asking a popular girl for a "date," to stage fright, to overt apprehension about a visit to the dentist, to a little girl crying because her doll is broken, just as well as to occasions which directly elicit courage or initiative or independence and which may be responded to more or less adequately. It is the overriding fear of all American parents that their child will turn into a sissy; it is the overriding fear of all Americans from the moment that they can understand language that they may be taken for a sissy; and a very great deal of American speech and activity, so often misinterpreted by non-Americans, is designed solely to avert this damning judgment. Particularly self-confident Americans may say "I guess I'm just a sissy. . . ." when they feel quite sure that they are not. When applied to adult males (but only in that case) the term also implies sexual passivity.

To prevent this dread development, the American child is constantly urged toward independence and activity and initiative, greatly praised for every real or reported manifestation of these qualities, reproved or punished for failure. And its independent activity in the neighborhood playground is a first and most important testing ground.

*   *   *

So far, in discussing the upbringing of the American child, I have avoided sex pronouns and, somewhat awkwardly, used the word "it"; unfortunately English lacks a single word for he-or-she, and it would have been necessary to use the phrase all the time, for the treatment given small boys and girls differs only slightly in degree, not at all in kind. There is, however, an important difference in effect. As was pointed out in the previous chapter, all Americans acquire a predominantly feminine conscience; and this faces the little boy with a dilemma which his sister does not experience. Because of the encapsulated mother, the little boy has doubts about his masculinity, whereas the little girl is reaffirmed in her femininity. To prove to himself, and to the world, that he is a real "he-man" (the reduplication in the term is in itself suggestive) the little boy has to be more strident, shout and boast more, call more attention to himself than his sister need. American children of both sexes are brought up very similarly, by and large face the same dilemmas, and acquire the same type of character; but all the overcompensations for insecurity—a great deal is demanded of American children, up to the limit of their powers— are far more developed in the boy.

The ideal American family consists of two children, an elder daughter and a younger son, generally known as "Sis" and "Buddy" (or "Junior"). This does not mean that this size of family, or order of birth, is statistically more common in the United States than in other countries of similar urbanization; but this is the typical composition when the average American family is pictured in illustration or advertisement, and very often in popular fiction and films. In narratives a third child, a still younger brother, is often introduced for dramatic effect.

In all societies everywhere the birth of a younger baby involves the older child in considerable psychological turmoil, if for no other reason, because the new arrival inevitably displaces the older child from the center of family love and attention. Different societies interpret this situation in different ways. Margaret

Mead has suggested that the typical American reaction of the child to the newborn baby is one of resentment, because the new arrival is permitted all the babyish ways which the older child has had to abandon in its forced progress—up to the limit of its strength—toward independence and adulthood. From this initial situation she derives "the bitterness toward all those who 'have it soft,' 'get by,' 'get away with murder,' a bitterness combined with envy."

With the exception of a single combination, the relationship between brothers and sisters is without deep intensity. They have no special obligations toward one another (except to "agree," not to squabble too much); outside the rural South, the brother is not expected to defend his sister's honor, nor is he responsible for her fortune, her marriage, or her children. In the vast majority of cases brothers and sisters scatter as soon as they leave home; typically they follow different pursuits, live in different localities, and, if they go to a university, go to different ones.

The one important exception occurs when two children of the same sex, particularly two boys, are born within a short interval of each other—at the most, two years. In this case the elder brother is likely to introduce the younger brother into his play group, and later his gang; and this has some regular and typical results. The younger brother is a member of a group in the majority older than he is, and with standards of daring and accomplishment beyond the level of his years. Fired by the standard he is set, the younger brother (the "kid brother") becomes extravagantly rash in his words and actions, confident that he will be saved from the dangerous results of his behavior by his older brother's protection, by his superior strength and wisdom.

As the child grows in independence and skills, its father becomes somewhat more important, particularly as an authority which can be opposed to that of the mother. Most mothers conscientiously try to build for their husbands the position of authority in the family, and tell their children to ask his permission; but they often override his decisions, on the ground that he is too severe or too lenient, that he doesn't make allowance for children or that he is spoiling them. Most American parents dislike accepting the onus of restricting their children's pleasure and amusement; and there is a very general tendency for the parent first approached to put the burden of decision on the other. Most children learn this early, and become adept at playing one parent against the other. In those households where the father controls the children's pocket money, a refused application from the father will often be made good by the mother from her domestic budget. In many families it seems as though the parents were in covert competition for their children's love.

In the September adjoining its sixth birthday every American child will go to its neighborhood school, with the insignificant exception of the very rich. This may well be in a different town or district from that in which it was born, for conscientious American parents will often, within the limits of possibility open to them, move their home to that neighborhood whose school offers the best opportunities to their offspring. Schools are rarely judged by scholastic standards or opportunities, for, within a given region, the variation is slight. They are judged by their size, by the splendor and modernity of their buildings, by the number and condition of the accessory structures—workshops, indoor gymnasiums, and the like— and often by the absence of Negro children, or too many children of the alien and foreign born. The town in which an American spends the greater part of his schooldays is known as his "home town."

At school the competition for success, by which the child can earn its parents' love and approval and rate itself in the world, is again partly formalized. In American schoolrooms scholastic performance is classified on a five-point scale, usually from A to E, though marks are sometimes used, and these grades are inscribed on the report cards which the child must take home monthly. Since C is the average for the child's peers, parents can see immediately how their child rates in this year's crop of young Americans, whether he is a credit to them and himself, and therefore worthy of unqualified love, or whether they have failed in their most important function.

School athletics are less important for the rating of young children, and, in a way, never very important for the vast majority of American children. All American boys are expected to enjoy unformalized sports, typified by the baseball game on the empty lot; but to "go out for" a school sport means to accept a quasi-professional status, to acknowledge athletic abilities above the average. Athletes as a class are admired, envied, and privileged; they represent their school against its neighbors and rivals; and all boys, at any rate, are meant to follow the fortune of their teams with the greatest enthusiasm and emotional involvement. Among the athletes themselves the competition for success, symbolized by the Letter, is extremely keen. But it is a matter of individual choice whether the boy will himself enter in this competition; extra praise and regard are given to those who successfully do so; but blame is not given to those who do not.

In the event of an inadequately equipped athlete engaging in a competition beyond his powers, the attitude of the noncompetitors and of those he competes with are strongly contrasting. The people who are not involved in the competition are likely to identify with this valiant "underdog," to admire and praise his courage, and get great vicarious satisfaction from any success against the mighty that he may achieve. In contrast, the competitors have little respect for a person "going out of his class" and are justified in using all their strength and skill to eliminate him.

As was stated earlier, the children find in the schoolteacher an authority who can nearly always be successfully opposed to the parents. The parents keep this acknowledged rival and superior under the closest scrutiny, demanding in her private life standards of conduct and moral rectitude far higher than those they apply to themselves or their neighbors. This supervision is formalized in the parent-teacher association (P.T.A.) in which the most civic-minded parents meet with the teachers at regular intervals to discuss the school and their children. Though often in fact aided by grants from the federal or state treasury, the school is regarded as created and paid for by the initiative and taxes of the local inhabitants; it is their creation, and it is their duty to see that it compares favorably with its rivals. The American public school is justifiably one of the chief sources of American civic pride.

The American school is, in the first instance, a social device, and an extremely successful one, for stamping the American character on children, whatever their background and origins may be; it is only secondarily an institution for implanting and transmitting knowledge. Scholastic achievement is one of the few spheres where American children are not pushed to the limit of their strength; compared with any country of Western Europe, the standard required at any given age is low. Most Americans attend school for more years than most Western Europeans, however. Classwork has a few distinctive features: training is given in public speaking by the use of recitations (spoken themes) as well as by essays; civics is an important subject, often made vivid by visits to neighboring factories, constructions, police courts, and the like; biology and science are taught early; study of the dead languages, if taught at all, normally only starts at high school (from the age of fourteen); European history is practically not taught at all; growing use is made of radio and films as adjuncts to teaching; vocational training starts early (again from high school) and is given in a great number of subjects, with very complete technical equipment in the bigger urban schools. Apart from this direct vocational training, American public-school education is less directed toward equipping the children for adult life (except for the development of Americanism) than toward making their childhood enjoyable and significant; under the influence of John Dewey, most American teachers believe that "children are people"; and much class time is given over to communal tasks and discussions with little direct relevance to later life.

ANDRE MAUROIS ON AMERICAN EDUCATION (1961) From Andre Maurois "A Frenchman Appraises United States Schools," *The Saturday Review,* vol. XLIV, pp. 54–55.

Any Frenchman who studies the structure of American education is at first much surprised. He beholds innumerable universities and colleges that seem prosperous and well attended; he is told that 30 percent of the youth get the benefit of a college education and that the proportion will soon reach 50 percent. Yet when he asks "What is the curriculum?" the answer is: "It all depends on the university you speak of. Which colleges do you mean?" He then realizes that many of those institutions are private, being administered either by a board of trustees or by a church, while others are controlled by the various states of the Union. He is informed that there is no uniform program; that in many places a student himself chooses, from a vast catalogue, the subjects he wishes to study, as he would make his own menu in a cafeteria; and also that a doctor's degree does not have the same value when conferred by a comparatively unknown university as it has when bestowed by Harvard or some other institution held in high repute.

How is that possible, the visiting Frenchman asks. Does not the Ministry of Education in Washington determine the programs of exams for the whole country?

When he is then told that Washington has nothing to do with education except for statistics and that the subsidies of the Federal Government are given through the states, his astonishment increases. He has been accustomed in his own country to a complete centralization. First the French Revolution, and later Napoleon, built the University of France, primary, secondary, and superior education, into one solid body, controlled by the Minister for National Education. Napoleon's ideal would have been to see all young Frenchmen of the same age doing at the same time all over the country the same Latin lesson or the same problem of geometry. The rigidity of the system does not in 1961 come quite up to Napoleon's dream, but the unity of programs remains complete. Whether a young man studies in Paris or in Caen, Grenoble or in Aix, he must study the same subjects and his diploma will have the same value as any other diploma. Every year a General Competition takes place between all French *lycée* (high schools). The best pupils of each *lycée* write on the same day on the same themes a French composition, a Latin version, an essay on philosophy, etc. The prizes are solemnly handed over, at the Sorbonne, by the President of the French Republic. On that day Napoleon's dream comes true and it often happens that small provincial towns outrank Paris.

Is French unity better than American variety? The advantage of the French system is to force upon all a basic culture without which it would be for a Frenchman impossible to get a bachelor's degree and to have access to higher education. Yet I realize the French plan would never work in the United States. You cannot impose on Mississippi a type of university that suits Massachusetts. Between populations, traditions, needs, the differences are too wide. America is a continent. Moreover, one cannot compare the American system, whose object is to give the same education to all children, with the French system, which, after each cycle, requires a successful examination before allowing the pupil to proceed. As to superior education, in France it is intended for a small intellectual elite. French universities are similar to American graduate schools. The first two years of an American university would be in France the last two years of a secondary school.

A second deep-seated difference between the two countries is this: In America, where education is meant to be essentially democratic, all school children, whatever their I.Q.s, are treated about the same way. I heard American teachers say, "Let us beware of being ostensibly partial to brilliant minds; slow-witted pupils might then acquire an inferiority complex." Their unconfessed desire is that the bottom boy should feel equal to the head boy. In some extreme cases a dunce may be told to stay in the same grade for a second year, but an American educator doesn't take such a decision without reluctance. The child might feel humiliated. The less gifted child is given easier work suitable to his interests and abilities.

In France, high school years are a permanent ordeal by examination. Every week there is a test, either in French composition, or history, or mathematics, and each boy is told his position on the list. The bottom ones will not get on to the next grade. The French baccalaureate is a difficult examination which at the end of the secondary education eliminates 40 to 70 percent of the candidates. Once a Frenchman has got his bachelor's degree, there begins the time of entrance examinations for the specialized schools which give access to all high positions in France. The *Ecole Polytechnique* and the *Ecole Centrale* remind one of MIT or Cal Tech. Big business in France is run mostly by former students of the *Ecole Polytechnique,* so-called X, and they surround themselves with other X. From the *Ecole Normale Superieure* come the best professors and lecturers in humanities and sciences; that school has an immense prestige. *The Ecole d'Administration* trains future ambassadors, administrators, treasury experts. To sum up, the first twenty-five years in the life of a Frenchman who has both ambition and talent resemble an obstacle course whose successive hurdles are competitive examinations. The good point about this plan is that most men in high positions possess real culture; the danger is that the student who shines in competition will not necessarily become an efficient man of action.

Whenever I explain the French organization to American educators, they reply: "We do it in a different way but we also select the best. In point of fact it is not easy to enter any of our really first-class universities. There is a long waiting list and it takes a brilliant school record to get in. Only *you* seem to throw back the mediocrities to outer darkness. *We* think that brilliant universities are needed for brilliant students and mediocre universities for mediocre students. In America bad students will be accepted by bad universities, where they will feel more comfortable and usurp nobody's place."

Let us add that one of the aspects of American education makes a great impression on a Frenchman; it is the social side of college life. A French university is not a small and self-sufficient society. It is a group of buildings where students attend lectures or work in a laboratory. The student body is not self-governing.

There are few social activities. Our students have more time for their studies; they are perhaps less prepared for "togetherness." While I was in America, I happened to take part in a debate with high school boys and girls fifteen or sixteen years old. I was deeply impressed by their ease and poise, their respect for the rules of public discussion, and the interest they took in current affairs.

Here we come to a third difference. Most French educators would say that current affairs are out of place at school. My own master, the philosopher Alain, used to say, "Education should be resolutely in arrears." He meant that the task of school and university is to transmit to the young generation the culture patiently accumulated by centuries. If in school one does not study Homer and Plato, Shakespeare and Molière, Dickens and Tolstoy, there is a good chance he will never read them at all. If one neglects history in favor of current affairs, first he will never know history, and second he will not understand current affairs. The part of schools is not to expedite current affairs but to initiate students in timeless affairs.

The British professor Whitehead remarked that "there can be no successful democratic society till general education conveys a philosophic outlook." In France the last year of a secondary education is mostly devoted to philosophy and for many students, assuming the professor of philosophy proves worthy of his subject, that is the most important year of all. I remember with gratitude how I then found in Alain much more than a professor; I mean a master. I am afraid in America philosophy is more or less left to specialists, whereas it should teach all men the art of thinking and the art of living. Technical power without moral power is dangerous. According to his philosophy—or his faith—man can use or misuse the new forces modern science places at his disposal. In times as difficult as ours men should be made worthy of their increased strength. A modern country needs: a) skilled workers able to apply the new techniques; b) research workers able to improve them; c) philosophers able to teach how to ally efficiency and wisdom. America produces, better perhaps than we do, the first two types. Maybe she doesn't attach enough social importance to the third type.

A heated debate has been taking place in France for some time between the champions of technical studies and those of classical studies. Before the French Revolution education was entirely in the hands of the Church. Jesuit colleges in the seventeenth and eighteenth centuries formed all great French writers; Greek and Latin were then the basis of education. The results proved good. Not only Corneille but also Voltaire was educated by the Jesuits. Today the need for scientists and technicians has become so urgent that more time must be given to scientific studies. It is possible, in a curriculum so heavily loaded with mathematics, to find time for ancient languages? Many doubt it, but surely some sort of literary culture is still necessary. In order to lead men, whether it be in industry or in public services, one must understand them, their feelings, and their passions. Where does one learn to know men if not in the works of philosophers? I once heard a great French administrator tell younger men: "You will never be able to govern France if you have not read Balzac." He was right. Moreover, a literary and artistic culture is necessary to enjoy all forms of leisure: theatre, travel, and music.

*   *   *

At to the difference between French and American students, I should sum up by saying that French students are generally one or two years ahead of American students in general culture, but that American students seem more unspoiled, keep a fresher mind, and know better how to get along with people. It would be madness to ask either nation to act or teach according to the tradition of the other.

THE HIGH SCHOOLS OF MICHIGAN (1962)   From John N. Wales, *Schools of Democracy* (Lansing, Mich., 1962), pp. 151–54.

It is time to summarise. This survey has led to the belief that in general the High Schools in Michigan are in the main doing the job for which they were designed, and doing a good job; they are serving the needs of the community, and they actively and accurately reflect the values and predilections of that community. Indeed, if there is a radical criticism, it is that they do this too accurately; they follow, they do not lead. And one is inclined to attribute the defects—a lack of intellectual strenuousness, a lack of scholarship, a lack of leadership—to the inherent contradiction latent in the movement which is popularly associated with the name of John Dewey, and which was concisely expressed in *Cardinal Principles.* It is suggested that the uncritical acceptance of comprehensiveness as essential to a democratic society; the direct attempt to inculcate citizenship and patriotism as a technique in promoting and preserving democracy; the substitution, in large measure, of practical activities and vocational courses for the more old fashioned basic humanities and natural sciences, are all based on fallacies, and that the democratic ideals of liberty and equality of opportunity, and the fulfillment of individual potentialities; could now be more efficiently and more logically served by a partial return to the ideas expressed by the Committee of Ten in 1892. Such a move would be no compromise of principle; it would indeed be only to do what Dewey was attempting to do forty years ago, to emphasise neglected aspects of education in a democracy, and to bring the High School more into line with the needs of the day. Indeed, as was noted in Chapter IV, there are signs that this movement has already begun.

The two most urgent such needs are leadership and scholarship. Suggestions for possible reforms and remedies have been discussed in a previous chapter, but there is one immediate step, practicable within the existing framework, which could have far-reaching results. It is setting-up, by the State Department of Public Instruction collaborating with the Michigan Educational Association and the Universities in Michigan, of a Schools Examination Board. The Board would be an independent body, concerned only with academic achievement. Its examinations would be annual, and at two levels, the first or ordinary level at Tenth Grade, as a result of which the pupil would be issued with a Certificate stating the subjects taken and the marks attained, whether he had reached pass level, and if so whether with distinction. The second examination would be at Twelfth Grade, and would be at advanced level. A Certificate of a Pass at this level, in a certain minimum number of required subjects, would be equivalent to University Matriculation, and would be accepted as such; a Distinction would indicate University Scholarship level, and on it State Scholarships would be awarded. The examinations would not be compulsory in any school, but would be open to any pupil, whether in a Public School or in a private institution, who desired to take them. If this system were instituted it would have the effect, in a measurably short time, of creating an impartial and gradually rising standard of attainment, of strengthening the teacher's position and improving standards of teaching, and of presenting parents, colleges and prospective employers with an objective picture which they could accept with confidence. If the State of Michigan were to lead the way in such an experiment, the eventual results throughout the nation could be incalculable.

I am all too well aware, in making these proposals, of a certain presumption—a presumption that has betrayed itself too often, much against my intentions, in many of the preceding pages. If I have appeared to be critical of certain aspects of the American system of education, it is partly because of the many criticisms openly made to me by teachers and administrators themselves within the system, and even more because the aims and ideals of American education are so good and so important that everything possible should be done to achieve them; if I have appeared critical of certain aspects of contemporary American society, it is because its virtues—its generosity and largeness of view, its zest and its potentialities—are so congenial to me that I would like only to see some of the weaknesses diminished, the two most conspicuous, as has been indicated, appearing to be a lack of leadership, and a tendency to set intellectual sights too low. But, when all is said and done, America is attempting to do something of unprecedented value, and unprecedented difficulty, to teach, in Dr. Margaret Mead's words, "boys and girls to live successfully, in a world that does not yet exist, in jobs that have not yet been created." The aims and standards of a dynamic society are necessarily different from those of a static one. In his book, *The Republic and the Person* Dr. Chalmers has probably said the last word that need be said:

> "By eliminating the ill-equipped, the European systems undoubtedly outstrip us in the quality of the average student's performance. That their ablest students are not one whit abler than ours, nor more numerous in proportion to the population, has been common knowledge among scholars for generations. And in spite of our own failure to reckon fairly the cost of legislating for all the opportunity and obligation to go to school, despite our failure adequately to pay the school bill, and other disappointments, the American school system has demonstrated in thousands of ways that it is appropriate for America."

American educators rightly resist any suggestion that America should return to the European model; whatever the next step in American education may be, it must come from within; it must reflect the magnanimity and the adventurousness of American society; it must be in the direction of realising more truly and more effectively the American ideals of equality of opportunity for all and of individual fulfillment. In surveying the American scene, I, as an English educator, can only wish that I could feel as confident as Dr. Chalmers about the direction of our own culture; I can only await, with some trepidation, what could be some very illuminating return comments of an American observer about schools in Great Britain. But now, my part is done; I have had my "blast," and I do not expect any walls to crumble at the sound of this very tentative trumpet.

A SOVIET EDUCATOR ON AMERICAN ELEMENTARY SCHOOLS

(1962)   From Soya Malkova, "In The Schools of America: Notes of a Soviet Educator," *Soviet Education*, vol. V, pp. 50–53, 56–59.

Meeting with American educators of various ranks, from ordinary teachers to heads of sections of the ministry of education (for the sake of simplicity we shall refer to the Department of Education, which is part of the Ministry [sic] of Health, Welfare and Education, we would pose the following question: "What is the basic problem facing American schools?" To this question everybody would reply in the same way: "Money."

The lack of sufficient funds is really the number one problem of American schools. The United States has a so-called decentralized system of school administration. This means, first, that the selection of textbooks, the drawing up of curriculums and other factors in the work of the school are matters that are resolved by the local community in which the school is located. Second, schools exist on funds that are collected as a tax on the local population. The school budget is made up of the following parts: 55% from the tax on the population; 41% from the state; and 4% from the Federal Government.

Until recent times this system of decentralization was lauded in every way. It was said to be the most democratic system. Only recently has the opinion been expressed that this system is more suitable for the eighteenth century than for the twentieth.

The division of American cities into poor and rich areas is very clearly seen. When showing us a city the Americans would usually say, "The rich live here." And we would see splendid residences, far from the dust and smoke of the city, in the suburbs, and hidden by clumps of trees. "And this is where the poor live." This could be guessed without explanations: ramshackle houses squeezed against each other, garbage containers under windows, laundry on the lines, and children playing right on the streets.

It is quite obvious that if schools exist on the basis of local resources, then the schools in wealthy areas are in better material circumstances than in poor areas. Actually, in the suburbs, to which businessmen and the highly paid intelligentsia have moved, the yearly expenditure for each pupil is twice that of the expenditure in the poor areas. This is what we were told at the National Education Association. It was enough to look at the exteriors of schools to sense the difference. In wealthy suburbs we saw magnificent schoolbuildings built in the contemporary style. This is usually a group of one-storey buildings connected by passages. These schools have plenty of light and air. Modern materials are used in construction; they are light, strong and beautiful. The construction of schoolbuildings in the United States is guided by the rule that it is better to spend more initially and then not have to expend money on current repairs. The planning of a school is well thought out. There are many rooms for various purposes. Classroom furniture is light and movable. Some schools have swimming pools. Americans show these schools with pride, and they have reason to do so. The buildings are really beautiful. However there is one "but." You will see such schools, as a rule, only in wealthy areas.

We visited a seventy-five-year-old school in the large city of Minneapolis. Three classes study in one room at the same time; a library of 200 books is located in a small storeroom. In other schools we saw pupils studying on the stage and in the corridors because there were not enough classrooms. According to official data, the schools do not have room for two million pupils. The situation is particularly bad in the southern states of the United States. We were shown a chart at the Ministry of Education that indicated the percentage of illiterate or partly literate in the adult population. The figure for the southern states is 20 to 25 percent.

Money is needed to build schools—much money. Local school communities cannot cope with this problem on their own. That is why the American public is now demanding, with greater frequency and persistence, that the Federal Government increase its share in the financing of schools. And not just schools. There is nothing in the United States that resembles our out-of-school institutions. The few centers for children that exist depend upon private contributions and experience an acute need for funds.

The Congress of the United States has more than once considered legislation for increasing school allocations. But it has been rejected every time: congressmen, half of whom are people with an income greater than fifty thousand dollars a year and a fifth of whom are millionaires, do not wish to spend money on public education.

In an Elementary School

I went to one elementary school, where I was very gladly received, nearly every day over a period of three weeks. The children became used to me and, when meeting me on the street, they would greet me as they would their own teachers with: "Hi, Mrs. Malkova!"

The school is a one-storey brick building in a poor area. The people who live in this area are Negroes, Puerto Ricans, and whites, all of them at the lowest rungs of the social ladder. The school has 750 children ranging in age from five to twelve years. Compulsory education in the United States begins at the age of six. But part of the children attend preparatory grades before enrolling in the 1st grade. These are called "kindergartens" in America. But they have very little in common with our kindergartens. The school that I visited had three preparatory grades. They function three to four hours a day. Looking through the glass door of the class, you can see tots drawing, listening to a teacher's story, or singing. These are "kindergartens"—preparation for formal instruction in the 1st grade.

The elementary school in the United States is usually of the six-year type and exists apart from the secondary school. One teacher teaches all subjects in each class. True, the pupils get a new teacher every year, since teachers specialize in a definite grade and do not "lead" pupils through the six years in a row.

The school has a good library with a large reading room. But it does not have workshops, study halls, or laboratories. All study activity takes place in the classroom.

Each classroom is an independent unit. It has chests for storing teaching aids and simple instruments, a wall closet for the children's clothing, shelves under the windows for textbooks and books, and also a wash basin.

The furniture in the classrooms consists of little tables and chairs which are grouped either in a semicircle or are scattered chaotically around the room. Each classroom reflects the tastes of the teacher. In some classes I saw small sofas with covers and a mountain of pillows, or tables covered by a white embroidered tablecloth. Everywhere the walls are decorated with the children's drawings, their various other efforts, posters entitled "Winter," "Our Breakfast," "What We Know About Animals," and so forth. The classrooms usually have two or three blackboards, and in front of the main one is the mandatory fixture in every American school—the national flag.

The school day begins at 8:30 A.M. The 1st and 2nd grades begin their classes a little earlier because there are two sessions of these grades. Once a week the school day begins with a general meeting of pupils—the assembly. All the children gather in the auditorium of the school, sing the national anthem, and swear the oath of allegiance to the flag. Then follows some kind of performance—the 6th grade depicts a scene from the "Life of Lincoln," the 4th grade relates the story of their trip to the zoo and the habits of the animals, and so forth. Sometimes a guest of the school addresses the assembly—which is what happened with me, for example.

The school day ends at 3:00 P.M. There is a thirty-minute lunch period in the middle of the school day. Most of the pupils eat in the school lunchroom. For thirty to forty cents they get a small carton of milk, a "hot dog" (that is what the Americans call their most popular food—a hot sausage on a bun), and jelly. School ends an hour earlier on Wednesdays. The school gives the churches a special period for religious instructions. Usually, however, school is let out at three o'clock. Only the prolonged-day groups remain. These groups now exist in a number of schools located in poor areas of large cities.

Special teachers take charge of the prolonged-day groups. Pupils get sandwiches and milk in the classroom itself and then special activities are organized with the children (music, dances, and handicrafts for the boys).

The 750 girls and boys in the school are assigned to classes according to a whole series of classifications. First of all, the school has a class for the mentally retarded children, a class for children with poor eyesight, two classes for the so-called emotionally disturbed children. The remaining children are assigned to classes in accordance with their "intelligence quotient". . . .

More than a half-century ago American pedagogy came to believe deeply in the theory of intellectual endowment and since that time has built its work on this theory. According to the theory, people are born with definite intellectual abilities and only one-fourth of the people can cope with intellectual activity. At that time, half a century ago, measurements were established—tests for measuring the intelligence quotient. The overwhelming majority of American schools now use these tests and assign pupils to various classes in accordance with the test results.

We examined dozens of tests that were being used in the schools. They included the following problems: find the words similar in meaning; insert the suitable word missing from the sentence; underline the number that does not fit into the given sequence of numbers; and so forth. Dozens of specialists, American and English, have proved convincingly that if the tests measure anything it is certainly not innate intelligence, but only the skills acquired by the child in classifying the systematizing, and his store of words.

Obviously, in taking these tests the best results are achieved by children from well-to-do families, where parents could afford to buy them toys and books, in short, to develop their children. A low intelligence quotient is received, as a rule, by children from poor and, particularly, Negro families. Many progressive educators in the United States with whom we spoke protest strongly against measuring the intelligence quotient of pupils, and consider this system faulty because it categorizes, without foundation, a large number of children as slow and deprives a great many children of an education.

Frankly, we Soviet educators were staggered by the harshness of this system. A youngster enters the 1st grade and takes his first step in school. But already in

October, on the basis of his test results, he has been labeled "slow" and assigned to a specific class.

The school referred to above has the following gradations in the 1st grade: 1-1, 1-2, 1-3, and so forth up to number 7. The "intellectually gifted children" are in the 1-1 and 1-2 sections, then follow the "average," and at the very end the "slow" children whose quotient was lower than ninety.

The labels "able" and "slow" have a tremendous influence on the status of the children and on the work of the teachers, even of those who are against the system. As a teacher once said to us: "I am against testing. But knowing the intelligence quotients of the children in my class, I cannot force myself to be unbiased. I still look at them through the prism of this confounded quotient." We saw what this system of classifying children by abilities leads to in practice when we attended classes.

"Here Are the Slow Children"

We heard this phrase from a teacher every time we prepared to attend a class with an index of 4, 5, or lower. The teacher conducts his class with this thought in mind. It is considered that the "slow" children are incapable of abstract thinking, that the teaching materials must be simplified for them, and that these materials must have a greater share of practical elements.

*   *   *

We were astounded by this, shall we say, mild, neutral position of the teacher in the class which we observed fairly frequently. As we noticed, the teacher seldom uses methods to force the pupil to work, to encourage and stimulate him. Being under the influence of the theory of innate endowments, the teacher does not attempt to somehow pull up the pupil, to give him complicated problems. His reasoning is simple: "What can you expect from this boy? He has an intelligence quotient of 75." The boy looks upon himself in the same way, since all of the children know whether they are "able" or "slow."

The indifference of teachers is also attributable to the fact that it is school practice to transfer all pupils to the next grade. At the end of the year the teacher effects not a transfer but a so-called reorganization of the class. He writes a report on each pupil, similar to the following: "Williams reads poorly. He is poor in arithmetic. But his quotient is 80. In the 2nd grade he should be placed in the 6 (or 7) index group." And there he will study in accordance with an even lower level syllabus, with very low demands on the quality of his knowledge.

We were invited to a conference of teachers and parents in New York where pressing school problems were discussed. In their speeches many said: "The elementary school is the root of all evils. It does not provide the basic knowledge. The children cannot read, write or count. They are not prepared to continue their studies in the secondary school."

To get a complete understanding of the American elementary school we must become familiar with yet another part of it—the work with "I.G.C."

I.G.C.

Those three letters—I.G.C.—were to be seen on classroom doors. They are constantly being mentioned in conversation by American teachers. The children also say: "We are from the I.G.C. class." They are the initial letters of three words—intellectually gifted children. According to American standards these are children with an intelligence quotient higher than 110 to 120. They are assigned to separate classes where the content and methods of instruction are very much different from the ones described above. Attending these classes and talking with the children gave us the impression that their knowledge is at the level of knowlege of our good pupils.

In the I.G.C. classes we saw real exercises and serious work in arithmetic and the native language. When at these classes we almost felt as if we were back in our own school. Class 4-1 had 22 pupils, including only seven Negroes. A spelling lesson was in progress. The teacher would pronounce a word and the pupils would name its letters. From time to time the teacher would ask them to make up a sentence with this or that word, change the tense of its verb, and explain the forming of tenses.

The pupils found the prefix and root of the word "triangle," and discussed the origin of the prefix. The teacher imperceptibly moved from grammar to mathematics. The pupils discussed various geometric figures and determined their properties.

Class 6-1 has 24 students, five of them Negroes. The arithmetic lesson is progressing at a quick tempo. The teacher reads the problem and the pupils make brief notes on their sheets. One boy is at the blackboard. Two or three minutes pass; several persons raise their hands and supply the answers. The next problem follows; brief notes; answers. There is no waiting for the late ones; the solutions are arrived at quickly, without explanations, without long notes, and almost orally. The syllabuses in I.G.C. classes are rich and serious. The teaching of mathematics, for instance, is conducted in accordance with a new syllabus, the basis of which is the theory of numbers. The teaching of arithmetic has been reorganized to accord with this theory, beginning with the 1st grade.

Foreign language instruction is introduced in the I.G.C. classes of the 3rd and 4th grades, with the broad utilization of television and radio. Independent work by pupils plays a large role in these classes.

Just as in the grades for the "slow," the teacher plans a series of integral themes for the year. But while studying these themes attention is concentrated on independent work in reading and the writing of reports and compositions.

Reference books, encyclopedias, and dictionaries are prominently displayed in these classes. The pupils utilize this literature in class or in the library when writing reports. Once a week a class is held in the library. The children are taught to use catalogues, to find needed information, make notes, etc.

Pupils in the higher—5th and 6th—grades, while studying the natural sciences, do two or three so-called projects per year. The project is a small "research" paper on a subject selected by the pupil and usually related to the syllabus. We saw finished projects by 6th-graders on the subjects of "Space," "Atomic Energy," "Man's Nervous System," and others. These reports present material gathered from books, reference works, and museums. They include charts, diagrams, drawings, and descriptions of small experiments conducted by the children. Bibliographic information is attached to the reports. It is interesting to note that American teachers, as a rule, do not evaluate the pupils' responses in the classroom. Only tests and independent "research" papers are evaluated.

The school year is divided into three or four periods. The evaluations of schoolwork are recorded on a special card for parents at the end of the year.

When one moves from a class for the "slow" to an I.G.C. class one gets a literally physical sense of the difference in the level of knowledge, the demands made by the teacher, and the atmosphere prevailing in the classroom. We also felt this difference sharply when we visited schools in the wealthy suburbs.

Montgomery County is one of the most fashionable suburbs around Washington. Here, in beautiful residences surrounded by green lawns, live highly-placed officials, businessmen, lawyers, and university professors. They have built schools for their children that match their residences. The teachers here are well qualified and children are not divided according to abilities. Only within the classroom are the children grouped according to progress in their studies. Thanks to the small number of pupils in each grade, the teacher can organize work with separate groups. For example, at an arithmetic lesson of the 5th grade nine pupils were working independently with problem sheets. The ten remaining pupils were working under the supervision of the teacher.

Learning to read is also fully individualized. There is no common textbook. Each pupil makes his own selection of a book to read. Having read it, he discussed it with the teacher, shows her his record of books read and the list of unfamiliar words that he is compiling. Each pupil must read thirty to forty books during the year. He draws illustrations for some books or makes a dramatic presentation to the class.

In the natural sciences each large topic is covered through the same sort of independent work as we had seen in the I.G.C. groups.

The teacher also behaves differently in these schools. He is active; he employs many methods to stimulate the pupil, to force him to work. The parents are sent not only the children's grades but also their work.

We observed the same kind of educational work in private schools. These are institutions where an education costs up to 2,000 dollars yearly. They are accessible only to children with very wealthy parents. There are no "slow" ones here either, and each child gets his needed share of attention and encouragement from the teacher.

17

EDUCATION
FOR
URBAN INDUSTRIAL
AMERICA,
1895–1918

The Urban Experience

DESCRIPTION OF THE TENEMENT CHILD (1890) From Jacob A. Riis, *How the Other Half Lives* (New York, 1890), pp. 179–83.

The problem of the children becomes, in these swarms, to the last degree perplexing. Their very number makes one stand aghast. I have already given instances of the packing of the child population in East Side tenements. They might be continued indefinitely until the array would be enough to startle any community. For, be it remembered, these children with the training they receive—or do not receive—with the instincts they inherit and absorb in their growing up, are to be our future rulers, if our theory of government is worth anything. More than a working majority of our voters now register from the tenements. I counted the other day the little ones, up to ten years or so, in a Bayard Street tenement that for a yard has a triangular space in the centre with sides fourteen or fifteen feet long, just room enough for a row of ill-smelling closets at the base of the triangle and a hydrant at the apex. There was about as much light in this "yard" as in the average cellar. I gave up my self-imposed task in despair when I had counted one hundred and twenty-eight in forty families. Thirteen I had missed, or not found in. Applying the average for the forty to the whole fifty-three, the house contained one hundred and seventy children. It is not the only time I have had to give up such census work. I have in mind an alley—an inlet rather to a row of rear tenements—that is either two or four feet wide according as the wall of the crazy old building that gives on it bulges out or in. I tried to count the children that swarmed there, but could not. Sometimes I have doubt that anybody knows just how many there are about. Bodies of drowned children turn up in the rivers right along in summer whom no one seems to know anything about. When last spring some workmen, while moving a pile of lumber on a North River pier, found under the last plank the body of a little lad crushed to death, no one had missed a boy, though his parents afterwards turned up. The truant officer assuredly does not know, though he spends his life trying to find out, somewhat illogically, perhaps, since the department that employs him admits that thousands of poor children are crowded out of the schools year by year for want of room. There was a big tenement in the Sixth Ward, now happily appropriated by the beneficent spirit of business that blots out so many foul spots in New York—it figured not long ago in the official reports as "an out-and-out hogpen"—that had a record of one hundred and two arrests in four years among its four hundred and seventy-eight tenants, fifty-seven of them for drunken and disorderly conduct. I do not know how many children there were in it, but the inspector reported that he found only seven in the whole house who owned that they went to school. The rest gathered all the instruction they received running for beer for their elders. Some of them claimed the "flat" as their home as a mere matter of form. They slept in the streets at night. The official came upon a little party of four drinking beer out of the cover of a milk-can in the hallway. They were of the seven good boys and proved their claim to the title by offering him some.

The old question, what to do with the boy, assumes a new and serious phase in the tenements. Under the best conditions found there, it is not easily answered. In nine cases out of ten he would make an excellent mechanic, if trained early to work at a trade, for he is neither dull nor slow, but the short-sighted despotism of the trades unions has practically closed that avenue to him. Trade-schools, however excellent, cannot supply the opportunity thus denied him, and at the outset the boy stands condemned by his own to low and ill-paid drudgery, held down by the hand that of all should labor to raise him. Home, the greatest factor of all in the training of the young, means nothing to him but a pigeon-hole in a coop along with so many other human animals. Its influence is scarcely of the elevating kind, if it have any. The very games at which he takes a hand in the street become polluting in its atmosphere. With no steady hand to guide him, the boy takes naturally to idle ways. Caught in the street by the truant officer, or by the agents of the Children's Societies, peddling, perhaps, or begging, to help out the family resources, he runs the risk of being sent to a reformatory, where contact with vicious boys older than himself soon develops the latent possibilities for evil that lie hidden in him. The city has no Truant Home in which to keep him, and all efforts of the children's friends to enforce school attendance are paralyzed by this want. The risk of the reformatory is too great. What is done in the end is to let him take chances—with the chances all against him. The result is the rough young savage, familiar from the street. Rough as he is, if any one doubt that this child of common clay have in him the instinct of beauty, of love for the ideal of which his life has no embodiment, let him put the matter to the test. Let him take into a tenement block a handful of flowers from the fields and watch the brightened faces, the sudden abandonment of play and fight that go ever hand in hand where there is no elbow-room, the wild entreaty for "posies," the eager love with which the little messengers of peace are shielded, once possessed; then let him change his mind. I have seen an armful of daisies keep the peace of a block better than a policeman and his club, seen instincts awaken under their gentle appeal, whose very existence the soil in which they grew made seem a mockery. I have not forgotten the deputation of ragamuffins from a Mulberry Street alley that knocked at my office door one morning on a mysterious expedition for flowers, not for themselves, but for "a lady," and having obtained what they wanted, trooped off to bestow them, a ragged and dirty little band, with a solemnity that was quite unusual. It was not until an old man called the next day to thank me for the flowers that I found out they had decked the bier of a pauper, in the dark rear room where she lay waiting in her pine-board coffin for the city's hearse. Yet, as I knew, that dismal alley with its bare brick walls, between which no sun ever rose or set, was the world of those children. It filled their young lives. Probably not one of them had ever been out of the sight of it. They were too dirty, too ragged, and too generally disreputable, too well hidden in their slum besides to come into line with the Fresh Air summer boarders.

With such human instincts and cravings, forever unsatisfied, turned into a haunting curse; with appetite ground to keenest edge by a hunger that is never fed, the children of the poor grow up in joyless homes to lives of wearisome toil that claims them at an age when the play of their happier fellows has just begun. Has a yard of turf been laid and a vine been coaxed to grow within their reach, they are banished and barred out from it as from a heaven that is not for such as they. I came upon a couple of youngsters in a Mulberry Street yard a while ago that were chalking on the fence their first lesson in "writin'." And this is what they wrote: "Keeb of te Grass." They had it by heart, for there was not, I verily believe, a green sod within a quarter of a mile. Home to them is an empty name. Pleasure? A gentleman once catechized a ragged class in a down-town public school on this point, and recorded the result: Out of forty-eight boys twenty had never seen the Brooklyn Bridge that was scarcely five minutes' walk away, three only had been in Central Park, fifteen had known the joy of a ride in a horse-car. The street, with its ash-barrels and its dirt, the river that runs foul with mud, are their domain. What training they receive is picked up there. And they are apt pupils. If the mud and the dirt are easily reflected in their lives, what wonder? Scarce half-grown, such lads as these confront the world with the challenge to give them their due, too long withheld, or——. Our jails supply the answer to the alternative.

THE SLUM IN CHICAGO (c. 1890)   From Jane Addams, *Twenty Years at Hull-House* (New York, 1911), pp. 98–99.

The policy of the public authorities of never taking an initiative, and always waiting to be urged to do their duty, is obviously fatal in a neighborhood where there is little initiative among the citizens. The idea underlying our self-government breaks down in such a ward. The streets are inexpressibly dirty, the number of schools inadequate, sanitary legislation unenforced, the street lighting bad, the paving miserable and altogether lacking in the alleys and smaller streets, and the stables foul beyond description. Hundreds of houses are unconnected with the street sewer. The older and richer inhabitants seem anxious to move away as rapidly as they can afford it. They make room for newly arrived immigrants who are densely ignorant of civic duties. This substitution of the older inhabitants is accomplished industrially also, in the south and east quarters of the ward. The Jews and Italians do the finishing for the great clothing manufacturers, formerly done by Americans, Irish and Germans, who refused to submit to the extremely low prices to which the sweating system has reduced their successors. As the design of the sweating system is the elimination of rent from the manufacture of clothing, the "outside work" is begun after the clothing leaves the cutter. An unscrupulous contractor regards no basement as too dark, no stable loft too foul, no rear shanty too provisional, no tenement room too small for his workroom, as these conditions imply low rental. Hence these shops abound in the worst of the foreign districts where the sweater easily finds his cheap basement and his home finishers.

The houses of the ward, for the most part wooden, were originally built for one family and are now occupied by several. They are after the type of the inconvenient frame cottages found in the poorer suburbs twenty years ago. Many of them were built where they now stand; others were brought thither on rollers, because their previous sites had been taken for factories. The fewer brick tenement buildings which are three or four stories high are comparatively new, and there are few large tenements. The little wooden houses have a temporary aspect, and for this reason, perhaps, the tenement-house legislation in Chicago is totally inadequate. Rear tenements flourish; many houses have no water supply save the faucet in the back yard, there are no fire escapes, the garbage and ashes are placed in wooden boxes which are fastened to the street pavements. . . .

A VISIT TO THE NORTH END OF BOSTON (1893)   From B. O. Flower,
Civilization's Inferno, Or Studies in the Cellar (Boston, 1893), pp. 30–35.

The scenes I am about to describe were witnessed on a sunless, dreary afternoon, the day being strangely in keeping with the environment of the exiles of society who dwell in the slums. The sobbing rain, the sad, low murmur of the wind under the eaves and through the narrow alleys, the cheerless, frowning sky above, were in perfect harmony with the pathetic drama of life I was witnessing. Everything seemed pitched in a minor key, save now and then there swelled forth splendid notes of manly heroism and womanly courage, as boldy contrasting with the dead level of life as do the full, rich notes of Wagner's noblest creation with the plaintive melody of a simple ballad sung by a shepard lad. My companion was a hero, old in the service of saving the children of the slums, a noble-minded Christian who imitates the great Galilean by mingling with the earth's outcasts to save them.

The first building we entered faced a narrow street. The hallway was as dark as the air was foul or the walls filthy. Not a ray or shimmer of light fell through transoms of sky-light. The stairs were narrow and worn. By the aid of matches we were able to grope our way along, and also to observe more than was pleasant to behold. It was apparent that the hallways or stairs were seldom surprised by water, while pure, fresh air was evidently as much a stranger as fresh paint. After ascending several flights, we entered a room of undreamed-of-wretchedness. On the floor lay a sick man. He was rather fine looking, with an intelligent face, bright eyes, and a countenance indicative of force of character. No sign of dissipation, but an expression of sadness, or rather a look of dumb resignation peered from his expressive eyes. For more than two years he had been paralyzed in his lower limbs, and also affected with dropsy. The spectacle of a strong man with the organs of locomotion dead is always pathetic; but when the victim of such misfortune is in the depths of abject poverty, his case assumes a tragic hue. There, for two years, he had lain on a wretched pallet of rags, seeing his faithful wife tirelessly sewing, hour by hour and day by day, and knowing full well that health, life and hope were hourly slipping from her. This poor woman supports the invalid husband, her two children and herself, by making pants for leading Boston clothiers. No rest, no surcease, a perpetual grind from early dawn often till far into the night; and, what is more appalling, outraged nature has rebelled; the long months of semi-starvation and lack of sleep have brought on rheumatism, which has settled in the joints of her fingers, so that every stitch means a throb of pain. Thus with one of the most painful diseases enthroned in that part of the body which must move incessantly from dawn till midnight, with two small children and a husband who is utterly powerless to help her, this poor woman struggles bravely and uncomplainingly, confronted ever by a nameless dread of pending misfortune. Eviction, sickness, starvation—such are the ever-present spectres, while every year marks the steady encroachment of disease, and the lowering of the register of vitality. Moreover, from the window of her soul falls the light of no star athwart the pathway of life.

The next place visited was in the attic of a tenement building even more wretched than the one just described. The general aspects of these houses, however, are all much the same, the chief difference being in the degrees of filth and squalor present. Here in an attic lives a poor widow with three children, a little boy and two little girls. They live by making pants at starvation wages. Since the youngest child was two and a half years old she has been daily engaged in overcasting the long seams of garments made by her mother. When we first called she had just passed her fourth birthday, and now overcasts from three to four pairs of pants every day. There, on a little stool, she sat, her fingers moving as rapidly and in as unerring a manner as an old experienced needle-woman. These three children are fine looking, as are most of the little Portuguese I visited. Their large heads and brilliant eyes seem to indicate capacity to enjoy in an unusual degree the matchless delight springing from intellectual and spiritual development. Yet the wretched halls of their little apartment practically mark the limit of their world; the needle their inseparable companion; their moral and mental natures hopelessly dwarfed; a world of wonderful possibilities denied then by an inexorable fate over which they have no control and for which they are in no way responsible. We often hear it said that these children of the slums are perfectly happy; that, not knowing what they miss, life is as enjoyable to them as it is to the young in more favorable quarters. I am satisfied however, that this is true only in a limited sense. The little children I have just described are already practically machines; day by day they engage in the same work, with much of the monotony characteristic of an automatic instrument propelled by blind force. When given oranges and cakes, a momentary smile illumined their countenances, a liquid light beamed from their eyes, only to be replaced by the solemn, almost stolid expression, which has become habitual even on faces so young. This conclusion was still more impressively emphasized by the following touching remark of a child of twelve years in another apartment, who was with her mother busily sewing. "I am forty-three years old to-day," remarked the mother, and said the good Samaritan present, "I shall be forty-two next week." "Oh dear," broke in the child, "I should think people would grow so TIRED of living so MANY YEARS." Was utterance ever more pathetic? She spoke in tones of mingled sadness and weariness, revealing in one breath all the pent-up bitterness of a young life condemned to a slavery intolerable to any refined or sensitive nature. Is it strange that people here take to drink? To me it is far more suprising that so many are sober. I am convinced that, in the slums, far more drunkenness is caused by abject poverty and inability to obtain work, than want is produced by drink. Here the physical system, half starved and often chilled, calls for stimulants. Here the horrors of nightmare, which we sometimes suffer during our sleep, are present during every waking hour. An oppressive fear weighs forever on the mind. Drink offers a temporary relief and satisfies the craving of the system; besides the environment invites dissipation and human nature at best is frail. I marvel that there is not more drunkenness exhibited in the poverty spots of our cities.

Among the places we visited were a number of cellars or burrows. We descended several steps into dark, narrow passageways, leading to cold, damp rooms, in many of which no direct ray of sunshine ever creeps. We entered one room containing a bed, cooking-stove, rack of dirty clothes and some broken chairs. On the bed lay a man who has been ill for three months with rheumatism. This family consists of father, mother, and a daughter in her teens, all of whom are compelled to occupy one bed. They eat, cook, live, and sleep in this wretched cellar and pay over fifty dollars a year rent. This is a typical illustration of life in this underground world.

In another similar cellar or burrow, we found a mother and seven boys and girls, some of them quite large, all sleeping in two medium-sized beds in one room; this apartment is also their kitchen. The other room is a storehouse for kindling wood the children gather and sell, a little store and living-room combined. Their rent is two dollars a week. The cellar was damp and cold; the air stiffling. Nothing can be imagined more favorable to contagion both physical and moral than such dens as these. Ethical exaltation or spiritual growth is impossible with such environment It is not strange that the slums breed criminals, which require vast sums yearly to punish after evil has been perpetrated; but to me it is an ever-increasing source of wonder that society should be so short-sighted and neglectful of the condition of its exiles, when an outlay of a much smaller sum would ensure a prevention of a large proportion of the crime that emanates from the slums; while, at the same time, it would mean a new world of life, happiness and measureless possibilities for the thousands who now exist in hopeless gloom.

In a small room fronting an interior court we found a man whose face bore the stamp of that "hope long deferred which maketh the heart sick." He is, I am informed, a strictly temperate, honest and industrious workman. Up to the time of his wife's illness and death, which occurred last summer, the family lived in a reasonably comfortable manner, as the husband found no difficulty in securing work on the sea. When the wife died, however, circumstances changed. She left six little children, one almost an infant. The father could not go to sea, leaving his little flock without a protector, to fall the victims of starvation, and since then he has worked whenever he could obtain employment of any kind. For the past six weeks he has been practically without work, and the numerous family of little ones have suffered for life's necessities. His rent is two dollars and a quarter a week.

DESCRIPTION OF A WORKING CHILD IN CHICAGO (1895) From Florence Kelley and Alzina P. Stevens, "Wage-Earning Children," as quoted in Richard T. Ely, ed., *Hull-House Maps and Papers* (New York, 1895), pp. 54–59.

The Nineteenth Ward of Chicago is perhaps the best district in all Illinois for a detailed study of child-labor, both because it contains many factories in which children are employed, and because it is the dwelling-place of wage-earning children engaged in all lines of activity.

The Ewing Street Italian colony furnishes a large contingent to the army of bootblacks and newsboys; lads who leave home at 2.30 A.M. to secure the first edition of the morning paper, selling each edition as it appears, and filling the intervals with blacking boots and tossing pennies, until, in the winter half of the year, they gather in the Polk Street Night-School, to doze in the warmth, or torture the teacher with the gamin tricks acquired by day. For them, school is "a lark," or a peaceful retreat from parental beatings and shrieking juniors at home during the bitter nights of the Chicago winter.

There is no body of self-supporting children more in need of effective care than these newsboys and bootblacks. They are ill-fed, ill-housed, ill-clothed, illiterate, and wholly untrained and unfitted for any occupation. The only useful thing they learn at their work in common with the children who learn in school, is the rapid calculation of small sums in making change; and this does not go far enough to be of any practical value. In the absence of an effective compulsory school-attendance law, they should at least be required to obtain a license from the city; and the granting of this license should be in the hands of the Board of Education, and contingent upon a certain amount of day-school attendance accomplished.

In this ward dwells, also, a large body of cash-children, boys and girls. Their situation is illustrated by the Christmas experience of one of their number. A little girl, thirteen years of age, saw in an evening paper of December 23rd last, an advertisement for six girls to work in one of the best-known candy stores, candidates to apply at seven o'clock the next morning, at a branch store on the West Side, one and a half miles from the child's home. To reach the place in time, she spent five cents of her lunch money for car-fare. Arriving, she found other children, while but one was wanted. She was engaged as the brightest of the group, and sent to a down-town branch of the establishment, at a distance of two and a quarter miles. This time she walked: then worked till midnight, paying for her dinner, and going without supper. She was paid fifty cents, and discharged with the explanation that she was only required for one day. No cars were running at that hour, and the little girl walked across the worst district of Chicago, to reach her home and her terrified mother at one o'clock on Christmas morning.[1] No law was violated in this transaction, as mercantile establishments are not yet subject to the provisions of the factory act.

Fortunately the development of the pneumatic tube has begun to supersede the cash-children in the more respectable of the retail stores; and a movement for extending the workshop law to the mercantile establishments would, therefore, meet with less opposition now than at any previous time. The need for this legislation will be acknowledged by every person who will stand on any one of the main thoroughfares of Chicago on a morning between 6.30 and 7.30 o'clock, and watch the processions of puny children filing into the dry-goods emporiums to run, during nine or ten hours, and in holiday seasons twelve and thirteen hours, a day to the cry, "Cash!"

In the stores on the West Side, large numbers of young girls are employed thirteen hours a day throughout the week, and fifteen hours on Saturday; and all efforts of the clothing-clerks to shorten the working-time by trade-union methods have hitherto availed but little. While the feeble unions of garment-makers have addressed themselves to the legislature, and obtained a valuable initial measure of protection for the young garment-workers, the retail-clerks, depending upon public opinion and local ordinances, have accomplished little on behalf of the younger clothing-sellers.

In dealing with newsboys, bootblacks, and cash-children, we have been concerned with those who live in the nineteenth ward, and work perhaps there or

[1]Incidentally it is of interest that this firm was one of the most liberal givers of Christmas candy to the poor.

perhaps elsewhere. We come now to the children who work in the factories of the nineteenth ward.

The largest number of children to be found in any one factory in Chicago is in a caramel works in this ward, where there are from one hundred and ten to two hundred little girls, four to twelve boys, and seventy to one hundred adults, according to the season of the year. The building is a six-story brick, well lighted, with good plumbing and fair ventilation. It has, however, no fire-escape and a single wooden stair leading from floor to floor. In case of fire the inevitable fate of the children working on the two upper floors is too horrible to contemplate. The box factory is on the fifth floor, and the heaviest pressure of steam used in boiling the caramels is all on the top floor. The little girls sit closely packed at long tables, wrapping and packing the caramels. They are paid by the piece, and the number of pennies per thousand paid is just enough to attract the most ignorant and helpless children in the city.[2] Previous to the passage of the factory law of 1893, it was the rule of this factory to work the children, for several weeks before the Christmas holidays, from 7 A.M. to 9 P.M., with twenty minutes for lunch, and no supper, a working week of eighty-two hours. As this overtime season coincided with the first term of the night-school, the children lost their one opportunity. Since the enactment of the factory law, their working week has consisted of six days of eight hours each; a reduction of thirty-four hours a week.

Health

It is a lamentable fact, well known to those who have investigated child-labor, that children are found in greatest number where the conditions of labor are most dangerous to life and health. Among the occupations in which children are most employed in Chicago, and which most endanger the health, are: The tobacco trade, nicotine poisoning finding as many victims among factory children as among the boys who are voluntary devotees of the weed, consumers of the deadly cigarette included; frame gilding, in which work a child's fingers are stiffened and throat disease is contracted; button-holing, machine-stitching, and hand-work in tailor or sweat shops, the machine-work producing spinal curvature, and for girls pelvic disorders also, while the unsanitary condition of the shops makes even hand-sewing dangerous; bakeries, where children slowly roast before the ovens; binderies, paper-box and paint factories, where arsenical paper, rotting paste, and the poison of the paints are injurious; boiler-plate works, cutlery works, and metal-stamping works, where the dust produces lung disease; the handling of hot metal, accidents; the hammering of plate, deafness. In addition to diseases incidental to trades, there are the conditions of bad sanitation and long hours, almost universal in the factories where children are employed.

The power of the Illinois inspectors, so far as they have any power to require that only healthy children shall be employed, and these only in safe and healthy

---

[2]The affidavits of the children afford an astonishing collection of unpronounceable names, Polish and Bohemian combinations of consonants, interspersed with Smith. As there is rarely an English-speaking child in this factory, the prevalence of the Smiths was a matter of perplexity, until it transpired that notaries, troubled by the foreign orthography, suggest that the children call themselves by a more manageable name. This widespread custom greatly increases the difficulty of prosecutions for violation of the factory law in establishments in which the employees are drawn from the foreign colonies. And in the caramel works, with its polyglot population, the work of fitting the affidavits to the children is as laborious as it is absurd.

places, is found in #4 of the Workshop and Factories Act, the last clause, already quoted. What may be accomplished under this section is indicated by the following report concerning medical examinations in the inspector's office, made for the boys by Dr. Bayard Holmes, of the College of Physicians and Surgeons; and for the girls by Dr. Josephine Milligan, resident physician at Hull House:—

During four months 135 factory children were given medical examinations in the office. The inspectors required these children to secure health certificates because they were undersized, or seemed to be ill, or were working in unwholesome shops, or at dangerous occupations. They were children sworn by their parents to be fourteen years of age, or over.

Each child was weighed with and without clothing; had eyes and ears tested; heart, lungs, skin, spine, joints, and nails examined; and forty measurements taken.

Of the 135 children, 72 were found sufficiently normal to be allowed to continue work. Of the 63 refused certificates, 53 were not allowed to work at all, and 10 were stopped working at unwholesome trades, as tobacco-stripping, grinding in cutlery factory, running machines by foot-power, and crimping cans; these were advised to look for more wholesome work.

DESCRIPTION OF A TYPICAL NEW YORK TENEMENT HOUSE

(**1903**)   From Robert W. DeForest and Laurence Veiller, eds., *The Tenement House Problem* (New York, 1903), pp. 7–10.

Some knowledge of the prevailing kind of New York tenement house must necessarily precede any consideration of its evils and their remedies. It is known as the "double-decker," "dumb-bell" tenement, a type which New York has the unenviable distinction of having invented. It is a type unknown to any other city in America or Europe.

Although the housing problem is one of the leading political questions of the day in England, the conditions which exist there are ideal compared to the conditions in New York. The tall tenement house, accommodating as many as 100 to 150 persons in one building, extending up six or seven stories into the air, with dark, unventilated rooms, is unknown in London or in any other city of Great Britain. It was first constructed in New York about the year 1879, and with slight modifications has been practically the sole type of building erected since, and is the type of the present day. It is a building usually five or six or even seven stories high, about 25 feet wide, and built upon a lot of land of the same width and about 100 feet deep. The building as a rule extends back 90 feet, leaving the small space of ten feet unoccupied at the rear, so that the back rooms may obtain some light and air. This space has continued to be left open only because the law has compelled it. Upon the entrance floor there are generally two stores, one on each side of the building, and these sometimes have two or three living rooms back of them. In the centre is the entrance hallway, a long corridor less than 3 feet wide and extending back 60 feet in length. This hallway is nearly always totally dark, receiving no light except that from the street door and a faint light that comes from the small windows opening upon the stairs, which are placed at one side of the hallway. Each

EDUCATION FOR
URBAN INDUSTRIAL
AMERICA
1895–1918

floor above is generally divided into four sets of apartments, there being seven rooms on each side of the hall, extending back from the street to the rear of the building. The front apartments generally consist of four rooms each and the rear apartments of three rooms, making altogether fourteen upon each floor, or in a seven-story house eighty-four rooms exclusive of the stores and rooms back of them. Of these fourteen rooms on each floor, only four receive direct light and air from the street or from the small yard at the back of the building. Generally, along each side of the building is what is termed an "air shaft," being an indentation of the wall to a depth of about 28 inches, and extending in length for a space of from 50 to 60 feet. This shaft is entirely enclosed on four sides, and is, of course, the full height of the building, often from 60 to 72 feet high. The ostensible purpose of the shaft is to provide light and air to the five rooms on each side of the house which get no direct light and air from the street or yard; but as the shafts are narrow and high, being enclosed on all four sides, and without any intake of air at the bottom, these rooms obtain, instead of fresh air and sunshine, foul air and semi-darkness. Indeed it is questionable whether the rooms would not be more habitable and more sanitary with no shaft at all, depending for their light and air solely upon the front and back rooms into which they open; for each family, besides having the foul air from its own rooms to breathe, is compelled to breathe the emanations from the rooms of some eleven other families; nor is this all, these shafts act as conveyors of noise, odors, and disease, and when fire breaks out serve as inflammable flues, often rendering it impossible to save the buildings from destruction.

A family living in such a building pays for four rooms of this kind a rent of from $12 to $18 a month. Of these four rooms only two are large enough to be deserving of the name of rooms. The front one is generally about 10 feet 6 inches wide by 11 feet 3 inches long; this the family use as a parlor, and often at night, when the small bedrooms opening upon the air shaft are so close and ill-ventilated that sleep is impossible, mattresses are dragged upon the floor of the parlor, and there the family sleep, all together in one room. In summer the small bedrooms are so hot and stifling that a large part of the tenement house population sleep on the roofs, the sidewalks, and the fire-escapes. The other room, the kitchen, is generally the same size as the parlor upon which it opens, and receives all its light and air from the "air shaft," or such a supply as may come to it from the front room. Behind these two rooms are the bedrooms, so called, which are hardly more than closets, being each about 7 feet wide and 8 feet 6 inches long, hardly large enough to contain a bed. These rooms get no light and air whatsoever, except that which comes from the "air shaft," and except on the highest stories are generally almost totally dark. Upon the opposite side of the public hall is an apartment containing four exactly similar rooms, and at the rear of the building there are, instead of four rooms on each side of the hallway, but three, one of the bedrooms being dispensed with. For these three rooms in the rear the rent is generally throughout the city from $10 to $15 a month. In the public hallway, opposite the stairs, there are provided two water-closets, each water-closet being used in common by two families and being lighted and ventilated by the "air shaft," which also lights and ventilates all the bedrooms. In the newer buildings there is frequently provided, in the hallway between the two closets, a dumb-waiter for the use of the tenants.

It is not to be wondered at, therefore, that with such a kind of tenement house repeated all over the different parts of this city, and forming practically the only kind of habitation for the great mass of the people, the tenement house system has become fraught with so much danger to the welfare of the community. The effect upon the city population of the form of congregated living found in our tenement houses is to be seen, not only in its results upon the health of the people, but upon their moral and social condition as well. The public mind is just now especially aroused over the manifestation of one special form of vice in tenement districts. It is not to be wondered at that vice in various forms should manifest itself in the tenements; the wonder is that there is not more vice in such districts. The tenement districts of New York are places in which thousands of people are living in the smallest space in which it is possible for human beings to exist—crowded together in dark, ill-ventilated rooms, in many of which the sunlight never enters and in most of which fresh air is unknown. They are centres of disease, poverty, vice, and crime, where it is a marvel, not that some children grow up to be thieves, drunkards, and prostitutes, but that so many should ever grow up to be decent and self-respecting. All the conditions which surround childhood, youth, and womanhood in New York's crowded tenement quarters make for unrighteousness. They also make for disease. There is hardly a tenement house in which there has not been at least one case of pulmonary tuberculosis within the last five years, and in some houses there have been as great a number as twenty-two different cases of this terrible disease. From the tenements there comes a stream of sick, helpless people to our hospitals and dispensaries, few of whom are able to afford the luxury of a private physician, and some houses are in such bad sanitary condition that few people can be seriously ill in them and get well; from them also comes a host of paupers and charity seekers. The most terrible of all the features of tenement house life in New York, however, is the indiscriminate herding of all kinds of people in close contact, the fact, that, mingled with the drunken, the dissolute, the improvident, the diseased, dwell the great mass of the respectable working-men of the city with their families.

DESCRIPTION OF "NURSERIES" IN THE COAL COUNTIES OF PENNSYLVANIA (1903)   From Francis H. Nichols, "Children of the Coal Shadow," *McClure's Magazine*, vol. XX, pp. 439–44.

The School of the "Breaker"

The company's nurseries for boys of the coal shadow are the grim black buildings called breakers, where the lump coal from the blast is crushed into marketable sizes.

In speaking of the events of his childhood, the average man is far more apt to refer to the time "when I was working in the breaker" than to any occurrence of his school-days. After being ground in heavy machinery in the cupola of the breaker, the broken coal flows down a series of chutes to the ground floor, where it is loaded on freight cars waiting to receive it. The chutes zigzag through the building, about three feet apart. Between them, in tiers, are nailed a series of planks; these serve as seats for the "slate-pickers." Mixed with the coal are pieces of slate rock which it is the duty of the slate-picker to detect as they pass him, and to throw into another chute which passes to the refuse heap below. A few of the slate-pickers are white-haired old men, superannuated or crippled miners who are no longer able to blast coal below ground, and who for the sake of a dollar a day pass their last years in the breaker; but an overwhelming majority in all the breakers are boys. All day long their little fingers dip into the unending grimy stream that rolls past them.

Dangers and Hardships of the Work

The coal so closely resembles slate that it can be detected only by the closest scrutiny, and the childish faces are compelled to bend so low over the chutes that prematurely round shoulders and narrow chests are the inevitable result. In front of the chutes is an open space reserved for the "breaker boss," who watches the boys as intently as they watch the coal.

The boss is armed with a stick, with which he occasionally raps on the head and shoulders a boy who betrays lack of zeal. The breakers are supposed to be heated in winter, and a steam pipe winds up the wall; but in cold weather every pound of steam is needed in the mines, so that the amount of heat that radiates from the steam pipe is not sufficient to be taken seriously by any of the breakers' toilers. From November until May a breaker boy always wears a cap and tippet, and overcoat if he possesses one, but because he has to rely largely upon the sense of touch, he cannot cover his finger-tips with mittens or gloves; from the chafing of the coal his fingers sometimes bleed, and his nails are worn down to the quick. The hours of toil for slate-pickers are supposed to be from seven in the morning until noon, and from one to six in the afternoon; but when the colliery is running on "full capacity orders," the noon recess is reduced to half an hour, and the goodnight whistle does not blow until half-past six. For his eleven hours' work the breaker boy gets no more pay than for ten.

The wages of breaker boys are about the same all over the coal regions. When he begins to work at slate picking a boy receives forty cents a day, and as he becomes more expert the amount is increased until at the end of, say, his fourth year in the breaker, his daily wage may have reached ninety cents. This is the maximum for an especially industrious and skillful boy. The average is about seventy cents a day. From the ranks of the older breaker boys are chosen door-boys and runners, who work in the mines below ground.

The number of boys who work in hard coal mines is imperfectly realized in the rest of the United States. According to the report of the Bureau of Mines of Pennsylvania for 1901, 147,651 persons were employed "inside and outside the mines of the anthracite region." Of these, 19,564 were classified as slate-pickers, 3,148 as door-boys and helpers, and 10,894 as drivers and runners.

The report makes no classification of miners by their ages, but I am convinced that 90 per cent of the slate-pickers, 30 per cent of the drivers and runners, and all of the door-boys and helpers are boys. In other words, a total of 24,023, or nearly one-sixth of all the employees of the anthracite coal mines, are children.

Age Certificates and What They Amount To

According to the mining laws of Pennsylvania, "no boy under the age of fourteen shall be employed in a mine, nor shall a boy under the age of twelve be employed in or about the outside structures or workings of a colliery" (*i.e.*, in a breaker). Yet no one who stands by the side of a breaker boss and looks up at the tiers of benches that rise from the floor to the coal-begrimed roof can believe for a minute that the law has been complied with in the case of one in ten of the tiny figures in blue jumpers and overalls bending over the chutes. The mine inspector and the breaker boss will explain that "these boys look younger than their ages is," and that a sworn certificate setting forth the age of every boy is on file in the office.

Children's age certificates are a criminal institution. When a father wishes to place his son in a breaker, he obtains an "age blank" from a mine inspector, and in its spaces he has inserted some age at which it is legal for a boy to work. He carries the certificate to a notary public or justice of the peace, who, in consideration of a fee of twenty-five cents, administers oath to the parent and affixes a notarial seal to the certificate.

Justifiable and Unjustifiable Perjury

According to the ethics of the coal fields, it is not wrong for a minor or his family to lie or to practise any form of deceit in dealing with coal-mine operators or owners. A parent is justified in perjuring himself as to his son's age on a certificate that will be filed with the mine superintendent, but any statement made to a representative of the union must be absolutely truthful. For this reason my inquiries of mine boys as to their work and ages were always conducted under the sacred auspices of the union.

Testimony "On the Level"

The interrogative colloquy was invariably something like this:

"How old are you?"

Boy: "Thirteen; going on fourteen."

Secretary of the Local: "On the level now, this is union business. You can speak free, understand."

Boy: "Oh, dat's a diffurnt t'ing altogether. I'm nine years old. I've been working since me fadder got hurted in th' explosion in No. 17 a year ago last October."

THE PROBLEM OF HUNGRY SCHOOL CHILDREN (1906) From John Spargo, *The Bitter Cry of the Children* (New York, 1906), pp. 57-60, 117-22.

Summarizing, briefly, the results of this investigation, the problem of poverty as it affects school children may be stated in a few lines. All the data available tend to show that not less than 2,000,000 children of school age in the United States are the victims of poverty which denies them common necessities, particularly adequate nourishment. As a result of this privation they are far inferior in physical development to their more fortunate fellows. The inferiority of physique, in turn, is responsible for much mental and moral degeneration. Such children are in very many cases incapable of successful mental effort, and much of our national expenditure for education is in consequence an absolute waste. With their enfeebled bodies and minds we turn these children adrift unfitted for the struggle of life, which tends to become keener with every advance in our industrial development, and because of their lack of physical and mental training they are found to be inefficient industrially and dangerous socially. They become dependent, paupers, and the procreators of a pauper and dependent race.

Here, then, is a problem of awful magnitude. In the richest country on earth hundreds of thousands of children are literally damned to lifelong, helpless, and debasing poverty. They are plunged in the earliest and most important years of character formation into that terrible maelstrom of poverty which casts so many thousands, ay, millions, of physical, mental and moral wrecks upon the shores of our social life. For them there is little or no hope of escape from the blight and curse of pauperism unless the nation, pursuing a policy of enlightened self-interest and protection, decides to save them. In the main, this vast sum of poverty is due to causes of a purely impersonal nature which the victims cannot control, such as sickness, accident, low wages and unemployment. Personal causes, such as ignorance, thriftlessness, gambling, intemperance, indolence, wife-desertion, and other vices or weaknesses, are also responsible for a good deal of poverty, though by no means most of it as is sometimes urged by superficial observers. There are many thousands of temperate and industrious workers who are miserably poor, and many of those who are thriftless or intemperate are the victims of poverty's degenerating influences. But whether a child's hunger and privation is due to some fault of its parents or to causes beyond their control, the fact of its suffering remains, and its impaired physical and mental strength tends almost irresistibly to make it inefficient as a citizen. Whatever the cause, therefore, of its privation, society must, as a measure of self-protection, take upon itself the responsibility of caring for the child.

There can be no compromise upon this vital point. Those who say that society should refuse to do anything for those children who are victims of their parents' vices or weaknesses adopt a singularly indefensible attitude. In the first place it is barbarously unjust to allow the sins of the parents to bring punishment and suffering upon the child, to damn the innocent and unoffending. No more vicious doctrine than this, which so many excellent and well-intentioned persons are fond of preaching, has ever been formulated by human perversity. Carried to its logical end, it would destroy all legislation for the protection of children from cruel parents or guardians. It is strange that the doctrinaire advocates of this brutal gospel should overlook its practical consequences. If discrimination were to be made at all, it should be in favor of, rather than against, the children of drunken and profligate parents. For these children have a special claim upon society for protection from wrongs in the shape of influences injurious to their physical and moral well-being, and tending to lead them into evil and degrading ways. The half-starved child of the inebriate is not less entitled to the protection of society than the victim of inhuman physical torture.

Should these children be excluded from any system of feeding adopted by the state upon the ground that their parents have not fulfilled their parental responsibilities, society joins in a conspiracy against their very lives. And that conspiracy ultimately and inevitably involves retribution. In the interests and name of a beguiling economy, fearful that if it assumes responsibility for the care of the child of inebriate parents, it will foster and encourage their inebriety and neglect, society leaves the children surrounded by circumstances which practically force them to become drunkards, physical and moral wrecks, and procreators of a like degenerate progeny. *Then* it is forced to accept the responsibility of their support, either as paupers or criminals. That is the stern Nemesis of retribution. Where an enlightened system of child saving has been followed, this principle has been clearly recognized. In Minnesota, for example, the state assumes the responsibility for the care of such children as a matter of self-protection. To quote the language of a report of the State Public School at Owatonna: "It is for economic as well as for humane reasons that this work is done. The state is thus protecting itself from dangers to which it would be exposed in a very few years if these children were reared in the conditions which so injuriously affect them." Whatever steps may be taken to punish, or make responsible to the state, those parents who by their vice and neglect bring suffering and want upon their children, the children themselves should be saved.

To the contention that society, having assumed the responsibility of insisting that every child shall be educated, and providing the means of education, is necessarily bound to assume the responsibility of seeing that they are made fit to receive that education, so far as possible, there does not seem to be any convincing answer. It will be objected that for society to do this would mean the destruction of the responsibility of the parents, That is obviously true. But it is equally true of education itself, the responsibility for which society has assumed. Some individualists there are who contend that society is wrong in doing this, and their opposition to the proposal that it should undertake to provide the children with food is far more logical than that of those who believe that society should assume the responsibility of educating the child, but not that of equipping it with the necessary physical basis for that education. The fact is that society insists upon the education of the children, not, primarily, in their interests nor in the interests of the parents, but in its own. All legislation upon child labor, education, child guardianship in general, is based upon a denial of proprietary rights to children by their parents. The child belongs to society rather than to its parents.

DESCRIPTION OF CHILD LABOR IN OYSTER AND SHRIMP CANNERIES IN THE SOUTH (1913)   From Lewis W. Hine, "Baltimore To Biloxi and Back," *Survey* vol. XXX, pp.167–72.

When we speak of child labor in oyster canning, we refer to the cooked or "cove" oysters, not to the raw ones. Children are not used in opening raw oysters for the sole reason that their fingers are not strong enough. Occasionally one finds young boys at work on the boats dredging for the oysters, but not many children work on the boats, for that is a man's job.

The two chief sections engaged in the work of canning oysters and shrimps are the Gulf Coast, from New Orleans eastward to Florida, and the Atlantic Coast of Maryland, the Carolinas, and Georgia. Maryland was the pioneer state, but it has already been outstripped by Mississippi, and several other states follow close in amount of annual output.

Every year about October, hundreds of Polish and Bohemian people (some authorities say thousands) are herded together by various bosses or "padrones" in Baltimore and other centers of the South, shipped over to the coasts by train and by boat and set up in shacks provided by the canning companies. We are told by one of the canners, "We give these people all the modern conveniences." The modern conveniences appear to be summed up in artesian wells. If there were no cold or wet weather in these parts, if waste and sewage were carried off, and if there were no crowding, these temporary quarters would be endurable; but in cold, or hot, or wet weather they are positively dangerous, especially to children. One row of dilapidated shacks that I found in South Carolina housed fifty workers in a single room house. One room sheltered eight persons, and the shacks were located on an old shell pile within a few rods of the factory, a few feet from the tidal marsh where odors, mosquitoes, and sand flies made life intolerable, especially in hot weather.

There is a prevailing impression that in the matter of child labor the emphasis on the labor must be very slight, but let me tell you right here that these processes involve work, hard work, deadening in its monotony, exhausting physically, irregular, the workers' only joy the closing hour. We might even say of these children that they are condemned to work.

Come out with me to one of these canneries at three o'clock some morning. Here is the crude shed-like building, with a long dock at which the oyster boats unload their cargoes. Near the dock is the ever present shell pile, a monument of mute testimony to the patient toil of little fingers. It is cold, damp, dark. The whistle blew some time ago, and the young workers slipped into their meager garments, snatched a bite to eat and hurried to the shucking shed. The padrone told me "Ef dey don't git up, I go and *git 'em up.*" See those little ones over there stumbling through the dark over the shell piles, munching a piece of bread, and rubbing their heavy eyes. Boys and girls, six, seven and eight years of age, take their places with the adults and work all day.

The cars are ready for them with their loads of dirty, rough clusters of shells, and as these shells accumulate under foot in irregular piles, they soon make the mere matter of standing one of physical strain. Notice the uncertain footing, and the dilapidated foot-wear of that little girl, and opposite is one with cloth fingers to protect herself from jagged shells—they call them "finger-stalls." Their fingers are often sore in spite of this precaution.

When they are picking shrimps, their fingers and even their shoes are attacked by a corrosive substance in the shrimp that is strong enough to eat the tin cans into which they are put. The day's work on shrimp is much shorter than on oysters as the fingers of the worker give out in spite of the fact that they are compelled to harden them in an alum solution at the end of the day. Morever, the shrimp are packed in ice, and a few hours handling of these icy things is dangerous for any child. Then, too, the mornings, and many of the days, are cold, foggy and damp.

The workers are thinly clad, but like the fabled ostrich, cover their heads and imagine they are warm. If a child is sick, it gets a vacation, and wanders around to kill time.

The youngest of all shift for themselves at a very early age. One father told me that they brought their baby, two months old, down to the shucking-shed at four o'clock every morning and kept it there all day. Another told me that they locked a baby of six months in the shack when they went away in the morning, and left it until noon, then left it alone again all the afternoon. A baby carriage with its occupant half smothered under piles of blankets is a common sight. Snuggled up against a steam box you find many a youngster asleep on a cold morning. As soon as they can toddle, they hang around the older members of the family, something of a nuisance, of course, and very early they learn to amuse themselves. For hours at a time, they play with the dirty shells, imitating the work of the grown-ups. They toddle around the shed, and out on to the docks at the risk of their lives.

A little older and they learn to "tend the baby." As a substitute for real recreation, this baby tending is pathetic.

Mary said, "I shucks six pots if I don't got the baby: two pots if I got him."

As soon as they can handle the oysters and shrimps, they are "allowed to help."

The mother often says, "Sure. I'm learnin' her de trade," and you see many youngsters beginning to help at a very early age. Standing on a box in order to reach the table, little Olga, five years old, was picking shrimps for her mother at the cannery I visited. Later in the day, I found her at home worn out with the work she had been doing, but the mother complained that Olga was "ugly." Little sympathy they get when they most need it! Four-year-old Mary was working irregularly through the day shucking about two pots of oysters. The mother is the fastest shucker in the place.

* * *

Are you surprised to find that many children seem dumb and can not understand our language?

"But we educate them" some canners tell us.

This is the way they do it. In the few places where I found any pretense to education the children shucked oysters for four hours before school. Then they went to school for half a day, returning at one o'clock for a hurried lunch. They worked for four hours more, five days in the week. On Saturday they put in an alleged half day consisting of eight or nine hours work. Is it any marvel that the school principal told me "It isn't satisfactory, but at least we are giving them some help in learning the language." They need the help. At another place, with two canneries, but two children were going to school, and the illiteracy of both adults and children was appalling.

"There is no compulsion about schooling here," the principal said.

The "vocational guidance" which most of them receive, year in and year out, is seen in the sheds where under the eagle eye of the boss, who watches to see that they do not shirk, and under the pressure of parental authority, they put in their time where it will bring tangible returns. One padrone told me:

"I keep 'em a-working all the year. In the winter, bring 'em down here to the gulf. In summer, take 'em to the berry fields of Maryland and Delaware. They don't lose many weeks' time, but I have a hard time to get 'em sometimes. Have to tell 'em all kinds of lies."

So here we have a certain kind of "scientific management" of child labor by means of which even the vacation time of the children is utilized.

"Why do they do it?"—that question comes to one over and over; what keeps these little ones at their uninteresting task? In the first place, their immigrant parents are frugal, even parsimonious, and every little helps. Then they think it keeps the children out of trouble, little realizing that they are storing up trouble when they grow up, handicapped by lack of education, broken physically, and with a distaste for work. Small wonder if they drift into the industrial maelstrom of cheap, inefficient labor, and float on as industrial misfits.

If we look at it from the employer's point of view, we find his chief justification is that children are needed because the goods are perishable, and must be put up immediately. You ask him if the children are not perishable, and he says he can't see that they are spoiled, "It doesn't hurt 'em. They're tough. I began myself at their age," and so on. It will be long years before these employers will be looking at this children's labor with a long-range finder, a problem to be met along with that of improved machinery. The children themselves are docile; they do as they are told; they are imitative, like to do what the rest are doing; they are easily stimulated by the idea of competing with other children; and they are very sensitive to criticism and ridicule. I do not, however, recall a single case of a child being whipped for not working. It can easily be seen that with the parents, or employers, and children against it, the task of liberation from this commercialized family peonage of immature workers is not an easy one.

On the Atlantic Coast more negroes are employed, than on the Gulf Coast, and they do not work the children very much, except where they have come under the influence of the immigrant workers. In almost every case, the bosses and padrones agree that the Baltimore workers are much more satisfactory than the Negroes. They say:

"There is no comparing them. The whites work harder, longer hours are more easily driven, and use the children much more."

The chief advantage of Negro help is that it saves the cost of transportation. Where it is necessary to get the work done promptly the immigrants are imported.

That this exploitation of the children is absolutely unnecessary is proven by the canneries that get along without them. It needs merely more efficient planning on the part of the managers, and better supervision on the part of the state. It is certainly a condition not to be endured when we consider the hardships involved—the long hours, the monotonous and tiring work, the irregular conditions of work and of life, the exposure, the unsanitary surroundings, the moral dangers, the lack of education, and the double exploitation of summer and winter.

One morning I found a little cannery worker setting about her endless job. At the end of the day as I passed near, human nature asserted itself. She asked me to photograph her dolly too, this oyster shucker.

The Immigrant Experience

THE CHILDREN OF THE JEWISH POOR (1892) From Jacob A. Riis, *The Children of the Poor* (New York, 1892), pp. 43–50.

The entire absence of privacy in their homes and the foul contact of the sweaters' shops, where men and women work side by side from morning till night, scarcely half clad in the hot summer weather, does for the girls what the street completes in the boy. But for the patriarchal family life of the Jew that is his strongest virture, their ruin would long since have been complete. It is that which pilots him safely through shoals upon which the Gentile would have been inevitably wrecked. It is that which keeps the almshouse from casting its shadow over Ludlow Street to add to its gloom. It is the one quality which redeems, and on the Sabbath eve when he gathers his household about his board, scant though the fare be, dignifies the darkest slum of Jewtown.

How strong is this attachment to home and kindred that makes the Jew cling to the humblest hearth and gather his children and his children's children about it, though grinding proverty leave them on a bare crust to share, I saw in the case of little Jette Brodsky, who strayed away from her own door, looking for her papa. They were strangers and ignorant and poor, so that weeks went by before they could make their loss known and get a hearing, and meanwhile Jette, who had been picked up and taken to Police Headquarters, had been hidden away in an asylum, given another name when nobody came to claim her, and had been quite forgotten. But in the two years that passed before she was found at last, her empty chair stood ever by her father's, at the family board, and no Sabbath eve but heard his prayer for the restoration of their lost one. It happened once that I came in on a Friday evening at the breaking of bread, just as the four candles upon the table had been lit with the Sabbath blessing upon the home and all it sheltered. Their light fell on little else than empty plates and anxious faces; but in the patriarchal host who arose and bade the guest welcome with a dignity a king might have envied I recognized with difficulty the humble pedlar I had known only from the street and from the police office, where he hardly ventured beyond the door.

But the tenement that has power to turn purest gold to dross digs a pit for the Jew even through this virtue that has been his shield against its power for evil. In its atmosphere it turns too often to a curse by helping to crowd his lodgings, already overflowing, beyond the point of official forbearance. Then follow orders to "reduce" the number of tenants that mean increased rent, which the family cannot pay, or the breaking up of the home. An appeal to avert such a calamity came to the Board of Health recently from one of the refugee tenements. The tenant was a man with a houseful of children, too full for the official scale as applied to the flat, and his plea was backed by the influence of his only friend in need—the family undertaker. There was something so cruelly suggestive in the idea that the laugh it raised died without an echo.

The census of the sweaters' district gave a total of 23,405 children under six years, and 21,285 between six and fourteen, in a population of something over a hundred and eleven thousand Russian, Polish, and Roumanian Jews in the three wards mentioned; 15,567 are set down as "children over fourteen." According to the record, scarce one-third of the heads of families had become naturalized citizens, though the average of their stay in the United States was between nine and ten years. The very language of our country was to them a strange tongue, understood and spoken by only 15,837 of the fifty thousand and odd adults enumerated. Seven thousand of the rest spoke only German, five thousand Russian, and over twenty-one thousand could only make themselves understood to each other, never to the world around them, in the strange jargon that passes for Hebrew on the East Side, but is really a mixture of a dozen known dialects and tongues and of some that were never known or heard anywhere else. In the census it is down as just what it is—jargon, and nothing else.

Here, then, are conditions as unfavorable to the satisfactory, even safe, development of child life in the chief American city as could well be imagined; more unfavorable even than with the Bohemians, who have at least their faith in common with us, if safety lies in the merging through the rising generation of the discordant elements into a common harmony. A community set apart, set sharply against the rest in every clashing interest, social and industrial; foreign in language, in faith, and in tradition; repaying dislike with distrust; expanding under the new relief from oppression in the unpopular qualities of greed and contentiousness fostered by ages of tyranny unresistingly borne. Clearly, if ever there was need of moulding any material for the citizenship that awaits it, it is with this; and if ever trouble might be expected to beset the effort, it might be looked for here. But it is not so. The record shows that of the sixty thousand children, including the fifteen thousand young men and women over fourteen who earns a large share of the money that pays for rent and food, and the twenty-three thousand toddlers under six years, fully one-third go to school. Deducting the two extemes, little more than a thousand children of between six and fourteen years, that is, of school age, were put down as receiving no instruction at the time the census was taken; but it is not at all likely that this condition was permanent in the case of the greater number of these. The poorest Hebrew knows—the poorer he is, the better he knows it—that knowledge is power, and power as the means of getting on in the world that has spurned him so long is what his soul yearns for. He lets no opportunity slip to obtain it. Day and night schools are crowded by his children, who are everywhere forging ahead of their Christian school-fellows, taking more than their share of prizes and promotions. Every synagogue, every second rear tenement or dark back yard, has its school and its school-master with his scourge to intercept those who might otherwise escape. In the census there are put down 251 Jewish teachers as living in these tenements, a large number of whom conduct such schools, so that, as the children form always more than one-half of the population in the Jewish quarter, the evidence is after all that even here, with the tremendous inpour of a destitute, ignorant people, and with the undoubted employment of child labor on a large scale, the cause of progress along the safe line is holding its own.

In all of her years in America, my mother never saw the inside of a
school. My father went only once, and that was when he took me and my two
younger brothers to *La Soupa Scuola* (the "Soup School"), as it was called among
the immigrants of my generation. We headed along Second Avenue in the direction
of 115th Street, my father walking in front, holding the hands of my two brothers,
while I followed along with a boy of my own age, Vito Salvatore, whose family had
arrived from Avigliano seven years before.

My long European trousers had been replaced by the short knickers of the time,
and I wore black ribbed stockings and new American shoes. To all outward
appearances I was an American, except that I did not speak a word of English.

Vito kept chanting what sounded like gibberish to me, all the while casting
sidelong glances in my direction as though nursing some delightful secret.

"Mrs. Cutter cut the butter ten times in the gutter!"

"What the devil are you singing—an American song?" I asked in the dialect of
our people.

"You'll meet the devil all right." And again, in English, "Mrs. Cutter cut the
butter ten times in the gutter! Only this devil wears skirts and carries a stick this
long. Wham, and she lets you have it across the back! This, my dear Narduccio, is
your new head teacher."

Was it possible? A woman teacher! "In Avigliano we were taught by men," I
bragged to my friend. "There was Maestro Mecca. Strong? When he cracked your
hand with his ruler it went numb for a week. And you are trying to scare me with
your woman teacher. . . ."

I spoke with pride. Already "yesterday" was taking on a new meaning. I was
lonely. I missed the mountains. I missed my friends at the shoemaker shop and my
uncles and the life I had always known. In the face of a strange and uncertain
future, Avigliano now loomed in a new and nostalgic light. Even unpleasant
remembrances had a fascination of their own. Who had felt the blows of Don
Salvatore Mecca could stand anything.

The Soup School was a three-story wooden building hemmed in by two five-
story tenements at 116th Street and Second Avenue. When Vito pointed it out I
experienced a shock. It appeared huge and impressive, I was ashamed to let him
know that in Avigliano our school consisted of only one room, poorly lighted and
poorly heated, with benches that hadn't been changed in fifty years. However, at
this moment something really wonderful happened to take my thoughts from the
poverty of our life in Avigliano.

Before entering the school, my father led us into a little store close at hand.
There was a counter covered by glass and in it all manner and kinds of sweets such
as we had never seen before. *"Candi!"* my father told us, grinning. "This is what is
called *candi* in America.

"C-a-n-d-y!" know-it-all Vito repeated in my ear.

We were even allowed to select the kind we wanted. I remember how I selected
some little round cream-filled chocolates which tasted like nothing I had ever eaten
before. It was unheard-of to eat sweets on a school day, even though this was a
special occasion. Anyway, the only candy I knew was *confetti*, the sugar-coated

almond confection which we had only on feast days or from the pocket of my uncle the priest on some very special occasion, and for which we kissed his hand in return. But today my father was especially happy. He ate a piece of candy too. The picture of us there on the street outside the Soup School eating candy and having a good time will never fade.

The Soup School got its name from the fact that at noontime a bowl of soup was served to us with some white, soft bread that made better spitballs than eating in comparison with the substantial and solid homemade bread to which I was accustomed. The school itself was organized and maintained by the Female Guardian Society of America. Later on I found out that this Society was sponsored by wealthy people concerned about the immigrants and their children. How much this organization accomplished among immigrants in New York City would be difficult to estimate. But this I do know, that among the immigrants of my generation and even later *La Soupa Scuola* is still vivid in our boyhood memories.

Why we went to the Soup School instead of the regular elementary public school I have not the faintest idea, except that possibly the first Aviglianese to arrive in New York sent his child there and everyone else followed suit—and also possibly because in those days a bowl of soup was a bowl of soup.

Once at the Soup School I remember the teacher gave each child a bag of oatmeal to take home. This food was supposed to make you big and strong. You ate it for breakfast. My father examined the stuff, tested it with his fingers. To him it was the kind of bran that was fed to pigs in Avigliano.

"What kind of a school is this?" he shouted. "They give us the food of animals to eat and send it home to us with our children! What are we coming to next?"

By the standards I had come to know and understand in Avigliano, the Soup School was not an unpleasant experience. I had been reared in a strict code of behavior, and this same strictness was the outstanding characteristic of the first of my American schools. Nor can I say, as I had indicated to Vito, that a blow from Mrs. Cutter ever had the lustiness of my old teacher, Don Salvatore Mecca. But what punishment lacked in power, it gained by the exacting personality of our principal.

Middle-aged, stockily built, gray hair parted in the middle, Mrs. Cutter lived up to everything my cousin Vito had said about her and much more. Attached to an immaculate white waist by a black ribbon, her pince-nez fell from her nose and dangled in moments of anger. She moved about the corridors and classrooms of the Soup School ever alert and ready to strike at any infringement of school regulations.

I was sitting in class trying to memorize and pronounce words written on the blackboard—words which had absolutely no meaning to me. It seldom seemed to occur to our teachers that explanations were necessary.

"B-U-T-T-E-R—butter—butter," I sing-songed with the rest of the class, learning as always by rote, learning things which often I didn't understand but which had a way of sticking in my mind.

Softly the door opened and Mrs. Cutter entered the classroom. For a large and heavy-set woman she moved quickly, without making any noise. We were not supposed to notice or even pretend we had seen her as she slowly made her way between the desks and straight-backed benches. "B-U-T-T-E-R," I intoned. She was behind me now. I could feel her presence hovering over me. I did not dare take my eyes from the blackboard. I had done nothing and could conceive of no possible reason for an attack, but with Mrs. Cutter this held no significance. She carried a short bamboo switch. On her finger she wore a heavy gold wedding ring. For an instant I thought she was going to pass me by and then suddenly her clenched fist with the ring came down on my head.

I had been trained to show no emotion in the face of punishment, but this was too much. However, before I had time to react to the indignity of this assault, an amazing thing happened. Realizing that she had hurt me unjustly, Mrs. Cutter's whole manner changed. A look of concern came into her eyes. She took hold of my arm, uttering conciliatory words which I did not understand. Later Vito explained to me that she was saying, "I'm sorry. I didn't mean it. Sit down now and be a good boy!"

Every day before receiving our bowl of soup we recited the Lord's Prayer. I had no inkling of what the words meant. I knew only that I was expected to bow my head. I looked around to see what was going on. Swift and simple, the teacher's blackboard pointer brought the idea home to me. I never batted an eyelash after that.

I learned arithmetic and penmanship and spelling—every misspelled word written ten times or more, traced painfully and carefully in my blankbook. I do not know how many times I wrote "I must not talk." In this same way I learned how to read in English, learned geography and grammar, the states of the Union and all the capital cities—and memory gems—choice bits of poetry and sayings. Most learning was done in unison. You recited to the teacher standing at attention. Chorus work. Repetition. Repetition until the things you learned beat in your brain even at night when you were falling asleep.

I think of the modern child with his complexes and his need for "self-expression"! He will never know the forceful and vitalizing influence of a Soup School or a Mrs. Cutter.

I vividly remember the assembly periods. A long narrow room with large windows at either end, long rows of hard benches without backs, and the high platform at one end with a piano, a large table, several chairs, and the American flag. There were no pictures of any kind on the walls.

Silence! Silence! Silence! This was the characteristic feature of our existence at the Soup School. You never made an unnecessary noise or said an unnecessary word. Outside in the hall we lined up by size, girls in one line and boys in another, without uttering a sound. Eyes front and at attention. Lord help you if you broke the rule of silence. I can still see a distant relative of mine, a girl named Miluzza, who could never stop talking, standing in a corner behind Mrs. Cutter throughout an entire assembly with a spring-type clothespin fastened to her lower lip as punishment. Uncowed, defiant—Miluzza with that clothespin dangling from her lip. . . .

The piano struck up a march and from the hall we paraded into assembly—eyes straight ahead in military style. Mrs. Cutter was there on the platform, dominating the scene, her eyes penetrating every corner of the assembly hall. It was always the same. We stood at attention as the Bible was read and at attention as the flag was waved back and forth, and we sang the same song. I didn't know what the words meant but I sang it loudly with all the rest, in my own way, "Tree Cheers for De Red Whatzam Blu!"

But best of all was another song that we used to sing at these assemblies. It was a particular favorite of Mrs. Cutter's and we sang it with great gusto, "Honest boys who never tread the streets." This was in the days when we not only trod the streets but practically lived in them.

THE AMERICANIZATION OF EDWARD BOK (c. 1900)   From *The Americanization of Edward Bok: The Autobiography of a Dutch Boy Fifty Years After* (New York, 1921), pp. 1–4, 8, 448–52.

The leviathan of the Atlantic Ocean, in 1870, was *The Queen,* and when she was warped into her dock on September 20 of that year, she discharged, among her passengers, a family of four from the Netherlands who were to make an experiment of Americanization.

The father, a man bearing one of the most respected names in the Netherlands, had acquired wealth and position for himself; unwise investments, however, had swept away his fortune, and in preference to a new start in his own land, he had decided to make the new beginning in the United States, where a favorite brother-in-law had gone several years before. But that, never a simple matter for a man who has reached forty-two, is particularly difficult for a foreigner in a strange land. This fact he and his wife were to find out. The wife, also carefully reared, had been accustomed to a scale of living which she had now to abandon. Her Americanization experiment was to compel her, for the first time in her life, to become a housekeeper without domestic help. There were two boys: the elder, William, was eight and a half years of age; the younger, in nineteen days from his landing-date, was to celebrate his seventh birthday.

This younger boy was Edward William Bok. He had, according to the Dutch custom, two other names, but he had decided to leave those in the Netherlands. And the American public was, in later years, to omit for him the "William."

Edward's first six days in the United States were spent in New York, and then he was taken to Brooklyn, where he was destined to live for nearly twenty years.

Thanks to the linguistic sense inherent in the Dutch, and to an educational system that compels the study of languages, English was already familiar to the father and mother. But to the two sons, who had barely learned the beginnings of their native tongue, the English language was as a closed book. It seemed a cruel decision of the father to put his two boys into a public school in Brooklyn, but he argued that if they were to become Americans, the sooner they became part of the life of the country and learned its language for themselves, the better. And so, without the ability to make known the slightest want or to understand a single word, the morning after their removal to Brooklyn, the two boys were taken by their father to a public school.

The American public-school teacher was perhaps even less well equipped in those days than she is to-day to meet the needs of two Dutch boys who could not understand a word she said, and who could only wonder what it was all about. The brothers did not even have the comfort of each other's company, for, graded by age, they were placed in separate classes.

Nor was the American boy of 1870 a whit less cruel than is the American boy of 1920; and he was none the less loath to show that cruelty. This trait was evident at the first recess of the first day at school. At the dismissal, the brothers naturally sought each other, only to find themselves surrounded by a group of tormentors who were delighted to have such promising objects for their fun. And of this opportunity they made the most. There was no form of petty cruelty boys' minds could devise that was not inflicted upon the two helpless strangers. Edward seemed to look particularly inviting, and nicknaming him "Dutchy" they devoted themselves at each noon recess and after school to inflicting their cruelties upon him.

Louis XIV may have been right when he said that "every new language requires a new soul," but Edward Bok knew that while spoken languages might differ, there is one language understood by boys the world over. And with this language Edward decided to do some experimenting. After a few days at school, he cast his eyes over the group of his tormentors, picked out one who seemed to him the ringleader, and before the boy was aware of what had happened, Edward Bok was in the full swing of his first real experiment with Americanization. Of course the American boy retaliated. But the boy from the Netherlands had not been born and brought up in the muscle-building air of the Dutch dikes for nothing, and after a few moments he found himself looking down on his tormentor and into the eyes of a crowd of very respectful boys and giggling girls who readily made a passageway for his brother and himself when they indicated a desire to leave the schoolyard and go home.

Edward now felt that his Americanization had begun; but, always believing that a thing begun must be carried to a finish, he took, or gave—it depends upon the point of view—two or three more lessons in this particular phase of Americanization before he convinced these American schoolboys that it might be best for them to call a halt upon further excursions in torment.

At the best, they were difficult days at school for a boy of six without the language. But the national linguistic gift inherent in the Dutch race came to the boy's rescue, and as the roots of the Anglo-Saxon lie in the Frisian tongue, and thus in the language of his native country, Edward soon found that with a change of vowel here and there the English language was not so difficult of conquest. At all events, he set out to master it.

*　　*　　*

We all have our pet notions as to the particular evil which is "the curse of America," but I always think that Theodore Roosevelt came closest to the real curse when he classed it as a lack of thoroughness.

Here again, in one of the most important matters in life, did America fall short with me; and, what is more important, she is falling short with every foreigner that comes to her shores.

In the matter of education, America fell far short in what should be the strongest of all her institutions: the public school. A more inadequate, incompetent method of teaching, as I look back over my seven years of attendance at three different public schools, it is difficult to conceive. If there is one thing that I, as a foreign-born child, should have been carefully taught, it is the English language. The individual effort to teach this, if effort there was, and I remember none, was negligible. It was left for my father to teach me, or for me to dig it out for myself. There was absolutely no indication on the part of teacher or principal of responsibility for seeing that a foreign-born boy should acquire the English language correctly. I was taught as if I were American-born, and, of course, I was left dangling in the air, with no conception of what I was trying to do.

My father worked with me evening after evening; I plunged my young mind deep into the bewildering confusions of the language—and no one realizes the confusions of the English language as does the foreign-born—and got what I could through these joint efforts. But I gained nothing from the much-vaunted public-school system which the United States had borrowed from my own country, and then had rendered incompetent—either by a sheer disregard for the thoroughness that makes the Dutch public schools the admiration of the world, or by too close a regard for politics.

Thus, in her most important institution to the foreign-born, America fell short. And while I am ready to believe that the public school may have increased in efficiency since that day, it is, indeed, a question for the American to ponder, just how far the system is efficient for the education of the child who comes to its school without a knowledge of the first word in the English language. Without a detailed knowledge of the subject, I know enough of conditions in the average public school to-day to warrant at least the suspicion that Americans would not be particularly proud of the system, and of what it gives for which annually they pay millions of dollars in taxes.

I am aware in making this statement that I shall be met with convincing instances of intelligent effort being made with the foreign-born children in special classes. No one has a higher respect for those efforts than I have—few, other than educators, know of them better than I do, since I did not make my five-year study of the American public school system for naught. But I am not referring to the exceptional instance here and there. I merely ask of the American, interested as he is or should be in the Americanization of the strangers within his gates, how far the public school system, as a whole, urban and rural, adapts itself, with any true efficiency, to the foreign-born child. I venture to color his opinion in no wise; I simply ask that he will inquire and ascertain for himself, as he should do if he is interested in the future welfare of his country and his institutions; for what happens in America in the years to come depends, in large measure, on what is happening to-day in the public schools of this country.

*   *   *

Whatever shortcomings I may have found during my fifty-year period of Americanization; however America may have failed to help my transition from a foreigner into an American, I owe to her the most priceless gift that any nation can offer, and that is opportunity.

As the world stands to-day, no nation offers opportunity in the degree that America does to the foreign-born. Russia may, in the future, as I like to believe she will, prove a second United States of America in this respect. She has the same limitless area; her people the same potentialities. But, as things are to-day, the United States offers, as does no other nation, a limitless opportunity: here a man can go as far as his abilities will carry him. It may be that the foreign-born, as in my own case, must hold on to some of the ideals and ideas of the land of his birth; it may be that he must develop and mould his character by overcoming the habits resulting from national shortcomings. But into the best that the foreign-born can retain, America can graft such a wealth of inspiration, so high a national idealism, so great an opportunity for the highest endeavor, as to make him the fortunate man of the earth to-day.

He can go where he will: no traditions hamper him; no limitations are set except those within himself. The larger the area he chooses in which to work, the larger the vision he demonstrates, the more eager the people are to give support to his undertakings if they are convinced that he has their best welfare as his goal. There is no public confidence equal to that of the American public, once it is obtained. It is fickle, of course, as are all publics, but fickle only toward the man who cannot maintain an achieved success.

A man in America cannot complacently lean back upon victories won, as he can in the older European countries, and depend upon the glamour of the past to sustain him or the momentum of success to carry him.. Probably the most alert public in the world, it requires of its leaders that they be alert. Its appetite for variety is insatiable, but its appreciation, when given, is full-handed and whole-hearted. The American public never holds back from the man to whom it gives; it never bestows in a niggardly way; it gives all or nothing.

What is not generally understood of the American people is their wonderful idealism. Nothing so completely surprises the foreign-born as the discovery of this trait in the American character. The impression is current in European countries—perhaps less generally since the war—that America is given over solely to a worship of the American dollar. While between nations as between individuals, comparisons are valueless, it may not be amiss to say, from personal knowledge, that the Dutch worship the gulden infinitely more than do the Americans the dollar.

I do not claim that the American is always conscious of this idealism; often he is not. But let a great convulsion touching moral questions occur, and the result always shows how close to the surface is his idealism. And the fact that so frequently he puts over it a thick veneer of materialism does not affect its quality. The truest approach, the only approach in fact, to the American character is, as Viscount Bryce has so well said, through its idealism.

It is this quality which gives the truest inspiration to the foreign-born in his endeavor to serve the people of his adopted country. He is mentally sluggish, indeed, who does not discover that America will make good with him if he makes good with her.

But he must play fair. It is essentially the straight game that the true American plays, and he insists that you shall play it too. Evidence there is, of course, to the contrary in American life, experiences that seem to give ground for the belief that the man succeeds who is not scrupulous in playing his cards. But never is this true in the long run. Sooner or later—sometimes, unfortunately, later than sooner—the public discovers the trickery. In no other country in the world is the moral conception so clear and true as in America, and no people will give a larger and more permanent reward to the man whose effort for that public has its roots in honor and truth.

"The sky is the limit" to the foreign-born who comes to America endowed with honest endeavor, ceaseless industry, and the ability to carry through. In any honest endeavor, the way is wide open to the will to succeed. Every path beckons, every vista invites, every talent is called forth, and every efficient effort finds its due reward. In no land is the way so clear and so free.

How good an American has the process of Americanization made me? That I cannot say. Who *can* say that of himself? But when I look around me at the American-born I have come to know as my close friends, I wonder whether, after all, the foreign-born does not make in some sense a better American—whether he is not able to get a truer perspective; whether his is not the deeper desire to see America greater; whether he is not less content to let its faulty institutions be as they are; whether in seeing faults more clearly he does not make a more decided effort to have America reach those ideals or those fundamentals of his own land which he feels are in his nature, and the best of which he is anxious to graft into the character of his adopted land?

It is naturally with a feeling of deep satisfaction that I remember two Presidents of the United States considered me a sufficiently typical American to wish to send me to my native land as the accredited minister of my adopted country. And yet when I analyze the reasons for my choice in both these instances, I derive a deeper satisfaction from the fact that my strong desire to work in America for America led me to ask to be permitted to remain here.

It is this strong impulse that my Americanization has made the driving power of my life. And I ask no greater privilege than to be allowed to live to see my potential America become actual: the America that I like to think of as the America of Abraham Lincoln and of Theodore Roosevelt—not faultless, but less faulty. It is a part in trying to shape that America, and an opportunity to work in that America when it comes, that I ask in return for what I owe to her. A greater privilege no man could have.

THE KINDERGARTEN AND THE IMMIGRANT CHILD (1903)   From Richard W. Gilder, "The Kindergarten: An Uplifting Social Influence in the Home and the District," National Education Association, *Journal of Proceedings and Addresses* (Wash., D.C., 1903), pp. 390–91.

You cannot catch your citizen too early in order to make him a good citizen. The kindergarten age marks our earliest opportunity to catch the little Russian, the little Italian, the little German, Pole, Syrian, and the rest and begin to make good American citizens of them. And your little American-born citizen is often in quite as much need of early catching and training.

The direct effect of the kindergarten upon the children is easy to grasp. The teachers will tell you that not only surly young ones soon succumb to the amiable environment, but that the difference in the average child is quickly perceived. The children are brought into a new social order; they are taught to have regard for one another, and they do acquire such regard—along with a new and highly valuable respect for law and order.

No one can speak of the kindergarten without including the work of the mothers' meeting and club, with library annex; the teaching there of games and of handiwork along with practical discussions on food, cooking, sleep, play, open air, cleanliness, health; on manners, housework, overstimulating of young children, and the like; sometimes with talks by physicians of incalculable benefit to uninstructed parents. A vital element of the kindergarten, too, is the visitation by the teachers in the homes of the children. Then there are the mothers' and fathers' visits to the kindergartens, and occasionally there are fathers' meetings also. Perhaps hitherto the father has been regarded too much as a negligible quantity in kindergarten work.

Home visitation, mothers' meetings, and social work are an integral part of the system, and with us are being constantly pressed farther and farther. Special efforts are made, too, to bring the children more into touch with nature; seeds are distributed and flowers raised; there are indoor gardens and outdoor gardens, visits to the parks, and play festivals in the parks. There is a loan collection of animals, and a movement is on foot to have a few animals kept for kindergarten purposes in some, at least, of the small parks of the city; this is, in fact, already done in one of our minor parks. The kindergarten work is by no means limited to the daily routine of exercises.

There is a very close bond between the kindergarten and the home; and the closest of all is, of course, the child itself. The first thing learned, perhaps, is cleanliness. Both the child and the mother soon learn that. In the case of the mother lack of hygiene means lack of knowledge; she is quick to learn and to profit by her new knowledge.

✻   ✻   ✻

Again, the success of the kindergarten method in the management of the child is a revelation to the parents. They naturally come to acquire new parental manners. One philosophical observer of the good effects of the kindergarten said lately: "I used to hit my Josie something awful, and now I don't."

The whole family comes under the influence of what I may call the kindergarten charm. A change comes over the little children. The kindergarten songs and games are introduced into the home. The father often is deeply interested, learns the songs, supplements the handiwork of the children. One father said to the mother: "Be sure and go to the meeting; when you get home you always act lively, as you did before we were married." Two mothers said to the same teacher, lately, that they dreaded promotion for their children, as they would "rather they would be trained than taught." "Many mothers laughingly informed me," one of the teachers says, "that no one of the various members of the family was exempt from the criticism of the table manners." This reversal as to the usual source of home instruction is, in the circumstances, necessary and helpful, and tends powerfully to social improvement. It often leads also, to be sure, to the inevitable tragedy, later in life, that comes from separation in sentiment, such as is depicted in Tourguéneff's *Fathers and Sons*; but in the case of a new national environment this cannot be helped; it is, in fact, wholesomely evolutionary. Kindergarten children are more willing and better assistants to their mothers than the older children who have not been in kindergarten. Tidiness in the home with regard to the children's playthings is the direct effect of the "putting away" in the kindergarten. Personal cleanliness as intimated, is the first note struck by the kindergarten—and it reverberates promptly in the home.

The influence of the kindergarten upon the child's home is unescapable. And if the individual child and the child's family are influenced, there is the beginning, at least, of an influence upon the district. We find that parents become so deeply interested in the kindergarten that they send one child there after another; and that, when the child grow up, the second generation is sure to be sent also. The growing-up and grown-up kindergarten children are apt to revisit the kindergarten, and keep up an intelligent interest in its work and sympathy with its spirit. The spell of the kindergarten remains upon them.

The social uplift is felt—first, by the child; second, by the family and, third, by the neighborhood. This is the contemporaneous influence; but if the direct influence upon the child is good, if certain social principles are deeply implanted in it at a highly susceptible age, surely the social uplift will not be confined to the few years that the child remains in the kindergarten; the training will naturally tend to good manners, good morals, and good citizenship in the years to come.

AN EDUCATOR ON THE NEW IMMIGRANTS (1909)   From Ellwood P. Cubberley, *Changing Conceptions of Education* (Boston, 1909), pp. 13–15.

During the middle years of the nineteenth century, large numbers of English came, in all a total of about three and one-half millions having arrived since 1820. Still later, large numbers of Scandinavians arrived, these going largely to the agricultural sections of the Northwest. In all, nearly two millions of Scandinavians have come to our shores.

While these people frequently settled in groups and retained for a time their foreign language, manners, and customs, they were nevertheless relatively easy to assimilate. All except the Irish came from countries where general education prevailed, and where progressive methods of agriculture, trade, and manufacturing had begun to supersede primitive methods. All were from race stock not very different from our own, and all possessed courage, initiative, intelligence, adaptability and self-reliance to a large degree. The willingness, good nature, and executive qualities of the Irish, the intellectual thoroughness of the German, the respect for law and order of the English, and the thrift of the Scandinavian have been good additions to our life.

About 1882, the character of our immigration changed in a very remarkable manner. Immigration from the north of Europe dropped off rather abruptly, and in its place immigration from the south and east of Europe set in and soon developed into a great stream. After 1880, southern Italians and Sicilians; people from all parts of that medley of races known as the Austro-Hungarian Empire,—Czechs, Moravians, Slovaks, Poles, Jews, Ruthenians, Croatians, Servians, Dalmatians, Slovenians, Magyars, Roumanians, Austrians; and Slavs, Poles, and Jews from Russia began to come in great numbers. After 1900, Finns from the north, driven out by Russian persecution; and Greeks, Syrians, and Armenians from the south, have come in great numbers to our shores.

These southern and eastern Europeans are of a very different type from the north Europeans who preceded them. Illiterate, docile, lacking in self-reliance and initiative, and not possessing the Anglo-Teutonic conceptions of law, order, and government, their coming has served to dilute tremendously our national stock, and to corrupt our civic life. The great bulk of these people have settled in the cities of the North Atlantic and North Central states, and the problems of proper housing and living, moral and sanitary conditions, honest and decent government, and proper education have everywhere been made more difficult by their presence. Everywhere these people tend to settle in groups or settlements, and to set up here their national manners, customs, and observances. Our task is to break up these groups or settlements, to assimilate and amalgamate these people as a part of our American race, and to implant in their children, so far as can be done, the Anglo-Saxon conception of righteousness, law and order, and popular government, and to awaken in them a reverence for our democratic institutions and for those things in our national life which we as a people hold to be of abiding worth.

JANE ADDAMS ON IMMIGRANTS AND THEIR CHILDREN IN CHICAGO

(**1911**)   From Jane Addams, *Twenty Years at Hull-House* (New York, 1911), pp. 231-44.

From our very first months at Hull-House we found it much easier to deal with the first generation of crowded city life than with the second or third, because it is more natural and cast in a simpler mold. The Italian and Bohemian peasants who live in Chicago, still put on their bright holiday clothes on a Sunday and go to visit their cousins. They tramp along with at least a suggestion of having once walked over plowed fields and breathed country air. The second generation of city poor too often have no holiday clothes and consider their relations a "bad lot." I have heard a drunken man in a maudlin stage, babble of his good country mother and imagine he was driving the cows home, and I knew that his little son who laughed loud at him, would be drunk earlier in life and would have no such pastoral interlude to his ravings. Hospitality still survives among foreigners, although it is buried under false pride among the poorest Americans. One thing seemed clear in regard to entertaining immigrants; to preserve and keep whatever of value their past life contained and to bring them in contact with a better type of Americans. For several years, every Saturday evening the entire families of our Italian neighbors were our guests. These evenings were very popular during our first winters at Hull-House. Many educated Italians helped us, and the house became known as a place where Italians were welcome and where national holidays were observed. They come to us with their petty lawsuits, sad relics of the *vendetta*, with their incorrigible boys, with their hospital cases, with their aspirations for American clothes, and with their needs for an interpreter.

An editor of an Italian paper made a genuine connection between us and the Italian colony, not only with the Neapolitans and the Sicilians of the immediate neighborhood, but with the educated *connazionali* throughout the city, until he went south to start an agricultural colony in Alabama, in the establishment of which Hull-House heartily cooperated.

Possibly the South Italians more than any other immigrants represent the pathetic stupidity of agricultural people crowded into city tenements, and we were much gratified when thirty peasant families were induced to move upon the land which they knew so well how to cultivate. The starting of this colony, however, was a very expensive affair in spite of the fact that the colonists purchased the land at two dollars an acre; they needed much more than raw land, and although it was possible to collect the small sums necessary to sustain them during the hard time of the first two years, we were fully convinced that undertakings of this sort could be conducted properly only by colonization societies such as England has established, or, better still, by enlarging the functions of the Federal Department of Immigration.

An evening similar in purpose to the one devoted to the Italians was organized for the Germans, in our first year. Owing to the superior education of our Teutonic guests and the clever leading of a cultivated German woman, these evenings reflected something of that cozy social intercourse which is found in its perfection in the fatherland. Our guests sang a great deal in the tender minor of the German folksong or in the rousing spirit of the Rhine, and they slowly but persistently pursued a course in German history and literature, recovering something of that poetry and romance which they had long since resigned with other good things. We found strong family affection between them and their English-speaking children, but their pleasures were not in common, and they seldom went out together. Perhaps the greatest value of the Settlement to them was in placing large and pleasant rooms with musical facilities at their disposal, and in reviving their almost forgotten enthusiasms. I have seen sons and daughters stand in complete surprise as their mother's knitting needles softly beat time to the song she was singing, or her worn face turned rosy under the hand-clapping as she made an old-fashioned courtsey at the end of a German poem. It was easy to fancy a growing touch of respect in her children's manner to her, and a rising enthusiasm for German literature and reminiscence on the part of all the family, an effort to bring together the old life and the new, a respect for the older cultivation, and not quite so much assurance that the new was the best.

This tendency upon the part of the older immigrants to lose the amenities of European life without sharing those of America, has often been deplored by keen observers from the home countries. When Professor Masurek of Prague gave a course of lectures in the University of Chicago, he was much distressed over the materialism into which the Bohemians of Chicago had fallen. The early immigrants had been so stirred by the opportunity to own real estate, an appeal perhaps to the Slavic land hunger, and their energies had become so completely absorbed in money-making that all other interests had apparently dropped away. And yet I recall a very touching incident in connection with a lecture Professor Masurek gave at Hull-House, in which he had appealed to his countrymen to arouse themselves from this tendency to fall below their home civilization and to forget the great enthusiasm which had united them into the Pan-Slavic Movement. A Bohemian widow who supported herself and her two children by scrubbing, hastily sent her youngest child to purchase, with the twenty-five cents which was to have supplied them with food the next day, a bunch of red roses which she presented to the lecturer in appreciation of his testimony to the reality of the things of the spirit.

An overmastering desire to reveal the humbler immigrant parents to their own children lay at the base of what has come to be called the Hull-House Labor Museum. This was first suggested to my mind one early spring day when I saw an old Italian woman, her distaff against her homesick face, patiently spinning a thread by the simple stick spindle so reminiscent of all southern Europe. I was walking down Polk Street, perturbed in spirit, because it seemed so difficult to come into genuine relations with the Italian women and because they themselves so often lost their hold upon their Americanized children. It seemed to me that Hull-House ought to be able to devise some educational enterprise, which should build a bridge between European and American experiences in such wise as to give them both more meaning and a sense of relation. I meditated that perhaps the power to see life as a whole, is more needed in the immigrant quarter of a large city than anywhere else, and that the lack of this power is the most fruitful source of misunderstanding between European immigrants and their children, as it is between them and their American neighbors; and why should that chasm between fathers and sons, yawning at the feet of each generation, be made so unnecessarily cruel and impassable to these bewildered immigrants? Suddenly I looked up and saw the old woman with her distaff, sitting in the sun on the steps of a tenement house. She might have served as a model for one of Michael Angelo's Fates, but her face brightened as I passed and, holding up her spindle for me to see, she called out that when she had spun a little more yarn, she would knit a pair of stockings for her goddaughter. The occupation of the old woman gave me the clew that was needed. Could we not interest the young people working in the neighboring factories, in these older forms of industry, so that, through their own parents and grandparents, they would find a dramatic representation of the inherited resources of their daily occupation. If these young people could actually see that the complicated machinery of the factory had been evolved from simple tools, they might at least make a beginning towards that education which Dr. Dewey defines as "a continuing reconstruction of experience." They might also lay a foundation for reverence of the past which Goethe declares to be the basis of all sound progress.

My exciting walk on Polk Street was followed by many talks with Dr. Dewey and with one of the teachers in his school who was a resident at Hull-House. Within a month a room was fitted up to which we might invite those of our neighbors who were possessed of old crafts and who were eager to use them.

We found in the immediate neighborhood, at least four varieties of these most primitive methods of spinning and three distinct variations of the same spindle in connection with wheels. It was possible to put these seven into historic sequence and order and to connect the whole with the present method of factory spinning. The same thing was done for weaving, and on every Saturday evening a little exhibit was made of these various forms of labor in the textile industry. Within one room a Syrian woman, a Greek, an Italian, a Russian, and an Irishwoman enabled even the most casual observer to see that there is no break in orderly evolution if we look at history from the industrial standpoint; that industry develops similarly and peacefully year by year among the workers of each nation, heedless of differences in language, religion, and political experiences.

And then we grew ambitious and arranged lectures upon industrial history. I remember that after an interesting lecture upon the industrial revolution in England and a portrayal of the appalling conditions throughout the weaving districts of the north, which resulted from the hasty gathering of the weavers into the new towns, a Russian tailor in the audience was moved to make a speech. He suggested that whereas time had done much to alleviate the first difficulties in the transition of weaving from hand work to steam power, that in the application of steam to sewing we are still in the first stages, illustrated by the isolated woman who tries to support herself by hand needlework at home until driven out by starvation, as many of the hand weavers had been.

The historical analogy seemed to bring a certain comfort to the tailor as did a chart upon the wall, showing the infinitesimal amount of time that steam had been applied to manufacturing processes compared to the centuries of hand labor. Human progress is slow and perhaps never more cruel than in the advance of industry, but is not the worker comforted by knowing that other historical periods have existed similar to the one in which he finds himself, and that the readjustment may be shortened and alleviated by judicious action; and is he not entitled to the solace which an artistic portrayal of the situation might give him? I remember the evening of the tailor's speech that I felt reproached because no poet or artist has endeared the sweaters' victim to us as George Eliot has made us love the belated weaver, Silas Marner. The textile museum is connected directly with the basket weaving, sewing, millinery, embroidery, and dressmaking constantly being taught at Hull-House, and so far as possible with the other educational departments; we have also been able to make a collection of products, of early implements, and of photographs which are full of suggestion. Yet far beyond its direct educational value, we prize it because it so often puts the immigrants into the position of teachers, and we imagine that it affords them a pleasant change from the tutelage in which all Americans, including their own children, are so apt to hold them. I recall a number of Russian women working in a sewing-room near Hull-House, who heard one Christmas week that the House was going to give a party to which they might come. They arrived one afternoon when, unfortunately, there was no party on hand and, although the residents did their best to entertain them with impromptu music and refreshments, it was quite evident that they were greatly disappointed. Finally it was suggested that they be shown the Labor Museum—where gradually the thirty sodden, tired women were transformed. They knew how to use the spindles and were delighted to find the Russian spinning frame. Many of them had never seen the spinning wheel, which has not penetrated to certain parts of Russia, and they regarded it as a new and wonderful invention. They turned up their dresses to show their homespun petticoats; they tried the looms; they explained the difficulty of the old patterns; in short, from having been stupidly entertained, they themselves did the entertaining. Because of a direct appeal to former experiences, the immigrant visitors were able for the moment to instruct their American hostesses in an old and honored craft, as was indeed becoming to their age and experience.

In some such ways as these have the Labor Museum and the shops pointed out the possibilities which Hull-House has scarcely begun to develop, of demonstrating that culture is an understanding of the long-established occupations and thoughts of men, of the arts with which they have solaced their toil. A yearning to recover for the household arts something of their early sanctity and meaning, arose strongly within me one evening when I was attending a Passover Feast to which I had been invited by a Jewish family in the neighborhood, where the traditional and religious significance of woman's daily activity was still retained. The kosher food the Jewish mother spread before her family had been prepared according to traditional knowledge and with constant care in the use of utensils; upon her had fallen the responsibility to make all ready according to Mosaic instructions that the great crisis in a religious history might be fittingly set forth by her husband and son. Aside from the grave religious significance in the ceremony, my mind was filled with shifting pictures of woman's labor with which travel makes one familiar; the Indian women grinding grain outside of their huts as they sing praises to the sun and rain; a file of white-clad Moorish women whom I had once seen waiting their turn at a well in Tangiers; south Italian women kneeling in a row along the stream and beating their wet clothes against the smooth white stones; the milking, the gardening, the marketing in thousands of hamlets, which are such direct expressions of the solicitude and affection at the basis of all family life.

There has been some testimony that the Labor Museum has revealed the charm of woman's primitive activities. I recall a certain Italian girl who came every Saturday evening to a cooking class in the same building in which her mother spun in the Labor Museum exhibit; and yet Angelina always left her mother at the front door while she herself went around to a side door because she did not wish to be too closely identified in the eyes of the rest of the cooking class with an Italian woman who wore a kerchief over her head, uncouth boots, and short petticoats. One evening, however, Angelina saw her mother surrounded by a group of visitors from the School of Education, who much admired the spinning, and she concluded from their conversation that her mother was "the best stick-spindle spinner in America." When she inquired from me as to the truth of this deduction, I took occasion to describe the Italian village in which her mother had lived, something of her free life, and how, because of the opportunity she and the other women of the village had to drop their spindles over the edge of a precipice, they had developed a skill in spinning beyond that of the neighboring towns. I dilated somewhat on the freedom and beauty of that life—how hard it must be to exchange it all for a two-room tenement, and to give up a beautiful homespun kerchief for an ugly department store hat. I intimated it was most unfair to judge her by these things alone, and that while she must depend on her daughter to learn the new ways, she also had a right to expect her daughter to know something of the old ways.

A RUSSIAN IMMIGRANT IN THE "PROMISED LAND" (1912) From Mary Antin, *The Promised Land* (Boston, 1912), pp. 26–27, 198–200, 203–5.

The knowledge of such things as I am telling leaves marks upon the flesh and spirit. I remember little children in Polotzk with old, old faces and eyes glazed with secrets. I knew how to dodge and cringe and dissemble before I knew the names of the seasons. And I had plenty of time to ponder on these things, because I was so idle. If they had let me go to school, now—But of course they didn't.

There was no free school for girls, and even if your parents were rich enough to send you to a private school, you could not go very far. At the high school, which was under government control, Jewish children were admitted in limited numbers,—only ten to every hundred,—and even if you were among the lucky ones, you had your troubles. The tutor who prepared you talked all the time about the examinations you would have to pass, till you were scared. You heard on all sides that the brightest Jewish children were turned down if the examining officers did not like the turn of their noses. You went up to be examined with the other Jewish children, your heart heavy about that matter of your nose. There was a special examination for the Jewish candidates, of course; a nine-year-old Jewish child had to answer questions that a thirteen-year-old Gentile was hardly expected to understand. But that did not matter so much. You had been prepared for the thirteen-year-old test; you found the questions quite easy. You wrote your answers triumphantly—and you received a low rating, and there was no appeal.

I used to stand in the doorway of my father's store, munching on an apple that did not taste good any more, and watch the pupils going home from school in twos and threes; the girls in neat brown dresses and black aprons and little stiff hats, the boys in trim uniforms with many buttons. They had ever so many books in the satchels on their backs. They would take them out at home, and read and write, and learn all sorts of interesting things. They looked to me like beings from another world than mine. But those whom I envied had their own troubles, as I often heard. Their school life was one struggle against injustice from instructors, spiteful treatment from fellow students, and insults from everybody. Those who, by heroic efforts and transcendent good luck, successfully finished the course, found themselves against a new wall, if they wished to go on. They were turned down at the universities, which admitted them in the ratio of three Jews to a hundred Gentiles, under the same debarring entrance conditions as at the high school,—especially rigorous examinations, dishonest marking, or arbitrary rulings without disguise. No, the Czar did not want us in the schools. . . .

In America, then, everything was free, as we had heard in Russia. Light was free; the streets were as bright as a synagogue on a holy day. Music was free; we had been serenaded, to our gaping delight, by a brass band of many pieces, soon after our installation on Union Place.

Education was free. That subject my father had written about repeatedly, as comprising his chief hope for us children, the essence of American opportunity, the treasure that no thief could touch, not even misfortune or poverty. It was the one thing that he was able to promise us when he sent for us; surer, safer than bread or shelter. On our second day I was thrilled with the realization of what this freedom of education meant. A little girl from across the alley came and offered to conduct us to school. My father was out, but we five between us had a few words of English by this time. We knew the word school. We understood. This child, who had never seen us till yesterday, who could not pronounce our names, who was not much better dressed than we, was able to offer us the freedom of the schools of Boston! No application made, no questions asked, no examinations, rulings, exclusions; no machinations, no fees. The doors stood open for every one of us. The smallest child could show us the way.

This incident impressed me more than anything I had heard in advance of the freedom of education in America. It was a concrete proof—almost the thing itself. One had to experience it to understand it. . . .

The apex of my civic pride and personal contentment was reached on the bright September morning when I entered the public school. That day I must always remember, even if I live to be so old that I cannot tell my name. To most people their first day at school is a memorable occasion. In my case the importance of the day was a hundred times magnified, on account of the years I had waited, the road I had come, and the conscious ambitions I entertained.

I am wearily aware that I am speaking in extreme figures, in superlatives. I wish I knew of some other way to render the mental life of the immigrant child of reasoning age. I may have been ever so much an exception in acuteness of observation, powers of comparison, and abnormal self-consciousness; none the less were my thoughts and conduct typical of the attitude of the intelligent immigrant child toward American institutions. And what the child thinks and feels is a reflection of the hopes, desires, and purposes of the parents who brought him overseas, no matter how precocious and independent the child may be. Your immigrant inspectors will tell you what poverty the foreigner brings in his baggage, what want in his pockets. Let the overgrown boy of twelve, reverently drawing his letters in the baby class, testify to the noble dreams and high ideals that may be hidden beneath the greasy caftan of the immigrant. Speaking for the Jews, at least, I know I am safe in inviting such an investigation.

Who were my companions on my first day at school? Whose hand was in mine, as I stood, overcome with awe, by the teacher's desk, and whispered my name as my father prompted? Was it Frieda's steady, capable hand? Was it her loyal heart that throbbed, beat for beat with mine, as it had done through all our childish adventures? Frieda's heart did throb that day, but not with my emotions. My heart pulsed with joy and pride and ambition; in her heart longing fought with abnegation. For I was led to the schoolroom, with its sunshine and its singing and the teacher's cheery smile; while she was led to the workshop, with its foul air, care-lined faces, and the foreman's stern command. Our going to school was the fulfilment of my father's best promises to us, and Frieda's share in it was to fashion and fit the calico frocks in which the baby sister and I made our first appearance in a public schoolroom.

I remember to this day the gray pattern of the calico, so affectionately did I regard it as it hung upon the wall—my consecration robe awaiting the beatific day. And Frieda, I am sure, remembers it, too, so longingly did she regard it as the crisp, starchy breadths of it slid between her fingers. But whatever were her longings, she said nothing of them; she bent over the sewing-machine humming an Old-World melody. In every straight, smooth seam, perhaps, she tucked away some lingering impulse of childhood; but she matched the scrolls and flowers with the utmost care. If a sudden shock of rebellion made her straighten up for an instant, the next instant she was bending to adjust a ruffle to the best advantage. And when the momentous day arrived, and the little sister and I stood up to be arrayed, it was Frieda herself who patted and smoothed my stiff new calico; who made me turn round and round, to see that I was perfect; who stooped to pull out a disfiguring basting-thread. If there was anything in her heart besides sisterly love and pride and good-will, as we parted that morning, it was a sense of loss and a woman's acquiescence in her fate; for we had been close friends, and now our ways would lie apart. Longing she felt, but no envy. She did not grudge me what she was denied. . . .

*　　*　　*

Father himself conducted us to school. He would not have delegated that mission to the President of the United States. He had awaited the day with impatience equal to mine, and the visions he saw as he hurried us over the sun-flecked pavements transcended all my dreams. . . . in his primary quest he had failed. There was left him the compensation of intellectual freedom. That he sought to realize in every possible way. He had very little opportunity to prosecute his education, which, in truth, had never been begun. His struggle for a bare living left him no time to take advantage of the public evening school; but he lost nothing of what was to be learned through reading, through attendance at public meetings, through exercising the rights of citizenship. Even here he was hindered by a natural inability to acquire the English language. In time, indeed, he learned to read, to follow a conversation or lecture; but he never learned to write correctly, and his pronunciation remains extremely foreign to this day.

If education, culture, the higher life were shining things to be worshipped from afar, he had still a means left whereby he could draw one step nearer to them. He could send his children to school, to learn all those things that he knew by fame to be desirable. The common school, at least, perhaps high school; for one or two, perhaps even college! His children should be students, should fill his house with books and intellectual company; and thus he would walk by proxy in the Elysian Fields of liberal learning. As for the children themselves, he knew no surer way to their advancement and happiness.

So it was with a heart full of longing and hope that my father led us to school on that first day. He took long strides in his eagerness, the rest of us running and hopping to keep up.

At last the four of us stood around the teacher's desk; and my father, in his impossible English, gave us over in her charge, with some broken word of his hopes for us that his swelling heart could no longer contain. I venture to say that Miss Nixon was struck by something uncommon in the group we made, something outside of Semitic features and the abashed manner of the alien. My little sister was as pretty as a doll, with her clear pink-and-white face, short golden curls, and eyes like blue violets when you caught them looking up. My brother might have been a girl, too, with his cherubic contours of face, rich red color, glossy black hair, and fine eyebrows. Whatever secret fears were in his heart, remembering his former teachers, who had taught with the rod, he stood up straight and uncringing before the American teacher, his cap respectfully doffed. Next to him stood a starved-looking girl with eyes ready to pop out, and short dark curls that would not have made much of a wig for a Jewish bride.

All three children carried themselves rather better than the common run of "green" pupils that were brought to Miss Nixon. But the figure that challenged attention to the group was the tall, straight father, with his earnest face and fine forehead, nervous hands eloquent in gesture, and a voice full of feeling. This foreigner, who brought his children to school as if it were an act of consecration, who regarded the teacher of the primer class with reverence, who spoke of visions, like a man inspired, in a common schoolroom, was not like other aliens, who brought their children in dull obedience to the law; was not like the native fathers, who brought their unmanageable boys, glad to be relieved of their care. I think Miss Nixon guessed what my father's best English could not convey. I think she divined that by the simple act of delivering our school certificates to her he took possession of America.

AN ITALIAN IMMIGRANT ON BECOMING PRINCIPAL OF A PUBLIC SCHOOL IN NEW YORK CITY (c. 1917)
From Angelo Patri, *A Schoolmaster of a Great City* (New York, 1921), pp. 24–32.

Now came my appointment as principal. I stretched my arms and said, "Free at last, my own master! I am limited only by my own vision."

I entered the new school, "My school," as I proudly called it. There it was, a big, massive structure towering like a fortress above the elevated lines, fronting a large public park, the airy rooms full of sunshine.

It did not look out into the back-yards of tenements. No smell of leaking gas stoves came in through the open windows. In other days, if I gazed out of a school window I looked into the homes of the neighbours—squalid, noisy homes they were. Whenever there was a quarrel, the loud shrieks and the bad language broke in upon the classroom recitation, and made the children blush and break into nervous laughter. They were ashamed of their parents and their neighbourhood.

This new school of mine seemed altogether different. I looked out of my office window at the trees on the hill beyond and watched them sway in the wind, like the restless backs of many elephants. I saw the open spaces, the sunlight, the park, and I rejoiced. These, I knew, were the teacher's best friends.

The day after my installation I went to my office ready to begin on "my school" and carry it up to the heights of power and efficiency. "My school" should come into its own. I do not remember now whether I intended to accomplish this in a day or a month, or a year, for as I sat thinking about it the half-past eight gong rang sharply, insistently. It brought me up-standing in the office door. I heard bell after bell beginning in the first room and follow in order from floor to floor, shrill out its call, cease, pass on its message to its neighbour in the next classroom to pass it along to the next, like a chain of energy linking up the classrooms for the day's work. I had never heard anything quite like that before.

Then came the measured rhythm of many feet. From six entrances the children surged through the halls and into their classrooms. I had a blurred impression of sound, and colour and motion and many, many children and teachers all going swiftly by. I saw no individual faces, no distinct forms, just the great mass surging past. Stunned and bewildered I stood where I was until I realised that a great silence had settled over the building. The big school had begun its day's work and begun it without me.

I sat down at my desk because I didn't know what else to do. The clerk came in with the mail. The former principal who was still in the building with the fifteen hundred children he was to take to the new school came in to arrange some details of administration. With him I went over the number of classes in the school, the teachers who were to go and stay, the district lines and the number of children to be transferred in and out. This done he walked out of the office.

I was about to gather myself together and take hold of "my school," and then the gong rang again. I heard doors roll, bells trill, sharp commands, rhythmic footsteps, and the great surge of sound and colour and motion passed me again, children going in, children going out. They moved in classes, eyes front, hats off. A mass of children coming in to take the places of the mass that was going out. There was no time lost, just a tramp, tramp, a roll of a door, as it opened, a click as it shut and then silence as before.

The next day was the same—and the next! I had not taken hold. I left the office and walked through the school, corridors, classrooms and playgrounds listening and watching, trying to get an idea here and there.

I passed the open door of a classroom and saw a teacher smiling down at a little boy and all the other little boys smiling sympathetically at both. I was glad and walked towards the teacher. Instantly the smile disappeared, her body grew tense, the little boy sat down and all the other little boys sat up stiff and straight and put their hands behind them.

I tried to say something pleasant but I saw they were afraid of me and I went away.

I went into another room and the teacher was intent upon a little book, she was marking, and at the same time telling a boy that she hoped he'd learn something about grammar before he died, but she doubted it.

Without lifting her eyes and so missing seeing me, she said, "Walter, analyse, 'Come here.' "

A boy whose thoughts were a long way off jumped up and said—"Simple declarative, Come is the subject—here is the predicate verb," and sat down.

The class laughed heartily and the teacher said as she marked his failure, "Fine— But you forgot something—Come is the subject, here is the predicate, the period is the object."

Everyone laughed. Walter shook himself and analysed the sentence correctly. Then they realised my presence and froze over. The teacher apologised for not having noticed my entrance saying she thought it was one of the boys and asking me to be seated but I saw she was uncomfortable and I left.

A teacher brought me a disciplinary case. Before she could tell me the trouble she burst into tears. When I tried to tell her there was nothing to cry about she but cried the harder.

Was she afraid of the new principal? Why should she be afraid of him? Yet the scene was somewhat familiar. Oh, I remembered—"You are wasting your time. You are wasting the children's time. You are totally unfit for this work. If I had a son he should not be in your class."

Was that it?

This was bad. The teachers did not want me in the classrooms. They cried when they came to the office.

I'd make friends with the children. But I could not get at them. They were in classes in the rooms—in masses in the yards and corridors. Only the occasional bad one stood out as an individual with whom I could come in personal contact.

"My Dream School" was not so easy.

I thought a great deal about the situation. I know now that in those first days I interpreted the school through my finger tips and eyes and ears rather than through my intellect. I saw and heard the disorderly boy. I ached physically and mentally over the weak teacher, I saw every mistake she made, I heard every faulty intonation of her voice and felt a sense of personal injury. Why was she like that? Why couldn't she be big and fine? And the strong teacher! Why weren't they all like that? That was the way I wanted them. They must all measure up to the best. I rather felt than saw the peaks and hollows.

But in this restless, uncertain sea of motion, noise, colour and gongs; of constant going up-stairs and down-stairs, one learned to "go slow" and watch and wait for his opportunity.

In my discouragement I told an older principal about my efforts and failures.

"What do you mean?" he said in a puzzled fashion. "I don't understand you."

"I've tried to have the teachers and children feel that I'm their friend, that I'm eager to help them but I don't seem to be able to get them to speak or act freely in my presence. They are afraid of me!"

"Afraid of you? Of course they are and they ought to be. The teachers and children are all right. You'll find them well trained. Take my advice if you want any peace of mind and keep them under your thumb."

These were not the exact words that had disheartened me years before, but the idea was the same, and I remembered and understood. There was little danger of forgetting. I came upon this blind obedience repeatedly. Obedience, the loyal obedience that was school tradition.

"Let's try to have the children come to school fresh and clean," said I one day to a group of teachers. "Praise those who come in clean blouses and with well brushed hair."

Shortly after this a mother came in to see me. She laid a little package on my desk.

"Please, I bring you back this shirt."

Startled, I echoed, "Shirt? What shirt?"

"This shirt that the teacher gave my Jonas."

"Tell me about it," I said.

"The teacher said if they were good and sat up tall so that they got 'A' from the Lady Principal she would give them a blouse. Jonas told me and I told him he should try hard and get a blouse. So he did. He tried and tried and got one. But this blouse I don't like. Never put a thin blouse on Jonas in February—only in April. I want you should take this back and give him a flannel one—a red one he likes."

Here she pulled the wrapping off a pretty little blue and white cotton blouse, and beamingly presented it to me.

Turning over her story in my mind I remembered she had said the "Lady Principal." I went in search of my assistant and handing her the blouse I said, "Do you know anything about that?"

"No, but maybe I would understand if you told me how you came by it."

I told her and she chuckled.

"Surely that's Miss North. You said to get the children to come in clean blouses so she talked to them daily and when I visited the room she showed me the boys I was to commend for neat appearance and encourage for their efforts to clean up."

"Let's go in and see the teacher," I suggested, still in the dark.

As we entered each little boy sat in the middle of his tiny bench, each held a primer carefully covered in brown paper with a red edged name-paster precisely fixed in the centre of the front cover; each wore a light coloured wash blouse—(I counted seven of the same sort as the one on my desk).

The sunshine came in through the windows and made little rainbows dance above the aquarium where the fishes looked as if they'd just been polished and put in their places.

AMERICANIZING THE IMMIGRANT ADULT (1909) From Sara R. O'Brien, *English for Foreigners* (Boston, 1909), pp. 24, 55, 76, 140, 149.

This is a tooth-brush.
It is my tooth-brush.
I take it in my hand.
I dip it in warm water.
I shall brush my teeth.
I brush my teeth.
I brush my teeth with this tooth-brush.
I brush all of my teeth.
I brush them every day.
I take this thread.
I shall clean my teeth with it.
I clean between my teeth with it.
My teeth are clean and white.
I take care of my teeth.
I take good care of my teeth.

✻   ✻   ✻

This is the family, in the sitting room.
The family is made up of the father, the mother, and the children.
That is the father who is reading.
The father is the husband.
That is the mother who is sewing.
The mother is the wife.
The father and the mother are the parents.
The sister is playing the piano.
The brother is standing beside her.
The family makes the home.

Copy: *There is no place like home.*

EDUCATION FOR
URBAN INDUSTRIAL
AMERICA
1895–1918

2173

*   *   *

A gentleman knows how to dress well. He doesn't buy clothes which he can't afford. He knows it is cheaper to pay cash for his clothes than to buy on credit.

A gentleman always wears clean clothes. He changes his clothes often. He airs the clothes which can't be washed. He knows that he must wear clean clothes to keep in good health. Unclean clothes bring disease to him, and may also bring disease into his home.

A gentleman is neat in his dress. He does not dress in loud colors. He likes better the kind of clothes which do not attract attention. It pays to dress neatly, for often a man is judged by his clothes.

*   *   *

Are you a citizen of the United States? The United States takes care of all its citizens and gives them many rights. A citizen has the right to life, liberty, and happiness. He has the right to buy and sell, to have a home, and to help in making the government under which he lives a good government. These rights of citizenship must be paid for by the men who enjoy them. A true citizen pays for his rights by obeying the laws, paying his taxes, and taking his part in protecting the government of the United States.

The law tells you what is best for you and for everybody else. You must obey the law, and you should help others to keep the law. A citizen obeys the laws because they are made by the people, for the good of all the people. A law-breaker not only hurts himself but others also. That is why the government must have courts of justice and jails. The only way to make good laws is by choosing the right men to make the laws.

A citizen pays his just taxes, and shares in the government of his city and country. He is interested in the public health, in education, and in all things that are for the good of the city and the state. He watches the work of all the City Departments, and knows how the public money is collected and spent. He earns his own living, and deals honestly with all men. He aids the poor and helpless, and does all he can to prevent cruelty to children and animals.

He is willing to pay for his rights even by giving up his life for his country, if necessary. Because he is a free citizen of his state and of the United States, he is ready at all times to serve his city, his state, and his country.

*   *   *

The American flag means liberty and justice for everybody. It is honored by all citizens on the land and on the sea. For it the soldiers of our army and the sailors of our navy are willing to fight and even to die.

The colors of the flag tell the story of the nation's freedom. Red is for bravery, white is for purity, and blue is for justice.

The stripes tell the number of the original states of the United States, and the stars tell the number of states now in the Union. How many stars has the flag now?

All Americans love the Stars and Stripes. Let us all respect the flag and be true to it.

Copy:—*America is another word for opportunity.*

DEMOCRACY AND THE MELTING POT (1915)   From Horace M. Kallen, "Democracy versus The Melting Pot," *Nation,* vol. C, pp. 190-94, 217-20.

Now it would seem that the preservation, though not the development, of any given type of civilization rests very largely upon these two conditions—like-mindedness and self-consciousness. Without them art, literature, culture in any of its nobler forms, appear to be unlikely: and colonial America had a culture—chiefly of New England—but representative enough of the whole British-American life of the period. Within the area of what we now call the United States this life was not, however, the only life. Similarly animated groups of Frenchmen and Germans in Louisiana and Pennsylvania regarded themselves as the cultural peers of the British, and because of their own common ancestry, their own like-mindedness and self-consciousness, they have retained a large measure of their individuality and spiritual autonomy to this day, after generations of unrestricted and mobile contract and a century of political union with the dominant British populations. . . .

In sum, when we consider that portion of our population which has taken root, we see that it has not merely stippled the country in small units of diverse ethnic groups. It forms rather a series of stripes or layers of varying sizes, moving east to west along the central axis of settlement, where towns are thickest; i.e., from New York and Philadelphia through Chicago and St. Louis, to San Francisco and Seattle. Stippling does not prevail even in the towns, where the variety of population is generally greater. Probably more than half of that population is either foreign-born or of non-British stock, yet even so, the towns are aggregations, not units. Broadly divided into the sections inhabited by the rich and those inhabited by the poor, this economic division does not abolish, it only crosses, the ethnic one. There are rich and poor little Italys, Irelands, Hungarys, Germanys, and rich and poor Ghettos. The common city-life, which depends upon like-mindedness, is not inward, corporate and inevitable, but external, inarticulate and incidental, a reaction to the need of amusement and the need of protection, not the expression of a homogeneity of heritage, mentality and interest. Politics and education in our cities thus often present the phenomenon of ethnic compromises not unknown in the former Austria-Hungary: concessions and appeals to "the Irish vote," "the Jewish vote," "the German vote," vary with concessions and appeals to "the business vote," "the labor vote," and "the woman vote"; occasionally there are compromise school-committees whose members represent each ethnic faction, until, as in Boston, one group grows strong enough to dominate the entire situation.

South of Mason and Dixon's line the cities exhibit a greater homogeneity. Outside of certain regions in Texas the descendants of the native white stock, often degenerate and backward, prevail among the whites, but the whites as a whole constitute a relatively weaker proportion of the population. They live among nine million negroes, whose own mode of living tends, by its mere massiveness, to standardize the "mind" of the poor white, of the proletarian south, in speech, manner and the other values of social living, and to determine the terrible pattern which, among other things, the fear of negro competition makes race-prejudice take. . . .

All immigrants and their offspring are by the way of undergoing "Americanization" if they remain in one place in the country long enough—say six or seven years. The general notion of "Americanization" appears to signify the adoption of the

American variety of English speech, American clothes and manners, the American attitude in politics. "Americanization" signifies, in short, the disappearance of the external differences upon which so much race-prejudice often feeds. It appears to imply the fusion of the various bloods, and a transmutation by "the miracle of assimilation" of Jews, Slavs, Poles, Frenchmen, Germans, Hindus, Scandinavians and so on into beings similar in background, tradition, outlook and spirit to the descendants of the British colonists, the "Anglo-Saxon" stock. Broadly speaking, these elements of Americanism are somewhat external, the effect of environment; . . .

Other things being equal, a democratic society which was to be a realization of the assumptions of the Declaration of Independence, supposing them to be true and socially operative, would be a leveling society such that all persons in it became alike either on the lowest or the highest plane. The outcoming of free social contacts should, according to "the laws of imitation," establish "equality" on the highest plane; for imitation is said to be of the higher by the lower, so that the cut of a Paris gown at $1,000.00 becomes imitated in department stores at $17.50, and the play of the rich becomes the vice of the poor. This process of leveling up through imitation is facilitated by the so-called "standardization" of externals. In these days of ready-made garments, factory-made furniture, refrigerating plants, "boiler-plate," movies and radio, it is almost impossible that the mass of the inhabitants of the United States should wear other than uniform clothes, use other than uniform furniture, utensils or eat anything but the same sorts of food, read anything but the same syndicated hokum, see anything but the same standardized romances and hear anything but the same broadcasted barbarisms. . . .

Immigrants appear to pass through four phases in the cause of being automatically Americanized. In the first phase they exhibit economic eagerness, the greedy hunger of the unfed. Since external differences are a handicap in the economic struggle, they "assimilate," seeking thus to facilitate the attainment of economic independence. Once the proletarian level of such independence is reached, the process of assimilation slows down and tends to come to a stop. The immigrant group is still a national group, modified, sometimes improved, by environmental influences, but otherwise a solitary spiritual unit, which is seeking to find its way out on its own social level. This search brings to light permanent group distinctions and the immigrant, like the Anglo-Saxon American, is thrown back upon himself and his ancestry. Then a process of dissimilation begins. The arts, life and ideals of the nationality become central and paramount; ethnic and national differences change in status from disadvantages to distinctions. All the while the immigrant has been uttering his life in the English language and behaving like an American in matters economic and political, and continues to do so. The institutions of the Republic have become the liberating cause and the background for the rise of the cultural consciousness and social autonomy of the immigrant Irishman, German, Scandinavian, Jew, Pole, or Bohemian. On the whole, the automatic processes of Americanization have not repressed nationality. These processes have liberated nationality, and more or less gratified it. . . .

Two genuine social alternatives are before Americans, either of which they may realize if they will. In social construction the will is father to the fact, for the fact is hardly ever anything more, under the grace of accident and luck, than the concord or conflict of wills. What do Amiercans *will* to make of the United States—a unison, singing the old British theme "America," the America of the New England School? or a harmony, in which that theme shall be dominant, perhaps among others, but one among many, not the only one? . . .

The mind reverts helplessly to the historic attempts at unison in Europe—the heroic failure of the pan-Hellenists, of the Romans, the disintegration and the diversification of the Christian church, for a time the most successful unison in history; the present-day failures of Germany and of Russia. In the United States, however, the whole social situation is favorable as it has never been at any time elsewhere—everything is favorable but the basic law of America itself, and the spirit of the American institutions. To achieve unison—it can be achieved—would be to violate these. For the end determines the means and the means transmute the end, and this end would involve no other means than those used by Germany in Poland, in Schleswig-Holstein, and Alsace-Lorraine; by Russia in the Jewish Pale, in Poland, in Finland; by Austria among the Slavs; by Turkey among the Arabs, Armenians and Greeks. Fundamentally it would require the complete nationalization of education, the abolition of every form of parochial and private school, the abolition of instruction in other tongues than English, and the concentration of the teaching of history and literature upon the English tradition. The other institutions of society would require treatment analogous to that administered by Germany to her European acquisitions. And all of this, even if meeting with no resistance, would not completely guarantee the survival as a unison of the older Americanism. For the program would be applied to diverse ethnic types under changing conditions, and the reconstruction that, with the best will, they might spontaneously make of the tradition would more likely than not be a far cry from the original. . . .

The attainment of the other alternative, a harmony, also requires concerted public action. But the action would do no violence to the ideals of American fundamental law and the spirit of American institutions nor to the qualities of men. It would seek simply to eliminate the waste and the stupidity of the social organization, by way of freeing and strengthening the strong forces actually in operation. Taking for its point of departure the existing ethnic and cultural groups it would seek to provide conditions under which each might attain the cultural perfection that is proper to its kind. The provision of such conditions has been said to be the primary intent of American fundamental law and the function of American institutions. And all of the various nationalities which compose the American nation must be taught first of all this fact, which used perhaps to be, to patriotic minds, the outstanding ideal content of "Americanism"—that democracy means self-realization through self-control, self-discipline, and that one is impossible without the other. . . .

Men may change their clothes, their politics, their wives, their religions, their philosophies, to a greater or lesser extent: they cannot change their grandfathers. Jews or Poles or Anglo-Saxons, in order to cease being Jews or Poles or Anglo-Saxons, would have to cease to be, while they could cease to be citizens or church members or carpenters or lawyers without ceasing to be. The selfhood which is inalienable in them, and for the realization of which they require "inalienable" liberty is ancestrally determined, and the happiness which they pursue has its form implied in ancestral endowment. This is what, actually, democracy in operation assumes. There are human capacities which it is the function of the state to liberate and to protect in growth; and the failure of the state as a government to accomplish this automatically makes for its abolition. Government, the state, under the democratic conception is, it cannot be too often repeated, merely an instrument, not an end. That it is often seized by the powers that prey, that it makes frequent mistakes and considers only secondary ends, surface needs, which vary from moment to moment, of course is obvious: hence the social and political messes government is always getting into. But that it is an instrument, flexibly adjustable to changing life, changing opinion and needs, the whole modern electoral organization and party system declare. And as intelligence and wisdom prevail over "politics" and special interests, as the steady and continuous pressure of the "inalienable" qualities and purposes of human groups more and more dominate the confusion of their common life, the outlines of a possible great and truly democratic commonwealth become discernible. Its form would be that of the federal republic; its substance a democracy of nationalities, cooperating voluntarily and autonomously through common institutions in the enterprise of self-realization through the perfection of men according to their kind. The common language of the commonwealth, the language of its great tradition, would be English, but each nationality would have for its emotional and involuntary life its own peculiar dialect or speech, its own individual and inevitable esthetic and intellectual forms. The political and economic life of the commonwealth is a single unit and serves as the foundation and background for the realization of the distinctive individuality of each *natio* that composes it and of the pooling of these in harmony above them all. Thus "American civilization" may come to mean the perfection of cooperative harmonies of "European civilization"—the waste, the squalor and the distress of Europe being eliminated—a multiplicity in a unity, an orchestration of mankind. As an orchestra every type of instrument has its specific *timbre* and *tonality* founded in its substance and form; as every type has its appropriate theme and melody in the whole symphony, so in society, each ethnic group may be the natural instrument, its temper and culture may be its theme and melody and the harmony and dissonances and discords of them all may make the symphony of civilization. With this difference: a musical symphony is written before it is played; in the symphony of civilization the playing is the writing, so that there is nothing so fixed and inevitable about its progressions as in music, so that within the limits set by nature and luck they may vary at will, and the range and variety of the harmonies may become wider and richer and more beautiful—or the reverse.

But the question is, do the dominant classes in America want such a society? The alternative is actually before them. Can they choose wisely? Or will vanity blind them and fear constrain, turning the promise of freedom into the fact of tyranny, and once more vindicating the ancient habit of men and aborting the hope of the world?

A CALL FOR A HIGHER IDEAL THAN THE MELTING POT (1916) From Randolphe Bourne, "Trans-National America," *Atlantic Monthly*, vol. CXVIII, pp. 86–87.

No reverberatory effect of the great war has caused American public opinion more solicitude than the failure of the "melting pot." The discovery of diverse nationalistic feelings among our great alien population has come to most people as an intense shock. It has brought out the unpleasant inconsistencies of our traditional beliefs. We have had to watch hard-hearted old Brahmins virtuously indignant at the spectacle of the immigrant refusing to be melted, while they jeer at patriots like Mary Antin who write about "our forefathers." We have had to listen to publicists who express themselves as stunned by the evidence of vigorous nationalistic and cultural movements, in this country among Germans, Scandinavians, Bohemians, and Poles, while in the same breath they insist that the alien shall be forcibly assimilated to that Anglo-Saxon tradition which they unquestioningly label "American."

As the unpleasant truth has come upon us that assimilation in this country was proceeding on lines very different from those we had marked out for it, we found ourselves inclined to blame those who were thwarting our prophecies. The truth became culpable. We blamed the war, we blamed the Germans. And then we discovered with a moral shock that these movements had been making great headway before the war even began. We found that the tendency, reprehensible and paradoxical as it might be, has been for the national clusters of immigrants, as they became more and more firmly established and more and more prosperous, to cultivate more and more assiduously the literatures and cultural traditions of their homelands. Assimilation, in other words, instead of washing out the memories of Europe, made them more and more intensely real. Just as these clusters became more and more objectively American, did they become more and more German or Scandinavian or Bohemian or Polish.

✳   ✳   ✳

To face the fact that our aliens are already strong enough to take a share in the direction of their own destiny, and that the strong cultural movements represented by the foreign press, schools, and colonies are a challenge to our facile attempts, is not, however, to admit the failure of Americanization. It is not to fear the failure of democracy. It is rather to urge us to an investigation of what Americanism may rightly mean. It is to ask ourselves whether our ideal has been broad or narrow—whether perhaps the time has not come to assert a higher ideal than the "melting-pot." Surely we cannot be certain of our spiritual democracy when, claiming to melt the nations within us to a comprehension of our free and democratic institutions, we fly into panic at the first sign of their own will and tendency. We act as if we wanted Americanization to take place only on our own terms, and not by the consent of the governed. All our elaborate machinery of settlement and school and union, of social and political naturalization, however, will move with friction just in so far as it neglects to take into account this strong and virile insistence that America shall be what the immigrant will have a hand in making it, and not what a ruling class, descendant of those British stocks which were the first permanent immigrants, decide that America shall be made. This is the condition which confronts us, and which demands a clear and general readjustment of our attitude and our ideal.

TEACHING THE ADULT IMMIGRANT (1916)   From Frank B. Lenz, "Education of the Immigrant," *Educational Review*, vol. LI, pp. 469–77.

Education of Immigrant Adults and Evening Schools for Foreigners

The education of the immigrant adult should begin on shipboard when these people have nothing to do but listen and learn. During the two weeks of passage they are particularly alive to the best ideals that we can give them. Trained social workers appointed by civil service examination should be selected to do this work. The worker could give classes in English every day; he could give talks on American government and citizenship. He should have a small library of books and pamphlets in various languages. He could act as guardian of these people against abuse from deck-hands. He could give stereopticon lectures. He could provide for concerts in which the foreigners themselves would take part. He could warn them against the dangers to which they are exposed in America. The greatest value in teaching them on shipboard lies in the fact that it arouses their interest in English and stimulates them to continue studying in the evening schools when they land.

Why is it necessary or even desirable to educate the immigrant adult? For two reasons: for our own protection and for the immigrant's benefit. Today the majority of immigrants coming to this country come to better their economic condition. Therefore it is our first business to teach him English—the colloquial English that will enable him to get on in life; to get a job, to keep it and then to get a better one; to find his way about the streets and to familiarize himself with American life.

If he is a married man he must be educated for the sake of his family. Too often we find that the cause of disrupted immigrant homes is due to the fact that the parents do not understand nor sympathize with their children who have been remoulded in our public schools. Children become ashamed of their parents' ways and lose the proper respect for them. Quarrels ensue and the older boys and girls leave home to work in the mill or factory.

Selection of Evening School Teachers

Teaching the adult immigrant is a wholly different problem from teaching the immigrant child. The evening schools should be entirely separate and under different management and supervision from the day schools. No teacher should teach in the evening schools who teaches all day in the public schools. The teacher who teaches adults should be healthy and vigorous. He should possess originality, resourcefulness, enthusiasm, perseverance and sympathy. He should know his students personally; he should be well versed in their occupations and interests in order to connect the lesson with their daily lives.

In my opinion it is unnecessary that the teacher be acquainted with the immigrant's own language. Last year with a class of Germans I began by letting them know that I had a slight acquaintance with their language. This proved to be a serious mistake, because I soon found that more German than English was spoken in the classroom. It became necessary for me to do a great deal of translating. The pupil should learn to think in English. The successful teacher is the one who makes the pupil the active person during the process of instruction. A short time ago I was reconfirmed in my opinion on this point when several Greeks came to me with complaints about the methods employed by one of their own countrymen in teaching English. They preferred to attend the Y.M.C.A. school where the teacher was unacquainted with their tongue.

The Method and Content of Instruction

First of all the teacher must not forget that his primary function is to teach English and not geography, mathematics or chemistry. He usually commences the evening's work with conversation. The subject of conversation should be based upon the foreigner's experience. It should be about his work, his home, his country or his business relations. What the teacher must do is to give the pupils English equivalents for what they know in their own language. He must teach them to express these words in such a way that they will be understood. Thus conversation will be made the basis of instruction. A drill in phonetics, concert reading and individual reading will lead up to conversation. The unaccustomed ear must be made accustomed to the sounds of our words and phases. Grammar should be taught in connection with each lesson, but it should at all times take a minor place on the program. Dry, formal technique will fail to hold the interest of any group. Spelling is the stumbling block of the foreigner. His language is generally phonetic while ours is not, hence the difficulty. Therefore we have the double task of breaking old habits and forming new ones.

Supplementary Activities

The organization of debating clubs, glee clubs, or orchestras in the class does much to establish a bond of sympathy among the pupils and between the teacher and the pupils. Talks by principals and visitors; musicales, recitations and theatricals go a long way toward the assimilation process. Sight-seeing trips to different parts of the city, to theatres and to libraries furnish excellent themes for conversation. Stereopticon lectures should be given whenever possible to impart information and to furnish topics of conversation. We can not afford to disregard the social life of the foreigner. Let his social education begin in the evening school—make the school a social center where he can come and bring his friends and feel that it in part belongs to him. Before anyone is acceptable to society he must be socially fit. The evening school can become a vital factor in socializing the immigrant.

❊   ❊   ❊

Domestic Education of the Immigrant

Domestic education would put particular emphasis upon the importance of educating immigrant women along the lines of sanitation, hygiene, foods, home nursing and sewing. Most immigrant women know very little about city life. For the most part they are of the peasant type; they have generally worked in the fields and have not lived in a city or close to neighbors. It becomes necessary to teach them the use of sinks, the care of toilets, the disposal of garbage, and other sanitary work. The immigrant mother must be taught the value of fresh air. She must be taught that fresh air will prevent sickness. It is a part of the domestic educator's duty to show her the relation between flies and disease. She must be taught how to ventilate her house and her clothing. The importance of personal cleanliness must be demonstrated to the mother and her family, but this often has to be done in the face of opposition and superstition. The nurse must personally demonstrate in the home of the immigrant how to bathe and keep a child clean. She must show the girls the folly of paint and powder and she must impress upon them the value of privacy, modesty and morality. Few immigrant women know food varieties and food values; nor do they know how to properly prepare a wholesome meal. Consequently meager and monotonous diets are served alike to all members of the family. Food selection should be taught by taking groups of buyers to the markets while food preparation should be taught in the home by a domestic science educator.

Many foreign women are totally ignorant of the methods of treating bruises, cuts or sprains. They are unable to render the simplest first aid to their children. They do not know the use of medicines nor do they know the parts of the body. I was told by a district nurse in Los Angeles of a case where a doctor was attending a sick Russian. He had prescribed hot pads and bandages to be applied to the chest of the patient but to his dismay on his return he found heavy poultices across the stomach of the sick man.

Prospective mothers are usually very ignorant as to how to care for themselves. The nurse who can gain entrance to the home can render more valuable service than can a male physician because of the fear of the latter.

Most immigrant women know how to sew a little but they need instruction in purchasing and in cutting materials. They must be taught how to select goods which are both durable and attractive. But all the work will be of but little avail unless the newcomer has a model to go by. How can we expect an immigrant family to know a decent American standard of living and home life when they are immediately rushed off to a tenement house in the crowded districts of the city? They find there nothing but low and vicious models. Can we wonder that they copy these very standards? There should be a model American home in every port of entry in America. Here the immigrant, and especially those who are detained for a few days, would get a correct impression of an American home. She would learn what a well-arranged and well-ordered home was by actual contact. And then there should be another model home in every foreign district of the cities, where lessons in cooking, cleaning, sewing and care of the baby, are given during the day and in the evening. The power of example is a big factor in the education and development of the youth and this is no less true in the case of adult immigrants for they are in the youthful stage of experience after arriving in America.

THE EDUCATION OF THE ADULT IMMIGRANT IN CLEVELAND, OHIO

(1916)   From Herbert Adolphus Miller, *The School and the Immigrant* (Cleveland, 1916), pp. 91–94.

It appears that the educational officials of the Cleveland school system are highly satisfied with the quality of the work done in the evening elementary schools. In the printed report for 1914, and again in that for 1915, the city superintendent and the supervisor of evening schools inform the public that "Our evening schools rank high as to quality and amount of work done, and are very much superior to nearly all of those in other cities in regularity of attendance and much lower in cost per capita."

It is impossible for the members of the Survey Staff to share the optimism of the superintendent and the supervisor in this matter. During the course of the Survey 66 visits have been made by five members of the Survey Staff to evening elementary classes. As a result the conclusion has been forced upon these observers that the work done in these classes is very far from ranking high in either quality or amount. While there are many enthusiastic teachers and hundreds of eagerly conscientious pupils, the classroom work exhibits an almost total lack of unified plan, matured method, and intelligent direction. The trouble is that the teaching methods have not been intelligently adapted to the needs and abilities of the pupils.

The typical characteristics of the work are well illustrated by that observed in five successive classrooms in one school visited in March, 1916. The pupils were almost entirely young foreign men of from 25 to 30 years of age. Many of them were employed in one of Cleveland's great steel manufacturing establishments. They were not illiterate, but they had almost no knowledge of English. They were all weary from their day's work and they kept awake only by the exercise of apparent effort.

In the first of the five classes a writing lesson was being conducted, and these husky laboring men were busily engaged in copying, "I am a yellow bird. I can sing. I can fly. I can sing to you."

In the second class the teacher was barely able to talk English and the work was almost entirely conducted by the translation method. The teacher made several fruitless attempts to get the pupils to speak English. He did this by telling them repeatedly, "Think the sentence in your own language and then try to translate it into English." After this had failed to produce satisfactory results, the teacher gave it up and had them read a selection about making pickles from cucumbers.

The third class was taught by a bright young foreigner who had apparently received a classical education. The work was conducted just as are many classes in Latin. The teacher spoke English almost perfectly, and although his pupils could neither speak nor understand it, he carefully explained to them about inflections, voices, moods, tenses, numbers, and persons. He then told them they that were to conjugate "to have" and "to be." After this was explained to them in their own language, the pupils all went to the board and began to write "I have, thou hast, he has." and "I am, thou art, he is,"etc. The teacher explained that "art" was the second person singular, indicative mood, present tense, of the substantive verb "be." After this the class had a reading lesson from the third reader about a robin that said, "God loves the flowers and birds too much to send the cold to freeze them."

In the fourth room the pupils had a reading lesson about "Little drops of water, Little grains of sand." They then had a spelling lesson of the words in the reading selection. The teacher was interested, vivacious, and expended a great amount of nervous energy in talking very rapidly and almost incessantly. She took up most of the time with her own activity and most of the pupils could not understand what she was talking about.

In the fifth and last class the teacher was also most voluble and talked more than all the students combined. It was a reading lesson and the 14 men present were engaged in reading a selection beginning:

Oh, baby, dear baby,
Whatever you do,

You are king of the home
And we all bend to you.

Similar examples might be multiplied from the written records of the work observed in the evening classes, and classes of the sort described may be seen by any one who will take the time to visit the evening schools of the city. Perhaps the most impressive characteristic of it all is that every teacher appears to be entirely free to teach whatever he pleases by any method that he wishes to use. The lessons assigned and the methods employed in the different rooms are astonishingly varied. There seems to be no effective supervision, no plan for improving the teachers in service, and no effort to find out which of the many methods used produces the best results.

New Theory

THE DEMANDS OF SOCIOLOGY UPON PEDAGOGY (1896)   From Albion W. Small, "Demands of Sociology upon Pedagogy," *Journal of Proceedings and Addresses* (Washington, D.C., 1896), pp. 178–81, 184.

Human experience is concerned with three knowable elements: First, man's material environment, inanimate, and animate; second, man himself as an individual, in all his characteristics, from his place in the animal kingdom, through his special physiology, psychology, and technology; third, man's associations or institutions. Sociology is the systematic attempt to reduce the reactions of these three elements—nature, man, institutions—to scientific form and expression. The inclusive reality which sociology finds comprehending both the processes and the products of these reactions is society, *i.e.*, individuals in association, within the conditions imposed by the material environment and modified by human achievement. The task set for each individual when he finds himself participant of this reality, is to accommodate himself to prevailing conditions in such a manner that he may both accomplish and enjoy a maximum share of the development which his stage in social evolution is empowered to accomplish.

This life task of men consequently sets the pedagogical task of teachers. The prime problem of education, as the sociologist views it, is how to promote adaptation of the individual to the conditions, natural and artificial, within which individuals live and move and have their being. It would not be in point to discuss here the relative place of action and cognition in progress toward this end. That belongs to pedagogical technology. I assume that both action and cognition are unchallenged means of modern pedagogy. With their proportions, and with the appropriate sequence at different stages of culture, sociology is not directly concerned. Sociology has no tolerance, however, for the pedantry that persists in carpentering together education courses out of subjects which are supposed to exercise, first, the perceptive faculty, then the memory, then the language faculty, then the logical faculty, etc., etc., etc. On the contrary, every represented contact of a person with a portion of reality sooner or later calls into exercise every mental power of that person, probably in a more rational order and proportion than can be produced by an artificial process. Our business as teachers is primarily, therefore, not to train particular mental powers, but to select points of contact between learning minds and the reality that is to be learned. The mind's own autonomy will look out for the appropriate series of subjective mental processes. In the second place, our business as teachers is to bring these perceptive contacts of pupil's minds with points of objective reality into true association with all the remainder of objective reality, *i.e.*, we should help pupils, first, to see things, and second, to see things together as they actually exist in reality. In other words, the demand of sociology upon pedagogy is that it shall stop wet-nursing orphan mental faculties, and find out how to bring persons into touch with what objectively is, as it is. The mind itself will do the rest.

In pursuance of this demand, sociology necessarily becomes an active partisan upon one of the pedagogical doctrines over which educators are divided, viz.: sociology denies that the rational center for the concentration of studies is any science or group of sciences. The rational center is the student himself. Personal adaptation to life means the given person's organization of his contacts with reality. In other words, pedagogy should be the science of assisting youth to organize their contacts with reality; and by this I mean to organize these contacts with reality by both thought and action, and for both thought and action.

Relatively the world stands still during the school-age of any person. The pupil himself changes visibly almost every day. The reality with which the pupil can have conscious contact is defined therefore by the pupil's own powers and opportunities. At each stage, however, himself on the one hand, and nature, men, institutions, on the other hand, are the subject and object of adjustment. A changing self has the task of adaptation to a surrounding frame of things, which daily displays new mysteries and complexities. The teacher's task is to help the individual understand this environment, of which the pupil for a long time seems to himself to be the center. It is the teacher's business to help the pupil understand this whole environment as it is related to himself. Presently, if the pupil's perceptions grow more penetrating and comprehensive, his own personal interests cease to seem the pivot on which the world of experience turns. His personality becomes extended, and at the same time his egoism gets balanced with the personal equation of others whose interests appear. The child finds the complement of his egoism in the family, the school, the group of playmates, the community, and at last, if his education is complete, in society at large. Yet, at each varying diameter of comprehension, life, of which the child is at first to himself the center and circumference, and later life as a whole, of which to the last the individual is to himself in the final resort the most interesting part—life, either individual or social, is the ever-present reality which summarizes all that men can positively know. This central and inclusive reality varies, in representation, from socially unrelated individual life to a conception of individual life enlarged by evolved social consciousness into a function of the more abiding reality. This human career, either as pursued for himself by the socially unconscious individual, or as a mingling of the individual with others associated by force of circumstances in pursuing purposes which none perfectly comprehend,—this life of men alike in nature, within conditions, imposing common limitations upon nature,—is the whole of man's range of positive experience and scientific observation. Sociology consequently demands of educators that they shall elaborate available aids, first, to perception by the individual of the relation of part to part in this inclusive reality—the life of men in society; second, that educators shall perfect influences to promote adjustment of individuals to their appropriate functions within this whole. The part of the problem which I have at present in mind is the proper direction and organization of the pupil's perceptions. So far as the subject-matter of sociology is concerned, everything knowable and worth knowing is a fact or a relation helping to make up this complexity which we call society or social life. The important claim of sociology in this connection is that this reality, like poverty, we have always with us. This reality as a connected whole, related to the pupil, is always the natural and rational means of education. A sequence of studies, in the sense that the pupil is to be enjoined from intelligent contact with portions of reality until other portions have had their turn, is a monstrous perversion of the conditions of education. All reality, the whole plexus of social life, is continually confronting the pupil. No "subject" abstracted from this actual whole is veracious to the pupil unless he is permitted to see it as a part of the whole. It is a misconstruction of reality to think and accordingly to act as though one kind of knowledge belongs to one age and another to another. The whole vast mystery of life, in all its processes and conditions, confronts the child as really as it does the sage. It is the business of the educator to help the child interpret the part by the whole. Education from the beginning should be an initiation into science, language, philosophy, art, and political action in the largest sense. When we shall have adopted a thoroughly rational pedagogy, the child will begin to learn everything the moment he begins to learn anything.

Am I demanding a pedagogy which presupposes one philosopher as teacher and another as pupil? Certainly. Every teacher ought to be a philosopher. Every child already is one till conventionality spoils him. More than that, he is also scientist, poet, and artist in embryo, and would mature in all these characters if we did not stunt him with our bungling. I would revive Rousseau's cry, "Return to nature!" but in a sense of which Rousseau never dreamed,—not nature in the burlesque of our ignorant preconceptions, but nature scientifically explored, nature, the universal law of which is to own the sway of rational mind.

I am not asserting that grammar, and geometry, and geography, and geology, and history, and economics, and psychology, and ethics, as such, should be taught in the nursery. I am asserting that in the cradle the child begins to be in contact with that nature and society of which all these are phases and products, and reports. Sociology demands for the child, from the cradle to his second childhood, opportunities for such frank contact with life that its various aspects will confide to him their mystery in its real relations with the other elements of life. Sociology demands of the tutors and governors who lead the child through the formal part of education, that they shall pilot Wilhelm Meister so discreetly through his years of apprenticeship that he shall learn his world at the smallest expense and with least cause for regret both to others and to himself. Whether this citizen of the world shall ever learn to construe life in terms of the conventional sciences is an entirely secondary matter. The main thing is that, from the beginning, he shall learn to know himself and his world truly—so far as he knows at all,—in all essential relations. This involves the learning of such sciences as he does acquire in the character of excerpts from the whole book of knowledge, not as self- sufficient knowledges.

I repeat that sociology values subjects of study for reasons quite different from those traditionally alleged. Physical, biological, and social science, with the products of human thought deposited in literature, are worthy of study not because they are tonics for various kinds of mental impotence, but because they are, and only in so far as they are, revealers of man himself and of the life of which he is both creator and creature.

Without alluding further to other departments of knowledge, I may apply what I have said to the subject-matter of the social sciences in particular.

Sociology demands with equal confidence: first, that for everybody the study of *society* shall begin with the nursing bottle, and continue so long as social relations continue; second, that for most people the study of *sociology* shall never begin at all. If the argument thus far has provoked expectation that I shall recommend the introduction of sociology into the curriculum of the lower schools, as the needed corrective of educational defects, the inference is decidedly at fault. Only exceptional pupils should study sociology earlier than their senior year in college, and probably these few would do better to defer the study till after taking the bachelor's degree. While sociology proper is not a desirable subject for young pupils, our educational methods will be miserably inadequate to their social function till every teacher, from the kindergarten on, is sufficiently instructed in sociology to put all his teaching in the setting which the sociological view-point affords. This implies, of course, that the function of education must one day be taken so seriously that only men and women who have more than the bachelor's preparation will be entrusted with its direction.

The study of society which we may reasonably demand in our schools and colleges today must and should be chiefly in connection with the subjects physiography, political geography, anthropology, ethnology, history, civics, and economics. The sociological demand with reference to these subjects is that instruction in them shall be rationalized in the same way that the teaching of geography has been reformed during my recollection. . . .

Sociology demands of educators, finally, that they shall not rate themselves as leaders of children, but as makers of society. Sociology knows no means for the amelioration or reform of society more radical than those of which teachers hold the leverage. The teacher who realizes his social function will not be satisfied with passing children to the next grade. He will read his success only in the record of men and women who go from the school eager to explore wider and deeper these social relations, and zealous to do their part in making a better future. We are the dupes of faulty analysis if we imagine that schools can do much to promote social progress until they are motived by this insight and this temper.

A CALL FOR SOCIAL EDUCATION (1902) From Jane Addams, *Democracy And Social Ethics* (New York, 1902), pp. 178–92, 208–16, 220.

As democracy modifies our conception of life, it constantly raises the value and function of each member of the community, however humble he may be. We have come to believe that the most "brutish man" has a value in our common life, a function to perform which can be fulfilled by no one else. We are gradually requiring of the educator that he shall free the powers of each man and connect him with the rest of life. We ask this not merely because it is the man's right to be thus connected, but because we have become convinced that the social order cannot afford to get along without his special contribution. Just as we have come to resent all hindrances which keep us from untrammelled comradeship with our fellows, and as we throw down unnatural divisions, not in the spirit of the eighteenth-century reformers, but in the spirit of those to whom social equality has become a necessity for further social development, so we are impatient to use the dynamic power residing in the mass of men, and demand that the educator free that power. We believe that man's moral idealism is the constructive force of progress, as it has always been; but because every human being is a creative agent and a possible generator of fine enthusiasm we are sceptical of the moral idealism of the few and demand the education of the many, that there may be greater freedom, strength, and subtilty of intercourse and hence an increase of dynamic power. We are not content to include all men in our hopes, but have become conscious that all men are hoping and are part of the same movement of which we are a part.

Many people impelled by these ideas have become impatient with the slow recognition on the part of the educators of their manifest obligation to prepare and nourish the child and the citizen for social relations. The educators should certainly conserve the learning and training necessary for the successful individual and family life, but should add to that a preparation for the enlarged social efforts which our increasing democracy requires. The democratic ideal demands of the school that it shall give the child's own experience a social value; that it shall teach him to direct his own activities and adjust them to those of other people. We are not willing that thousands of industrial workers shall put all of their activity and toil into services from which the community as a whole reaps the benefit, while their mental conceptions and code of morals are narrow and untouched by any uplift which the consciousness of social value might give them.

We are impatient with the schools which lay all stress on reading and writing, suspecting them to rest upon the assumption that the ordinary experience of life is worth little, and that all knowledge and interest must be brought to the children through the medium of books. Such an assumption fails to give the child any clew to the life about him, or any power to usefully or intelligently connect himself with it. This may be illustrated by observations made in a large Italian colony situated in Chicago, the children from which are, for the most part, sent to the public schools.

The members of the Italian colony are largely from South Italy,—Calabrian and Sicilian peasants, or Neapolitans from the workingmen's quarters of that city. They have come to America with the distinct aim of earning money, and finding more room for the energies of themselves and their children. In almost all cases they mean to go back again, simply because their imaginations cannot picture a continuous life away from the old surroundings. Their experiences in Italy have been those of simple outdoor activity, and their ideas have come directly to them from their struggle with Nature,—such a hand-to-hand struggle as takes place when each man gets his living largely through his own cultivation of the soil, or with tools simply fashioned by his own hands. The women, as in all primitive life, have had more diversified activities than the men. They have cooked, spun, and knitted, in addition to their almost equal work in the fields. Very few of the peasant men or women can either read or write. They are devoted to their children, strong in their family feeling, even to remote relationships, and clannish in their community life.

The entire family has been upheaved, and is striving to adjust itself to its new surroundings. The men, for the most part, work on railroad extensions through the summer, under the direction of a *padrone*, who finds the work for them, regulates the amount of their wages, and supplies them with food. The first effect of immigration upon the women is that of idleness. They no longer work in the fields, nor milk the goats, nor pick up faggots. The mother of the family buys all the clothing, not only already spun and woven but made up into garments, of a cut and fashion beyond her powers. It is, indeed, the most economical thing for her to do. Her house-cleaning and cooking are of the simplest; the bread is usually baked outside of the house, and the macaroni bought prepared for boiling. All of those outdoor and domestic activities, which she would naturally have handed on to her daughters, have slipped away from her. The domestic arts are gone, with their absorbing interests for the children, their educational value, and incentive to activity. A household in a tenement receives almost no raw material. For the hundreds of children who have never seen wheat grow, there are dozens who have never seen bread baked. The occasional washings and scrubbings are associated only with discomfort. The child of such a family receives constant stimulus of most exciting sort from his city street life, but he has little or no opportunity to use his energies in domestic manufacture, or, indeed, constructively in any direction. No activity is supplied to take the place of that which, in Italy, he would naturally have found in his own surroundings, and no new union with wholesome life is made for him.

Italian parents count upon the fact that their children learn the English language and American customs before they do themselves, and the children act not only as interpreters of the language, but as buffers between them and Chicago, resulting in a certain almost pathetic dependence of the family upon the child. When a child of the family, therefore, first goes to school, the event is fraught with much significance to all the others. The family has no social life in any structual form and can supply none to the child. He ought to get it in the school and give it to his family, the school thus becoming the connector with the organized society about them. It is the children aged six, eight, and ten, who go to school, entering, of course, the primary grades. If a boy is twelve or thirteen on his arrival in America, his parents see in him a wage-earning factor, and the girl of the same age is already looking toward her marriage.

Let us take one of these boys, who has learned in his six or eight years to speak his native language, and to feel himself strongly identified with the fortunes of his family. Whatever interest has come to the minds of his ancestors has come through the use of their hands in the open air; and open air and activity of body have been the inevitable accompaniments of all their experiences. Yet the first thing that the boy must do when he reaches school is to sit still, at least part of the time, and he must learn to listen to what is said to him, with all the perplexity of listening to a foreign tongue. He does not find this very stimulating, and is slow to respond to the more subtle incentives of the schoolroom. The peasant child is perfectly indifferent to showing off and making a good recitation. He leaves all that to his schoolfellows, who are more sophisticated and equipped with better English. His parents are not deeply interested in keeping him in school, and will not hold him there against his inclination. Their experience does not point to the good American tradition that it is the educated man who finally succeeds. The richest man in the Italian colony can neither read nor write—even Italian. His cunning and acquisitiveness, combined with the credulity and ignorance of his countrymen, have slowly brought about his large fortune. The child himself may feel the stirring of a vague ambition to go on until he is as the other children are; but he is not popular with his schoolfellows, and he sadly feels the lack of dramatic interest. Even the pictures and objects presented him, as well as the lanuage, are strange.

If we admit that in education it is necessary to begin with the experiences which the child already has and to use his spontaneous and social activity, then the city streets begin this education for him in a more natural way than does the school. The South Italian peasant comes from a life of picking olives and oranges, and he easily sends his children out to pick up coal from railroad tracks, or wood from buildings which have been burned down. Unfortunately, this process leads by easy transition to petty thieving. It is easy to go from the coal on the railroad track to the coal and wood which stand before a dealer's shop; from the potatoes which have rolled from a rumbling wagon to the vegetables displayed by the grocer. This is apt to be the record of the boy who responds constantly to the stimulus and temptations of the street, although in the beginning his search for bits of food and fuel was prompted by the best of motives.

The school has to compete with a great deal from the outside in addition to the distractions of the neighborhood. Nothing is more fascinating than that mysterious "down town," whither the boy longs to go to sell papers and black boots, to attend theatres, and, if possible, to stay all night on the pretence of waiting for the early edition of the great dailies. If a boy is once thoroughly caught in these excitements, nothing can save him from over-stimulation and consequent debility and worthlessness; he arrives at maturity with no habits of regular work and with a distaste for its dulness.

On the other hand, there are hundreds of boys of various nationalities who conscientiously remain in school and fulfill all the requirements of the early grades, and at the age of fourteen are found in factories, painstakingly performing their work year after year. These later are the men who form the mass of the population in every industrial neighborhood of every large city; but they carry on the industrial processes year after year without in the least knowing what it is all about. The one fixed habit which the boy carries away with him from the school to the factory is the feeling that his work is merely provisional. In school the next grade was continually held before him as an object of attainment, and it resulted in the conviction that the sole object of present effort is to get ready for something else. This tentative attitude takes the last bit of social stimulus out of his factory work; he pursues it merely as a necessity, and his very mental attitude destroys his chance for a realization of its social value. As the boy in school contracted the habit of doing his work in certain hours and taking his pleasure in certain other hours, so in the factory he earns his money by ten hours of dull work and spends it in three hours of lurid and unprofitable pleasure in the evening. Both in the school and in the factory, in proportion as his work grows dull and monotonous, his recreation must become more exciting and stimulating. The hopelessness of adding evening classes and social entertainments as a mere frill to a day filled with monotonous and deadening drudgery constantly becomes more apparent to those who are endeavoring to bring a fuller life to the industrial members of the community, and who are looking forward to a time when work shall cease to be senseless drudgery with no self-expression on the part of the worker. It sometimes seems that the public schools should contribute much more than they do to the consummation of this time. If the army of school children who enter the factories every year possessed thoroughly vitalized faculties, they might do much to lighten this incubus of dull factory work which presses so heavily upon so large a number of our fellow-citizens. Has our commericialism been so strong that our schools have become insensibly commercialized, whereas we supposed that our industrial life was receiving the broadening and illuminating effects of the schools? The training of these children, so far as it has been vocational at all, has been in the direction of clerical work. It is possible that the business men, whom we in America so tremendously admire, have really been dictating the curriculum of our public schools, in spite of the conventions of educators and the suggestions of university professors. The business man, of course, has not said, "I will have the public schools train office boys and clerks so that I may have them easily and cheaply," but he has sometimes said, "Teach the children to write legibly and to figure accurately and quickly; to acquire habits of punctuality and order; to be prompt to obey; and you will fit them to make their way in the world as I have made mine." Has the workingman been silent as to what he desires for his children, and allowed the business man to decide for him there, as he has allowed the politician to manage his municipal affairs, or has the workingman so far shared our universal optimism that he has really believed that his children would never need to go into industrial life at all, but that all of his sons would become bankers and merchants?

Certain it is that no sufficient study has been made of the child who enters into industrial life early and stays there permanently, to give him some offset to its monotony and dulness, some historic significance of the part he is taking in the life of the community.

*   *   *

We constantly hear it said in educational circles, that a child learns only by "doing," and that education must proceed "through the eyes and hands to the brain"; and yet for the vast number of people all around us who do not need to have activities artificially provided, and who use their hands and eyes all the time, we do not seem able to reverse the process. We quote the dictum, "What is learned in the schoolroom must be applied in the workshop," and yet the skill and handicraft constantly used in the workshop have no relevance or meaning given to them by the school; and when we do try to help the workingman in an educational way, we completely ignore his everyday occupation. Yet the task is merely one of adaptation. It is to take actual conditions and to make them the basis for a large and generous method of education, to perform a difficult idealization doubtless, but not an impossible one.

*   *   *

As the poet bathes the outer world for us in the hues of human feeling, so the workingman needs some one to bathe his surroundings with a human significance—some one who shall teach him to find that which will give a potency to his life. His education, however simple, should tend to make him widely at home in the world, and to give him a sense of simplicity and peace in the midst of the triviality and noise to which he is constantly subjected. He, like other men, can learn to be content to see but a part, although it must be a part of something.

It is because of a lack of democracy that we do not really incorporate him in the hopes and advantages of society, and give him the place which is his by simple right. We have learned to say that the good must be extended to all of society before it can be held secure by any one person or any one class; but we have not yet learned to add to that statement, that unless all men and all classes contribute to a good, we cannot even be sure that it is worth having. In spite of many attempts we do not really act upon either statement.

FLORENCE KELLEY ON CHILD LABOR LAWS (1903)   From "An Effective Child Labor Law." *Annals of the American Academy of Political and Social Science,* vol. XXI, pp. 440–44.

An effective child-labor law rests primarily upon certain definite prohibitions among which are the following:

Labor is Prohibited

(1) for all children under the age of fourteen years,

(2) for all children under sixteen years of age who do not measure sixty inches and weigh eighty pounds,

(3) for all children under sixteen years of age who cannot read fluently and write legibly simple sentences in the English language.

(4) for all children under the age of sixteen years, between the hours of 7 p. m. and 7 a. m., or longer than eight hours in any twenty-four hours.

(5) for all children under the age of sixteen years in occupations designated as dangerous by certain responsible officials.

Of the foregoing prohibitions Number 1 is in force in a number of states so far as work in factories, stores, offices, laundries, etc., is concerned. In New York and Massachusetts recent statutes restrict, though they do not yet prohibit outright, work in the street occupations for children under the age of fourteen years. The movement in this direction gained marked headway during the past winter. Number 2 is not yet embraced in any statute, but is vigorously advocated by many physicians and others practically acquainted with working children. Number 3 has long been the law in New York State, and is of the highest value to the immigrant children so far as it is enforced. Number 4 is in force in Ohio. Number 5 is in force in Massachusetts.

The Child

Effective legislation requires that before going to work the child satisfy a competent officer appointed for the purpose, that it
(1) is fourteen years of age, and

(2) is in good health, and

(3) measures at least sixty inches and weighs eighty pounds, and

(4) is able to read fluently and write legibly simple sentences in the English language, and

(5) has attended school a full school year during the twelve months next preceding going to work.

The Parent

Effective child-labor legislation requires that the parent
(1) keep the child in school to the age of fourteen years, and

(2) take oath as to the exact age of the child before letting it begin to work, and

(3) substantiate the oath by producing a transcript of the official record of the birth of the child, or the record of its baptism, or some other religious record of the time of the birth of the child, and must

(4) produce the record of the child's school attendance, signed by the principal of the school which the child last attended.

The Employer

Effective child-labor legislation requires that the employer before letting the child begin to work,

(1) obtain and place on file ready for official inspection papers showing
    (a) the place and date of birth of the child substantiated by
    (b) the oath of the parent corroborated by
    (c) a transcript of the official register of births, or by a transcript of the record of baptism, or other religious record of the birth of the child, and by
    (d) the school record signed by the principal of the school which the child last attended, and by
    (e) the statement of the officer of the Board of Education designated for the purpose, that he has approved the papers and examined the child.

(2) After permitting the child to begin work, the employer is required to produce the foregoing papers on demand of the school-attendance officer, the health officer and the factory inspectors.

(3) In case the child cease to work, the employer must restore to the child the papers enumerated above.

(4) During the time that the child is at work, the employer must provide suitable seats, and permit their use so far as the nature of the work allows; and must

(5) post and keep posted in a conspicuous place, the hours for beginning work in the morning, and for stopping work in the middle of the day; the hours for resuming work and for stopping at the close of the day; and all work done at any time not specified in such posted notice constitutes a violation of the law. The total number of hours must not exceed eight in any one day or forty-eight in one week.

The Officials

Effective legislation for the protection of children requires that the officials entrusted with the duty of enforcing it

(1) give their whole time, not less than eight hours of every working day, to the performance of their duties, making night inspections whenever this may be necessary to insure that children are not working during the prohibited hours;

(2) treat all employers alike, irrespective of political considerations, of race, religion or power in a community;

(3) prosecute all violations of the law;

(4) keep records complete and intelligible enough to facilitate the enactment of legislation suitable to the changing conditions of industry.

The School

The best child-labor law is a compulsory education law covering forty weeks of the year and requiring the consecutive attendance of all the children to the age of fourteen years. It is never certain that children are not at work, if they are out of school. In order to keep the children, however, it is not enough to compel attendance,—the schools must be modified and adapted to the needs of the recent immigrants in the North and of the poor whites in the South, affording instruction which appeals to the parents as worth having, in lieu of the wages which the children are forbidden to earn, and appeals to the children as interesting and attractive. These requirements are so insufficiently met in the great manufacturing centres of the North, that truancy is in several of them, at present, an insoluble problem. No system of child-labor legislation can be regarded as effective which does not face and deal with these facts.

The evolution of the vacation school and camp promises strong reinforcement of the child-labor laws; which are now seriously weakened by the fact that the long vacation leaves idle upon the streets children whom employers covet by reason of the low price of their labor, while parents, greedy for the children's earnings and anxious lest the children suffer from the life of the streets, eagerly seek work for them. Nothing could be worse for the physique of the school child than being compelled to work during the summer; and the development of the vacation school and vacation camp alone seems to promise a satisfactory solution of the problem of the vacation of the city child of the working class.

A CALL FOR A NEW EDUCATION FOR THE IMMIGRANT CHILD

(1908)   From Jane Addams, "The Public School and the Immigrant Child," *Journal of Proceedings and Addresses* (Washington, D.C., 1908), pp. 99–102.

I am always diffident when I come before a professional body of teachers, realizing as I do that it is very easy for those of us who look on to bring indictments against results; and realizing also that one of the most difficult situations you have to meet is the care and instruction of the immigrant child, especially as he is found where I see him, in the midst of crowded city conditions.

And yet in spite of the fact that the public school is the great savior of the immigrant district, and the one agency which inducts the children into the changed conditions of American life, there is a certain indictment which may justly be brought, in that the public school too often separates the child from his parents and widens that old gulf between fathers and sons which is never so cruel and so wide as it is between the immigrants who come to this country and their children who have gone to the public school and feel that they have there learned it all. The parents are thereafter subjected to certain judgment, the judgment of the young which is always harsh and in this instance founded upon the most superficial standard of Americanism. And yet there is a notion of culture which we would define as a knowledge of those things which have been long cherished by men, the things which men have loved because thru generations they have softened and interpreted life, and have endowed it with value and meaning. Could this standard have been given rather than the things which they see about them as the test of so-called success, then we might feel that the public school has given at least the beginnings of culture which the child ought to have. At present the Italian child goes back to its Italian home more or less disturbed and distracted by the contrast between the school and the home. If he throws off the control of the home because it does not represent the things which he has been taught to value he takes the first step toward the Juvenile Court and all the other operations of the law, because he has prematurely asserted himself long before he is ready to take care of his own affairs.

We find in the carefully prepared figures which Mr. Commons and other sociologists have published that while the number of arrests of immigrants is smaller than the arrests of native born Americans, the number of arrests among children of immigrants is twice as large as the number of arrests among the children of native born Americans. It would seem that in spite of the enormous advantages which the public school gives to these children it in some way loosens them from the authority and control of their parents, and tends to send them, without a sufficient rudder and power of self-direction, into the perilous business of living. Can we not say, perhaps, that the schools ought to do more to connect these children with the best things of the past, to make them realize something of the beauty and charm of the language, the history, and the traditions which their parents represent. It is easy to cut them loose from their parents; it requires cultivation to tie them up in sympathy and understanding. The ignorant teacher cuts them off because he himself cannot understand the situation, the cultivated teacher fastens them because his own mind is open to the charm and beauty of that old-country life. In short, it is the business of the school to give to each child the beginnings of a culture so wide and deep and universal that he can interpret his own parents and countrymen by a standard which is world-wide and not provincial.

The second indictment which may be brought is the failure to place the children into proper relation toward the industry which they will later enter. Miss Arnold has told us that children go into industry for a very short time. I believe that the figures of the United States census show the term to be something like six years for the women in industry as over against twenty-four years for men, in regard to continuity of service. Yet you cannot disregard the six years of the girls nor the twenty-four years of the boys, because they are the immediate occupation into which they enter after they leave the school—even the girls are bound to go thru that period—that is, the average immigrant girls are—before they enter the second serious business of life and maintain homes of their own. Therefore, if they enter industry unintelligently, without some notion of what it means, they find themselves totally unprepared for their first experience with American life, they are thrown out without the proper guide or clue which the public school might and ought to have given them. Our industry has become so international, that it ought to be easy to use the materials it offers for immigrant children. The very processes and general principles which industry represents give a chance to prepare these immigrant children in a way which the most elaborated curriculum could not present. Ordinary material does not give the same international suggestion as industrial material does.

Third, I do not believe that the children who have been cut off from their own parents are going to be those who, when they become parents themselves, will know how to hold a family together and to connect it with the state. I should begin to teach the girls to be good mothers by teaching them to be good daughters. Take a girl whose mother has come from South Italy. The mother cannot adjust herself to the changed condition of housekeeping, does not know how to wash and bake here, and do the other things which she has always done well in Italy, because she has suddenly been transported from a village to a tenement house. If that girl studies these household conditions in relation to the past and to the present needs of the family, she is undertaking the very best possible preparation for her future obligations to a household of her own. And to my mind she can undertake it in no better way. Her own children are mythical and far away, but the little brothers and sisters pull upon her affection and her loyalty, and she longs to have their needs recognized in the school so that the school may give her some help. Her mother complains that the baby is sick in America because she cannot milk her own goat; she insists if she had her own goat's milk the baby would be quite well and flourishing, as the children were in Italy. If that girl can be taught that the milk makes the baby ill because it is not clean and be provided with a simple test that she may know when milk is clean, it may take her into the study not only of the milk within the four walls of the tenement house, but into the inspection of the milk of her district. The milk, however, remains good educational material; it makes even more concrete the connection which you would be glad to use between the household and the affairs of the American city. Let her not follow the mother's example of complaining about changed conditions; let her rather make the adjustment for her mother's entire household. We cannot tell what adjustments the girl herself will be called upon to make ten years from now; but we can give her the clue and the aptitude to adjust the family with which she is identified to the constantly changing conditions of city life. Many of us feel that, splendid as the public schools are in their relation to the immigrant child, they do not understand all of the difficulties which surround the child—all of the moral and emotional perplexities which constantly harass him. The children long that the school teacher should know something about the lives their parents lead and should be able to reprove the hooting children who make fun of the Italian mother because she wears a kerchief on her head, not only because they are rude but also because they are stupid. We send young people to Europe to see Italy, but we do not utilize Italy when it lies about the schoolhouse. If the body of teachers in our great cities could take hold of the immigrant colonies, could bring out of them their handicrafts and occupations, their traditions, their folk songs and folk lore, the beautiful stories which every immigrant colony is ready to tell and translate; could get the children to bring these things into school as the material from which culture is made and the material upon which culture is based, they would discover by comparison that which they give them now is a poor meretricious and vulgar thing. Give these children a chance to utilize the historic and industrial material which they see about them and they will begin to have a sense of ease in America, a first consciousness of being at home. I believe if these people are welcomed upon the basis of the resources which they represent and the contributions which they bring, it may come to pass that these schools which deal with immigrants will find that they have a wealth of cultural and industrial material which will make the schools in other neighborhoods positively envious. A girl living in a tenement household, helping along this tremendous adjustment, healing over this great moral upheaval which the parents have suffered and which leaves them bleeding and sensitive—such a girl has a richer experience and a finer material than any girl from a more fortunate household can have at the present moment.

I wish I had the power to place before you what it seems to me is the opportunity that the immigrant colonies present to the public school: the most endearing occupation of leading the little child, who will in turn lead his family, and bring them with him into the brotherhood for which they are longing. The immigrant child cannot make this demand upon the school because he does not know how to formulate it; it is for the teacher both to perceive it and to fulfil it.

AN EDUCATION TO ELIMINATE "LAGGARDS" IN THE SCHOOLS
(1909) From Leonard P. Ayres, *Laggards In Our Schools: A Study of Retardation And Elimination In City School Systems* (New York, 1909), pp. 3–7.

Conditions

In every school there are found some children who are older than they should be for the grades they are in. These children constitute serious problems for the teachers. They are misfits in the classes, require special attention if they are to do satisfactory work and render more difficult the work with the other children. These children are known as over-age or retarded children. They are found in all school system but are by no means equally common in all systems. In this regard there is an enormous variability among cities. In Medford, Massachusetts, only 7 per cent of the children are retarded according to the standard adopted, while in Memphis, Tennesee, among the colored children 75 per cent are retarded. All of the other cities studied fall between these two extremes. On the average about 33 per cent of all of the pupils in our public schools belong to the class "retarded." This gives an idea of the magnitude of the problem with which we are dealing. It is not at all a problem concerning a few under-developed or feeble minded children. It is one affecting most intimately perhaps 6,000,000 children in the United States.

Wherever we find that the retarded children constitute a large part of all of the school membership we find that many of the children do not stay in the schools until they complete the elementary course. Children who are backward in their studies and reach the age of fourteen (which is generally the end of the compulsory attendance period) when they are in the fifth or sixth grade instead of in the eighth, rarely stay to graduate. They drop out without finishing. The educational importance of this fact is great. We are apt to think of the common school course as representing the least amount of schooling that should be permitted to anyone, but the fact remains that a large part of all of our children are not completing it. As retardation is a condition affecting all of our schools to some extent, so too elimination, or the falling out of pupils before completing the course, is an evil found everywhere but varying greatly in degree in different localities. In Quincy, Massachusetts, of every hundred children who start in the first grade eighty-two continue to the final grade. In Camden, New Jersey, of every hundred who start only seventeen finish. The other eighty-three fall by the wayside. The general tendency of American cities is to carry all of their children through the fifth grade, to take one-half of them to the eighth grade and one in ten through the high school.

In the current discussion of retardation two claims have repeatedly been put forward by those who seek to show that retardation is not a serious matter and that in any event the responsibility of the school for existing conditions is small. These claims are, first, that if we find many over-age children in the schools it is because they enter at comparatively advanced ages; and secondly, that even if some children do progress slowly they are in a measure offset by an equal or greater number who make rapid progress.

Our studies have thrown light on both of these contentions. The children who are retarded on account of late entrance are found to be only a small part of all of the retarded children. In New York City where children enter school on the average later than they do in many other cities, the retarded children whose backwardness is due to late entrance are found to constitute less than one-third of all. Since retardation is ascribable to only two conditions, late entrance and slow progress, and since late entrance is found to be only a small factor, slow progress, however caused, is proved to be the great factor in bringing about the existing condition.

*　　*　　*

The contention that the children who make slow progress are in a measure counterbalanced by a substantially equal number who make rapid progress is found to rest on an even slighter basis of fact. Taking the average of the conditions found in our city schools the figures show that for every child who is making more than normally rapid progress there are from eight to ten children making abnormally slow progress. In the lower grades, before the process of elimination enters to remove the badly retarded children, the average progress of the pupils is at the rate of eight grades in ten years. These conditions mean that our courses of study as at present constituted are fitted not to the slow child or to the average child but to the unusually bright one.

If the lower grades of our schools contain many children who are not going ahead at the normal rate, this means that there are large numbers of pupils who are doing the work of the grades they are in for the second or third time. These children are repeaters. The study of the figures from different cities reveals the importance of this class from both the educational and economic view points. The computations show that in the schools of Somerville a little more than 6 per cent of the children are repeaters. From this figure the records of the cities range upwards until we reach Camden, New Jersey, with 30 per cent of the children in the repeating class. The average percentage is a little over 16. This means that in the country as a whole about one-sixth of all of the children are repeating and we are annually spending about $27,000,000 in this wasteful process of repitition in our cities alone.

Causes

When we seek to analyze the causes which are responsible for the conditions which have been discussed we find the field a difficult one. There is no one cause for retardation nor can we say that any one cause is preponderant. Late entrance is a potent factor, irregular attendance is another. In both cases time lost through illness plays an important part. Certain physical defects are responsible for a part of the backwardness. On the basis of the investigation conducted in New York we can say that in general children suffering from the physical defects which are recorded in that city by the school physicians make nearly 9 per cent slower progress than do the children who are found on examination to have no defects. Children having some sorts of defects, adenoids for instance, are retarded still more.

The study of the bearing of nationality on school progress has been fruitful. In general there is little relation between the percentage of foreigners in the different cities and the amount of retardation found in their schools. Some of our most foreign cities make very good records, while in some of our most American cities school conditions are very bad indeed. In the country as a whole there are more illiterates proportionately among native whites of native parents than among native whites of foreign parents and school attendance is more general among the latter than among the former.

In the New York investigation it was shown that there are decided differences between the different races in the matter of school progress. There the Germans made the best records, followed by Americans, Russians, English, Irish, and Italians in that order. Everywhere that investigations have been made it has been conclusively shown that ignorance of the English language is a handicap that is quickly and easily overcome and has little influence on retardation.

Several other branches of the investigation have brought to light conditions of great educational importance, as for instance an inquiry into the effects of different rates of promotion on the number of times the average child fails during his course, which demonstrated that we are training our children well in failure.

Another point on which important facts have been secured is the old question whether the child who enters school at say the age of eight or nine makes more rapid or slower progress than the one who enters at the age of five.

Perhaps no more important set of facts has been brought to light than those relating to the relative standing of the two sexes. We have always known that fewer boys than girls go to the high school but we have not before known that there is 13 per cent more retardation among boys than among girls and 13 per cent more repeaters among boys than among girls, or that the percentage of girls who complete the common school course is 17 per cent greater than the percentage of boys. *These facts mean that our schools as at present constituted are far better fitted to the needs of the girls than they are to those of the boys.*

There is another thing that has been proved; namely, that these conditions which have been discussed are neither of recent origin nor are they growing worse. Conditions are slowly improving in most places but not in all and not rapidly. They are not improving so rapidly that we have any grounds for feeling that if let alone they will care for themselves.

Remedies

The possible remedies for the conditions which have been discussed may be divided into two classes, legislative and administrative.

If children are to progress regularly through the grades they must be present in the schools. This means that we must have better compulsory attendance laws and better provision for their enforcement. If we are to enforce the attendance laws we must know where the children of school age are. Therefore, we must have better laws for taking the school census and better methods for utilizing the returns. If we are to have all of our children complete the common school course we must have an agreement which is now commonly lacking between the length of the school course and the length of the compulsory attendance period. It is a curious anomaly that we commonly have school courses eight or nine years in length and compel attendance for six years only.

The administrative reforms which must be brought about consist mainly of more thorough and better medical inspection, courses of study which will more nearly fit the abilities of the average pupil, more flexible grading, and, most important of all, a better knowledge of the facts. We must have better school records and we must learn to interpret them more intelligently. It is far from creditable that in hardly a city in the country can the school authorities tell how many pupils begin school each year, or how fast they advance, or what proportion finish or why they fall out, or where and why they lose time.

AN ANSWER TO THE PROBLEMS OF CHILD LIFE (1912) From Robert
Hunter, *Poverty* (New York, 1912), pp. 200–03, 209–10, 260.

These present-day problems of the child—the cities, the coming of immigrants, the collapse of home life, the yardless tenement—are all due to one underlying cause. There has been an entire revolution in industry during the last century, and nearly all the social problems of child life have grown up as a result of this revolution. The best thought of this entire period has been given to industrial development,—to economy, wealth, profits, and wages. That the needs of the child have been overlooked, if not entirely forgotten, in the readjustment of society to the new conditions, cannot be questioned. At the risk of a slight interruption in the discussion of the problems of child life, perhaps it would be well to trace the recent changes in life which have occurred, for the purpose of showing their effect on the child and the present necessity of important readjustments of old institutions to these changes and of new social institutions to satisfy the needs of the child.

* * *

When this [industrial] revolution brought into the world large cities and a new industrial life, it, at the same time, destroyed what has been described as the Home. In our largest cities *this* home no longer exists. The economic development of the last hundred years has destroyed it and left in its stead a mere shadow of what once was the source of all things essential to the world. The mills, factories, abattoirs, breweries, and bakeries took from the home the various trades; the state supplied the defence, and the city the water supply; the sanitarian, the surgeon, and the alienist took precaution against disease and replaced home remedies by skilled practice and medical science; the sick have hospital care, the schools undertake the instruction of the child, and the factory, etc., the technical training. The home is now a few rooms in a crowded tenement or apartment house. The fields have diminished to commons, the commons to yards, and the yards to courts and light shafts; the tenement has become yardless. Little or nothing has replaced the social losses of the home, and the same may be said of the possibilities for recreation, which were lost with the fields and commons. A few settlements have endeavored to supply opportunities for keeping alive the neighborhood feeling; a few playgrounds have come to supply the recreative needs; but the losses have been serious and as yet there are no sufficient substitutes. The rapidity with which this revolution has occurred is almost unbelievable. There are men now living who have seen the working out of the whole industrial process.

✻   ✻   ✻

These problems of child life are school problems. They sum themselves up in the questions: Are we to have the school ignore this larger work of education and remain a sort of dispensary of learning—an inflexible missionary of the three R's? Will it, because of financial embarrassment, be forced to give itself only half-heartedly and slovenly to these new problems of education, or is it to take, as its responsibility, the entire problem of child life and master it? If the school does not assume this responsibility, how shall the work be done? The reason for the present neglect of these vital matters is, it seems to me, ignorance rather than unconcern. The city fathers do not appreciate the new social needs, and the teachers, as a class, are lacking in a knowledge of industrial history and social evolution. They have not realized that the home is passing away and that, unless the school takes the child, he is left to the street. They have specialized in philosophy, pedagogy, and psychology. They have isolated themselves from contact with those in poverty. I could not wish for a better example of these facts than that furnished by a principal, who said recently (according to the daily papers): "With all the play centres provided by the Board of Education, crime is on the increase. The parents are anxious for some agency to take their children day or night. Don't mistake this for love of education. It is *parental selfishness that is throwing the burden, and the righteous burden, of the home upon the schools.*" It is almost inconceivable that a principal in our schools should know so little of the problems of the city child. He apparently does not know the tenement,—the yardless, homeless tenement,—and one fears that he may not know the rudiments of his obligations as an educator. But if he were the only one in ignorance, we should be fortunate indeed. As a matter of fact the Police Magistrates, the Board of Education, the Board of Estimate and Apportionment, as well as the teachers seem to be entirely unconscious of this industrial revolution which has entirely altered the conditions of child life, and they look upon these new problems as a result of parental selfishness, and upon the increase of juvenile crime as a result of parental neglect, and so on, never seeming to realize that the whole thing is a product of social evolution, and that the charge of neglect must rest upon the community and the school, and not, in most cases, upon the parent.

✻   ✻   ✻

The world must ever change, and for the benefit of the child must come the change beyond the change. But, in order that the little one may be nobler than his father, one change is just now imperatively necessary and presses upon us. The factory in displacing the home workshop has made no provision for the proper manual and industrial education of the child. The tenement in displacing the home and the common has made no provision for the child's play. The school must take upon itself these new responsibilities, both of which are educational problems, and both of which the school, more than any other public agency, is fitted to master. An awakening to the necessity of assuming the new duties should not be delayed, for the yardless tenement is multiplying, the children must be kept from the factory, and the little ones of the street may even now be counted by the million.

LILLIAN WALD CALLS FOR "SOCIALIZED PARENTAL CONTROL"

(1915) From Lillian D. Wald, *The House on Henry Street* (New York, 1915), pp. 105–11.

The first public school established in New York City (Number 1) is on Henry Street. Number 2 is a short distance from it, on the same street, and Number 147 is at our corner. Between their sites are several semi-public and private educational institutions, and from School No. 1 to School No. 147 the distance is not more than three-quarters of a mile.

It is not unnatural, therefore, that the school should loom large in our consciousness of the life of the child. The settlement at no time would, even if it could, usurp the place of school or home. It seeks to work with both or to supplement either. The fact that it is flexible and is not committed to any fixed programme gives opportunity for experimentation not possible in a rigid system, and the results of these experiments must have affected school methods, at least in New York City.

Intelligent social workers seize opportunities for observation, and almost unconsciously develop methods to meet needs. They see conditions as they are, and become critical of systems as they act and react upon the child or fail to reach him at all. They reverse the method of the school teacher, who approaches the child with preconceived theories and a determination to work them out. Where the school fails, it appears to the social workers to do so because it makes education a thing apart,—because it separates its work from all that makes up the child's life outside the classroom. Great emphasis is now laid upon the oversight of the physical condition of children from the time of their birth through school life; but the suggestion of this extension of socialized parental control did not emanate from those within the school system.

Cooking has been taught in the public schools for many years, and the instruction is of great value to those who are admitted to the classes; but appropriations have never been sufficient to meet all the requirements, and the teaching is given in grades already depleted by the girls who have gone to work, and who will perhaps never again have leisure or inclination to learn how to prepare meals for husband and children,—the most important business in life for most women.

The laboratory method employed in the schools never seemed to us sufficiently related to the home conditions of vast numbers of the city's population; and, therefore, when the settlement undertook, according to its theory, to supplement the girls' education, all the essentials of our own housekeeping—stove, refrigerator, bedrooms, and so on—were utilized. But neither were single bedrooms and rooms set apart for distinct purposes entirely satisfactory in teaching domestic procedure to the average neighbor and the leader finally developed out of her knowledge of their home conditions the admirable system of "Housekeeping Centers" now sustained and administered by a committee of men and women on which the settlement has representation.

A flat was rented in a typical Henry Street tenement. Intelligence and taste were exercised in equipping it inexpensively and with furniture that required the least possible labor to keep it free from dirt and vermin. Classes were formed to teach housekeeping in its every detail, using nothing which the people themselves could not procure,—a tiny bathroom, a gas stove, no "model" tubs, but such as the landlord provided for washing. Cleaning, disinfecting, actual purchasing of supplies in the shops of the neighborhood, household accounts, nursing, all the elements of homekeeping, were systematically taught. The first winter that the center was opened the entire membership of a class consisted of girls engaged to be married,— clerks, stenographers, teachers; none were prepared and all were eager to have the homes which they were about to establish better organized and more intelligently conducted than those from which they had come. When one young woman announced her betrothal she added, "And I am fully prepared because I have been through the Housekeeping Center."

Other centers have been established by the committee in different parts of the city. Dr. Maxwell, Superintendent of Schools, always sympathetic and ready to fit instruction to the pupils' needs, has encouraged the identification of these housekeeping centers with the schools. Whenever an enterprising principal desires it, the teachers of the nearby housekeeping center are made a part of the school system. Perhaps we may some day see one attached to every public school; and I am inclined to believe that, when institutions of higher learning fully realize that education is preparation for life, they too will wonder if the young women graduates of their colleges should not, like our little girl neighbors, be fitted to meet their great home-making responsibilities.

Out of the experience of the originator of the housekeeping centers "Penny Lunches" for the public schools have been inaugurated, and provide a hot noonday meal for children. The committee now controlling this experiment has inquired into food values, physical effects on children, relation to school attendance, and so on.

The schools in a great city have an additional responsibility, as many of the pupils are deprived of home training because of extreme poverty or the absence of the mother at work, and a measure of failure may be traced to an imperfect realization of the conditions under which pupils live, or to a lack of training on the part of some of the teachers. The Home-and-School Visitor, whose duties are indicated in her title, is charged to bring the two together, that each may help the other; but there are few visitors as yet, and the effect upon the great number of pupils in attendance (over 800,000 in New York) is obviously limited.

We are not always mindful of the fact that children in normal homes get education apart from formal lessons and instruction. Sitting down to a table at definite hours, to eat food properly served, is training, and so is the orderly organization of the home, of which the child so soon becomes a conscious part. There is direction toward control in the provision for privacy, beginning with the sequestered nursery life. The exchange of letters, which begins with most children at a very early age, the conversation of their elders, familiarity with telegrams and telephones, and with the incidents of travel, stimulate their intelligence, resourcefulness, and self-reliance.

Contrast this regulated domestic life with the experience of children—a large number in New York—who may never have been seated around a table in an orderly manner, at a given time, for a family meal. Where the family is large and the rooms small, and those employed return at irregular hours, its members must be fed at different times. It is not uncommon in a neighborhood such as ours to see the mother lean out of the fourth- or fifth- story window and throw down the bread-and-butter luncheon to the little child waiting on the sidewalk below—sometimes to save him the exertion of climbing the stairs, sometimes because of insufficient time. The children whose mothers work all day and who are locked out during their absence are expected to shift for themselves, and may as often be given too much as too little money to appease their hunger. Having no more discretion in the choice of food than other children of their age, they become an easy prey for the peddlers of unwholesome foods and candies (often with gambling devices attached) who prowl outside the school limits.

G. STANLEY HALL ON ADOLESCENCE AS "A NEW BIRTH" (1905)   From
G. Stanley Hall, *Adolescence* (New York, 1905), vol. I, pp. 1–3.

Adolescence is a new birth, for the higher and more completely human traits are now born. The qualities of body and soul that now emerge are far newer. The child comes from and harks back to a remoter past; the adolescent is neo-atavistic, and in him the later acquisitions of the race slowly become prepotent. Development is less gradual and more saltatory, suggestive of some ancient period of storm and stress when old moorings were broken and a higher level attained. The annual rate of growth in height, weight, and strength is increased and often doubled, and even more. Important functions previously non-existent arise. Growth of parts and organs loses its former proportions, some permanently and some for a season. Some of these are still growing in old age and others are soon arrested and atrophy. The old moduli of dimensions become obsolete and old harmonies are broken. The range of individual differences and average errors in all physical measurements and all psychic tests increases. Some linger long in the childish stage and advance late or slowly, while others push on with a sudden outburst of impulsion to early maturity. Bones and muscles lead all other tissues, as if they vied with each other, and there is frequent flabbiness or tension as one or the other leads. Nature arms youth for conflict with all the resources at her command—speed, power of shoulder, biceps, back, leg, jaw,—strengthens and enlarges skull, thorax, hips, makes man aggressive and prepares woman's frame for maternity. The power of the diseases peculiar to childhood abates, and liability to the far more [simple] diseases of maturity begins, so that with liability to both it is not strange that the dawn of the ephebic day is marked at the same time by increased morbidity but diminished rates of mortality. Some disorders of arrest and defect as well as of excessive unfoldment in some function, part, or organ may now, after long study and controversy, be said to be established as peculiar to this period, and diseases that are distinctly school- and city-bred abound, with apparently increasing frequency. The momentum of heredity often seems insufficient to enable the child to achieve this great revolution and come to complete maturity, so that every step of the upward way is strewn with wreckage of body, mind, and morals. There is not only arrest, but perversion, at every stage, and hoodlumism, juvenile crime, and secret vice seem not only increasing, but develop in earlier years in every civilized land. Modern life is hard, and in many respects increasingly so, on youth. Home, school, church, fail to recognize its nature and needs and, perhaps most of all, its perils. The cohesions between the elements of personality are loosened by the disparities of both somatic and psychic development, and if there is arrest at any stage or in any part before the higher unity is achieved there is almost sure to be degeneration and reunion on a lower level than before. One of the gravest dangers is the persistent ignoring by feminists of the prime importance of establishing normal periodicity in girls, to the needs of which everything else should for a few years be secondary.

The functions of every sense undergo reconstruction, and their relations to other psychic functions change, and new sensations, some of them very intense, arise, and new associations in the sense sphere are formed. Haptic impressions, appetite for food and drink, and smell are most modified. The voice changes, vascular instability, blushing, and flushing are increased. Sex asserts its mastery in field after field, and works its havoc in the form of secret vice, debauch, disease, and enfeebled heredity, cadences the soul to both its normal and abnormal rhythms, and sends many thousand youth a year to quacks, because neither parents, teachers, preachers, or physicians know how to deal with its problems. Thus the foundations of domestic, social, and religious life are oftenest undermined. Between religion and love God and nature have wrought an indissoluble bond so that neither can attain normality without that of the other. Secondary sexual qualities are shown to have an ever-widening range, and parenthood to mean more with every upward step of development. The youth craves more knowledge of body and mind, that can help against besetting temptations, aid in the choice of a profession, and if his intellect is normal he does not vex his soul overmuch about the logical character of the universe or the ultimate sanction of either truth or virtue. He is more objective than subjective, and only if his lust to know nature and life is starved does his mind trouble him by in-growing. There are new repulsions felt toward home and school, and truancy and runaways abound. The social instincts undergo sudden unfoldment and the new life of love awakens. It is the age of sentiment and of religion, of rapid fluctuation of mood, and the world seems strange and new. Interest in adult life and in vocation develops. Youth awakes to a new world and understands neither it nor himself. The whole future of life depends on how the new powers now given suddenly and in profusion are husbanded and directed. Character and personality are taking form, but everything is plastic. Self-feeling and ambition are increased, and every trait and faculty is liable to exaggeration and excess. It is all a marvelous new birth, and those who believe that nothing is so worthy of love, reverence, and service as the body and soul of youth, and who hold that the best test of every human institution is how much it contributes to bring youth to the ever fullest possible development, may well review themselves and the civilization in which we live to see how far it satisfies this supreme test.

WILLIAM JAMES ON THE MEANING OF PRAGMATISM (1907) From
William James, *Pragmatism: A New Name for Some Old Ways of Thinking* (New York, 1907), pp. 141–48.

Some years ago, being with a camping party in the mountains, I returned from a solitary ramble to find every one engaged in a ferocious metaphysical dispute. The *corpus* of the dispute was a squirrel—a live squirrel supposed to be clinging to one side of a tree-trunk; while over against the tree's opposite side a human being was imagined to stand. This human witness tries to get sight of the squirrel by moving rapidly round the tree, but no matter how fast he goes, the squirrel moves as fast in the opposite direction, and always keeps the tree between himself and the man, so that never a glimpse of him is caught. The resultant metaphysical problem now is this: *Does the man go round the squirrel or not?* He goes round the tree, sure enough, and the squirrel is on the tree; but does he go round the squirrel? In the unlimited leisure of the wilderness, discussion had been worn threadbare. Every one had taken sides, and was obstinate; and the numbers on both sides were even. Each side, when I appeared, therefore appealed to me to make it a majority. Mindful of the scholastic adage that whenever you meet a contradiction you must make a distinction, I immediately sought and found one, as follows: "Which party is right," I said, "depends on what you *practically mean* by 'going round' the squirrel. If you mean passing from the north of him to the east, then to the south, then to the west, and then to the north of him again, obviously the man does go round him, for he occupies these successive positions. But if on the contrary you mean being first in front of him, then on the right of him, then behind him, then on his left, and finally in front again, it is quite as obvious that the man fails to go round him, for by the compensating movements the squirrel makes, he keeps his belly turned towards the man all the time, and his back turned away. Make the distinction, and there is no occasion for any further dispute. You are both right and both wrong according as you conceive the verb 'to go round' in one practical fashion or the other."

Although one or two of the hotter disputants called my speech a shuffling evasion, saying they wanted no quibbling or scholastic hair-splitting, but meant just plain honest English "round," the majority seemed to think that the distinction had assuaged the dispute.

I tell this trivial anecdote because it is a peculiarly simple example of what I wish now to speak of as *the pragmatic method.* The pragmatic method is primarily a method of settling metaphysical disputes that otherwise might be interminable. Is the world one or many?— fated or free?—material or spiritual?—here are notions either of which may or may not hold good of the world; and disputes over such notions are unending. The pragmatic method in such cases is to try to interpret each notion by tracing its respective practical consequences. What difference would it practically make to any one if this notion rather than that notion were true? If no practical difference whatever can be traced, then the alternatives mean practically the same thing, and all dispute is idle. Whenever a dispute is serious, we ought to be able to show some practical difference that must follow from one side or the other's being right.

A glance at the history of the idea will show you still better what pragmatism means. The term is derived from the same Greek word $\pi\rho\acute{\alpha}\gamma\mu\alpha$, meaning action, from which our words "practice" and "practical" come. It was first introduced into philosophy by Mr. Charles Peirce in 1878. In an article entitled "How to Make Our Ideas Clear," in the *Popular Science Monthly* for January of that year Mr. Peirce, after pointing out that our beliefs are really rules for action, said that, to develop a thought's meaning, we need only determine what conduct it is fitted to produce: that conduct is for us its sole significance. And the tangible fact at the root of all our thought-distinctions, however subtle, is that there is no one of them so fine as to consist in anything but a possible difference of practice. To attain perfect clearness in our thoughts of an object, then, we need only consider what conceivable effects of a practical kind the object may involve—what sensations we are to expect from it, and what reactions we must prepare. Our conception of these effects, whether immediate or remote, is then for us the whole of our conception of the object, so far as that conception has positive significance at all.

This is the principle of Peirce, the principle of pragmatism. It lay entirely unnoticed by any one for twenty years, until I, in an address before Professor Howison's Philosophical Union at the University of California, brought it forward again and made a special application of it to religion. By that date (1898) the times seemed ripe for its reception. The word "pragmatism" spread, and at present it fairly spots the pages of the philosophic journals. On all hands we find the "pragmatic movement" spoken of, sometimes with respect, sometimes with contumely, seldom with clear understanding. It is evident that the term applies itself conveniently to a number of tendencies that hitherto have lacked a collective name, and that it has "come to stay."

✳   ✳   ✳

It is astonishing to see how many philosophical disputes collapse into insignificance the moment you subject them to this simple test of tracing a concrete consequence. There can *be* no difference anywhere that doesn't *make* a difference elsewhere—no difference in abstract truth that doesn't express itself in a difference in concrete fact and in conduct consequent upon that fact, imposed on somebody, somehow, somewhere, and somewhen. The whole function of philosophy ought to be to find out what definite difference it will make to you and me, at definite instants of our life, if this world-formula or that world-formula be the true one.

There is absolutely nothing new in the pragmatic method. Socrates was an adept at it. Aristotle used it methodically. Locke, Berkeley, and Hume made momentous contributions to truth by its means. Shadworth Hodgson keeps insisting that realities are only what they are "known as." But these forerunners of pragmatism used it in fragments: they were preluders only. Not until in our time has it generalized itself, become conscious of a universal mission, pretended to a conquering destiny. I believe in that destiny, and I hope I may end by inspiring you with my belief.

Pragmatism represents a perfectly familiar attitude in philosophy, the empiricist attitude, but it represents it, as it seems to me, both in a more radical and in a less objectionable form than it has ever yet assumed. A pragmatist turns his back resolutely and once for all upon a lot of inveterate habits dear to professional philosophers. He turns away from abstraction and insufficiency, from verbal solutions, from bad *a priori* reasons, from fixed principles, closed systems, and pretended absolutes and origins. He turns towards concreteness and adequacy, towards facts, towards action and towards power. That means the empiricist temper regnant and the rationalist temper sincerely given up. It means the open air and possibilities of nature, as against dogma, artificiality, and the pretence of finality in truth.

At the same time it does not stand for any special results. It is a method only. But the general triumph of that method would mean an enormous change in what I called in my last lecture the "temperament" of philosophy. Teachers of the ultra-rationalistic type would be frozen out, much as the courtier type is frozen out in republics, as the ultramontane type of priest is frozen out in protestant lands. Science and metaphysics would come much nearer together, would in fact work absolutely hand in hand.

Metaphysics has usually followed a very primitive kind of quest. You know how men have always hankered after unlawful magic, and you know what a great part in magic *words* have always played. If you have his name, or the formula of incantation that binds him, you can control the spirit, genie, afrite, or whatever the power may be. Solomon knew the names of all the spirits, and having their names, he held them subject to his will. So the universe has always appeared to the natural mind as a kind of enigma, of which the key must be sought in the shape of some illuminating or power-bringing word or name. That word names the universe's *principle*, and to possess it is after a fashion to possess the universe itself. "God," "Matter," "Reason," "the Absolute," "Energy," are so many solving names. You can rest when you have them. You are at the end of your metaphysical quest.

But if you follow the pragmatic method, you cannot look on any such word as closing your quest. You must bring out of each word its practical cash-value, set it at work within the stream of your experience. It appears less as a solution, then, than as a program for more work, and more particularly as an indication of the ways in which existing realities may be *changed*.

Theories thus become instruments, not answers to enigmas, in which we can rest. We don't lie back upon them, we move forward, and, on occasion, make nature over again by their aid. Pragmatism unstiffens all our theories, limbers them up and sets each one at work. Being nothing essentially new, it harmonizes with many ancient philosophic tendencies. It agrees with nominalism, for instance, in always appealing to particulars; with utilitarianism in emphasizing practical aspects; with positivism in its disdain for verbal solutions, useless questions and metaphysical abstractions.

All these, you see, are *anti-intellectualist* tendencies. Against rationalism as a pretension and a method pragmatism is fully armed and militant. But, at the outset, at least, it stands for no particular results. It has no dogmas, and no doctrines save its method. As the young Italian pragmatist Papini has well said, it lies in the midst of our theories, like a corridor in a hotel. Innumerable chambers open out of it. In one you may find a man writing an atheistic volume; in the next some one on his knees praying for faith and strength; in a third a chemist investigating a body's properties. In a fourth a system of idealistic metaphysics is being excogitated; in a fifth the impossibility of metaphysics is being shown. But they all own the corridor, and all must pass through it if they want a practicable way of getting into or out of their respective rooms.

No particular results then, so far, but only an attitude of orientation, is what the pragmatic method means. *The attitude of looking away from first things, principles, "categories," supposed necessities; and of looking towards last things, fruits, consequences, facts.*

So much for the pragmatic method! You may say that I have been praising it rather than explaining it to you, but I shall presently explain it abundantly enough by showing how it works on some familiar problems. Meanwhile the word pragmatism has come to be used in a still wider sense, as meaning also a certain *theory of truth*. I mean to give a whole lecture to the statement of that theory, after first paving the way, so I can be very brief now. But brevity is hard to follow, so I ask for your redoubled attention for a quarter of an hour. If much remains obscure, I hope to make it clearer in the later lectures.

One of the most successfully cultivated branches of philosophy in our time is what is called inductive logic, the study of the conditions under which our sciences have evolved. Writers on this subject have begun to show a singular unanimity as to what the laws of nature and elements of fact mean, when formulated by mathematicians, physicists and chemists. When the first mathematical, logical, and natural uniformities, the first *laws*, were discovered, men were so carried away by the clearness, beauty and simplification that resulted, that they believed themselves to have deciphered authentically the eternal thoughts of the Almighty. His mind also thundered and reverberated in syllogisms. He also thought in conic sections, squares and roots and ratios, and geometrized like Euclid. He made Kepler's laws for the planets to follow; he made velocity increase proportionally to the time in falling bodies; he made the law of the sines for light to obey when refracted; he established the classes, orders, families and genera of plants and animals, and fixed the distances between them. He thought the archetypes of all things, and devised their variations; and when we rediscover any one of these his wondrous institutions, we seize his mind in its very literal intention.

But as the sciences have developed further, the notion has gained ground that most, perhaps all, of our laws are only approximations. The laws themselves, moreover, have grown so numerous that there is no counting them; and so many rival formulations are proposed in all the branches of science that investigators have become accustomed to the notion that no theory is absolutely a transcript of reality, but that any one of them may from some point of view be useful. Their great use is to summarize old facts and to lead to new ones. They are only a man-made language, a conceptual shorthand, as some one calls them, in which we write our reports of nature; and languages, as is well known, tolerate much choice of expression and many dialects.

Thus human arbitrariness has driven divine necessity from scientific logic. If I mention the names of Sigwart, Mach, Ostwald, Pearson, Milhaud, Poincaré, Duhem, Ruyssen, those of you who are students will easily identify the tendency I speak of, and will think of additional names.

Riding now on the front of this wave of scientific logic Messrs. Schiller and Dewey appear with their pragmatistic account of what truth everywhere signifies. Everywhere, these teachers say, "truth" in our ideas and beliefs means the same thing that it means in science. It means, they say, nothing but this, *that ideas (which themselves are but parts of our experience) become true just in so far as they help us to get into satisfactory relation with other parts of our experience*, to summarize them and get about among them by conceptual short-cuts instead of following the interminable succession of particular phenomena. Any idea upon which we can ride, so to speak; any idea that will carry us prosperously from any one part of our experience to any other part, linking things satisfactorily, working securely, simplifying, saving labor; is true for just so much, true in so far forth, true *instrumentally*. This is the "instrumental" view of truth taught so successfully at Chicago, the view that truth in our ideas means their power to "work," promulgated so brilliantly at Oxford.

Messrs. Dewey, Schiller, and their allies, in reaching this general conception of all truth, have only followed the example of geologists, biologists and philologists.

In the establishment of these other sciences, the successful stroke was always to take some simple process actually observable in operation—as denudation by weather, say, or variation from parental type, or change of dialect by incorporation of new words and pronunciations—and then to generalize it, making it apply to all times, and produce great results by summating its effects through the ages.

The observable process which Schiller and Dewey particularly singled out for generalization is the familiar one by which any individual settles into *new opinions*. The process here is always the same. The individual has a stock of old opinions already, but he meets a new experience that puts them to a strain. Somebody contradicts them; or in a reflective moment he discovers that they contradict each other; or he hears of facts with which they are incompatible; or desires arise in him which they cease to satisfy. The result is an inward trouble to which his mind till then has been a stranger, and from which he seeks to escape by modifying his previous mass of opinions. He saves as much of it as he can, for in this matter of belief we are all extreme conservatives. So he tries to change first this opinion, and then that (for they resist change very variously), until at last some new idea comes up which he can graft upon the ancient stock with a minimum of disturbance of the latter, some idea that mediates between the stock and the new experience and runs them into one another most felicitously and expediently.

This new idea is then adopted as the true one. It preserves the older stock of truths with a minimum of modification, stretching them just enough to make them admit the novelty, but conceiving that in ways as familiar as the case leaves possible.

JOHN DEWEY ON EDUCATION (1897)   From John Dewey, "My Pedagogic Creed," *School Journal*, vol. LIV, pp. 77–80.

Article I—What Education Is

I believe that all education proceeds by the participation of the individual in the social consciousness of the race. This process begins unconsciously almost at birth, and is continually shaping the individual's powers, saturating his consciousness, forming his habits, training his ideas, and arousing his feelings and emotions. Through this unconscious education the individual gradually comes to share in the intellectual and moral resources which humanity has succeeded in getting together. He becomes an inheritor of the funded capital of civilization. The most formal and technical education in the world cannot safely depart from this general process. It can only organize it or differentiate it in some particular direction.

I believe that the only true education comes through the stimulation of the child's powers by the demands of the social situations in which he finds himself. Through these demands he is stimulated to act as a member of a unity, to emerge from his original narrowness of action and feeling, and to conceive of himself from the standpoint of the welfare of the group of which he belongs. Through the responses which others make to his own activities he comes to know what these mean in social terms. The value which they have is reflected back into them. For instance, through the response which is made to the child's instinctive babblings the child comes to know what those babblings mean; they are transformed into articulate language and thus the child is introduced into the consolidated wealth of ideas and emotions which are now summed up in language.

I believe that this educational process has two sides—one psychological and one sociological; and that neither can be subordinated to the other or neglected without evil results following. Of these two sides, the psychological is the basis. The child's own instincts and powers furnish the material and give the starting point for all education. Save as the efforts of the educator connect with some activity which the child is carrying on of his own initiative independent of the educator, education becomes reduced to a pressure from without. It may, indeed, give certain external results, but cannot truly be called educative. Without insight into the psychological structure and activities of the individual, the educative process will, therefore, be haphazard and arbitrary. If it chances to coincide with the child's activity it will get a leverage; if it does not, it will result in friction, or disintegration, or arrest of the child nature.

I believe that knowledge of social conditions, of the present state of civilization, is necessary in order properly to interpret the child's powers. The child has his own instincts and tendencies, but we do not know what these mean until we can translate them into their social equivalents. We must be able to carry them back into a social past and see them as the inheritance of previous race activities. We must also be able to project them into the future to see what their outcome and end will be. In the illustration just used, it is the ability to see in the child's babblings the promise and potency of a future social intercourse and conversation which enables one to deal in the proper way with that instinct.

I believe that the psychological and social sides are organically related and that education cannot be regarded as a compromise between the two, or a superimposition of one upon the other. We are told that the psychological definition of education is barren and formal—that it gives us only the idea of a development of all the mental powers without giving us any idea of the use to which these powers are put. On the other hand, it is urged that the social definition of education, as getting adjusted to civilization, makes of it a forced and external process, and results in subordinating the freedom of the individual to a preconceived social and political status.

I believe that each of these objections is true when urged against one side isolated from the other. In order to know what a power really is we must know what its end, use, or function is; and this we cannot know save as we conceive of the individual as active in social relationships. But, on the other hand, the only possible adjustment which we can give to the child under existing conditions, is that which arises through putting him in complete possession of all his powers. With the advent of democracy and modern industrial conditions, it is impossible to foretell definitely just what civilization will be twenty years from now. Hence it is impossible to prepare the child for any precise set of conditions. To prepare him for the future life means to give him command of himself; it means so to train him that he will have the full and ready use of all his capacities; that his eye and ear and hand may be tools ready to command, that his judgment may be capable of grasping the conditions under which it has to work, and the executive forces be trained to act economically and efficiently. It is impossible to reach this sort of adjustment save as constant regard is had to the individual's own powers, tastes, and interests—say, that is, as education is continually converted into psychological terms.

In sum, I believe that the individual who is to be educated is a social individual and that society is an organic union of individuals. If we eliminate the social factor from the child we are left only with an abstraction; if we eliminate the individual factor from society, we are left only with an inert and lifeless mass. Education, therefore, must begin with a psychological insight into the child's capacities, interests, and habits. It must be controlled at every point by reference to these same considerations. These powers, interests, and habits must be continually interpreted—we must know what they mean. They must be translated into terms of their social equivalents—into terms of what they are capable of in the way of social service.

Article II—What the School Is

I believe that the school is primarily a social institution. Education being a social process, the school is simply that form of community life in which all those agencies are concentrated that will be most effective in bringing the child to share in the inherited resources of the race, and to use his own powers for social ends.

I believe that education, therefore, is a process of living and not a preparation for future living.

I believe that the school must represent present life—life as real and vital to the child as that which he carries on in the home, in the neighborhood, or on the playground.

I believe that education which does not occur through forms of life, or that are worth living for their own sake, is always a poor substitute for the genuine reality and tends to cramp and to deaden.

I believe that the school, as an institution, should simplify existing social life; should reduce it, as it were, to an embryonic form. Existing life is so complex that the child cannot be brought into contact with it without either confusion or distraction; he is either overwhelmed by the multiplicity of activities which are going on, so that he loses his own power of orderly reaction, or he is so stimulated by these various activities that his powers are prematurely called into play and he becomes either unduly specialized or else disintegrated.

I believe that as such simplified social life, the school life should grow gradually out of the home life; that it should take up and continue the activities with which the child is already familiar in the home.

I believe that it should exhibit these activities to the child, and reproduce them in such ways that the child will gradually learn the meaning of them, and be capable of playing his own part in relation to them.

I believe that this is a psychological necessity, because it is the only way of securing continuity in the child's growth, the only way of giving a back-ground of past experience to the new ideas given in school.

I believe that it is also a social necessity, because the home is the form of social life in which the child has been nurtured and in connection with which he has had his moral training. It is the business of the school to deepen and extend his sense of the values bound up in his home life.

I believe that much of present education fails because it neglects this fundamental principle of the school as a form of community life. It conceives the school as a place where certain information is to be given, where certain lessons are to be learned, or where certain habits are to be formed. The value of these is conceived as lying largely in the remote future; the child must do these things for the sake of something else he is to do; they are mere preparation. As a result they do not become a part of the life experience of the child and so are not truly educative.

I believe that the moral education centers upon this conception of the school as a mode of social life, that the best and deepest moral training is precisely that which one gets through having to enter into proper relations with others in a unity of work and thought. The present educational systems, so far as they destroy or neglect this unity, render it difficult or impossible to get any genuine, regular moral training.

I believe that the child should be stimulated and controlled in his work through the life of the community.

I believe that under existing conditions far too much of the stimulus and control proceeds from the teacher, because of neglect of the idea of the school as a form of social life.

I believe that the teacher's place and work in the school is to be interpreted from this same basis. The teacher is not in the school to impose certain ideas or to form certain habits in the child, but is there as a member of the community to select the influences which shall affect the child and to assist him in properly responding to these influences.

I believe that the discipline of the school should proceed from the life of the school as a whole and not directly from the teacher.

I believe that the teacher's business is simply to determine on the basis of larger experience and riper wisdom, how the discipline of life shall come to the child.

I believe that all questions of the grading of the child and his promotion should be determined by reference to the same standard. Examinations are of use only so far as they test the child's fitness for social life and reveal the place in which he can be of the most service and where he can receive the most help.

Article III—The Subject-Matter of Education

I believe that the social life of the child is the basis of concentration, or correlation, in all his training or growth. The social life gives the unconscious unity and the background of all his efforts and of all his attainments.

I believe that the subject-matter of the school curriculum should mark a gradual differentiation out of the primitive unconscious unity of social life.

I believe that we violate the child's nature and render difficult the best ethical results, by introducing the child too abruptly to a number of special studies, of reading, writing, geography, etc., out of relation to this social life.

I believe, therefore, that the true center of correlation on the school subjects is not science, nor literature, nor history, nor geography, but the child's own social activities.

I believe that education cannot be unified in the study of science, or so called nature study, because apart from human activity, nature itself is not a unity; nature in itself is a number of diverse objects in space and time, and to attempt to make it the center of work by itself, is to introduce a principle of radiation rather than one of concentration.

I believe that literature is the reflex expression and interpretation of social experience; that hence it must follow upon and not precede such experience. It, therefore, cannot be made the basis, although it may be made the summary of unification.

I believe once more that history is of educative value in so far as it presents phases of social life and growth. It must be controlled by reference to social life. When taken simply as history it is thrown into the distant past and becomes dead and inert. Taken as the record of man's social life and progress it becomes full of meaning. I believe, however, that it cannot be so taken excepting as the child is also introduced directly into social life.

I believe accordingly that the primary basis of education is in the child's powers at work along the same general constructive lines as those which have brought civilization into being.

I believe that the only way to make the child conscious of his social heritage is to enable him to perform those fundamental types of activity which make civilization what it is.

I believe, therefore, in the so-called expressive or constructive activities as the center of correlation.

I believe that this gives the standard for the place of cooking, sewing, manual training, etc., in the school.

I believe that they are not special studies which are to be introduced over and above a lot of others in the way of relaxation or relief, or as additional accomplishments. I believe rather that they represent, as types, fundamental forms of social activity; and that it is possible and desirable that the child's introduction into the more formal subjects of the curriculum be through the medium of these activities.

I believe that the study of science is educational in so far as it brings out the materials and processes which make social life what it is.

I believe that one of the greatest difficulties in the present teaching of science is that the material is presented in purely objective form, or is treated as a new peculiar kind of experience which the child can add to that which he has already had. In reality, science is of value because it gives the ability to interpret and control the experience already had. It should be introduced, not as so much new subject-matter, but as showing the factors already involved in previous experience and as furnishing tools by which that experience can be more easily and effectively regulated.

I believe that at present we lose much of the value of literature and language studies because of our elimination of the social element. Language is almost always treated in the books of pedagogy simply as the expression of thought. It is true that language is a logical instrument, but it is fundamentally and primarily a social instrument. Language is the device for communication; it is the tool through which one individual comes to share the ideas and feelings of others. When treated simply as a way of getting individual information, or as a means of showing off what one has learned, it loses its social motive and end.

I believe that there is, therefore, no succession of studies in the ideal school curriculum. If education is life, all life has, from the outset, a scientific aspect, an aspect of art and culture, and an aspect of communication. It cannot, therefore, be true that the proper studies for one grade are mere reading and writing, and that at a later grade, reading, or literature, or science, may be introduced. The progress is not in the succession of studies but in the development of new attitudes towards, and new interests in, experience.

I believe finally, that education must be conceived as a continuing reconstruction of experience; that the process and the goal of education are one and the same thing.

I believe that to set up any end outside of education, as furnishing its goal and standard, is to deprive the educational process of much of its meaning and tends to make us rely upon false and external stimuli in dealing with the child.

*   *   *

Article V—The School and Social Progress

I believe that education is the fundamental method of social progress and reform.

I believe that all reforms which rest simply upon the enactment of law, or the threatening of certain penalties, or upon changes in mechanical or outward arrangements, are transitory and futile.

I believe that education is a regulation of the process of coming to share in the social consciousness; and that the adjustment of individual activity on the basis of this social consciousness is the only sure method of social reconstruction.

I believe that this conception has due regard for both the individualistic and socialistic ideals. It is duly individual because it recognizes the formation of a certain character as the only genuine basis of right living. It is socialistic because it recognizes that this right character is not to be formed by merely individual precept, example, or exhortation, but rather by the influence of a certain form of institutional or community life upon the individual, and that the social organism through the school, as its organ, may determine ethical results.

I believe that in the ideal school we have the reconciliation of the individualistic and the institutional ideals.

I believe that the community's duty to education is, therefore, its paramount moral duty. By law and punishment, by social agitation and discussion, society can regulate and form itself in a more or less haphazard and chance way. But through education society can formulate its own purposes, can organize its own means and resources, and thus shape itself with definiteness and economy in the direction in which it wishes to move.

I believe that when society once recognizes the possibilities in this direction, and the obligations which these possibilities impose, it is impossible to conceive of the resources of time, attention, and money which will be put at the disposal of the educator.

I believe that it is the business of every one interested in education to insist upon the school as the primary and most effective interest of social progress and reform in order that society may be awakened to realize what the school stands for, and aroused to the necessity of endowing the educator with sufficient equipment properly to perform his task.

I believe that education thus conceived marks the most perfect and intimate union of science and art conceivable in human experience.

I believe that the art of thus giving shape to human powers and adapting them to social service, is the supreme art; one calling into its service the best of artists; that no insight, sympathy, tact, executive power, is too great for such service.

I believe that with the growth of psychological service, giving added insight into individual structure and laws of growth; and with growth of social science, adding to our knowledge of the right organization of individuals, all scientific resources can be utilized for the purposes of education.

I believe that when science and art thus join hands the most commanding motive for human action will be reached; the most genuine springs of human conduct aroused and the best service that human nature is capable of guaranteed.

I believe, finally, that the teacher is engaged, not simply in the training of individuals, but in the formation of the proper social life.

I believe that every teacher should realize the dignity of his calling; that he is a social servant set apart for the maintenance of proper social order and the securing of the right social growth.

I believe that in this way the teacher always is the prophet of the true God and the usherer in of the true kingdom of God.

JOHN DEWEY ON THE PLACE OF READING IN PRIMARY EDUCATION

(1898)   From John Dewey, "The Primary Education Fetich," *Forum,* vol. XXV, pp. 315–17.

It is some years since the educational world was more or less agitated by an attack upon the place occupied by Greek in the educational scheme. If, however, Greek occupies the place of a fetich, its worshippers are comparatively few in number, and its influence is relatively slight. There is however, a false educational god whose idolaters are legion and whose cult influences the entire educational system. This is language-study—the study not of foreign language, but of English; not in higher but in primary education. It is almost an unquestioned assumption of educational theory and practice both, that the first three years of a child's school-life shall be mainly taken up with learning to read and write his own language. If we add to this the learning of a certain amount of numerical combinations, we have the pivot about which primary education swings. Other subjects may be taught; but they are introduced in strict subordination.

The very fact that this procedure, as part of the natural and established course of education, is assumed as inevitable,—opposition being regarded as captious and revolutionary,—indicates that, historically, there are good reasons for the position assigned to these studies. It does not follow, however, that because this course was once wise it is so any longer. On the contrary, the fact, that this mode of education was adapted to past conditions, is in itself a reason why it should no longer hold supreme sway. The present has its claims. It is in education, if, anywhere, that the claims of the present should be controlling. To educate on the basis of past surroundings, is like adapting an organism to an environment which no longer exists. The individual is stultified, if not disintegrated; and the course of progress is blocked. My proposition is, that conditions—social, industrial, and intellectual—have undergone such a radical change, that the time has come for a thoroughgoing examination of the emphasis put upon linguistic work in elementary instruction.

The existing status was developed in a period when ability to read was practically the sole avenue to knowledge, when it was the only tool which insured control over the accumulated spiritual resources of civilization. Scientific methods of observation, experimentation, and testing were either unknown or confined to a few specialists at the upper end of the educational ladder. Because these methods were not free, were not capable of anything like general use, it was not possible to permit the pupil to begin his school career in direct contact with the materials of nature and of life. The only guarantee, the only criterion of values, was found in the

EDUCATION FOR URBAN INDUSTRIAL AMERICA 1895–1918

ways in which the great minds of the past had assimilated and interpreted such materials. To avoid intellectual chaos and confusion, it was necessary reverently to retrace the steps of the fathers. The *régime* of intellectual authority and tradition, in matters of politics, morals, and culture, was a necessity, where methods of scientific investigation and verification had not been developed, or were in the hands of the few. We often fail to see that the dominant position occupied by book-learning in school education is simply a corollary and relic of this epoch of intellectual development.

Ordinary social conditions were congruent with this intellectual status. While it cannot be said that, in the formative period of our educational system in America, authority and tradition were the ultimate sources of knowledge and belief, it must be remembered that the immediate surroundings of our ancestors were crude and undeveloped. Newspapers, magazines, libraries, art-galleries, and all the daily play of intellectual intercourse and reaction which is effective to-day were non-existent. If any escape existed from the poverty of the intellectual environment, or any road to richer and wider mental life, the exit was through the gateway of books. In presenting the attainments of the past, these maintained the bonds of spiritual continuity and kept our forefathers from falling to the crude level of their material surroundings.

When ability to read and write marked the distinction between the educated and the uneducated man, not simply in the scholastic sense but in the sense of one who is enslaved by his environment and one who is able to take advantage of and rise above it, corresponding importance attached to acquiring these capacities. Reading and writing were obviously what they are still so often called—the open doors to learning and to success in life. All the meaning that belongs to those ends naturally transferred itself to the means through which alone they could be realized. The intensity and ardor with which our forefathers set themselves to master reading and writing, the difficulties overcome, the interest attached in the ordinary routine of school-life to what now seems barren,—the curriculum of the three R's,—all testify to the motive-power these studies possessed. To learn to read and write was an interesting, even exciting thing; it made such a difference in life.

It is hardly necessary to say that the conditions, intellectual as well as social, have changed. There are undoubtedly rural regions where the old state of things still persists. With reference to these, what I am saying has no particular meaning. But, upon the whole, the advent of quick and cheap mails, of easy and continuous travel and transportation, of the telegraph and telephone, the establishment of libraries, art-galleries, literary clubs, the universal diffusion of cheap reading-matter, newspapers and magazines of all kinds and grades,—all these have worked a tremendous change in the immediate intellectual environment. The values of life and of civilization, instead of being far away and correspondingly inaccessible, press upon the individual—at least in cities—with only too much urgency and stimulating force. We are more likely to be surfeited than starved: there is more congestion than lack of intellectual nutriment.

The capital handed down from past generations, and upon whose transmission the integrity of civilization depends, is no longer amassed in these banks termed books, but is in active and general circulation, at an extremely low rate of interest. It is futile to try to conceal from ourselves the fact that this great change in the intellectual atmosphere—this great change in the relation of the individual to accumulated knowledge—demands a corresponding educational readjustment. The significance attaching to reading and writing, as primary and fundamental instruments of culture, has shrunk proportionately as the immanent intellectual life of society has quickened and multiplied. The result is that these studies lose their motive and motor force. They have become mechanical and formal, and out of relation—when made dominant—to the rest of life.

JOHN DEWEY ON THE "NEW EDUCATION" (1899) From John Dewey, *The School and Society* (Chicago, 1899), pp. 19–33.

We are apt to look at the school from an individualistic standpoint, as something between teacher and pupil, or between teacher and parent. That which interests us most is naturally the progress made by the individual child of our acquaintance, his normal physical development, his advance in ability to read, write, and figure, his growth in the knowledge of geography and history, improvement in manners, habits of promptness, order, and industry—it is from such standards as these that we judge the work of the school. And rightly so. Yet the range of the outlook needs to be enlarged. What the best and wisest parent wants for his own child, that must the community want for all of its children. Any other ideal for our schools is narrow and unlovely; acted upon, it destroys our democracy. All that society has accomplished for itself is put, through the agency of the school, at the disposal of its future members. All its better thoughts of itself it hopes to realize through the new possibilities thus opened to its future self. Here individualism and socialism are at one. Only by being true to the full growth of all the individuals who make it up, can society by any chance be true to itself. And in the self-direction thus given, nothing counts as much as the school, for, as Horace Mann said, "Where anything is growing, one former is worth a thousand reformers."

Whenever we have in mind the discussion of a new movement in education, it is especially necessary to take the broader, or social view. Otherwise, changes in the school institution and tradition will be looked at as the arbitrary inventions of particular teachers; at the worst transitory fads, and at the best merely improvements in certain details—and this is the plane upon which it is too customary to consider school changes. It is as rational to conceive of the locomotive or the telegraph as personal devices. The modification going on in the method and curriculum of education is as much a product of the changed social situation, and as much an effort to meet the needs of the new society that is forming, as are changes in modes of industry and commerce.

It is to this, then, that I especially ask your attention: the effort to conceive what roughly may be termed the "New Education" in the light of larger changes in society. Can we connect this "New Education" with the general march of events? If we can, it will lose its isolated character, and will cease to be an affair which proceeds only from the over-ingenious minds of pedagogues dealing with particular pupils. It will appear as part and parcel of the whole social evolution, and, in its more general features at least, as inevitable. Let us then ask after the main aspects of the social movement; and afterwards turn to the school to find what witness it gives of effort to put itself in line. And since it is quite impossible to cover the whole ground, I shall for the most part confine myself to one typical thing in the modern school movement—that which passes under the name of manual training, hoping if the relation of that to changed social conditions appears, we shall be ready to concede the point as well regarding other educational innovations.

I make no apology for not dwelling at length upon the social changes in question. Those I shall mention are writ so large that he who runs may read. The change that comes first to mind, the one that overshadows and even controls all others, is the industrial one—the application of science resulting in the great inventions that have utilized the forces of nature on a vast and inexpensive scale: the growth of a world-wide market as the object of production, of vast manufacturing centers to supply this market, of cheap and rapid means of communication and distribution between all its parts. Even as to its feebler beginnings, this change is not much more than a century old; in many of its most important aspects it falls within the short span of those now living. One can hardly believe there has been a revolution in all history so rapid, so extensive, so complete. Through it the face of the earth is making over, even as to its physical forms; political boundaries are wiped out and moved about, as if they were indeed only lines on a paper map; population is hurriedly gathered into cities from the ends of the earth; habits of living are altered with startling abruptness and thoroughness; the search for the truths of nature is infinitely stimulated and facilitated and their application to life made not only practicable, but commercially necessary. Even our moral and religious ideas and interests, the most conservative because the deepest-lying things in our nature, are profoundly affected. That this revolution should not affect education in other than formal and superficial fashion is inconceivable.

Back of the factory system lies the household and neighborhood system. Those of us who are here today need go back only one, two, or at most three generations, to find a time when the household was practically the center in which were carried on, or about which were clustered, all the typical forms of industrial occupation. The clothing worn was for the most part not only made in the house, but the members of the household were usually familiar with the shearing of the sheep, the carding and spinning of the wool, and the plying of the loom. Instead of pressing a button and flooding the house with electric light, the whole process of getting illumination was followed in its toilsome length, from the killing of the animal and the trying of fat, to the making of wicks and dipping of candles. The supply of flour, of lumber, of foods, of building materials, of household furniture, even of metal ware, of nails, hinges, hammers, etc., was in the immediate neighborhood, in shops which were constantly open to inspection and often centers of neighborhood congregation. The entire industrial process stood revealed, from the production on the farm of the raw materials, till the finished article was actually put to use. Not only this, but practically every member of the household had his own share in the work. The children, as they gained in strength and capacity, were gradually initiated into the mysteries of the several processes. It was a matter of immediate and personal concern, even to the point of actual participation.

We cannot overlook the factors of discipline and of character-building involved in this: training in habits of order and of industry, and in the idea of responsibility, of obligation to do something, to produce something, in the world. There was always something which really needed to be done, and a real necessity that each member of the household should do his own part faithfully and in cooperation with others. Personalities which became effective in action were bred and tested in the medium of action. Again, we cannot overlook the importance for educational purposes of the close and intimate acquaintance got with nature at first hand, with real things and materials, with the actual processes of their manipulation, and the knowledge of their social necessities and uses. In all this there was continual training of observation, of ingenuity, constructive imagination, of logical thought, and of the sense of reality acquired through first-hand contact with actualities. The educative forces of the domestic spinning and weaving, of the saw-mill, the grist-mill, the cooper shop, and the blacksmith forge, were continuously operative.

No number of object-lessons, got up as object-lessons for the sake of giving information, can afford even the shadow of a substitute for acquaintance with the plants and animals of the farm and garden, acquired through actual living among them and caring for them. No training of sense-organs in school, introduced for the sake of training, can begin to compete with the alertness and fullness of sense-life that comes through daily intimacy and interest in familiar occupations. Verbal memory can be trained in committing tasks, a certain discipline of the reasoning powers can be acquired through lessons in science and mathematics; but, after all, this is somewhat remote and shadowy compared with the training of attention and of judgment that is acquired in having to do things with a real motive behind and a real outcome ahead. At present, concentration of industry and division of labor have practically eliminated household and neighborhood occupations—at least for educational purposes. But it is useless to bemoan the departure of the good old days of children's modesty, reverence, and implicit obedience, if we expect merely by bemoaning and by exhortation to bring them back. It is radical conditions which have changed, and only an equally radical change in education suffices. We must recognize our compensations—the increase in toleration, in breadth of social judgment, the larger acquaintance with human nature, the sharpened alertness in reading signs of character and interpreting social situations, greater accuracy of adaptation to differing personalities, contact with greater commercial activities. These considerations mean much to the city-bred child of today. Yet there is a real problem: how shall we retain these advantages, and yet introduce into the school something representing the other side of life—occupations which exact personal responsibilities and which train the child with relation to the physical realities of life?

When we turn to the school, we find that one of the most striking tendencies at present is toward the introduction of so-called manual training, shop-work, and the household arts—sewing and cooking.

This has not been done "on purpose," with a full consciousness that the school must now supply that factor of training formerly taken care of in the home, but rather by instinct, by experimenting and finding that such work takes a vital hold of pupils and gives them something which was not to be got in any other way. Consciousness of its real import is still so weak that the work is often done in a half-hearted, confused, and unrelated way. The reasons assigned to justify it are painfully inadequate or sometimes even positively wrong.

If we were to cross-examine even those who are most favorably disposed to the introduction of this work into our school system, we should, I imagine, generally find the main reasons to be that such work engages the full spontaneous interest and attention of the children. It keeps them alert and active, instead of passive and receptive; it makes them more useful, more capable, and hence more inclined to be helpful at home; it prepares them to some extent for the practical duties of later life—the girls to be more efficient house managers, if not actually cooks and sempstresses; the boys (were our educational system only adequately rounded out into trade schools) for their future vocations. I do not underestimate the worth of these reasons. Of those indicated by the changed attitude of the children I shall indeed have something to say in my next talk, when speaking directly of the relationship of the school to the child. But the point of view is, upon the whole, unnecessarily narrow. We must conceive of work in wood and metal, of weaving, sewing, and cooking, as methods of life not as distinct studies.

We must conceive of them in their social significance, as types of the processes by which society keeps itself going, as agencies for bringing home to the child some of the primal necessities of community life, and as ways in which these needs have been met by the growing insight and ingenuity of man; in short, as instrumentalities through which the school itself shall be made a genuine form of active community life, instead of a place set apart in which to learn lessons.

A society is a number of people held together because they are working along common lines, in a common spirit, and with reference to common aims. The common needs and aims demand a growing interchange of thought and growing unity of sympathetic feeling. The radical reason that the present school cannot organize itself as a natural social unit is because just this element of common and productive activity is absent. Upon the playground, in game and sport, social organization takes place spontaneously and inevitably. There is something to do, some activity to be carried on, requiring natural divisions of labor, selection of leaders and followers, mutual cooperation and emulation. In the schoolroom the motive and the cement of social organization are alike wanting. Upon the ethical side, the tragic weakness of the present school is that it endeavors to prepare future members of the social order in a medium in which the conditions of the social spirit are eminently wanting.

The difference that appears when occupations are made the articulating centers of school life is not easy to describe in words; it is a difference in motive, of spirit and atmosphere. As one enters a busy kitchen in which a group of children are actively engaged in the preparation of food, the psychological difference, the change from more or less passive and inert recipiency and restraint to one of buoyant outgoing energy, is so obvious as fairly to strike one in the face. Indeed, to those whose image of the school is rigidly set the change is sure to give a shock. But the change in the social attitude is equally marked. The mere absorption of facts and truths is so exclusively individual an affair that it tends very naturally to pass into selfishness. There is no obvious social motive for the acquirement of mere learning, there is no clear social gain in success thereat. Indeed, almost the only measure for success is a competitive one, in the bad sense of that term—a comparison of results in the recitation or in the examination to see which child has succeeded in getting ahead of others in storing up, in accumulating the maximum of information. So thoroughly is this the prevalent atmosphere that for one child to help another in his task has become a school crime. Where the school work consists in simply learning lessons, mutual assistance, instead of being the most natural form of cooperation and association, becomes a clandestine effort to relieve one's neighbor of his proper duties. Where active work is going on all this is changed. Helping others, instead of being a form of charity which impoverishes the recipient, is simply an aid in setting free the powers and furthering the impulse of the one helped. A spirit of free communication, of interchange of ideas, suggestions, results, both successes and failures of previous experiences, becomes the dominating note of the recitation. So far as emulation enters in, it is in the comparison of individuals, not with regard to the quantity of information personally absorbed, but with reference to the quality of work done—the genuine community standard of value. In an informal but all the more pervasive way, the school life organizes itself on a social basis.

Within this organization is found the principle of school discipline or order. Of course, order is simply a thing which is relative to an end. If you have the end in view of forty or fifty children learning certain set lessons, to be recited to a teacher, your discipline must be devoted to securing that result. But if the end in view is the development of a spirit of social cooperation and community life, discipline must grow out of and be relative to this. There is little order of one sort where things are in process of construction; there is a certain disorder in any busy workshop; there is not silence; persons are not engaged in maintaining certain fixed physical postures; their arms are not folded; they are not holding their books thus and so. They are doing a variety of things, and there is the confusion, the bustle, that results from activity. But out of occupation, out of doing things that are to produce results, and out of doing these in a social and cooperative way, there is born a discipline of its own kind and type. Our whole conception of school discipline changes when we get this point of view. In critical moments we all realize that the only discipline that stands by us, the only training that becomes intuition, is that got through life itself. That we learn from experience, and from books or the sayings of others *only* as they are related to experience, are not mere phrases. But the school has been so set apart, so isolated from the ordinary conditions and motives of life, that the place where children are sent for discipline is the one place in the world where it is most difficult to get experience—the mother of all discipline worth the name. It is only where a narrow and fixed image of traditional school discipline dominates, that one is in any danger of overlooking that deeper and infinitely wider discipline that comes from having a part to do in constructive work, in contributing to a result which, social in spirit, is none the less obvious and tangible in form—and hence in a form with reference to which responsibility may be exacted and accurate judgment passed.

The great thing to keep in mind, then, regarding the introduction into the school of various forms of active occupation, is that through them the entire spirit of the school is renewed. It has a chance to affiliate itself with life, to become the child's habitat, where he learns through directed living; instead of being only a place to learn lessons having an abstract and remote reference to some possible living to be done in the future. It gets a chance to be a miniature community, an embryonic society. This is the fundamental fact, and from this arise continuous and orderly sources of instruction. Under the industrial *régime* described, the child, after all, shared in the work, not for the sake of the sharing, but for the sake of the product. The educational results secured were real, yet incidental and dependent. But in the school the typical occupations followed are freed from all economic stress. The aim is not the economic value of the products, but the development of social power and insight. It is this liberation from narrow utilities, this openness to the possibilities of the human spirit that makes these practical activities in the school allies of art and centers of science and history.

*　　*　　*

In educational terms, this means that these occupations in the school shall not be mere practical devices or modes of routine employment, the gaining of better technical skill as cooks, sempstresses, or carpenters, but active centers of scientific insight into natural materials and processes, points of departure whence children shall be led out into a realization of the historic development of man.

JOHN DEWEY ON THE SCHOOL AS SOCIAL CENTER (1902)   From John
Dewey, "The School as a Social Center," National Education Association, *Journal of
Proceedings and Addresses* (Washington D.C., 1902), pp. 373–80.

In this paper I shall confine myself to the philosophy of the school as a
social center. But at the same time I do not feel that the philosophical aspect of the
matter is the urgent or important one. The pressing thing, the significant thing, is
really to make the school a social center; that is, a matter of practice, not of theory.
Just what to do in order to make the schoolhouse a center of full and adequate
social service, to bring it completely into the current of social life,—such are the
matters I am sure which really deserve the attention of the public and that occupy
your own minds.

It is possible, however, and conceivably useful to ask ourselves: What is the
meaning of the popular demand in this direction? Why should the community in
general, and those particularly interested in education in especial, be so unusually
sensitive at just this period of this need? Why should the lack be more felt now than
a generation ago? What forces are stirring that awaken such speedy and favorable
response to the notion that the school as a place of instruction for children is not
performing its full function—that it needs also to operate as a center of life for all
ages and classes?

*   *   *

As I have already intimated, the older idea of the school was that its primary
concern was with the inculcation of certain facts and truths from the intellectual
point of view, and the acquisition of certain forms of skill. When the school became
public or common, this notion was broadened to include whatever would make the
citizen a more capable and righteous voter and legislator; but it was still thought
that this end would be reached along the line of intellectual instruction. To teach
children the Constitution of the United States, the nature and working of various
parts of governmental machinery, from the nation through the state and county
down to the township and the school district, to teach such things was thought to
prepare the pupil for citizenship. And so some fifteen or twenty years ago, when the
feeling arose that the schools were not doing all that they should be doing for our
life as a whole, this consciousness expressed itself in a demand for a more thorough
and extensive teaching of civics. To my mind the demand for the school as a social
center bears the same ratio to the situation which confronts us to-day, as the
movement for civics bore to the conditions of half a generation ago. We have
awakened to deeper aspects of the question; we have seen that the machinery of
governmental life is after all but a machinery, and depends for its rightness and
efficiency upon underlying social and industrial causes. We have lost a good deal of
our faith in the efficacy of purely intellectual instruction.

Some four specific developments may be mentioned as having a bearing upon
the question of the school as a social center. The first of these is the much increased
efficiency and ease of all the agencies that have to do with bringing people into
contact with one another. Recent inventions have so multiplied and cheapened the
means of transportation, and the circulation of ideas and news through books,
magazines and papers, that it is no longer physically possible for one nationality,

race, class or sect to be kept apart from others, impervious to their wishes and beliefs. Cheap and rapid long-distance transportation has made America a meeting place for all peoples and tongues of the world. The centralization of industry has forced members of classes into the closest association with, and dependence upon each other. Bigotry, intolerance, or even an unswerving faith in the superiority of one's own religious and political creed are much shaken when individuals are brought face to face with each other, or have the ideas of others continuously and forcibly placed before them. The congestion of our city life is only one aspect of the bringing of people together which modern inventions have induced.

That many dangers result from sudden dislocations of people from the surroundings—physical, industrial and intellectual—to which they have become adapted; that great instability may accompany this sudden massing heterogeneous peoples, goes without saying. On the other hand, these very agencies present instrumentalities of which advantage may be taken. The best as well as the worst of modern newspaper is a product. The organized public library with its facilities for reaching all classes of people is an effect. The popular assembly and lyceum is another. No educational system can be regarded as complete until it adapts itself into the various ways in which social and intellectual intercourse may be promoted; and employs them systematically, not only to counteract dangers which these same agencies are bringing with them, but so as to make them positive causes in raising the whole level of life.

Both the demand and the opportunity are increased in our large cities by the commingling of classes and races. It is said that one ward in the city of Chicago has forty different languages represented in it. It is a well-known fact that some of the largest Irish, German and Bohemian cities in the world are located in America, not in their own countries. The power of the public schools to assimilate different races to our institutions, through the education given to the younger generation, is doubtless one of the most remarkable exhibitions of vitality that the world has ever seen. But, after all, it leaves the older generation still untouched; and the assimilation of the younger can hardly be complete or certain as long as the homes of the parents remain comparatively unaffected. Indeed, wise observers in both New York City and Chicago have recently sounded a note of alarm. They have called attention to the fact that in some respects the children are too rapidly, I will not say Americanized, but too rapidly de-nationalized. They lose the positive and conservative value of their own traditions, their own native music, art and literature. They do not get complete initiation into the customs of their new country, and so frequently left floating and unstable between the two. They even learn to despise the dress, bearing, habits, language and beliefs of their parents—many of which have more substance and worth than the superficial putting on of the newly adopted habits. If I understand aright, one of the chief motives in the development of the new labor museum at Hull House has been to show the younger generation something of the skill and art and historic meaning in the industrial habits of the older generations—modes of spinning, weaving, metal working, etc., discarded in this country because there was no place for them in our industrial system. Many a child has awakened to an appreciation of admirable qualities hitherto unknown in his father or mother for whom he had begun to entertain a contempt. Many an association of local history and past national glory had been awakened to quicken and enrich the life of the family.

In the second place, along with the increasing intercourse and interaction, with all its dangers and opportunities, there has come a relaxation of the bonds of social discipline and control. I suppose none of us would be willing to believe that the movement away from dogmatism and fixed authority was anything but a movement in the right direction. But no one can view the loosening of the power of the older religious and social authorities, without deep concern. We may feel that in time independent judgement, with the individual freedom and responsibility that go with it, will more than make good the temporary losses. But meantime there is a temporary loss. Parental authority has much less influence in controlling the conduct of children. Reverence seems to decay on every side, and boisterousness and hoodlumism to increase. Flippancy toward parental and other forms constituted authority waxes, while obedient orderliness wanes. The domestic ties themselves, as between husband and wife as well as in relation to children, lose something of their permanence and sanctity. The church, with its supernatural sanctions, its means of shaping the daily life of its adherents, finds its grasp slowly slipping away from it. We might as well frankly recognize that many of the old agencies for moralizing mankind, and of keeping them living decent, respectable and orderly lives, are losing in efficiency—particularly, those agencies which rested for their force upon custom, tradition, and unquestioning acceptance. It is impossible for society to remain purely a passive spectator in the midst of such a scene. It must search for other agencies with which it may repair the loss, and which may produce the results which the former methods are failing to secure. Here, too, it is not enough for society to confine its work to children. However much they may need the disciplinary training of a widened and enlightened education, the older generation needs it also. Besides, time is short—very short for the average child in the city school. The work is hardly more than begun there, and unless it is largely to go for naught, the community must find methods of supplementing it and carrying it further outside the regular school channels.

In the third place, the intellectual life, facts and truths of knowledge are much more obviously and intimately connected with all other affairs of life than they ever have been at any previous period in the history of the world. Hence a purely and exclusively intellectual instruction means less than it ever meant before. And, again, the daily occupations and ordinary surroundings of life are much more in need of interpretation than ever they have been before. We might almost say that once there was a time when learning related almost wholly to a world outside and beyond that of the daily concerns of life itself. To study physics, to learn German, to become acquainted with Chinese history, were elegant accomplishments, but more or less useless from the standpoint of daily life. In fact, it is just this sort of idea which the term "culture" still conveys to many minds. When learning was useful, it was only to a comparatively small and particularly select class in the community. It was just something that the doctor or lawyer or clergyman needed in his particular calling, but so far away from and above the mass of mankind that it could only awaken their blind and submissive admiration. The recent public lament regarding the degradation of the teacher's calling is, to my mind, just a reminiscence of the time when to know enough to be a teacher was something which of itself set off the individual in a special class by himself. It fails to take account of the changes which have put knowledge in common circulation, and made it possible for every one to be a teacher in some respect unto his neighbor.

*　　*　　*

On the other hand, life is getting so specialized, the divisions of labor are carried so far, that nothing explains or interprets itself. The worker in a modern factory who is concerned with a fractional piece of a complex activity, present to him only in a limited series of acts carried on with a distinct portion of a machine, is typical of much in our entire social life. The old worker knew something of his process and business as a whole. If he did not come into personal contact with all of it, the whole was so small and so close to him that he was acquainted with it. He was thus aware of the meaning of the particular part of the work which he himself was doing. He saw and felt it as a vital part of the whole, and his horizon was extended. The situation is now opposite. Most people are doing particular things of whose exact reasons and relationships they are only dimly aware. The whole is so vast, so complicated, so technical, that it is next to out of the question to get any direct acquaintanceship with it. Hence we must rely upon instruction; upon interpretations that come to us through conscious channels. One of the great motives for the flourishing of some great technical correspondence schools of the present day is not only the utilitarian desire to profit by preparation for better positions, but an honest eagerness to know something more of the great forces which condition the particular work one is doing, and to get an insight into those broad relations which are so partially, yet tantalizingly, hinted at. The same is true of the growing interest in forms of popular science, which forms a marked portion of the stock in trade of some of the best and most successful of our modern monthly magazines. This same motive added much to the effectiveness of the university extension movement, particularly in England. It creates a particular demand for a certain type of popular illustrated lecture. Unless the lives of a large part of our wage earners are to be left to their own barren meagerness, the community must see to it by some organized agency that they are instructed in the scientific foundation and social bearings of the things they see about them, and of the activities in which they are themselves engaging.

The fourth point of demand and opportunity is the prolongation under modern conditions, of continuous instruction. We have heard much of the significance of prolonged infancy in relation to education. It has become almost a part of our pedagogical creed that premature engagement in the serious vocations of life is detrimental to full growth. There is a corollary to this proposition which has not yet received equal recognition. Only where social occupations are well defined, and of a pretty permanent type, can the period of instruction be cut short at any particular period. It is commonly recognized that a doctor or a lawyer must go on studying all his life, if he is to be a successful man in his profession. The reason is obvious enough. Conditions about him are highly unstable; new problems present themselves; new facts obtrude. Previous study of law, no matter how thorough and accurate the study, did not provide for these new situations. Hence the need of continual study. There are still portions of country where the lawyer practically prepares himself before he enters upon his professional career. All he has to do afterward is to perfect himself in certain finer points, and get skill in the manipulation of what he already knows. But these are the more backward and unprogressive sections, where change is gradual and infrequent, and so the individual prepared once is prepared always.

* * *

[The school] must provide, at least, part of that training which is necessary to keep the individual properly adjusted to a rapidly changing environment. It must interpret to him the intellectual and social meaning of the work in which he is engaged; that is, must reveal its relations to the life and work of the world. It must make up to him in part for the decay of dogmatic and fixed methods of social discipline. It must supply him compensation for the loss reverence and influence of authority. And, finally, it must provide means for bringing people and their ideas and beliefs together, in such ways as will lessen friction and instability and introduce deeper sympathy and wider understanding.

In what ways shall the school as a social center perform these various tasks? To answer this question in anything like detail is to pass from my alloted sphere of philosophy into that of practical execution. But it comes within the scope of a theoretical consideration to indicate certain general lines. First, there is mixing people up with each other; bringing them together under wholesome influences, and under conditions which will promote their getting acquainted with the best side of each other. I suppose whenever we are framing our ideals of the school as a social center, what we think of is particularly the better class of social settlements. What we want is to see the school, every public school, doing something of the same sort of work that is now done by a settlement or two scattered at wide distances through the city. And we all know that the work of such an institution as Hull House has been primarily, not that of conveying intellectual instruction, but of being a social clearing house. It is a place where ideas and beliefs may be exchanged, not merely in the arena of formal discussion,—for argument alone breeds misunderstanding and fixes prejudice,—but in ways where ideas are incarnated in human form and clothed with the winning grace of personal life. Classes for study may be numerous, but all are regarded as modes of bringing people together, of doing away with barriers of caste, or class, or race, or type of experience that keep people from real communion with each other.

The function of the school as a social center in promoting social meetings for social purposes, suggests at once another function—provision and direction of reasonable forms of amusement and recreation. The social club, the gymnasium, the amateur theatrical representation, the concert, the stereopticon lecture,—these are agencies the force of which social settlements have long known, and which are coming into use wherever anything is doing in the way of making schools social centers. I sometimes think that recreation is the most overlooked and neglected of all ethical forces. Our whole Puritan tradition tends to make us slight this side of life, or even condemn it. But the demand for recreation, for enjoyment, is one of the strongest and most fundmental things in human nature. To pass it over is to invite it to find its expression in defective and perverted form. The brothel, the saloons, the low dance house, the gambling den, the trivial, inconsiderate and demoralizing associations which form themselves on every street corner, are the answer of human nature to the neglect, on the part of supposed moral leaders, of this factor in human nature. I believe that there is no force more likely to count in the general reform of social conditions than the practical recognition that in recreation there is a positive moral influence which it is the duty of the community to take hold of and direct.

In the third place, there ought to be some provision for a sort of continuous social selection of a somewhat specialized type—using "specialized," of course, in a relative sense. Our cities carried on evening schools long before anything was said or heard of the school as a social center. These were intended to give instruction in the rudiments to those who had little or no early opportunities. So far they were and are good. But what I have in mind is something of a more distinctly advanced and selective nature. To refer once more to the working model upon which I am pretty continuously drawing, in the activities of Hull House we find provision made for classes in music, drawing, clay modeling, joinery, metal working, and so on.

There is no reason why something in the way of scientific laboratories should not be provided for those who are particularly interested in problems of mechanics or electricity; and so the list might be continued. Now the obvious operation of such modes of instruction is to pick out and attract to itself those individuals who have particular ability in any particular line. There is a vast amount of unutilized talent dormant all about us. Many an individual has capacity within himself of which he is only dimly conscious, because he has never had an opportunity for expressing it. He is not only losing the satisfaction of employment, but society suffers from this wasted capital. The evils of unearned increment are as nothing beside those of the undiscovered resource. In time, I am confident the community will recognize it as a natural and necessary part of its own duty—quite as much as is now giving instruction to little children—to provide such opportunities for adults as will enable them to discover and carry to some point of fulfillment the particular capacities that distinguish them.

In conclusion, we may say that the conception of the school as a social center is born of our entire democratic movement. Everywhere we see signs of the growing recognition that the community owes to each one of its members the fullest opportunity for development. Everywhere we see the growing recognition that the community life is defective and distorted, excepting as it does thus care for all its constituent parts. This is no longer viewed as a matter of charity, but as a matter of justice—even of something higher and better than justice—a necessary phase of developing and growing life. Men will long dispute about material socialism, about socialism considered as a matter of distribution of the material resources of the community; but there is a socialism regarding which there can be no such dispute—socialism of the intelligence and of the spirit. To extend the range and the fullness of sharing in the intellectual and spiritual resources of the community is the very meaning of the community. Because the older type of education is not fully adequate to this task under changed conditions, we feel its lack, and demand that the school shall become a social center. The school as a social center means the active and organized promotion of this socialism of the intangible things of art, science and other modes of social intercourse.

THE DEWEYS ON EDUCATION FOR WAGE EARNERS (1915) From John
Dewey and Evelyn Dewey, *Schools of To-Morrow* (New York, 1915), pp. 303–6, 308, 313–16.

The conventional type of education which trains children to docility and obedience, to the careful performance of imposed tasks because they are imposed, regardless of where they lead, is suited to an autocratic society. These are the traits needed in a state where there is one head to plan and care for the lives and institutions of the people. But in a democracy they interfere with the successful conduct of society and government. Our famous, brief definition of a democracy, as "government of the people, for the people and by the people," gives perhaps the best clew to what is involved in a democratic society. Responsibility for the conduct of society and government rests on every member of society. Therefore, every one must receive a training that will enable him to meet this responsibility, giving him just ideas of the condition and needs of the people collectively, and developing those qualities which will insure his doing a fair share of the work of government. If we train our children to take orders, to do things simply because they are told to, and fail to give them confidence to act and think for themselves, we are putting an almost insurmountable obstacle in the way of overcoming the present defects of our system and of establishing the truth of democratic ideals. Our State is founded on freedom, but when we train the State of to-morrow, we allow it just as little freedom as possible. Children in school must be allowed freedom so that they will know what its use means when they become the controlling body, and they must be allowed to develop active qualities of initiative, independence, and resourcefulness, before the abuses and failures of democracy will disappear.

The spread of the realization of this connection between democracy and education is perhaps the most interesting and significant phase of present educational tendencies. It accounts for the growing interest in popular education, and constitutes a strong reinforcement to the arguments of science and psychology for the changes which have been outlined. There is no doubt that the text-book method of education is well suited to that small group of children who by environment are placed above the necessity of engaging in practical life and who are at the same time interested in abstract ideas. But even for this type of person the system leaves great gaps in his grasp of knowledge; it gives no place to the part that action plays in the development of intelligence, and it trains along the lines of the natural inclinations of the student and does not develop the practical qualities which are usually weak in the abstract person. For the great majority whose interests are not abstract, and who have to pass their lives in some practical occupation, usually in actually working with their hands, a method of education is necessary which bridges the gap between the purely intellectual and theoretical sides of life and their own occupations. With the spread of the ideas of democracy, and the accompanying awakening to social problems, people are beginning to realize that every one, regardless of the class to which he happens to belong, has a right to demand an education which shall meet his own needs, and that for its own sake the State must supply this demand.

Until recently school education has met the needs of only one class of people, those who are interested in knowledge for its own sake, teachers, scholars, and research workers. The idea that training is necessary for the man who works with his hands is still so new that the schools are only just beginning to admit that control of the material things of life is knowledge at all. Until very recently schools have neglected the class of people who are numerically the largest and upon whom the whole world depends for its supply of necessities. One reason for this is the fact that democracy is a comparatively new thing in itself; and until its advent, the right of the majority, the very people who work with their hands, to supply any of their larger spiritual needs was never admitted. Their function, almost their reason for existence, was to take care of the material wants of the ruling classes.

❊   ❊   ❊

If schools are to recognize the needs of all classes of pupils, and give pupils a training that will insure their becoming successful and valuable citizens, they must give work that will not only make the pupils strong physically and morally and give them the right attitude towards the state and their neighbors, but that will as well give them enough control over their material environment to enable them to be economically independent. Preparation for the professions has always been taken care of; it is, as we have seen, the future of the worker in industry which has been neglected. The complications of modern industry due to scientific discoveries make it necessary for the worker who aspires to real success to have a good foundation of general education on which to build his technical skill, and the complications of human nature make it equally necessary that the beginner shall find his way into work that is suited to his tastes and abilities. . . .

It is fatal for a democracy to permit the formation of fixed classes. Differences of wealth, the existence of large masses of unskilled laborers, contempt for work with the hands, inability to secure the training which enables one to forge ahead in life, all operate to produce classes, and to widen the gulf between them. Statesmen and legislation can do something to combat these evil forces. Wise philanthropy can do something. But the only fundamental agency for good is the public school system. Every American is proud of what has been accomplished in the past in fostering among very diverse elements of population a spirit of unity and of brotherhood so that the sense of common interests and aims has prevailed over the strong forces working to divide our people into classes. The increasing complexity of our life, with the great accumulation of wealth at one social extreme and the condition of almost dire necessity at the other makes the task of democracy constantly more difficult. The days are rapidly passing when the simple provision of a system in which all individuals mingle is enough to meet the need. The subject-matter and the methods of teaching must be positively and aggressively adapted to the end.

There must not be one system for the children of parents who have more leisure and another for the children of those who are wage-earners. The physical separation forced by such a scheme, while unfavorable to the development of a proper mutual sympathy, is the least of its evils. Worse is the fact that the over bookish education for some and the over "practical" education for others brings about a division of mental and moral habits, ideals and outlook.

The academic education turns out future citizens with no sympathy for work done with the hands, and with absolutely no training for understanding the most serious of present day social and political difficulties. The trade training will turn future workers who may have greater immediate skill than they would have had without their training, but who have no enlargement of mind, no insight into the scientific and social significance of the work they do, no education which assists them in finding their way on or in making their own adjustments. A division of the public school system into one part which pursues traditional methods, with incidental improvements, and another which deals with those who are to go into manual labor means a plan of social predestination totally foreign to the spirit of a democracy.

The democracy which proclaims equality of opportunity as its ideal requires an education in which learning and social application, ideas and practice, work and recognition of the meaning of what is done, are united from the beginning and for all. Schools such as we have discussed in this book—and they are rapidly coming into being in large numbers all over the country—are showing how the ideal of equal opportunity for all is to be transmuted into reality.

JOHN DEWEY ON EDUCATION AS GROWTH (1916)   From John Dewey,

Democracy and Education (New York, 1916), pp. 59-61.

When it is said that education is development, everything depends upon *how* development is conceived. Our net conclusion is that life is development, and that developing, growing, is life. Translated into its educational equivalents, this means (*i*) that the educational process has no end beyond itself; it is its own end; and that (*ii*) the educational process is one of continual reorganizing, reconstructing, transforming.

1. Development when it is interpreted in *comparative* terms, that is, with respect to the special traits of child and adult life, means the direction of power into special channels: the formation of habits involving executive skill, definiteness of interest, and specific objects of observation and thought. But the comparative view is not final. The child has specific powers; to ignore that fact is to stunt or distort the organs upon which his growth depends. The adult uses his powers to transform his environment, thereby occasioning new stimuli which redirect his powers and keep them developing. Ignoring this fact means arrested development, a passive accommodation. Normal child and normal adult alike, in other words, are engaged in growing. The difference between them is not the difference between growth and no growth, but between the modes of growth appropriate to different conditions. With respect to the development of powers devoted to coping with specific scientific and economic problems we may say the child should be growing in manhood. With respect to sympathetic curiosity, unbiased responsiveness, and openness of mind, we may say that the adult should be growing in childlikeness. One statement is as true as the other.

Three ideas which have been criticized, namely, the merely privative nature of immaturity, static adjustment to a fixed environment, and rigidity of habit, are all connected with a false idea of growth or development,—that it is a movement toward a fixed goal. Growth is regarded as *having* an end, instead of *being* an end. The educational counterparts of the three fallacious ideas are first, failure to take account of the instinctive or native powers of the young; secondly, failure to develop initiative in coping with novel situations; thirdly, an undue emphasis upon drill and other devices which secure automatic skill at the expense of personal perception. In all cases, the adult environment is accepted as a standard for the child. He is to be brought up *to* it.

Natural instincts are either disregarded or treated as nuisances, as obnoxious traits to be suppressed, or at all events to be brought into conformity with external standards. Since conformity is the aim, what is distinctively individual in a young person is brushed aside, or regarded as a source of mischief or anarchy. Conformity is made equivalent to uniformity. Consequently, there are induced lack of interest in the novel, aversion to progress, and dread of the uncertain and the unknown. Since the end of growth is outside of and beyond the process of growing, external agents have to be resorted to to induce movement towards it. Whenever a method of education is stigmatized as mechanical we may be sure that external pressure is brought to bear to reach an external end.

2. Since in reality there is nothing to which growth is relative save more growth, there is nothing to which education is subordinate save more education. It is a commonplace to say that education should not cease when one leaves school. The

point of this commonplace is that the purpose of school education is to insure the continuance of education by organizing the powers that insure growth. The inclination to learn from life itself and to make the conditions of life such that all will learn in the process of living is the finest product of schooling.

When we abandon the attempt to define immaturity by means of fixed comparison with adult accomplishments, we are compelled to give up thinking of it as denoting lack of desired traits. Abandoning this notion, we are also forced to surrender our habit of thinking of instruction as a method of supplying this lack by pouring knowledge into a mental and moral hole which awaits filling. Since life means growth, a living creature lives as truly and positively at one stage as at another, with the same intrinsic fullness and the same absolute claims. Hence education means the enterprise of supplying the conditions which insure growth, or adequacy of life, irrespective of age. We first look with impatience upon immaturity, regarding it as something to be got over as rapidly as possible. Then the adult formed by such educative methods looks back with impatient regret upon childhood and youth as a scene of lost opportunities and wasted powers. This ironical situation will endure till it is recognized that living has its own intrinsic quality and that the business of education is with that quality.

Realization that life is growth protects us from that so-called idealizing of childhood which in effect is nothing but lazy indulgence. Life is not to be identified with every superficial act and interest. Even though it is not always easy to tell whether what appears to be mere surface fooling is a sign of some nascent as yet untrained power, we must remember that manifestations are not to be accepted as ends in themselves. They are signs of possible growth. They are to be turned into means of development, of carrying power forward, not indulged or cultivated for their own sake. Excessive attention to surface phenomena (even in the way of rebuke as well as of encouragement) may lead to their fixation and thus to arrested development. What impulses are moving toward, not what they have been, is the important thing for parent and teacher.

EDWARD L. THORNDIKE ON ANIMAL INTELLIGENCE (1898) From
Edward L. Thorndike, *Animal Intelligence* (London, 1911), pp. 26–29, 241–44.

After considerable preliminary observation of animals' behavior under various conditions, I chose for my general method one which, simple as it is, possesses several other marked advantages besides those which accompany experiment of any sort. It was merely to put animals when hungry in inclosures from which they could escape by some simple act, such as pulling at a loop of cord, pressing a lever, or stepping on a platform. (A detailed description of these boxes and pens will be given later.) The animal was put in the inclosure, food was left outside in sight, and his actions observed. Besides recording his general behavior, special notice was taken of how he succeeded in doing the necessary act (in case he did succeed), and a record was kept of the time he was in the box before performing the successful pull, or clawing, or bite. This was repeated until the animal had formed a perfect association between the sense-impression of the interior of that box and the impulse leading to the successful movement. When the association was thus perfect, the time taken to escape was, of course, practically constant and very short.

If, on the other hand, after a certain time the animal did not succeed, he was taken out, but *not fed*. If, after a sufficient number of trials, he failed to get out, the case was recorded as one of complete failure. Enough different sorts of methods of escape were tried to make it fairly sure that association in general, not association of a particular sort of impulse, was being studied. Enough animals were taken with each box or pen to make it sure that the results were not due to individual peculiarities. None of the animals used had any previous acquaintance with any of the mechanical contrivances by which the doors were opened. So far as possible the animals were kept in a uniform state of hunger, which was practically utter hunger. That is, no cat or dog was experimented on, when the experiment involved any important question of fact or theory, unless I was sure that his motive was of the standard strength. With chicks this is not practicable, on account of their delicacy. But with them dislike of loneliness acts as a uniform motive to get back to the other chicks. Cats (or rather kittens), dogs and chicks were the subjects of the experiments. All were apparently in excellent health, save an occasional chick.

By this method of experimentation the animals are put in situations which call into activity their mental functions and permit them to be carefully observed. One may, by following it, observe personally more intelligent acts than are included in any anecdotal collection. And this actual vision of animals in the act of using their minds is far more fruitful than any amount of history of what animals have done without the history of how they did it. But besides affording this opportunity, for purposeful and systematic observation, our method is valuable because it frees the animal from any influence of the observer. The animal's behavior is quite independent of any factors save its own hunger, the mechanism of the box it is in, the food outside, and such general matters as fatigue, indisposition, etc. Therefore the work done by one investigator may be repeated and verified or modified by another. No personal factor is present save in the observation and interpretation. Again, our method gives some very important results which are quite uninfluenced by *any* personal factor in any way. The curves showing the progress of the formation of associations, which are obtained from the records of the times taken by the animal in successive trials, are facts which may be obtained by any observer who can tell time. They are absolute, and whatever can be deduced from them is sure. So also the question of whether an animal does or does not form a certain association requires for an answer no higher qualification in the observer than a pair of eyes. The literature of animal psychology shows so uniformly and often so sadly the influence of the personal equation that any method which can partially eliminate it deserves a trial.

Furthermore, although the associations formed are such as could not have been previously experienced or provided for by heredity, they are still not too remote from the animal's ordinary course of life. They mean simply the connection of a certain act with a certain situation and resultant pleasure, and this general type of association is found throughout the animal's life normally. The muscular movements required are all such as might often be required of the animal. And yet it will be noted that the acts required are nearly enough like the acts of the anecdotes to enable one to compare the results of experiment by this method with the work of the anecdote school. Finally, it may be noticed that the method lends itself readily to experiments on imitation.

*　　*　　*

Laws Of Behavior In General

Behavior is predictable. The first law of behavior, one fraction of the general law of the uniformity of nature, is that with life and mind, as with mass and motion, the same cause will produce the same effect,—that *the same situation will, in the same animal, produce the same response,—and that if the same situation produces on two occasions two different responses, the animal must have changed.*

Scientific students of behavior will, with few exceptions, accept this law in theory, but in practice we have not fully used it. We have too often been content to say that a man may respond in any one of several ways to the same situation, or may attend to one rather than another feature of the same object, without insisting that the man must in each case be different, and without searching for the differences in him which cause the different reactions.

The changes in an organism which make it respond differently on different occasions to the same situation range from temporary to permanent changes. Hunger, fatigue, sleep, and certain diseases on the one hand, and learning, immunity, growth and senility on the other, illustrate this range.

Behavior is predictable *without recourse to magical agencies.* It is, of course, the case that any given difference between the responses of an animal to the same situation depends upon some *particular* difference in the animal. Each immunity, for example, has its detailed representation in an altered condition of the blood or other bodily tissue. In general the changes in animal which cause changes in its behavior to the same situation are fully enumerated in a list of the bodily changes concerned. That is, whatever changes may be supposed to have taken place in the animal's vital force, spiritual essence, or other magical bases for life and thought, are useless for scientific explanation and control of behavior.

No competent thinker probably doubts this in the case of such changes as are referred to by hunger, sleep, fatigue, so-called 'functional' diseases and immunity, and those who do doubt it in the case of mental growth and learning seem to represent an incomplete evolution from supernatural, or rather infrascientific, thinking. There may be in behavior a surplus beyond what would be predictable if the entire history of every atom in the body was known—a surplus necessarily attributable to changes in the animal's incorporeal structure. But scientific thinkers properly refuse to deliberately count upon such a surplus.

Every response or change in response of an animal is then the result of the interaction of its original knowable nature and the environment. This may seem too self-evident a corollary for mention. It should be so, but, unfortunately, it is not. Two popular psychological doctrines exist in defiance of it. One is the doctrine that the movements are really random, they occur by virtue of some force that works at random. If the movements are really the result of the action of the environment on the animal's nature, they are never random. A baby twiddles his thumbs or waves his legs for exactly the same sort of reason that a chick pecks at a worm or preens its wing.

The other doctrine which witnesses to neglect of the axiom that behavior is the creation of the environment, acting on the animal's nature, is the doctrine that the need for a certain behavior helps to create it, that being in a difficulty tends in and of itself to make an animal respond so as to end the difficulty.

The truth is that to a difficulty the animal responds by whatever is inherited and acquired nature has connected with the special form of difficulty and that in many animals the one response of those thus provided which relieves the difficulty is selected and connected more firmly with that difficulty's next appearance. The difficulty acts only as a stimulus to the animal's nature and its relief acts only as a premiun to the connection whereby it was relieved. The law of original behavior, or the law of instinct, is then that *to any situation an animal will, apart from learning, respond by virtue of the inherited nature of its reception-, connection- and action-systems.*

The inquiry into the laws of learning to be made in this essay is limited to those aspects of behavior which the term has come historically to signify, that is, to intellect, skill, morals and the like.

For the purposes of this essay it is not necessary to decide just what features of an animal's behavior to include under intellect, skill, morals and the like. The statements to be made will fit any reasonable dividing line between behavior on the one side and mere circulation, digestion, excretion and the like on the other. There should in fact be no clear dividing line, since there is no clear gap between those activities which naturalists have come to call behavior and the others.

The discussion will include: First, a description of two laws of learning; a second, an argument to prove that no additional forces are needed—that these two laws explain all learning; and third, an investigation of whether these two laws are reducible to more fundamental laws. I shall also note briefly the consequences of the acceptance of these laws in one sample case, that of the study of mental evolution.

Provisional Laws of Acquired Behavior or Learning

The Law of Effect is that: *Of several responses made to the same situation, those which are accompanied or closely followed by satisfaction to the animal will, other things being equal, be more firmly connected with the situation, so that, when it recurs, they will be more likely to recur; those which are accompanied or closely followed by discomfort to the animal will, other things being equal, have their connections with that situation weakened, so that, when it recurs, they will be less likely to occur. The greater the satisfaction or discomfort, the greater the strengthening or weakening of the bond.*

The Law of Exercise is that: *Any response to a situation will, other things being equal, be more strongly connected with the situation in proportion to the number of times it has been connected with that situation and the average vigor and duration of the connections.*

THORNDIKE AND WOODWORTH ON THE TRANSFER OF TRAINING
(1901)   From Edward L. Thorndike and Robert S. Woodworth, "The Influence of Improvement in One Mental Function on the Efficiency of Other Functions," as quoted in *Psychological Review,* vol. VIII, pp. 248–51, 394–95.

Our chief method was to test the efficiency of some function or functions, then to give training in some other function or functions until a certain amount of improvement was reached, and then to test the first function or set of functions. Provided no other factors were allowed to affect the tests, the difference between the test before and the test after training measures the influence of the improvement in the trained functions on the functions tested.

It is possible to test the general question in a much neater and more convenient way by using, instead of measures of a function before and after training with another, measures of the correlation between the two functions. If improvement in one function increases the efficiency of another and there has been improvement in one, the other should be correlated with it; the individuals who have high rank in the one should have a higher rank in the other than the general average. Such a result might also be brought about by a correlation of the inborn capacities for those functions. Finding correlation between two functions thus need not mean that improvement in one has brought increased efficiency in the other. But the absence of correlation does mean the opposite. In an unpublished paper Clark Wissler, of Columbia University, demonstrates the absence of any considerable correlation between the functions measured by the tests given to students there. Naomi Norsworthy, of Teachers College, has shown (the data were presented in part at the Baltimore meeting; the research is not yet in print) that there is no correlation between accuracy in noticing misspelled words and accuracy in multiplication, nor between the speeds; that there is little or no correlation between accuracy and speed in marking on a printed page misspelled words, words containing *r* and *e*, the word *boy*, and in marking semicircles on a page of different geometrical figures.

Perhaps the most striking method of showing the influence or lack of influence of one function on another is that of testing the same function-group, using cases where there are very slightly different data. If, for instance, we test a person's ability to estimate a series of magnitudes differing each from the next very slightly, and find that he estimates one very much more accurately than its neighbors on either side, we can be sure that what he has acquired from his previous experience or from the experience of the test is not improvement in the function-group of estimating magnitudes but a lot of particular improvements in estimating particular magnitudes, improvements which may be to a large extent independent of each other.

The experiments, finally, were all on the influence of the training on efficiency, on ability as measured by a single test, not on the ability *to improve*. It might be that improvement in one function might fail to give in another improved ability, but succeed in giving ability to improve faster than would have occurred had the training been lacking.

The evidence given by our experiments makes the following conclusions seem probable:

It is misleading to speak of sense discrimination, attention, memory, observation, accuracy, quickness, etc., as multitudinous separate individual functions are referred to by any one of these words. These functions may have little in common. There is no reason to suppose that any general change occurs corresponding to the words 'improvement of the attention,' or 'of the power of observation,' or 'of accuracy.'

It is even misleading to speak of these functions as exercised within narrow fields as units. For example, 'attention to words' or 'accurate discrimination of lengths' or 'observation of animals' or 'quickness of visual perception' are mythological, not real entities. The words do not mean any existing fact with anything like the necessary precision for either theoretical or practical purposes, for, to take a sample case, attention to the meaning of words does not imply equal attention to their spelling, nor attention to their spelling equal attention to their length, nor attention to certain letters in them equal attention to other letters.

The mind is, on the contrary, on its dynamic side a machine for making particular reactions to particular situations. It works in great detail, adapting itself to the special data of which it has had experience. The word *attention*, for example, can properly mean only the sum total of a lot of particular tendencies to attend to particular sorts of data, and ability to attend can properly mean only the sum total of all the particular abilities and inabilities, each of which may have an efficiency largely irrespective of the efficiencies of the rest.

Improvement in any single mental function need not improve the ability in functions commonly called by the same name. It may injure it.

Improvement in any single mental function rarely brings about equal improvement in any other function, no matter how similar, for the working of every mental function-group is conditioned by the nature of the data in each particular case.

The very slight amount of variation in the nature of the data necessary to affect the efficiency of a function-group makes it fair to infer that no change in the data, however slight, is without effect on the function. The loss in the efficiency of a function trained with certain data, as we pass to data more and more unlike the first, makes it fair to infer that there is always a point where the loss is complete, a point beyond which the influence of the training has not extended. The rapidity of this loss, that is, its amount in the case of data very similar to the data on which the function was trained, makes it fair to infer that this point is nearer than has been supposed.

The general consideration of the cases of retention or of loss of practice effect seems to make it likely that spread of practice occurs only where identical elements are concerned in the influencing and influenced function.

The particular samples of the influence of training in one function on the efficiency of other functions chosen for investigation were as follows:

1. The influence of certain special training in the estimation of magnitudes on the ability to estimate magnitudes of the same general sort, *i.e.*, lengths or areas or weights, differing in amount, in accessory qualities (such as shape, color, form) or in both. The general method here was to test the subject's accuracy of estimating certain magnitudes, *e.g.*, lengths of lines. He would, that is, guess the length of each. Then he would practice estimating lengths within certain limits until he attained a high degree of proficiency. Then he would once more estimate the lengths of the preliminary test series. Similarly with weights, areas, etc. This is apparently the sort of thing that happens in the case of a tea-taster, tobacco-buyer, wheat-taster or carpenter, who attains high proficiency by judging magnitudes or, as we ambiguously say, in delicacy of discriminating certain sense data. It is thus like common cases of sense training in actual life.

2. The influence of training in observing words containing certain combinations of letters (*e.g.*, s and e) or some other characteristic on the general ability to observe words. The general method here was to test the subject's speed and accuracy in picking out and marking certain letters, words containing certain letters, words of a certain length, geometric figures, misspelled words, etc. He then practiced picking out and marking words of some one special sort until he attained a high degree of proficiency. He was then re-tested. The training here corresponds to a fair degree with the training one has in learning to spell, to notice forms and endings in studying foreign languages, or in fact in learning to attend to any small details.

3. The influence of special training in memorizing on the general ability to

memorize. Careful tests of one individual and a group test of students confirmed Professor James' result. These tests will not be described in detail.

These samples were chosen because of their character as representative mental functions, because of their adaptability to quantitative interpretations and partly because of their convenience. Such work can be done at odd times without any bulky or delicate apparatus. This rendered it possible to secure subjects. In all the experiments to be described we tested the influence of improvement in a function on *other functions closely allied to it.* We did not in sense-training measure the influence of training one sense on others, nor in the case of training of the attention the influence of training in noticing words on, say, the ability to do mental arithmetic or to listen to a metaphysical discourse.

✳   ✳   ✳

When one undergoes training in estimating certain magnitudes he may improve in estimating others from various causes. Such training as was described in our previous paper gives one more accurate mental standards and more delicacy in judging different magnitudes by them. In the case of estimations of magnitudes in terms of unfamiliar standards such as grams or centimeters, the acquisition of the mere idea of what a gram or centimeter is, makes a tremendous difference in all judgments. This will be seen in the case of N.'s estimation of areas. She was told that an inch was 2.54 centimeters, and with that as practically the sum of her knowledge of the size of a centimeter made judgments of a certain inaccuracy. The mere examination for two minutes of areas 1, 10, 50 and 100 sq. cm. in size reduced this inaccuracy to 38 per cent. of what it had been. The acquisition of definite ideas is thus an important part of the influence of improvement in one function on the efficiency of other functions. Even this, however, may not be operative. With some subjects in some cases the new ideas or the refinement of old ideas produced by the training seem impotent to influence judgments with slightly different data.

It is hard to prove whether or not or to what extent the delicacy in judging by means of such ideas in the case of one set of data is operative with the different data used in the test series. Surely it sometimes is not.

The training might also give ideas of how to estimate most successfully habits of making the judgments in better ways, of making allowance for constant errors, of avoiding certain prejudices. These habits might often concern features in which the function trained and the functions tested were identical. For instance, the subjects who judged areas of various shapes made their judgments before training by looking at the 10, 25 and 100 sq. cm. areas given them as guides; after training they never looked at these but used the mental standards acquired. This habit is a favorable one, for a person can look at a 25 sq. cm. area in the shape of a square and still think various-shaped areas from 30 to 50 sq. cm. are under 30. The mental standard works better.

The training might give some mysterious discipline to mental powers which we could not analyze but could only speak of vaguely as training of discrimination or attention. If present, such an effect should be widely and rather evenly present, since the training in every case followed the same plan. It was not.

For functions so similar and for cases so favorable for getting better standards and better habits of judging the amount of improvement gotten by training in an allied function is small. Studies of the influence of the training of similar functions in school and in the ordinary course of life, so far as we have made such, show a similar failure to bring large increases of efficiency in allied functions.

EDWARD L. THORNDIKE ON THE CONTRIBUTION OF PSYCHOLOGY TO EDUCATION (1910) From Edward L. Thorndike, "The Contribution of Psychology to Education," *Journal of Educational Psychology,* vol. I, pp. 5–8.

Psychology is the science of the intellects, characters and behavior of animals including man. Human education is concerned with certain changes in the intellects, characters and behavior of men, its problems being roughly included under these four topics: Aims, materials, means and methods.

Psychology contributes to a better understanding of the aims of education by defining them, making them clearer; by limiting them, showing us what can be done and what can not; and by suggesting new features that should be made parts of them.

Psychology makes ideas of educational aims clearer. When one says that the aim of education is culture, or discipline, or efficiency, or happiness, or utility, or knowledge, or skill, or the perfection of all one's powers, or development, one's statements, and probably one's thoughts, need definition. Different people, even amongst the clearest-headed of them, do not agree concerning just what culture is, or just what is useful. Psychology helps here by requiring us to put our notions of the aims of education into terms of the exact changes that education is to make, and by describing for us the changes which do actually occur in human beings.

Psychology helps to measure the probability that an aim is attainable. For example, certain writers about education state or imply that the knowledge and skill and habits of behavior which are taught to the children of today are of service not only to this generation and to later generations through the work this generation does, but also to later generations forever through the inheritance of increased capacity for knowledge and skill and morals. But if the mental and moral changes made in one generation are not transmitted by heredity to the next generation, the improvement of the race by direct transfer of acquisitions is a foolish, because futile aim.

Psychology enlarges and refines the aim of education. Certain features of human nature may be and have been thought to be unimportant or even quite valueless because of ignorance of psychology. Thus for hundreds of years in the history of certain races even the most gifted thinkers of the race have considered it beneath the dignity of education to make physical health an important aim. Bodily welfare was even thought of as a barrier to spiritual growth, an undesirable interferer with its proper master. Education aimed to teach it its proper place, to treat it as a stupid and brutish slave. It is partly because psychology has shown the world that the mind is the servant and co-worker as well as the master of the body, that the welfare of our minds and morals is intimately bound up with the welfare of our bodies, particularly of our central nervous systems, that today we can all see the eminence of bodily health as an aim of education.

To an understanding of the material of education, psychology is the chief contributor.

Psychology shares with anatomy, physiology, sociology, anthropology, history and the other sciences that concern changes in man's bodily or mental nature the work of providing thinkers and workers in the field of education with knowledge of the material with which they work. Just as the science and art of agriculture depend upon chemistry and botany, so the art of education depends upon physiology and psychology.

A complete science of psychology would tell every fact about every one's intellect and character and behavior, would tell the cause of every change in human nature, would tell the result which every educational force—every act of every person that changed any other or the agent himself—would have. It would aid us to use human beings for the world's welfare with the same surety of the result that we now have when we use falling bodies or chemical elements. In proportion as we get such a science we shall become masters of our own souls as we now are masters of heat and light. Progress toward such a science is being made.

Psychology contributes to understanding of the means of education, first, because the intellects and characters of any one's parents, teachers and friends are very important means of educating him, and, second, because the influence of any other means, such as books, maps or apparatus, cannot be usefully studied apart from the human nature which they are to act upon.

Psychology contributes to knowledge of methods of teaching in three ways. First, methods may be deduced outright from the laws of human nature. For instance, we may infer from psychology that the difficulty pupils have in learning to divide by a fraction is due in large measure to the habit established by all the thousands of previous divisions which they have done or seen, the habit, that is, of "division—decrease" or "number divided—result smaller than the number." We may then devise or select such a method as will reduce this interference from the old habits to a minimum without weakening the old habits in their proper functioning.

Second, methods may be chosen from actual working experience, regardless of psychology, as a starting point. Thus it is believed that in the elementary school a class of fifteen pupils for one teacher gives better results than either a class of three or a class of thirty. Thus, also, it is believed that family life is better than institutional life in its effects upon character and enterprise. Thus, also, it is believed that in learning a foreign language the reading of simple discussions of simple topics is better than the translation of difficult literary masterpieces that treat subtle and complex topics. Even in such cases psychology may help by explaining *why* one method does succeed better and so leading the way to new insights regarding other questions not yet settled by experience.

Third, in all cases psychology, by its methods of measuring knowledge and skill, may suggest means to test and verify or refute the claims of any method. For instance, there has been a failure on the part of teachers to decide from their classroom experience whether it is better to teach the spelling of a pair of homonyms together or apart in time. But all that is required to decide the question for any given pair is for enough teachers to use both methods with enough different classes, keeping everything else except the method constant, and to measure the errors in spelling the words thereafter in the two cases. Psychology, which teaches us how to measure changes in human nature, teaches us how to decide just what the results of any method of teaching are.

So far I have outlined the contribution of psychology to education from the point of view of the latter's problems. I shall now outline very briefly the work being done by psychologists which is of special significance to the theory and practice of education and which may be expected to result in the largest and most frequent contributions.

It will, of course, be understood that directly or indirectly, soon or late, every advance in the sciences of human nature will contribute to our success in controlling human nature and changing it to the advantage of the common weal. If certain lines of work by psychologists are selected for mention here, it is only because they are the more obvious, more direct and, so far as can now be seen, greater aids to correct thinking about education.

The first line of work concerns the discovery and improvement of means of measurement of intellectual functions. (The study of means of measuring moral functions such as prudence, readiness to sacrifice an immediate for a later good, sympathy, and the like, has only barely begun.) Beginning with easy cases such as the discrimination of sensory differences, psychology has progressed to measuring memory and accuracy of movement, fatigue, improvement with practice, power of observing small details, the quantity, rapidity and usefulness of associations, and even to measuring so complex a function as general intelligence and so subtle a one as suggestibility.

The task of students of physical science in discovering the thermometer, galvanometer and spectroscope, and in defining the volt, calorie, erg, and ampere, is being attempted by psychologists in the sphere of human nature and behavior. How important such work is to education should be obvious. At least three-fourths of the problems of educational practice are problems whose solution depends upon the *amount* of some change in boys and girls. Of two methods, which gives the *greater* skill? Is the gain in general ability from a "disciplinary" study so great as to outweigh the loss in specially useful habits? Just how much more does a boy learn when thirty dollars a year is spent for his teaching than when only twenty dollars is spent? Units in which to measure the changes wrought by education are essential to an adequate science of education. And, though the students of education may establish these units by their own investigations, they can use and will need all the experience of psychologists in the search for similar units.

The second line of work concerns race, sex, age and individual differences in all the many elements of intellect and character and behavior.

How do the Igorottes, Ainus, Japanese and Esquimaux differ in their efficiency in learning to operate certain mechanical contrivances? Is the male sex more variable than the female in mental functions? What happens to keenness of sensory discrimination with age? How do individuals of the same race, sex and age differ in efficiency in perceiving small visual details or in accuracy in equaling a given length, or in the rapidity of movement? These are samples of many questions which psychologists have tried to answer by appropriate measurements. Such knowledge of the differences which exist amongst men for whatever reason is of service to the thinker about the particular differences which education aims to produce between a man and his former self.

These studies of individual differences or variability are being supplemented by studies of correlations. How far does superior vividness and fidelity in imagery from one sense go with inferiority in other sorts of imagery? To what extent is motor ability a symptom of intellectual ability? Does the quick learner soon forget? What are the mental types that result from the individual variations in mental functions and their inter-correlations? Psychology has already determined with more or less surety the answers to a number of such questions instructive in their bearing upon both scientific insight into human nature and practical arrangements for controlling it.

The extent to which the intellectual and moral differences found in human beings are consequences of their original nature and determined by the ancestry from which they spring, is a matter of fundamental importance for education. So also is the manner in which ancestral influence operates. Whether such qualities as leadership, the artistic temperament, originality, persistence, mathematical ability, or motor skill are represented in the germs each by one or a few unit characters so that they "Mendelize" in inheritance, or whether they are represented each by the cooperation of so many unit characters that the laws of their inheritance are those of "blending" is a question whose answer will decide in great measure the means to be employed for racial improvement. Obviously both the amount and the mode of operation of ancestral influence upon intellect and character are questions which psychology should and does investigate.

The results and methods of action of the many forces which operate in childhood and throughout life to change a man's original nature are subjects for study equally appropriate to the work of a psychologist, a sociologist or a student of education, but the last two will naturally avail themselves of all that the first achieves.

EDWARD L. THORNDIKE'S "LAWS OF LEARNING" (1912)   From Edward L. Thorndike, *Education: A First Book* (New York, 1912), pp. 7, 60, 71, 90–92, 95–99.

The Need of Education

Man improves education as he improves any other human activity—by openminded thought about it, by learning the results of existing forms of it, by experimenting with other forms, and by clearing up and making reasonable our notions of what changes we should make in human beings and of how we should make them. Such impartial scientific study of man's efforts to change himself for the better has been receiving more and more attention within the past twenty years. In the case of school education, for instance, the actual changes wrought in boys and girls by this or that form of education are being measured, old and new methods are being tested by experiment in the same spirit of zeal and care for the truth that animates the man of science, and the educational customs which have been accepted unthinkingly by "use and want" are being required to justify themselves to reason.

Such scientific study faces five problems or groups of problems, namely, those of:

1. *The aims of education.* What changes should be made in human beings by schools and other educating forces?
2. *The material or subjects of education.* What is the original nature of the human beings whom we have to change? What are the principles or laws of human nature and behavior that we need to know in order to change men for the better?

EDUCATION FOR
URBAN INDUSTRIAL
AMERICA
1895–1918

2243

3. *The means and agents of education.* What forces are at our command in the task of producing and preventing changes in human beings?
4. *The methods of education.* How should these means and agents be brought to bear upon the subjects of education so as best to realize its aims?
5. *The results of education.* What have been the actual effects of different methods, means, and agents acting upon different kinds of human beings?

* * *

Intellect and Character Are Due to Intelligible Causes

No response of any human being occurs without some possibly discoverable cause; and no situation exists whose effect could not with sufficient knowledge be predicted. Things do not happen by mere chance in human life any more than in the fall of an apple or in an eclipse of the moon. The same situation acting on the same individual will produce, always and inevitably, the same response. If on different occasions it *seems* to produce different responses, it is because the individual has changed in the meantime and is not the same creature that he was. At the bottom of the endless variety of human nature and circumstance there are laws which act invariably and make possible the control of human education and progress by reason. So the general rule of reason applies to education: *To produce a desired effect, find its cause and put that in action.*

* * *

The original equipment of the central or average or typical human being consists, over and above his strictly physical, chemical and physiological nature, in tendencies to respond to certain situations by certain sensations, feelings and acts. These tendencies may be called the original mental make-up of man as a species.

When the situation is simple, the response uniform and the connection between the two close and hard to modify, the tendency is usually called a reflex. Thus, since the original make-up of man leads him to respond to bright light entering the eye by contracting the pupil, doing so promptly and surely and rather unalterably, the tendency is called the pupillary reflex. When the situation is more complex, the response more variable and the connection between the two more easily modified, the tendency is called an instinct. Thus the tendency of man to respond to the situation—*unfamiliar large animals approaching him rapidly with open jaws*—by trembling, running and hiding, is called one of the instincts of fear. When the situation is very complex, the response very variable and the bond between them very modifiable, the words 'capacity,' 'predisposition' and the like are often used instead of instinct. Thus the fact that man as a species by original nature has tendencies which, when the proper situations are provided, grow into thought, speech and music, would be expressed by such terms as 'the capacity for reasoning,' 'the predisposition toward articulation, imitation and the other factors in speech,' and 'musical capacity.'

Such is the original stuff of human nature, out of which the circumstances of life and training have fashioned each of us. As the potter must know his clay, the musician his instrument or the general the raw recruits out of whom he hopes to make a disciplined force, so education has to reckon with these unlearned tendencies. To change men's wants for the better, we must heed what conditions originally satisfy and annoy them, since the only way to create an interest is by grafting it on to one of the original satisfiers. To enable men to satisfy their wants more fully, the crude curiosity, manipulation, experimentation and irrational interplay of fear, anger, rivalry, mastery, submission, cruelty and kindliness must be modified into useful, verified thought and equitable acts.

The task of education is to make the best use of this original fund of tendencies, eradicating its vicious elements, wasting the least possible of value that nature gives, and supplying at the most useful time the additions that are needed to improve and satisfy human wants. This task is complicated by the fact that original tendencies are often 'delayed'—that is, appear only when a certain stage of mental growth is reached—so that education has to wait perhaps longer than it wishes before it can count upon them. It is further complicated by their transitoriness. Many tendencies appear for a time, but wane if not given exercise and reward; so that education has to strike while the iron is hot. If the response is sought too early, effort is wasted; if it is sought too late, the effort may fail altogether. It is further complicated by the discords between the behavior to which original nature prompts and the behavior which the welfare of man in his present civilized state requires. Man's original equipment dates far back and adapts him, directly, only for such a life as might be led by a family group of wild men among the brute forces of land, water, storm and sun, fruits and berries, animals and other family groups of wild men. But man has created a new world, in which his original nature is often at a loss and against which it often rebels.

Some original tendencies should be cherished almost as they are. Some must be rooted out of children—by withholding the situations that would call them forth so that they die a natural death from lack of exercise; or by making their exercise result in pain and discomfort; or by substituting desirable habits in place of them. The great majority of original tendencies, however, should neither be preserved in their exact original form, nor be altogether annihilated, but should be so modified and redirected as to further the improvement and satisfaction of men's wants under the conditions of humane and rational living.

Thus the indiscriminate manipulation of objects is modified into instructive play with sandpiles, blocks or ball; and later into the intelligent use of tools, pencil, pen, typewriter, engine, printing-press and the like. Thus the satisfyingness which originally accompanies notice and approval by anybody is redirected to form special attachments to the approval of parents, teachers, one's own higher nature, and heroes, living and dead, who are chosen as ideal judges. Thus the original incitement of 'another trying to get the food or victory or admiration which we crave' is replaced gradually by rivalry with others in all work and play, then by rivalry with our own past records or with ideal standards. Thus out of 'collecting and hoarding at random whatever is handy and attractive to the crude interests in color, glitter and novelty,' habits of intelligent scientific collecting and arranging may be formed, and the interest in collecting may be made a stimulus to getting knowledge about the objects collected. Thus the original interests, the tendencies to be satisfied by and annoyed by, to like and dislike, are turned into acquired interests in efficient workmanship, kindly fellowship, the welfare of one's family, friends, community and nation, and finally into the love of truth, justice and the happiness of mankind as a whole.

*   *   *

The Material for Education: The Learning Process
THE LAWS OF HABIT FORMATION

All the changes that are produced in human intellect, character and skill happen in accord with, and as the result of, certain fundamental laws of change. The first is the Law of Exercise, that, other things being equal, *the oftener or more emphatically a given response is connected with a certain situation, the more likely it is to be made to that situation in the future.* Thus, by repeatedly inducing a child to respond to the question, 'How many are four and two?' by saying, 'Six,' a bond is formed between that situation and that response. This law may be more briefly stated as: 'Other things being equal, *exercise strengthens the bond between situation and response.*'

This law needs no comment. It is the most commonly recognized law of human behavior. The need is rather of emphasis upon the other things which may be unequal. Chief among them are the *consequences of the response,* whose power in learning is recognized by the Law of Effect.

The Law of Effect is that, other things being equal,[1] *the greater the satisfying-ness of the state of affairs which accompanies or follows a given response to a certain situation, the more likely that response is to be made to that situation in the future.* Conversely, the greater the discomfort or annoyingness of the state of affairs which comes with or after a response to a situation, the more likely that response is *not* to be made to that situation in the future. Suppose, for example, that when a child responds to the situation, *being asked, 'How many are four and two?* by saying 'Six,' he is always given kind looks, candy and the approval of his fellows. Suppose, on the contrary, that he always received rebukes, blows and jeers. This law may be stated more briefly as: *Satisfying results strengthen, and discomfort weakens, the bond between situation and response.*

Old connections between situation and response are weakened, and new connections are created, only by some force. Human nature does not do something for nothing. The satisfyingness and annoyingness of the states of affairs which follow the making of the connection are the chief forces which remodel man's nature. Education makes changes chiefly by rewarding them. The prime law in all human control is to get the man to make the desired response and to be satisfied thereby.

The Law of Effect is the fundamental law of learning and teaching. By it a crab learns to respond to the situation, *two paths,* by taking the one, choice of which has in the past brought food. By it a dog will learn to respond to the situation, *a white box and a black box,* by neglecting the latter if opening it in the past has been promptly followed by an electric shock. By it animals are taught their tricks; by it

[1] The other things that are involved are, besides the law of exercise already described, the closeness with which the satisfaction or discomfort is connected with the connection it is to influence, and the readiness of the response to be connected with the situation. Each of these factors is of great importance, but their explanation belongs in a special volume on educational psychology.

babies learn to smile at the sight of the bottle or the kind attendant, and to manipulate spoon and fork; by it the player at billiards or golf improves his game; by it the man of science preserves those ideas that satisfy him by their promise, and discards futile fancies. It is the great weapon of all who wish—in industry, trade, government, religion or education—to change men's responses, either by reinforcing old and adding new ones, or by getting rid of those that are undesirable.

EDWARD L. THORNDIKE ON EDUCATIONAL MEASUREMENT

(1918)   From Edward L. Thorndike, "The Nature, Purposes, and General Methods of Measurements of Educational Products," as quoted in National Society for the Study of Education, *Seventeenth Yearbook, Part II. The Measurement of Educational Products* (Bloomington, Ill., 1918), pp. 7, 16, 18–20, 24.

Whatever exists at all exists in some amount. To know it thoroughly involves knowing its quantity as well as its quality. Education is concerned with changes in human beings; a change is a difference between two conditions; each of these conditions is known to us only by the products produced by it—things made, words spoken, acts performed, and the like. To measure any of these products means to define its amount in some way so that competent persons will know how large it is, better than they would without measurement. To measure a product well means so to define its amount that competent persons will know how large it is, with some precision, and that this knowledge may be conveniently recorded and used. This is the general *Credo* of those who, in the last decade, have been busy trying to extend and improve measurements of educational products.

We have faith that whatever people now measure crudely by mere descriptive words, helped out by the comparative and superlative forms, can be measured more precisely and conveniently if ingenuity and labor are set at the task. We have faith also that the objective products produced, rather than the inner condition of the person whence they spring, are the proper point of attack for the measurer, at least in our day and generation.

This is obviously the same general creed as that of the physicist or chemist or physiologist engaged in quantitative thinking—the same, indeed, as that of modern science in general. And, in general, the nature of educational measurements is the same as that of all scientific measurements.

In detail, however, there are notable differences. An educational product, such as a composition written, a solution of a problem in arithmetic, an answer to a question about history, a drawing of a house or the performance of an errand, is commonly a complex of many sorts of things. The task of measuring it seems more like measuring a house or an elephant than it is like measuring a length or a volume or a weight. A complete measurement of, say, a composition might include an exact definition of its spelling, its usage of words, its usage of word forms, its wit, its good sense and so on and on; and each of these might again be subdivided into a score or more of component elements.

What we do, of course, is to make not such a complete measurement of the total fact, but to measure the amount of some feature, *e.g.*, the general merit of the composition or the richness of its vocabulary, just as physical science does not measure the elephant, but his height, or his weight, or his health, or his strength of pull. Every measurement represents a highly partial and abstract treatment of the product. This is not understood by some of our critics who object to tests and scales because of their limited point of view. The critic's real point should be that an educational product commonly invites hundreds of measurements, as we all well know. It should be noted also that single measurements are still in a sense complex, being comparable to volume, wattage or the opsonic index, rather than to length, weight or temperature.

In the second place, the zeros of the scales for the educational measures and the equivalence of their units are only imperfectly known. As a consequence, we can add, subtract, multiply and divide educational quantities with much less surety and precision than is desirable. Indeed, in any given case, the sense in which one educational product is twice as good or as desirable as another, or in which one task is twice as hard as another, or in which one improvement is twice as great as another, is likely to be a rather intricate and subtle matter, involving presuppositions which must be kept in mind in any inferences from the comparison.

In some cases so little is known of units of amount that we do not even try to equate distances along the scale, but simply express relative size in terms of arbitrarily chosen units and reference points. This is the case, for example, with the most commonly used measurement in psychology and education, that due to applying the Binet-Simon tests.

Nobody need be disturbed at these unfavorable contrasts between measurements of educational products and measurements of mass, density, veolocity, temperature, quantity of electricity, and the like. The zero of temperature was located only a few years ago, and the equality of the units of the temperature-scale rests upon rather intricate and subtle presuppositions. At least, I venture to assert that not one in four of, say, the judges of the supreme court, bishops of our churches, and governors of our states could tell clearly and adequately what these presuppositions are. Our measurements of educational products would not at present be entirely safe grounds on which to extol or condemn a system of teaching reading or arithmetic, but many of them are far superior to the measurements whereby our courts of law decide that one trademark is an infringement on another. . . .

The purpose of measurements of educational products is in general to provide somebody with the knowledge that he needs of the amount of some thing, difference or relation. The "somebody" may be a scientific worker, a superintendent of schools, a teacher, a parent or a pupil. He may need a very precise or only an approximate measure, according to the magnitude of the difference which he has to determine. He may need it for guidance in many different sorts of decisions and actions.

Some of the most notable uses concern the values of studies in terms of the changes produced by them, the effects of different methods of teaching, and the effects of various features of a school system, such as the salary scale, the length of the school day and year, the system of examining and promoting pupils, or the size of class. There are many problems under each of these heads, and each of these problems is multifarious according to the nature, age, home life and the like of the pupils, and according to the general constitution of the educational enterprise, some small feature of which is being studied.

Another important group of uses concerns inventories of the achievements of certain total educational enterprises such as our educational surveys must become if they are to carry authority with scientific men. The total educational enterprise may be the work of a teacher, of a school, of an orphanage, of a prison, of a system of schools, or the like.

Another important group of uses centers around the problem of giving the individual pupil the information about his own achievement and improvement which he needs as a motive and a guide. It is interesting to note that the first of the newer educational scales, which was expected to be used chiefly by scientific investigators of the teaching of handwriting, now hangs on the wall of thousands of classrooms as a means for pupils to measure themselves. There are many other purposes, and important ones, such as the detection and removal of gross prejudices on the part of teachers in their own evaluations of certain educational aims and products. These, however, cannot be described here.

The superintendents, supervisors, principals and teachers directly in charge of educational affairs have been so appreciative of educational measurements and so sincere in their desire to have tests and scales devised which they can themselves apply, that the tendency at present is very strong to provide means of measurement which are concerned somewhat closely with school achievements, and which can be used by teachers and others with little technical training. There is also a tendency, because of this need for a large number of measurements in the case of educational problems, to try to devise tests which can be scored by persons utterly devoid of judgment concerning the products in question.

LEWIS TERMAN ON THE THEORY AND PRACTICE OF INTELLIGENCE TESTING (1916)   From Lewis M. Terman, *The Measurement of Intelligence* (Boston, 1916), pp. 19–21, 36–40, 65–68, 72–73, 114–16, 140–41.

Another important use of intelligence tests is in the study of the factors which influence mental development. It is desirable that we should be able to guard the child against influences which affect mental development unfavorably; but as long as these influences have not been sifted, weighed, and measured, we have nothing but conjecture on which to base our efforts in this direction.

When we search the literature of child hygiene for reliable evidence as to the injurious effects upon mental ability of malnutrition, decayed teeth, obstructed breathing, reduced sleep, bad ventilation, insufficient exercise, etc., we are met by endless assertion painfully unsupported by demonstrated fact. We have, indeed, very little exact knowledge regarding the mental effects of any of the facts just mentioned. When standardized mental tests have come into more general use, such influences will be easy to detect wherever they are really present.

Again, the most important question of heredity is that regarding the inheritance of intelligence; but this is a problem which cannot be attacked at all without some accurate means of identifying the thing which is the object of study. Without the use of scales for measuring intelligence we can give no better answer as to the essential difference between a genius and a fool than is to be found in legend and fiction.

Applying this to school children, it means that without such tests we cannot know to what extent a child's mental performances are determined by environment and to what extent by heredity. Is the place of the so-called lower classes in the social and industrial scale the result of their inferior native endowment, or is their apparent inferiority merely a result of their inferior home and school training? Is genius more common among children of the educated classes than among the children of the ignorant and poor? Are the inferior races really inferior, or are they merely unfortunate in their lack of opportunity to learn?

Only intelligence tests can answer these questions and grade the raw material with which education works. Without them we can never distinguish the results of our educational efforts with a given child from the influence of the child's original endowment. Such tests would have told us, for example, whether the much-discussed "wonder children," such as the Sidis and Wiener boys and the Stoner girl, owe their precocious intellectual prowess to superior training (as their parents believe) or to superior native ability. The supposed effects upon mental development of new methods of mind training, which are exploited so confidently from time to time (e.g., the Montessori method and the various systems of sensory and motor training for the feeble-minded), will have to be checked up by the same kind of scientific measurement.

In all these fields intelligence tests are certain to play an ever-increasing role. With the exception of moral character, there is nothing as significant for a child's future as his grade of intelligence. Even health itself is likely to have less influence in determining success in life. Although strength and swiftness have always had great survival value among the lower animals, these characteristics have long since lost their supremacy in man's struggle for existence. For us the rule of brawn has been broken, and intelligence has become the decisive factor in success. Schools, railroads, factories, and the largest commercial concerns may be successfully managed by persons who are physically weak or even sickly. One who has intelligence constantly measures opportunities against his own strength or weakness and adjusts himself to conditions by following those leads which promise most toward the realization of his individual possibilities.

All classes of intellects, the weakest as well as the strongest, will profit by the application of their talents to tasks which are consonant with their ability. When we have learned the lessons which intelligence tests have to teach, we shall no longer blame mentally defective workmen for their industrial inefficiency, punish weak-minded children because of their inability to learn, or imprison and hang mentally defective criminals because they lacked the intelligence to appreciate the ordinary codes of social conduct.

*　　*　　*

The Binet scale is made up of an extended series of tests in the nature of "stunts," or problems, success in which demands the exercise of intelligence. As left by Binet, the scale consists of 54 tests, so graded in difficulty that the easiest lie well within the range of normal 3-year-old children, while the hardest tax the intelligence of the average adult. The problems are designed primarily to test native intelligence, not school knowledge or home training. They try to answer the question, "How intelligent is this child?" How much the child has learned is of significance only in so far as it throws light on his ability to learn more.

Binet fully appreciated the fact that intelligence is not homogeneous, that it has many aspects, and that no one kind of test will display it adequately. He therefore assembled for his intelligence scale tests of many different types, some of them designed to display differences of memory, others differences in power to reason, ability to compare, power of comprehension, time orientation, facility in the use of number concepts, power to combine ideas into a meaningful whole, the maturity of apperception, wealth of ideas, knowledge of common objects, etc.

The tests were arranged in order of difficulty, as found by trying them upon some 200 normal children of different ages from 3 to 15 years. It was found, for illustration, that a certain test was passed by only a very small proportion of the younger children, say the 5-year-olds, and that the number passing this test increased rapidly in the succeeding years until by the age of 7 or 8 years, let us say, practically all the children were successful. If, in our supposed case, the test was passed by about two thirds to three fourths of the normal children aged 7 years, it was considered by Binet a test of 7-year intelligence. In like manner, a test passed by 65 to 75 per cent of the normal 9-year-olds was considered a test of 9-year intelligence, and so on. By trying out many different tests in this way it was possible to secure five tests to represent each age from 3 to 10 years (excepting age 4, which has only four tests), five for age 12, five for 15, and five for adults, making 54 tests in all.

The following is the list of tests as arranged by Binet in 1911, shortly before his untimely death:—

Age 3:
    1. Points to nose, eyes, and mouth.
    2. Repeats two digits.
    3. Enumerates objects in a picture.
    4. Gives family name.
    5. Repeats a sentence of six syllables.

Age 4:
    1. Gives his sex.
    2. Names key, knife, and penny.
    3. Repeats three digits.
    4. Compares two lines.

Age 5:
    1. Compares two weights.
    2. Copies a square.
    3. Repeats a sentence of ten syllables.
    4. Counts four pennies.
    5. Unites the halves of a divided rectangle.

Age 6:
    1. Distinguishes between morning and afternoon.
    2. Defines familiar words in terms of use.
    3. Copies a diamond.
    4. Counts thirteen pennies.
    5. Distinguishes pictures of ugly and pretty faces.

Age 7:
    1. Shows right hand and left ear.
    2. Describes a picture.
    3. Executes three commissions, given simultaneously.
    4. Counts the value of six sous, three of which are double.
    5. Names four cardinal colors.

Age 8:
1. Compares two objects from memory.
2. Counts from 20 to 0.
3. Notes omissions from pictures.
4. Gives day and date.
5. Repeats five digits.

Age 9:
1. Gives change from twenty sous.
2. Defines familiar words in terms superior to use.
3. Recognizes all the pieces of money.
4. Names the months of the year, in order.
5. Answers easy "comprehension questions."

Age 10:
1. Arranges five blocks in order of weight.
2. Copies drawings from memory.
3. Criticizes absurd statements.
4. Answers difficult "comprehension questions."
5. Uses three given words in not more than two sentences.

Age 12:
1. Resists suggestion.
2. Composes one sentence containing three given words.
3. Names sixty words in three minutes.
4. Defines certain abstract words.
5. Discovers the sense of a disarranged sentence.

Age 15:
1. Repeats seven digits.
2. Finds three rhymes for a given word.
3. Repeats a sentence of twenty-six syllables.
4. Interprets pictures.
5. Interprets given facts.

Adult:
1. Solves the paper-cutting test.
2. Rearranges a triangle in imagination.
3. Gives differences between pairs of abstract terms.
4. Gives three differences between a president and a king.
5. Gives the main thought of a selection which he has heard read.

It should be emphasized that merely to name the tests in this way gives little idea of their nature and meaning, and tells nothing about Binet's method of conducting the 54 experiments. In order to use the tests intelligently it is necessary to acquaint one's self thoroughly with the purpose of each test, its correct procedure, and the psychological interpretation of different types of response.

In fairness to Binet, it should also be borne in mind that the scale of tests was only a rough approximation to the ideal which the author had set himself to realize. Had his life been spared a few years longer, he would doubtless have carried the method much nearer perfection.

By means of the Binet tests we can judge the intelligence of a given individual by comparison with standards of intellectual performance for normal children of different ages. In order to make the comparison it is only necessary to begin the examination of the subject at a point in the scale where all the tests are passed successfully, and to continue up the scale until no more successes are possible. Then we compare our subject's performances with the standard for normal children of the same age, and note the amount of acceleration or retardation.

Let us suppose the subject being tested is 9 years of age. If he goes as far in the tests as normal 9-year-old children ordinarily go, we can say that the child has a "mental age" of 9 years, which in this case is normal (our child being 9 years of age). If he goes only as far as normal 8-year-old children ordinarily go, we say that his "mental age" is 8 years. In like manner, a mentally defective child of 9 years may have a "mental age" of only 4 years, or a young genius of 9 years may have a mental age of 12 or 13 years.

An extended account of the 1000 tests on which the Stanford revision is chiefly based has been presented in a separate monograph. This chapter will include only the briefest summary of some of those results of the investigation which contribute to the intelligent use of the revision.

The question as to the manner in which intelligence is distributed is one of great practical as well as theoretical importance. One of the most vital questions which can be asked by any nation of any age is the following: "How high is the average level of intelligence among our people, and how frequent are the various grades of ability above and below the average?" With the development of standardized tests we are approaching, for the first time in history, a possible answer to this question.

Most of the earlier Binet studies, however, have thrown little light on the distribution of intelligence because of their failure to avoid the influence of accidental selection in choosing subjects for testing. The method of securing subjects for the Stanford revision makes our results on this point especially interesting. It is believed that the subjects used for this investigation were as nearly representative of average American-born children as it is possible to secure.

The intelligence quotients for these 1000 unselected children were calculated, and their distribution was plotted for the ages separately. The distribution was found fairly symmetrical at each age from 5 to 14. At 15 the range is on either side of 90 as a median, and at 16 on either side of 80 as a median. That the 15- and 16-year-olds test low is due to the fact that these children are left-over retardates and are below average in intelligence.

The I Q's were then grouped in ranges of ten. In the middle group were thrown those from 96 to 105; the ascending groups including in order the I Q's from 106 to 115, 116 to 125, etc.; correspondingly with the descending groups. . . .

The symmetry for the separate ages was hardly less marked, considering that only 80 to 120 children were tested at each age. In fact, the range, including the middle 50 per cent of I Q's, was found practically constant from 5 to 14 years. The tendency is for the middle 50 per cent to fall (approximately) between 93 and 108.

Three important conclusions are justified by the above facts:—

1. Since the frequency of the various grades of intelligence decreases *gradually* and at no point abruptly on each side of the median, it is evident that there is no definite dividing line between normality and feeble-mindedness, or between normality and genius. Psychologically, the mentally defective child does not belong to a distinct type, nor does the genius. There is no line of demarcation between either of these extremes and the so-called "normal" child. The number of mentally defective individuals in a population will depend upon the standard arbitrarily set up as to what constitutes mental deficiency. Similarly for genius. It is exactly as if we should undertake to classify all people into the three groups: abnormally tall, normally tall, and abnormally short.

2. The common opinion that extreme deviations below the median are more frequent than extreme deviations above the median seems to have no foundation in fact. Among unselected school children, at least, for every child of any given degree of deficiency there is another child as far above the average I Q as the former is below. We have shown elsewhere the serious consequences of neglect of this fact.

3. The traditional view that variability in mental traits becomes more marked during adolescence is here contradicted, as far as intelligence is concerned, for the distribution of I Qs is practically the same at each age from 5 to 14. For example, 6-year-olds differ from one another fully as much as do 14-year-olds.

*   *   *

The validity of the intelligence quotient. The facts presented above argue strongly for the validity of the I Q as an expression of a child's intelligence status. This follows necessarily from the similar nature of the distributions at the various ages. The inference is that a child's I Q, as measured by this scale, remains relatively constant. Re-tests of the same children at intervals of two to five years support the inference. Children of superior intelligence do not seem to deteriorate as they get older, nor dull children to develop average intelligence. Knowing a child's I Q, we can predict with a fair degree of accuracy the course of his later development.

The mental age of a subject is meaningless if considered apart from chronological age. It is only the ratio of retardation or acceleration to chronological age (that is, the I Q) which has significance.

It follows also that if the I Q is a valid expression of intelligence, as it seems to be, then the Binet-Simon "age-grade method" becomes transformed automatically into a "point-scale method," if one wants to use it that way. As such it is superior to any other point scale that has been proposed, because it includes a larger number of tests and its points have definite meanings.

*   *   *

Of the 1000 children, 492 were classfied by their teachers according to social class into the following five groups: *very inferior, inferior, average, superior,* and *very superior.* A comparative study was then made of the distribution of I Q's for these different groups.

The data may be summarized as follows:—

1. The median I Q for children of the superior social class is about 7 points above, and that of the inferior social class about 7 points below, the median I Q of the average social group. This means that by the age of 14 inferior class children are about one year below, and superior class children one year above, the median mental age for all classes taken together.

2. That the children of the superior social classes make a better showing in the tests is probably due, for the most part, to a superiority in original endowment. This conclusion is supported by five supplementary lines of evidence: (a) the teachers' rankings of the children according to intelligence; (b) the age-grade progress of the children; (c) the quality of the school work; (d) the comparison of older and younger children as regards the influence of social environment; and (e) the study of individual cases of bright and dull children in the same family.

3. In order to facilitate comparison, it is advisable to express the intelligence of children of all social classes in terms of the same objective scale of intelligence. This scale should be based on the median for all classes taken together.

4. As regards their responses to individual tests, our children of a given social class were not distinguishable from children of the same intelligence in any other social class.

The school work of 504 children was graded by the teachers on a scale of five grades: *very inferior, inferior, average, superior,* and *very superior.* When this grouping was compared with that made on the basis of I Q, fairly close agreement was found. However, in about one case out of ten there was rather serious disagreement; a child, for example, would be rated as doing *average* school work when his I Q would place him in the *very inferior* intelligence group.

When the data were searched for explanations of such disagreements it was found that most of them were plainly due to the failure of teachers to take into account the age of the child when grading the quality of his school work. When allowance was made for this tendency there were no disagreements which justified any serious suspicion as to the accuracy of the intelligence scale. Minor disagreements may, of course, be disregarded, since the quality of school work depends in part on other factors than intelligence, such as industry, health, regularity of attendance, quality of instruction, etc.

*   *   *

Influence of social and educational advantages. The criticism has often been made that the responses to many of the tests are so much subject to the influence of school and home environment as seriously to invalidate the scale as a whole. Some of the tests most often named in this connection are the following: Giving age and sex; naming common objects, colors, and coins; giving the value of stamps; giving date; naming the months of the year and the days of the week; distinguishing forenoon and afternoon; counting; making change; reading for memories; naming sixty words; giving definitions; finding rhymes; and constructing a sentence containing three given words.

It has in fact been found wherever comparisons have been made that children of superior social status yield a higher average mental age than children of the laboring classes. The results of Decroly and Degand and of Meumann, Stern, and Binet himself may be referred to in this connection. In the case of the Stanford investigation, also, it was found that when the unselected school children were grouped in three classes according to social status (superior, average, and inferior), the average I Q for the superior social group was 107, and that of the inferior social group 93. This is equivalent to a difference of one year in mental age with 7-year-olds, and to a difference of two years with 14-year-olds.

However, the common opinion that the child from a cultured home does better in tests solely by reason of his superior home advantages is an entirely gratuitious assumption. Practically all of the investigations which have been made of the influence of nature and nurture on mental performance agree in attributing far more to original endowment than to environment. Common observation would itself suggest that the social class to which the family belongs depends less on chance than on the parents' native qualities of intellect and character.

The results of five separate and distinct lines of inquiry based on the Stanford data agree in supporting the conclusion that the children of successful and cultured parents test higher than children from wretched and ignorant homes for the simple reason that their heredity is better. The results of this investigation are set forth in full elsewhere.[1]

*   *   *

It would, of course, be going too far to deny all possibility of environmental conditions affecting the result of an intelligence test. Certainly no one would expect that a child reared in a cage and denied all intercourse with other human beings could by any system of mental measurement test up to the level of normal children. There is, however, no reason to believe that *ordinary* differences in social environment (apart from heredity), differences such as those obtaining among unselected children attending approxmately the same general type of school in a civilized community, affects to any great extent the validity of the scale.

A crucial experiment would be to take a large number of very young children of the lower classes and, after placing them in the most favorable environment obtainable, to compare their later mental development with that of children born into the best homes. No extensive study of this kind has been made, but the writer has tested twenty orphanage children who, for the most part, had come from very inferior homes. They had been in a well-conducted orphanage for from two to several years, and had enjoyed during that time the advantages of an excellent village school. Nevertheless, all but three tested below average, ranging from 75 to 90 I Q.

The impotence of school instruction to neutralize individual differences in native endowment will be evident to any one who follows the school career of backward children. The children who are seriously retarded in school are not normal, and cannot be made normal by any refinement of educational method. As a rule, the longer the inferior child attends school, the more evident his inferiority becomes. It would hardly be reasonable, therefore, to expect that a little incidental instruction in the home would weigh very heavily against these same native differences in endowment.

*   *   *

As elsewhere explained, the mental age alone does not tell us what we want to

[1] See *The Stanford Revision and Extension of the Binet-Simon Measuring Scale of Intelligence.* (Warwick and York, 1916.)

know about a child's intelligence status. The significance of a given number of years of retardation or acceleration depends upon the age of the child. A 3-year-old child who is retarded one year is ordinarily feeble-minded; a 10-year-old retarded one year is only a little below normal. The child who at 3 years of age is retarded one year will probably be retarded two years at the age of 6, three years at the age of 9, and four years at the age of 12.

What we want to know, therefore, is the ratio existing between mental age and real age. This is the intelligence quotient, or I Q. To find it we simply divide mental age (expressed in years and months) by real age (also expressed in years and months). The process is easier if we express each age in terms of months alone before dividing. The division can, of course, be performed almost instantaneously and with much less danger of error by the use of a slide rule or a division table. One who has to calculate many intelligence quotients should by all means use some kind of mechanical help.

Native intelligence, in so far as it can be measured by tests now available, appears to improve but little after the age of 15 or 16 years. It follows that in calculating the I Q of an adult subject, it will be necessary to disregard the years he has lived beyond the point where intelligence attains its final development.

Although the location of this point is not exactly known, it will be sufficiently accurate for our purpose to assume its location at 16 years. Accordingly, any person over 16 years of age, however old, is for purposes of calculating I Q considered to be just 16 years old. If a youth of 18 and a man of 60 years both have a mental age of 12 years, the I Q in each case is $12 \div 16$, or .75.

The significance of various values of the I Q is set forth elsewhere. Here it need only be repeated that 100 I Q means exactly average intelligence; that nearly all who are below 70 or 75 I Q are feeble-minded; and that the child of 125 I Q is about as much above the average as the high-grade feeble-minded individual is below the average. For ordinary purposes all who fall between 95 and 105 I Q may be considered as average in intelligence.

PAUL HANUS ON EFFICIENCY IN SCHOOL MANAGEMENT (1913) From Paul Hanus, "Improving School Systems by Scientific Management—Underlying Principles," National Education Association *Journal of Proceedings and Addresses* (Ann Arbor, Mich., 1913), pp. 248–49, 253–56, 259.

The efficient management of a public-school system depends on the following conditions:

1. A clear conception on the part of all concerned with its work of the purposes for which the school system exists—of its aims.

2. A clear conception of the difference between the functions of the board of education and those of its staff, and actual differentiation between them in practice; i.e., centralization of authority and responsibility for: (A) effective lay control in the board; (B) business and professional management in the board's staff of employees.

3. Complete accountability of the board to the people for the work done and the money expended under its direction.

4. A general manager and executive for the whole enterprise appointed by the

board, whose authority is commensurate with his responsibility—the city superintendent of schools.

5. A competent staff of employees for the educational activities and for the business affairs of the school system directly responsible to the general manager.

6. Complete accountability of the general manager and thru him of the staff to the board of education for the proper performance of the duties with which they are charged.

7. Habitual and well-organized self-examination within the school system; including adequate objective appraisal by the staff of results achieved, and well-conducted experiments to confirm or refute educational opinion within and without the school system.

8. Co-operation under leadership thruout the school system itself, and of the school system and the community.

* * *

Accountability [of the local board] in respect to the educational affairs of the school system covers: (1) adequate provision for the educational needs of the community . . . and (2) the success actually and progressively achieved by the school system in educating all the children of the city in accordance with their capacities and needs. The success is measured by its ability to hold all children exclusive of the mentally defective in elementary schools, vocational schools, and high schools, beyond the upper limit of the compulsory attendance age; the proportion of such pupils of normal age completing or failing to complete a course of study in these schools; the efficiency of the compulsory attendance service in preventing as well as curing irregularity of attendance and truancy; and its success in discovering, segregating, grading, and caring for mentally defective children of school age.

Accountability, both financial and educational, cannot be satisfactorily discharged without brief, compact, adequate, and perfectly lucid statistical summaries of the facts reported on. That such statistical summaries are worthless unless they are truthful and easily interpreted not only by members of the board but also by any intelligent person who considers them seriously goes without saying. That school statistics now often conceal rather than reveal the facts is a serious handicap to efficient educational management. That school statistics, like other statistics, may be misused by designing persons is also true. Nevertheless accurate and readily interpretable school statistics constitute one of the most valuable means of self-examination a school system can use; and self-examination with a view to learning and setting forth the truth is a very important step toward the progressive improvement of school systems, i.e., toward efficient management.

Finally, effective lay control by the board of education requires the complete independence of the board of education from the city government.

* * *

Efficient management of the school system requires, as we have seen, the centralization of responsibility for all executive details, including professional management, in the staff, with the city superintendent at the head as general manager. Such executive and professional management requires:

Constant, alert, and courageous endeavor to secure for the people the education their children should have, i.e., *to secure the schools needed for the appropriate education of all the children.*

Adequate and appropriate means of determining the qualifications of well-trained and otherwise satisfactory workers for the educational staff, and for the business staff of the school system.

The appointment of duly qualified members of the staff thru the general manager, and their assignment to duty, including transfers, by him. No preference should be shown for home candidates as such in any appointments.

Promoting the progressive usefulness of the staff, and insuring their tenure of office during efficiency and good behavior, and removing unsatisfactory members from the service.

Appropriate promotion of members of the staff to posts of increased responsibility and emolument. But such appointments should not be limited to persons already members of the staff.

Retiring satisfactory members of the staff when they become disabled or superannuated, with suitable retiring allowances.

Organizing the staff for the performance of the several functions to be discharged.

Supervising the performance of these functions, and reporting thereon to the board.

Promoting co-operation under leadership thruout the school system itself, as well as promoting co-operation of the school system with the community.

Hence, as general manager of the board's affairs, it is the duty of the city superintendent, with the help of the staff: (a) To show the board of education what schools and how many of each kind are required and where they should be built to realize the educational aims for which the school system exists. The people want good schools, but not being technically conversant with the problems involved cannot themselves plan the details of such schools; nor do they know what material equipment—buildings, grounds, and teaching apparatus—the schools require, nor where such schools should be located. (b) To secure a properly qualified supervisory force for the organization, administration, and supervision of the schools. (c) To secure an efficient teaching corps for all the schools; and to recommend the salaries to be paid them, together with the conditions for tenure, promotion, and retirement with or without retiring allowances. (d) To formulate courses of study for the several schools, together with suggestions as to methods of teaching. (e) To select textbooks, apparatus, and all other teaching resources. (f) To define standards of achievement as to quality and quantity of work done by pupils in harmony with varying individual and local needs thruout the school system. (g) To define similar standards of achievement for the work done by teachers and supervisory offiers. (h) To carry on habitual, well-organized self-examination within the school system, by means of (1) carefully collected and properly organized educational statistics showing progressively what educational results are actually achieved in every branch of the service; (2) investigation involving experimental verification or refutation of educational opinion within and without the school system, or at least a search for the method of such objective appraisal of educational opinion and of the results achieved; and (3) a system of office records for the educational affairs of the school system that can be made to yield to the staff, to the board, and to the public, truthful, clear, prompt, and adequate information on any aspect of the work—to yield this information at any time, but especially in the annual report of the superintendent and the board. (i) To secure a staff of properly qualified officers and employees for the business affairs of the school system, i.e., a staff to purchase sites, build buildings, and equip them and care for them properly when built; to purchase all kinds of supplies and to secure their prompt distribution to the schools, and an adequate and properly qualified office force. (j) To provide a system of records and accounts for the business affairs of the school system as for its educational affairs.

*   *   *

We have found the principles of efficient management of a school system to be:

A clear conception of the purposes for which the school system exists—the work it has to do.

An equally clear conception on the part of all concerned with this work of the nature, scope, and limits of each branch of the service, i.e., of the board, and the staff.

Centralization of authority and responsibility for effective lay control in the board; and for professional and business management in the staff.

Complete accountability of the staff to the board and of the board to the people.

Habitual, well-organized self-examination to determine the results actually achieved, including experimental verification or refutation of educational opinion within and without the school system.

A system of clear, adequate, incontestable, and accessible records of the educational results progressively achieved, for the information of the staff, the board, and the public.

A similar system of financial records or accounts for the same purpose.

Co-operation thruout the school system, under the leadership of the superintendent and the supervisory staff, in both the professional and the business affairs; co-operation of these branches of the service with each other and with the teachers; and co-operation of the community with the school system.

J. FRANKLIN BOBBITT ON COST-ACCOUNTING IN EDUCATION
(1915) From J. Franklin Bobbitt, "High-School Costs," *School Review*, vol. XXIII, pp. 505–6.

Accurate cost-accounting lies at the foundation of all successful business management. In railroad administration, for example, it is known that under usual normal conditions locomotive repair-cost should average about six cents per mile-run; lubricating oils should cost about eighteen cents per hundred miles for passenger locomotives, and about twenty-five cents for freight locomotives; and so on for each item involved in the entire management. With these cost-standards at hand, derived from wide general practice, if a railroad manager finds at the end of the year that locomotive repairs average fifteen cents per mile-run, then it is quite evident upon the surface that something is wrong somewhere. The railroad is paying too high wages to labor; it is getting too little labor for the amount expended; its labor force is working under adverse conditions; there is graft in the repair department; or the entire outfit of locomotives is in a sad state of depreciation. When the cost runs so high above standard, something needs to be investigated, and either shown to be the result of unusual conditions, or corrected. If, on the other hand, the repair-cost is running at three cents per mile on an average, and if unusual conditions do not exist, then it appears probable that locomotives are being left to depreciate too rapidly. Cost-accounting is thus seen to be one method of diagnosing the situation and locating irregularities of management.

In operating a high-school, expenditures need to be made for many things— general administration, supervision, instruction, fuel, janitors, light, power, library, etc. For each of these, standard unit-costs are needed for judging the efficiency of the management. If it is known, for example, that satisfactory instruction in high-school English can be had for fifty dollars per thousand student-hours, and that this price represents the norm of practice, then those responsible for high-school management have a standard of judgment that can be used for measuring the efficiency of their practices. If instruction in this subject is costing them $75 per 1,000 student-hours, and they are aiming at results of only the usual sort, it is evident that they are wasting money, and that administrative adjustments need to be made. If they are getting this commodity for $30 per thousand student-hours, then it is probable that they are practicing so great an economy as seriously to injure the quality of the work.

There can be nothing final about such standards of practice; and they need to be set up anew each year. They afford a fact-basis of judgment, however, that is superior to mere arbitrary opinions as to what ought to be invested in the thing in question.

REPORT OF THE COMMITTEE ON ECONOMY OF TIME ON THE MINIMUM ESSENTIALS IN ELEMENTARY SCHOOL SUBJECTS

(1915)   From H. B. Wilson, "Introduction." National Society for the Study of Education, *Fourteenth Yearbook: Part I, Minimum Essentials In Elementary School Subjects,* (Chicago, 1915,) pp. 9–16.

This report to the National Department of Superintendence by its committee on Economy of Time in Elementary and Secondary Education, made with the assistance of a number of co-operating investigators, constitutes the fourth large effort within the last two decades by some branch of the National Education Association to examine and improve the curriculum of the public schools. Attention was first directed to the high-school curriculum in the report of the Committee of Ten. The report of the Committee of Fifteen was concerned with the training of teachers and the organization of city schools, but it also gave large attention to the correlation of the studies of the elementary schools. The report of the Committee of Twelve on Rural Schools, in its treatment of instruction and discipline, discussed the course of study, accepting the report of the Committee of Fifteen on the several branches of the course of study.

The present report on the minimum essentials in certain subjects of the elementary curriculum is one result of an effort to develop a program for economizing time in public-school education. The attack on this large problem was begun in the National Council of Education in 1903 under the leadership of

President Emeritus James H. Baker[1] The most significant result thus far of the work of the Committee from the Council is the report on "Economy of Time in Education," published in 1913 as *Bulletin 38* of the Bureau of Education. Upon the initiative of the Council committee the Department of Superintendence authorized the appointment of a committee of five at the meeting of the Department in Mobile in February, 1911. The earlier efforts of this committee were directed toward arriving at an understanding of the meaning and scope of the problem and in enlisting the co-operation of those who can aid in a fundamental way in its solution.

Preliminary reports defining in outline form the scope of the problem and the possible lines of attack in its solution were made at the meetings of the Department in St. Louis in 1912 and in Philadelphia in 1913. At the meeting of the Department one year ago in Richmond, two typical reports on English and arithmetic were presented as illustrative of the type of studies which the committee had come to believe should be made in all subjects, in the interest of determining the proper content for the subjects of study in the elementary curriculum. The Department responded to the presentation of these reports and to the projected plan for treating all subjects in the elementary curriculum similarly most enthusiastically by recommending that an appropriation sufficient to defray the expenses of such a piece of work be made, and guaranteeing the provision of the same in case the Executive Committee of the National Education Association found it impossible to appropriate the money from funds at its disposal.

While the Department committee was made responsible by a resolution adopted at the meeting of the Department in St. Louis in 1912 for studying possible ways of economizing time both in the elementary and in secondary schools, our attention thus far has been mainly directed, and in this report is wholly directed, to the study of elementary-school problems, reserving until a later time the study of such problems in the secondary field as are vitally related.

In the report referred to above the Council Committee on Economy of Time in Education brought forcibly to the attention of the country the desirability of shortening the period of formal education. The following proposals pertinent to the purposes of the Department Committee on Economy of Time in Education are quoted . . .

1. The contemporary judgment is that the period of general education should be shortened at least two years.

4. In the elementary and secondary period, economy through selection, elimination, vital methods, relation to modern life, would yield much better results and little or nothing would be lost by the proposed change in time.

8. To define the form of discussion, the following divisions of the entire period of general and special education are proposed:

Elementary education...6–12
Secondary education (2 divisions—4 years and 2 years) 12-18

[1] The chief initial impetus toward the movement for economizing time in education, probably antedating somewhat the attack on the problem by the National Council, was given by the late President William R. Harper, of the University of Chicago, before a notable gathering at the University in the autumn of 1902, where he read a brief paper proposing a scheme for saving two years of time in the completion of a college course. Participating in this discussion were the late Superintendent Louis Soldan, of St. Louis, and Professor John Dewey. See "Shortening the Years of Elementary Schooling," by John Dewey, *School Review*, II, 17, January, 1903.

College .... 18–20 or 16–20
University (graduate school and professional schools) 20–24

Preceding their statement of conclusions, the committee said:

> When by economy—this does not mean more cramming, but less—as much can be accomplished in the elementary and secondary schools and in the first two years of college as is now done in the full sixteen years, the last two years of college can count toward graduate and professional degrees and two years in the whole period can be saved.

Upon the general thesis that the period of formal education should be shortened there appears to be fairly general agreement. Where and how this shortening is to take place is, however, not so generally agreed upon. The committee of the Council believes that the greatest waste in education is in the elementary schools and has recommended that the period of elementary education be reduced to six years, maintaining that the essential knowledge, habits, ideals, and attitudes for individual and social needs can be and should be acquired in that time. This attitude on the part of the Council was evidenced in the resolution proposed by Professor Suzzallo of the committee of the Council in closing his address before the meeting of the Department of Superintendence at Mobile, as follows:

> The main requirement at this point in our progress is to investigate the waste in the elementary schools and to make definite proposals for eliminating the archaic and least useful materials of the course of study and to propose more economic methods of teaching. To this end I move that the Department of Superintendence appoint a committee of five on Economy of Time in Elementary Education, this committee of five to co-operate with the general Committee on Economy of Time in Education.

The same attitude is further indicated in the following quotations from the report of the Council:

> We approach now the question of saving time in the elementary period or of accomplishing more within the time. . . . The committee agrees that there is much waste in elementary education and that the elementary period should be from six to twelve. Nearly all our correspondents are emphatic regarding waste and the importance of shortening the entire period of general education. Saving of time can be made in the following ways:
>
> 1. The principle of selection is, first: Choose the most important subjects and the most important topics; make a distinction between first-rate facts and principles and tenth-rate; prune thoroughly, stick to the elements of a subject; do not try to teach everything that is good; confine the period of elementary education to mastering the tools of education. This does not prevent inspirational work, which is a demand on the skill of the teacher rather than on time. A great secret of education is to accomplish a maximum of training with a minimum of material. This is especially true of formal subjects; it is true also of inspirational subjects, in that after a general survey of the field emphasis should be placed upon a few selected points. Under the conditions above enumerated the formal elementary period can end in six years.

The committee of the National Department of Superintendence is not yet committed to the thesis that it is necessary or desirable to shorten the period of elementary education. It does, however, agree with the Council committee that there is great waste in elementary education and that either the period should be shortened or that more should be accomplished in the' time allotted, or both. Economy of time in elementary education may mean either a shortening of the period of formal education or the more economical use of the time required, whatever it may be, in order that the maximum accomplishment in knowledge and skill may result. It is the latter conception of educational economy that is the more fundamental. The significant problem, then, is not what can be done to accomplish in six years what now requires eight years, but what can be done in the elementary schools of our democracy to secure that degree of accomplishment in knowledge, character, and skill essential to equip those who finish the elementary schools with an intense desire and the training necessary to make the greatest possible additional personal growth and with the disposition and ability to contribute to the welfare of society. Society is still depending primarily upon the elementary schools to furnish not only the tools of knowledge but also those facts, concepts, and principles essential in a democracy to common discussion and to the collective consideration of common problems. The training of the elementary schools must supply the requisite basis for "mutual intercourse, mutual understanding, and mutual sympathy," which are absolutely essential to a successful democracy. It is from the point of view of insuring that the schools supply this common basis for conference and intercourse that the determination of the indispensable content for each subject of study is paramount significance. We must determine what the absolute essentials are in the equipment of our citizenship that they may discuss and confer on a sufficiently high level to insure the progressive evolution of our democratic society. By concentrating our teaching efforts upon these essentials, their thorough teaching and permanent fixation will be insured in the minimum time.

Our first objective, therefore, is not merely time gain. If gain is accomplished, it must issue because the efficiency can be secured in less time. Saving of time is undoubtedly desirable if it can be secured without sacrificing efficiency. The saving of time will not only result in less cost to the taxpayers for the maintenance of the public schools but it will likewise result in increasing the earning power of those who graduate from these schools, owing to their earlier entrance into remunerative occupations.

Economy in time under either conception may be attained (1) by the elimination of nonessential subjects or subject-matter and by including only such additional significant material as is clearly vital in realizing the ends of elementary education; (2) by the improvement in methods of teaching and learning; (3) by the organization of the whole school system and the course of study so that each part may be taken at the optimal time in the child's development. In view of the objectives in appointing the committee from the Department of Superintendence, attention is first devoted to (1) in this report. For logical reasons also (1) should be treated first.

The ideally constructed course of study for the elementary schools in the interest of providing adequate general education is one stripped of all content not essential to the needs of modern life and organized so as to harmonize with the child's growth in capacity and experience. Its presentation with due regard to the most efficient methods of teaching and learning must be assumed, of course, if it is to secure the largest possible results. With reference to this task Professor Dewey says the problem is "selection of the kind, variety, and due proportion of subjects answering most definitely to the dominant needs and powers of presentation that will cause the selected material to enter vitally into growth."[1] Again he says: "The selection and grading of material in the course of study must be done with reference to the proper nutrition of the dominant directions of activity in a given period. The difficulty is in seeing just what materials and methods, in what proportion and arrangement, are available and helpful at a given time."[2]

[1] See Dewey "The Psychology of the Elementary Curriculum" in *The School and the Child*.
[2] *Op. cit.*

Before the question can be convincingly answered whether the period of elementary education can be shortened, it would seem necessary to determine the minimum standard curriculum selected and organized to meet fully the general aims or purposes of elementary education, specifying a minimum essential content for each subject of this standard curriculum. Whether the aims of the elementary school can be satisfactorily realized in six years or not, or in what time they can be realized, can be discovered only after such a determination has been made. In other words, we must work out a minimum content for each subject of study, holding in mind those standards of attainment which good teaching should seek to approximate. With this tentatively accomplished, we shall have a basis for determining the standard time required for executing such a course of study.

Whatever time may ultimately prove to be necessary, the fundamental questions are: (1) What subjects are essential constituents of the elementary curriculum? (2) What is the absolutely essential content in each subject? It is the second question on which the Department committee and the co-operating investigators have been working during the past year. The results of these investigations follow in this Yearbook. It is perhaps unnecessary to point out what a careful reading will render evident, that in the time available it was impossible to make the reports more than partial and tentative. Not only do the results submitted need the testing of use and criticism, but much more work remains to be done.

The formulation of a minimum essential content for any school subject is a complex problem and is beset with theoretical and practical difficulties. Various methods of procedure may be adopted: (1) An examination may be made of representative curricula the country over to determine the consensus of experience and practice as to the topics to be included, time to be alloted, etc. (2) Subject-matter to be included and time allotments may be determined on the basis of judgments of superintendents, principals, teachers, subject-matter experts, and students of education. (3) An examination may be made of progressive experiments designed to secure economy in time either by elimination or by improvements in methods and organization. (4) Each part or each subject may be subjected to some more fundamental educational criteria or tests of inclusion, emphasis, or exclusion. Until there are definitely established and accepted standards of attainment based on individual capacities and social needs, the determination or minimum essentials by any method is a difficult problem.

Is it possible to arrive at a definition of the function of the elementary school which will be generally accepted? And more especially, is it possible to derive from such a definition acceptable fundamental principles which may guide in determining the minimum essentials in school subjects? Apparently our leaders in education agree that the function of the elementary school is to provide those educational opportunities necessary to insure, with the assistance of the other institutions of society, the acquisition on the part of elementary-school children of those habits, skills, knowledges, ideals, and prejudices which must be made the common property of all, that each may be an efficient member of a progressive democratic society, possessing the power of self-support and self-direction, the capacity and disposition for co-operative effort, and, if possible, the ability to direct others in positions of responsibility requiring administrative capacity.

The selection of subject-matter for any given period must be made with reference to the capacities and interests of children at this period and with reference to common social needs. Ultimately, the content and emphasis in each subject of study is determined by society's judgement in reference to its needs, while the organization of this content and the methods which shall be employed in teaching children are determined by the nature, ability, and interests of the children to be taught.

Two general principles of inclusion of subject-matter may therefore be formulated thus: (1) Whatever is included in any subject for any age must be reasonably comprehensible by children of that age. (2) Whatever is included must minister to the social needs common to ordinary American children. Corresponding principles of elimination may be formulated thus: (1) Subject-matter too difficult for the majority of normal children without undue expenditure of time and energy must be excluded. (2) Subject-matter that is not essential for at least the majority of children must be excluded. The fixing of minimum essentials upon any other basis than the abilities and social needs of the majority of children leads at once into difficulties. A curriculum or a content for any subject based on the ability and needs common to all normal children gives an impossible low standard. One based on the capacities and needs of 75 per cent of children is likewise too low to be useful. On the other hand, a minimum standard which is adjusted to the capacities of but 50 per cent of children is a misnomer.

The only escape from the dilemma is a graduated series of essentials progressing from the skills and abilities necessary for all normal children up through those that are desirable for all normal children, if they can be attained. The great variability in individual capacities and the possibly equally great variability in individual needs for effective social adjustment make any other basis of selection impossible.

If it is impossible to discover from educational theory fundamental tests for exclusion or inclusion, we are driven to the method of determining minimum essentials on the basis of the best current practices and experimentation which give satisfactory results. Those results are satisfactory which meet adequately the common needs of life in society. This in the main is the method employed in the investigations upon which the following reports in the Yearbook are based.

ESTABLISHMENT OF THE NATIONAL SOCIETY FOR THE PROMOTION OF INDUSTRIAL EDUCATION (1906)   From National Society for the Promotion of Industrial Education, *Bulletin No. 1* (New York, 1907), pp. 13–14.

A meeting to effect a permanent organization of the Society for the Promotion of Industrial Education was called to order, Dr. James P. Haney, presiding, at four p. m., on Friday, November 16th, at Cooper Union. There were present about 250 persons, among whom were prominent business men and educators from the cities of New York, Chicago, Boston, Philadelphia, Springfield, Ill.; Milwaukee; Menominee, Wis.; Buffalo; Cincinnati, Raleigh, N. C. Many of the smaller cities of New England and the Middle East were also represented.

Brief remarks as to the general projects of the Society were called for by the Chairman, and responded to by Mr. Keyes of Hartford, Dr. MacAlister of Philadelphia, Mr. Stout of Menominee, President Winston of Raleigh, Mr. Campbell of Buffalo, Mr. Geier of Cincinnati, Miss Howes of Boston and Mrs. Woolman of New York. Each of the speakers emphasized the value of an organization that should unite the various advocates of industrial training and provide opportunities for discussion and propaganda.

A suggested form of constitution was then submitted in typewritten form to the meeting and its consideration taken up by sections. After some discussion and certain modifications and amendments, the document herein printed was adopted as a whole. A resolution was adopted that the Board of Managers be instructed to take steps to bring about the incorporation of the Society under the laws of the State of New York, if this were found to be practicable. A further resolution provided that all persons present at the organization meeting who signed application blanks should be charter members of the Society. The Executive Committee was, in addition, authorized to make such verbal changes in the constitution as it should deem proper, without making changes in the meaning of the document.

Immediately after the adoption of the section of the constitution, relating to officers, a nominating committee was appointed by the chair, consisting of Messrs. C. F. Warner, Louis Rouillion and F. E. Mathewson. This committee, after the adoption of the constitution as a whole, submitted the following nominations:

President, Dr. Henry S. Pritchett.

Vice-President, Mr. M. W. Alexander.

Treasurer, Mr. V. Everit Macy.

Members of the Board of Managers for *three years*—Mr. M. P. Higgins, Mr. John Mitchell, Prof. C. R. Richards, Dr. James P. Haney, Mr. Robert A. Woods, Mr. Charles F. Warner, Mr. Anthony Ittner, Mrs. Mary Morton Kehew, Mr. W. F. Pfahler.

Members of Board of Managers for *two years*—Mr. F. A. Vanderlip, Mr. Fred W. Sivyer, Mr. Charles A. Moore, Dr. Elmer E. Brown, Mr. Leslie W. Miller, Mr. F. J. McNulty, Miss Jane Addams, Mr. Louis Rouillion, Mr. Walter M. Wood.

Members of Board of Managers for *one year*—Mr. Frederick P. Fish, Mr. Wm. D. Huber, Mr. James P. Munroe, Mr. Fred J. Miller, Mrs. B. B. Munford, Mr. W. W. Atterbury, Mr. E .P. Bullard, Jr.; Mr. J. Ernest G. Yalden, Mr. Henry Bruere.

A motion was passed instructing the Secretary to cast one ballot for this list of nominations. This was done and the persons named were declared elected to the respective offices.[1]

A motion was made and adopted that Prof. C. R. Richards be requested to serve as acting secretary for the Society until the meeting of the Board of Managers. The meeting then adjourned.

At 8 o'clock on the evening of the same day, a general meeting was held in the assembly hall of Cooper Union. President Nicholas Murray Butler of Columbia University presided in the absence of Dr. Henry S. Pritchett, President-elect of the Society. Dr. Butler was introduced by Mr. Milton P. Higgins, president of the Committee on Organization.

[1] Owing to their inability to serve, certain members elect of the Board of Managers declined office. The vacancies so created were later filled by the Board of Managers.

ORGANIZED LABOR ON INDUSTRIAL EDUCATION (1915)   From Samuel Gompers, "Industrial Education and the American Federation of Labor," Emily Robinson, ed., *Vocational Education* (New York, 1921), pp. 159–62.

An argument, I take it, is not required of me in support of industrial education, nor any exposition of the purposes or ideals of industrial education. You know what industrial education is and what are its purposes and ideals. The question in your minds is perhaps with reference to myself as a representative of organized labor. Do I know what industrial education is, and what are its purposes and ideals? But as my personal knowledge is of very little consequence to anyone, except as a sort of reflex of the knowledge of the millions of workers, the question is, in fact, does organized labor understand what industrial education is, and what are its purposes and ideals? Finally, if it does understand these purposes and ideals, does it approve of them? And will it cooperate sincerely in the development of tried and proven rational schemes of industrial education?

A great part of my life and energy has been devoted to combating wrong-headed notions about the attitude of organized labor with reference to every sort of social and economic question. These questions have increased in number and in variety with the development of industrial civilization. The need for efficient industrial education for our boys and girls is now more urgent than ever before. Nor is the need of educational training for greater efficiency confined to the factory or the shops; it is manifest in the home life, and in demands for instruction in domestic economy. The factory system and modern industrial organization have resulted in such high specialization that only what have been referred to tonight as the tag-ends of industry have been left to women in the homes, and in modern industrial establishments the subdivision of labor has gone on to such a degree that workers perform the same set task a thousand, or ten thousand, or a hundred thousand times a day. The same task is automatically repeated again and again without knowledge of its relation to the rest of the industry for the sole purpose of gaining time and speed. I repeat that if ever industrial education was essential it is essential today. We cannot turn back the wheels of industry, but we can make the knowledge and the effectiveness of the workers such that they will have some comprehension of the entire article produced and of every branch of the production.

In the work I have sometimes felt that the presumption is always against labor—that it is always assumed as a matter of course that labor is by a sort of "natural depravity" and strange blindness, opposed to everything, including everything that is for its own interest. Sometimes it is assumed that this opposition is due to pernicious temperament on the part of labor leaders, and sometimes that it is due to simple ignorance and incapacity to understand complex social conditions. The workers are essentially honest and sincere, and let me assure you, the degree of their ignorance is not so great as the presumptuous and supercilious often assume it to be.

It may be difficult to cram into twenty minutes' time all that may be necessary to say with reference to the attitude of organized labor toward industrial education, but I shall endeavor to comply with the limit set.

You should know that organized labor does not oppose the development of industrial education in the public schools. Indeed, that would not at all fairly indicate the attitude of organized labor. I say to you that the organizations constituting the American Federation of Labor have been for years engaged in the work of systematically providing industrial education to their members. This instruction has been given thru the medium of the trade union journal and schools established and maintained by them. Organized labor, I repeat, is not opposed to industrial education. It is eager to cooperate actively in instituting industrial education in our public schools. The workingman has too little time, and can therefore take but little interest in any other sort of education.

You will agree with me that there is absolutely no reason why labor, organized or unorganized, should oppose the sort of industrial education proposed here in Richmond, and I can assure you that labor does not oppose anything without good reason. When it has good reason to oppose so many things why should it oppose anything without reason?

Organized labor has opposed and will continue to oppose some enterprises which have been undertaken in the name of industrial education. It has opposed and will continue to oppose the exploitation of the laborer even when the exploitation is done under the name of industrial education. It may continue to regard with indifference, if not with suspicion, some private schemes of industrial education. With regard to such enterprises where they are instituted by employers, organized labor is from Missouri—it will have to be shown that the given enterprise is not a means of exploiting labor—a means of depressing wages by creating an over supply of labor in certain narrow fields of employment.

Organized labor cannot favor any scheme of industrial education which is lop-sided—any scheme, that is to say, which will bring trained men into any given trade without regard to the demand for labor in that trade. Industrial education must maintain a fair and proper apportionment of the supply of labor power to the demand for labor power in every line of work. Otherwise its advantages will be entirely neutralised. If, for example, the result of industrial education is to produce in any community a greater number of trained machinists than are needed in the community, those machinists which have been trained cannot derive any benefit from their training, since they will not be able to find employment except at economic disadvantages. Under these conditions industrial education is of no advantage to those who have received it, and it is a distinct injury to the journeymen working at the trade who are subjected to a keen competition artificially produced. Industrial education must reach the needs of the worker as well as the requirements of the employer.

I can see that in some respects the most difficult task before industrial education is that of maintaining an equilibrium of supply and demand of efficient artisans, and equilibrium as nearly perfect as is physically possible. . . .

THE BATAVIA (NEW YORK) PLAN (1912) From John Kennedy, "The Batavia Plan After Fourteen Years of Trial," "The Elementary School Teacher," vol. XII, pp. 449–51, 458–59.

The plan is in full operation, here and is well stated on its fourteenth year of use. It may therefore be said to have stood the test of time. Its popularity at the outset was instantaneous. The people understood it at once, and applauded it. It never had to fight its way. It is a reform without martyrs. At present I see no abatement of its popularity, and we know of families that moved into town because of it.

Our plan has the two-teacher phase and the one-teacher phase. In rooms containing more than fifty children we have two teachers, one giving class instruction continuously to classes reciting alternately, and the other giving individual attention all the time to slow and backward children. In rooms containing less than fifty children we have but one teacher. But this teacher gives half her periods of time to the needs of individuals. This phase of the plan permits its extension and use under all conditions. It has furnished the solution for the problem of individualizing the high school. We have a general individual teacher in the high school; and in addition to that each teacher there gives half of his or her periods to individualing. This is the polity at present.

I have observed many and varied results springing from the use of this plan. Some of those results have been surprising, and all have been gratifying. I cannot hope to go into them all; but will mention some.

When a crowd are assembled it is either uplift or crush for the individual. We are confident that our plan has secured the inspiration and warded off the danger.

Where there is inequality of condition the crowd becomes a tangled mass. The attempt to move a tangled mass is overstrain. Overstrain has its inevitable goal in breakdown. Under our plan we beleive there is no strain. Our teachers are becoming more vigorous from year to year.

Worry of any kind has its goal in breakdown, if not in death. And few people are aware how contagious a thing nervous debility is. Nerves are responsive to nerves. We feel that worry has been eliminated here, and that our children are calm, composed, safe and vigorous.

Sanitation should be the first care of school management. Under our plan it seems to me that our schools have become not only sanitary but salubrious. That is, schools properly individualed become conducive to the recovery of impaired or lost health. I have come to feel that the "pale student" is a contradiction in terms. Energy is a red-blooded matter. If a student is becoming pale ask immediately what is the matter with the school?

Interested occupation is preoccupation; and all know that preoccupation in good things is the best safeguard against the approach of evil things. It is my belief that our plan tends toward absorbed preoccupation in the good work of getting an education. This is not only a negative safeguard, but it is also a positive promotive of character by supplying high aims.

I have implied already that our order and discipline have greatly improved. They have greatly improved; and it is the right kind of order; it is the order that not only permits business to proceed; it is the order that is an atmosphere that nourishes the growth of character. Where energy is expended in securing a semblance of order, the same energy must be employed in maintaining it. There is tension that is depleting and depressing all around.

Our individual teaching has enabled us to move our grades. They do not now sink down by their own weight. Our children all move forward and arrive on time. The quick one no longer marks time; he sets the pace for the rest of them; and the rest line up on him. There is no longer any retardation. There is no longer any necessity for skipping grades in order to get on. We always allow an individual to gain a grade where it is to his advantage to do so. But there is a marked difference between gaining grades and skipping them. The gainer of a grade needs individual attention; and under our plan he gets it. Let no one suppose that the individualing is done only with children of questionable capacity. There are numerous circumstances that send our brightest pupils at times to the individual table.

It is here that we get the benefit of schooling. The child's first incentive is to line up with his fellows. When he gets the warhorse spirit in him his career is made. He works first for his line; then he works because of enjoyment in his work, and at last he works for grand remote aims. When his acquisitive powers are trained, and when he can see the goal of life, he may then work out his own salvation in the solitude of home. The soldier and the war-horse are trained to dress on the standard. And so it should be in schools. The school classes and grades should move forward in lines dressed at right angles to the line of advancement—no obliquity; no dragging; all crowding on the standard; and all champing the bit.

*   *   *

The immediate goal of the individual teaching is to put the pupil into a condition to react against the sweep of the class, and to enable him to appropriate the benefits of class-membership and class instruction. Knowledge is not the aim at the individual table; it is power, initiative, vigor. It is not a taking of him off his feet; it is a putting of him on his feet. He cannot get his lessons at the individual table; he can only get his power there; so there is no coaching. This means, of course, that the pupil cannot offer himself as a subject for individual attention. Every pupil knows that he must recite his own preparation. If he does not recite well his case receives such attention as it merits. A plan that aims at vigor puts no premium on laziness or cowardice.

Our individual teacher does nothing but ask questions. It is no refuge for an evader to run up against a questioner. No one is rendered weak or dependent by being asked a question. The question meets the needy one at a crisis of his life, and proves his salvation. The question picks him from in front of the car of Juggernaut; the question saves him from being a victim offered up to Moloch.

Justice is defined as the giving unto each human being his right. The rights of an individual are exactly coextensive with his needs. Needs, rights, and duties are correlative terms, covering the same exact subject or object-matter. Duty is what is *due* from us, and what we *ought* to do is what we *owe* to do. If anyone suffers any restriction of his right someone is delinquent in the discharge of his duty. Someone is either *insolvent,* or he is disregardful of his obligations. Children have many debtors because they have many needs; but there are few on whom they have as great and as sacred claims as on their teacher.

My own convictions after fourteen years' experience with this plan are a result that may possibly be of interest. I offer them for what they are worth. I like our children as they are. I believe that they are susceptible of a fine education if we subject them to the dual process of individual attention and class stimulus. I believe that either of these processes will break down without the sustaining aid of the other. But in due combination I think they are invincible. But the combination, like other wholesome compounds, must have its quantitative formula. The combination of individual and class instruction that gives a potency is the proportion of one to one. It is a formula easily remembered. It is *HO* without any subscribed exponents or indices whatever. By *HO* combined in due proportion we live; by either taken separately we die. Believing as I do in the feasibility of universal education, I feel confident that our republic can endure, and that free institutions will remain the blessed possession of men.

DESCRIPTION OF THE PROJECT METHOD (1918)   From William Heard
Kilpatrick, "The Project Method." *Teachers College Record*, vol. XIX, pp. 319–23.

The word 'project' is perhaps the latest arrival to knock for admittance at the door of educational terminology. Shall we admit the stranger? Not wisely until two preliminary questions have first been answered in the affirmative: First, is there behind the proposed term and waiting even now to be christened a valid notion or concept which promises to render appreciable service in educational thinking? Second, if we grant the foregoing, does the term 'project' fitly designate the waiting concept? Because the question as to the concept and its worth is so much more significant than any matter of mere names, this discussion will deal almost exclusively with the first of the two inquiries. It is indeed entirely possible that some other term, as 'purposeful act', for example, would call attention to a more important element in the concept, and, if so, might prove superior as a term to the word 'project'. At the outset it is probably wise to caution the reader against expecting any great amount of novelty in the idea here presented. The metaphor of christening is not to be taken too seriously; the concept to be considered is not in fact newly born. Not a few readers will be disappointed that after all so little new is presented.

A little of the personal may perhaps serve to introduce the more formal discussion. In attacking with successive classes in educational theory the problem of method, I had felt increasingly the need of unifying more completely a number of important related aspects of the educative process. I began to hope for some one concept which might serve this end. Such a concept, if found, must, so I thought, emphasize the factor of action, preferably wholehearted vigorous activity. It must at the same time provide a place for the adequate utilization of the laws of learning, and no less for the essential elements of the ethical quality of conduct. The last named looks of course to the social situation as well as to the individual attitude. Along with these should go, as it seemed, the important generalization that education is life—so easy to say and so hard to delimit. Could now all of these be contemplated under one workable notion? If yes, a great gain. In proportion as such a unifying concept could be found in like proportion would the work of presenting educational theory be facilitated; in like proportion should be the rapid spread of a better practice.

But could this unifying idea be found? Here was in fact the age-old problem of effective logical organization. My whole philosophic outlook had made me suspicious of so-called 'fundamental principles'. Was there yet another way of attaining unity? I do not mean to say that I asked these questions, either in these words or in this order. Rather is this a retrospective ordering of the more important outcomes. As the desired unification lay specifically in the field of method, might not some typical unit of concrete procedure supply the need—some unit of conduct that should be, as it were, a sample of life, a fair sample of the worthy life and consequently of education? As these questionings rose more definitely to mind, there came increasingly a belief—corroborated on many sides—that the unifying idea I sought was to be found in the conception of wholehearted purposeful activity proceeding in a social environment, or more briefly, in the unit element of such activity, the hearty purposeful act.

It is to this purposeful act with the emphasis on the word purpose that I myself apply the term 'project'. I did not invent the term nor did I start it on its educational career. Indeed, I do not know how long it has already been in use. I did, however, consciously appropriate the word to designate the typical unit of the worthy life described above. Others who were using the term seemed to me either to use it in a mechanical and partial sense or to be intending in a general way what I tried to define more exactly. The purpose of this article is to attempt to clarify the concept underlying the term as much as it is to defend the claim of the concept to a place in our educational thinking. The actual terminology with which to designate the concept is, as was said before, to my mind a matter of relatively small moment. If, however, we think of a project as a pro-ject, something pro-jected, the reason for its adoption may better appear.

Postponing yet a little further the more systematic presentation of the matter, let us from some typical instances see more concretely what is contemplated under the term project or hearty purposeful act? Suppose a girl makes a dress. If she did in hearty fashion propose to make the dress, if she planned it, if she made it herself, then I should say the instance is that of a typical project. We have a wholehearted purposeful act carried on amid social surroundings. That the dressmaking was purposeful is clear; the purpose once formed dominated each succeeding step in the process and gave unity to the whole. That the girl was wholehearted in the work was assured in the illustration. That the activity proceeded in a social environment is clear; other girls at least are to see the dress. As another instance, suppose a boy undertakes to get out a school newspaper. If he is in earnest about it, we again have the effective purpose being the essence of the project. So we may have a pupil writing a letter (if the hearty purpose is present), a child listening absorbedly to a story, Newton explaining the motion of the moon on the principles of terrestrial dynamics, Demosthenes trying to arouse the Greeks against Philip, Da Vinci painting the *Last Supper*, my writing this article, a boy solving with felt purpose an 'original' in geometry. All of the foregoing have been acts of individual purposing, but this is not to rule out group projects: a class presents a play, a group of boys organize a base-ball nine, three pupils prepare to read a story to their comrades. It is clear then that projects may present every variety that purposes present in life. It is also clear that a mere description of outwardly observable facts might not disclose the essential factor, namely the presence of a dominating purpose. It is equally true that there can be every degree of approximation to full projects according as the animating purpose varies in clearness and strength. If we conceive activities as ranging on a scale from those performed under dire compulsion up to those into which one puts his 'whole heart', the argument herein made restricts the term 'project' or purposeful act to the upper portions of the scale. An exact dividing line is hard to draw, and yields indeed in importance to the notion that psychological value increases with the degree of approximation to 'wholeheartedness'. As to the social environment element, some may feel that, however important this is to the fullest educative experience, it is still not essential to the conception of the purposeful act as here presented. These might therefore wish to leave this element out of the defining discussion. To this I should not object if it were clearly understood that the resulting concept—now essentially psychological in character— generally speaking, demands the social situation both for its practical working and for the comparative valuation of proffered projects.

With this general introduction, we may, in the first place, say that the purposeful act is the typical unit of the worthy life. Not that all purposes are good, but that the worthy life consists of purposive activity and not mere drifting. We scorn the man who passively accepts what fate or some other chance brings to him.

We admire the man who is master of his fate, who with deliberate regard for a total situation forms clear and far-reaching purposes, who plans and executes with nice care the purposes so formed. A man who habitually so regulates his life with reference to worthy social aims meets at once the demands for practical efficiency and of moral responsibility. Such a one presents the ideal of democratic citizenship. It is equally true that the purposeful act is not the unit of life for the serf or the slave. These poor unfortunates must in the interest of the overmastering system be habituated to act with a minimum of their own purposing and with a maximum of servile acceptance of others' purposes. In important matters they merely follow plans handed down to them from above, and execute these according to prescribed directions. For them another carries responsibility and upon the results of their labor another passes judgment. No such plan as that here advocated would produce the kind of docility required for their hopeless fate. But it is a democracy which we contemplate and with which we are here concerned.

As the purposeful act is thus the typical unit of the worthy life in a democratic society, so also should it be made the typical unit of school procedure. We of America have for years increasingly desired that education be considered as life itself and not as a mere preparation for later living. The conception before us promises a definite step toward the attainment of this end. If the purposeful act be in reality the typical unit of the worthy life, then it follows that to base education on purposeful acts is exactly to identify the process of education with worthy living itself. The two become then the same. All the arguments for placing education on a life basis seem, to me at any rate, to concur in support of this thesis. On this basis education has become life. And if the purposeful act thus makes of education life itself, could we reasoning in advance expect to find a better preparation for later life than practice in living now? We have heard of old that "we learn to do by doing," and much wisdom resides in the saying. If the worthy life of the coming day is to consist of well-chosen purposeful acts, what preparation for that time could promise more than practice now, under discriminating guidance, in forming and executing worthy purposes? To this end must the child have within rather large limits the opportunity to purpose. For the issues of his act he must—in like limits— be held accountable. That the child may properly progress, the total situation—all the factors of life, including comrades—speaking, if need be through the teacher, must make clear its selective judgment upon what he does, approving the better, rejecting the worse. In a true sense the whole remaining discussion is but to support the contention here argued in advance that education based on the purposeful act prepares best for life while at the same time it constitutes the present worthy life itself.

A more explicit reason for making the purposeful act the typical unit of instruction is found in the utilization of the laws of learning which this plan affords. I am assuming that it is not necessary in this magazine to justify or even explain at length these laws.

INDIVIDUALIZED INSTRUCTION (1918)   From Frederic Burk, "Individualized Instruction vs. the Lockstep System," *American City*, vol. XVIII, pp. 327–30.

Those who have ever stood in a penitentiary and watched the line of prisoners marching in lockstep to their cells never forget the scene—each prisoner with hands clasping the shoulders of the man in front; the line closely packed so that it marches solidly as one man, with no power to vary the rate of gait, all individuality lost. Yet we know the individual is there—the man who fell and he who merely stumbled, the boy who a short time ago buckled on his armor to conquer the world, and he who was conquered ere he was born—all now leveled by common degradation to this ignominious equality of man. This is the lockstep—the physical lockstep of our prisons, handed down by tradition from ages when humanity did not think.

We have the mental lockstep in our schools, handed down by the same tradition from the same ages. From nine until three, every mental and physical act of every pupil, if the regulations of the class method of instruction could be carried out ideally, must be performed in unison, by external direction and dictation of the teacher. Each must work over lessons which he has already learned, because others have failed in them, and he must hasten forward with foundation lessons unlearned, because the others cannot wait longer for him. All must learn the arithmetic of shingling—little girls as well—not because all will be shinglers, but because some one might be. So also with selling stock and buying bonds, banking, surveying, horse trading, and many other vocational and avocational pursuits presented by the one course.

The unbreakable unit is the class; for if the system is to be maintained at all, no variation in the absolute uniformity can be permitted. If, by accident, one pupil makes a movement or a sound out of unison, thinks by a different route, shortens or lengthens the established time, or puts down his left foot when he should put down his right, the whole system is thrown out of gear.

Of course, it is untrue that any two children are enough alike to keep profitably in unison for five minutes, much less for a school year or for the school course. By driving, in lockstep, over the same course of study a Napoleon and a Verdi, a Francis Bacon and a Man with the Hoe, a Rembrandt and an Edison, a Byron and a Burbank, we obtain, not education, but the caricature of it.

Those who fall out of the lockstep are many. There is no means provided, nor any possible, whereby these can regain the step. A few fall behind because they are naturally slow; some stumble over a single difficulty, and before they can recover they are left behind; some are absent, and when they return they cannot catch up; many rebel and fret because there are so many waits, and become disciplinary outlaws. School statistics tell the story: 12 to 20 per cent annually fail of promotion; one-third of all the pupils in city schools have lost one, two, three or more years; over 50 per cent enter life without an elementary schooling. The full significance cannot be told. We do not know what it means to the personal problems of livelihood and to social advantages, to health and disease, to crime and citizenship, to social and civic progress, to generations unborn, that considerably over half the nation's youth go out into life without the rudiments of an education.

*   *   *

EDUCATION FOR
URBAN INDUSTRIAL
AMERICA
1895–1918

Individual Schooling in Operation

Some five years ago the State Normal School at San Francisco introduced an individual system into the elementary department maintained to train its students as teachers. The beginning was made very simply. No lessons were assigned, and the pupils were informed that each might do as much as he could, that the teachers would help pupils to study, and that when a pupil reached the standard of the grade in thoroness in any subject, he would be given his certificate of promotion to the next grade in that subject.

The main room is like a study hall. The pupils, each as a rule intent upon his own work, are making the best possible use of their time. Concentration is characteristic. Some are studying texts or reference material, and some may be working upon written tests of work completed. The teachers are giving help when necessary, or testing pupils who have completed a topic or section of work. If a pupil shows he has thoroly mastered the topic, he will proceed with the next; if he shows lack of clear comprehension in some features, these deficiencies will be indicated and the teacher will give him work to repair these deficiencies. Usually the repair work is different from the original and approaches the difficulty from some new angle.

The Program Plan

For each subject during the day there is allotted a certain definite period, in no case exceeding thirty minutes. During these periods all pupils, except as later stated, pursue the given subject for the allotted time, and then, upon signal, change to another subject. The exceptions—and there are many—are due to the fact that some pupils forge ahead in some subjects and fail to bring up in others. In such cases, the amount of time per day a pupil is permitted to study the advanced topic is curtailed, and this time is given to the lagging subjects. The program system is, however, giving way to the self-reliant system.

The Self-Reliant System

Pupils who have shown good judgment in the management of their school work are put on a self-reliant basis. . . . Under the program system, a pupil may be called upon to change his subject just as he has warmed up to it or is in the midst of an important solution. The "self-reliant" pupil is responsible for the adjustment of his time, so that he does not run far ahead of his grade in some subjects while he lags in others. Placed upon their own responsibility, pupils who have seemed to resist all attempts to be forced to improve their composition or writing, or who have been supposed to be "slow," have remedied their shortcomings remarkably.

Rates of Progress

Pupils vary widely in rates of progress. As a rule, in most subjects the fastest pupil accomplishes in one month what the slowest requires five months to accomplish, while the others are very evenly distributed between these extremes. Each pupil varies very much in his progress, and there are few who are continuously rapid, continuously slow or continuously medium. While the system has not been in operation long enough to have records completing the entire eight grades, the rates indicate that the variation for completing these eight elementary grades will lie between five and seven years; that is, if all pupils entered the elementary school at six years of age, they will be ready for the high school between the ages of eleven and thirteen.

Thoroness and Discipline

Individual instruction is necessarily more thoro than class instruction. Each pupil masters by himself all the work necessary to reach the grade standard as shown by thoro tests; if he is weak in any place, he is given repair exercises until he is thoro. Under an individual system, pupils vary *in the time* required to complete a unit of work, but they are practically identical in thoroness in results; under the class system the time is uniform, but they vary *in thoroness*.

The usual disciplinary problems disappear. The issue of obedience has rarely occasion to arise between teacher and pupil, and consequently the tension upon both teacher and pupil is relieved. . . .

*   *   *

Introducing Individual Teaching into Rural and City Schools

To introduce an individual system of education into our public schools, we must start with the realization that, just as the class system has built special and complex machinery, so now in introducing a principle diametrically opposed, we must expect to invent and construct new and entirely different machinery. The course of study must be remodeled so that the basis of promotion shall be standards of ability or knowledge.

THE RURAL SCHOOL

The individual plan can be introduced into most rural schools with ease. Rural schools usually have an attendance of less than twenty-five pupils distributed over all grades, and the large majority of them study alone while the teacher is conducting class recitations. Pupils are not promoted out of the room except to graduate. Originally the rural schools were conducted upon an individual plan, with the crudest conditions of teachers, texts and management. Yet the bone and sinew of America's progress have come out of them. The class recitation is superfluous folly in rural schools, for there are usually only two to half a dozen pupils in the class. By cutting out the recitation, in which the teacher wastes almost the entire day, she can give her time to supervising the study of her pupils and their progress individually, and can set apart proper times for special exercises in oral discussion.

*   *   *

The Question of Cost

The question upon the lips of everyone who for the first time considers the project of introducing the individual system is: "How can one teacher teach fifty pupils . . .?" . . . The individual plan is too expensive."

There is an absurd fallacy contained in this question. For illustration, the schooling cost of carrying a class of fifty pupils thru one grade, if the average time is twelve months, is just double what it would be if these fifty pupils were carried thru the same grade with the same thoroness in an average of six months. We could double the number of teachers in a school *with no addition to the cost of schooling,* provided that by so doing we cut the time for schooling one-half.

If we put fifty pupils into a class under lockstep operation, all fifty will be in the same grade all of the year, and seven to ten of them will be there the following year or even longer. But under an individual plan, our data show, a few will be promoted in two months, and others continuously thereafter until, during the last two months, only a half-dozen or so will remain of the fifty. Since the pupils pass thru the school in less time, there will be in attendance at one time only a few more than one-half the total number usual under the class system. The same number of pupils receive schooling, and there would be no financial reason for reducing the number of teachers. But instead of fifty pupils per teacher, there would be only twenty-five to thirty. We should need only little more than half the number of buildings, half the interest upon the money invested in them; half the upkeep and repairs, half the janitors, half the heat, etc. In short, individual instruction, if our data upon the rates of progress are correct, will reduce the cost of our present class schooling considerably over one-half, and at the same time decrease the existing ratio of pupils per teacher nearly one-half. If after these reductions it is still found profitable to employ even more teachers in order to obtain the greatest rapidity of progress consistent with increased thoroness, there are ample means available from these savings.

It is true that in the first years of establishing an individual system we should probably find it necessary to employ more teachers in order to work off the accumulated laggardism of the class system. But we could not legitimately charge this cost as an extra expense. Schooling will never be placed upon a sound financial basis until the fallacy of the current notion that the school cost depends upon the number of pupils who may be crowded upon one teacher without regard to the time they use her services in completing a grade shall be entirely done away with.

CARDINAL PRINCIPLES OF SECONDARY EDUCATION (1918) From U.S.

Bureau of Education, *Cardinal Principles of Secondary Education: A Report of the Commission on the Reorganization of Secondary Education, Appointed by the National Education Association, Bulletin No. 35* (Washington, D.C., 1918), pp. 7–11, 18–27, 32.

I. The Need for Reorganization

Secondary education should be determined by the needs of the society to be served, the character of the individuals to be educated, and the knowledge of educational theory and practice available. These factors are by no means static. Society is always in process of development; the character of the secondary-school population undergoes modification; and the sciences on which educational theory and practice depend constantly furnish new information. Secondary education, however, like any other established agency of society, is conservative and tends to resist modification. Failure to make adjustments when the need arises leads to the necessity for extensive reorganization at irregular intervals. The evidence is strong that such a comprehensive reorganization of secondary education is imperative at the present time.

1. *Changes in society.*—Within the past few decades changes have taken place in American life profoundly affecting the activities of the individual. As a citizen, he must to a greater extent and in a more direct way cope with problems of community life, State and National Governments, and international relationships. As a worker, he must adjust himself to a more complex order. As a relatively independent personality, he has more leisure. The problems arising from these three dominant phases of life are closely interrelated and call for a degree of intelligence and efficiency on the part of every citizen that cannot be secured through elementary education alone, or even through secondary education unless the scope of that education is broadened.

*　　*　　*

The responsibility of the secondary school is still further increased because many social agencies other than the school afford less stimulus for education than heretofore. In many vocations there have come such significant changes as the substitution of the factory system for the domestic system of industry; the use of machinery in place of manual labor; the high specialization of processes with a corresponding subdivision of labor; and the breakdown of the apprentice system. In connection with home and family life have frequently come lessened responsibility on the part of the children; the withdrawal of the father and sometimes the mother from home occupations to the factory or store; and increased urbanization, resulting in less unified family life. Similarly, many important changes have taken place in community life, in the church, in the State, and in other institutions. These changes in American life call for extensive modifications in secondary education.

2. *Changes in the secondary-school population.*—In the past 25 years there have been marked changes in the secondary-school population of the United States. The number of pupils has increased, according to Federal returns, from one for every 210 of the total population in 1889–90, to one for every 121 in 1899–1900, to one for every 89 in 1909–10, and to one for every 73 of the estimated total population in 1914-15. The character of the secondary-school population has been modified by the entrance of large numbers of pupils of widely varying capacities, aptitudes, social heredity, and destinies in life. Further, the broadening of the scope of secondary education has brought to the school many pupils who do not complete the full course but leave at various stages of advancement. The needs of these pupils can not be neglected, nor can we expect in the near future that all pupils will be able to complete the secondary school as full-time students.

At present only about one-third of the pupils who enter the first year of the elementary school reach the four-year high school, and only about one in nine is graduated. Of those who enter the seventh school year, only one-half to two-thirds reach the first year of the four-year high school. Of those who enter the four-year high school about one-third leave before the beginning of the second year, about one-half are gone before the beginning of the third year, and fewer than one-third are graduated. These facts can no longer be safely ignored.

3. *Changes in educational theory.*—The sciences on which educational theory depends have within recent years made significant contributions. In particular, educational psychology emphasizes the following factors:

(a) *Individual differences in capacities and aptitudes among secondary-school pupils.* Already recognized to some extent, this factor merits fuller attention.

(b) *The reexamination and reinterpretation of subject values and the teaching methods with reference to "general discipline."*—While the final verdict of modern psychology has not as yet been rendered, it is clear that former conceptions of "general values" must be thoroughly revised.

(c) *Importance of applying knowledge.*—Subject values and teaching methods must be tested in terms of the laws of learning and the application of knowledge to the activities of life, rather than primarily in terms of the demands of any subject as a logically organized science.

(d) *Continuity in the development of children.*—It has long been held that psychological changes at certain stages are so pronounced as to overshadow the continuity of development. On this basis secondary education has been sharply separated from elementary education. Modern psychology, however, goes to show that the development of the individual is in most respects a continuous process and that, therefore, any sudden or abrupt break between the elementary and the secondary school or between any two successive stages of education is undesirable.

The foregoing changes in society, in the character of the secondary-school population, and in educational theory, together with many other considerations, call for extensive modifications of secondary education. Such modifications have already begun in part. The present need is for the formulation of a comprehensive program of reorganization, and its adoption, with suitable adjustments, in all the secondary schools of the Nation. Hence it is appropriate for a representative body like the National Education Association to outline such a program. This is the task entrusted by that association to the Commission on the Reorganization of Secondary Education.

II. The Goal of Education in a Democracy

Education in the United States should be guided by a clear conception of the meaning of democracy. It is the ideal of democracy that the individual and society may find fulfillment each in the other. Democracy sanctions neither the exploitation of the individual by society, nor the disregard of the interests of society by the individual. More explicitly—

The purpose of democracy is so to organize society that each member may develop his personality primarily through activities designed for the well-being of his fellow members and of society as a whole.

This ideal demands that human activities be placed upon a high level of efficiency; that to this efficiency be added an appreciation of the significance of these activities and loyalty to the best ideals involved; and that the individual choose that vocation and those forms of social service in which his personality may develop and become most effective. For the achievement of these ends democracy must place chief reliance upon education.

Consequently, education in a democracy, both within and without the school, should develop in each individual the knowledge, interests, ideals, habits, and powers whereby he will find his place and use that place to shape both himself and society toward ever nobler ends.

III. The Main Objectives of Education

In order to determine the main objectives that should guide education in a democracy it is necessary to analyze the activities of the individual. Normally he is a member of a family, of a vocational group, and of various civic groups, and by virtue of these relationships he is called upon to engage in activities that enrich the family life, to render important vocational services to his fellows, and to promote the common welfare. It follows, therefore, that worthy home-membership, vocation, and citizenship demand attention as three of the leading objectives.

Aside from the immediate discharge of these specific duties, every individual should have a margin of time for the cultivation of personal and social interests. This leisure, if worthily used, will recreate his powers and enlarge and enrich life, thereby making him better able to meet his responsibilities. The unworthy use of leisure impairs health, disrupts home life, lessens vocational efficiency, and destroys civic-mindedness. The tendency in industrial life, aided by legislation, is to decrease the working hours of large groups of people. While shortened hours tend to lessen the harmful reactions that arise from prolonged strain, they increase, if possible, the importance of preparation for leisure. In view of these considerations, education for the worthy use of leisure is of increasing importance as an objective.

To discharge the duties of life and to benefit from leisure, one must have good health. The health of the individual is essential also to the vitality of the race and to the defense of the Nation. Health education is, therefore, fundamental.

There are various processes, such as reading, writing, arithmetical computations, and oral and written expression, that are needed as tools in the affairs of life. Consequently, command of these fundamental processes, while not an end in itself, is nevertheless an indispensable objective.

And, finally, the realization of the objectives already named is dependent upon ethical character, that is, upon conduct founded upon right principles, clearly perceived and loyally adhered to. Good citizenship, vocational excellence, and the worthy use of leisure go hand in hand with ethical character; they are at once the fruits of sterling character and the channels through which such character is developed and made manifest. On the one hand, character is meaningless apart from the will to discharge the duties of life, and, on the other hand, there is no guarantee that these duties will be rightly discharged unless principles are substituted for impulses, however well-intentioned such impulses may be. Consequently ethical character is at once involved in all the other objectives and at the same time requires specific consideration in any program of national education.

This commission, therefore, regards the following as the main objectives of education: 1. Health. 2. Command of fundamental processes. 3. Worthy home-membership. 4. Vocation. 5. Citizenship. 6. Worthy use of leisure. 7. Ethical character.

The naming of the above objectives is not intended to imply that the process of education can be divided into separated fields. This can not be, since the pupil is indivisible. Nor is the analysis all-inclusive. Nevertheless, we believe that distinguishing and naming these objectives will aid in directing efforts; and we hold that they should constitute the principal aims in education.

VI. Recognition of the Objectives in Reorganizing
High-School Subjects

Each subject now taught in high schools is in need of extensive reorganization in order that it may contribute more effectively to the objectives outlined herein, and the place of that subject in secondary education should depend upon the value of such contribution. In Section IV of this report various references have been made to needed changes. For fuller treatment the reader is referred to reports of this commission dealing with the several subjects. These reports indicate important steps in such modifications. In each report the commission attempts to analyze the aims in terms of the objectives; to indicate the adaptation of methods of presentation to the aims accepted; and to suggest a selection of content on the basis of aims and methods.

VII. Education as a Process of Growth

Education must be conceived as a process of growth. Only when so conceived and so conducted can it become a preparation for life. . . .

* * *

We recommend a reorganization of the school system whereby the first six years shall be devoted to elementary education designed to meet the needs of pupils of approximately 6 to 12 years of age; and the second six years to secondary education designed to meet the needs of pupils of approximately 12 to 18 years of age.

XI. Division of Secondary Education into Junior and Senior Periods

The six years to be devoted to secondary education may well be divided into two periods which may be designated as the junior and senior periods. In the junior period emphasis should be placed upon the attempt to help the pupil to explore his own aptitudes and to make at least provisional choice of the kinds of work to which he will devote himself. In the senior period emphasis should be given to training in the fields thus chosen. This distinction lies at the basis of the organization of junior and senior high schools.

In the junior high school there should be the gradual introduction of departmental instruction, some choice of subjects under guidance, promotion by subjects, prevocational courses, and a social organization that calls forth initiative and develops the sense of personal responsibility for the welfare of the group.

In the senior high school a definite curriculum organization should be provided by means of which each pupil may take work systematically planned with reference to his needs as an individual and as a member of society. The senior high school should be characterized by a rapidly developing social consciousness and by an aptitude of self-reliance based upon clearly perceived objectives.

Under ordinary circumstances the junior and senior periods should each be three years in length so as to realize their distinctive purposes. In sparsely settled communities where a senior high school can not be maintained effectively, the junior high school may well be four years in length, so that the pupils may attend school nearer to their homes for one more year.

The commission is not unmindful of the desirability, when funds permit, of extending secondary education under local auspices so as to include the first two years of work usually offered in colleges, and constituting what is known as the "junior college," but it has seemed unwise for the commission to attempt to outline the work of this new unit.

XII. Articulation of Secondary Education with Elementary Education

Admission to high school is now, as a rule, based upon the completion of a prescribed amount of academic work. As a result many over-age pupils either leave school altogether or are retained in the elementary school when they are no longer deriving much benefit from its instruction. Should a similar conception of the articulation of the two schools continue after the elementary program has been shortened to six years, similar bad results will persist. Experience in certain school systems, however, shows that the secondary school can provide special instruction for over-age pupils more successfully than the elementary school can. *Consequently we recommend that secondary schools admit, and provide suitable instruction for, all pupils who are in any respect so mature that they would derive more benefit from the secondary school than from the elementary school.*

XIII. Articulation of Higher Education with Secondary Education

In view of the important role of secondary education in achieving the objectives essential in American life, it follows that higher institutions of learning are not justified in maintaining entrance requirements and examinations of a character that handicap the secondary school in discharging its proper functions in a democracy.

As stated in Section XII of this report, the secondary school should admit all pupils who would derive greater benefit from the secondary than from the elementary school. With the demand of democratic society for extended liberal and vocational education for an ever-increasing number of persons, the higher institutions of learning, taken as a whole, are under a similar obligation with reference to those whose needs are no longer met by the secondary school and are disposed to continue their education. The conception that higher education should be limited to the few is destined to disappear in the interests of democracy.

The tradition that a particular type of education, and that exclusively nonvocational in character, is the only acceptable preparation for advanced education, either liberal or vocational, must therefore give way to a scientific evaluation of all types of secondary education as preparation for continued study. This broader conception need not involve any curtailment of opportunities for those who early manifest academic interest to pursue the work adapted to their needs. It does, however, mean that pupils who, during the secondary period, devote a considerable time to courses having vocational content should be permitted to pursue whatever form of higher education, either liberal or vocational, they are able to undertake with profit to themselves and to society.

*   *   *

XV. The Specializing and Unifying Functions of Secondary Education

1. *Their significance.*—The ideal of a democracy, as set forth in Section II of this report, involves, on the one hand, specialization whereby individuals and groups of individuals may become effective in the various vocations and other fields of human endeavor, and, on the other hand, unification whereby the members of that democracy may obtain those common ideas, common ideals, and common modes of thought, feeling, and action that make for cooperation, social cohesion, and social solidarity.

Without effective specialization on the part of groups of individuals there can be no progress. Without unification in a democracy there can be no worthy community life and no concerted action for necessary social ends. Increasing specialization emphasizes the need for unification, without which a democracy is a prey to enemies at home and abroad.

2. *The specializing function.*—Secondary education in the past has met the needs of only a few groups. The growing recognition that progress in our American democracy depends in no small measure upon adequate provision for specialization in many fields is the chief cause leading to the present reorganization of secondary education. Only through attention to the needs of various groups of individuals as shown by aptitudes, abilities, and aspirations can the secondary school secure from each pupil his best efforts. The school must capitalize the dominant interest that each boy and girl has at the time and direct that interest as wisely as possible. This is the surest method by which hard and effective work may be obtained from each pupil.

Specialization demands the following provisions in secondary education:

(*a*) *A wide range of subjects.*—In order to test and develop the many important capacities and interests found in pupils of secondary-school age, the school should provide as wide a range of subjects as it can offer effectively.

(*b*) *Exploration and guidance.*—Especially in the junior high school the pupil should have a variety of experience and contacts in order that he may explore his own capacities and aptitudes. Through a system of educational supervision or guidance he should be helped to determine his education and his vocation. These decisions should not be imposed upon him by others.

(*c*) *Adaptation of content and methods.*—The content and teaching methods of every study should be adapted to the capacities, interests, and needs of the pupils concerned. In certain studies these factors may differ widely for various groups of pupils, e.g., chemistry should emphasize different phases in agricultural, commercial, industrial, and household-arts curriculums.

(*d*) *Flexibility of organization and administration.*—Flexibility should be secured by "election" of studies or curriculum, promotion by subjects from the beginning of the junior high school, possible transfer from curriculum to curriculum, provision for maximum and minimum assignments for pupils of greater and less ability, and, under certain conditions, for the rapid or slow progress of such pupils.

(*e*) *Differentiated curriculums.*—The work of the senior high school should be organized into differentiated curriculums. The range of such curriculums should be as wide as the school can offer effectively. The basis of differentiation should be, in the broad sense of the term, vocational, thus justifying the names commonly given, such as agricultural, business, clerical, industrial, fine-arts, and household-arts curriculums. Provision should be made also for those having distinctively academic interests and needs. The conclusion that the work of the senior high school should be organized on the basis of curriculums does not imply that every study should be different in the various curriculums. Nor does it imply that every study should be determined by the dominant element of that curriculum. Indeed any such practice would ignore other objectives of education just as important as that of vocational efficiency.

3. *The unifying function.*—In some countries a common heredity, a strongly centralized government, and an established religion contribute to social solidarity. In America, racial stocks are widely diversified, various forms of social heredity come into conflict, differing religious beliefs do not always make for unification, and the members of different vocations often fail to recognize the interests that they have in common with others. The school is the one agency that may be controlled definitely and consciously by our democracy for the purpose of unifying its people. In this process the secondary school must play an important part because the elementary school with its immature pupils can not alone develop the common knowledge, common ideals, and common interests essential to American democracy. Furthermore, children of immigrant parents attend the secondary school in large and increasing numbers; secondary education comes at a stage in the development of boys and girls when social interests develop rapidly; and from the secondary school the majority of pupils pass directly into participation in the activities of our society.

The unifying function calls for the following provisions in secondary education:

(*a*) Studies of direct value for this purpose, especially the social studies and the mother tongue, with its literature.

(*b*) The social mingling of pupils through the organization and administration of the school.

(*c*) The participation of pupils in common activities in which they should have a large measure of responsibility, such as athletic games, social activities, and the government of the school.

4. *Specialization and unification as supplementary functions.*—With increasing specialization in any society comes a corresponding necessity for increased attention to unification. So in the secondary school, increased attention to specialization calls for more purposeful plans for unification. When there was but little differentiation in the work within the secondary school, and the pupils in attendance were less diversified as to their heredity and interests, social unification in the full sense of the term could not take place.

The supplementary character of these functions has direct bearing upon the subjects to be taken by secondary-school pupils. To this end the secondary school should provide the following groups of studies:

(*a*) *Constants*, to be taken by all or nearly all pupils. These should be determined mainly by the objectives of health, command of fundamental processes, worthy home-membership, citizenship, and ethical character.

(*b*) *Curriculum variables*, peculiar to a curriculum or to a group of related curriculums. These should be determined for the most part by vocational needs, including, as they frequently do, preparation for advanced study in special fields.

(*c*) *Free electives*, to be taken by pupils in accordance with individual aptitudes or special interests, generally of a nonvocational nature. These are significant, especially in preparation for the worthy use of leisure.

The constants should contribute definitely to unification, the curriculum variables to specialization, and the free electives to either or both of these functions.

In the seventh year, that is the first year of the junior high school, the pupil should not be required to choose at the outset the field to which he will devote himself. For those who do not at this time have a definite purpose, opportunity should be given to gain some experience with several significant types of work, such as some form of industrial arts, gardening or other agricultural activity, typewriting or problems drawn from business, household arts for girls, and for at least a part of the pupils some work in a foreign language.

*　　*　　*

It may be found feasible to organize several such subjects or projects into short units and to arrange the schedule so that every pupil may take several of them. The work thus offered may and should be of real educational value, in addition to its exploratory value.

In the two following years of the junior high school, some pupils should continue this trying-out process, while others may well devote one-fourth to one-half of their time to curriculum variables. Pupils who will probably enter industry at the end of the ninth grade may well give as much as two-thirds of their time to vocational preparation, but they must not be permitted to neglect preparation for citizenship and the worthy use of leisure.

In the senior high school the relative proportion of these three groups of subjects will vary with the curriculum. Pupils who are to enter a gainful occupation before the completion of the senior high school may well devote a large proportion of their time to the curriculum variables, especially during their last year in school.

In brief, the greater the time allowed for curriculum variables, the more purposeful should be the time devoted to the constants in order that the school may be effective as an agency of unification. Above all, the greater the differentiation in studies, the more important becomes the social mingling of pupils pursuing different curriculums.

The supplementary character of the specializing and unifying functions has a direct bearing also upon the type of high school best suited to the needs of democratic society, as discussed in the next section.

XVI. The Comprehensive High School as the Standard Secondary School

The comprehensive (sometimes called composite, or cosmopolitan) high school, embracing all curriculums in one unified organization, should remain the standard type of secondary school in the United States.

Junior high schools must be of the comprehensive type, whatever policy be adopted for the senior high schools, since one of the primary purposes of the junior high school is to assist the pupil through a wide variety of contacts and experiences to obtain a basis for intelligent choice of his educational and vocational career. In the judgment of the commission senior high schools and four-year high schools of the older organizations should, as a rule, be of the comprehensive type for the following reasons:

1. *For effectiveness of vocational education.*—When effectively organized and administered . . . the comprehensive high school can make differentiated education of greater value to the individual and to society, for such value depends largely upon the extent to which the individual pursues the curriculum best suited to his needs. This factor is of prime importance, although frequently ignored in discussions regarding the effectiveness of vocational and other types of differentiated education.

In a system of special-type schools many influences interfere with the wise choice of curriculum. Thus many pupils choose the high school nearest to their homes, or the school to which their friends have gone or are going, or the school that provides the most attractive social life or has the best athletic teams. Still others are unwisely influenced by the notions of neighbors and friends of the family. After entering a special-type school, many pupils drop out because the work is not adapted to their needs, while comparatively few transfer to another school.

In a comprehensive school the influences interfering with a wise choice of curriculum may be reduced to a minimum. When an unwise choice has been made the pupil may be greatly aided in discovering a curriculum better adapted to his needs because he can see other work in the school, talk with school companions, and confer with teachers who are able to give him expert advice regarding such curriculums. When such a pupil has found a curriculum better adapted to his needs, he can be transferred to it without severance of school relationships and, what seems to him, the sacrifice of school loyalty.

Moreover, pupils in comprehensive schools have contacts valuable to them vocationally, since people in every vocation must be able to deal intelligently with those in other vocations, and employers and employees must be able to understand one another and recognize common interests. Similarly, teachers in comprehensive schools have a better opportunity to observe other curriculums and are thereby better able to advise pupils intelligently.

Summarizing under this head, the well-organized comprehensive school can make differentiated education of greater value than can the special-type school, because it aids in a wise choice of curriculum, assists in readjustments when such are desirable, and provides for wider contacts essential to true success in every vocation.

2. *For unification.*—When administered by a principal who himself recognizes the social value of all types of secondary education and inspires a broad spirit of democracy among teachers and pupils, the comprehensive high school is a better instrument for unification. Through friendships formed with pupils pursuing other curriculums and having vocational and educational goals widely different from their own, the pupils realize that the interests which they hold in common with others are, after all, far more important than the differences that would tend to make them antagonistic to others. Through school assemblies and organizations they acquire common ideas. Through group activities they secure training in cooperation. Through loyalty to a school which includes many groups they are prepared for loyalty to State and Nation. In short, the comprehensive school is the prototype of a democracy in which various groups must have a degree of self-consciousness as groups and yet be federated into a larger whole through the recognition of common interests and ideals. Life in such a school *is a natural and valuable preparation for life in a democracy.*

3. *For objectives other than vocation.*—A comprehensive high school can provide much more effectively for health education, education for the worthy use of

leisure, and home-making education than a number of smaller special-type schools can.

The most effective health education requires adequate equipment and instructors competent to diagnose health needs and direct health activities. Expenses and difficulties of duplication of such facilities in every smaller special-type school are almost prohibitive. Preparation for the worthy use of leisure is best achieved when there is a wide variety of activities from which pupils may select, such as arts and crafts clubs, literary and debating societies, and musical organizations. All of these require for their success enthusiastic leadership such as can best be secured from a large faculty. Girls in all curriculums should have the advantages of work in household arts under efficient directors and with adequate equipment. Such conditions are most readily provided in the comprehensive school where there is a strong department of household arts.

With the establishment of a special-type high school it frequently happens that various important phases of education are neglected or minimized in the other schools of that system.

4. *For accessibility.*—In cities large enough to require more than one high school it is desirable to have each school so located as to serve a particular section of the city, thereby reducing the expense and loss of time involved in travel on the part of pupils. The proximity of the school to the homes results also in greater interest in education on the part of pupils and parents, and consequently increases the drawing and holding power of the school.

5. *Adaptation to local needs.*—In recommending the comprehensive high school as the standard secondary school the commission recognizes that in large cities where two or more high schools are needed it is not always possible to provide every curriculum in each high school, such a practice being precluded by the fact that certain curriculums would thereby enroll in the several schools too few pupils to permit economical organization and administration. In such cases a few curriculums may well appear in selected comprehensive schools or even in a single school only, while other curriculums appear in every school.

The commission also recognizes the impracticability of offering every curriculum in every small rural high school. In such cases it is desirable that a curriculum for which the number of pupils does not warrant such duplication should be offered in selected schools, and that pupils needing that curriculum should go to those schools. This plan is substantially the same as that recommended for the large city.

6. *Effective organization of curriculums in comprehensive high schools.*— Finally, the commission recognizes that in the past relatively ineffective instruction has been afforded in some comprehensive schools. This has been due in part to the fact that everywhere vocational education has been passing and is still passing through a period of experimentation. The commission believes, however, that the most serious defect in vocational education in the comprehensive high school has been due to a lack of proper organization and administration. Effective vocational education can not be secured when administered like so many accidental groupings of subjects. To remedy this situation the commission recommends that each curriculum, or group of closely related curriculums, in the large comprehensive high school be placed under the supervision of a director whose task it shall be to organize that curriculum and maintain its efficiency. The curriculum directors must work under the general direction of the principal, who must be the coordinator of all the activities of the school. Especially is it necessary that each director shall be selected with the same care that would be exercised in choosing the principal of a special-type school enrolling as many pupils as are enrolled in the curriculum or

curriculums under his direction. In medium-sized high schools unable to employ directors for the various curriculums, the teachers should be organized into committees to consider the problems of the various curriculums, all working under the direction of the principal.

Unless the various curriculums are effectively organized and administered, and unless the democratic spirit pervades the school, the comprehensive high school is in danger of failure; with these factors present, it has every promise of success.

XVII. Recognition of the Objectives in Organizing the School

The objectives must determine the organization, or else the organization will determine the objectives. If the only basis upon which a high school is organized is that of the subjects of study, each department being devoted to some particular subject, there will result an over-valuation of the importance of subjects as such, and the tendency will be for each teacher to regard his function as merely that of leading the pupils to master a particular subject, rather than that of using the subjects of study and the activities of the school as means for achieving the objectives of education. . . .

*   *   *

It is the firm belief of this commission that secondary education in the United States must aim at nothing less than complete and worthy living for all youth, and that therefore the objectives described herein must find place in the education of every boy and girl.

Finally, in the process of translating into daily practice the cardinal principles herein set forth, the secondary school teachers of the United States must themselves strive to explore the inner meaning of the great democratic movement now struggling for supremacy. The doctrine that each individual has a right to the opportunity to develop the best that is in him is reinforced by the belief in the potential, and perchance unique, worth of the individual. The task of education, as of life, is therefore to call forth that potential worth.

While seeking to evoke the distinctive excellencies of individuals and groups of individuals, the secondary school must be equally zealous to develop those common ideas, common ideals, and common modes of thought, feeling, and action, whereby America, through a rich, unified, common life, may render her truest service to a world seeking for democracy among men and nations.

New Practices

FIRST DAYS AT HULL HOUSE (1887)   From Jane Addams, *Twenty Years at Hull House* (New York, 1911), pp. 101–7.

In the very first weeks of our residence Miss Starr started a reading party in George Eliot's "Romola," which was attended by a group of young woman who followed the wonderful tale with unflagging interest. The weekly reading was held in our little upstairs dining room, and two members of the club came to dinner each week, not only that they might be received as guests, but that they might help us wash the dishes afterwards and so make the table ready for the stacks of Florentine photographs.

Our "first resident," as she gayly designated herself, was a charming old lady who gave five consecutive readings from Hawthorne to a most appreciative audience, interspersing the magic tales most delightfully with recollections of the elusive and fascinating author. Years before she had lived at Brook Farm as a pupil of the Ripleys, and she came to us for ten days because she wished to live once more in an atmosphere where "idealism ran high." We thus early found the type of class which through all the years has remained most popular—a combination of a social atmosphere with serious study.

Volunteers to the new undertaking came quickly; a charming young girl conducted a kindergarten in the drawing-room, coming regularly every morning from her home in a distant part of the North Side of the city. Although a tablet to her memory has stood upon a mantel shelf in Hull-House for five years, we still associate her most vividly with the play of little children, first in her kindergarten and then in her own nursery, which furnished a veritable illustration of Victor Hugo's definition of heaven,—"a place where parents are always young and children always little." Her daily presence for the first two years made it quite impossible for us to become too solemn and self-conscious in our strenuous routine, for her mirth and buoyancy were irresistible and her eager desire to share the life of the neighborhood never failed, although it was often put to a severe test. One day at luncheon she gayly recited her futile attempt to impress temperance principles upon the mind of an Italian mother, to whom she had returned a small daughter of five sent to the kindergarten "in quite a horrid state of intoxication" from the wine-soaked bread upon which she had breakfasted. The mother, with the gentle courtesy of a South Italian, listened politely to her graphic protrayal of the untimely end awaiting so immature a wine bibber; but long before the lecture was finished, quite unconscious of the incongruity, she hospitably set forth her best wines, and when her baffled guest refused one after the other, she disappeared, only to quickly return with a small dark glass of whisky, saying reassuringly, "See, I have brought you the true American drink." The recital ended in seriocomic despair, with the rueful statement that "the impression I probably made upon her darkened mind was, that it is the American custom to breakfast children on bread soaked in whisky instead of light Italian wine."

That first kindergarten was a constant source of education to us. We were much surprised to find social distinctions even among its lambs, although greatly amused with the neat formulation made by the superior little Italian boy who refused to sit beside uncouth little Angelina because "we eat our macaroni this way,"—imitating the movement of a fork from a plate to his mouth,—"and she eat her macaroni this way," holding his hand high in the air and throwing back his head, that his wide-open mouth might receive an imaginary cascade. Angelina gravely nodded her little head in approval of this distinction between gentry and peasant. "But isn't it astonishing that merely table manners are made such a test all the way along?" was the comment of their democratic teacher. Another memory which refuses to be associated with death, which came to her all too soon, is that of the young girl who organized our first really successful club of boys, holding their fascinated interest by the old chivalric tales, set forth so dramatically and vividly that checkers and jackstraws were abandoned by all the other clubs on Boys' Day, that their members might form a listening fringe to "The Young Heroes."

I met a member of the latter club one day as he flung himself out of the House in the rage by which an emotional boy hopes to keep from shedding tears. "There is no use coming here any more, Prince Roland is dead," he gruffly explained as we passed. We encouraged the younger boys in tournaments and dramatics of all sorts, and we somewhat fatuously believed that boys who were early interested in adventurers or explorers might later want to know the lives of living statesmen and inventors. It is needless to add that the boys quickly responded to such a program, and that the only difficulty lay in finding leaders who were able to carry it out. This difficulty has been with us through all the years of growth and development in the Boys' Club until now, with its five-story building, its splendid equipment of shops of recreation and study rooms, that group alone is successful which commands the services of a resourceful and devoted leader.

The dozens of younger children who from the first came to Hull-House were organized into groups which were not quite classes and not quite clubs. The value of these groups consisted almost entirely in arousing a higher imagination and in giving children the opportunity which they could not have in the crowded schools, for initiative and for independent social relationships. The public schools then contained little hand work of any sort, so that naturally any instruction which we provided for the children took the direction of this supplementary work. But it required a constant effort that the pressure of poverty itself should not defeat the education aim. The Italian girls in the sewing classes would count that day lost when they could not carry home a garment, and the insistence that it should be neatly made seemed a super-refinement to those in dire need of clothing.

As these clubs have been continued during the twenty years they have developed classes in the many forms of handicraft which the newer education is so rapidly adapting for the delight of children; but they still keep their essentially social character and still minister to that large number of children who leave school the very week they are fourteen years old, only too eager to close the schoolroom door forever on a tiresome task that is at last well over. It seems to us important these children shall find themselves permanently attached to a House that offers them evening clubs and classes with their old companions, that merges as easily as possible the school life into the working life and does what it can to find places for the bewildered young things looking for work. A large proportion of the delinquent boys brought into the juvenile court in Chicago are the oldest sons in large families whose wages are needed at home. The grades from which many of them leave school, as the records show, are piteously far from the seventh and eighth where the very first instruction in manual training is given, nor have they been caught by any other abiding interest.

In spite of these flourishing clubs for children early established at Hull-House and the fact that our first organized undertaking was a kindergarten, we were very insistent that the Settlement should not be primarily for the children, and that it was absurd to suppose that grown people would not respond to opportunities for education and social life. Our enthusiastic kindergartner herself demonstrated this with an old woman of ninety, who, because she was left alone all day while her daughter, cooked in a resturant, had formed such a persistent habit of picking the plaster off the walls that one landlord after another refused to have her for a tenant. It required but a few weeks' time to teach her to make large paper chains, and gradually she was content to do it all day long, and in the end took quite as much pleasure in adorning the walls as she had formerly taken in demolishing them. Fortunately the landlord had never heard the aesthetic principle that the exposure of basic construction is more desirable than gaudy decoration. In course of time it was discovered that the old woman could speak Gaelic, and when one or two grave professors came to see her, the neighborhood was filled with pride that such a wonder lived in their midst. To mitigate life for a woman of ninety was an unfailing refutation of the statement that the Settlement was designed for the young.

On our first New Year's Day at Hull-House we invited the older people in the vicinity, sending a carriage for the most feeble and announcing to all of them that we were going to organize an Old Settlers' Party.

ST. GEORGE'S EPISCOPAL CHURCH (N.Y.C.) AND THE EDUCATION OF THE CHILDREN OF THE POOR (c.1890) From William S. Rainsford, *The Story of a Varied Life* (Garden City, N.Y., 1922), pp. 234–43.

I had a notice board fixed to the stone pillars of the chruch porch. It read: "Come in, rest and pray." Many such can be seen in New York now. Ours was the first and it did steady work, that notice board! It spoke to the passer-by of what the church sood for. . . .

The church, did not stand on a thoroughfare. For what we were attempting it was not well-placed, for it faced a quiet square and no great thoroughfare ran near us. But into the square came some of the drifting element of the East Side, some "bums," some tired and disheartened folk, and they read our sign, and sometimes came in. They soiled a few cushions, they stole a few church books, but they were never shown the door. Of course they did not come to the church services. Such beaten folk had got too far from any church for that. But some of them began to show interest in us—and on a cold day, to a badly clothed man, it was a pleasant place. On Sundays I stood at the church door till a few minutes before the services opened. I also got back to the door as soon after the belssing was given as I could.

In August, 1884, I rented, at $5 a day, a large room back of a saloon at 253 Avenue A, between 15th and 16th streets. I persuaded some of the small local storekeepers to display placards I had printed asking the neighbours to come to a religious service on Sunday afternoon. The only entrance was through the saloon where, in spite of the Sunday closing law, an active trade in drinks of many sorts, all of them strong, was always going on, and a rough crowd was smoking and playing billiards and cards. A questionable environment it seemed for a "baby mission," but the thing in its favour that decided me was that there was no stand-offishness about it. Here was a meeting place of the people I was after, a meeting place of their own choosing and making, not one that the church made and thrust on them. I had walked many, many miles in those dirty swarming streets (where women and children hung in midsummer out of windows and doors in a way that made you think they were pushed out from inside), looking for a place, before I found what I wanted. No. 253 Avenue A suited me well.

Since that beginning in the little Baptist chapel in Bethnal Green almost twenty years before, I had made a good many experiments in the missionary field, but as I made my way, that hot August afternoon, to the saloon in Avenue A, I felt I was on ground absolutely unknown to me. Of what was going to happen I had no idea whatever. . . .

I found the room almost full of children and rough boys, a few poor women, and no men except those whose heads were occasionally thrust through the door dividing us from the saloon, and who were evidently interested only in what a figure these new adventurers into the tenement region would cut. A babel of voices greeted our entering. The boys were on their feet, rushing after each other all around the place—a regular "follow-my-leader" scramble. The girls were there too for a lark, and took their fair share in raising a row. It was a youthful but an exceedingly tough looking crowd.

I called them to order and tried to speak. This brought things to an immediate crisis. Those boys formed a flying wedge. It was well and promptly done, and I was knocked flat on the floor. It was all play, rough play—no viciousness in it, but play with a definite purpose. They knew the purpose; and certainly they won the first round. When I got up from the floor we had a lively time of it, singling out the leaders and getting them inside.

As you can imagine, after this beginning the rest of the proceedings were somewhat disturbed. When we had locked up the room and turned homeward the neighborhood gave us another taste of its quality. I had hardly reached the street when I found that behind me quite a procession of youngsters had formed. They fell into line and where I went they went, joining in a sort of chant as they marched which ran: "Won't he be a comfort to his mummy when he's grown up?"

That first hot afternoon taught me afresh a lesson. I was prepared to learn. To the young I must look for my allies. "Tis they who are ready to follow a leader. St. George's future on the East Side depended on its sucess or its failure in winning the confidence of its neglected little ones.

Here I had my first real meeting with the living thing Jacob Riis afterward immortalized as "Tony," and I love to remember that Riis first saw Tony pasting the ugly old stained-glass windows of St. George's (the lower ones) with mud. If we had things to teach Tony, Tony certainly had much to teach us. His home a slum tenement, no room or little room for him at school, no understanding of him when he did get a place in school, and when he broke from school's unsympathetic and most unnatural restraint, then a bad law, shamefully administered, which tied his wild, vivid boyhood up with older and vicious criminals, in a prison for truants. No place to play but the street, and no peace in the street for the ubiquitous "cop," his natural enemy. Everything that stood for order and for property, the policeman, the landlord, the church, all were against him. Even in the parks he was faced with "Keep off the grass." So there was nothing left him but the gutter.

Yes, as I got up that afternoon with very considerable difficulty and delay from the accumulated dirt of that squalid room back of the saloon on Avenue A, my heart went out to those romping ragamuffins who had thrown me on the floor. What a dirty and neglected crew they were, and yet what infinite possibilities! What abundant life was packed away under their ragged jackets! I had started out intending to reach their fathers and mothers, and *here the children had pushed in between*. Though they may not have been aware of it, they had a purpose. They wanted to see and know if we had anything to give them worth while; if to their so empty and neglected lives we could bring anything better than they had been accustomed to.

I shook as much of the filth off my clothes as I could and went home with much to think about. . . .

The effect that little school had (we opened it first on Sunday afternoons, then in the mornings as well) on the whole work of the church was profound. It illustrated and explained our purpose as nothing else could. The place came to serve as a common meeting ground, a modest bridge across which East Siders who had given up all church life did seek and find a place in the great congregation composed of all sorts and conditions of men. But win and hold that meeting ground took intelligent, self-denying, and regular work; and for giving it, a debt is due to that first little band of volunteers who so promptly came to my call.

THE UNIVERSITY (OF CHICAGO) ELEMENTARY SCHOOL (1896)   From John Dewey, "The University School," *University Record,* vol. I, pp. 417–19.

The University School[1]

The attention of those interested in educational experiments is called to the school conducted under the auspices of the Pedagogical Department of The University of Chicago. The school is located at 5714 Kimbark Avenue, and there are at present thirty-two pupils enrolled, their ages ranging from six to twelve years. There are two regular teachers employed, Miss Clara Mitchell, a graduate of and former teacher in the Chicago Normal School, and Miss Katharine Camp, a graduate of the University of Michigan and recently in charge of the science in the Normal Department of Pratt Institute. Miss Camp will have charge of the science work, amd Miss Mitchell of the history and literature particularly. There is also a

[1] Report of an Address by Head Professor Dewey before the Pedagogical Club, Saturday, October 31, 1896.

regular instructor in carpentry and woodwork, and one in music, and in addition there are some assistants from the classes in pedagogy.

Especial attention is paid to matters of health. The children have the use of the University gymnasium and the advantage of instruction by Miss Anderson of the woman's gymnasium, who also undertakes a careful study of the physical needs of each child. The prominence of manual training in its different forms secures an ample variety of the activities requisite for physical and mental well-being. When the season is favorable, excursions to the museums, parks, places of geographic or natural interest in the country, and to typical industries in the city are undertaken as often as seems necessary.

The conception underlying the school is that of a laboratory. It bears the same relation to the work in pedagogy that a laboratory bears to biology, physics, or chemistry. Like any such laboratory it has two main purposes: (1) to exhibit, test, verify, and criticise theoretical statements and principles; (2) to add to the sum of facts and principles in its special line. It is obvious, however, that a laboratory requires a building and an equipment, but this laboratory has as yet few of the facilities needed for the work it has undertaken. It is in the condition in which chemical and other laboratories were some years ago when the need of experimental work was first becoming apparent. Visitors should bear this fact in mind.

As it is not the primary function of a laboratory to devise ways and means that can at once be put to practical use, so it is not the primary purpose of this school to devise methods with reference to their direct application in the graded school system. It is the function of some schools to provide better teachers according to present standards; it is the function of others to create new standards and ideals and thus to lead to a gradual change in conditions. If it is advisable to have smaller classes, more teachers and a different working hypothesis than is at present the case in the public schools, there should be some institution to show this. This the school in question hopes to do, and while it does not aim to be impractical, it does not aim primarily to be of such a character as to be immediately capable of translation into the public school.

The hypothesis underlying this experiment is that of the school as a social institution. Education outside the school proceeds almost wholly through participation in the social or community life of the groups of which one is a member. Through language and personal contact the intellectual and moral resources of the whole group are effectively, if unconsciously, transmitted to each member and put at his disposal. Moreover each individual does certain things (in the way of play and work) along with others, and thereby learns to adjust himself to his surroundings and also gains control of his own special powers.

The work here outlined is based on the assumption that the more formal education of the school does not depart from the same general course that the unconscious adjustment follows, but organizes it. The school is a special social community in which the too complex social environment is reduced and simplified; in which certain ideas and facts concerning this simplified social life are communicated to the child; in which, also, the child is called upon to undertake not all kinds of activity, but those specially selected on the ground of peculiar adaptation to the child.

This simplified social life should reproduce, in miniature, the activities fundamental to life as a whole, and thus enable the child, on one side, to become gradually acquainted with the structure, materials, and modes of operation of the larger community; while, upon the other, it enables him individually to express himself through these lines of conduct, and thus attain control of his own powers.

The fundamental activities (as well as those with which the child has been most in contact) are those connected with the home as the center of protection, shelter, comfort, artistic decoration, and food supply. Hence the school work aims to center upon these activities, and, so far as possible, enables the child to reproduce them in a gradual, orderly, and social way, in his own experience. Hence the educational importance attached to manual training, cooking, etc. They are not regarded as special accomplishments to be separately mastered, but rather as the media through which the child may gain social experience, and also as furnishing the most natural centers about which the materials of knowledge may be gathered and communicated to the child. It is intended to apply this same general idea to each branch of instruction. With the activities of the home as a point of departure, the different subjects taught in the ordinary school are the necessary products of this working out of the fundamental forms of social action. A large part of the educational waste comes from the attempt to build a superstructure of knowledge without a solid foundation in the child's relation to his social environment. In the language of correlation, it is not science, or history, or geography that is the center, but the group of social activities growing out of the home relations. It is beginning with the motor rather than with the sensory side. Since so much is said about sense training in the new education, it is well to ask under what stimulus the senses act. Attention itself is selective. The eye of the animal is alive to those things only which have a relation to its activities,—the getting of food or the escape from danger. The child, too, is attentive to what relates to his activities,—in other words, to what interests him, hence the senses get their stimulus from the motor side, from what the child wishes to do. It is not necessary to make up a set of stimuli to hold his attention or get him interested when he is using the saw or plane. His senses are on the alert, since he must use them in order to do something. This is the psychological reason for beginning with the child's activities. On the social side they introduce the child to the world of human relations; on the individual side they reveal him to himself as a factor in those relations.

The mode in which the common school studies are developed from these social activities is easily seen. Reading, writing, and spelling are usually taught too soon, since the brain centers called into exercise by these studies are not sufficiently developed to make their use pleasurable and profitable. It is one of the great mistakes of education to make reading and writing constitute the bulk of the school work the first two years. The true way is to teach them incidentally as the outgrowth of the social activities at this time. Thus language is not primarily the expression of thought, but the means of social communication. By its use the child keeps track of his work from day to day; by it he gives to others the results of his own special activity, and his own consciousness is widened by knowing what others have thought and done in the same lines. If language is abstracted from social activity, and made an end in itself, it will not give its whole value as a means of development. When the same reading lesson is given to forty children and each one knows that all the others know it, and all know that the teacher knows it, the social element is effectively eliminated. When each one has something individual to express, the social stimulus is an effective motive to acquisition. It is not claimed that by the method suggested, the child will learn to read as much, nor perhaps as readily in a given period as by the usual method. That he will make more rapid progress later when the true language interest develops, and that the break in the continuity of the child's life will be prevented, can be claimed with confidence.

Number is another of the trinity of fetishes of primary work. With the home activities as the basis of school work there is a constant demand for measurement in carpentry, cooking and sewing. The child may not learn as much of number as by the study of the multiplication table, but he will get an idea of what number really is, instead of the mere technique of number as is the case at present. The children who have been taught abstract relations only cannot translate them into the concrete form required by practical life. If they began with the practical activities, there would be no such difficulty. A teacher in a cooking school stated that it took her adult students nearly a month to get true ideas of measurement. Could any one doubt their knowledge of the multiplication table or fractions? If number is taught not as number, but as a means through which some activity undertaken on its own account may be rendered more orderly and effective, it assumes a different aspect, and affords insight into the ways in which man actually employs numerical relations in social life.

The relation of science to the activities of life is equally vital. In the history of the race, science is the outgrowth of the race activities, and not the result of investigation undertaken for its own sake. Thus the child is repeating the race experience when his activities lead him into the path of knowledge. Cooking leads to botany, chemistry, and the related sciences; the coal used leads to geology and geography, and ultimately to botany also. Carpentry and sewing lead likewise to a knowledge of materials, and the processes of construction, all of which gives a practical insight into the arts of life and their relation to man. All this work will form the avenue of approach to history in its true sense, since history should begin with the conquest of nature by man. Beginning with the life of primitive man living in trees or caves, the additional elements are gradually introduced until the child has the key by means of which he can interpret the complex social life he sees about him. History as simplified social life gives a proper foundation for teaching the literature of any period. Hiawatha or the Iliad should only be given in connection with a study of the social life of the people represented in the respective poems.

One of the main educational questions under consideration at the present time is the proper organization of the subject-matter of the curriculum, and the relation of the subjects mentioned to other means of expression, such as drawing, coloring and modeling. On the hypothesis given above, it is evident that an organizing principle has been found, and that each study has its essential function in the educational unity. The hypothesis is not to be accepted as proved but needs testing and verifying under different conditions and circumstances. Of the value of careful experiment along this line there can be no question.

DESCRIPTION OF A DAY AT THE UNIVERSITY ELEMENTARY SCHOOL

(1900)   From Laura L. Runyon, "A Day with the New Education," *Chautauquan,* vol. XXX, pp. 589–92.

"My dear," said my husband one morning—in the tone of voice he reserves for notifying me that a contagious disease has broken out in the neighborhood, or that he has discovered signs of total depravity in one of the children—"I think we are making a mistake in sending the children to the public school."

I had used those identical words to him on several successive mornings, after I had stayed awake for hours trying to decide whether to let the children go on getting only a fiftieth part of the attention of a teacher in the public schools, or to hire a university student to tutor them in his odd moments, at $1.50 an hour. But I never like to irritate my husband early in the morning, so I restrained the "Just what I told you," and said calmly:

"What have you to suggest?"

"I hear that all the professors at the university are sending their children to the Dewey school."

I had heard of the Kosminski and the Ray schools in South Park, Chicago, where we had recently moved, and so asked if this were a new one, named after the admiral.

"Oh dear, no!" said my husband. "Mead says it's one of the greatest movements of the century. It's a primary school run by a university, with Dr. Dewey, the psychologist, to direct it. Its real name is 'The University Elementary School,' but every one calls it the Dewey school, because Dr. Dewey is working out some psychological principles of education."

Now I recollected that one of my neighbors, to whom I had expressed my dissatisfaction with public schools, had sent me some books concerning a new plan of education. I got them and found them to be, "My Pedagogical Creed," and "The School and Society," both by Prof. John Dewey, head of the Department of Psychology and Pedagogy in the University of Chicago. I wondered if the new school were a "finishing" school, and if Dr. Dewey had discovered a way to abbreviate the amount of knowledge a child must have to be respectable, so that it could be learned in the elementary grade. I determined to visit the school.

I have always found it best to do things while they are in my mind; so I started immediately after breakfast and arrived at the school before work had begun.

None of the children seemed to have any books as they came up. I didn't see even a geography or a reader among the older children. One little girl had a live alligator in a box; a small boy was carrying a large Indian blanket in from a carriage; one child had a basket of fruit, and another a package which I heard him tell the teacher contained "sandwiches." As he gave them into her charge, a smaller boy who had been following him, asked pleadingly, "Aren't you going to invite me, George?"

I concluded that this must be an off day with the school; but thought that I might as well stay and see them start,—they seemed to be having such a good time.

At nine o'clock a bell rang, and the children went to various rooms, where I saw some one was marking their attendance. I was surprised to find that there were not more than ten children with any one teacher; and that instead of the absolute silence I had considered the proper beginning of school, the children merely took their places in what seemed to be a recognized order, and continued their conversation. Then the "leader" was given a program for the day.

I concluded that not all were going to the picnic and that I would stay and see what I could. I followed the children to the gymnasium, where seats were arranged for the morning exercises, which consisted chiefly of singing. One or two groups of children were asked to sing their "Group Song." Upon inquiry I was told that the charming little melody and the words of the songs I heard were composed by the children who sang them. All the "leaders" as they took their groups to various rooms after the singing seemed to have programs for the day; and I concluded that the picnic had been postponed, and felt sorry for the children with the sandwiches and fruit.

Upstairs I found a group of children about ten years old engaged in setting up electric bells. I recognized one of the children as a boy from our neighborhood, and wondered if I could get him to fix our bell, since we had had a sign "Please knock; bell don't ring" on the door for two days while waiting for the repair man.

A group of younger children had a sheepskin from which they were taking the wool. They spread the wool out thin with their hands and let the dirt fall out, then pulled the fibers straight and wound them on a stick which they called their "distaff." One little girl who had her distaff full was spinning the wool into yarn with the help of a spindle she said she "made in the shop." Around the room were primitive looms being "warped" by the children, and I was shown designs of their own which were to be woven into small blankets. In another room I found one of the large old-fashioned looms of which I had heard, but had never seen before. Two of the older boys were at work "setting it up" as they called it.

Everywhere the children were busy, but the morning was half gone and I had heard nothing that reminded me of a school except a class talking Latin as I passed. I had heard a class discussing whether John Smith or George Washington were the greater man, and another group, with a relief map, trying to decide where it would be best to erect forts to protect the English colonies from the French aggressions from the north and west. But I always know at home when the children get on those subjects that they are *not* studying their lessons. I wondered why the teacher did not tell them, if she thought it worth while, and then have them bound states and name the capitals and principal cities. In all the classes the children talked—sometimes two at once; but with a freedom of expression and an ability to stick to the point which surprised me.

I met one of the teachers in the hall and besought her to tell me about the school: whether they had days, or hours, when they really used books; whether Dr. Dewey believed children ought to learn how to read, write and cipher, or whether the new education was a preparation for Tolstoy's socialism. She said that Dr. Dewey believed the time spent in an elementary school on reading, writing and arithmetic could be more profitably spent; that an average child could learn these in doing other things.

She directed me to a class in primitive life where the children had spent some weeks in working out, with the aid of the teacher, what the earliest people must have done when they had no clothing, or food, or shelter, or means of defense. She told me how they had thought of a spear by fastening a stick between the split ends of a club; how they had made bowls out of clay, and discussed caves as the first homes, and skins as the first clothing. How they had moulded in clay their ideas of man and animals in those days, and had become so interested that they had begged to write a report of their work for the school paper. This report had been dictated to the teacher, as none of the class could write. It was then typewritten and all read what the whole group had agreed should be their record of work.

As I passed the room where the little girl with the alligator was, I observed the whole class absorbed in reading a similar report of their work, while the alligator in its box was unnoticed. When a child did not know a word, he was quite as likely to ask one of the other children to help him as to appeal to the teacher.

I had seen "gymnasium" on the program and concluded I would visit that and perhaps find the physical training my little folks needed. But I did not get so far, for as I passed through the dining-room the boy I had seen with the sandwiches and the girl with the fruit were setting the table. Each had a high white apron on and said they were the "waiters," and that this was their "day for the group luncheon;" that the rest of the group were cooking in the kitchen.

I found my way to the kitchen, which I had previously mistaken for the laboratory, with its rows of gas fixtures and asbestos mats. I learned that earlier in the morning the group had had a cooking lesson in which they experimented with the food given them. Each child had cooked one-third of a cup of flaked wheat in two-thirds of a cup of water. Each had calculated how much water he would need if he cooked half a cup, and then one child was told to find out how much he would need for the whole group and to cook it, while other tasks were assigned to the rest. Some were cooking a food which they had missed by absence, or which they had failed to cook properly. One child was making cocoa for all; another was making out a tabular statement showing the proportion of water needed for each of the various preparations of wheat, oats and corn they had studied.

I thought how Fred worried over his fractions, and here were children two years younger working out the number of cupfuls of water and cereal that would be needed for a family of three, five or eight, on the basis of the number for which one-third of a cupful would be sufficient.

The teacher told me that after they had used various weights and measures until they were familiar with them, they arranged them in tables for convenient reference; that after they had added by threes, fives, sevens, etc., they arranged these in the multiplication tables.

As I went back through the dining-room to the reception-room where one of the teachers had promised to answer some of my questions, the children sat down to the luncheon they had prepared. The sandwiches and fruit appeared, and the small boy who had begged an invitation was there, as a guest. A teacher had also been invited, and served the cereal brought her by the waiters.

From time to time during the morning, a line from Dr. Dewey's book had come into my mind: "Education is a process of living; not a preparation for future living."

The teacher who had consented to enlighten me said that Dr. Dewey had no thought of training cooks or factory hands, but that he believed there was an educational value in handling the raw materials from which our food, clothing and comforts are derived, and a mental training in reinventing each stage of the process of these industries. Then she told me how one group of children had begun by twisting the wool in their hands to spin it into thread, as the earliest primitive people must have done; how the stick on which they had wound the hand-twisted wool dropped to the ground, twirling about and twisting the end of the thread held in the hand; and how this idea had been developed into the top-shaped spindle I had seen. They had then invented hand-cards for getting the fibers straight, then the idea of the spinning-wheel and the reel. They had also worked out the loom from the simple form of two sticks between which the warp was stretched to the more complex machinery. This had been done by the teacher putting in the simplest way exactly the difficulty to be overcome; and then the children worked out the way to overcome it.

The teacher further pointed out to me that in cooking their luncheons they not only learned to use fractions and weights and measures, as I had seen, but incidentally learned a great deal about chemistry. They estimated in percentage the amount of water and starch in a potato; they tried the effect of the juice of the tomato and of vinegar on milk, and decided that the curdling was due to an acid, and then found that soda would neutralize the acid and that it could be used to prevent curdling in their tomato bisque soup.

"But all this has been found out by past generations," I said. "Why not give the children the results; why require them to repeat the process?"

"*Because the process is the valuable part.* All universities now have laboratories in order that the students may perform their own experiments, rather than watch the professor do them; we merely carry out the same idea in the elementary period. The children have to read and write and manipulate figures and construct in order to do other things in which they are interested; and because what they desire to accomplish appeals to them as of real value, they are willing to do the less interesting work connected with it. Or take any one of our textile industries: the child has always thought of cloth as a thing by itself, with no history back of it beyond the store from which it was purchased. Under the guidance of the teacher he sees it reduced to its first elements, then reconstructed by himself, and cloth has become a new thing to him, bringing to his mind the lives of many people and many occupations. Moreover, he has learned a method of investigation which he can apply to any subject."

I was convinced, and entered my children; but asked, just as a matter of curiosity, "Isn't it very expensive to have a teacher for so few children?"

"Yes, but the university and some friends of the school who are interested in seeing the experiment carried through until the children enter college are helping us. Of course we hope some day to have an endowment," she said with a smile.

DESCRIPTION OF P.S. 188 ON NEW YORK'S EAST SIDE (1900)   From "The Largest Public School in the World," *The New York Times,* November 25, 1900.

Public School No. 188 is the largest public school in the world. In the great play yard in the central court the children were romping about so noisily that the two men had to cease talking. They could not hear each other. Then, of a sudden a gong sounded, and the hubbub was hushed. The boys on one side of the yard, the girls on the other, fell into lines, each representing a class and slowly and noiselessly, save for the shuffling of feet, they marched away to their classrooms. "You won't believe it, perhaps, but that little army you have just seen contained five thousand children, or as many as attend all the schools in the entire State of Nevada. Under this roof there are a quarter of a thousand more pupils than in all Columbia University. Indeed, there are seats enough for the students of Yale, Brown, Amherst, and Bowdoin combined."

Following the boys upstairs, the two men met Mr. Mandel, the principal, whose face brightened as soon as he was asked if they might visit the classrooms. "I guess you won't have time to go into all of them," he said, as he led the way. "You see there are ninety-six altogether." Turning through a door the visitors found themselves confronted by forty lads poring over a history lesson. In the teacher's chair a boy had been left in charge. "A small-sized republic," remarked the principal. "You see how well they can govern themselves. They have elected this president to administer affairs in the interim."

"They do maintain good decorum to be sure," said the writer, "although there must be some tough rowdies among them. They doubtless go to school because they have to, and so when they get through the slums will swallow them up again. I suppose there is hardly one of them who has in view any definite vocation."

"I'd be glad to take a census of the class to find out," said Mr. Mandel, and, turning to the teacher, who had just returned, he asked him to call the roll. Of the thirty-nine present, only one was undecided as to his life work. Eleven wanted to take up various business careers. Nine intended to be lawyers, six civil engineers, three dentists, three doctors, two teachers and one each for the various callings of mechanic, engraver, designer of clothes, and electrical engineer. Of the thirty-nine, the majority were Jewish. On inquiry the teacher found that the reason why six had chosen civil engineering was because they had watched the construction of the Williamsburg Bridge. The engineers who directed the work, who "bossed the *dagoes*," as one Irish boy put it, had made many of the youth of the neighborhood ambitious to rise to a like position of wisdom and authority. The average age of the boys of this class was fourteen. They will be graduated next February.

Across the hall the visitors found a class hard at work at English composition. It was made up of pupils who contrasted strongly with those they had just left. They were four or five years younger and showed more clearly the influence of their home life. Their faces were dirtier, their hair more snarled, and their clothes more ragged.

"We haven't had as much opportunity to bring out what is best in these little fellows," Mr. Mandel explained.

The subject of the essays was, "My Vacation." And when they were handed in they showed that nearly all of the class had spent the summer in East Side streets. One spoke of an "outing" in Central Park, and another had gone "camping" in the Bronx. A third devoted his whole composition to a baseball game. It, to him, was the most important happening in the last two months. The teacher read it aloud as follows: "During vacation our team and another team arranged a game of baseball. It was to be played at 6th Street dock for $2. The game started and it was the ending of the fifth inning. The score was in favor of the other side, 7 to 0 when the pitcher went to pieces and we hit him for ten runs and won out by 10 to 7."

A hand was waving wildly in the rear of the room, and as soon as its possessor was recognized by the teacher a voice resounded shrilly, "I tell youse about dat game. I wuz on the side dat lost. Each side put up a dollar. We wuz beat cuz dey bribed our pitcher."

The writer of the composition hotly denounced this as a falsehood, and words would have led to blows had not the teacher interposed. Meanwhile the sociologist nodded his head thoughtfully and to his friend muttered, "No wonder our politics and commercial methods are corrupt. Ah, ha, I'll put this in my book."

"No city in the world spends as much as New York for education. Even London takes second rank," was the response. "With 2,000,000 more inhabitants London appropriates several million dollars less a year for schools than we do. In 1900 that city spent for 500,000 pupils $16,988,000, or a little more than two-thirds New York's appropriation for an enrollment of 555,000." Mr. Mandel brought the conversation to a close by leading the visitors into another classroom. "This is the foreign class of boys," he explained. "Here we take them almost out of the steamships. When we have sifted this class throughly, we will leave not one who can speak the English language." As it happened, the teacher had just asked all those who could speak English to stand up. Only two rose to their feet. One, a bright-eyed, black-haired lad of fourteen, said he had just arrived from Jerusalem but that he had studied English there in an institution called the Zionist Normal Polytechnic Kindergarten College. He said he could also speak German, Hebrew, Spanish, and Arabic. The second pupil said he had picked up enough English to understand most Americans because of having lived two months in London. He was a Jew boy also, and was born in Russia. The two lads were told that they would be assigned to other classes, and then the lesson proceeded. The teacher was endeavoring to make her pupils understand the words "open" and "shut." She would go to the door, and swinging it back, say, "I open the door." Closing it she would say, "I shut the door." Then, retreating to her chair, she would point to some pupil and give the command, "You, open the door." This done, she would address another boy with, "You, shut the door." After the class had apparently caught the meaning of the new words, the teacher put it to another test. Nodding to a little Hungarian and closing the door at the same time, she asked, "Now what do I do?" In his reply the lad showed that he had already imbibed a little English from his East Side playmates, for he shouted at the top of his voice, "You shut up. You shut up."

Mr. Mandel accordingly turned the visitors over to his assistant, Mr. Radik, as guide, who, as he led the way, chanced to say:"I suppose you have inspected our carpenter shop. We are quite proud of it."

"No, we haven't seen that," replied the author. "Who works in it, the janitor?"

Mr. Radik was so taken back by this utterance that he grasped the first door knob he came to as if for support. Then he explained that the carpenter shop was a regular classroom, where all the students had instruction the last two years of their course. Opening the door, he disclosed to view a score of boys each at a bench and at work making tabourets. "The finished product will adorn many an East Side parlor," said Mr. Radik. "Some of them show an unusually high degree of skill. Each student works from an original design. There is no opportunity for one to copy from another."

The class of foreign girls was hard at work learning such words as "head," "hand," and "foot" when the visitors arrived. After this drill the teacher took a crayon and, holding it up, said slowly, "I have a piece of chalk." Pupil after pupil took the chalk and repeated the same words. "Now," said the teacher, "I am going back to our old lesson," and patting the head of a little girl, she asked her what part of the body it was. With a serious, almost sad, look the child faced the class, and tapping her curly locks she said, "Dis ist my piece of head." But her classmates never showed the slightest trace of a smile. Even if any of them noticed the mistake, the language was all too foreign and too strange to contain any humor.

All of the thirty-three girls were Hebrews. Twenty were born in Russia, seven in Hungary, and six in Austria. Half had arrived in New York in the last six months and had fled from Russia to escape the torch and the saber. Several of the girls were thirteen or fourteen years old, and, according to their teachers, they were proficient in arithmetic and Russian literature. "But do they appreciate the opportunities of this country?" asked the author. "Ask that little one whom you call Rosie how she regards America." In Yiddish the teacher asked the question, and Rosie's answer, translated, was, "I love sweet America. They are kind to me here."

THE SCHOOL NURSE IN NEW YORK CITY (1903) From Lina L. Rogers, "A Year's Work for Children in New York Schools," *American Journal of Nursing*, vol. IV, pp. 181–84.

In a paper on "Medical School Inspection" printed in the New York *Medical Journal*, February 10, 1900, the following statement occurs, "The objective point in the system is *exclusion*." Now, in the same month in 1903, the system has undergone such changes that the objective point is quite the reverse—namely, *to keep the child in school*, and at the same time have the treatment carried on systematically until a cure is effected. This is due to the presence of nurses in the schools.

*   *   *

Under the old regulation, when the teacher sent a child suffering from some contagious disease, such as ringworm, to the doctor, and he excluded the child from school, their duties were finished. The child possibly took his card home and no attention was paid to it, and when needed it could not be found. He, in the meantime, played with the other children on the street until he got well or until the truant officer found him.

Now, instead of being sent out of school he is taken to the nurse, who promptly washes the sore spot with a tincture of green soap and water and applies a coating of flexible collodion. After this kind of treatment for a few days the "ring" disappears entirely. The collodion having stopped the spread of contagion, he is practically as safe as the others.

*   *   *

By means of the card system now in use it is almost impossible for the children to be neglected if everyone does his duty. The diseases are arranged in code form, each disease having its own particular number. These numbers are placed on an index card, which also has dates, when ordered under treatment, when under treatment, exclusion, readmission, and also the class and room number and school. This is signed by the Medical Inspector and left on file for the use of those requiring this information. The routine inspection is made once a week by the doctor, who goes into the class-room, stands with his back to a window, and as the children pass before him he looks at the eyes, throat, hands, and hair of each individually. On other days at an appointed time he visits the school, and those who have returned after an absence of several days, or any who have the slightest indication of any contagious disease, or who have returned after being excluded by the doctor, are sent to him. Those who can be cared for by the nurse are sent at once to her, the others being either returned to their class-rooms or sent home, as the case demands.

*   *   *

During the one hundred and twenty school days from January until June, when vacation began, the number of treatments given was one hundred and thirty-five thousand eight hundred and fifty-four, there being twenty-three thousand one hundred and ninety-one children with different diseases. To show from what children suffer most I will quote a few figures for the Borough of Manhattan alone, where there are sixteen nurses: Contagious eye diseases, sixty-five thousand nine hundred and eighty-seven; pediculosis, fifty-five thousand six hundred and thirty-one; ringworm, six thousand and fifty-seven; eczema, two thousand two hundred and eighty-five; scabies, one hundred and sixty-three; miscellaneous, five thousand seven hundred and thirty-one, which includes anything not on the code, such as cuts, wounds, etc.

Trachoma . . . is not treated at any time by the nurses. The simple washing out of the eye has very little effect on the disease, if any, and is a source of contagion unless the strictest precautions are observed. The acute conjunctivitis and the purulent forms are thoroughly cleansed with a boracic-acid solution, and besides this treatment in school the mother is visited and a practical demonstration is given with the advice to repeat the treatment at regular times.

Eczema, scabies, and impetigo are treated according to the schedule given [by the New York City Department of Health]. Pediculi succumb readily to the kerosene and sweet-oil. The potassium carbonate aids in getting off the oils and dirt. The vinegar when heated and applied loosens the "nits," when they can be brushed or drawn off with a piece of cloth. This means a lot of labor for the mother, but as they are anxious for the children to be clean every effort is made. That the work is needed is seen by the many requests from teachers and doctors asking for nurses in schools where they have none.

While much has been done, there is still more to be done. We hope to have every school in the city supplied with a room and other essentials, as well as having a nurse. Not the least part of the education is the instruction given to the mothers in the homes in cleanliness and the smaller details of nursing.

It is hoped that other cities may find it a part of their educational system which they cannot neglect, and that in a very short time the work will be universal.

PARENT-TEACHER ASSOCIATIONS AND THE PUBLIC SCHOOLS
(1907)   From Fannie Fern Andrews, "Parents' Associations And The Public Schools," *Charities and the Commons*, vol. XVII, pp. 335–36.

The formation of parents' associations connected with the schools is a part of the wider movement for the social utilization of the school plant. . . . This movement began with the kindergarten, which established the custom of holding mothers' meetings. In these meetings, the mothers and kindergartner talk over the children and discuss the functions of the home as related to those of the school. In many places, this mutual cooperation between kindergartner and mother has grown, until regularly organized mothers' clubs have been formed. These have much advantage over the mothers' meetings; for permanent organization brings with it permanent interest. Mothers' meetings and mothers' clubs, however, have not been limited to the kindergarten; they are also found in connection with the higher grades of the school. Moreover, the idea has grown until the mothers' clubs have developed into parents' meetings and parents' clubs or parents' associations, as they are called. Fathers, as well as mothers, have become interested in the work. These associations are not compulsory, but have generally been formed at the pleasure of the school principal, either by his own personal efforts or at the suggestion of parents or citizens.

Several women's organizations have become interested in this movement, and have been of material assistance to teachers and parents in getting them together. Probably the body which has accomplished the most in this direction is the National Congress of Mothers, which has for one of its chief aims the formation of mothers' clubs and parent-teacher associations. It has a state organizer in nearly every state in the Union, and many hundreds of clubs formed under its direction are doing most commendable work. Their object is, according to Article II of the constitution: "To bring into closer relation the home and the school; that parents and teachers may intelligently cooperate in the education of the child." Each association joins the National Congress of Mothers, which provides helpful literature on subjects of interest to parents and teachers, and also offers suggestive programs and speakers. . . .

Work of the Boston Associations. The parent-teacher associations, which perhaps come nearer than any others to the general idea of bringing school and community together, are those in Boston, which were established by the conference committee on moral education. The first was organized in May, 1905. . . .

"Its aims," says the annual report, "are threefold: to bring the home and the school together; to instruct the parents concerning the care of their children; and to promote the social interests of the neighborhood. To accomplish the first object, efforts have been made to acquaint the parent with the teacher's work in developing the child intellectually, physically and morally; and, on the other hand, to explain to the teacher the problems with which the parent has to deal. This has been brought about through talks, given by teachers and parents at the monthly meetings of the association, and by means of teas, held after every meeting where parents and teachers come together in a social way for interchange of thoughts.

These talks, which the report goes on to describe, seem remarkably comprehensive and pointed. Among those given by the teachers were brief explanations of the course of study and the aims of the teacher in physical and moral training, with particular emphasis on the necessity of cooperation between teachers and parents. Other topics were: Specific Instances in which the Parent can Cooperate with the Teacher; Cleanliness in the Schoolroom; How Children Spend their Evenings, and Cigarette Smoking among School Children.

Among the subjects presented by the parents, were: Fighting among boys, gambling, cigarette smoking, novel reading, theater going, spending pennies for cheap candy, playing in the street, etc. In consequence of some of these talks, a committee was appointed to find out what evening opportunites for amusement or education in the neighborhood were open to boys and girls. At a subsequent meeting this committee reported and recommended that the teachers inform their pupils of the places where they might go for healthful amusement and instruction.

At another meeting, one of the mothers spoke of the filthy condition of some of the streets, yards and vacant lots in the neighborhood, declaring "that dirt and disorder lower the morals of the children," and a committee was subsequently appointed to make an investigation, and to recommend improvements. "Through these talks," the report says, "the parents have become more familiar with the teacher's problems, and the teacher has learned to interpret the child from the parent's point of view."

Instructing the fathers and mothers. Not only, however, have these meetings brought the home and school into happy cooperation, they have also fulfilled the second object of this association; namely, "to instruct the parents concerning the care of their children." The main address at each meeting was devoted to such instruction. During the year, there were five lectures on the physical development of the child and two on the moral welfare. Three of these on the physical development were given by the medical inspector of the district. These lectures have proved an efficient agency for giving medical instruction to the parents. That they have helped the medical inspector in the performance of his duties, thereby making inspection a live issue in this community, is proved by personal testimony. . . .

The enthusiasm in all these associations is gratifying. "Why haven't we had them before?" is constantly being asked. The mothers are glad to assume much of the responsibility in carrying on the work, and take a great deal of pride in making the teas pretty and attractive. Too much cannot be said of the value of the teas. Here, everybody is expected to speak to everybody else, and over a cup of tea, which seems to have a magic charm for producing cordiality and geniality, the teachers and parents mingle; grievances vanish, and many a hard boy or girl has been converted into a helpful, conscientious pupil as a result of a friendly chat at one of these teas. . . .

The whole result of this work in Boston seems to demonstrate conclusively that these organizations supply a real need in the educational system. What these associations have done in their own localities indicates what similar organizations may do for the other school districts. Being a part of the general movement for the social utilization of the schools, and having a definite, distinct function to perform in this movement, they should not spring up by chance; nor should their activities be left to the accidental enthusiasm of a teacher or parent. The underlying principles of every parent-teacher association should be alike; they should aim to elevate the intellectual and social life of the community. It is evident, of course, that the specific problems of each association will be peculiar to the district in which it has been fromed. What would elevate one neighborhood might have no application whatever to another. It suggests itself, therefore, that there should be some recognized authority in every city to organize and guide parent-teacher associations. Logically, every school district of the city should be represented in such an organization, which shall deal with the intellectual and social problems peculiar to the district.

Since these associations are so intimately connected with the school system, they would most naturally come under the direction of the school committee, which is the guiding force in all the other forms of educational endeavor. The school committee should use its good offices to create among the parents and teachers of a school district a sentiment in favor of establishing a forum for the exchange of ideas on the intellectual and social development of the district. And further they should provide the facilities for the consummation of the plan. Schoolhouses should be placed at the disposal of parent-teacher associations; lecture service should be provided out of the school funds, and such printed matter as constitution and by-laws, invitations to meetings and annual reports should be issued by the school committee at the request of the association. There are many other ways in which a school committee can further such organizations—by furnishing the facilities for the tea, or the paraphernalia for an entertainment—without assuming a controlling attitude. The parent-teacher association would become a preeminently democratic institution—an organizer of enlightened public opinion on all educational matters. The combined force of all these associations in a city would constitute an educational support, invaluable to a body chosen by the people to watch over and direct their educational interests.

THE "VISITING TEACHER" (1910) From Public Education Association of New York City, "The Visiting Teacher," pamphlet, no pagination.

AN OLD PRACTICE

The teacher of a country school knows the home of every pupil. It has always been an essential part of the kindergarten idea that the kindergartner shall have a close acquaintance with the family of each child. But in a city school the teacher has large classes, little time, lives far from the neighborhood, and therefore home cooperation must be gained through the visits of a special teacher. The function of such a teacher is to prevent waste and to make school work effective. Such a teacher works as part of the school system by removing or modifying disorganizing conditions which affect individual pupils or families and through them injure the school system as a whole. With their assistance the system functions more effectively and more economically. The experience of several years proves this.

PROBLEM NOT SOLVED BY OTHER AGENCIES

The *Attendance Officer* attempts cure only.

The *School Nurse* takes health cases only.

The *Average Grade Teacher* has neither time, energy nor training.

The *Visiting Teacher* prevents the habit.

The *Visiting Teacher* considers the whole child.

The *Visiting Teacher* has training and experience both in teaching and in practical sociology.

COMMON PROBLEMS AND THEIR SOLUTION

Irregular attendance develops loss of interest, truancy and repetition of grade. Truant schools are expensive.

Misbehavior in the classroom wastes time that should be spent by teacher and children on regular work, distracts attention, and is a bad example.

Poor scholarship retards the child's advance through the grades, stifles his ambition, wastes his school opportunities, and delays the progress of the class.

Child labor stunts growth, robs youth of normal development, and produces unskilled workers.

The *Visiting Teacher* goes to the child's home, takes time to discover the cause, removes it when possible and by persistent attention establishes regularity. Prevention through a visiting teacher costs less than cure through truant schools, if indeed you get the cure.

The *Visiting Teacher* advises the parents, supplies needed out-of-school activities, gains the child's friendship and acquaints the school with the cause of the trouble.

The *Visiting Teacher* interprets to the home the demands of the school, encourages the child, interests the family in the child's home study, and explains the home difficulties to the teacher.

The *Visting Teacher* persuades parents to keep the child in school, and by so doing conserves mental and physical vitality, and sends forth a more intelligent and efficient workman.

THE FIRST MONTESSORI SCHOOL IN AMERICA (1912)   From Anne E. George, "The First Montessori School In America," *McClure's Magazine,* vol. XXXIX pp. 103–10.

My interest in the Montessori System was the natural outcome of my experience as a primary teacher. It had been my good fortune to work in schools where the fundamental Montessori idea, that of mental liberty, of development from within, was a ruling principle.

In the Chicago Latin School the little children have a separate building, which, strange as it may seem, has always been called by Miss Vickary the "Children's House." Years ago she substituted little tables and movable chairs for stationary desks and benches, furnished abundant and convenient blackboard space, and in every way endeavored to create an environment suited to the needs of little children. In such surroundings and under such guidance it is not surprising that my work tended more and more toward individual freedom. With a class of six-year-old children such freedom must express itself in action more than through abstract lessons. This meant, of course, much "hand work," and for years I had realized that the manipulation of materials ordinarily at hand required a great deal of direction and interpretation by the teacher before they became of value to the child. This direction did not do much toward making the children independent, and I found myself constantly discarding material as too difficult for the first grade. We did achieve order and discipline with activity to a great extent, but I felt that this control came more or less as a response to my wishes, and was not an outgrowth of the actual work done by the children.

About this time a friend wrote to me from Italy of a wonderful woman, a physician, Maria Montessori, who had not only seen the real need in primary education—an opportunity for self-development and for self-mastery in the child,—but who had been able, through her peculiar genius, to evolve a practicable system. Miss Risser's description of the schools where little children moved about happily, each absorbed in his own business in life, aroused in me a deep interest. The sense-training games of which she told seemed to represent the simple preparatory exercises for which I had been seeking in my effort to make hand work of real value to very little children.

This letter made such an impression upon me that I went to Italy to learn something of the method at first hand. Dr. Montessori took me to her schools, showing me in detail how she gave her lessons. The impression made by those mornings has stayed with me and has been my guide in all my work since Dr. Montessori's simplicity was a revelation. Whenever we entered a classroom, I distinctly felt that a new and sweeter spirit pervaded the place, and that the children were, in an indescribable way, set free. Yet there was order in everything. With a straightforwardness often stripped entirely of words, Maria Montessori taught, or, to use her own word, "directed," her children. She treated the children, not as automations, but as individual human beings. She never forced her personality or her will upon them, and made none of the efforts to attract and interest which I had often made use of.

In an eight months' course which I took with Dr. Montessori the following year, I obtained the schooling in her method that prepared me for my work in this country. The first American Montessori school was established under the auspices of Mr. Frank A. Vanderlip and several of his friends and neighbors at Tarrytown, New York.

The American Casa dei Bambini

Externally, Dr. Montessori's Casa dei Bambini bore little resemblance to this first American school. She made her first experiments in the model tenements of the San Lorenzo district in Rome—a section which has the same relation to the Eternal City that the East Side has to New York. She drew her children from the homes of poverty and squalor and too frequently of ignorance and vice. The American Montessori school, on the other hand, had its headquarters in a beautiful house overlooking the Hudson. My children all came from cultured families, whose greatest ambition it was to give their children everything possible in the way of education and rational enjoyment. We recognized, however, that these external differences had no special bearing upon the Montessori idea. That, superficially, there are marked differences between two sets of children with such diverse environments, goes without saying, Naturally, children who have been conscientiously nurtured from their birth develop greater dependence upon those nearest them and upon each other than those who have had to shift for themselves from the time when they were babies.

But, after all, these differences are only on the surface. The fundamental impulses and aspirations of childhood are the same in the San Lorenzo quarter of Rome as on the Hudson. All children have essentially the same minds, the same hearts, the same natures. From the first, therefore, I had no idea of "adapting" an exotic product to American conditions. I had observed Montessori work from day to day in Rome, and my only ambition was to do for American children precisely what she had done for Italians.

The children had their school-room in a part of the piazza closed in with glass. They understood from the very beginning that this was their room. There was nothing in it that they did not own and could not use—the light rugs, the little movable tables at which they worked, the little wicker chairs, the blackboards adjusted to their height, and the Montessori materials placed in order upon low book-shelves. The odd dozen children who were suddenly given this inheritance were fairly representative of childhood at its best. Nearly all were under five—the youngest was hardly three, none, of course, had ever been to school before. They represented all varying grades of intelligence and character. There were those who were exceedingly highstrung and disorganized, others who were unresponsive and methodical, others who had so little muscular control that they could hardly get out of a chair without knocking it over. There were some so quiet and unaggressive that they could hardly be forced to leave their corners, others so fond of applause that they constantly demanded the center of the stage. There were many brilliant minds; like all American children, however, nearly all had been unconsciously over-stimulated.

My problem was to take these children, place them in this school-room with the Montessori materials, and, with as little positive direction as possible, lead them, largely through the development of the senses, into the knowledge and the use of their intellectual powers as well as to normal physical control. The average person does not comprehend the extent to which little children are enveloped in a mental fog. It is, after all, the senses that keep us in intelligent contact with our environment; but little children have these senses developed only in rudimentary fashion. Only by training does the human animal learn to use his sense of touch—the little child scarcely knows the difference between rough and smooth and cold and warmth. He does not see the external world in clear and definite outlines; to his blurred vision there is little difference between a square and a round object. My duty was to lift the children out of the confused mass of impressions in which they moved and make them see the the world in its accurate proportions, According to the Montessori philosophy, self-control comes, not through any particular inward and spiritual grace, but through the control of the senses. Montessori recognizes that these senses are, in many ways, man's richest inheritance; that he who has them completely developed and under control rules his own body, and consequently his mind; and that their mastery should be an essential preliminary to all education. That the spiritual life is touched and awakened in a surprising and beautiful way has been to me the most evident, though the most mysterious, result of the method. And through this sense development I hoped to bring out each separate individuality, to create an independent and self-reliant human being. Children, just like adults, tend to lean upon one another; there is a natural gravitation from the younger to the older, from the weaker to the stronger. Human nature being what it is, this sense of dependence, to a certain extent, is inevitable, both in children and grown-ups; but all have defined characteristics and abilities, which, given a fair opportunity, will disclose themselves.

I gave no lessons just at first, but limited our use of the materials to exercises in which the children learned to carry the various objects from shelf to table and to replace them again in the established order. They were told that as soon as they understood the use of the materials they would be quite free to take them, and put them back again. A very widespread misconception seems to be that in the Montessori schools children are at once given full access to all the exercises and are allowed to select any object that attracts them. An instant's thought will show that such a course would lead to license, to anarchy, and never to liberty. The child is, indeed, allowed to make mistakes, and the teacher must for the most part withhold her hand and make no direct correction; but—and here lies the point which is often overlooked—the child is not allowed to make mistakes that arise from immaturity or from a failure to understand what he is to do with the material.

This indicates the teacher's duty. First, she must from her observation be able at the beginning to present the materials to the child in a sequence which for him is a logical one. Once started upon the road to intellectual independence, he will indicate clearly what this sequence should be. And, second, she must be very sure, before leaving the child to use the material alone, that he has understood her lesson as an explanation of what he is to do with the objects. It was at first frequently necessary frankly to take from a child's hands a game of which he knew the use, but which was beyond his powers.

Great Confusion and Disorder at First

The first weeks of the school were very discouraging, and any teacher who will pause and consider my problem will see that it must necessarily have been so. I felt with painful acuteness that Montessori spoke truly when she said: "These first days of disorder, though they reveal much to the teacher, are yet a most trying and difficult time!"

Order Comes Out of Confusion

As soon as the children found their objects of interest, disorder disappeared. They found more entertainment in their blocks, their colors, and in their stairs than they did in mental vagabondage. They now had a new and serious purpose in life, and with this power of concentration came a real independence. Children who had previously hung upon each other, their nurses, or their parents now struck out for themselves. Of their own volition they found a practical application in the buttoning and tying games, and began to dress and undress themselves. Others who had not yet mastered the art of feeding themselves now began to resent the assistance of their nurses and to it themselves. In the school-room they continually showed their growing independence by ceasing to imitate one another.

There was one little three-year-old girl, in particular, who had been dependent upon a precocious sister of five. Whatever the older sister did the younger implicitly imitated. If one had a blue crayon, the younger must have a blue crayon too. The younger could not even eat her toast unless her older sister ate hers at the same time. This went on for some time, when suddenly the little girl became interested in the "pink tower" and began to work independently at it. One day Jean, the older sister, saw with amazement that Dorothy was busily engaged with this new toy. "Why, sister," she said, "I am filling in a circle and your are making a tower!" For the younger child the act amounted to a declaration of independence; she now began her real life as an individual, and ceased to be merely the little sister of a very precocious child.

These children all showed that pride of discovery that comes to all men and women when they have really done something themselves. They would jump up and throw their arms around my neck when they had independently mastered such simple things as the cylinder, or the buttoning and tying frames. "I did it all myself!" "You didn't know I could do it, did you?" "I have done it better to-day than I did yesterday!" And with this new independence came real discipline, of which perhaps the finest evidences were the respect for work as work and a consideration for the rights of others. If a child wanted a particular object which one of his classmates was using, instead of snatching it from his hand, he would wait quietly by until the latter had finished with it.

*　　*　　*

Learning to Write with the Sandpaper Letters

And so, in the course of several months, these children, who began with the most rudimentary sense perceptions, acquired a reasonably complete control of their eyes, their hands, and their muscles. In other words, they were becoming intelligent and educated individuals. And now they began to manifest interest in those wonderful toys which have most impressed the popular imagination—the sandpaper alphabet. This has already been described in MCCLURE'S MAGAZINE. Briefly it consists of separate script letters, cut out of sandpaper and pasted on small individual cardboards. Its use at first is merely another lesson in the sense of touch. The children move the index-finger along the letter, just as they move the same finger along the sandpaper strips on the "smooth" and "rough" tablets. The teacher carefully teaches them to trace these letters in the proper way, beginning and ending at the same points as one does in ordinary writing. In this way the child not only learns almost unconsciously the shape of the letters, but the muscles acquire the necessary exercise for the precise movements required. In the Montessori schools, the child acquires the physical skill demanded for the production of written words long before he makes any attempt at writing. We teach him the phonetic value of each letter as he traces it. As the index-finger moves along the *t*, we make the usual phonetic sound of this consonant and get him to repeat it. In a short time the average child has mastered the whole alphabet.

In applying this method to the beginnings of reading and writing, I have, of course, had to face the problem presented to us all by the unphonetic character of our English language. I make no attempt here to outline my experiments, for I do not feel that they have gone far enough to be of any great value. I will only say that, so far, I have followed with great success the ordinary phonetic methods, substituting for the blackboard drill on word-families a set of cards upon which the phonograms, cut in sandpaper, are mounted. The children learn these as they did the letter sounds, and eagerly make spontaneous use of them, tracing over and over again -*ing*, -*at*, -*ate*, and so on, giving the sound and readily forming words by placing the separate letters before these groups. The word and sentence method, which I have always used with great success will, I believe, grow naturally out of these lessons when we begin our silent reading lessons and make use of the blackboard.

"Explosions into Writing"

I made no attempt to force this wonderful Montessori alphabet upon my Tarrytown children. Whenever I thought that a child was prepared for it, I would perhaps quietly call it to his attention. If he showed interest, then I let him have it; if not, he returned at once to the other materials. A boy who originally rebelled against entering the class at all was one of those who made the most rapid progress. At first he was exceedingly nervous and discouraged; but the work had not gone on many months before he had himself under fairly good control. Through at first he could scarcely use his fingers, in a couple of months he took up the sandpaper letters, and learned the alphabet in two days. Soon he could pick out the letters for practically every sound, and, under my direction, put them together so as to make almost any simple word. One day, when I used the word "plant," he looked up and said: "That word has a p and an a and an n and a t in it." Finally, after more exercise of this sort, he felt the "explosive impulse," went to the blackboard without any prompting from me, and wrote his name. He followed this up by writing other words that were associated with his every-day life—"gun," "daddy," "dog," "cat," "red," and so on. He accomplished these wonders about four months after his first day at school. It so happened that on this day he did something else which he had hitherto disdained— went with the other children into the rhythm exercise. In his delight with these accomplishments, he ran up to me, threw his arms around my neck, and cried: "I can skip and I can write, and I just love school!"

The American children do not, as a rule, display the same enthusiasm about writing as the Italians. Probably the reason is that writing strikes them as quite a normal human proceeding; they have seen people doing it from their earliest recollection, while the Italian children have not. One of my brightest little girls, suddenly feeling the impulse, went to the board one day and wrote several little words and a number of letters. "Oh, see what Caroline has done!" cried one of her schoolmates. "Oh, yes, I can write the letters," she replied in a casual fashion. The next day she went to the board of her own accord and wrote the word "silence." She turned quietly and said: "I can write "silence." Another child jumped up and rushed to the blackboard to get a closer view, whereupon, to her consternation, Caroline rubbed it out. "Oh, it was just something I wrote," she said simply. "I can write it again." And she did so.

Several other have "exploded" in the same way. My children do not write with the same facility as Montessori's. However, I have had them only half a day, whereas the Case dei Bambini hold sessions all day long. Moreover, at the present writing the Tarrytown children have had only about five months' schooling. Before the term is out, and before most of them have reached their fifth year, I confidently expect that most of them will have reached the writing stage in their development.

✻   ✻   ✻

The finest results of this first American experiment, however, are not necessarily these more showy accomplishments, but the development of individuality in the children—the mastery of self, the growth of independence, and the recognition and use of the senses. I have been able, likewise, to dispose of the criticism which is most frequently brought against the Montessori system. The Italian educator, it is said, makes the mistake of bringing the children too closely to the earth, as distinguished from other methods which encourage imagination and deal in fairies and knights and imaginative games. Dr. Montessori makes the children see the world as it really is. To her a block is a block, not a castle; the hands and fingers are anatomical structures, not pigeons; the children learn real geometrical forms by their right names—triangles, squares, circles, ovals—and not as symbolic abstractions. Does this not entirely crush the imaginative instinct, it is asked, and so destroy one of the qualities most essential to moral and intellectual growth? So far as I have observed, my Montessori children still have their imaginative faculties unimpaired. They are just as much interested in birds, trees, flowers, snow, and in people as the children of the kindergarten. The imagination plays little part in the Montessori schools in Italy, simply because imagination is not the predominant quality of the Italian mind, and never has been. The basic purpose of the Montessori method is to bring out whatever is in the child, and, since the Italian is not naturally imaginative, that quality does not appear. On the other hand, the American child is highly imaginative, and, according to its very genius, the Montessori system does not destroy this quality, but causes it to flower. I have had plenty of story-telling in my school, but in this, as in everything, I have followed the Montessori idea. The children have not been compelled to form a circle and listen to the story, whether they wished to or not. I have said, "Now I am going to tell a story; any one who wishes may come over here and listen." Often all would come, and often three or four remained at work. Occasionally those who came would leave in the middle of the story and occupy themselves in other ways. I made no attempt to recall or hold them, because I wished to see what stories interested different children. The child reveals himself in this just as he does in everything.

DESCRIPTION OF THE CITY AND COUNTRY SCHOOL OF NEW YORK CITY (c. 1912)   From Caroline Pratt, *I Learn from Children* (New York, 1948), pp. 27–30.

Turning back from my fifteen-year-old Pete in the shop toward childhood's beginnings, I came again to the little boy running his railroad system on the nursery floor. I had dreamed of a child world in which railroads and city streets, farms and factories, the stuff of which the real world is made, could be brought down to children's scale so that they might grasp it. I had envisioned a community of children who could in their own way, through the child activity which we misguidedly call play, reproduce this world and its functioning. Such a community of little individuals, equals in size and strength and understanding as adults are equals in their own adult communities, would learn not only physical truths about the world, but social truths as well, the all-important truths of people with many individual differences who must live and work with each other.

Certainly this was a harder way to teach children the unity of human endeavor than having them sit in a circle for half an hour at the beginning of the school day. To a traditional educator it was madness to turn children loose as I proposed to do.

But to me it was criminal to bind them. I had no faith in mystical circles; my faith was in children.

In its physical terms the plan was simplicity itself: a goodly floor space, basic materials for play, and many children using them together. Out of these modest ingredients I thought I could create a school for little children.

Simple as were my needs, I had to wait until the spring of 1913 before I could get them satisfied. A friend then offered me a small sum of money for expenses if I could find a place to work.

I went to Miss May Matthews, the head of Hartley House, a settlement on the West Side, and told her what I proposed to do. All I needed was a room. I would provide the materials and find the children.

She was quickly responsive to my plan, and offered me the assembly room; but with the stipulation that everything must be picked up and put away at the end of each session. This was nearly fatal: how could any really good play scheme be developed, if we had to destroy it each time and begin from the beginning when we came again? But she was helpless. There was no way she could find to give me the exclusive use of the settlement's main assembly room. Pioneer teachers who are today trying to introduce block play into public-school classrooms—with this handicap among the many they must cope with—may sympathize with my frustration.

On the half-a-loaf principle I decided to make a try. I had thought so much about what I wanted to do that I had to take whatever opportunity was offered to see it in action.

So, with whatever restrictions, I had my floor space. Next was the crucial point in my plan, the materials. Crayons and paper, scissors and paste were obvious. What I sought was something so flexible, so *adaptable,* that children could use it without guidance or control. I wanted to see them build a world; I wanted to see them re-create on their own level the life about them, in which they were too little to be participants, in which they were always spectators.

I knew children yearned to do this, and did it whenever they were allowed, with whatever materials they could lay their hands on. They moved dining-room chairs together to make trains; they set up housekeeping on the beach and baked pies out of sand; they towed coal barges of shingles laden with pebbles. And I had seen children playing with blocks at Teachers College, when the gifted Patty Hill had charge of the Kindergarten there.

She had designed the blocks herself, for the children in her classes to use during their free periods. They were not a part of her teaching program, but I had watched what the children had done with them during those short play periods when they could do what they liked. To me those play periods seemed the most important part of the school day.

Of all the materials which I had seen offered to children ("thrust upon" would better fit the situation), these blocks of Patty Hill's seemed to me best suited to children's purposes. A simple geometrical shape could become any number of things to a child. It could be a truck or a boat or the car of a train. He could build buildings with it from barns to skyscrapers. I could see the children of my as yet unborn school constructing a complete community with blocks.

But would they? There was something more they needed, a body of information. The little railroader on the nursery floor had evidently picked up information about railroads from observation and experience, and his wise parents had left him free to digest what he had seen, to take it into himself, and then to translate it into physical terms which he could handle. He had been allowed the freedom to gather together whatever he needed to reproduce in his own way what he knew. He was reconstructing a part of his world in which he was most interested.

Just as he had learned to walk and to talk by experiment, he was now carrying his method on to new fields of learning. He was learning about the world, thinking about it, reasoning about it, accepting this, rejecting that, putting it together and making it work.

Children have quite a body of information, more than adults generally guess. I am not talking about information which has been told them or read to them and which, parrot-like, they repeat, to the admiration of the same misguided adults. I mean the information which they have gained by their own efforts, firsthand, often unconsciously. What the groceryman and the milkman bring, what goes on inside the home, in the street or, for country children, on the farm—all this is most exciting knowledge, unless they have been sidetracked by having read to them stories of such sensational content that everything they are familiar with seems tame.

The child is already possessed of a method of learning, which served him well in babyhood. And he has gathered for himself a small body of related information. He needs only opportunity to go on with his education.

THE MONTESSORI EDUCATIONAL ASSOCIATION (1913) From Montessori Educational Association pamphlet (Washington, D.C., n.d.), no pagination.

WILLIAM KNOWLES COOPER
Secretary, Young Men's Christian Association

WILLIAM M. DAVIDSON
Superintendent, Washington Public Schools

MRS. DOROTHY CANFIELD FISHER
Author of "The Montessori Mother"

JOHN B. LARNER
Attorney-at-Law, Washington, D. C.

MRS. J. GIRVIN PETERS

MISS EDITH C. WESTCOTT
Principal, Western High School, Washington, D. C.

MISS MARGARET WOODROW WILSON

Director of Montessori Work
MISS ANNE E. GEORGE
Translator of "The Montessori Method"

The Montessori Educational Association

PURPOSE

The Montessori Educational Association was formed, as stated in the Articles of Incorporation, "to promote and develop in America the educational movement based on the principles and theories of Dr. Montessori, and to assist in the establishment and maintenance of schools for children and schools of observation and practice conducted according to said principles."

ORIGIN OF THE ASSOCIATION

The organization is the outcome of the enthusiasm aroused in the parents by the success of Miss George's application of the Montessori method to American children.

In 1911 the first Montessori school in America was opened in Tarrytown, N.Y., under the direction of Miss Anne E. George, Dr. Montessori's first American pupil, and the translator of her book. This school, made possible by the far-sighted interest of Mr. and Mrs. Frank A. Vanderlip, soon showed that the method which had been so brilliantly successful with Italian children was equally applicable to those of America, and Miss George received urgent calls to open schools in several cities. But patriotic motives induced her to accept an invitation to the Capital city, where in October, 1912, she opened a school in the house of Mrs. Alexander Graham Bell. The parents of the children enrolled in this class were so impressed with the results that they became convinced of the value of this method for educational purposes. They determined not only to establish this school on a permanent basis, but to put forth every effort to extend the same benefit to other children. To this end they have formed a national association, with headquarters in Washington. Among the incorporators of the Association are the active members of the Montessori

American Committee, a voluntary committee formed in 1912 at the request of Dr. Montessori.

SCHOOLS OF OBSERVATION AND PRACTICE

In this spirit they propose to establish in Washington, under Miss George's direction, free schools in connection with social settlements, for the purpose of providing training classes and furnishing the inspiration and special technique necessary to Montessori teachers.

These schools will at all times be open to observation. In such a laboratory educators from all over the country will be able to appraise the value of the method, and experimental psychologists will have a field for research.

A MONTESSORI BULLETIN

The Association expects to issue a bulletin of information upon all matters of special interest to its members. This bulletin, though modest in its beginning, may grow into a publication of importance; but even in the simplest form it will be of great value to members.

A BUREAU OF INFORMATION

One function of the Association will be to serve as a clearing-house for information about all matters connected with the Montessori method of education.

THE MONTESSORI PRINCIPLE

This Association appeals to all who share the almost universal feeling that there is need of some improvement in our present school system. Of late years the cry "Teach to the individual" has been growing more and more insistent. It is becoming more apparent every day that an education which attempts to force all human beings into the same mould, without regard to their individual capacities, cannot develop the full powers of each: may even in some cases smother or distort them. There is a great waste of time expended in useless work and of energy misdirected. Much of this waste may be avoided if the child can be trained at the formative age to the best use of his faculties.

This the Montessori method claims to do, and the justice of the claim has been demonstrated to the satisfaction of all who have watched Miss George's work this winter. It has been found that this method develops the child's individuality, while inculcating habits of concentration, order, forbearance, and steadiness. The result is that the child goes out from this training with a mind capable of effective application to any work that lies before him.

The fundamental idea is that the child should be allowed to develop naturally along the lines indicated by its own individuality. There is no real development but self-development; there is no real control but self-control. Therefore the child must be allowed complete liberty of thought and action, except insofar as it is harmful in itself or to others. This does not mean undirected, unemployed liberty, which would soon result in license. Here it is that the material comes into use. Children cannot remain idle when surrounded by so many interesting objects. The first period of chaos, when restless, undisciplined children hurry from one toy to another, soon gives way to quiet, long-sustained work, increasing interest, and quick responsiveness to direction. It is the teacher's office to aid and encourage the efforts which the children originate.

Though the children work always independently of each other, at the same time they are taught to respect the rights of others, and there inevitably grows up the community spirit induced by similar interests and accomplishments. This community spirit and the feeling of responsibility is further fostered by the little luncheons served by the children themselves, and self-control is developed to a remarkable degree.

As all our knowledge of outside things is gained through our senses, great stress is laid on the equal development of all of these. This is accomplished by a series of toys carefully prepared by Montessori to develop all five senses, particularly that of touch, which she considers as important as that of sight or of hearing. Very quickly through these "sense stimuli," as they are called, a co-ordination before unknown becomes apparent. The child acquires the full use of all his faculties, bodily and mental. Reading and writing are learned unconsciously, as a natural result of the child's interest in the form and sound of letters, and here he is aided by his sense of touch. Thus the development of the mind keeps pace with that of the body, and takes place naturally, absolutely without forcing, through the rational and happy employment and cultivation of all faculties.

That these statements are not merely theories has been already proved to the satisfaction of all who have watched the progress of the school during the past year. The parents who have seen their children develop into self-reliant little persons, happy and sweet-tempered in their relations with their companions, capable of unusual concentration and full of independence and the capacity to initiate their own amusements, can feel only gratitude for the opportunity which has made this possible. If the method which has worked so well with a few fortunate ones can be applied to the education of children generally throughout the country, will it not make for mental and moral progress everywhere? Then to diffuse the knowledge and extend the benefits of this system among all American citizens becomes the highest kind of social service.

MEMBERSHIP

A large membership from all parts of the United States and Canada is desired. The annual dues are $2. Any person in sympathy with the purpose of the Association is eligible to membership. Members will be elected by the Board of Trustees from names which have been favorably reported by the Membership Committee. Any person duly elected a member may, upon payment of the sum of $50, become a life member, and shall thereafter be exempt from payment of dues. Any person contributing the sum of $100 or more to the support of the Association shall become a patron.

CRITICISM OF THE MONTESSORI SYSTEM (1914) From William Heard
Kilpatrick, *The Montessori System Examined* (Boston, 1914), pp. 61–67.

We have passed in review the principal features of the Montessori theory and practice. Good points and bad have appeared. Before attempting a summation of the several valuations made, it may be well to ask, Where among other systems of education does this one belong? What is the relation of Madam Montessori to the world's educational thinkers?

When the surmise was made in the first chapter that Pestalozzi formed the background of Madam Montessori's educational philosophy, one might better have said that it was the Rousseau-Pestalozzi-Froebel group which formed that background, although there are more distinct marks of Pestalozzianism than of the others. This group of educational thinkers are differentiated from others by the presence of several characteristics which we find also in the Montessori theory. The revolutionary attitude, the feeling that one is breaking with customary practice, while certainly present, need hardly be mentioned, as this is an element found to a greater or less degree in all reformers. More to the point are: (1) a belief that the child nature is essentially good; (2) that the educational process is fundamentally an unfolding of what was given at birth; (3) a consequent belief in liberty as the necessary condition of this development; (4) the utilization of sense-experiences as means to bringing about the development; (5) a tendency to accept the faculty psychology; (6) the consequent tendency to emphasize the disciplinary aspect of sense-training; and finally (7) the emphasis upon nomenclature in connection with sense-experiences. While not all of these are found with distinctness in the writings of each one of the group, they either are so present or have been drawn as corollaries by followers. They are likewise present in the Montessori theory. When we consider that each of these characteristic doctrines, while containing a greater or less amount of truth, still has needed to be strictly revised in order to square with present conceptions; when we further consider that Madam Montessori's own conception of these doctrines has needed an almost identical revision; when we still further consider that Madam Montessori has confessedly been most influenced by Seguin, whose ideas were first published in 1846; when we consider, in particular, that Madam Montessori still holds to the discarded doctrine of formal or general discipline,—in the light of all these, we feel compelled to say that in the content of her doctrine, she belongs essentially to the mid-nineteenth century, some fifty years behind the present development of educational theory.

If we compare the work of Madam Montessori with that of such a writer and thinker as Professor Dewey, we are able to get an estimate of her worth from still a different point of view. The two have many things in common. Both have organized experimental schools; both have emphasized the freedom, self-activity, and self-education of the child; both have made large use of "practical life" activities. In a word, the two are cooperative tendencies in opposing intrenched traditionalism. There are, however, wide differences. For the earliest education, Madam Montessori provides a set of mechanically simple devices. These in large measure do the teaching. A simple procedure embodied in definite, tangible apparatus is a powerful incentive to popular interest. Professor Dewey could not secure the education which he sought in so simple a fashion. Madam Montessori was able to do so only because she had a much narrower conception of education, and because she could hold to an untenable theory as to the value of formal and systematic sense-training. Madam Montessori centered much of her effort upon devising more satisfactory methods of teaching reading and writing, utilizing thereto in masterly fashion the phonetic character of the Italian language. Professor Dewey, while recognizing the duty of the school to teach these arts, feels that early emphasis should rather be placed upon activities more vital to child-life which should at the same time lead toward the mastery of our complex social environment. Madam Montessori, in a measure following Pestalozzi, constantly uses logically simple units as if they were also the units of psychological experience. In reading and writing, it is the letter and the single sound, not the word or thought connection, that receive attention. Sense-qualities are taught preferably in isolation, apart from life situations. She speaks also of leading the child "from sensations to ideas . . . and to the association of ideas." Professor Dewey insists that the experience is the unit, and that the logically simple units emerge for consciousness by differentiation from the experience. Things, as a rule, are best taught, then, in connection with what is for the child a real experience, when they enter as significant parts into such an experience; and this because learning is essentially the differentiation and organization of meanings. It is, of course, to be borne in mind that a child experience is vastly different from the adult experience. What to a child is a whole satisfying experience, to us may be very fragmentary and disconnected.

But there are even more comprehensive contrasts. Madam Montessori hoped to remake pedagogy; but her idea of pedagogy is much narrower than is Professor Dewey's idea of education. His conception of the nature of the thinking process, together with his doctrines of interest and of education as life,—not simply a preparation for life,—include all that is valid in Madam Montessori's doctrines of liberty and sense-training, afford the criteria for correcting her errors, and besides, go vastly farther in the construction of educational method. In addition to this, he attacked the equally fundamental problem of the nature of the curriculum, saw it as the ideal reconstruction of the race achievement, and made substantial progress toward a methodology of its appropriation. This great problem of the curriculum, it can almost be said, Madam Montessori has, so far, not even seen. While this is no adequate recital of Professor Dewey's contributions, it suffices, in connection with what has been previously said, to show that they are ill advised who put Madam Montessori among the significant contributors to educational theory. Stimulating she is; a contributor to our theory, hardly, if at all.

Is this, then, the final judgment of Madam Montessori's contribution? The question of a permanent contribution turns on whether there have been presented original points of view capable of guiding fruitfully educational procedure. What novel and original ideas have we found that could at the same time bear the scrutiny of criticism? The scientific conception of education is certainly valid. Madam Montessori may, in a way, have come upon it herself; but no one could say that the world did not have a fuller conception of it prior to her. The most that can be claimed on this point is that her advocacy and example have proved stimulating. Her doctrine of education as unfolding is neither novel nor correct. In the doctrine of liberty she has made no theoretical contribution; though probably her practice will prove distinctly valuable. Our kindergartens and primary schools must take account of her achievement in this respect. Her doctrine of auto-education will at most provoke thought; the term is good, the idea old. Her utilization of "practical life" activities, more specifically her solution of early tenement-house education, must prove distinctly suggestive. It may well turn out that the Casa dei Bambini is after all her greatest contribution. The sense-training which to her seems most worth while, we decline to accept except in a very modified degree. The didactic apparatus we reject in like degree. Her preparation for the school arts should prove very helpful in Italy. It is possible that her technique of writing will prove useful everywhere. If so, that is a contribution. With this the list closes. We owe no large point of view to Madam Montessori. Distinguishing contribution from service, she is most a contributor in making the Casa dei Bambini. Her greatest service lies probably in the emphasis on the scientific conception of education, and in the practical utilization of liberty.

PRESS DISPATCHES ON THE JUNIOR HIGH SCHOOL IN SOMERVILLE, MASSACHUSETTS AND ROCHESTER, NEW YORK (1914) From *The Elementary School Journal,* vol. XV p. 115.

---

1. Somerville, Mass.

One of the greatest changes in the course of study is at the Forster School. Here has been established what is termed a junior high school. The program of studies is so arranged for the pupils of the sixth, seventh, and eighth grades as to give them the opportunity to take studies that will enable them to decide what higher courses they wish to take up later on. In this way it gives the pupils instruction in foreign languages at an age when study can be more easily carried on. The school is to be in charge of Joseph A. Ewart, the present master. The course taken by the pupils in this school does not prevent them from taking a different course after they enter the high school. The courses will comprise preparatory, commercial, manual arts, and grammar courses, all of which courses will devote approximately two-thirds of the time to the regular studies of the curriculum and one-third to the differential courses.

In the preparatory course this year Latin will be taught, but no modern language will be taken up. In the commercial course typewriting will be offered in connection with elementary bookkeeping and business arithmetic. In the manual arts course the handwork will be a practical nature, while in the household arts course for girls the course in cooking will aim to give the girls practice in making articles of food that would be serviceable for family use. Each of the courses will be so planned and so taught as to connect with corresponding courses in the high school.

2. Rochester, New York

Rochester, N.Y., is about to establish a reorganized school system under which it will operate junior and senior high schools.

The new system is classified in this way:

a) Elementary schools, each containing a kindergarten and six grades.

b) Junior high or intermediate schools, each consisting of three grades, the seventh, eighth, and ninth.

c) Senior high, or high schools, each consisting of three grades, the tenth, eleventh, and twelfth.

The number of grades is not changed, but there is a new stopping-point.

It is claimed that in arranging the two courses—one leading to completion of the senior high-school course and the other the junior—there will be no interference with the continuance through the former of the graduates of the latter, if they elect to remain in school. But it is also insisted that a better course can be outlined for those who expect to quit school with the ninth grade—and a majority do it—if plans are made with that result in view.

CHARLES H. JOHNSTON ON THE JUNIOR HIGH SCHOOL MOVEMENT
(1916)   From Charles Hughes Johnston, "The Junior High School," National Education Association, *Addresses And Preceedings . . . 1916*, vol. LIV, 1916 pp. 145–46.

The junior-high-school movement is sweeping the country. It marks a general educational reawakening, renaissance, reconstruction. This Association has made it first a field of investigation, then a propaganda and slogan, now a constructive program for development. The Department of Superintendence has embodied it in its resolutions. The United States Bureau stands committed to it. Many state departments are making it state wide. Large cities are adopting it wholesale. Small cities in impressive numbers and with impressive administrative originality are making their own ingenious adjustments to the idea. Surveyors of all kinds can think of no recommendable school policy that does not specifically incorporate junior-high-school features. Local city politics finds it useful, popular. All sorts propagandists like it. Cooperating agencies affiliating with public schools (library associations, for example) see in it something promising. University departments of education and normal schools and all other agencies for preparing teachers are finding new aspects of professional preparation for this type of teaching, new educational ideals toward which to point the intending teacher. Textbook houses, with expected enterprise, are announcing a new junior-high-school series of textbooks, heralding, they claim, an education with new and invigorating ingredients. Teachers employment agencies have begun to use the new term and to recommend for positions those with the newly required qualification. Standing "expert" commissions of inquiry (your own national Commission on the Reorganization of Secondary Education and the North Central Association Commission on Unit Courses and Curriculums) are preparing large areas, in fact the whole country, for the intricate kinds of inner readjustments the adoption of this fundamental change in school policy calls for. There are now educational courses in our colleges and normal schools dealing with junior-high-school education, and given by "experts." There is a literature, a terminology, a lingo, a cult, an educational philosophy, an educational party.

What is meant by the "junior high school"? One writer thinks the junior high school is a school made up of the upper grades (seventh and eighth) and the lowest grade (ninth) of the present high school, and "organized after the plan of a high school as regards curriculum, nature, and method of recitation, instruction, and supervision." This, the author says, is the "real junior high school—the school of tomorrow." Another says it is a school of these same grades or even of the seventh and eighth grades "which offers regular high-school subjects" and also "prevocational education" whose purpose of existence is "congregation and segregation"; congregation from many surrounding elementary schools and segregation from them into a new atmosphere where indeed, for educational purposes, different groups of these pupils can be given different trainings in certain subjects. Neither of these definitions is at all adequate to the variety of junior high schools in existence, to the distinguishing purpose of the junior high schools, or to what should characterize the ideal junior high school. Beginning the junior high school in the narrow but correct sense as a special institution, we should say that it is that portion or department of the public-school system above the sixth elementary grade, including the seventh and eighth, and usually the ninth also, which is organized under a distinctive internal management with a special principal and teaching staff, or under a six-year secondary-school department divided into a junior and a senior high school of three years each with one general management. Such a school in these first three years would provide for departmental teaching, partially differentiated curriculums, and for prevocational instruction, for a system of educational advice and guidance, and for supervised study. No defintion which merely says it is an institution which shifts the seventh and eighth grade boys from elementary school to high school properly represents the ideal of this school.

P. S. 26, INDIANAPOLIS: THE SCHOOL AS SOCIAL SETTLEMENT

(1915)   From John Dewey and Evelyn Dewey, *Schools of To-Morrow* (New York, 1916) pp. 207-15.

The supervising principal of public school No. 26 in Indianapolis is trying an experiment unlike any other known to us in an effort to make his plant a true school; that is, a place where children of his neighborhood shall become healthy, happy, and competent both economically and socially, and where the connection of instruction with the life of the community shall be directly recognized both by children and parents. Mr. Valentine's school is located in the poor, crowded colored district of the city and has only colored pupils. It is not an attempt to solve the "race question" nor yet an experiment suited only to colored people. There is nothing in the school not entirely practical in any district where the children come from homes with limited resources and meager surroundings. A visitor when leaving this school can not fail to wish that such ventures might be started in all our great cities,—indeed in any community where people need to be aroused to a sense of their needs, including the fact that if they are to contribute to the best interests of the community, they must be taught how to earn a living, and how to use their resources for themselves and their neighbors both in leisure time and in working hours. Mr. Valentine's school is a school for colored children only in the sense that the work has been arranged in relation to the conditions in the neighborhood; these modify the needs of the particular children who are the pupils. Yet the success of the experiment would mean a real step forward in solving the "race question" and peculiar problems of any immigrant district as well. Mr. Valentine is not interested in illustrating any theories on these points, but in making up for gaps in the home life of the pupils; giving them opportunities to prepare for a better future; in supplying plenty of healthy occupation and recreation; and in seeing to it that their school work reacts at once to improve neighborhood conditions.

Mr. Valentine's school is really a social settlement for the neighborhood, but it has a decided advantage over the average settlement, for it comes in contact with all the children living within its district for a number of hours each day, while most settlements reach the children for only a few scattered hours each week. The school has a larger influence than most settlements because it is a public institution for which the people who use it are paying their share; they feel that their relation to it is a business one, not a matter of philanthropy. Because of this businesslike relation the school is able really to teach the doctrines of social welfare. In any settlement the work is always handicapped by the fact that the people who make use of it feel that they are receiving something for which they do not pay, that something is being done for them by people who are better off financially than they are. But giving a community facilities that it lacks for special classes and recreation through the public school of the district put the work on a different basis. The school is really the property of the people of the district; they feel that they are more or less responsible for what is done there. Any wider activites that a school may undertake are to a certain extent the work of the people themselves; they are simply making use of the school plant for their own needs.

The neighborhood around Mr. Valentine's school is one of the poorest in Indianapolis, and once had a bad reputation for lawlessness and disorder as well. The school had struggled along for years with little or no support from the community as a whole or from individual parents. The per cent of truancy was high, and a large number of cases were sent to the juvenile court each year. The children took no interest in their work as a whole, and cases of extreme disorder were not infrequent; one pupil tried to revenge himself on his teacher for a merited punishment with a butcher's knife, in another case it was necessary to arrest a boy's father as a lesson to the neighborhood. Besides this attitude of hostility and of unwilling attendance, the school had to contend with immoral surroundings which finally made it necessary to do something to isolate the school building from neighboring houses. Finally the school board bought the tract of land and wooden tenements around the school building. It was at first proposed to tear down the old buildings, but the authorities were persuaded to turn them over to the school for its use. The school now found itself the possessor of a large playground and of three frame tenements in the worst possible condition, the board having stipulated that this added property should mean no further expense to the city after its purchase and the cleaning up of the grounds. It was decided to use the buildings for social and industrial purposes. One of them was fitted up by the pupils and neighbors interested as a manual training building. In this there is a carpenter shop, a sewing room, and a room for the class in shoemaking. Each grade devotes a regular number of hours a week to hand work, and has an opportunity to join other industrial classes after school. The immediate practical appeal of the work is never lost sight of, and the work is arranged to fit the needs of the individual pupil.

The carpenter shop is open all day, and there are classes for the girls as well as for the boys. Pupils are at liberty to go into the shop and work whenever they have any free time. The work is not confined to exercises to train the child in the use of tools, but each pupil makes something that he needs or wants, something that will be of real use to him. Processes and control of tools are taught the pupil by means of the piece of work he is doing. This is the keynote to all the industrial work done in the school. The more remote end of teaching the child processes which will be useful to him later is not lost sight of, but material is always used which has some immediate value to the child or to the school. The boys have learned carpentry work by making things that were needed in the school building—tables, cupboards, and bookcases—and by doing some of the repairing on the building. The girls have learned to sew by making clothes for themselves, for their brothers and sisters, and by making curtains and linen for the school. They have learned to cook by making soup for hot lunches for the school and the neighbors, and by cooking a whole meal for their own class. Besides the cooking and sewing department for the girls, there is a class in millinery and in crocheting. These two classes are conducted from the commercial point of view, to teach the girls to do something that will enable them to earn some money. In the millinery class the pupils start by making and trimming hats for themselves, so that they learn the different processes in the trade. The girls in the class who show the most skill are then allowed to take orders from friends and neighbors and trim or make hats for them. Besides the cost of the material the buyer pays a very small sum for the work, and this goes into the school treasury. The millinery class has done quite a business in the neighborhood, and turned out some very successful hats. Crocheting is taught as a trade, and any girl who wishes to make some money has an opportunity to learn how to make lace, table doilies, and all sorts of crocheted articles, like hoods, etc., which will sell. As the girls are learning, they are working on something which they can use for themselves or in their homes.

The work for the boys is arranged in the same way. Besides the carpenter work and the repairing there is a boys' cooking class, a shoe-repairing department, and a tailoring shop. The cooking class is even more popular with the boys than with the girls. In the shoe-repairing shop, which holds classes after school hours, the boys learn to mend their own shoes. A professional cobbler is the teacher, and the mending must be neatly done. The boys begin work on their own old shoes and as they progress in skill, are allowed to bring shoes from home to be repaired, or to mend for the girls and for the younger boys in the schools, who, however, pay a small sum for the work. The tailoring department is run on the same plan, to teach habits of personal neatness and of industry through giving the pupils work that results in neatness and gives some manual skill and control of tools. The class is taught by a tailor, and the boys learn to patch and mend their own clothers, as well as to sponge and press them. Attendance is entirely voluntary, and the class meets after the regular school work is over. Knowing how to keep themselves tidy has resulted in a very marked improvement in the appearance and habits of the boys in the class, and has had an influence not only on the whole school, but on the neighborhood as well. The boys no longer resent the attempts of the teachers to influence them towards cleanliness and neatness, for they have become conscious of the advantages of these habits.

The cooking and domestic science classes are taught in one of the tenements turned over to the school without having been repaired, although the cooking equipment was supplied by the city. All the other work on the building—cleaning, painting, repairing, furnishing, and decorating—was done and paid for by the pupils of the school with help from the neighborhood clubs that use the building. There is a large cooking room, a demonstration dining and sitting room, and two bedrooms. The girls not only learn to cook real meals, but they learn how to serve them, and then how to take care of the demonstration house. The domestic science classes include lessons in buying, the comparative costs and values of food, something of food chemistry and values, and large quantity cooking. This work is done in connection with the soup kitchen. A group of girls have charge of the kitchen long enough to really learn about the work. They plan the menu and do the buying, cooking and serving of the soup, selling it for three cents a bowl to the pupils of the school and to neighbors. They keep all the accounts and not only have to make all their expenses, but are expected to make some profit for the use of the school as well. They have made enough profit in one year to furnish most of the demonstration house. Aside from teaching how to do housework thoroughly and easily, the purpose of the house is to furnish an example of what can be done to make one of the regular frame tenements of the district comfortable and attractive, without more expense than most of the people now put into their homes. The house is very simply furnished, with cheap and strong things, in plain colors that are easily kept clean; the painting and papering was done by the pupils. The sewing class has made all the curtains and linen for the house, and made furniture by covering boxes, etc. Besides the class work that goes on in the building, the rooms are also used as a social center for the girls of the school.

VOCATIONAL EDUCATION IN THE GARY, INDIANA SCHOOLS

(1915)   From Randolph S. Bourne, "Appentices to the School," *New Republic*, vol. II, pp. 302-4.

Vocational training in the schools of Gary means that whatever work is necessary in the way of repairing, conserving, beautifying or enhancing the facilities, is done by the school itself. These large, lavishly equipped modern school-buildings require a force of mechanics to keep them in repair. Their shops are the industrial and manual shops for the school. The children work in them with skilled union workmen, who are employed not primarily as "manual training" teachers, but as assistants to the building superintendent. The mechanics teach by allowing the children to help them as apprentices. They earn their salaries by repair and construction work, while the children who desire it get an incomparable vocational training at practically no cost to the town. Where the ordinary trade-school must have large classes to make the enterprise pay, the Gary vocational work may be done with the smallest groups, for the shops are paying for themselves anyway.

Manual training takes on quite a new meaning as you move about, watching the boys in the carpenter-shop making desks or tables, or cabinets for the botany collections, or book-racks for the library, sending them on to the paint-shop when they have finished; boys in the sheet-metal shop hammering zinc for the roof; young electricians repairing bells; a couple of plumbers tinkering with pipes; little groups of serious and absorbedly interested boys in the foundry and forge and pattern-making shop, all cooperating like the parts of a well-ordered factory. There was obviously enough real work to keep busy for his hour a day every child who desired training in a trade. Where school and workshop are thus fused, the need for "continuation" and "cooperative" courses—where the boy alternates between shop or factory and school—disappears. The child has the advantages of both.

The ordinary school, and even the specialized vocational school, is rarely doing more in its industrial, manual, or domestic science work than playing a rather dreary game with toys. There could scarcely be a greater contrast between the real shops of the Gary schools and those ordinary "shops" and kitchens with their dozens of little machines at which at a given time the entire class does its little stereotyped "stunt." In Gary the domestic science room is a real kitchen in which the daily luncheon is prepared and served at cost to the teachers and pupils who desire it. The cook is a real cook, and the girls come in as observers, helpers or workers, just as the boys go into the shops. The nearest approach to a luxury is the pottery shop, but this is itself perhaps the best symbol of that fusion of the artistic and the practical that is the Wirt genius. What are you to say when you walk into the art studio and find half a dozen girls and boys high on a scaffolding painting a frieze which they have themselves designed, while others are at work on stained-glass designs to go in varnished paper on the panels of the door?

There is a genial, joyous quality about all the work that gives every room a charm—the foundry with its deep shadows, the smooth gray pottery shop with its turning wheels and bright glazed jugs, the botany room with its mass of greenery. Even the history room at Emerson School had the atmosphere which comes from concentrated interest and the slow accretion of significant material. Emerson itself is a spacious and dignified building with innumerable little touches of taste that one usually associates only with the high schools of exceptionally wealthy and cultivated suburban communities. It is a delightful paradox that so beautiful a life should appear to be lived where every activity seems to be motivated by direct utilitarian application. I said that you have to plough your mind up to understand this kind of school. Certainly I have never seen a place which more nearly permitted to seem real that old ideal of the joy of work which we imagine must have existed back in guild days. It may be left to the imagination what children trained in such a school are likely to have to say to the industrial society in which we live.

The practical work of the school is only limited by local school needs, but the shoeless condition of some of the Froebel children inspired the starting of a shoe shop were old shoes were made over. Both Emerson and Froebel have a printery from which come all the blanks, reports, programs, etc., used in the school, as well as the bulletins and papers by which the various classes are tempted to preserve the good things they write. The commercial pupils have charge of all the accounting and bookkeeping as well as the supplies. The children who work in the shops are paid in checks, which are calculated on the basis of prevailing union wages for the working-time. This provides opportunities for a banking system, which is also in charge of the commercial class. In the Jefferson School the boiler-room is an integral part of the machine-shop.

The botany class was responsible for the beautiful and elaborate conservatory at the entrance of the Emerson School, and for the window hot-house in the botany room, where practical experiments are made. The botanists also have charge of the shrubs and trees on the grounds, and the vegetable gardens which they work communistically all through the summer. Their study of food and textile products ramified into the domestic science work, just as the zoology study was fused with physiology. This latter class had a playground zoo, with foxes and coyotes, raccoons and prairie-dogs, about whose habits and adventures they were preparing a brochure, which was already in press at the printery. When I stepped into the zoology laboratory itself. I found that I was in an even more animated zoo. Crows, chickens and pigeons in cages at the back of the room were lusty with vociferous greeting. The imperturbability of the children amidst this racket showed me how well aware they were that this was the way a zoology room ought to behave.

Such a school, where the child works almost unconsciously into a vocation which appeals to him as neither play nor drudgery, is far more "vocational" than even the specialized school. The child, beginning so young in shop or laboratory, and assimilating the work very gradually, is able to lay deep foundations of interest and skill. The Gary school is distinctly unspecialized. In a sense it gives a completely "liberal education." The child emerges a skillful amateur. The industrial and scientific work no more "train" him to take a definite place in the industrial world than the cultural work trains him to be a college professor. But he does leave school well equipped to cope with a dynamic, rapidly changing industrial society which demands above all things versatility, and which scraps methods and machines as ruthlessly as it does men. Only the man of rounded training and resourcefulness who can turn his hand quickly to a variety of occupations has much chance of success. Our public school, in spite of its fancied "liberal" curriculum, has really been turning out only very low-grade specialists. It has made no effort to produce the type of mind most needed today—the versatile machinist, the practical engineer, the mind that adapts and masters mechanism. This is probably the best intellectual type our society produces. This exactness, resourcefulness, inventiveness pragmatic judgment of a mechanism by its product, the sense of machinery as a means, not an end, are exactly the qualities that society demands in every profession or trade.

The Gary school is the first I have seen that promises to cultivate this kind of intelligence. It frankly accepts the machine not in the usual sense of the vocational schools, as an exacting master that the child is to learn docilely to obey, but as the basis of our modern life, by whose means we must make whatever progress we may will. The machine seems to be a thing to which society is irrevocably pledged. It is time the school recognized it. In Gary it is with the child from his earliest years. It is the motive of his scientific study. The physics teacher at the Emerson School told me that he thought the fascinating and irresponsible automobile and done more to educate the younger male generation than most of the public schools. Tinkering with an automobile was a whole scientific training.

I dropped into his physics class, and found a dozen twelve-year-old girls and their nine-year-old "helpers" studying the motor-cycle. With that fine disregard for boundaries which characterizes Gary education, the hour began with a spelling lesson of the names of the parts and processes of the machine. After the words were learned, the mechanism was explained to them as they pored over it, and their memory of vaporization, evaporation, etc., called into play. The motor-cycle was set going, the girls described its action, and the lesson was over, as perfect a piece of teaching as I have ever heard. The intense animation of that little group was all the more piquant for having as a background the astounded disapprobation of three grave school superintendents from the East.

To these physics classes the ventilating, heating and electric systems in the schools are all textbooks. The climate is studied. The shops provide many physics problems. There was a class of boys having explained to them the physical principles of various types of machines. The impetuous rush of those little boys as they were sent into the maching-shop to take apart a lawn-mower, a bicycle, and a cream-separator, and the look of elation on their faces, would alone make Gary unforgettable to me. It was evident that this was indeed a different kind of school.

DEWEY ON THE GARY, INDIANA SCHOOL PLAN (1915)   From John Dewey and Evelyn Dewey, *The Schools of To-Morrow* (New York, 1916), pp. 175–84, 187–95.

A great deal has been written lately about the public school system at Gary, Ind., with special reference to the novel features of school administration that are being worked out there, or else with emphasis on the opportunities for industrial training. But the biggest idea there is the one behind these new features. It is the social and community idea. Mr. Wirt, the superintendent of schools, has had an opportunity to make the schools of the steel town almost from the very beginning of the town, and he has wanted to do it right. He did not visit the most famous schools all over the country or send for the best school architect; instead he stayed right at home, and forgetting what had or had not been done in other places, he tried to make the best possible schools for Gary. The question he tried to answer was this: What did the Gary children need to make them good citizens and happy and prosperous human beings, and how could the money available for educational purposes supply all these needs? The industrial features of his schools will be taken up later, but it may be well to point out in passing that they were not instituted to turn out good workers for the steel company, nor to save the factories the expense of training their own workers, but for the educational value of the work they involved. In the same way it would be a mistake to consider the Gary schools simply as an attempt to take the unpromising immigrant child and turn him into a self-supporting immigrant, or as an attempt to meet the demand of an industrial class for a certain sort of training.

Mr. Wirt found himself the superintendent of schools in an American town, responsible for thousands of children coming from all sorts of surroundings. It was his problem to take care of them for a number of years in such a way that at the end of the time each child would be able to find his own job and do it successfully, whether this was feeding a machine or managing a business, whether it was taking care of a family or working in an office, or teaching school. His problem is not to give the special information each one may need for the details of his work, but to keep the natural interests and enthusiasms of childhood, to enable each pupil to gain control of his mind and body, and to insure his being able to do the rest for himself. To be successful as a human being and an American citizen, is the goal that the public schools of the country have set for their pupils: earning a living forms part of this ideal, and follows as a matter of course if the larger training is successful. There are many factors to be considered in deciding on the best ways of reaching this goal: such as the individual peculiarities of every child that goes to school; the people that will teach; the neighborhood in which the child lives; and the larger community which pays for the schools. Mr. Wirt's plan takes advantage to their full value of the contributions each one has to make to the whole scheme. Each factor is a contributory asset; without it the others could not perform their work; therefore it means a weak spot in the result if anything is overlooked.

A tremendous waste in the organization of the ordinary public school appears at the first glance to a critic who is seeking to spend the school taxes with the greatest possible benefit to the children and to the taxpayers. The entire school equipment of building, yard, and supplies stands empty for half of every school day, besides summer vacation and Saturdays. The buildings are expensive and for the greater part of the time are not in use at all. This is an extravagance in itself, but when we consider the way the average child who goes to public school in town or city spends the hours when he is not in school, and the very incomplete education he gets during the school hours, we begin to realize just how serious this extravagance is. Mr. Wirt decided to keep the schools open all day in Gary, so that the children would not be forced to spend the greater part of their time playing in the alleys and on crowded street corners, exposed to all the dangers to health and morals that such places offer for the loiterer. Still the buildings would be closed for many hours a day and for many weeks, and he decided that the people who built the buildings—the tax-payers—ought to have a chance to use them for public purposes during this time, so the Gary schools have evening school, Saturday classes, and summer sessions. This makes the up-keep of the buildings much more expensive than having them open for a few months only, therefore some way of running the plant more economically must be discovered.

Children can not sit still all day at their desks as they do for five hours in most schools; therefore other things must be provided for them to do if they are to keep well and busy during eight hours of school. The Gary buildings obtain this necessary economy by using a building for twice as many pupils as the ordinary building is supposed to be able to take care of. There are two schools in every house, one from eight to three and the other from nine to four, and each takes its turn at the regular classrooms during alternate hours, the remaining half of the day being spent in the various occupations that make Gary unique. In this way enough money is saved to equip shops and pay extra teachers for the subjects that supplement the regular curriculum, and to pay for the extra sessions. Thus with taxes of ordinary size the people of Gary get schools that utilize the children's time, and give them increased facilities for learning, besides offering the adults of the community opportunities for special courses in evening school. At present in Gary the number of adults using the school buildings is greater than the number of children, though of course the number of hours they attend school is much shorter. By having two duplicate schools in every building one half the usual cost per classroom is saved, and enough money to supply healthy activities for the children for eight hours a day and to keep the schools open evenings, holidays and Sundays for adults is obtained.

Each building is equipped with a gymnasium, swimming pool, and playground, and has physical directors that are in attendance for the entire eight hours. Physical training is as much a part of the regular school work as anything else, and besides the work that is part of every pupil's program there are two hours a day when the playground is open for the children to use as they please. Instead of going to the streets to play, the children stay in the school and use the play opportunities it offers. For the most part the physical training takes the form of supervised play and apparatus work. Experimentation has shown here as in so many other places that the pupils are not really interested in the formal group exercises, and that they go through with them under compulsion and so lose most of the benefit. So for the gymnastic drill, swimming pool, tennis courts, and apparatus are largely substituted. The directors see that the individual gets the special exercise that he needs so that the work does not lose its orderliness or effectiveness, and besides getting physical development suited to his needs, every child has a healthy and pleasant place to play or otherwise spend his time outdoors.

The Gary pupil is expected to gain physically during the school year just as he is expected to keep up with his grade in his other work. Each child is examined by a doctor, and the pupils who are not strong enough for the strain of the classroom work are not sent home to do nothing until they are stronger, but are kept in school and given a program suited to their strength, their classroom time is cut down to a minimum, and they spend most of the day on the playground or in the gymnasium, doing the sort of things the doctor says they need to get strong. The physical growth of the pupils is just as important as the mental, and by devoting the same care to it that is given to the child's progress through the grades, the schools go a long way towards making themselves a small community which gives every opportunity for a normal and natural life.

The schools are open eight hours a day, but the grade teachers teach for only six hours, while the physical directors are on duty for the whole time. Four hours of each school's time is given to the regular classroom work or laboratories, and one hour for the auditorium and one hour for "application" or play. Then there are the other two hours when the children may use the play facilities if they wish, and they all do use them. By rotating the classes the number of teachers does not have to be increased, and the pupils get the benefit of teachers especially trained for the subject they are teaching. By dividing each school into groups of pupils the classes are smaller than in most public schools. For the first two hours in the morning—from 8:15 to 10:15—one school has the use of the classrooms, studios, shops and laboratories, one group in a recitation room for the first hour and in the shops for the second, the second group beginning with the shop work. The other school uses the playground for the first hour and attendance is not compulsory, for the second hour one group goes to the auditorium and the other remains on the playground for systematic gymnastics or has an "application" period. Then at 10:15 the first school goes to the auditorium and playgrounds for its work and the second school takes possession of the class and shop rooms for two hours. Grades one to five have two hours daily in regular classrooms for formal instruction in language, history, literature, and mathematics. Grades six to twelve have three hours daily for this formal instruction. The additional hour is taken from the play and application periods. Grades one to five have one hour of laboratory work in science or shop work in industrial training, thirty minutes for music or literature, and thirty minutes for physical training. Grades six to twelve have the entire two hours for shop work in industrial training, laboratory work in science, or music and drawing.

By this scheme of alternation of classes and schools twice the number of children that are usually cared for in one building are taken care of in smaller classes by teachers who are specialists in their subjects. For besides the industrial teachers, there are teachers for French, German, history, mathematics, literature, music, art, nature study, and the sciences. This additional efficiency is paid for by the saving on buildings effected by the two school systems. Each grade room is used by at least four different classes, so each child does not have a desk where he keeps his things and belongings, but has a locker for his books and changes his classroom at the end of the hour. No one teacher is responsible for one set of pupils, but for her own work, and in the same way the pupils are responsible for themselves. Obviously such a scheme as this requires a real spirit of cooperation among the pupils and teachers, and also good business management.

*　　*　　*

In discipline, in social life, and in the curriculum the Gary schools are doing everything possible, in cooperation with church and home, to use to the best educational purpose every resource of money, organization and neighborhood influence. The school is a small community in its discipline, and a democratic one. The work is so well arranged that the children want to go to school; there is no need to drag them with truant officers or overawe them by a show of stern authority. Once in the school building they feel at home and take the same interest and responsibility in the work that they take in their own homes.

*　　*　　*

Another difficult problem for the public schools in an industrial community with a foreign population is to keep the children in school after the legal age at which they may leave. The Gary schools go about this just as they attack the question of public health, not by making more rules or trying compulsion, but by getting the children themselves to help, by making the schools so obviously useful for each individual that he wants to stay. There are no "High Schools" in Gary! A pupil goes to school in one building from the day he enters kindergarten until he is ready for college or until he goes into business or the factory. There is no graduation with a celebration and a diploma at the end of the eighth grade. When a pupil begins the ninth grade his program deviates from the plan of previous years, but otherwise there is nothing done to make the child think he has gone as far as he needs, that from now on he will simply be getting frills and luxuries. The teachers do not change. The same history, language and literature teachers conduct all the grades; and in the shops the pupils get a chance to learn some one thing thoroughly. The pupils do not look forward to the last four years of school with dread of a hard and useless grind, they look at it as a continuation of their school life, getting harder from year to year as their own ability increases. And especially they regard this period as an opportunity to get training whose immediate value they can see. The arguments of the school to persuade the pupils to stay in school are practical, telling arguments, things the children can see. The school press prints from time to time bulletins explaining to the pupils and their parents the opportunities that the Gary schools offer in the way of general education and of special training. These bulletins give statistics and information about the opportunities in the different fields of work; they show the boys and girls in figures the relative positions and salaries of high-school graduates and those who leave school at fourteen—as they appear one, two, or ten years after leaving school. Business men come to the schools and tell the students what the chances for graduates and non-graduates are in their business and why they want better educated employees. Statistics of Gary pupils are kept and shown to the pupils. The usual break between the eighth grade and high school does not exist, and, therefore, parents do not think it necessary to take their children out of school. They find that the sacrifices they have made to keep the children in can be kept up for a few years more. If children are going to learn a trade better by staying in school than by leaving, and if children are keen to continue in school with definite plans for the future, even the most poverty-stricken parent is unwilling to thwart the advantage of his children. It is well known that in big cities where the proportion of pupils who leave school at fourteen is overwhelming, and where the usual reason given is that the parents need the financial help of the children, the real reason for defection is the indifference of the pupils themselves to school. The almost invariable answer given by the child to the question, "Why did you leave school?" is, "Because I did not like it." This fact taken with the poverty at home is enough to make them leave school at the first chance. Give the child work that he recognizes as interesting and valuable and a chance to play, and his hatred of school will speedily be forgotten.

The inflexibility of the ordinary public school tends to push the pupils out of school instead of keeping them in. The curriculum does not fit them, and there is no way of making it fit without upsetting the entire organization of the school. One failure sets a pupil back in all his work, and he soon gets the feeling that his own efforts are not important, because the school machinery works on at the same rate, regardless of any individual pupil or study. Indifference or dislike is almost surely the result of feeling that work is making no impression, that the machine for which he is working is not after all affected or dependent upon his work. In Gary organization has been made to fit each individual child, and is flexible enough so that even the most difficult pupil can not upset its working. The child and the school get along together. We have explained in an earlier paragraph how the two-school system works so that an individual can spend more or less time on any one subject, or can drop it altogether. The child who is weak physically spends much of his time on the playground, while the child who is weak in arithmetic or geography can take these lessons with both schools or even with a grade below, and hundreds of children in the same building can make the same sort of change in their program without disturbing the orderly conduct of the school routine. A pupil who is stronger in one subject than in the rest of his work, can take that subject with a higher grade. The pupil who is losing interest in school and falling behind in most of his studies, or who is beginning to talk of leaving, is not punished for this lack of interest by being put still further back. His teachers find out in what he is good and give him plenty of time to work at it, and to get ahead in it so that his interest in his work is stimulated. If he later wakes up to an interest in the regular school program, so much the better. Every facility is given him to catch up with his grade in all the work. If this awakening does not come, the boy or girl has still been kept in school until he or she learned some one thing, probably the one most suited to the pupil's ability, instead of leaving or failing entirely by being held back in everything until even the one strong faculty died and the pupil was without either training or the moral stimulus of success.

The school program is reorganized every two months and the pupil may change his entire program at any one of these times, instead of having to struggle along for half a year with work that is too hard or too easy or not properly apportioned. For administrative convenience the schools still keep the grade classifications, but pupils are classified not according to the grade number, but as "rapid," "average," and "slow" workers. Rapid pupils finish the twelve years of school at about sixteen years of age, average workers at eighteen, and slow workers at twenty. This classification does not describe the quality of work done. The slow marker may be a more thorough scholar than the rapid worker. The classification is used not to distinguish between the abilities of scholars, but to take advantage of the natural growth of the child by letting his work keep abreast with it. The rapid child moves as quickly as possible from grade to grade instead of being held back until his work has no stimulus for him, and the slow worker is not pushed into work before he is ready for it. Does this flexible system work successfully or does it result in easy-going, slap-dash methods? We have only to visit the schools and see the pupils hard at work, each one responsible for his own movements through the day, to be convinced that the children are happy and interested; while from the point of view of the teacher and educator, the answer is even more positively favorable, when we consult the school records. Fifty-seven per cent. of all the school children in Gary who are thirteen years old are in the seventh grade or above it. This is a better showing than most industrial communities can make, and means that the majority of all the Gary school children go through school at about the same rate as the average pupil who is preparing for college. Even more remarkable than this are the figures regarding the pupils who have gone on to higher schools or colleges after leaving the Gary schools. One-third of all the pupils that have left the Gary schools during the eight years of their existence are now in the state university, in an engineering school, or a business college. When we remember that the population of Gary is made up principally of laborers in the steel mills, and is sixty per cent. foreign born, and compare with this the usual school history of the second generation in this country, we realize how successful Mr. Wirt has been in making a system which meets the needs of the pupils, a system that appeals to the community as so good that they want to go on and get more education than mere necessity requires.

The motive back of these changes from the routine curriculum is always a social one. Mr. Wirt believes that if the social end of the school is properly emphasized the pedagogical will take care of itself. . . .

*　　*　　*

The older children learn responsibility and cooperation from having to look out for the little people, and the latter learn an astonishing amount about the subject from waiting on, watching, and asking questions of the older pupils. Both grades find out what is going on in the school and get thereby a large feeling of fellowship, while the interest of the lower one grows and finds reasons for staying in school.

THE GARY SYSTEM IN NEW YORK CITY (1917)　　From Mary Graham Bonner, "School Riots And the Gary System," *The Outlook*, vol. CXV, pp. 334–35.

W as it politics, Socialism, and Tigerism that was stirring the children to riot in the Bronx against the Gary schools? To children politics in themselves could mean nothing. But were they being urged on to striking, excitement, and rebellion by any insidious motives that they were too young to understand?

For many blocks I walked, inquiring of every one the way to Public School 50. All knew. It was the most recent school to be of interest. It was exciting—this rioting—and they were either directly or indirectly tremendously interested. The first lad I saw carried a club. He was a round-faced, chubby boy, with high color, sparkling eyes, and naturally good spirits.

"What is the reason for the strike?" I asked; "and were you one of the rioters?"

He looked at me for a moment doubtfully. He had heard of detectives. He had so recently seen patrol wagons, and he wanted to be quite safe—even if he did carry a club ready to smash windows. I assured him I had no power, so he spoke quite willingly.

"Yes ma'am," he said, "I was one of the rioters. And I'm on my way to another school now where lots of the fellows have gone to start a new riot. Gee! They're great!"

"Do you like the Gary system?" I asked.

"No; they make me walk up and down stairs too much," he said. He was so corpulent a little chap that I thought in his individual case walking up and down stairs might have no ill effect.

"It was just this morning we started," the lad continued. "All the fellows did—and sure I was one of them."

I questioned him more, but out of all his talk I could gather only one adverse opinion to his school life—he had had to walk up and down stairs twice a day. Also it was great fun to riot in the morning instead of doing sums.

I talked to another child, a block away. A small girl she was, with big brown eyes and a soft, delicate voice.

"I like the Gary system," she said, "but my mother took me away from school to-day. She said those rough boys would kill me."

"Does your mother like the system?" I asked.

"Yes, ma'am," she answered. "My mother thinks the Gary system is nice. But the other parents don't. They are speeching up the street. They're speeching so you can scarce hear them. Each mother's speeching, about her own children and no one is listening to any one else. It's terrible, ma'am, and the Gary system is so nice."

"Do the teachers like it?" I asked. I had heard they opposed the longer hours, and I felt that many (not the great majority, but many) were so misplaced. It was as though surgeons cared not for the outcome of their operations nor for the good of their patients, but only for the pay and to have their patients get out of the ether in a hurry. So many were teaching for "something to do to earn money." Not because they loved their work, nor because there was so much money in it. But it was a way to pay for their clothes and support themselves until a nice man came along and they could sit at home and not have to get up every morning when the alarm went off.

"They didn't like it at all," the child continued, "up to this morning. But this morning they got hurted—some of them—and I guess they don't hate anything that much."

I talked to group after group of parents as I walked to the school. I talked to policemen who were standing around with many of the small boys. The policemen carried clubs, the small boys carried sticks and improvised clubs. They were thoroughly enjoying themselves—at least the boys were."

I asked them of the opposition to the Gary plan. "Sure, every one in this part of the city is against it," they said. "Most of them are Socialists."

"Politics?" I queried. I received no answer.

I saw the principal of Public School No. 50. To speak the truth, indeed. I repeat again that I saw him. He would do no "speeching." He would talk to me after November's first week had gone by, he said. I had been told he was against the Gary plan. I informed him of this knowledge, but he would say nothing.

Again I questioned: "How about politics?" But he would not answer.

On the principal's desk I saw the Hylan button. "Going to vote for Hylan?" I asked. He looked a trifle astonished and said:

"Oh, the District Attorney put that there."

I left. He was not going to tell me anything—not now when politics were at such a keen and critical point. And out into the street I went. I looked up at the school. Windows broken and laughing children rioting. How irrelevant! How incongruous, and yet how pitiful! Fighting for something they did not clearly understand. Child after child told me that they had to walk up and down stairs in the Gary plan.

The mother were indeed "speeching." At the street corners groups had grown into crowds, and angry voices were protesting, protesting, protesting—against what they weren't quite so sure.

I had taken a young friend with me—the wife of a man who had given up a splendid and promising law practice for the sake of his country. I heard her telling a group that her husband had not received his pay on time—but he understood this was war.

"Yes, war time," they flung back. "What do we know of war?"

"I guess it's hit us all," I said.

"Hit us!" one woman yelled at me. "Prices hit us. But Mitchel with his swelled head goes around with a high hat and has the money. It's all his fault, this talk of war, and he keeps the money."

"Did the children riot of their own accord?" I asked.

"No," admitted one woman. "They were put up to it. But I don't blame them. What do they learn there? Nothing but to be slaves of the rich. Yes, there'll be two classes in this town, the rich and the poor, the Rockefellers and we—their slaves."

And so that was at the back of it. Into the lives of these children, into their homes, into their parents' lives, had come politics. Of that I felt convinced. The fact that children would have an opportunity such as they had never had before, an opportunity to be something else besides sweatshop workers, to do something else besides slave and toil and grow old and die, a chance to live—to live and to have the opportunities of the rich children in private schools, to have a life's work they wanted, to be trained for what they had talent—none of this had entered their heads.

Never had I made a speech before, never had I spoken in public; but here were crowds of people—crowds of parents opposing a system because their children would be owned by the Rockefeller Foundation, they thought. Their children would have to toil for the rich. There had been two big factors at work, and at work with a vengeance; Socialism and the Tiger's paw had clutched them. They were amazed at what I had to tell them of what vocational work meant, and of what the Gary system would mean for them. For a long time they felt that there was some ulterior motive in my talk. I must have been paid by some political party or I must be one of the rich. "Where's your automobile?" one surly youth shrieked at me. Nevertheless, I continued to argue. I told them of the school farther up in the Bronx which had had the Gary system for several years and where it had worked such marvels. I told of the visits I had paid to parents up there and of their enthusiasm. And I told them what vocational training meant—a chance for every boy and girl under the stars to be free—free and to live—to be of some importance.

"Mitchel, Mitchel," they sneered. "The man with the tall hat and the swelled head, who likes the rich to rule and who makes the prices go up higher."

I heard a woman late that evening talk. Her speech started with the Gary system. She assured her auditors that Mr. Mitchel was at the root of it all—she had been told by folks who knew.

"Yes," she shrieked at the mob before her, "they want our children to work for the rich, so that fine ladies can ride in automobiles and have us for their servants. And then they talk of Liberty bonds. We'll tell them that we won't subscribe to their bonds until they make the prices of sugar and flour and potatoes different. It's a rich man's war—let him pay for it. And it's Mitchel's war. Win this war, he thinks, and bring in the Gary system, and the world will be owned by the rich, and he can still wear his high hat."

As I listened and talked alternately, as I walked from corner to corner, from neighborhood to neighborhood, I discovered indeed what it was all about—why these children had been rioting. They had not liked walking up and down stairs, to be sure. And some of their teachers had not liked the change in routine, and had, for this reason, encouraged criticism. But back of these children, back of these parents, stands the giant specter of Tammany Hall and the uncompromising pacifists who, simply to win votes for their respective candidates, are attacking a system of education which will give every child, not only a chance to be "created equal," but to live "equal," and so escape the sweatshops of his parents' early days. The pity of it is that the children have been dragged into this kind of political warfare without a knowledge on their part of what is being done to them. What condemnation too severe can be visited upon politicians who dare to prostitute our public school system in this way?

EVALUATION BY THE GENERAL EDUCATION BOARD OF THE GARY, INDIANA SCHOOLS (1918) From Abraham Flexner and Frank P. Bachman, *The Gary Schools: A General Account* (New York, 1918), pp. 196–206.

In bringing this volume to a close, it is perhaps worth while to sum up briefly the pros and cons of a complicated situation.

On the credit side of the ledger must be placed the fact that Gary has adopted, and taken effective steps towards providing facilities for, a large and generous conception of public education. Had Gary played safe, we should find there half a dozen or more square brick "soap-box" buildings, accommodating a dozen classes, each pursuing the usual book studies, a playground, with little or no equipment, perhaps a basement room for manual training, a laboratory, and a cooking room for girls. Provided with this commonplace system, the town would have led a conventional school life—quiet, unoffending, and negatively happy—doing as many others do, doing it about as well as they do it, and satisfied to do just that. Instead, it adopted the progressive, modern conception of school function, formulated its conception in clear terms and with all possible expedition provided facilities adequate to the conception. The adoption and execution of this policy required administrative courage and civic liberality. In one sense there was nothing revolutionary in it, for not a few schoolmen have adopted this broad conception of public education. But Gary not only adopted this conception in theory—it made realization possible by providing in its main schools the physical conditions needed for its execution. The Froebel and the Emerson schools are not simply fine buildings, that in their environment startle the visitor—they are instruments formed to embody and realize a distinct educational idea. Even the temporary makeshifts required by the exigencies of the situation show an intelligent and serious effort to do what is feasible in the same direction for children unable to attend the well equipped central schools. The extended curriculum is therefore a reality at Gary, and the general movement toward enrichment of the curriculum has been stimulated by Gary's example.

On the credit side of the ledger belongs also Gary's contribution to school organization. There can be no question that a modern plant, consisting of classrooms, shops, gymnasium, laboratories, and auditorium, can be operated on the Gary type of organization so as to accommodate a considerably larger number of children than the same plant operated on the conventional plan. Indeed, the Gary type of organization anticipates such unsatisfactory and deplorable makeshifts, as "part-time," by providing on purely educational grounds for the intensive use of all school facilities. Thus, without waiting to be driven by pressure of large numbers,

Gary has developed a type of school organization which permits the effective instruction of the maximum number of children in a plant having modern facilities. From this point of view, the Gary organization is perhaps the most fruitful suggestion yet contributed toward the practical solution of the administrative problems involved in realizing a broad conception of public education.

Finally, Gary has attempted to practice democratic theory in school conduct and discipline. It is a common-place that arbitrary or military discipline is alien to the American spirit. Cooperation, representing the willing subordination of the individual in the endeavor to achieve necessary and desirable ends, must somehow be procured. In various ways—in classroom, corridors, auditorium, shop, etc.—Gary appeals to the cooperative spirit, relies on it, believes in it, gives it something to do—at times perhaps unwisely and to excess. In any event, the schools are rich in color and movement, they are places where children live as well as learn, places where children obtain educational values, not only through books, but through genuine life activites. The Gary schools make a point not only of the well known measurable abilities, but of happiness and appreciation, which cannot be measured, even though they may be sensed. It does not follow that Gary obtains no results from these efforts, merely because the outcome of its efforts in classroom work is unsatisfactory. The final results of appreciation and stimulus are too subtle, too remote, too readily obscured or augmented by other factors in experience or environment to be themselves definitely appraised. But evidence that appeals to the appreciative instincts is not made in vain is encountered now here, now there, in the activities, interests, and attitudes of teachers and children alike.

There are, it is clear, two distinct bodies of material employed at Gary, each having its appropriate method of approach: first, definite subjects, that have in the last resort to be "learned" in such wise that the pupil may attain and demonstrate a reasonable degree of mastery; next, aesthetic or other activities, giving wholesome pleasure at the time and tending to establish higher levels of need and taste. The traditional pedagogue concentrates on the first group and relentlessly organizes the subjects contained within it. The philosopher, insisting that at its best education supplies the means of natural growth, emphasizes the second group, not infrequently revolting from systematic presentation and precise results. A really effective school will undoubtedly harmonize the two. It will set up high and definite standards of workmanship for tasks that represent desired skills—spelling, arithmetic, cooking, sewing, or what not—endeavoring to reach these by employing well thought out and well wrought out methods of procedure; it will also provide a variety of experiences of a stimulating and appreciative character, without being overmuch concerned at the moment to decide why they are good, or what good they do, then or thereafter. One gets at Gary the impression of confusion in this matter. The auditorium, for example, embodies largely the stimulating and appreciative experiences that cannot be closely followed up. But the type of procedure that is natural to the auditorium not infrequently invades the shops, the cafeteria, and the classrooms, as if the passive absorption adapted to the auditorium were a generally applicable educational method.

We thus pass to the debit side of the account. The readers of this volume already know that the execution of the Gary plan is defective. It is of course true that no public school system thus far critically studied has been pronounced satisfactory—satisfactory in the sense that it meets current and reasonable standards of efficiency. It would therefore be manifestly unfair to demand that Gary should fully embody and practically succeed with every item of its varied and extensive program. A good many extenuating considerations may be fairly urged—the newness of the community, the complexities due to the character of the population, the breadth of the conception, the enormous difficulty of obtaining a teaching and supervising staff competent to execute the plan. But after making every possible allowance, it remains to be admitted that in respect to administration and instruction Gary might fairly have been expected to make a better showing.

Fundamentally, the defect is one of administration. No scheme will execute itself. Precisely because the Gary scheme is complicated, extensive, and at some points novel, uncommonly watchful administrative control is requisite. Such control does not exist. In consequence, results appear to be largely taken for granted. Illustrations in proof of this statement may be drawn from many of the preceding chapters. For example, the present organization assumes that satisfactory educational results are obtained when the plant consists half of regular classrooms and half of special facilities, and these facilities are kept in continuous use. As the plan works out, the groups assembled at Gary in the auditorium or on the playground are large or small, composed of a single grade or many grades, according to the requirements of a schedule constructed on this basis. It would, of course, be most convenient if this somewhat mechanical arrangement proved educationally effective. But does it? Not, in our judgment, without certain cautions and qualifications which Gary has thus far neglected. The "duplicate" school organization should therefore be viewed as an experiment to be watched and modified rather than assumed as a principle according to which a school schedule may be arbitrarily arranged.

The execution of the Gary plan is again defective in respect to educational supervision. To be sure, teaching and discipline in harmony with the Gary idea are to be found; side by side, however, are also teaching and discipline of old-fashioned type. Of course, this is inevitable. No consistently modern scheme could be completely realized at this time, because the materials have not as yet been created, the teachers have not yet been trained. Criticism is warranted, not because crudities and inconsistencies occur, but because the agencies which ought to be concerned over this situation have failed to take hold of it vigorously. Consequently in the so-called "old line" branches, the fundamental necessities of education, Gary execution falls short of usual performance. In reaching out for something new, Gary has too lightly parted with certain essential and established values, without being aware of the loss it has inadvertently made.

Not even in those branches to which Gary has given impetus and development—the so-called special activities—has a high or even satisfactory standard been reached. An excellent spirit pervaded the playgrounds, gymnasiums, shops, laboratories, and household arts departments. But high—even satisfactory—standards of workmanship did not rule. Some boys and girls did well; some did ill; concerted effort to procure generally good work, conscientious insistence upon excellent performance are only spasmodically in evidence. Not that teachers and principals do not want good work; they plainly do. But that patient and close attention to details by which alone good work can be obtained was far too irregular to be effective. Here, as elsewhere, one cannot avoid the conclusion that a large and generous scheme, distinguished by intelligence and vision in conception, falls too far short in the execution.

Attention has been called to the ways in which pupils participate in responsible activities—record keeping, etc. Such participation is admirably calculated to give a flavor of reality to school life. What ought, however, to be a credit item is converted into a debit because the absence of proper accountability results in slipshod work that must do the pupils positive damage. Records characterized by poor spelling, arithmetical inaccuracies, and grave omissions pass unchallenged. Not only is the immediate educative effect lost, but the child tends to become habituated to inferior performance. Thus, once more sound conception is frustrated by ineffective execution.

Could the Gary scheme be acceptably executed without additional expenditure? If not, how much more would have to be spent? Or can results of higher quality be obtained on the present outlay only by attempting less? We are unable to say. These questions cannot be finally answered until the present administrative and supervisory officers either conceive their functions somewhat differently or exercise them more effectively. Unquestionably, the mere process of gearing up the present organization would substantially improve results; for which reason it would be unwise either to curtail opportunities or largely to increase expenditure until the existing system has shown what it can accomplish when on the alert.

An eminent surgeon, accounting for his success in treating a recalcitrant wound, recently remarked of the hospital with which he is associated: "Here we try things." He did not mean that he and his associates follow a hit-or-miss policy. He was, in point of fact, describing an arduous, rigorous, exacting, and at the same time strictly accountable procedure. They canvass their resources, select in a critical way the moves which may reasonably be expected to prove beneficial, and with the most scrupulous care watch the outcome, determining the next procedure on the basis of ascertained results. They "try things," but they "try things" intelligently and critically.

It is a severe criticism of much of our current education that it does not "try things." This modern world of ours is in many ways a new world, with new peoples facing new problems and new opportunities. We tell ourselves again and again that only through education can safe and happy adjustments be reached; no one pretends that education has yet found these adjustments. Nevertheless, educational inertia is all but invincible. Only here and there in the person of this or that teacher or principal or supervisor does it "try things." And the moment it is proposed to "try things"—the only method by which progress can be made—the forces of conservatism organize to check and discredit progressive enterprise.

It is to the substantial and lasting credit of Gary that it has had the courage, liberality, and imagination to "try things." Nor have things been tried blindly and recklessly. The social situation to be dealt with has been thoughtfully analyzed; the resources at our disposal have been intelligently marshaled. That is, Gary did not act in ignorance of the situation to be met; it did not employ ill adjusted tools. It has failed only in caution and criticism. Hence, while things have been tried, results have not been carefully checked. Disappointment was inevitable, but it is disappointment that does not necessarily imply fundamental error.

It is not difficult to understand why self-criticism was overlooked. Education has for centuries too largely consisted of exercises habitually practised, partly for known and obvious, partly for unknown, ends. It made little practical difference whether the end was known or unknown, because in neither case were schoolmen accustomed to examine results carefully in order to ascertain what their efforts and processes achieved. In failing to scrutinize results, Gary simply did as others did. There is also another consideration. The Gary scheme was conceived in enthusiasm. The temperament of the reformer is not usually associated in the same individual with the temperament of the critic. The two must, however, be brought together. The innovator must formulate his purposes clearly and concretely; and his results must be measured in the light of his professed aims. If innovation is carried on in this critical spirit, conservatism will also have to submit to assay.

The theory of which Gary is an exemplification is derived from the facts and necessities of modern life. The defects of Gary cannot therefore simply throw us back on the meager type of education appropriate enough to other conditions. Gary's experience up to this time means merely that further efforts, at Gary and elsewhere, more clearly defined, more effectively controlled, must be made in order, if possible, to accomplish Gary's avowed object—the making of our schools adequate to the needs and conditions of current life.

THE IDEAL SCHOOLS OF MENOMONIE, WISCONSIN (1904) From Adele Marie Shaw, "The Ideal Schools of Menomonie," *The World's Work*, vol. VII, pp. 4541–42.

These grammar-school lads that I saw were at work in a self-reliant, businesslike fashion upon a hickory step-ladder, a whitewood medicine-cabinet, a birch towel-roller, an oak piano-stool, red-birch inkstands, foot-stools, salt-boxes, collar and cuff boxes, plate-racks picture-frames, and waste-baskets.

Care is taken to suit the instruction to the environment. I was attracted by a particularly smooth, strong sled. "We make sleds usually in the late fall," Mr. Bauersfeld explained. "Sleds and snow-shovels—and skees. When the band-saws break in a mill near by Mr. Stout gets them for us, and the sleds are shod with the best of steel." Everywhere I saw this inventive economy using old material in new ways. Some of the boxes were constructed from worn-out desk-tops.

"We make kites in the spring," Mr. Bauersfeld went on, "sometimes seventeen different kinds; and then we have a kite day and race airships on the kite-strings. They get a good deal of practice in mechanics out of the rigging of their airships," he twinkled.

Beyond the carpentry-room there was a little recitation-hall. A long work-counter allowed space for any practical demonstration the conductor of the classes wanted to use. From that and from a tool-room as complete and systematic as any library, with classified nails and classified saws, and from a fireproof vault where varnishes are stored which the pupils use in learning the arts of stains, fillers, shellac, and French polishing I emerged to see more *results*.

In this school Mr. Stout works out an occasional problem outside the curriculum. Once he asked a class of boys at the beginning of a year to "make something" quite independently. "Make anything you want to," he said. They wrestled faithfully, and the results were atrocious but interesting. Mr. Stout had found out what was in their minds. The objects were locked up and forgotten till the end of the year. Then they were produced, and great was the mirth of the class over their own work. They learned since making these articles how to appreciate grace of outline as well as mechanical perfection. They could no longer conceive such crudities.

The material for this woodwork is bought in the rough, green lumber, and the instructors reduce it to any shape they wish. I looked at a mass of oak and birch and some slabs of red cherry that will some day be the superintendent's desk. It was carefully set up in the dry-kiln, the hot air circulating between the planks. Close at hand was the planning-mill, where blocks and boards are cut by the instructors into any shape desired. The economy and utility of this way of purchasing is evident even to a novice.

From the wood-working department I went into the iron-working rooms. I had spent much time in the immense forge-shop, where twenty-two "down-draft forges" were busy, and I had wandered in the din of anvils, and peered into hooded fires, and been startled by a trip-hammer controlled by a high-school boy of fifteen. I had gone somewhat breathless through a kind of royal machine-shop, where striplings were handling giganitc forces with a steady concentration that made the air alive. I had given to the extradordinary equipment of the mechanical drawing-room a more intelligent and less thrilled attention. I was ready for more lathes and draughting-boards. But I was not prepared for the foundry.

The pit and the crane, the bucket-ladle capable of producing a two-ton casting, the melting-room with its brass furnace, its "cupola" for iron, its floor of removable iron plates, its iron loading-stage beneath the floor, were vital with the sense of human mastery over material. In the faces of the boys bent over the machines this mastery had been plain—the tension of their work blended with the fine content-ment of power rightly applied.

This was the work of the boys. The girls study "domestic science" in a department of six large sunny and well-arranged rooms.

DOMESTIC SCIENCE

The real interest in this work to a quick-witted girl is furnished in the pleasure of acquiring knowledge in the study of fabrics and textiles, manufactures and materials, in the working out of an original problem. A girl is given a group of foods to be reduced to their food elements by the study of scientific tables. If in the group (designed perhaps for a breakfast) the girl finds a food whose nourishing elements exist in an equal amount in a cheaper material, then the substitution is made and the cost reduced. To a group of girls is frequently given the preparation of one or two or three meals the cost of whose raw materials shall not exceed a definite amount. These meals are served to invited guests, chiefly father and mothers, and the entertainers take turns in acting as hosts and waiters.

One of these meals I saw in the process of serving. A high-school girl had been given a dollar, out of which she was to provide for twenty-five people. Here is the record:

Cream Tomato Soup
Croûtons

Veal Loaf   Potatoes

Bread and Butter
Milk

Tomatoes, 12 cents; veal, 40; potatoes, 14; bread, 15; milk, 15; butter, 10. Total, $1.06. Twenty-seven people served.

Deftness and a trim and accurate handling of materials, with the brain planning behind the work, are the objects for which the department labors under Miss Laura G. Day. Home experiments are recorded methodically, so that at the end of the year every child has card-catalogued her independent struggles. The children are known and their homes are known. Deception is practically impossible.

THE COUNTRY SCHOOL OF THE FUTURE (1905) From Liberty Hyde Bailey, *The Outlook to Nature* (New York, 1905), pp. 177–85.

A prominent school man said to me recently, "Practically no one goes from the high schools into the trades." This may be because so few of our youth go through the high school, or because high schools are not in direct vibration with the trades. My friend meant to infer the latter. No doubt education should be supremely natural, and it can be natural only when it makes use of the forces and objects in the neighborhood. The principal of an old academy told me last fall that he was planning to teach dairying in the school, both as a scholarship study and as a means of aiding the industry of the community. I asked him how he could teach it without a laboratory and apparatus. "I have the ideal laboratory," he replied, "because it is an actual enterprise: it is the creamery yonder." I recognized that he was a prophet.

The science-teaching, as I have said, developed the laboratory. Of course the laboratory is fundamental, yet it is not sufficient if we are to teach also by means of affairs. It is only a collection of materials with which to work,—formerly dead things, but now live things. We cannot teach affairs in collection-laboratories: we must have actual shops, actual enterprises, actual fields, actual gardens,—not the materials brought to the pupil, but the pupil taken to the materials. Even the farm and the shop may be made means of education.

"Object lessons" are excellent means of developing observation, but the "objects" are largely make-believe or are taken out of their natural place and thereby lose much of their meaning. The new "nature-study" tries to place the pupil with the objects and phenomena as they occur in nature; and so far as it does this, it is fundamental and abiding. The persistency with which nature-study is treated as if it were object-teaching or mere laboratory-teaching, shows how difficult it is to extend the sphere of the school beyond the schoolhouse.

The education designed by the Land Grant Act was essentially technical and professional. For many years the result was largely information-teaching; but the experimental era is now passing, and, while still intensely practical, this teaching is developing greater scholarship value. The general elementary schools cannot teach trades or professions; but they can use the materials of trades and professions as one of the aids to scholarship, and while doing so they will give such a "set" toward the occupations as will attract all youth and will at the same time make them more efficient in their own behalf and also in behalf of civilization.

In an agricultural community, for example, all the farms of the neighborhood will afford training in the elements of failure and success. There is no reason why the pupils should not know why and how a man succeeds with his orchard or dairy or factory, as well as to have the cyclopedia information about the names of capes and mountains, dates, and the like; and why should not every good farmer explain his operations to the pupils? Such work, if well done, would vitalize the school and lift it clean out of the ruts of tradition and custom. It would make a wholly new enterprise of the school, rendering it as broad and significant and native as the community itself, not a puny exotic effort for some reason dropped down in the neighborhood. When the public schools begin to touch experience and pursuits in a perfectly frank and natural way, we may hope that persons who have money to give for education will bestow some of it on elementary and country schools, where it will reach the very springs of life.

It will be seen that all this is a much larger idea than manual training alone. Good as manual training is, it will inevitably lead to something that articulates directly with the lives of the pupils and the needs of the community. It is now passing from the make-believe into the real, from mere hand-training into actual applied problems.

All this constitutes the new "industrial education,"—an education that uses the native objects and affairs of the community as means of training in scholarship, setting the youth right toward life, making him to feel that schooling is as indigenous and natural as any other part of his life, that he cannot afford to neglect schooling any more than he can neglect the learning of a business or occupation, that schooling will aid him directly in his occupation, that the home and school and daily work are only different phases of his own normal development, and that common duties may be made worthy of his ideals. Unfortunately, the term "industrial education" is ordinarily understood to mean direct training for the trades; therefore it would be a great gain to a clear understanding of the subject if some other term could be used for this new and pedagogically sound idea. The term nature-study will not answer the purpose, for this is commonly understood to cover what we know as "nature," not including industries and affairs. In my own mind, the term nature-study is large enough, for I think of "nature," in this relation, as expressing the natural method of education, whereby the pupil is educated at first in the terms of the world he lives in; but the term has been so long used with another signification that it cannot be pressed into service for the larger and fuller idea. "Environmental education" has been suggested; but this would always have to be explained, it sounds pompous and theoretical, and the environment is usually considered to comprise only the "natural" surroundings and not the parts established therein by man. I wish we might say "natural education," but this is indefinite and would always be disputed. For the time being, therefore, I see no better term than industrial education, with the reservation that it mean much more than commercial education, or than manual and technical skill for use in the arts and trades,—that it mean true education in aiding mental development, supplying usable information, affording manual and physical training, developing sympathy with the work of the world, arousing enthusiasm for service.

I cannot forbear to say a word about this last category,—enthusiasm. I find myself with a constantly growing feeling that much of our educational practice suppresses exuberance and spontaneity, and crushes out originality. This is particularly true of the older types of formal education. The pupil or student is so continuously overawed, or at least over-mastered, by the opinions of others, as expressed in books and literatures, that he hesitates to express an opinion of his own, lest it shall not fall into the well-worn ruts. More than this, educational practice has been so dominated by the bogy of "mental discipline" that enthusiasms have been neglected. Yesterday a man said to me that he had taken the botany in a great university but graduated without love of plants, and had taken the astronomy without having learned the glory of the heavens.

The new natural or industrial education should do much to correct all this, for it puts the pupil into touch with living questions and in line for service, and it develops the value of evidence and of proof. The activities cannot be contained in books nor smother by "authority." They put the man to work; and they should leave him possessed of his natural spontaneousness.

THE RURAL SCHOOL AS SOCIAL CENTER (1907)   From Kenyon L. Butterfield,
Chapters In Rural Progress (Chicago, 1907), pp. 122–30, 133–35.

. . . not only is there a feeling that the pupil in school can be brought into
closer touch with the life of the community, but that the school as an institution
can be made more useful to the community as a whole. This double thought has
been expressed in the phrase, "Make the school a social center," and practically it is
being slowly worked out in numerous city schools. How far can this idea be
developed in the contry school?

The purpose of this chapter is not to deal in the theory of the subject, nor to
argue particularly for this view of the function of the school, but rather to try to
show some methods by which the rural school and the farm community actually can
be brought into closer relations. In this way we may perhaps indicate that there is a
better chance for co-operation between the rural school and the farm community
than we have been accustomed to believe, and that this closer relation is worth
striving for. Five methods will be suggested by which the rural school can become a
social center. Some of these have already been tried in rural communities, some of
them have been tried in cities, and some of them have not been tried at all.

1. The first means of making the rural school a social center is through the
course of study. It is here that the introduction of nature-study into our rural
schools would be especially helpful. This nature-study when properly followed
approves itself both to educators and to farmers. It is a pedagogical principle
recognized by every modern teacher that in education it is necessary to consider the
environment of the child, so that the school may not be to him "a thing remote and
foreign." The value of nature-study is recognized not only in thus making possible
an intelligent study of the country child's environment, but in teaching a love of
nature, in giving habits of correct observation, and in preparing for the more
fruitful study of science in later years. Our best farmers are also coming to see that
nature-study in the rural schools is a necessity, because it will tend to give a
knowledge of the laws that govern argiculture, because it will teach the children to
love the country, because it will show the possibilities of living an intellectual life
upon the farm. Nature-study, therefore, will have a direct influence in bringing the
child into close touch with the whole life of the farm community.

But it is not so much a matter of introducing new studies—the old studies can be
taught in such a way as to make them seem vital and human. Take, for instance,
geography. It used to be approached from the standpoint of the solar system. It now
begins with the schoolhouse and the pupils' homes, and works outward from the
things that the child sees and knows to the things that it must imagine. History,
writing, reading, the sciences, and even other subjects can be taught so as to
connect them vitally and definitely with the life of the farm community. To quote
Colonel Parker, who suggests the valuable results of such a method of teaching:

> It would make a strong, binding union of the home and the school, the farm methods
> and the school methods. It would bring the farm into the school and project the school
> into the farm. It would give parent and teacher one motive in the carrying out of which
> both could heartily join. The parent would appreciate and judge fairly the work of the
> school, the teacher would honor, dignify and elevate the work of the farm.

The study of the landscape of the near-by country, the study of the streams, the study of the soils, studies that have to do with the location of homes, of villages, the study of the weather, of the common plants, of domestic animals—all of these things will give the child a better start in education, a better comprehension of the life he is to live, a better idea of the business of farming, a better notion about the importance of agriculture, and will tend to fit him better for future life either on the farm or anywhere else, than could any amount of the old-fashioned book knowledge. Is it not a strange fact that so many farmers will decry book knowledge when applied to the business of farming, and at the same time set so much store by the book learning that is given in the common arithmetic, the old-fashioned reader, and the dry grammar of the typical school? Of course anyone pleading for this sort of study in the rural schools must make it clear that the ordinary accomplishments of reading, writing, and ciphering are not to be neglected. As a matter of fact, pupils under this method can be just as well trained in these branches as under the old plan. The point to be emphasized, however, is that a course of study constructed on this theory will tend to bring the school and the community closer together, will make the school of more use to the community, will give the community more interest in the school, while at the same time it will prepare pupils to do their work in life.

2. A second way of making the rural school a social center is through the social activities of the pupils. This means that the pupils as a body can co-operate for certain purposes, and that this co-operation will not only secure some good results of an immediate character, results that can be seen and appreciated by everyone, but that it will teach the spirit of co-operation—and there is hardly anything more needed today in rural life than this spirit of co-operation. The schools can perform no better service than in training young people to work together for common ends. In this work such things as special day programmes, as for Arbor Day, Washington's Birthday, Pioneer Day; the holding of various school exhibitions; the preparation of exhibits for country fairs, and similar endeavors, are useful and are being carried out in many of our rural schools. But the best example of this work is a plan that is being used in the state of Maine, and is performed through the agency of what is called a School Improvement League. The purposes of the league are: (1) to improve school grounds and buildings; (2) to furnish suitable reading-matter for pupils and people; (3) to provide works of art for schoolrooms. There are three forms of the league, the local leagues organized in each school; the town leagues, whose membership consists of the officers of the local leagues; and a state league, whose members are delegates from the town leagues and members of the local leagues who hold school diplomas. Any pupil, teacher, school officer, or any other citizen may join the league on payment of the dues. The minimum dues are one cent a month for each pupil, for other members not less than ten cents a term. But these dues may be made larger by vote of the league. Each town league sends a delegate to the meeting of the state league. Each league has the usual number of officers elected for one term. These leagues were first organized in 1898 and they have already accomplished much. They have induced school committees to name various rural schools for distinguished American citizens, as Wahington, Lincoln, and so forth. They give exhibitions and entertainments for the purpose of raising funds. Sometimes they use these funds to buy books for the schoolroom. The books are then loaned to the members of the league; at the end of the term this set of books is exchanged for another set of books from another school in the same township. In this way, at a slight expense, each school may have the use of a large number of books every year. The same thing is done with pictures and works of art, these being purchased and exchanged in the same way. Through the efforts of the

league schoolhouses have been improved, inside and out, and the school grounds improved. It is not so much the doing of new things that has been attempted by this league. The important item is that the school has been *organized* for these definite purposes, and the work is carried on systematically from year to year. It needs no argument to show the value of this sort of co-operation to the pupil, to the teacher, to the school, to the parents, and ultimately to the community as a whole.

3. A third method is through co-operation between the home and the school, between the teacher and pupils on one side, and parents and taxpayers on the other side. Parents sometimes complain that the average school is a sort of mill, or machine, into which their children are placed and turned out just so fast, and in just such condition. But if this is the case, it is partly the fault of the parents who do not keep in close enough touch with the work of the school. It is not that parents are not interested in their children, but it is rather that they look at the school as something separate from the ordinary affairs of life. Now, nothing can be more necessary than that this notion should be done away with. There must be the closest co-operation between the home and school. How can this co-operation be brought about? Frequently parents are urged to visit the schools. This is all right and proper, but it is not enough. There must be a closer relation than this. The teacher must know more about the home life of her pupils, and the parents must know far more about the whole purpose and spirit, as well as the method, of the school. A great deal of good has been done by the joint meeting of teachers and school officers. It is a very wise device, and should be kept up. But altogether the most promising development along this line is the so-called "Hesperia movement," described in another chapter. These meetings of school patrons and teachers take up the work of the school in a way that will interest both teachers and farmers. They bring the teachers and farmers into closer touch socially and intellectually. They disperse fogs of misunderstanding. They inspire to closer co-operation. They create mutual sympathy. They are sure to result in bringing the teacher into closer touch with community life and with the social problems of the farm. And they are almost equally sure to arouse the interest of the entire community, not only in the school as an institution and in the possibilities of the work it may do, but also in the work of that teacher who is for the time being serving a particular rural school.

4. A fourth method is by making the schoolhouse a meeting-place for the community, more especially for the intellectual and aesthetic activities of the community. A good example of this kind of work is the John Spry School of Chicago. In connection with this school there is a lecture course each winter; there is a musical society that meets every Tuesday evening; there is a men's club that meets every two weeks to discuss municipal problems and the improvement of home conditions; there is a women's club to study for general improvement and social service; there is a mothers' council meeting every two weeks; there is a literary and dramatic society, meeting every week; composed of members of high-school age, and studying Shakespeare particularly; there is a dressmaking and aid society meeting two evenings a week, to study the cutting of patterns, garment-making, etc.; a food-study and cooking club, also meeting two evenings a week; an inventive and mechanical club, meeting two evenings a week, and tending to develop the inventive and mechanical genius of a group of young men; an art club; and a boy's club, with music, games, reading-lessons, reading of books and magazines, intended for boys of fourteen or fifteen years of age. These things are all under the direction of the school, they are free, they are designed to educate. It will not be feasible for the rural school to carry out such a programme as this, but do we realize how large are the possibilities of this idea of making the rural school a

community center? No doubt one of the advantages of the centralized rural school will be to give a central meeting-place for the township, and to encourage work of the character that has been described. Of course, the Grange and farmers' clubs are doing much along these lines, but is it not possible for the district school also to do some useful work of this character? Singing-schools and debating clubs were quite a common thing in the rural schools forty years ago, and there are many rural schools today that are doing work of this very kind. Is there any reason, for example, why the country schoolhouse should not offer an evening school during a portion of the winter, where the older pupils who have left the regular work of the school can carry on studies, especially in agriculture and domestic science? There is need for this sort of thing, and if our agricultural colleges, and the departments of public instruction, and the local school supervisors, and the country teachers, and the farmers themselves, could come a little closer together on these questions the thing could be done!

5. Fifth and last, as a method for making the school a social center, is the suggestion that the teacher herself shall become something of a leader in the farm community. The teacher ought to be not only a teacher of the pupils, but in some sense a teacher of the community. Is there not need that someone should take the lead in inspiring everyone in the community to read better books, to buy better pictures, to take more interest in the things that make for culture and progress? There are special difficulties in a country community. The rural teacher is usually a transient; she secures a city school as soon as she can; she is often poorly paid; she is sometimes inexperienced; frequently the labor of the school absorbs all her time and energy. Unfortunately these things are so, but they ought not to be so. And we shall never have the ideal rural school until we have conditions favorable to the kind of work just described. The country teacher ought to understand the country community, ought to have some knowledge of the problems that the farmers have to face, ought to have some appreciation of the peculiar conditions of farm life. Every teacher should have some knowledge of rural sociology. The normal schools should make this subject a required subject in the course, especially for country teachers. . . .

* * *

The programme needed to unite rural school and farm community is then, first, to enrich the course of study by adding nature-study and agriculture, and about these co-ordinating the conventional school subjects; second, to encourage the co-operation of the pupils, especially for the improvement of the school and its surroundings; third, to bring together for discussion and acquaintance the teachers and the patrons of the school; fourth, so far as possible to make the schoolhouse a meeting-place for the community, for young people as well as for older people, where music, art, social culture, literature, study of farming, and in fact, anything that has to do with rural education, may be fostered; and fifth, to expect the teacher to have a knowledge of the industrial and general social conditions of agriculture, especially those of the community in which her lot is cast.

NATIONAL COMMISSION ON A NEW COUNTRY LIFE EDUCATION

(1911) From *Report of the Commission on Country Life* (New York. 1911), pp. 121–25.

The subject of paramount importance in our correspondence and in the hearings is education. In every part of the United States there seems to be one mind, on the part of those capable of judging, on the necessity of redirecting the rural schools. There is no such unanimity on any other subject. It is remarkable with what similarity of phrase the subject has been discussed in all parts of the country before the Commission. Everywhere there is a demand that education have relation to living, that the schools should express the daily life, and that in the rural districts they should educate by means of agriculture and country life subjects. It is recognized that all difficulties resolve themselves in the end into a question of education.

The schools are held to be largely responsible for ineffective farming, lack of ideals, and the drift to town. This is not because the rural schools, as a whole, are declining, but because they are in a state of arrested development and have not yet put themselves in consonance with all the recently changed conditions of life. The very forces that have built up the city and town school have caused the neglect of the country school. It is probable that the farming population will willingly support better schools as soon as it becomes convinced that the schools will really be changed in such a way as to teach persons how to live.

The country communities are in need of social centers,—places where persons may naturally meet, and where a real neighborhood interest exists. There is difference of opinion as to where this center should be, some persons thinking it should be in the town or village, others the library, others the church or school or grange hall. It is probable that more than one social center should develop in large and prosperous communities. Inasmuch as the school is supported by public funds and is therefore an institution connected with the government of the community, it should form a natural organic center. If the school develops such a center, it must concern itself directly with the interests of the people. It is difficult to make people understand what this really means, for school-teaching is burdened with tradition. The school must express the best cooperation of all social and economic forces that make for the welfare of the community. Merely to add new studies will not meet the need, although it may break the ground for new ideas. The school must be fundamentally redirected, until it becomes a new kind of institution. This will require that the teacher himself be a part of the community and not a migratory factor.

The feeling that agriculture must color the work of rural public schools is beginning to express itself in the interest in nature-study, in the introduction of classes in agriculture in high-schools and elsewhere, and in the establishment of separate or special schools to teach farm and home subjects. These agencies will help to bring about the complete reconstruction of which we have been speaking. It is especially important that we make the most of the existing public school system, for it is this very system that should serve the real needs of the people. The real needs of the people are not alone the arts by which they make a living, but the whole range of their customary activities. As the home is the center of our civilization, so the home subjects should be the center of every school.

The most necessary thing now to be done for public school education in terms of country life is to arouse all the people to the necessity of such education, to coordinate the forces that are beginning to operate, and to project the work beyond the schools for youth into continuation schools for adults. The schools must represent and express the community in which they stand, although, of course, they should not be confined to the community. They should teach health and sanitation, even if it is necessary to modify the customary teaching of physiology. The teaching should be visual, direct and applicable. Of course, the whole tendency of the schools will be ethical if they teach the vital subjects truthfully; but particular care should be taken that they stand for the morals of the pupils and of the communities.

We find a general demand for federal encouragement in educational propaganda, to be in some way cooperative with the states. The people realize that the incubus of ignorance and inertia is so heavy and so widespread as to constitute a national danger, and that it should be removed as rapidly as possible. It will be increasingly necessary for the national and state governments to cooperate to bring about the results that are needed in agricultural and other industrial education.

The consideration of the educational problem raises the greatest single question that has come before the Commission, and which the Commission has to place before the American people. Education has now come to have vastly more significance than the mere establishing and maintaining of schools. The education motive has been taken into all kinds of work with the people, directly in their homes and on their farms, and it reaches mature persons as well as youths. Beyond and behind all educational work there must be an aroused intelligent public sentiment; to make this sentiment is the most important work immediately before us. The whole country is alive with educational activity. While this activity may all be good, it nevertheless needs to be directed and correlated, and all the agencies should be more or less federated.

The Federal Government and Education

CALL FOR THE FIRST WHITE HOUSE CONFERENCE ON CHILDREN
(**1908**)   From *Proceedings of the Conference on the Care of Dependent Children, 1909*
(Washington D.C., 1909), pp. 17–18.

December 22, 1908

Hon. Theodore Roosevelt,

President of the United States,
Washington, D.C.

Dear Mr. President: In your message to Congress December 6, 1904, urging the establishment of a juvenile court for the District of Columbia, you said:

> No Christian and civilized community can afford to show a happy-go-lucky lack of concern for the youth of to-day; for, if so, the community will have to pay a terrible penalty of financial burden and social degradation in the tomorrow.

Congress promptly responded and enacted an excellant juvenile court law. The wisdom of this step has already been proven by the work of the court.

Generally speaking, the cause of the delinquent child has been well advanced. Juvenile courts have been established in many States; a considerable number of probation officers have been appointed; many of the juvenile reformatories are progressing along well established lines of modern thought and are supported by generous appropriations from the public treasury; detention homes have been opened in many cities to keep children out of jail; parental schools are being established for the training of truants and unruly school children.

The State has dealt generously with her troublesome children; but what is she doing for those who make no trouble but are simply unfortunate? There are a large number of these children for whom there is need of special activity and interest. Some are orphans or half-orphans; some are abandoned by heartless parents; some are victims of cruelty or neglect. They are not delinquents; they are accused of no fault; they are simply destitute or neglected.

Destitute children certainly deserve as much consideration and help as those who, by reason of some alleged delinquency, enforce the attention of the State and become objects of its care; but only a few States have defined responsibility for this class of children. Their care and protection is left in many localities to the fidelity of volunteer agencies without requiring proper standards of method or efficiency and without definite responsibility to the State or the community.

Unfortunately there has not been as frequent interchange of ideas and experiences among the officials of orphan asylums, with consequent progress, as among those who work for delinquents.

These dependent children are cared for in different ways. According to a special bulletin of the United States Census there were in orphan asylums and kindred institutions on December 31, 1904, not less than 92,887 children. In addition to these there were probably some 50,000 dependent children in family homes under supervision.

In many States, however, little or no child-saving work is done, and in many States the organizations are greatly handicapped by the lack of appreciation and of adequate support.

It is of the highest importance to the welfare of this vast number of future citizens that all child-saving work shall be conducted on a high plane of efficiency; that in the placing of children in families the utmost care shall be taken to exclude all undesirable applicants; that every precaution shall be taken in the subsequent supervision of the children to prevent neglect, overwork, insufficient education, or inadequate moral and religious training, of each individual child and to fit it for active and creditable citizenship.

The problem of the dependent child is acute; it is large; it is national. We believe that it is worthy of national consideration. We earnestly hope, therefore, that you will cooperate in an effort to get this problem before the American people.

If a conference could be arranged, under your auspices, in Washington, some time in January, to which leaders of this particular phase of child-caring work could be invited, it would, in our judgment, greatly advance the cause of the dependent child. Such a conference could formulate a plan for your consideration, pointing out ways whereby you could specially help by recommending to Congress certain legislation and in other ways.

Hoping for your favorable consideration of this matter, we are,

Very respectfully,

Homer Folks,
Secretary, New York States Charities Aid
Association.

Hastings H. Hart,
Superintendent Illinois Children's Home and
Aid Society,
Chairman, Study of Child Placing,
Russell Sage Foundation.

John M. Glenn,
Secretary and Director, Russell Sage
Foundation.

Thomas M. Mulry,
President, St. Vincent de Paul Society
of the United States.

Edward T. Devine,
Editor Charities and The Commons,
General Secretary, Charity Organizing Society,
Professor of Social Economy, Columbia
University.
Julian W. Mack,
Judge Circuit Court, of Chicago, Ill.,
Ex-President, National Conference of Jewish
Charities.
Charles W. Birtwell,
General Secretary, Boston Children's Aid
Society.
Theodore Dreiser,
Editor of the Delineator.
James E. West,
Secretary, National Child-Rescue League.

ACT TO ESTABLISH THE CHILDREN'S BUREAU (1912)   From *Act of April*
9, 1912 (37 Stat., 79) as Amended by Act of March 4, 1913 (37 Stat., 736).

An Act To establish in the Department of Labor a bureau to be
known as the Children's Bureau

Be it enacted by the Senate and House of Representatives of the United
States of America in Congress assembled, That there shall be established in the
Department of Labor a bureau to be known as the Children's Bureau.[1]

SEC. 2. That the said bureau shall be under the direction of a chief to be
appointed by the President, by and with the advice and consent of the Senate, and
who shall receive an annual compensation of five thousand dollars. The said bureau
shall investigate and report to said department upon all matters pertaining to the
welfare of children and child life among all classes of our people, and shall
especially investigate the questions of infant mortality, the birth rate, orphanage,
juvenile courts, desertion, dangerous occupations, accidents and diseases of children,
employment, legislation affecting children in the several States and Territories. But
no official, or agent, or representative of said bureau shall, over the objection of the
head of the family, enter any house used exclusively as a family residence. The chief
of said bureau may from time to time publish the results of these investigations in
such manner and to such extent as may be prescribed by the Secretary of Labor.

SEC. 3. That there shall be in said bureau, until otherwise provided for by law,
an assistant chief, to be appointed by the Secretary of Labor, who shall receive an
annual compensation of two thousand four hundred dollars; one private secretary to
the chief of the bureau, who shall receive an annual compensation of one thousand
five hundred dollars; one statistical expert, at two thousand dollars; two clerks of
class four; two clerks of class three; one clerk of class two; one clerk of class one;

[1]Transferred from Department of Commerce and Labor to Department of Labor by act
approved March 4, 1913.

one clerk, at one thousand dollars; one copyist at nine hundred dollars; one special agent, at one thousand four hundred dollars; one special agent, at one thousand two hundred dollars; and one messenger, at eight hundred and forty dollars.

SEC. 4. That the Secretary of Labor is hereby directed to furnish sufficient quarters for the work of this bureau at an annual rental not to exceed two thousand dollars.

SEC. 5. That this act shall take effect and be in force from and after its passage. Approved, April 9, 1912.

ON INFANT CARE (1914)   From Mrs. Max West, *Infant Care,* U.S. Children's Bureau, publication no. 8 (Washington, D.C., 1914), pp. 59–61.

Habits are the result of repeated actions. A properly trained baby is not allowed to learn bad habits which must be unlearned later at great cost of time and patience to both mother and babe. The wise mother strives to start the baby right.

＊　　＊　　＊

In order to establish good habits in the baby, the mother must first be aware what they are, and then how to induce them. Perhaps the first and most essential good habit is that of regularity. This begins at birth, and applies to all the physical functions of the baby—eating, sleeping, and bowel movements. The care of a baby is readily reduced to a system unless he is sick. Such a system is not only one of the greatest factors in keeping the baby well and in training him in a way which will be of value to him all through life, but reduces the work of the mother to the minimum and provides for her certain assured periods of rest and recreation.

As a sample of what is meant by a system in baby care the following plan is suggested, which may be variously modified to suit particular cases:

6 a.m., baby's first nursing.
Family breakfast; children off to school.
9 a.m., baby's bath, followed by second nursing.
Baby sleeps until noon.
12 to 12.30, baby's noon meal.
Out-of-door airing and nap.
3 to 3.30 p.m., afternoon nursing.
Period of waking.
6 to 7 p.m., baby's supper and bed.

It is quite feasible to have the baby's night meal at 11.30 or 12 o'clock, in order to give the mother a chance to spend an occasional evening in pleasant recreation.

＊　　＊　　＊

The rule that parents should not play with the baby may seem hard, but it is without doubt a safe one. A young, delicate, or nervous baby especially needs rest and quiet, and however robust the child much of the play that is indulged in is more or less harmful. It is a great pleasure to hear the baby laugh and crow in apparent delight, but often the means used to produce the laughter, such as tickling, punching, or tossing makes him irritable and restless. It is a regrettable fact that the few minutes of play that the father has when he gets home at night, which is often almost the only time he has with the child, may result in nervous disturbance of the baby and upset his regular habits.

The mother should not kiss the baby directly on the mouth, nor permit others to do so, as infections of various kinds are spread in this way. She needs also to be cautioned about rocking the baby, jumping him up and down on her knee, tossing him, shaking his bed or carriage, and, in general, keeping him in constant motion. All these things disturb the baby's nerves and make him more and more dependent upon these attentions. But this is not to say that the baby should be left alone too completely. All babies need "mothering," and should have plenty of it. When the young baby is awake he should frequently be taken up and held quietly in the mother's arms, in a variety of positions, so that no one set of muscles may become overtired. An older child should be taught to sit on the floor or in his pen or crib during part of his waking hours, or he will be very likely to make too great demands upon the mother's strength. No one who has not tried it realizes how much nervous energy can be consumed in "minding" a baby who can creep or walk about, and who must be continually watched and diverted, and the mother who is taking the baby through this period of his life will need to conserve all her strength, and not waste it in useless forms of activity.

CHILDREN'S BUREAU CALLS FOR MINIMUM STANDARDS OF SCHOOL HEALTH (1919)
From U.S. Children's Bureau, *Standards of Child Welfare, a Report of the Children's Bureau Conferences May and June, 1919* (Washington, D.C., 1919) p. 438.

---

1. Proper location, construction, hygiene and sanitation of schoolhouse; adequate room space—no overcrowding.

2. Adequate playground and recreation facilities, physical training, and supervised recreation.

3. Open-air classes and rest periods for pre-tubercular and certain tuberculous children, and children with grave malnutrition. Special classes for children needing some form of special instruction due to physical or mental defect.

4. Full-time school nurse for not more than 1,000 children to give instruction in personal hygiene and diet, to make home visits to advise and instruct mothers in principles of hygiene, nutrition, and selection of family diet, and to take children to clinics with permission of parents.

5. Adequate space and equipment for school medical work and available laboratory service.

6. Part-time physician with one full-time nurse for not more than 2,000 children, or full-time physician with two full-time nurses for 4,000 children for:

(a) Complete standardized basic physical examinations once a year, with determination of weight and height at beginning and end of each school year; monthly weighing wherever possible.

(b) Continuous health record for each child to be kept on file with other records of the pupil. This should be a continuation of the preschool health record which should accompany the child to school.

(c) Special examinations to be made of children referred by teacher or nurse.

(d) Supervision to control communicable disease.

(e) Recommendation of treatment for all remediable defects, diseases, deformities, and cases of malnutrition.

(f) Follow-up work by nurse to see that physician's recommendations are carried out.

7. Available clinics for dentistry, nose, throat, eye, ear, skin, and orthopedic work; and for free vaccination for smallpox and typhoid.

8. Nutrition classes for physically subnormal children, and the maintenance of midmorning lunch or hot noonday meal when necessary.

9. Examination by psychiatrist of all atypical or retarded children.

10. Education of school child in health essentials.

11. General educational work in health and hygiene, including education of parent and teacher, to secure full cooperation in health program.

REPORT OF THE COMMISSION ON NATIONAL AID TO VOCATIONAL EDUCATION (1914)   From 63d Cong., 2d Sess., *House Document no. 1004,* pp. 12–13, 22–23.

While many different kinds and grades of vocational education will always be required, the kind most urgently demanded at the present time is that which will prepare workers for the more common occupations in which the great mass of our people find useful employment.

There is a great and crying need of providing vocational education of this character for every part of the United States—to conserve and develop our resources; to promote a more productive and prosperous agriculture; to prevent the waste of human labor; to supplement apprenticeship; to increase the wage-earning power of our productive workers; to meet the increasing demand for trained workmen; to offset the increased cost of living. Vocational education is therefore needed as a wise business investment for this Nation, because our national prosperity and happiness are at stake and our position in the markets of the world can not otherwise be maintained.

The social and educational need for vocational training is equally urgent. Widespread vocational training will democratize the education of the country: (1) By recognizing different tastes and abilities and by giving an equal opportunity to all to prepare for their life work; (2) by extending education through part-time and evening instruction to those who are at work in the shop or on the farm. Vocational training will indirectly but positively affect the aims and methods of general education: (1) By developing a better teaching process through which the children who do not respond to book instruction alone may be reached and educated through learning by doing; (2) by introducing into our educational system the aim of utility, to take its place in dignity by the side of culture and to connect education with life by making it purposeful and useful. Industrial and social unrest is due in large measure to a lack of a system of practical education fitting workers for the callings. Higher standards of living are a direct result of the better education which makes workers more efficient, thus increasing their wage-earning capacity.

An overwhelming public sentiment shows the need for vocational education in this country. The testimony in this behalf comes from every class of citizenship, from the educator, the manufacturer, the trades-unionist, the business man, the social worker, and the philanthropist. Every State superintendent of public instruction declared that its rapid extension was required for many different reasons in his State and great national educational, civic, industrial, and commercial organizations, representing more than 12,000,000 people, have repeatedly gone on record as believing that a system of vocational education was absolutely necessary to the future welfare of the nation.

While recognizing that training for all the different vocations is important and desirable, agricultural and trade and industrial education are most in need of national encouragement at the present time. The best way to aid the States in giving these kinds of vocational training is through grants for the preparation of efficient teachers and grants for the part payment of their salaries.

National grants are required for the salaries and the training of vocational teachers: (1) To help to solve a problem too large to be worked out extensively and permanently save by the whole nation; (2) to help the States, with their widely varying resources, to carry the cost of giving vocational education and thereby to make this education possible in those States and localities already burdened with the task of meeting the requirements of general education; (3) to equalize among the States the large and unequal task of preparing workers whose tendency to move from State to State is making training for a life work a national as well as a State duty; (4) to give interest and prestige in the States to the work of preparing our youth for useful and productive service.

National grants for agricultural, and trade and industrial education are justified: (1) By the urgency of the demand for the effective training of our workers, which the States can not meet in time without Federal encouragement and aid; (2) by the interstate and national character of the problem, due to its nation-wide interest and importance; (3) by abundant precedent, in appropriations by Congress throughout our entire history, for educational purposes, and in cooperation between the Federal Government and the States, where team play was necessary to handling matters that could not be as well handled by the States alone; (4) by the successful results to the Nation as well as to the States of previous grants for educational purposes.

After six years of consideration of the question by Congress and the country an overwhelming public sentiment favors national grants. The favorable opinions given at the hearings and in answer to questions sent out by the commission to educators, employers and employees, and educational, civic, industrial, agricultural, and commercial organizations national in their scope, were practically unanimous.

The States are facing many new and difficult questions in connection with the efforts to develop agricultural, trade and industrial, commercial, and home economics education. One of the most valuable ways in which the National Government could aid the States in this work would be by national grants expended through Federal agencies for studies, investigations, and reports furthering the efforts of the States to place the work of their vocational schools on a scientific and business-like basis. As a Nation we are singularly lacking in this kind of information. European countries have gained much advantage over us because they are already in possession of this knowledge.

This help can best be secured from the Government. We can not rely upon individuals or national organizations to gather it. The States can not well deal individually with the matter. The work must be done by the National Government to secure the best results. If the Government makes grants to be expended in cooperation with the States for the benefit of any kind of vocational education, every consideration requires that the moneys expended in the venture should be accompanied with all the helpful knowledge that the Federal Government has gleaned or can glean from its studies.

We have become a great industrial as well as a great agricultural nation. Each year shows a less percentage of our people on the farms and a greater in the cities.

Our factory population is growing apace. Our future as a nation will depend more and more on the success of our industrial life, as well as upon the volume and quality of our agricultural products. It has repeatedly been pointed out that the time is not far distant when our rapidly increasing population will press hard upon an improved agriculture for its food supply, and force our industries to reach out over the entire world for trade wherewith to meet the demands for labor of untold millions of bread winners.

In volume of output the United States leads the four great manufacturing nations of the world. More than a billion and a half of people outside of these four countries are largely dependent upon them for manufactured articles. "The rewards offered in this world trade are beyond comprehension. They are to be measured in money, in intellectual advancement, in national spirit, in heightened civilization." Yet we have only begun to invade this market, where we find our competitor too often in possession of the field and strongly entrenched against us.

It is true that we have a large foreign trade in manufactured articles, but of our exports a very large proportion consists of crude materials. German, French, and English exports represent on the average a much greater value in skill and workmanship than do those from our own ports. Less than one-third of the volume of our foreign commerce is made up of manufactures ready for consumption. A very large proportion consists of raw and semi-raw materials, such as lumber, cotton, meat, coal, oil, and copper bar, to secure which we have robbed our soil and the earth beneath our feet of the riches we have been foolish enough to regard as inexhaustible. The statistics of our foreign commerce show that the proportion of these raw products, in the total volume of our exports, has been declining during the past three decades, and that the maintenance and development of our foreign trade is coming to depend each year to a greater extent upon our ability to compete with foreign nations in the products of skilled labor,—upon our ability to "sell more brains and less material."

The volume of our foreign trade has in the past depended upon the exploitation of a virgin soil and of our other natural resources. In this crude work we have had no competitors. Our profit has been the profit of the miner working in a rich soil. The volume and profitableness of our trade in the future, however, must depend much more largely upon the relative skill and efficiency of the vocationally-trained artisans of England, France, and Germany. Our products will find a market in foreign countries only in those lines of industrial activity in which the labor is as efficient and as well trained as the labor of the countries with which we must compete.

The battles of the future between nations will be fought in the markets of the world. That nation will triumph, with all that its success means to the happiness and welfare of its citizenship, which is able to put the greatest amount of skill and brains into what it produces. Our foreign commerce, and to some extent our domestic commerce, are being threatened by the commercial prestige which Germany has won, largely as the result of a policy of training its workers begun by the farseeing Bismarck almost half a century ago.

France and England, and even far-off Japan, profiting by the schools of the Fatherland, are now establishing national schools of vocational education. In Germany, within the next few years, there will probably be no such thing as an untrained man. In the United States probably not more than 25,000 of the eleven or twelve million workers in manufacturing and mechanical pursuits have had an opportunity to acquire an adequate training for their work in life.

THE SMITH-LEVER ACT (1914)   From 63d Cong., 2d Sess., Chap. 79 (1914), pp. 372–73.

Be it enacted by the Senate and House of Representatives of the United States of America in Congress assembled, That in order to aid in diffusing among the people of the United States useful and practical information on subjects relating to agriculture and home economics, and to encourage the application of the same, there may be inaugurated in connection with the college or colleges in each State now receiving, or which may hereafter receive, the benefits of the Act of Congress approved July second, eighteen hundred and sixty-two, entitled "An Act donating public lands to the several States and Territories which may provide colleges for the benefit of agriculture and the mechanic arts" (Twelfth Statutes at Large, page five hundred and three), and of the Act of Congress approved August thirtieth, eighteen hundred and ninety (Twenty-sixth Statutes at Large, page four hundred and seventeen and chapter eight hundred and forty-one), agricultural extension work which shall be carried on in cooperation with the United States Department of Agriculture: *Provided,* That in any State in which two or more such colleges have been or hereafter may be established the appropriations hereinafter made to such State shall be administered by such college or colleges as the legislature of such State may direct: *Provided further,* That, pending the inauguration and development of the cooperative extension work herein authorized, nothing in this Act shall be construed to discontinue either the farm management work or the farmers' cooperative demonstration work as now conducted by the Bureau of Plant Industry of the Department of Agriculture.

SEC. 2. That cooperative agricultural extension work shall consist of the giving of instruction and practical demonstrations in agriculture and home economics to persons not attending or resident in said colleges in the several communities, and imparting to such persons information on said subjects through field demonstrations, publications, and otherwise; and this work shall be carried on in such manner as may be mutually agreed upon by the Secretary of Agriculture and the State agricultural college or colleges receiving the benefits of this Act.

SEC. 3. That for the purpose of paying the expenses of said cooperative agricultural extension work and the necessary printing and distributing of information in connection with the same, there is permanently appropriated, out of any money in the Treasury not otherwise appropriated, the sum of $480,000 for each year, $10,000 of which shall be paid annually, in the manner hereinafter provided, to each State which shall by action of its legislature assent to the provisions of this Act . . . .

THE SMITH-HUGHES ACT (1917)   From Senate Bill no. 703, *64th Cong., 2d Sess., chap. 114 (1917), pp. 929–31, 934–35.*

CHAP. 114—An Act To provide for the promotion of vocational education; to provide for cooperation with the States in the promotion of such education in agriculture and the trades and industries; to provide for cooperation with the States in the preparation of teachers of vocational subjects; and to appropriate money and regulate its expenditure.

Be it enacted by the Senate and House of Representatives of the United States of America in Congress assembled, That there is hereby annually appropriated, out of any money in the Treasury not otherwise appropriated, the sums provided in sections two, three, and four of this Act, to be paid to the respective States for the purpose of cooperating with the States in paying the salaries of teachers, supervisors, and directors of agricultural subjects, and teachers of trade, home economics, and industrial subjects, and in the preparation of teachers of agricultural, trade, industrial, and home economics subjects; and the sum provided for in section seven for the use of the Federal Board for Vocational Education for the administration of this Act and for the purpose of making studies, investigations, and reports to aid in the organization and conduct of vocational education, which sums shall be expended as hereinafter provided.

SEC. 2. That for the purpose of cooperating with the States in paying the salaries of teachers, supervisors, or directors of agricultural subjects there is hereby appropriated for the use of the States, subject to the provisions of this Act, for the fiscal year ending June thirtieth, nineteen hundred and eighteen, the sum of $500,000; for the fiscal year ending June thirtieth, nineteen hundred and nineteen, the sum of $750,000; for the fiscal year ending June thirtieth, nineteen hundred and twenty, the sum of $1,000,000; for the fiscal year ending June thirtieth, nineteen hundred and twenty-one, the sum of $1,250,000; for the fiscal year ending June thirtieth, nineteen hundred and twenty-two, the sum of $1,500,000; for the fiscal year ending June thirtieth, nineteen hundred and twenty-three, the sum of $1,750,000; for the fiscal year ending June thirtieth, nineteen hundred and twenty-four, the sum of $2,000,000; for the fiscal year ending June thirtieth, nineteen hundred and twenty-five, the sum of $2,500,000; for the fiscal year ending June thirtieth, nineteen hundred and twenty-six, and annually thereafter, the sum of $3,000,000. Said sums shall be allotted to the States in the proportion which their rural population bears to the total rural population in the United States, not including outlying possessions, according to the last preceding United States census: *Provided,* That the allotment of funds to any State shall be not less than a minimum of $5,000 for any fiscal year prior to and including the fiscal year ending June thirtieth, nineteen hundred and twenty-three, nor less than $10,000 for any fiscal year thereafter, and there is hereby appropriated the following sums, or so much thereof as may be necessary, which shall be used for the purpose of providing the minimum allotment to the States provided for in this section: For the fiscal year ending June thirtieth, nineteen hundred and eighteen, the sum of $48,000; for the fiscal year ending June thirtieth, nineteen hundred and nineteen, the sum of $34,000; for the fiscal year ending June thirtieth, nineteen hundred and twenty, the sum of $24,000; for the fiscal year ending June thirtieth, nineteen hundred and twenty-one, the sum of $18,000; for the fiscal year ending June thirtieth, nineteen hundred and twenty-two, the sum of $14,000; for the fiscal year ending June thirtieth, nineteen hundred and twenty-three, the sum of $11,000; for the fiscal year ending June thirtieth, nineteen hundred and twenty-four, the sum of $9,000; for the fiscal year ending June thirtieth, nineteen hundred and twenty-five, the sum of $34,000; and annually thereafter the sum of $27,000.

Sec. 3. That for the purpose of cooperating with the States in paying the salaries of teachers of trade, home economics, and industrial subjects there is hereby appropriated for the use of the States for the fiscal year ending June thirtieth, nineteen hundred and eighteen, the sum of $500,000; for the fiscal year ending June thirtieth, nineteen hundred and nineteen, the sum of $750,000; for the fiscal year ending June thirtieth, nineteen hundred and twenty, the sum of $1,000,000; for the fiscal year ending June thirtieth, nineteen hundred and twenty-one, the sum of $1,250,000; for the fiscal year ending June thirtieth, nineteen hundred and twenty-two, the sum of $1,500,000; for the fiscal year ending June thirtieth, nineteen hundred and twenty-three, the sum of $1,750,000; for the fiscal year ending June thirtieth, nineteen hundred and twenty-four, the sum of $2,000,000; for the fiscal year ending June thirtieth, nineteen hundred and twenty-five, the sum of $2,500,000; for the fiscal year ending June thirtieth, nineteen hundred and twenty-six, the sum of $3,000,000; and annually thereafter the sum of $3,000,000. Said sums shall be allotted to the States in the proportion which their urban population bears to the total urban population in the United States, not including outlying possessions, according to the last preceding United States census: *Provided,* That the allotment of funds to any State shall be not less than a minimum of $5,000 for any fiscal year prior to and including the fiscal year ending June thirtieth, nineteen hundred and twenty-three, nor less than $10,000 for any fiscal year thereafter, and there is hereby appropriated the following sums, or so much thereof as may be needed, which shall be used for the purpose of providing the minimum allotment to the States provided for in this section: For the fiscal year ending June thirtieth, nineteen hundred and eighteen, the sum of $66,000; for the fiscal year ending June thirtieth, nineteen hundred and nineteen, the sum of $46,000; for the fiscal year ending June thirtieth, nineteen hundred and twenty, the sum of $34,000; for the fiscal year ending June thirtieth, nineteen hundred and twenty-one, the sum of $28,000; for the fiscal year ending June thirtieth, nineteen hundred and twenty-two, the sum of $25,000; for the fiscal year ending June thirtieth, nineteen hundred and twenty-three, the sum of $22,000; for the fiscal year ending June thirtieth, nineteen hundred and twenty-four, the sum of $19,000; for the fiscal year ending June thirtieth, nineteen hundred and twenty-five, the sum of $56,000; for the fiscal year ending June thirtieth, nineteen hundred and twenty-six, and annually thereafter, the sum of $50,000.

That not more than twenty per centum of the money appropriated under this Act for the payment of salaries of teachers of trade, home economics, and industrial subjects, for any year, shall be expended for the salaries of teachers of home economics subjects.

SEC. 4. That for the purpose of cooperating with the States in preparing teachers, supervisors, and directors of agricultural subjects and teachers of trade and industrial and home economics subjects there is hereby appropriated for the use of the States for the fiscal year ending June thirtieth, nineteen hundred and eighteen, the sum of $500,000; for the fiscal year ending June thirtieth, nineteen hundred and nineteen, the sum of $700,000; for the fiscal year ending June thirtieth, nineteen hundred and twenty, the sum of $900,000; for the fiscal year ending June thirtieth, nineteen hundred and twenty-one, and annually thereafter, the sum of $1,000,000. Said sums shall be allotted to the States in the proportion which their population bears to the total population of the United States, not including outlying possessions, according to the last preceding United States census: *Provided,* That the allotment of funds to any State shall not be less than a minimum of $5,000 for any fiscal year prior to and including the fiscal year ending June thirtieth, nineteen hundred and nineteen, nor less than $10,000 for any fiscal year thereafter. And there is hereby appropriated the following sums, or so much thereof as may be needed, which shall be used for the purpose of providing the minimum allotment provided for in this section: For the fiscal year ending June thirtieth, nineteen hundred and eighteen, the sum of $46,000; for the fiscal year ending June thirtieth, nineteen hundred and nineteen, the sum of $32,000; for the fiscal year ending June thirtieth, nineteen hundred and twenty, the sum of $24,000; for the fiscal year ending June thirtieth, nineteen hundred and twenty-one, and annually thereafter, the sum of $90,000.

SEC. 5. That in order to secure the benefits of the appropriations provided for in sections two, three, and four of this Act, any State shall, through the legislative authority thereof, accept the provisions of this Act and designate or create a State board, consisting of not less than three members, and having all necessary power to cooperate, as herein provided, with the Federal Board for Vocational Education in the administration of the provisions of this Act.

*　　*　　*

SEC. 10. That any State may use the appropriation for agricultural purposes, or any part thereof allotted to it, under the provisions of this Act, for the salaries of teachers, supervisors, or directors of agricultural subjects, either for the salaries of teachers of such subjects in schools or classes or for the salaries of supervisors or directors of such subjects under a plan of supervision for the State to be set up by the State board, with the approval of the Federal Board for Vocational Education. That in order to receive the benefits of such appropriation for the salaries of teachers, supervisors, or directors of agricultural subjects the State board of any State shall provide in its plan for agricultural education that such education shall be that which is under public supervision or control; that the controlling purpose of such education shall be to fit for useful employment; that such education shall be of less than college grade and be designed to meet the needs of persons over fourteen years of age who have entered upon or who are preparing to enter upon the work of the farm or of the farm home; that the State or local community, or both, shall provide the necessary plant and equipment determined upon by the State board, with the approval of the Federal Board for Vocational Education, as the minimum requirement for such education in schools and classes in the State; that the amount expended for the maintenance of such education in any school or class receiving the benefit of such appropriation shall be not less annually than the amount fixed by the State board, with the approval of the Federal board as the minimum for such schools or classes in the State; that such schools shall provide for directed or supervised practice in agriculture, either on a farm provided for by the school or other farm, for at least six months per year; that the teachers, supervisors, or directors of agricultural subjects shall have at least the minimum qualifications determined for the State by the State board, with the approval of the Federal Board for Vocational Education.

SEC. 11. That in order to receive the benefits of the appropriation for the salaries of teachers of trade, home economics, and industrial subjects the State board of any State shall provide in its plan for trade, home economics, and industrial education that such education shall be given in schools or classes under public supervision or control; that the controlling purpose of such education shall be to fit for useful employment; that such education shall be of less than college grade and shall be designed to meet the needs of persons over fourteen years of age who are preparing for a trade or industrial pursuit or who have entered upon the work of a trade or industrial pursuit; that the State or local community, or both, shall provide the necessary plant and equipment determined upon by the State board, with the approval of the Federal Board for Vocational Education, as the minimum requirement in such State for education for any given trade or industrial pursuit; that the total amount expended for the maintenance of such education in any school or class receiving the benefit of such appropriation shall be not less annually than the amount fixed by the State board, with the approval of the Federal board, as the minimum for such schools or classes in the State; that such schools or classes giving instruction to persons who have not entered upon employment shall require that at least half of the time of such instruction be given to practical work on a useful or productive basis, such instruction to extend over not less than nine months per year and not less than thirty hours per week; that at least one-third of the sum appropriated to any State for the salaries of teachers of trade, home economics, and industrial subjects shall, if expended, be applied to part-time schools or classes for workers over fourteen years of age who have entered upon employment, and such subjects in a part-time school or class may mean any subject given to enlarge the civic or vocational intelligence of such workers over fourteen and less than eighteen years of age; that such part-time schools or classes shall provide for not less than one hundred and forty-four hours of classroom instruction per year; that evening industrial schools shall fix the age of sixteen years as a minimum entrance requirement and shall confine instruction to that which is supplemental to the daily employment; that the teachers of any trade or industrial subject in any State shall have at least the minimum qualifications for teachers of such subject determined upon for such State by the State board, with the approval of the Federal Board for Vocational Education: *Provided,* That for cities and towns of less than twenty-five thousand population, according to the last preceding United States census, the State board, with the approval of the Federal Board for Vocational Education, may modify the conditions as to the length of course and hours of instruction per week for schools and classes giving instruction to those who have not entered upon employment, in order to meet the particular needs of such cities and towns.

SEC. 12. That in order for any State to receive the benefits of the appropriation in this Act for the training of teachers, supervisors, or directors of agricultural subjects, or of teachers of trade, industrial or home economics subjects, the State board of such State shall provide in its plan for such training that the same shall be carried out under the supervision of the State board; that such training shall be given in schools or classes under public supervision or control; that such training shall be given only to persons who have had adequate vocational experience or contact in the line of work for which they are preparing themselves as teachers, supervisors, or directors, or who are acquiring such experience or contact as a part of their training; and that the State board, with the approval of the Federal board, shall establish minimum requirements for such experience or contact for teachers, supervisors, or directors of agricultural subjects and for teachers of trade, industrial, and home economics subjects; that not more than sixty per centum nor less than twenty per centum of the money appropriated under this Act for the training of teachers of vocational subjects to any State for any year shall be expended for any one of the following purposes: For the preparation of teachers, supervisors, or directors of agricultural subjects, or the preparation of teachers of trade and industrial subjects, or the preparation of teachers of home economics subjects.

THE
PROGRESSIVE ERA,
1919–1929

Americanization

THE AMERICANIZATION OF THE IMMIGRANTS: COMPULSION OR PERSUASION? (1920) From Frank V. Thompson, *The Schooling of the Immigrants* (New York, 1920), pp. 11–15, 152–54.

In a contemplated program of Americanization, the important decision that confronts us is whether we shall proceed by means of a policy of compulsion or by one of persuasion. Shall we insist that the stranger who has entered our land shall by force of law and compulsion acquire our language, conform to our major customs, become naturalized, and renounce all prior allegiance, or shall we attempt to persuade him to adopt American customs, and to use our language, by pointing out the moral obligation, by furnishing convenient means in the way of free instruction, and perhaps by granting privileges which may be withheld from the non-citizen? A no less important question may be raised as to whether or not the compulsion, if adopted, shall be employed in the case of those who are already here or only in the case of those who may come in the future.

It is desirable at this point merely to raise these issues and not to attempt a commitment. Americanization is one of the issues raised by the war. A realization of past shortcomings is keen in time of war and we hasten to make amends. Emergencies are usually met by compulsory measures, and the recent war emergency has increased the tendency to meet all situations by such means. The situation has its dangers as well as its advantages, and there may be a danger in formulating our program of Americanization at this moment, as we may incline to extreme measures. Having gone too slowly before, we may now be tempted to go too fast. Having undertaken too little till now, we may undertake too much; from no regulation we may jump to over-regulation, from a policy of *laissez-faire* and individualism to ordinance and autocracy. We are beginning to realize that the spirit of autocracy is not peculiar to any one race or country, and is potential at least in the freest of governments and present somewhere in the instincts of all of us. It is only when this spirit controls and dominates that the resulting government is denominated an autocracy and the individual an autocrat. It is the principle of democracy always to make decisions on the theory that there are two sides to every question and some good on each side. Autocracy and Bolshevism agree in method, at least, in that under either of these, decisions are made from but one point of view, with no admission that there can be an opposite standpoint.

We may suspect the so-called 100-per-cent Americans of holding autocratic views with regard to a proper program of Americanization. With undoubted zeal and single-minded purpose they would within a brief period of time compel all non-

English-speaking immigrants, those here now as well as those to come, to acquire the English language; they would compel the taking out of citizenship papers and conformity in dress, manners, and mode of living to the standard of native Americans. They would by edict abolish the Little Italies, the Little Hungaries, and the ghettos. They would have the recent comers abandon former dreams, hopes, and aspirations, and feel, act and live in the ways that are natural to the native born, who have been more fortunate in environment and circumstances. They demand, in fact, a revolution in the life of the foreign-born individual. The native who makes this demand is unconscious of the evolution which several generations have produced in himself. If Americanism is primarily a mode of thinking and feeling, the compulsionist is forced to maintain the theory that habits of thinking and feeling can be manufactured by force and decree.

Those who would limit compulsion to immigrants who are to come in the future, and who may be duly notified of the new condition, make a stronger case than the compulsionists who would resort to an *ex post facto* procedure and require those who are already here to conform to a regulation not obtaining at the time of their coming. The recent literacy amendment to our immigration laws (May, 1917) imposes nothing retroactive. The imposition of an additional amendment requiring literacy in the English language for those who wish to enter our country, a literacy to be acquired within a limited number of years subsequent to entrance, would have the virtue of a contract known in advance.

Opposed to the compulsionist is the advocate of voluntary nationalization. At the present time he is little less embarrassed than is the compulsionist. His system does not seem to have got anywhere. Most of our communities have not set up provisions for the education of the immigrant, and where communities have done so there is always the disappointing discrepancy between the number of those who are attracted and those who we wish might be. A curious paradox seems involved in estimating the advantages of either method: to democratize our newer brethren we must resort to autocratic procedures; the democratic method does not promise to democratize. But the democratic method at least has permitted the immigrant to Americanize himself. There has been going on an automatic process of Americanization which our democratic methods has permitted and encouraged; while it is regrettable that there is so large a number of non-English-speaking immigrants among us, it is also surprising and pleasing that the greater proportion of our foreign born have sought and acquired that which we have not forced upon them.

* * *

There is much to be said to the credit of the bilingual school for the cause of Americanization. The criticism has often justly been made of the public school that it effects a false Americanization by a too rapid process of change from old landmarks to new. The tragedy of the child of foreign parentage suddenly turning in contempt against the Old World speech and ways of his father and mother has been noted by many commentators. Acquiring the gloss and veneer or smartness of Americanism without an appreciation of its deeper meaning is not true Americanization. Americanization must be consistent with the commandment, "Honor thy father and thy mother." The sudden breaking away from the old landmarks of race, religion, and custom has never resulted in good citizenship in the new relations. The bilingual school in many instances has been the bridge in Americanization and made assimilation gradual and consequently sound. We are attempting no praise for the bilingual school that refuses to make concessions or, worse, which inculcates suspicion or distrust of American institutions. The bilingual school which instills the new allegiance without relinquishing old associations can be and usually is an effective institution for the development of citizenship. There is a danger, of course, that the bilingual school will preserve indefinitely something like a dual allegiance. That the bilingual school promises to do this thing is feared by many, but the complaint of the immigrant is that the children break away from traditions of the parents too fast, that they insist on becoming Americans too soon; foreign-born parents attest that their children prefer English to the native tongue in spite of all conserving influences.

In Europe the bilingual school has been accused of maintaining the dual relationship indefinitely. Let us remember, however, that this result has usually followed where the state has sought to obliterate the languages and customs of subject nationalities; where there has been no compulsion, assimilation has usually taken place. Wherever the nation has attempted to force conformity or assimilation, the coerced races have sullenly resisted and maintained a distinctive individuality; witness Poland under the triple yoke of Germany, Russia, and Austria. May we not take a leaf for ourselves out of Old World experiences?

PROBLEMS OF EDUCATING THE IMMIGRANT ADULT IN PASSAIC, NEW JERSEY (1920)   From U.S., Bureau of Education, *Bulletin No. 4, 1920,* pp. 15-21.

Relation of the Present Social and Industrial Conditions of Passaic to the Problem of Adult Education.

It is obvious from the foregoing facts that, inasmuch as the foreign born make up the majority of the people of Passaic, the first task of the public school in the matter of adult education is to meet the needs of the foreign-born adults. Let us consider what is already being done in this direction and what is the attitude of the people most concerned in the matter of adult education.

According to the reports of the board of education, 3,116 people attended evening classes for the teaching of English from 1915 to 1919, but the average daily attendance for each of those years was only 249 pupils per year, as shown in the following table:

Enrollment and average attendance in public evening schools.

Attendance	1915–16	1916–17	1917–18	1918–19	Total
Pupils enrolled	1,211	582	580	743	3,116
Average attendance	468	203	188	137	249

During the past year considerable effort has been put forth by various agencies outside the schools to increase the number of classes in English. Both the Young Men's Christian Association and the Young Women's Christian Association have had classes, but considering all the agencies, both inside and outside the schools, is still obvious that only a small fraction of the people who are not able to speak English are receiving instruction in English. The most significant point about the figures of attendance at the public schools is that, although 3,116 people entered evening school in the four years from 1915 to 1919, the average attendance for those years was only 996, or about one-third of the number who entered. But since the same 996 people did not attend regularly, it follows that not even one-third of the people who entered had full-time instruction. In other words, the classes in English in the public evening schools are not attracting many pupils, and they are failing to hold them after they get the people to the schools.

It should be pointed out that this situation is not peculiar to Passaic. The city of Passaic is fortunate in having a progressive and up-to-date school system. It is also to be congratulated upon the fact that the city has the modern type of school buildings, which makes possible a socialized school for both children and adults, and these school buildings (Nos. 10 and 12) are situated in the section of the city where social centers are most needed. Passaic, with its progressive school policy, can develop an excellent system of adult education; the fact that the board of education has asked for a survey of the situation is evidence that it is interested in future accomplishments, not in defense of past failures. The fact is, however, that Passaic is in much the same position in regard to the development of adult education in which other cities of large numbers of students. a teaching force willing and eager to do its part, a large adult population, mostly foreign born, to whom the right kind of adult education would be a boon, and only a small number of people attending the evening classes.

Recently, since the interest in Americanization work, there has been a tendency throughout the country for various civic bodies, boards of trade, Young Men's Christian Associations, Young Women's Christian Associations, civic clubs, etc., to get together, form a committee, and lay out plans for increasing attendance at classes for the teaching of English; but the attendance still remains entirely out of proportion to the number of people to be reached. It is now generally recognized that one reason for this fact is that the group of people taking the initiative, praiseworthy as are their efforts, are, after all, not the group of people most concerned in the matter; that is, the men and women who attend or would be likely to attend such classes in the public schools. The bureau, therefore, in making the survey, followed its usual custom of endeavoring to find out from the people themselves, through their different clubs, foreign groups, and labor organizations, why they did not attend the evening schools and what kind of courses they would be interested in taking.

One of the first things revealed by the investigation was that the people, through their different nationality groups, had already started classes for teaching themselves English. This was particularly interesting in view of the fact that a number of public citizens interested in the subject of Americanization had stated as one of the reasons why so few people took courses in English that "foreigners do not want to learn English." We are convinced that this is an erroneous impression, for in no case was there found any objection to learning English, and in many cases real eagerness to learn. It was found that the labor organization that had by far the largest number of foreign born, the Passaic Local of the Amalgamated Textile Workers of America, was already starting classes in English and citizenship and was planning to have classes in history, economics, etc. Such efforts, of course, are in line with the general movement among workers to start educational courses through trade-union colleges, workers' institutes, etc. Evidently, then, it was true in Passaic, as in other cities, that there was a desire on the part of the people for courses in English, and in a good many instances for more than the elementary courses in English. Why, then, were they not attending the evening schools in greater numbers?

What the People Say in Regard to the Evening Schools.

The following are some of the reasons given by the men and women themselves. Poles, Russians, Hungarians, Bohemians, Austrians, as to why they did not attend evening school:

"How can I? I work at night."

"I work now during the day, but my wife works at night and I have to stay at home to take care of the children."

"I tried it; I learned to read and write some, but not to speak English."

"It is childish. We keep saying all the time, 'this is a desk;' 'this is a door.' I know it is a desk and a door. What for keep saying it all the time?"

"My teacher, she was very nice young lady, but very young. She does not understand what I want to talk about or know about."

"7.30 p. m. to 9.30 p. m. is too long; you get home too late. You get out of work at 5, then get out of school at 9.30, and it's 10.30 before you get to bed, and that's too late for a spinner. A spinner can't take changes."

"They treat you like a child because you don't know English."

"Too tired."

In each of the interviews the people were asked if they would be more likely to come if they had teachers of their own nationality to teach them English. The response was immediate; their faces would light up as they replied, "Yea; that is different. Then we will not get discouraged in the beginning."

If these criticisms are carefully studied, it will be found that most of the fundamental reasons for the present failure in evening school instruction are touched upon in them. The criticisms are of three kinds—those that have to do with the method of instruction in the school; the attitude toward the foreign born, and conditions outside the school which make attendance difficult.

English Not Taught As A Means Of Social Communication.

In the first place, investigation proved that it was true that the method of instruction did not sufficiently take into consideration the people who were being taught. The recitation was not a "social recitation," and the inductive method was not used as a means of developing the course.

In the Passaic schools, at the time of the investigation, there were 395 pupils enrolled in the evening schools. There were 22 nationalities represented. The men and women enrolled were working during the day in 51 different establishments, the largest number being employed in the textile industry. Their ages ranged from 19 to 45 and over.

These pupils were grown men and women who, after a hard day's work, were giving up their evenings to come to school in order to learn to *communicate* in English. Yet, upon the whole, the chief criticism to be made of the evening school instruction is that the *English language was not being taught for purposes of communication*. The criticism of the workers that they were taught to read and write, but not to speak, was well-founded criticism. Oral language is more important for the average person than the written or printed work; yet the large part of time in the classroom was taken up in reading and writing. And it should be mentioned at this point that there was little evidence of any sensitiveness to the sound of words on the part of the teachers. Pupils were permitted to enunciate badly, making the same mistake over and over again, without correction. There was a most unfortunate habit of reading in chorus. This is, of course, a discredited method, particularly so in teaching adults a foreign language, since the best pupils lead in the chorus and the others are merely confirmed in their own bad habits of enunciation. There was almost no attempt to use the dramatic method of teaching; that is, having the pupils act out the written selections. There was almost no encouragement to discussion and little attempt to draw out the pupils and let them assist in carrying on the lesson. On the contrary, there was a very close adherence to the textbook, and at the same time a failure to follow the suggestions in the textbook as to methods of teaching. For example, in a lesson on "The newspaper," the directions were that the teacher should have newspaper, and the pupils should read it, but as there was no newspaper in the class the lesson lost most of its value.

Also, it can not be denied that there was a tendency to treat the members of the class as though they were children. The attitude was kindly, but the tone of voice was not that of an equal addressing equals. Often the context of the lesson or the method of questioning was nothing short of absurd when it was remembered that it was adults who were receiving instruction; as, for example, "How many different things are there in the sky?" The answer was, "The sun, moon, stars, and clouds." Aside from the fact that the answer is not what might be called a comprehensive list of the "things in the sky," the lesson was taught without any graphic representation to insure that the pupils attached the right words to the right objects. Or again, in one class the read selections on "A coal mine," "The iron and steel industry," and "A packing house." Although there were men in the class who doubtless knew far more about these industries than the teacher, and although discussion on any one of them might have been used as a basis for testing how far the men had developed the art of communicating their ideas in English, no attempt was made to do anything but read each selection and pass on to the next.

The most serious criticism, however, was that with few exceptions there was no attempt at individual instruction. The pupils were taught as a class, instead of being divided into small groups and allowed to progress according to their ability. There was little use of the inductive method in determining the needs of each individual in the class and in developing his power of communication.

As it happens, the best teaching of English which was observed was in a class of workers taught by an organizer of one of the labor organizations. The enunciation was not always correct, but the spirit in the class was that of equals working out a problem together. There was the most thorough individual instruction, and an alertness on the part of the teacher in finding out the difficulties of each pupil and helping him to solve them. The men were working hard, even doing home work for each lesson, and there was an atmosphere of mutual helpfulness that was most inspiriting.

Relation of Hours of Work to Evening School Instruction

But even if the instruction was of the best possible type, there is another reason for the present failure to secure large numbers in evening schools for which the school is not responsible in any way, and which no amount of attraction on the part of the school can offset. We refer to the hours of work in the average industry and the prevalence of night work. Over and over again, as we have pointed out, when the workers were asked why they did not attend evening schools, the answer was a shrug and "How can I? I have night work," or "My wife works at night, I take care of the children." Consequently, we secured the hours of work of every person in the evening schools at the time of the investigation (with the exception of two small classes). Infomation was obtained from 207 pupils. They were in 41 different types of work. Of the 207 pupils, 136, or 65.7 per cent, worked from 8 hours to 8 hours and 40 minutes. Of these, 104 worked an 8 hour and 40-minute day, and the 48-hour week is the present standard in the textile industry of Passaic. It is an interesting fact that, of all the 395 who enrolled in evening schools this year, 54.2 per cent of those who stated their employment (304) were workers in the textile industry. A third of those from whom the hours were secured worked 9 hours and over. Twenty-six worked 9 hours, and 34 worked from 9 to 10 hours.

It is only the exceptional person who, after a 10-hour day, will come to evening school for 2 hours' hard work on learning a new language. Nor can it be expected that large numbers of those having an 8-hour and 40-minute day will have the energy to attend school in the evening. But even this is not as great a handicap as the intermittent night work which unexpectedly cuts into the attendance in classes throughout the school, taking a dozen workers from one class, half a dozen from another, etc. The pupils in evening school when asked about night work, replied "Any time may work nights," "Last year worked nights 12 weeks straight," "I work two weeks day work, one week night work," or "May go on night shift next week, or overtime to 6 or 7 o'clock," or "I work four weeks day work, one week night work," or "Can't tell when we are going to have night work."

That was the point; they couldn't tell when they were going to have night work, and this uncertainty plays havoc with the administration of the school. No factory with a working force, say of 2,000, would undertake to get out production if suddenly 500 left one week and didn't come back for four weeks, and 200 more left just before the 500 came back, and didn't come back for 12 weeks, etc. Administratively, it would be an impossible proposition, and yet that is exactly the administrative proposition that is being put up to the schools at the present time. There is a great deal of agitation for the teaching of English and the extension of adult education, but the schools can not be expected to function successfully in this matter when industrial conditions undermine the effectiveness of the work of the schools, as is the case at present.

Recognizing this fact the bureau took up with the manufacturers in Passaic the question of releasing the workers during the day without loss of pay to attend classes in English in the public schools. At least two of the largest woolen manufacturers have already agreed to release their workers who wish to learn English at 4.30 in the afternoon with pay from 4.30 to 5 (which is the end of the dya shift in the woolen mills) on consideration that the workers will give until 5:30 to the lessons. The proposition was also taken up with the workers, and although not all the nationalities could be seen, those groups who were interviewed stated that they considered, the proposition fair and would be glad to attend the public schools to learn English from 4:30 to 5:30 p. m. Passaic is to be congratulated upon

THE PROGRESSIVE ERA
1919–1929

the fact that it has manufacturers and workers who are willing to make this arrangement, and also that it has schools sufficiently near the mills to make such an arrangement feasible.

Method of Approach to The Problem of Adult Education Psychologically Unsound.

But even this arrangement will not succeed unless the whole method of attracting people to the public schools is changed. The chief lesson to be learned from the interviews with the different nationalities and from the study of the social and industrial conditions is that the present method of approaching the problem of adult education is psychologically unsound; that is, the tendency has been to work out plans *for* the people, not *with* them. It is the old story of endeavoring to work changes from the top down instead from the bottom up. Such a method can not produce enduring results, since no plan for educational progress can be ultimately successful until it has its roots in the intelligent understanding of the masses of the people. If the schools are to function in the lives of the people, they must be sensitive to the people's needs, but that is not possible except by establishing a means of connection with the people so that they may make their needs and desires known.

This is true in general for the whole country, but its application to a city like Passaic is particularly obvious. In the early days in this country, the school was a social gathering place for the people, and all the people in the community knew that the schools belonged to them and were for their use. But at the present time the case is different. In a city like Passaic, where the large number of people are foreign born and from countries which do not have public school systems founded on the same principles as those of America, the bulk of the people who should be attending the schools have no comprehension of the fact that the schools belong to the people and should grow and change in accordance with their needs. They do not even know that if a certain number of people ask for a course in any subject, the schools must provide such a course. The school is to them a public institution which spells authority; they do not think of it as a place to go for recreation and instruction and inspiration. They do not think of it as a place in which they can expand and grow, but rather as a place in which they must conform, and above all they do not think of it as *their* institution which they are responsible for developing until it adequately meets the needs of all the people.

ISAAC BERKSON ON THE VALUE OF ETHNIC GROUPS (1920)   From Isaac B. Berkson, *Theories of Americanization: A Critical Study* (New York, 1920). pp. 128–32.

Multiple Cultural Loyalty

Those who have broken with the group usually consider themselves "broadminded." The loyalty to a minority ethnic group is often conceived of as narrowing. When the allegiance had been given blindly and exclusively to the family tradition, this may be true. But when it is given intelligently and with discrimination, without yielding the allegiance to the State and culture it represents, the double loyalty becomes a powerful force toward humanization.

The knowledge of another language, another history, and another point of view, is in itself a liberalizing influence. All additional knowledge is protection against indoctrination—a freeing of the mind. Knowledge of other peoples is not necessarily an allegiance. One may know very much about German philosophy and literature and yet not approve of them. Nevertheless, in the literature and culture of every developed nation humane elements will be found—interests and thoughts which conceive of life not from the narrow nationalistic point of view, but from the broadly human, universal outlook. Knowledge of these brings with it an appreciation which is psychologically an incipient loyalty. In so far as we have a love for foreign and ancient literature and languages, we have the beginnings of an allegiance towards them. When this appreciation reaches out into the plane of action, when in addition to the intellectual and aesthetic appreciation there is involved also the emotional appreciation imperative to further these activities, then a loyalty has come into being. When the notion of duty enters, then the allegiance has been pledged. And it is here, where emotions and actions are involved, that a multiple loyalty becomes especially significant.

For emotions and actions are subject to conflict, and conflict tends to be resolved into harmony. The need of furthering two distinct cultures must lead to an elimination of those elements which are mutually incompatible and to the emphasis upon those elements in each which have a universal interest. Each group culture contains within it elements of an international character, and attention must be centered upon these if both loyalties are to be retained. As in the individual, the variety of conflicting instincts and emotions must lead to a process of elimination, modification and development resulting in the creation of a rational philosophy and mode of life, so too, allegiance to more than one social group must lead to a larger view of life because it brings more knowledge and appreciation, but especially because the loyalties are under the necessity of rationalization.

It was not because thay had a double allegiance that hyphenated Americans were odious. It was because in their case the hyphen was a pretense or considered to be so, and used in order to hide the actual fact of a single rival allegiance to a foreign government. Had they been true hyphenates, owing equal allegiance to both peoples and really equally interested in the welfare of both, they would have been led to judge not from prejudice, but from the rule of right. And from the moral viewpoint at least, there could be nothing better. It is just the presence of true hyphenates, men who loved other nations as they did this, that gave our purposes in the war aims more truly human and less selfish than could otherwise have been possible.

The significance of a double allegiance, it should be noted, is greater than twice a single allegiance. Double here means multiple. The knowledge of an additional language and culture and the understanding of another people means not only a personality richer by so much. It means rather what an additional dimension does in spatial relations. It gives perspective. It opens up the mind to a new concept; there are other nations than one's own. The change of view is of significance not only for the additional nationality for which the interest is aroused but for the whole mental outlook. It prevents the mind from falling into the natural tendency of imagining that one's own culture is the only culture worthy of the name, and one's own countrymen, the only real humans. Interest in another nationality must go far toward giving one an international, as against a provincial outlook. Differences are seen more readily in their proportion; it is understood that humanity can speak in other languages, express itself in other cultures, exist in other physiognomies.

True universalization, colloquially called "broadmindedness," can come only through the multiplication of loyalties, not through the suppression of them, just as true spirituality comes from the addition of interests which must be harmonized, not through suppression of instincts. This is especially true in the present condition of society. There is no International Country to which we might give our allegiance. We must give it to the existing nations which are all particularistic. Otherwise we turn out in practical life to be disloyal, however conscientiously we may be true to our dreams. We cannot speak a universal language. We may speak one tongue or many. We cannot be everywhere. We must be in one place or in many places. Universalization cannot be promoted by abolition of nations (they cannot be abolished by fiat, nor can an international humanity be created by fiat) but by the multiplication of the number of nations toward which we feel sympathetic, leading to an emphasis upon the international elements in each nation.

There is, of course, the well recognized danger in such a multiplication of allegiance. It sometimes permits a *double and sinister political* allegiance to mask under the cover of a *cultural interest*. Sometimes, too, the humane interest may lead to a political allegiance conflicting with patriotism. When this leads to the ascendancy of right as against selfish national prejudice, then it cannot be considered as anything but beneficial. When it leads to the loyalty to a foreign government as against right, it is reprehensible. But the chances for such an unrighteous foreign allegiance are small under the influence of our own environment, provided that our scheme of education is such as is assumed here where every child must attend the public schools. When such a disloyal foreign allegiance does occur, it must be treated as a separate problem. We do not maintain that people should not heed their conscience, because that may lead to the conscientious objector, who is, as we think, unreasonable in his plea of conscience and, in effect, though not in motive, disloyal. We do not suppress individuality because its expression sometimes leads to selfishness. Nor should we suppress the double cultural allegiance which is essentially humanizing because under present conditions where war is possible (in itself a most irrational condition in civilized society) it may at times create difficulties.

Multiple cultural allegiance is in itself a force tending to remove the likelihood of war. The notorious fact that international science, art and religion were of little avail in stemming the tide of war and the surprising ease with which savants, social workers and ministers found it possible to lose sight of universal interests, even to turn chauvinists, should warn us against expecting too much from merely ideal bonds. One's closest friends are still for the most part in one's own country; and control of military and police forces, of education, of the means of forming public opinion and of a multitude of other conditions gives the national government a stranglehold upon the lives of its citizens. Nevertheless, the ever-present danger of conflict between nation and nation can be overcome only by a multiplication of international ties until they become numerous and strong enough to bear the strain of national separatism. A League of Nations can become effective only in so far as it is an expression of a community of international interest and is based securely upon a multiplicity of interdependences. The further development of communication, the growth of economic interdependence, the multiplication of many forms of international societies and above all revision of education so that it may make apparent, not obscure, the existence of these many interdependences must precede any lasting peace. Important among these interrelationships is the consciousness of kinship rising out of the multiple cultural allegiance. Is is significant that the presence of foreign ethnic groups gave us great concern during the war. Only the conviction that the Central Powers had violated the peace of the world could break the force of this international bond. On the other hand, our best evidence that double allegiances are not fatal comes from the experience of the war. The presence of hyphenated Americans did not prevent us from winning the war. Perhaps it even aided us for it forced us to become clear as to our purposes. How could the many conflicting loyalties of our variegated population be met? Only by a stand that was above national prejudice could we be united for the tremendous undertaking. The multiple loyalty enhances the quality of patriotism and raises it to the level of an international interest.

Loyalty to a minority ethnic group, in addition to enriching the general culture, promotes the spiritualization of the individual's aims and purposes, It tends to make his outlook more universal, his perspective international, his approval to lie on the plane of intelligent conscious justification. He remains near to those intimacies of close family relationship which seem basic to a real human touch and understanding; but he must still maintain an open mind towards divergences. His sympathies remain deep while they are broadened. Understanding the keen and intense woes and joys that are possible when one lives in close proximity to those with whom one feels an emotional and almost sensous consciousness of kind, the sympathies are broadened and extended to a reach of international scope, where the unities are broadly humane, and the kinship is on the plane of the intelligent.

These are general values which arise out of a multiple allegiance. In addition, each particular group will contribute in accordance with its own gifts and culture. No association of men capable of social coherence and self-consciousness and tending to maintain its identity midst conditions which naturally would disintegrate them can be conceived of as being altogether without a culture. How much each group can contribute will depend upon the excellence of its cultural accomplishments. The whole range of contribution may extend from cooking recipes, quaint melodies and legends, through customs, conventions, folkways, to language, literature, ethics, social organization and religion. To describe these even briefly for the Jewish group alone would require volumes and the work of many masters. In the following pages it is the intention not to attempt to evaluate Judaism or describe the Jewish heritage, but to present several ideas which will give some hint of the depth and meaning of Jewish life.

HENRY PRATT FAIRCHILD ON THE MELTING POT MISTAKE

(**1926**) From Henry Pratt Fairchild, *The Melting-Pot Mistake* (Boston, 1926), pp. 205–20.

W e have seen how viciously false is the statement that citizenship makes the foreigner a part of America. Equally false is the assertion that the foreigner lives and works in America, and the implication that the act of becoming a "part of America" is-to use the vernacular-strictly "up to him." The only way to become a part of America is to live in America for an extended period of time. But the immigrant does not live in America. So what is he to do, and what are we to do?

The outstanding fact in this connection is that as a result of a century and a half of immigration there have been built up within the physical boundaries of what is called America extensive and deeply entrenched offshoots of numerous foreign nationalities. These are most conspicuous, and probably most frequent, in our great cities, and any one who has participated in any form of social case work has inevitably become familiar with them. But they exist in equally well-developed forms in the less crowded sections of the country devoted to agriculture, mining, and other extractive pursuits. In a certain section of Nebraska, a generation ago, one could drive for miles without meeting an adult who could speak English, and "Dutch Bohunk" was a customary epithet of opprobrium among the native American children of the town. Similar situations exist all over the land, furnishing conclusive refutation of the common argument that "distribution" can be relied upon to solve all the evils of immigration.

These "foreign colonies," as they are commonly called, are living evidences of the tenacity of nationality. They show how vigorously every individual clings to his own original national traits, how choice and dear they seem to him, and how difficult it is for him to change them even if he wishes. There are many sections of the United States in which even the third generation of immigrants does not speak English.

The persistence of nationality, and the revolutionary nature of the transformation involved in a change of nationality, can hardly be comprehended by one who has never been called upon to undergo such a process. For the average native-born American, whose life has been spent continuously in the congenial atmosphere of his own nationality, perhaps there is no better means of illustrating the change that is involved in a movement from one part of the United States to another, such as tens of thousands of Americans have experienced. Take, for example, the case "of a young man who has been brought up in a strictly Puritanical community, and, in his early twenties, let us say, moves to a community with a less rigid code. He has been trained not to paly cards, not to dance, not to smoke, perhaps not to attend the theater or play pool or billiards. He has been made to believe that these things are wrong, and so he does actually regard them as wrong. Yet in his new environment he sees the very best people doing all of these things without any compunction or even any sense of their being questionable. Their code is different from his. Such a person goes through a very difficult and trying transition period. If he has a good intellect and if his moral sentiments are healthy and sound, he usually works his way out all right. But in the meantime his pathway is surrounded with many pitfalls."[1] Even in a country as closely unified as the United States there are many varying social environments. The change from one to another is always a soul-trying experience, yet it is as nothing compared to that which every immigrant must undergo who actually moves into America.

Illustrations of the nature of the contrasts between diverse nationalities and the difficulty of harmonizing them, might be multiplied almost indefinitely. Some have already been given. A few more may be added to emphasize the true nature of the experience which we demand of the immigrant when we call upon him to be assimilated.

Two young men, an Englishman and an American, both teachers in schools in a

[1]Quoted from the author's *Elements of Social Science*, page 115.

Turkish city and therefore familiar with a variety of national institutions, were sitting at one of the outdoor tables in front of a cafe in Athens. There passed by an officer of the Greek army in uniform in the company of a civilian apparently of humble status. The young Englishman was struck by the incident, and commented upon it.

"You would never see anything like that in England."

"Why not?" inquired the American.

"Because in England the officers come from the aristocratic families, and would not condescend to walk on the streets with a common man. It's a very good system too, because it creates a profound respect for the officers on the part of the enlisted men.

"But it can not be nearly as effective as the American system," said the other, "where the officers are chosen for ability or distinguished conduct. That is a much more powerful basis for respect than mere birth."

The point was argued at length, with of course no change in the ideas of either disputant. Now the ancestors of the American and the Britisher might well have been kinsmen and neighbors in some English village not so many generations ago, yet their views on this fundamental subject were as wide apart as the poles. Ask yourself, proud descendant of old Pilgrim lineage, how long you would have to live in England before you became convinced that the system of a hereditary aristocracy was a sounder basis for military graduation than individual ability and achievement. Yet in other respects, these two young men were vastly closer to each other than they were to their Greek and Armenian pupils, who simply could not conceive, for instance, how their teacher could innocently take a walk in the country alone with a young woman.

One of the recent characteristic expressions of the American nationality is the attempt to secure the suppression of the use of alcoholic beverages by national legislation. It is a unique and courageous adventure, and the American people certainly ought to have the opportunity to try it out, in accordance with established American institutions and constitutional procedure, without the interference of millions of persons whose traditional attitude toward both the use of alcoholic drinks and constitutional and representative government is so distinctly foreign that they can not possibly even comprehend the character and spirit of this undertaking. Yet there can be no doubt that the alien elements in this country form one of the most serious obstacles, not to the success of the Prohibition Movement—upon which genuine Americans hold very divergent opinions—but to the legitimate prosecution of the experiment in democratic government which the Eighteenth Amendment and the Volstead Act represent. In spite of all that is said about the "machinations of an organized minority," there can be no doubt that these two measures were carried out in strict conformity to the established legal procedure of the United States. But the enforcement of them is immeasurably hampered by the activities of countless individuals who are completely indifferent to American institutions and completely unresponsive to American public opinion. The situation has been humorously described in the following words: "Many of these people simply fail to get the idea of prohibition. Thousands of them think it was put into force by executive decree of President Wilson. I have heard them talk about it for hours and advocate a twenty-four hour national strike in protest, believing that thus they can force President Harding to rescind the decree. To try to explain the theory of prohibition to a group of Italian workmen is very much like trying to explain to you, the reader, that in Siberia people walk on their ears. In other words, it sounds interesting, but it does not 'get over.' A friend of mine, a Red Cross worker during the war, related to me his futile effort to explain American prohibition to an Italian Senator in Italy. The Senator listened with attention for three quarters of an hour and then asked 'But what kind of wine do they drink now?' The fact that they are not supposed to drink wine at all simply failed to register with him. It was inconceivable. People of this type, who are otherwise law-abiding and patriotic and well-intentioned, protect bootleggers and otherwise violate the Volstead Act with the same faith in the justice of their actions that a group of Middle Western Americans would have in evading a law that prohibited them from planting corn.[2]

It is significant that most of the bootleggers, at least as far as one can judge from ordinary evidence—statistics do not seem to be available—appear to be foreigners. Doubtless a handsome proportion, if not the majority, of their patrons are native-born Americans. But this does not alter the case. It seems that one of the features of the American nationality in its immediate phase is a nice distinction between patronizing a bootlegger and being a bootlegger. If there were not abundant non-Americans who were quite willing to be bootleggers, the trade would almost certainly fall off markedly. It can not be purely by chance that a map of "wetness" in the United States is almost a replica of a map showing the distribution of the foreign-born. All of this, be it remembered, is not an argument for or against Prohibition, but an illustration of the difficulty of expressing the national will in an experimental policy when national unity does not exist.

These special national loyalties and affiliations persist for many generations, even when the individual descendants of the original immigrants are almost completely assimilated. Group feeling as expressed in group pride is one of the most enduring of all human sentiments. Mention has already been made of the elaborate exposition called "America's Making." This was conceived as means of promoting a better understanding, not only between the various groups of foreigners—an aspect of the Americanization problem, by the way, all too frequently neglected. Doubtless many useful results were accomplished in this direction. But behind the scenes, according to the newspaper reports, some lively and incongruous displays of group jealousy marred the serene atmosphere of the enterprise. These clashes were largely caused by rival claims as to the group affiliation of certain prominent Americans of various early periods. It is significant that antagonism was sharpest not among the representatives of the new immigration, who are presumably least completely assimilated, but among the Scotch and the Irish. An Irishman, checking over the list of notables displayed in the Scotch booth, was outraged to find a number of persons included whom he claimed as pure Irish. The chairman of the Scotch group, however, maintained that "the Scotch-Irish of the north of Ireland always have been and always will be Scotch regardless of where they make their home." The Welsh also entered the controversy by claiming President Monroe, who was listed in both the Welsh and the Scotch booths. Even as these words are being written the newspapers print an account of a journey of the President of the United States halfway across the continent to take part in a great "Norse" celebration, in commemoration of the completion of one hundred years of Norwegian settlement in this country. Doubtless the celebrants are all loyal and patriotic, yet the vivid consciousness of their foreign origin is a definite factor in American national disunity, just as it is in the case of any other group similarly inspired.

All of this may seem very trivial and inconsequential to the native American

[2]C. T. Crowell, "How Prohibition Works," *Independent and Weekly Review*, Jan. 14, 1922.

who has never been thrown into the stress of conflicting nationalities. But nationality is largely a matter of things that are in themselves trivial, but nevertheless have a profound effect in creating group feeling. A whimsical presentation of this truth has been given by Mr. Clarence Day, Jr., in a sketch which deserves to be quoted in full, but of which this paragraph must stand as representative.

" 'Why is it,' " the old explorer was wondering, " 'that men care so for trifles? Even death and danger won't stop us, or make us less fussy. In a country where a man knows that he's likely to be killed any day, in the middle of his career, he ought to have a little sense of proportion. But life's not safe a minute in Kiboa, for instance, and have they any sense? Not a bit. People there are exactly as finicky as everywhere else. They spend most of their time being preoccupied with meaningless nothings. I did more for those Kiboans than I have ever done for any tribe since—I stamped over two fever epidemics and taught them how to build mill wheels—and yet, at their great banquet to celebrate the lives I had saved, they were horrified because I used the wrong stick to eat with at table. There were two sticks, a prong and a flat one. I ate peas with the flat one. I should have use the prong. Well, that ended me. They still tried to be grateful, but it was painful to them—I had turned out low caste.' "[3]

It would be the gravest mistake to conclude, however, that nationality is all a matter of nonessentials or superficialities. There should, indeed, be no doubt on that point at this stage of our discussion. Nationality includes all the deepest, dearest, most inalienable, and most unquestioned elements in the social inheritance of every individual. This can be appreciated by recalling that the moral code itself is a part of nationality. It is true that there are certain fundamental resemblances among the moral codes of all civilized peoples, and even of barbarous or savage peoples, just as there are basic physical resemblances among all the races of man. But this is only because, nationally as well as racially, men are much more alike than they are different. Nevertheless, it is the differences that divide men into groups, and differences in moral codes are as nearly insuperable as any barrier that exists. During the unreflective and uncritical years of character formation the authority of the moral code of one's own particular group is absolute. Consequently, by the time one reaches an age of analytical comparison the sway of one's own code has become so firmly established that it is almost impossible, by the exercise of any processes of reasoning, to emancipate one's self from it. You may convince yourself that in some particular respect the code of France, or Turkey, or Japan is higher, or more rational, or more conducive to human well-being than your own. But it is quite a different thing to make yourself feel comfortable when you begin to pattern your conduct after that code. A remarkable illustration of these truths was furnished by the case of the young Albanian who killed his countryman, Essad Pasha, in Paris in 1920. In the course of the trial the fact was brought out that Essad Pasha had previously been instrumental in causing the death of the father of his slayer. According to Albanian law and social usage it was not only the right, but also the duty, of the younger man to pursue the man who had killed his father, until he had accomplished his death. The remarkable feature of the case is that although the crime was committed on the French soil, and the case was tried before a Frech court, the decision was that the young Albanian was governed by the Albanian code,

[3]*The New Republic*, October 18, 1922, page 198.

and hence in committing what we would call a murder he not only *thought* he was right but he *was* right. He was therefore acquitted.

The process of Americanization, then, for the immigrant is infinitely more difficult than for the native because the former, during the years before his arrival in the United States, has already acquired more or less completely a foreign nationality. This nationality is dissimilar in most respects, and absolutely contradictory and inconsistent in many respects, to the American nationality. Yet to the foreigner it is his natural and authoritative spiritual tradition and social environment. He may hold a critical attitude toward certain aspects of it, just as most Americans are dissatisfied with some phases of the American nationality, but taken as a whole it represents to him truth, beauty, goodness, morality, justice, propriety, efficiency, custom, order, and—home. Let the critical and self-satisfied American of native birth reflect that in the process of Americanization this whole spiritual endowment must be abandoned, and another taken it its place, and it may help him dimly to perceive how tragic, how soul-wracking must be the experience of assimilation, though probably no one who has actually gone through it can appreciate the stress and tragedy involved.

The Motion Pictures

THE MOTION PICTURE IN EDUCATION (1922)   From Will H. Hays,
"Improvement of Moving Pictures," National Education Association *Journal of Proceedings and Addresses* (Boston, 1922), pp. 252–57.

The National Education Association holds its convention in the home of its ancestors. We remember the law passed in Massachusetts in 1647 which required each town of 50 householders to "appoint one to teach all such children as shall resort to him, to write and read," and I approach your venerable family tree with a consistent humility, inasmuch as this instrument of education, the motion picture, has hardly reached the age of a high-school graduate. In a little over fifteen years it has grown from a naked idea until today it is the principal amusement of the great majority of all our people and the sole amusement of millions, one of the greatest industries in America, having an investment in real estate, studios, and equipment of nearly $500,000,000, with probably $50,000,000 paid annually in salaries, $200,000-000 spent annually in production, and $800,000,000 spent annually for admissions.

A few years ago such a meeting as this would have been impossible. You would not have felt that you were warranted in taking time to discuss the motion picture in education. But today the educators of the country are appreciating its value, and it has been with peculiar pleasure that I have noted this interest as evidenced by the invitation that brings me here to the National Education Association.

There has been some query as to just what this new effort which the industry is making at this time is all about. It is simply that these men who make and distribute pictures have associated themselves together to do jointly those things in which they are mutually but non-competitively interested, having as the chief purposes of such association two great objectives—and I quote verbatim from the formal articles of association, which have been filed at Albany: "establishing and maintaining the highest possible moral and artistic standards in motion picture production, and developing the *educational* as well as the entertainment *value* and the general usefulness of the motion picture."

This is the legal statement of a legal purpose by a legally organized body. It creates no super-court autocratically to pass upon pictures, nor does it place anyone in the attitude, and most certainly I shall not be placed in the attitude, of being the judge of the morals of those who are in the industry. The purposes of the association are stated in its articles, and no articles of association breathing a more important message could well be found.

The importance of the association's first great purpose, "to establish and maintain the highest possible moral and artistic standards in motion picture production" and the fact that its realization is now progressing can not be overestimated. And there is no group in this country more interested than are you teachers in its consummation. While this is true, you, of course, have a special interest in the second great objective, that is—"to develop the educational as well as the entertainment value and general usefulness of the industry"—and for the attainment of both ends I want your sympathetic cooperation.

The motion picture is essentially a source of amusement, and its importance in that regard is measured only by the imperative necessity of entertainment for our people. In all the big cities and maple-shaded towns and villages which comprise America there are perhaps fifteen thousand motion-picture theaters and in those theaters fifteen million seats. Taking into account at least two performances a day and applying the collected statistics, we estimate that within every twenty-four hours between Maine and California twenty millions men, women, and children look for an hour or two on the motion-picture screen. They come with no preoccupation; not out of duty nor out of solicitation, but just in that mood of reception and relaxation, in that state of mind and emotion which a master psychologist, a great teacher, would want them to come, having the desire to make the strongest possible impression upon them. U.S. Commissioner of Education John J. Tigert said recently, "Within the celluloid film lies the most powerful weapon for the attack against ignorance that the world has ever known."

Obviously, it is true that the influence of the motion picture on our National life is, indeed, absolutely limitless—its influence on our taste, its influence on our conduct, its influence on our aspirations, its influence on our youth, and its consequent immeasurable influence on our future. And so its integrity must—and shall—be protected just as we protect the integrity of our churches, and its quality must—and shall—be developed just as we develop the quality of our schools.

I wonder if you realize, you teachers and all those who have at heart the general welfare—what the motion picture means to the youth of this country? I approach this subject not merely from the viewpoint of the men who have millions of dollars invested in the business, but from the viewpoint of the fathers and mothers who have millions of children invested in the business. We say 20,000,000 a day see motion pictures. Possibly half of this number are children.

Above everything else perhaps is our duty to youth. To teachers I do not have to say that this industry must have toward that sacred thing, the mind of a child, toward that clean, virgin thing, that unmarked slate, the same sense of responsibility, the same care about the impressions made upon it that the clergyman, or the most inspired teacher of youth would have.

So certainly is the improving of this industry a matter of immediate concern to everyone, that I earnestly ask and hope to receive the advice and cooperation of the public. Too much can not be expected too soon, either in the raising of the morals and artistic standards or in the development of the educational value. There can be no overnight miracle, but preferred attention is being given to purposes of the association right now in the pictures which are now being made. Every day there is opportunity in the studios to take that action at the place and at the only place where effective action can be taken. Responsibility for these pictures now being made by the members of our association can not be avoided. They will be the proof either of our honesty of purpose or of our failure. They will be the proof either of our ability to correct our evils ourselves or of our inability to run our own business. The members of this association, acting on that definite knowledge, are doing everything in their power at this moment to live up to their professions, and the pictures will soon show the results of their efforts.

While asking for your aid and cooperation I would like to ask, too, that you judge us by our actual performances rather than by any promises we may make. We are building this industry for years to come—for generations to come, and though our progress may perhaps be slow at the beginning, the results, we are confident will be permanent and certain.

It has been said repeatedly that certain objectionable pictures which have been made are the class of pictures the public wanted, this deduction being based upon box-office receipts. One way for you to help us make good pictures is very easy, and that is by refusing to patronize bad pictures. I am not suggesting an alibi for the motion-picture business; I am only emphasizing that this is not a one-man's job, nor the job of one group; it is the multitude's job; in doing it there is work for all. One of the largest producers has told me that in his opinion the outstanding financial successes in the last eighteen months have been clean pictures. I may not know thoroughly the picture business, but I do know thoroughly the American public, and I know that its manhood and womanhood is sound and will support clean pictures. And the American public is the real censor for the motion picture, just as it is for the press and the pulpit.

May I refer a minute to this question of censorship, which is an incident in the matter? The people of this country, of course, are against censorship fundamentally—are against censorship of press, against censorship of pulpit, and against censorship of pictures. But just as certainly, my friends, is this country against wrong doing—and the demand for censorship will fail when the reason for the demand is removed. As we move toward the consummation of the objects of our association so in like degree will recede all demands for censorship.

I am against political censorship, of course, because political censorship will not do what is hoped for it in the last analysis. The motion-picture business objects to political censorship for one great reason—because the motion-picture business is an American business. But there is one place and one place only where the evils can be eliminated and the good and great advantage of motion pictures retained, and that is at the point where and when the pictures are made. And it *can* be done then and there, make no mistake about that. There is no twilight zone in the matter. Right is right and wrong is wrong, and men know right from wrong. The corrections *can* be made, real evil *can* and must be kept out, the highest standards of art, taste, and morals *can* be achieved, and it is primarily the duty of the producers to do it.

I reiterate, it can not be done in a moment. It can not be done without the aid and support of the public, and that support I know you will give. And with the raising of the moral and artistic standard comes the development of the educational value of the motion picture. You are not unmindful of the great educational value of the entertainment picture as such. It must be the purpose of the industry to strive continually to make presentations historically correct and give authentic portrayals of customs, costumes, and habits.

In addition to the general educational value of entertainment pictures, we are together concerned, of course, with two additional phases, first the pedagogic picture and then the picture which is semi-educational and semi-entertainment. It must be that the motion picture is a distinct contribution to visual instruction. The quick way to the brain is through the eye. Scientific tests which have been made and which are being made and with which you are familiar seem to prove the value of the motion picture in the classroom.

The producers are interested in this educational work. They realize its importance and the industry is eager to help. Up to the present time it has been easy for producers to meet the requirements of the educational field, for the demand for strictly instructional classroom films has been small. Films are costly and unless a single film can be used over and over it can not be made without great loss. If educational films are to be produced accurately and in sufficient numbers, better methods of distribution must be worked out. Again those who produced the films were not trained educators and therefore unable to produce pedagogically sound films, while at the same time the educators, whose advice has been available, have too often proved unable to adapt themselves to the peculiar technical demands of screen production. Before great progress can be made there must be some method worked out to bring together the men and women who are skilled in the methods and mechanics of picture production.

Much has been done with the motion picture already as an instrumentality of instruction, but the surface has hardly been scratched. Certainly the educators of the country are awakening to its possibilities. Four non-commercial magazines are or recently have been in existence, dedicated to the discussion of the problems of visual education. Various museums of natural history have used films for lecture purposes in small museums and public schools.

The educational value has been appreciated and tried out in various directions. Recently the Amerian City Bureau inaugurated a film service on municipal and civic subjects. In Washington representatives of the National Academy of Science, the American Association for the Advancement of Science, The National Research Council, and the Scripps Interests are joined to promote science service which, among other things, seeks to educate the popular mind by putting into screen form stories of scientific discovery and invention. The Society for Visual Education has produced many films of educational nature. Professors in many schools and colleges are talking of filming the materials of their courses and Yale is said to have under production 100 reels showing its famous Chronicles of America.

The Society of Visual Education prepares and distributes motion-picture films, which will be pedagogically sound textbook supplements for the use of teachers. Besides this Association and the Visual Instruction Department of your own organization, there are two other groups of educators in the motion-picture field— the National Academy of Visual Instruction and the Visual Instruction Association of America. An incomplete list shows twenty-eight colleges and universities which have organized departments for the distribution of films. At least seventeen of our largest educational institutions are giving courses to their students on the use of the motion picture for visual instruction. Several large universities are conducting scientific research into motion-picture problems. The best material ever produced in the study of the psychology of reading has come through the motion pictures of the eye, which have been taken by the Department of Education of the University of Chicago. Again, our knowledge of the processes by which children learn to write has been greatly increased through motion pictures, photographs of hand movements taken by the same university.

Thirty-four cities, including New York, Chicago, Cleveland, Detroit, Indianapolis, Los Angeles, and San Francisco, are now using pedagogical films in their classrooms and assembly halls. New York spent approximately $10,000 for this purpose last year, while Los Angeles spent $25,000. There are probably about 10,000 projecting machines installed in schools and churches. If methods can be found for easy payments on machines and effective methods for distribution of films, this field will grow with great rapidity.

The motion-picture industry will cooperate with the National Education Association fully to that end. On behalf of our organization I offer to your association all of our facilities to aid in your experimentation. There is already a great demand for pedagogic pictures. I propose that we jointly study tnat demand and that we jointly find ways and means of supplying it. Let a committee be appointed of this association made up of the very best talent within your ranks; let them meet with the great producers of the country and find ways to use our facilities. We ask you to aid us and to let us aid you in the study of the whole problem of the use of the motion picture as a direct pedagogic instrument. Let us together find the means of making pedagogic pictures which are scientifically, psychologically, and pedagogically sound. Not only can we take care of the demand which now obtains but the great demand which is imminent and which will certainly come, must be met, and met by the producers with a supply that measures up to the ideas of the educators of the country.

It can never be said again, and I think it has been suggested, that the producers do not want to furnish educational pictures. The producers want to serve America. They know that there is no more important and lasting service which they can perform than to aid you in the actual educating of the youth of the country by this new means and make yet more efficient if possible the work which you, the teachers, are doing in the fulfilment of your noblest and most useful of all professions.

Nor will you be unmindful of the great good done by this industry. The motion picture has carried the silent call for virtue, honesty, ambition, hope, love of country and of home to audiences speaking twenty different languages but all understanding the universal language of pictures. There may be fifty different languages spoken in this country, but the picture of a mother is the same in every language. It has brought to narrow lives a knowledge of the wide, wide world; it has been the benefactor of uncounted millions. It is the poor man's pleasure; grand opera for the well-to-do, but pictures for the man who works with his hands. As we serve the leisure hours of the masses with right diversions, so do we rivet the girders of society.

Those who are responsible for this industry do not minimize their responsibility, nor would they shirk it. With your help and the help of thinking people in this country in supporting the good pictures, we can accomplish the purpose of this association. The motion picture industry accepts the challenge in the demand of the American people for a higher quality of art and interest in its entertainment. The industry accepts the challenge in the demand of the American youth that its pictures shall give to them the right kind of entertainment and instruction.

We accept the challenge in the righteous demand of the American mother that the entertainment and amusement of that youth shall be worthy of their value as a most potent factor in the country's future. We accept the challenge in the proper demand of the educators of the country that the full instructional value of motion pictures shall be developed and used. We accept full responsibility. It is a service and "service is the supreme commitment of life." It is a service which needs the very best from all, and I have great faith in its fulfilment.

Psychology, Mental Hygiene
and Social Work

EDUCATIONAL APPLICATIONS OF PSYCHOANALYSIS (1920) From Wilfrid
Lay, *Man's Unconscious Conflict* (New York, 1920), pp. 265–66, 271–74, 279–80.

Thinking that is directed only according to the plans of the modern
systems of education fails, through its not taking into account the results of the
symbolisation that the Unconscious is continually forming so as to push up from the
depths below the expression of its craving.

We have shown by means of illustrations how some of the most commonplace
actions of everyday life are the symbolic expressions of primal cravings misunderstood and misapplied by the conscious life. In the actual training given by teachers
in schoolrooms very little if any of this symbolism is recognised and the pupils are
wrenched to fit a Procrustean bed instead of having their personalities developed
according to the characteristics with which nature endowed them. If figs are not
gathered of thorns, it is impossible to expect a certain kind of result from the
classical type of training. But every child has a feeling of inferiority before any
educational task, whether it be arithmetic or history or Latin, and the sense of
mastery, which is especially strong in boys, should be employed by the teacher in all
school work, for we now know that it is as inevitable as sunshine, and that the
young person is bound to get it out of some source, even out of his own body, or
abuse of his own mind. If the example in arithmetic is not solved, the pupil is much
more likely to take his gratification from the dream-life of the moving-picture
shows, where anything that human desire can conceive is represented as a visual
reality, but it is equally true that so great a gratification may be derived from the
successful performance of a school task that it will completely satisfy the craving of
the individual, in fact produce a craving for more satisfaction of the same nature.
That is what we call getting thoroughly interested in arithmetic or in history or in
any branch of school work.

*   *   *

Mention has already been made of the book *Die Psychanalytische Methode* by
Oscar Pfister,[1] which is devoted to the application of the psychoanalytic procedure
to the problems of education. There is no other book dealing directly with this

[1]Leipzig and Berlin, 1913, viii+512 pp.

subject in English. It is also quite out of the question to give anything like a thorough treatment of even a single phase of the subject in a chapter in a general review of so large a topic as I have attempted to deal with in the present volume.

There are, however, a number of general considerations which no one having anything to do with education can afford to ignore. The first and most important fact that should be recognised by teachers and others interested in education is the unconscious resistance on the part of the pupil to everything that the teacher represents. This resistance may be coexistent with the most polite acquiescence, the result of a strong home training, and with the most excellent ability,—both of which, to be sure, make the friction between pupil and teacher less,—but both of these qualities are quite independent of the natural unconscious resistance to the authority of the teacher. The necessity for the outward show of authority is of course greater in schools where the classes are large, and where for that reason there seems to be less opportunity for elasticity, and where the authority of the teacher is correspondingly exaggerated. In smaller schools where more of the teacher's attention is secured for each pupil, there is still found a great proportion of the authority element in spite of the possibly stronger feeling of *camaraderie* between teachers and pupils. Indeed, it is one of the compensations of the ambivalence of the educational situation that some smaller schools, in order to defend themselves against a supposed laxity in the performance of their functions, stiffen their curriculum and increase their paternalistic authority for the purpose of raising their standard of scholarship.

Now, this paternalistic trend of education necessarily proceeds from the view of education as a transmitting of the experience of the race to the individual. It is implied that the teacher has a better and wider experience than the pupil and that his object is to make the pupil see that it will be better for him to avail himself of this accumulated knowledge, for the uplift of the race. Right here the teacher is faced with the unconscious resistance of the pupil in the fact that the pupil's Unconscious, seeking always for a means of increasing his sense of superiority, so as to remove the painful feeling of inferiority which is the cause of all fables, is sure that at bottom it knows better than the teacher, better than the father, better in fact than all the world, when it sets itself up as an authority. The school, the teachers and the work are to the Unconscious of the child of any age barriers set up between it and the following of its own bent, which as we have seen is for phantastic as opposed to directed thinking.

B. The Father-Image

The school has for a long time been looked at as *in loco parentis*, or as taking, for the time during which the child is in school, the place of the parent. As the vast majority of teachers in this country are women, it might be supposed that the parent represented by the school is the mother. A little reflection, however, will show that this is a mistake. The unmarried women suited by nature for successful class management in large schools are usually those who show to some extent an overweighting of the masculine end of their bisexuality. In order to deliver their message, which is essentially a message of masculine to feminine, they inevitably though unconsciously themselves assume at least a modicum of the masculine element of authority.

It is necessary here to recall what has been found by psychoanalysis concerning the father-image. To the Unconscious of the child, school and all it represents, no matter how sweetly the work is sugar-coated with the different "activities,"—athletic, literary, dramatic, etc.,—is a father-image. Every unconscious trend of the adolescent human (and remember how many of us are ourselves, in our Unconscious, merely adolescent and not adult) revolts, because it is infantile and archaic, from any restrictions upon the natural expression of its cravings. And the school is not only a representative of society, like the endopsychic censor, and of the restrictions of society upon the free play of the manifestation of the child's unconscious craving, but is in most cases a more highly organised system than society itself. Nowhere do restrictions bristle more threateningly than in school. This is particularly true of large schools where much red tape has to be unwound.

It is inevitable, however, that this should be so. The child cannot be left to follow its own phantasies, which would lead it deeper and deeper into introversion. The boy and the girl must be taken, as few parents take them, and impressed with the difference between the pleasure-pain principle and the reality principle. That is the great, we might almost say the only, task of the teacher,—to make a man out of a boy, to make a woman out of a girl. There must needs be a sacrifice of all that the child unconsciously holds dear. All its regressive, autistic tendencies must be combated on every hand, and it must be led gently and continuously to an appreciation of the value of directed thinking.

＊　　＊　　＊

The antagonism between teacher and pupil is a natural one resting on and being caused not only by the unconscious element in the pupil but also by that of the teacher. If the pupil can get the teacher by the ears, whether done coarsely, as in the hoarse voice of an uncivilised street arab in the schools of a great city, or gently and with refined elegance of language in some girls' boarding school, it is a pulling over of the teacher by the child to the child's thought material. Actually there ought to be enough mental material at the disposal of the teacher to weigh so much both in the teacher's estimation and in the pupil's that no room could be found for any antagonism. Disorder in a schoolroom is always the indication of a vacuum being filled. There is generally a vacuum in the minds of most pupils which needs filling in the right way. It is impossible for the child to fill it properly in a schoolroom except with ideas directed by the teacher. If the teacher is full of unanalysed complexes it will be much easier for the pupil to throw him off the track. This is especially true of the power-complex which is most likely to be found in the teacher, for the petty power exercised in the schoolroom must, as Pfister suggests, furnish an unconscious attraction to many persons, leading them to adopt this calling, just as the vocation of locomotive engineer, fireman or policeman furnishes an attraction to children of a much younger age.

＊　　＊　　＊

The Unconscious of the pupil, always looking out for a chance to get its satisfaction from a sense of power, instinctively tries it out on any teacher that is either new to the school or new to the pupil. It seems as if no work was to be done *for* a new teacher until a trial of strength was had between the Unconscious of the teacher and those of the pupils. There arise in this connection some very painful scenes in which the teacher and the pupil are really making love to each other, but in archaic modes. The view of the matter which psychoanalysis forces upon us may be illustrated by an analysis of the situation in which for some form of classroom disorder a pupil has become offensive to the teacher. The unsocial nature of the pupil's overt acts is rarely brought home to him. He is probably told repeatedly that while he is making noises, or even while he is merely inattentive, he is impeding the work of the school. But while he may verbally admit it, he is at heart unconvinced. . . .

WILLIAM WHITE ON CHILDHOOD AND MENTAL HYGIENE
(1920)   From William A. White, "Childhood: The Golden Period for Mental Hygiene," *Mental Hygiene*, vol. IV, pp. 261–67.

If it is true that defects in the character make-up can be explained as originating in traits which were acquired in early childhood as reactions to certain factors in the child's environment, then the way is opened for an attempt to prevent such undesirable traits by an understanding of the child and a modification or elimination of those environmental factors which produce such results. For example, we all know many persons who are afraid of lightning, yet Watson tells us that in all the babies he has worked with he has never seen a reaction of fear to sudden flashes of light.[1]

If the fatalistic ways of thinking engendered by the theories of heredity can be put aside, then we find another reason for considering that the period of childhood offers the golden opportunity for mental hygiene and for realizing that this is the period upon which effort must finally be centered in the development of a program of prevention.

What are the points of attack for the development of such a program?

First, there must be a real understanding and development of child psychology. This development must be along the lines of behaviorism, a study of what the child is trying to do in terms of the child psyche. Here, as elsewhere in dealing with children, the tendency has been to think of the child as if it were a small adult and to project upon it those types of explanation which we as adults have found satisfying in our own personal experience. A behavioristic child psychology must get away from this tendency and get at the original data from first-hand observation. Such a study of the development of types of reaction, a study of the primitive instincts and their unfolding in the more complex reactions as development progresses, is of the first importance.

Second, an understanding of the nature of the child's relations to its environment, particularly its personal environment and specifically to the members of the family, is also essential. Its relation to the family situation begins from the moment of birth, and from the symptoms that later develop in the psychoses we have come to learn how important those relations are for conditioning the later reactions for

[1]On the other hand, he tells us that loud noises will produce the reaction of fear in very young children. As the lightning is usually followed by thunder, the flash itself is soon reacted to by fear on the principle of the conditioned reflex. Watson, John B.: *Practical and Theoretical Problems in Instinct and Habits* in *Suggestions of Modern Science Concerning Education*. (New York, 1918)

better or for worse. The fact has too long escaped notice that the family situation contains within itself certain elements of a disruptive nature.[2] It is as essential that the child should ultimately escape from its bondage to the family as it is that it should, during a certain period, be a part of that family and more or less subject to its direction. The complex interplay of these attractions and repulsions needs to be more fully studied as they express themselves in the symbolic mosaic at the psychological level.

And thirdly, a full understanding of all these matters must reach their application in education. Here again the effort has too often been to project upon the child something which we as adults think desirable rather than to understand the equipment of the child and then try to develop that equipment in the best possible way. Education has been largely empirical and too much confined to teaching; it needs to be developed as a scheme for assisting and guiding the developing personality, based upon a real understanding of the principles involved and the equipment.

And finally, inasmuch as it cannot be expected that the child is going to acquire all this information and then apply it to itself, it is essential to develop some means whereby such information can be translated into effectiveness. The child is so intimate and so all-pervading an element in our social structure that any organized effort to influence it profoundly in its development must needs touch every part of that structure. The obviously more important points of attack, however, are the home and the school, of which places probably the home offers the least encouragement. The relations between parents and children are governed for the most part by crude instinct and it would hardly seem that we either have organized knowledge in a sufficiently practical form or means at our disposal to alter this situation materially or even to interfere with it on a large scale, except in a superficial way, with anything like a sure touch. To be sure, much can be done by the trained social worker, but this is usually in cases where trouble already exists, and even such approaches must come largely through the schools. That this is so is perhaps unfortunate, for there are of necessity many problems that cannot be touched in this way except perchance through the family physician, who should become more and more a reliable source of information, advice, and strength as the teaching of psychiatry and kindred subjects broadens out in the medical schools. Take, for example, the problem of the unwelcome child—the impregnation which was accidental and not desired, the months of childbearing endured without joy, the pains of parturition that are borne in bitterness, and finally the child to be the recipient of all this accumulated feeling of resentment.[3] "What is the later story of such a life?" "How could it be modified to advantage?" are the immediate questions, but perhaps of greater significance is the query how the problem of the unwelcome child relates itself to one of the burning questions of the day—birth control and the use of contraceptive measures. Man's antipathetic tendencies, as well as his creative purposes, are sublimated and refined in the course of cultural

[2] For a discussion of these elements, see my *Mental Hygiene of Childhood.*

[3] These remarks are not intended to apply to phenomena usually considered under the designation "maternal impressions." I am referring only to the attitude of the mother toward a child that was not desired. Such an attitude conditions a feeling of inferiority which may be a serious handicap throughout life. A similar situation is produced when there are several children one of which is a favorite of the parents. In such a relationship the child feels keenly his inferiority in the family situation, as does the unwelcome child.

evolution. The viable child is no longer plunged head down in a vase of water—the germ cells are not permitted in conjunction.

The school seems, therefore, to be the most practical place to work for results, although of course a great deal of knowledge must be acquired about the child before it is of school age. Work of this character we are trying to plan in Washington in connection with a private charity which ministers to the infant, helping the mother during her pregnancy and the child for the first six years. Arrived at the school, however, the teacher becomes the surrogate for the parent and perhaps in many ways, not only by education, but because of emotional detachment, is better calculated to be of real service than the parent. If the teachers, with the machinery of the schools, are going to be of real value, it will mean that the education in the normal school will have to be broadened, the final result of which will be somewhat older, more mature, better teachers, better paid.

All our approaches to the understanding of defective psychological adjustments point indubitably to childhood as the period when things first go wrong, and the indication is therefore clear that this is the period which must be studied and modified to prevent the failures of later life. A great mass of evidence has been accumulated which goes to show that serious breaks in adjustment do not ordinarily occur without the cooperation of some lack of balance in the personality make-up, that they are rarely to be satisfactorily accounted for by the influence of extraneous circumstances alone. This evidence has been accumulated from the study of actual breaks as we see them in our patients—breaks which we have come to look at only as end results. The studies which have been made of delinquents show this very well indeed—how, for example, the young man who has finally come to a long-term sentence in prison will almost invariably show, if a careful survey of his past life is made, a long series of conduct anomalies which make the final outcome not only understandable, but often quite inevitable. I have in mind a recent case that came under my observation. A negro ran amuck, broke into several dwellings, and in one shot and killed a young woman. He was convicted of murder in the first degree and sentenced to be hanged. A behavioristic survey of this man disclosed the fact that he had shown traits of lack of control, impulsive and irresponsible conduct from his early youth, that he early began to drink and to take drugs, that he had been arrested and served sentences upon many occasions for both major and minor offenses, that there was all through his career a tendency to indulge in acts of violence and acts that were calculated to jeopardize the safety and the lives of others. The final homicide was the logical outcome of such a career, and at this late date execution seems rather a confession of impotence in dealing with this antisocial problem. No really intelligent plan had ever been brought to bear upon the problem he presented, but he was allowed to pursue his course to its logical outcome; whereupon society washes its hands of him finally and for all time. From the standpoint of responsibility, it might well be questioned which was the more responsible—the society that permitted all this or the defective youth who went his way.

One of the most important issues in mental hygiene, then, as I see it, is to correlate the sick adult with the knowledge we have that his illness is traceable in its beginnings to his early life. I have already indicated that this must be done by a more developed knowledge of the psychology of childhood, which is reflected in the home, in the school, and in the principles and methods of education. While all of this is true, we need not to lose sight of the fact that much work which is at present being carried on has mental hygiene implications, some very directly. Such work as the Child Bureau is doing in attempting to determine the minimum requirements of food, clothing, wages, etc., is obviously important. We must first have a live child if we are to have any problem at all. Efforts to improve the environment, even with reference to such obvious features as food, clothes, and ordinary sanitation, however, are not lacking in their general effect upon the mind of the developing child. Recent observations in the devastated countries of Europe have shown how quickly destitution, which takes all the joy out of life, is reflected in the mental make-up of the children. Here also come in such problems as the care of the pregnant woman, child labor, sex education, school sanitation, and more specifically the problems of the atypical child and juvenile delinquency, all of which can be better dealt with in proportion to our increased knowledge of child psychology, while such social problems as marriage and divorce, and, as already indicated, birth control, have very direct bearings. All of these several factors will be seen to have their bearings when it is realized that the child is not a finished product, but the result of influences which play upon it from all these sources. It is a product of the past through heredity, of the innumerable elements, largely personal, of its environment, of its instincts as they work out in relation to that environment, of social and family traditions, and of the social standards of its time and place, and all of the various approaches indicated can be made more effective in the light of such knowledge. I am minded at this point to compare the broad behavioristic program that I have indicated with the restricted scheme that is spanned only too often by the Binet-Simon scale. This scale, as devised by its originators, may be a very valuable tool in the hands of a skilled observer, but as the "be all and end all" of child psychology it may become quite as vicious in its results as the fatalism inspired by the false theories of heredity I have already mentioned.

And finally, inasmuch as many of the breaks, perhaps most of them, occur in the adolescent period or the period of early adulthood, it would, to my mind, be of inestimable value if some help could be systematically extended to the youth when, if he has not as yet broken, the symptoms of final disaster are quite apt to be discoverable. This might easily be done while he is still in school or college, if there could be connected with each such institution an adviser skilled in matters psychological and sympathetic and understanding of the problems of the young. This is a matter to which Dr. Paton has called special attention. I feel sure that such an adviser, connected with our large universities, would soon establish a large and useful clinic to which a great number of the student body would resort for advice and assistance in dealing with their life problems as they are beginning to unfold at this most critical period of life. It is of the utmost necessity that not only should our schools and colleges be equipped to offer instruction in any branch of learning desired, but that the individual should be consulted as to his equipment, his personal tendencies and desires, his difficulties and shortcomings, as well as his special aptitudes and opportunities. Unless this is done, the big educational machines will go on grinding out their regular proportion of failures. When it is done, those failures can be minimized and it may be found that not a few may profitably be turned away from a higher education to a life of greater usefulness in some other direction.

This is the sort of effort that is calculated to adjust the educational machine to the needs of the individual. To-day that machine offers a fixed structure into which the individual is fed, to come out well or ill in proportion to his capacity to meet the requirements. The means I suggest would have the effect of helping to adjust the educational opportunities to the needs of the individual and would be a movement towards individualizing the student just as we have learned in psychiatry that any material advances in therapeutic efficiency must come along with a further individualizing of our patients.

These are some of the directions in which my thought is led by a consideration of the mental hygiene of childhood. If we are to produce a better race of adults, we must be able to control the influences which go to mold the adult character. A practical program in this field seems to me to be possible, and to offer a decidedly more workable scheme than an effort to go back of the returns with the eugenist and control the material. The more we know of what can be accomplished with the material given us, the better position we will be in to undertake the control of what that material shall be.

SOCIAL WORK IN THE PUBLIC SCHOOLS (1923) From Anna B. Pratt,
"Should the Visiting Teacher be a New Official?" *Journal of Social Forces,* vol. I, pp. 3–5.

In June, 1921, "A Survey by the National Association of Visiting Teachers and Home and School Visitors" reported only 28 cities having 91 workers. That same year the Commonwealth Fund of New York in its "Program for the Prevention of Delinquency" offered to pay two-thirds of the salary of a visiting teacher for a three-year period in thirty different communities in the United States, and at the same time they offered, through the New York School of Social Work, fifteen yearly scholarships of $1,200 each for the training of such workers. This year they are giving $16,000 to the White-Williams Foundation of Philadelphia for the further training of school counselors. These awards of the Commonwealth Fund were made after a very careful study of the work in different communities. The fund found that social work in the schools tended to reduce juvenile delinquency. After a recent survey of the juvenile courts there has also come a recommendation for social work in the public schools. Dr. Thomas Eliot, of Northwestern University, made "a study of the unofficial treatment of predelinquent children for the juvenile courts committee of the National Probation Association." Among others, he quoted Judge Samuel D. Levy of the Children's Court of the City of New York as saying: "The problem of delinquency and anti-social conduct of children should have its intensive study in the schools, commencing in the kindergarten." In conclusion the committee suggests that "a resolution be considered registering their approval of the principle of assumption by the educational system of educational responsibility for the study and treatment of malbehavior problems as primarily educational or reeducational problems."

In 1919, the White-Williams Foundation of Philadelphia had an opportunity to study some of these reeducational problems in one of the disciplinary schools. In six months the counselor there worked with 65 boys, 35 of whom were on probation and 50 had been visited by various social agencies. This opportunity to compare the work of the court, an outside agency, and the school showed the advantage of seeing the boy every day and of working with the home from the angle of the school. If the probation officer visited the home the boy was often absent; if the boy reported to the probation officer, he had none of the child's background by which he could judge of the accuracy of his report. The counselor found, by comparing notes with the probation officer, that she often had a very different picture of the child from the one which the probation officer had and as hers was gained by daily contact and by home visits, it seemed to be the more accurate of the two. With the social agencies, if there was a family crisis, the boy as an individual often escaped notice. If they did center their attention upon him, they had the same problem which the court had.

This study led the foundation to feel that if these boys in the disciplinary school could have been reached in the regular grades by a social worker in the schools instead of from social agencies or courts, in many instances the trouble might have been averted. It was therefore decided to transfer the counselor to a grade school that she might try to discover these problems in their incipient stage.

Two years before, the foundation had placed two counselors in the eighth grade of two public schools to guide vocationally the children before they left school. These counselors had found that it was impossible to separate the child's work life from his school and social life. It was necessary to know the background of each child as well as his interests and abilities before advising him about the kind of school that he should enter after graduation from the grades or whether he should go into business or industry. At the same time these counselors discovered that the children most needing advice were escaping attention by leaving school from the earlier grades. Here the problems of retardation and behavior were so interwoven with the vocational problem that it was impossible to separate them.

The crux of the problems of education, reeducation in disciplinary schools and vocational counseling revealed themselves to the counselor as one and the same— the necessity for knowing the whole child, his home life, his community life and his work life, as well as his school life. Only when he is known on all these sides and when he is adjusted to them, can he become adjusted in his school life. Part of this latter adjustment involves the teacher's recognition of the child as an individual. To approximate total adjustment in all his relationships is the function of the social worker. Recently the chief of the Bureau of Compulsory Education in Philadelphia, who has sponsored the work of the counselors there since its beginning, brought out this point in addressing a meeting of principals. "It is true," he said, "that there is someone supposed to perform each of the separate functions of the school counselor or visiting teacher; the medical department for health; the attendance department for attendance and some cases of conduct; the vocational departments in many schools for vocational information; teachers and principals for behavior, but each of these sees only one thing that is the matter with the child and tries to handle it. The counselor knows the child—all of him—his assets as well as his liabilities; and it is for this reason that his function is unique and duplicates no other in the school system."

As the name implied, in the beginning of social work in the schools, the connecting of home and school through home visiting was thought by many to be the main feature of this new school function. Such mutual understanding is very necessary but it is only a tool to be used in the child's adjustment. For this reason some who are doing the work are dissatisfied with the older names of home and school visiting and visiting teaching and are using school counseling as more descriptive of the kind of treatment called for by the problems which the principals and teachers refer.

These problems as set down in the Visiting Teachers' Survey in 1921 are six; mal-adjustment in scholarship; adverse home conditions; irregular attendance; misconduct; lateness, and the physical conditional of the children. In Philadelphia the problems of educational and vocational guidance are added. Underlying the other problems and often their cause is the adverse home condition. This is most often misunderstood and therefore misinterpreted by the teacher. Children may come to school ragged and dirty, even when the father earns a sufficient wage, if he spends his money in drink or if the mother is shiftless and wastes the greater part of it. Because the teachers do not know what is back of the apparent poverty, they often lessen the responsibility of the parents by helping the children out of their own pockets. Even if they do know the cause they have not the time to labor with the parents. A teacher who valued the help of the school counselor referred such a problem to her. George was fifteen years of age in the backward grade at school. He had a dulled, overworked look and often at school in the afternoon fell asleep. He was being excused from school by special arrangement every Monday because his help was badly needed in the family. His mother who called at school to secure this permission, bore out the general impression of extreme poverty and need. The home when visited was found to be very dirty and poorly furnished on one of the poorest streets. The father was out of work and when possible the mother was getting temporary work cleaning. The boy had been working not only Mondays but after school hours, often till 9 p. m. The mother was staunch in her assertion that the father worked whenever he could get it and that he could fine none at the time on account of the employment situation. Talks with people who were acquainted with the family, with employers and with social agencies who had previously known them, showed that the father had worked only intermittently for years, though he was capable of making $30 a week, and that he could have steady work if he would stay sober. The counselor saw the father and partly through contact established and partly through threats of reporting the situation, secured his promises to go to work and give the boy a chance in school. He even agreed for a time to keep him from working the legitimate number of hours after school, so that he might show what the boy could do. The boy formerly worked in a coal yard and his teacher watches the conditon of his hands to see whether or not he has resumed work. So far the father is keeping his promise and the counselor is seeking an improvement in the boy's studies and an increased interest, not only in school but in things in general and in plans for the future.

When scholarship is poor, there seems less excuse for referring a child to a social worker. The teacher may struggle on for days, dealing only with the situation as it presents itself in the classroom, while a social worker who studies the whole child may be able to put her finger on a physical or home condition that will quickly solve the problem.

For several weeks one small boy had been refusing to do anything that the teacher asked; he was sullen and would not answer a question. The counselor studied his school record and found just before he had begun to bother the teacher he had failed in arithmetic. She also discovered that, months before, the school physician had advised glasses, but the nurse's note telling of the situation had failed to reach the boy's home. His father was a bookkeeper and told the counselor how anxious he was that Frank should succeed in mathematics. He had no patience with his failure. The counselor saw that Frank was proud and suspected that his misbehavior was a defense reaction. As soon as the father heard that the doctor had ordered glasses he took Frank to the oculist and found that the boy's vision was so poor that he could not see the board. Glasses quickly remedied the difficulty and Frank finally confessed to the counselor: "I felt terrible about failing, but I didn't want anyone to know it." When the teacher understood what was really behind the sullen face, she co-operated with the counselor and the father in winning back the boy's self-respect. Very soon Frank was not only a success in arithmetic, but also a leader in all his work. The counselor's study of the various sides of the boy, her bringing together of the different people interested in him and her understanding of child psychology brought results which the teacher, single-handed, could not secure.

If the progressive educators accomplish their purpose in adapting the school to the child, many of the problems of our schools will be solved by the teacher. The small classes will give the teachers time to visit and they will be able to help the ordinary individual when his problem is a simple one. Unfortunately there are today still and will probably continue to be in every classroom in spite of better education the exceptional individuals, with very difficult home lives, that require the careful handling that can be given only by a counselor who is trained in social and behavior problems, and whose whole time is devoted to the work.

The courses in social work which will probably be in the future curricula of the normal schools and colleges, will make the teachers more keenly alive to such problems, but they will not qualify them to become social case workers any more than the present courses in hygiene and psychology have made them doctors or psychologists. As they now refer abnormal health and mental problems to these specialists, so they will demand the help of social workers for their serious social and behavior problems. This will make the need of a social worker in the school of tomorrow as great as it is in the school of today. Those who are studying the matter are already convinced that in the school of today the school counselor has a place that is not filled by any other school official.

THE PUBLIC SCHOOL AND THE BACKWARD CHILD (1923)   From Stanley Powell Davies, *Social Control of the Feeble-Minded* (New York, 1923), pp. 171–76, 185.

Waverley and Rome have been taken as examples of what the institution can do and is doing in the social reconstruction of its inmates. The institution as we have seen, receives only a fraction of the cases of mental deficiency existing in the general population. It receives, moreover, the more difficult of these cases, those who by reason of gross defect, troublesome behavior, or unfavorable home conditions, cannot continue in community life. The institution is also frequently called upon at present to receive individuals who so far as personal conduct and social surroundings are concerned, might well remain in the community, but who are sent to the institution because there is no other place where they can receive the specialized training suited to their limited mental capacities. It is for the education of this latter class of children that the public school is coming to recognize its responsibility.

Since the first special classes for backward children were established in the public schools of Cleveland in 1878, there has been developing gradually, but very gradually, the idea that the public school is an agency charged with the task of educating all the children of the community according to their several and special capacities, and that it has as great a duty therefore to provide training for the backward or defective child in accordance with his capabilities as for the normal or exceptional child in accordance with his capabilities.

When the age of six is reached, the public school can begin to function in dealing with this problem. One of its primary tasks in that connection is that of identification. The demand for a complete census of the feebleminded has frequently been made from time to time as a preliminary to an adequate State program for dealing with this problem. To obtain such a census at the present time of all the feebleminded in the population of all ages has been shown to be practically impossible. Estimates of the number of such persons there have been, but anything like complete identification of defective individuals has proved to be too stupendous a task for present resources. If we lack such important information for the present generation, we can begin to get it in full detail for the rising generation, through the public school. That agency can identify for us defective individuals, whose identity can be made a matter of record for future use, if necessary, at any time throughout the life of the individual.

The identification, however, must be for some purpose, and once the defective children of a given group are known, the public school should stand ready to give those children the type of training best suited to their needs. The public school is the one agency capable of dealing with this problem in a complete way at a time when effort will be most effective. It is easy enough to set up a prescribed academic curriculum (based on the theoretic but non-existent average child) and require all children to conform to that or drop behind and repeat grades until they do. Such a system means, however, for the defective child that after the first few grades he reaches a point where can go no further; it means shame and discouragement in being "left behind" with younger pupils; it means every incentive to truancy with its ready concomitants of delinquency and crime. It means "putting in time" and wasted years, only to drop out of school, as soon as the working age is reached, a failure and without any training with which to face the world. In many instances such a school program means, moreover, that the defective boy or girl is hustled off to the institution because he is in the way around the school and retards the progress of other pupils. In other words, the whole program is calculated to make social outcasts of the mentally defective boy or girl, to ostracize them from society. And society pays for this; either by supporting those persons for the rest of their days in an institution, or in the larger bill of crime, delinquency, pauperism, and social degeneracy of those who are left to drift.

We have seen that the institution never has been and probably never will be large enough to receive more than a fraction of the mental defectives in the population. Nor is it desirable that mental defectives should be institutionalized if they can be taught to live industrially useful, socially acceptable lives outside the institution. The responsibility of the public school as a universal, educational agency is clear. The training of mental defectives is an educational problem as truly as that of normal children. It is only a different kind of education. By an appropriate course of instruction, the public school should stand ready to give every backward and effective child who is amenable to special class instruction (and most of them are), the kind of training needed to equip him for an independent, self-respecting citizenship. The institution should be called upon to receive only the more extreme cases who are either too low-grade or too troublesome in behavior to be capable of special class instruction and those whose home conditions are so unfavorable as to make institutional care advisable. The rank and file of those who fall below the standard of normality as determined by the intelligence tests are rightly the responsibility of the public school.

There are some of those who have come closest to these backward children in the public school work who more and more hesitate to call them subnormal or defective. True, by ordinary academic standards or by the criterion of the intelligence test, they fall short. But these workers have come to think of them as merely "differently minded" or "hard-minded." In other words, while their failure to keep up with the ordinary class work is apparent, they reveal not infrequently ability along practical and mechanical lines, and sometimes, unusual ability. It is in this direction, as is well known, that special class instruction tends. It places the emphasis on industrial and technical training. Dr. Henry H. Goddard has written: "The one thing that fits all these children, the one thing that draws out whatever is to be drawn out of them, is training of the hand,-manual training, industrial training. These things such children can do with wonderful success; in this they are interested; this they can do with great joy; it arouses in them a feeling of satisfaction at accomplishing something."[1]

Summarizing opinion on this point, Miss Meta L. Anderson writes: "The experts all agree apparently on the kind of work most worth-while to teach defective children, and it is on this curriculum approved by experts that the work in the classes for defectives should be based. Therefore, the following subjects should be included in the course of study for the classes for defectives: habits of personal cleanliness, sense training, manual training, physical training, vocational and industrial training, gardening, academic work; also speech training in so far as it is found to be at all worth-while."[2]

The theory seems to be sound. The practice is somewhat more difficult. The manual work taught in the school is apt to consist of those things that give good, general development training, but are not specifically useful in an occupational way after the child graduates at the working age from the special class. This is particularly true of the boys' training. They are taught such things as basket-and brush-making, chair-caning, rug-weaving, toy-making and other kinds of wood-working, which are excellent enough in themselves but are not usually wage-earning occupations at which the boy can find a job when he gets out. In other words, as we have observed from the list of occupations which the boys from the Waverley institution have found, the boy is more likely to get a job as machinist's or plumber's helper, packer, teamster, machine-tender in a spinning room and various kinds of factory work more or less skilled, painter, barber, etc. The fact that most of the boys graduating from the special classes today are compelled to find unskilled work does not necessarily indicate that many of them are not capable of doing skilled work but simply that they have not had the training for it. Those who are engaged in special class teaching are for the most part well aware of this problem of making the vocational instruction more practical but it remains a problem how to work this out in connection with school instruction

✻   ✻   ✻

Present indications are that the public school before many years will be so organized to deal with backward and defective children that it will become the largest and most important single agency devoted to the work of developing the feebleminded for economic and social usefulness. It is far better that the backward

[1] Meta L. Anderson, *Education of Defectives in the Public Schools* p. 12.
[2] *Ibid*, p. 12.

child should not be separated from the normal life of the home and the community in order to receive the specialized training that he needs. Where the public school work for these children is well developed both from the standpoint of intra-school provision and extra-school and post-school supervision, the results as in New York and Cincinnati, indicate how well the public school can meet this problem. In the future the institution will continue to have an important function to serve but only for those lower-grade or extremely difficult cases that cannot reasonably be retained in the school and for those who must be removed from a bad home environment.

JOHN B. WATSON ON THE MATTER OF LEARNED BEHAVIOR VERSUS INHERITED (1925) From John B. Watson, *Behaviorism* (New York, 1925), pp. 74–75, 79–82.

Introduction

In the next few lectures we shall talk about how man is equipped to behave at birth—a subject that touches the very heart of human psychology.

When the array of facts about any subject is not very complete it is only human nature to announce a thesis, that is, state what one is going to try to prove and then try to prove it by a logical argument. I am in that position. I have not the full complement of facts about the so-called 'instinctive' nature of man—I do not know who has; hence, please look upon my next few lectures both as logical presentations of what facts there are in the case and as a thesis which I am trying to defend. I shall present my thesis first.

The Thesis Presented

Man is an animal born with certain definite types of structure. Having that kind of structure, he is forced to respond to stimuli at birth in certain ways (for example: breathing, heart beat, sneezing, and the like. A fairly full list I shall give you later on). This repertoire of responses is in general the same for each of us. Yet there exists a certain amount of variation in each—the variation is probably merely proportional to the variation there is in structure (including in structure, of course, chemical constitution). It is the same repertoire now that it was when the *genus homo* first appeared many millions of years ago. Let us call this group of reactions man's *unlearned behavior*.

In this relatively simple list of human responses there is none corresponding to what is called an 'instinct' by present-day psychologists and biologists. There are then for us no instincts—we no longer need the term in psychology. Everything we have been in the habit of calling an 'instinct' today is a result largely of training— belongs to man's *learned behavior*.

As a corollary from this I wish to draw the conclusion that there is no such thing as an inheritance of *capacity, talent, temperament, mental constitution* and *characteristics*. These things again depend on training that goes on mainly in the cradle. The behaviorist would *not* say: "He inherits his father's capacity or talent for being a fine swordsman." He would say: "This child certainly has his father's slender build of body, the same type of eyes. His build is wonderfully like his father's. He, too, has the build of a swordsman." And he would go on to say: "—and his father is very fond of him. He put a tiny sword into his hand when he was a year of age, and in all their walks he talks sword play, attack and defense, the code of duelling and the like." A certain type of structure, plus early training—*slanting*—accounts for adult performance.

*   *   *

Differences in Structure and Differences in Early Training Will Account
For All Differences in Later Behavior

A while ago I said that granting individual variation in structure we could find no real proof that man's unlearned repertoire of acts has differed through the ages or that he has ever been either more or less capable of putting on complex training than he is in 1925. The fact that there are marked individual variations in structure among men has been known since biology began. But we have never sufficiently utilized it in analyzing man's behavior. In this lecture I want to utilize another fact only recently brought out by the behaviorists and other students of animal psychology. Namely, that *habit formation starts in all probability in embryonic life and that even in the human young environment shapes behavior so quickly that all of the older ideas about what types of behavior are inherited and what are learned break down.* Grant variations in structure at birth and rapid habit formation from birth, and you have a basis for explaining many of the so-called facts of inheritance of "mental" characteristics. . . .

*   *   *

Our conclusion, then, is that we have no real evidence of the inheritance of traits. I would feel perfectly confident in the ultimately favorable outcome of careful upbringing of a *healthy, well-formed baby* born of a long line of crooks, murderers and thieves, and prostitutes. Who has any evidence to the contrary? Many, many thousands of children yearly, born from moral households and steadfast parents become wayward, steal, become prostitutes, through one mishap or another of nurture. Many more thousands of sons and daughters of the wicked grow up to be wicked because they couldn't grow up any other way in such surroundings. But let one adopted child who has a bad ancestry go wrong and it is used as incontestable evidence for the inheritance of moral turpitude and criminal tendencies. As a matter of fact, there has not been a double handful of cases in the whole of our civilization of which records have been carefully enough kept for us to draw any such conclusions—mental testers, Lombroso, and all other students of criminality to the contrary notwithstanding. As a matter of fact adopted children are never brought up as one's own. One cannot use statistics gained from observations in charitable institutions and orphan asylums. All one needs to do to discount such statistics is to go there and work for awhile, and I say this without trying to belittle the work of such organizations.

I should like to go one step further now and say, "Give me a dozen healthy infants, well-formed, and my own specified world to bring them up in and I'll guarantee to take any one at random and train him to become any type of specialist I might select—doctor, lawyer, artist, merchant-chief and, yes, even beggar-man and thief, regardless of his talents, penchants, tendencies, abilities, vocations, and race of his ancestors." I am going beyond my facts and I admit it, but so have the advocates of the contrary and they have been doing it for many thousands of years. Please note that when this experiment is made I am to be allowed to specify the way the children are to be brought up and the type of world they have to live in.

ON DELINQUENT PARENTS (1927) From Miriam Van Waters, *Parents on Probation* (New York, 1927), pp. 4–6.

We have grown so accustomed to dealing with children as if they were the only delinquents. Let us imagine the situation reversed. Then we would deal with parents under the familiar headings: delinquent parents, causation and treatment; types of offending, dependent, defective, and neglected parents; parents in unfit homes; parents in relation to jobs, companions, friends, teachers, clergymen, social workers and newspaper men; parents who have been given probation and made good; those who do not deserve probation and ought to be institutionalized in reformatories, hospitals, or prisons. Viewing the innumerable faults of parents, their responsibility for the sufferings of children who come to courts and clinics, we might conclude they are tolerated in the community only because we have no other place to put them.

It is wise to place parents on probation. Probation is a word which may be used in two senses. A nurse or civil service employee is a probationer when he is permitted to carry a limited responsibility and to practice the arts of his profession under supervision, but is thought not ready yet for a final appointment. Parents are in this class. No one seems satisfied with their performance. Their ability to do the whole job is questioned and the modern world is constantly devising new ways to assist them, or to encroach upon their field of activity. Probation also may be used to describe the status of one who has been identified as an offender, but is thought worthy of help from science, religion and social work, provided he will cooperate in a plan for his own welfare and the protection of the community.

Probation used in this sense implies no stigma. The past of the offender has been scrutinized and "forgotten"; it is referred to only as a means for better understanding; he begins life fresh from to-day—this is all any honest person can ask.

Parents in their own eyes are actually on probation. They face self-criticism, criticism from their children, from grandparents, ministers, doctors, psychologists, press, criminologists, teachers and neighbors. This in no way differentiates them from the rest of the world. All our established institutions are on probation and seeking to justify themselves. Criticism of others, and a sense of dissatisfaction for all that goes on in the world is the rule to-day . . . the general verdict appears to be that other people ought to do their jobs better.

If parents are alarmed at the thought of being on probation let them remember that it is a highly favorable status from which to readjust. Probation is not a sentence; it is not an acquittal. The probationer always has a subsequent history. To be allowed to live in the open air in a world so fascinating, so full of change, motion, laughter, tears, to be permitted at all to take part in the thrilling spectacle of the twentieth century with its barbarism, savagery and civilization so strangely mingled, to have brought a child forth at this particular time when human beings are on the eve of a tremendous renaissance, due to our discoveries and rediscoveries in human behavior, ought to make the parent nerve himself. Like the sturdy child who raises his face stained with tears and says to the judge: "Sure, I'll make good," so to-day parents should face the super-parent, which is mankind, with a resolute intent to demonstrate that faith and trust in them have not been misplaced.

One warning always should be given by the court in granting probation. It is true that the probationer is entitled to all the help available from doctors, psychiatrists and social workers, but his most important task is to make his own decisions. He will be fussed over a great deal, given all manner of advice, much of it contradictory; there will be people seeking to enslave, pamper and exploit him. If he has the independence of judgment to save his soul under these conditions, he is a good man. So the parent, in accepting probation will be flooded with advice and admonitions. Those unfortunate fathers and mothers who entrust the rearing of their children entirely to specialists prolong their tutelage and rob themselves of the lifeblood of their task. Parents, in the long run, like any other delinquents, must be their own probation officers.

MENTAL HYGIENE IN INFANCY (1930)   From Marion E. Kenworthy, "Social Maladjustments In the Intellectually Normal," *Mental Hygiene,* vol. XIV, pp. 837–40.

If this subject were to be handled adequately its vastness would require consideration of many more details than the scope of this paper permits. When one considers the many ramifications of human adjustment presented in the problems of social adaptation in the intellectually normal, the possibilities for exploration are practically limitless. It is not my intention here to suggest that the manifestations of social and emotional maladjustment as found in the group of the intellectually normal differ essentially from the difficulties of adjustment found in the groups whose intellectual endowment is classed as superior or inferior. Proof that such a concept is not valid can be found if one but parallels the emotional deviations in the neurotic and psychotic breakdowns of those of normal and superior endowment with like breakdowns of those in the feebleminded group. And if one must accept the premise that all humans, regardless of their level of intelligence, are capable of becoming so emotionally jammed as to develop a neurotic or psychotic disorder, it is not difficult to assume that many of the milder forms of deviation may likewise exist. While recognizing the validity of this concept, the focus of this paper is the study of those individuals whose intelligence range, measured in terms of intelligence quotient, lies in the scale between the points 90 and 110.

Since the roots of adult emotional difficulties are found in childhood, it is pertinent to discuss the many angles of experience in the early years upon which the adult personality is built. The adjustment of an individual is admittedly the product of all the experiences that have played upon the three levels of his inherited equipment. If one attempted to watch a stage performance in which three distinct scenes were being enacted at the same time one would find the task well-nigh impossible. Yet the child, from the beginning, lives out his life's performance upon the three-level stage of his physical, intellectual, and emotional endowment.

It is not surprising, then, that for so many generations past parents have been so largely unaware of the meaning of most of the child's reactions to life. In the first few months the parents are preoccupied with the feeding, bathing, and general physical care of the baby and are too frequently ignorant of the intellectual and emotional values involved in the learning and feeling processes that are being enacted under their very eyes, in response to the thousands of new experiences coming to the young child. These parental blind spots are still fostered by certain so-called scientific groups through statements such as, "Personality does not begin to develop until after the age of two", "Concern yourself in the early years with keeping your baby physically healthy and the rest will take care of itself", and so on.

As our technique in handling the behavior problems and emotional maladjustments of children becomes more effective, the vital importance of the experiences of the first two years becomes more vivid. In order to study cause-and-effect relationships in the behavior of an individual at any point in his career, we must recognize the need for a clear-cut picture of his trends of satisfaction and dissatisfaction. We cannot depend upon a capacity to verbalize these feeling-values even by the adult, because of the conflicts involved. From the child, living in an environment so largely controlled by an adult kind of authority, it is folly to expect admission of satisfaction in experiences that are identified by the child as forbidden. It is clear that many of those very satisfactions which are most deeply involved in the symptomatic behavior of an individual are often unrecognized by him as having such value, particularly that is generally accepted as asocial. It is easy to see why the individual frequently has no conscious awareness of the satisfying qualities of the neurotic and psychotic trends. The very recognition of them would tend to dissipate the pleasurable values of the experience by the development of conflicts, and would destroy some of the satisfaction for which the symptoms were originally created.

Whether one is concerned primarily with child guidance or with adult psychiatric practice, one constantly meets with the manifold evidence of early experiences that, if properly handled could have contributed to the constructive emotional growth of the individual but that, unrecognized or mishandled, have deterred this growth.

For example, one of the first adjustments to reality after the birth of the baby with which the average parent is concerned is found in the nursing experience. In the event that the child shows a quick reaction to the nursing contact—establishes a good oral rhythm, swallows without choking, and nurses persistently—little real thought is given to the significance of all of the elements involved in such a successful experience. If we evaluate it purely from the physical level, such a satisfactory performance suggests a good neuromuscular organism. Interpreted from the angle of the intellectual equipment, it suggests a so-called normal endowment, for by the very performance the child indicates its capacity to register sensory motor responses sufficiently well to establish a nursing habit unfalteringly. Interpret this on the emotional level and we see that the child who establishes a normal nursing rhythm easily thus gains a ready satisfaction. In an ideal situation the pleasurable elements in the nursing contact are manifold. Not only is the child's physical hunger satisfied, but also the upper oral segmental cravings are released, especially in the cases where the mother's breast and nipple formation are good, the milk flow is normal, etc. These rhythmic movements of the lips and tongue become identified early as a source of pleasure and satisfaction. It is a common observance that the baby when half-wakened will soothe itself back to sleep by the repetition of rhythmic lip movements as if at the breast. If one had to choose the most important facet of the child's experience and the one that, if improperly handled, could make for more emotional maladjustment than any other at this period of the child's life, one would stress the need for proper handling of the nursing situation. In the event that the feeding experience is incomplete in its satisfaction, either because of faulty physical equipment of the mother, inadequate milk supply, too rapid flow of milk, as in many cases, the more intangible negatives furnished the child by the mother's attitudes of unresponsiveness and rejection—in this event, a whole series of feeling tones of a more unsatisfying kind are prone to develop.

We repeatedly find very early in these children who are deprived on either physical or the emotional level, a development of substitute pleasures. One of the most common is that of thumb-sucking. If the latter develops, it should suggest to us at once that this behavior response is due to the child's need for finding a means of completing his segmental cravings for pleasure, which are not being met in a more natural way.

Since we are interested in a program of prevention, obviously our attention will be directed toward discovering the causes of this deviation. The quick and ready relinquishing of these symptomatic patterns by the baby when the causes of dissatisfaction are removed suggests the value of more awareness on the part of the parents of the importance of causation. Thumb-sucking treated by threats, punishment, artificial restraint, and so forth, is not cured. The parent who attacks the problem in this way is not only failing to recognize the causes of the behavior but is also unaware of the underlying feeling tones of dissatisfaction that already exist. Thus the punishment restraint to which the child is exposed only augments the negative values already established and the consequent emotional damage that inevitably follows.

At the nursing level the mother satisfies the child's need for love and sense of being wanted, as well as his physiological hunger cravings. A denial of the breast before the child has gained the impulse to wean himself is prone to produce problems that are not only intensive but extensive in their effects upon the child's integration. Constructive but satisfying ways of preparing the child for the next step in growing up are available. Since the possibility of sudden withdrawal of the breast is always possible, either through illness or failure of sufficient nutritive value of the milk or through loss of the supply, the first constructive step is accomplished by introducing the use of a bottle at least once a day from the beginning. In this way it is identified as a source of satisfaction at the same time as the breast, and, if the mother holds the child in the same relative position during the bottle feeding as at breast feeding, little negative value seems to be produced. The introduction of new and pleasing foods such as orange or prune juice by spoon feeding accomplishes a more ready acceptance of the next step, in establishing more mature food habits. The pleasurable element of the taste would seem to offset the displeasure of the new reality. Taking the last few drops from the cup, if made an adventure by the mother's enthusiasm, helps to make the transition to the more grown-up levels with a minimum of dissatisfaction and conflict.

One could give many examples of mishandling at this period, if space permitted. It may, however, suggest the extent of the problem to realize that cases of tongue-sucking, clothes-sucking, retention of food in the mouth, refusal of solid foods, with gagging or vomiting, food fadism, and in some cases even stammering are frequently associated with inadequate handling at this level.

Further evidences of this lack of understanding and faulty handling are found in many of the other early experiences to which the child is exposed. If one bears in mind that the child reacts to every experience, whether physical or intellectual, with a feeling response, the attitudes and methods of approach used by parents in meeting the issues of sphincter control, sleeping habits, cleanliness, etc., are bound to reflect themselves in the child's own attitudes of acceptance or rejection. One might postulate here that experiences of all kinds which possess predominant elements of satisfaction are always more readily acceptable than those in which unsatisfying values predominate. In the latter the immediate impulse is to deny or withdraw from repetition.

Progressive Education—Theory

THE CHILD AS ARTIST (1919)   From Floyd Dell, *Were You Ever a Child?* (New York, 1919), pp. 100–2, 107–9.

In this matter, most decidedly, we need expert advice. Let us start with Beauty. The one who best understands Beauty is undoubtedly the Artist. Let us call in the Artist. . . . Will you question him, or shall I? You prefer to do it yourself, I see. Very well, then—but please try to get to the point as soon as possible!

THE QUESTIONER. What we want to know is this: is it possible to teach the child to become an artist?

THE ARTIST. He is an artist already.

THE QUESTIONER What do you mean!

THE ARTIST. Just what I say. The child is an artist; and that artist is always a child. The greatest periods of art have always been those in which artists had the direct, naive, unspoiled vision of the child. The aim of our best artists today is to recover that vision. They are trying to see the world as children see it, and to record their vision of it as a child would do. Have you ever looked at children's drawings—not the sort of things they are taught to do by mistaken and mischievous adults, but the pictures that are the natural expressions of their creative impulses? And haven't you observed that modern paintings are coming to be more and more like such pictures?

THE QUESTIONER. Well—er, yes, I had noticed something of the kind! But is that sort of thing necessarily art? I mean—well, I don't want to attempt to argue with you on a subject in which you are an expert, but—

THE ARTIST. Oh, that's all right! The modern artist is ready to discuss art with anybody—the more ignorant of the subject, the better! You see, we want art to cease to be the possession of a caste—we want it to belong to everybody. As a member of the human race, your opinions are important to us.

THE QUESTIONER. That is very kind of you. I fear it is rather in the nature of a digression, but, since I may ask without fear of seeming presumptuous,—*are* those horrid misshapen green nudes of Matisse, and those cubical blocks of paint by I-forget-his-name, and all that sort of thing—are they your notion of what art should be?

THE ARTIST. Mine? Oh, not at all! They are merely two out of a thousand contemporary attempts to recover the naive childlike vision of which I spoke. If you will compare them with a child's drawing, or with a picture by a Navajo Indian, or with the sketch of an aurochs traced on the wall of his cave by one of our remote ancestors, you will note an essential difference. Those artists were not trying to be naive and childlike; they *were* naive and childlike. The chief merit of our modern efforts, in my personal opinion, is in their quality as a challenge to traditional and mistaken notions of what art should be—an advertisement, startling enough, and sometimes maliciously startling, of the artist's belief that he has the right to be first of all an artist.

THE QUESTIONER. Now we are coming to the point. What *is* an artist?

THE ARTIST. I told you, a child. And by that, I mean one who *plays* with his materials—not one who performs a set and perhaps useful task with them. A creator—

THE QUESTIONER. But a creator of what? Not of Beauty, by any chance?

THE ARTIST. Incidentally of Beauty.

THE QUESTIONER. There we seem to disagree. If those horrid pictures—

THE ARTIST. What I am about to tell you is the only really important thing about art. Unfortunately, the facts at issue have never been studied by first-class scientific minds, and so they lack a proper terminology to make them clear. In default of such a scientific terminology, we are forced to use the word "rhythm" in the special sense in which artists understand it. You speak of the movements of a dance as being rhythmic. The artist understands the word to refer to the relation of these movements to each other and above all to the emotion which they express. And to him the whole world is a dance, full of rhythmic gestures. The gesture of standing still, or of being asleep, is also rhythmic; the body is itself a gesture—he will speak of the rhythm of the line of a lifted arm or a bent knee. Trees that lift their branches to the sky, and rocks that sleep on the ground have their rhythms— every tree and every rock its own special rhythm. The rhythm of a pine tree is different from that of a palm—the rhythm of granitic rocks different from that of limestone. So far the matter is simple enough. But the relations of these rhythms to each other are also rhythmic. These relations are in fact so manifold that they constitute a chaos. But in this chaos each person feels a different rhythm; and, according as he has the power, transmits his sense of it to us through a rhythmic treatment of his medium. In the presence of his work, we feel what he has felt about the world; but we feel something more than that—we feel also the rhythm of the struggle in the artist between his impulse to command and his impuse to obey. Our own impulses of vanity and of reverence go out to welcome his power and his faithfulness. And just as there are gay rhythms and sad rhythms in the gesture of movement, so there are magnificent rhythms and trivial rhythms in the gesture of a soul facing the chaos of the world. What has he found worth while to play with, and how has he played with it? What kind of creator is he? Ability to feel and express significant rhythm—that is nine-tenths of art.

THE QUESTIONER. But my dear fellow, how are we to teach all this to children?

THE ARTIST. Very simply: by giving them a knife and a piece of wood.

THE QUESTIONER. Well, really!

THE ARTIST. And crayons and clay and singing-games and so forth.—But perhaps you prefer to show them pictures of alleged masterpieces, and tell them, "This is great art!" They will believe you, of course; and they will hate great art ever afterwards—just as they hate great poetry, and for the same excellent reason: because, presented to them in that way, it is nothing but a damned nuisance. Yet the child who enjoys hearing and telling a story has in him the capacity to appreciate and perhaps to create the greatest of stories; and the child who enjoys whittling a block of wood has in him the capacity to appreciate and perhaps to create the greatest art!

THE GREENWICH VILLAGE IDEA (c.1919)   From Malcolm Cowley, *Exile's Return* (New York, 1934), pp. 59–62.

Greenwich Village was not only a place, a mood, a way of life: like all bohemias, it was also a doctrine. Since the days of Gautier and Murger, this doctrine had remained the same in spirit, but it had changed in several details. By 1920, it had become a system of ideas that could roughly be summarized as follows:

1. The idea of salvation by the child.—Each of us at birth has special potentialities which are slowly crushed and destroyed by a standardized society and mechanical methods of teaching. If a new educational system can be introduced, one by which children are encouraged to develop their own personalities, to blossom freely like flowers, then the world will be saved by this new, free generation.

2. The idea of self-expression.—Each man's, each woman's, purpose in life is to express himself, to realize his full individuality through creative work and beautiful living in beautiful surroundings.

3. The idea of paganism.—The body is a temple in which there is nothing unclean; a shrine to be adorned for the ritual of love.

4. The idea of living for the moment.—It is stupid to pile up treasures that we can enjoy only in old age, when we have lost the capacity for enjoyment. Better to seize the moment as it comes, to dwell in it intensely, even at the cost of future suffering. Better to live extravagantly, gather June rosebuds, "burn my candle at both ends. . . . It gives a lovely light."

5. The idea of liberty.—Every law, convention or rule of art that prevents self-expression or the full enjoyment of the moment should be shattered and abolished. Puritanism is the great enemy. The crusade against puritanism is the only crusade with which free individuals are justified in allying themselves.

6. The idea of female equality.—Women should be the economic and moral equals of men. They should have the same pay, the same working conditions, the same opportunity for drinking, smoking, taking or dismissing lovers.

7. The idea of psychological adjustment.—We are unhappy because we are maladjusted, and maladjusted because we are repressed. If our individual repressions can be removed—by confessing them to a Freudian psychologist—then we can adjust ourselves to any situation, and be happy in it. (But Freudianism is only one method of adjustment. What is wrong with us may be our glands, and by a slight operation, or merely by taking a daily dose of thyroid, we may alter our whole personalities. Again, we may adjust ourselves by some such psycho-physical discipline as was taught by Gurdjieff. The implication of all these methods is the same—that the environment itself need not be altered. That explains why most radicals who became converted to psychoanalysis or glands or Gurdjieff[1] gradually abandoned their political radicalism.)

8. The idea of changing place.—"They do things better in Europe." England and Germany have the wisdom of old cultures; the Latin peoples have admirably preserved their pagan heritage. By expatriating himself, by living in Paris, Capri or

[1]George Ivanovich Gurdjieff, a Russian living in France, had worked out a system of practical mysticism based largely on Yoga. His chief disciple was A. E. Orage, the editor of the New English Weekly. In the spring of 1924, when Orage was in New York, he gained a great many converts, chiefly among older members of the Greenwich Village set.

the South of France, the artist can break the puritan shackles, drink, live freely and be wholly creative.

All these, from the standpoint of the business-Christian ethic then represented by the Saturday Evening Post, were corrupt ideas. This older ethic is familiar to most people; but one feature of it has not been sufficiently emphasized. Substantially, it was a production ethic. The great virtues it taught were industry, foresight, thrift, and personal initiative. The workman should be industrious in order to produce more for his employer; he should look ahead to the future; he should save money in order to become a capitalist himself; then he should exercise personal initiative and found new factories where other workmen would toil industriously, and save, and become capitalists in their turn.

During the process many people would suffer privations: most workers would live meagerly and wrack their bodies with labor; even the employers would deny themselves luxuries that they could easily purchase, choosing instead to put back the money into their business; but after all, our bodies were not to be pampered; they were temporary dwelling places, and we should be rewarded in Heaven for our self-denial. On earth, our duty was to accumulate more wealth and produce more goods, the ultimate use of which was no subject for worry. They would somehow be absorbed, by new markets opened in the West, or overseas in new countries, or by the increased purchasing power of workmen who had saved and bettered their position.

That was the ethic of a young capitalism, and it worked admirably, so long as the territory and population of the country were expanding faster than its industrial plant. But after the war the situation changed. Our industries had grown enormously to satisfy a demand that suddenly ceased. To keep the factory wheels turning, a new domestic market had to be created. Industry and thrift were no longer adequate. There must be a new ethic that encouraged people to buy, a consumption ethic.

It happened that many of the Greenwich Village ideas proved useful in the altered situation. Thus, self-expression and paganism encouraged a demand for all sorts of products—modern furniture, beach pajamas, cosmetics, colored bathrooms with toilet paper to match. Living for the moment meant buying an automobile, radio or house, using it now and paying for it tomorrow. Female equality was capable of doubling the consumption of products—cigarettes, for example—that had formerly been used by men alone. Even changing place would help to stimulate business in the country from which the artist was being expatriated. The exiles of art were also trade missionaries: involuntarily they increased the foreign demand for fountain pens, silk stockings, grapefruit and portable typewriters. They drew after them an invading army of tourists, thus swelling the profits of steamship lines and travel agencies. Everything fitted into the business picture.

ACCOUNT OF THE BEGINNINGS OF THE PROGRESSIVE EDUCATION ASSOCIATION (1919)
From Stanwood Cobb, "The Romance of Beginnings."
Progressive Education, vol. VI, pp. 66–73.

The last educational decade, to the description of which this anniversary number of PROGRESSIVE EDUCATION is devoted, has been one of the most significant periods in the history of education. The war, with its cataclysmic and immensely evolutionary stimulus in all departments of human thought and action, did not fail also to accelerate the progress of marked innovations already taking place in the educational world. Intelligent leaders everywhere, both lay and professional, began to ask themselves the question, "Is education all right?"—and decided in the negative. As to what the failings were and how they could be remedied, a mass of revolutionary educational literature created during these ten years offers a vast body of intelligent and liberal opinion. Not the least significant in this new educational thought and literature is the part contributed by the Progressive Education Association which had the good fortune to take its birth at the beginning of this eventful decade.

"Could you ever have believed," I am sometimes asked, "that the Progressive Education Association would grow from such humble beginnings to the proportions and success it now enjoys?"

"Progressive Education," I answer, "has only begun to tap the potential human resources of America."

The Progressive Education Association was founded upon the realization that there were thousands of parents and teachers throughout the country who were dissatisfied with the prevailing type of education, and were ready and waiting for something better. It has been through reaching out to these parents and teachers and bringing news and information concerning what seems to us the most advanced type of education yet evolved, that our success is due.

But this task is only in its infancy; for the number of people who are looking for a more adequate education are not six thousand (our present membership) but nearer six hundred thousand. Greater efforts lie ahead of us than behind. If we have had any significant success up to the present, this is only an inspiration toward the future achievement of reaching every intelligent forward-looking parent and teacher in the country, and enrolling them in the great enterprise of bringing better education to our children.

What is "progressive education"? This forward movement, toward greater freedom and interest and joy in school-life, characterized by Dr. Charles W. Eliot as "the most significant movement in American education today," is described in a leaflet by Morton Snyder "as a part of the great liberal trend in human affairs, akin to other movements in the realms of public health, industrial relations, social conditions, and international affairs. It is an alliance between the sciences and idealism: the expression of a new attitude toward childhood and youth.

"It is not a plan; it is a spirit. It is an appreciation of the nature of young people and of the sound conditions under which they grow most richly and most beautifully. Freedom, interest, sympathy, trust, health—these are the essentials. It has created schools in which teachers and students work together happily, under wholesome, stimulating conditions, living in the fullest sense the life of today to be ready for tomorrow."

And now to recount simply and briefly, at the request of our editor, the story of the early days of the association. It was in the winter of 1918–1919 that a group of educators and lay people deeply interested in the new education met almost weekly at the home of Mrs. Laura C. Williams, in Washington, D. C. for the purpose of furnishing a focus to the then scattered and ununified attempts at educational reform going on in different parts of the country. The task facing the little group of organizers was to attempt to fuse scattered links into one chain, so to speak.

In order to do this, two things had first to be accomplished; first, to work out a minimum set of principles which should prove truly descriptive of the various educational experiments then going on; and secondly to choose a name under which to subsume all these new movements in education.

Neither task was easy. It took the whole group weeks of labor—in which Eugene R. Smith, then head of the Park School, Baltimore, made the most significant contribution—to evolve the set of seven principles for which our association has since vouched. And it took hours of discussion to select a name which would prove provocative and yet soundly descriptive. We thought of several different terms, but finally chose the term "progressive." This word, although it has met with some criticism, has proved successful in that it is now being accepted by the general public, and is in current usage, in books, magazines, newspapers, and popular reference, to designate the new education in this country. EDUCATION.

The next step, after selecting our principles and our name, was to actually organize an association. This we did by arranging a preliminary meeting to arouse interest, and then an organization meeting, held in the Washington Public Library, March 15, 1919, at which the following people spoke: Dr. Otis W. Caldwell, Eugene R. Smith, Marietta L. Johnson, Anne E. George, and the writer. Membership cards were passed around at the end of the meeting—which had proved most enthusiastic—and when all was ended, we gathered together in considerable excitement and trepidation to count results, for on the outcome of this evening hinged our very existence. Eighty-five members, and eighty-five dollars! On this modest beginning, plus several hundred dollars generously donated by Mrs. Williams, we launched our slender enterprise.

All secretarial work at this time was voluntary. And when the writer, having meanwhile founded a school of his own, became unable to function as executive secretary, Mrs. Milan V. Ayres, one of the group of organizers of the Progressive Education Association, stepped into the breach and for several years generously contributed most earnest and wholehearted work to the growth of the association, using her own home as office.

Our chief means of adding to our membership in those simple halcyon days was by drawing heavily upon the interest and zeal of our existing members for new names. With every receipt to a new member we enclosed, with a card of thanks, a blank asking for additional names of friends who might be interested. These lists came back to us in generous numbers; and the creation of this endless chain, as one might call it, kept our association alive and growing.

Mrs. Ayres did not, however, confine her secretarial work to the merely formal receipt and acknowledgement of dues. In answer to inquiries or wherever special interest was shown by members, she wrote personal letters. As her own interest and zeal for the movement which we were endeavoring to propagate were strong, her correspondence helped to kindle and keep alive in the hearts of our membership a sincere spirit of devotion and service to the cause of progressive education.

The general interest and zeal of our members in these early years is shown by the fact that a majority of them gave more than the modest sum of one dollar which we had decided upon as a minimum membership. Many gave $2, $3, $5, or $10; and some even larger amounts.

Many friendly, enthusiastic letters were received. The kind which pleased us most read like this: "I have been contributing regularly to over thirty different organizations. I am, for certain reasons, now discontinuing these contributions to all except the Progressive Education Association. This, to my mind, is the cause the most productive of benefit to future generations." These letters showed clearly what the association meant to parents and teachers scattered over the country, who were feeling their way toward these progressive principles but were not aware of a definite movement in this direction. New schools of an experimental nature had been founded under separate and unrelated auspices, some as a result of the influence of Francis W. Parker, some as a result of Dewey's writings, some built upon the educational reform principles of Marietta L. Johnson, and some modeled after the Park School of Baltimore which was founded by Professor Hans Froelicher directly upon the educational principles of Rousseau, Pestalozzi, and Froebel. These schools did not then in general realize themselves to be—what they in reality were—integral parts of a common educational movement. Professor Froelicher later wrote us, "I did not even know at the time we organized the Park School that there were other schools of similar educational aim. I did not learn this until I was brought in contact with your association in its first year of organization."

It must not be thought, however, that either our purpose or our effort was confined to a group of private schools. Nothing could be further from the truth. Our aim from the very beginning had in it little of modesty. We aimed at nothing short of reforming the entire school system of America. And from our inception we came in touch not only with a private school clientele, but with public school teachers, supervisors, principals and superintendents in all parts of the country. Our membership today clearly demonstrates the fact that we serve the public schools of the country in larger aggregate numbers than we do the private schools.

The fact that in the literature of the association the doings of progressive private schools preponderate, will not, we hope, lead the casual observer to the impression that we are more interested in the private than in the public school. It so happens that, for obvious reasons, some of the most significant experimental work in education is being done in the small private school, which is flexible and easily deployed—a sort of skirmish cavalry, so to speak, in the great frontal attack of the new education upon the forces of tradition, of routine, of mediocrity, and bureaucracy. Moreover, the actual facts can easily be gathered from this group of schools, whereas to properly set forth each progressive situation in our vast public school systems would call for special investigators and a large outlay of money. We hope, however, to make some contribution along this line, as soon as we can secure the necessary funds.

We had nothing to offer our members in these early days except a modest little bulletin published—à la Elbert Hubbard—every now and then. But it was not what we offered our members that called forth their zeal, but rather what we asked from them—a bit of service to the cause of better education. Or it may be viewed in this light, that we offered them an opportunity to stand shoulder to shoulder in a brotherhood fighting for the principles of freedom, activity, interest, and joy in the education of children.

Never since has interest and enthusiasm prevailed over so high a percentage of our membership. It sometimes seems that our very growth has somewhat minimized effort on the part of our membership; and the fact that they now receive in the magazine more value than the cost of their membership, tends to make them recipients rather than bestowers of bounty. We must never forget that, after all, the purpose of our association is to enlist concerted effort for the dissemination of those educational ideals in which we so heartily believe that to us the association takes on the nature of a cause. It is not therefore subscribers to a magazine that we seek, so much as members of and contributors to a humanitarian movement for the benefit of the world's children.[1]

[1]With this sentiment, I may say, our editor heartily concurs.

In the first year of our existence I proposed a convention. "But how can we hold a successful convention with no funds, and a tiny membership?" was the query of one of the more cautious members of the Executive Committee.

"Nothing is easier," I replied. "As for expenses, all we need is a modest hall, and a few dollars for programs and mailing expense. As for attendance, there is no law against local interest furnishing most of the audience."

In this the cautious member acquiesced somewhat hesitantly, but with such generous spirit that she later furnished the material means which made possible a very successful convention, held in Washington April 9th and 10th, 1920. Angelo Patri came down from New York and gave us the finest address I have ever heard him give, and generously donated his services. Marietta L. Johnson also gave us what I consider, without exception, the best of the many talks I have heard her make. Frank D. Slutz of the Moraine Park School fired us with his earnest message. Other speakers were: Dr. Frank F. Bunker, of the Federal Bureau of Education; Colonel Bernard Lentz, Originator of the Recruit Educational Centers; and Persis K. Miller, progressive principal of Public School 76, Baltimore. All of these speakers not only made no charge, but did not even present bills for expenses!

The convention, as regards enthusiasm and zeal, was a great success. A splendid, earnest, harmonious spirit prevailed. Moreover, we progressives were now meeting with each other face to face, and becoming concretely aware of our fellow-membership in a brotherhood which stood for progress. Thus began that series of national conferences which, held annually, except for the year 1924, have proved such an important factor in the growth and sense of solidarity of our association. They have been successively held in Dayton, Baltimore, Chicago, Philadelphia, Boston, Cleveland, New York. Here we all gather together, bring our interest and our problems, get to know one another, and carry away a sense of brotherhood and of enthusiasm which is a very vital factor in the new education movement.

A second important stage in the growth of the association was reached when it succeeded in enlisting the interest and earnest cooperation of Mrs. Avery Coonley, who had been for years contributing to the movement of the new education by the organization and maintenance of laboratory schools of her own in the suburbs of Chicago. Having recently (and fortunately for us) moved to Washington, she joined whole-heartedly in the work of the association at that propitious moment when the departure of Mrs. Ayres for Chicago made it necessary for us to engage paid secretarial service—a need which Mrs. Coonley now helped us to meet.

It was not until a year later, however, that there occurred an event—the result of her generous interest—which raised the association to a new level of recognition and influence. Remarked Mrs. Coonley one day to a small group of us, à propos of nothing at all: "You know, the Women's Party have been asking me to furnish them with legal talent for their coming campaign. But I think I would rather put that amount of money into a magazine for Progressive Education."

How our hearts sang within us! A magazine, which should do for education what the Geographical Magazine had done for geography, had been a dream as yet unrealized. Nor had we ever asked or hinted for it. And now, just like that, it was a "fait accompli"! In the twinkling of an eye, the magazine stepped into the arena of existence! A mere word uttered in a taxicab on the way to a dinner does not make a magazine, you may say! Ah, little then do you realize the power of an idea. Yes, it is true to state that our magazine sprang into existence in a taxicab! All else were mere details of growth and adjustment.

Not unimportant details, however. A wrong choice of editor would have been fatal. But we struck right the very first time. Gertrude Hartman was the name Mrs. Coonley suggested, and after an interview, Gertrude Hartman was selected. The eminent rightness of this choice has been made apparent, I think; for under her editorship the magazine has won wide-spread recognition as an interpreter of the educational progress of the day.

In planning the content and format of the magazine a publication committee consisting of Mr. Avery Coonley, Miss Lucia Morse, and the writer, worked in conjunction with the editor earnestly and long. Mrs. Coonley—and we all heartily concurred—wished to have the new magazine appear in a form dignified and attractive, as befitted the exponent of what we all believed to be the ideal type of education. After almost settling upon an excellent printer, Mrs. Coonley was informed of another printer esteemed as the most artistic in the country. Should we not have the house of Norman A. Munder print our magazine?

"Yes, I think it would be fine to have Mr. Munder," said Mrs. Coonley. "And wouldn't it be well to have Frederick Goudy (the world's leading type designer) design our cover, and the make-up of the inside pages?"

Thus it happened that the first number of Progressive Education was hailed as the most artistic and perfectly printed magazine in the country. This outer success in make-up and cover design has been no slight factor in the appeal our magazine has made from its inception.

It is fitting to pay here a word of tribute to the many busy educators who have so generously contributed articles to the magazine, thereby making it really the mouth-piece of the new work that is being carried on. Their willingness to pool their experiences for the common good is indicative of the cooperative, social spirit which is characteristic of the new educational point of view.

Shortly after the magazine was launched we moved our office from its cramped quarters in an inconvenient part of Washington to 10 Jackson Place, a suite of rooms commanding a view of the beautiful Lafayette Park. Here in the reception room well stocked with books and magazines on progressive education and beautifully furnished through the generosity of Mrs. Coonley, many visitors come to learn of the work of the association, and here are held the monthly meetings of the executive committee, which has functioned earnestly and enthusiastically throughout these ten years of the association's existence.

During the first two years in their new quarters, Miss Lucia Morse, having a leave of absence from the directorship of the Junior Elementary School at Downers Grove, generously donated her services to the association-office. Her daily work during this time and her right judgment in solving the many problems that arose during those years of up-building were vital factors in the success of our association.

Miss Morse contributed her services during a period in which we were searching for a paid executive capable of conducting the executive and the business side of the association, yet preferably an educator well versed in progressive education. These qualifications were hard to find combined in one person. But the association was fortunate in finally securing Mr. Morton Snyder, who had been for some years head of the Scarborough School. Mr. Snyder showed great ability in organizing the work of the Association, in expanding the membership, and in increasingly acquainting the public with "progressive education." Upon his withdrawal last June to take the head of the Rye Country Day School, the association was again fortunate in securing in Mr. J. Milnor Dorey, who had been associated with Mr. Snyder at

Scarborough School, a man admirably combining educational and business-executive qualifications.

I must not omit mention of one other person propitiously important to our association, President Charles W. Eliot. In our first year a consultation as to who should be our president had resulted in this revered educator as our natural first choice. But would he accept? Was he interested in, or favorable to, the new education? We thought he was.

The task of approach was delegated to me, and after making an appointment by mail with some preliminary hint of our purpose in seeing him and some literature of our association, I went up to Cambridge with mingled trepidation and hopes. Ushered into the presence of Dr. Eliot, who had known my father and who now greeted me with simple dignity and kindliness, I did not find it difficult to present my errand.

"I am sorry, I cannot consent to be your president," was his kindly-put but firm answer. "I am not able to travel to attend committee meetings, and I should not want to be a 'dummy' president."

"Then would you be willing to become our Honorary President?"

Dr. Eliot reflected for a moment, then answered with directness and simplicity, "Yes, I believe in your principles and aims, I believe in the kind of education you advocate, and I shall be glad to serve as your honorary president."

You can imagine what a great satisfaction it was to us, that our association had won the approval of Dr. Eliot. And, of course, his name lent dignity and strength to our organization, which at that time had more of zeal and enthusiasm than of prestige in the eyes of the educational world.

In 1926 the death of Dr. Eliot, full of years and honors, left a vacancy in our honorary presidency, which in endeavoring to fill the association—again with a bit of trepidation—solicited him whose philosophy is the foundation and inspiration of educational reform in this country—John Dewey. With what sympathy and whole-heartedness Dr. Dewey has given not only his name but his assistance to the association, his significant address at our 1928 New York Convention bears ample witness.

Nor must we be unmindful of the generous aid contributed by our presidents, the first of whom, Arthur E. Morgan, 1921–1923, accepted this responsibility at a time when he was extremely busy not only with the affairs of the Moraine Park School which he had previously organized, but also with Antioch College, of which he had just been made president. Our next president, Eugene R. Smith, 1923–1925, of the Beaver Country Day School, we had always naturally looked to as one of the fulcral points of progressive education. During his presidency he assisted greatly in making the Boston Convention a significant success, both as to size, enthusiasm, and subsequent progressive influence. Francis M. Froelicher, our third president, 1925–1927, was then head of the Oak Lane Country Day School, Philadelphia, and has subsequently become the head of Avon-Old-Farms, where he is more than ever helping to make educational history.

Thus we have traced the fortunes of the Progressive Education Association from its modest beginnings to the present. If I have told my tale rightly it will be seen as a great cooperative endeavor enlisting the work and interest of a large number of people, lay as well as professional. The association has, in the first decade of its existence, succeeded in becoming the clearing-house for the new education movement in this country, as the organized expression of certain evolutionary forces working in education and in the adult attitude toward the child. It is founded upon the pioneer educational work of a host of educators and laymen who, having visioned a new ideal of education, have not hesitated to undertake the arduous work of giving to their dreams a significant, concrete form. The association has given to these various and hitherto unconnected educational enterprises "a local habitation and a name," so that all might realize themselves as part of the great forward movement of education.

How much remains to be done! Our association, only just now entering its teens, is gaining strength for the great task that lies ahead. Thousands of parents and educators are yet to be enlightened as to the nature and values of progressive education. It is our responsibility to carry this message to all the parents and teachers of the country in the hope of extending to all the children of all the people of this great land those educational advantages which are now enjoyed by only a few scattered groups of especially fortunate children here and there through the country.

STANWOOD COBB,
President.

THE PRINCIPLES OF THE PROGRESSIVE EDUCATION ASSOCIATION
(1924) From *Progressive Education*, vol. I, pp. 1–2.

A Statement of the Principles of Progressive Education

I. Freedom to Develop Naturally

The conduct of the pupil should be governed by himself according to the social needs of his community, rather than by arbitrary laws. Full opportunity for initiative and self-expression should be provided, together with an environment rich in interesting material that is available for the free use of every pupil.

II. Interest, the Motive of All Work

Interest should be satisfied and developed through: (1) Direct and indirect contact with the world and its activities, and the use of the experience thus gained. (2) Application of knowledge gained, and correlation between different subjects. (3) The consciousness of achievement.

III. The Teacher a Guide, Not a Task-Master

It is essential that teachers should believe in the aims and general principles of Progressive Education and that they should have latitude for the development of initiative and originality.

Progressive teachers will encourage the use of all the senses, training the pupils in both observation and judgment; and instead of hearing recitations only, will spend most of the time teaching how to use various sources of information, including life activities as well as books; how to reason about the information thus acquired; and how to express forcefully and logically the conclusions reached.

Ideal teaching conditions demand that classes be small, especially in the elementary school years.

IV. Scientific Study of Pupil Development

School records should not be confined to the marks given by the teachers to show the advancement of the pupils in their study of subjects, but should also include both objective and subjective reports on those physical, mental, moral and social characteristics which affect both school and adult life, and which can be influenced by the school and the home. Such records should be used as a guide for the treatment of each pupil, and should also serve to focus the attention of the teacher on the all-important work of development rather than on simply teaching subject matter.

V. Greater Attention to All that Affects the Child's Physical Development

One of the first considerations of Progressive Education is the health of the pupils. Much more room in which to move about, better light and air, clean and well ventilated buildings, easier access to the out-of-doors and greater use of it, are all necessary. There should be frequent use of adequate playgrounds. The teachers should observe closely the physical condition of each pupil and, in co-operation with the home, make abounding health the first objective of childhood.

VI. Co-operation Between School and Home to Meet the Needs of Child-Life

The school should provide, with the home, as much as is possible of all that the natural interests and activities of the child demand, especially during the elementary school years. These conditions can come about only through intelligent co-operation between parents and teachers.

VII. The Progressive School a Leader in Educational Movements

The Progressive School should be a leader in educational movements. It should be a laboratory where new ideas, if worthy, meet encouragement; where tradition alone does not rule, but the best of the past is leavened with the discoveries of today, and the result is freely added to the sum of educational knowledge.

WALTER LIPPMANN'S CRITIQUE OF INTELLIGENCE TESTS

(1922)   From "A Future for the Tests," *New Republic,* vol. XXXIII, pp. 9–11.

How does it happen that men of science can presume to dogmatize about the mental qualities of the germplasm when their own observations begin at four years of age? Yet this is what the chief intelligence testers, led by Professor Terman, are doing. Without offering any data on all that occurs between conception and the age of kindergarten, they announce on the basis of what they have got out of a few thousand questionnaires that they are measuring the hereditary mental endowment of human beings. Obviously this is not a conclusion obtained by research. It is a conclusion planted by the will to believe. It is, I think, for the most part unconsciously planted. The scoring of the tests itself favors an uncritical belief that intelligence is a fixed quantity in the germplasm and that, no matter what the environment, only a predetermined increment of intelligence can develop from year to year. For the result of a test is not stated in terms of intelligence, but as a percentage of the average for that age level. These percentages remain more or less constant. Therefore, if a child shows an IQ of 102, it is easy to argue that he was born with an IQ of 102.

There is here, I am convinced, a purely statistical illusion, which breaks down when we remember what IQ means. A child's IQ is his percentage of passes in the test which the average child of a large group of his own age has passed. The IQ measures his place in respect to the average at any year. But it does not show the rate of his growth from year to year. In fact it tends rather to conceal the fact that the creative opportunities in education are greatest in early childhood. It conceals the fact, which is of such far-reaching importance, that because the capacity to form intellectual habits decreases as the child matures, the earliest education has a cumulative effect on the child's future. All this the static percentages of the IQ iron out. They are meant to iron it out. It is the boast of the inventors of the IQ that "the distribution of intelligence maintains a certain constancy from five to thirteen or fourteen years of age, *when the degree of intelligence is expressed in terms of the intelligence quotient.*" The intention is to eliminate the factor of uneven and cumulative growth, so that there shall be always a constant measure by which to classify children in class rooms.

This, as I have pointed out, may be useful in school administration, but it can turn out to be very misleading for an unwary theorist. If instead of saying that Johnny gained thirty pounds one year, twenty-five the next and twenty the third, you said that measured by the average gain for children of his age, Johnny's weight quotients were 101, 102, 101, you might, unless you were careful, begin to think that Johnny's germplasm weighed as much as he does today. And if you dodged that mistake, you might nevertheless come to think that since Johnny classified year after year in the same position, Johnny's diet had no influence on his weight.

The effect of the intelligence quotient on a tester's mind may be to make it *seem* as if intelligence were constant, whereas it is only the statistical position in large groups which is constant. This illusion of constancy has, I believe, helped seriously to prevent men like Terman from appreciating the variability of early childhood. Because in the mass the percentages remain fixed, they tend to forget how in each individual case there were offered creative opportunities which the parents and nurse girls improved or missed or bungled. The whole more or less blind drama of childhood, where the habits of intelligence are formed, is concealed in the mental test. The testers themselves become callous to it. What their footrule does not measure soon ceases to exist for them, and so they discuss heredity in school children before they have studied the education of infants.

But of course no student of human motives will believe that this revival of predestination is due to a purely statistical illusion. He will say with Nietzsche that "every impulse is imperious, and, as *such*, attempts to philosophize." And so behind the will to believe he will expect to find some manifestation of the will to power. He will not have to read far in the literature of mental testing to discover it. He will soon see that the intelligence test is being sold to the public on the basis of the claim that it is a device which will measure pure intelligence, whatever that may be, as distinguished from knowledge and acquired skill.

This advertisement is impressive. If it were true, the emotional and the worldly satisfactions in store for the intelligence tester would be very great. If he were really measuring intelligence, and if intelligence were a fixed hereditary quantity, it would be for him to say not only where to place each child in school, but also which children should go to high school, which to college, which into the professions, which into the manual trades and common labor. If the tester could make good his claim, he would soon occupy a position of power which no intellectual has held since the collapse of theocracy. The vista is enchanting, and even a little of the vista is intoxicating enough. If only it could be proved, or at least believed, that intelligence is fixed by heredity, and that the tester can measure it, what a future to dream about! The unconscious temptation is too strong for the ordinary critical defences of the scientific methods. With the help of a subtle statistical illusion, intricate logical fallacies and a few smuggled obiter dicta, self-deception as the preliminary to public deception is almost automatic.

The claim that we have learned how to *measure hereditary intelligence* has no scientific foundation. We cannot measure intelligence when we have never defined it, and we cannot speak of its hereditary basis after it has been indistinguishably fused with a thousand educational and environmental influences from the time of conception to the school age. The claim that Mr. Terman or anyone else is measuring hereditary intelligence has no more scientific foundation than a hundred other fads, vitamins and glands and amateur psychoanalysis and correspondence courses in will power, and it will pass with them into that limbo where phrenology and palmistry and characterology and the other Babu sciences are to be found. In all of these there was some admixture of primitive truth which the conscientious scientist retains long after the wave of popular credulity has spent itself.

So, I believe, it will be with mental testing. Gradually under the impact of criticism the claim will be abandoned that a device has been invented for measuring native intelligence. Suddenly it will dawn upon the testers that this is just another form of examination, differing in degree rather than in kind from Mr. Edison's questionnaire or a college entrance examination. It may be a better form of examination than these, but it is the same sort of thing. It tests, as they do, an unanalyzed mixture of native capacity, acquired habits and stored-up knowledge, and no tester knows at any moment which factor he is testing. He is testing the complex result of a long and unknown history, and the assumption that his questions and his puzzles can in fifty minutes isolate abstract intelligence is, therefore, vanity. The ability of a twelve-year-old child to define pity or justice and to say what lesson the story of the fox and crow "teaches" may be a measure of his total education, but it is no measure of the value or capacity of his germplasm.

Once the pretensions of this new science are thoroughly defeated by the realization that these are not "intelligence tests" at all nor "measurements of intelligence," but simply a somewhat more abstract kind of examination, their real usefulness can be established and developed. As examinations they can be adapted to the purposes in view, whether it be to indicate the feeble-minded for segregation, or to classify children in school, or to select recruits from the army for officers' training camps, or to pick bank clerks. Once the notion is abandoned that the tests reveal pure intelligence, specific tests for specific purposes can be worked out.

A general measure of intelligence valid for all people everywhere at all times may be an interesting toy for the psychologist in his laboratory. But just because the tests are so general, just because they are made so abstract in the vain effort to discount training and knowledge, the tests are by that much less useful for the practical needs of school administration and industry. Instead, therefore, of trying to find a test which will with equal success discover artillery officers, Methodist ministers, and branch managers for the rubber business, the psychologists would far better work out special and specific examinations for artillery officers, divinity school candidates and branch managers in the rubber business. On that line they may ultimately make a serious contribution to a civilization which is constantly searching for more successful ways of classifying people for specialized jobs. And in the meantime the psychologists will save themselves from the reproach of having opened up a new chance for quackery in a field where quacks breed like rabbits, and they will save themselves from the humiliation of having furnished doped evidence to the exponents of the New Snobbery.

A Postscript

This discussion has already provoked a lengthy correspondence which suggests the advisability of summarizing at this point the conclusions arrived at in the series of articles. The argument which I am prepared to defend is as follows:

1. The statement that the intelligence of the American nation has been measured by the army intelligence tests has no foundation. Generalizations, like those of Mr. Lothrop Stoddard, that "the average mental age of Americans is only about fourteen" are in the strictest sense of the word nonsense.

2. There is reason to hope that for the purpose of more homogeneous

classification of school children the intelligence tests may be of some practical benefit if administered with scepticism and sympathy.

3. This benefit is in great danger of being offset by dangerous abuse if the claims of the intelligence testers are not purged of certain fundamental assumptions.

4. The most important of these fundamental assumptions are:

    (a) that the intelligence test measures "intelligence,"

    (b) that "intelligence" is fixed by heredity, and that the intelligence test reveals and measures hereditary intelligence.

5. The attempt to construct a universal test of native intelligence on these assumptions may be an interesting theoretical experiment, but the claim that such a test exists, or is likely soon to exist, is scientifically unsound, is designed to lead to social injustice and to grave injury to those who are arbitrarily classified as predestined inferiors or superiors.

6. The claim that a universal test of native intelligence exists is not only unfounded and harmful, but it is also stultifying to the practical development of the tests themselves. Instead of aiming at a universal test of hereditary intelligence, psychological research should be directed towards the development of a multitude of specific tests for the use of administrators, industrial, scholastic or military, as the case may be, who have to deal with the practical problem of selecting and classifying groups of people. The aim should be to test, not the capacity of the germplasm of John Smith, for that cannot by any knowledge we possess be distinguished from his training, but the specific fitness of John Smith at this moment to do the work of the eighth grade, to run a freight locomotive or to sell medium priced automobiles. For tasks of modern life are much too varied to be measured by a single and universal test. One series of tests for intelligence is as meaningless as would be the attempt to measure time, space, weight, speed, color, shape, beauty, justice, faith, hope and charity, with a footrule, a pound scale and a speedometer.

FRANKLIN BOBBIT ON CURRICULUM MAKING (1924)   From Franklin Bobbitt, *How to Make a Curriculum* (Boston, 1924), pp. 7–17, 32–33.

For a number of years the world has been in a state of unusual unrest. Social currents have been moving in strange, threatening and often disastrous ways. They have carried us far from where we were only a few years ago. And the present speed of change indicates that we have yet far to go.

Because of the social changes, education must shift its ground in fundamental ways. It must perform functions which it has not hitherto attempted; and discontinue labors no longer serviceable.

It is easy to make changes. There are many who delight in any kind of change, and feel that they are making progress when they are making changes. But merely shifting position is not necessarily progress. There are more ways of going wrong than of going right. The *status quo* is usually better than changes in wrong directions. Curriculum-making must find guiding principles which will lead it with all the certainty that is possible in right directions.

It is helpful to begin with the simple assumption, to be accepted literally, that education is to prepare men and women for the activities of every kind which make up, or which ought to make up, well-rounded adult life; that it has no other purpose; that everything should be done with a view to this purpose; and that nothing should be included which does not serve this purpose.

Education is primarily for adult life, not for child life. Its fundamental responsibility is to prepare for the fifty years of adulthood, not for the twenty years of childhood and youth.

When we know what men and women ought to do along the many lines and levels of human experience, then we shall have before us the things for which they should be trained. The first task is to discover the activities which ought to make up the lives of men and women; and along with these, the abilities and personal qualities necessary for proper performance. These are the educational objectives.

The plan to be employed is activity-analysis. The first step is to analyze the broad range of human experience into major fields. The lines can be drawn in any number of ways. Each curriculum-making group will make the divisions that seem best to it for its purposes. The following is a classification that has been found serviceable:

1. Language activities; social intercommunication.
2. Health activities.
3. Citizenship activities.
4. General social activities—meeting and mingling with others.
5. Spare-time activities, amusements, recreations.
6. Keeping one's self mentally fit—analogous to the health activities of keeping one's self physically fit.
7. Religious activities.
8. Parental activities, the upbringing of children, the maintenance of a proper home life.
9. Unspecialized or non-vocational practical activities.
10. The labors of one's calling.

While the curriculum-maker may desire to analyze the field along entirely different lines, he will be careful to see that his analysis omits no portion of the broad range of desirable human experience. Many matters will be taken care of through the normal processes of living, and without any systematic educational labor. Other matters will be left to non-scholastic agencies. But in the original analyses of human experience, the whole field should be viewed in order that the portions which belong to the schools may be properly seen, within themselves, and in relation to the whole.

The major fields of human action having been defined, the second step is to take them, one after the other, and analyze them into their more specific activities. In this analysis, one will first divide his field into a few rather large units; and then break them up into smaller ones. This process of division will continue until he has found the quite specific activities that are to be performed.[1]

At all stages of the analyses, attention should be fixed upon the *actual activities of mankind.* In part the analyses will be made on the basis of simple observation. This is all that is needed so long as there is virtual unanimity on the part of all objective-minded analysts of the situation. This will largely be the case with the major units, and their larger subdivisions. As the analyses approach the units that

[1]For detailed information relative to these analyses, see Charters, *Curriculum Construction,* chaps. IV–IX.

are minute, numerous, and interrelated with each other, and especially when accuracy demands quantitative definition, careful scientific assembling of the facts becomes necessary.

The activities once discovered, one can then see the objectives of education. These latter are the *abilities* to perform in proper ways the activities. The two are cognate, but not identical. For brevity, it is possible to state the two together in the way shown subsequently in this chapter.

In the following list of objectives, the several major fields are divided into their principal subdivisions. We have not here attempted to go into the more minute subdivisions. We have held, in the main, to those which represent the practically unanimous judgment of some twenty-seven hundred well-trained and experienced adults. In a number of cases, however, where the field is complex or obscure, the items represent only majority approval. They are still upon the level of hypothesis and require further study and analysis. They are attempts to define regions of fields which we know exist, but the details of which are yet obscure. We cannot ignore these regions simply because our knowledge of them is incomplete. We must define them as best we can for working purposes; and then further clarify our vision through the two methods of scientific research and of dealing practically with them. It is well to have a proportioned vision of the whole field even though many spots be obscure and problematical.

The following[2] is presented merely to illustrate the *kind* of statement of objectives that appears to be needed—on this particular level of generality. The curriculum-making group will formulate its own statement on the basis of its understanding of the realities.

Major Objectives of Education

I. SOCIAL INTERCOMMUNICATION

1. Ability to use language in all ways required for proper and effective participation in the community life.

2. Ability effectively to organize and present orally one's thought to others: (a) In conversation; (b) In recounting one's experiences; (c) In more serious or formal discussion; (d) In oral report; (e) In giving directions; (f) To an audience.

3. Ability to pronounce one's words properly.

4. Ability in speech to use the voice in ways both agreeable and effective.

5. Command over an adequate reading, speaking and writing vocabulary.

6. Ability to use language which is grammatically correct.

7. Ability effectively to organize and express one's thought in written form: (a) Memoranda; (b) Letters; (c) Reports, news items or articles, systematic discussion of questions; (d) Giving directions; (c) Written addresses.

8. Ability to write with proper legibility, ease, and speed.

9. Ability to spell the words of one's writing vocabulary.

---

[2]This statement of objectives has grown up gradually through twelve years of cooperative effort on the part of some fifteen hundred members of graduate classes in "The Curriculum" conducted by the writer at the University of Chicago. Recently the list was critically examined by some twelve hundred high-school teachers in Los Angeles, and again revised. It was then used as a basis for determining the objectives of the several junior and senior high-school departments in the recent curriculum labors in that city. It is still, of course, but a tentative draft. It will require revision and re-revision re-revision on the basis of accurate scientific analyses of detailed portions of the field as these accumulate. Or it may be entirely discarded in favor of a different plan, should a more serviceable one be offered.

10. Ability to use good form, order, and arrangement in all of one's written work: margins, spacing, alignment, paragraphing, capitalization, punctuation, syllabication, abbreviation, etc.

11. Ability to understand the oral expression of others.

12. Ability to read the written or printed expression of others with proper ease, speed, and comprehension.

13. Ability to use dictionary, encyclopædia, atlas, handbooks, card catalogues, reader's guides, indexes, and other library and reference helps in finding facts or materials wanted.

14. Ability to read and interpret facts expressed by commonly used types of graphs, diagrams, and statistical tables.

15. Ability to express facts by means of graphs, diagrams, and statistical tables.

16. Ability to use maps with ease and understanding.

17. Ability to read drawings, and to prepare simple drawings or designs.

✻　　✻　　✻

II. MAINTENANCE OF PHYSICAL EFFICIENCY

101. Ability to control one's dietary in such ways as to make one's food contribute in maximum measure to one's physical well-being.

102. Ability to keep the body mechanism properly oxygenated.

103. Ability to utilize muscular exercise as a lifelong means of maintaining a high level of physical vitality.

104. Ability and disposition throughout life to engage with pleasure and profit in a varied repertory of games, sports, athletics, outdoor recreations, etc., such as swimming, skating, hiking, rowing, riding, tennis, golf, ball games of various kinds, running games, dancing, fishing, hunting, canoeing, motoring, camping, athletic events, etc.

105. Ability and disposition to engage in a variety of unspecialized practical labors which contribute to one's repertory of physical experiences.

106. Ability to employ setting-up exercises for corrective or emergency purposes when nothing better is available.

107. Ability to carry one's self and to move and act with ease, grace, and precision.

108. Ability to maintain postures conducive to the best physical functioning.

109. Ability to make one's various mental and emotional states and activites contribute in maximum degree to one's physical functioning.

110. Ability to make one's sleep contribute in maximum measure to the development and maintenance of a high level of physical vitality.

111. Ability to relax physically and mentally at proper times and in proper ways.

112. Ability to protect one's self from micro-organisms; and to deal with them and their products effectively in case of attack.

113. Ability to take proper precautions against the spread of disease.

114. Ability to protect from dust, smoke, and noxious gases.

115. Ability rightly to control the factors involved in the maintenance of body temperatures.

116. Ability to dress in ways that promote the physical well-being in maximum degree.

117. Ability and disposition to maintain personal cleanliness.

118. Ability to provide the most favorable conditions for the elimination from the tissues, organs, and body in general of all harmful or needless substances and agents.

119. Ability to control one's relations to sunlight so as to secure maximum benefits therefrom.

120. Ability to secure that variety or diversity of physical experiences necessary for maximum well-being.

121. Ability to draw up an individual program of work, play, rest, sleep, meals, etc., best suited to one's physical nature and capacity.

122. Ability to avoid preventable accidents.

123. Ability to deal with conditions produced by many kinds of common accidents.

124. Ability to care for the teeth.

125. Ability to care for the eyes.

126. Ability to care for nose, ear, and throat.

127. Ability to care for the skin.

128. Ability to keep the heart and blood vessels in normal working condition.

129. Ability to care for the hair and scalp.

130. Ability to care for the nails.

131. Ability to care properly for the feet.

132. Ability to control sex-functions in the interests of physical and social well-being.

133. The ability to keep reasonably well-informed, in the degree to be expected of the layman, as to the discoveries of science in the fields of health conservation and promotion.

134. Ability alone or in cooperation with physicians and nurses to deal effectively with many kinds of disorders.

135. Ability to care for the sick,—so far as laymen need this ability.

136. Ability to take the protective, precautionary, or remedial steps necessary to protect one's self or family from common ailments.

137. Ability wisely to utilize the services of physicians, nurses, dentists, and other specialists in health and physical upbuilding and maintenance.

138. Ability within one's occupational field to cooperate effectively in providing wholesome working conditions.

139. Ability to perform one's civic functions in cooperating with and in the social support and control of public agencies engaged in promoting the general physical welfare.

*　　*　　*

III. EFFICIENT CITIZENSHIP

201. Ability to think, feel, act, and react as an efficient, intelligent, sympathetic, and loyal member of the large social group—that group that is prior to differentiation and within which social differentiation occurs. Large-group or citizenship consciousness. Sense of membership in the total social group, rather than in some special class. Large-group local consciousness when dealing with local problems; large-group state consciousness when dealing with state responsibilities; large-group national consciousness when dealing

with national matters; large-group world-consciousness when dealing with mankind's responsibilities for world cooperation and management.

202. Ability and disposition to view the specialized or functional groups and agencies, not as independent entities, but as service arms of the general social whole, without which they could not exist.

203. The ability of the citizen to do his individual share in performing those social functions for which all citizens are equally responsible in the establishment, organization, maintenance, protection, oversight, and control of the specialized groups and agencies into which society is differentiated for effectiveness of action. The young citizen-in-training is to acquire those abilities which, when adulthood is reached, will enable him to perform the following things in connection with the several specialized social agencies:

(a) Sharing fully in an informed and impelling public opinion, which looks to the general welfare in its control of each service agency.

(b) Setting up in public opinion and maintaining the standards of result to be achieved by each service agency.

(c) Seeing that each service agency aims at the standards of results to be achieved.

(d) Seeing that the service agency employs procedures which are effective in producing the desired results and which are economical in social costs.

(e) Seeing that the material working conditions necessary for the most effective and economical procedures are supplied.

(f) Seeing that each service agency is provided with personnel and organization of the kind required by the procedures to be employed; and properly rewarded.

(g) Directly or indirectly selecting or approving the selection of the personnel of the agency.

(h) Supplying the funds necessary for the efficient, and in all ways proper, conduct of the agency.

(i) Currently or periodically examining, directly or through publicity reports, or both, into the results achieved by the agency, and the degree of economy employed.

(j) Where results achieved and degree of economy employed comply with standards of expectation, approving and properly rewarding the labors of those who have thus given good service.

(k) Where results do not reach the standards of expectation, or where there has been waste, finding the causes of the deficiency, and removing them as expeditiously as practicable.

204. Ability to organize and use social facts effectively in arriving at conclusions.

205. The ability to use general principles in analyzing and considering economic, political, and other social problems.

206. Ability to protect one's self from social, economic, and political fallacies, illusions, misrepresentations, petty-mindedness, fragmentary-mindedness, sentimentality, selfish prejudices, and the like, through one's continual reliance upon facts and principles.

207. Ability to discern the character and the extent of one's social obligations and duties in the amount and character of things done for one by other individuals, groups and agencies.

208. Ability to discern one's individual rights in the quantity of one's services to the general group. Ability to read one's rights as things earned.

209. Ability to see social relations so clearly as to discern the *duties* of others, individuals and groups, within the social whole.

210. Ability to see social relations so clearly as to discern the *rights* of others within the social whole.

211. Disposition of the citizen as consumer to avoid waste.

212. A sufficient knowledge of the laws which one is expected to obey.

213. An understanding and appreciation of the social-service labors and sacrifices which have brought our institutions and social procedures to their present high levels of development.

214. Ability to organize and express one's ideas clearly and effectively in the discussion, formal or informal, of social problems.

215. Ability wisely to choose a specialized occupation in which one can give good service to one's self, to one's family, and to society.

*   *   *

IX. UNSPECIALIZED PRACTICAL ACTIVITIES

801. Ability to use all common kinds of measuring devices: measures of lengths, area, volume, capacity, weight, time, value, temperature, specific gravity, etc.

802. Ability to sharpen, adjust, clean, lubricate, replace worn or broken parts, and otherwise keep household and garden tools and appliances in good order and good working condition.

803. Ability to make repairs, adjustments and additions to the house and its equipment.

804. Ability to make repairs, adjustments, and sometimes to construct household furniture or other equipment.

805. Ability to participate intelligently in the original planning of one's home.

806. Ability to operate household equipment.

807. Ability to keep the house, premises, and equipment clean and sanitary.

808. Ability to keep the house in good order.

809. Ability to care for and operate the electrical system and appliances in one's home; and to make simple repairs, adjustments, or replacements.

810. Ability to protect the home from fire.

811. Ability to perform the operations involved in the care of the premises and garden.

812. Ability to care for pets or other live animals.

813. Ability to perform the various activities involved in traveling and outdoor life.

814. Ability wisely to select garments.

815. Ability to design, select the materials, make, mend and alter clothing.

816. Ability to care for one's clothing.

817. Ability to perform the laundry and other cleaning activities of the home.

818. Ability to perform the various activities involved in providing the family with food.

819. Ability to perform the several activities involved in a proper care of the person.

820. An amateur ability to do productive, creative, or interpretative work in the field of the fine arts. (Semi-specialized.)

821. Ability to perform the simple business operations involved in the conduct of personal and family affairs.

*   *   *

The first step in curriculum-making is to decide what specific educational results are to be produced.

The results to be produced should be stated in human terms. Most of them are human abilities of one kind or another. Operating within these as factors are personal qualities and characteristics of many kinds.

The objectives should be stated in definite terms. When so stated, it is possible for educationists to know with certainty at what they are aiming. It is also possible for parents and students to understand.

The objectives should be stated, so far as their nature will permit, in the everyday language of common sense. They should be easily intelligible to everybody concerned, especially to parents and pupils.

General unanalyzed objectives are to be avoided. For the ten major divisions of human action, it would be possible to state ten corresponding abilities. These would be so general as to be practically useless for curriculum-making. "Ability to care for one's health," for example, is too general to be useful. It must be reduced to particularity: ability to manage the ventilation of one's sleeping-room, ability to protect one's self against micro-organisms, ability to care for the teeth, and so on.

Objectives that are only vague high-sounding hopes and aspirations are to be avoided. Examples are: "Character building," the "harmonious development of the individual," "social efficiency," "general discipline," "self-realization," "culture," and the like. All of these are valid enough; but too cloud-like for guiding practical procedure. They belong to the visionary adolescence of our profession, not to its sober and somewhat disillusioned maturity.

MENTAL HYGIENE AND EDUCATION (1926)   From Elizabeth A. Irwin and Louis Marks, *Fitting the School to the Child* (New York, 1926), pp. 118–19, 130–31.

Education should not consist of acquiring information but of acquiring experience. A youngster may grow up in an environment rich with educational possibilities and yet be entirely shut off by the attitude of the people around him. Just as the child in the home of an ignorant farmer may grow up without any acquaintance whatever with the plant and animal life about him, so the city child is apt to know nothing of the industrial processes and the other occupational features of his own environment. As soon as the child enters the school, it begins to separate him from reality. Many a six-year-old does not know the names of the garments he wears and the food he eats. Yet he is crammed with columns of spelling words and rows of figures without regard to whether this mental food is analogous to milk or pickles. The modern science of nutrition has far outrun the science of education. It emphasizes not only the quantity of food but its quality and kind.

Furthermore, the unscientific pabulum of the school is administered on an unscientific schedule. Why do we have to hurry things along so fast? If adding is hard at seven years, why not leave it till nine? If reading is hard at six, why not teach it at eight or nine? There is enough educational experience that is wholesome for six- or seven-year-old children, without overdrawing their account with life in advance. It is like paying a high price for strawberries in February when you can have them abundantly in June at moderate cost. This hot-house forcing is characteristic not only of one subject in the curriculum but practically of all of them.

Shall Reading Be Learned at Six

It is almost impossible for a normal child not to learn to read before he is ten if he is exposed to books by those who value them. On the other hand, it is often torture for an imaginative child of six or seven years of age to sit through period after period of "was" and "he" and "go" and other abstract symbols. The irksome drill of the reading class is not really for the good of the child, but serves chiefly to allay the fears of parents who are in a panic lest their children may turn out at ten to be illiterate. They seem to need reassurance all along the line by a series of universal signals that their children are as well equipped as other children are. If Willie can read as well as Johnnie, then Willie's mother can look Johnnie's mother in the face without shame; and it is the exceptional father who does not love to take his nine-year-old daughter's letter from his pocket and exhibit it to his business friends.

For such reasons, the child is subjected for several hours every week to stories of Johnnie Jack Rabbit in words of one syllable and endless repetitions concerning the adventures and misadventures of Gruby-Gruntum and Toby-Trottum, until, if he has any mind at all, he learns to close it when the reading book is opened. Is not literature a broader foundation for culture than this parrot-like drill, made necessary by trying to teach the child to read two or three years before it is easy for him?

✳   ✳   ✳

What the Young Child Should Learn

Young children should learn to use their bodies and muscles; to be gentle, polite, and curious. They should learn to ask questions and be interested in the answers. They should collect and classify things. They should learn languages; if there is need of learning languages, the period under ten years is the time when this is most readily done. Music may be learned almost unconsciously by little children. Why are not rhythm of motion and sound, dancing and singing and beating a drum more appropriate to seven years than the stereotyped abstractions of academic lessons?

Many children acquire a permanent dislike for literature, music, or mathematics through the shortsighted policy of the school which forces these subjects upon them while they are still unprepared for them. The difficulty of the conceptual material or the adult point of view leads the child to dislike the subject all the rest of his life.

From simple dislike it is a short step to the feeling that one has no aptitude. We are constantly meeting adults who say that they have no appreciation for music or that they always hated mathematics. Such attitudes are often traceable to wrong methods of teaching and to associations formed in childhood and now grown to such proportion that they form a real adult disability.

The child should learn in school the art of sociability. The faults of an educational system based on the three R's are so manifest that intelligent parents sometimes raise the question, why send the child to school anyway? Cannot the well-educated parent, though an amateur, do better by his child than the professional teacher? But the school is not merely a place where lessons are learned and recited; it is preëminently the place where the young individual learns to make social adjustments to other individuals of his own generation. Since the family has grown smaller, the social contacts of the schoolroom have become more important than ever. The school provides this opportunity and is in this respect unique. There is no substitute. It is possible to educate a child ideally from the intellectual point of view, and yet to educate him in such a way that he is wholly set apart from his fellows. The parents of gifted children especially have this danger to consider. While genius has existed in isolation and has made historic contributions to civilization, there are few parents who would deliberately choose to educate a child for solitude. A person's adjustment to other people depends to a large extent on sharing with them a common mental background. Even the public school curriculum, with all its faults, has at least this social value. It supplements the more specific social value of the human contacts made in school.

✳   ✳   ✳

The Emotional Education of the Child

The school should above all things be a place for children to get the habit of being happy. Has anyone ever yet read the record of a crime which was committed by a contented and happy person? We have been forced to the conclusion that many of the so-called problem cases of every school would be no longer problems if we realized the effect of our school curriculum upon the pupils. The children often develop antagonisms to teacher, subject, and school because they are bored. How many healthy, normal, grown-up people would patiently stand the daily grind of a so-called education which they did not understand or which did not give some play to their natural and instinctive desire for self-expression?

It is true that Rousseau stressed the value of natural instincts, that Pestalozzi attempted to put his theories into practice, that Herbart spoke of character as the desideratum of education, and that Froebel was dominated by the idea of free development; yet while we speak and think in terms of these great reformers, the schools in practice have never yet succeeded in catching up with the spirit of these leaders. One of our high schools has taken for its motto, "more happiness in education." It is not enough, however, that such well-intentioned slogans should be adopted by the school. They may prove as sterile of results as the inspired teachings of our educational geniuses. This is sure to be the case, as long as they remain, from the teacher's point of view, in the domain of pure theory and sentiment.

The school has this to gain from an alliance with mental hygiene: that happiness in education need not remain merely a pious hope but may be translated into a technique of living. The educator can no longer evade his responsibility for the emotional development of the child on the ground that a science and technique are lacking. Already the beginnings of such a science and technique are in existence and are widely applied in the cases of people with pathological tendencies. The improvement as well as the utilization of this technique rests largely with the schools where the emotional education of the normal child is more neglected than that of his erratic brother. The school has assumed that the emotional development of the normal child could be taken for granted, but that his intellectual development should be subjected to ceaseless prodding and surveillance. What education chiefly needs is that we shall take more for granted in regard to the child's intellectual development, and take more thought about teaching him the art of happy and productive living.

HUGHES MEARNS ON THE SIGNIFICANCE OF THE CREATIVE SPIRIT IN EDUCATION (1926) From Hughes Mearns, "The Creative Spirit and Its Significance for Education," in Gertrude Hartman and Ann Shumaker, eds., *Creative Expression.* . . (New York, 1926), pp. 13–16.

That is the title . . . suggested by the editor. My own preference was "All God's Chillun Got Wings" until I remembered that all God's chillun are not permitted to use them. I visit many schools which, in spite of a modern cheerfulness and a seeming acquiescence of pupils, are to me places where the wings of God's children are gradually and painlessly removed. High marks are given to them who know least about flying; future advancement is open only to those who keep their feet always on the ground. When the creative spirit strives here and there to flutter, it becomes an activity that must be practiced in stealth, rarely with full approval of the authorities.

In *Creative Expression* one sees the creative spirit in action, sometimes in full flight; and these are but representatives of myriad activities; hundreds of illustrations had to be left out for lack of space and only the pictorial could be shown, for the creative spirit is something more than a product in clay and canvas: it is dancing, rhythmic living, a laugh, a flash of the mind, strength of control, swiftness of action, an unwritten poem, a song without words; it is life adding its invisible living cells to more and abundant life. But these pictures will serve; for the object is to tempt the unbeliever to loiter a moment at the shrine of the true gods. Our argument may not move him, but the grace of our service may win him into the faith.

To the unbeliever, then, I address myself when I would tell of the creative spirit and its varied manifestations; and also, of course, to those who believe but would have their faith strengthened. The creative impulse is more easily observed in young children but the housewife who bakes unerringly without book or recipe knows it; the carpenter fashioning a cupboard to his own notion of shape and line, the office man given free sway in the phrasing of a sales advertisement, the lawyer playing upon the mood of judge and jury, these practice it without knowing it; my true love's letter is the perfect product of instinctive artistry; all our adult ways of interacting one with another, in short, call on the creative spirit, and our life is artistic or dull in proportion to our creative gifts. But adults are in the main wingless; convention, tribal taboos, mechanistic living, long years of schooling, something has stilled the spirit within or walled it securely. It is to children we must go to see the creative spirit at its best; and only to those children who are in some measure uncoerced.

Outwardly it is harmony; a unity of eye, hand, bodily muscles, mind; a concentration upon the object of desire that sets the world aside. It is frequently balked by the need of special information or of special skill; these are the obstructions that it must surely overcome or the heart's desire is not achieved and the spirit dies; these, too, are the strategic places where the wise teacher is at hand with just the right assistance. But of that later; the outward picture concerns us now. Not only is there harmony of mind and body but there is the closest connection between the thing conceived as worthy to be done and the media necessary—brush, paint, wood, metal, clay, blocks, script, tool, machine.

It flourishes, of course, in what we call play, but mindful of our religious inheritances, in which play has been conceived as touched with evil, I hasten to note concrete illustrations of play that has taken on all the characteristics of work: a butterfly collection occupying five steady years which brought technical knowledge of family and species, of habitat, environment, breeding, and culture, of correspondence with other collectors and with foreign sales agents, and an ability to present orally to an assembly of several hundred children and adults the serious business of preparing such a collection and to lead the discussion that followed with the skill of experience; a study of biological specimens that led an elementary-school boy first to museums and then to summer school (Wood's Hole) until all unwittingly the avocation put him so far outside the role of pupil that an ornithologist and later a marine biologist claimed that they must talk to the lad as a colleague and defer to him in his special scientific field; an elementary-school boy who constructed photostatic apparatus and motion-picture cameras from lard cans found on the village refuse pile and from odds and ends picked up at rummage sales; a young artist who built herself a five thousand dollar studio through a persistently applied scheme of savings, earning, and commercial borrowings.

Illustration of such activity is at hand in every classroom including the college classroom if one has the skill to look for it. The common ingredient in each case, that which makes it different from formal instruction, is that the "urge to do" is self-engendered; it seeks its own way to fulfillment; it is not stopped by time, space, apparatus, or by teachers or school administrators, although because of the last two it may often conceal every outward trace of interest in the thing that occupies the main tracts of the mind, in this regard behaving like a conquered people in the presence of the ruling race. It may even at these times assume a cautious stupidity; for neither to the unsympathetic nor to the arrogant and unfeeling will it confess an interest in the inner dream. Under unfriendly questioning it may even deny, and thus through clumsiness and inexpertness get into the coil of adult morality.

II

When the creative spirit is at work, not only are body and mind cooperating with instinctive harmony to secure the desired result, but the language art is functioning at a high degree of excellence. A child may speak haltingly in classroom recitation, or in a school "composition" write with despairing inadequacy, who in the midst of a bit of self-initiated artistry, the making of a toy motor boat, a radio set, a cartoon, or a poem, will talk with the effectiveness of an inspired expert. In his own language and idiom, of course, and provided you do not bring with you the flavor of the impossible linguistic standards of adult perfection. You may ask questions then, if you are not of the forbidding sort; and if you have an ear for right rhythmic speech you may have cause to marvel at the language sense that these youngsters really have; and you may wonder why we as teachers do not take advantage of the gifts that children have in this line instead of damming—both spellings apply here— their utterance through our insistence on the use of an alien tongue.

The claim for "lessons" and "home assignments" is that they teach persistence, but who can equal the persistence of children when engaged in creative work? Ask the mothers and fathers who have tried to keep up with the demands of their offspring for continuous attention to a loved story or game! And the work which they set for themselves is not stopped by the ending of the day; it carries over, day after day, until the accomplished end is reached. The astonishing paintings that decorate Miss Keelor's room (second grade) were not done at a sitting. Day by day they grew. She has just told me the history of one remarkable water color of an autumn orchard, how the house and the trees and the far-off hills came slowly to their present places in the picture and then one morning a shy voice confided, "I was thinking about it last night in bed, so I put some apples on the tree as well as on the ground, for, of course, they all wouldn't have fallen off, would they? And the red apples are so pretty I wanted more of them." A teacher has just dropped in to tell me of a remarkable speech delivered from a most unexpected source at a recent Lincoln Day assembly. "It was done with such ease and masterfulness," he said, "with the modesty of a trained speaker, and yet it was the boy's first serious public appearance. We found out that he had been at work for weeks in various libraries. He had concentrated on a bibliography that no teacher would have had the heart to give any one as an assignment, even in the old days; and no one knew he was at it! He saturated himself with material like an expert research student, and then calmly talked out of full knowledge. The school is so thrilled by it that they are thinking of naming him for the most responsible position in the vote of the pupils, chairman of the Student Council, a most coveted office, I tell you, and never held but by the all-around best man in the place!"

"And no one knew he was at it!" That is a quality that must not be missed, in which regard these young artists are one with the older artist. The same artist-shyness is here, the same fear of spoiling the picture through the wrong word from outside; even suggestions, the artist knows, are dangerous until the work is finished. And flattery can knock one out of the humor—shatter the inspiration—as well as dispraise, or stupid misunderstanding, or nagging (parents and teachers, elder sisters, and governesses, please take notice!), or that unfeeling looking-over-the-shoulder which has dished many a promising canvas. Artists and children hide from onlookers until enough of the work is done to insure a possible completion (that's why they should have their own rooms, studios, workshops). But they work cheerfully enough among their own kind; so in some schools the artistic work is done out of hours and teachers never hear of it; but in the schools that are represented in *Creative Expression* one senses that the artist has been protected from the cold eye of the outsider. "I'm painting that red barn," I heard a Woodstock celebrity once say to a group of gushing ignorants, "but if you ask me what I am painting, I shall have to go fishing for a week." He was bitter with a sense of outrage at their unfeeling impertinence in hovering over him, but all they said was, "Isn't he just *screamingly* funny! And don't you *love* it! It *is* the barn you're painting, isn't it? I'm just *crazy* about it!" And as he folded up his work he remarked hopelessly, "I'm off! Fishing it is!"

But at the right moment they want praise like any other artist. Or, rather, they want what the artist-student calls a "crit." "Oh," cried one of Miss Keelor's little boys, "you didn't hang mine up!" It was a moment of real torture. Miss Keelor brought the painting out slowly (while, no doubt, she thought hard) and looked at it again. "I didn't think it had enough in it," she explained, but not with an air of really knowing. "So much space here," she mused, and then looked at the pictures of the others. He looked too and understood. "I could do some more!" He caught the idea eagerly, explaining spiritedly new thoughts that began to come to him with a rush. And away he went, satisfied with the judgment.

And at other times, just like real artists, they are dismayed at praise. You hang their pictures; they are grieved. "It is not good enough," they say in real distress and go sturdily to work to make a better one to take its place. Every one who has been intimate with gifted poets and painters knows how difficult it is to get them to pack their work off to magazines or to exhibitions. To go through the agony of such necessary business is one of the last things learned by the professional; and more often than not it is his prudent and practical wife who supplies the needed motivation.

III

This then is the torrential force that comes unbidden out of the mysterious recesses of personality and fashions things out of wood, color, fabric, clay, and words; the thing that dances, sings, leads a dozen dramatic reincarnations; the thing that drives a small child into profound research or sets him digging into a difficulty with the energy of a dog at a woodchuck hole; whose ways are sure, whose outcome is beauty. Not that I would say that the conscious end is beauty. Children seem to be driven by an inner necessity of putting forth something; that it shall turn out to be beautiful is not their concern; their impulse at its best is to place something in the outside world that is already (or almost ready) in their inside world of perceiving, thinking, feeling; they measure their success or failure by the final resemblance of the thing done to the thing imagined. And in their best moments they seem to know exactly what to do: the muscles ripple in perfect harmony to the right touch, line, blow; in painting the brush is swung fearlessly and surely, in pottery the punches and patches are thumbed without hesitation. In this regard they are in tune again with the professional artist. Experience has loosened his fears; he trusts his instinct for level, balance, the swift adjustings of his medium and his materials to satisfy those flashing demands from within.

One needs to emphasize here that the modern discovery of the child as artist—a very ancient bit of knowledge, of course—is coincident with the realization of the beauty of primitive art generally. The child is a genuine primitive. He needs little or no instruction, but he must have materials and his surroundings must be such as to call his effort worthy; he is susceptible to condemnation and will give up all his precious art and lose one of the most gracious of nature's gifts—for, alas, it may be easily lost—if his overlords command. The art of the uncivilized tribes, ancient and modern, is just that untutored art of our own children. And now that we are treasuring every trace of the craft of the primitive peoples, the native art in Africa, Mexico, Egypt, the South Seas, it is fitting that our educational leaders should be rediscovering with joy and understanding the work of our own young "natives."

WILLIAM HEARD KILPATRICK DISCUSSES THE MEANING OF
SUBJECT-MATTER (1926)   From William Heard Kilpatrick, *Foundations of Method* (New York, 1926), pp. 27–278. 283.

"**A**s useful as is the term experience for your purpose, I think you used a phrase even better."

"What was that?"

"Ways-of-behaving. To me this is even a more obvious common denominator to child and subject-matter than is the notion of experience. The child is, if he is anything, a bundle of 'ways-of-behaving.' As you yourself said, the race-experience has preserved for us the best ways-of-behaving that have thus far been devised. Then child and subject-matter are both alike ways-of-behaving. The child's ways are small, crude, erring, perhaps, when we compare them with the best ways-of-behaving of the best among us; but they clearly belong on the same scale, as you have just brought out."

"That sounds good, but let's look more closely. The combination 7x8 = 56 is subject-matter. How is it a way-of-behaving? Did you not too hastily include all subject-matter in your assertion?"

"I think not. Consider a case where 7x8 = 56 actually belongs. I buy seven eight-cent stamps. I could pay for them separately, paying in at the stamp window eight cents seven distinct times—I mean in seven separate and distinct payments. That would be 7x8. But that is too much trouble. Thanks to our race experience (for many uncivilized tribes do not know so much arithmetic) instead of seven separate and distinct operations of paying eight cents each I make one paying operation of fifty-six cents. This race experience subject-matter way-of-behaving is much neater and more expeditious."

"I had never thought of that before. And do all the things that we teach our children show the same thing? How about geography?"

"It too, properly considered, consists of ways-of-behaving. I was in Detroit and learned to my regret that a certain train upon which I was relying did not, on account of the change to daylight saving time, get me into New York soon enough to meet an engagement. No other through train passing Detroit would do as well. Then came my geography. How about the Lake Shore road? Many trains between Chicago and New York pass that way, and the distance from Detroit down could not be great. There must surely be a road that would make the connection. Search disclosed such a connecting road with a satisfactory schedule of trains. A fast train to New York was caught and the engagement met. Here geographical knowledge actually meant a way-of-behaving. It told me where to look." "Would you be willing to say that all subject-matter in the curriculum really works this way?"

"I am quite willing to say that all ought to work this way; that anything which does not so work has no place in the curriculum."

"This is one way then of criticizing a curriculum?"

"Indeed it is, and trenchant criticism it gives too. Much curriculum content I fear could not stand it."

"You would have to interpret behavior rather broadly, would you not, in order to include all desirable learnings under the head of ways-of-behavior?"

"No more broadly than behavior properly extends. To me behavior is as broad as life; it specifically includes all ways of reacting in life to life situations. So far as I can see that will include all we need."

"A moment ago you used this conception as a criterion for criticising the curriculum. I am wondering if it is equally valuable as a criterion for judging learning."

"What have you in mind?"

"I mean so as to decide whether a thing has been learned. We have said this in several different ways before. I should like now to say that nothing has been learned until it has been made over into an actual way-of-behaving. Much school learning seems to me to be merely for show purposes, chiefly for show on examination day. To me this is a degradation of the notion of learning, a prostitution of it. Nothing has been learned till it is there and disposed to serve as an actual way-of-behaving."

"Wouldn't that condemn many schools and teachers?"

"I think it would, but it is no less valuable for all that. In fact I think our schools are often off the track. They seem not to know what they are about or why. If everybody saw that subject-matter is good only and because it furnishes a better way-of-behaving and that learning means acquiring actually that way-of-behaving—if every one saw these things, we should have, as we ought to have, a different kind of schools."

"Does this have any bearing on education as a preparation for life?"

"This conception helps us to understand one previously discussed, the continuous reconstruction of experience. To learn anything as a new way of behaving is of course to reconstruct experience. If we demand that the way-of-behaving be got only as it is immediately needed, we shall have the continuous remaking of experience; and this of course is life itself, living now—the opposite of education as a mere preparation for future living."

"And you really mean that you wish everything the child learns to reappear soon as a new way of behaving? Everything—arithmetic, geography, history, spelling?"

"That is exactly what I mean. I should wish each thing to be learned when and because it was needed as a way-of-behaving right then and there. If it comes into the child's life because it is thus needed, I think it will sooner and more frequently and more vitally be called on to serve again in that child's life."

"Do you mean there should be no variation from this, none whatever? Remember how many inferior teachers we have."

"I told you what I should wish. In this world we often are compelled to take less than we wish."

*   *   *

"It seems to me that you have defined study, learn, teach, and subject-matter as if they belonged to life, not to school. Is this intentional or have you other definitions that apply to school?"

*   *   *

"Life has been foremost not only here but everywhere else when we have sought the better education. To me education is of life, for life, and by and through life; and life is of and for education. So the saying is true that education is life."

"You spoke of new conceptions of study and learn and subject-matter. What differences do you see between the old and the new as regards these?"

"Chiefly this, as it seems to me. The old conception, seldom found within the past seventy-five years one hundred per cent pure, was this. Childhood is, in itself and apart from adult activities, a waste period. Education as a preparation for adult life is thus a good way of utilizing this otherwise wasted period. To do this we (a) study adult life and see what it needs. After laying aside the things that will be learned without our consideration we take the remainder and organize them into an order suitable for learning. This is a curriculum. (b) We divide this curriculum into suitable portions of 'subject-matter' ('lessons') and assign these (under a penalty) for learning. This with testing named below constitutes 'teaching.' (c) The child undertakes to avoid the penalty by getting to the place where he can show that he has learned. The effort to get to this desired place or state is 'study,' and the typical way is to memorize a printed page. (d) When the child can avoid the penalty by answering our tests, chiefly 'reciting' what he has memorized, we count that he has learned. (e) If we carry the matter far enough we hope that the child will keep what he has thus 'learned' in the 'storehouse of his memory' till the day of need arises, and that he will then look within, choose what he needs, and apply it."

"The whole thing then has in the past been based on an extreme notion of preparation for future living."

"Yes, so it seems to me."

PLASTIC ART IN EDUCATION (1926)   From Willy Levin, "Plastic Art," as quoted in Gertrude Hartman and Ann Shumaker, eds., *Creative Expression* . . . (New York, 1926), pp. 27–29.

Archipenko, the great sculptor, has said very cleverly, "Art begins where Nature ends." These words really express almost entirely my philosophy of art. The impressions we get in our everyday life, worked over in our minds with the help of our senses and our inner self, make the foundation of art. Nature is only a means for us to bring out what is in us.

Before I begin to speak about the creative ability of children and how I help them create, I must say that I am not a professional teacher, but primarily an artist whom life has thrown into a teacher's profession, and very interesting I find, is the study of a child's creative soul. But please overlook it if my technical terms are not professional.

During my five-years' experience with children in clay modeling, I have become convinced that every child can create, and the fewer standards we force upon them the richer will be the creative results obtained. The only standards I recognize for them in using certain materials are: technique, which grows with the child; proportion and movement, when they get to be ten years of age, and form after that age. In short, I give them some crude elements of fundamentals when they are old enough not only to understand but to experience them, and the expression of this living-through of the thing is the creation. A child does not reason, does not recognize rules; it wants to do a thing, it does it. It is the teacher's task to draw out of them just the one right thing which is the creation.

A child see things differently, therefore it expresses itself differently from grownups, it is personal, it is an expressionist; it feels strongly and impulsively, and goes away from nature instinctively, that is, it exaggerates—which really is the aim of all art. To force our conceptions upon children is to suppress them, to kill their imagination, their spontancity, to take away their creative ability: this is what happens in the old school, and what makes the greatest difference between the old and the progressive school in teaching art.

The ability of children to create differs; some are naturally more artistic than others, have natural feeling for proportion, for composition, and so on, due to certain circumstances in life, such as heredity, environment and others.

I also have been asked to tell how I work with the children to get results. This is the hardest thing to do, because it can't be formulated. You have to feel the thing the child wants to do, to think their thoughts, in short to become a child yourself, and to be able to do so, you must have the soul of a child, and unless it is so and only so, you can't get results.

I often have been asked the questions: "Do you give children models to copy?" "Do you tell them what to make?" No, the only help I give in choosing the subject (if they don't come full of ideas themselves) is to go through their class program with them which suggests subjects to the children. Another thing I sometimes do is to let them squeeze the clay and develop the forms suggested by it. In modeling figures (by figures I mean animals as well as human figures) children always begin with the details of the figure and by and by produce the whole. They make the feet first or the head, putting in the eyes, nose, and mouth, which seem to them the most important; even in pottery they often make the cover of a dish before they make the dish. I let the small children go ahead in this way, showing them only how to work the parts together so they don't fall apart in drying. But when they are about nine years old, I ask them to make the whole figure at once, or to produce the biggest part of the figure first. I get this result through the question: "Which is the biggest part of the figure?" They usually say the body, though occasionally I have answers like the head or the feet. Here the question of proportion comes in for the first time. I ask them to compare their own heads with their own bodies, and ask which is larger. When they are about eleven years of age they begin to model figures in movement. I have them make primitive armatures. They continually try out the pose themselves, in order to experience, to feel the movement. The understanding of form-construction grows with the growth of the child's mentality. When I feel that the child can understand form, I explain the construction of the human body to them in an elementary way. I show them the big forms of the body and the joints, to make them understand that twisting or bending of the parts can only be done at the places where joints exist. But they only model movement, not form. I have noticed that children instinctively compose their designs well; they have a natural feeling for balance. They show it mostly in getting their designs into a tile. They experience it still more in modeling groups, in which I encourage them when they are older, as it takes them into composition in a wider sense.

Our materials are clay, which can be fired, and plasteline, which does not harden. In order to preserve the objects modeled in this medium, they have to be cast in plaster of paris. Besides figure work we do a great deal of pottery. We use the Indian Coil method in building by hand, for the children often find their own individual ways. Some who have patience enough learn how to use the primitive Kick Wheel. I fire their pottery and figures when they are technically well made. We put colored glazes on, and the children learn something about changes of materials going through a firing process. I let the little ones paint their clay things with water colors. They learn how to use their brushes on clay, but I seldom fire their work, nor do they glaze it.

By the time the children are eight years old they make finished products. For decoration of these, we use besides colored glazes, underglazes, colored clays, et cetera, and as they grow older, they learn many other techniques of decoration.

In my opinion, the best medium for little children to work in is clay; it hardens enough so it can be painted or varnished. It is very important to make them knead their clay before they begin to model. Besides learning the technique of preparing clay, it develops their finger muscles. For older children clay is advisable only with the purchase of a kiln. It is too disappointing to children who have worked hard at a vase or a bowl or at any other piece of pottery, not to be able to finish the article; that is: to fire it in a kiln, glaze it and fire it again to make it waterproof.

THE SECRETARY OF THE PROGRESSIVE EDUCATION ASSOCIATION EXPLAINS PROGRESSIVE EDUCATION (1927)   From Morton Snyder. "What Is Progressive Education?" National Education Association, *Journal of Proceedings and Addresses* (Washington, D.C., 1927), pp. 235–36.

American education, in harmony with America itself, is changing before our eyes. Indeed, it always will be changing. As new conditions arise, our education must fit young people to meet them; furthermore, it must anticipate future conditions harmful to humanity and prepare young people to prevent these; more important still, it must imagine future conditions helpful to humanity and prepare young people to create these better conditions. It would be as absurd to expect schools to remain as they are at a given moment as to expect children not to mature. An unchanging educational plan would be a denial of education itself, a repudiation of the principle of growth.

The reconstruction under way throughout American education is based upon four fundamental facts. (1) The resources of America make it possible to give each individual the chance best to serve his fellows through the fullest development of his own powers. (2) America turns with growing confidence to education as the natural field for the working out of her humanitarian ideals; from malleable childhood may come a better world. (3) In education, as everywhere else, science has been the chief ally of altruism. The discoveries of the laboratories have made possible the intelligent carrying out of our generous impulses. (4) Human knowledge has increased so rapidly that we must now set up a new definition of the educated person and a new technic for developing such a being.

School, even at its best, it not a natural situation, but is a device created by grownups for the purpose of assisting young people quickly to adjust themselves to "civilization." Educational leaders today are concerned with reducing the artificiality of school to a minimum so that childhood and youth may have the chance for natural growth. There are many experiments to this end, some radical, some cautious. They have this common ideal; they think of school and college as an adventure rather than simply as a discipline; they think of intellectual experience as one of creative thinking rather than of mere learning what others have thought;

they think of the atmosphere and relation of school as that of home and the world rather than that of an institution. This is the spirit in which our newer schools are conceived and administered. Certain characteristics are reasonably clearly defined; they will be found in an increasing number of public and private schools, from kindergarten to university, all over the country.

1. We have come to understand that the schools are for the children, not the children for the schools. We have stopped forcing children into molds and are reorganizing buildings, furnishings, courses of study, methods, and discipline to fit pupils as they are, not as we grownups think they ought to be.

2. A major consideration is health—of body, of mind, of spirit. Buildings and equipment, the daily routine of work and of play, physical examinations and supervision—these assure the first. More sensible requirements and more skilful methods are producing mental health. The substitution of encouragement for despair, of naturalness for fear—this is giving us a spiritual soundness that many of us never knew in our own school days.

3. Naturally, there is freedom—not a license and disorder, just freedom, the same that young people have in any well-managed home. There is freedom to move about, to talk quietly, to ask questions, to give honest answers—to be oneself without fear of being punished. Without this neither the body nor the spirit can grow. But also courtesy and fair play—let us not forget these.

4. Interest has taken the place of dictation. The things studied and the things done are what children may be reasonably expected to want to do, not something that grownups have always required but which bear no relation to children themselves. Consider cube root! Whoever heard of it outside the textbook? What child wants to? Why should he?

5. Profitable, enthusiastic group activity! No more passive learning from a book, sitting still, waiting to be called on and hoping to be overlooked. Today, children work together to accomplish something they all want to see finished—a problem in arithmetic, a play, a piece of construction. Whatever it is, it's co-operative work, not going it alone.

6. But while groups afford the means of discussion, individuals are the real objects of interest. We have learned to accept in school what we have always known outside, that no two people are alike and that it's not only impossible to make them alike, but wrong to try to do so. One is bright, another slow; one a housekeeper, another an artist; one lively, another quiet. Each has a right to be himself, and the school has no right to undertake to make all alike.

7. A most important factor is the new relationship between teachers and pupils. The good teacher is now the one who puts friendliness in place of authority, who secures enthusiasm in place of mere obedience. The good disciplinarian is no longer the master who keeps a roomful still by one look from his eye, but the one who keeps everyone happily busy.

8. Creativeness, the proper expression of the inborn desire to make something. Boys and girls today are encouraged to make, to create—anything, everything, to satisfy their soul's ambitions. It may be a story to a picture, a layercake or a boxtrap, a poem or an automobile. There are two great reasons for this: we shall develop whatever talent there is. And a heart's desire will be satisfied.

9. The world has come to school and school has gone out into the world. No more barren rooms; classrooms have become museums; outside interests are brought to school to be shared with classmates. And school goes downtown, or to the concert, to the art museum, to the park, to the mill, to the woods anywhere where there is something to see and to learn.

10. Esthetics, the arts—call it what you will—beauty has been given a higher seat in the scheme of things. Dramatics and poetry, music in all its forms, including dancing, drawing and painting, modeling, wookwork, jewelry—all have come to stay.

11. The mechanics of school have been reduced to subordinate importance, or, in small schools, largely eliminated. Textbooks, examinations, tests and measurements, marks, promotion, classifications, punishments, penalties assignments, the timetable—these are inconspicuous conveniences of the modern school.

12. An outstanding characteristic of the progressive movement is that parents are as active as teachers. A new spirit of intelligent and helpful co-operation is evident in progressive schools, whether public or private.

But the new education is more than a matter of materials and manners. A common criticism of the old is that there has been so much of accepting information and so little questioning and of thinking. We must train youth to imagine, to think forward, to anticipate conditions, to discard old idols, when need be. This attitude does not disregard the past. The past is accepted as evidence, but is denied the authority of law. Present-day interests receive larger attention. Young people's questions on socialism, pacifism, internationalism, and sex are being intelligently answered, and the questioners given the means and method for coming to sound conclusions. Learning has come to be understood as an experience which involves the creation of something in the mind. The benefits arise from the reality of the enterprise and from the sense of accomplishing something truly worthwhile.

Innovations are not accomplished without criticism. The critics of the new regime say: (1) There is too much emphasis on interest and too little on duty. (2) There is too much freedom and too little control. (3) It puts too much faith in human nature and assumes too much native power among young people. The progressive is not advocating a doctrine of ease or of laxity; he merely believes it better to secure a supreme effort through interest than an indifferent one through sense of duty; the doctrine of interest is not a surrender to ease, but an assurance of zeal. As to freedom, none but the extremest radical concedes youth the right to do as it pleases on all occasions, or credits it with the ability to decide all problems wisely; the liberal favors all the freedom possible at the moment, with more in prospect. As to faith in human nature and its power, the progressive asks merely that school shall not create artificial barriers to the natural development of power.

The new regime has not been in effect long enough to give opportunity for scientific testing of results. Presently we shall have statistical comparisons between the new and the old. But favorable evidence is not wanting. The graduates of progressive elementary schools do well in high school; in the course of events they successfully pass college entrance examinations; finally, they maintain good standing in college. Details and the names of schools and of colleges could be given in support of this statement. The testimony may be summarized in the single generalization, backed by much data, that at every level children who have come through the new schools compare favorably with those from the old.

They compare favorably not only in technical, measurable aspects of education, but in the even more important human values which make up life. They are more selfreliant, with greater initiative and capacity for selfdirection. They are better read and better informed, with more alert powers of reasoning and judgment. Health shows in their faces and in their bearing, inducing naturalness and confidence, enthusiasm and satisfaction. School has become "a real show" and children are finding new joy in attending.

The new ideals are meeting with a growing response from the thoughtful public, made up, as it is, of parents and intelligent laymen, who, having come up through the old regime, desire something better for the children of tomorrow, and of teachers and administrators concerned to grow and to improve their schools. The increasing evidence of this response is found in the numbers of new private schools everywhere springing up, and, more important still, in the changes actually taking place at all levels in our public schools. The process of adjustment moves from the bottom upward, from primary to intermediate, to junior high school, to senior high school. Now the colleges are introducing reforms which are but the application of principles already in effect in the lower schools.

To sum it all up, the new school movement is at once a protest and a vision. It has effectively challenged the authority, the repression, the barrenness of an educational procedure which was at odds with nature and which in practise defeated many of its own purposes. It has created schools in which teachers and students work together happily, under conditions physically and mentally wholesome, in a richly stimulating environment, living in the fullest sense the life of today to be ready for tomorrow.

"THE NEW ARTICLES OF FAITH" (1928)   From Harold Rugg and Ann Shumaker, *The Child-Centered School* (New York, 1928), pp. 55–67.

---

i

FREEDOM

And the first of these articles of faith is freedom. "Free the legs, the arms, the larynx of a child," say these advocates of the new education, "and you have taken the first step towards freeing his mind and spirit."

Hence the revolution in school furniture, schedules of work, all the paraphernalia of administration. Fixed seats nailed to the floor, lock-step precision, rigidity, conformity, are disappearing. In their places are coming the informal, intimate atmosphere—the air of happy, cheerful living. Light, movable tables and chairs that may be shoved aside at any time to make room for work or play; children moving freely about, talking with one another, leaving the room to go to other parts of the building relatively at their own discretion. The fixed, elaborate machinery of mass education is being abandoned: large classes; emphasis upon grades; housing in stereotyped, barrack-like buildings; adherence to strict time schedules; the oppressive silence of restraint; the labored compulsion—all the stringent coercion of the old order is passing.

The new freedom reveals itself, therefore, in an easier, more natural group life. At great expense to itself it maintains mere corporal's guards of classes—ten, twelve, fifteen, rarely over twenty pupils—in sharp contrast to the huge regiments of the formal, graded school. Thus the formal question-and-answer recitation is giving way to the free interchange of thought in group conferences and progress through individual work.

Freedom to develop naturally, to be spontaneous, unaffected, and unselfconscious, is, therefore, the first article of faith.

What is this new freedom based upon? Nothing less than the reorientation of the entire school around the child. These schools are child-centered institutions in contrast to the teacher-centered and principal-centered schools of the conventional order. They believe that the ability to govern one's self grows only through the practice of self-government. They have learned wisely the lesson of democracy in the western world; namely, that no people, however potentially able, will learn how to carry on its collective affairs except under freedom to practice self-government. Wherever adult societies have imposed democratic forms of government on a people uneducated in democracy, chaos has resulted. Throughout a century of national history in America our schools have adopted the form and the catch slogans of democracy, but never its true technique.

In this respect, however, another day has come in the new schools. These schools believe that boys and girls should share in their own government, in the planning of the program, in the administering of the curriculum, in conducting the life of the school. In the elementary division of some of these schools, during an informal morning discussion period, children, with the teacher as a wise but inconspicuous adult member of the group, consider together what they are to undertake during the day. The routine needs of the school, as well as the lesson assignments, the planning of excursions and exhibits, and the criticism of reports are taken over by the pupils. This is, indeed, a revolution in educational procedure and stands in sharp contrast to the conventional mode of conducting a school.

The difference in amount of work done by teachers and pupils respectively under these two plans of work—the pupil-initiating plan vs. the teacher-initiating plan—is conspicuous. In the formal school of today the teacher still does the thinking, planning, and initiating. Pupils are passive, quiescent, generally uninterested if not actively antagonistic. Learning is at a low ebb, if not at a standstill. In the child-centered school, however, pupils are alive, active, working hard, inventing, organizing, contributing original ideas, assembling materials, carrying out enterprises. As individuals and as social groups pupils grow, and they grow in the capacity to govern themselves, to organize machinery for handling their collective affairs, as well as in individual capacity for creative self-expression. So it is that the true theory of democracy is being put into practice in these new schools.

This centering of responsibility and initiative in the pupil brings into the forefront the child's own needs. His immediate interests are to furnish the starting point of education, according to the new schools. But, even of the most rebellious reformers, few advocate that the entire work of the school be based solely upon these naïve and spontaneous interests of children. However, the last twenty-five years of experimentation have undoubtedly contributed no more revolutionary articles of faith than that involved in this reorientation of the school about the child.

Freedom, pupil initiative—therefore, the active school.

Naturally, from the free atmosphere in which pupil initiative plays the chief role it is but a next step to pupil activity. In these free, child-centered schools, therefore, pupils are active—physically active, mentally active, artistically active. There is a large amount of actual physical exertion, of overt bodily movement, of a wide variety of sensory contacts, of the type of energy-release which is ordinarily designated as play. Hence the terms, "activity schools," "play schools," and so on.

Education is to be based on child experience—experience not only in the physical sense but in the intellectual and emotional sense too. Thus do these child-centered schools want experience to be real. They depend as little as possible upon described experience. The wiser among their leaders know, of course, that in the adult world much real experience is abstract, described, vicarious, verbal. Therefore the child who is growing toward adulthood will appropriate to his uses an increasingly larger amount of described experience. In the higher reaches of the school, indeed, many described experiences must be made the very center of educational development. However, as far as possible, and predominantly in the lower years of the child-centered schools, real life is reproduced in physical miniature. Excursions are made into the neighborhood, the community. The scholastic environment is extended outward to include *realia* of a variegated sort, and within the school itself plants, animals, tools, materials, machines, are provided to stimulate activity and to give rise to interests which will require activity in their development. Much free play is permitted for the experiences in self-direction it affords.

Now the most deep-seated tendency in human life is movement, impulse, activity. The new schools, therefore, are experimenting vigorously with this fundamental psychological law—that the basis of all learning is reaction. That they are making a contribution is unquestioned.

In the formal schools the conditions of true growth were exactly reversed. One found outward quiet, orderliness, apparent concentration, little physical movement. Actually, however, this condition was one of restlessness, of much inner activity—a continual mutiny against the aims of the school. The iron rule of the school succeeded only in inhibiting the outward symptoms of inattention. There was fidgeting, uneducative scattering of interest and attention, and little conscious reflection on the matters in hand.

The new schools, with freedom of activity and movement, with apparent lack of concentration, produce nevertheless a much more truly educative absorption. The newer education regards the active child as the truly growing child. Not activity for activity's sake—energy exploding in random movements—but activity which is a growing toward something more mature, a changing for the better. The true criterion of educative activity is prolonged attention and concentrated effort. Such then is the activity which the new education writes into its articles of faith.

Freedom, not restraint.

Pupil initiative, not teacher initiative.

The active, not the passive, school.

There is a fourth new article of faith—child interest as the orienting center of the school program.

In the formal schools, even in those of today, the program of the child's education is organized about school subjects. Not so in the new schools. We find a new educational vocabulary exponential of a unique educative program. Compare the schedules of the new and the old schools. What a difference! The logically arranged subjects of the past—reading, writing, arithmetic, spelling, geography, history—are replaced by projects, units of work, creative work periods, industrial arts, creative music, story hour, informal group conferences, and other vastly intriguing enterprises.

This curriculum does not look well on paper. It is a chaos of irregular time allotments. School principals might have a difficult time trying to fit the orderly movement of a large school into it. But it does give promise of active learning.

The new school is setting up a program of work which has a personal connection with the immediate life of the child. It starts from his needs and interests. The units of the new program approximate as nearly as possible what to the children are real-life situations. Hence the new school organizes its program around the centers of interest rather than around academic subjects. Wherever school subjects, however, coincide with life needs, then the new centers of interest coincide with the old school subjects; for example, the subjects of reading and creative music, the story hour. But because the formal school subjects were the product of academic research interests, most of them do not coincide with life interests, either of children or of adults. Hence in the new educational order they must go. This new plan of organizing the curriculum around units of pupil activity gives greater promise of widespreading, educational achievement for the pupil than does the dry, intellectualized, logical arrangement of subjects-to-be-learned of the old school. It is vitalized by interesting and purposeful activity that has an intimate connection with the child's personal life.

That the new schools are evolving an educational program in which school subjects are rejected in favor of broader and more integrative centers of work is illustrated also in the tendency to organize materials in a few broad departments of knowledge. The old school organized knowledge into many minute, disparate, academic departments. In the upper grades of some of the new schools the initiating center of organization is the interest of the child in some contemporary institution or problem. In the lower grades the focus is the immediate school scene. In the higher grades the emphasis shifts to adult society; in the foreground always stand the fundamental movements or trends, the crucial institutions or problems of contemporary life.

All this does not mean that the new school entirely avoids school subjects, but the subjects in these schools differ materially from those of the formal school. The new-school subjects represent new departmentalizations of knowledge which include a broad view of race experience rather than mere devitalized definitions and long lists of factual enumerations. They are concerned at bottom with big concepts, themes, movements, that explain broad, fundamental phases of human life.

The old school spent its time and energy in drilling pupils into a state of passable efficiency in minimal essentials. The new school treats these minimal essentials, which are largely skills, as by-products of the educative situation. Usually it has succeeded in teaching them much more adequately than the old school, and in less time.

v

CREATIVE SELF-EXPRESSION

"I would have a child say not, 'I know,' but, 'I have experienced.' "

Education as conformity *vs.* education as creative self-expression, adaptation and adjustment *vs.* creative experience—these are some of the phrases which are recurring with accumulating momentum in the discussions of the new education.

We find as sharp a contrast in theory between the old and the new at this point in our analysis as in our consideration of other aspects. The spirit of the old school was centered about social adjustment, adaptation to the existing order. The aim of conventional education was social efficiency. Growth was seen as increasing power to conform, to acquiesce to a schooled discipline; maturity was viewed from the standpoint of successful compliance with social demands.

In the new school, however, it is the creative spirit from within that is encouraged, rather than conformity to a pattern imposed from without. The success of the new school has been startling in eliciting self-expression in all of the arts, in discovering a marvelously creative youth. The child as artist, poet, composer, is coming into his own.

This success is due not so much to the changed viewpoint concerning the place of art in education as to the whole new theory of self-expression, the emphasis on the place of creative originality in life. Art in the new school is permitted; in the old it was imposed. The new school assumes that every child is endowed with the capacity to express himself, and that this innate capacity is immensely worth cultivating. The pupil is placed in an atmosphere conducive to self-expression in every aspect. Some will create with words, others with light. Some will express themselves through the body in the dance; others will model, carve, shape their ideas in plastic materials. Still others will find expression through oral language, and some through an integrated physical, emotional, and dramatic gesture. But whatever the route, the medium, the materials—each one has some capacity for expression.

The artist in Everyman's child is being discovered, not only in the unusual, the gifted, the genius; the lid of restraint is being lifted from the child of the common man in order that he may come to his own best self-fulfillment. The new schools are providing "drawing-out" environments in sharp contrast to the "pouring-in" environments of the old.

Art in the new schools is naïve, neo-primitive. The child is permitted to set his own standards as he works. The "masters" are not set out to be worshiped respectfully—they are admired in the frank and critical spirit of intimate companionship. Appreciation of the finished works of genius is best built up, say the new schools, by first encouraging the creative products of the child's own pen, voice, brush. The emphasis is not upon finished work, skill, and technical perfection, but upon the release of the child's creative capacities, upon growth in his power to express his own unique ideas naturally and freely, whatever the medium.

✳ ✳ ✳

The leaders of our schools are confronted by no more important and overwhelming problem than that of providing an environment by which each child can learn to live with others and yet retain his personal identity. To live with others, learn how to adjust himself to them, and yet grow in the confident knowledge that he, like each of them, is a unique individuality, a rare personality; to live with others and yet grow in the assurance that he too is superior, that he, and he alone, is distinctive in some trait or traits and that he has something unique to contribute to the groups in which he lives. How are the new and the old schools trying to solve this problem?

The old school, with its mass-education machinery, seemed to treat children in social groups, to develop social attitudes, but in reality it sacrificed the individual to mythical group needs. Social contacts during school hours were dominated by an arbitrary authority—the teacher—and had to conform to a rigid formality in order that discipline might be maintained. The old school, therefore, left the child entirely unaided in coping with social situations. Under mass education—hyper-intellectual, hyper-individualistic—with pupils isolated in seats, no opportunity was offered to practice cooperative living except in the undirected out-of-school contacts. The child was not assisted in learning to work effectively with a group at a common interest. A false notion of individuality was erected; namely, that superiority could be asserted only through personal competition. The old school over-emphasized competition because it was a convenient, effective, and inexpensive device for attaining greater effort from pupils. However, it was often used at the cost of successful social living.

The new school, on the other hand, encourages the child to be a distinct personality, an individualist, to believe in his ability—but of course not to an unjustifiable degree. It sets up situations which provide constant practice in cooperative living. It encourages activities in which he can make a personal contribution to group enterprises; in which he has social experiences, graded to fit his level of social development; in which he feels himself an accepted and respected member of a society of which he himself approves.

The new school bridges the gap, therefore, between the development of individuality on the one hand and successful social participation on the other by insisting that the true development of the individual and the fulfillment of personality are best attained as one expresses himself most successfully and adequately with others and *toward* others.

How does the new school propose to secure this cooperative endeavor?

It does so by means of a wide variety of group activities. Dramatics which require concerted effort toward a common goal; assemblies through which frequent interchange of mutually interesting ideas takes place; student committees and clubs managing student affairs; miniature social organizations and group games—these are some of the social situations which the new school deliberately encourages. The group dance also is coming into its own as a vehicle for more than rhythmic physical development. Indeed, rhythmics gives promise of usurping the place in the lower school that has formerly been given to competitive athletics. Active experience in grace and physical poise, as an agency for the education of personality of each and every individual, is the aim, rather than development of a few stellar performers with the mass remaining mere passive, untransformed observers.

The new school has no extracurricular activities. These group activities are a regular and important part of school life—they are not a side issue indulged in at the end of the day or week as unrelated recreation or relief from the real business of the school.

Again, where the old school maintained a noisy silence as the ideal schoolroom atmosphere, the new removes the ban from speech, encourages communication as a vehicle for social understanding and personal development. Indeed the new school has gone so far in this respect as to be accused at times of being garrulous. However, it is well known that practice in the free use of language, with guidance, helps to develop qualities desirable for successful social living. Fluent, natural speech is the basis for effective self-expression and mutual understanding.

In ways like these the new school is evolving its informal real-life organization, encouraging common aims and purposes, the interpenetration of minds, producing in the school a life of happy intimacy—creating a "wholesome medium for the most complete living."[1]

JOHN DEWEY ON PROGRESSIVE EDUCATION AND THE SCIENCE OF EDUCATION (1928)   From John Dewey, "Progressive Education And The Science of Education." *Progressive Education*, vol. V, pp. 197–204.

 W hat is Progressive Education? What is the meaning of experiment in education, of an experimental school? What can such schools as are represented here do for other schools, in which the great, indefinitely the greater, number of children receive their instruction and discipline? What can be rightfully expected from the work of these progressive schools in the way of a contribution to intelligent and stable educational practice; especially what can be expected in the way of a contribution to educational theory? Are there common elements, intellectual and moral, in the various undertakings here represented? Or is each school going its own way, having for its foundation the desires and preferences of the particular person who happens to be in charge? Is experimentation a process of trying anything at least once, of putting into intermediate effect any "happy thought" that comes to mind, or does it rest upon principles which are adopted at least as a working hypothesis? Are actual results consistently observed and used to check an underlying hypothesis so that the latter develops intellectually? Can we be content if from the various progressive schools there emanate suggestions which radiate to other schools to enliven and vitalize their work; or should we demand that out of the cooperative undertakings of the various schools a coherent body of educational principles shall gradually emerge as a distinctive contribution to the theory of education?

Such questions as these come to mind on the occasion of such a gathering as this. The interrogations expressed are far from all inclusive. They are one-sided, and intentionally so. They glide over the important questions that may be asked about

[1]Tippett, James S., and Others. *Curriculum Making in an Elementary School*, (Boston, 1927), p. 8.

what these schools are actually doing for the children who attend them; how they are meeting their primary responsibility that to the children themselves and their families and friends. The one-sided emphasis is, as was said, intentional. The questions are shaped to take another slant; to direct attention to the intellectual contribution to be expected of progressive schools. The reasons for this one-sidedness are close at hand. It is natural that in your own exchange of experiences and ideas the question slurred over should be prominent. And that pupils in progressive schools are themselves progressing, and that the movement to establish more progressive schools is progressing, I have no doubt. Nor do I think that the old question, once a bugaboo, as to what will happen when the pupils go to college or out into life, is any longer an open one. Experience has proved that they give a good account of themselves; so it has seemed to me that the present is a fitting time to raise the intellectual, the theoretical problem of the relation of the progressive movement to the art and philosophy of education.

The query as to common elements in the various schools receives an easy answer up to a certain point. All of the schools, I take it for granted, exhibit as compared with traditional schools, a common emphasis upon respect for individuality and for increased freedom; a common disposition to build upon the nature and experience of the boys and girls that come to them, instead of imposing from without external subject-matter and standards. They all display a certain atmosphere of informality, because experience has proved that formalization is hostile to genuine mental activity and to sincere emotional expression and growth. Emphasis upon activity as distinct from passivity is one of the common factors. And again I assume that there is in all of these schools a common unusual attention to the human factors, to normal social relations, to communication and intercourse which is like in kind to that which is found in the great world beyond the school doors; that all alike believe that these normal human contacts of child with child and of child with teacher are of supreme educational importance, and that all alike disbelieve in those artificial personal relations which have been the chief factor in isolation of schools from life. So much at least of common spirit and purpose we may assume to exist. And in so far we already have the elements of a distinctive contribution to the body of educational theory: respect for individual capacities, interests and experience; enough external freedom and informality at least to enable teachers to become acquainted with children as they really are; respect for self-initiated and self-conducted learning; respect for activity as the stimulus and centre of learning; and perhaps above all belief in social contact, communication, and cooperation upon a normal human plane as all-enveloping medium.

These ideas constitute no mean contribution: It is a contribution to educational theory as well as to the happiness and integrity of those who come under the influence of progressive schools. But the elements of the contribution are general, and like all generalities subject to varied and ambiguous interpretations. They indicate the starting point of the contribution that progressive schools may make to the theory or science of education, but only the starting point. Let us then reduce our questions to a single one and ask, What is the distinctive relation of progressive education to the science of education, understanding by science a body of verified facts and tested principles which may give intellectual guidance to the practical operating of schools?

Unless we beg the question at the outset assuming that it is already known just what education is, just what are its aims and what are its methods, there is nothing false nor extravagant in declaring that at the present time different sciences of education are not only possible but also much needed. Of course such a statement goes contrary to the idea that science by its very nature is a single and universal system of truths. But this idea need not frighten us. Even in the advanced sciences, like those of mathematics and physics, advance is made by entertaining different points of view and hypotheses, and working upon different theories. The sciences present no fixed and closed orthodoxy.

And certainly in such an undertaking as education, we must employ the word "science" modestly and humbly; there is no subject in which the claim to be strictly scientific is more likely to suffer from pretence, and none in which it is more dangerous to set up a rigid orthodoxy, a standardized set of beliefs to be accepted by all. Since there is no one thing which is beyond question, education, and since there is no likelihood that there will be until society and hence schools have reached a dead monotonous uniformity of practice and aim, there cannot be one single science. As the working operations of schools differ, so must the intellectual theories devised from those operations. Since the practice of progressive education differs from that of the traditional schools, it would be absurd to suppose that the intellectual formulation and organization which fits one type will hold for the other. To be genuine, the science which springs from schools of the older and traditional type, must work upon that foundation, and endeavor to reduce its subject-matter and methods to principles such that their adoption will eliminate waste, conserve resources, and render the existing type of practice more effective. In the degree in which progressive schools mark a departure in their emphasis from old standards, as they do in freedom, individuality, activity, and a cooperative social medium the intellectual organization, the body of facts and principles which they may contribute must of necessity be different. At most they can only occasionally borrow from the "science" that is evolved on the basis of a different type of practice, and they can even then borrow only what is appropriate to their own special aims and processes. To discover how much is relevant is of course a real problem. But this is a very different thing from assuming that the methods and results obtained under traditional scholastic conditions form the standard of science to which progressive schools must conform.

For example it is natural and proper that the theory of the practices found in traditional schools should set great store by tests and measurements. This theory reflects modes of school administration in which marks, grading, classes, and promotions are important. Measurement of I.Qs and achievements are ways of making these operations more efficient. It would not be hard to show that need for classification underlies the importance of testing for I.Qs. The aim is to establish a norm. The norm, omitting statistical refinements, is essentially an average found by taking a sufficiently large number of persons. When this average is found, any given child can be rated. He comes up to it, falls below it, or exceeds it, by an assignable quantity. Thus the application of the results make [s] possible a more precise classification than did older methods which were by comparison hit and miss. But what has all this to do with schools where individuality is a primary object of consideration, and wherein the so-called "class" becomes a grouping for social purposes and wherein diversity of ability and experience rather than uniformity is prized?

In the averaging and classificatory scheme some special capacity, say in music, dramatics, drawing, mechanical skill or any other art, appears only one along with a large number of other factors, or perhaps does not appear at all in the list of things tested. In any case, it figures in the final result only as smoothed down, ironed out, against a large number of other factors. In the progressive school, such an ability is a distinctive resource to be utilized in the cooperative experience of a group; to level it down by averaging it with other qualitites until it simply counts in assigning to the individual child a determinate point on a curve is simply hostile to the aim and spirit of progressive schools.

Nor need the progressive educator be unduly scared by the idea that science is constituted by quantitative results, and, as it is often said, that whatever exists can be measured, for all subjects pass through a qualitative state before they arrive at a quantitative one; and if this were the place it could be shown that even in the mathematical sciences quantity occupies a secondary place as compared with ideas of order which verge on the qualitative. At all events, quality of activity and of consequence is more important for the teacher than any quantitative element. If this fact prevents the development of a certain kind of science, it may be unfortunate. But the educator cannot sit down and wait till there are methods by which quality may be reduced to quantity; he must operate here and now. If he can organize his qualitative processes and results into some connected intellectual form, he is really advancing scientific method much more than if, ignoring what is actually most important, he devotes his energies to such unimportant by-products as may now be measured.

Moreover, even if it be true that everything which exists could be measured—if only we knew how—that which does not exist cannot be measured. And it is no paradox to say that the teacher is deeply concerned with what does not exist. For a progressive school is primarily concerned with growth, with a moving and changing process, with transforming existing capacities and experiences; what already exists by way of native endowment and past achievement is subordinate to what it may become. Possibilities are more important than what already exists, and knowldege of the latter counts only in its bearing upon possibilities. The place of measurement of achievements as a theory of education is very different in a static educational system from what it is in one which is dynamic, or in which the ongoing process of growing is the important thing.

The same principle applies to the attempt to determine objectives and select subject-matter of studies by wide collection and accurate measurement of data. If we are satisfied upon the whole with the aims and processes of existing society, this method is appropriate. If you want schools to perpetuate the present order, with at most an elimination of waste and with such additions as enable it to do better what it is already doing, then one type of intellectual method or "science" is indicated. But if one conceives that a social order different in quality and direction from the present is desirable and that schools should strive to educate with social change in view by producing individuals not complacent about what already exists, and equipped with desires and abilities to assist in transforming it, quite a different method and content is indicated for educational science.

While what has been said may have a tendency to relieve educators in progressive schools from undue anxiety about the criticism that they are unscientific—a criticism levelled from the point of view of theory appropriate to schools of quite a different purpose and procedure—it it not intended to exempt them from responsibilty for contributions of an organized, systematic, intellectual quality. The contrary is the case. All new and reforming movements pass through a stage in which what is most evident is a negative phase, one of protest, of devation, and innovation. It would be surprising indeed if this were not true of the progressive educational movement. For instance, the formality and fixity of traditional schools seemed oppressive, restrictive. Hence in a school which departs from these ideals and methods, freedom is at first most naturally conceived as removal of artificial and benumbing restrictions. Removal, abolition are, however, negative things, so in time it comes to be seen that such freedom is no end in itself, nothing to be satisifed with and to stay by, but marks at most an opportunity to do something of a positive and constructive sort.

Now I wonder whether this earlier and more negative phase of progressive education has not upon the whole run its course, and whether the time has not arrived in which these schools are undertaking a more constructively organized function. One thing is sure: in the degree in which they enter upon organized constructive work, they are bound to make definite contributions to building up the theoretical or intellectual side of education. Whether this be called science or philosophy of education, I for one, care little; but if they do not intellectually organize their own work, while they may do much in making the lives of the children committed to them more joyous and more vital, they contribute only incidental scraps to the science of education.

The word organization has been freely used. This word suggests the nature of the problem. Organization and administration are words associated together in the traditional scheme, hence organization conveys the idea of something external and set. But reaction from this sort of organization only creates a demand for another sort. Any genuine intellectual organization is flexible and moving, but it does not lack its own internal principles of order and continuity. An experimental school is under the temptation to improvise its subject-matter. It must take advantage of unexpected events and turn to account unexpected questions and interests. Yet if it permits improvisation to dictate its course, the result is a jerky, discontinuous movement which works against the possibility of making any important contribution to educational subject-matter. Incidents are momentary, but the use made of them should not be momentary or short-lived. They are to be brought within the scope of a developing whole of content and purpose, which is a whole because it has continuity and consecutiveness in its parts. There is no single subject-matter which all schools must adopt, but in every school there should be some significant subject-matters undergoing growth and formulation.

An illustration may help make clearer what is meant. Progressive schools set store by individuality, and sometimes it seems to be thought that orderly organization of subject-matter is hostile to the needs of students in their individual character. But individuality is something developing and to be continuously attained, not something given all at once and ready-made. It is found only in life-history, in its continuing growth; it is, so to say, a career and not just a fact discoverable at a particular cross section of life. It is quite possible for teachers to make such a fuss over individual children, worrying about their peculiarities, their likes and dislikes, their weaknesses and failures, so that they miss perception of real individuality, and indeed tend to adopt methods which show no faith in the power of individuality. A child's individuality cannot be found in what he does or in what he consciously likes at a given moment; it can be found only in the connected course of his actions. Consciousness of desire and purpose can be genuinely attained only toward the close of some fairly prolonged sequence of activities. Consequently some organization of subject-matter reached through a serial or consecutive course of doings, held together within the unity of progressively growing occupation or project, is the only means which corresponds to real individuality. So far is organization from being hostile to the principle of individuality.

Thus much of the energy that sometimes goes to thinking about individual children might better be devoted to discovering some worthwhile activity and to arranging the conditions under which it can be carried forward. So far is the principle of working toward organization of knowledge not hostile to the principles of progressive education that the latter cannot perform its functions without reaching out into such organization.

An exaggerated illustration, amounting to a caricature, may perhaps make the point clearer. Suppose there is a school in which pupils are surrounded with a wealth of material objects, apparatus, and tools of all sorts. Suppose they are simply asked what they would like to do and then told in effect to "go to it," the teacher keeping hands—and mind, too—off. What are they going to do? What assurance is there that what they do is anything more than the expression, and exhaustion, of a momentary impulse and interest? The supposition does not, you may say, correspond to any fact. But what are the implications of the opposite principle? Where can we stop as we get away from the principle contained in the illustration? Of necessity—and this is as true of the traditional school as of a progressive—the start, the first move, the initial impulse in action, must proceed from the pupil. You can lead a horse to water but you can't make him drink. But whence comes his idea of what to do? That must come from what he has already heard or seen; or from what he sees some other child doing. It comes as a suggestion from beyond himself, from the environment, he being not an originator of the idea and purpose but a vehicle through which his surroundings past and present suggest something to him. That such suggestions are likely to be chance ideas, soon exhausted, is highly probable. I think observation will show that when a child enters upon a really fruitful and consecutively developing activity, it is because, and in as far as, he has previously engaged in some complex and gradually unfolding activity which has left him a question he wishes to prove further or with the idea of some piece of work still to be accomplished to bring his occupation to completion. Otherwise he is at the mercy of chance suggestion, and chance suggestions are not likely to lead to anything significant or fruitful. . . .

I hardly need remind you that I have definitely limited the field of discussion to one point: the relation of progressive education to the development of a science of education. As I began with questions, I end with one: Is not the time here when the progressive movement is sufficiently established so that it may now consider the intellectual contribution which it may make to the art of education, to the art which is the most difficult and the most important of all human arts?

A CONTRIBUTION TO A SYMPOSIUM: "THE NEW EDUCATION TEN YEARS AFTER" (1930)   From Margaret Naumburg, "The Crux of Progressive Education," *The New Republic,* vol. LXII, pp. 145–46.

The new attitude in education is not a denial of the living values inherent in the past, but an attempt to refocus education from the standpoint of the present. It is now beginning to be recognized that education should not be concerned with the mere accretion of information. This truth has been forced upon us by the unmanageable accumulation of facts that science has poured into our laps in one generation. No human lap, it was soon found, was large enough to hold all the data concerning any single subject in the world of today. So man was forced at last to realize that children could no longer be taught in school to carry bulging loads of irrelevant facts. These had then, of necessity, to be thrown overboard, so far as education is concerned, and relegated to their proper place as one of the instruments of existence but not as an end in themselves. As a second step, the world began, in the light of modern science, to seek again for the meaning and purpose of existence and the relative place of man in this unexpected and unexplored conglomerate of worlds.

In short, education is being forced back to its essential function of dealing with human life in all its fluid forms. Immediately, then, the emphasis shifts. If life, more life, is to be the core of education, school organization and curriculum must also be shifted to a subordinate place. Individual children, in all their human variety, must be the living center of our changing schools, and the crux of the problem of our new education moves from controlling the machinery of organization and the collection of facts to creating a living organism, a new society, within the school itself. Such transformation only becomes possible as we begin to study and understand the interaction between the life of the individual and that of the group. This is the essential problem of the new education. And the degree of socialization or individualization current in each country must be balanced by the introduction of the opposite approach.

America's coming-of-age has had to be achieved through the growth of group consciousness. A series of interlocking social, civic, business and cultural organizations has sustained the practical needs and spiritual hunger of widespread millions. Just because America is so group-minded, any questioning as to the positive value of this constant and limited herd life is sure to be a source of irritation. We are still so imbued with a purely group psychology, so completely identified with mass action and reaction, that it is not possible even for our leaders to be aware how typically American this is. Unable to see ourselves as others do, we can scarcely expect to realize how deeply our group ways separate us from the crystallized individualism of Europe.

We may now be in the throes of growing up, but America as a whole is not self-conscious enough to guess it. She faces Europe today with the false pride of a superior adult among a crowd of impractical children. The American bond salesman, with his social evenings of radio talks, prize fights and Kiwanis gatherings, would merely scoff at the suggestion that America had something to learn before it could catch up to the integrated and independent "I" psychology of the European. Our instinctive faith in the power of groups to change the face of the world is still so unchallenged that we are incapable, as a nation, of realizing the strength that may yet lie in a more individualized life.

Since we are a nation of doers, it is much easier to discover the concrete objectives of our many group movements than any conscious formulation of the values from which they spring. For us, activity is more sure and clear than motive. We are generally too busy fostering the factions and subfactions of our own pet organizations to have time to be concerned with the why and the whither. And that is just where many Europeans achieve detachment. They are able to consider more fearlessly and realistically the significance of values. They dare more often to discuss the uniqueness or limitations of their respective countries, even though they may still prefer their own to ours. To many a Spaniard, Frenchman or German such questions exist as vital problems, to be grappled with thoroughly in order to help the growth and development of their own land, This far less true in America, where economic prosperity has deluded us into an ignorant assurance in fields where Europe is still our superior.

Since the War, many of the leading spirits of Europe have turned with inquiry and concern toward America. Recent economic and social changes have made them aware of the inadequacy of their more individualistic approach to life. And this right-about-face is most obvious in the attitude of progressive leaders in the new education in Germany and Austria. So conscious are these educators, struggling to democratize their schools, of our American development in social education, that they are making their schools programs more concrete, according to the principles of the "Project Method." They are also increasing our type of self-initiated group activities, in order to combat what they regard as the peculiarly nationalistic individualism of their pupils.

It is almost impossible for those who have not recently visited these schools to realize the change that is taking place there. In Germany and Austria the break with the regime has allowed the mass to split off into many separate and self-assertive factions. There is, in consequence, much eagerness now to take over and adopt our native outlets of social response, as a method of rechanneling the marked individualism of European youth.

To Professor Dewey, of course, all Europe turns for an authentic and complete expression of this socialized concept of education. Dr. Dewey has given the perfect formulation of the American ideal of group consciousness. While he has in the past said relatively little as to the role of individualism in the play of this group life, he has, in a recent series of articles in The New Republic, taken a firm and unmistakable stand as to the relation of individualism to the society of today and tomorrow, though he reiterates his faith in group consciousness as the lever of our future social state.

For Dr. Dewey, individualism can never be that condition of matured and separate growth still discoverable in the old culture of Europe; nor can it apparently be expressed for him in the germinating strength of those who spend their lives in such seclusion as brings forth art and science for the benefit of society as well as of themselves. For to him the individualism of the past is inevitably tied to the laissez-faire economics of Big Business; and this he dismisses briefly as unproductive to the group of our future social order. The new individualism as he foresees it is something quite different. "Assured and integrated individuality," he says, "is the product of social relationships and publicly acknowledged functions."

Here Dr. Dewey is being the American of Americans. Is this the best that the future holds for a more complete and integrated individualism? A dull and gloomy picture, this technological utopia, to those of us who still hope for a richer and socially balanced individualism—the flowering of a more equitable society. In this new world, if man is no longer pitted against man in the purely economic struggle for existence, man will vie with man to create and construct for others as well as himself. A more integrated society would give fuller life to its people; and more highly integrated individuals would in return add strength and power to their own social group. This process of correlating the individual and society would not remain, as in the past, one of conflict and opposition, but would be an opportunity for mutual sustenance. To reduce the power of centered individual development is ultimately to reduce the strength of society. For it is precisely these cross currents of force, derived from the impacts and interactions of groups and individuals, that bring forth visions and build new worlds for the future.

In his essay on Don Quixote and Hamlet, the Spanish writer, Salvador de Madariaga, has admirably stated the extremes of conflict that the individual faces in the society of all ages. He takes Don Quixote as the typical Spaniard, "because he seeks to impress his world on the world," and Hamlet as the typical Englishman, "because he feels in his inner self the pressure of the community." "While the activity of Don Quixote, unused by social life, manifests itself in adventures, outwardly moving spirals which end in falls and disaster and nothingness, the passivity of Hamlet, imposed on him by social life, manifests itself in soliloquies, inwardly moving spirals which screw themselves into him a quest seeking his soul's mystery. And as in both cases there is a lack of balance between the conflicting claims of the individual and society, both the Spanish individual who tyrannizes society and the English individual whom society tyrannizes, go through the world with wistfulness in their eyes."

But this wistfulness exists in the eyes of individuals throughout the world, of all ages and all times, when they come into conflict with the demands of their social group. To ignore this as the essence of human life seems a puzzling omission in Dr. Dewey's description of his uniformly responsive individualism of the future.

When Senor Madariaga has aligned the Spanish nature with Don Quixote and the English with Hamlet, he has universalized two opposing types that roam the world. Originally, perhaps, pure representatives of racial or national attitudes, they have a wider significance today. For the speeding up of the world contacts has reduced the barrier of time and space, and now makes it necessary for us to recognize all types reacting in society, in terms of their human rather than their national aspects.

The crux of education lies, as I have said, in the balance of individual and group values. For the immediate future, the European educator will find that his problem is to adjust the individual to the values of group life; whereas for the American, the problem will be to avoid too great emphasis on group life, and develop an individualism that is socially responsive.

Progressive Education—Practice

"HABIT CLINICS" FOR PRE-SCHOOL CHILDREN (1922)   From Douglas A. Thom, "Habit Clinics for Children of the Pre-School Age," *American Journal of Psychiatry*, vol. LXXIX, pp. 31–36.

The function of the habit clinic is to deal with those children who are developing during the pre-school age—that is, between the ages of two and five years—undesirable methods of meeting the daily problems with which they are confronted, to further the formation of habits that will tend toward the proper development of the child and its best interest, to determine in so far as possible the basis of undesirable habits and unhealthy methods of reaction, and to institute proper training and treatment to overcome such habits. In brief, the habit clinic has for its objective the healthy development of the mental aspect of the child's life, beginning at a time when methods of prevention rather than of cure can be utilized.

We do not feel it necessary to seek justification for the organization of these clinics in some vague, ill-defined hope that they may tend toward the prevention of mental disease; we feel that their existence is justified by the immediate results obtained. A neurotic child or one struggling with some undesirable habit problem, who is finding it difficult to make early adaptations and to face every-day problems in a normal, healthy manner, may very easily become the dominant member of the household and not infrequently be the direct or indirect cause of much family strife. All too frequently such a child becomes the economic hazard or the social menace that eventually leads to the disintegration of the home. Such a child not only demands, but usually gets, a disproportionate share of the parents' time, to the neglect of the other children and their consequent jealousy, envy, and resentment. Although no claim is made at this time that there is any relation between these undesirable habits in childhood and the mental breakdowns of later life, it is not difficult to see that these infantile reactions closely resemble the psychoneurotic manifestations in adult life and that a fundamental lack of inhibitions may be the dominating characteristic in a delinquent career.

We all appreciate that the success or failure of the individual to adapt himself in a manner satisfactory to those with whom he is associated may depend upon numerous and varied factors, all very intricate and involved and frequently closely interwoven with one another—bad bodily health dependent, perhaps, upon some simple problem of nutrition or an improper balance between the glands of internal secretion, a nervous system incapable of functioning in a normal manner, and the less well-defined inherent defects that prevent the normal development of the instinctive and emotional life of the individual.

Although one or more of the foregoing factors may be present in a great majority of the cases that are "failing to make the grade," we cannot ignore the fact that often the stumbling block is not within the individual himself, but in the environment in which he is reared—that there is a group of cases, however large or small we cannot say at this time, who become the victims of their environment rather than of their heredity, their economic or social failure having its origin in the mental conflicts of childhood and in the development of unhealthy methods of dealing with mental problems. It is obvious, therefore, that it will be greatly to the advantage of the particular individual concerned and of those with whom he is to come in contact in future years if such conflicts can be unearthed and such unhealthy methods of reaction corrected at the age of five instead of at thirty. Whatever view one may hold regarding the fundamentals of character and personality, we are, I think, all agreed that there are certain instincts, "innate tendencies," natural inclinations or propensities—call them what you will—which are lying dormant in the individual from birth ready to be called into service, usually at the necessary time and with the necessary force to meet the best needs of the individual. The stimuli that actuate these forces may come either from within the individual or from the environment, and it is for the purpose of attempting to guide, to inhibit, or to stimulate these instinctive forces which may be underdeveloped or overdeveloped or imperfectly developed, that we study the mental life of the child, utilizing behavior as the medium of interpretation. . . .

The home represents the workshop in which these personalities are being developed, and the mental atmosphere of the home can be very easily contaminated. The ever-changing moods of the parents, colored by their indifference, their quarrels, depressions, and resentments, and shown by their manner of speech and action, are decidedly unhealthy; so, too, are the timidity of a mother, the arrogance of a father, and the self-consciousness of a younger sister, and the egotism of an older brother. Under such conditions we find a mental atmosphere as dangerous to the child as if it were contaminated by scarlet fever, diphtheria, or typhoid. On the other hand, cheerfulness, affection, kindly consideration, cleanliness, a manner and speech that are not forbidding, but show interest in the questions of the child, frankness and honesty in answering questions with the idea of developing freedom in speech and action not inhibited by fear of punishment or silent contempt—all these things play a part in the development of the personality of the child that cannot be overestimated. The environment is found to be mirrored in the character of the child, regardless of what its heredity may be.

THE DALTON PLAN (1922)   From Helen Parkhurst, *Education on the Dalton Plan* (New York, 1922), pp. 19–24, 34–44.

Freedom is the first principle of the Dalton Laboratory Plan. From the academic, or cultured point of view, the pupil must be made free to continue his work upon any subject in which he is absorbed without interruption, because when interested he is mentally keener, more alert, and more capable of mastering any difficulty that may arise in the course of his study. Under the new method there are no bells to tear him away at an appointed hour and chain him pedagogically to another subject and another teacher. Thus treated, the energy of the pupil automatically runs to waste. Such arbitrary transfers are indeed as uneconomic as if we were to turn an electric stove on and off at stated intervals for no reason. Unless a pupil is permitted to absorb knowledge at his own rate of speed he will never learn anything thoroughly. Freedom is taking his own time. To take someone else's time is slavery.

The second principle of the Dalton Laboratory Plan is co-operation or, as I prefer to call it, the interaction of group life. There is a passage in Dr. John Dewey's *Democracy and Education* which admirably defines this idea. "The object of a democratic education," he writes, "is not merely to make an individual an intelligent participator in the life of his immediate group, but to bring the various groups into such constant interaction that no individual, no economic group, could presume to live independently of others."

Under the old educational system a pupil can and often does live outside his group, touching it only when he passes in company with his fellows over the common mental highway called the curriculum. This easily ends in his becoming antisocial, and if so he carries this handicap with him when he leaves school for the wider domain of life. Such a pupil may even be "an intelligent participator" in the life of his form or class, just as a teacher may be. But a democratic institution demands more than this. Real social living is more than contact; it is co-operation and interaction. A school cannot reflect the social experience which is the fruit of community life unless all its parts, or groups, develop those intimate relations one with the other and that interdependence which, outside school, binds men and nations together.

Conditions are created by the Dalton Laboratory Plan in which the pupil, in order to enjoy them, involuntarily functions as a member of a social community. He is accepted or rejected by this community according as his functioning, or conduct is social or the reverse. The law operates in school just as it does in the world of men and women. To be effective this law must not be imposed, but unwritten, an emanation as it were of the atmosphere breathed by the community. The value of community life lies in the service it renders in making each free individual composing it perpetually conscious that he, as a member, is a co-worker responsible to, and for, the whole.

This constitutes a problem in school procedure. It should be so organized that neither pupil nor teacher can isolate themselves, nor escape their due share in the activities and in the difficulties of others. We all know the teachers who hang up their personality each morning as they hang up their coats. Outside school these people have human interests and human charm which they do not dare to exhibit when with their pupils lest they should in so doing seem to abrogate their authority. The Dalton Laboratory Plan has no use for the parade of such fictitious authority, which is restrictive, not educative. Instead of promoting order it provokes indiscipline. It is fatal to the idea of a school as a vital social unit.

Equally, from the pupil's point of view, is the child when submitted to the action of arbitrary authority and to immutable rules and regulations, incapable of developing a social consciousness which is the prelude to that social experience so indispensable as a preparation for manhood and womanhood. Academically considered, the old system is just as fatal as it is from the social point of view. A child never voluntarily undertakes anything that he does not understand. The choice of his games or pursuits is determined by a clear estimate of his capabilities to excel in them. Having the responsibility of his choice his mind acts like a powerful microscope, taking in and weighing every aspect of the problem he must master in order to ensure success. Given the same free conditions his mind would act on the problems of study in exactly the same way. Under the Dalton Laboratory Plan we place the work problem squarely before him, indicating the standard which has to be attained. After that he is allowed to tackle it as he thinks fit in his own way and at his own speed. Responsibility for the result will develop not only his latent intellectual powers, but also his judgment and character.

But in order that he may accomplish this educative process—in order that he may be led to educate himself—we must give him an opportunity to survey the whole of the task we set. To win the race he must first get a clear view of the goal. It would be well to lay a whole twelvemonth's work before the pupil at the beginning of the school year. This will give him a perspective of the plan of his education. He will thus be able to judge of the steps he must take each month and each week so that he may cover the whole road, instead of going blindly forward with no idea either of the road or the goal. How so handicapped can a child be expected to be interested in the race even to desire to win it? How can a teacher hope to turn out a well-equipped human being unless he takes the trouble to study the psychology of the child? Both for master and for pupil a perception of their job is essential. Education is, after all, a co-operative task. Their success or failure in it is interlocked.

Children learn, if we would only believe it, just as men and women learn, by adjusting means to ends. What does a pupil do when given, as he is given by the Dalton Laboratory Plan, responsibility for the performance of such and such work? Instinctively he seeks the best way of achieving it. Then having decided, he proceeds to act upon that decision. Supposing his plan does not seem to fit his purpose, he discards it and tries another. Later on he may find it profitable to consult his fellow students engaged in a similar task. Discussion helps to clarify his ideas and also his plan of procedure. When he comes to the end the finished achievement takes on all the splendour of success. It embodies all he has thought and felt and lived during the time it has taken to complete. This is real experience. It is culture acquired through individual development and through collective co-operation. It is no longer school—it is life.

Not only will this method of education stimulate the deepest interest and the highest power in a student, but it will teach him how to proportion effort to attainment. In his book upon the principles of war General Foch says: "Economy of forces consists in throwing all the forces at one's disposition at a given time upon one point." So the child's attack upon his problem of work should be facilitated by allowing him to concentrate all his forces upon the subject that claims his interest at one particular moment. He will in this case not only do more work, but better work too. The Dalton Laboratory Plan permits pupils to budget their time and to spend it according to their need.

"The secret of education," so Emerson tells us, "lies in respecting the pupil. It is not for you to choose what he shall know, what he shall do. It is chosen and fore-ordained and he alone holds the key to his own secret. By your tampering and thwarting and too much governing he may be hindered from his end and kept out of his own. Respect the child. Wait and see the new product of nature. Nature loves analogies but not repetitions. Respect the child. Be not too much his parent. Trespass not on his solitude."

*　　*　　*

The Plan in Practice

I come now to a consideration of the Dalton Laboratory Plan in its practical application to the problem of education. Perhaps in order to clear the ground it is well to begin by indicating what it is not.

The Dalton Laboratory Plan is not a system or a method, which through ages of use has petrified into a monotonous and uniform shape, to be branded on to succeeding generations of pupils as sheep are branded on going into a fold. It is not a curriculum, which, all too often, is simply the machine by means of which the brand is stamped upon the individuals caught in the meshes of the system. Practically speaking, it is a scheme of educational reorganization which reconciles the twin activities of teaching and learning. When intelligently applied it creates conditions which enable the teacher to teach and the learner to learn.

In order to apply the scheme it is not necessary or even desirable to abolish classes or forms as units of organization in the school, nor the curriculum as such. The Dalton Laboratory Plan preserves both. Each pupil is classified as a member of a form, and for each form a maximum and a minimum curriculum is drawn up. But at its inception it lays the whole work proposition before the pupils in the shape of a contract job. The curriculum is divided up into jobs and the pupil accepts the work assigned for his class as a contract. Though dispensed with above middle school, the younger children may sign a definite contract which is returned to each individual as soon as his job is completed.

"I———, pupil of———standard form, contract to do the———assignment.

Date and signature———."

As every month of the year has its own assigned work, a contract-job for any one form comprises a whole month's work. For convenience we arrange the different parts of the curriculum under the heading of major and minor subjects:

Major Subjects	Minor Subjects
Mathematics	Music
History	Art
Science	Handiwork
English	Domestic Science
Geography	Manual Training
Foreign Languages, etc.	Gymnastics, etc.

The first category of subjects is not more important than the other, but they are classified as "major" because they are used as the basis of promotion in most schools, and college entrance examinations thus necessitate that more time should be given to them. The value of the minor subjects lies in their expansive influence upon the student. The study of them creates a response to beauty and also an increased power of expression. But if in the lower school, which includes children ranging from eight to twelve years, foreign languages are not required as a basis for promotion, they should be classified as minor subjects for lower-school pupils.

For the purpose of simplifying the initial application of the Dalton Laboratory Plan, I recommend that it should be applied firstly to major subjects alone. As the new scheme becomes familiar it can gradually be extended to the minor subjects. Take, for example, a school wherein the major subjects for Form II are Mathematics, Science, History, Geography, English, and French. The first contract-job for a pupil belonging to that form would be a block of the year's curriculum comprising a month's work in each of these major subjects. In the United States we reckon a school month as twenty days. The contract would therefore cover the ground divided as below:

TWENTY DAYS—FORM II CONTRACT JOB

1 month of French	1 month of English	1 month of Science	1 month of Mathematics	1 month of Geography	1 month of History

This diagram represents a required standard of work for the performance of which each pupil in Form II would contract. Though the standard is the same, the pupils are not. As their mental legs must be of different lengths, their rate of speed in study must vary also. Some may not even need the twenty days for their contracted work; others may not be able to get it done in that time. It is of the essence of the Dalton Laboratory Plan that pupils should progress each at his own rate, for only so can the work be assimilated thoroughly. Thus each pupil must be allowed to organize his method of working as he thinks best. Unfortunately at the outset we cannot assume that these pupils know how to work, though as the new plan is put into operation they will gradually learn to organize both their time and work to better and better advantage. But efficiency means speed, and speed will only be attained when good habits of work are established. It takes time to counteract the habit of dependence bred in the pupil by constantly telling him what to do, when and how to do it. This system made him a servant, occasionally an efficient servant, but always dependent on orders. And though the reorganization of school machinery is quickly effected the response of the pupil to the changed conditions is not always as rapid. It is the business of the teacher to see that the adjustment proceeds, however slowly. The process can be helped by making the divided curriculum clear, and by seeing that the pupil grasps the whole scope and nature of the work he contracts to accomplish. Unless he understands what is required of him his organization of his time will be defective.

By giving his task in the form of a contract for whose execution he feels himself responsible, we give the work dignity and him the consciousness of a definite purpose. This feeling is increased if we make him aware of our confidence in his desire and in his power to execute it. A pupil must not, however, be permitted to continue the study of any major subject beyond the limits of the month's assignment unless he has completed his contract in every subject. He must not be allowed to work up to a higher standard than his form average in one or two subjects and fall below it in the rest of them. This would merely give him an opportunity of evading progress in those studies in which he is weak and lose to him the value of correlated and vitalized subjects. Uniformity of standard insures that he will so organize his time that most of it will be devoted to overcome his individual weaknesses and difficulties. The plan teaches him to *budget his time* so that it is sufficient to his needs and to have him go slowly and thoroughly. In this way he will be well prepared for each succeeding step. His subject diet will be well balanced and his culture will be well rounded.

The amount of any monthly assignment is a part and a very vital part of the teacher's problem. A good curriculum should be so balanced and co-related that neither too much nor too little is included in the contract-job. In the lower school not more should be required than the pupils can easily accomplish by a wise division of their time. That a ten-year-old child should learn all that a normal child of his age can learn is the ideal to set before us. A study of child psychology is necessary if we are to reorganize the machinery of education so that it corresponds to his powers and satisfies his needs at every age.

Turning from the pupil to the school building, it is evident that the Dalton Laboratory Plan exacts the establishment of laboratories, one for each subject in the curriculum, though with a small teaching staff two subjects may be studied in a single laboratory. A specialist in that particular subject, or subjects, should be in charge of each laboratory whose relation to the scheme I will deal with later on. For the moment I want to emphasize the point that these laboratories are the places where the children experiment—where they are free to work on their jobs, not places where they are experimented upon.

The text-book library of the school must be distributed among these laboratories according to subject. It is of course essential that the necessary books should be always accessible to every student—a supply of scientific books in the science laboratory, history books in the history laboratory, and so on. With regard to these books, it is well to have a few standard text-books and to increase as far as possible the number of reference books. Do not be afraid of including in the school library books that are designed for adult readers, the kind of books which have hitherto been found rather on home, than on school, bookshelves. Remember that no book can be too well written to interest a child. The dry terseness of the ordinary school manual, devoid of any literary quality, is responsible for half the distaste of learning so characteristic of the average school boy or girl. It is at school that our future men and women should become acquainted with those literary treasures which are the common heritage of humanity. And regarded merely as a mine of information, nothing could be more valuable in the development of the pupil's intelligence than the opportunity thus given him of comparing the different views of different authors on the subject he is studying.

Among the impediments to true education which is ruthlessly abolished by the Dalton Laboratory Plan is the time-table. Even to the teacher the time-table is a bugbear. How often have I heard head masters and mistresses complain of the difficulty of dividing time so that no member of the teaching staff should feel his special subjects slighted! As a result the time-table is usually compiled rather in the interest of the instructors than of the pupils. To the latter the time-table is nothing less than a curse. Its banishment is in fact the first step towards his liberation.

Let us assume that in a given school laboratory time for all classes or forms extends from 9 to 12 o'clock every morning. Under the Dalton Plan this three-hour period is devoted to the study of the major subjects—Geography, History, Mathematics, Science, English, and French. Before setting out to organize their time themselves each pupil consults his teacher, who, under the new plan, has become a subject specialist, or adviser. Together they go over the pupil's contract work, classifying his subjects as strong and weak. Those subjects which a child loves and enjoys studying will usually be found among his strong subjects. The subjects he is weak in are almost invariably those which he finds difficult to understand and assimilate, chiefly because he has not hitherto been able to give enough time to them.

For the sake of clarity I will take a concrete example. Mary Smith is a member of Form II. When, with the aid of her adviser, she has sorted out her subjects, we will suppose that they fall into the two following categories:

Weak Subjects	Strong Subjects	
Mathematics	English	Geography
French	History	Science

In relation to the three hours' laboratory time at her disposal we may express her individual needs by the following equation:

THREE HOURS' LABORATORY TIME

Mathematics + French = English + History + Geography + Science
(Weak Subjects)   (Strong Subjects)

Having accepted her contract-job she must keep the whole job in mind, and being weak in French and Mathematics she needs to devote as much time to them as to her four strong subjects. But if the time-table were in force, Mary, despite her difficulties, would only be allowed as long for her Mathematics and French as the other pupils in Form II, many of whom might be strong in them. Can a more complete condemnation of the time-table be found than this simple demonstration of its working?

Emancipated from its tyranny, Mary's equation will change as she eliminates antipathy to, or weakness in, those subjects. But as long as her problem can be expressed in the terms of the above equation, she should devote half of her three available hours every day to Mathematics and French, and only the remaining half to the other four subjects. If she is stronger in French than in Mathematics then the one-and-one-half hours should be divided accordingly.

Mary will, however, be free to choose which subject she will take up first, and she will go into the laboratory consecrated to that subject. Having chosen it at the moment when her interest in it is keen, she will do better work and do it more quickly too. Once in the laboratory Mary proceeds to study as an individual, but if she finds other members from Form II there she works with them. This is the rule of the laboratory under the Dalton Plan. It subdivides and reduces the large class group and it creates a small group of pupils doing intensive work, which stimulates discussion and exercises social influence. The educative value of such small groups is immense in giving an atmosphere to the laboratory, in providing occasions for social adjustment and experience. It provides invaluable play of mind upon mind. As Mary has entered that laboratory voluntarily, and can leave it for another when she feels inclined, no problems of discipline arise. Her mind comes in with her and goes out with her, disciplined by interest in the subject, harnessed—the whole of it— to her job. No time is wasted, for though the general time-table has gone Mary has, in consultation with her adviser, made a time-table for herself. This is very important, especially in the case of the younger children, in order to inculcate the value of time. To spend it in supplying our mental and moral needs is to put it to the wisest use.

It is also essential to Mary that she should realize exactly what progress she is making in the subject of her choice. For this purpose I invented the graph device before alluded to. As it merits a chapter to itself I will only now refer to it casually as a part of the laboratory equipment and procedure. There are three sets of graphs. The first provides each special teacher and adviser with the means of following the other members of the class. It also enables the pupil himself to compare his progress with that of his classmates. But Mary has also her own contract-job graph, on which she records her daily progress. The third graph pictures the progress of the class or form a whole, as well as the individual progress.

So that the pupil should never lose sight of the job in its entirety, progress is measured in weeks of work accomplished. Mary has six major subjects with four weeks of work on each of them. Her contract thus entails twenty-four weeks of work. On the weekly graph she is therefore marked, not in each separate subject, but in the number of weeks' work done out of the total required, week by week.

In this manner a pupil advances steadily, job by job, through the curriculum of his class. If in a school year of nine or ten months he only finishes eight jobs on account of absence or illness, he begins the ninth job in the following year. The clever child may, on the contrary, accomplish in one year the work mapped out to cover eighteen months. Often the slow, apparently less intelligent, child gains in rapidity, and in any case he builds well and soundly at his own natural rate.

DESCRIPTION OF A "CONDUCT CURRICULUM" AT THE KINDERGARTEN AT TEACHERS COLLEGE, COLUMBIA UNIVERSITY

(**1923**)   From Patty Smith Hill, Introduction to Agnes Burke et al., *A Conduct Curriculum for Kindergarten and First Grade* (New York, 1923), pp. xi–xvii.

As early as 1905 Teachers College made it possible for an experiment to be initiated in the kindergarten of the Speyer School with children from three or four to six years of age. The group with which this was tried was in charge of Miss Luella A. Palmer, Director of the public school kindergartens of Greater New York, who was at that time a graduate student in this department. The experiment started in 1905 was one of the earliest attempts in any field of education to apply the principles of democracy to school organization. To provide conditions suitable for training in the beginnings of self-government, wide opportunities were offered the children for learning from each other, through their own experience, emphasis being laid upon the initiation and execution of their own purposes and plans. While this 1905 experiment was timid as compared with the later experiments which grew out of it, choices and decisions were turned over to the children whenever possible to do so without waste of time and effort. A conscious attempt was also made to work out a technique of teaching, built upon a new conception of the teacher as a guide rather than as a dictator. The teacher was conceived of as the mature member of a social group of immature beings, in which her wider experience, wiser judgment, greater knowledge and technique were to be at the disposal of the children, when she or they felt the need of adult direction.

Few observers were interested, since the procedure seemed radical in the extreme, as compared with the conservative and formal kindergartens and first grades of the day. For this reason, it was deemed advisable to defer the continuation of this venture until 1915, when better conditions were afforded in the kindergarten and playground of the Horace Mann School. Much wider interest was awakened by this second attempt. This increased interest was manifested in a request, coming from both parents and school, for the continuation of this type of organization in the first grade. To promote its success, one of the teachers, who had participated in the previous experiment in the kindergarten, was selected to carry on similar work with the same group of children in the first grade.

The second trial of this experiment found us far more courageous, as the 1905 attempt had convinced us that even young children were far more capable of learning self-government than we had dreamed. One of the most marked results of these opportunities for learning self-direction was the decreasing necessity for teacher-administered discipline and punishment. Not only those teachers who participated, but the majority of those who observed consecutively, were convinced that a social organization based upon wisely directed liberty was the only medium in which habits of self-direction and social co-operation could be established. In this way the school served as a laboratory of democracy, in which the technique of democratic citizenship could be gradually acquired.

Even in 1915, however, this form of social organization impressed the more conservative pedagogical minds as radical and wasteful. In order, therefore, to justify the results of such training through some more convincing evidence than the mere enthusiasm of those who were conducting the experiment, it was realized that some method of recording daily work must be devised. Up to this time few systematic efforts had been made to record the progress of young children. With no precedent at our disposal, we decided to appoint special observers to make records of what they considered typical outcomes in the individual and social behavior of the group. These were listed as carefully as the scientific training of teachers at that time permitted, and the results were tabulated. The observers, disagreeing in minor details, unanimously agreed that this freer organization offered conditions in which the children learned initiative, independence, perseverance, concentration, and social co-operation such as the old order had never provided.

It was then discovered that these records of the children's progress served, not only as a statement of what had actually transpired, but as standards of possible attainment through the more freely organized work and play.

Some of the captions used in this early record sheet under which we classified the attainments of the children were: ability to initiate purposes and plans, ability to persevere or "stick to one's job" in spite of difficulties, ability to lead and follow intelligently, ability to give fair criticism to self and others and finally to profit by such criticism.

This method of recording children's progress, improved in form from year to year, was used from 1915 to 1921. At this juncture the need for the criticism and direction of a highly trained psychologist was recognized. The difficulty lay in finding an expert willing to do pioneer work in the psychology of these early years. When criticism was asked, psychologists invariably pointed out that little help could be given, because the captions under which the records were made dealt almost exclusively with non-measurable qualities, those not sufficiently objective to induce psychologists to attempt to scale or measure them. While the qualities, as such, were approved and acknowledged as of unquestioned worth, they were too vague, too indefinite, to warrant attempts at scientific measurement. It was agreed that some more objective outcomes must be found before further attempts could be made to measure the progress of young children.

At this stage of the experiment, the department secured the services of Doctor Agnes Rogers, who directed us in the process of breaking up the captions of our previous records into the more specific abilities and habits involved.

After working with some three or four hundred leaders in kindergarten and primary education, specific habits which the majority agreed that young children should form were listed and a tentative "Habit Inventory" was published. This was used as the basis of further study and experiment, not only in the kindergarten and first grade of the Horace Mann School, but with groups of children under the direction of the teachers co-operating with Doctor Rogers in the inventory and habit scale.

As this inventory was used, the observers noted, not only the obvious improvement and acceleration of habit-formation with the children, but also that the supervisors and classroom teachers began to think of all instruction in terms of desirable changes in thought, feeling, or conduct; in other words, in terms of changed behavior due to a changed nervous system. As was but natural, changes in behavior were appreciated first in the realm of moral and social conduct. But as the study proceeded, the conception of behavior grew to include, not only those technical activities listed as conduct, but all those changes in thought and feeling, directly or indirectly, immediately or remotely, leading to and influencing behavior.

In order to clarify our own thinking in the use of psychological terms and in listing these changes in the child's behavior, whether in the realm of thought and feeling, in appreciation, attitudes, and ideals, or in the more overt modifications in conduct, some definition of the technical differences in these phenomena had to be agreed upon. Recourse was had to Doctor Edward L. Thorndike's writings and the following conception of behavior accepted:

"I use it to refer to those activities of thought, feeling, and conduct in the broadest sense which an animal—here, man—exhibits, which are omitted from discussion by the physics, chemistry, and ordinary psychology of to-day, and which are referred by popular usage to intellect, character, skill, and temperament. Behavior, then, is not contrasted with, but exclusive of, conscious life."

Two results of accepting this point of view followed: first, all outward evidences of ability to appreciate the beauty of music, art, or literature were considered of too great importance to omit in our records of desirable changes; second, subject-matter, as such, was thought of in terms of activities and experiences leading to desirable changes in thought and feeling, or in conduct. As a consequence, instead of making our "Habit Inventory" an appendix to the curriculum, then in use with its subject-matter, knowledge and technique, we found ourselves gradually transforming the curriculum, as a whole, by applying the principles of habit formation to all of the school subjects. Thus the proper conduct of the three R's or the correct technique of the fine and industrial arts became as evident as the so-called moral or social conduct. Each school subject was studied from the viewpoint of the desirable improvements in thought, feeling, and conduct which might thereby be stimulated and established in habits of behavior. Thus the activities of each subject were listed in one column; opposite were listed the desired changes which should grow out of these activities.

This has proved a difficult task for laymen to attempt, and it has been a project requiring unremitting labor for many months on the part of the department, as a whole, and the committee in particular. Faulty though this first presentation may be, it has at least set up definite aims and objectives to the teachers of young children, laying the emphasis, not on knowledge or appreciation, as such, but on desirable changes or improvements in these—in the changed nervous system which leads to habits of behavior, finally culminating in character.

This step forward from a "Habit Inventory" at large to the study of each aspect of the curriculum, not as a formal school subject, but as a social situation rich in activities and experiences leading to the formation of desirable habits, avoids a danger which we had realized from the first; that is, of teaching habits out of their organic relation to situations. From the first we had feared that habits might be taught arbitrarily, separated from social situations which give rise to the necessity for their formation. When conduct is acquired in a social situation, it not only takes on meaning but is likely to be associated in the mind of the child with a sense of satisfaction or pleasure. For this reason, the child, as well as the teacher, must be helped to a realization of the necessity for the conduct desired. This possibility is increased if the conduct set as the objective is acquired in experience, in a situation, the conduct itself serving, not only as an aim, but as a desirable and economical solution of the problem involved in the experience.

When the child, as well as the teacher, is thus made conscious of the acquired conduct as a happy means of solving individual or group problems, the result is associated with satisfaction. It is a psychological law that any activity which is not associated with a sense of satisfaction may be lost. In other words, it is not likely to be repeated except when dictated by external authority. The economy of learning conduct in experience may be illustrated with any habit selected from the "Habit Inventory"; for example, one of the habits listed was the proper technique or conduct of crossing the street, a habit of tremendous importance in safeguarding the lives of little children in large cities. In the curricula of the past, the knowledge and conduct involved in this habit would find no place; or, if considered worthy of a place in the curriculum, it would have been presented to the child as a matter of information, leaving the application to mere chance. In this curriculum, however, this desirable conduct is not presented as unapplied knowledge, or taught out of the experience which calls for it. The school excursion would be selected as the best social situation for teaching the child "Safety First." Here is the medium in which this particular knowledge, ideal or conduct can be learned with the minimum of time and effort on the part of both teacher and child.

In making this curriculum one group of teachers started with the subject or situation, listing the inherent activities and conducts desired; the other group approached from the standpoint of the specific habit of conduct listed in the inventory, searching for the natural situations in which to set the habit to be formed. Thus, whether one started with the inventory or with the situation, the outward result was the same; but in school practice it makes a vast difference whether the teacher views a habit as something to be taught at any time, or under any conditions, or as a form of activity organically related to an experience or situation in which the *raison d'être* for learning arises.

No attempt is here made to present a curriculum as a whole, with the specific story to be told or read, the song to be sung, the game to be played, etc. Instead, an effort has been made to set up the different objectives, when the song is sung or listened to, the story read or told, which, if attained, will lead to changes in thought, feeling, and conduct in each of these situations.

While improvement in conduct leading to habit is our most fundamental aim in making this curriculum, changes in thought and feeling, changes in appreciation, ideals, and attitudes, have not been omitted. Though the knowledge and ideals involved are not listed separately, it should be noted that they usually appear under the heading of activities or outcomes. A separate, more specific and detailed listing of the knowledge and ideals involved in these activities and conducts is being attempted as this, the first of a series of monographs on the education of young children, goes to press.

Since the technical meaning of conduct is better understood by the classroom teacher than that of behavior, we are venturing to call this a "Conduct Curriculum," though a "Curriculum of Behavior" might be technically more correct. Psychologists will pardon this verbal change, if by the use of the term we get over to the public the idea that education must set as its objective the *changed child*—the child in which desirable changes in thought, feeling, and conduct are sought and achieved day by day, until habit and character have been established.

THE ELEMENTARY SCHOOL OF THE SCHOOL OF EDUCATION AT
THE UNIVERSITY OF MISSOURI (1924)   From Junius L. Meriam, *Child Life And The Curriculum* (New York, 1931), pp. 14–18.

Initial steps. The school opened in 1905, enrolling pupils in the first three grades. The director of the school had not then formulated his problem, but, his previous experience in public-school work had opened up the content of the curriculum as *the* important field for study in elementary education.

The problem of the curriculum. For the first two years rearrangement of the traditional subjects was studied. This was unsatisfactory. It was not sufficiently constructive. In the fall of 1907 a tentative outline of a course for eight grades had been formulated as a basis for more constructive study. The content of this course— or, more appropriately, series of studies—was taken directly from the out-of-school interests and activities of children, but at first was without any organization. Before the close of the year the studies had been arranged for convenience in four groups, as now outlined in Chapter Seventeen. While this four-group arrangement has been maintained since that time, the subdivisions have been very flexible and have not been allowed to crystallize in a fixed organization.

The curriculum has been the central problem for professional study. All problems of school management and methods have been regarded as strictly subordinate and have therefore been given only incidental attention. This study of management and method is the more effective as it is made subservient to the larger problem of the curriculum; management and method are means of accomplishing the work outlined in the curriculum.

Administration and supervision. The immediate direction of this school has, from its beginning, been the work of the professor of school supervision in the School of Education. He has been allowed large liberty in governing the policy of the school. His advisers have been chiefly the teachers in this school and those in public schools who have cooperated with him or who have been students at the university. Hundreds of visiting teachers and many parents have made suggestions.

Supervision of the school has been, first, in preparation of outlines such as those given in Chapter Seventeen. Teachers are expected to study these outlines, not to follow them. Each teacher is allowed great freedom in her own schedule, management, and method. The curriculum and the policy of the school encourage this. Supervision is given by frequent conferences with individual teachers, rather than through regular teachers' meetings.

The teachers. The school of about one hundred pupils is taught by four teachers devoting full time, and usually a fifth teacher, a graduate student with previous experience as teacher, who devotes one-half time to the school. No specific qualifications are required of these teachers. Most of them have had experience in public schools. Some have had professional training; some have had none at all. The endeavor has been to appoint no one who was not open to come into full sympathy with the principles and policies of the school. One serious interruption of the work has been the frequent change of teachers. Low salaries, marriage, and inability to advance the professional study have occasioned these changes to a greater degree than is current in public schools.

The pupils and organization. The pupils come largely from the district in which the school is situated. Some come from other sections of the little city of Columbia, and a few come from near-by rural districts. No selection is evident save as the small annual tuition fee of ten dollars prevents some from attending. The school admits children six years of age into the first grade.[1] Seven grades are provided, and work is being prepared for the eighth grade. The school is organized into grades of the traditional type. However, these grades are really groups of children who are advanced from grade to grade on the basis of a year's work rather than the completion of the work assigned to a given grade. In the main, each of four teachers has two consecutive grades. The two grades form one large group and work together as one, so are as possible. There is no departmental work as organized in many schools.

Building and furnishings. The five-thousand-dollar frame building is unique in its construction. The building is 50 feet long and 50 feet wide, two stories high, and has a basement. One half of the first floor is called the Fountain Room. An aquarium 14 feet long, 5 feet wide, and 3 feet deep, with a fountain at the south end of the room, gives it the name. This aquarium is the center for studies in nature and becomes a pleasing bit of schoolroom decoration. Around the walls of the Fountain Room are exhibit cases, where the work of all the pupils is exhibited. This exhibit is continual and not for special occasions. As new projects are completed they take the place of the old. This room serves as an auditorium. There are no seats. None are needed, except for visitors. When there is to be an assembly the pupils come from their rooms, each bringing his chair. At the close of these frequent, but not daily, assemblies, the pupils take their chairs with them and the floor is again free for folk dancing and games. This Fountain Room is the social center of the school and is the most serviceable room in the building.

On the second floor at the top of the open stairway is the library, 25 feet by 35 feet in area. Here the upper-grade pupils do most of their work.

There are four classrooms or workrooms, one on the first floor and three on the second. These rooms are supplied with chairs and tables easily moved about by pupils, instead of the formal school desks screwed to the floor.

Equipment. Except for the library, the meager equipment is a surprise to the many visitors. The library contains about twenty-five hundred volumes, besides about one hundred boxes of clippings and pictures. These books, with scarcely a duplicate, are a substitute for texts.

A museum of illustrative material collected from various industrial establishments and other sources contributes to the work done. Boys in bench work and girls in domestic science do their work in the high-school building. The Elementary School is not provided with any shop or science apparatus. With an excellent library and full liberty for excursions and field work, school work is not seriously handicapped because of meager equipment.

Leading features. 1. The school does not study reading, writing, arithmetic, and others of the traditional subjects. Subjects for study are taken directly from life outside of school.

2. The school does not use textbooks, but has an extensive library to supplement studies made on excursions and field trips.

3. The school has no recitations for testing students on assignments previously made. Conferences are held irregularly, though usually daily, in which pupils pool

[1]Until September, 1918, the school provided no kindergarten because of lack of schoolroom space, of funds for maintenance, and of time for study of this preelementary stage of schooling. Since September, 1918, the sixth and seventh grades have been organized with the ninth grade into a junior high school.

their findings made in the library or upon special observation. These conferences seldom drag, inasmuch as in the study of timely topics pupils have much to report.

4. No assignments are made as lessons to be prepared. Assignments are replaced by developing, in these conferences, new problems or new material on old problems. Opportunities are pointed out, rather than tasks assigned. The former is more conducive to industrious application than the latter.

5. No final examinations or irregular tests are used to discover what the pupil has done or to spur him on to further accomplishment. Daily work is a sufficient test, and cooperative study of teacher and pupil is more effective than any artificial stimulus.

THE ETHICAL CULTURE SCHOOL, NEW YORK CITY (1925)   From Agnes De Lima, *Our Enemy The Child* (New York, 1925), pp. 126–31.

The Ethical Culture School, established in 1878, was founded by Dr. Felix Adler as a free kindergarten for the children of working people, but it grew rapidly into a full graded school to which children were admitted from all social strata. Children are not excluded because of race, religion, or color—a rare policy in a private school—and scholarships, affording either full or partial tuition extended to over two-fifths of the enrollment, cut down economic barriers. In admitting children, however, preference is usually given to those with a high record of scholarship and a high intelligence rating—at least 115—and once admitted, pupils are expected to meet the exacting requirements of the school's course of study. The result of this policy is that the school serves primarily a rather narrowly specialized intellectual type, and necessarily excludes many children whose special talents lie outside the range of measurability of the scales, or who lack ability to perform difficult academic work.

Some of these pupils are permitted to remain and take a modified course leading to a certificate instead of a diploma, but they are regarded rather as lost souls by the administration. In discussing them recently Superintendent Lewis said:

> For them the thought of the world bearing on human progress so far as it is bound up in ethics, literature, history, science, and foreign languages is very largely a sealed book. Facts they can often grasp and reproduce, but the relations of facts and reasoning generally in the abstract data of language are often beyond their capacity. Hence they do not seem to me to be those best qualified by nature to attain the school's highest aims. . . . They are not those whose intelligence can be raised to a point where they can cope successfully with the burning problems now facing mankind.

The avowed purpose of the school is to train ethical leaders, "reformers" of society, and its officers are proud of the fact that a larger proportion of its graduates than of any other school are engaged in teaching, research, or some type of social service. The ideal of service to society is held constantly before the pupils by means of formal ethics instruction as well as by numerous activities on behalf of the community.

A prevocational arts course has been established in the last two years of high school for those children who show special artistic ability. It is the ultimate hope of the school to offer similar courses to those specially endowed in music, in home-making, mechanical ingenuity, and science. Even here, however, the emphasis is placed upon academic standing and intellectual capacity, for Superintendent Lewis does not believe the course will be successful with students who do not possess at least average general intelligence in addition to special talent, nor would he give preference to the dull but talented student over the bright and equally talented one.

While all the children of the middle and upper school are thus held to the requirements of a conventional curriculum, the attempt is made through psycho-logical study of each child to provide a rounded range of activities, mental, physical, and social. This is important, for precociously intellectual children are frequently emotionally infantile, or unable to respond normally to social situations.

Some years ago an experiment was made in the primary grades of the Ethical Culture School by Miss Mabel Goodlander to test out some of the more progressive theories of education.[1] No changes were made in size of class or in room space, but complete freedom was given in the selection of materials, use of class time, and employment of special teachers. Miss Goodlander's aim was "to create a free social environment where children in cooperation with others of the same age might make a beginning in democratic living under conditions more like life outside school than commonly considered appropriate for the school regime." Children as well as teacher were at liberty to sit where convenient, talk and move about freely so long as they did not annoy others, and to work or play either as individuals or in groups. Although the teacher directed the class when necessary, the children were mainly engaged in projects of their own.

It is one of Miss Goodlander's cardinal beliefs that the teacher must never dominate the situation. "We must learn," she says, "to appreciate more sympathet-ically each child's point of view, and we should be willing to accept his judgment in many things frankly and sincerely even when it differs from our own."

As regards curriculum the emphasis was shifted from formal studies to constructive work and play, to expression in varying art forms, and to first-hand knowledge of social and industrial activities related to the child's life. The three R's were mastered, but Miss Goodlander waited until the interest of the children in them had been naturally aroused.

Miss Goodlander carried her experiment forward with the same group for four years, and then started with a new class. According to Superintendent Lewis the experiment was a success, tests showing that as compared with two parrallel divisions Miss Goodlander's group met the school's requirement in formal work and excelled in ability to observe, initiate, and carry projects through; in cooperation it was superior to one group and inferior to another.

In the fall of 1924 a branch of the Ethical Culture School was opened in the West Seventies under the direction of Miss Goodlander, who can now more thoroughly test out and develop her earlier experiment. The classes are housed in a large old fashioned dwelling which admits of a sense of intimacy and naturalness so important for young children especially. The grades are limited to the first four, and the kindergarten and the class registers are kept down to fifteen. The groups are therefore small enough for the development of individual ability, but large enough to encourage social and cooperative activities. The program is extremely flexible,

[1] See Mabel R. Goodlander, "Education Through Experience." *Bulletin No. 10*, New York Bureau of Educational Experiments.

the children are allowed much freedom in choosing and directing their own work, in shop, play and the arts, no less than in the more formal subjects. The classes stay all day, and have plenty of time outdoors both in the park and nearby, and visiting places of interest in the city. Even all day Saturday trips to the country are planned. The children are fitted to take their places in the succeeding grades of the parent school, which it is to be hoped will gradually become more freed from traditional practices and outlook.

MENTAL HYGIENE CLINICS IN THE PUBLIC SCHOOLS OF
MINNEAPOLIS (1925)   From Smiley Blanton, "The Function of the Mental Hygiene Clinic in the Schools and Colleges," *The Child, The Clinic and the Court* (New York, 1925), pp. 93–96.

When Dr. Healy took his first court case of a patient suffering from severe behavior difficulty, he laid the foundation for the study of even the mildest cases: for it is obvious that if the behavior-difficulties of a severe type are caused by something, and can be helped by a careful social and psychiatric study, then the simple problems of behavior which occur in the ordinary normal child are also capable of being similarly treated. Or, again, we may say if man's behavior on any level is caused by something, and can be modified, then the behavior on every level must be caused by something, and can be modified.

Dr. Healy's clinic, and similar clinics, established the fact that behavior must be considered as a symptom—a symptom just as fever is a symptom. For example, it does not help us to treat stealing as stealing, or temper-tantrums, or negativism, or truancy, without considering the causes that lie back of this behavior. If we may consider, then, behavior as a symptom and that behavior, on all levels, is caused by something, it seems to be that it logically follows that we could wisely undertake the treatment of behavior-difficulties at the very earliest moment. It was with this viewpoint in mind that we established the child behavior clinic in connection with the Minneapolis schools.

There were two possibilities open: to establish a clinic for the purpose of treating children with severe behavior-difficulties, children who have definitely broken with the social system; or to take cases with difficulties of mild type, so mild that hitherto they have been considered as perfectly normal reactions to children, not worthy of treatment and usually considered discipline problems. The latter was our choice.

It seemed to us that the public school was the best place for such a clinic, designed for preventive work in mental hygiene, since all the children of the community pass through the public schools. The public schools have done a good deal already towards caring for those who have poor intelligence, and who have various handicaps, such as the deaf, the blind, the crippled; but practically nothing has been done to care for those children with beginning behavior-difficulties, many of whom are children of superior intelligence. The ideal that we had for our clinic was to care for those children with average or superior intelligence, who have behavior-difficulties of the very mildest type. For example, the irritable, moody, pilfering, negative, too-suggestible child, the child who has not yet learned to control his temper, who is not able to adjust himself to the group, who is too sensitive or too "bumptious," who does not show the proper interest in his studies, who is too much attached to his parents, or antagonistic toward them. These, and a host of other slight behavior-difficulties, are treated in the clinic.

We do not assume that children with these mild behavior-difficulties are going to have mental breakdowns, but we do know that they would not be able to realize their highest possibilities; that without guidance they would go through life working at fifty to seventy-five per cent efficiency.

Let me describe the organization of our clinic, its staff and equipment. The Minneapolis School Board has given us the wing of a children's hospital where there is an open-air school. We have a psychologist, Dr. Goodenough, who has spent several years with Dr. Terman working with exceptional children. The psychological tests are given in order to establish the intelligence quotient, and also to bring out the special abilities and disabilities and mental reactions. So far as possible we try to establish an emotional quotient as well as an intelligence quotient. We have three psychiatric social workers: Miss Hester Crutcher, Miss Alice Leahy and Miss Sue Mason. These workers had been teachers before they went into psychiatric social work, so they are thoroughly familiar with the school problems. We have also working with the clinic twenty visiting teachers and ten corrective speech teachers, who work with the cases after they have passed through the clinic.

A part of the work of the Child Guidance Clinic is to organize a course in mental hygiene for high school students, juniors and seniors. This year one course will be given, an elective course, which will be limited to one hundred students. If this plan works out, we hope to be able to introduce such courses in mental hygiene in other high schools. The course will consist of sixteen lectures and credits will be given for the course. Students will write their life histories, and those that need advice will be met personally and their problems will be talked over.

Another phase of the clinic's work will be the establishment of behavior clinics in the kindergartens. A Behavior Chart has been worked out, which the kindergarten teacher will fill out for each child. After this is done the charts will be looked over and those children that need to be seen will be given help. The parents will be asked to come in and talk over the situation with the social worker and the teacher. After six months another Behavior Chart will be filled out for each child. In this way the child's progress can be ascertained. We hope to have such behavior clinics established in all the kindergartens of the city.

A third phase is a course in mental hygiene for teachers and a course for parents.

Cases are referred to the clinic by the teachers or by the parents. Although the clinic is in the public schools, it also takes pre-school cases, which are referred by the parents direct. The clinic also serves the juvenile court. No clinic could care for all the cases so there is need of a plan to care for such cases as cannot be taken by the clinic.

It might be interesting to give a few average cases as they come to the clinic, with the symptoms that brought them.

ACTING THINGS OUT AT THE SHADY HILL (CAMBRIDGE, MASS.) SCHOOL (1926)   From Gertrude Hartman and Ann Shumaker, eds., *Creative Expression* . . . (New York, 1926), pp. 178–81.

The morning at the Shady Hill School begins with the informal gathering together of all the children for what is known as Assembly. It is the time when one group shares with the rest some interesting piece of class work they have done. Often the medium of expression is a dramatic presentation. Such an important sounding term, however, does not at all represent the spirit in which these Assemblies are prepared and given. Carried over from classroom work, the costuming is often simply a spear or a crown, and the setting merely one end of the Assembly room, helped out by properties and burlap covered screens. We try to do away with a curtain and to make as few shifts of scene as possible, and these quite openly.

One of the rich fields for dramatization is poetry. This year two interesting and very different things were done by the children of the seventh grade (eleven years old). The idea of acting out certain poems in *Now We Are Six* came from one of the girls. So I brought a copy of the book to school, and in our hour of poetry time, read aloud. The book was just closed when the silence of rapt attention was broken by the many eager suggestions the children had for "illustrating" Milne's poems. Different ones told their choices for the different parts and then these were assigned by thoughtful voting. The next hour that the children had for English, they spent on their dramatization, learning the poems by heart and acting them out. They worked individually or in groups till they felt they had something to present to the rest of the class from whom they asked and accepted comments. Such real people were Christopher Robin, Poole, Alexander Beetle, and the rest, that not a thought was given to costumes or scenery, those more artificial things which help heighten illusion, till the very morning of the presentation to the school in Assembly. Then there was a brown fur coat for Poole, two hats and school bags for doctors, a bench and a blanket for a bed, an empty bottle and spoon, a gray wooden box and a broom handle for a fishing pole. Nor was anything more needed, for the members of the grade were really living in the book. Now they were ready to give to their audience the same joy as they had had when first they heard the poems. In all they spent two hours in preparation for a twenty-minute assembly, that has not yet been forgotten.

This same group of seventh-grade children did a second and very different piece of work in dramatizing Masefield's poem, *Spanish Waters*. I read this to them because they had asked for another poem that they might act out. Listening carefully they realized that there was only one real play character, the old tired man who was remembering back to the days when he had been a pirate, seizing gold on the ships that sailed through Spanish Waters. And it seemed to him that again he heard the waters;

> Like a slow sweet piece of music from the gray forgotten years
> Telling tales, and beating tunes—

The children were able to enter into the old pirate's mood, seeing with him his pictures from the past. It was their suggestion that, besides showing the old man, they could act out two tableaux, the landing of the pirates at sunset and the carrying the treasure inland, and the burying of these chests by the moon's ghastly light. These pictures of necessity required action, and it was planned that all motions should, as much as possible, be in accord with the rhythm of the poem.

Because so much of the beauty of Spanish Waters lay in the pictures, the children wanted to have some suggestion of costumes and scenery. To create the semblance of pirates they all wore bandannas, gay belts, and neckerchiefs. They carried chests in which they had stowed a string of beads, a few coins, or a silver cup—the treasure. Yet these chests so weighted them down that their steps were slow and their bent backs ached. They stumbled over imaginary tree trunks and plowed their way through sucking quagmires. In the background, "a mile off Nigger Head," lay a large model of a sailing ship.

Certain devices were necessary to keep the whole piece together. The remembered music of the Spanish waters suggested to the minds of the children that two of their number should play off stage, one at the piano, and the other at the 'cello. So there was music before and after each picture, making possible the drawing of the gray blanket curtains, behind which electric light bulbs were changed, from red to blue, and pirates shifted places. Meanwhile the worn old man, his head in his hands, listened, as he sat on a box to one side of the closed curtains. The music over, they parted, and once more the old pirate saw his visions of the glorious days on Spanish waters.

The fields of history and literature are closely connected, and much material available for dramatization may be found therein. The fourth grade of last year, in preparation for a study of Homer's Odyssey, had parts of the Iliad read aloud to them. The swing, and forceful simplicity of the language, fired their imagination, as they followed the Greek heroes through the battles of the Trojan War. Each child identified himself with one of the characters and lived with him his adventures.

Particularly vivid is the incident of the Trojan camp when Odysseus and Diomedes creep spying to the Trojan lines to get information and hostages. On the way they meet Dolon, one of the enemy, who is out on a like reconnoitering expedition for the Trojans. They kill him and after a sudden, swift visitation on the enemy the two Greeks return unharmed to their own camp.

The dramatic suspense of the whole scene was intense, and as the reading stopped, there was silence for a moment. "I wish I could be Dolon," "Oh! I want to be Odysseus," "Let me be Diomedes," came in quick succession.

The room was at once converted into an imaginary plain in Troy; the watch fires of the Greek camp flickering in opposition to the dull glow of those of the Trojans on the other side, Each character took his place and the group started in to reenact the scene, extemporizing where memory failed. The rhythm of the language had fixed itself in the children's minds so that it carried over almost entirely. There was no costuming; a book served for a shield; invisible swords were brandished and sweaters were heavy armor.

After the initial attempt there was a storm of criticism, each child suggesting action and words to be substituted or speeches to be entirely changed. Certain parts were read again, the children listened intently and reconstructed their own ideas.

The next time the character's parts were reassigned. New interpretation brought new problems. With a unified group conception acting as the driving force, the class demanded the reading over once more. When several more such trials had been made the children who had best taken their parts were chosen and the incident was acted for the final time to everyone's satisfaction.

The whole dramatization took perhaps an hour. It was done without preparation for an audience and so impelling was the children's desire to give this scene that the result reflected the vividness and strength of the original. Also the whole historical incident was impressed on each individual in a far more real and lasting way than any objective presentation could have done it.

This year's fourth grade found dramatic possibilities in their study of Egypt, which served as an introduction to the story of Greek civilization. For three weeks they became archeologists and excavators. With the help of a book of photographs the class would approach the outside of a tomb, choose the place to dig, and, as the pages turned, bring to light one treasure after another.

One day the teacher suggested acting what they had been pretending. The children were delighted and went into the study to make their own plan. Everyone began to tell what he would find. After a noisy half hour they returned having decided in what order each would come and what he would find. So far the finding of the tomb was to be all imaginary. The teacher suggested the possibility of making an actual tomb enclosed with the burlap screens. This idea was seized upon. For several days, about three and a half hours in all, children, without any outside help, worked over large sheets of brown paper with brushes and paints until they had made the decorations for the walls of the tomb. To dress the mummies who were to be inside the tomb, they copied from a book headdresses, the costumes of two guards, and a little mummified monkey they found.

Since the first day of planning the class felt this scene should be shown to the rest of the school, so one morning exercise was set aside for "The Discovery of an Egyptian Tomb." The school was informed that Grade IV had gone out with some of the Harvard unit and hoped to discover something of importance. These searchers were now before the school, with real picks and shovels. Pretending to dig, they unearthed an imaginary scarab, a bit of a broken tear bottle and jewels. Then a hole led them to pull away some rocks, and screens, and there, in the stillness of centuries, stood a silent group surrounded by a blaze of color. On the walls in red and blue and yellow were obelisks, river boats, desert scenes, hieroglyphics, and real Egyptian numerals. Two rigid guards stood faithfully watching over the prostrate mummies of a Pharaoh, his Queen, and son. The royal family were tightly wrapped and wore brilliant headdresses. Beside the boy squatted the mummy of his pet monkey. After a long look at these riches the tomb was covered up again until the archeologists should return to remove certain treasures to the school museum.

I feel sure that almost every kind of class work may be illuminated by dramatizing. Most little children act things out quite naturally and if they are encouraged to keep it up they are spared self-consciousness in acting, even at the self-conscious age in living. When a class acts for itself there is of course no audience. That is the time when most creative things are done, before repetition has established a way of doing. At this stage the play is an experience being lived for the first time, not a known thing being shared with onlookers. Once a form is established, however, it seems to kindle the actors to have an audience. The bothersome conventions of having to speak louder at assembly than in the classroom, of having to keep from standing behind each other and so forth, seem to be more than compensated for by the heightened excitement of having more people to draw under the spell of the situation. All the above examples are of rapid dramatizing where the purpose was to make vivid a piece of class work. There is another kind of acting experience that we try to give our children once in a year— that is, taking part in the production of a play that is as finished in speech and action, in costumes and setting, as they can make it. A sense of workmanship comes from such a long-time piece of work, where the best skill of grown-ups and children is requisitioned, that sometimes lasts as an unforgettable experience. By their nature, however, these great events can happen only very seldom. Meanwhile on a week day, in almost any classroom, one can be acting things out.

ART AND THE CHILD AT WALDEN SCHOOL, N. Y. C. (1926)   From Florence Cane. "Art In The Life Of The Child," in Gertrude Hartman and Ann Shumaker, eds., *Creative Expression* (New York, 1926), pp. 42-46.

The world of art is truly a cosmos. It contains within it the whole drama of life. The creative process is life itself revealing all its phases: conception and growth, play and work; its problems, conflicts, failures, overcomings, and achievements. Therefore art may hold within it possibilities for the development of the child in relation to life far more important than the possibilities for the development of the artist. Too often man has identified himself with his art in a false way: pinned his ego on his art and said, "If my art is great, I will be great." I do not believe this to be true. On the contrary, I believe that man is like a tree and art is one of the fruits of that tree. The fruit is a measure of that tree's worth. The quality of the painting inevitably develops if the child develops as an individual, and equally the child grows with his growth as a painter. Therefore the direction of my teaching has been towards the liberation and growth of the child's soul through play and work and self-discipline involved in painting.

The play spirit is the primary one. The creative impulse is born of it and without play art cannot exist. Art always starts in play, otherwise it is not art, and it must preserve this element or lose its purity. I mean play in the sense that it springs from an inner wish for satisfaction of the true self. In early youth this satisfaction seems to be completely achieved.

> Heaven lies about us in our infancy
> Shades of the prison house begin to close
>   Upon the growing boy.

As the child matures, the possibility of complete achievement slips away from him, but in his effort to approximate it the element of work enters in. His search for truth and beauty drives him on to infinite labor. This labor must always be related to the play—the inner wish to express the unattainable—or it is no longer art and contains neither beauty nor truth. When outer standards enter, such as the desire to please, to be accepted, to receive praise and fame, the shrine is desecrated and art takes flight. In the play aspect lies the instinctive, irrational, and unconscious; the black as well as the white; the grotesque and crude as well as the beautiful; the wild as well as the controlled. Its outpouring is like the unfolding of life; it brings with it release and joy. Perhaps it is the recognition of both these values that makes this work vital. The young child is uncritical and easily pleased; endless fantasies stream forth; their projection through the painting makes a channel for the subjective life, builds in the child a faith in himself and forms the beginning of his own center. Man is born with the creative impulse and this impulse may become the means of revealing and developing the self. The work side being a continuation and development of the play becomes more conscious and directed; it brings in its train strength and power, the ability to conquer difficulties, and achieve a completed thing.

Though I speak of work and play as two aspects they occur in the same work of art and one must do nothing to separate them. In the play side lies the instinctive creative impulse that must be cherished above all else; in the work side lies the searching need for perfection, the development of the material thrown up by the first. The first is like the birth of life, the second is its overcoming and transforming. This must come in natural stages adapted to the individual needs of each student. Infinite care must be taken to do nothing that may stifle the creative impulse.

Creation is a process like life itself. It rises out of a state of quiet, a sacred spot where the miracle is born. Out of the dark, the unconscious, a spring wells forth, and like a stream cutting its own bed through the meadow it flows. After this process a detachment sets in and the artist views, judges, and develops according to his taste and maturity. In the young child or a great genius a state of unity may exist and the two processes occur at the same time. Because of this simple unity in the young child painting is play for him and he is better off with almost no teaching. The creative fantasy must be respected and allowed free play a long time before any laws of art can be brought to the child without harm. The expression of feeling or the representation of objects as they appear to the comprehension of the child are essential to the building of an inner honesty and a faith in his own powers. A flower may appear larger to a child than himself. He should be permitted to make it so without comment. For if he gives up belief in his own concept for that of the adult's, a conformity may begin which leads to sterility. If, however, his ideas and feelings are permitted to flow freely regardless of whether they appear clear or confused to the adult, they will satisfy him. As he makes these fantastic patterns and forms he gains empirical experience. In placing colors next to each other often enough he discovers harmony; in interlacing lines he finds rhythm; and in opposing masses he learns balance. So in this early period there is little teaching except to show the child how to take care of the material and to use his body freely as he paints.

But when he grows older a change gradually takes place in him. At about ten or eleven years he is no longer so easily pleased. He becomes critical. The thing projected in canvas does not conform to the inner image and the child becomes dissatisified. But his desire to achieve in his painting what he imagines drives him on to a search for truth. He enters a new period, the second stage of creation. He no longer merely plays; he works. At this time teaching is needed. The teacher must give the children whatever technical help they require individually as the need appears, but more important than that she must keep them related to their own center, the source, continually leading them back to themselves for the answer whenever possible. All through the years when they are acquiring technique she must see to it that the door to their imagination is kept open. The greatest harm that teachers of art can do is to let the acquiring of technique postpone or exclude creation. Form is man's language for expressing his spirit and if the spirit slips away the form is empty and dead.

Building on these observations the general plan of art in the Walden School is somewhat as follows: The young children from two to ten are given free use of materials: crayons and large paper, water-colors, post-card colors, and clay. They draw, or paint, or model, at will—just as they play with blocks or toys. As it is a free spontaneous impulse and only followed as such, it will be impractical to have a special teacher come in regularly. So the class teacher has care of the children in art as well as in their regular work. I go in at the beginning of the year a few times and give the class teacher my point of view. The teachers, furthermore, obtain their own creative experience by learning to paint in a special class for teachers. The teachers' class is an interesting development that has grown out of our experimentation. A number of teachers wanted to paint and asked me whether they could. I consented to try the experiment. Now many of them come regularly and are doing very interesting work; and it actually does have an immediate liberating effect on the work of their children.

I begin by giving the child carefully chosen materials, materials that respond well. The crayons must be soft enough to mark easily, not to require pressure, and yet not so soft they will smudge. Paper must be good enough in quality to take the strokes well and hold them. If it is too coarse the child's efforts are often balked. Water colors must be moist in order to respond. Brushes must be large to help keep the work free. There is always a tendency to cramp and niggle. In using post-card colors for young children, if they are to help themselves and keep the work clean, a systematic plan must be made. I give each child a china palette with the divisions for the colors. The large jars of colors stand in a row on a table covered with oil cloth. In front of each large jar stands a small empty jar with a wooden mustard spoon. The child can help himself to a color with this spoon, place it on his palette, replace the spoon in the empty jar, ready for the next child to use. By this method the problem of waste and mixed colors is done away with. I teach the children such practical details as the need to dip the brush in water before using a new color, to change the water frequently when it gets muddy, to start work on the upper part of the paper first so as to avoid smearing, or in using crayons the need of keeping them sharp and clean. All such small details are the means towards giving the child the power to express what he wants. Often discouragement comes from simply not knowing how to keep the colors clear or the brushes clean. A class teacher who does not paint herself may be unaware of the importance of these matters. I want to cultivate in the child a love of his tools, such as good craftsmen always have. It builds something in the child. The care he gives his materials reflects in his painting and then in his life. In learning to make his strokes with care he finds he needs a supple brush; the washing of it properly is therefore closely related to good work.

Next as to the free use of his body: If the child is working in a standing position I see that he is well balanced so that he may sway easily from one foot to the other. One should be able to dramatize a gesture, as a dancer or an actor would. For the arms I try to teach large gestures with the shoulder as a working point. So often the children cramp themselves and use only the finger muscles. I tell them that all their joints, the wrists, elbow, and shoulder are pivots to work from as reliable as the center of a compass. When they draw I want them first to feel the line they are going to make and then trust the arm to do it. Here may be found the difference between fear and faith, and the line shows it. Let the child mark two points far apart on the paper and join them with a curve. There are two ways: if he tries timidly to guide the line in a cramped fashion it will be poor and uncertain because it is determined by fear; but if he swings it in freely trusting the arm, the line will assume a beautiful strong curve and express the organic use of the whole being.

Having given the child his materials, I trust him to do what he wants and let him continue to draw or paint as long as his interest lasts. To the extent he is content with his work I am assured the thing projected on paper corresponds to the image within. One little girl of five said of her painting, "It looks the way you feel inside."

At the ages of ten or eleven the plan changes. The children leave their classroom and come to me in the studio. All of their work is more differentiated now and is being carried beyond mere spontaneous impulse. Here they are given oil paints, or colored inks, or linoleum, or wood blocks, or clay. Besides the direct painting we are trying to develop some of the practical arts. The students have decorated rooms, not only mural painting, but all the workman side—the scraping, crack filling, and ordinary painting. They also decorate lockers and doors, and paint screens. They have printed a magazine and illustrated it with their own wood blocks. They have put on plays and made their own costumes and scenery. The competent, confident way in which they tackle these jobs assures us that the undirected early work is bearing its fruit.

Having sketched the general plan of art in the school I will outline my approach to the work. I believe that art is a search for the unattainable and that craft work is a search for the attainable. The difference, if clearly realized, defines the approach. Since it is the unattainable, the immortal thing we seek, naturally it is within the child's own soul the source is found. It is because I have this faith in children and build their faith that they respond as they do. It is for this reason that I do not volunteer criticism. I feel it is a violation of the creative process for one human being to interrupt or direct another. Who knows what the vision of the worker is, except the worker himself, and how can a teacher be of use except at the point of dissatisfaction when the worker has reached an impasse? Therefore I wait until I am asked for help. It is not only what is taught but when that is important. I never lessen the child's self-criticism. I must ask him what he thinks is poor and by questioning find out what he meant to do; then show him how he failed, and find a way to come nearer to his conception. It calls for all one's understanding and all one's technique, for with the right direction—not correction—the child should move on; a new door should be opened where he will perceive more directly, or feel more deeply, or think more clearly.

I never suggest a subject; it is always the children's choice. If one says occasionally she doesn't know what to paint I talk with her until I draw out of her a hidden wish for something she wanted to do but was afraid she couldn't. It is very interesting to observe how the interest will flag if they attempt to paint something they don't really care about; but if they attempt something that is really dear to them, no matter how difficult it is, the necessary energy is there. That is why it is so important for them to choose their own subject.

THE PHILOSOPHY OF THE WINNETKA, ILLINOIS, CURRICULUM

(1926)   From Carleton Washburne, "The Philosophy of the Winnetka Curriculum," in National Society for the Study of Education, *Twenty-sixth Yearbook, Part I*, (Bloomington, Ill., 1926), pp. 219-28.

The Winnetka curriculum is based upon four hypostases: Every child has a right to master those knowledges and skills which he will probably use in life; every child has a right to live naturally, happily, and fully as a child; human progress depends on the development of each individual to his full capacity; the welfare of human society requires the development of a strong social consciousness in each individual.

It is a comparatively simple matter to determine what knowledges and skills are commonly needed. Scientific investigations of the demands of society in this field are well under way. It is becoming possible to build the knowledge-and-skill part of the curriculum upon research. The Winnetka schools have contributed their share to such research.

We, in Winnetka, have made an exhaustive study of the common allusions to persons and places in periodical literature, recognizing that in order to read intelligently a person must have familiarity with these persons and places.[1] We have made comparative analyses of the vocabulary studies of others, to determine what words children are most likely to need to spell.[2] We have made statistical studies of primary reading books to find what phonograms are most useful to children learning to read,[3] and have analyzed the 10,000 commonest words in the English language to discover the syllables which occur so commonly as to demand instant recognition.[4] With others, we have measured the speed and accuracy possessed by successful, intelligent men and women in various arithmetical processes, as a guide to the degree of skill children are likely to need.[5]

As a result of such studies of our own, and of studies of the same general type made by others, we have, as far as possible, built the knowledge-and-skill part of our curriculum on the known needs of society.

If a certain bit of knowledge or skill is necessary to practically every normal person, every child should have an opportunity to master it. There should not be excellent grasp for some, good for others, fair for others, and poor for still others—there should be real mastery for every child. The wide differences that are known to exist among children make it obvious that this mastery cannot be obtained by all children—or any group of children—in the same length of time and with the same amount of practice. Hence it is necessary to provide varying amounts of time and varying amounts of instructional material for different children.

To do this under ordinary public school conditions, the Winnetka Schools, following Frederic Burk's lead,[6] have developed their individual instruction technique. This consists of re-stating the knowledge-and-skill curriculum in terms of very definite units of achievement; preparing complete diagnostic tests to cover all of these units; and preparing self-instructive, self-corrective practice materials.

[1]Washburne, Carleton: "Basic facts needed in history and geography" and "Building a fact course in history and geography," Chapters XIII and VI, *Twenty-Second Yearbook* of this Society, Part II, 1923; Pendleton, Charles, and Washburne, Carleton, "The fact basis of a history, geography, and civics curriculum," *Journal of Educational Research*, October, 1923; Mohr, Louise, and Washburne, Carleton, "The Winnetka social science investigation," *Elementary School Journal*, December, 1922.

[2]Washburne, Carleton, "A spelling curriculum based on research," *Elementary School Journal*, June, 1923.

[3]Vogel, Mabel; Jaycox, Emma; and Washburne, Carleton, "A basic list of phonics for Grades I and II, *Elementary School Journal*, February, 1923.

[4]Washburne, Carleton, "The Commonest Syllables," *Journal of Educational Research*, October, 1926.

[5]Washburne, Carleton, "Social Needs in Arithmetic." *Elementary School Journal*, September, 1926.

[6]Ward, Mary A., and others, "Individual System as Developed in the San Francisco State Teachers College." *Twenty-Fourth Yearbook* of this Society, Part II.

When these three things have been done, it is not at all difficult to allow each child to work as long on any unit of the curriculum as is necessary to master it.[7]

The grade subdivisions of the knowledge-and-skill curriculum in Winnetka are based upon statistical records of the amount the slowest, normal, diligent child can accomplish in a year. We consider it unfair and demoralizing to set up standards which some children are doomed never to meet. A normal probability curve of achievement in a common essential is an admission of flat failure on the part of the school or the teacher. To set a standard, presumably based on a social need, and then so to teach that very few children achieve it, that the bulk of them are consigned to mediocrity, and others to failure, is inexcusable inefficiency.

Each year, therefore, for the past six years, the teachers of each grade in Winnetka have met with me in May or June and gone over the accomplishments of all the children in each subject. The records of children proved by intelligence tests to be subnormal have been, for this purpose, ignored. So have the records of children who are known to have loafed, who have obviously not tried to get their work done, and of those who have been absent for more than two weeks. The records of all other children have been analysed, and if any normal child, with an I.Q. over 95, who has attended school regularly and worked diligently, has not reached standard in a certain subject, the standard has been immediately lowered. Or, if any such child has not been able to complete all the units of work assigned to his grade in any subject, uncompleted units have been pushed up into the next grade higher.

Conversely, if the slowest, normal, diligent child in a certain subject has completed more units of work than we had considered practicable for a year's work in his grade, additional units have been pulled down from the grade above and made a part of the lower grade's curriculum.

In this way, after repeated adjustments based on each year's careful record of every child's progress, we have gradually found, experimentally, how many units of work and what standards of achievement are attainable by all normal, diligent children in a year's time in each grade.

Attacking the same problem from another angle, we have made, or are making, grade-placement studies to determine what sort of material is suitable for children of various stages of school progress. One such study consisted of measuring the spelling ability of several thousand children in and about Chicago, then finding what commonly needed words were relatively easy to spell and what ones relatively hard, for children of each degree of ability.[8] Another involved finding what books are read and liked by children of different ages and degrees of reading ability in thirty-four American cities.[9] Another, growing out of this, consists of analysing the measurable differences between books liked in various grades.[10] Still another consists of writing material for children of certain grades and known reading ability, then testing their comprehension; rewriting the parts that have failed to get across, and re-testing, until the material is made suitable.[11]

[7]Washburne, Carleton, "A Program of Individualization,"*Twenty-Fourth Yearbook* of this Society, Part II, and bibliography therein.

[8]Washburne, Carleton: "A Spelling Curriculum Based on Research." *Elementary School Journal*, June, 1923.

[9]Washburne, Carleton, and Vogel, Mabel: *Winnetka Graded Book List*, American Library Association, 1926.

[10]Washburne, Carleton: "Measurable Differences in Books Suitable for Different Grades. *Elementary English Review*, April, 1926.

[11]Still in progress—to be published.

This whole field of grade-placement is relatively unworked. A curriculum is not scientific or efficient unless it is based on known needs and is so constructed as to involve the presentation of suitable subject matter in the right order and at the right stage of a child's development, as determined by research.

Through at least partially scientific selection of subject matter, through such scientific studies as we have been able to make of the best methods and times for the presenting of subject matter, and through the technique of individual instruction and progress, the Winnetka schools are finding that it is possible to teach the commonly needed knowledges and skills in about half of the school day—and to teach them in such a way that every normal child, temporarily at least, achieves mastery.[12]

This leaves half the school day clear—usually half the morning and half the afternoon—for the other phases of the curriculum.

Every child has the right to live naturally, happily, and fully as a child. In *human* life, childhood is in itself an important phase. *Biologically,* childhood may be mere preparation for the reproductive stage, and all life beyond that stage may be mere waste. But humanly, the whole span of life is worth while. The reproductive stage is often the stage of struggle and turmoil from which one looks back longingly to the care-free happiness of childhood or to the peace and contemplation of later life. Childhood in itself is a beautiful section of life, and children should be given a chance for free, full living.

Homes are built primarily for adults. The mother who said, "Helen, go and see what John is doing and tell him not to," is quite typical. The present nursery-school movement is bringing to our attention the need for places built and planned for children. The playground movement has for years been trying to provide opportunities for happy child life.

We try to make the Winnetka schools happy, attractive places for children to be in. What Bobbitt calls the "play-level" of the curriculum has a respected place in our schools. We believe in colorfulness, coziness, hominess in our classrooms; in an opportunity for spontaneity. We want children to *want* to come to school.

There is, however, a more far-reaching purpose back of the activities of that part of the day which is freed from academic subject matter. We are attempting to develop each child's individuality, each child's special interests and abilities, as fully as possible. And we are trying to train him in the use of his own particular abilities for the welfare of others, to instill in him a fundamental sense of his dependence upon and responsibility for the group of which he is a part—a group which gradually enlarges until it embraces all mankind.

The group cannot progress—mankind cannot evolve—except as each individual develops and as each individual *varies* from the average. Schools in the past have been largely concerned with making people alike, with giving them the *same* knowledges and skills. There is a place for this—we don't want originality in spelling, for instance—but if we really succeeded in a complete standardization of education, we would produce a race of Robots. And progress would cease. In so far as we can find and develop in each child, on the other hand, those capacities which are different, in so far as we can encourage self-expression and creation, we are making for human evolution.

Creative work consequently occupies a vital place in the curriculum of the

[12]Washburne, Carleton; Vogel, Mabel; and Gray, William S. *A Survey of the Winnetka Public Schools.* Public School Publishing Company, 1926.

Winnetka Schools. We are attempting to provide both stimulus and opportunity for each child to contribute something new. Instead of suppressing variation, we are trying to encourage and develop it, so that each child as an individual, different from all other individuals, may grow to his full stature.

No individual can develop fully, however, except as the society of which he is a part develops. Each individual must, for his own ultimate welfare, contribute to the welfare of the group.

The part of the curriculum most necessary in the present stage of human development, therefore, is neither the acquisition of knowledges and skills nor the opportunity for happy, childlike living, important as we believe both of these things to be. It is the attempt to give children a deep and abiding sense of the fact that in the world's good is one's own, and that in one's own is the world's.

This is akin to what Bobbitt calls "large-group consciousness"—it is a realization of the interdependence of man on man, of the organic unity of the human race.

These terms all sound abstract and far out of the realm of childhood. They sound 'high brow.' Yet unless we can make them real in the lives of the coming generations, there is little hope for the survival of civilization. Mankind to-day is like an uncoordinated baby with a sharp knife in its hand. Science has given us knowledge which is as capable of destroying the race as it is of upbuilding it. And the spiritual development—the sense of social responsibility—of mankind has not kept pace with its knowledge. To help mankind to coordinate—to train it in cooperation while it is still in our schools—is our one great hope, and our greatest responsibility.

The worst of it is that the science of education has scarcely touched this aspect of education. We have to grope our way blindly. And meanwhile the baby has the knife!

The efforts of the Winnetka Public Schools to develop a social consciousness include provision for a wide variety of cooperative activities in which each child must merge his personal good in the common weal, and also many activities in which each child may develop fully his own individuality.

Dramatizations offer one field for cooperative activities; for the writing of the plays, the planning and making of the costumes and scenery, the advertising and managing of occasional public performances, give children opportunities to develop their own special capacities, and to contribute these to the group enterprise.

The preparation of the school paper—some writing for it, some drawing, some making stereotypes from the drawings, some carving woodcuts, some soliciting advertisements, some handling the business end, some setting type, some running the presses, some taking charge of distribution—give a large number of children a chance to develop their own particular abilities and at the same time to cooperate in a common activity.

Team games on the playground, ensemble playing in the orchestra or band, or in the harmonica bands of the lower grades—these and dozens of other activities are selected and planned with the primary purpose of training children to live socially, of making each child realize that the welfare of the group depends upon each member of the group contributing the best that is in him.

Another, and not dissimilar line of social development comes through our self-governing assemblies. The assemblies and the business meetings within each classroom are training in citizenship—training in social acting and thinking.

The social studies, which are often the basis for many of the socialized activities, probably offer the most direct training in social consciousness. Our history and geography from the beginning are world history and geography. Our emphasis throughout the grades is on the underlying unity of man. Both the factual side of the work in the middle grades and the problem side stressed in the junior high school are constructed and taught from the point of view of developing a social consciousness in the children.

Finally, the subconscious development of a social sense through the various activities, and the generalized social consciousness brought out in the treatment of the social studies, are made definite and personal through discussions both in class and between the teacher and each child, and through a system of rating each child's development.

The report card used in the Winnetka schools shows on one side the pupil's progress in mastering commonly needed knowledges and skills, on the other side his progress in developing certain attitudes and habits essential for social living. A section of this latter part of the "goal card" is reproduced herewith. The remainder of it deals, in the same way, with orderliness, work spirit, self-reliance, initiative, and special interests or abilities.

Group Spirit	Period						Period					
	1st	2nd	3rd	4th	5th	6th	1st	2nd	3rd	4th	5th	6th
Has marked ability to co-operate with the group in both work and play. Shows consideration for others. Is helpful in all activities.												
Is able at most times to co-operate with the group and contributes his share to the betterment of the work or play activities.												
Shows the usual amount of ability to co-operate with the group both in work and in play. Shows an average degree of consideration for others. Is helpful when his own interests are not too greatly concerned.												
Slow to co-operate with the group. Shows only a slight degree of consideration for others. Seldom is very helpful, often hinders.												
Does not co-operate with the group in work or play. Is selfish and violates the rights of others.												

Each 6-week period a check mark is placed opposite the paragraph that most nearly describes the attitude of the child. This is done by the teacher in consultation *with* the child himself. We have found this rating helpful both to the child and the teacher. The child learns self-analysis and sees definitely an ideal toward which to work. The teacher is obliged to consider the attitude of each pupil and to see where each needs developing.

There are progressive educators who would have us merge our underlying principles in an "activities curriculum" so that children's mastery of knowledges and skills would grow naturally out of childlike, social situations. This sounds good; but we seriously doubt whether it can be done without damaging each type of activity.

Socialized activities demand that the whole group work together. Knowledge-and-skill mastery requires that different children proceed at different rates. Some of the social problems children need to attack and some of the knowledges and skills they need to learn are not really childlike, and cannot therefore be taught through child-like activities.

Our observation has been that schools which attempt to develop all their knowledge-and-skill subjects from childlike activities, often do a 'sloppy' job in giving the children mastery of the tool subjects, and sometimes distort the so-called 'childlike' activities in an attempt to bring in knowledge and skills.

There seems no valid reason for supposing that all types of activity should correlate or that the same methods should be applied to all types of learning. It can be shown that children can master knowledges and skills happily and satisfactorily without tying these up to projects. And it has yet to be proved that children who do so master them are unable to apply them to life situations. Our own experience has been that if children are at the same time living full lives, and if the materials of instruction are so prepared as to show the children the relation of their knowledges and skills to real situations, there is no unusual difficulty about 'carry-over.'

Nor do we find any signs of split personality or divided self that some people have feared might result from giving children mastery of subject matter individually, and social training in groups.

The ordinary, natural life of any person is divided into different parts. At a certain time we eat breakfast. A little later we may be reading the world news. Then we may be doing our particular job. In the evening we may be amusing ourselves at the theater, or a dance, or in our home. These activities are unrelated. Each fills one need in our lives. And we don't suffer from the lack of correlation.

In Winnetka, we feel that the development of the social consciousness is too important a thing to be used as a mere means to the end of mastering knowledges and skills—or to be distorted in an effort to include all necessary knowledges and skills. Insofar as the socialized activities *incidentally* shed light on the tool subjects, or give application to these subjects, we are glad to recognize the relation. But we do not feel that we can safely trust to such incidental relationships to give our children the necessary mastery of the tool subjects.

It would be a mistake, on the other hand, to assume that in practice the knowledge-and-skill subjects, the creative activities, and the socializing activities are in water-tight compartments. While we feel that each requires different treatment in the curriculum, the children don't know that we are making any such distinctions. The school day, in actuality, shows a constant inter-play among all functions. The play activities, creative work, and socializing activities merge to such an extent as to be often undistinguishable the one from the other. When a socializing activity calls for certain knowledge or skill, the social and individual parts of the work merge. Certain parts of the day are largely, although not exclusively, devoted to individual mastery of tool and fact subjects. Other parts throw the emphasis upon self-expressive and socialized activities—upon group and creative work. But sharp lines are not drawn.

In our *thinking*, however, in our selection of subject matter and activities, in our equipment and planning, the three functions of the curriculum stand out in bold contrast. The underlying philosophy of the Winnetka curriculum demands that every normal child master the knowledges and skills he is going to need in life; that every child be given a chance to live happily and richly as a child; that every child be given an opportunity to develop fully his own individuality; and that all children be brought to the fullest possible realization that in the world's good is one's own, and in one's own good is the world's.

MARIETTA JOHNSON ON ORGANIC EDUCATION (1927) From Marietta Johnson, "The Educational Principles of the School of Organic Education . . .," as quoted in National Society for the Study of Education, *Twenty-sixth Yearbook, Part I* (Bloomington, Ill., 1927), pp. 349–51.

We believe the educational program should aim to meet the needs of the growing child. We believe that childhood is for itself and not a preparation for adult life. Therefore, the school program must answer the following questions:

What does the child of any particular age need to minister to the health of his body, to preserve the integrity of the intellect, and to keep him sincere and unselfconscious of spirit?

The answers to these questions will constitute the curriculum of the school, and as we grow in understanding of the nature and needs of childhood, the curriculum will change.

We believe that all children need music; therefore we give the younger children singing and dancing and singing games and all sorts of rhythmic work. As the children grow older, this work becomes folk dancing and folk singing, with reading of notes, singing harmonies, and learning to play an instrument at about ten or twelve years of age.

Time is given to dramatics throughout the school life.

*   *   *

We believe that all children need creative handwork. This is the fundamental method of thinking. Therefore, all sorts of material are provided for self-expression. For the very young children, merely making things of clay and sand and using blocks may be sufficient. Later, this develops into real projects, using tools and art and craft materials. The creative handwork continues through all ages up to college. We believe it should continue through the college program. Handwork should grow out of, or be related to, work in history, literature, etc., as far as possible.

We believe that all childhood needs stories. The stories for the very young children would naturally take the form of folklore, and fables, and fairy tales; later on, the form of history, literature, and geography, after learning to read at about eight or nine years of age. This reading work would also result in composition and the study, perhaps, of grammar in the high-school period. The literature, history, and geography stories begun in the early years, would be replaced by the study of history, literature, and science as such in the high-school and college years.

The speech centers are developed very young. A child may learn a language other than his own at an early age, whereas he should not be obliged to read his own until he is eight or nine years of age. We would, therefore, give the children some experience in using a foreign language, such as Spanish or French.

All children need fundamental conceptions of number. The work of measuring, weighing, estimating, counting, begun in the early years, would naturally require the use of figures at about eight or ten, when the mechanics of number would be acquired with great delight. Later, the applied problems, and still later, the abstract problems, which are enjoyed during the high-school and college years.

In order to preserve unselfconsciousness in growth, no grades or marks should be given and no intellectual tasks set by the teacher. The children should be grouped according to chronological age. The teacher should provide suitable work for the group, with individual variation where necessary. The child should not do as he pleases; he does not know what is good for him. In order to preserve the unity of his intellectual and emotional life, intellectual work should accompany and follow sincere interest and desire, and the reward for all learning should be the inner satisfaction and the consciousness of power which comes through understanding.

All children should have free play, so every daily program should include much time in the open, much time in free, self-prompted occupations, and some time to dream. The fullest social association should be given.

We believe that education is life, growth; that the ends are immediate; that the end and the process are one. We believe that all children should have the fullest opportunity for self-expression, for joy, for delight, for intellectual stimulus through subject matter, but we do not believe that children should be made self-conscious or externalized by making subject matter an end. Our constant thought is not what do the children learn or do, but what are the "learning" and the "doing" doing to them.

We believe all children need Nature—not so much for facts as for experience and attitude. The Nature walks and talks of the little children would develop into serious Nature Study, gardening, and science of the older groups.

Every schoolroom must be a health center. In the measure that the school provides activities and exercises which tend to produce a sound, accomplished, beautiful body, an intelligent, sympathetic mind, a sweet, sincere spirit, it is educational. In the measure that it does not, it is not educational, however informational it may be.

We believe that society owes all children guidance, control, instruction, association, and inspiration—right conditions of growth—throughout the growing years until physical growth is completed. No child may know failure—all must succeed. Not "what do you know," but "what do you need," should be asked, and the *nature* of childhood indicates the answer.

THE BEAVER COUNTRY DAY SCHOOL, BROOKLINE, MASSACHUSETTS

(1927)   From Eugene R. Smith, "The Principles of Curriculum-Making In The Beaver Country Day School," in National Society For The Study of Education, *Twenty-Sixth Yearbook, Part I* (Bloomington, Illinois, 1927), pp. 323–25.

Leaving this discussion of general principles, let us consider some of the more specific arrangements that result from them.

The social science central subject includes, as we have said, history, geography, civics, and current events. It might be said to be woven of two continuous threads of thought, one concerned with the pupils themselves, their surroundings, and their communities, from the smallest up to the United States and North America; the other taking up that which is more remote in time and place, and developing into a study of the world in general. In each one of the threads are involved the divisions already mentioned. The method for the study of those things immediate to the children, and particularly of those concerning their own country, is natural spiral as well as cumulative. The more important matters recur from year to year, each time with new and broader emphasis. The other thread is largely progressive, although of necessity repetition and enlargement must enter in from time to time. The thread concerned with the United States is thinner in the early stage, centering around holidays and other civic events, and coming often from likenesses and contrasts rather than from directly planned attack. Later on, it increases until it becomes the main thread, with the other as its adjunct.

In the three primary years, the children respond very strongly to primitive life, possibly because it is less complex and more easily understood by them than is present-day civilization, and so can be more easily used as material for imagination. Possibly also, because it to some extent parallels and interprets their own experiences in reaching out for the foundational things of life. This response is particularly strong in regard to the fundamental needs of food, clothing, and shelter. This second thread, therefore, takes the pupils into the lives of early uncivilized, or little civilized, peoples. Geography is accordingly little more than a condition of life until the third grade, where the more important land and water divisions and other geographical units become somewhat familiar.

The early civilizations, including those of Egypt, Palestine, and Greece, are used in the fourth year, with increasing consideration of geography in its relation to peoples and their problems. Much connection between this and the home-country thread comes out here through industrial and other comparisions. For example, the making of paper from papyrus may stimulate investigation of paper making to-day, clothing problems then and now may be compared, or the progress of the art of various countries may be traced.

In the fifth year, we found a very strong interest in the history of Europe, strongest perhaps in the period of chivalry. Consequently, Roman history is followed by mediaeval history and leads up to the European foundations for the study of United States history. The geography of Europe naturally accompanies its history, but since earlier Roman history gives an impetus for the study of Africa, the continent precedes Europe. The study of Africa, once started, naturally goes beyond what is needed for the Roman period and its general aspects are completed at this time.

The period of American exploration opens the sixth year, bringing in the continents of South and North America as a necessary accompaniment. The geography of the Oriental countries is studied almost as a separate subject, taken to complete the view of the world. Yet in many ways, it also connects with, and contrasts with, other parts of the social studies.

The first years of the junior high school probe rather deeply into present-day life, centering study about our own problems, but following our trade relations, our transportation, and our foreign affairs into all corners of the globe. It is expected that at the end of the eighth year the pupils shall have considerable knowledge and wide interests in regard to mankind, the conditions affecting his progress, and his problems, past and present.

The social sciences of the later years of the course are necessarily college preparatory histories, for which current outlines and textbooks are the foundation.

The mathematics is not hurried in the early primary years, coming in the first and second classes rather as a response to practical needs and game interests than as a superimposed task. Gradually, it takes a larger part in the curriculum, following the recommendations of various psychologists and committees and particularly the report of the National Committee. In this, as in all of the tool subjects, progress is regularly tested by standardized tests, which are used not only for diagnostic purposes, but also as a safeguard to the maintenance of curriculum standards and completeness.

The formal English is based on the usage necessary at each stage of progress: that usage is both oral and written, and comes partly from other subjects and partly from the inspiration of each pupil's reading in poetry and prose. Literature increases its proportion of the time as the pupils grow older. Oral English is required throughout the high school and much opportunity is given for presiding at meetings, writing and presenting plays, and other practical language applications.

The academic subjects for the last four years are to a large extent determined by college entrance requirements, although their content is sometimes modified or supplemented to suit individual or group needs. These requirements are, of course, considered as minimal essentials, rather than complete outlines. . . .

LUCY SPRAGUE MITCHELL ON NEW YORK CITY'S LITTLE RED SCHOOL HOUSE (1929)
From Lucy Sprague Mitchell, *Two Lives: The Story of Wesley Clair Mitchell and Myself* (New York, 1953), pp. 413–19.

I stopped teaching at City and Country School and joined Elisabeth Irwin in her experiment in the Little Red School House, telling everyone that I wanted the experience of working in a public school, which was true. My financial support I withdrew slowly and carefully on an announced schedule of gradually reduced contributions covering ten years. Later I gave them a five-year notice that I could no longer give them the buildings rent-free, and Robin and I moved out of the part that we had occupied for seventeen years. In the end, the school bought the six houses I had remodeled. Financially, the venture had cost me something like a third of all my capital, which certainly would have shocked my business-minded father. But I was content. The school was a going concern with the teachers gradually taking on more responsibility. I had enough money left for some less costly experiments. I had had years of good experience in teaching and educational thinking and was ready and eager for work with people like Elisabeth Irwin and Harriet Johnson and all the Bureau staff. I left the City and Country School with relief. I fancy that Caroline, too, was relieved not to have a person around who persistently wanted to work on ideas that she turned up. Caroline had enough ideas of her own.

Within the following seven years in which I taught at the Little Red School House, I did work out my history-geography program with children. This was one of many opportunities that Elisabeth Irwin gave me. It was through her that I got my first chance to work in a public school—the goal that I never lost sight of. I entered the public-school system—but by a side door. I joined the staff of the Little Red School House in February, 1929, when it began its experiment within a public school. I took some written examinations and an oral examination with Dr. Louis Marks, received a teaching certificate and became the kindergarten teacher. The experiment was financed by the Public Education Association. The plan approved by the Board of Superintendents was: for the first year, the staff of the Little Red School House was to take over the curriculum planning and the teaching of kindergarten, first and second grades, and to train the regular public-school teachers assigned to these classes in our thinking about children and our teaching methods; in succeeding years our staff was to carry these children up through sixth grade, and each year add the new kindergarten children, so that eventually we should be in charge of the curriculum and the teaching of all the children in the school. The children, when they reached third grade, were to be tested in academic skills and subject matter in the "courses of study." Except for that, we were allowed an absolutely free hand in subject matter and teaching techniques.

The school in which this experiment was tried had been chosen because it had a falling registration and because it was supposed to be typically "American"—that is, the children came from families with a wide variety of national backgrounds. Nearly all these families were in the low-income bracket; many mothers as well as fathers worked.

The school was an old building—ugly and run-down, dark basement used for play space, screwed-down desks and all the other stigmata of our earlier school buildings *plus* an outdoor toilet used by the kindergarten boys since the law required separate toilets for boys and girls, and only one was available for the kindergarten. In the name of "modesty," these little four- and five-year-old boys were unbuttoned in their room and with flapping trousers proceeded downstairs and out into the back yard where, through the winter months, the water pipes often were frozen so that the toilet would not flush. Later, we received permission to have kindergarten boys and girls use the same toilet near their room at different times. Also the desks were removed from first- and second-grade rooms and replaced by tables and chairs.

Before school started in February, 1929, the Little Red School House staff got to work with paintbrushes. We painted everything we were allowed to—chairs and tables, toys, orange crates (for individual cubbies, blocks and toys). We hung bright curtains, which partly hid the varnished golden oak woodwork. We took down the pictures of "cute" clean children picking flowers or clattering over cobblestones in wooden shoes (interpretation of modern Netherlands for second grade), and as soon as the children's crayons and showcard color paints had got into action, we covered the walls with their gay crude paintings. In each of our five rooms—one kindergarten, two first and two second grades—we installed a workbench for the children with a few small but genuine tools which we ourselves used to knock together rough shelving. Elisabeth Irwin with her ample figure and gay, witty tongue sailed around watching her enthusiastic paint-daubed crew, bringing us supplies of orange crates and old lumber gathered from neighborhood stores in her Ford, which usually held her two dogs as well as this loot. That first year we had no help from the public-school teachers in "getting ready." The paint was dry and our weary staff thoroughly cleaned with turpentine when school opened. Some two hundred children and five confused public-school teachers entered their transformed rooms.

The teachers were more confused than the children—at least in my kindergarten class, even though most of the children were entering school for the first time. For they, I felt, had been rather heavily conditioned in their expectations of what school would be like by their parents and older brothers or sisters. As part of my job, I kept full records during these three years, both of the groups of children I taught and of every child, records which I studied and analyzed but never published. These records included what the group as a whole and what each child did in block-building, drawing, painting and carpentry; verbatim notes of group discussions; accounts of trips with preparatory and follow-up activities and discussions; many records of spontaneous conversations and many stories dictated to me by children; diary accounts of such activities as dramatic play and, with older children, map-making.

When I took over the kindergarten, I had thirty-nine children, four and five years old. When I said to the principal that I thought twenty-five was the legal limit, she told me not to worry as fourteen children were not on the morning registry but simply allowed to come as a convenience to parents. None of these children had ever handled blocks or tools; they had never been allowed to play on the floor or to get dirty in school. The little girls, in particular, were warned to keep their dresses clean. My first move was to ask the mothers to send overalls for school use. I called the children "little workers." The whole official curriculum—some twenty-six courses of study, parts of which I had to follow—was based on the assumption right down to the four- and five-year-old level, that children learn through words. For instance, the curriculum demanded that kindergarten children learn the names of three flowers. The regular kindergarten teacher taught them "rose," "daisy," "tulip." One day I brought a tulip into the classroom. Some children said it was a tulip, but more said it was a rose or a daisy. As a further check I took the class for a walk through the flower section of the old Jefferson Market, then on Sixth Avenue near the school. The children applied the names they had learned indiscriminately to *all* flowers.

Words are symbols. Yet here were young children being trained to use word symbols without knowing what the symbols stood for, words that carried no images with them. In all areas the situation with older children was much the same: in arithmetic, they were being trained to use symbols of numbers without any number concept behind the symbols; in maps, they were being trained to use lines and color symbols without knowing the realities of mountains, political boundaries, etc., which these symbols stood for. In our whole educational practices, perhaps our whole culture, had not the learning of words and other symbols been substituted for learning through experience about the things for which these symbols stood? Did we not all talk about "democracy," "freedoms," "equality," "work," etc., etc., without having any real experience, any genuine concepts behind these big words? Were we not all "saluting the flag" in some way, instead of living the principles of which the flag was supposed to be the symbol? Of course, this was not a new idea to me. Still it was a shock to find to what an extent teachers were being trained to substitute words for real experiences and real thinking, and curricula were being written on the assumption that using a name meant understanding the thing named.

I began to study my records of what my kindergarten (and later the older children) did in their play and said in their spontaneous conversations, trying to separate what they had learned by experience from words they had been taught to say. A few examples will show the gulf between learning by experience and learning by words alone.

We went to the open Gansvoort Farmers Market where the farmers brought their farm produce in trucks and wagons and sold them. By the time we got our thirty-nine little kindergarten children to the market, most of the farmers had left. One man, however, stood by his wagon of turnips. I whispered to the front children that this man was a farmer. The word passed from one excited child to child. "It's a farmer! It's a farmer!" I was never sure what they expected a farmer to be but certainly not something that looked just like a man. This farmer was a pleasant person who liked children. He told them dramatically how yesterday he picked the turnips on his farm, packed them in baskets and in the early morning drove his horse and wagon from his farm, across the Hudson on a ferry, to the market. It was so early, he said, that the electric lights were still on. Then he gave us three or four turnips. Those turnips stood on the teacher's desk for several days. The children handled them and talked about the farmer. One day we gathered for a discussion in a big circle, with the turnips on a small table in the middle. I asked, "Where did the farmer get his turnips?" Edgar, wildly waving his hand, said, "From the A and P." And not a child thought otherwise. The children had seen a farmer but not a farm.

On another trip to the live fowl Gansvoort market, we saw a big bird walking about his box cage. "He's a turkey," said Tom. Stella burst into shrill laughter. "No, he can't be," she said. "Turkeys don't have feathers." Was she judging by plucked turkeys in a meat market, or by chocolate turkeys?

So it went. These children brought up on a city street had had practically no experience with live animals or growing things. We were not allowed to have a pet in the room. In outdoor play, we used a tiny separate yard with a stone sidewalk and a few patches of earth. One day after a rain, the children discovered two angleworms. They became our prized pets.

In their room the children had small toy horses. They put the horses to bed, covered them with blankets; they brought them milk and sometimes a steak for dinner. "What do horses eat?" asked the kindergarten teacher. "Hay," said Rosalind, and continued to feed her horse milk. A livery stable was something that in those days could be found in the city. We visited one—saw the horses that worked at night delivering vegetables from the markets on the docks to retail stores and slept or rested in the morning. In their stalls some horses were sleeping lying down, some standing up. Some were eating hay. The livery man led out a horse and gave him a drink of water from the trough. He put one child after another on the horse's back (I hanging on to the child) and led the horse around. It was an overwhelming experience.

Gradually the play with blocks developed stables with stalls and watering trough. The horses were fed some dried grass that I brought for hay. The horses were taken to the market (built with blocks by other children).

The rough wagons made at the bench were filled with vegetables (painted balls of clay) and pulled by the horses to stores built by another group of children. Housewives emerged from their block houses, bought vegetables at the stores and returned to cook them for their doll children. Group play based on shared experience. Human geography based on neighborhood work. A city program developed by city children from their here and now world.

The here and now program developed for kindergarten and first grade children was adequate and satisfying to these young children. But the subject matter in the curriculum for the older children (we eventually went up through the fourth grade) went beyond the here and now. Their interest, too, had begun to expand to faraway and long-ago things and people. Even the first graders were no longer satisfied to have apples begin in a refrigerator car or chickens on the market pier. Where do apples and chickens come from?—began to be a typical question. The whole staff of the Little Red School House decided these city children must be given some real country and farm experience and as a part of the school—not just in a summer camp where only a few children could go. So we launched a June program in the country which has ever since been a part of the program of the Little Red School House. The first experiment was with twenty-six kindergarten children, most of whom were then six years old, and some of the younger children in the first grade. Elisabeth Irwin arranged for us to use a settlement camp which would otherwise have been empty through June, and she and two mothers went along to manage the practical end—cooking, supplies and the like. Rhoda Harris, who was to have these children next year, and I went as teachers.

Perhaps these children were too young—not too young for a farm experience, but too young to leave their mothers. Certainly many of the children were emotional for the first days. Before the month was out, however, every one of them had adapted to the strange place and strange substitutes for mothers.

"Adapting" meant many things. I found out one new relationship that it meant when we got ready for the first night. I was to sleep in a room with twelve children whom I had taught. I had them help me make up their beds and then mine. Then we laid out their twelve pajamas and I unpacked and laid out mine on my bed. Anne watched me completely puzzled. She came over and examined my night clothes. She was obviously struggling with a new idea. Finally it came out. Slowly she asked, "Do teachers *sleep?*"

The High School

THE SELECTIVE CHARACTER OF AMERICAN SECONDARY
EDUCATION (1922)   From George S. Counts, *The Selective Character of American
Secondary Education* (Chicago, 1922), pp. 141–48.

In view of the foregoing analysis it is clear that we in America have not
abandoned in practice the selective principle in secondary education, even though
we have established a free public high school in almost every community in the
country. It is not strictly in accord with the facts to say that "a public high school
differs from an elementary school chiefly in the age of its children." It is true that
children in high school are on the average somewhat older than those in the
elementary school, yet, as a matter of fact, there is not very much difference in the
ages of pupils enrolled in the eighth grade and those in the first year of the high
school. High-school students, even today and in spite of the amazing growth of the
high-school enrolment since 1880, are a highly selected group. And this difference is
just as important as the difference in age. Secondary education is not education for
adolescence, as elementary education is education for childhood, but rather
education for a selected group of adolescents, as we have seen in the preceding
chapters, and as we shall note again now in summary.

Parental Occupation And The Public High School

There is a close relation between parental occupation and the privileges of
secondary education. If we examine the entire high-school population, we find
certain occupational groups very well and others very poorly represented, in
proportion to their numbers in the general population. Among the former are the
five great non-labor groups with professional service occupying the most advanta-
geous position, followed by the proprietors, commercial service, managerial service,
and clerical service. At the other end of the series are the lower grades of labor with
common labor almost unrepresented and personal service, miners, lumber-workers,
and fishermen, and the miscellaneous trades and machine operatives in the
manufacturing and mechanical industries, occupying somewhat better positions in
the order named. The other occupational groups are found between these two
extremes. Next to the non-labor groups are the printing trades and the public
service, followed by the machine trades, transportation service, and the building
trades. In general, the order here given reflects the social and economic status of the

occupation, its educational and intellectual standards, and the stability of employment.

Not only do these various occupational classes exhibit different degrees of representation in the high school at the beginning of the course, but those very groups that are under-represented in the Freshman year have the smallest ratio of Seniors to Freshmen. In fact, the representation of an occupation in the first year of the high school is at the same time a fairly accurate measure of its tendency to persist through the fourth year. Consequently, the differences among the groups become more and more pronounced in the successive years of the school. The student population gradually becomes more and more homogeneous as the source from which it is drawn becomes more narrow, until by the time the Senior year of the high school is reached, the student body exhibits a distinctly class character. Here the representatives of the laboring classes are few indeed in proportion to their number in the general population, and the lower grades of labor have practically disappeared. This is brought out in striking fashion by the data from Mt. Vernon in which the sixth grade is contrasted with the last year of the high school.

Evidence in corroboration of these conclusions, drawn from a study of the high-school population, is derived from the investigation of groups of children of high-school age not in high school in Seattle and Bridgeport. In the former city, a study of 514 children of high-school age at work showed a social composition very different from that of the high-school population. Here, four great labor groups—the building trades, common labor, machine trades, and transportation service—contribute over 60 per cent of the children. The situation is just the reverse of that found in the high school. In Bridgeport a similar condition is found. In the evening high school of that city the sons and daughters of the laboring classes constitute the great majority of the enrolment with the machine trades in the lead, followed by the miscellaneous trades, common labor, and the building trades. In the trade school the situation is about the same except that the representation of the laboring classes is yet larger and common labor forges ahead of the miscellaneous trades to second place. Apparently the children of the laboring classes are destined to follow in the footsteps of their fathers. This representation of the labor groups is still further increased in that group of educational unfortunates enrolled in the compulsory continuation classes in which common labor holds first place, accounting for over one-fourth of the entire registration.

These differences in the extent of educational opportunity are further accentuated through the choice of curricula. As a rule, those groups which are poorly represented in the high school patronize the more narrow and practical curricula, the curricula which stand as terminal points in the educational system and which prepare for wage-earning. And the poorer their representation in high school, the greater is the probability that they will enter these curricula. The one-and two-year vocational courses, wherever offered, draw their registration particularly, from the ranks of labor. This tendency is considerably more pronounced among the girls than among the boys. The former seem to be peculiarly bound by the social class from which they come. One is surprised at the unmistakable class character of the girls' college preparatory course in a high school such as that in Bridgeport. Furthermore, the thesis may be cautiously advanced that these differences appear somewhat more clearly in the East than in the West, but it is hardly safe to generalize on the basis of returns from four cities.

A study of expectations following graduation, as given by the students, indicates that this selective principle continues to operate beyond the period of secondary education. Those classes which are least well represented in the last year of the high school will apparently be yet less well represented in the colleges and universities. And, as in the case of the choice of curricula, this tendency is more marked among the girls than among the boys, in the East than in the West.

The Public High School And The Cultural Level

Parental occupation, as one index of cultural level, exhibits a close relation to educational opportunity. The same is true of the possession of a telephone in the home, according to the returns from Bridgeport and Mt. Vernon. In the former city, it was found that telephones are two and one-half times as frequent in the homes of high-school students as in those of children attending the trade school, and seven times as frequent as in the homes of the children in the compulsory continuation classes. Furthermore, the percentage of telephones increases decidedly from year to year in the high school. Thus we find but 39.7 per cent of the students in the Freshman year coming from homes with telephones, whereas in the Senior year, this percentage is 60.3. There are also wide differences among the curricula in this respect. In the case of the girls, telephones are almost twice as frequent in the homes of those who are enrolled in the college preparatory as in the homes of those taking the commercial course. And these curricular differences are less marked among the boys than among the girls as was observed in the study of the parental occupation. Data from Mt. Vernon, including returns from the sixth grade, support in every particular these conclusions drawn from the Bridgeport study.

The Public High School And Family Influences

All the evidence brought to light in this study points to the importance of the family as a powerful factor in determining attendance at high school. The mortality of parents of high-school students is found to be considerably below the expectation for children of high-school age, and does not increase perceptibly from the Freshman to the Senior year. In fact, according to the returns from Mt. Vernon, the mortality of parents is appreciably higher among sixth-grade children than among students in the last year of the high school. An examination of the various groups of children of high-school age not in high school shows a much higher mortality of parents here than among high-school students. In the case of young people attending the evening high school in Bridgeport, the mortality of parents is extraordinarily high, more than two and one-half times as high as among those attending the day high school. Unquestionably the disorganization of the home through the death of a parent is reflected in the diminution of the opportunities of secondary education.

While the evidence is neither quite so clear nor quite so objective, apparently the engaging in remunerative employment on the part of the mother acts in the same way as the death of a parent. Comparisons made among the groups studied usually hold in the one case as in the other. Yet, it must not be forgotten that the working mother is usually just one element in a complex social situation.

The influence of the size of the family on educational opportunity is not altogether clear. On the average, those elements in the population who do not patronize the high school have larger families than those who do, but there is no evidence to indicate that the size of the family itself is a determining factor; for the number of brothers and sisters is no smaller among Seniors than among Freshmen, and the very large families have just as high representation in the last as in the first year of the high school. Likewise the very small families do not apparently increase their representation in the later years of the high school.

The order of birth seems to be a matter of more importance, although the complexity of the situation is hardly compatible with any but the most cautious of statements. Our clearest evidence, drawn from the four groups studied in Bridgeport, indicates that the firstborn has somewhat more limited chances of securing a high-school education than the lastborn child. It is on him particularly that the burden of family support is likely to fall, if one or more of the children must help to bear it.

The Public High School And The Immigrant

Returns from Bridgeport and Mt. Vernon indicate very clearly that children of native parentage attend the public high school in proportionately much larger numbers than do children of immigrant parentage. There are certain immigrant groups, however, that approximate, if they do not surpass, the native stock in their zeal for secondary education, altogether apart from the social and economic handicaps under which the immigrant labors. Among these, probably the Russian Jews stand at the top, followed by the Irish, the Germans, and the peoples of the British Empire. At the other extreme are the Italians, the Poles, and the races of the old Austro-Hungarian Empire who patronize the high school in exceedingly small measure. Disregarding the record of the Russian Jews, it may be stated as a general principle that the farther east and south we go in Europe, as the source of our immigrants, we find less interest in secondary education.

The well-known tendency among our own people for the girls to patronize the high school in greater numbers than the boys is reversed among certain immigrant stocks. Thus, while in the Bridgeport High School there are but 74 boys of native parentage to every 100 girls, among the Italians this ratio of boys to girls is 154. This social trait, if such it may be called, varies much from group to group. Beginning with the Irish who exhibit the American trait in approximately its native strength of sending girls rather than boys to high school, the proportion of boys steadily increases as we pass east and south into Europe. Among the peoples of the "new" immigration the right of the girl to a secondary education is not recognized as on a parity with that of the boy.

In choice of curricula the girls of immigrant stock are clearly less inclined toward the college preparatory course than are the girls of native parentage. Curiously enough the reverse is true of the boys, but, since the boys of American parentage are exceptionally well represented in the scientific course, which in reality is a college preparatory course, no large significance should be attached to this difference between the foreign and native stock.

The Public High School And The Negro

While for the country as a whole the proportion of negroes of high-school age to be found in our high schools is very small, in the city of St. Louis they do about as well as the whites. A study of the student population in the negro high school of this city helps us to understand the difficulties that stand in the way of educational achievement on the part of members of this race. The fathers of the students in this high school are for the most part engaged in manual labor, and the lower and less respectable grades of manual labor, particularly personal service and common labor.

The negro family exhibits a large measure of disorganization, as indicated by such crude and unsatisfactory phenomena as a deceased parent or a working mother. In the high-school population of St. Louis the parental mortality for the negro children is well over twice as high as for the children of white stock, and the frequency of the working mother is between five and six times as great for the students of the one as for those of the other race. All of which makes it safe to conclude that nowhere else in the nation is there a similarly large representation of any other race living on the same social and economic level that is sending as large a proportion of its children to high school as the negroes of St. Louis.

The negroes exhibit in a pronounced fashion the American trait of sending a larger proportion of their girls than of their boys to high school. In choice of curricula, the negro girls differ from their white sisters chiefly in avoidance of the two-year commercial curriculum and in their very frequent selection of the home economics course. The negro boys avoid the general and concentrate on the manual training course. Following graduation, the negro girls expect to attend normal school and enter professional service in much larger numbers than do the whites. And they are not apparently looking forward to clerical service in proportionate numbers. Surprisingly, in the case of the boys, the only important difference between the two races is the much larger expectation of college attendance on the part of the negroes. It should be kept in mind, however, that these conclusions are based altogether on statements by the students, and consequently require considerable discounting.

The Public High School And Psychological Selection

Not only is the high-school population selected sociologically, but it is selected psychologically as well. Children of high-school age not in high school, whether they be in the evening high school, the trade school, or the continuation classes, show a lower intelligence rating on the average than do those in high school. But there is much overlapping in the distribution of ability for the two groups. There is much excellence out of, as well as much mediocrity in, the high school. The trade-school population shows a particularly wide distribution of ability.

In the high school itself the traditional academic curricula draw a higher type of ability, on the average, than do the newer and vocational curricula. Here also, however, the overlapping of the distributions is pronounced, and perhaps even more significant than the average difference.

The children from the laboring classes exhibit ability of practically as high grade as do those from the other occupational groups. This is probably due to the much greater elimination of children of labor parentage. Likewise the children of immigrants do about as well on the tests as do the children of native stock.

Firstborn make records somewhat superior to the records of lastborn children. This is probably to be explained in terms of greater elimination and thus more rigid selection among the former. The intelligence score also varies inversely with the size of the family. The explanation here is apparently to be found in the limitation of births among the more foresighted elements in the population.

THE PROGRESSIVE
ERA
1919–1929

2509

In the population of the private secondary school, which charges a considerable tuition fee which is fundamentally college preparatory in its function, we probably have as accurate a picture as we can get today of the sources from which the private academy drew its students before the rise of the free public high school. While this picture is certainly not accurate to the details, the general outlines in all probability do not falsify the facts.

Taking the student populations of Exeter Academy and the University of Chicago High School, we find the laboring classes practically absent, in contrast to a representation of 29 per cent in the public high school. Furthermore, these two schools draw almost three-fourths of their students from two occupational groups—the proprietors and professional service. Also almost 90 per cent of these students are of native parentage. Thus, while we may say that public secondary education is still highly selective, it is obvious that it has been and might be much more so. . . .

*   *   *

Little need be said in conclusion. The story that has been told in the foregoing pages is not a new one. Misfortune, as well as fortune, passes from generation to generation. The children of unfortunate parentage are unfortunate, assuming here that the current secondary education is worth to the individual some fraction of its cost. The ancient adage, "To them that hath shall be given," is true today as in olden times. When not preserved through the operation of biological forces, the inequalities among individuals and classes are still perpetuated to a considerable degree in the social inheritance. While the establishment of the free public high school marked an extraordinary educational advance, it did not by any means equalize educational opportunity; for the cost of tuition is not the entire cost of education, or even the larger part of it. Education means leisure, and leisure is an expensive luxury. In most cases today this leisure must be guaranteed the individual by the family. Thus secondary education remains largely a matter for family initiative and concern, and reflects the inequalities of family means and ambition.

HIGH SCHOOLS FOR INDUSTRIAL AMERICA (1929)   From George S. Counts, *Secondary Education For Industrialism* (Cambridge, Mass., 1929), pp. 2, 50–55, 58–60, 67–70.

In at least one respect the historian of the future will, I think, find our attack upon the problem of education gravely deficient. He will see us extremely busy with many things, some of which are important; but he will be amazed at the absence of any vigorous and concerted effort to discover the educational implications of the new industrial civilization which is rapidly overwhelming and transforming the traditional social order. He will see, as we apparently do not, that we have been literally precipitated into a new world: a world which with a ruthless and relentless energy is destroying inherited values, creeds, and faiths; a world which is demanding new social arrangements, a new legal code, a new ethics, a new aesthetics, a new religion, and even a thorough-going revision of our ideas regarding the nature of man. He will see us in this strange fantastic industrial society repeating formulae handed down from an agrarian age when we should be searching with tireless effort for formulae suited to the world as it is; he will see us preoccupied with educational techniques and the minutiae of school-keeping when we should be wrestling with the basic problems of life; he will see us greatly agitated over the construction of an algebra test or a marking scale, when we should be endeavoring to make the school function in the building of a new civilization.

✳ ✳ ✳

Our secondary school has already responded in many ways to those profound changes which have transformed the social order. During the past generation the public high school has modified its program—if not fundamentally, at least with great rapidity. The extraordinary expansion of the curriculum, the almost feverish search for subjects, the readiness with which new devices are tried and abandoned, the general lack of confidence in any particular educational formula, and the eagerness with which we scan the horizon for the coming of the true prophet of salvation, would all seem to be inspired by a more or less conscious recognition of the demolition of the social foundations upon which the older program of secondary education rested.

More significant, however, than the enrichment of the curriculum, the development of pupil activities, and the movement for structural reorganization indeed underlying and motivating these changes, was the revolutionary advance in attendance. We are all familiar with the fact that since 1890 the number of boys and girls attending our secondary schools has grown at an ever more rapid rate. Thirty-eight years ago there were probably not more than 300,000 pupils in these institutions, while today the total is certainly as much as four and one-half millions and perhaps not far from five millions. Almost within the span of a single generation attendance at a secondary school has ceased to be a rare privilege and instead has become an opportunity or almost a right enjoyed by half of the nation's adolescent members. Indeed in many communities practically all children of appropriate age are in high school.

This truly extraordinary phenomenon, without precedent, I think, in the history of education, should be ranked among the great social movements of our dynamic age. It has brought into the secondary school children from practically all social classes and all levels of ability; it has rendered obsolete much of the theory and many of the practices of the secondary school of the past; it has raised a whole series of new problems and plunged the secondary school into one of the most critical periods of its history; it has shattered the traditional molds of secondary education and opened the way to bold experimentation along new lines; it has broken the ties which bound the secondary school to the privileged classes and to the aristocratic ideal in social life; it has given us a new conception of secondary education—the conception that it is the function of the public high school to meet the educational needs of adolescence as it is the function of the elementary school to meet the needs of childhood.

Why have boys and girls crowded into the secondary school in such multitudes? This is not a question of purely theoretic interest. On the contrary, it is a question of crucial importance, because the answer that we give to it will largely determine our attitude towards numerous problems which we face in the secondary school today. If we find that the expansion of the high school is a product of the efforts of our own profession, we may assume that what we have done we can at least in part undo. If such an explanation is supported by the facts, we might, after deciding that the admission of boys and girls from the less favored social classes and from the lower levels of ability is undesirable, proceed to restore the selective secondary school of tradition. If, on the other hand, we conclude that the movement is the fruit of the operation of forces over which we have relatively little control, then for better of for worse we must accept a *fait accompli*. In this latter event our major task would be that of adjusting programs and policies to the new conditions which have been set by society.

From statements already made in this lecture, as well as from my other writings, it perhaps is evident that I am definitely inclined towards the second of these two opposing views. While conceding that the enrichment of the high-school curriculum, the modification of promotion arrangements, and the introduction of new methods of instruction have probably accelerated the democratization of the secondary school, I am confident that the real forces at work are of a much more fundamental character. According to the historical record of a generation ago our profession as a whole neither advocated nor even anticipated the extraordinary changes that were about to transform the secondary school. To be sure, here and there towards the close of the nineteenth century prophetic individuals, . . . were able to penetrate the future and see the faint outlines of coming events; but the great mass of teachers and administrators were more effective in perpetuating tradition than in creating a new type of institution. In fact I would be quite willing to defend the thesis that for the most part they opposed rather than supported the attack of the populace upon the ancient citadel of aristocracy. Such a statement should, of course, be interpreted neither as condemnation nor as approval, but if true, merely as statement of fact.

Why then has the high-school population grown at such a surprising rate? To this question there is no simple answer. The movement suggests some great natural phenomenon, such as the avalanche down the mountain side, the increase of an animal species after the discovery of a new food supply, or the migration of a people following the conquest of some natural barrier. Great events, though often precipitated by relatively feeble happenings, can be adequately explained only in terms of equally great causes. So if we should endeavor, in a single sentence, to account for the growth of the high school, we would say that it is the product of a new social order—the resultant of a whole series of forces and conditions which we call industrial civilization. And by industrial civilization we do not refer merely to the appearance of great cities and huge economic combinations but rather to the coming of highly integrated society which holds within its close embrace metropolitan center and rural hamlet, industrial enterprise and vegetable garden, shop and field and factory.

But let us turn to a more specific answer to our query. This answer will lead us into the heart of the problem of the relation of the secondary school to industrialism, and at the same time will prepare the ground for a consideration of that reconstruction of the theory of secondary education which industrial civilization is now demanding.

If we may assume for the moment that in general the expansion of the high school is essentially a response to the appearance of a new type of civilization, what are the particular elements in that civilization which would seem to have been significant? To my mind there are seven factors which, working in close union, have been largely responsible for bringing the secondary school into the fourth great creative period of its history since the fall of the ancient empires. The rapid democratization of secondary education in our time may be traced to the presence of certain social ideals in the United States, the prior extension of the opportunities of elementary education, the appearance of a highly integrated society, the growing complexity of civilization, the increase in wealth and income, the decrease in the death rate, and the decline of the birth rate. A brief examination of each of these factors will reveal its bearing on the question at hand.

*   *   *

This is not the place for the development of a theory of secondary education which takes into account the fact of the new social order. Yet I cannot refrain altogether from giving positive illustration to my thought. Let me therefore center attention on two questions raised by industrialism which are of peculiar urgency and which indicate the type of thinking required by the present situation. The one pertains to the position of labor in society and the other to the status of the individual. The one leads to the consideration of a conflict with the old aristocratic tradition in secondary education, and the other to an evaluation of one of the most important elements in our rural heritage.

The tradition of secondary education in the western world is an aristocratic tradition. Generally the secondary school has prepared the favored few for the privileged positions in the social order, and in some societies, such as our own, it has served as a short cut to aristocracy for poor but gifted boys and girls. In either case attendance at this institution has carried great social prestige and has suggested to the popular mind separation of the individual from the rank and file of humanity and identification with the source of respectability and power. As long as registration in the institution was highly restricted, either by natural or artificial barriers, tradition was in harmony with the facts. But with the extraordinary expansion of the public high school in recent years a serious conflict has arisen. Both parents and children continue to do homage to the occupations of aristocratic lineage and to regard the high school as a means of access to these callings.

In meeting this situation there are three possible courses of action. We may follow the present policy of drift and trust to the slow and cruel operation of economic forces to bring about a readjustment among the occupations; we may accept the current occupational hierarchy as a sort of divine dispensation—a position actually taken by some of our most confirmed intelligence testers—and arbitrarily limit admission to the more favored vocations to boys and girls of superior talents; or we may pursue the really courageous course and fashion an educational and social philosophy which exalts all forms of socially useful labor and which accepts the challenge of the fundamental social reconstruction of society in the light of a rational ideal. If we should choose the third of these possibilities, as I hope we may, our entire profession would have to go to school; and the subject of study would be our industrial civilization.

The second issue which I wish to discuss with you has to do with the status of the individual under industrialism. Until we have faced this issue squarely and in all of its implications, the intelligent formulation of a program of training for home membership, preparation for vocational life, or education for civic and social responsibilities will be impossible. Should we endeavor to perpetuate the tradition of individualism—the product of great distances, extreme isolation, and primitive social organization—or should we seek deliberately to construct an ideal which is more in harmony with the character of a highly integrated social order? As we praise the virtues of individualism are we not moving inevitably towards some form of collectivism? Unless controlled in the light of some theory of human worth is there not grave danger that this will result in severe regimentation and the consequent subordination of the individual to social mechanism? Such regimentation as is appearing today may not be the necessary concomitant of collectivism but rather the natural product of a vast competitive society in which, by the turn of the wheel of fortune, great masses of individuals are forced to obey the will of a single man. The incongruity of the present situation becomes apparent when we realize that under industrialism practically all tasks from making shoes to managing an educational system are cooperative tasks. And our great failures, whether in the sphere of industrial production or in the conduct of government, may be traced to inability to work together for the general good. May this not be due to a clash between our inherited tradition of individualism and the demand for collective behavior in a society which is essentially cooperative? So here again we are faced with the choice between the policy of drift and the policy of shaping an educational theory in the light of the facts of a new civilization.

In concluding this lecture I wish to direct your attention again to the social limits within which educational theory must work. If educational thought is to be effective in modifying practice, it must keep close to society. To what extent the school can influence the direction of social evolution is perhaps an open question; but certainly if it is to achieve this result it must articulate with its own age. Moreover, that it can in any fundamental sense create the impulses which drive society onward, is highly improbable. In a word, the school cannot build a Utopia. It is for this reason that much of the so-called progressive education of our time is progressive only in name and aspiration. The major weakness of this movement is that it lacks a solid social foundation. A school cannot become socially progressive by mere resolve. Unless it reaches down into the sub-stratum of society and taps the deep-flowing currents of social life, it can only be another pedagogical experiment, of interest to the academician but destined for an early grave. The founding of a progressive educational movement is as difficult as the founding of a progressive political party, and for much the same reasons. If it is not rooted in some profound social movement or trend, it can be but an instrument of deception. In spite of all of the well-intentioned efforts of intellectuals, society stubbornly chooses its own roads to salvation.

If these conclusions are sound, then we may assume that we have in the public high school today all of the conditions which are necessary for a genuinely progressive and creative educational movement. Through it the impulses of a new civilization are surging; through it the aspirations of a new society are seeking expression. If the high school courageously accepts the opportunity which has thus been thrust in its path, it may become a mighty cultural instrument for civilizing and humanizing this barbarous uncouth giant of industrialism that now bestrides the world. But perhaps we as school teachers dare not take up the challenge which has been thrown to us. In the past we have belonged to a timid race and have usually taken orders from our superiors. And we are now being asked to go out into the world and grapple with realities, to understand and harness powerful social forces, to participate in the decision of what is right and what is wrong, even to assume some responsibilities of leadership in the building of a new civilization. This to my mind is the meaning of industrialism for secondary education.

ROBERT AND HELEN LYND ON THE THINGS CHILDREN LEARNED IN THE HIGH SCHOOLS OF MIDDLETOWN (1924)

From Robert and Helen M. Lynd, *Middletown* (New York, 1924), pp. 188–97, 206–11.

The school, like the factory, is a thoroughly regimented world. Immovable seats in orderly rows fix the sphere of activity of each child. For all, from the timid six-year-old entering for the first time to the most assured high school senior, the general routine is much the same. Bells divide the day into periods. For the six-year-olds the periods are short (fifteen to twenty-five minutes) and varied; in some they leave their seats, play games, and act out make-believe stories, although in "recitation periods" all movement is prohibited. As they grow older the taboo upon physical activity becomes stricter, until by the third or fourth year practically all movement is forbidden except the marching from one set of seats to another between periods, a brief interval of prescribed exercise daily, and periods of manual training or home economics once or twice a week. There are "study-periods" in which children learn "lessons" from "text-books" prescribed by the state and "recitation-periods" in which they tell an adult teacher what the book has said; one hears children reciting the battles of the Civil War in one recitation period, the rivers of Africa in another, the "parts of speech" in a third; the method is much the same. With high school come some differences; more "vocational" and "laboratory" work varies the periods. But here again the lesson-text-book-recitation method is the chief characteristic of education. For nearly an hour a teacher asks questions and pupils answer, then a bell rings, on the instant books bang, powder and mirrors come out, there is a buzz of talk and laughter as all the urgent business of living resumes momentarily for the children, notes and "dates" are exchanged, five minutes pass, another bell, gradual sliding into seats, a final giggle, a last vanity case snapped shut, "In our last lesson we had just finished"—and another class is begun.

All this ordered industry of imparting and learning facts and skills represents an effort on the part of this matter-of-fact community immersed in its daily activities to endow its young with certain essential supplements to the training received in the home. A quick epitome of the things adult Middletown has come to think it important for its children to learn in school, as well as some indication of regions of pressure and change, is afforded by the following summary of the work in Grades I and VII in 1890 and in 1924:

1890	*GRADE I*	1924
Reading		Reading
Writing		Writing
Arithmetic		Arithmetic
Language		Language
Spelling		Spelling
Drawing		Drawing
Object Lessons (Science)		Geography
Music		Music
		Civic Training
		History and Civics
		Hygiene and Health
		Physical Education

Reading	Reading
Writing	Writing
Arithmetic	Arithmetic
Language	Language
Spelling	Spelling
Drawing	Drawing
Music	Music
Geography	Geography
Object **Lessons** (Science)	Civic Training
Compositions and Declamation	History and Civics
	Manual Arts (Boys)
	Home Economics (Girls)
	Physical Education

In the culture of thirty-five years ago it was deemed sufficient to teach during the first seven years of this extra-home training the following skills and facts, in rough order of importance:[1]

   a. The various uses of language. (Overwhelmingly first in importance.)
   b. The accurate manipulation of numerical symbols.
   c. Familiarity with the physical surroundings of peoples.
   d. A miscellaneous group of facts about familiar physical objects about the child—trees, sun, ice, food, and so on.
   e. The leisure-time skills of singing and drawing.

Today the things for which all children are sent to school fall into the following rough order:

   a. The same uses of language.
   b. The same uses of numerical figures.
   c. Training in patriotic citizenship.
   d. The same familiarity with the physical surroundings of peoples.
   e. Facts about how to keep well and some physical exercise.
   f. The same leisure-time skills of singing and drawing.
   g. Knowledge and skills useful in sewing, cooking and using tools about the home for the girls, and, for the boys, an introductory acquaintance with some of the manual skills by which the working class members get their living.

   Both in its optional, non-compulsory character and also in its more limited scope the school training of a generation ago appears to have been a more casual

---

[1]The state law of 1865 upon which the public school system rests provided for instruction in "orthography, reading, writing, arithmetic, English, grammar, and good behavior," and the minutes of the Middletown School Board for 1882 (the only minutes for a decade on either side of 1890 which describe the course of study in detail) affirm that "reading, writing, and arithmetic are the three principal studies of the public schools, and if nothing more is possible, pupils should be taught to read the newspapers, write a letter, and perform the ordinary operations of arithmetic."

adjunct of the main business of "bringing up" that went on day by day in the home. Today, however, the school is relied upon to carry a more direct, if at most points still vaguely defined, responsibility.

✻   ✻   ✻

When we approach the high school, however, the matter-of-fact tendency of the city to commandeer education as an aid in dealing with its own concerns becomes more apparent. Caught less firmly than the elementary school in the cake of tradition and now forced to train children from a group not heretofore reached by it, the high school has been more adaptable than the lower school. Here group training no longer means the same set of facts learned on the same days by all children of a given grade. The freshman entering high school may plan to spend his four years following any one of twelve different "courses of study";[2] he may choose the sixteen different yearly courses which will make up his four years of training from a total of 102.[3] All this is something new, for the 170 students who were going to high school in the "bursting days of boom" of 1889–90 had to choose, as Middletown high school students had done for thirty years, between two four-year courses, the Latin and the English courses, the sole difference between them being whether one did or did not take "the language." The number of separate year courses open to them totaled but twenty.

The facts and skills constituting the present-day high school curriculum present a combination of the traditional learning reputed to be essential to an "educated" man or woman and newer applied information or skills constantly being inserted into the curriculum to meet current immanent concerns. Here, too, English, the successor in its varied forms of the language work in the grades, far outdistances all competitors for student time, consuming 22 per cent. of all student hours. It is no longer compulsory throughout the entire four years as it was a generation ago; instead, it is required of all students for the first two years, and thereafter the earlier

---

[2]Courses Three to Twelve inclusive have a uniform first-year group of required and elective subjects. Four subjects are taken each half of each year, of which two or three are required and the rest selected from among a list offering from two to nine electives, according to the course and the year. The indispensables of secondary education required of every high school student are:

One year of English for those taking Courses One through Six.
Three years of English for those taking Courses Seven through Twelve.
One year of algebra.
One year of general history.
One year of American history.
One-half year of civics.
One-half year of sociology.
One year of science.
One-half year of music.
One-half year of gymnasium.

This constitutes a total of ten required and six elective one-year courses or their equivalents during the four years for the academic department (Courses One through Six) and nine required and seven elective courses for those in the vocational department (Courses Seven through Twelve).

[3]The year unit rather than the term or semester unit is taken here as the measure of the number of courses, since it furnishes the only basis of comparison with 1890. When different subjects make up one year's course they are almost invariably related, e.g., civics and sociology, zoology and botany.

literary emphasis disappears in seven of the twelve courses, being replaced in the third year by commercial English, while in the fourth year it disappears entirely in five courses save as an optional subject. Both teaching and learning appear at times to be ordeals from which teachers and pupils alike would apparently gladly escape: "Thank goodness, we've finished Chaucer's *Prologue!*" exclaimed one high school English teacher. "I am thankful and the children are, too. They think of it almost as if it were in a foreign language, and they *hate* it."

Latin, likewise, though still regarded by some parents of the business class as a vaguely significant earmark of the educated man or woman, is being rapidly attenuated in the training given the young. It is not required of any student for even one year, though in one of the twelve courses it or French is required for two years. Gone is the required course of the nineties taken by over half of the high school students for the entire four years and enticingly set forth in the course of study of the period as "Latin, Grammar, Harkness: Begun-Completed. Latin, Reader, Harkness: Begun-Completed. Latin, Virgil, Harkness: Begun-Completed." The "Virgil Club's" annual banquet and the "Latin Wedding" are, however, prominent high school social events today, and more than one pupil confessed that the lure of these in the senior year helped to keep him through four years of Latin. Although Latin is deader than last summer's straw hat to the men joshing each other about Middletown's Rotary luncheon table, tradition, the pressure of college entrance requirements, and such incidental social considerations as those just mentioned still manage to hold Latin to a place of prominence in the curriculum: 10 per cent. of all student hours are devoted to Latin, as against but 2 per cent. each to French and Spanish;[4] only English, the combined vocational courses, mathematics, and history consume more student hours.

The most pronounced region of movement appears in the rush of courses that depart from the traditional dignified conception of what constitutes education and seek to train for specific tool and skill activities in factory, office, and home. A generation ago a solitary optional senior course in bookkeeping was the thin entering wedge of the trend that today controls eight of the twelve courses of the high school and claimed 17 per cent. of the total student hours during the first semester of 1923–24 and 21 per cent. during the second. At no point has the training prescribed for the preparation of children for effective adulthood approached more nearly actual preparation for the dominant concerns in the daily lives of the people of Middletown. This pragmatic commandeering of education is frankly stated by the president of the School Board: "For a long time all boys were trained to be President. Then for a while we trained them all to be professional men. Now we are training boys to get jobs."

Unlike Latin, English, and mathematics in that they have no independent, honorific traditions of their own, these vocational courses have frankly adopted the canons of office and machine shop: they must change in step with the coming of new physical equipment in machine shops and offices, or become ineffective.[5] A

[4]Since the World War German has not been taught in Middletown.

[5]This conformity to existing conditions is accentuated by the necessity of bidding for union support and falling in with current trade union practices. The attitude of the unions toward this school training varies all the way from that of the carpenters whose president attends the evening classes and who start a high school trained boy with a journeyman's card and corresponding wages to that of the bricklayers and plasterers who start a high school vocational graduate at exactly the same wage as an untrained boy.

recently organized radio class shows the possibility of quick adaptability to new developments. More than any other part of the school training, these vocational courses consist in learning *how* rather than learning *about.* Actual conditions of work in the city's factories are imported into the school shops; boys bring repair work from their homes; they study auto mechanics by working on an old Ford car; they design, draft, and make patterns for lathes and drill presses, the actual casting being done by a Middletown foundry; they have designed and constructed a house, doing all the architectural, carpentry, wiring, metal work, and painting. A plan for providing work in a local machine shop, alternating two weeks of this with two weeks of study throughout the year, is under discussion.

Under the circumstances, it is not surprising that this vocational work for boys is the darling of Middletown's eye—if we except a group of teachers and of parents of the business class who protest that the city's preoccupation with vocational work tends to drag down standards in academic studies and to divert the future college student's attention from his preparatory courses.[6] Like the enthusiastically supported high school basket-ball team, these vocational courses have caught the imagination of the mass of male tax-payers; ask your neighbor at Rotary what kind of schools Middletown has and he will begin to tell you about these "live" courses. It is not without significance that vocational supervisors are more highly paid than any other teachers in the school system.

Much of what has been said of the strictly vocational courses applies also to work in bookkeeping and stenography and in home economics. The last-named, entirely new since 1890, is devised to meet the functional needs of the major group of the girls, who will be home-makers. Beginning in the seventh and eighth years with the study of food, clothing, and house-planning, it continues as an optional course through the high school with work in dressmaking, millinery, hygiene and home nursing, household management, and selection of food and clothing. As in the boys' vocational work, these courses center in the more obvious, accepted group practices; much more of the work in home economics, for example, centers in the traditional household productive skills such as canning, baking, and sewing, than in the rapidly growing battery of skills involved in effective buying of ready-made articles. The optional half-year course for the future business girl in selection of food and clothing, equipping a girl "to be an intelligent consumer," marks, however, an emergent recognition of a need for training in effective consumption, as does also the class visiting of local stores to inspect and discuss various kinds of household articles. In 1925 a new course in child care and nutrition was offered in one of the grade schools; while it consists almost entirely in the study of child

---

[6]Many Middletown people maintain that the coming of vocational work to the high school has tended greatly to lower its standing as a college preparatory school. More than one mother shook her head over the fact that her daughter never does any studying at home and is out every evening but gets A's in all her work. It is generally recognized that a boy or girl graduating from the high school can scarcely enter an eastern college without a year of additional preparatory work elsewhere.

Leading nationally known universities in neighboring states gave the following reports of the work of graduates in the Middletown high school: In one, of eleven Middletown students over a period of fifteen years, one graduated, none of the others made good records, four were asked to withdraw because of poor scholarship; of the four in residence in 1924, two were on probation, one was on the warned list, and one was doing fair work. In another, of five Middletown students in the last five years, one did excellent work, one fair, two did very poor work and dropped out after the first term, one had a record below requirement at the time of withdrawal. In a third, of eight Middletown students in the last five years, one was an excellent student, four were fair, and three were on probation. The single Middletown student in a fourth university attended for only a year and was on probation the entire time.

feeding rather than of the wider aspects of child care, it is highly significant as being the first and sole effort on the part of the community to train women for this fundamental child-rearing function. Standard women's magazines are resorted to in these courses for girls as freely as technical journals are employed in the courses for boys.

Second only in importance to the rise of these courses addressed to practical vocational activities is the new emphasis upon courses in history and civics. These represent yet another point at which Middletown is bending its schools to the immediate service of its institutions—in this case, bolstering community solidarity against sundry divisive tendencies. A generation ago a course in American history was given to those who survived until the eighth grade, a course in general history, "covering everything from the Creation to the present in one little book of a hundred or so pages," followed in the second year of the high school, and one in civil government in the third year. Today, separate courses in civic training and in history and civics begin with the first grade for all children and continue throughout the elementary school, while in high school the third-year course in American history and the fourth-year course in civics and sociology are, with the exception of the second-year English course, the only courses required of all students after the completion of the first year. Sixteen per cent. of the total student hours in the high school are devoted to these social studies—history, sociology, and civics—a total surpassed only by those of English and the combined cluster of vocational, domestic science, manual arts, and commercial courses.

※　　※　　※

Accompanying the formal training afforded by courses of study is another and informal kind of training, particularly during the high school years. The high school, with its athletics, clubs, sororities and fraternities, dances and parties, and other "extracurricular activities," is a fairly complete social cosmos in itself, and about this city within a city the social life of the intermediate generation centers. Here the social sifting devices of their elders—money, clothes, personal attractiveness, male physical prowess, exclusive clubs, election to positions of leadership—are all for the first time set going with a population as yet largely undifferentiated save as regards their business class and working class parents. This informal training is not a preparation for a vague future that must be taken on trust, as is the case with so much of the academic work; to many of the boys and girls in high school this is "the life," the thing they personally like best about going to school.

The school is taking over more and more of the child's waking life. Both high school and grades have departed from the attitude of fifty years ago, when the Board directed:

> "Pupils shall not be permitted to remain on the school grounds after dismissal. The teachers shall often remind the pupils that the first duty when dismissed is to proceed quietly and directly home to render all needed assistance to their parents."

Today the school is becoming not a place to which children go from their homes for a few hours daily but a place from which they go home to eat and sleep.[7]

[7]This condition is deplored by some as indicative of the "break-up of the American home." Others welcome it as freeing the child earlier from the domination of parents and accustoming him to face adjustments upon the success of which adult behavior depends. In any event, the trend appears to be in the direction of an extension of the present tendency increasingly into the grades.

ABRAHAM FLEXNER'S CRITIQUE OF THE HIGH SCHOOL (1930) From
Universities: American, English, German (New York, 1930), pp. 46-52.

The American college reproduced the English college as it existed "at a time when the university in England was eclipsed by its constituent colleges." It was, and has to this day remained, a teaching institution, largely at the secondary level. We cannot, however, understand the secondary school work of the American college or university, unless we understand the American high school. And this is no easy task, for the American high school is greatly lacking in uniformity, varying in size, for example, from a staff of three or four teachers—and most American high schools belong to this category—to a staff of a hundred teachers or more. Amazing to relate, also, the staff of three will offer courses of study that on paper bear much resemblance in respect of substance and extent to the courses offered by the staff numbering a hundred. At one time viewed as the people's college, the high school is apparently coming to be a place where an increasingly large segment of American youth can get a little knowledge of almost every imaginable subject, practical, often in the most trivial sense, or cultural, sometimes in the best sense. Subject-matter, like Latin, mathematics, or history, and skills, like typewriting or cooking, are ingeniously combined on an utterly fallacious theory into "units," "points," and "counts"; and when by a simple arithmetical process enough "points" have been accumulated and enough hours and years been consumed in the process, the pupil has received "a four-year high school education." Calculation by means of arithmetically added "points" serves, unintentionally, greatly to reduce intellectual effort. The four-year course is first broken up into bits; it is easier to master bits than to master a whole; the credits accumulate from year to year. "*Divide et impera.*" The prevailing philosophy of education tends to discredit hard work. Individuality must be respected. Undoubtedly. The child's creative possibilities must be allowed to unfold. Certainly. But by the time several such considerations have come into play, discipline through effort has been relegated to a very subordinate position.

The high school used to be a sieve of a certain kind. But American democracy objects to sieves. Would not selection and distribution of students on the basis of industry, ability, and capacity to go forward on intellectual lines be democratic? Most certainly, yes. Yet the high school cannot be democratic in this sense. It is, on the contrary, a kind of bargain-counter on which a generous public and an overworked and underpaid teaching staff display every variety of merchandise— Latin, Greek, science, agriculture, business, stenography, domestic arts—leaving the student, with such advice and direction as he may get from teachers, parents, and college matriculation requirements, free to piece together, under restrictions that sometimes amount to much and sometimes to little, a course of study that by the end of four years will yield "counts" or "units of credit" enough to win a diploma or to enable him to satisfy the entrance requirements of the college of his choice. In this little matter, the university is not above helping him; as if the university did not have enough to do anyway, institutions like Wisconsin and Chicago offer extension or home study courses of high school grade which prepare for regular matriculation, though no particular standard is set up for the extension or home study students.

Undoubtedly the free American high school has its good points. Sir Michael Sadler has recently declared that it is the most important single contribution to modern social life. It represents a laudable ambition—the ambition to keep children from drifting into blind alleys, industrially or economically. It is part of the great American melting pot; it is socially and physically wholesome. And the social development of American youth represents a solid contribution to educational philosophy and practice, for if American youth can be kept sane and wholesome, we may avoid the social rift which is the great problem with which German educators are wrestling today. The importance of identifying school and society needed emphasizing a generation ago, as Professor Dewey perceived; it needs no reiteration today. "Americans are boys," says Professor de Madariaga, including even the grown-ups. The schools could well for the present direct their emphasis to another quarter. Of course, there are even now high schools and high school teachers that value brains and scholarship; high schools admirably equipped and well conducted; and in any event it is a great and hitherto unheard of achievement to keep the door open for all classes of the population for four years—from thirteen to seventeen—as the high school does. But the high school is too elementary, too broken up, and too miscellaneous to constitute for most students anything more than an elementary education. As to the quality of the achievement, no nation has ever so completely deceived itself. The present United States Commissioner of Education has just assured the assembled superintendents of the entire country that the whole world is following in the wake of the United States; have we not introduced the radio and the "talkies" into the schools? Is not the percentage of the school population attending high schools several times as large as that in any other country? But what would happen to these statistics if the incompetently manned schools were dropped, as they should be, and if dabbling at cooking and typewriting were not reckoned as of equal importance with history or literature or science? Taxation for education has indeed gone forward by leaps and bounds; buildings and equipment have generally improved. None the less there are few states and still fewer large cities— though fortunately there are a few—in which the conduct of education is not tainted by politics and favouritism. And the largest cities are the worst. The schools of New York and Chicago are bedraggled in the mire. There are, I have gladly admitted, here and there men and women on the superintending and teaching staffs who are cultivated and well educated. In strange ways, industry, ability, a fine spirit, and scholarship occasionally appear in a sea of mediocrity and incompetence; but it is unpardonable misrepresentation to attribute these characteristics to even a considerable portion of the rapidly changing teaching staff. In a vague way the general public wants education and believes in it; but of its difficulties and severities it has no comprehension. The inferiority of the product becomes obvious later, when a discriminating college professor or employer takes his lamp, like Diogenes, and starts the search for a high school or college graduate, who can write and spell, and who is master of the elements of mathematics, a science, or a modern language. There is no need to be surprised at this showing. It could not have been very different; trained teachers and intelligent parents supporting them could not possibly have been procured within a generation in a country teeming with material attractions; perhaps one ought not even to be discouraged; nor would one be, if one saw anything like a concerted effort on the part of the leading universities to uphold the essentially intellectual character of the educative process.

It is urged and rightly that the American high school cannot imitate the continental secondary school; it cannot concern itself merely with a limited group in pursuit of certain definite and highly respected ends. An increasingly large body of boys and girls wish a high school education, and they wish it for an ever greater variety of purposes. In a democratic country, this demand cannot and must not be ignored. But our school men fail, I think, to perceive another point. Let us grant that our high schools must do some things, with which European schools are not yet so deeply concerned. It is also true that European schools do something with which we Americans need to be greatly concerned. In our efforts to satisfy the varied and changeable tastes and needs of the many, we have for the time being to a considerable degree lost sight of the importance of solid and coherent—though not inflexible—training of the able. We have tried to include in the high school curriculum—we shall later learn that universities are liable to the same criticism—every kind of subject and activity, intellectual, vocational, and technical. It cannot be done; or it can only be done at the expense of genuine education. Thus the American high school is neither intelligent, selective, nor thorough; and it is the high school graduates of a given June—mostly untrained, mostly unselected, mostly equipped with discursive knowledge in a score of subjects, many of which possess no intellectual and practically no vocational value—it is these high school graduates of June, plus those furnished by extension and correspondence courses, who become the college students of the following autumn.

19

A NEW
ORIENTATION
FOR
EDUCATION,
1930–1950

The Depression

NEWS ACCOUNTS OF UNDERNOURISHED SCHOOL CHILDREN IN CHICAGO (1931) From *The New York Times*, April 8, 1931; June 18, 1931.

CHICAGO, April 8.—A group of University of Chicago faculty members warns against the ravages of undernourishment among children in the public schools. It appears that principals and teachers in many schools have for several months been contributing from their salaries in order to provide free lunches for hungry children. Allowances have been made to the schools from the fund raised by the Governor's Commission on Unemployment, but the money has been insufficient to meet the need.

Meantime, the Board of Education announces that it has exhausted its fund for the payment of teachers and other educational purposes. This fact, however, has not prevented it issuing an elaborate report on the schools at a cost of $13,000, which is generally regarded as a campaign document contributed to the cause of Mayor [William H.] Thompson.

CHICAGO, June 18.—Shortly after a check-up of the city schools revealed today that 11,000 hungry children were being fed by teachers, Superintendent William J. Bogan dispatched a plea to Frank Loomis, secretary of Governor Emmerson's Relief Committee, pleading "for God's sake, help us feed these children during the Summer."

Mr. Bogan originally appealed to the Governor's committee for $100,000 to feed hungry school children. Today his letter asked for "at least $10,000." The Governor's committee sent a group of social investigators to study the situation.

In the meantime teachers are seriously handicapped by the failure of the Board of Education to pay them. Collections taken up among the more fortunate children have also aided in feeding those not so fortunate.

HUNGRY CHILDREN (1932)   From *The New York Times,* December 18, 1932.

Even those with little imagination know how no employment or underemployment, the failure of banks and building and loan associations have affected many children whose parents faced the future self-reliant and unafraid a few years ago. In the millions of homes which have escaped the abyss of destitution fear of what may still happen is destroying the sense of security which is considered necessary for the happiness and well-being of children.

Great effort has been made to prevent suffering. Last year probably more than a billion dollars was expended by public and private agencies for the relief of the unemployed. Although this is probably some eight times as much as was spent for relief in normal times, no one who has been going in and out of the homes of the unemployed in large urban centres or in the single-industry towns and mining communities has reported that it has been adequate to insure shelter, clothes and reasonably adequate diet for all needy children. . . .

Although the death rate [of infants and children] is low, there is much evidence that the health of many children is being adversely affected by the prolonged depression. For example, hospitals and clinics report an increase in rickets among children; in New York City, where relief for the unemployed has probably been more nearly adequate than in any other of the largest cities, the city Health Department reports that 20.5 per cent of the school children examined were suffering from malnutrition in 1932. . . .

Undernourishment is even more widespread in areas of extreme depression, where the available relief has been quite inadequate, such as the coal-mining communities and "one-industry towns," where there has been little or no work for several years, or in districts where the depression has been added to the economic losses brought by flood and drought.

In a recent report of the Surgeon General of the Public Health Service on the rural health work in the drought-stricken areas in 1931, the reports of the health officers as to health conditions in the counties are summarized. Here one finds the health officers of Alabama and Arkansas, for example, reporting for county after county an increase in pellagra due to inability to purchase the necessary food; and "dietary diseases" and widespread undernourishment were frequently referred to in the reports for these and other States. The bulletin, "Health Briefs," of the Tennessee Health Department for August of this year says that "the increase in deaths from pellagra that has been forecast since the beginning of the reduced economic conditions is now beginning to show on the tally sheets of vital statistics." . . .

Recently the director of the Child Hygiene Division of the Children's Bureau was called into a conference to discuss how the reduced relief budgets should be expended so as to insure the health of the children. Protective foods for children include milk, fruits, some fresh vegatables, and eggs, and the problem was how to purchase these as well as the foods that supply energy for a family of five when the total income is $11 a month. Some families are managing to exist on a smaller per capita than $2 a month, but at the cost of greatly lowered vital capacity and resistance to disease.

It is the future effects of undernourishment among children that are to be feared. As Dr. William H. Welch has put it, "The ground lost by undernourishment in childhood may never be regained." That many children have suffered such losses during the past three years is certain. . . .

NEWTON BAKER ON THE CHILD NOMADS OF THE DEPRESSION

(1932) From Newton D. Baker, "Homeless Wanderers Create a New Problem for America," *The New York Times*, December 11, 1932.

A curious social phenomenon has developed out of the present depression. All over the country hordes of young people and entire families are found wending their way along the highways and byways. They are the people whom our postoffices label "address unknown," and whom we call transients, lacking a more adequate term by which to describe them. Every group in society is represented in their ranks, from the college graduate to the child who has never seen the inside of a schoolhouse. Expectant mothers, sick babies, young childless couples, grim-faced middle-aged dislodged from lifetime jobs—on they go, an index of insecurity, in a country used to the unexpected. We think of the nomads of the desert—now we have the nomads of the depression.

At least 25,000 families in our country and more than 200,000 boys and young men are reported by the United States Children's Bureau and the National Association of Travelers' Aid Societies as recruits in the present transient army. Because of the difficulties which lie in the way of a "head-to-head" census, these figures are generally conceded as telling only a part of the story. The actual count, beyond doubt, is several times the reported figures. One thing we know positively: that is, this army is gaining rapidly in numerical strength.

One-quarter of the present transient army, we are told, is made up of boys ranging between 16 and 21 years of age. Girls flock to the city in numbers, but the desire to travel long miles across country has not as yet proved as contagious to them as it has to their brothers.

Russia's experience with her vagabond youth should prove a warning to us. The shelterless, or bezprizorni, as they were called, came into being after the overthrow of the Russian monarchy in 1917 and increased so rapidly that they were estimated in a few years' time to number from 2,000,000 to 3,000,000 boys and girls. This army of children, many of them as young as 10 years, terrorized whole villages and cities and became known for their murders, robberies and other acts of violence. The "wild children of Russia" the press termed them. . . .

The reasons which have made our transient youth take to the road seem mild in comparison with those which caused the Russian children's exodus. The quest for jobs, the lure of adventure, escape from broken, unhappy or poverty-stricken homes or personality difficulties are the causes behind most youthful flights in America. The average young American transient of today, we are told by social workers and others who come into daily contact with him, is a normal boy from a substantial family. He differs from the hobo of yesterday in that his goal is apt to be a "chance to work" not an escape from it. In contrast to the bezprizorni, a considerable proportion of our boys have had high school educations, while most of the wild children of Russia, we are told, were unable to read or write.

Of the 7,512 transients served by the Salvation Army in Washington, D.C., during the first quarter of 1932, it was found that 1,866 had had an eighth-grade education, 260 had been in high school and 258 were college trained.

Reports submitted on the transient seem to agree that he is on the whole an honest, self-respecting person. Railroads record few thefts as a result of recent transient migrations. Communities through which they pass connect them with only occasional misdemeanors or crimes.

America's vagabonds, however, share this quality in common with Russia's wild children: having tasted the poison of a wandering life they find it difficult to give it up. In all probability the bezprizorni, when they first started out, were a harmless group of young people also, but finding it impossible to secure food and shelter by honest means, they resorted to other methods. No doubt they were helped in their activites by criminals and degenerates of their country just as the social workers report our transients are being contaminated today.

It is impossible to travel across any country, to live in box cars or "jungles," as the camp sites near the railroad yards are called, or even in municipal shelters, without meeting men whose influence is destructive. All too easily impressionable young people thrown into these environments without home guidance or direction pick up the vices and crimes of the underworld—gambling, stealing, drug addiction, prostitution and sexual perversion. . . .

The health hazards of the road are also many for the transient. Often he arrives in town sick from exposure or lack of food. Last winter in one Western city thirty-five men and boys were removed from box cars seriously ill, some in advanced stages of pneumonia. One railroad alone reported fifty men and boys killed and more than 100 crippled along its route. Hospitals treat the transient only if he is seriously ill. The demands for free care on these institutions are so great and their resources so limited that, unless it is a case of absolute necessity, they feel that their first obligation lies to the needy sick of their own community.

The drifting family in our country about whom we hear so much less than the transient youth has but one reason generally for its vagabondage, and that is the loss of a job by its breadwinner. Unable to find work or to continue the rent or payments on the home, the family piles itself into the old car and takes to the highway. Its philosophy, if any exists, probably runs like this: "We know what to expect if we stay at home, but who knows what our luck may be further on?"

Human nature is such that almost anyone will give a handout once with some little grace, but continuous handouts day after day are often not so generously bestowed. So we have the family making its way as best it can, looking for the elusive job, the unexpected stroke of luck or the pot of gold at the end of the rainbow, and as a rule ending its pilgrimage in some remote spot miles away from the starting place, miserable and destitute.

The children of these families perhaps suffer most of all. They are dazed, bewildered bits of humanity driven from town to town by a strange force called a "depression," which has upset the stability of their past and is dangerously threatening the safety of their future.

So suddenly has the seriousness of the transient problem thrust itself upon us and so rapidly has it increased in size that it may be said to have taken the average American community completely by storm. Busily coping with welfare and relief problems of their own and pondering how the multitude can be fed on the loaves purchasable with their limited resources, communities have been inclined to consider the transient as some other city's problem. And so, what is one city's problem today, by a system of "passing on," becomes another city's difficulty tomorrow. . . .

We are all interested in reducing budgets—personal, municipal, State and national—but it is well to remember that ruthlessly slashing essential services is both a costly and hazardous undertaking. If there is any doubt in our mind of the seriousness the present transient problem brings with it, we have only to turn to Russia for a somewhat similar tragedy for which that government paid dearly.

The question which every American community faces today and which demands an immediate answer is, can we afford to permit permanent injury to the character of this generation of youth?

SENATE HEARING ON PAYLESS PAYDAYS FOR TEACHERS IN CHICAGO

(1932)   From "Federal Corporation in Unemployment Relief. Hearing Before a Subcommittee of the Committee on Manufacturers," *U.S. Senate, 72nd Cong., 1st Sess., May 9, 1932* (Washington, D.C., 1932), pp. 48–51.

SENATOR COSTIGAN. What is your name?

MR. WILSON. Irvin A. Wilson.

SENATOR COSTIGAN. Are you president of the Chicago Principals Club?

MR. WILSON. I am president of the Chicago Principals Club, and am here officially representing that organization.

SENATOR COSTIGAN. Have you a statement for the committee?

MR. WILSON. I have no statement. I will speak from notes, Mr. Chairman.

SENATOR COSTIGAN. Please proceed.

MR. WILSON. In the first place, gentlemen of the committee, the credit of the Chicago board of education has completely collapsed. The taxes which are now in process of collection on the penalty date, which was the 1st of June, were collected only to the extent of less than 50 per cent.

SENATOR WHEELER. You say the financial structure has completely collapsed. How much of that has been due to the misapplication of funds by those in charge of the school board, if any?

MR. WILSON. I should say a very small part of it from that standpoint alone. It is pretty largely from the fact which Mr. Stillman brought out. In a period of two years no taxes whatever have been collected, and we have been borrowing money for the last several years at least a year ahead, and for the last three or four years two years ahead in order to meet expenses.

SENATOR WHEELER. One hears so much these days about the corruption and crookedness of city officials and school boards, that I was wondering as to the making of money of those interested in school boards on private contracts—I was wondering how much, if any, you had knowledge of in Chicago; just in a general way, without specific instances, has there been much of that?

MR. WILSON. The schools have recently been surveyed by Dr. George D. Strayer, of Columbia University, and in his survey report just submitted to the board of education this week, he makes several recommendations for economy in the board of education, and the board of education already ahead of that survey put into operation a great many economies under the present stress period of financial depression.

SENATOR WHEELER. I hope an aroused public opinion will come about in Chicago and other large cities that are suffering from lack of funds, against these thieving public officials who have been responsible to some extent, at least, in breaking down the finances of the cities, counties, and States of our country.

MR. WILSON. I want to address myself, gentlemen, to two or three things. In the middle of February the Chicago Principals Club, in order to acquaint the people of Chicago with the critical financial situation facing the school people, sent a questionnaire to each of the 14,000 teachers in the city. We had replies from 263 of the city's schools, and from 6,315 teachers, covering their own financial situation, beginning from the first of last May, when salaries ceased to come through on time.

Over the period of the last 13 months the Chicago school system has paid in cash to school employees only 5 months out of 13.

SENATOR COSTIGAN. When you refer to the 1st of last May, what year have you in mind? Is that of this year?

MR. WILSON. The 1st of May, 1931. These are some of the results we have on the questionnaire.

The teachers of Chicago, 3,177 of those teachers, out of 6,315, reported a total loss of $2,367,000 in bank failures. Two thousand eight hundred and sixty-nine of those teachers reported a loss of time of $621,293, because of personal illness, this at a time when salaries were not forthcoming.

SENATOR WHEELER. How many lost money by investing in the Insull Securities Cos. in Chicago?

MR. WILSON. I imagine a large number of them did that. Two thousand two hundred and seventy-eight reported losses to the extent of $7,800,000, by lapsed life insurance policies, as the result of this critical financial situation. Seven hundred and fifty-nine lost their homes, lost an equity in the homes which they were buying. There were large amounts due on rent and food, doctors' and dentists' bills, and all those things.

Insurance companies have loaned teachers at Chicago on their policies, $1,128,000. Many of the teachers had been forced to allow their life insurance policies to lapse. Eight hundred and five teachers reported having gone to what we call the loan sharks and procured money to the extent of $232,000, and were therefore paying an interest rate equal to a maximum of 42 per cent a year on that.

I want to say to you that the situation of the Chicago school teachers has been critical for the past year. A year ago we went into the summer vacation period with two months' back salary unpaid. This year, unless something unexpected happens in the next few days, we will go into the summer vacation with six months' unpaid salaries.

Twenty million dollars to-day is owing the teachers, 14,000 teachers, of Chicago. That is an average of $1,400 for each teacher in the Chicago school system that that community owes to the teachers. If every citizen in the United States were assessed an equal tax, that would bring in the stupendous total of $150,000,000,000, enough to operate the entire public-school system of the United States of America for three-quarters of a century.

SENATOR WHEELER. I did not get that statement.

MR. WILSON. Each teacher in Chicago is owed by that community $1,400; each of the 14,000 teachers. If every citizen in the United States were assessed an equal tax, that would bring in the stupendous total of $150,000,000,000, which would be enough to operate the entire public-school system of the United States for three-quarters of a century. That is the load, gentlemen, the Chicago public-school teachers are carrying to-day. That is the load the Chicago public-school teachers have carried almost continuously for the past 12 months.

I say to you that we have reached the breaking point. I believe that it is impossible for the Chicago school situation to go on as it is without some form of relief. We can not see any relief immediately ahead in the city. We are appealing to you as representatives of the United States Government, because we believe that education is fundamental to the preservation of the ideals of this Nation.

We are certain that anything that wrecks, cripples the school system of this Nation can not but have an effect upon the citizenship in all times. We believe the second largest city in the country, with such a school situation that we are certain is absolutely unique and tremendously dangerous, tremendously serious; we believe that that situation if permitted to continue will finally result in but one thing, the complete collapse of the Chicago public-school system, which would be a blot upon the good name, not only of that city, but upon the records of this Nation.

We believe that education and citizenship must go hand in hand. We believe that anything that interferes with the proper carrying out of the educational system of this Nation will finally have its effect upon the citizenship and upon the State as a whole.

This we believe to be a real crisis, a crisis that demands the most expert thinking, the most expert acting, and the most expert remedy. We are, therefore, appealing to you wholly on the ground that the United States of America can not afford to permit 500,000 boys and girls to remain out upon the streets of the second largest city in this Nation. We are certain that is imminent unless some relief comes, and comes immediately.

Certainly the ideals of America support public education. We believe that that city of ours is supporting public education. We are willing to make any sacrifice, and we have made all sacrifices in order that the schools of that city be kept open during the past year.

SENATOR COSTIGAN. Mr. Wilson, the problem of the boys on the street is further complicated, is it not, because many of them belong to families the members of which have long been and still are unemployed?

MR. WILSON. Absolutely. That is a very, very important point in connection with that.

SENATOR WHEELER. What has the appeal been to the bankers out there to take up these warrants?

MR. WILSON. The warrants which are now given to teachers—I have a half of one month's salary in my pocket at the present time that I have not been able to dispose of, that I would have to dispose of, if I were putting it on the market to-day, at 12 to 20 per cent discount. That is the answer of the bankers.

SENATOR WHEELER. Will the bankers take these warrants?

MR. WILSON. The bankers will not take the warrants at all. You have to sell them through private investment companies.

SENATOR WHEELER. They will not take them at all?

MR. WILSON. Not at the present time.

SENATOR WHEELER. Why will they not take them? What is the excuse they will not take them, the reason for it?

MR. WILSON. Very largely because of the muddle the tax situation is in, out of which we have not emerged in Chicago.

SENATOR WHEELER. But eventually it seems to me the city of Chicago, certainly the people of the city of Chicago, are not going to let the complete city government collapse there.

I want to remind you that the Congress of the United States has passed a reconstruction bill for the purpose of helping the bankers of the country. We have passed the Glass-Steagall bill for the purpose of helping the bankers of the country, and to keep the banks open, and we have passed other legislation, all of it with the idea of helping the big banks of the country, and it seems to me that when a community is in the situation that you have described, that at least there ought to be patriotism enough among your bankers in Chicago to take up these warrants and keep it going until such time as your tax muddle is straightened out.

MR. WILSON. Of course, as a matter of fact, over the last several years the bankers have carried the situation completely, but when this so-called tax strike came on, and with less than 50 per cent of the taxes due, and on which the penalty date began June 1, with less than 50 per cent of those taxes paid, the bankers find it impossible to carry the situation longer.

CHEAPER EDUCATION (1933)   From Avis D. Carlson, "Deflating The Schools," *Harper's,* vol. CLXVII, pp. 705–13

During the first two years of the depression the schools did business about as usual. By September, 1931, the strain was beginning to tell. Salary cuts were appearing even in large towns, and the number of pupils per teacher had definitely increased. Building programs had been postponed. In a few communities school terms had been considerably shortened, and in others some of the departments and services were being lopped off. But, on the whole, the school world wagged on pretty much as usual.

During the 1932–33 term the deflation gathered momentum so rapidly that many communities had to close their schools. By the end of last March nearly a third of a million children were out of school for that reason. But the number of children affected, shocking as it is, does not tell the story so vividly as does the distribution of the schools. Georgia had 1,318 closed schools with an enrollment of 170,790, and in Alabama 81 per cent of all the children enrolled in white rural schools were on an enforced vacation. In Arkansas, to cite the case of another sorely pressed State, over 300 schools were open for sixty days or less during the entire year. By the last of February more than 8,000 school children were running loose in sparsely settled New Mexico. And over a thousand West Virginia schools had quietly given up the struggle.

These are, of course, States which for one reason or another have always lagged educationally. But consider the case of Ohio, which formerly was near the other end of the procession. According to authentic information, some of it compiled by the Cleveland Plain Dealer and some by the State Director of Education, practically every school in the State had to shorten its term. Numbers of county schools shut down at the end of seven months. Findlay and Cuyahoga Falls, towns of 20,000 population, closed after seven months. Akron worried on a little longer, to the first week in May, owing its teachers $330,000. During the first part of the year the Dayton schools were open only three days a week. Youngstown closed three weeks earlier than usual, with a half million dollars in overdue salaries on its books. Every school in Carroll County clipped a month from its term.

In various other American communities where the schools continued open to the end of their 1923–33 term, it was only because teachers went stoutly on with their work even when they knew that salaries would not be forthcoming at the end of the month. The Chicago situation is so well known that there is no need to discuss it. But the average citizen who read of it somehow got the notion that it was unique. It was unique only in the size of the town and the length of time the drama had dragged on. Scattered throughout the nation last year were hundreds of school districts in which the Chicago plan of issuing tax-anticipation warrants which finally became uncashable worked out to its bitter end. In Oklahoma scores of teachers cashed only one or two warrants all year. In the whole of Apache County, Arizona, not a single warrant was cashed. In Mississippi, Northern Minnesota, Idaho, South Dakota, Alabama, Ohio, and probably other States that I do not know about, some of the rural teachers managed to exist by "boarding around" at the homes of their patrons, much as in the days of The Hoosier Schoolmaster. If the schools had been on a pay-as-you-go basis there is no estimating how many of them would have been closed during a greater part of the year. . . .

Some governmental expenditures are more essential than others, of course, and some are less wastefully made than others. But the average taxpayer is never disposed to investigate and make discriminations. Recently he has been in such straits that he is less than ever inclined to pause for discrimination. He may suspect or know that certain branches of his local government are shot with waste and graft of the most flagrant sort and that others are outworn and useless; but in that field he is either indifferent or convinced of his helplessness. He surely knows that an enormous bonded indebtedness is involving a staggering annual bill for "fixed charges"—but the capitalistic system being what it is, he supposes that fixed charges must remain fixed and sacrosanct. So far as he can see, there is only one thing he can do. He can kick and kick hard about all these governmental trimmings like county nurses and school gymnasiums which have been growing up under his eyes in the last twenty years. Use the knife, legislator, send it deep!

Thus adjured, the legislator has responded nobly.

Take the case of Iowa. In that home of fat cornfields and distraught corn growers, 95 per cent of the cost of the public schools came from the property tax. As farm prices have dropped, banks closed, and delinquent taxes mounted, the strain has become unbearable. If any State in the Union should have been interested in modernizing its tax system, that State was Iowa. The 1933 legislature brought forth much legislation. But an analysis of the 32 new laws that affect the schools shows that all but one were concerned solely with economy. The millage levies were limited to 80 per cent of the 1930 level. Agriculture, home economics, and manual training were taken from the list of required subjects, and kindergartens were made optional instead of mandatory. The appropriations for the State department of public instruction were reduced by 30 per cent. Permission was given for the discontinuance of junior colleges, and regulations were laid down for the disestablishment of county high schools. A flat minimum salary of $40 a month was fixed for teachers, regardless of their training or experiences—which, interestingly enough, is just about half the annual minimum income the government has assigned to industrial workers. Every conceivable kind of budget whittling was done, but nothing whatever was accomplished in the way of correcting the basic tax trouble.

Kansas, true to her genius for engaging in reforms on a heroic scale, had an economy legislature that really did things. None of the Iowan attention to small details in economy sullied their record. In spite of words of caution from the governor, they kept their eyes on the main job. They made a four-million-dollar cut in State appropriations, a large share of which must be borne by the State schools. They ordered the tax commission to reduce real property values 20 per cent, and they sternly limited school levies. And, to make all things doubly sure, they required every governmental agency to tot up its indebtedness, issue bonds to cover it, and forthwith go on a strict "cash basis." Having started from scratch, it must stay absolutely within its income. No more tax-anticipation warrants for Kansas.

Naturally such a legislative job is received in various ways. The taxpayers' associations that forced it are jubilant. School boards are bewildered. No one knows what to count upon, because the amount of delinquent taxes is nowadays unpredictable.

In smaller communities over the State the situation is still [August] uncertain. The "cash basis" system comes particularly hard just at this moment, for Kansas is going through one of the worst drouths in her drouth-ridden history. Two years of twenty-five cent wheat followed by a year of drouth make a sad combination for Kansas. Out through the wheat country great level fields are being foreclosed by the thousands. In the eastern part of the State, where diversified farming is practiced, the condition is no better. Naturally, then, taxes dribble into the courthouses in slow, thin streams. In the face of all this some rural school boards have decided that it is not worth while trying to open their schools. More than one rural teacher has contracted to teach for $35 a month, which in an eight months' school year means an annual income of $280. How many books and magazines these teachers, who are supposed to form the cultural leadership of rural Kansas, can afford to buy during the next year is open to any one's estimate. Their teaching will consist of a plodding sort of routine drill—when they are not worrying about the problem of how to replace the shoes which have just sprung leaks.

In general, the urban districts have the choice between cutting down to the Three R's, putting the teachers on a subsistence level, or shortening the term. At Horton, a town of about 4,000, the superintendent and teachers were hired at a rate of $50 a month. In a typical countyseat town of 3,500 the plan is to eliminate the kindergarten, school nurse, and one grade school, cut salaries sharply again, then run along until near the holidays, when the officials will say to the teachers, "We have only so much money on hand. If you want to prorate it among yourselves, well and good. If not, you'll have to go." The assumption back of this plan is that on the present crowded teacher market it will always be possible to get teachers no matter what salary is offered.

In other States the school legislation may not have been so extreme, but much of it was to the same point. In Idaho the appropriations for all educational institutions were reduced from 20 to 39 per cent of the 1931 level. In Oregon the teachers' minimum salary law was invalidated for two years. In Wyoming the legislature provided for the distribution of the government royalty fund (derived from mineral leases on federal lands) for a six months' term instead of eight months. In Michigan a severe tax limitation law was passed. In Delaware there was proposed a measure which would make it unlawful to employ any person to teach art, music, or athletics.

In Arkansas, where the school situation was last year so bad that in late November a tourist driving across the State saw few rural schools open, the legislature set itself to the task of relieving the schools. The line of reasoning was apparently thus: "In the good old days when the schools were in politics we did not have such messes as this. Therefore we will return them to the politicians, and incidentally save some money on them." Accordingly, the offices of County Board of Education and County Superintendent were abolished. The powers and duties of the former were vested in that picturesque institution, the County Court, and the powers and duties of the latter in a county examiner appointed by the county judge. This county examiner is required to remain in active teaching service, and for his extra-professional chore is to be paid a fee of $650 a year! Another backward step of the same sort was taken in the abolition of the State Board of Education and throwing of the office of State Superintendent back into State politics.

In Oklahoma an economy measure requires the adoption of text books for a period of ten years. On a mad-hatter arrangement like that a whole generation of children would have grown up without knowing that the state of Poland exists or that the form of government in Russia has changed! Another interesting new law establishes a schedule of maximum salaries for schools which are to have State aid. According to this schedule the teachers with the lowest permissible training and experience are to be limited to $40 a month, while the upper limit for an experienced, college graduate, elementary teacher is $85, or an annual income of $680, if State funds can hold out for eight months. An inexperienced high school teacher with an A.M. is entitled to $90. The most any such teacher can ever get with no matter how many years of experience is exactly $100. . . .

In general, there are four points at which a Board of Education sitting down to work out its annual budget may apply the knife: in building and repairs, in text books and classroom equipment, in salaries, and in services and curricula.

The first need not detain us long. It is no longer available at all as a method of economy. At the onset of the depression building programs were abandoned and repairs reduced to a minimum that in many a town will prove a costly economy in the long run, if not an actual danger to life and limb. The results of this three-year stretch of thrift are beginning to be apparent. Since the average school district had spent heavily for building during the decade before 1930 (to compensate for the war years when no construction went on and to accord with the general spirit of "bigger and better") probably no great harm has yet been done by this halt in building. But depression or no depression, the school population continues to increase by more than 200,000 a year. Present building equipment will not long continue to house a family that grows so rapidly. In many city systems room-shortage is already an acute problem. In fact the 1932–33 term saw about 250,000 children attending school on a part-time basis for lack of school rooms and approximately 150,000 others housed in temporary or portable shacks. To enjoy the Century of Progress one must forget that the eccentric metropolis which stages the show used seven hundred tin shacks in housing its school-children last year and has just junked its entire junior high school system in order to gain classroom space for the senior high schools.

The next items to be considered by our hypothetical Board in desperate search for something to reduce are text books and classroom equipment. Here, too, economy was early in the game carried as far as it could be without serious injury to the quality of instruction offered. It is safe to say that whatever further reduction is being made for the 1933–34 term does offer that injury. With a million more pupils than in 1930, the sale of textbooks had dropped off 30 per cent by the beginning of 1933. Such a contrast in figures can only mean that youngsters are using dog-eared, dirty books, crudely defaced and probably with missing pages. A fine chance they have to learn to respect books! It can also only mean that many schools are already seriously crippled by the lack of books. Supplementary readers and reference books fall to pieces after a while, and if they are not replaced, instruction in the courses which depend upon them must cease.

And now the Board comes to salaries. Three courses are open. Salaries may be cut all round, teachers may be released, or at the worst both devices may be resorted to. The first method was the one most often chosen in 1932–33. According to a study made last spring by the United States Office of Education, teachers' salaries had already dropped from 12 to 43 per cent—besides, of course, the discount levied by bankers who cashed the warrants. This fall salaries fell sharply again. In many regions the teachers are now literally on a subsistence level. Throughout the country as a whole the classroom teachers who still have jobs, who are paid in cash and with some degree of regularity, and who have an annual income of as much as $1200 may count themselves among the plutocrats of the profession. The rise of commodity prices, which the administration is so assiduously fostering, will materially add to the troubles of the pedagogues. . . .

In preceding depression years new teachers were not hired, but this year has seen a wave of actual releases. Chicago has trimmed her teaching force by more than a thousand. With the $2,200,000 cut Boston is making from last year's budget many teachers will surely have to be eliminated. So small a city as Tulsa has had to let 60 go. In villages and cities everywhere the teaching force is smaller this year than in 1930, when the school population was about a million less than this year. To the cynic who asks, "What of it?" one has to reply that Mark Hopkins on the end of a log may be only a romantic ideal, but Susan Smith facing 50 or 60 pupils in a room designed to seat 35 or 40 comfortably is so far at the other extreme that it is nonsense to think she can do much teaching.

And finally, the Board approaches the items most loaded with emotional dynamite: services and curricula. Here enter for attention the celebrated "fads and frills" about which every critic of the public schools is so deeply exercised. Now a fad or a frill seems to be anything in the school system which was not there thirty years ago. Last year the schools began reluctantly to relinquish them, in other words, to retreat to the educational customs of 1900. This year a veritable axe has descended upon them. Night schools and special schools for physically and mentally handicapped children have been eliminated or drastically curtailed. At the present rate of mortality, kindergartens will soon be a thing of the past. Supervisors are being blown out like chaff in the wind. Health services are being abandoned and visiting teachers becoming a luxury few cities can afford. Many towns have eliminated music entirely and others have greatly reduced their offerings. Art, home economics, manual training, physical education, trade and vocational classes, and even foreign languages are all being eliminated or curtailed.

NEWS ACCOUNT OF ORGANIZATION OF UNEMPLOYED COLLEGE GRADUATES (1932)   From *The New York Times,* July 27, 1932.

Organization of the Association of Unemployed College Alumni was announced yesterday after a meeting of graduates of nine Eastern colleges at the offices of the League for Industrial Democracy. Estimating the number of unemployed alumni in this city alone at more than 10,000, the association made public a plan of action designed to enlist members throughout the country.

In a statement prepared at the meeting the group pointed out that since June, 1929, it has become increasingly difficult for university graduates to obtain positions. Distress consequent upon unemployment was more acute among college-trained men and women, according to the announcement, because of their relatively high standards of living and education. . . .

Colleges represented at the meeting included Columbia, Harvard, New York University, Vassar, Hunter, City College, Swarthmore, Columbia Law School and New York Dental School.

COLLEGE STUDENTS DURING THE DEPRESSION (1933)   From Gilbert Love, "College Students Are Beating The Depression," in *School and Society*, XXXVII (June 10, 1933), pp. 749–5l.

Across the campus of Oklahoma A. and M. College moved a weird procession. At the front was an ancient open flivver, sufficiently battered to be termed "collegiate." In its front seat were two boys; in its back seat a bale of hay. There followed another car, differing from the first only in the number and kind of dents in its fenders and body. It was also manned by two boys. Its back seat was occupied by a large crate of protesting poultry. Then came a fifth boy leading a Jersey cow. The cow refused to be influenced by the obvious impatience of the motorized portion of the procession, so it was hours later when the strange group finally arrived in front of a house on the outskirts of the college town. The poultry was given a back yard coop in which to live and, presumably, to lay eggs. The cow was tethered in an adjoining field. Then from some recesses in the battered hulls of the flivvers the boys pulled out some 200 quarts of canned fruits and vegetables and a dozen cured hams. With meat and vegetables in the cellar and prospective eggs and milk in the back yard, the five were ready for higher education.

College students have probably developed more ingenious ways of beating the depression than any other group in America. Using their wits to earn money or cooking their own meals and living in shacks to save it, Joe College and Betty Co-ed are getting educated in spite of technological unemployment, bank moratoria, impoverishment of agriculture and a general scarcity of cash. For instance:

Two male students at Ohio State University have started a "dog laundry." They call for Fido, Bruno or Towser, take him to their "plant" and return him all nicely bathed, combed and manicured. . . .

A Notre Dame student who found that all the regular "hashing," janitorial and secretarial jobs were taken when he arrived in South Bend, created a business for himself by becoming a campus guide. He spends his Sundays at the entrance to the university, picking up groups of visitors and taking them to points of interest around the famous school.

A student at Western Reserve University, Cleveland, has been able to hold a comparatively lucrative position right through the depression because he is becoming accustomed to hold-ups. The large gasoline station at which he is night attendant has been robbed three times by gunmen.

A couple of husky freshmen at West Virginia University who probably didn't know the difference between a casserole and a wash tub when they left home, have been going to school on less than $1.60 a week apiece by renting a back bedroom with a small stove in it and cooking cheap but nourishing foods.

Eight boys at the University of Washington are getting their meals at very small cost by cooking them in a basement and "taking in" several other students as boarders.

An examination of a single small school reveals the wide variety of occupations that students have taken up to support themselves. In Duquesne University, Pittsburgh, one student is an undertaker's helper, one a railroad fireman, one a laborer in a steel mill, one cuts granite tombstones and another sells newspapers. A student who has become an expert on glass works a regular eight-hour shift in a glass factory 40 miles from Pittsburgh and "commutes" to take a full-time course at Duquesne. A pharmacist who has changed his mind about professions is keeping his corner drug store to pay his way through a law course. An enterprising student buys old text-books from sophomores and sells them to freshmen. An athletic young man is serving as first aid instructor for a coal company. One Duquesne student is reputed to hold 27 odd jobs on the campus and in the city. Among other things he is editor-in-chief of the school newspaper and official announcer at the major league baseball games at Forbes Field.

The student wage-earners at Duquesne are mostly male. But, throughout the country, girls are showing as much initiative and courage as their masculine fellow-students in making their own way. Take Northwestern co-eds, for example. One girl living in a Northwestern cooperative dormitory earns her expense money by remodeling hats and dresses, washing and waving hair and doing any odd mending wanted. Two girls have become so well known for their adeptness at catering that they can not take care of all the calls they receive from hostesses in Evanston and near-by sections of Chicago. Another girl is housekeeper—"home manager" would be more accurate—in a household in which there is a grandmother who is so seriously ill that she must have two nurses, a father and mother who must be away on business most of the time, and three small children who are left in Evanston to attend school. An exclusive apartment hotel employs a co-ed as hostess in its tea room. For working about four hours a day the girl is given a luxurious apartment, maid service and meals. Another girl makes several hundred dollars a year by tinting photographs for an out-of-town company.

Student occupations at the University of Pennsylvania, Philadelphia, range all the way from historical research to handling boats. A recent survey disclosed the fact that students were engaged in 84 kinds of gainful activity. Dish washing, furniture moving, painting, tutoring, pantry work, scraping floors and soda dispensing seem to be favorites, if numbers are any indication. To take care of some of the students who could not find work in Philadelphia, the student placement service started an automobile washing and polishing establishment on the campus.

The University of Pennsylvania took action at the start of the present school year to turn over as many campus jobs as possible to students. As a result, collegians are now acting as night watchmen, janitors, secretaries, mail carriers, switchboard operators, locker room attendants, technicians and clerks. Students have also been appointed to act as gate men and ushers at athletic contests and to handle all parking on university grounds. They handle trunks in the dormitories at the beginning and end of each academic year and have been authorized to sell certain articles at service stands placed in university buildings.

As a matter of fact, schools everywhere are taking heroic measures to help their students through the period of economic difficulty.

Costs at the University Commons, University of Kentucky, have been reduced to such an extent that students can now live there for $3.50 a week. Through the intervention of the dean of men at West Virginia University, the standard rate of board charged in private homes near the university has been reduced from $7 to $4 a week.

At the University of Pittsburgh a number of boys are being allowed to live rent-free in unused garages and other buildings near the campus. And, although it was not officially sanctioned by the university, a group of athletes lived for several months last winter in a drafty campus building used for dressing room purposes.

Officials of Carthage College, in Illinois, let a miner pay his daughter's tuition in coal this past winter. At Notre Dame 300 students are earning their board by waiting on tables in the dormitory dining halls. They are so numerous that they serve a meal to their 2,000 fellow students in 20 minutes.

Statistics compiled last fall indicate that fully half the men and one fourth of the women attending the nation's 48 land-grant colleges are working for at least part of their funds. More than 13,000 men and 3,000 girls in these colleges are earning all their expenses. Their total earnings are $7,000,000 a year.

At the University of Wisconsin, three fifths of the students earned part of their expenses during the last school year, and 23 per cent were wholly self-supporting. At Yale, during the last school year, students earned $553,701. The institution contributed another $683,378 in scholarships and loans.

When the economic depression is finally over and commendations for valor are being passed around, some sort of special recognition should be given the student who, with only enough money to last until June if he spent but 35 cents a day for food, quit a $100 a month job because it was keeping him from his studies.

UNEMPLOYED COLLEGE GRADUATES (1934)   From *School and Society*, vol. XXXIX, p. 307.

Thousands of college graduates, many with high-grade professional training, are among the ranks of the unemployed, as disclosed in a recent survey conducted by the American College Personnel Association. Under the direction of Dr. Esther Lloyd-Jones, assistant professor of education at Teachers College, Columbia University, and Clyde R. Miller, director of the Bureau of Educational Service, the study embraced fifty-four colleges and universities located in every section of the United States. The confidential records of these fifty-four institutions revealed that at the present time 21,974 men and women holding degrees from these colleges are without positions.

"The figures revealed by this survey do not pretend to completeness," Mr. Miller reports. "They include only those individuals who have notified the appointment bureaus of their colleges that they are without work. Scores of colleges are not included in the association, and the appointment bureaus of the member colleges have no information concerning the status of large numbers of their alumni who have not communicated with them. It is safe to say that at the present time hundreds of thousands of college graduates are unemployed. Many of them are technically trained men and women of proven ability and splendid achievement."

Many professions are represented, the teaching profession leading with 12,420 unemployed. Engineers are next in rank, listing 2,845 unemployed graduates, the larger number being electrical, mechanical and civil engineers. Business graduates also suffer greatly, the survey showed, as 2,436 business executives are unemployed.

Over 100 different occupations are listed, together with the number of unemployed graduates in each field. Some of the most frequent groups include architects, agriculturalists, bankers, chemists, educational administrators, dietitians, journalists, librarians, social workers, salesmen, laboratory technicians. religious educators, advertising men, draftsmen, artists and biologists.

Of the colleges and universities which listed unemployed alumni, the Ohio State University has the greatest number, with 2,097. The University of Chicago has 1,798; the University of Illinois, 1,445; Teachers College, Columbia University, 1,255; Princeton University, 450; the Carnegie Institute of Technology, 844, New York University, 575; the University of Minnesota, 528; Temple University, 687; the College of the City of New York, 550.

YOUTH AND THE SCHOOL DURING THE DEPRESSION (1938)   From American Council on Education, *Youth Tell Their Story* (Washington, D.C., 1938), pp. 67–73.

There are many kinds of educational surveys, differing primarily in the manner of approach. Among others, there is the survey that studies educational programs by going to the schools, to the teachers and superintendents. And there is the one that approaches education from the angle of those who are going, or who have gone, through the educational mill.

A Commission-sponsored survey of the Baltimore and the Maryland school systems has already been made by Frank W. Wright and Payson Smith, who adopted the first approach. They went direct to the schools, talked with teachers and superintendents, and studied school records and reports. The result was an interesting and valuable report on the educational program in the state, followed by sympathetic evaluations and pertinent recommendations.

The present study of the educational program follows the second approach. It is believed that such an approach yields results that are less distinctly local in character, and uncovers conditions more likely to be found elsewhere in the United States. Provided always that the sample of the youth studied is essentially national in character, the facts uncovered can be accepted as having national implications. And, as previously indicated, it is with the national implications, and not the local peculiarities, that the staff of the Commission is primarily concerned.

So, in approaching this vitally important area of the youth's school life, we went, as usual, to the youth themselves. . . . When the last Federal census was taken in 1930, 19 per cent of the youth of America between the ages of 16 and 24 were in schools or colleges. In our sample, the percentage of school youth was 19.4, a difference of only 0.4 per cent. While going through these school data, it will be well to remember therefore that about four out of every five youth considered were permanently out of school.

So far as these out-of-school youth are concerned, our interest will be to discover what the schools have done, what the youth's reactions to their past education have been, and what, if anything, there was in the economic, domestic, or social conditions under which they lived that tended to affect, for better or worse, the quality and quantity of the education they received. . . .

Summary of Factors Affecting the Amount of Schooling Youth Receive

In what appears to be the order of their importance, the outstanding factors that affect the amount of schooling youth receive are enumerated below:

The occupation of the father. The largest variations in the schooling youth had received were found to be associated with the father's usual occupation. This held true for the Negro as well as the white youth, as well as for each sex group within the races.

Race is placed second and above sex. An accurate evaluation of the importance of the race factor is complicated because Negro youth, especially in the rural areas, have fathers whose usual occupation is either farm laborer, farm tenant, or unskilled laborer. Thus it is impossible to determine exactly how much of the relatively low grade attainment of Negro youth is due to some "race difference" and how much is the result of the fact that a large proportion of Negroes are in economically weak occupations.

Sex. Sex differences appear regardless of how the data are analyzed. Within the races, within occupations, within the different age groups, and within the various localities, the female youth in general have higher median grades.

Why Do Youth Leave School?

So far, we have been concerned chiefly with an analysis of the factors that seem to influence the youth's school progress as measured by the grade he has attained. Our purpose has been to discover these factors, and to attempt to measure their relative potency. At this point, we consider briefly the factors operating to terminate a youth's formal education, as revealed by the reasons for leaving school that were given by the youth themselves.

Youth's Reasons for Leaving School

The following table presents an analysis of the reasons given by young people for leaving school.

Reason given	Percentage of youth
Economic reasons	54.0
Lack of family funds	34.1
Desire to earn own money	15.7
Needed to work at home	4.2
Lack of interest in school	24.6
Lack of interest	20.6
Disciplinary trouble	2.2
Subjects too difficult	1.8
Feeling of completion upon graduation	13.2
Poor health	3.2
To marry	3.0
Other reasons	2.0
Total	100.0
Number of youth	10,858

The responses analyzed in Table 18 indicate that, for every twenty-five youth who have left school,

Ten left because of economic need
Six left because of lack of interest or because of maladjustment
Four left because they wanted to earn their own money
Three left because they considered their education completed upon graduation
Two left for other reasons such as marriage, health, etc.

The outstanding reason given by the youth for leaving school was the financial inability of their parents to keep them there. In fact, almost four out of every ten (38 per cent) of the out-of-school youth indicated that they would have preferred to remain in school, but that lack of family funds, or the need for their services at home, prevented their continuing.

It is also significant that a fourth of the youth said they left school because of a lack of interest or because of their inability to adjust themselves to the school program. This 25 per cent is probably an understatement, as undoubtedly a large proportion of those who said they dropped out because they wanted to earn money for themselves did so because the attraction of economic independence was greater than that of the school program.

The fact that 13.2 per cent said they had left school because they considered their education complete upon graduation does not mean, of course, that only 13.2 per cent actually completed the grades in the various school levels. All it means is that this proportion left school at the completion of the elementary, secondary, or college level because they felt that the education they had received was adequate to meet their needs.

In so far as the matter of leaving school at undesirably low levels is the direct result of inadequate funds, it is obvious that the remedy lies deeper than any improvement or extension of the educational programs. If society is interested in broadening and deepening the educational backgrounds of all its young people, it seems quite clear that the first move is to make further schooling possible for them by some local, state, or Federal subsidizing program, a beginning of which has already been made by the National Youth Administration.

As indicated above, about 40 per cent of our youth would go farther in school if the opportunity were provided them. An analysis of the responses of the twelfth grade graduate suggests that almost half (46.8 per cent) failed to proceed to a higher educational level because of a lack of family funds. Almost as large a proportion (42.7 per cent) of the youth employed on relief projects gave the same reason.

It seems obvious that before the schools can effectively participate in any solution of the national youth problem opportunities for attending them must be provided. In other words, it would seem that society's first job is to change the nature of "equality of educational opportunity" from that of a noble jingle to an established and effective reality.

Are Schools Adapted to the Needs and Interests of Youth?

Four out of every ten youth assert that they leave school because their parents cannot continue to send them. For them, the solution is primarily a matter of providing opportunities that don't exist. For a large proportion of the remainder, the solution is more definitely a matter of so adjusting our school programs as to make them sufficiently attractive to compete with other things. Our data reveal that, with several groups of youth, unsatisfactory school adjustment—by which is meant a combination of lack of interest, disciplinary difficulties, and too difficult subjects—is a more general reason for leaving school than a lack of family funds. So far as the youth's own statements of why he left school can be accepted as the real reasons, all of this indicates that, for large groups of youth, the schools simply have failed to function as a genuine force. The fact that relatively high percentages of youth giving lack of interest as their reason for dropping out were found among those who left school at the upper high school level, as well as among those who left at the elementary level, indicates that all along the line the schools, as they are now set up, are adapted to neither the needs nor the interests of large numbers of our young people.

For youth who are preparing for professional vocations, it appears that the holding power of the schools is exceedingly strong. Less than 5 per cent of young people found to be engaged in professional work stated that they left school because they lacked interest. Somewhat the same situation is true for youth discovered in office and sales work, as only 14 per cent of the youth so engaged gave lack of interest as their reason for dropping out.

Three hundred and forty-two (about 3 per cent) of the out-of-school youth gave marriage as their reason for leaving. Of this number, a substantial proportion

A NEW
ORIENTATION
FOR EDUCATION
1930–1950

2545

dropped out of school at relatively low levels. In fact, over half the married boys (52.4 per cent) and almost half the married girls (42.3 per cent) were found to have received no more than an elementary school education. This naturally raises the question as to what schools are doing to help these youth meet the obligations and problems which marriage is certain to force upon them. If there is an economic justification for providing vocational training for youth who will have to earn their own living at a comparatively early age, there would seem to be an equally sound social justification in providing young people with at least a basic knowledge of the obligations and problems of marriage. That youth themselves consider this a part of the school's job is indicated by their opinion that sex education should be made a regular part of the school program.

What to Do About It

An analysis of the reasons given by youth as to why they left school tends, in a general way, to support the conclusions that grew out of our analysis of the data on the school progress they had made. The first move should be one of providing adequate educational opportunities for all the youth who are capable and who are desirous of taking advantage of them.

The second step in increasing the extent to which the schools can effectively participate in the solution of the youth problem concerns those youth who, though provided by their parents with adequate opportunity, chose to leave school at relatively low levels. For these, the approach is clearly one of adapting school programs to their interests and needs. Youngsters, like horses, can be led to water, but only thirst will make them drink. . . .

Do Out-of-School Youth Want Vocational Training?

This question was asked only of youth who had left school. They were asked if they would take vocational training if it were made available. As used by the interviewer, the term "vocational training" meant training for any job. It included training in the professions and arts, as well as in business and trades. For the majority (60 per cent) the answer was "yes."

As suggested in one of our introductory paragraphs, the questions asked of our young people were generally such as to exclude any temptation to make false or inaccurate responses. In this particular question, however, there is clearly an encouragement of wishful thinking. That six out of every ten of the out-of-school youth are, in fact, genuinely desirous of further vocational training is, we suspect, open to question. We doubt, therefore, if this 60 per cent can be taken as an indication of the potential demand by out-of-school youth for free public vocational training.

It is believed, however, that these data reveal that there is a real demand for more vocational training. Many young people have learned, especially during the past few years, what usually happens when, to a prospective employer's question, "What can you do?" they answer, "Anything." What usually happens is that they get no job. These and similar experiences have led them to believe that training for a specific type of work is very often not only desirable but necessary.

An element of wishful thinking is also apparent in many of the responses to the second half of the question: If so, for what kind of job would you like to be trained?

An examination [reveals] that out of every twenty-five youths expressing a desire for vocational training,

Nine desired training for one of the professions
Six desired training for business or commercial work
Six desired training in trades and crafts
Two desired training in domestic and personal service
Two desired training in other unclassified fields.

About all that some of these data show is that vocations, like the grass that grows in pastures, usually look greener on the other side of the fence. This is somewhat dramatically illustrated by the responses of farm youth. About one out of fourteen wanted training in agriculture.

Yet, even when due weight is given to human nature's ancient enthusiasm for variety and change, there still remain in these expressed preferences for vocational courses some implications that are worthy of sober consideration.

More than five out of every six out-of-school youth who wanted training wanted it in one of the professions, in business, or in the skilled trades. For the out-of-school group as a whole, 36 per cent wanted training in the professions. It will be remembered that the median grade attainment of this group was the completion of the ninth grade.

These two facts—the outstanding preference for professional training, and the generally low grade attained—can, and probably do, mean two things. They mean that this younger generation aspires in the traditional manner of all younger generations. It wants to do bigger and better things. They also mean that, for some reason or other, there has been precious little realism injected into the thinking of a large proportion of our young people about the jobs that are available and the services they are qualified to perform. In view of the almost complete absence of vocational guidance from their school experiences, at least a part of the responsibility for this dearth of realism can justly be laid at the doorstep of the schools.

Among the hopeful and constructive facts that the data in Table 20 reveal is the very real demand for training in trades and crafts. In spite of the denials from certain labor leaders, there is a considerable body of evidence to suggest that, if there is such a thing as an unfilled labor demand, it exists in certain kinds of skilled trades. The fact that half of the 1,000 youth who were found to be employed on unskilled jobs desired some kind of vocational training, and that half this number (49.6 per cent) wanted training in some trade or craft, is not only a refreshing item of realism, but a definitely hopeful sign.

A NEW
ORIENTATION
FOR EDUCATION
1930-1950

2547

The Federal Government and Education

REPORT ON EDUCATION FOR FAMILY LIFE (1930) From White House
Conference on Child Health and Protection, *White House Conference, 1930, Addresses and
Abstracts of Committee Reports* (Washington, D.C., 1930), pp. 147–51.

The surest means of meeting social maladjustment is by education. The
very fact that there is, at present, a conflict between family tradition and active
social and economic forces is an indictment of our education in the immediate past.
It has either not kept up with the times in furthering adjustment to changing
conditions, or it has not provided the insight necessary for resistance to the
operation of inimical forces.

As industrialism and efficiency are carried over into education, it is important
that vocational competency should not be stressed to the neglect of education for
living. There is need of widespread teaching of ethics and human values, of training
in artistic appreciation and creative expression, in the use of time, in the art of
living, and in human relationships. Such training would shift our sense of values,
provide for profitable use of leisure time, and add to human happiness.

In addition, guidance and specific instruction should be provided in preparation
for family life, ultimate marriage and parenthood, and specific training in mental
hygiene and human behavior for all those individuals who touch the home or the
child in a professional capacity. The need for such training is gradually being
recognized and courses are already being provided in various professional schools.
Such an educational program to be effective would have to be carried on over a
long period of time, and there would perhaps always be necessity for supplementary
training for parents to help them meet the actual problems of child rearing as they
arise.

From the point of view of the sociologists a definite challenge is given: "Is the
time not ripe to lay the foundations of a new and separate science of the family?"
The present trend in the evolution of home economics would seem to indicate its
possibility. Beginning with the application of science to the technology of the arts
of the household as they related to food, clothing, and shelter, in the science of
home economics it has been found that after all the home could not be made
satisfactory, however good its material conditions, without a knowledge of the
child, and unless the psychology of the child was given a place in its field of
knowledge. Finally, when child guidance was attempted, it was found that the

child's behavior is chiefly conditioned by his life in the subtle complex of personal relations which we call the family. Knowledge of the family and of its intricacies and relations has become the central problem in a scientific study of the home. Home economics education should play a significant rôle in lifting the level of family living through furnishing information to direct family consumption, and knowledge and skills for the management of the surviving household activities. And it has a special challenge to develop the individual to see these activities not as ends in themselves but in relation to the promotion of wholesome family life.

Parental Education

Parent education is a means by which all the problems facing family life are brought into conscious consideration, traditions are evaluated in the light of present-day living, and new techniques and methods of adjustment are evolved.

While preschool laboratories, nursery schools and clinics have been analyzing the problems of parents and the needs of children, various educational organizations and institutions have been developing facilities for making this information available to parents through organization of parent study groups, conferences, lectures, radio talks, and a vast amount of popular literature. The projects were developed under many different types of institutions and agencies. National programs were developed by various national organizations. State-wide programs were inaugurated in state universities and departments of education. Cities developed their own local programs to provide facilities for the education of parents. The National Council of Parent Education was organized for the purpose of coördinating and exercising leadership in the field.

Heredity, problems arising in the social and educational development of the child, his health, special problems of behavior, home management, religious education, and vocational guidance are the topics most frequently discussed by parent study groups. The informal discussions which characterized the early study groups still play a conspicuous part in the modern parent education movement. In addition to these, there have been recently a large number of lectures and round-tables on special topics given in connection with schools for parents, parent institutes, and conferences. The radio is also being used increasingly.

Child guidance clinics and consultation centers are appreciating the necessity of working with the parent as well as with the child in bringing about a satisfactory readjustment. In addition, various agencies in related fields, churches, religious and lay educational organizations, juvenile courts, children's aid societies, community centers, health clinics, and such home visiting agents as the visiting nurse, the family social worker, and the visiting teacher, are educating parents informally as part of their work of education, prevention, adjustment, and rehabilitation.

Recommendations

Further research is important in the field of the family. Only on the basis of research can an adequate science of the family be established, and the problems of marital and parent-child relationships be treated. One specific research recommendation, growing out of the studies of this Committee, is that provision be made for standardizing those scales for family relationships and home atmosphere tentatively formulated for the White House Conference.

Further research is needed on the social and economic factors affecting family life today. The relation of these factors to the family is worthy of the same careful consideration that has been given to the conditions of production in relation to industry and commerce.

Institutions or research centers to study family relationships and processes of family life, as well as the economic and social factors operating upon the family today, should be established.

Family consultation centers should be established with a staff composed of specialists in home economics, housing, social work, law, psychiatry, psychology, and sociology. These centers should be prepared to give advice and information on the different problems of family life.

Special attention should be paid to Italians, Mexicans, and other immigrant groups, who come into the cities from rural backgrounds and who need help in adjusting themselves to the conditions of American urban life.

Special attention should also be paid to the Negro family in order that it may attain that economic security necessary for stable family life, and may be assisted to the attainment of high ideals of family life.

Instruction should be provided by schools and colleges to further the satisfactions of intelligent participation in family life and to prepare for courtship, marriage, and parenthood.

In view of the responsibilities and obligations being laid upon the family as the primary agency for child health and protection, as revealed by the recommendations of the various sub-committees of the White House Conference, this Committee strongly recommends that various educational associations and organizations and the educational departments of the different states be requested to study the possibilities for organizing parent education as part of the systems of public instruction, and that the professional groups and organizations concerned with children also be asked to study their opportunities and obligations for parent education.

THE CHILDREN'S CHARTER (1930)   From U.S. Children's Bureau, *The Story of the White House Conferences on Children and Youth* (Washington, D.C., 1967), pp. 11–12.

The Children's Charter

PRESIDENT HOOVER'S WHITE HOUSE CONFERENCE ON CHILD HEALTH AND PROTECTION, RECOGNIZING THE RIGHTS OF THE CHILD AS THE FIRST RIGHTS OF CITIZENSHIP, PLEDGES ITSELF TO THESE AIMS FOR THE CHILDREN OF AMERICA

I For every child spiritual and moral training to help him to stand firm under the pressure of life

II For every child understanding and the guarding of his personality as his most precious right

III For every child a home and that love and security which a home provides; and for that child who must receive foster care, the nearest substitute for his own home

IV For every child full preparation for his birth, his mother receiving prenatal, natal, and postnatal care; and the establishment of such protective measures as will make child-bearing safer

V For every child health protection from birth through adolescence, including: periodical health examinations and, where needed, care of specialists and hospital treatment; regular dental examinations and care of the teeth; protective and preventive measures against communicable diseases; the insuring of pure food, pure milk, and pure water

VI For every child from birth through adolescence, promotion of health, including health instruction and a health program, wholesome physical and mental recreation, with teachers and leaders adequately trained

VII For every child a dwelling-place safe, sanitary, and wholesome, with reasonable provisions for privacy; free from conditions which tend to thwart his development; and a home environment harmonious and enriching

VIII For every child a school which is safe from hazards, sanitary, properly equipped, lighted, and ventilated. For younger children nursery schools and kindergartens to supplement home care

IX For every child a community which recognizes and plans for his needs, protects him against physical dangers, moral hazards, and disease; provides him with safe and wholesome places for play and recreation; and makes provision for his cultural and social needs

X For every child an education which, through the discovery and development of his individual abilities, prepares him for life; and through training and vocational guidance prepares him for a living which will yield him the maximum of satisfaction

XI For every child such teaching and training as will prepare him for successful parenthood, home-making, and the rights of citizenship; and for parents, supplementary training to fit them to deal wisely with the problems of parenthood

XII For every child education for safety and protection against accidents to which modern conditions subject him—those to which he is directly exposed and those which, through loss or maiming of his parents, affect him indirectly

XIII For every child who is blind, deaf, crippled, or otherwise physically handicapped, and for the child who is mentally handicapped, such measures as will early discover and diagnose his handicap, provide care and treatment, and so train him that he may become an asset to society rather than a liability. Expenses of these services should be borne publicly where they cannot be privately met

XIV For every child who is in conflict with society the right to be dealt with intelligently as society's charge, not society's outcast; with the home, the school, the church, the court and the institution when needed, shaped to return him whenever possible to the normal stream of life

XV For every child the right to grow up in a family with an adequate standard of living and the security of a stable income as the surest safeguard against social handicaps

XVI For every child protection against labor that stunts growth, either physical or mental, that limits education, that deprives children of the right of comradeship, of play, and of joy

XVII For every rural child as satisfactory schooling and health services as for the city child, and an extension to rural families of social, recreational, and cultural facilities

XVIII To supplement the home and the school in the training of youth, and to return to them those interests of which modern life tends to cheat children, every stimulation and encouragement should be given to the extension and development of the voluntary youth organizations

XIX To make everywhere available these minimum protections of the health and welfare of children, there should be a district, county, or community organization for health, education, and welfare, and full-time officials, coordinating with a state-wide program which will be responsive to a nationwide service of general information, statistics, and scientific research. This should include:

(a) Trained, full-time public health officials, with public health nurses, sanitary inspection, and laboratory workers
(b) Available hospital beds
(c) Full-time public welfare service for the relief, aid, and guidance of children in special need due to poverty, misfortune, or behavior difficulties, and for the protection of children from abuse, neglect, exploitation, or moral hazard

FOR EVERY CHILD THESE RIGHTS, REGARDLESS OF RACE, OR COLOR, OR SITUATION, WHEREVER HE MAY LIVE UNDER THE PROTECTION OF THE AMERICAN FLAG.

THE MINIMUM ESSENTIALS OF A SCHOOL PROGRAM(1930)   From White
House Conference On Child Health and Protection, *White House Conference, 1930,
Addresses and Abstracts of Committee Reports,* (Wash., D. C., 1930), pp. 189–90.

Recommendations

In order that the health of the whole child shall be protected and promoted, the
Committee on The School Child recommends that:

The home protect and promote the health of the preschool child so that he will
enter upon his school life in sound health, free from remediable defects.

School buildings and surroundings be provided which meet recognized standards
in construction and equipment, and in their adequate maintenance and operation.

Home and school cooperation in the detection and correction of remediable
defects, in the prevention and control of communicable disease, in the program of
health instruction conducted by the school, and in all other phases of the school
health program.

The school year be so organized that there will be no diminishing efficiency or
accumulation of fatigue on the part of the child from day to day or month to
month.

The summer vacation period be so utilized as to show the best attainable care of
the whole child; and this not only that the children then be best served, but that the
experimentation may point the way to a remaking of the school curriculum as well.

The curriculum be built around the interests, needs, and abilities of the child
with adequate provision for the mentally gifted and the handicapped.

Every student teacher in training be required to pursue courses that will enable
her to understand the child as a whole and to promote his physical, mental,
emotional, and social health.

"In-service" training be provided by school superintendents for their teachers,
supervisors, principals, physicians, nurses, and other health specialists, so that they
can more intelligently carry out their respective duties in relation to the school
health program.

Budget provision be made by boards of education for the school health program,
sufficient to insure the essentials in the best programs now conducted in progressive
schools, with the expectation that in the near future there will be need and
justification for the expenditure annually of at least 10 per cent of the educational
budget for the inclusive school health program. Of even greater importance than a
fixed percentage of the budget is that primary emphasis be placed upon the fullest
practical realization of a comprehensive and satisfactory health program in the
schools which will justify the expenditure of all that it costs.

More definite criteria for school health work be formulated as a basis for the
development of better tests and instruments for surveying and evaluating the
relative work and efficiency of the many materials and procedures employed.

Equalization of opportunity be sought in all schools, by all possible means, for
all school children, so that they may achieve the best health of which they are
capable; this to apply to all schools, whether urban or rural, to Negro Schools,
Indian Schools, and all other types of schools in the United States and in the schools
of the territories.

Provisions be made for full-time utilization of the school plant for desirable
leisure time activities of youth; that boards of education arrange such coordination

between playground and recreation authorities of the community and the school directors of such activities that gymnasium facilities, playgrounds, shops, craft studios, and other portions of the school plant be made available to all children under competent supervision in the afternoons, in the evenings where desirable, on Saturday and portions of Sunday when not in conflict with religious observance; where necessary, restrictive legislation, limiting the use of the school plant be repealed.

Legislation by the state be not too specific, but mandatory in requirement that schools shall make necessary provisions in space, buildings, and equipments, in health services, instruction and supervision, to secure the fundamental objectives in health and protection of all children in the schools; legislation also to provide, in enabling acts, legal sanctions for progressive health programs adopted by local communities.

DESCRIPTION OF THE NATIONAL YOUTH ADMINISTRATION

(**1938**) From Betty and Ernest K. Lindley, *A New Deal for Youth: The Story of the National Youth Administration* (New York, 1938), pp. 156–63.

The American dream of equal educational opportunity has never fully materialized—not even in the elementary schools. The gap between aspiration and fact has been the widest at the college level. Even at the state institutions, laboratory fees, books, and incidentals are more costly than in the high schools, and most students must meet the additional expense of board and lodging away from home. A bridge of scholarships and loan funds has carried a few promising but poor young people across the gap. A wider bridge has been built by the energetic and ambitious youths who have worked their way through college. Entirely or partly self-supporting students have been respected members of undergraduate communities. They have not been unknown even at the high-tuition private colleges catering chiefly to the children of families in the upper-income brackets.

For a decade before the great depression the difficulty of working one's way through college had been increasing somewhat. Between 1920 and 1930 college attendance more than doubled. Many colleges are situated in small communities where the number of part-time jobs did not increase in proportion to the number of students seeking them. Nor, on the average, was there a decrease in the cost of a college education to the individual student.

With the advent of the depression, the number of students partly or entirely dependent on their own earning capacities sharply increased, and the number of jobs open to them sharply decreased. Most institutions made all the concessions that their own often dwindling resources permitted to promising students with little or no money. Some of the State universities were able to provide living quarters in limited quantity at extremely low cost. Some university cafeterias sold balanced dinners to needy students at ten or twelve cents. Yet this scale of living was beyond the means of many youth. At one State university, the authorities found that one young man had been trying to feed himself on fifty cents a week and that another was sleeping during a cold winter in an old automobile parked on the edge of town.

Yet these ambitious young people hung on grimly. Many of them would have been no better off anywhere else. At the colleges they could suffer undernourishment in attractive surroundings; and in the classrooms and college libraries they could at least find warmth. Thousands of other capable young people remained in idleness at home because they could not scrape together even enough money for incidental fees at the least expensive colleges.

In spite of all that was done, the enrollment in colleges and universities dropped about 10 per cent between 1932 and 1934, and would have dropped further if the Federal Government had not begun to supply aid to needy students in February 1934. If this drop had meant a weeding out of the least fit, perhaps it could have been considered as not undesirable. But it was not. It meant only the loss of some of those who lacked financial means and could not find the jobs with which to pay for their own education.

With the creation of the Civilian Conservation Corps various educators began to suggest that a small amount of money be made available to help young people to go to college. Until the unused capacity of the colleges was filled, it obviously was less expensive to keep youths in college than to put them in CCC camps. Indeed, there was no cheaper way to keep a large number of people of college age off the labor market and usefully occupied. And for those capable of benefiting from a higher education, this way probably held the greatest promise of gain for society as a whole.

These considerations led President Roosevelt to approve the use of enough Federal relief money to help approximately 75,000 young people to attend college during the second half of the college year 1933–34. With a slight expansion this aid was continued by FERA during the next college year and since then has been provided through NYA.

The principal terms of the college aid program have remained unchanged since the program was instituted in February 1934. In return for work, the Federal Government pays to a needy student a maximum of $20 a month during the college year. The average of payments within any institution may not exceed $15 a month. Every bona fide non-profit-making and tax-exempt institution which requires a high school diploma or the equivalent as the minimum for entrance is eligible to participate. Each is given as a quota a percentage of its enrollment of regular students.

Unlike the work program for out-of-school youth, NYA college student aid has never been restricted to youth from relief families. The colleges and universities themselves select the students to be aided. The Federal Government requires that these students possess the ability to do good scholastic work, that they be regular students carrying at least three-fourths of the normal academic schedule, and that they be unable to enter or remain in college without Federal assistance. The institutions themselves also arrange and supervise the work which these youths do to earn their Federal wage checks. The pay is at the hourly rates for comparable work in the college or community. The chief Federal requirements are that this work be useful and that it be work not formerly done by regular employees or which could be done out of regular budgets.

Under NYA the college aid program has been expanded to include graduate students under the age of 25. The graduate students are permitted to earn a maximum of $40 a month each. For two years, graduate aid was segregated, and the graduate students assisted in any one institution were allowed to earn up to an average of $30 a month. During 1937–38, graduate aid was lumped with college aid. While an individual graduate student may still earn up to $40 a month, the funds allotted to any institution are sufficient to permit average earnings for college and graduate students combined of only $15 a month. A small special fund has been created for Negro graduate students.

Approximately 98 per cent of the eligible institutions, including junior colleges and normal schools, have participated in the student aid program. Most of the handful of exceptions are privately controlled colleges with limited enrollments and high tuition. A few institutions in this class accepted Federal aid for a year or two but have now dropped it. Others continue to take advantage of it, but in many cases not to the full extent of their quotas. . . .

For a limited number of students, NYA aid pays all, or substantially all, expenses during the college year. Before Federal aid was established, the University of Iowa had provided dormitory space in a field house, where 100 students were sheltered for $1.00 a week each. Subsequently this university assisted in the organization of 10 co-operative houses for a total of 300 young men and women. During 1935–36, these co-operative house charged $15 a month for board and room, and at the end of the year were able to refund approximately one month's board to each participating student. Several State institutions have assisted in making similar provision for a few students with little money. At the University of Idaho two years ago, more than 200 students paid for all their living expenses, fees, and necessary incidentals with $18 a month each.

NYA students who live at home while going to college, as many do in the cities, often are able to pay most or all of their fees and incidental expenses from NYA earnings. For the great majority, however, NYA earnings will pay only from 50 per cent to as little as 10 per cent of their expenses. At the tax-supported institutions the NYA assistance usually meets from 25 to 60 per cent of the total expenses of students who do not live at home. At the privately controlled colleges the percentage is lower.

In some cases, NYA aid is used to supplement scholarships. At the privately controlled institutions most scholarships are only rebates, in part or in whole, of tuition fees. Where scholarships exist at tax-supported institutions, they are usually only of small sums. In the whole country, the number of scholarships that pay all the essential expenses of a college student is negligible. Without assistance from NYA or other sources, many students would be unable to avail themselves of scholarships.

In many cases, NYA aid is combined with money from home, or another job, or a scholarship, or all three. A brilliant Negro student at the University of Illinois won a small scholarship. He also found a job which gave him his meals. His father, a railroad laborer earning $90 a month, sent him $6 a month. Yet, without aid from still another source, he would not have had enough to pay his expenses. The difference was made up by an NYA job as a laboratory assistant in the Department of Natural History. A student at Vanderbilt University was able to pay for his education by the combination of a scholarship, summer work, $300 in loans from the student loan fund, and an NYA job. These illustrations could be multiplied many times. In most institutions, NYA assistance is under the direction of the same officials who handle other student aid funds, including the parceling out of part-time jobs. In many cases the fitting and joining and penny-by-penny calculation which college personnel officials put into the allocation of aid to needy students would excite the admiration of an efficiency engineer.

Almost one-third of the students receiving NYA college aid are from families with annual incomes of $999 or less. Three-fourths are from families having annual incomes of $1999 or less. About 16 per cent are from families whose incomes are

$2000 or more, and for 8.2 per cent the size of the family income is unknown. More than 55 per cent are from families containing five or more persons, and more than 34 per cent are from families of six or more. Three out of five are boys. Negroes and other racial minorities make up 5.8 per cent.

THE EDUCATIONAL PROGRAM OF THE C.C.C. (1935)   From Frank Ernest Hill, *The School In The Camps: The Educational Program of the Civilian Conservation Corps* (New York, 1935), pp. 11, 29, 34–37, 65.

The organization of the C.C.C. makes its head, Robert Fechner, and his office directly responsible to the President. But the actual work is carried on under the Director by a number of Government agencies. In the case of most of the camps there are four agencies chiefly concerned. The Department of Labor selects the greater part of the enrollees through staffs supplied by the various states. The Army establishes and administers the camps, taking charge of construction of buildings, supply of clothing and food, the regulation of conduct (including penalties and discharges), and the promotion of health and welfare. The Department of Agriculture, through the Forestry and Soil Erosion Service, helps select sites and plans and supervises work in about 68 per cent of the camps. The Department of the Interior through the Park Service performs the same functions for camps in the National Parks, and in state, county, and city parks, and also contributes the services of the Office of Education.

This is a division of function sufficiently complex, yet it is well to keep it in mind as the essential one affecting camp organization, and as an arrangement comparatively simple.

However, if we wish to serve precision and completeness, a much more complicated pattern must be envisaged. For example, the Veterans' Administration selects the 33,000 veterans who at present occupy about 140 of the camps. Again, the Office of Indian Affairs selects the men, administers 77 camps not included in the 1,648 "regular" ones which were functioning March 1, and directs the work for a quota of 14,000 Indians.

*   *   *

Camp Badger, or Camp F-360, in the Ninth Corps Area lies in Fresno County, California. The nearest town is Dunlap, some nineteen miles west and several thousand feet below it, for the camp is high above sea level, on National Forest land not far from the General Grant National Park.

Camp Badger is in one respect better equipped educationally than the majority of C.C.C. camps. It has a three-room schoolhouse. This is a building sufficiently rude, with one large room and two smaller ones. The camp adviser's office makes additional space for records and consultation.

When it is not occupied by a class, the large room is used as a reading center. It is furnished with a number of camp-made tables and benches. In the middle of one of the longer sides is a small platform with a desk, and a portable blackboard stands behind it. The two smaller rooms also have blackboards and benches. The rooms are fairly well lighted. The reading room contains the camp library.

In addition to these rooms, the kitchen is used for a class in cooking, and a little darkroom has been built for a class in photography. A journalism class issues the *Badger Hill Billy* and the camp possesses a mimeograph for putting out this six-page paper.

This equipment is in many ways above the average for C.C.C. camps. The schoolhouse is an advantage which many do not possess. There are no statistics on schoolhouses; from inquiry and observation I should estimate that not 200 of the 1,700 camps were fortunate enough to have them this spring. However, perhaps forty per cent of the camps have at least one room devoted solely to education. Sometimes this may be merely the office of the adviser which can be used for small classes. Perhaps a third have not even these facilities. They use the mess hall, the recreation hall, the officers' lounge, the forester's quarters (for classes taught by the superintendent or his foremen), the camp shop for classes in motors or mechanical work, and even a corner of the barracks. There are a hundred devices used to secure space and isolation. At Camp Rip Van Winkle, at Tannersville, New York, the stage of the recreation hall was curtained off, and provided space for two classes. A small schoolhouse was in process of completion here, however. In southern California and the Southwest generally the drying rooms are not essential to the camps, and these are being converted into space for education.

✻   ✻   ✻

At Camp A-2, at Bellsville, Maryland, I found the adviser doing the most careful job of relating visual education to class work which I encountered: indeed, this was the only camp where anything like an intensive experiment came to my attention. He had secured films on such subjects as Clearing Land, American Roads, and C.C.C. Erosion Work, and reported that a number of subjects assisted in clarifying class work.

Every camp has its radio. On occasions this may have an educational aspect.

The above discussion will indicate that educational facilities in the camps are still in a highly formative state. There has been a constant demand from all parts of the country for shops and schoolhouses, better classroom equipment, more books, more projectors. Exactly what action will be taken on these matters under the 1935 appropriation has not yet been announced.

The teaching force which functions in the schoolrooms of the Corps is a large one. There were 16,142 persons offering instruction in June, 1935, to 172,962 men who desired it. This constitutes one instructor for every 10 men. Of the total, 1,346 were educational advisers, 1,266 assistant educational advisers (enrollees), 2,829 Army officers, 4,235 from the technical staffs, 4,121 enrollees, 1,048 F.E.R.A. or E.E.P.teachers, 292 regular teachers, and 1,005 were classified as "others."

The character of the teaching force varies greatly. It may be assumed safely that 9,000 of them at least (most of the advisers, officers, and technical staff, and some of the teachers) hold college degrees, and that another 1,500 (the rest of the teachers) have special preparation for teaching. Many of the enrollees who teach have had college work; a few are college graduates.

✻   ✻   ✻

Courses in the Educational Program everywhere are classified as Elementary, High School, Vocational, College, or General. But this classification does not fully cover activities related to schooling, as the monthly Educational Report itself indicates. For purposes of discussion I shall make what seems to me a more comprehensive and exact grouping: Academic (Elementary, High School, and College), Arts and Crafts (usually included with music and drama under "General"), Vocational (High School, or College), and Instruction on the Job. These, with lectures and showing of films and organized sport,—all of which may have a definitely educative quality—make up the total of school effort.

To get a sense of the character of this work in action, one must clearly recognize what has already been set forth by statistics and comment: the miscellaneous educational background of the enrollees. To meet this background practically, most camp programs must cover at least a twelve years' difference in preparation. Certain practices have been developed to do this.

The classification, Elementary, High School, and College, is one device. This definitely groups enrollees. A man with a sixth grade education can not logically (though occasionally he may in practice!) take a course in political science set at college freshman level. And in one respect all corps areas go further: the illiterates and near-illiterates are grouped by themselves, and in an informal manner are dealt with by grade. In the Eighth Corps Area I found this practice being extended. Precise grading was followed in a number of camps which I visited in eastern Texas, the canvas curtains or separate rooms of the really spacious school quarters giving privacy to each of the eight groups which were maintained. These groups were taught by F.E.R.A. teachers, who were mostly women, and thus the conditions of the public school class were to a considerable extent reproduced.

However, beyond the eighth grade in all sections of the country a certain looseness of grouping exists. This is not the case where courses are being taken in nearby high schools or colleges, or in the camp itself, for school credit. But there are thousands of courses, probably half of the total, where entrance requirements are loose, and men with varying school backgrounds listen and discuss the subject matter of the course. It is hard to shut a man with seventh grade education from a course in American history, even though high school graduates may make up the bulk of the registration. A large class in soil erosion is almost bound to cover an eight-year difference in scholastic preparation on the part of its members. A motor mechanics or cooking or woodworking group will often show as great a variety. Naturally, when much of the work is manual as in these latter cases, the poorly educated enrollee, if his native intelligence is good, will sometimes show to as much advantage as the one with the high school training.

But there is, of course, a difference between teaching even tool-sharpening or tree identification to a mixed group, and teaching it to a group that has prepared for college work. The instructor's method must be simpler in the first case, and the material he presents will be different also. In practice, the mixed group has set its stamp upon C.C.C. teaching. Many courses are planned consciously for men with approximately ninth grade schooling—the average training in the C.C.C. Most men with seventh or eighth grade work behind them have had sufficient experience to rise to the ninth grade level; for those who are above it the material is usually new, and there is always the opportunity for discussion and reading. Also, the enrollee either adjusts himself to his class or leaves it, and the group ends by being fairly homogeneous.

For anyone who wishes to get a clear idea of the miscellaneous (and most typical) C.C.C. course, an examination of the correspondence courses in the Ninth

Area Correspondence Extension Service will be helpful. This school was organized by the corps area adviser, and all of the ten courses which were being taken on March 1, 1935, by 17,593 enrollees were aimed at the capacities of what might be thought of as an average C.C.C. man and were worked out on the basis of an extensive knowledge of camp types and attitudes.

Each of these courses consists of twelve lessons. The subjects are Auto Mechanics, Business English, Diesel Engine, Elementary Aeronautics, Forestry, How to Read a Blueprint, How to Study, Journalism, Practical Photography, and Psychology. Other courses are in preparation. The Correspondence Extension Service is under the California Department of Education, administered by the Bureau of Vocational Rehabilitation with the use of F.E.R.A. funds. However, its staff of forty-odd writers, typists, and clerks works in direct association with the Corps Area Office.

These correspondence courses are sometimes taken by individuals under the direction of the camp adviser. Sometimes they are taught by the adviser or one of his teachers as regular camp courses, additional material being incorporated by the instructor when desired. I use them here as examples of typical C.C.C. teaching, both because they have proved their great adaptability to work in camp, and because they represent the most tangible evidence available as to the character of this work. The method of presentation in these courses is simple and concise, and professes to do no more than prepare the way for further study. The first lesson in the Diesel Engine course states: "Neither a correspondence course such as this nor one short Diesel school course can classify you as a "Diesel engineer" or as an expert capable of telling at once what is wrong with a Diesel engine." Such instruction will simply send the enrollee "into the Diesel field more fully equipped and ready to gain further practical knowledge in the work."

Most C.C.C. courses not taken for high school or college credit are keyed to this simplicity of purpose and material. It is realized fully that enrollees are coming and going, that the period of sustained work in a given subject is likely to be brief. So the subject is generally thought of as covering approximately a three months' period, or less. The men will be in camp for that time; also, the short period will bring them to the end of an effort, even if the accomplishment is modest. "I try to change my program pretty thoroughly every three months," one successful adviser told me. "Sometimes we go on with the same subjects, but we give them new names. If we have had 'Motor Mechanics' covering chiefly the theory and operation of engines, we continue our work under 'Garage Practice', or some such title."

Many corps area advisers give such practices a conscious direction by encouraging camp advisers to break the various subjects attempted into small units. I noted this tendency in the Second, Third, Sixth, and Seventh Corps Areas especially. Is a course in cooking projected? Very well, let it first be a course in kitchen management: what a kitchen should have, how the furnishings and utensils should be placed and cared for. Then a study in the care, preparation, and treatment of meats, then one for vegetables and salads, etc. By this division a greater thoroughness can be made possible, as well as a greater simplicity. Such units are easy to plan, they can be covered in six weeks, and they concentrate the enrollee's attention on a specific field of practice. With each unit completed, he receives a certificate from the camp, and gets a sense of having accomplished something. This is the more valuable because the enrollee student has a limited time for study and class work, usually in periods after a hard day's work. He goes more willingly if knowledge is approached in short, definite stages. The tendency to organize in small units is well suited to classes like The Care of Tools, Blueprint Reading, The Use of a Slide Rule, etc.

*   *   *

The defects of the C.C.C. are important, and their importance has been recognized by the Government agencies associated with the camps. A continuous battle has been in process to better the physical quality of the camps, improve the caliber of officers, and develop higher standards in the C.C.C. classes. Definite and in some cases dramatic progress has been made toward a higher standard. What will be achieved a year or more from now is of course an aspect of the future.

If we wish to get a sense of this possible future, and also fully to understand the present, we must look even more carefully than we have at the more successful aspects of the Educational Program. For achievement is potentially a norm. If one hundred camps establish and maintain a high level of performance, that becomes standard practice which a thousand others must aim at. And only from the positive work done can we get a sense of how far this adventure in education may go, and what value its going there may hold.

The positive contribution of the Educational Program as I see it, may be summarized under the following accomplishments:

1. The creation by the Army of an administrative background friendly to the concept of the camp educational program and of power to make it effective.

2. The development of educational values in the work projects by the technical staffs.

3. The coordination of authority in the best camps, which brings Army, education, and technical services together in cooperative effort.

4. A remarkable degree of success, through the foregoing means and the methods and practice of the Educational Program in addition, in reaching a type of young man seldom reached by other agencies.

5. The creation of a new type of curriculum that may have value for education beyond the camps as well as in them.

6. The creation of a new type of teaching force with similar possibilities.

7. The development of a training method of particular value for
   a. Its creative relationship of instructor to student.
   b. Its close relationship of study to life.

8. The demonstration of new possibilities for improving both school work and adult education in American communities.

GEORGE COE ON THE CIVILIAN CONSERVATION CORPS (1935)   From George A. Coe, "What Kind of School Is a CCC Camp?" in *Social Frontier,* vol. I, pp. 24–26.

Of all the numerous types of relief devised since the onset of the depression, the Citizens Conservation Corps is by all odds the best—the best for bodily health and vigor, and especially the best for mental health and balance.

Moreover, the camps have provided something more than relief; they have had an educational fringe from the beginning, and now, under the inspiration of former Commissioner Zook and the leadership of Dean Marsh, education is becoming a definite aim and a planned activity. Each camp has an educational adviser who is under broad instructions to get acquainted with the needs and the aspirations of the young men, and then to employ on their behalf whatever means and agencies are available in the local situation. Each adviser starts, as it were, "from scratch." He is not encumbered by precedents nor by formal orders from supervisors, nor are any of the mechanics of "school" obligatory. If the resulting programs have a patchwork appearance, they have also the virtues of adaptation to the pupils informality, the experimental attitude, and all-'round plasticity. Such programs, or something to be developed out of them, will surely be a growing feature of the camps, however long or short their future may be. In fact, the main problem of their future is an educational one. Considered as relief, their efficiency is unquestionable; considered as schools, however, the kind and degree of their value remain to be determined.

The Need for Educational Appraisal

That an immediate educational appraisal of the CCC is needed should be evident. The Department of Superintendence implies as much when, without naming the Corps, it asks for an adequate program of work "and education" for our masses of unemployed youth. Already in various parts of the country research men are beginning to consider what outcomes should be expected from camp experience, and testing processes are being tentatively applied. Meantime, the popularity of the camps is so great that hasty proposals are being made with respect to their future. The Society of American Foresters, and Mr. Silcox, the head of our Forestry Service, have recommended that, in the interest of our forests, the camps be made a permanent feature of American life. On grounds broader than this there is a widespread belief that a year of camp life would be a wholesome experience for American youth generally, and that the present CCC camps furnish the right nucleus for such a development. The idea of learning through camping, already popularized by the Christian Associations, the Boy Scouts, and other agencies, is thus developing into a movement for a unique addition to our school system— unique on this continent, though not without partial precedents in Europe. Finally, from the head of our army comes the suggestion that military training be added to the present camp programs to the end of enlarging our reserve force. Each of these proposals for expansion carries within itself the danger of relegating education to the realm of wishful thinking, or at most to the status of a rather hit-or-miss by-product of a generous impulse. Any experienced teacher who inspects a CCC camp with the question in mind of its actual and possible effects upon growth in knowledge, attitudes, and habits will discover far more problems than solutions.

Any discerning eye, it is true, will delight in some features of CCC camp experience. To take part in making one's own habitation comfortable, sanitary, and neat; to build a playground and then use it oneself; to make the yard and the approaches to the camp attractive; to make flower-beds or rock gardens; to indulge such hobbies as photography, nature-study, and the building of radio receivers; to have regular hours; to adjust oneself to a cooperative group; to be in intimate contact with beauty in nature—all this means that important educational forces already are at work. It must be remembered, too, that each of these young men actually earns $30 a month by self-respecting toil, that $25 of this amount is paid directly by the government to his parents or to his dependents, and that the remainder may be spent as one will. For all this no educator can fail to be thankful. But can any educator forget that these young men are parts of a far larger human world; that this is the period in life in which, if ever, they will develop an active interest in and knowledge of this larger world; that their present experience of hardship and of uncertainty as to their future makes them peculiarly ready to inquire into the realities of life and of society, and that even so short a period as six months to a year just now may well be the decisive factor in determining their significance as adult citizens?

What, then, is a CCC Camp considered as a school? In particular, do the camps contain the essential elements of a permanent educational plan? Can we, if we so desire, build a new unit of our school system upon what we already have here? The conditions for health and morale during a few months of economic distress are here, to be sure; but what about the other conditions and processes of education? Let us use our eyes.

Paucity of Equipment and Inadequacy of Staff

The equipment of the camps is equipment for temporary relief, not for teaching and learning. The forest can be used for teaching forestry, of course, and such maintenance-operations as cooking and truck-driving, but these few occupations are of concern to only a small minority, and normal facilities for any other systematic teaching are not present even in skeleton form. The primary requirement of space for teaching and learning is not met. The educational adviser must use unadapted parts of mess halls and any available corner where men or materials can be assembled. So rudimentary a requirement as sufficient and proper illumination for evening study cannot be taken for granted. The basic physical fact is that a CCC camp is a temporary barracks for "feeding and sleeping" young men who must have immediate relief.

The endeavor to make these relief camps into educational camps has begun at the right point, namely, the installing at each camp of an educational adviser with almost *carte blanche* discretion as to program. But the adviser faces the stark fact that expenditure for his salary is not matched by financial provision for other imperative requirements—books, for example. He may have to wriggle to obtain gifts of books, or loans from public libraries—loans that are cautiously or reluctantly made because the administrative arm of the librarian is not long enough to reach to the camp. One can find camp "libraries" that contain nothing but one or two daily newspapers, piles of donated magazines, and less than half a dozen works of any kind upon the bookshelf. This, for the mental nourishment of two hundred young Americans! Materials and tools for laboratory and shop work are similarly scant. As for teachers, the adviser has to rely upon three unsteady sources: uncompensated speakers and leaders who may be enlisted in near-by communities; educated young men who happen to be found in the camp, and unemployed teachers who are receiving educational relief. Of these last only a few are provided, and the fluctuations in available public funds make even this resource a wavering one. Some of the most vital courses have here or there been dropped because relief funds are contracting.

Incidental Nature of Educational Program

The young men are required to spend seven or more hours daily at road-building, erosion-prevention, fire-prevention, and the like. There are available for systematic instruction and study only such energy and inclination as remain after a day's labor. That road-building itself has educational value need not be questioned, but to assume that effective cultural, civic, and vocational study requires only such left-over time and energy would be absurd.

The "enrolees" are not required to attend any classes, nor to do any studying, nor to meet any standards or take any tests. Naturally so, for the CCC is essentially a scheme of work-relief, and only incidentally and as an afterthought a scheme for schooling young men. If this situation has the advantage of putting the educational adviser upon his mettle because he must make courses attractive, it has the disadvantage—especially in view of the compulsory seven-hour work day—of representing education as a "take-it-or-leave-it" extra. Some camp commandants are willing to put pressure upon the young men, as by granting certain privileges only to those who attend educational classes, but such measures only accentuate the inherent maladaptation of the situation to the aims of education.

Military Administration and Educational Aims

The educational adviser is a subordinate official even in his own specialty—subordinate to a man who pursues a very different specialty. That the army officers who are in charge are not educators is not to their discredit, nor is it surprising that some of them flounder when they make decisions that affect teaching and learning. Indeed, there is something less than fairness in a system that subjects them to tests for which their training and experience have not prepared them. They are there as part of an emergency measure; they are required to do as best they can something that had to be done suddenly. The results are as good as we had any right to expect. It appears that in the by and large these military men, after some natural hesitation, are loyally supporting the new educational scheme. Some at least of the higher officers are strenuously for it. Yet the fact remains that military men are required to supervise a type of civilian service for which they have not been trained. If the camps are to become a permanent part of our school system, the present method of administering them will need to be changed, and undoubtedly it will be changed by making it either more specifically military in type or else more specifically civil. We shall have either camps managed by military men for military purposes (even though educational phraseology be employed), or else school camps managed by educators for purposes of civil education, general and vocational. Between the military and the civil we shall have to choose.

The question just raised leads on to a deeper one. We have not merely to determine who shall supervise a school, the meaning of "school" being agreed upon, but also to decide whether the old American meaning of the term shall be fundamentally transformed. Sleepily to assume that the present drive for militarizing the CCC means nothing more than adding a new frill to an old educational garment is to accept a cultural revolution without knowing that one is doing it. It is to surrender at this important point the definitely civil basis and control that hitherto have been taken for granted in our school system. This is not a merely theoretical or "academic" issue even for the present camps; if the camps are to become a permanent part of our school system, the issue is overwhelmingly practical and overwhelmingly important. What is to be the specific and basic difference between our camps and those of Hitler's Germany? There, too, a year in a work camp is looked upon as wholesome for youths; it is "educational" in the there-accepted sense of "education." But the all-controlling aim is that of Fascism. The *Arbeitsdienst* is intended to fuse the youth of Germany into a particular kind of national unity, namely, the kind that unquestioningly and unanimously accepts political and economic orders from above just as a soldier accepts military orders. Hitler's scorn of democracy and of the whole idea of popular rule underlies his work-camp scheme. This is why it is military in tone and method. By the same sign, our own public education, to the extent that it becomes basically military, will promote the narrow virtues of the soldier, not the virtues of a citizen of a democracy going freely about his daily duties. It is not unfair to add that there are some Americans who hold essentially Fascist conceptions of government, and that many Americans are unawake to the almost world-wide growth of the plant that has flowered in Italy and Germany.

Comprehensive Planning versus Scratching the
Surface

The 360,000 young men now in these camps are only a minor fraction of those who have equal need of such help. Moreover, there are no camps for young women. What, then, do the proponents of a permanent system have in mind? Do they envisage camp education for only the present fraction of distressed young men, or for all distressed young men, or for all young men, or for all youth of both sexes? If the purpose is education, why not provide a year in the forest for all alike? But this, even if the age of eligibility were reduced from the present 18–25 to 18–22 or 17–21, would require a more than thirty-fold multiplication of present facilities! Moreover, these facilities would have to be transformed from lath and building-paper to permanent materials, and buildings and equipment for education would have to be added. Even if a less inclusive plan should be adopted, the erection of durable structures for housing, feeding, and education would be crushingly expensive; and, when all was done and ready, the camps, as educational units, would largely duplicate our high schools and junior colleges.

Beyond the question of financial cost there emerge also problems that concern educational validity. For example, is prolonged segregation from the society of women wholesome at this period in a young man's career? Is this the way to promote growth towards normal family life? Indeed, is it certain that a prolonged stay in the forest is altogether favorable for social growth in general? Can we assume that the values of a short vacation in the wilds will attach to a period several times as long, or that other social values than those of a vacation can readily be imported into such far places? The difficulty of carrying on vocational education at a distance from the varied industries of the country seems to be rather obvious. As for cultural and civic growth, the centers of population, large and small, appear as yet to be the most favorable environment. For it is in these centers that the issues that most involve culture, character, and citizenship become most visible; it is here that the original material for study most abounds. That is, the present sites of our high schools and junior colleges are distinctly better than the forests for educational purposes that permanent camps would have to pursue.

The short of the matter is that the CCC, though wisely conceived as a means of emergency relief, is only beginning to acquire social and educational perspectives.

The camps will endure, supposedly, as long as the necessity for mass relief continues. Whether this period be long or short, the educational advisers who under present conditions can create only a few fragments of education, should be provided with the means and the personnel for something more systematic and organized. It is fortunate that Commissioner Studebaker has announced that he sees here a great educational opportunity. Yet we may as well realize that the CCC cannot offer, either economically or educationally, very much beyond palliatives for a fractured youth-experience. Only preposterously naive thinking can take the camps as a guide to a permanent system.

The Elementary School

ON TEACHING CHILDREN TO READ (1931)   From Mabel Vogel Morphett and Carleton Washburne, "When Should Children Begin to Read," in *Elementary School Journal*, vol. XXXI, pp. 496–503.

In tracing back to their origins the reading difficulties of some children and their distaste for the subject, the Department of Educational Counsel in Winnetka found that in several instances the children's mental ages on entering the first grade had been low and that discouragement had resulted from their first attempts to learn to read. This discouragement sometimes resulted in a mental set against reading, which lasted for years and which hampered all their school work. The research department, therefore, with the aid of the primary-grade teachers, set about the task of discovering the period in the mental development of children when, as a rule, there is the best chance of their learning to read readily.

In September, 1928, all Winnetka first-grade children, 141 in number, were given the Detroit First-Grade Intelligence Test. The eight first-grade teachers were not told the mental ages of the children and attempted to teach all of them to read. The method, in accordance with the Winnetka technique, was largely individual, so that the slow children did not retard the fast ones. In February, 1929, the reading progress of these children was measured for the purpose of determining the amount of progress made by children at each mental level.

In order that the reading progress might be measured, the first large teaching unit was divided into definite steps, which were measurable by the teachers. Twenty-one steps took the children through the beginning reading materials. Each further step represented the reading of a primer or first reader. Reading progress was measured by the number of these steps which the child had completed by February.

In addition to these progress steps the sight-word score of each child was measured. Each child in Winnetka is required to know at least 139 words at sight before passing from first-grade reading to second-grade reading. These words are those most frequently used in primers and first readers. The children were tested individually with flash cards, and the number of words recognized by each child was recorded as his sight-word score. In some cases the children knew some of the second-grade sight words as well as the 139 first-grade words. In such cases the score was the total number of first- and second-grade words recognized.

The first-grade teachers, all of whom had had several years of experience with the reading materials, agreed that children who seemed ready for reading from the beginning of the year had usually completed at least thirteen progress steps and knew at least thirty-seven sight words by February. Therefore, thirteen progress steps and thirty-seven sight words were accepted as the measure of the minimum degree of satisfactory progress.

The Detroit First-Grade Intelligence Test and the Stanford Revision of the Binet-Simon Scale were used to determine the mental ages of children. The Detroit tests were given to all first-grade children entering in September. The Stanford-Binet test was given later in the year, and the mental ages were calculated as of September, 1928, In this way comparison between the mental ages determined by the Detroit and Stanford-Binet tests was made possible.

Table I gives the correlations which were found between the sight-word scores and intelligence and between reading progress and intelligence. Since the data proved to be non-linear, the correlation ratios rather than the correlation coefficients are given. When the relation between reading progress and intelligence was calculated, it was necessary to use the rank method of figuring correlations since the intervals of progress were not necessarily of equal difficulty. The correlations show that there is a fairly high degree of relationship between mental age and reading progress. The Detroit test shows more relation to progress than does the Stanford-Binet test. Of the three measures of intelligence—mental age, average of the mental and chronological ages, and intelligence quotient—mental age shows the greatest degree of relationship although the differences are slight. In all the calculations that follow, mental age alone is used as the method of figuring intelligence.

The scores were next divided into groups based on the children's mental ages in September. The percentage of children of each mental age making satisfactory progress (thirteen steps or more) and the percentage making satisfactory sight-word scores (thirty-seven or more) were determined. Tables II and III show the results.

Table II shows that a small percentage of children who began reading with a mental age of less than six years were able to achieve satisfactory reading progress but that for the group having a mental age between six years and six years and six months there was a sharp rise in the percentage making satisfactory progress. This fact is shown graphically in Figure I. The curves for the Stanford-Binet and the Detroit tests are essentially alike, although final flattening occurs later on the Stanford-Binet curve.

*　　*　　*

The curve of the results on the Stanford-Binet test seems to indicate that children would gain considerably in speed of learning if they could wait until they had attained a mental age of seven years and six months before beginning to read. However, the curve of the results of the Detroit test shows that the children with mental ages of six years and six months made progress practically as satisfactory as that of the children with higher mental ages. Since the results of the Detroit test show a higher correlation with reading progress than do the results of the Stanford-Binet test and since the Detroit test is more practicable to administer than the Stanford-Binet test, it seems reasonable to use the Detroit test as a basis for determining children's readiness for reading. The mental level of six years and six months is the breaking point in the curve, that is, the point beyond which there is very little gain in postponing the teaching of reading. This break is evident to some extent on the Stanford-Binet curve and markedly true on the curve of Detroit test scores.

Figure 2 points to the same conclusion—that it pays to postpone beginning reading until a child has attained a mental age of six years and six months. If this practice is followed, 78 per cent of the children may be expected to make satisfactory general progress, and 87 per cent of the children may be expected to make satisfactory progress in learning sight words.

A similar study was carried on during the school year 1929–30 for the purpose of checking the results of the 1928–29 experiment.

* * *

All children who were mentally six years of age or more were taught reading from the beginning of the year. The previous study made it seem futile to try to teach younger children, but a few with lower mental ages were taught reading for the purpose of the experiment. Mental ages were determined this time by the Detroit First-Grade Intelligence Test and the Pintner-Cunningham Primary Mental Test.

At the end of the year (June, 1930) the children were tested on the sight-word list and the Gray Standardized Oral Reading Check Test. A child was considered to have made satisfactory progress if he knew the entire sight-word list (139 words) and read the Gray test in fifty seconds or less with three errors or less. This standard has been set by Gray for Grade 1. Table IV gives the number of children of each mental age and the percentage of children at each mental level making satisfactory scores in both sight words and oral reading. Figure 3 makes the data of Table IV graphic. As in Figures 1 and 2, the percentage of children who learned to read satisfactorily is greatest at the mental ages of six years and six months and of seven years. The curve for sight-word scores breaks at the mental age of six years and six months, while the curve on the Gray Standardized Oral Reading Check Test breaks at the mental age of seven.

The second year's experiment, therefore, in which a different set of children, different teachers, a different method of determining mental age, and a different method of determining progress were used and in which a whole year's work instead of a half year's was taken as the measure of progress confirms the experiment of the first year.

Summary

1. Correlations between mental age and ability to learn to read, as measured by reading progress and sight-word scores, showed a fairly high degree of relationship. The correlations ranged from .50 to .65.

2. The correlations between mental age and reading progress were somewhat higher when mental age was measured by the Detroit First-Grade Intelligence Test than when mental age was measured by the Stanford Revision of the Binet-Simon Scale.

3. Mental age alone showed a larger degree of correlation with reading progress than did the intelligence quotient or the average of mental and chronological ages.

4. When the Detroit test was used as a basis for determining mental-age groups, the children who had a mental age of six years and six months made far better progress than did the less mature children and practically as satisfactory progress as did the children of a higher mental age.

5. When mental age was measured by the Stanford Revision of the Binet-Simon

Scale, the children with a mental age of six years and six months again made very much better progress in reading than did those of less maturity, but they made less satisfactory progress than did those whose mental age was six months greater. The gain in ability up to six years and six months of mental age, however, was much greater than the subsequent gain.

6. A repetition of the experiment in 1929–30 with different teachers, different children, and different tests confirmed the earlier experiment in all its basic conclusions.

7. Consequently, it seems safe to state that, by postponing the teaching of reading until children reach a mental level of six and a half years, teachers can greatly decrease the chances of failure and discouragement and can correspondingly increase their efficiency.

THE CASE AGAINST HOMOGENEOUS GROUPING (1931)   From Alice V. Keliher, *A Critical Study of Homogeneous Grouping* (New York, 1931), pp. 161–63.

Present standardized tests of intelligence which are employed in schools do not measure the broad scope of intelligent behavior. Present standardized measures of learnings do not measure the broad scope of learning. Since neither measure is an adequate measure of the whole functioning of the individual in that particular line, the combination of these measures is not an adequate nor a relevant basis for grouping. Therefore, these bases, in representing only a part of the whole individual, and in averaging the individual's variations, are not acceptable bases for action which of necessity concerns and affects the whole individual, as does segregation into "bright," "average," and "dull" groups.

As To Homogeneous Grouping; Its Desirability and Possibility

When the total range of an individual's variations is considered, great reduction of variations by sorting individuals into groups which are relatively stable is impossible. The variations may be suppressed and unnoticed, but they are present.

The sorting of individuals into "homogeneous" groups does not produce the expected reduction of variations even in measured traits.

A high regard for homogeneity as a general phase may lead to mediocrity.

When the broad ranges of behavior are considered, an individual is not consistent within his own abilities.

When the narrow ranges of academic skills are considered, a high degree of specificity in these skills is found within each individual.

A group of individuals may be homogeneous in one narrow trait and not be homogeneous in other traits. Therefore, a "general homogeneity" with which the whole range of traits would coincide is an impossibility.

Since determination of needs, and especially determination of which individuals have like needs, cannot be made in advance without an unjustifiable determinism, there appears no basis for consistent differentiation of curricula of the elementary grades.

In the light of the high variability of specific abilities within the individual, consistent differentiation of curricula which would provide for the many needs of individuals within a single track is impossible.

The prescription of a body of subject matter and skills to be acquired by all groups, with enrichment to fill the "time saved" by the brighter children, means that those skills are counted as the common essentials of the educational program and their attainment is reckoned to be of more importance than is the creative expression of intelligence.

Creative abilities and appreciations are also highly variable within an individual and, therefore, a consistent differentiation of curricula would not provide for these varying traits. . . .

Conclusions Less Certain but in Accord with Evidence

Discouragement and suppression are not so likely to result if children are functioning in a heterogeneous, noncompetitive group. Therefore, so far as these attitudes are concerned, claims that grouping homogeneously is superior to grouping heterogeneously are questionable; the practical question seems to be the elimination of the competitive element.

Children do discern the reasons for their segregation into groups and attribute their placement in most cases to a "general level" of ability. This is a harmful concept for the individual since a general level does not exist, and the individual's supposition that it does exist is likely to cause him to neglect, repress, or remain in ignorance of abilities which are not called out in the routine of an academic school day.

The differentiation of curricula may easily lead to the fixing of environmental conditions which, in turn, may fix the possibilities of development for the child.

So far as one can study the heretofore unmeasured consequences of homogeneous grouping, there are serious attitude hazards which must be investigated further. The writer concludes that segregation has dangers for mental health, and, therefore, in the light of these dangers, homogeneous grouping is not desirable.

WILLIAM HEARD KILPATRICK ON THE ACTIVITY MOVEMENT

(1934)   From William Heard Kilpatrick, "Definition of the Activity Movement To-Day," as quoted in National Society for the Study of Education, *Thirty-third Yearbook, Part II* (Bloomington, Ill., 1934), pp. 63–64.

VI. Summary

In conclusion, the following summary seems authorized by a study of the definitions and of the table:

1. There is on the whole an essential unity of theory in the activity movement, though this is seen with varying degrees of clearness and consistency.

2. The term 'activity' as the unit conception of the activity program seems best

A NEW
ORIENTATION
FOR EDUCATION
1930–1950

2573

understood as a unitary sample of actual child living as nearly complete and natural as school conditions will permit.

3. In keeping with this conception of 'activity,' the educative process takes on appropriate meaning. Study and learning become natural and inherent within the life process: study as the effort of intelligence to deal adequately with the situation at hand; learning as summing up the varied internal effects upon the child of the experiences as such—intellectual, emotional, physical, all inherently interrelated.

4. As to how to determine the content and succession of the activities, a difference of opinion appears. Some would have the teacher and authorities plan these in general outline in advance, though all would have the pupils exercise considerable responsibility in planning them in detail. Probably the larger number and the general spirit would expect the successive activities to emerge under teacher-guidance from the developing experience process itself; and in this the more satisfactorily the fruitful suggestions can come from the pupil's own intelligent thought, the more successful has been the work of the teacher.

5. There is difference of opinion as to the degree in which some customary content of fact and skill and knowledge should be fixed and acquired independently of the activities themselves. Probably a large majority accept a certain body of such common content as necessary somehow to be got. There is difference of opinion as to how much of this will come inherently through the activities. A clear majority seem to think that some repetitive drill must supplement the ordinary work of the activities. Such additional drill, some would give before the inherent need arises; probably a larger number would in general give it only after the need has been felt.

6. There is difference of statement, though less surety of position, as to the retention of the traditional subject divisions. Some seem still to think of activities as means of teaching the customary subjects. Probably most are still subject-division conscious (partly from habit, partly from outside demand) and are anxious that their pupils advance according to these ordinary standards. The clear spirit of the movement, however, is to think of the essential educative process as moving independently of traditional subject divisions. The clear intent is to put the growth of the child before the learning of any specified subject matter.

7. The activity movement, considered simply from the theory side, is restricted to the 'method' aspect of education. True enough, arising as it apparently did out of a democratic regard for the individual, it has its appropriate social implications; but, even so, for fulness of practice it needs to be complemented by an adequate social theory founded (it seems safe to say) on the careful study of the social situation. In this sense, the activity conception by itself does not and cannot suffice for a complete curriculum theory.

HAROLD RUGG ON THE ACTIVITY SCHOOL (1936) From Harold Rugg, *American Life and the School Curriculum: Next Steps Toward Schools of Living* (Boston, 1936), pp. 367–70.

2574

But come with me into another kind of school and note the manner in which group activities are employed.

Here is a fourth-grade group, conducting its early-morning group discussion. A nine-year-old boy is in the chair; the teacher sits in the circle as one member of the group. The chairman of the farm excursion committee reports the plans for the trip that is to be taken to the country the next day. The members of the group make notes of the time and place of starting and things to bring. Another committee member distributes a mimeographed copy of the outline of observation and study that the class had jointly made during the preceding days, with the guidance of the teacher. There is a further discussion, some minor changes, and final approval of the outline. Assistant guides are appointed. Other business comes up. The chairman of the library committee then reminds the group that cards must be filled out and filed for all books taken away from the library. The teacher asks for reports on the progress made by individuals on their separate projects. The bulletin-board committee reminds the group of two important newspaper clippings just posted.

In another room a seventh-grade group is conducting the meeting of the junior-senior-high-school assembly. A thirteen-year-old girl presides over a vigorous debate from the floor, taken part in by a dozen boys and girls. At its close a program of music and a short talk illustrated by a motion picture are presented by representatives from the seventh-grade group.

In the social-science discussion room the social-problems club of the twelfth grade is having a vigorous meeting on the significance to America and to Russia of Japan's advance into northern China and Mongolia. Maps and charts hang on the walls. The tables are piled high with reference books and magazines, bulletins and pamphlets. Folders full of statistical facts supply definite data for critical discussion. Here is the group consideration of a vast amount of individual student research. The teacher, though not presiding, is an alert, subtle questioner and assistant guide to the discussion.

At noon the work of the busy lunchroom is largely done by students; they do most of preparing the meal, serving it, handling the money and accounts, cleaning up, maintaining order, and the like. Are there teachers, professional cooks, and managers to co-operate? Yes, of course, for this is an *educational* institution.

In the afternoon we pass from one alert group to another. In a large laboratory some ninth-graders are building a miniature replica of the water-purification plant of the city. "It works!" one boy proudly exclaims, drawing pure drinking water from the outlet.

In a shop a fifteen-foot motor launch is getting its final coat of paint. Beside it several boys are tuning up a motor. Some others are working with a homemade radio. Engineering books and blueprints are being studied by several others.

In the Student Council Office the high-school court, with its elected judge, jury, and prosecuting officers, and its teacher adviser, reviews the cases of real problems of discipline that are brought before it.

The School Council, composed of elected representatives from every group of pupils from the primary grades to the high school, and from the staff, is holding its weekly meeting to consider and decide questions of policy and administration.

In the school-newspaper office the editorial-board members are carrying on their individual and group tasks.

In the music wing the band and orchestra and glee club meet for practice and discussion. The cast of the senior-high play are working with juvenile playwrights and stage director on their new script.

❄   ❄   ❄

At five o'clock several hundred young people and parents assemble in the auditorium for an illustrated lecture and discussion of some new scientific discoveries by the university's archaeological expedition in the Near East.

We return to the school after dinner in the evening. The place is ablaze with light. In the auditorium a group of several hundred grownups and high-school students are holding a community forum on the topic, "If world war comes can America keep out?" In the panel, on the platform, both parents and high-school students take part in the vigorous debate which has been launched by an ex-army officer and a professor of European history from the university.

Meanwhile the laboratories, studios, shops, and library of the school are busy places. There are some young people of high-school age, but most of those present are grownups. In the elementary principal's office is a child-study class of mothers and fathers. In the fine-arts studios a score of adults are painting or modeling. A poetry class is reading and talking and having coffee together in a seminar room. Stage sets for a play are being built in one of the shops by another group.

Have we not had enough of illustrations to show the active group character of life in the new school? Here are no marching or sitting companies of young robots, automatically responding to orders from above. Here are live, dynamic groups of young people and old people *living together*. Here is a community of face-to-face groups, interpenetrating one another's minds, learning to co-operate by co-operating, learning social control by practicing social control, learning what government is by governing themselves, growing in aesthetic appreciation by creating original art products.

The Social Reconstructionists

GEORGE COUNTS ON SCHOOLS AND A NEW SOCIAL ORDER
(1932)   From George S. Counts, *Dare the School Build a New Social Order?* (New York, 1932), pp. 1–4, 9–12.

I

Like all simple and unsophisticated peoples we Americans have a sublime faith in education. Faced with any difficult problem of life we set our minds at rest sooner or later by the appeal to the school. We are convinced that education is the one unfailing remedy for every ill to which man is subject, whether it be vice, crime, war, poverty, riches, injustice, racketeering, political corruption, race hatred, class conflict, or just plain original sin. We even speak glibly and often about the general reconstruction of society through the school. We cling to this faith in spite of the fact that the very period in which our troubles have multiplied so rapidly has witnessed an unprecedented expansion of organized education. This would seem to suggest that our schools, instead of directing the course of change, are themselves driven by the very forces that are transforming the rest of the social order.

The bare fact, however, that simple and unsophisticated peoples have unbounded faith in education does not mean that the faith is untenable. History shows that the intuitions of such folk may be nearer the truth than the weighty and carefully reasoned judgments of the learned and the wise. Under certain conditions education may be as beneficent and as powerful as we are wont to think. But if it is to be so, teachers must abandon much of their easy optimism, subject the concept of education to the most rigorous scrutiny, and be prepared to deal much more fundamentally, realistically, and positively with the American social situation than has been their habit in the past. Any individual or group that would aspire to lead society must be ready to pay the costs of leadership: to accept responsibility, to suffer calumny, to surrender security, to risk both reputation and fortune. If this price, or some important part of it, is not being paid, then the chances are that the claim to leadership is fraudulent. Society is never redeemed without effort, struggle, and sacrifice. Authentic leaders are never found breathing that rarefied atmosphere lying above the dust and smoke of battle. With regard to the past we always recognize the truth of this principle, but when we think of our own times we profess the belief that the ancient roles have been reversed and that now prophets of a new age receive their rewards among the living.

That the existing school is leading the way to a better social order is a thesis which few informed persons would care to defend. Except as it is forced to fight for its own life during times of depression, its course is too serene and untroubled. Only in the rarest of instances does it wage war on behalf of principle or ideal. Almost everywhere it is in the grip of conservative forces and is serving the cause of perpetuating ideas and institutions suited to an age that is gone. But there is one movement above the educational horizon which would seem to show promise of genuine and creative leadership. I refer to the Progressive Education movement. Surely in this union of two of the great faiths of the American people, the faith in progress and the faith in education, we have reason to hope for light and guidance. Here is a movement which would seen to be completely devoted to the promotion of social welfare through education.

Even a casual examination of the program and philosophy of the Progressive schools, however, raises many doubts in the mind. To be sure, these schools have a number of large achievements to their credit. They have focused attention squarely upon the child; they have recognized the fundamental importance of the interest of the learner; they have defended the thesis that activity lies at the root of all true education; they have conceived learning in terms of life situations and growth of character; they have championed the rights of the child as a free personality. Most of this is excellent, but in my judgment it is not enough. It constitutes too narrow a conception of the meaning of education; it brings into the picture but one-half of the landscape.

If an educational movement, or any other movement, calls itself progressive, it must have orientation; it must possess direction. The word itself implies moving forward, and moving forward can have little meaning in the absence of clearly defined purposes. We cannot, like Stephen Leacock's horseman, dash off in all directions at once. Nor should we, like our presidential candidates, evade every disturbing issue and be all things to all men. Also we must beware lest we become so devoted to motion that we neglect the question of direction and be entirely satisfied with movement in circles. Here, I think, we find the fundamental weakness, not only of Progressive Education, but also of American education generally. Like a baby shaking a rattle, we seem to be utterly content with action, provided it is sufficiently vigorous and noisy. In the last analysis a very large part of American educational thought, inquiry, and experimentation is much ado about nothing. And, if we are permitted to push the analogy of the rattle a bit further, our consecration to motion is encouraged and supported in order to keep us out of mischief. At least we know that so long as we thus busy ourselves we shall not incur the serious displeasure of our social elders.

The weakness of Progressive Education thus lies in the fact that it has elaborated no theory of social welfare, unless it be that of anarchy or extreme individualism. In this, of course, it is but reflecting the viewpoint of the members of the liberal-minded upper middle class who send their children to the Progressive schools—persons who are fairly well-off, who have abandoned the faiths of their fathers, who assume an agnostic attitude towards all important questions, who pride themselves on their open-mindedness and tolerance, who favor in a mild sort of way fairly liberal programs of social reconstruction, who are full of good will and humane sentiment, who have vague aspirations for world peace and human brotherhood, who can be counted upon to respond moderately to any appeal made in the name of charity, who are genuinely distressed at the sight of *unwonted* forms of cruelty, misery, and suffering, and who perhaps serve to soften somewhat the bitter clashes of those real forces that govern the world; but who, in spite of all their good qualities, have no deep and abiding loyalties, possess no convictions for which they would sacrifice over-much, would find it hard to live without their customary material comforts, are rather insensitive to the accepted forms of social injustice, are content to play the role of interested spectator in the drama of human history, refuse to see reality in its harsher and more disagreeable forms, rarely move outside the pleasant circles of the class to which they belong, and in the day of severe trial will follow the lead of the most powerful and respectable forces in society and at the same time find good reasons for so doing. These people have shown themselves entirely incapable of dealing with any of the great crises of our time—war, prosperity, or depression. At bottom they are romantic sentimentalists, but with a sharp eye on the main chance. That they can be trusted to write our educational theories and shape our educational programs is highly improbable.

Among the members of this class the number of children is small, the income relatively high, and the economic functions of the home greatly reduced. For these reasons an inordinate emphasis on the child and child interests is entirely welcome to them. They wish to guard their offspring from too strenuous endeavor and from coming into too intimate contact with the grimmer aspects of industrial society. They wish their sons and daughters to succeed according to the standards of their class and to be a credit to their parents. At heart feeling themselves members of a superior human strain, they do not want their children to mix too freely with the children of the poor or of the less fortunate races. Nor do they want them to accept radical social doctrines, espouse unpopular causes, or lose themselves in quest of any Holy Grail. According to their views education should deal with life, but with life at a distance or in a highly diluted form. They would generally maintain that life should be kept at arm's length, if it should not be handled with a poker.

If Progressive Education is to be genuinely progressive, it must emancipate itself from the influence of this class, face squarely and courageously every social issue, come to grips with life in all of its stark reality, establish an organic relation with the community, develop a realistic and comprehensive theory of welfare, fashion a compelling and challenging vision of human destiny, and become less frightened than it is today at the bogies of *imposition* and *indoctrination*. In a word, Progressive Education cannot place its trust in a child-centered school.

This brings us to the most crucial issue in education—the question of the nature and extent of the influence which the school should exercise over the development of the child. The advocates of extreme freedom have been so successful in championing what they call the rights of the child that even the most skillful practitioners of the art of converting others to their opinions disclaim all intention of molding the learner. And when the word indoctrination is coupled with education there is scarcely one among us possessing the hardihood to refuse to be horrified. This feeling is so widespread that even Mr. Lunacharsky, Commissar of Education in the Russian Republic until 1929, assured me on one occasion that the Soviet educational leaders do not believe in the indoctrination of children in the ideas and principles of communism. When I asked him whether their children become good communists while attending the schools, he replied that the great majority do. On seeking from him an explanation of this remarkable phenomenon he said that Soviet teachers merely tell their children the truth about human history. As a consequence, so he asserted, practically all of the more intelligent boys and girls adopt the philosophy of communism. I recall also that the Methodist sect in which I was reared always confined its teachings to the truth!

The issue is no doubt badly confused by historical causes. The champions of freedom are obviously the product of an age that has broken very fundamentally with the past and is equally uncertain about the future. In many cases they feel themselves victims of narrow orthodoxies which were imposed upon them during childhood and which have severely cramped their lives. At any suggestion that the child should be influenced by his elders they therefore envisage the establishment of a state church, the formulation of a body of sacred doctrine, and the teaching of this doctrine as fixed and final. If we are forced to choose between such an unenlightened form of pedagogical influence and a condition of complete freedom for the child, most of us would in all probability choose the latter as the lesser of two evils. But this is to create a wholly artificial situation: the choice should not be limited to these two extremes. Indeed today neither extreme is possible.

I believe firmly that a critical factor must play an important role in any adequate educational program, at least in any such program fashioned for the modern world. An education that does not strive to promote the fullest and most thorough understanding of the world is not worthy of the name. Also there must be no deliberate distortion or suppression of facts to support any theory or point of view. On the other hand, I am prepared to defend the thesis that all education contains a large element of imposition, that in the very nature of the case this is inevitable, that the existence and evolution of society depend upon it, that it is consequently eminently desirable, and that the frank acceptance of this fact by the educator is a major professional obligation. I even contend that failure to do this involves the clothing of one's own deepest prejudices in the garb of universal truth and the introduction into the theory and practice of education of an element of obscurantism. In the development of this thesis I shall examine a number of widespread fallacies which seem to me to underlie the theoretical opposition to all forms of imposition. Although certain of these fallacies are very closely related and to some extent even cover the same territory, their separate treatment will help to illuminate the problem.

✻ ✻ ✻

III

If we may now assume that the child will be imposed upon in some fashion by the various elements in his environment, the real question is not whether imposition will take place, but rather from what source it will come. If we were to answer this question in terms of the past, there could, I think, be but one answer: on all genuinely crucial matters the school follows the wishes of the groups or classes that actually rule society; on minor matters the school is sometimes allowed a certain measure of freedom. But the future may be unlike the past. Or perhaps I should say that teachers, if they could increase sufficiently their stock of courage, intelligence, and vision, might become a social force of some magnitude. About this eventuality I am not over sanguine, but a society lacking leadership as ours does, might even accept the guidance of teachers. Through powerful organizations they might at least reach the public conscience and come to exercise a larger measure of control over the schools than hitherto. They would then have to assume some responsibility for the more fundamental forms of imposition which, according to my argument, cannot be avoided.

That the teachers should deliberately reach for power and then make the most of their conquest is my firm conviction. To the extent that they are permitted to fashion the curriculum and the procedures of the school they will definitely and positively influence the social attitudes, ideals, and behavior of the coming generation. In doing this they should resort to no subterfuge or false modesty. They should say neither that they are merely teaching the truth nor that they are unwilling to wield power in their own right. The first position is false and the second is a confession of incompetence. It is my observation that the men and women who have affected the course of human events are those who have not hesitated to use the power that has come to them. Representing as they do, not the interests of the moment or of any special class, but rather the common and abiding interests of the people, teachers are under heavy social obligation to protect and further those interests. In this they occupy a relatively unique position in society. Also since the profession should embrace scientists and scholars of the highest rank, as well as teachers working at all levels of the educational system, it has at its disposal, as no other group, the knowledge and wisdom of the ages. It is scarcely thinkable that these men and women would ever act as selfishly or bungle as badly as have the so-called "practical" men of our generation—the politicians, the financiers, the industrialists. If all of these facts are taken into account, instead of shunning power, the profession should rather seek power and then strive to use that power fully and wisely and in the interests of the great masses of the people.

The point should be emphasized that teachers possess no magic secret to power. While their work should give them a certain moral advantage, they must expect to encounter the usual obstacles blocking the road to leadership. They should not be deceived by the pious humbug with which public men commonly flatter the members of the profession. To expect ruling groups or classes to give precedence to teachers on important matters, because of age or sex or sentiment, is to refuse to face realities. It was one of the proverbs of the agrarian order that a spring never rises higher than its source. So the power that teachers exercise in the schools can be no greater than the power they wield in society. Moreover, while organization is necessary, teachers should not think of their problem primarily in terms of organizing and presenting a united front to the world, the flesh, and the devil. In order to be effective they must throw off completely the slave psychology that has dominated the mind of the pedagogue more or less since the days of ancient Greece. They must be prepared to stand on their own feet and win for their ideas the support of the masses of the people. Education as a force for social regeneration must march hand in hand with the living and creative forces of the social order. In their own lives teachers must bridge the gap between school and society and play some part in the fashioning of those great common purposes which should bind the two together.

This brings us to the question of the kind of imposition in which teachers should engage, if they had the power. Our obligations, I think, grow out of the social situation. We live in troublous times; we live in an age of profound change; we live in an age of revolution. Indeed it is highly doubtful whether man ever lived in a more eventful period than the present. In order to match our epoch we would probably have to go back to the fall of the ancient empires or even to that unrecorded age when men first abandoned the natural arts of hunting and fishing and trapping and began to experiment with agriculture and the settled life. Today we are witnessing the rise of a civilization quite without precedent in human history—a civilization founded on science, technology, and machinery, possessing the most extraordinary power, and rapidly making of the entire world a single great society. Because of forces already released, whether in the field of economics, politics, morals, religion, or art, the old molds are being broken. And the peoples of the earth are everywhere seething with strange ideas and passions. If life were peaceful and quiet and undisturbed by great issues, we might with some show of wisdom center our attention on the nature of the child. But with the world as it is, we cannot afford for a single instant to remove our eyes from the social scene or shift our attention from the peculiar needs of the age.

In this new world that is forming, there is one set of issues which is peculiarly fundamental and which is certain to be the center of bitter and prolonged struggle. I refer to those issues which may be styled economic.

✳   ✳   ✳

Our generation has the good or the ill fortune to live in an age when great decisions must be made. The American people, like most of the other peoples of the earth, have come to the parting of the ways; they can no longer trust entirely the inspiration which came to them when the Republic was young; they must decide afresh what they are to do with their talents. Favored above all other nations with the resources of nature and the material instrumentalities of civilization, they stand confused and irresolute before the future. They seem to lack the moral quality necessary to quicken, discipline, and give direction to their matchless energies. In a recent paper Professor Dewey has, in my judgment, correctly diagnosed our troubles: "the schools, like the nation," he says, "are in need of a central purpose which will create new enthusiasm and devotion, and which will unify and guide all intellectual plans."

This suggests, as we have already observed, that the educational problem is not wholly intellectual in nature. Our Progressive schools therefore cannot rest content with giving children an opportunity to study contemporary society in all of its aspects. This of course must be done, but I am convinced that they should go much farther. If the schools are to be really effective, they must become centers for the building, and not merely for the contemplation, of our civilization. This does not mean that we should endeavor to promote particular reforms through the educational system. We should, however, give to our children a vision of the possibilities which lie ahead and endeavor to enlist their loyalties and enthusiasms in the realization of the vision. Also our social institutions and practices, all of them, should be critically examined in the light of such a vision.

WILLIAM HEARD KILPATRICK ON EDUCATION AND THE SOCIAL CRISIS (1932) From *Education And The Social Crisis: A Proposed Program* (New York, 1932), pp. 78–80.

We now conclude the special work on the profession of education. It has, first of all, broadened its own outlook beyond mere school-keeping to include a concern for significant educative effects wherever found. The profession will endeavor to use educative procedures to improve any such bad effects and to promote the better. In particular, considering the great significance of the present economic and social situation the profession will join forces with other agencies in the effort to bring about such study of this situation as will mean an increasingly intelligent planning of the social and economic processes to the end that life may be better for all.

As a first step in such a program the profession must remake its own outlook so as to acquire one and all a truly social point of view. It should then undertake to secure the intelligent study of the social situation both in school and in the adult world in the light of the best that is known, that life may begin at once to be better. Life it must view as one continuous process, with education as the effort at its intelligent direction. Each period of life will show its problems. The aim of education will be to help those of each period so to study its problems that they will more surely act intelligently in both private and public affairs. All must come to expect social changes and adjust their thinking accordingly. If we are to meet the conforming situation, all must wish the common good. All must learn to criticize intelligently both existing and proposed institutions. And all must seek, each for himself, a unified outlook on life in place of the conflicts all too common within because they are so deeply at work without.

In particular, in order to help best in the adult world, a new and much more inclusive education must be planned with the aim of reaching all classes of the population in a serious study of life's problems and this in the hope that early steps may be taken to improve our institutional life. Such study among adults should help the schools greatly, partly in relieving the schools of the now impossible task of trying to give an education which will supposedly last for the rest of life. It should further help the schools by making parents and the community in general more intelligent as to what should go on in school and therefore more willing to have the schools undertake a really social program.

The school as we know it must be remade to a more social point of view. Now the aim is too often so to equip each pupil that he may the better get ahead of others. Content and method will need remaking. Much of what is now taught is too largely conventional and all too remote from life. The idea that education consists in the acquisition of stated subject-matter must give way to the study of problems vital within the lives of the young people and to the undertaking of enterprises significant within the community. Only in such way can we hope to get the needed intelligent thinking about social affairs or build adequate social attitudes. As far as the age of the pupils will permit they must become intelligently critical of our, and their, social life and institutions. It is, of course, true that there can be but inefficient social education by the school so long as the institutions of the social and economic world work directly against the effort of the school. But we can do better than we have been doing. With adults working to change our institutions for the better, there will come a better day for the school. When elders are critical of social life about us, that life will have less power to mis-educate the young. As fast as that social life can be changed, the school can become in its own processes more effectively educative. Working thus simultaneously with old and young we may hope to hasten the better day.

Rainbow & Door

BOYD BODE ON SOCIAL RECONSTRUCTION AND THE SCHOOLS

(1933) From Boyd Bode, "The Confusion in Present-Day Education," as quoted in William Heard Kilpatrick et al., *The Educational Frontier* (New York, 1933), pp. 26–31.

In brief, a survey of our economic development would seem to indicate that equality of opportunity does not mean what it meant a hundred years ago. In those earlier days the argument that free competition among individuals served to develop desirable qualities or traits had some plausibility. But now great industrial and economic units have come upon the scene, and in them the individual tends to become submerged. Our "American way of life" has disappeared or, at any rate, is fast disappearing; and no appeals or sentimental attachment to the past can alter that fact. Genuine loyalty to the past does not mean opposition to change, but an active concern for the kind of change that will reconstruct what is valuable in our tradition so as to suit present conditions.

If equality of opportunity is to be preserved, the purposes or aims of our economic and industrial organizations must be widened so as to include other considerations besides that of pecuniary profit. If, for example, the idea of public interest could become sufficiently powerful to secure action with reference to the elimination of depressions, of economic insecurity, of unemployment, and of undesirable methods of selling and advertising, our whole national psychology would undergo a corresponding change. Since these matters are of direct concern to the average citizen, whether he happens to be an employee under the organizations immediately concerned or a member of the general public, they would be discussed in the newspapers, on the platform, and at the dinner-table; we should gradually acquire the habit of regarding our economic and industrial life from the standpoint of public interest. This wide participation by the Russian people in the Five-Year Plan; and a similar analogy would exist with respect to the relation between our schools and the rest of the social order. Translated into social terms, the escape from compartmentalization would mean an attempt to reconstruct the social pattern, which would then become a matter of common concern to the school and to the public outside the school.

The analogy can be pushed still another step. A democratic procedure, like Russian communism, involves a definite creed or point of view, and, like all creeds, it "loads the dice" in certain respects. It assumes at the outset, for example, that cooperation, sharing, creative activity, are desirable qualities, and so it advocates the type of school organization with which progressive education has made us familiar. Second, it holds that all the values which enter into the process of reconstruction or reinterpretation must stand on their own merits with no special protection from the outside. In other words, it holds that the outcome of the reinterpretation must not be determined in advance so as to ensure special privileges for certain values as against the rest. This too is a definite creed, which could hardly expect to meet with universal acceptance.

This statement, however, of the presuppositions which determine democratic procedure in education also brings to light the distinctive feature that differentiates this procedure from the rest. This distinctive feature consists in the dictum that the individual must be permitted and encouraged to do his own thinking, to formulate his own social philosophy. It concedes in advance the possibility that some individuals will use the intellectual freedom which is accorded them to draw the conclusion that such freedom is reprehensible and a danger to society. Or, to state it differently, the reconstruction of values, without antecedent special privileges to any of them, may lead to the belief the certain values should be protected, that conclusions should be predetermined, that, in short, the democratic procedure is all wrong. Such an outcome might be considered regrettable from the standpoint of the school, but it could not be ruled out in advance without stultifying the whole idea of democratic procedure.

This implication of democratic procedure, it may be noted, has a direct bearing on the idea of "participation." In the Russian scheme, participation in the main means cooperation in the realization of a program that is laid out in advance. In our own schools the terms *participation* and *social* all too frequently limited in the same way. Pupils are encouraged to participate or to be social by exhibiting a spirit of helpfulness. There is, however, a different and in some ways far deeper meaning of these terms. If we take these terms to refer to the *search* for a program, i.e., if we take them to mean sensitiveness to values and an active concern for the reconciliation and conservation of conflicting values, the individual acquires a certain new distinctiveness. We are then forced to take special note of the fact that this reconstruction of values is something that the individual must do for himself. The reconstruction may be socially motivated to any degree, yet it remains a personal matter. Participation may easily degenerate into a form of herd action, in which the finest fruits of education are lost to sight.

At present the day may seem far distant when the school and the general public will be engaged extensively in matters of common concern. Meanwhile the school must do what it can to relate its activities to the larger concerns of the social order. The best hope for the school, in this connection, is to become more sensitive than it has been in the past to the need of reexamining our national tradition. In stressing the interdependence of individuals in this modern world, something can be done, even in the lower grades, toward pointing out the need for widening our purposes in industrial and economic enterprises and for reconstructing our conception of the universe in which we live. With regard to this latter point, certain contrasts could be introduced to prepare for a better understanding of our tradition. Thus Franklin's proof that lightning is electricity and acts in strict conformity to natural laws gains a large measure of its significance from the fact that people previously held, and to some extent still hold, a widely different view on this subject. The same may be said regarding the evidence that diseases are "natural" phenomena. Or, again, the suggestion arising from the progressive remaking of our physical and social environment that intelligence should be entrusted with the task of recreating our standards of conduct and of values in accordance with changing conditions is a subject of violent disagreement. These illustrations serve to provide a clue to the determination of both subject-matter and method, and also to suggest how the continuity of the school with the social order, upon which our progressive schools have rightly placed so much emphasis, may be widened and directed. Eventually this growing insight should culminate in the comprehension of the basic conflicts that are to be found in every major domain of life—in religion, in economics, in government, and in the field of private and social conduct.

As was stated previously, the primary concern of a democratic educational procedure is to stimulate a reconstruction of our beliefs and habits in the light of their mutual relationships rather than to predetermine the nature of this reconstruction. The reconstruction will gravitate naturally and inevitably toward a philosophy of life or a social outlook, and it will take place with such assistance and encouragement as the schools can provide, but not according to any prescribed pattern. In a scheme of this kind we find clues for the selection of subject-matter and for methods of teaching. Can it also be claimed that such a scheme will provide a basis for social progress? It is obvious that a program of this kind, if really carried out, would not lead in every case to the same kind of social outlook. On the contrary, differences in attitude or points of view that exist among our population would tend to become more sharply accentuated and defined. But since a common program of some kind seems to be necessary, how can we hope that this kind of education would contribute to it?

*   *   *

The objection is plausible but has no finality. The differences in attitude or points of view to which reference was made above have always existed among our population. These differences, however, have not prevented the nation—except in the matter of economic-industrial development—from moving, on the whole, in the direction of a richer and more significant democracy. The evidence of this trend is to be found in the nature of the development exhibited by governmental functions. By and large, this development shows a growing concern for the welfare of the common man. Recognition of the rights of the common man is the basic article in our national faith, a faith that has hitherto proved more potent than our differences and disagreements. Is there any reason to suppose that this faith will be less dynamic if it becomes conscious of its larger implications and opportunities, if it gains a vision of a world in which its dream has become a reality?

It may be repeated that the kind of education which has been discussed here would doubtless carry people further apart in some respects, that it would emphasize certain differences in points of view. The point is that it would also do much toward cultivating common understandings and purposes. The time was when a liberal education meant the possession of a common body of knowledge and a common outlook on life. That time has gone by. About the only common element in present-day liberal education is that the same number of credits may be counted toward graduation. Liberal education has ceased to emphasize the possession of such a common tradition. To inherit the tradition of democracy, for example, is not like inheriting the classical tradition; it is more like inheriting a lawsuit. Yet this disturbing fact offers the opportunity of regaining, in a different form, the sense of solidarity among educated persons which is so largely lacking at the present time. All education, whether "liberal" or "technical," should help to create a sense that our traditions require reconstruction and thus provide community of understandings and interests, regardless of its content. In so doing it widens the area of common purposes by weakening the antagonisms that spring from complacent short-sightedness and from stupid loyalties to the past. Real education humanizes men. It does so, however, not by moulding them into unthinking acceptance of preestablished patterns, but by stimulating them to a continuous reconstruction of their outlook on life.

It is in this need for reconstruction that we find the new educational frontier. At present educators are insensitive to this need, in direct proportion to their pretensions of scientific impeccability or to their sentimental absorption in the development of the individual child. A new emphasis is necessary if scientific method in education and the concept of individuality are to become meaningful. It is necessary if education is to make its proper contribution toward safeguarding the future. Without the clarity of vision that such education can bestow, there is imminent danger that class interests will brush aside the common good, or that in the storm and stress of conflict we shall lose our way and follow after strange gods. As our national faith gains a clearer understanding of itself, it will be deepened and strengthened and the genius of the American people will be set free to make its distinctive contribution to the welfare and happiness of mankind.

JOHN DEWEY AND JOHN L. CHILDS ON EDUCATION AND SOCIAL PREFERENCE (1933) From John Dewey and John L. Childs, "Education Involves Social Preference," in William Heard Kilpatrick et al., *The Educational Frontier* (New York, 1933), pp. 290–91.

Our position implies that a philosophy of education is a branch of social philosophy and, like every social philosophy, since it requires a choice of one type of character, experience, and social institutions, involves a *moral* outlook. Education, as we conceive it, is a process of social interaction carried on in behalf of consequences which are themselves social—that is, it involves interactions between persons and includes shared values. A frequent objection to this view rests upon a misunderstanding. It asserts that this conception fails to grasp the basic value of individuality. The reverse is the case. *Social* cannot be opposed in fact or in idea to *individual.* Society *is* individuals-in-their-relations. An individual apart from social relations is a myth—or a monstrosity. If we deal with actual individuals, and not with a conceptual abstraction, our position can be also formulated in these terms: Education is the process of realization of integrated individualities. For integration can occur only in and through a medium of association. Associations are many and diverse, and some of them are hostile to the realization of a full personality, they interfere with it and prevent it. Hence *for the sake of individual development,* education must promote some forms of association and community life and must work against others. Admit that education is concerned with a development of individual potentialities and you are committed to the conclusion that education cannot be neutral and indifferent as to the kind of social organization which exists. Individuals develop not in a remote entity called "society" at large but in connection *with one another.* The conditions of their association with one another, of their participation and communication, of their cooperation and competition, are set by legal, political, and economic arrangements. In the interest, therefore, of education—not of any preconceived "ism" or code—the fact is emphasized that education must operate in view of a deliberately preferred social order.

WILLIAM HEARD KILPATRICK ON TEACHER TRAINING FROM THE SOCIAL POINT OF VIEW (1933)   From William Heard Kilpatrick et al., *The Educational Frontier* (New York, 1933), pp. 257.

If conscious education is to go forward under a new social vision, a new social emphasis will be necessary in the professional preparation of teachers and other educators. This becomes even the more necessary because for some two decades now the dominant stress in study and research has been laid upon the scientific and impersonal aspects of education, with a resulting accumulation of techniques and procedures which largely ignore any social outlook and bearing. Indeed the net effect has often been anti-social in that many have been led to believe that a scientific and statistical treatment of facts as such would supply all needed direction and aim. The inadequacy and impossibility of such a position is elsewhere herein discussed. It must suffice at this point to say that an adequate stress upon general and social considerations is now long overdue. The new social situation thus gives renewed emphasis and adds besides its own peculiar demands.

GEORGE S. COUNTS ON THE LAUNCHING OF THE SOCIAL FRONTIER (1934)   From "Orientation," *Social Frontier*, vol. I, pp. 3–4.

American Society, along with world society, is passing through an age of profound transition. This fact has been proclaimed with ever greater emphasis and frequency by the march of ideas and events since the Civil War and particularly since the opening of the present century. It is proclaimed in the advance of science, technology, and invention, in the growing mastery of natural forces, in the changing forms of economy and government, in the increasing instability of the whole social structure, in the swelling armaments and the intensification of international rivalries, and in the wars, revolutions, and social calamities which seem to have become the order of the day throughout the world. Also it is proclaimed in the obsolescence of inherited conceptions of human relationships, in the decline of faith in traditional moral and religious doctrines, in the popularity of cults of cynicism and disillusionment, and in the appearance of revolutionary political theories, philosophies, and programs.

While the transition presents many facets, in its basic terms in the United States it is a movement from a simple agrarian and trading economy to a highly complex urban and industrial order with agriculture transformed into single-crop specialties. Since the days of Andrew Jackson the nation has evolved out of a loose aggregation of relatively self-contained rural households and neighborhoods into a vast society marked by minute differentiation of structure and function, close integration of parts, and common dependence on a far-flung productive and distributive mechanism whose operation requires an ever increasing measure of cooperation, general planning, and unified direction. In a word, for the American people the age of individualism in economy is closing and an age of collectivism is opening. Here is the central and dominating reality in the present epoch.

This fact means that the nation has entered a period freighted with unmeasured opportunities and responsibilities—a period when, in the words of Emerson, "the old and the new stand side by side, and admit of being compared; when the energies of all men are searched by fear and by hope; when the historic glories of the old can be compensated by the rich possibilities of the new era." In the years and decades immediately ahead the American people will be called upon to undertake arduous, hazardous, and crucial tasks of social reconstruction: they will be compelled to make some of the grand choices of history, to determine in which direction they are to move, to make decisions which will deeply affect the life of their country for generations and indeed for centuries—decisions concerning the incidence of economic and political power, the distribution of wealth and income, the relations of classes, races, and nationalities, and the ends for which men and women are to live. Moreover, owing to the revolutionary conquest of mechanical energy during the past one hundred years, the American people stand today on the threshold of unprecedented and unimagined potentialities of material and spiritual development. Also they stand in the imminent presence of economic collapse, political reaction, cultural regimentation, and war. They must choose among the diverse roads now opening before them. In particular they must choose whether the great tradition of democracy is to pass away with the individualistic economy to which it has been linked historically or is to undergo the transformation necessary for survival in an age of close economic interdependence.

In the making of these choices persons and institutions engaged in the performance of educational functions will inevitably play an important role. To the extent that they operate in the real world they will make their influence felt. Indeed, even if they should pursue a policy of evasion, in actual fact they would be throwing their influence on the side of outmoded anarchy and disorder. Whatever course they pursue they will either retard or hasten the adjustment to the new realities, they will either make easy or difficult the transfer of the democratic ideal from individual to social foundations. They will be called upon, not only to bring the heritage of knowledge, thought, and attitude abreast of general social advance, but also to make broad choices concerning alliances to be consummated, values to be preserved, interests to be defended, social goals to be striven for.

Already a few voices have been raised within the ranks of educational workers in acceptance of the challenge of social reconstruction. But as yet these voices are too timid to be effective, too tentative to be convincing, and too individual to speak a language of clear-cut purpose. They belong to persons who singly and in isolation have captured this or the other meaning of unfolding events. Before these persons, and perhaps countless others who have thus far remained inarticulate, can hope to become a positive creative force in American society and education, they must come into closer communication, clarify their thought and purposes, draw like-minded individuals into their ranks, and merge isolated and discordant voices into a mighty instrument of group consensus, harmonious expression, and collective action. To contribute to the achievement of this object THE SOCIAL FRONTIER is being launched.

The journal makes no pretense to absolute objectivity and detachment, knowing such a goal to be impossible of achievement in that realm of practical affairs to which education belongs and in which positive decisions must be made. It represents a point of view, it has a frame of reference, it stands on a particular interpretation of American history. It accepts the analysis of the current epoch presented above and outlined in greater detail in *Conclusions and Recommendations, Report on the Social Studies* of the Commission of the American Historical Association.

THE SOCIAL FRONTIER assumes that the age of individualism in economy is closing and that an age marked by close integration of social life and by collective planning and control is opening. For weal or woe it accepts as irrevocable this deliverance of the historical process. It intends to go forward to meet the new age and to proceed as rationally as possible to the realization of all possibilities for the enrichment and refinement of human life. It will nurse no fantasies of returning to the simple household and neighborhood economy of the time of Thomas Jefferson; it will seek no escape from the responsibilities of today, either by longing for a past now gone beyond recovery or by imagining a future bearing the features of Utopia. It proposes to take seriously the affirmation of the Declaration of Independence that "all men are created equal" and are entitled to "life, liberty, and the pursuit of happiness." Also it proposes, in the light of this great humanist principle applied to the collective realities of industrial civilization, to pass every important educational event, institution, theory, and program under critical review. Finally, it will devote its pages positively to the development of the thought of all who are interested in making education discharge its full responsibility in the present age of social transition. Its editorial staff and board of directors hope that it will help fight the great educational battles—practical and theoretical—which are already looming above the horizon. And they trust that it will engage in the battles of the twentieth and not of the eighteenth century.

THE SOCIAL FRONTIER acknowledges allegiance to no narrow conception of education. While recognizing the school as society's central educational agency, it refuses to *limit* itself to a consideration of the work of this institution. On the contrary, it includes within its field of interest all of those formative influences and agencies which serve to induct the individual—whether old or young—into the life and culture of the group. It regards education as an aspect of a culture in process of evolution. It therefore has no desire to promote a restricted and technical professionalism. Rather does it address itself to the task of considering the broad role of education in advancing the welfare and interests of the great masses of the people who do the work of society—those who labor on farms and ships and in the mines, shops, and factories of the world.

A NEW FRAME OF REFERENCE FOR THE TEACHING OF SOCIAL STUDIES (1934) From American Historical Association, Report of the Commission on the Social Studies, *Conclusions and Recommendations of the Commission* (New York, 1934), pp. 10, 16–18, 30–31, 34–39.

---

12. In the light of its assumptions about the nature and the functions of the social sciences, about the value of scholarship and the limitations of the scientific method, the Commission proceeds now, in the further development of its frame of reference, to indicate what it deems to be the factors in American life—the social and economic realities of time and place—which necessarily condition the selection

and formulation of any educational program in the social sciences for the present and proximate future.

C. NECESSARILY CONDITIONING FACTORS IN
AMERICAN LIFE

1. The very fact that the Commission is charged with making recommendations concerning education in the social sciences *within the United States* conditions necessarily the Commission's selection and formulation of a program. For the American nation is an entity with distinctive aspects, traditions, and usages— geographical, economic, political, social, and cultural—of perduring vigor and strength, which must be taken into account if social science instruction is to be something more than abstract, if it is to be properly concrete, realistic, and serviceable.

*   *   *

8. Under the moulding influence of socialized processes of living, drives of technology and science, pressures of changing thought and policy, and disrupting impacts of economic disaster, there is a notable waning of the once widespread popular faith in economic individualism; and leaders in public affairs, supported by a growing mass of the population, are demanding the introduction into economy of ever-wider measures of planning and control.

9. Cumulative evidence supports the conclusion that, in the United States as in other countries, the age of individualism and *laissez faire* in economy and government is closing and that a new age of collectivism is emerging.

10. As to the specific form which this "collectivism," this integration and interdependence, is taking and will take in the future, the evidence at hand is by no means clear or unequivocal. It may involve the limiting or supplanting of private property by public property or it may entail the preservation of private property, extended and distributed among the masses. Most likely, it will issue from a process of experimentation and will represent a composite of historic doctrines and social conceptions yet to appear. Almost certainly it will involve a larger measure of compulsory as well as voluntary co-operation of citizens in the conduct of the complex national economy, a corresponding enlargement of the functions of government, and an increasing state intervention in fundamental branches of economy previously left to the individual discretion and initiative—a state intervention that in some instances may be direct and mandatory and in others indirect and facilitative. In any event the Commission is convinced by its interpretation of available empirical data that the actually integrating economy of the present day is the forerunner of a consciously integrated society in which individual economic actions and individual property rights will be altered and abridged.

11. The emerging age is particularly an age of transition. It is marked by numerous and severe tensions arising out of the conflict between the actual trend toward integrated economy and society, on the one side, and the traditional practices, dispositions, ideas, and institutional arrangements inherited from the passing age of individualism, on the other. In all the recommendations that follow, the transitional character of the present epoch is recognized.

A NEW
ORIENTATION
FOR EDUCATION
1930–1950

* * *

Chapter III. Philosophy and Purpose in Education[1]

1. Education is a form of action on the part of some particular social group; it is not a species of contemplation removed from social life and relationships.

2. Education always expresses some social philosophy, either large or small, involves some choices with respect to social and individual action and well-being, and rests upon some moral conception.

3. Conceived in a large and clarified frame of reference, education is one of the highest forms of statesmanship: a positive and creative attack upon the problems generated by the movement of ideas and interests in society.

4. Finding its immediate expression in individuals, education so conceived is concerned with the development of rich and many-sided personalities capable of co-operating in a social order designed to facilitate the creation of the largest possible number of rich and many-sided personalities.

EDUCATION AN EXPRESSION OF A PARTICULAR GEOGRAPHICAL AND CULTURAL SETTING

1. Being a form of social action, education always has a geographical and cultural location; it is therefore specific, local, and dynamic, not general, universal, and unchanging; it is a function of a particular society at a particular time and place in history; it is rooted in some actual culture and expresses the philosophy and recognized needs of that culture. Contemporary American society of course is of vast proportions and manifests wide-reaching economic and cultural ramifications extending to the most distant parts of the world.

* * *

4. In two respects education will be challenged: (a) the emerging economy will involve the placing of restraints on individual enterprise, propensities, and acquisitive egoism in agriculture, industry, and labor and generally on the conception, ownership, management, and use of property, as the changing policies of government already indicate; and (b) the emerging economy, by the reduction of hours of labor and other measures, promises to free the ordinary individual from the long working day, exhausting labor and economic insecurity, thus providing him with opportunities for personal development far greater and richer than those enjoyed under the individualistic economy of the eighteenth and nineteenth centuries.

5. The implications for education are clear and imperative: (a) the efficient functioning of the emerging economy and the full utilization of its potentialities require profound changes in the attitudes and outlook of the American people, especially the rising generation—a complete and frank recognition that the old order is passing, that the new order is emerging, and that knowledge of realities and

[1] In the present chapter the Commission has directed its attention toward the formulation of the philosophy and purpose of education as a whole, as well as toward the problem of the teaching of the social sciences themselves. In attempting this larger task, it desired, first, to place the subject of its special concern in the general setting, and, second, to bring the findings of the social sciences to bear upon the total educational undertaking.

capacity to co-operate are indispensable to the development and even the perdurance of American society; and (b) the rational use of the new leisure requires a cultural equipment which will give strength and harmony to society instead of weakness and discord.

6. Conversely, continued emphasis in education on the traditional ideas and values of economic individualism and acquisitiveness will intensify the conflicts, contradictions, maladjustments, and perils of the transition.

GENERAL APPLICATIONS

1. Organized public education in the United States, much more than ever before, is now compelled, if it is to fulfill its social obligations, to adjust its objectives, its curriculum, its methods of instruction, and its administrative procedures to the requirements of the emerging integrated order.

2. If the school is to justify its maintenance and assume its responsibilities, it must recognize the new order and proceed to equip the rising generation to co-operate effectively in the increasingly interdependent society and to live rationally and well within its limitations and possibilities.

3. It thus follows that educators are called upon to examine critically the frame of reference under which they have been operating, and to proceed deliberately to the clarification and affirmation of purpose in the light of the changed and changing social situation and in the light of those facts and trends which remain compelling, irrespective of individual preferences.

4. Educators stand to-day between two great philosophies of social economy: the one representing the immediate past and fading out in actuality, an individual-ism in economic theory which has become hostile in practice to the development of individuality for great masses of the people and threatens the survival of American society; the other representing and anticipating the future on the basis of actual trends—the future already coming into reality, a collectivism which may permit the widest development of personality or lead to a bureaucratic tyranny destructive of ideals of popular democracy and cultural freedom.

5. If education continues to emphasize the philosophy of individualism in economy, it will increase the accompanying social tensions. If it organizes a program in terms of a philosophy which harmonizes with the facts of a closely integrated society, it will ease the strains of the transition taking place in actuality. The making of choices cannot be evaded, for inaction in education is a form of action.

6. Within the limits of an economy marked by integration and interdependence, many possibilities, many roads stand open before education. The making of choices by either evasion or positive action also cannot be avoided in the development of an educational program.

7. The road which the Commission has chosen and mapped in the preceding chapter is one which, it believes, will make possible the most complete realization, under the changed conditions of life, of the ideals of American democracy and cultural liberty: the recognition of the moral equality and dignity of all men; the abolition of class distinctions and special privileges; the extension to every individual, regardless of birth, class, race, religion, or economic status, of the opportunity for the fullest development of his creative capacities, his spiritual qualities, his individuality; the encouragement of social inquiry, inventiveness, and tolerance; the protection of all liberties essential to defense against the exercise of brute power; the development of resistance to appeals to racial and religious

passion and prejudice; the establishment of those standards and securities set forth in *A Charter for the Social Sciences in the Schools.*

8. Such an affirmation of human values in education, the Commission holds, is peculiarly imperative in a society moving toward economic planning and control. Recognizing the necessity of living in an integrated economy and aware that such economy may be made to serve either some privileged minority or the entire population, the Commission deliberately presents to education, and affirms the desirability of, an economy managed in the interests of the masses, as distinguished from any class or bureaucracy.

9. From this point of view, a supreme purpose of education in the United States, in addition to the development of rich and many-sided personalities, is the preparation of the rising generation to enter the society now coming into being through thought, ideal, and knowledge, rather than through coercion, regimentation, and ignorance, and to shape the form of that society in accordance with American ideals of popular democracy and personal liberty and dignity.

IMMEDIATE IMPLICATIONS FOR THE ORGANIZATION
AND CONDUCT OF THE SCHOOL SYSTEM

1. In the integrated society now emerging the ideal of individual, institutional, and local advancement will of necessity give way increasingly to considerations of general, national, and world welfare.

The High School

GOODWIN WATSON ON THE RECONSTRUCTED HIGH SCHOOL OF THE FUTURE (1935)   From Goodwin Watson, "A Program for American Youth," as quoted in Samuel Everett, ed., *A Challenge to Secondary Education* (New York, 1935), pp. 153–59.

The secondary school here presented is intended primarily for all pupils from about thirteen years of age to about twenty years of age, but essentially the same organization will serve also the adults of the community. This school assumes some six years of happy experience in elementary school, during which time pupils have acquired a good foundation of health, have developed many interests, have learned to speak, to read and to write reasonably well, have made friends, explored a little of the worlds of nature, men and books, have developed the ability to go places, to use money, to take care of themselves in all ordinary circumstances, and to observe the simple amenities of our culture. The schooling here outlined will complete what may be thought of as the intensive period of schooling for almost all citizens. A small group—perhaps 20 per cent of those who finish this secondary school—will enter universities and professional schools. The remainder of the pupils will get jobs, establish homes, and will participate in continuing adult education activities throughout life. As adults they may come back often to the same advisers, shops, libraries, gymnasia, laboratories, etc., which they learned to use during their secondary-school experience.

Scholarships will make it possible for every pupil, without economic handicap, to profit by this program at least until he is eighteen years of age.

*   *   *

What Do They Learn?

Since the curriculum consists of improved and enriched ways of carrying on normal adolescent life, it is organized in categories which are forms of individual and social functioning.

The most important "functional divisions" of the curriculum may well be:

1. Keeping physically fit
2. Keeping mental and emotional balance
3. Increasing ability to find and to use needed information from books

4. Choosing vocations
5. Developing the ability to earn a living (for some, this may include preparation for entrance to professional schools)
6. Maintaining desirable social relationships
7. Exploring leisure-time possibilities
8. Developing skill in some avocational pursuits, hobbies, recreations
9. Creating beauty in surroundings, dress, and objects of art
10. Acquiring understanding of, and at-home-ness in, the world of nature
11. Learning discrimination and taste in novels, stories, plays, poems, movies, radio programs, etc.
12. Purchasing and saving wisely
13. Establishing a home
14. Bringing up children
15. Becoming able to interpret current events as reflected in the news
16. Serving the community, state, nation, and world society, as a good citizen
17. Working out a satisfying philosophy of life

The potential curriculum in each of the seventeen areas includes all of the individual and community activities which contribute to the designated goal. The curriculum for any individual, at any particular time, includes a selection from the vast collection of possibilities, of those activities which he and his adviser agree are important for his community and for him.

The most pressing problems today, for our community life, are those related to the economic crisis. Start where we will, with health, housing, crime prevention, better movies, or the need for more serenity—we find it impossible to go far because of the economic impasse. Education, recreation, art and research are distorted in the attempt to hold together a self-defeating system. It is likely that units in almost any area will come back again and again to the common problem of building a new social order.

The individual needs are more variable. Some, with technical interests, will need competence in building a short-wave radio, or in the accurate procedures of quantitative chemical analysis. Others will be concerned with the equally complex and less well understood techniques of social control in running a club or conducting a campaign. Editing a school paper which interprets community, national and world events in terms of their meaning for the pupils of this school, is a creative enterprise bearing little relationship to most high-school journalism. Dramatic groups engaged in making realistic, vivid, and artistically impressive the struggle to build a better world will have accepted a more vital task than is usually faced by these groups. Thus many individuals, with widely varying talents and interests, will all be contributors to a common purpose.

While every curricular unit may be stated in terms of an activity toward some goal, this should not be interpreted to mean narrow, superficial, short-sighted, opportunistic, direct action. On the contrary, awareness of many purposes in each activity is essential. We want to do, but to do we must understand; and to have pride in what we do, we must exercise taste, skill, and patience in the work. The success or failure of this type of school may depend upon securing proper breadth and penetration in the development of each unit. There is no more serious problem for advisers than to determine how thoroughly background should be developed, how rigorously the investigations should be made, how extensively the ramifications should be followed. Probably there will be a few situations in which there is danger of giving more time and effort than a particular question warrants. Much more frequently the error has appeared to be in the other direction. Interests have been so casual and superficial as to be too easily satisfied.

Teachers have often depended upon requirements and schedules to compel long attention to a given area of material and have neglected to develop techniques for stimulating the pupils to plough deeper into matters on their own initiative. When the courses and requirements and hours of time-serving have failed, as they must inevitably fail, to produce qualities of intellectual stamina, there was a plea for a selection of students who didn't need to be trained, or for extension of the compulsory methods which had already shown their inadequacy.

Part of the virtue of the program here suggested is that it puts the responsibility for thoroughness, mastery, competence and scholarship back where it belongs, on the teacher-pupil-problem relationship. The teacher must help the pupil to feel the problem itself which can be met only after due effort on his part. Both teacher and pupil should be constantly aware of ideals of workmanship and habits of attack which will continue beyond the demands of the immediate situation. Certainly there is this much left in the old doctrine of formal discipline.

An aid to determining how thoroughly each project should be undertaken comes from the opportunity to test out results in living. A curse of much present education is that it so seldom connects with the real out-of-school situation. Even if it takes off from a springboard of some "life situation" it may sail on and on through the heights of theory, never coming down to earth again. The units and methods of the proposed program are planned to give pupils a chance to try out ideas in practice. One test of whether a matter has been studied far enough is whether there has been achieved a competence that works in actuality.

If some pupils are studying French to gain an enjoyment of modern French literature, no test can be more appropriate than their own degree of ease and enjoyment in such reading. If a group undertakes to help the community raise a better quality of fruit for its own use, the proper test is in the improved harvest. If there is a need to explode the widely accepted fallacy that machines have taken away jobs, so that there is no longer work that needs to be done, the editorials in the papers, the speeches of citizens in public forums, the conversations around home fireplaces, will show when the campaign has been successful. Whether the purpose be great and remote, or immediate and personal, there is a test in life itself. Is it desired to gain weight or to reduce weight? One test (not the only one) of the completion of the project is the attainment of the desired condition. Is the purpose to get more chance to play tennis? Then the project is not complete until through all the activities of discussion, investigation, planning, securing cooperation, etc., the new tennis court is in shape to use. For many adolescents the rigorous demands of an actual paid job are essential. The obstacles of life constitute an appreciable barrier to slovenly methods. When study ends in a term paper it runs a danger of arranging facts by wishful thinking; when the demands of nature and society must be met, good intentions alone, or bluffing, or snap judgments, are likely to bring obvious failure.

What Takes the Place of Textbooks?

The "content" of the traditional school could be found largely in the books—one text for each subject. As the schools have progressed these resources have expanded to include several texts for a given course, reference libraries, laboratories, city museums, points to be visited by excursions, newspapers, magazines, radio programs, telephone conversations with experts, etc. The proposed program continues this expansion. Not only any resources that can be brought into the school buildings but any aids which pupils can find in the life and institutions of the community, are to be included. The library will, of course, be of great importance and should include the factual material bearing on all the functional divisions. Resources for health will be found, in part, in the city health department and sanitation services, in the medical profession, in hospitals, diet kitchens, homes, as well as on the school staff. Resources for vocational matters will include any business, agricultural, industrial, or professional enterprises which are willing to take on apprentices or observers (under educational control). Resources for recreation will include the homes of pupils, the playgrounds, and parks, the theatres and concerts, the woods and lakes of the surrounding region. Travel should be encouraged whenever distant settings can better meet some need. Whatever aids to living can be afforded by the total environment belong in the curriculum.

Guides for the use of this rich background of facilities will constitute a rich "library of possibilities." Each unit guide will deal with a given project or problem. Each will tell how other groups have gone at such an endeavor, their successes and failures. The guides will be in constant revision by the groups of pupils who use them. Additions will be made, weaknesses revealed. Such modifications might well be reported to a single clearing-house and made quickly available to all other schools.

The guides will be written for the pupils. They will be as nearly as possible self-teaching. The suggestions will aim to stimulate the initiative of the pupils rather than to give cook-book directions.

There will be several hundred guides to unit projects under each functional division of the curriculum. Some may be used by every pupil, others by most pupils, still others by only a few. New guides will be added constantly as individuals and groups develop new projects of possible significance beyond their own school. The clearing-house referred to will distribute monthly catalogs of newly developed materials and each school can add in accord with its need and resources.

The unit guides will carry enough content material—facts, selected statements of viewpoint—to make possible a first level understanding of the matter in hand. But they will be useful chiefly as guides, pointing to fuller treatment in books, magazines, and other resources.

THE NEW RURAL HIGH SCHOOL (1935) From C. Maurice Wieting, "The Rural High School," as quoted in Samuel Everett, ed., *A Challenge to Secondary Education* (New York, 1935), pp. 105–11.

Social conditions among the rural population have altered more since the World War than ever before in a like period of time throughout American history. Prior to this conflict the American farmer considered his wellbeing as dependent on local economic conditions. Now he clearly sees his dependence upon international trade.

In frontier days the rural school was a local institution established to teach the young the fundamental skills of reading, writing, and arithmetic. This knowledge enabled the youth to keep track of his accounts, write his name, and read a few books.

Life was fairly simple in an agricultural region. Land was plentiful and free. The young man married at an early age, settled on a piece of land, and lived in a rough house on the prairie. He worked long hours at manual labor coming home in the evening fatigued and ready to retire. Contacts with other individuals were infrequent, and freedom to act according to desire was possible to a high degree.

Education in this type of society played a relatively minor role. When work was to be done, the boys stayed out of school. Few pupils finished even the elementary school, and most communities made no provision for secondary education.

Today fundamental changes have taken place in rural life. Invention has made possible labor-saving devices which shorten the hours of work for the farmer. Free land is gone, and there is no longer room for expansion. The World War stimulated production and then, with its close, cut off the demand. Low prices paid to farmers for the last fifteen years are an indication of the lack of effective demand.

The Agricultural Adjustment Act further illustrates the trend of the times. The restriction of production that has taken place has meant an increase of leisure time for those who are engaged in farming. For many young men growing up today farming offers little opportunity. High land values and low farm prices do not encourage him to engage in agriculture. On the other hand, mass unemployment in the industrial centers now keeps him from leaving the farm for the city. The result is that a generation of farm youth is now growing up without any clear idea of what the future will hold. Instead of dropping out of school at an early age, an increasing percentage of rural boys and girls graduate from the secondary schools.

The history of rural secondary schools has been a story of constant struggle for establishment and support. In the Middle West few high schools were built, but academies were established as a part of college training. Gradually schools were built in rural centers, until today universal secondary education is possible, in theory if not in fact, in all parts of the United States.

In the early academy the curriculum was based upon the entrance requirements of the college. Latin, Greek, mathematics, grammar, and rhetoric were required. When the high school separated from the college physically it often retained the same course of study. History and science had to fight for a place in the school but were included.

The greatest indictment against the present school system in rural areas is that it has not revised its curriculum to meet changing economic and social conditions. Times have changed rapidly, but the cultural lag of the school has conspired to keep education static. English, mathematics, and formal science are still the basic subjects in most high schools.

It is impossible to outline a blueprint of the future, but the indications are that we will have a planning society. Under the working of the Agricultural Adjustment Act farmers are coming together collectively to decide about matters of production. The next step may well be the consideration of other problems. The cooperative movement in marketing and purchasing has grown remarkably in the United States.

John W. Studebaker, United States Commissioner of Education, insists that the establishment of local forums is the only certain method of adult education possible. If this fact is accepted then a different conception of all education must be evolved. Education becomes something vital and part of everyday life.

This fundamental shift in the conception of education can be traced to the pioneer work of John Dewey, and men like William H. Kilpatrick who have followed his philosophy. Education is understood as a process of training the entire child. It is not a preparation for life in the future, but the living of life itself. Put into actual practice, this philosophy means the elimination of many traditional subjects and a radical shift in the method of teaching those which are retained. Child life, child capacities, and child outlook must determine the application of adult philosophy of social ideals.

What is taught in the rural school should be modified by the activity that is dominant in each locality. In Iowa, where the raising of corn is the chief occupation of the community, children will have an outlook on life conditioned by this environment. In the South, where cotton is the main crop, other social and economic factors will determine community life. It is the duty of the school curriculum to be flexible enough to interpret social and economic factors of the rural community.

No person can safely assume that any one community or any one state is just like another. In the past many schools have taken courses of study from urban centers and installed them in toto in rural schools. This practice of slavish imitation has been most unfortunate. Rural children have suffered from the imposition of a type of education in no wise fitted for their needs.

Analysis of the local community is an important duty of the persons wishing to revise a rural school curriculum. Likewise there must be an analysis of state and national trends and an understanding of how these changes will affect rural education. It should be conceived as the duty of the school to keep abreast with social change and to lead in the evaluation of new movements.

Many people insist that the school does not have the right to lead in social change since schools are supported by the status quo. The stronger argument, however, is that it is the duty of the school to interpret the trends of the time and advocate changes which will lead to better social conditions. But in this connection the realistic administrator must recognize the inherent conservatism of rural peoples. During the past decade liberalism and even radicalism have leavened this viewpoint. Experiments in rural education in many scattered communities and a few states do indicate progress.

METHOD OF DEVELOPING AND USING THE PROPOSED CURRICULUM

No curriculum for any school can be formulated in advance by any person or group of persons. The techniques of curriculum construction can be suggested by experts and they can help in the development of rough outlines, but the most effective courses of study are those written by teachers who will eventually use them.

An understanding of the basic philosophy underlying the curriculum must be developed in the school system. Perhaps the best way to do this would be through a series of teachers meeting under the direction of the superintendent or the curriculum director. But before any curriculum construction is undertaken there should be a thorough analysis of all of the economic and social conditions which bear upon the lives of those in the community. This will involve an intensive study of modern problems, their recent trends, and an honest attempt to look into the future.

In a typical rural community this approach would involve an understanding of farming, credit, religion, recreation, racial traits, community history, political parties, and countless other matters. Every teacher on the staff would have to contribute a share in building toward this complete understanding. Added to this intensive study of local conditions there should be an understanding and comprehension of modern educational literature. This suggests that the group meetings shall consider all problems in the light of the best educational practice.

Curricula representing the best productions of other communities should be studied and analyzed. Teachers interested in certain subjects should specialize in their own field. Mastery of basic subject matter and ability to write good materials is essential. A standard form of writing and arranging the materials should be adopted before any production takes place. Indeed the most difficult job in most curriculum revision programs is to keep teachers from rushing into actual writing before they develop a sound background. When tentative material for instruction has been developed it should be taught in a class experimentally. Then it should be reviewed and rewritten before it is put into more permanent form.

Along with this program of curriculum construction must go to a planned publicity campaign. The public must be informed of the advantages of a better course of study. They must be educated to the change that is considered desirable.

An important step is putting the curriculum into effect in the school system. Since under the philosophy here outlined an activity program is demanded it may be necessary to reorganize the entire schedule of the school. Hour periods should be at a minimum and longer periods should be planned when possible. Creative work should be encouraged by the teacher who acts as an adviser to a willing pupil. This demands a radical departure from the traditional concept of the teacher as master and the pupil as slave.

While many rural schools have a dearth of physical equipment within the plant they will find that the community offers a wide field for study. Wide use can be made of the local community through excursions of many different kinds. Local men and women can, moreover, be encouraged to contribute their knowledge and enthusiasms in many aspects of the work of the school.

In vocational courses the classes can spend part of their time going on judging trips, visiting model farms, inspecting homes and hospitals. Materials distributed by the State Agricultural College can be used as the basis for study and report. Farm leaders and local business men are often willing and flattered to be asked to present materials to a high-school class.

A study of local marketing conditions can best be made by an actual visit to the railroad, the trucking depot, wholesale houses, and retail stores. Money and banking will have new interest when officers of a bank explain the workings of their institution. Understanding of propaganda and the workings of new agencies can be stimulated by a visit to town newspapers. Practical instruction in bookkeeping can be obtained by visiting a merchant and observing his methods of keeping records.

Lawyers, doctors, and professional men of all kinds will be glad to assist in this type of education.

*   *   *

THE CORE-CURRICULUM PLAN IN VIRGINIA (1935)   From Sidney B. Hall and Fred M. Alexander, "The Core Curriculum Plan In A State Program," as quoted in Samuel Everett, ed., *A Challenge to Secondary Education* (New York, 1935), pp. 25–29.

Summary

The philosophy growing out of the analysis of the basic considerations outlined in the beginning of this chapter, and adopted as a guide for the development of the new secondary-school curriculum, is expressed briefly in the following statements:

1. The curriculum consists of all the experiences of pupils under the influence of the school.

2. Education is the development of personality.

3. Progress is realized through guiding social change by intelligent human effort and choice.

4. All education has its orientation in the ideals of the culture and of the epoch in which it exists (American secondary education has its orientation in the ideals of democracy).

PRINCIPLES OF EDUCATION

The following principles of education are based upon the foregoing philosophy and may be used as guides for the development of the secondary-school curriculum:

1. The school is an agency of society for its perpetuation and recreation.

2. Growth processes in individuals and in society are resultants of continuing interaction between individuals and society.

3. Individuals differ in interests, abilities, attitudes, appreciations and understandings, habits and skills, and in capacity to learn.

4. Growth is continuous.

5. All learning comes through experience.

6. An individual tends to avoid experiences that annoy and to seek experiences that satisfy.

7. The school can serve as a creative institution only as it succeeds in controlling through its curriculum the experience of learners so that cultivated, integrated, and individualized personalities are developed.

THE SCOPE OF THE CORE CURRICULUM

It is apparent that the aims of education derived from the ideals of a continuously changing democratic society cannot be realized through the study of separate subjects consisting of inert facts. No social event, no social institution can be compartmentalized exclusively as historical, economic, or political. Subjects represent an organization for specialized, advanced study. The alternative to the subject organization as the basis for the scope of the core curriculum is a plan which will enable students to discover how the movements and forces of society have and are still modifying social life.

❖   ❖   ❖

Centers of Interest

The major functions of social life enumerated above should serve as integrating centers for the developing experiences of students. They will provide the growing individual with opportunities for reaching out into the broad areas of human experience and into the major fields of knowledge where he may gather the materials necessary for his development. To be socially useful, these experiences must be related; they should have continuity. For each year the learner should increase the area, depth, and number of his experiences consistent with his ability. Guides, therefore, are needed for the organization of instruction for each year of the secondary school. The determining factors for selecting these guides for the organization of instruction are the interests, abilities, and needs of the pupils, and the agencies, institutions, and forces in society that modify the major functions of social life.

With these criteria as bases an analysis was made to determine the forces and agencies in society to be used as guides for organizing instruction in the secondary school. The following forces, institutions, and agencies that modify the major functions of social life were set up:

1. GRADE VIII . . . Adaptation of our living through nature, social and mechanical inventions, and discoveries

2. GRADE IX . . . Agrarianism and industrialism and their effects upon our living

3. GRADE X . . . Effects of changing culture and changing social institutions upon our living

4. GRADE XI . . . Effects of a continuously planning social order upon our living

❖   ❖   ❖

Core Fields

The following broad fields of knowledge are selected as core fields: social studies, language arts, science for the four years of the secondary school, and general mathematics for the first year. These core fields embrace man-to-man relationships, man-to-nature relationships, and include the arts to an extent in social studies and language arts. Within each broad field subject-matter lines are disregarded so that pupils may develop unitary experiences in their study of human relations. The purpose here is to set the stage for integration.

For all pupils in the secondary school a core curriculum organized around these fields is set up. Provision is made in the core-curriculum plan to provide opportunity for those pupils whose needs make it desirable for them to elect the study of specialized organized bodies of knowledge such as foreign languages, mathematics, etc.

In a society as heavily oriented towards the future and the next generation as Middletown, a study of the way it trains its young offers one of the surest means of penetrating beneath the surface of life to its dominant values. Middletown cares about its children. They symbolize to the parent generation a path of release from certain of life's frustrations and a large share of this adult generation's hope of the future. Some people have exclaimed, "What a crass culture!" after reading the earlier study of Middletown; but one who knows the city would always insist, "Certainly not in its hopes and plans and sacrifices for its children!" For Middletown reaches with eagerness, albeit an eagerness tempered with caution and apprehension over the unfamiliar, for what it conceives to be for its children's good. If adult Middletown sees its own hope for the immediate future as lying in hard work and making money, it has been wont to see in education the Open Sesame that will unlock the world for its children.

Middletown has accordingly been emotionally ready for change of a "conservatively progressive" sort in its schools. Whether a community actually effects changes in its institutional habits, and where the changes occur, depends, however, upon a congeries of factors in addition to this general emotional receptivity. These factors include a community's wealth, the relative urgency with which its different problems press upon it, the tenacity of its traditions, the presence or absence of strong local personalities with an interest in a particular change, the rate of change in the larger culture surrounding it, and the development in this larger culture of clearly defined and easily transmittable yardsticks by which such relative lags as may exist in local procedures can be recognized. . . .

*   *   *

In 1927–28 the Middletown schools embarked upon a ten-year program of school planning and reorganization. Taking off squarely from the platform of industrial "planning" ardently sponsored in those pre-New Deal days by the then Secretary of Commerce, and later President, Hoover, and commending the "many startling results" being accomplished by engineering intelligence applied to industrial problems, the Middletown school administrators pointed to the sweeping character of current social change, quoting Owen D. Young to the effect that "Our chief problem is no longer to adjust ourselves to a well-defined system, but to change"; they noted that "Municipal planning has not received as great attention as industrial planning, which no doubt accounts for much of its lack of progress in rendering an increased service with a decreased cost"; and they then installed a Research Department and began to plan. Central to this ten-year planning and reorganization program was the redefinition of the philosophy of education in Middletown, and central to the latter was the emphasis upon the individual child:[1]

"During the past few years of educational endeavor in [Middletown], the Board

[1] The quotations in the paragraph above and the long quotation that follows are from a review of progress at the conclusion of the first five years of the ten-year plan. They are contained in the opening pages of a 105-page report on Educational Planning in the [Middletown] Public Schools, issued by the Department of Educational Research in 1933.

of Education and its school administrators . . . have faced the problem of selecting the educational philosophy on which to build. . . .

"The philosophy on which school authorities have attempted to build in [Middletown] may be made a bit clearer by first briefly contrasting it with that of the past. Our philosophy of education in America has been largely that of the pioneer. Prior to the last century, and during much of the nineteenth century, our philosophy was very largely nationalistic and aristocratic. We now believe in the education of the masses. We have spent too much time in transplanting to America the theories, practices, and educational traditions of European education.

"Educational tradition from Europe furnished us with much that is out-worn and ineffective. There are still many disciples of aristocratic European traditions. From the beginning of time until recent years, world change has developed slowly. As a result, knowledge was traditionally handed down. Such a process became authoritative and the accepted basis of knowledge. Many held to such a traditional philosophy and advocated that to learn is basically acquisition and acceptance on authority.

"Ours is a different philosophy. *It advocates that the aim of education should be to enable every child to become a useful citizen, to develop his individual powers to the fullest extent of which he is capable, while at the same time engaged in useful and lifelike activities. . . . We believe in the doctrine of equal educational opportunity for every child to develop according to his abilities, interests, and aptitudes.* [Italics ours.]

"In planning the educational work in [Middletown] in recent years, the Board of Education and school officials have tried to operate on the above basic philosophy of American Education. . . . The plan as at first laid out was to extend over a period of about ten years. The first five-year period has passed and it is the function of this Bulletin to briefly review what has been accomplished to date . . . and to look into the immediate future. ". . . While we do not desire [in the pages which follow in this Bulletin] to point to spectacular improvements, we do believe that the comparisons made will show a distinct advance from the practices of an earlier period. . . . The elements of the educational plan along which progress in varying degrees has been made, and upon which further thought and effort must be spent, are the following:

1. The personnel organization.
2. The gradual reorganization of the [Middletown] City Schools.
3. The reorganization and rearranging of curricular offerings in terms of pupil needs.
4. The revision of the courses of study and the development of technique of course-of-study construction.
5. The use of the appraisal and city-wide testing program.
6. Guidance program for counseling boys and girls of junior and senior high-school age.
7. The upgrading of teaching personnel.
8. Child accounting and holding power of the schools.
9. Budgetary procedure and the study of school costs and trends.
10. A survey of school sites.
11. Landscape plans for the school grounds.
12. A survey of school buildings."

Here speaks not the voice of the businessmen of Middletown's school board but that of the professional school of education, whose influence in the 1920's was pervading all American education and whose spirit had taken on flesh and fresh authority in Middletown in its own successful Teachers College.

In 1930 the Central High School adopted a new curriculum "devoted to the principle that the schools should fit the needs of the individual pupil instead of forcing the child to fit himself to the standard curriculum, as has been the practice in the past." Such radical changes in subjects taught, in methods of teaching, and in habits of teachers, as a literal putting into practice of such an educational credo involves, would require, according to some Middletown teachers, more knowledge of individual needs than at present exists, and more time to discover and meet these needs than administrators imagine. But, in response to this slogan, there is apparent today in the high school a slow diminution in the traditional emphasis upon factual courses and more emphasis upon exploratory work around main problems, supposedly closer to student needs. In chemistry, for example, individual supervised laboratory work is diminishing the role of class lectures. Mathematics is increasingly "shop math." There is, also, in the high school as in the grades, more grouping of students by ability, with more freedom and rapidity of progress for the more intelligent. Some of the abler children in the high school are receiving at the hands of unusual teachers a type of free-ranging training in social studies, wider than anything apparent in 1925, that is generally recognized in Middletown as answering these children's urgent questions and at the same time extending their horizon far beyond their local concerns.

This new emphasis upon the development of the individual student, coming at the same time as the new problems raised by the heavy increase in the high-school and college populations, has forced Middletown into a revaluation of the role of "an education." With the high school and even the college no longer serving as a screen sifting out the "scholars" from the "nonscholars" even as roughly as they did before the World War, and with secondary education become a mass experience, the feeling has grown that education must not only be good but must be good for something—to the individual and to society. Otherwise, a culture believing so firmly in things, "paying their way" and being "worth what they cost" finds it hard to justify the increased cost to the taxpayers of the delay in children's "settling down to work" and the encouragement of "children's wild ideas" which prolonged education entails. "Culture," in the literary sense, is a luxury to most of these hard-working folk whose children are now pressing into the schools, and they want something more tangible—a better job, the ability to earn more money—as at least one dependable outcome of "an education." As a partial answer to this problem, a "guidance program" has been inaugurated as a part of Middletown's new educational planning.

Compaſſes

ON MEETING THE NEEDS OF ADOLESCENTS (1939)   From V. T. Thayer et al., *Reorganizing Secondary Education* (New York. 1939), pp. 44–50.

Four Crucial Areas of Needs

Studies of adolescents suggest that their needs group themselves roughly into four areas: immediate social relationships, wider social relationships, economic relationships, and—closely related to all of these—personal living. It is on the basis of needs in these aspects of living that the discussion of this volume is phrased.

Why needs are best classified in terms of relationships. Needs are phrased in terms of the individual's functioning relationships with the groups in which he lives primarily because they are conceived as both personal and social in nature. The personality of the individual is formed only through functioning relationships with others, and its needs cannot be met without them. Parental relationships have survival value for the infant and are essential for the development of his personality. As the individual grows through childhood and adolescence, other persons and groups come to play a similar if less portentous role in his life, while he himself becomes a more active factor. From a helpless infant, then, he grows into an active personality which interacts with other personalities in ways that are more or less constructive both for his own further development and for the growth and happiness of all concerned.

In recognizing that the relationship between the individual and his group is circular in nature, education for participation in various types of group life is in a position to avoid the relatively sterile task of preparing young people merely to meet rigid, predefined, unevaluated social demands. This book therefore discusses educational processes appropriate to the adolescent's development in terms of his functioning relationships in various types of groups—his part in face-to-face personal contacts and in economic and wider social life. It takes account both of his current relationships as an adolescent and of those in which he is about to become involved as he approaches adulthood; but concern with his future activities and participations does not transcend concern with his present problems as he now feels them.

Why needs in these areas are crucial. Needs in the areas of immediate social relationships, of wider social and economic relationships, and of personal living are held to be crucial on pragmatic grounds primarily. Interpretative scrutiny of case-history material reveals that the individual meets his severest problems in these areas, and that it is in these areas that social forms require most profound reconstruction. The family and other face-to-face groups are confused as to standards, ideals, and member roles. Economic life is profoundly disturbed. Valid and growth-fostering ways of managing wider social cooperation under modern conditions remain still to be found. Individuals are bewildered and unhappy in consequence, and the full possibilities in personal living are not realized.

Yet the schools, which are supposed to prepare young people for effective living, have neglected these areas in favor of handing down materials that had a genuine place only in another order. There was a time when the induction of the young person into social and economic life took place directly as he grew up in its midst. There was no need for the school as an intermediary agency. Manners and methods of procedure were traditional, and the standards and ideals of relationships quite universal. The school's job in that day was to hand down an inherited culture which had become too complicated for immediate absorption by tradition or through activities shared with elders. Schools merely speeded up the process by which the young came into possession of certain aspects of the cultural heritage.

But now there is no agency as well adapted as the school to launch the young person properly into the complexities of personal, social, and economic relationships, with all of their demands for reconstruction in terms of human values. The time is ripe, therefore, for the school to examine its resources for educating the adolescent for creative participation in these relationships.

Though it cannot be said that all the group participations of the individual in modern industrial society are represented in these particular areas, it may be said that those that are so represented constitute the major part of his life and are at the moment most heavily fraught with possibilities for good or evil; they are most influential in determining the individual's happiness, and most in need of creative reconstruction. It is true, of course, that individuals are members of groups of varying socio-economic status, for example, as well as constituents of social or economic society. Even though class consciousness is not so acute in America as it is in Europe, it is probably on the increase. Individuals also belong to distinctive national, subcultural, and religious backgrounds, and share relationships in numbers of other groups, some of them less significant or less definable than these. None of the problems and values to which these types of group cohesiveness give rise are to be neglected, but they may all be subsumed under the categories suggested. And for purposes of educational planning it seems expedient to use these more general areas for the present. In the course of history other relationships may come to be predominant over these and require further appropriate revision in the curriculums and procedures of the secondary schools.

Interconnections among these areas; the values of distinguishing among them. It must be recognized that personal living, participation in economic life, and in narrower and wider social relationships cannot be strictly segregated, the one from the other. In the actual functioning of the individual, they may not be distinct; any one activity may well involve relationships that are at once personal, economic, and social.

The fact that the economic and political are closely related in the contemporary American scene needs no elaboration. Also, the individual has personal experience and face-to-face contacts as well as wider relationships and responsibilities when he shares in economic production or assumes civic responsibility, for example. This is true even though the economic or civic group of which he is a part is complex, and its other members often remote. Even with modern technology and extreme specialization of labor, a man working in a factory that employs five thousand people is still in close contact with the members of the hiring division, the foreman, and the other men at the bench; he has immediate personal relationships with all of them. And though he is physically removed from the West African native who collects the raw materials he uses or even from the workers in other departments of his plant, the effects of his distant relationships with them are always eventually in some sense personal in nature. The immediate and personal cannot be strictly separated from wider and more remote forms of participation in a highly organized and interrelated society.

Moreover, a person always takes with him the same attitudes, prejudices, ideals, and characteristic ways of going about things, no matter what the activity in which he engages and no matter what the group in which he takes part. There is an essential consistency in the personality; new experiences are always approached in the context of patterns of relationship already built up. A man does not change his make-up on the way from home to factory, though he may, for example, overreact with rebellion in one setting to compensate for his extreme submissiveness in another. Further, with new insights and new motivations, adults as well as adolescents sometimes take on new and for them uncharacteristic attitudes and go about the solution of one problem or another in a way new to them. But once the new way has been learned, it is likely to begin to carry over into future behavior. There is a continuity of the personality in all of its relationships, no matter how they may be classified, and any discussion of educational processes for differentiated types of social participation must give this continuity proper emphasis.

There is still another way in which experience amalgamates participation in various types of relationship. Life within the family or any other intimate group whose cohesiveness is based largely upon mutual liking or respect among its members is deeply affected by economic, social, and civic conditions. The crippling effects of increased economic insecurity on the development of desirable family relationships need not be detailed. Improvement in the life of smaller and more intimate groups is in many ways dependent upon improvement in the life of wider and more diffuse groups. Conversely, individuals who achieve stability in their more intimate relationships are on the whole better able to play constructive roles in their wider social and economic relationships.

Still further, for many individuals, functioning in one or another of these areas of relationship bears almost the whole of the burden of living. For some, economic undertakings constitute the most vital part of the personal life. Mothers frequently find their task in the home all-absorbing and all-challenging. Political activity often provides both satisfying personal relationships and opportunity to play a part in economic reconstruction. And so on.

Nevertheless, separation of the relationships of the individual into distinguishable categories is not only convenient but significant for the purposes of secondary education. The individual is aware of doing different things as he functions in one or another relationship and is conscious of the fact that he requires different knowledges, skills, and techniques in each. It is true that presiding at the family dinner table and keeping books for a plumbing concern both involve personal relationships; that the same person, with his integrated patterns of submission and aggressiveness, love and hate, functions in both. Likewise it is true that the working atmosphere in which he keeps the books may affect the way in which he behaves towards his children as he presides at the dinner table, and that the degree of serenity in his home has its influence both upon his personal life and the mechanics of his bookkeeping. Yet the individual recognizes a difference between functioning in the family and on the job, between working at the office and performing his more distinctive functions as a citizen, like voting or sitting on a neighborhood noise-abatement committee. He needs different skills, operates with different purposes in mind, has greater or less choice in one or the other, and finds in each a different place in the configuration of authority (being the head of the table, the last on the bookkeeping staff, and somewhere halfway down the line at the committee meeting).

In this awareness of difference on the part of the participant himself lies one principle of validity for the separateness of these categories of group relationships. The relatively different operational skills, knowledges, and techniques which he requires in each are a second reason. The limits laid upon his participation constitute a third: the adolescent is now a family member, but he is still looking forward to marriage and a family of his own. He still does not work for a living, and is not yet permitted to enter into all of the rights and responsibilities of citizenship.

A fourth reason why the individual makes distinctions among his functions in various group relationships may lie in the way these functions are themselves separately institutionalized in contemporary society. Except for the skills involved, the primitive father might not distinguish between the economic occupation of gathering food and the ritual of its consumption in the family group. But in complex societies the functions of living are carried on in different places, with different persons, under different sets of conditions. Moreover, the standards and ideals governing these separately institutionalized relationships change at different rates. Authoritarianism in the factory is still rampant. Health is a foremost consideration in the family, but only a minor consideration in industries concentrating on keeping down the costs of production. Standards of personal honesty and integrity in political life are notoriously lower than those in the decent home. The aggressive competitiveness characteristic of business and politics would never be tolerated in more personal associations. These variant standards complicate the problem of adjustment for the individual. This holds specially true for the adolescent who is just coming into contact with the conflicting standards and ideals of the out-of-home-and-school world.

In brief, then, though the meeting of a need in any one area is not without its effects upon the needs of the individual in other areas, there is good reason to distinguish among these areas in educational planning. This is not to be taken to mean that the school is to be departmentalized into these areas, but only that they provide a valid approach in studying and comprehending student needs.

Conclusion

In conclusion, it may be said that using needs as a basis for revising educational goals and processes does not mean tabulating desires and inclinations and drawing up definitive lists of experiences through which they may be met; neither does it mean specifying particular knowledges, skills, and attitudes now lacking in the student and contriving efficient methods for inculcating them. Instead it means seeking clues to the desirable reconstruction of the whole self in the adolescent's personality. The logically dual meaning of the word *need* proves of value in that it refers simultaneously to two requirements: one, that education take cognizance of the wishes and desires of each individual as they express themselves at the time when he is to be confronted with an educational situation; and the other, that it treat these wishes and desires in ways to effect desirable changes in them.

DEFINING DESIRABLE DIRECTIONS OF GROWTH FOR HIGH SCHOOL YOUTH (1939) From V. T. Thayer et al., *Reorganizing Secondary Education* (New York, 1939), pp. 52, 63–66, 86.

Toward what type of personality is it desirable that the adolescent grow? What comprehensible standards should be set for his growth in order that ultimate human values may be conserved and enhanced as he comes into direct contact with an educationally indifferent cultural, social, and economic environment?

In seeking the desirable directions of growth to be fostered by education on the secondary level, it is essential to recall that the school and home do not control and manipulate the adolescent's significant experiences to the degree that they do those of the child. His world becomes increasingly the social world in general, and he can no longer be protected from its inconsistent, conflicting, and confused demands. There is less and less shelter for him against the evil effects of social indifference, political corruption, economic exploitation, ugliness in the relationships between persons, confusion in standards, conflict in ideals. The personal, social, economic, and civic life into which he is emerging is not designed and controlled for the development of the young person, but often to quite other ends; yet he continues to learn from his accruing experience in an environment that is often patently destructive.

*　　*　　*

Desirable Directions of Growth and the Democratic Tradition

DIRECTION FOR THE GUIDANCE OF EDUCATIONAL GROWTH IN THE DEMOCRATIC TRADITION

In seeking guiding principles appeal must always be made to long experience among many people. It is only through living that the individual learns to live. It is only through testing, trying out, rejecting, and selecting that man as a group defines the basic values worthy of pursuit. In seeking ultimate values in personal experience, then, both the student and the school may well look to an experience in selection and evaluation wider than their own, to the cherished values of the culture which surrounds them. To be acceptable, these values must be germane to the individual's aspirations. They must be harmonious with certain fundamental educational insights in regard to his nature and potentialities. And they must be closely related to the basic allegiances of the society in which both the individual and the school find their being and their worth. It is here proposed that the values of the democratic tradition best meet all these requirements.

The American public school has always been conceived as a democratic institution; public education has been heralded from the time of the founding fathers as a necessary instrumentality for the maintenance of other democratic institutions. This was largely because, from the beginning, the success of democracy was seen to rest upon the intelligence of the common man. The fact that the free secondary school has been open to all in this country as nowhere else has contributed to its democratic aura. Today the secondary school enrolls a larger proportion of the appropriate age range than ever in its history, and now the preservation of democratic institutions calls for effective intelligence on the part of the common man as never before. But the school requires a rededication to its task as an instrumentality for the maintenance of democracy.

The rededication is necessary because democracy itself is threatened, and because the old ways in which the schools once served it are no longer adequate. In the first place, verbal allegiance and democratic slogans are not magic passwords to annihilate threats like the current concentration of wealth and power, or to call forth out of nothingness solutions to problems like insecurity and unemployment. Second, the open door of the school can no longer assure economic opportunity. Third, sheer knowledge and skill alone do not provide the creative intelligence required for action to save democracy in jeopardy and reinterpret it in terms of current conditions. And it has been upon these three no longer reliable bulwarks that the school's effort as an institution in the service of democracy has depended.

It is important to note that the proposal to set desirable directions of growth in terms of the democratic tradition is alien neither to what the school has always conceived as its function nor to the sustaining society in which both school and individual must find their ultimate worth. ". . . The conviction that personality is the center of value and that all social organizations get their significance from their promise to enhance the individual: to guarantee the sacredness of his person, to safeguard his rights, to extend his opportunities"[1]—this has been stated as the keystone of the democratic tradition. So stated, without further analysis for the moment, this tradition is not only at home in the American scene but meets the other criteria for a satisfactory guide in seeking acceptable directions of growth. It embodies the predominant elements in any worthy conception of the ultimate purposes of education and carries the whole weight of the individual's search for validity in the activities of his life. Further, it implies the reciprocal process of the individual in interaction with his society, in that the individual can find his sense of worth only through participation in his social medium, on the one hand, while on the other, the medium must be of a sort to offer opportunities that foster an increasing sense of worth on his part.

Further, there is nothing static about the basic conception of the worth of the individual in the democratic tradition. This worth continues to be jeopardized after one fashion or another—by chattel slavery, by wage slavery, by the limitation of the right to speak freely, by the corporate state, by threat of annihilation through war or through maldistribution of goods. But even more significant is the fact that the worth of the person is capable of infinite enhancement. When all the jeopardies to life, the insecurities concerning the physical wherewithal of existence and the right to the full product of one's labor—when the whole current plague of threats to the individual's abundance in life has been removed, even still his worth and dignity may continue to be enhanced. New vistas can be opened through the ever new freedom he is capable of handling, the ever new activities in which he may engage, his increasing abilities to manage life in ways ever more satisfying and rewarding.

To this central notion of the worth of the individual and its locus in his interaction with the mores and institutions of his time there are many subdivisions and an almost infinite number of fronts of advance. Ways must be devised for instituting the processes that promise its realization in the interaction going on between living individuals and the particular economic, civic, and social conditions of their times. The ideal itself must be implemented, fostered, enriched through particular experience in particular situations. But the basic conception stands as a direction finder, a point of reference, for the values to be sought throughout the intricacies of an always changing, ever evolving configuration of oncoming events.

The school in search of the directions of growth to be fostered in the personality, then, can do no better than to look to the cherished ideals of a democratic society, and to the current conditions now threatening them or offering wider opportunity for their realization. The person equipped to forestall these threats and realize these opportunities will not merely be conserving a verbal allegiance. He will be realizing an aspiration born of long experience of many

[1]T. V. Smith, *The Promise of American Politics* (Chicago, University of Chicago Press, second edition, 1936), p. 48.

groups; he will be finding ways and means to his own sense of worth and validity in existence, and simultaneously achieving the only tenable ultimate goal of education itself: such control over his experience as will make further experience of increasing value to himself and others.

Further, if the individual accepts this conception as his own ideal, he is not proclaiming for himself a note which resounds only in the stars; his is not a goal remote from prevailing if unrealized allegiances. Having genuine roots in national experience and historical aspirations, it permits of further growth and flowering through cultivation. And in it, as a part of the tradition of his own people, the young person may find some sense of security, some background, some firm foundation in support of his own endeavor.

*　　*　　*

Teaching is purposeful and effective only when the objectives of teaching are clearly in mind, and when subject-matter and method are clearly seen as instrumental to these ends. But the teacher will always have to remember that intellectual and emotional factors, insight and feeling, understanding and allegiance are one in the action of the person. What is called for is an integrated personality emotionally geared to creative participation in a democracy, sensitive with reference to the factors involved in complex situations, intelligent in adapting action to realize the democratic values at stake, and with a firm intellectual grasp on these values themselves.

Conclusion

In summary, then, it is suggested that reorganization in secondary schools take its departure from an identification of the needs of young people. Meeting needs adequately involves helping the student to reconstruct and reorganize his own inner life so as to cope more effectively with his surroundings. Toward this end, both the student and his guide, the teacher, require a sense of direction, some ideal of the ultimate goals of action. Acceptable goals are found in the concept of a democratic way of life and behavior consistent with the three strands of the democratic tradition—the worth of the individual, a reciprocal relationship between the individual and his group, and the free play of intelligence as a method of resolving problems and conflicts.

ACCOUNT OF THE "EIGHT-YEAR STUDY" (1942)   From Wilford M. Aiken, *Adventure in American Education: The Story of the Eight-Year Study* (New York, 1942), pp. 12–15, 110–13.

The plan of co-operation between schools and colleges provided that a small number of representative secondary schools, to be selected by the Directing Committee of the Commission, would be released from the usual subject and unit requirements for college admission for a period of five years,[1] beginning with the class entering college in 1936. Practically all accredited colleges and universities agreed to this plan. Relatively few colleges require candidates to take College Entrance Board Examinations. In such cases, these examinations were waived by all except Harvard, Haverford, Princeton, and Yale. These four men's colleges, with this one reservation, accepted the proposal and agreed to co-operate. The Directing Committee was especially appreciative of the full co-operation of the women's colleges.

It was agreed that admission to college during the experimental period would be based upon the following criteria:

A. Recommendation from the principal of the co-operating secondary school to the effect that the graduating student (a) is possessed of the requisite general intelligence to carry on college work creditably; (b) has well-defined, serious interests and purposes; (c) has demonstrated ability to work successfully in one or more fields of study in which the college offers instruction.

B. A carefully recorded history of the student's school life and of his activities and interests, including results of various types of examinations and other evidence of the quality and quantity of the candidate's work, also scores on scholastic aptitude, achievement, and other diagnostic tests given by the schools during the secondary school course.

It is intended that the tests used will be of such character that the results submitted to the colleges will give a more adequate and complete picture of the candidate than is given by methods now in use. A special Committee on Records is now at work endeavoring to determine:

1. what information the college needs for wise selection and guidance of students;
2. how that information can best be secured;
3. in what form it should be recorded and presented to the colleges.

The co-operating colleges will not be obliged to admit under this agreement all such students as meet the new requirements. However, during the experimental period and from the limited group of cooperating schools, the colleges agree to accept students under this plan without regard to the course and unit requirements now generally in force for all students, and without further examination. The colleges, for this period, agree, also, that students applying for admission under the new requirements will be considered without discrimination in comparison with students applying from other schools where present requirements are in effect.

The Directing Committee approached the task of selecting the secondary schools to participate in the Study by asking school and college officials in strategic positions in various parts of the country to recommend schools which would contribute to the improvement of secondary education if given the opportunity provided by this agreement with colleges and universities. About two hundred schools were suggested. Every member of the Committee then occupied a full-time, responsible post. No one was free to give the time necessary for careful investigation, but acting as wisely as possible under the circumstances, the Committee chose twenty-eight schools which seemed well-qualified to promote the purpose of the Study. Later two California schools were added.

In making selection, the Committee decided to include both private and public schools, large and small schools, and schools representing different sections of the United States. But the chief concern of the Committee was to choose competent

2614   [1]This period was later extended to eight years.

schools which were dissatisfied with the work they were doing and eager to inaugurate exploratory studies and changes which could not be undertaken without the freedom granted by the colleges. The schools[2] finally chosen to co-operate in the Study are:

Altoona Senior High School
   Altoona, Pennsylvania
Baldwin School
   Bryn Mawr, Pennsylvania
Beaver Country Day School
   Chestnut Hill, Massachusetts
Bronxville High School
   Bronxville, New York
Cheltenham Township High
   School
   Elkins Park, Pennsylvania
Dalton Schools
   New York, New York
Denver Senior and Junior High
   Schools
   Denver, Colorado
Des Moines Senior and Junior
   High Schools
   Des Moines, Iowa
Eagle Rock High School
   Los Angeles, California
Fieldston School
   New York, New York
Francis W. Parker School
   Chicago, Illinois
Friends' Central School
   Overbrook, Pennsylvania
George School
   George School, Pennsylvania
Germantown Friends School
   Germantown, Pennsylvania
Horace Mann School
   New York, New York

John Burroughs School
   Clayton, Missouri
Lincoln School of Teachers
   College
   New York, New York
Milton Academy
   Milton, Massachusetts
New Trier Township High
   School
   Winnetka, Illinois
North Shore Country Day
   School
   Winnetka, Illinois
Radnor High School
   Wayne, Pennsylvania
Shaker High School
   Shaker Heights, Ohio
Tower Hill School
   Wilmington, Delaware
Tulsa Senior and Junior High
   Schools
   Tulsa, Oklahoma
University of Chicago High
   School
   Chicago, Illinois
University High School
   Oakland, California
University School of Ohio State
   University
   Columbus, Ohio
Winsor School
   Boston, Massachusetts
Wisconsin High School
   Madison, Wisconsin

The schools began their new work in the fall of 1933. Each developed its own plans and decided for itself what changes should be made in curriculum, organization, and procedure. The Directing Committee had decided that the independence and autonomy of each school must be carefully guarded. It thought that significant developments could come only out of each school's sincere attempt to serve better the boys and girls in its own community. The Directing Committee

[2]In 1936, one of the original 28, Pelham Manor, withdrew with the consent and approval of the Directing Committee.

attempted through its membership, through sub-committees, and through specialists in the fields of evaluation, records and reports, and curriculum to render every possible assistance sought by the schools, but to avoid any tendency to dictate thought or action. That policy gave to the schools the freedom and responsibility which belong to them. Without preventing essential unity of purpose, this thoroughly democratic procedure has led to desirable variety in organization and procedure.

*   *   *

Altogether, 1475 pairs of students were studied—those entering college in 1936, for four years; those entering in 1937, for three; those entering in 1938, for two; and the class entering in 1939, for one year. A vast amount of data was accumulated, and the Staff gave their summers and most of 1941 to analysis of the collected information.

What did they discover?

The Graduates of the Thirty Schools Succeed

In the comparison of the 1475 matched pairs, the College Follow-up Staff found that the graduates of the Thirty Schools

1. earned a slightly higher total grade average;
2. earned higher grade averages in all subject fields except foreign language;
3. specialized in the same academic fields as did the comparison students;
4. did not differ from the comparison group in the number of times they were placed on probation;
5. received slightly more academic honors in each year;
6. were more often judged to possess a high degree of intellectual curiosity and drive;
7. were more often judged to be precise, systematic, and objective in their thinking;
8. were more often judged to have developed clear or well-formulated ideas concerning the meaning of education—especially in the first two years in college;
9. more often demonstrated a high degree of resourcefulness in meeting new situations;
10. did not differ from the comparison group in ability to plan their time effectively;
11. had about the same problems of adjustment as the comparison group, but approached their solution with greater effectiveness;
12. participated somewhat more frequently, and more often enjoyed appreciative experiences, in the arts;
13. participated more in all organized student groups except religious and "service" activities;
14. earned in each college year a higher percentage of non-academic honors (officership in organizations, election to managerial societies, athletic insignia, leading roles in dramatic and musical presentations);

15. did not differ from the comparison group in the quality of adjustment to their contemporaries:
16. differed only slightly from the comparison group in the kinds of judgments about their schooling;
17. had a somewhat better orientation toward the choice of a vocation;
18. demonstrated a more active concern for what was going on in the world.

The College Follow-up Staff has this to say about these findings:

> Some of these differences were not large, but wherever reported, they were consistent for each class. It is apparent that when one finds even small margins of difference for a number of large groups, the probability greatly increases that the differences cannot be due to chance alone.
>
> *It is quite obvious from these data that the Thirty Schools graduates, as a group, have done a somewhat better job than the comparison group whether success is judged by college standards, by the students' contemporaries, or by the individual students.*

When these results began to emerge, the Directing Committee and school Heads asked whether this creditable showing might be due to the graduates of those of the Thirty Schools which had not departed greatly from traditional patterns and ways of college preparation. To answer this question the College Staff analyzed the records of the graduates of the six participating schools in which least change had taken place and the records of the graduates of the six schools in which the most marked departures from conventional college preparatory courses had been made. Each of these groups was studied in relation to its respective comparison group.

*   *   *

This investigation revealed that

> The graduates of the most experimental schools were strikingly more successful than their matchees. Differences in their favor were much greater than the differences between the total Thirty Schools and their comparison group. Conversely, there were no large or consistent differences between the least experimental graduates and their comparison group. For these students the differences were smaller and less consistent than for the total Thirty Schools and their comparison group.

The College Follow-up Staff comments on these facts as follows:

> If the proof of the pudding lies in these groups, and a good part of it does, then it follows that the colleges got from these most experimental schools a higher proportion of sound, effective college material than they did from the more conventional schools in similar environments. If colleges want students of sound scholarship with vital interests, students who have developed effective and objective habits of thinking, and who yet maintain a healthy orientation toward their fellows, then they will encourage the already obvious trend away from restrictions which tend to inhibit departures or deviations from the conventional curriculum patterns.

THE HARVARD COMMITTEE ON SECONDARY EDUCATION (1945) From
General Education In A Free Society, Report of the Harvard Committee (Cambridge, Mass.,
1945), pp. 167–77.

The fact that an educational institution grants a diploma on the basis of
the completion of courses and the passing of examinations does not imply that its
aim is wholly to impart learning. As we suggested in the second chapter, learning is
also for the sake of cultivating basic mental abilities; in short, to foster the powers
of reason in man. The ability to think in accordance with the facts and with the
laws of inference, to choose wisely, to feel with discrimination is what distinguishes
man from the animals and endows him with intrinsic worth. Yet reason, while an
end, is a means as well—a means to the mastery of life. The union of knowledge and
reason in the integrated personality—this is the final test of education. We are not
now denying the central position of reason or of knowledge as ministering to
reason; we are only urging that reason is or must strive to become a master of a
highly complex inner kingdom consisting of many and diverse members, all of
which go into the making of a complete man. To put the matter bluntly, the
educational process has somewhat failed of its purpose if it has produced the merely
bookish youth who lacks spirit and is all light without warmth. But to leave the
matter in these terms is to make for dangerous confusion; we must safeguard our
statement from the misunderstandings to which it is exposed. What are some of the
important qualities, over and above intellectual ability, which are necessary for an
integrated and sound human being?

The school will be concerned with the health of its pupils, both physical and
mental. The human body must be healthy, fit for work, able to carry out the
purposes of the mind. Mental health has two forms. The first is social adjustment, an
understanding of other people and a responsiveness to their needs with its
counterpart of good manners. The second is personal adjustment, the individual's
understanding of himself, his poise and adequacy in coping with real situations.
Obviously the two are inseparable.

While traditionally man has been viewed as primarily a rational animal, recent
thinking has called attention to his unconscious desires and sentiments which
becloud and sometimes sway his reason. To be sure, classical philosophers
recognized the existence of the passions, but they tended to regard the latter as
alien intrusions and an unwanted complication. Yet passions, although dangerous
because primitive and even savage, are a source of strength if properly guided; they
supply the driving forces for achievement. Lord Bryce once said that if government
were in the hands of the young many mistakes would be made, but if government
were run by old men nothing would be done. According to the ancient myth, reason
is the charioteer that directs but is not the horse that pulls the chariot. In the
complete man we look for initiative, zest and interest, strength of resolution,
driving power. In a free society much of improvement, in or outside government,
comes from the initiative and the dogged perseverance of private citizens; and the
clash of ambitions in the struggle for the rewards of life, when regulated by the
rules of fair play and a concern for the common good, is a source of social progress.

The danger in the preceding account is that the various components of the
human person might be wrongly viewed as isolated elements or faculties, each
leading an autonomous existence. For instance, reason is not a faculty operating
separately from interest and zest. Without a zeal for knowledge, without the

impulse of curiosity, the thinker will remain lazy and unproductive. And yet, while ordinarily the perfection of one human power depends on the parallel development of the other powers, there are important and unpredictable exceptions. It is not true, for example, that a healthy body is always necessary for the existence of a vigorous mind. There are cases of great men in the arts and the sciences who, all their lives, fought against sickness; there have been persons eminent in a special field who were not rounded individuals. Human personality is enough of a mystery to preclude our making sweeping and rigid prescriptions.

Furthermore, the concept of the whole man is not adequate as an aim of education. The innate drives, the sentiments and force of will, are neutral, capable of developing in either direction, and may become antisocial unless they are "moralized," unless they are made to serve as tools in the hand of duty. The complete man must be a good man. Moral character arises from the molding of the native powers to ideal aims. The final secular good is the dedication of the self to an ideal higher than the self—the devotion to truth and to one's neighbor.

So far we have been dealing with general objectives. But teachers naturally ask what should be done in the school to implement these aims. We wish to make it clear that to adopt the above list of the human power is not at all to be committed to a comparable list of courses, as a part of formal instruction. There may or may not be courses in subjects such as health or manners, depending on the circumstances. Our point is that in a proper scheme of general education the mind will acquire the capacity to meet various particular and concrete problems in matters of health, human relationships, and the like. In this view the education of the mind leads to a maturing of the whole person. On any other view, the obvious danger is that schools will set for themselves so inclusive an objective, or perhaps one should say so many objectives, that their central and essential contribution will be neglected. The schools cannot do everything. When they attempt too many tasks, they sometimes fail to do any of them well. Other social institutions are concerned with helping the individual develop personal competence, while the schools have the special and major responsibility of furthering the growth of intellectual abilities. Our discussion of the qualities which go to make up the complete man is based upon the assumption that though these qualities are of the utmost importance, though they are, indeed, vital to the future well-being of our society, they are not the sole responsibility of the schools, and their cultivation must not stand in the way of developing those qualities for which the school bears the primary burden of responsibility.

However, the emotions and the will cannot be trained by theoretical instruction alone. Doubtless the three areas of knowledge, each in its own fashion, raise and discuss problems of human value. Yet values cannot be learned solely from books. Consider the case of social adjustment. Thinking is a solitary process, and in so far as education cultivates intellectual skills it is producing individualists. To be sure, thinking is stimulated by discussion with other people, but in the last resort one has to make up one's mind by oneself. Yet living is a cooperative process. Social adjustment is not something that just happens in the individual with the passing of years. One must learn to get along with other people just as one learns to use complex sentences. But the task of learning to get along with people is infinitely more difficult. Little children do not know how to get along with each other; a teacher or some other adult must constantly control the situation. If adults lived with each other after the fashion of children and regulated their disputes as children do, we should never have had a free society. The child has much to learn before he can behave as an equal among equals or cooperate with strangers for a common purpose. While the family and the neighborhood teach many of the preliminary lessons, the main task is really tackled in the training ground of actual situations, especially those of adolescence and adult living.

But while we admit that general instruction is not enough for our purpose, we also call attention to the fact that the school as it stands is equipped to exercise an influence over its pupils through media other than formal teaching. The school is an organization in which a certain way of life is practiced. The pupil acquires a habit by the process of unconscious absorption; no sermon need be preached. A word of ridicule uttered by another pupil may produce the desired effect. Furthermore, the teacher can and does exert an influence on the student by his example as well as by what he says on the platform. In our specialized society the teacher may think it enough to teach a subject. But impressionable young people get from a teacher much more than subject matter. They judge every action. In some respects the young are exceedingly intolerant; they expect in their teachers perfection to which they themselves do not aspire but which they want to see exemplified in all those in authority over them. Teachers should be more aware of their influence in matters unrelated to their subject.

Finally, in the school the pupil takes part in the various activities. No one who has examined the early histories of schools and colleges with the tales of "cows in the chapel" and "rioting on the common" can have much regret that students now have more legitimate outlets for their exuberance. Nonetheless, it is true that we may pursue a good thing too far and encourage a tone of anti-intellectualism. Or we may, particularly in urban schools, provide insufficient activities, inducing mere bookishness.

Ideally, as the name implies, activities should mean putting into practice the theory of the classroom. In the previous chapter we stressed the importance of the ability to make relevant judgments. Activities provide a means by which the abstract skills imparted in the classroom are made relevant to concrete choices and actions. The educational value of activities, such as it is, comes from the fact that habituation and experience are necessary for the development of any skill, including intellectual skills. Student government, within limits, is valuable in shaping the quality of later citizenship. It is only when the student faces the actual difficulties of governing by democracy that he begins to appreciate the complexity of a free society. To learn to resist pressure, to discover the power of a minority, to have free speech used against one, to prescribe rules and then to abide by them, is training of the first order for democratic living. The connection of the activities with the curriculum is easy to show in the case of the French Club, the Debating Society, the Glee Club, and the Forum. It is harder to illustrate when we come to managerial offices and to athletics. Yet there is no doubt that decisiveness, initiative, and cooperativeness can be stimulated in the student who has to cope with problems encountered in the running of an organization or in team play.

✳   ✳   ✳

Have we exhausted all the potentialities of the school in the preceding account? No, not wholly. When the curriculum, the pervasive atmosphere of the school, and the activities, having done their best, still fall short of expected results, then the school must have recourse to types of instruction in specific subject matters. There is a difference between implicit and explicit instruction. By the former we mean indirect instruction, as when a student acquires skills of thought and communication from courses in general education, or acquires initiative and resourcefulness from his participation in sports. The normally intelligent youth will be able to draw his own conclusions, carrying over into particular cases the spirit of his whole training. But there are those who must be told specifically and explicitly. For instance, while many pupils will be able to absorb relevant knowledge about health from the general course in biology and other allied courses, others will need explicit instruction in personal hygiene. Again, while some will learn manners by contagion from the established practices of the school, there will be others who will have to be told the rules of polite behavior in so many words. A school serving a community of first-generation immigrants may have to introduce courses on the American way and on American standards of living. However, such explicit instruction should be regarded as remedial and as peripheral to the curriculum. Because the circumstances vary, no uniform list of such special courses can be given, but some suggestions may be made.

Education is not complete without moral guidance; and moral wisdom may be obtained from our religious heritage. By law and by custom little sectarianism is now to be found in the great body of American schools and colleges. However, much of the best tradition of the West is to be found in the distillations of the prophets, in the homilies and allegories of an earlier age, and in Biblical injunctions. These are not the property of a sect or even of Christians; they constitute the embodiment of experience on the ethical plane which is, or should be, the heritage of all.

It is clear that physical health is a gift bestowed by heredity and confirmed for the individual by the care given to him in his early years. But the role of the school in the development of health may be decisive. Although the first responsibility in this matter rests with the family and the community, in some places the schools must assume the task of giving direct instruction in health, personal or civic. For many young people the elementary facts about diet, rest, exercise, drugs, and disease will have to be learned away from home if they are to be learned at all. Such instruction may make the difference between a debilitated and a healthy community. The subject may take time from other pursuits of more central intellectual importance. But no educational or social system is sound unless it rests on solid physical foundations.

In an earlier section we spoke of the importance of shop training for students who intend to go into scientific or technological work. Such experience is important for the general education of all. Most students who expect to go to college are now offered an almost wholly verbal type of preparatory training, while hand training and the direct manipulation of objects are mainly reserved for the vocational fields. This is a serious mistake. The bookish student needs to know how to do things and make things as much as do those students who do not plan to take further intellectual training. The direct contact with materials, the manipulation of simple tools, the capacity to create by hand from a concept in the mind—all these are indispensable aspects of the general education of everyone. In some schools pupils receive such training in the elementary grades. Other students gain such experience outside of school; but for those who have had no experience in the use of tools, a high-school course may offer the only possibility.

In modern society, where few children automatically follow their fathers' vocations, the school must inevitably give some help in choosing a career. Any treatment of American society should acquaint students with many sides of the conditions which they will have to face. Yet some students will need more detailed information about the requirements and possibilities of various kinds of work.

Formal course instruction is of doubtful value for this purpose, which can be better served by individual guidance and by the provision of suitable reading in the school library.

Beyond the knowledge of future work, the student needs an experience in actual work. Clearly the school itself cannot be expected to provide this experience in any formal way. Yet it is beneficial for all, even more so for those who expect to enter business or one of the professions than for those who will engage in some form of manual or craft work. It is important that this experience be of such a kind as to contribute to the total productivity of society, although it need not be manual labor. In other words, it is desirable that it be genuine, rather than made, work. We repeat that we are thinking here not of any formal school requirement but of what is necessary for the maturing of a young person.

It is obvious that our account of education in its bearing on the entire human being presupposes a general theory of human nature and of human values. It is equally obvious that in the nature of the case such a theory had to be assumed rather than explicitly formulated in this report. A contrast with current tendencies may help clarify our views. In a natural reaction against the inherited type of formal and bookish learning, educational practice has tended to swing to the opposite extreme and to replace the traditional courses of the curriculum with highly specific and practical courses. The danger here is that training is being substituted for education. More recently a reaction to the reaction has appeared, which would place great books in a central, even monopolistic, position and which tends to identify education exclusively with cultivating the ability to think. We have taken a position somewhere between these two. We have stated that education looks to the whole man and not to his reason alone; yet we have maintained that the whole man is integrated only in so far as his life is presided over by his reason. While we thus regard the cultivation of the mind as the chief function of the school, we view reason as a means to the mastery of life; and we define wisdom as the art of living. We have stressed the importance of the trait of relevance; and we have urged that, while in school, the pupil should be helped to see beyond conceptual frameworks and make concrete applications. Yet since the school by its nature cannot reproduce the complexity of actual life, a merely functional approach to teaching is inadequate also.

An extreme and one-sided view easily calls attention to itself and gains fervent adherents; but a balanced view is apt to be less immediately striking. Reasonableness does not lead to exciting conclusions because it aims to do justice to the whole truth in all its shadings. By the same token, reasonableness may legitimately hope to attain at least to part of the truth.

ON MEETING THE NEEDS OF YOUTH (1944)   From National Education Association, Educational Policies Commission, *Education for All American Youth: A Further Look* (Washington, D.C., 1952), p. 215.

2622   In the spring of 1944, the commission issued its first statement on educational needs.[1] There is not space to reproduce the entire statement, but the summary of ten "imperative educational needs of youth" carries the heart of the document and is particularly important because it was used as the basis for much of the program planning in secondary schools.

1. All youth need to develop salable skills and those understandings and attitudes that make the worker an intelligent and productive participant in economic life. To this end, most youth need supervised work experience as well as education in the skills and knowledge of their occupations.

2. All youth need to develop and maintain good health and physical fitness.

3. All youth need to understand the rights and duties of the citizens of a democratic society, and to be diligent and competent in the performance of their obligations as members of the community and citizens of the state and nation.

4. All youth need to understand the significance of the family for the individual and society and the conditions conducive to successful family life.

5. All youth need to know how to purchase and use goods and services intelligently, understanding both the values received by the consumer and the economic consequences of their acts.

6. All youth need to understand the methods of science, the influence of science on human life, and the main scientific facts concerning the nature of the world and of man.

7. All youth need opportunities to develop their capacities to appreciate beauty in literature, art, music, and nature.

8. All youth need to be able to use their leisure time well and to budget it wisely, balancing activities that yield satisfactions to the individual with those that are socially useful.

9. All youth need to develop respect for other persons, to grow in their insight into ethical values and principles, and to be able to live and work cooperatively with others.[2]

10. All youth need to grow in their ability to think rationally, to express their thoughts clearly, and to read and listen with understanding.[3]

ON EDUCATION FOR ALL AMERICAN YOUTH (1944)   From National Education Association, Educational Policies Commission, *Education for All American Youth* (Washington, D.C., 1944), pp. 234–38.

These were the two major questions: What are the learning experiences which all boys and girls should have in common? And how may these be organized so as to be most effective? There were many discussions of these questions, which we shall not attempt to recount. In the end, most of the staff accepted the statement

[1]See: "The Imperative Needs of Youth of Secondary School Age," *Bulletin of the National Association of Secondary-School Principals*, Vol. 31, No. 145, March 1947. See also: *Life Adjustment Education for Every Youth.* Washington, D.C.: U.S. Office of Education, Federal Security Agency, 1948.

[2]See: National Education Association and American Association of School Administrators, Educational Policies Commission. *Moral and Spiritual Values in the Public Schools.* Washington, D.C.: the Commission, 1951.

[3]See also the statements on "How Youth Differ" and "What Youth Have in Common," on pages 26–30.

of "imperative educational needs of youth" as the basis for defining the "common studies" of secondary education and were ready to move to the problem of organization.

Here several possibilities were considered. One was to set up one or more separate required courses for each of the "common studies"—citizenship, family life, health, consumer economics, science, English, literature, and the arts. Another was to have a single course covering all the experiences deemed necessary for all pupils, which would be continuous throughout the years of high school and community institute for two or more periods daily. A third possibility was some combination of the first two—a basic course to include most of the "common learnings," supplemented by special courses in certain fields.

The first plan had the advantage of simplicity of scheduling, because courses would be set up in single period units for either a semester or a year. It followed the traditional pattern with which pupils and teachers alike were acquainted. In effect, it would simply substitute, for some of the currently required semester and year courses, other courses with a somewhat different and more useful content. The range of knowledge required of individual teachers would be somewhat wider than in conventional courses, but not greatly so. . . .

The second plan—a continuous course using two or more hours daily throughout the upper secondary schools—was advocated on the ground that people's daily work, their civic interests, their family life, their leisure-time activities, the things they think about, and their ways of thinking are all bound up together, each influencing the other. Therefore, it was said, learning in these fields will be more effective and more closely tied to the imperative needs of life if teachers and students are able to deal with all aspects of a given subject, to study problems as they are found in life outside the school, and to keep aware of interrelations which cut across conventional subjectmatter lines.

Someone cited housing as an example. In home economics, he said, pupils study about planning and furnishing their own homes. Questions relating to public planning of housing developments, government subsidies, and low-cost credit appear in "American Problems" courses. Courses in physics and chemistry frequently include units on science applied to houses and their equipment. History classes often study the types of houses characteristic of various periods in national development. Courses on health have their units on "building homes for health." In mathematics, one finds lessons on computing interest charges and amortization of home loans. In art—but why go on? For nowhere—so ran the argument—*nowhere*, under the conventional organization of courses, is it possible to study the subject of housing in its *entirety*. Yet today the paramount problem for fully one-fifth of the families in American City is that of getting a home to live in, within the family means, which will serve all the members of the family in all the ways a home can and should serve them. And within five years, the same problem will rank among those at the top for the majority of the boys and girls in classes today. Why not make it possible, this advocate of the new-type course concluded, for a teacher and a class to turn all their time and all their energies to an all-round study of housing? Why not develop the habit of attacking large problems and using information drawn from a number of subjectmatter fields?

Some of the most persuasive arguments came from teachers who had already been doing some experimenting in this field—combining two, or occasionally three, classes, usually literature and social studies, with science or art added now and then. They and others pointed out these advantages:

Under the proposed comprehensive course, students can better understand the relations between the different things they are learning. For example, the impact of science on industry and urban life can be better understood when science and social studies are part of the same course. In like manner, literature is better understood in relation to the life of the times in which it was written and which it portrays, and in turn it throws light upon the history of those times.

Within the broad areas planned for the year, classes can begin their work in any year with the problems and purposes of which students are most keenly aware at the time. This gets the class off to an active start at zestful, purposeful learning. The skilful teacher will not be worried if these beginnings deal with the relatively simple and sometimes transient affairs of everyday life. For he knows that when once the processes of interested, purposeful learning are under way, they can be guided toward the more complex and enduring needs of youth.

Learning experiences which are important, but which do not require a large amount of time, can be included in the proposed course more readily than in a curriculum organized along the conventional semester-unit lines; for example, brief, intensive work on the improvement of study habits, or on the budgeting of time, or on the recreational resources of the neighborhood.

The proposed course would permit the adaptation of learning experiences in some fields to changing interests and outlooks as students become more mature. For example, during the three years from fifteen to eighteen there are marked shifts in the attitudes of students toward family relationships as boys and girls become less conscious of themselves as children, more conscious of themselves as potential husbands, wives, and parents. So also with interest in occupations. The tenth-grade student is interested in the choice of a possible occupational field and in planning a course to get him ready for a job that is still faraway. Three years later, he is likely to be concerned about the job that is just ahead—how to get it and hold it, requirements and conditions of work, industrial and labor relations, and the like. Given the comprehensive course, the learnings about family life and occupations could be distributed throughout the three years and matched to the changing interests of learners.

Greater flexibility in use of time would be possible and with it types of learning experiences that were impracticable under the system of single-period courses. When any problem or project required special attention for a week or a month, nearly the full triple or double period could be used for that purpose. Field trips and firsthand studies of the community would be feasible because of the longer blocks of time.

Most important of all, each teacher in the proposed course would have fewer *different* pupils and more time to work with and observe each pupil in a wider variety of situations. Therefore, it was said, let the teachers of these new "Common Learnings" courses serve also as counselors to their students. Such an arrangement would dovetail exactly with the recommendations already made that more adequate provision should be made for guidance and that most student counseling should be done by teachers.

The proposal was widely discussed before any action was taken. Some feared, as they said, a "soft pedagogy"—an aimless shifting from one point of transient interest to the next without sustained intellectual effort. In reply it was pointed out that the needs to be met would be clearly defined by the staff for each year of the course. There, to be sure, the planning-in-advance-for-everybody would end. Within the broad outlines of each year's work, each teacher and class would be free to plan and organize their own learning. But planning and organizing, in itself, is an act which requires no mean intellectual effort.

*   *   *

Some feared the danger of superficiality. Classes, they said, would "gallop off in all directions at once" and fail to learn anything thoroughly. The reply was made that here, as everywhere, the quality of learning would depend upon skilful teaching. Orderly sequences of learning might be expected in this course, quite as much as in single-subject courses. But there would be various types of sequences, each deliberately chosen by teacher and class because it seemed best suited to the task at hand. Sometimes the class would follow the method of scientific inquiry to conduct an experiment or solve a problem. Sometimes it would trace the relations of cause and effect through the events of history. Sometimes it would follow the logic of organized bodies of knowledge. And sometimes the order of learning would be that appropriate to growth in appreciations. To be able to choose a sequence of learning appropriate to one's aim is again an intellectual achievement.

Finally, there were some who feared—quite mistakenly, as it turned out—that this course would put an end to the systematic study of bodies of knowledge, such as the sciences, mathematics, history, and languages. This objection was withdrawn, however, when it was shown that there would be ample time in the total school program for any student who wished to do so, to complete all the courses in subject fields required for admission to college or university, even by those institutions which still held to their prewar requirements. Moreover, it was asserted, the conventionally required subjects would appear in the new course, insofar as they were needed to meet the common needs of all youth. English language, literature, history, and science would certainly be found among the "Common Learnings," though possibly in unaccustomed settings.

ON LIFE ADJUSTMENT EDUCATION IN THE HIGH SCHOOL
(1946) From U.S. Bureau of Education, *Life Adjustment Education for Every Youth, Bulletin no. 22* (Washington, D.C., 1951), pp. 8–10, 16–19, 21–23.

The question may well be raised, "What is Life Adjustment Education?" To some people the term has suggested a particular device or prescription, an emphasis on conformity to a specific pattern, or even a startling new pronouncement designed to cure the ills of education. At present the Commission on Life Adjustment Education for Youth offers no new pronouncements; rather it proposes to do something about the pronouncements which already have been made.

In the United States during the past 30 years there has been an increasing tendency to measure the effectiveness of curricula by how fully they provide experience in present living and experiences which prepare for the activities of living. There also has been an increasing emphasis on evaluating the effectiveness of instruction in terms of the extent to which it influences behavior. These trends are reflected in the yearbooks and other publications of organizations representing higher education as well as elementary and secondary education. Through the study of hundreds of educational analyses, surveys, experiments, and reports of commissions, school workers have acquired a sharper understanding of what is vital and meaningful in the preparation of youth for the job of living.

National committees have been developing and extending basic theses for the past 30 years, and they have made progress in clarifying thought and securing consensus. It is the conviction of the Commission that there is available such a wealth of sound theory by which to achieve effective educational programs that at this time the great need is for action which translates the theory into school practice.

The Commission on Life Adjustment Education for Youth is unique in that its major responsibility is that of translating into action recommendations contained in reports which other commissions or committees have made. The reports which the Commission would implement are those which have been issued by responsible professional groups such as the Commission on the Reorganization of Secondary Education, the American Youth Commission, the Committee on Orientation of the National Association of Secondary-School Principals, and the Educational Policies Commission.[1] These groups have set forth concepts of secondary education which are accepted generally and broadly by leaders in all fields of American education. The Commission believes they are so commonly held that they can serve as a basis of agreement for the development of a program of action for the education of all American youth.

The Commission defines Life Adjustment Education as that which better equips all American youth to live democratically with satisfaction to themselves and profit to society as home members, workers, and citizens.

It is concerned with ethical and moral living and with physical, mental, and emotional health.

It recognizes the importance of fundamental skills since citizens in a democracy must be able to compute, to read, to write, to listen, and to speak effectively. It emphasizes skills as tools for further achievements.

It is concerned with the development of wholesome recreational interests of both an individual and social nature.

It is concerned with the present problems of youth as well as with their preparation for future living.

---

[1] *Cardinal Principles of Secondary Education,* issued by the Commission on the Reorganization of Secondary Education in 1918.

Issues of Secondary Education. Bulletin of the Department of Secondary-School Principals. Report of the Committee on Orientation. January 1936.

Functions of Secondary Education. Bulletin of the Department of Secondary-School Principals. Report of the Committee on Orientation. January 1937.

Secondary Education for Youth in Modern America, written by Prof. Harl R. Douglass for the American Youth Commission of the American Council on Education in 1937.

The Purposes of Education in American Democracy, issued by the Educational Policies Commission in 1938.

That All May Learn, written by B. L. Dodds for the Implementation Committee of the National Association of Secondary-School Principals, 1939.

What the High Schools Ought To Teach, prepared for the American Youth Commission of the American Council on Education in 1940.

Education and Economic Well-Being in American Democracy, issued by the Educational Policies Commission in 1940.

Education for All American Youth, published by the Educational Policies Commission in 1944.

Planning for American Youth, published by the National Association of Secondary-School Principals, 1944.

It is for all American youth and offers them learning experiences appropriate to their capacities.

It recognizes the importance of personal satisfactions and achievement for each individual within the limits of his abilities.

It respects the dignity of work and recognizes the educational values of responsible work experience in the life of the community.

It provides both general and specialized education, but, even in the former, common goals are to be attained through differentiation both as to subject matter and experience.

It has many patterns. For a school, a class, or a pupil it is an individual matter. The same pattern should not be adopted in one community merely because it was effective in another. It must make sense in each community in terms of the goals which are set and the resources which are available.

It emphasizes deferred as well as immediate values. For each individual it keeps an open road and stimulates the maximum achievement of which he is capable.

It recognizes that many events of importance happened a long time ago, but holds that the real significance of these events is in their bearing upon life of today.

It emphasizes active and creative achievements as well as adjustment to existing conditions; it places a high premium upon learning to make wise choices, since the very concept of American democracy demands the appropriate revising of aims and the means of attaining them.

It is education fashioned to achieve desired outcomes in terms of character and behavior. It is not education which follows convention for its own sake or holds any aspect of the school as an end in itself rather than a means to an end.

Above all, it recognizes the inherent dignity of the human personality.

The concepts of education which would be translated into action by schools working with the Commission on Life Adjustment Education for Youth are widely understood and accepted by educational leaders in America. Practice has lagged considerably behind this understanding and acceptance of theory. The Commission hopes that through its efforts it may be instrumental in narrowing the gap between theory and practice.

*   *   *

Events Leading to the National Conference

ORIGIN AND NATURE OF THE RESOLUTION

In January 1944, the Vocational Education Division of the U.S. Office of Education undertook a study of Vocational Education in the Years Ahead. This study covered a period of 1 1/2 years. There was a working committee of 10 persons; this was supplemented by a reviewing committee and a consulting committee. More than 150 persons participated in the study.

On May 31 and June 1, 1945, a final conference was held at the Wardman Park Hotel in Washington, D.C. At that meeting many problems were presented relating to a life-adjustment program of education for that major group of youth of secondary-school age not now being appropriately served by preparation for college or by training for a specific vocation. According to Dr. J. C. Wright, at that time assistant commissioner for Vocational Education, and chairman of the Conference on Vocational Education in the Years Ahead, but few solutions to the grave and persisting problems were offered by the group assembled.[2]

Near the close of that meeting the chairman asked Dr. Charles A. Prosser, well-known leader in education and for many years director of Dunwoody Institute, Minneapolis, Minn., to summarize the conference. As a part of his summarization, Dr. Prosser presented what has now become an historic resolution.[3] This resolution recognized the need for a more realistic and practical program of education for those youth of secondary-school age for whom neither college-preparatory offerings nor vocational training for the skilled occupations is appropriate. It contained a request for the U.S. Commissioner of Education "to call at some early date a conference or a series of regional conferences between an equal number of representatives of general education and of vocational education—to consider this problem and to take such initial steps as may be found advisable for its solution." The resolution was unanimously adopted by the consulting committee.

* * *

THE FIVE REGIONAL CONFERENCES

From the beginning, this enterprise has been a joint undertaking of the Division of Secondary Education and the Division of Vocational Education. A U.S. Office of Education committee composed of representatives from both divisions prepared the agenda and made other plans for the five regional conferences. The first and pilot conference was held in April 1946, in New York City; the second in Chicago the following June; the third in Cheyenne in late September of the same year; the fourth a week later in Sacramento; and the fifth and final regional conference was held in Birmingham in November 1946.

Membership of each of these conferences was composed of leaders from the fields of vocational education and of general secondary education; there were approximately 25 participants in each conference; they included principals of secondary schools, State directors and supervisors of vocational education, superintendents of school systems, staff members of State departments of education, administrators and professors from institutions which prepare teachers, directors of curriculum and instruction, directors and research specialists in pupil personnel services, and officers of national organizations of workers in these several areas. They came from what may be accurately described as every geographical region, including 35 States and the District of Columbia.

Careful reports on the deliberations of each of these conferences were prepared

---

[2] From an address by J. C. Wright before the American Vocational Association at its fortieth annual convention, St. Louis, Mo., December 6, 1946.

[3] Original form of Prosser Resolution:
  It is the belief of this conference that, with the aid of this report in final form, the vocational school of a community will be able better to prepare 20 percent of the youth of secondary-school age for entrance upon desirable skilled occupations; and that the high school will continue to prepare another 20 percent for entrance to college. We do not believe that the remaining 60 percent of our youth of secondary school age will receive the life-adjustment training they need and to which they are entitled as American citizens—unless and until the administrators of public education with the assistance of the vocational education leaders formulate a similar program for this group.
  We therefore request the U.S. Commissioner of Education and the assistant commissioner for Vocational Education to call at some early date a conference or a series of regional conferences between an equal number of representatives of general and of vocational education—to consider this problem and to take such initial steps as may be found advisable for its solution.

for distribution to the conferees and other interested persons and organizations. Many suggestions were developed concerning (1) the characteristics of the group with whom the resolution is concerned; (2) the types of offerings and educational experiences which should be devised to meet their needs; and (3) the organizational rearrangements in schools, school districts, and State systems which will be necessary if the ideals of the resolution are to be achieved.

Without question the regional conferences validated the existence and importance of the problem referred to in the resolution. Each conference recommended that the U.S. Office of Education sponsor a national conference to develop a plan of action aimed at a continuing and concerted attack on this problem.

The work of the regional conferences consisted primarily of exploratory discussions of the problems inherent in the resolution and of possible ways of reaching solutions to them. Some time was spent in considering the nature of the youth with whom the resolution was concerned, the characteristics they have in common, if any, and the means by which they can be identified. In addition, attention was devoted to the question of what would constitute a suitable program of education for those particular youth and to the question of how the changes in schools and school systems which are indicated thereby can be accomplished.

It was the consensus of those participating in the regional conferences:

1. That secondary education today is failing to provide adequately and properly for the life adjustment of perhaps a major fraction of the persons of secondary-school age.

2. That public opinion can be created to support the movement to provide appropriate life adjustment education for these youth.

3. That the solution is to be found in the provision of educational experiences based on the diverse individual needs of youth of secondary-school age.

4. That a broadened viewpoint and a genuine desire to serve all youth is needed on the part of teachers and of those who plan the curriculums of teacher-training institutions.

5. That local resources must be utilized in every community to a degree as yet achieved only in a few places.

6. That functional experiences in the areas of practical arts, home and family life, health and physical fitness, and civic competence are basic in any program designed to meet the needs of youth today.

7. That a supervised program of work experience is a "must" for the youth with whom the resolution is concerned.

8. That one of the principal barriers to the achievement of the ideals of the resolution is the multiplicity of small, understaffed, and underfinanced school districts in this Nation.

9. That an intimate, comprehensive, and continuous program of guidance and pupil personnel services must constitute the basis on which any efforts to provide life adjustment education must rest.

The regional conferences served their purposes well. It was the groundwork laid at these conferences which made possible the considerable accomplishments of the National Conference. Incidentally, they proved beyond all question that those who have been primarily engaged in vocational education and those whose work has been largely in the field of general secondary education can work together in harmony and can make outstandingly significant contributions by joint endeavor.

＊　　＊　　＊

The Principal Purpose of the National Conference on Life Adjustment Education
(Prosser Resolution)

Throughout all its planning sessions and in connection with the preparation of all the materials described in the foregoing section, the committee in charge of arrangements was guided by the fact that the developments to that date revealed that there was one inevitable and compelling purpose to be achieved by the National Conference.

The five regional conferences had validated the existence and importance of the problem referred to in the resolution. Certain clarifying interpretations had been developed by the committee in collaboration with Dr. Prosser. A group of specialists in the Office of Education had studied the findings of the regional conferences and the pronouncements or common understandings which already had been given wide currency by national educational organizations, and had prepared therefrom a statement concerning the meaning and implications of the resolution on which general agreement at the National Conference was expected. As the many implications of the resolution were gradually uncovered and followed to their conclusions, both the importance and difficulty of the task of bringing about the many changes and improvements in school offerings which were indicated thereby became increasingly apparent.

*　　*　　*

The two general sessions on the opening day provided opportunity for the conferees to hear Dr. Charles A. Prosser, father of the resolution, and provided also for a "briefing session" at which the cochairmen provided instruction and answered questions regarding committee activities. The major portion of conference time was devoted to committee discussion and action. After the committees had been in session three times, provision was made for a general session at which preliminary committee reports were heard and discussed. This device made it possible for committees to so refine their recommendations that the conference was able to take action on the completed reports at the final session with a minimum of revision.

In opening the conference, Dr. Galen Jones, cochairman, stated that—

> We are convened here to consider a problem which is of central importance in education and which, we will all agree I am sure, is central to the perpetuation and improvement of the American way of life. That approximately one hundred persons in key positions of leadership in American education have arranged to give these several days to planning a program of action attests to the value and possibilities of this conference.

In commenting upon the motives which had compelled the participants to make a place for this conference in their busy schedules, Dr. Jones said,

> We are all earnestly concerned with accelerating the realization of the ideal of functional education for all youth. That a significant proportion of the youth of secondary-school age are not yet being appropriately and adequately served by sound programs of education is of great concern to all of us—it undoubtedly is the reason which has driven each one of us to be present here today. Another genuine source of motivation for most of us has been the realization that this conference provides a medium for cooperative attack on this persisting problem by *all* of those interested in various aspects of secondary education.

As the revised committee reports were heard one by one on the final day, it became increasingly apparent that this conference had exceeded all possible expectations cherished by even the most optimistic member of the committee on arrangements. Here were clarifying statements concerning all aspects of the resolution—what it meant, what would be involved in its realization, what stood across the road leading to the solution of its problems, and the like. Here were clearly defined activities which needed to be conducted at national, State, and local levels; and here were carefully delineated plans for administering these activities. Here were proposals for establishing, financing, and managing a continuing organization to stimulate and guide the conduct of such activities. Here were feasible, practical, workable devices for uniting all interested groups for a concerted effort on behalf of the Nation's neglected youth.

*　　*　　*

That the author of the resolution was highly pleased with the accomplishments of his fellows was evident from his inspiring remarks with which the conference was closed. He said, in part:

We have been talking here these past few days about all our hopes for the years ahead. Never in all the history of education has there been such a meeting as this one in which you have participated so loyally, so faithfully, and with such great productivity. Never was there such a meeting where people were so sincere in their belief that this was the golden opportunity to do something that would give to all American youth their educational heritage so long denied. What you have planned is worth fighting for—it is worth dying for.

Because of what you have done, we are on the eve of a system of education which looks after all American youth—those who go to college and those who do not; those who enter skilled occupations and those who do not.

I have thoroughly enjoyed the small part I have played in all this. I have never seen a group so sincere, never so much earnest thinking and earnest achievement. This is prophetic of the thinking and achievements which we are going to do in the days, weeks, and years which lie ahead.

I am proud to have lived long enough to see my fellow schoolmen design a plan which will aid in achieving for every youth an education truly adjusted to life. You dare not rest the case now, however. We have no proof that this plan will "deliver the goods." We must prove it by the work of the institutions we expect to establish for consummating our dream. Yes, it is a dream—man's big dream. If we go all the way back to primitive man and follow him down through the ages, he has always had this grand dream, dimly seen, before him. That you will bring its realization into the bright light of today and tomorrow I have no doubt. God bless you all!

ELMTOWN'S HIGH SCHOOL (1949)   From August B. Hollingshead, *Elmtown's Youth* (New York, 1949), pp. 168–80.

The high school curriculum is organized around three courses: college preparatory, general, and commercial.[1] Enrollment in each course is related very significantly to class position:[2] that is, each course acts either to attract or repel students in the different prestige classes. In 1941, the class I's and class II's concentrated on the college preparatory (154 per cent) and ignored the commercial course. Fifty-one per cent of the class III's were in general, 27 per cent in the college preparatory, and 21 per cent in the commercial course. The class IV's entered the general (58 per cent) and commercial courses (33 per cent) and avoided the college preparatory; only 9 per cent were in it. The pattern for the class V's was similar to the class IV's, except that 38 per cent were in the commercial and 4 per cent in the college preparatory course.

The prestige bias in the different courses is particularly clear among the girls. For instance, 12 of the 14 class II girls (86 per cent) enrolled in the college preparatory course; none in the secretarial division of the commercial course; and only one in the general-commercial course, and one in the general course. Sixty-two per cent of the girls from class IV and 38 per cent from class III were concentrated in the commercial course, particularly in the secretarial division. Since most girls trained in the secretarial division find jobs as secretaries and clerks in Elmtown's offices after graduation, the high school provides these girls with specialized terminal education.

The elementary curriculum trains children on the assumption that they will enter high school, and the high school in turn is oriented principally toward the preparation of students to enter college. Neither educational level is looked upon as terminal by the school administrators and teachers, yet one-third of the potential pupils never reach the high school, and of those who start less than one-half finish. Between 1935 and 1942, one-third of the adolescents who reached 18 each year graduated from high school, and, of this group, only 15 to 18 per cent left Elmtown to pursue some form of additional training. Less then one-half of the latter group went to a college or university. The remainder entered nurse's training, or took secretarial courses, business, Diesel-engine, air-conditioning, photographic, or other specific vocational training. Thus, although the high school represented the end of formal education for at least 4 out of 5 of its graduates, the curricular emphasis was on the college preparatory student.

This condition undoubtedly is related to the values assigned by students and teachers to the college preparatory course in contrast to the general and commer-

[1] The college preparatory course is designed to meet the entrance requirements of Home State University. It prescribes 4 years of English; 1 of United States history; 2 of mathematics; 2 of physics, chemistry, or biology; and 2 of foreign language. The general course requires six units: 3 of English, 1 of United States history, 1 of mathematics, 1 in some kind of science, and allows 10 units of electives. The commercial course is divided into two sections, general-commercial and secretarial-commercial. Both require 3 years of English, 1 of United States history, 1 of practical mathematics, and 1 of general science. The remaining units are in specialized subjects, such as bookkeeping, shorthand, typing, and commercial law.

[2] Specific enrollment figures by class and course are given in Table X of the Appendix. In the tables and discussion of four class I boys are combined with the class II's and treated as class II's in all but a few special incidents.

cial courses. A senior girl summarized the prevailing views of the college preparatory students when she said:

> If you take a college preparatory course, you're better than those who take a general course. Those who take a general course are neither here nor there. If you take a commercial course, you don't rate. It's a funny thing, those who take college preparatory set themselves up as better than the other kids. Those that take the college preparatory course run the place. I remember when I was a freshman, mother wanted me to take home economics, but I didn't want to. I knew I couldn't rate. You could take typing and shorthand and still rate, but if you took a straight commercial course, you couldn't rate. You see, you're rated by the teachers according to the course you take. They rate you in the first 6 weeks. The teachers type you in a small school and you're made in classes before you get there. College preparatory kids get good grades and the others take what's left. The teachers get together and talk, and if you are not in college preparatory you haven't got a chance.

The students may reflect the attitudes held generally by the teachers, but we believe that the favorable prestige assigned to the college preparatory course is connected functionally with the fact that the majority of class II youngsters were enrolled in it. If a person wants to "rate," especially among the girls, it is wise to enroll in the college preparatory course.

*　　*　　*

Because the academic teachers believe that college preparatory students have more ability, are more interested, and do better work than those in the general course, they prefer to teach the former group. Although these contentions may be true, more probably teachers of the college preparatory group satisfy their desire to see the students reflect the academic values they hold. These teachers look upon students in the general course as persons who have nothing better to do with their time, are mediocre in ability, lack motivation and interest. Students in the commercial courses are believed to be lower in ability than those in the general course.

Ten teachers are in the academic and five in the vocational group. The vocational teachers differ from the academic teachers in their estimates of student ability, as they do in most things relative to the school; they believe that students specializing in their courses are as bright as the rest of the lot. These divergent beliefs between the two groups are in part a defense of their own interests and in part a result of the thinly veiled animosity that prevails between the academic and the vocational teachers. Each teacher in the vocational subjects—agriculture, home economics, shop, band, and secretarial science—has an especially equipped room. Teachers in the traditional subjects—English, algebra, geometry, Latin, French, chemistry, physics, and history—believe that too much money is spent out of the limited school budget to equip these rooms. They are correct in their argument that more money is invested in this equipment than in all the rest of the school; moreover, it is comparatively new, whereas the academic teachers have to use equipment that dates as far back as 1890. Salary differences between the two groups is another potent source of friction, since the highest salaries are paid to the vocational and the lowest to the academic teachers. The cleavage between the academic and non-academic interests enter into every aspect of school life—

curriculum, grades, student government, athletics, and the cliques in which one participates.

*   *   *

Behind the stark figures of grades received in courses and scores made on intelligence tests lies the Elmtown social system. The culture complex associated with classes I, II, and III trains boys and girls to respond positively to competitive situations such as that presented by examinations and intelligence tests. Experience imbues them with a need for personal achievement that is expressed in their constant search for success, teaching them from infancy to face each new situation aggressively and to overcome it to the best of their ability. When they take a test, whether it is arithmetic or intelligence, they normally try to do their best on it, for their ego is on trial and they must make good, and they generally do. On the other hand, the class V adolescent has been subjected to a family and class culture in which failure, worry, and frustration are common. He has not been trained at home to do his best in school. His parents have not ingrained in him the idea that he must make good grades if he is to be a success in life. Moreover, the class system as it functions in the school does not help him to overcome the poor training he has received at home and in the neighborhood. We believe that such factors as these have as much influence on the differences observed in the test scores as "native intelligence," but this is essentially an impression—an impression, however, based on evidence accumulated in Elmtown.

The motivation of the adolescents toward high school and education in general is related, we believe, in a direct way to the grades they receive, but this relationship was not measured. This educational motivation is derived from the student's experiences in his class and family culture. The class I and II boys and girls know that high grades are necessary if they are to achieve the educational goal set for them by their family and class. Parents, friends of parents, brothers, sisters, and relatives who have been outstanding students in Elmtown High have set precedents they are urged to follow; for most, high school is merely a preparatory step for college. Then too, parents and relatives, who have achieved prominent positions in the community, expect them to be leaders. Stimulated by this interest and these examples, they generally respond by aiming for greater achievement. A by no means negligible element is a teacher's expectation that the class I and II child will "make good"; and she helps him realize this goal for, after all, his parents "help" a teacher or cause "trouble" very easily. These factors react in subtle ways to produce high grades and leadership in extracurricular activities in classes I and II.

Class III children tend to come from families who are either in relatively prominent, secure positions or who are insecure "climbers" who have achieved their positions within recent years after a long period of hard work. The latter group of parents normally are anxious to see their children achieve more in life than they have; consequently they place great emphasis upon grades and extracurricular activities. They would like to see their children go to college, at the very least into nurse's training, business school, or some type of short, direct training beyond high school. The secure parents do not have such strong desires for their children as the "climbers," but they want them to have a high school education. Approximately one-fifth of the parents in both groups realize they will not be able to send their children to college; these parents assume that the high school will give their children the last formal training they will receive. Class III children who aspire to climb the social ladder take the same courses as the class I's and class II's, groom themselves in a similar manner, join the same clubs, try to work into their cliques, and follow the same leisure time activities. Some two-thirds, however, are content to drift along, associate with other unambitious class III's or with the class IV's. They are not particularly interested in good grades, extracurricular activities, or training beyond high school. In passing, we may note that these children do not exhibit the tensions the ambitious upwardly mobile ones do.

Class IV students carry into the school situation attitudes they receive from their parents. A prevailing attitude in this class is: "No matter what you want to do or would like to do, the children from the 'rich families' and the teachers won't let you do it." The great majority of their parents did not attend high school, and a goodly segment of these people have little appreciation of the work the school is doing or what the child will get out of it. To many parents, high school is a needless drain on family finances, and they think that the boy and girl ought to be working. For a small majority the high school provides their children an opportunity to receive at relatively little expense to them some type of vocational training. The children from these families tend to enroll in the secretarial, agriculture, shop and homemaking courses. Some of these parents have a blind, almost pathetic, faith that education will enable their children to gain something from life that was denied to them.

✳   ✳   ✳

Family Influence, Grades, And Prizes.

In the Elmtown social system the school is used on occasion by ambitious parents to further their own designs. The two upper classes generally assume that good grades, school prizes, student offices, and prominence in scholastic affairs are their natural due. New teachers soon learn from their associations with other teachers, townspeople, parents, and adolescents "who is who" and what one should or should not do to avoid trouble. Trouble, a constant fear among the high school teachers, takes many forms which range from adverse reports by students to their parents to threats in Board meetings to dismiss so-and-so for such-and-such. Teachers, if they are successful, act judiciously in their relations with the children of the powerful; on appropriate occasions they look the other way. Teachers experienced in the system warn newcomers about this boy or that girl. Narratives, gossip, a hint here, a warning there, remarks in faculty meetings, give the teacher some understanding of the situation.

When controls implicit in the class system do not suffice to give persons in the two higher classes what they desire for their children, direct pressures are applied. A family struggling to maintain favorable prestige relies upon the children to bring home good grades, and, if the family is in a position to exert pressure on the school, it sees that they do receive high grades. Dozens of stories were told by Elmtowners of occurrences of this kind, not once or twice, but repeatedly. Two members of the Board were accused of bringing direct pressure on certain teachers to give their children high grades. Another member suggested that the President of the Board fire a certain teacher because he had made his daughter stay after school to complete an assignment.

It is believed widely in classes IV and V, and to a somewhat lesser extent in class III, that the grades a student receives are determined by the position of his parents in the social structure rather than by his ability or his industriousness. This belief is not without foundation, as is generally the case when one encounters a persistent belief illustrated by one story after another, over a number of years of questionable grading practices in relation to the children of prominent families.

Second Thoughts

ISAAC KANDEL ON THE SCHOOL AND A NEW SOCIAL ORDER
(1933) From Isaac L. Kandel, "Can the School Build a New Social Order?" *Kadelphian Review*, vol. XII, pp. 150–53.

That our schools can do more than they have done in the past to develop in pupils a critical attitude, but a critical attitude warranted only by mastery of knowledge, to weigh evidence, and to arrive at judgments cannot be denied. Can the school, however, go beyond this and throw its classrooms open for the discussion of controversial issues on which the greatest intellects of the day have so far failed to reach decisions? To what extent would society permit its schools to discuss critically not the workings of government but the character of existing political and social orders; it may even allow its schools to analyze the shortcomings and defects of our present economic order, but how long would the schools be allowed to advocate the substitution of a new order? Such limitations on what is claimed to be the right to professional freedom may be deplored, but so long as the educational situation remains as it has always been and is, teachers must enter the profession with a full knowledge of the limitations which society places upon them. No doubt there are aspects of education in which the teaching profession may rightly protest against external interference, but in the long run most social and national systems establish schools for the preservation of their culture. . . .

The school, then, cannot build a new social order nor should teachers combine as a group to penetrate from within. This is not a matter of courage or cowardice; it is a question of fact which all history of education has proved and which the study of any educational system, even the most radical and revolutionary, confirms. The school can only build the social order which society desires and derives its coloring from the social scene; it does not create or modify it but strengthens and gives reality to it. This condition does not detract from the task which teachers can perform and that is to devote more attention to the meaning of the culture and ideals, the hopes and ambitions which society expects to attain through the school, to discover the reasons for the break in gauge between school and society, to analyze the causes for the failure of the school to fulfill the duties which it has professedly assumed, in a word, to make the public more conscious of the ideals which it fundamentally does desire for its children, to dignify and ennoble them.

For the teachers as a profession there still remains the imperative duty of visualizing and giving reality to the dream of America, to discover whether there is an American culture which can furnish ideals and reality for the school; without this, preoccupation with methods and curricula, with techniques and devices for the improvement of the school, and with developing a so-called science of education, is meaningless. Without embarking on a utopian vision of a new social order, the American school still has much to achieve, if it can instil into the minds of the growing generation ideals of freedom and quality, tolerance and open-mindedness, and an attitude of criticism and intellectual sensitiveness to the situation as it is, based not on sentiment and theory but on ascertained facts and knowledge; if it can cultivate enlightenment based not on scepticism but on inquiry and thought; and if it can develop an ideal of individualism which recognizes that one's own interest lies not in success at the expense of others but insistently demands a sense of social responsibility and cooperation.

❊ ❊ ❊

In this sense, because these are fundamentally American ideals, the school can build the social order; in a constituted society the social order is changed by a slow process whose manifestations are incalculable; the school reflects social demands but does not initiate social change. A new education can be developed when the public has determined what the nature of the new America will be; to reverse the process would be to plough the sands. This is not a counsel of despair nor does it mean that education and the school have no concern with social progress; it does, however, mean that they are confronted with the task of discovering how social progress can best be promoted within the fabric of society as it now is. It might be well to recall the words of Thomas Arnold when he undertook the reform of Rugby. "Another system," he said, "may be better in itself, but I am placed in this system and am bound to try what I can make of it."

THE DILEMMA OF THE HIGH SCHOOL (1934)   From Isaac L. Kandel, *The Dilemma of Democracy* (Cambridge, Mass., 1934), pp. 6–19.

No nation has a better system of education than it deserves, or, to put it another way, every educational system reflects the character of the society which it is established to serve, a fact which is ignored by those latter-day reformers who, insisting on a new role for the school, would make it the starting point for social reconstruction. Hence it is not surprising to find that the fundamental principles of democracy are misinterpreted in the American schools as they have been misinterpreted in American society. Liberty has been converted into a doctrine of freedom which seeks to make of each individual at all ages the measure of all things and refuses through unfounded fear of indoctrination and its supposed consequences to set up any standards or values as a guide for the growth of the individual into a free personality. Equality has been confounded with identity, and the same institution seeks to be all things to all men and at their own level. Fraternity may inspire certain community, particularly athletic, activities, but has not been generalized into a dominating ideal as the mainspring of sympathy, tolerance, and cooperation in the interests of the common weal.

Even if we were not confronted by a crisis of such dimensions as the present, it would still be the duty of educators, as professional experts in the field, to discover standards, to interpret honestly and to promote those ideals in which a society professes to have faith. In face of the challenge which is today hurled at the school from all sides, educators would be recreant in their duty if they failed to answer it and if, with all the faith that they have in the institutions of democracy, they neglected to discover wherein school and society have failed and to consider how the school, at any rate, may be improved within the fabric that society has chosen.

It is not necessary, however, to go abroad to find a challenge to our educational system. The depression has served as the occasion for launching attacks on American education such as it has rarely known in its history, attacks which, if successful, would go far to undermine the very foundations upon which this system has been painfully built up since the establishment of the Republic. There are those, for example, who question whether the returns of our educational enterprise are commensurate with the constantly mounting cost in terms of better-prepared individuals and citizens and of a better society in which to live; there are others who would abolish free tuition in the high schools and would introduce fees, a form of criticism which always emanates from groups whose children would never suffer from the change; others again charge the schools with padding the curriculum with useless lumber, the fads and frills of education; still another group, and that within the profession, would cast out all that has been traditionally associated with secondary education and would not only provide still more room for what the lay critics regard as fads and frills but would even add some of their own. There is, in fact, widespread unrest throughout the country both on the quantity and the quality of secondary education. In these conditions Dr. Flexner would find ample material for another volume to answer his original question, Do Americans Really Value Education?[1]

Progress and reform cannot, however, be expected unless we face the real facts in the situation courageously, unflinchingly. As one examines the ever-growing volume of literature on education, and particularly in that branch in which Inglis showed his mastery, one cannot escape the impression that there is a lack of leadership and educational statesmanship, due to a certain tendency to demagogy, a certain readiness to bow to the common man who pays for the support of the school, a certain worship of what is at best a pseudo-science, and a consequent absence of a philosophy of secondary education which faces democracy as it is and does not build on some imaginary Utopia which is not yet born.

The challenge to democracy, from within and without, affects no part of our educational system so seriously as it affects the secondary school. The scope of elementary education is fairly well defined by what might in general terms be called the homogeneity of its clientele and the limited range of its activity. Without denying the tremendous importance of universal elementary education and its achievements wherever it has been introduced, we must admit that its function still remains that of introducing boys and girls in the early stages of their education to the fundamentals and the gateways of knowledge. Experts may quarrel as to the exact nature of the content of an elementary-school curriculum or as to the best methods of instruction, but there is at least a certain unanimity about the branches of human knowledge to which the pupils may properly be introduced.

When, however, we enter upon the field of secondary education, all certainty must be surrendered except on one point. If the practices of the world, including

[1] *Do Americans Really Value Education?* Harvard University Press, 1927.

the United States, are examined, there is no certainty as to the age when what is called secondary education should begin. No one, except the pedantic traditionalist, can today anywhere define the term secondary education. The situation is further complicated by the gradual differentiation of interests which manifests itself among pupils of secondary-school age, a differentiation due in part to innate capacities, in part to home conditions, and in part to the local or national environment. Finally, there is today, despite some expansions since the last quarter of the nineteenth century, complete uncertainty as to what the curricula of secondary education should be.

The point which I excepted, the point on which all but a very small, yet a very vociferous group are agreed, is that on the American tradition of free secondary education there can be no uncertainty. It is a tradition which in theory is as old as the Republic and in practice only fifty years younger. It is today the most important guarantee of that equality of opportunity, the strongest pillar on which democracy rests. The principle of giving every boy and girl a chance was accepted in this country before other countries, not excluding the most advanced, had even established the right of every child to a free elementary education. Nothing in the American system of public education has impressed the foreigner so much as the provision of free secondary education which leads every boy and girl on a broad highway from the kindergarten to the university. Any attempt to put the clock back would not only be foolish but would be doomed to failure, for it would be made at a time when all the leading countries of the world are seeking to increase opportunities for the education of their adolescents beyond the elementary age.

National interest, it is now universally recognized, demands the same common education for all, whether in the same school or not depends upon strength of class consciousness in a country,—up to the age of entrance on the next stage. A common education would guarantee not only a community of ideas but an absence of privilege, which exists when the early years of schooling are deliberately directed to prepare the few to enter the secondary school. This part of the program of educational reform on which most countries have embarked, the movement known as the ecole unique in France, the Einheitsschule in Germany, and secondary education for all or the education of the adolescent in England, is simple; much more difficult is the next task of providing equality of opportunity for further education.

It is recognized generally that an elementary education furnishes an inadequate preparation for life in the complex society of today whether viewed as a preparation for citizenship and its problems, or for vocational purposes, or even for mere understanding of the world as it is. Further, the greatest menace which confronts modern societies comes from the unemployment of youth left to itself and without any educational supervision. Finally, nations have begun to realize that in an exclusive system of secondary education, a vast amount of talent is lost at a time when the world calls for the leadership of the best minds wherever they can be found. Although the arguments for increasing the opportunities for education are recognized and accepted, no country is ready to accept the American experiment of one institution for all at the secondary level.

Thus at the very beginnings of a movement for democratizing educational opportunities those countries which are concerned in it because they are inspired by the demands of justice to all individuals irrespective of their social grade, or by national self-interest, or by the need of caring for unemployed youth, refuse to adopt the American high school as the model to be followed. Their arguments are interesting:—The single school which seeks to cater to the needs of all cannot meet the needs of the individual so well as the school specially designed for this purpose. The single school which offers an indiscriminate mixture of vocational, semi-vocational, and varied academic courses not only cannot successfully meet all the standards but it tends to ignore the differences in the content, method, and organization peculiar to each. It is curious that those American educators who, in order to corroborate the American ideal, point to the tendencies in the European countries to increase the opportunities of education so that no one who is capable of profiting thereby will be deprived of an education beyond the elementary stage, refuse to follow the European discussions of the subject further. There is a realization in these discussions that increased educational opportunities must be followed inevitably by increased differentiation of types of courses, but there is a grave fear, which is widespread, that to increase the size of schools in order to provide for a greater variety of courses would be detrimental to the individuality of the courses and the personality of the pupil, and that the inevitable result would be a leveling downwards. It is far from my intention to recommend the adoption of European patterns for the American system of education; if anything stands out in the study of comparative education it is that educational systems cannot be transplanted, that they spring out of conditions which are peculiarly embedded in national cultures. This does not preclude the educator, however, from examining the variety of solutions offered for the same problem in order to discover the dominant motive. If foreign systems of education have in the past rested upon class distinctions, as has been supposed but as has never been wholly true, the tendency today is to give to each an education according to his ability. The ideal of equality of opportunity is accepted, but, with the American practice definitely in mind, it is intended to avoid what is regarded as identity of opportunity. What must be conserved above all in education is quality. In concentrating on these fundamental ideas, quality in education and the meaning of equality, I can at least evade the charge, which is too facile, of comparing the worst in American with the best in European education. An educational system cannot, after all, be characterized as unique because of its youth or its age, or because of the size of its schools, or because of the number of choices offered to its pupils, or because an occasional pupil is inspired by an occasional teacher, whom he meets in the accident of choices, to change his mind about entering college. It is none of these things; it is the quality of the process and the results attained which render a system unique, whether it be education or any other human institution.

WILLIAM C. BAGLEY ON THE ACTIVITY MOVEMENT (1934)   From
William C. Bagley, National Society for the Study of Education, *Thirty-third Yearbook, Part II* (Bloomington, Ill., 1934), pp. 77–78.

The activity program, . . . I should regard as a valuable and legitimate supplement to a program of systematic and sequential learnings. As a substitute for systematic and sequential learning the activity program . . . is pitiably inadequate, as the Soviet experience so abundantly demonstrates.

The theory underlying the activity program . . . is fundamentally fallacious in the conception of freedom that it implies. The freedom of the immature child to choose what he or she will or will not learn is utterly insignificant in comparison with freedom from want, fear, fraud, and superstition—a type of freedom which is won only by a systematic and effortful mastery of the lessons that man has learned as he has traversed his rough road upward from the savage and the brute.

Again the theory is totally blind to two fundamental facts. In the first place it fails to recognize that one of the factors differentiating mankind from other animal species is the ability to work systematically and persistently in the face of immediate desire or impulse or interest. In the second place, the theory implicitly denies the plain biological significance of the period of immaturity—namely, the inescapable need of the human offspring for control, guidance, instruction, and discipline as a basis for the responsibilities of adulthood.

The theory is perilous because it deliberately belittles the importance and significance of that part of the social heritage which, among all of the factors that separate civilized man from *Homo neanderthalensis*, is at once the most precious and the most difficult for each generation to acquire—the heritage, namely, of knowledge, skill, ideals, and standards.

I can conceive of no set of assumptions, which when made the sole basis of an educational program and carried out consistently, would more certainly intensify individualism and enthrone a glorified hedonism.

BOYD BODE ON INDOCTRINATION (1935)   From Boyd Bode, "Education And Social Reconstruction," *The Social Frontier*, vol. II, (January, 1935), p. 22.

There is a sense, undoubtedly, in which all education is indoctrination. Whether all education is to be so labelled is chiefly a matter of taste. The important thing for present purposes is that the point at issue relates to the independent reconstruction of the confused and contradictory beliefs which every normal individual acquires by virtue of his membership in the social order. If this latter kind of education is to be called indoctrination, it is indoctrination of a distinctive kind. It is indoctrination in the belief or attitude that the individual has the right to a choice of beliefs. Stated negatively and in terms of paradox, it is indoctrination in the belief that the indoctrination of beliefs is wrong. For practical purposes it would be better to limit the term indoctrination to practices which deny to the individual the right to choose for himself.

It is a curious circumstance that it has become necessary to argue, as against proposed democratic reforms of education, for the right of the individual to choose his own beliefs, and for faith in the intelligence of the common man. The desire to predetermine beliefs indicates a lack of such faith. The remedy for the shortcomings of the progressive education movement is not to prescribe beliefs, but to specify the areas in which reconstruction or reinterpretation is an urgent need. If this point is covered, we can afford to take the position that the teacher has fulfilled his obligations if he provides the conditions for sincere and careful thinking, without assuming responsibility for the outcome. Faith in democracy requires submission to this test, without hedging or qualifications. If we profess to trust the intelligence of the common man, we cannot refuse to risk the application of the test. To borrow a political expression, the way to resume is to resume. If such faith in intelligence is not justified by the results, we can only conclude that our belief in democracy was a mistake. On the other hand, if this belief has a solid foundation, we may expect that the general drift will be towards the view that ideals and values must have their origin in everyday experiences and activities and must be held subject to revision in the light of changing conditions. In proportion as we achieve the insight that a solution of the conflicts inherent in our modern life requires the elimination of the dualism which lies back of them, we shall build for ourselves a distinctively democratic system of education and a distinctively democratic form of civilization.

It remains to add that, from this point of view, the bearing of education on social reconstruction is indirect rather than direct. It is never detached or neutral. Its raw material comes in large part from the mass of incoherent and discordant tendencies which we designate collectively as the status quo. Its proposal to carry through an appeal to intelligence is in itself a declaration of partisanship. Its method is intended to give a first-hand experience and thus a realizing sense of what is meant by the democratic conception of continuous growth and the enrichment of life. And, finally, its aim to cultivate in each pupil an independent social outlook gives promise of providing a basis for effective participation in giving direction to social change.

PROGRESSIVE EDUCATION AT THE CROSSROADS (1938)   From Boyd Bode,
Progressive Education at the Crossroads (New York, 1938), pp. 9–27.

The strongest and most evangelistic movement in American education at the present time is the movement known as progressive education. A visitor to our schools ordinarily has no difficulty in recognizing a so-called progressive school. He can usually tell the difference the moment he opens the door. The progressive school cultivates an atmosphere of activity and freedom which is all its own. In academic language, the progressive school is a place where children go, not primarily to learn, but to carry on a way of life.

The Progressives' Paradox

In spite of this distinctiveness, however, our visitor, if he is a reflective person, is likely to have peculiar difficulty in defining a progressive school. Any trait or aspect which he may select as a distinguishing characteristic presently turns out to have significant limitations. In other words, we seem to encounter a variety of contradictions when we try to state the qualities of such a school.

It emphasizes freedom, yet it also attaches major importance to guidance and direction. It plays up method, but it is also critical of the content of the more conventional curriculum. It places the individual at the center of the stage; yet it perpetually criticizes the competitive character of the present social order, which indicates that it rejects the philosophy of individualism. It insists that intelligence must be permitted to operate freely; yet it seldom alarms its constituents, who, in the case of private schools, are generally the more prosperous element in society. It commonly regards the college as the citadel of its enemy; yet its chief business is often preparation for college. It holds that learning takes place through doing; yet physical activity tapers off sharply as we go up the educational scale. To the earnest observer all this is very confusing.

These real or apparent contradictions naturally invite the conclusion that the progressive movement draws its chief inspiration from a certain sentimentality about children. This sentimentality, so it appears, leads to a lot of unedifying fussiness, which is camouflaged as "respect for personality," but is not intended to be really subversive. There is no intention of changing the established values of society beyond the point of spreading more sweetness and light. With respect to these values the teachers in our progressive schools are frequently as conventional as the buttons on the sleeve of a man's coat.

A New Organizing Principle

Such a conclusion, however, would be a bit too simple. The continuing vitality of the progressive movement is evidence that it is based on something of larger significance. The emphasis of progressive education on the individual, on the sinfulness of "imposition," and on the necessity of securing free play for intelligence, whether rightly or wrongly applied, is a reflection of the growing demand, outside of the school, for recognition of the common man. Similarly the confusion in progressive education is a reflection of the confusion in the outside world resulting from this demand.

We are gradually discovering that the admission of the common man to the status of full recognition means more than an extension of privilege. It is not on a par, for example, with opening the doors of an art gallery to all comers, instead of merely to the chosen few. In its application to industry this recognition obviously means an extensive revision of our conception of property rights and of the function of government. As applied to organized religion it means a shift of emphasis from eternal salvation to progress through social control. In relation to the values of scholarship and esthetic appreciation it means a transformation of these values so that they will not remain a detached occupation for a leisure class and for specialists, but will become incorporated in the affairs of everyday experience. In brief, the recognition of the common man—which is what we call democracy— introduces a point of view which is so far-reaching in its implications as to make democracy a distinctive and competing way of life.

Unless progressive education is content to be simply a method which is available to any teacher and for any purpose, it had better play out its string and become the exponent of that specific way of life for which the name "democracy" is perhaps as good as any. The refusal to take this step would leave progressive education with no guiding principle except random interests and hypothetical needs, and so would justify most of the hard things that have been said about it by its critics. On the other hand, taking this step means that the question of reorganizing or reinterpreting the established values and institutions of our civilization must receive major attention. These values took their character and form in large part at a time when the common man had not yet secured a prominent place in the picture. As was intimated a moment ago, there is considerable ground for the suspicion that our concern for the common man will evaporate into idle words and sentiments, unless we gain some perception of what is required to give the common man his proper share in our social and cultural heritage. To leave our conception of this heritage unchanged means that in our attempts to "socialize" the school population we are really practicing "imposition" on the sly.

In a word, the rise of the common man is the disturbing factor, both on the social and on the educational level. As long as he remained submerged, the situation was comparatively simple. It was commonly taken for granted that the higher cultural values were not for him. It was even supposed that he was too earth-earthy to appreciate them. This supposition was refuted as he gained wider opportunities, but it also appears that his scale of values is somewhat different from that of the aristocratic class by which he was ruled so long in the past. This difference is making itself felt in certain areas, such as industrial relations and organized religion, although it is not any too clear as yet just what kind of reorganization in ideals and practice is required in these areas by the application of the principle of democracy. What reorganization the principle of democracy calls for in the field of education is perhaps even more obscure. This problem must be faced, however, if we are to arrive at a significant and defensible conception of the meaning of the progressive movement in education.

❊   ❊   ❊

The Choice Required

Progressive education is confronted with the choice of becoming the avowed exponent of democracy or else of becoming a set of ingenious devices for tempering the wind to the shorn lamb. If democracy is to have a deep and inclusive human meaning, it must have also a distinctive educational system.

Since the whole weight of tradition is on the side of absolutes which are abstractions that served to maintain an aristocratic form of society, such a system must have direct and constant reference to the conflict between the aristocratic and the democratic ways of life. It must have a psychology based on the conception of knowledge and truth as functions in the control of experience—the kind of psychology which is pointed toward in what is sometimes called "organismic" psychology. It must have a theory of values which has as its center the continuous improvement of human living through voluntary reciprocity or the constant widening of common interests and common concerns. Lastly, it must undertake to point out how the acceptance of such a standard for growth and progress requires continuous and frequently extensive reconstruction or revision of traditional beliefs and attitudes, in accordance with growing insight and changing circumstances. In a word, progressive education must become clearly conscious of the implications contained in its basic attitude and to use these implications as a vantage point from which to reorganize its thinking and its procedures.

JOHN DEWEY ON THE NEW EDUCATION (1938) From John Dewey,
Experience And Education (New York, 1938), pp. 9–11, 68, 92–96.

The general principles of the new education do not of themselves solve any of the problems of the actual or practical conduct and management of progressive schools. Rather, they set new problems which have to be worked out on the basis of a new philosophy of experience. The problems are not even recognized, to say nothing of being solved, when it is assumed that it suffices to reject the ideas and practices of the old education and then go to the opposite extreme. Yet I am sure that you will appreciate what is meant when I say that many of the newer schools tend to make little or nothing of organized subject-matter of study; to proceed as if any form of direction and guidance by adults were an invasion of individual freedom, and as if the idea that education should be concerned with the present and future meant that acquaintance with the past has little or no role to play in education. Without pressing these defects to the point of exaggeration, they at least illustrate what is meant by a theory and practice of education which proceeds negatively or by reaction against what has been current in education rather than by a positive and constructive development of purposes, methods, and subject-matter on the foundation of a theory of experience and its educational potentialities.

It is not too much to say that an educational philosophy which professes to be based on the idea of freedom may become as dogmatic as ever was the traditional education which is reacted against. For any theory and set of practices is dogmatic which is not based upon critical examination of its own underlying principles. Let us say that the new education emphasizes the freedom of the learner. Very well. A problem is now set. What does freedom mean and what are the conditions under which it is capable of realization? Let us say that the kind of external imposition which was so common in the traditional school limited rather than promoted the intellectual and moral development of the young. Again, very well. Recognition of this serious defect sets a problem. Just what is the role of the teacher and of books in promoting the educational development of the immature? Admit that traditional education employed as the subject-matter for study facts and ideas so bound up with the past as to give little help in dealing with the issues of the present and future. Very well. Now we have the problem of discovering the connection which actually exists *within* experience between the achievements of the past and the issues of the present. We have the problem of ascertaining how acquaintance with the past may be translated into a potent instrumentality for dealing effectively with the future. We may reject knowledge of the past as the *end* of education and thereby only emphasize its importance as a *means*. When we do that we have a problem that is new in the story of education: How shall the young become acquainted with the past in such a way that the acquaintance is a potent agent in appreciation of the living present? . . .

Visitors to some progressive schools are shocked by the lack of manners they come across. One who knows the situation better is aware that to some extent their absence is due to the eager interest of children to go on with what they are doing. In their eagerness they may, for example, bump into each other and into visitors with no word of apology. One might say that this condition is better than a display of merely external punctilio accompanying intellectual and emotional lack of interest in school work. But it also represents a failure in education, a failure to learn one of the most important lessons of life, that of mutual accommodation and adaptation. Education is going on in a one-sided way, for attitudes and habits are in process of formation that stand in the way of the future learning that springs from easy and ready contact and communication with others. . . .

Because the studies of the traditional school consisted of subject-matter that was selected and arranged on the basis of the judgment of adults as to what would be useful for the young sometime in the future, the material to be learned was settled upon outside the present life-experience of the learner. In consequence, it had to do with the past; it was such as had proved useful to men in the past ages. By reaction to an opposite extreme, as unfortunate as it was probably natural under the circumstances, the sound idea that education should derive its materials from present experience and should enable the learner to cope with the problems of the present and future has often been converted into the idea that progressive schools can to a very large extent ignore the past. If the present could be cut off from the past, this conclusion would be sound. But the achievements of the past provide the only means at command for understanding the present. Just as the individual has to draw in memory upon his own past to understand the conditions in which he individually finds himself, so the issues and problems of present *social* life are in such intimate and direct connection with the past that students cannot be prepared to understand either these problems or the best way of dealing with them without delving into their roots in the past. In other words, the sound principle that the objectives of learning are in the future and its immediate materials are in present experience can be carried into effect only in the degree that present experience is stretched, as it were, backward. It can expand into the future only as it is also enlarged to take in the past.

If time permitted, discussion of the political and economic issues which the present generation will be compelled to face in the future would render this general statement definite and concrete. The nature of the issues cannot be understood save as we know how they came about. The institutions and customs that exist in the present and that give rise to the present social ills and dislocations did not arise overnight. They have a long history behind them. Attempt to deal with them simply on the basis of what is obvious in the present is bound to result in adoption of superficial measures which in the end will only render existing problems more acute and more difficult to solve. Policies framed simply upon the ground of knowledge of the present cut off from the past is the counterpart of heedless carelessness in individual conduct. The way out of scholastic systems that made the past an end in itself is to make acquaintance with the past a *means* of understanding the present. Until this problem is worked out, the present clash of educational ideas and practices will continue. On the one hand, there will be reactionaries that claim that the main, if not the sole, business of education is transmission of the cultural heritage. On the other hand, there will be those who hold that we should ignore the past and deal only with the present and future.

That up to the present time the weakest point in progressive schools is in the matter of selection and organization of intellectual subject-matter is, I think, inevitable under the circumstances. It is an inevitable as it is right and proper that they should break loose from the cut and dried material which formed the staple of the old education. In addition, the field of experience is very wide and it varies in its contents from place to place and from time to time. A single course of studies for all progressive schools is out of the question; it would mean abandoning the fundamental principle of connection with life-experiences. Moreover, progressive schools are new. They have had hardly more than a generation in which to develop. A certain amount of uncertainty and of laxity in choice and organization of subject-matter is, therefore, what was to be expected. It is no ground for fundamental criticism or complaint.

It is a ground for legitimate criticism, however, when the ongoing movement of progressive education fails to recognize that the problem of selection and organization of subject-matter for study and learning is fundamental. Improvisation that takes advantage of special occasions prevents teaching and learning from being steretyped and dead. But the basic material of study cannot be picked up in a cursory manner. Occasions which are not and cannot be foreseen are bound to arise wherever there is intellectual freedom. They should be utilized. But there is a decided difference between using them in the development of a continuing line of activity and trusting to them to provide the chief material of learning.

WILLIAM C. BAGLEY'S ESSENTIALIST PLATFORM (1938)   From William C. Bagley, "An Essentialist's Platform for the Advancement of American Education," *Educational Administration and Supervision*, vol. XXIV, pp.248–56.

The Problem and the Platform

❊   ❊   ❊

It is particularly unfortunate that American education should be unnecessarily weak at a time when the situation both at home and abroad is critical in the last degree.

The American people are facing an economic problem which both in nature and in magnitude is without an even remotely similar precedent in all history. In the richest country in the world, two thirds of the world's unemployment is now concentrated. In the midst of potential abundance, the cogs in the wheels of production, distribution, exchange, and consumption have lamentably failed to mesh.

It is the indicated and imminent task of the present dominant generation to solve this problem under whatever expert guidance at the hands of the economist and the social engineer it may find and accept. The student of education must cooperate with all other citizens in this task. It is his own specific duty, however, to consider the problems in his field that are bound to arise in the changes that seem now to be inevitable, regardless of the form which the solution of the present desperate economic situation may take—this with one exception, for if in desperation the American people discard democracy and yield to a dictator the sincere student of education will have no function and consequently no duty. The yes-man and the rubber-stamp will take his place. He will be a luxury without a purpose; and the dictators have standardized a simple but effective technique for liquidating luxuries of this sort.

We shall assume, however, that "it can't happen here" and that, whatever may be the new economic and social order, the political order based upon representative government and the Bill of Rights will persist. Hence a primary function of American education will be to safeguard and strengthen these ideals of American democracy, with especial emphasis upon freedom of speech, freedom of the press, freedom of assembly, and freedom of religion. It is clear enough now that whenever any one of these is permitted to collapse, the whole democratic structure will topple like a house of cards. These, then, are among the first essentials in the platform of the Essentialist.

Democracy is now distinctly on trial. It is under criticism and suspicion. Every weakness will be watched for and welcomed by its enemies. Inevitably the future will bring competition if not clashes and conflicts with the now militantly anti-democratic peoples. Democratic societies cannot survive either competition or conflict with totalitarian states unless there is a democratic discipline that will give strength and solidarity to the democratic purpose and ideal. If the theory of democracy finds no place for discipline, then, the theory will have before long only historical significance. French education, much closer to the danger, has recognized this imperative need. Still unswerving in fidelity to the ideals of democracy, and still giving its first emphasis to clarity of thought and independence in individual thinking as the time-honored objective of French education, it recognizes no less the fundamental importance of social solidarity in the defense of democracy.

American educational theory long since dropped the term "discipline" from its vocabulary. Today its most vocal and influential spokesmen enthrone the right even of the immature learner to choose what he shall learn. They condemn as "authoritarian" all learning tasks that are imposed by the teacher. They deny any value in the systematic and sequential mastery of the lessons that the race has learned at so great a cost. They condone and rationalize the refusal of the learner to attack a task that does not interest him. In effect they open wide the lines of least resistance and least effort. Obedience they stigmatize as a sign of weakness. All this they advocate in the magic names of "democracy" and "freedom."

Now, obviously, the freedom of the immature to choose what they shall learn is of negligible consequence compared with their later freedom from the want, fear, fraud, superstition, and error which may fetter the ignorant as cruelly as the chains of the slave-driver—and the price of this freedom is systematic and sustained effort often devoted to the mastery of materials the significance of which must at the time be taken on faith.

This problem is far more than merely personal or individual in its reference. A democratic society has a vital, collective stake in the informed intelligence of every individual citizen. That a literate electorate is absolutely indispensable not only to its welfare but to its very survival is clearly demonstrated by the sorry fate that so speedily overtook every unschooled and illiterate democracy founded as a result of the War that was to "make the world safe for democracy."

And literacy in this sense means, of course, far more than the mere ability to translate printed letters into spoken words; it means the development and expansion of ideas; it means the basis for intelligent understanding and for the collective thought and judgment which are the essence of democratic institutions. These needs are so fundamental to an effective democracy that it would be folly to leave them to the whim or caprice of either learner or teacher.

Among the essentials of the Essentialist, then, is a recognition of the right of the immature learner to guidance and direction when these are needed either for his individual welfare or for the welfare and progress of the democratic group. The responsibility of the mature for the instruction and control of the immature is the biological meaning of the extended period of human immaturity and necessary dependence. It took the human race untold ages to recognize this responsibility. It is literally true that until this recognition dawned man remained a savage. Primitive societies, as numerous students have observed (and their testimony seems to be unanimous), pamper and indulge their young. Freedom of children from control, guidance, and discipline is with them a rule so nearly universal that its only brief but significant exception during the nearly universal savage ceremonies marking the adolescent onset of maturity is regarded as the first faint beginning of consciously directed human education.

It would be futile to deny that control and discipline may be stupid and brutal and used for unworthy ends. It would be futile to deny the need for the development of self-discipline and for the relaxation of external discipline with the growth of volitional maturity. But all this does not alter the fundamental truth that freedom must go hand in hand with responsibility, and that responsible freedom is always a conquest, never a gift.

An effective democracy demands a community of culture. Educationally this means that each generation be placed in possession of a common core of ideas, meanings, understandings, and ideals representing the most precious elements of the human heritage.

There can be little question as to the essentials. It is by no means a mere accident that the arts of recording, computing, and measuring have been among the first concerns of organized education. They are basic social arts. Every civilized society has been founded upon these arts, and when these arts have been lost, civilization has invariably and inevitably collapsed. Egypt, Asia Minor, and Mesopotamia are strewn with the ruins of civilizations that forgot how to read and write. Contemporary civilization, for the first time in history, has attempted to insure its continuance by making these arts in so far as possible the prerogative of all.

Nor is it at all accidental that a knowledge of the world that lies beyond one's immediate experience has been among the recognized essentials of universal education, and that at least a speaking acquaintance with man's past and especially with the story of one's own country was early provided for in the program of the universal school. Widening the space horizon and extending the time perspective are essential if the citizen is to be protected from the fallacies of the local and the immediate.

Investigation, invention, and creative art have added to the heritage, and the list of recognized essentials has been extended and will be farther extended. Health instruction and the inculcation of health practices are now basic phases of the work of the lower schools. The elements of natural science have their place. Neither the fine arts nor the industrial arts are neglected.

We repeat that there can be little question as to the essentials of universal education. As Charles A. Beard has so well said: "While education constantly touches the practical affairs of the hour and day, and responds to political and economic exigencies, it has its own treasures heavy with the thought and sacrifice of the centuries. It possesses a heritage of knowledge and heroic examples—accepted values stamped with the seal of permanence."

A specific program of studies including these essentials should be the heart of a democratic system of education. In a country like ours with its highly mobile population there should be an agreement as to the order and grade-placement of subjects and especially of crucial topics. There is no valid reason for the extreme localism that has come to characterize American education. There is no valid reason for the failure of the American elementary school to lay as firm a foundation in the fundamentals of education as do the elementary schools of other democracies.